THE CAMBRIDGE HISTORY OF
IRELAND

This final volume in *The Cambridge History of Ireland* covers the period from the 1880s to the present. Based on the most recent and innovative scholarship and research, the many contributions from experts in their field offer detailed and fresh perspectives on key areas of Irish social, economic, religious, political, demographic, institutional and cultural history. And they do so by situating the Irish story, or stories – for much of these decades two Irelands are in play – in a variety of contexts, Irish and Anglo-Irish, of course, but also European, Atlantic and, latterly, global. The result is an insightful 'take' on the emergence and development of Ireland during these often turbulent decades. Copiously illustrated, with special features on images of the 'Troubles' and on Irish art and sculpture in the twentieth century, this volume will undoubtedly be hailed as a landmark publication by the most recent generation of historians of Ireland.

THOMAS BARTLETT was born in Belfast, and is a graduate of Queen's University Belfast. He has held positions at the National University of Ireland Galway, then as Professor of Modern Irish history at University College Dublin, and most recently as Professor of Irish history at the University of Aberdeen, until his retirement in 2014. He is a member of the Royal Irish Academy and his previous publications include *Ireland: A History* (Cambridge University Press, 2010).

THE CAMBRIDGE HISTORY OF
IRELAND

GENERAL EDITOR

THOMAS BARTLETT, professor emeritus of Irish history,
University of Aberdeen

This authoritative, accessible and engaging four-volume history vividly presents the Irish story – or stories – from c.600 to the present, within its broader Atlantic, European, imperial and global contexts. While the volumes benefit from a strong political narrative framework, they are distinctive also in including essays that address the full range of social, economic, religious, linguistic, military, cultural, artistic and gender history, and in challenging traditional chronological boundaries in a manner that offers new perspectives and insights. Each volume examines Ireland's development within a distinct period, and offers a complete and rounded picture of Irish life, while remaining sensitive to the unique Irish experience. Bringing together an international team of experts, this landmark history both reflects recent developments in the field and sets the agenda for future study.

VOLUMES IN THE SERIES

VOLUME I
600–1550
EDITED BY BRENDAN SMITH

VOLUME II
1550–1730
EDITED BY JANE OHLMEYER

VOLUME III
1730–1880
EDITED BY JAMES KELLY

VOLUME IV
1880 to the Present
EDITED BY THOMAS BARTLETT

THE CAMBRIDGE HISTORY OF
IRELAND

*

VOLUME IV
1880 to the Present

*

Edited by

THOMAS BARTLETT

University of Aberdeen

CAMBRIDGE
UNIVERSITY PRESS

University Printing House, Cambridge CB2 8BS, United Kingdom

One Liberty Plaza, 20th Floor, New York, NY 10006, USA

477 Williamstown Road, Port Melbourne, VIC 3207, Australia

314–321, 3rd Floor, Plot 3, Splendor Forum, Jasola District Centre, New Delhi – 110025, India

79 Anson Road, #06-04/06, Singapore 079906

Cambridge University Press is part of the University of Cambridge.

It furthers the University's mission by disseminating knowledge in the pursuit of
education, learning, and research at the highest international levels of excellence.

www.cambridge.org
Information on this title: www.cambridge.org/9781107113541
DOI: 10.1017/9781316286470

First published 2018
Reprinted 2018

Printed in the United Kingdom by TJ International, Padstow, Cornwall

A catalogue record for this publication is available from the British Library

ISBN – 4-Volume Set 978-1-107-16729-2 Hardback
ISBN – Volume I 978-1-107-11067-0 Hardback
ISBN – Volume II 978-1-107-11763-1 Hardback
ISBN – Volume III 978-1-107-11520-0 Hardback
ISBN – Volume IV 978-1-107-11354-1 Hardback

Cambridge University Press has no responsibility for the persistence or accuracy of URLs
for external or third-party internet websites referred to in this publication, and does not
guarantee that any content on such websites is, or will remain, accurate or appropriate.

Contents

v

Contents

Contents

Illustrations

Photographic Essay Illustrations

Tables and Charts

Maps

Contributors

THOMAS BARTLETT is Professor Emeritus of Irish History at the University of Aberdeen and General Editor of the Cambridge History of Ireland.

GUY BEINER is Senior Lecturer in History at Ben-Gurion University of the Negev. He is the author of *Remembering the Year of the French: Irish Folk History and Social Memory* (Madison, University of Wisconsin Press, 2009).

JOHN BEW is Professor in History and Foreign Policy in King's College London. His publications include *Citizen Clem: a Life of Attlee* (Oxford University Press, 2016).

PAUL BEW is Professor Emeritus of Politics at Queen's University Belfast. Among his many books is *Ireland: the Politics of Enmity* (Oxford University Press, 2007). He was made a life Peer in 2007.

CAITRIONA CLEAR is Senior Lecturer in History at NUI Galway. Among her many publications is *Social Change and Everyday Life in Ireland, 1850–1922* (Manchester, Manchester University Press, 2007).

CATHERINE COX is an Associate Professor in History at UCD. Her publications include *Negotiating Insanity in the Southeast of Ireland* (Manchester, Manchester University Press, 2012).

MARY E. DALY is Professor Emerita in Irish History at UCD. She is a former President of the Royal Irish Academy. Among her many publications is *The Slow Failure: Population Decline and Independent Ireland, 1920–76* (Madison, University of Wisconsin Press, 2006).

ANNE DOLAN is an Associate Professor of History at Trinity College Dublin. Her *Commemorating the Irish Civil War: History and Memory, 1923–2000* (Cambridge, Cambridge University Press) was published in 2003.

TERENCE DOOLEY is Director of the Centre for the Study of Historic Irish Houses and Estates, within the Department of History, at Maynooth University. His *The Decline and Fall of the Dukes of Leinster, 1872–1948* (Dublin, Four Courts Press) was published in 2014.

LINDSEY EARNER-BYRNE lectures in History in UCD. She is the author of *The Letters of the Catholic Poor: Poverty in Ireland, 1920–1940* (Cambridge University Press, 2017).

DAVID FITZPATRICK is Fellow Emeritus of Trinity College Dublin. His most recent book is *Descendancy: Irish Protestant Histories since 1795* (Cambridge University Press, 2014).

ROY FOSTER is Professor Emeritus of Irish History at Oxford University. His publications include a two-volume biography of W. B. Yeats and *Vivid Faces: The Revolutionary Generation in Ireland, 1890–1923* (London, W. W. Norton and Co., 2015).

BRIAN GIRVIN is an Honorary Professor in the School of Social and Political Sciences at the University of Glasgow. He edited (with G. Murphy) *Continuity, Change and Crisis in Contemporary Ireland* (London, Routledge, 2010).

ALVIN JACKSON is Sir Richard Lodge Professor of History at the University of Edinburgh. His *The Two Unions: Ireland, Scotland and the Survival of the United Kingdom, 1707–2007* was published by Oxford University Press in 2012.

MATTHEW KELLY is Professor of Modern History at Northumbria University. He published *The Fenian Ideal and Irish Nationalism, 1882–1916* (Boydell and Brewer, Woodbridge) in 2006.

MICHAEL KENNEDY is Executive Editor of the *Documents of Irish Foreign Policy Series* published under the auspices of the Royal Irish Academy.

FEARGHAL MCGARRY is Professor of Modern Irish History at Queen's University Belfast. His *The Rising: Ireland Easter 1916* was published by Oxford University Press in 2010.

Conor Mulvagh is a lecturer at UCD working on Commemoration and the Irish Revolutionary Decade (1912–1923). He is the author of *The Irish Parliamentary Party at Westminster, 1900–1918* (Manchester, Manchester University Press, 2016).

Paula Murphy is Professor Emerita in Art History at UCD. Her publications include *Sculpture, 1600–2000*, volume 3 in the *RIA Art and Architecture of Ireland* series (London and New Haven, Yale University Press) 2014.

Brian Ó Conchubhair is Associate Professor of Irish Language and Literature at the University of Notre Dame, Indiana. His publications include *Fin de Siècle na Gaeilge: Darwin, an Athbheochan agus smaointeoireacht na hEorpa* (An Clóchomhar, 2009).

Daithí Ó Corráin is a lecturer in History at Dublin City University. His *Rendering to God and Caesar: the Irish Churches and the Two States in Ireland* (Dublin, Four Courts Press) was published in 2006.

Gearóid Ó Tuathaigh is Professor Emeritus in History at NUI Galway. Among his many publications is *The GAA and Revolution in Ireland 1913–1923* (Cork, Collins Press, 2016).

John O'Hagan is Professor Emeritus of Economics at Trinity College Dublin. He edited (with C. Newman) *The Economy of Ireland: National and Sectoral Policy Issues* (Dublin, Gill & Macmillan, 12th edition 2014).

Eunan O'Halpin is the Bank of Ireland Professor of Contemporary Irish History at Trinity College Dublin. His most recent monograph is *Spying on Ireland: British Intelligence and Irish Neutrality during the Second World War* (Oxford, Oxford University Press, 2008).

Philip Ollerenshaw is an Associate Professor of History at the University of the West of England. His *Northern Ireland in the Second World War* (Manchester, Manchester University Press) was published in 2013.

Susannah Riordan is a lecturer in Irish History in UCD. She edited (with Catherine Cox) *Adolescence in Modern Irish History* (Dublin, UCD Press, 2015).

PAUL ROUSE is a lecturer in Irish History in UCD and the author of *Sport in Ireland: A History* (Oxford University Press, 2015).

ROBERT J. SAVAGE is Professor of the Practice of History at Boston College. He is the author of *The BBC's Irish Troubles: Television, Conflict and Northern Ireland* (Manchester, Manchester University Press, 2015).

General Acknowledgements

As General Editor of the Cambridge History of Ireland, I wish to express my gratitude to all those who assisted in bringing these four volumes to publication. My fellow editors, Brendan Smith, Jane Ohlmeyer and James Kelly have been unstinting with their time and unwavering in their determination to bring their respective volumes to completion as expeditiously as possible. John Cunningham offered vital editorial support at key points in this process. The team at Cambridge University Press, headed by Liz Friend-Smith, supported initially by Amanda George and latterly by Claire Sissen and Bethany Thomas, has been at all times enthusiastic about the project. It has been a great pleasure working with them. My thanks to the often unsung archivists whose documentary collections were freely drawn upon by the contributors in all volumes, to those who helped source images, and to those who drew the informative maps. Lastly, my warmest thanks to all the contributors who gave freely of their expertise in writing their chapters, and for their patience in awaiting publication of their efforts.

Thomas Bartlett, MRIA
General Editor, The Cambridge History of Ireland

Acknowledgements

In editing this volume, I have incurred many debts. My thanks to my fellow editors, Brendan Smith, Jane Ohlmeyer and James Kelly for their collegiality, solidarity and support in what was in every respect a collaborative venture. My thanks to John Cunningham for his editorial assistance. In editing volume 4, I sought advice from Nicholas Canny, Gearóid Ó Tuathaigh, James Smyth, Patrick Griffin, Kevin Whelan and Eamon Duffy, none of whom, be it said, are responsible for the final outcome. The team at Cambridge University Press, headed by Liz Friend-Smith, has been a pleasure to work with. As always, my thanks to the archivists who freely made available the documents on which these chapters draw. A special debt of gratitude is owed to Mary Broderick at the National Library of Ireland, and to Christian Dupont at the Burns Library in Boston College, for their assistance in sourcing images for this volume. Lastly, my thanks to the contributors for their patience during the completion of this volume and for their good humour in responding to my editorial interventions.

Thomas Bartlett
University of Aberdeen

Abbreviations and conventions

AOH	Ancient Order of Hibernians
BH	Bobbie Hanvey Photographic Archive, J. J. Burns Library, Boston College
BL	British Library
BMH	Bureau of Military History
CIÉ	Córas Iompair Éireann (Irish Transport Authority)
CRE	Commission for Racial Equality
DDA	Dublin Diocesan Archives
DÉ	Dáil Éireann
DIFP	Documents on Irish Foreign Policy (Royal Irish Academy)
DMP	Dublin Metropolitan Police
DUP	Democratic Unionist Party
EEC	European Economic Community
EU	European Union
FDI	Foreign Direct Investment
GAA	Gaelic Athletic Association
GHQ	General Head Quarters
GPO	General Post Office, Dublin
IAA	Irish Architectural Archive
IAOS	Irish Agricultural Organisation Society
ICA	Irish Country Women's Association
ICD	Irish Catholic Directory
IDA	Industrial Development Authority
IF	*Irish Freedom*
IHA	Irish Housewives' Association
IHS	*Irish Historical Studies*
IMA	Irish Medical Association
IMMA	Irish Museum of Modern Art

INTO	Irish National Teachers' Organisation
IPP	Irish Parliamentary Party
IRA	Irish Republican Army
IRB	Irish Republican Brotherhood
NAI	National Archives of Ireland
NARA	National Archives Records Administration
NESC	National Economic and Social Council
NGI	National Gallery of Ireland
NICRA	Northern Irish Civil Rights Association
NILP	Northern Ireland Labour Party
NIO	Northern Ireland Office
NLI	National Library of Ireland
NUI	National University of Ireland
PRONI	Public Record Office of Northern Ireland
RIC	Royal Irish Constabulary
RUC	Royal Ulster Constabulary
SAS	Special Air Service
SDLP	Social Democratic and Labour Party
SMA	Society for African Missions
SPIL	Society for the Preservation of the Irish Language
SSISI	Statistical and Social Inquiry Society of Ireland
TCD	Trinity College Dublin
TD	Teachta Dála (Dáil Deputy)
TNA	The National Archives, London
UCD	University College Dublin
UCDDA	UCD Department of Archives
UDA	Ulster Defence Association
UDL	Union Defence League
UDR	Ulster Defence Regiment
UIL	United Irish League
USC	Ulster Special Constabulary
UVF	Ulster Volunteer Force

General Introduction

The aims of this four-volume History of Ireland are quite straightforward. First, we seek to offer students, and the general reader, a detailed survey, based on the latest research, of the history of the island from early medieval times to the present. As with other Cambridge histories, a chronological approach, in the main, has been adopted, and there is a strong narrative spine to the four volumes. However, the periods covered in each volume are not the traditional ones and we hope that this may have the effect of forcing a re-evaluation of the familiar periodisation of Irish history and of the understanding it has tended to inspire. A single twist of the historical kaleidoscope can suggest – even reveal – new patterns, beginnings and endings. As well, among the one hundred or so chapters spread over the four volumes, there are many that adopt a reflective tone as well as strike a discursive note. There are also a number that tackle topics that have hitherto not found their way into the existing survey literature. Second, we have sought at all times to locate the history of Ireland in its broader context, whether European, Atlantic or, latterly, global. Ireland may be an island, but the people of the island for centuries have been dispersed throughout the world, with significant concentrations in certain countries, with the result that the history of Ireland and the history of the Irish people have never been coterminous. Lastly, the editors of the individual volumes – Brendan Smith, Jane Ohlmeyer, James Kelly and myself – have enlisted contributors who have, as well as a capacity for innovative historical research, demonstrated a talent for writing lucid prose. For history to have a social purpose – or indeed any point – it must be accessible, and in these volumes we have endeavoured to ensure that this is the case: readers will judge with what success.

Thomas Bartlett, MRIA
General Editor, The Cambridge History of Ireland

Preface

THOMAS BARTLETT

The period 1880–2016 in Irish history defies easy categorisation or simple generalisation. The historian surveying these years cannot but be left with an abiding sense of incompleteness. Issues such as sovereignty, land, language, religion, migration, culture and identity – that were troubling, even vexatious, at the end of the nineteenth century – remain unresolved though partly reformulated and stand surrounded by uncertainties in the second decade of the twenty-first century. The self-government – independence or 'Home Rule', the desire to 'take control' – that was the preferred objective of a large majority of Irish voters in the 1880s was conceded north and south by 1922, but it was done in a fragmented way and led to a fractured island. The 'sovereignty' acquired by the two Irelands that emerged from 'the decade of revolution', 1913–1923, was not at all what the 'South' (or Irish Free State) sought nor was it indeed what the 'North' (or Northern Ireland) desired. The partition of the island was viewed – at least *officially* in the Irish Free State – as an outrage that had, hopefully temporarily, halted the onward march of the Irish nation; by contrast, partition was seen almost immediately in Northern Ireland – at least by its Protestant majority, Northern Catholics were not at all enthusiastic – as the best possible outcome in that it guaranteed Unionist hegemony into the foreseeable future. In the event, the Irish Free State, set up following the Anglo-Irish War of 1919–1921, successfully extended its sovereignty during the interwar years, a process marked by the ratification of a new Irish constitution of 1937, Bunreacht na hÉireann, and culminating in the restoration of the 'Treaty ports' which had remained under British control, in 1938. However, the 'recovery' of the six counties of Northern Ireland proved impossible. The declaration of a republic in 1949 completed the process but the national sovereignty of the twenty-six counties was soon reduced by Ireland's accession to the European Economic Community (EEC) in 1973, and diminished further by the country's embrace of the concept of 'shared sovereignty' as the EEC morphed into the nascent European [political] Union (EU). For the most part, this evolution was broadly welcomed by the Irish public, but in the neighbouring island – Britain – which had joined 'Europe' at the same time as Ireland, it met with growing unease climaxing in the 'Brexit' vote of June 2016 to leave the EU altogether and 'take back control'. Northern Ireland (and Scotland, but not Wales) voted to remain in the EU, thus raising once again the threat of the break-up of the United Kingdom. Issues of sovereignty are destined to remain as uncertain into the future as they were in the 1880s.

Behind the issue of sovereignty lay questions of state formation and state survival. Both Northern Ireland and the Irish Free State were born out of war – civil, guerrilla or sectarian, on occasion a combination of all three – and, for many decades, both bore the scars of the conflicts attendant on their birth. Such circumstances were hardly propitious for survival, let alone thriving – as many states in Europe, post-1918, demonstrate. And yet, the two states survived, despite numerous challenges – sometimes economic, sometimes violent – the relationship between them currently can best be described as one of guarded engagement, much different to, and generally welcomed after, the frozen hostility that prevailed for much of the twentieth century. However, it would be foolish to claim, given a certain rapprochement between North and South and a joint commitment to the 'peace process' to end the 'Troubles' in the North, that Irish history has liberated itself from the centuries of ideological antagonism that long gave it definition. Low, perhaps very low, intensity conflict will continue for decades – the paramilitaries haven't gone away, you know – and the conditions for conflict remain. The unpredictable impact of the economic cycle may be compounded if the Brexit vote has the negative impact on Northern Ireland's economy that some predict; and, indeed, given the gloomy forecasts for the entire global economy, it may be that Ireland, North and South, is in for some stormy economic times.

If the quest for sovereignty has remained unfinished business, and relationships between North and South are far from cordial, those other vectors of the Irish story – land, language, religion – equally have proved disconcertingly elusive of resolution. True, the Land Question was *almost* solved under British rule but politicians in the new entities of Northern Ireland and the Irish Free State were constantly faced with rural discontent and they found plenty of agrarian issues demanding their attention. In addition, just as the

Land Question was indissolubly linked to Irish emigration, the failure to end, or even control for most of the twentieth century, the annual exodus of mostly rural dwellers – a flight not just from the land, but from Ireland itself – bore witness to the incompleteness of the supposed resolution of the Land Question. Similarly, the Language Question, the matter of the restoration of the Irish language as the vernacular of the people – a key objective for many of the revolutionary generation – has proved a disappointment. Notwithstanding many inducements, financial resources and patriotic exhortations, the decline of Irish has continued. Curiously, in the early decades of the twenty-first century, government-sponsored efforts are being made in Northern Ireland to revive 'Ulster-Scots', closely linked to the Scottish dialect of Lallans: initial signs are that the outcome here will not be all that different to that of the Irish language. So far as religion – a bedrock of Irish identity – is concerned, the decades from 1880 to 2016 could easily be styled 'The ascendancy and descendancy of the Catholic Church in Ireland', or some comparable formulation. The Catholic Church and its clergy and bishops until the 1960s, and perhaps beyond, exercised and enjoyed an influence that was without parallel in Europe (Spain under Franco and Portugal under Salazar are the only possible exceptions) and was likely only approached in some countries in South America. The church's views on a very broad range of issues – not just faith and morals – were eagerly sought, listened to attentively and frequently heeded by public representatives. Visually, the evidence for this dominance – to take just two vignettes – can be seen at the Eucharistic Congress of 1932, and at the funeral in 1940 of Archbishop Byrne, on both of which occasions large areas of Dublin, notably O'Connell Street and the surrounding area, were closed down in order to facilitate religious worship and public displays of Catholic allegiance. Such scenes are unimaginable in 2016. The Catholic Church's authority and influence, in decline since the 1960s, had fallen to an all time low by the second decade of the twenty-first century – a consequence of systemic weaknesses, secularisation and modernisation exacerbated by numerous cover-ups of the sexual and physical abuse of minors. When in August 2016 the Archbishop of Dublin, Diarmuid Martin, referred to the 'poisonous atmosphere' at St Patrick's College, Maynooth, the premier seminary for the formation of Irish priests since the 1790s, and drew attention to what he saw as a sexualised sub-culture at that institution, his strictures generated less surprise than expected: strikingly, anxiety, concern or outrage were rarely expressed by an Irish public that had long given up on, and had ceased to be shocked by, anything emanating from the once all-dominant Catholic Church in Ireland.

What of the Irish people during these decades? It is tempting to insist that, of course, they are better off now, that real progress has been made in diminishing poverty, that the standard of living is much improved, that the state and the state's institutions, and Irish society, North and South, are more caring, more tolerant or at least more humane than a hundred years ago; but it has proved to be a long road to arrive at this point, one paved with misguided intentions, flawed perspectives and heartless legalism. The promise of independence, of 'Sinn Féin' (=ourselves) the war-cry of the revolutionary generation, aspiring to take control, to do things right, proved illusory: women generally, children from poorer backgrounds, the socially marginal, the demographically surplus, the sexually deviant, the natural outsider, the writer, the artist, the maverick – unless monied – found Ireland, North and South, a cold house for much of the twentieth century; in many instances they still do.

Is this too bleak an assessment? Gaiety and laughter, fun and romance were not absent during these decades; gloom, doom and despond were not universal. Competitions organised by the Gaelic Athletic Association, at the national as well as the parish level, generated fervent enthusiasm, while music in the home after dark, dancing at the crossroads, horse-racing on the sands, conviviality in the pubs, the pleasures of radio listening and the cinema, and the consolations of religious worship were features of what have been dubbed, in deference to the French, '*les années noires*', the dark decades of Irish history. Together these activities brought much pleasure to the Irish people. No history that fails to recognise this reality or realities can truly be assessed as offering a rounded picture. And yet, conveying the realities of twentieth-century Irish life – the poverty and squalor, alongside the pride and contentment, the misery and separation jostling warmth and conviviality, the galling failure and triumphant success, the generosity with the hypocrisy is a taxing task.

Perhaps it was only in a petri dish occupied by these opposites that Irish literary talent could be incubated? Is it altogether accidental that Ireland during these decades produced four Nobel Prize winners in literature (William Butler Yeats 1865–1939), Samuel Beckett (1906–1989), George Bernard Shaw (1856–1950), and Seamus Heaney (1939–2013); five, if James Joyce (1882–1941) is accorded honorary status? By contrast, Scotland, with a similar population, though not with a similar violent recent history, had none. (Poland, Russia, Sweden, Spain, the United States and the United Kingdom all had similar numbers of Nobel laureates for literature, but all had multiples of the Irish population.) The story of twentieth-century Ireland is one of opposites: murder, mayhem and atrocity compete with high ideals, high mindedness and sacrifice, small differences – what foot does he dig with? – with ethnic exclusiveness: in short, great hatred with little room. These contrasts proved fertile soil for Irish writers. Beckett in *Waiting for Godot* has Vladimir asking: 'Well? What do we do'; 'Do nothing' answers Estragon, 'it's safer that way': his reply captured the suffocating atmosphere of Ireland in the mid-twentieth century. 'You coasted along' wrote John Hewitt (not, alas, a Nobel winner), similarly evoking successive Unionist governments' failure to adapt, evolve, or accommodate the nationalists in Northern Ireland in the years before the Troubles literally blew up.

The organisation of this volume requires explanation. The opening chapter by Ó Tuathaigh offers a road map through the entire period, and succeeding chapters dwell in depth on the highways and byways signposted therein. Thus the revolutionary tradition, constitutional politics, Unionist mobilisation and cultural revival in the years before 1914 are addressed by, respectively, Kelly, Mulvagh, Jackson, Foster and Ó Conchubhair. Social conditions and the Land Question are looked at afresh by Clear and Dooley, while Fitzpatrick explores the tangled story of Ireland and the Great War. McGarry offers a contemporary account of the revolutionary decade, while the history of the two Irelands during the inter-war period is discussed by Dolan and Riordan, concluding with Ollerenshaw drawing on recent research to describe the impact of World War II on both Northern Ireland and the Irish Free State. Post-war Irish politics and the fortunes of the Irish economies, North and South, are addressed by Girvin and O'Hagan: and war and peace in Northern Ireland during the tumultuous last decades of the twentieth century is the subject of a chapter by John and Paul Bew. There then follow a series of chapters that seek to take a long view of key issues and developments over the entire period, 1880–2016: family, and philanthropic and state institutions (Earner-Byrne, Cox), Irish foreign policy (Kennedy), media (Savage), the Catholic Church (Ó Corráin), memory and remembrance (Beiner), sport and leisure (Rouse), emigration (Daly) and art and architecture (Murphy). Lastly, O'Halpin offers some reflections on the tortuous course of Irish history since the 1880s, as Ireland evolved – some might prefer 'lurched' or 'staggered' – from an embedded, if discontented, member of the British Empire in 1880, to an embedded, if potentially unsettled, member of the European Union in 2016.

It will be seen at once that this is not a conventional, nor be it said, exhaustive, history of twentieth-century Ireland. Cumulatively, the historians in this volume have sought to convey the texture of Irish life in all its complexity over these decades and to highlight what they see as the key determinants of change and continuity. The picture that emerges cannot be a complete one, but rather it offers a fuller, more nuanced interpretative narrative of Ireland from the 1880s to the present than is currently available.

MAP 1. Map of Ireland.

Introduction: Ireland 1880–2016: Negotiating Sovereignty and Freedom

GEARÓID Ó TUATHAIGH

Introduction

By the late 1870s the effects of the Great Famine seemed to have worked themselves through the structure of the Irish economy and the fabric of Irish society. The drastic demographic check (of 1845–1855) had settled into what would remain an enduring pattern until the 1960s, with emigration rates generally outstripping the natural rate of population growth, resulting in a continuous population decline that was unique in Europe. Moreover, the high portion of the young and single in the emigrant outflow strengthened the conservative bias in many areas of Irish social and cultural life.[1]

The structure of the Irish economy had also taken firm shape. The balance of Irish agriculture (the bedrock of the economy) had shifted decisively towards grassland production. The range of successful, export-orientated manufacturing output was narrow and agri-related, with beer, whiskey, biscuits and a few niche luxury products prominent; otherwise, the manufacturing dispersed throughout the urban centres of the south and west was principally serving local demand. The commercial role of Dublin was important (as principal hub of trade with Britain and of wholesale distribution countrywide), with lesser port towns serving a similar role more locally. The underlying trends were clear: Ireland was firmly embedded in an increasingly integrated UK economy, with a well-developed communications system, and with rising literacy, as the adoption of English (and the abandonment of Irish) as the main vernacular advanced irreversibly.[2] The major exception to this profile was the north-east corner of Ulster, an expanding industrial enclave, based, from the mid-nineteenth century, on shipbuilding and a cluster of related industries that eclipsed linen as the mainstay of a local industrial zone

---

1 J. J. Lee, *The Modernisation of Irish Society, 1848–1918* (Dublin: Gill & Macmillan, 1973), 1–35.
2 C. Ó Gráda, *Ireland. A New Economic History 1780–1939* (Oxford University Press, 1994), 213–376.

that saw Belfast become the only recognisably industrial Victorian British city in Ireland.

By 1880 the Catholic Church in Ireland was reaching a position of remarkable cultural dominance over much of the country. An increasingly confident Catholic bourgeoisie, in town and country, fortified in its social and cultural influence by the thinning out through the Famine and post-Famine emigration of the rural underclass, supported the authority of an expanding establishment of religious personnel and institutional infrastructure (schools and health facilities as well as places of worship). The rich associational culture generated by this Catholic community was marked by a growing insistence on conformity, not only in relation to church teaching and religious observance, but also in social mores and behaviour. Its confidence was also the confidence of a missionary church, expanding throughout the Anglophone world.[3]

In Ulster, evangelical Protestant revivalism from the 1850s produced a heightened religious sense that rivalled the Catholic version. Allowing for clear distinctions between the Presbyterian and the Episcopal communities (in theology and devotional practice, and also in social and cultural life), the more fundamental cleavage was between Catholic and Protestant, running 'to a greater or lesser extent' through all spheres of social life.[4]

The extent to which Ireland seemed increasingly securely integrated into the British state and empire is striking. The economies of both islands were fully integrated. The pull of cultural integration was strong. A centrally administered system of elementary education resulted in rising levels of literacy in English. The Protestant hold on the higher reaches of the Irish administration remained strong (fuelling resentment among educated Catholics), but throughout the British Empire there were few impediments to profitable employment for ambitious Irish people in search of a career – in the army, civil service, professions, the stage and journalism, domestic service, nursing, and, at the lower end of the scale, the unskilled.[5]

3 P. Corish, *The Irish Catholic Experience: A Historical Survey* (Dublin: Gill & Macmillan, 1985), 192–258; D. W. Miller, *Church, State and Nation in Ireland, 1898–1921* (Pittsburgh, PA: University of Pittsburgh Press, 1973).

4 B. M. Walker, *Ulster Politics: The Formative Years, 1868–1886* (Belfast: Ulster Historical Foundation, 1989); for the contested world of sport, see P. Rouse, *Sport and Ireland: A History* (Oxford University Press, 2015), 149–242.

5 On Catholic social mobility pre-1914, see S. Pašeta, *Before the Revolution: Nationalism, Social Change and Ireland's Catholic Elite, 1879–1922* (Cork: Cork University Press, 1999); F. Campbell, *The Irish Establishment 1879–1914* (Oxford University Press, 2009); also, K. Jeffery (ed.), *An Irish Empire? Aspects of Ireland and the British Empire* (Manchester: Manchester University Press, 1996).

The closing years of the nineteenth century saw a strong reaction against this seemingly inexorable 'assimilationist' trend in Irish life. Across a broad cultural front – language, literature, arts and crafts, sport and, ultimately, politics – a cohort of activists stirred to challenge what they denounced as provincial and derivative and to advocate the cultivation of native (indigenous, authentic, Irish) cultural modes. Arnoldian Celticism and dollops of anti-modernist romanticism were strong ingredients. The anti-colonialist impulse – resentment at condescension – featured in the writings and propaganda of many of the challenging collectivity of cultural activists who produced a bumper crop of ideas, organisations and cultural works in the decades from 1880 to the eve of the Great War. Creativity, self-confidence and self-respect were watchwords of all the revivalist groups – against passivity, slack imitation and low self-esteem.[6]

Home Rule and its Critics

There is a sense in which a demand for some form of self-government may seem the natural political corollary of this broad wave of activism for confident, creative national development along 'Irish lines'. But the wave of cultural revivalism may also be read as a critique of the inadequacy or incompleteness of the demand for 'Home Rule', articulated as a claim for the restoration of the rights of an 'historic Irish nation', even as the remaining marks of distinct nationhood were being eroded and abandoned apace. This was the argument of Douglas Hyde and the Gaelic League and of the propagandists of the Irish-Ireland movement. But it also reflected an instinct of many cultural activists (whatever their position on the political or constitutional issue) that Catholicism should not be the default, defining characteristic of 'Irishness'.[7]

The solid electoral support for Home Rule (more than 80 per cent of the Irish parliamentary seats at all general elections in Ireland from 1885 to 1910) was a strong indication of general nationalist sentiment rather than

---

6 P. J. Mathews, *Revival: the Abbey Theatre, Sinn Féin, the Gaelic League and the Co-operative Movement* (Cork: Cork University Press for Field Day, 2003); R. F. Foster, *Vivid Faces: The Revolutionary Generation in Ireland 1890–1923* (London: Allen Lane, 2014); D. Kiberd and P. J. Mathews (eds.), *Handbook of the Irish Revival: An Anthology of Irish Cultural and Political Writings 1891–1922* (Dublin: Abbey Theatre Press, 2015).
7 Mathews, *op.cit.*; also T. G. McMahon, *Grand Opportunity. The Gaelic Revival and Irish Society, 1893–1910* (Syracuse: Syracuse University Press, 2008).

a stated preference for a specific constitutional formula. As Conor Cruise O'Brien perceptively remarked:

> The Irish electorate which voted for Home Rule did not consist of men who, having considered all possible constitutions for Ireland, decided that autonomy within the empire was the best solution. It consisted of men who wanted independence, who were assured by men whom they trusted that Home Rule was the best they could get, and re-assured, by the opposition of men whom they disliked, that Home Rule must be worth having. If the Unionist Ascendancy said that Home Rule was trafficking with treason and marching through rapine to the disintegration of the Empire, then Home Rule sounded all right.[8]

Likewise, it may be said that Irish unionist sentiment (especially in Ulster) clearly encompassed rational fears regarding what an Irish legislature with even limited powers might become – a stepping stone to a separatist Irish state with a triumphant Catholic majority and an inclination towards economic interventions (e.g., protectionist measures) that would jeopardise the economic prosperity of Ireland's few major exporting manufacturers, and, in particular, of east Ulster's industrial enclave. Moreover, unionist anxiety that Home Rule would be the harbinger of Rome rule had a rational basis, given the rise of ultramontanism and the visible evidence of Irish episcopal ambitions in, for example, the sphere of education. But Ulster unionist sentiment also reflected a more visceral anti-Catholicism, on theological grounds, but also on grounds of conscience, ethno-cultural historical fears and prejudices, seasoned with an ingrained colonial-settler sense of cultural superiority. With the progressive Ulsterisation of unionist militancy and resistance to Home Rule from the early twentieth century, this deep-seated instinct became crucial in mobilising popular Protestant opinion.[9]

Varieties of nationalism, socialism and (principally through the suffrage issue) early feminism – singly or in combination – provided the ideological passion for the Irish revolutionary 'generation of 1914', dedicated to achieving personal freedom and creating the 'good society'.[10] Self-help, creativity and innovation were their watchwords. Thus, in an Irish context, the 'vivid faces'

---

8 C. Cruise O'Brien (ed.), *The Shaping of Modern Ireland* (London: Routledge & Kegan Paul, 1960), 2.

9 A. Jackson, *The Ulster Party: Irish Unionists in the House of Commons, 1884–1911* (Oxford: Oxford University Press, 1989); P. Bew, *Ideology and the Irish Question: Ulster Unionism and Irish Nationalism 1912–1916* (Oxford: Oxford University Press, 1994), 1–70.

10 R. Wohl, *The Generation of 1914* (London: Weidenfeld and Nicolson, 1980); For an Irish family portrait, see D. McMahon (ed.), *The Moynihan Brothers in Peace and War 1909–1918: Their New Ireland* (Dublin and Portland, OR: Irish Academic Press, 2004).

open to the prospect of revolution (and active in organisations dedicated to radical, if not necessarily revolutionary, change in the cultural and political disposition of the country) were to be found in the Gaelic League, in literary and drama circles and in a host of more explicitly political causes and campaigns, as well as in suffragist, trade union and philanthropic organisations and activities.[11] Poets, artists, intellectuals and journalists featured prominently, but they were not the whole story of an impatient national revivalism. A rising cohort of the educated lower middle class anxious to 'move up' and a cadre of local leaders formed in the land struggles of 1879–1886, in the councils of the Gaelic Athletic Association, and, after 1899, in elected local government bodies, constituted its vital sinews.[12]

Yet, for all this energy and the profusion of ideas and talents, the commanding heights of not only the political but also the economic and social landscape of Edwardian Ireland were firmly held by the respectable bourgeois property-owners, in all parts of the island and among all denominations. The success of the Land League – the Land Acts of 1881–1906 leading to peasant-proprietorship – provided a solid foundation for an essentially conservative rural society, with a bourgeois leadership integrating comfortable farmers, shopkeepers, merchants, professions, commercial interests, journalists and clergy.[13] Land-hungry smallholders and the shrinking army of landless labourers could do little but swell the emigrant ranks or wait on ameliorative measures from the government or the church. There were, however, competing voices and visions. A whiff of Jacobinism clung to the clandestine Fenians. More robustly, on the left, the new trade unionism among the unskilled and the socialist message had gained a promising foothold within elements of the Irish working classes by the early twentieth century.[14]

And yet, the Catholic bourgeoisie was the dominant social formation for which the Home Rule party was the natural political vehicle. It stood for a firm commitment to constitutional politics, with a dash of literary Fenianism in its rhetoric, and an essentially conservative position on property, law and order, and social attitudes and behaviour. For all the personal rivalries and rancour that bedeviled the ranks of the Irish parliamentarians at Westminster

---

11 Foster, *op. cit.*, particularly 31–177.
12 *Ibid.* Also, T. Garvin, *Nationalist Revolutionaries in Ireland 1858–1928* (Oxford: Oxford University Press, 1987); P. Maume, *The Long Gestation: Irish Nationalist Life 1891–1918* (Dublin: Gill & Macmillan, 1999).
13 For the classic account of the 'challenging collectivity', see S. Clark, *Social Origins of the Irish Land War* (Princeton, NJ: Princeton University Press, 1979).
14 D. Nevin (ed.), *Trade Union Century* (Cork and Dublin: Mercier Press, 1994); E. O'Connor, *Syndicalism in Ireland, 1917–23* (Cork: Cork University Press, 1988).

(and among their supporters at home) there was a powerful imperative to keeping the 'politics of community' dominant, rather than allowing more divisive issues (notably class, but also other 'divisive' issues, such as women's suffrage) to intrude.[15]

The exception to this general profile was Ulster. Ulster was not uniformly different to the other provinces in its ethno-religious profile: Ulster's distinction was that it was in religious identities a more evenly divided province (44 per cent Catholic, 53 per cent Protestant in 1911). Communal politics were also paramount here, and the Protestant tenant farmers in Ulster were no less purposeful than those elsewhere during the land agitation in demanding the best deal available for themselves. But from the emergence of Home Rule, and certainly from its Parnellite triumph in the 1880s, two distinct communities, with opposing political positions, hardened and moved progressively into two mutually exclusive and totalising narratives of identity and political objective.

The associational culture – and not only through the Orange Order membership and the Catholic Ancient Order of Hibernians, but also direct church-centred religious and social practice – reinforced the underlying reality of two distinct confessional communities. In areas where economic competition or congested urban settlement and dislocation were most marked, confessional division sometimes descended into sectarian conflict. The Protestant bourgeoisie had, through the Orange and other loyal orders, a mechanism for ensuring the primacy of 'community' politics over alternative sirens of identity or interests. The 'politics of community' would endure, indeed solidify, proving resistant to sporadic challenges from cross-community, class-based initiatives and interventions, and comfortably keeping mainstream trade union-based or political labour firmly in its subordinate place into the post-1922 decades.[16]

Cultural and civic activism with a cross-community dimension was not entirely absent in Ulster.[17] But from at least the turn of the century the

---

15 For the continuing disruptive force of agrarian radicalism (notably land redistribution), see P. Bew, *Conflict and Conciliation in Ireland 1890–1910: Parnellites and Radical Agrarians* (Oxford: Oxford University Press, 1987); F. Campbell, *Land and Revolution: Nationalist Politics in the West of Ireland 1891–1921* (Oxford: Oxford University Press, 2005).

16 For a detailed examination of early tensions, see H. Patterson, *Class Conflict and Sectarianism: The Protestant Working-class and the Belfast Labour Movement, 1868–1920* (Belfast: Blackstaff Press, 1980).

17 For Protestant interest in the Gaelic Revival, see J. Bardon, *A History of Ulster* (Belfast: Blackstaff Press, 1992), 419–23; also D. Ó Doibhlin (ed.), *Duanaire Gaedhilge Róis Ní Ógáin* (Dublin: An Clóchomhar, 1995).

political polarisation that saw the strengthening of a distinct Ulster union-ist voice (distinct, that is, from the more dispersed southern unionists), was reflected in every sphere of life. Its early institutional forms anticipated the later partition realities. Thus, when Irish university education was reconfig-ured (from the old Royal University) in 1908, the new structure established a National University of Ireland with constituent colleges in Cork, Dublin (the old Catholic University) and Galway: but in Belfast, the stand-alone university was titled the Queen's University, Belfast.[18] If the Catholic bourgeoisie was the dominant element within the nationalist front, from 1905 the more asser-tive Ulster Protestant bourgeoisie took the initiative within Ulster unionism from the older landed leadership, intent on forging communal solidarity and harnessing to effective political purpose the more elemental sectarian pas-sions of 'the Orange street'.[19]

The Impact of the Great War, and its Aftermath

The introduction of the third Home Rule Bill in 1912 precipitated a succes-sion of political (and in time, military) shocks in Ireland that would last until 1923. The militarisation of political and, briefly in Dublin, industrial confron-tation happened quickly, with the founding of the Ulster Volunteer Force, the Citizen Army and the Irish Volunteers, all established during 1913. All were established with a declared defensive purpose. However, in common with a surging wave of militarisation across the continent of Europe (whether through state-controlled armies or an assortment of embryonic revolution-ary militias), the Irish volunteers were enthused by much heady rhetoric on the pure nobility of manly soldiering, and a corresponding contempt for the trimming and trading of the politics of persuasion and compromise, charac-teristic of representative parliamentary government.[20]

This surging wave crested in 1914. The outbreak of war transformed the political landscape in Ireland. It allowed the intractable problem of Ulster to be deferred until the war's end, and it provided the opening for both Redmond and Carson to establish firm *bona fides* for their preferred (if clearly

---

18 T. Dunne (ed.), *The National University of Ireland 1908–2008* (Dublin: UCD Press, 2008); T. W. Moody and J. C. Beckett, *Queen's Belfast 1845–1949: The History of a University* (London: Faber and Faber, 1959).
19 A. Jackson, *Ireland 1798–1998* (Oxford: Blackwell, 1999), 215–44; T. Bowman, *Carson's Army: The Ulster Volunteer Force 1910–1922* (Manchester: Manchester University Press, 2007).
20 See Foster, *Vivid Faces*, 221–57.

incompatible) solutions to the impasse; by urging their respective volunteer corps to join the war effort. However, for all Redmond's authority he faced opposition: a minority voice, but a vital one. A cluster of anti-recruitment groups openly campaigned against the war. Not all of these were pacifists. The socialists led by Connolly opposed a capitalist war between rival greedy empires and called for international solidarity between the working classes in resisting war. And the clandestine Irish republican movement – the Irish Republican Brotherhood – on both sides of the Atlantic was intent, as its revolutionary credo decreed, on using the war (and 'England's difficulty') as Ireland's opportunity to stage an armed revolt against British rule and to establish an Irish republic by force of arms.

The 1916 Rising was a relatively minor military episode, with fatalities no higher than 470 (the majority, civilians). However, the British response to the Rising was the trigger for a decisive shift in public opinion among the nationalist population, a shift on which the leaders of the Rising had gambled. The execution of fifteen of the leaders and the arrest of more than 3,500 others, many of whom had been active in cultural nationalist movements but had no connection with the Rising, had a significant impact on public opinion. As details of the lives (and bearing in death) of the rebel leaders became known, admiration for their ideals and character, if not yet retrospective approval of their actions, spread widely.[21]

The British mistakenly named the Rising a 'Sinn Féin' rebellion, thereby ensuring that 'Sinn Féin' now became a flag of convenience for all advanced nationalists who were prepared to praise the courage and ideals of the 1916 leaders and endorse the separatist cause for which they died. The end of 1917 (with the return of the interned prisoners and a new burst of organising) saw the launch of a reorganised Sinn Féin, with the surviving Rising commandant, Éamon de Valera, as president. The resurgent Sinn Féin placed itself at the head of the pan-nationalist opposition to the threat of conscription in Ireland during 1918. But the nationalist demand for 'self-determination', bought in blood by the 1916 sacrifice, had now moved on from Home Rule; for some, it had now moved to a non-negotiable republic.[22]

Ulster unionists had also paid heavily in blood for their devotion to empire and the cause of the Union, notably at the Somme in July 1916. They were no more accommodating regarding Home Rule in late 1916 or during 1917 than

---

21 On the Rising, see C. Townshend, *Easter 1916: The Irish Rebellion* (London: Allen Lane, 2005); F. McGarry, *The Rising. Ireland: Easter 1916* (Oxford University Press, 2010).

22 M. Laffan, *The Resurrection of Ireland. The Sinn Féin Party 1916–1923* (Cambridge University Press, 1999).

they had been during 1913–1914. The war years polarised further nationalist and Ulster unionist positions. With the general election at the end of 1918, under an enlarged electorate, the victory of Sinn Féin throughout most of nationalist Ireland set the bar high for the constitutional status of the Irish national state that was now being demanded. However, the Ulster unionists, with a majority of the seats in Ulster, were no less firm in their resolve to remain within the union. Some form of partition settlement was now inevitable. The issue, as indeed it had been since 1913, was its territorial extent and the duration of 'Ulster's' exclusion from an Irish Home Rule state.[23]

In January 1919, the inaugural meeting of the secessionist assembly (Dáil Éireann) in Dublin, attended by elected Sinn Féin deputies, reaffirmed the already declared Irish Republic, established a rival apparatus of government, and sent delegates to seek recognition of the Irish State at the peace talks in Paris. The opening of the Dáil was also accompanied by the first military action against crown forces (a few policemen) by the reconstituted Irish Volunteers (or Irish Republican Army – IRA as it became known). The War of Independence (1919–1921) was a guerilla campaign, prosecuted unevenly across limited areas of the country by IRA volunteers against crown forces. It was not a war that lent itself to a decisive victory for either side. The political pressures to find a solution were considerable, on both sides. Public opinion at home and abroad (notably in the United States and the dominions, where constituencies of the Irish diaspora were exercised by events in the homeland) pressed the British government to reach an accommodation. The IRA capacity to fight was not inexhaustible.[24] The elected Dáil may have succeeded in raising finance and maintaining a rudimentary apparatus of public administration and justice, but it was a constant challenge for it to gain the unequivocal recognition of its authority from the military leadership of the IRA. Moreover, given the nature of the guerilla campaign in the unsettled conditions of 1919–1921, the military leadership enjoyed primacy of authority over the political. In fact, for a solid core of die-hard republicans, the vesting of ultimate authority in the army command was the only cast-iron protection of the republic against backsliding by compromising politicians.[25] This

23 *Idem., The Partition of Ireland, 1911–1925* (Dundalk: Dublin Historical Association, 1983).

24 The revolutionary years are best covered in C. Townshend, *The Republic. The Fight for Irish Independence, 1918–1923* (London: Allen Lane, 2013); D. Ferriter, *A Nation and not a Rabble: The Irish Revolution 1913–1923* (London: Profile Books, 2015); P. Hart, *The I.R.A. at War 1916–1923* (Oxford University Press, 1993).

25 For close study of military/civilian tension, see T. Garvin, *1922: The Birth of Irish Democracy* (Dublin: Gill & Macmillan, 1996).

suspicion of the tribe of politicians was not unique to militant Irish republicans in the aftermath of the Great War, nor would it be confined to the short revolutionary interval of 1919–1921. On the contrary, the tortuous issue of the relationship of the army of the republic (the IRA) to the evolving (and democratically endorsed) structures of Irish government after 1922, would cast a long shadow on Irish politics and insurrectionary action for the rest of the century.[26]

If the establishment of an Irish Free State represented the best that could be wrested from Britain in 1921, it was clearly, in territorial extent and constitutional status, considerably less than the Irish republic for which the martyrs of 1916 had died. Yet, when Civil War erupted in 1922/23 it was not (as was feared and highly possible during 1913–1916) a military conflict between armed UVF and armed Irish Volunteers, but a split within Sinn Féin and the IRA on the constitutional status of the Irish national 'state' to be established as a result of the Anglo-Irish Treaty. Partition scarcely featured in the bitter Dáil debate on the Treaty. The British government had already taken what would prove to be the decisive step in resolving the 'Ulster Question' left over from the autumn of 1914, with the Government of Ireland Act in 1920, establishing two subsidiary 'Home Rule' parliaments (with limited devolved functions under Westminster control) in Ireland; one in Belfast for six counties in Ulster and the other in Dublin for the remaining 26 counties. The offer fell well short of the minimum the Sinn Féin-controlled Dáil would accept (to say nothing of republican militants in the IRA leadership). In July 1921 a truce opened the way for the negotiations that would conclude with the Treaty of December 1921 and the establishment of a 26-county Irish Free State with dominion status.

So far as the issue of Partition was concerned, by the end of 1921 the bird had flown. The Ulster Unionists maximised the territory they could take, consistent with a secure, permanent majority for unionist dominance, and established in Belfast the devolved administration provided for in the 1920 Act. The priority was security, not only against the external 'threat', but, more urgently, security against the enemy within. This enemy was, in effect, the Catholic, nationalist minority (about a third of the population), lodged

---

26 For historical context, see M. Mulholland, 'Political Violence', in R. Bourke and Ian McBride (eds.), *The Princeton History of Modern Ireland* (Princeton, NJ: Princeton University Press, 2016), 382–402; for the republican mindset, see R. W. White, *Ruairí Ó Brádaigh: The Life and Politics of an Irish Revolutionary* (Indianapolis, IN: University of Indiana Press, 2006).

against its wishes in Northern Ireland, severed from the larger 'majority' nationalist community on the island of which it felt itself an integral part.[27]

The establishment by the new northern administration of a special constabulary force – in effect, a Protestant citizen militia – enforced at a local level the majoritarian will upon which the northern state had been established. The threat posed by the IRA was no doubt real, but it was exaggerated by the Belfast regime, not only during 1920–1922 but also at regular intervals in later decades. Collins may have been prepared to countenance covert support for IRA actions within the six counties; but the strains of the War of Independence in the most active areas of the other three provinces, followed by the bitter internecine conflict of the Civil War, meant that the Dublin government was unable to provide any practical support (militarily or in any other way) to the nationalist minority in Northern Ireland.[28]

The sorry chapter of the Boundary Commission, provided for in the Treaty as a sop to nationalists, closed in 1925 with an agreement between Dublin and London to abide by the territorial status quo. Neither government had the appetite to pursue the matter further.[29] The Border, for all the nationalist protests, was a reality accepted by both governments and by the Ulster unionist leadership. The northern nationalist minority would have to live with it. And so too would the smaller unionist minority within the Irish Free State. Though many southern unionists had reluctantly come to accept the inevitability of Home Rule – and of some form of Partition – before the outbreak of war in 1914, the impact of the events of 1916 and the subsequent turn of Irish nationalism in a more separatist direction from 1917, followed by the trauma of the War of Independence and Civil War years (in which many southern Protestants/unionists, with traditional loyalty to the crown and its forces, suffered reprisals, intimidation and destruction of property) sapped the morale of the southern Protestant community. War losses, the trauma of the independence struggle, and anxiety at what lay in store, took its toll on the southern unionists, prompting some to uproot and leave.[30] Those who remained had to accept, as had the nationalists in the north, that by 1925

---

27 E. Phoenix, *Northern Nationalism: Nationalist Politics, Partition and the Catholic Minority in Northern Ireland 1890–1940* (Belfast: Ulster Historical Foundation, 1994); M. Harris, *The Catholic Church and the Foundation of the Northern Ireland State* (Cork: Cork University Press, 1993).

28 On the issue of early recognition of Northern Ireland by nationalists, regarding the payment of teachers' salaries, see Phoenix, *op.cit.*, 209–12.

29 J. J. Lee, *Ireland 1912–1985: Politics and Society* (Cambridge: Cambridge University Press, 1989), 140–50.

30 A. Bielenberg, 'Exodus: The Emigration of Southern Irish Protestants during the Irish War of Independence and the Civil War', *Past and Present*, 218 (February 2013), 199–233.

Partition was firmly established. The minorities on both sides of what was now an international border had to come to terms with their new reality. It was a fate they shared with millions of others in post-war Europe.

By the early 1920s irredentism was rife from the Baltic to the Balkans, with ethnic minorities trapped on the 'wrong' side of the boundaries of many new states. In the light of the historical experience of several of these European minorities in later decades, it is reasonable to ask whether the fate of the Irish minorities under Partition was the worst that could have befallen them. Disappointed, disaffected and fearful many of them undoubtedly were in the aftermath of 1922. But what mattered now was how they would be treated in their new situation, and whether (and to what extent) they might be reconciled to these new circumstances.

Conservative Paths, 1922–1965

The years after 1922 saw both Irish states consolidate their authority and establish effective law and order after the turbulence of the revolutionary decade. A fusion of confessional and political loyalties was the dominant feature of the mutually exclusive national identities proclaimed by the two states and incorporated in their symbols, public rhetoric and rituals. The laws and regulations of each state, allowing for their very different competences, reflected confessional majoritarianism in each case. In both states, constitutional status was the presiding imperative of government policy; in both, the politics of community identity prevailed.[31]

The decades following the end of the Civil War were marked in the Irish Free State by the relentless enlargement of Irish sovereignty, from the stretching of dominion status in the 1920s through de Valera's more aggressive measures in the 1930s, the 1937 constitution (establishing a republic in all but name) and the assertion of unfettered sovereignty through maintaining neutrality in World War II.[32] The formal declaration of a republic (and the final departure from the Commonwealth) in 1949 caused little excitement in Anglo-Irish relations, though it prompted the British government headed by Clement Atlee to pass the Ireland Act, guaranteeing that Northern Ireland would not cease to be a part of the UK until its parliament should decide

---

31 For a sharp comparative analysis, see D. Fitzpatrick, *The Two Irelands 1912–1939* (Oxford University Press, 1998).

32 For a sympathetic commentary, see D. Ferriter, *Judging Dev* (Dublin: Royal Irish Academy, 2007), esp. 123–93.

so.[33] Moreover, the determination to establish a distinct Irish 'voice' in international affairs was evident from the outset, in forceful contributions at the League of Nations and later, from 1955, at the United Nations (UN).[34] As for Northern Ireland, its status within the UK was never threatened after 1925. De Valera's march to the republic and continuing anti-partitionist rhetoric in the south served to fortify unionist resolve and the 1949 Act merely copper-fastened the constitutional status quo.

The two states were, essentially, confessional in character, but with marked differences. Craig explicitly proclaimed the Protestant character of the northern state, with his reference to a 'Protestant parliament and a Protestant state'.[35] The Unionist dominance (the very basis of the Northern Ireland state) reached, in time, into all aspects of political, economic and social life: the manipulated electoral system; the broadcasting media; sabbatarianism in restricting access to recreation facilities; preferential or exclusive dealings in public housing allocation, and in all areas of public expenditure in which political influence could be deployed. Security against the 'enemy within' was the province of an almost exclusively Protestant formation, the Ulster Special Constabulary, and, in addition, there was the exclusive dominance of the public or civic sphere by the symbols and rituals of the majority.[36]

The associational culture of the nationalist minority was marked by its own symbols (flags and emblems, names of sporting clubs), and republican and moderate nationalist politics asserted an alternative version of identity and political allegiance.[37] This tight communal politics did not go uncontested. Social distress and unemployment spikes, notably in the 1930s, produced occasional flurries of labour- or class-based politics. But these never

---

33 I. McCabe, *A Diplomatic History of Ireland, 1948–49: The Republic, the Commonwealth and NATO* (Dublin: Irish Academic Press, 1991).

34 M. Kennedy, *Ireland and the League of Nations 1919–1946* (Dublin and Portland, OR: Irish Academic Press, 1996); J. M. Skelly, *Irish Diplomacy at the United Nations 1945–1965: National Interests and the International Order* (Dublin and Portland, OR: Irish Academic Press, 1997); M. Kennedy and J. M. Skelly (eds.), *Irish Foreign Policy 1919–1966* (Dublin: Four Courts Press, 2000).

35 Northern Ireland House of Commons Debates, Official Report (Belfast: HMSO), vol. 34, col. 1095 (24 April 1934).

36 B. Follis, *A State under Siege: The Establishment of Northern Ireland, 1920–1925* (Oxford University Press, 1995); M. Farrell, *Northern Ireland: The Orange State* (London: Pluto, 1980); P. Buckland, *The Factory of Grievances: Devolved Government in Northern Ireland, 1921–1939* (Dublin: Gill & Macmillan, 1979).

37 Harris, *op. cit.*; for the long view, see M. Elliott, *The Catholics of Ulster: A history* (London: Allen Lane, 2000), and a case-study, A. C. Hepburn, *A Past Apart: Studies in the History of Catholic Belfast, 1856–1956* (Belfast: Ulster Historical Foundation, 1996).

posed a sustained electoral challenge or the threat of insurgency.[38] The communal politics of rival ethno-religious identities was normally strong enough (not least when manipulated by local political leadership) to drown out any clamour for class solidarity.

The southern state was formally more open and inclusive of all religious persuasions, guaranteeing religious freedom and citizens' equality through a written constitution, boasting a Protestant scholar (Douglas Hyde) as its first president, and with official republican rhetoric continuously invoking the tradition of Protestant nationalists and the ideals of the United Irishmen. The practices of the central government of the state were not infected with sectarian bias, though clearly there were incidents of jobbery at local level. Yet, the confessional character of the state was unmistakable in daily life.[39]

The constitution and statute law reflected Catholic moral and social teaching in sensitive areas, such as marriage and the family, contraception and family planning, and censorship (print and cinema). Indeed, social cohesion, such as it was, was the outcome of high levels of conformity to the social values and teaching of the Catholic Church. This was not surprising. Constituting over 90 per cent of the population of the Irish national state, with overwhelming control of schools and commanding a network of church-run hospitals and charitable institutions, the Catholic Church infrastructure gave it enormous influence on all aspects of life. Politicians – for the most part – were deferential or politically attentive to the wishes and the warnings of bishops. A formidable network of organised Catholic laity exercised a wide supervisory and morally vigilant role in the main arteries of social life – from charitable organisations to library committees – ensuring that all such bodies, public or voluntary, would do 'the right thing' by the church.[40]

Sexual behaviour and women's reproductive capacity were the most sensitive areas in which Catholic Church teaching sought to exercise control of public policy and morals. And yet, however strong the obedience of the Catholic laity to church teaching and clerical direction – and the legislators must be included here – the level of conformity and the social conservatism

---

38 See P. Devlin, *Yes, We Have No Bananas: Outdoor relief in Belfast 1920–1939* (Belfast: Blackstaff Press, 1981).

39 For a measured southern Protestant critique, see W. B. Stanford's pamphlet, *Faith and Faction in Ireland Now* (Dublin and Belfast: APCK, 1946); Hubert Butler provided a humane, free-thinking witness – see J. McGuire and J. Quinn (eds.), *Dictionary of Irish Biography*, volume 2 (Cambridge University Press, 2009), 121–3.

40 The standard is J. H.Whyte, *Church and State in Modern Ireland 1923–1971* (Dublin: Gill & Macmillan, 1971); for a trenchant commentary, T. Inglis, *Moral Monopoly: The Rise and Fall of the Catholic Church in Modern Ireland* (2nd edn., Dublin: Gill & Macmillan, 1998).

of Irish society in the decades following the establishment of the Irish Free State is unimaginable in the absence of continuing emigration from the state in these decades. From the 1930s, Britain was the destination for the great majority of these emigrants. This 'safety valve' decanted, inter alia, surplus labour from an underperforming economy; potential political dissenters; social 'problems' (such as single mothers) who could not be discreetly locked away in charitable institutions at home; the sexually and socially frustrated; and writers and artists.[41]

This clericalist and, for many, claustrophobic climate faced sharp criticism, often framed in terms of betrayal of the liberation hopes and aspirations of the revolutionary generation. Not all dissident writers went into exile, nor all socialist republicans, activists for women's rights or Protestant libertarians. The official leadership of the Protestant minority (the bishops, business and professional classes) offered their honest views to government when consulted. But mostly they followed a quietist route so far as the confessional character of the new state was concerned, probably relieved that their generally elevated socio-economic status was not threatened. In size and circumstance, the southern Protestant minority was very different to the Catholic minority in the north.[42]

Perhaps the most notable casualty of this subordination of 'freedoms' to sovereignty was the manner in which women – vitally present in the revolutionary wave in a host of causes – were decisively constrained in exercising an active public role and relegated, in so far as state rules and practices could ensure, to the domestic sphere of childrearing and homemaking. There was spirited – but for the most part unavailing – opposition to this reduced role from a succession of women's groups, and from the more radical elements of the trade union movement. But it would be the 1970s before the mapping of new contours of freedom and equality for women (as had been the revolutionary legacy) would be energetically renewed.[43]

---

41 M. E. Daly, *The Slow Failure. Population Decline and Independent Ireland 1920–1973* (Madison, WI: University of Wisconsin Press, 2006); E. Delaney, *Demography, State and Society: Irish Migration to Britain 1921–1971* (Liverpool: Liverpool University Press, 2000).

42 A. Ford, J. McGuire and K. Milne (eds.), *As by Law Established: The Church of Ireland since the Reformation* (Dublin: Lilliput Press, 1995); R. B. McDowell, *Crisis and Decline: The Fate of the Southern Unionists* (Dublin: Lilliput Press, 1997); J. White, *Minority Report: The Protestant Community in the Republic of Ireland* (Dublin: Gill & Macmillan, 1975).

43 R. C. Owens, *A Social History of Women in Ireland* (Dublin: Gill & Macmillan, 2005); M. O'Dowd and M. Valiulis (eds.), *Women and Irish History; Essays in Honour of Margaret McCurtain* (Dublin: Wolfhound Press, 1997).

In 1918 Irish labour elected to 'wait' on the resolution of the national question. It would continue to wait. The trade union movement, for all its chronic splintering, retained an all-island structure. However, both unions and political labour had to accommodate to the communal politics dominant in both jurisdictions. Labour in the Dáil edged successive centrist governments a little to the left – in terms of social welfare and equality issues. Occasional bursts of social protest in the streets (for example, unemployment and tax marches) testified to continuing radical vitality, north and south, but never threatened to precipitate a decisive realignment of politics along class lines.[44]

In terms of state-building, economic policy and the creation of social and cultural order, the exercise of sovereignty by the Irish national state was also markedly conservative. There was little innovation (apart from new nomenclature) in the structures of government and administration: the Whitehall model (including the primacy of the Department of Finance) was generally followed. As it was under the Union, so it would remain – a highly centralised apparatus of government and administration.[45] However, and revealingly, the new state abolished the 'Poor Law' system and decided to establish a preponderantly unarmed police force.

Perhaps the most ambitious initiative undertaken by the southern government, in seeking to realise the national regeneration agenda of the revolutionary era, was the commitment to restore the Irish language as the main vernacular. Given the historical circumstances of its decline and its perilous state by the end of the nineteenth century, and given Ireland's geo-cultural location on the superhighway of the Atlantic Anglophone world of the twentieth-century mass media, this was a daunting ambition. Concentrating on teaching the language in the schools, modest progress was made over many decades in producing cohorts of competent secondary bilinguals and in generating a lively literature in modern Irish. But the lack of a coherent strategy for turning acquired competence into general use, and the relentless erosion of the base-communities of native speakers, sapped early enthusiasm and, for many, belief in the achievability of the aim. Relentless political

---

44 F. Lane and D. Ó Drisceoil (eds.), *Politics and the Irish Working Class 1830–1945* (Basingstoke: Palgrave Macmillan, 2005); N. Puirséil, *The Irish Labour Party 1922–73* (Dublin: UCD Press, 2007); E. O'Connor, *A Labour History of Ireland, 1824–2000* (Dublin: UCD Press, 2nd edn., 2011).

45 R. Fanning, 'Britain's Legacy: Government and Administration', in P. J. Drudy (ed.), *Ireland and Britain since 1922* (Cambridge: Cambridge University Press, 1986), 45–64.

exhortation bred cynicism and resentment that by the end of the 1950s was but an aspect of a wider disillusion with the fruits of sovereignty.[46]

In neither of the Irish states did the economy perform impressively in the decades after Partition. For Northern Ireland the halcyon days of its nineteenth-century industrial staples were past by the 1920s, though the exceptional war-time demands (1939–1945) brought a temporary recovery. International trading conditions and the inexorable shrinking of Britain's imperial reach had serious consequences for the British economy and pre-sented difficult economic challenges to Northern Ireland leaders through the 1950s and 1960s. Those tasked with attracting new industry had to contend not only with international competition but also with the particular politi-cal and religious imperatives operating in the north's divided society. Living standards in Northern Ireland, however, were not dependent on the state of the economy. From the late 1920s, following the alteration of the basis for Northern Ireland's contribution to the UK exchequer, maintaining living standards there at UK levels (in welfare, health, education, infrastructure, communications) required continuous subsidies from London. This became especially important after 1945 with the establishment of the 'Welfare State' across the UK.[47]

The economic policy of the Irish Free State of the 1920s was largely one of free trade: minimally disruptive of the existing structure of the economy and trade, with agricultural exports for the British market the bedrock. Monetary and fiscal policy were tightly conservative. A notable exception to the gen-eral fiscal caution was the massive state-sponsored hydroelectric plant on the Shannon sanctioned in 1925. This interventionist tendency – on a case-by-case basis, where a recognised national strategic need had been identified – would be a feature of successive Irish governments in later decades, and would result in a varied portfolio of state and semi-state bodies.

The great obsession of the de Valera governments after 1932 was the Holy Grail of self-sufficiency. Import substitution would underpin the establish-ment of an Irish manufacturing base, under Irish ownership. The protection-ist surge in economic policy from 1932 was at its most intense in the early years, when it was exacerbated by the tariff war with Britain resulting from de

---

46 For perspectives on the language question, B. Ó Cuív (ed.), *A View of the Irish Language* (Dublin: Government Stationery Office, 1969) and for revisionist views, C. Nic Pháidín and S. Ó Cearnaigh (eds.), *A New View of the Irish Language* (Dublin: Cois Life, 2008).

47 On the economy of both states in the twentieth century, see A. Bielenberg and R. Ryan, *An Economic History of Ireland since Independence* (London: Routledge, 2013); also useful is K. A. Kennedy, T. Giblin and D. McHugh, *The Economic Development of Ireland in the Twentieth Century* (London and New York: Routledge, 1988).

Valera's decision to unilaterally suspend payment of the land annuities debt due to Britain under the 1922 Treaty. This short tariff war was severely disruptive of the Irish economy. But already by 1935, the Coal-Cattle pact signalled a realisation that Ireland needed to import coal and that Britain wanted to buy Irish cattle. The annuities dispute was settled in 1938, but a protectionist regime was maintained throughout the de Valera era, and into the 1960s. Modest increases in industrial employment and the creation of a (mainly unambitious) native entrepreneurial cohort did not provide the basis for sustaining even modest economic growth.[48]

The shortages and rationing during the war years revealed starkly the unattainability of the goal of self-sufficiency. Some reconsideration of economic strategy was urgently needed. But in the aftermath of 1945 – with major new initiatives launched for European recovery – what is remarkable is how tardy, protracted and piecemeal the reconsideration and redirection of Irish economic policy turned out to be. Political volatility was as much a consequence as a cause of the indifferent political response to the economic challenges of the post-war decade. There was no shortage of voices demanding a radical new direction in the affairs of the state, including calls for an Irish version of the economic planning approach being adopted for post-war reconstruction in several European states (France, Italy). Moreover, the immediate post-war decade or so was punctuated by a series of initiatives in Irish economic policy that clearly acknowledged the areas where more focused action was to be undertaken and new structures established: in promoting exports, industrial investment, tourism, the fishing industry, management and industrial standards.[49] But these significant initiatives, crucial for the future direction of the Irish economy from the late 1950s, were not part of a coherent economic strategy, and throughout the fifties the Irish economy lurched from one crisis to another: with overall stagnation, deflationary dips in output and employment, and a crisis of confidence that saw net emigration of more than 400,000 in the decade. The fruits of political sovereignty had turned badly sour.[50] The forces resisting a more coherent radical approach included not

---

48 For interpretative perspectives, see M. E. Daly, *Industrial Development and Irish National Identity 1922–1939* (Dublin: Gill & Macmillan, 1992), and J. K. Jacobsen, *Chasing Progress in the Irish Republic* (Cambridge: Cambridge University Press, 1994). Also Lee, *Ireland 1912–1985*, 175–328.

49 Key initiatives included, Institute for Industrial Research & Standards (1946), Industrial Development Authority (1949), Córas Tráchtála (1951), Bord Iascaigh Mhara [=Irish Fishery Board] (1952), Bord Fáilte [=Irish Tourism Board] (1952), Irish Management Institute (1952), and Ireland joining the IMF in 1957.

50 T. Garvin, *News from a New Republic: Ireland in the 1950s* (Dublin: Gill & Macmillan, 2010); D. Keogh, F. O'Shea and C. Quinlan (eds.), *The Lost Decade: Ireland in the 1950s* (Cork and Dublin: Mercier Press, 2004).

only such predictable vested interests as inefficient protected industries and hyper-cautious civil servants, but also those for whom the concept of 'planning' was freighted with Soviet collectivist meaning.[51]

Radical corrective action could not be delayed indefinitely. Already in 1948/9 the decision to accept reconstruction loans from the Marshall Aid programme demanded some measure of planning.[52] The crisis of the 1950s finally forced a more expansive and ambitious economic new departure. The Lemass–Whitaker initiatives of 1958–1966 – with the launch of a series of economic plans – brought a degree of coherence to the articulation of a new direction in economic policy, whatever the shortcomings and inconsistencies of the actual plans themselves. Whether or not the initiative fully merits the description of a 'new departure' in economic strategy, it certainly reset the discourse of patriotism and national objectives, away from self-sufficiency and exhortations on Irish cultural identity and towards economic development and rising living standards.[53]

Taken with other developments – the inauguration of a national television service, the reciprocal visits of Seán Lemass and Terence O'Neill, the opening of access to free secondary education – there is a sound case for seeing the period 1958–1966 as a critical hinge on which the modern Irish state turned: from 'Ireland her own' to a more open engagement with, and address to, external forces (for exports, investment and ideas). Impatient explorations of the scope for enhanced individual freedoms, choices, opportunities and life-chances emerged to challenge the valorisation of frugal comfort, the hallowed deference to seniority and the cloying embrace of stability that, to many, had come to mean simply stagnation.

New Directions: Post-1960s Ireland

By the later 1960s the future trajectory of Irish society – in ideology, economy, politics and cultural direction – was becoming more clearly discernible. The eclipse of the vision and the values of 'de Valera's Ireland' was neither abrupt

---

51 M. E. Daly, *Sixties Ireland: Reshaping the Economy, State and Society* (Cambridge: Cambridge University Press, 2016) discusses these forces in detail; a more favourable view of post-war thinking is G. Murphy, *In Search of the Promised Land: The Politics of Post-War Ireland* (Cork and Dublin: Mercier Press, 2009).

52 B. Whelan, *Ireland and the Marshall Plan 1947–1957* (Dublin: Four Courts Press, 2000).

53 The positive view of the Lemass era is in Lee, *Ireland 1912–1985*; and in B. Girvin and G. Murphy (eds.), *The Lemass Era: Politics and Society in the Ireland of Seán Lemass* (Dublin: UCD Press, 2005); For a trenchant revisionist view, see M. E. Daly, *Sixties Ireland*. Also, R. Savage, *A Loss of Innocence? Television and Irish Society* (Manchester: Manchester University Press, 2010).

nor total. Yet, the underlying direction of the society and the economy had decisively shifted from protectionist self-sufficiency (however modified) to an aspiring small 'open' trading economy and a society avidly open to external cultural stimuli (still overwhelmingly from the Anglophone world). Not all sectors of Irish society embraced this new departure with equal ardour: but the new leadership cadre of 'modernisers' (in politics, the bureaucracy, business, the media and, fitfully, the universities) overwhelmingly espoused the aspiration for Ireland to join the European 'Common Market' (EEC).[54]

The fact that the Irish economy was inextricably linked to the British economy meant that Ireland's ambition to join the EEC was conditional on British entry. In the event it would be 1973 before Ireland and Britain gained membership of the EEC. In the Irish plebiscite on entry, a large majority (83 per cent) voted in favour of entry. Clearly, the new horizons of Irish ambition (articulated principally in terms of economic prosperity) enjoyed popular endorsement. Sovereignty would henceforth be shared. The new European setting in which both Ireland and Britain were now lodged would place both states, at least formally, on an equal footing.

There would be no dramatic repudiation of traditional national objectives: the reunification of the country and the restoration of the Irish language. But the first was quietly folded into the thawing of North–South relations signalled by the Lemass–O'Neill talks. De Valera's departure from political leadership had also opened the way for the official retreat from the aim of restoring Irish as the principal national language. From the early 1960s the declared objective of state policy was a conveniently imprecise commitment to bilingualism. The relegation of the 'language question' to the margins of real political debate would be a relentless process in the decades that followed, even as the actual communities of Irish-speakers showed continuing vigour in establishing new (largely urban) networks of Irish-language schools and a lively presence in popular mass media.[55]

From the outset Irish enthusiasm for the European project was principally powered by concrete expectations, namely the prospect of economic support for achieving higher living standards. Moreover, it was further claimed that the European setting would encourage wider comparative cultural perspectives. In the early years, Irish confidence seemed justified by the price supports delivered through the Common Agricultural Policy (CAP) and, more

---

54 D. J. Maher, *The Tortuous Path: The Course of Ireland's Entry into the EEC, 1948–1973* (Dublin: Institute of Public Administration, 1986).

55 Nic Pháidín and Ó Cearnaigh, *New View of the Irish Language*, 27–42.

modestly, by structural and regional funds. In a tight club of nine states dedicated to 'convergence', Ireland had obvious entitlements. However, the optimism that informed the strong Irish vote of 1972 was not without a lining of anxiety.

The opening up of the Irish market – in successive phases up to the completion of the Single Market – accelerated the demise of the more inefficient manufacturing firms established under the protectionist regime from the 1930s. More significantly, the relentless enlargement of the EEC (later EU), by the accession of generally poorer countries, put pressure on the CAP and European budgets and reduced Ireland's influence and entitlements. Enlargement altered the geo-political balance of the EU, and from the 1990s a reunited Germany inexorably began to exercise its natural weight. Changes in governance and voting systems – responding to the strains and complexity of continuous and rapid enlargement – further diminished Ireland's influence.

Anxiety at this shifting balance – and at the intrusions of a bureaucratic behemoth – led over time to a cooling of Irish enthusiasm for the European project. And yet, despite rejection by Irish voters of the Lisbon and Nice Treaties at the first time of asking, Ireland, having bought into the European idea, would not succumb to buyer's remorse. Ireland marched in step with each move to the creation of the Single Market and, crucially, the adoption of the single currency. In electing to adopt the Euro in 2002, the Irish government surrendered control of exchange rates and monetary policy, two of the principal competences historically vested in a sovereign national state. To this relentless voluntary surrender of sovereignty, only a minority of republican-socialist groups made regular protest.[56]

Perhaps the most vital economic advantage conferred by Ireland's steadfast commitment to the 'open' economy from the 1960s, was its attractiveness to the inward flow of Foreign Direct Investment (FDI), particularly from the USA. Indeed, with the tightening of the European Single Market framework in the late twentieth century, Ireland became a singularly attractive portal to the EU for US firms with a global or transnational reach, with favourable Irish corporate tax rates enhancing language and labour skill advantages. The Irish government minister who mused that, in terms of business culture and values, Ireland was 'closer to Boston than to Berlin' ('can-do' individualism versus collectivist social democracy), drew attention to the essential point, that from the 1970s Ireland had sought to face simultaneously east to

---

56 The social scientist, A. Coughlan, and the publications of the Irish Sovereignty Movement, provided consistent opposition to ever-deepening European union.

continental Europe and west to the US, in seeking to maximise its opportunities and secure its future prosperity.[57] The successes of the Irish diaspora – spectacularly so in the case of Irish America – provided invaluable leverage (and global prominence) for Ireland, the benefits of which extended beyond gains in tourism or an 'edge' in attracting inward investment.

Whatever the cost-benefit verdict might be, in strictly economic terms, on Ireland's EU experience, a combination of external shocks (including oil crises and accelerating global trade liberalisation) and poor management of the economy at home, generated a series of economic crises in the 1970s and 1980s, triggering a depressingly familiar reflex in the 1980s with a net emigrant outflow of about 500,000.[58] Severe corrective action and a series of neo-corporatist 'national agreements' between all the economic and social partners prepared the economy to take advantage of favourable international conditions and to achieve impressive economic growth in the 1990s and into the early years of the new century.

It might have been expected that British–Irish relations, in good shape in the mid-1960s, would have found much common ground for cooperation within the EEC. This optimistic prospect was seriously threatened, during the three decades after 1968, by violent civil strife in Northern Ireland, which extended sporadically into the Republic and into English cities, and beyond.[59] The 'Troubles' in Northern Ireland from the late 1960s did not originate in the fundamental terms of an internecine or inter-state conflict over sovereignty. A civil rights and equality campaign for the Catholic minority – deploying the repertoire of demonstrations, marches, sit-ins and meetings then characteristic of radical civil rights movements on both sides of the Atlantic – provoked resistance from die-hards within the Unionist government and, more crucially, from popular loyalism supported by 'their' police. The reformers in Stormont, under pressure from London, moved to implement reforms, but the centre could not hold and violence increased.

The escalating confrontation on the ground congealed before long into a recognisably elemental shape: with the re-emergence within Catholic/nationalist areas of a hitherto moribund IRA, initially as poorly armed defenders of

---

57 Address of Tánaiste, Mary Harney T. D. to the American Bar Association (meeting in Dublin) on 21 July 2000 – text in R. Aldous (ed.), *Great Irish Speeches* (London: 2007), 184–5.
58 For 1970s, D. Ferriter, *Ambiguous Republic. Ireland in the 1970s* (London: Profile Books, 2012); R. F. Foster, *Luck and the Irish: A Brief History of Change 1970–2000* (London: Allen Lane, 2007).
59 M. Mulholland, *The Longest War* (Oxford University Press, 2002); T. Hennessey, *Northern Ireland: The Origins of the Troubles* (Dublin: Gill & Macmillan, 2005).

their communities and later, as they became militarily more formidable and more ruthless, as a force dedicated to subverting the northern state and forcing a British 'withdrawal'. The British government, when finally moved to exert its ultimate authority, suspended the local administration (Stormont), sent in the army to restore public order, and undertook direct rule in Northern Ireland, while seeking to devise a new viable local administration that would enjoy cross-community support and ensure peace and an acceptable measure of political stability. As for the Irish government, a general sympathy in the south for the predicament of the nationalist/Catholic minority – and eruptions of popular outrage at particularly emotive episodes (Bloody Sunday, hunger strikes) – did not ultimately dislodge the steady pursuit by Dublin of essentially the same objective as London – an acceptable, inclusive cross-community administration in Northern Ireland, but – a crucial proviso – with Dublin's role as guarantor of such a settlement formally recognised. In the event, the search for such a new dispensation would be protracted.

The strategy of the British military and security chiefs predictably reverted to the fundamental role of defeating the terrorist threat to the state by all available means – including the dark arts of counter-insurgency. The republican and loyalist paramilitaries continually crossed new limits of ruthlessness. What resulted was almost three decades of violence, punctuated by a litany of atrocities and a noxious polarisation of the two communities that affected all aspects of life: bombings, abductions, assassinations, shootings, population displacement, torture, hunger strikes, internment without trial, intimidation and arson; together with contamination of the criminal justice system and serious trespass on civil liberties in all jurisdictions of the archipelago.

The oscillation between an emphasis on security priorities and the search for a political solution raised recurring difficulties in British–Irish relations, in which the personalities of political actors and their attention to the exigencies of domestic politics regularly queered the diplomatic pitch. Then, after many false starts, and the intervention of an assortment of intermediaries, the groundwork was completed for the Belfast Agreement of 1998. The careful choreography of the final elaborate accommodations required direct American mediation: but the political and diplomatic will, determination and capacity of key echelons of the establishment in Dublin and London, and the readiness of the main political leaders in Northern Ireland to commit to compromise, were crucial. Clearly evident in the accommodations were the lessons that had been painfully learned during the conflict. Acceptance of the principle of consent was the foundation stone of the settlement, symbolised by the simultaneous endorsement of the Agreement north and south.

The Belfast Agreement (with later refinements that brought the more irreconcilable elements of Paisleyite loyalism within the consensual arc) left the constitutional position of Northern Ireland under London authority fundamentally unchanged. The deletion (supported by 94 per cent of southern voters) from the 1937 constitution of Articles two and three – claiming sovereignty over the entire island – and their substitution by an aspiration for unification by consent of the people, was a crucial concession to unionist demands. However, the structures of power-sharing, joint citizenship and cross-border institutions signalled the end of simple majoritarianism; and the formal recognition of the Irish government as co-guarantor of the Agreement was elevated by the lodging of the Agreement as an international treaty at the UN.[60] The impact of the 'Troubles' had generated an intense, difficult and often bitter reassessment of traditional nationalist assumptions on re-unification and the Ulster problem, at the end of which parsing the dogma of sovereignty had yielded to guaranteeing equality and exploring new modalities of peaceful cohabitation within Northern Ireland and throughout the archipelago.[61]

Social Change

While the northern conflict absorbed huge energies and resources from all parties in Ireland, the wheels of the world did not stop turning. In fact, in the closing decades of the twentieth century the social climate and character of Irish society turned decisively in a liberal direction, with secularisation and urbanisation as key drivers. External influences – ideological and cultural – contributed to the shift: Western feminism, medical and media advances, the magnetic pull of cities worldwide. The impact of various European institutions (directives and court rulings) in such areas as women's rights and wider employment rights, was frequently the source or the catalyst of change in domestic law in Ireland in the decades from the 1970s.

But domestic agents of change were also central to setting the agenda and forcing the pace. These included a cohort of feminist activists, well embedded

---

60 A sharply critical commentary on the road to the 1998 Agreement is provided in P. Bew, *Ireland: The Politics of Enmity 1789–2006* (Oxford University Press, 2007), 486–555.

61 For assessments of the Belfast Agreement based on theoretical work on power-sharing by A. Lijphart, see J. McGarry and B. O'Leary, *The Northern Ireland Conflict: Consociational Engagements* (Oxford University Press, 2004), and *Understanding Northern Ireland: Colonialism, Control and Consociation* (London and New York: Routledge, 2009).

in media and effective in finding key arteries of political advocacy. More conventional organisational channels were also vital. The Commission on the Status of Women (1970) was a harbinger of the kind of vital groundwork (facts, figures and recommendations, experts and energetic lobbyists) on which the incremental progress of the following decades would depend. More dramatic episodes symbolised and accelerated the shift in status and in the public role of women. Mary Robinson's election as president in 1990 (liberal, human rights lawyer and prominent advocate of women's rights) made a powerful statement – domestically and internationally – on the direction of social change in Ireland.[62]

The political debate on sensitive issues of social change in these decades was regularly bruising. But for all the divisive rancour that marked the demand for legislative change during several of these campaigns, the tide of public opinion running in a liberal direction was not for turning: legalisation of contraception (1979) – initially on a restrictive basis, later relaxed; criminalisation of marital rape (1990); decriminalisation of homosexual acts (1993); divorce (1995); same-sex marriage (2015).

The dramatic weakening of the influence of the Catholic Church in Ireland was, of course, crucial to the direction and pace of change in these areas of individual choice and social values and behaviour, given the church's established 'moral monopoly' in these areas. The cumulative effect of declining vocations, widening employment opportunities through improved access to education, the changing realities 'on the ground', as it were, with regard to the behaviour of young people, the effect of cultural waves from the USA and the UK, mediated through mass media – all combined in shifting the ground. The enormous damage to the authority and standing of the Catholic Church, internationally but with particular ferocity in Catholic Ireland (with its far-flung spiritual empire among the Irish diaspora and in its missionary network), inflicted by the tsunami of sexual scandals and revelations of institutional abuse and cover-up, unquestionably hastened the pace of liberal change and unnerved the party of resistance from the 1990s.[63]

---

62 L. Connolly and T. O'Toole, *Documenting Irish Feminisms: The Second Wave* (Dublin: Woodfield Press, 2005).

63 L. Fuller, *Irish Catholicism since 1950: The Undoing of a Culture* (Dublin: Gill & Macmillan, 2004); For a lively personal perspective, see M. Kenny, *Goodbye to Catholic Ireland* (London: Sinclair-Stevenson, 1997); on the obsessive issue, see D. Ferriter, *Occasions of Sin: Sex and Society in Modern Ireland* (London: Profile Books, 2012).

Significantly, the enduring strength of religious convictions was much in evidence in Northern Ireland, where traditional Catholic teaching on sexual matters found common cause with a robustly conservative Protestant evangelical constituency, in opposition to key elements of the liberal agenda: for example, on homosexuality ('save Ulster from sodomy') and same-sex marriage. But, in truth, the central preoccupation in Northern Ireland over three decades with finding a solution to violent conflict and the constitutional question seriously retarded considered public discussion of economic modernisation and wider issues of social and cultural change. Moreover, giving substance in general social intercourse to the ideas of parity of esteem and shared responsibility embodied in the formal structures of government – in effect, normalising everyday life – would inevitably prove challenging, notwithstanding the reasonable expectation of a peace dividend for the economy. Ingrained attitudes rarely change suddenly. Legacy issues of the years of violence left dark shadows and rituals of assertion of local territorial control (and defence) continued to retain their potential to inflame.

There has been a severe assessment of the 'performance' of the independent Irish state in its first six decades – in terms of economic growth, living standards and population retention – compared to other small western and northern European nation states.[64] Among the more challenging cultural explanations suggested for this failure has been the persistence of a post-colonial intellectual dependency syndrome (specifically, a dependence on British models and ideas unsuited to dynamic state-building).[65] Yet, given the historical experience of many European states, large and small, in these decades, one may ask whether an Irish state that maintained peace, parliamentary democracy and the rule of law, and that, while ideologically secure within the Western camp, earned a reputation in international bodies as an honest broker and a dedicated contributor to peace-keeping, might not also merit a column of credit.[66] Emigration, Catholic conservatism and a dispersed property-owning middle class ensured the long dominance of cautious

---

64 Lee, *Ireland 1912–1985*, is the principal critic, 511–687; but B. Girvin's assessment of Ireland's 'performance' employs different comparators, *Between Two Worlds* (Dublin: Gill & Macmillan, 1989); see also Jacobsen, *op.cit.*

65 Lee, *op.cit.*; Girvin, *op.cit.* identifies Ireland as a semi-peripheral state, between the First and Third World; for the case against a colonialist reading of the Irish historical experience, see S. Howe, *Ireland and Empire: Colonial Legacies in Irish History and Culture* (Oxford University Press, 2001).

66 Acknowledgement of the achievement of stable democracy comes in J. Prager, *Building Democracy in Ireland. Political Order and Cultural Integration in a Newly Independent Nation* (Cambridge University Press, 1986).

centrist politics, in which the valorisation of its insurrectionary moment of origin was reserved for comforting state rhetoric and ritual.

The combined impact of trade liberalisation and Ireland's European odyssey in search of prosperity, together with the severe self-examination forced by the northern conflict, created the need, the cultural climate and the policy framework for the 'reinvention of the republic'.

Conclusion

By the start of the new millennium relations between Ireland and Britain, at all levels, had reached extravagant cordiality, with reciprocal official gestures of respect (the official visits of Queen Elizabeth II to Ireland – the first reigning monarch since independence to do so – and of the Irish President to the UK); full Irish government involvement in World War I ceremonies – a recognition of shared sites of memory and mourning.[67] A note of nostalgia for the Redmondite legacy was evident in the centenary commemorations of the revolutionary events of 1913–1916 in Ireland.[68] The world of popular culture – mass media, sport, music, fashion – was utterly permeable within the archipelago. The 'Troubles' – notably the bombing of targets in Britain – made life difficult for sections of working-class Irish in British cities, with sharp hostility at times of particular danger: but with the ending of violence, relations quickly improved.

However, what became strikingly clear, once the Agreements had established stability in Northern Ireland and restored Anglo-Irish relations to a state of amity, was the extent to which globalisation in the early twenty-first century had transformed not only the economic prospects but, more profoundly, the deeper relevance of small national states to the lives of their citizens. The accelerating trade globalisation from the 1980s, combined with the revolution in communications technology, and the ever-increasing speed and sophistication of international financial transactions, resulted in the emergence of global conglomerates with resources effectively beyond the regulatory capacity of even the most powerful democratic 'open' states, not to speak of such relative minnows as Ireland.

---

67 J. Horne (ed.), *Our War: Ireland and the Great War* (Dublin: RIA, 2008); J. Horne and E. Madigan (eds.), *Towards Commemoration: Ireland in War and Revolution, 1913–1923* (Dublin: RIA, 2013).

68 The principal defender of Redmond's legacy was the former Taoiseach, John Bruton: see the article by S. Collins in the *Irish Times*, 16 August 2014, and also the *Irish Independent*, 17 January 2016.

More particularly, the healthy expansion of the Irish economy in the later 1990s lurched in the early years of the new century into a property-based bubble, with a ballooning of state and personal debt. The 2008 global banking and credit crisis shattered the Irish banking system and plunged the Irish economy into crisis. The corrective medicine prescribed for Ireland by the International Monetary Fund, the European Commission and the European Central Bank – enforced as a 'programme' by a team or 'troika' from these institutions – drove the Irish economy into severe contraction and left a massive debt burden for later generations. The crisis – and the remedy prescribed – was a cruel demonstration of how vulnerable the small 'open' economy of Ireland was to seismic global shocks, and how very limited was the influence of Ireland, or its claims for special consideration, when the interests of larger states within the EU (notably Germany) and of powerful financial institutions were involved.

Taking the corrective medicine of sharp austerity enabled Ireland to exit the 'troika' programme just in time for the centenary anniversary of the 1916 Rising, enabling the Taoiseach to claim that Ireland had recovered its 'economic sovereignty'.[69] But, in truth, the crisis merely highlighted what, at least from the Maastricht Treaty of 1992, had become an invincible fact of life: that the notion of national sovereignty in the context of ever-deepening European (EU) integration and global trade liberalisation bore little resemblance to what nationalists had understood it to mean (and to promise) a century earlier.

This chastening experience, in the context of global trade liberalisation and the flexing of muscles by large states, was not, of course, unique to Ireland. Indeed, the cooling of Ireland's ardour for the European project was some way short of the full tide of Euroscepticism surging through several EU states by the second decade of the new century. The UK – where, for historical reasons, Euroscepticism was particularly deeply embedded – finally saw these anxieties and disillusionment come to a head in a plebiscite in the summer of 2016, in which the slogan 'take back control of our country' proved a powerful call. By a 52 per cent to 48 per cent vote, Britain decided to leave the EU, the first state ever to so decide since the launch of the European project.

It was ironic that the British (more correctly English) longing for the restoration of national sovereignty was accompanied by Irish pleas to the UK voters to reject the sirens of national sovereignty ('little Englandism') and to stay with the project and structures of shared sovereignty and a common

---

69 Ireland exited the bailout programme (supervised by the 'troika') in December 2013.

destiny within the European (EU) family. In short, in 2016 Irish leaders were warning their English neighbours against a too narrow version of national 'Home Rule' and against the danger of jeopardising the clear benefits of membership of a larger [European] 'union'.[70]

As the new century advanced, Ireland's changing social complexion served to further highlight the receding world of protectionism, cultural no less than economic. By the second decade of the twenty-first century, Ireland's population growth over the previous two decades had introduced new immigrants from the EU states of eastern Europe, in addition to a migrant minority from Africa and Asia; making it increasingly less likely that future explorations of Irish identity would be conducted on essentialist ethno-cultural terms. Indeed, this had already become apparent in the work of Irish creative artists – in literature, theatre, cinema and the fine arts. Freedom to explore no longer required exile; there were no incarcerating nets (nationality, language or religion) from which Irish artists might feel – as Joyce had felt in 1912 – impelled to flee.

In 1885 Parnell declared that 'no man has the right to fix the boundary of the march of a nation'.[71] The quest for an independent Irish state was fuelled by a deep sense of historical injustice and by an optimistic belief in the creative possibilities of national sovereignty. On the other hand, Ulster unionist resolve in resisting this proposition was based on the claim that this shared historical memory was not theirs, and by a conviction that their well-being, prosperity and particular ethno-religious identity were best protected by continuing membership of the British state and empire.

The story of both Irish states after 1922 demonstrated that concepts of national sovereignty and boundaries (in the abstract or embodied in structures and institutions) are neither fixed nor permanent, but subject to revision, accommodation and renegotiation, in response to the ever-changing contours of power in the world and to the basic unheroic needs of people everywhere to live in a tolerable state of peace and comfort.

---

70 See, for example, report of the Taoiseach's speech, *Irish Examiner*, 21 June 2016. Other prominent Irish public figures likewise urged the UK voters to vote to remain in the EU.
71 Speech at Cork, 21 January 1885.

PART I

*

IRELAND 1880–1923

1

Radical Nationalisms, 1882–1916

MATTHEW KELLY

The Liberal–Home Rule Nexus

'We were probably the most conservative-minded revolutionaries that ever put through a successful revolution.'[1] So wrote Kevin O'Higgins, Minister for Justice in the first government of the Irish Free State, in 1923. This strangely transactional phrasing signalled the intention of a prominent politician of the new state to treat the existing political settlement, as secured by the victory of the Free State in the Irish Civil War, as final and to govern according to conventional parliamentary principles. O'Higgins would doubtless have preferred to be a minister in a 32-county Irish republic, but the uncompromising way he fulfilled his ministerial brief, particularly with respect to active republicans, made him in the eyes of republicans a potent symbol of illegitimate state authority. His assassination by the IRA in July 1927 was cruel evidence that for some, the revolution had yet to be 'put through'. Nonetheless, by the 1930s, conservative-minded revolutionaries – or their children – dominated Ireland's two largest political parties and the active republican minority would find de Valera's Fianna Fáil governments ready to carry on where O'Higgins had left off. Despite the formal commitments of both Fianna Fáil and Cumann na nGaedheal, later Fine Gael, to the establishment of a 32-county Irish republic, neither showed much inclination to disrupt the status quo and, crucially, both took the view that the state had a right to a monopoly on violence.

This was new; in the decades before the revolution, the constitutional nationalists associated with the Home Rule movement had not taken such a rigid view. During the Land War, they had helped create a permissive environment where non-violent collective action could segue into either physical resistance against the agents of the state or clandestine violence against the

---

1 R. F. Foster, *Vivid Faces. The Revolutionary Generation in Ireland* (London: Allen Lane, 2014), 25.

property and representatives of the landlord class. As for revolutionary nation-alism, the Home Rule leadership often implied that circumstances might arise that would render physical force legitimate, though this was postponed until such a time as it had been conclusively proved that the British state was unable to respond to the reasonable demands of Ireland's elected representa-tives. These ambiguities reflected the distinct configuration of British-Irish politics established in the 1880s, particularly following Gladstone's adoption of Home Rule in late 1885. Gladstone pitched his new commitment as the proper response to the democratically and constitutionally expressed demand of a distinct national group within the Union. His idea that Irish nationalism was politically legitimate and partly the product of British mis-governance of Ireland was strictly conditional: the Irish *were* one of Europe's 'strug-gling nationalities', but their political demands were only legitimate when expressed through established constitutional channels. Having already spo-ken of the need to 'govern Ireland according to Irish ideas', in the aftermath of Fenian outbreaks of 1867 Gladstone had declared that his 'mission was to pacify Ireland' and, in the 1880s, he was careful to insist that the Irish had earned the right to self-government through good behaviour.[2] At the same time, Gladstone argued the Union would only endure if the over-mighty English recognised how the widening of the franchise created new political nations and learned to respond with grace to the constitutionally expressed demands of the Irish, Welsh and Scottish.[3] As such, Gladstone's vision for a new constitutional settlement for the UK represented both a challenge to par-liamentary majoritarianism and posited a fundamental rethink of the com-munal and electoral bases of UK politics.

Gladstonian principle was never more political than in response to Ireland. The purpose of his Irish policy was to marginalise revolutionary nationalism and radical agrarianism, thereby diminishing the state's dependence on coer-cion and allowing it to govern through consistently liberal means. As such, the positive or principled case made for Irish Home Rule should not obscure its negative or functional purposes.[4] Much the same can be said of the min-istrations of constructive unionism, that effort of the Salisbury and Balfour

---

2 Quoted in H. C. G. Matthew, *Gladstone 1809–1898* (Oxford University Press, 1997), 147, 194.

3 M. Kelly, 'Irish Nationalism', in D. Craig and J. Thompson (eds.), *Languages of Politics in Nineteenth-Century Britain* (Basingstoke: Palgrave Macmillan, 2013), 211–13.

4 In the aftermath of Fenian attacks in 1867, Gladstone privately wrote that 'our purpose & duty is to endeavour to draw a line between the Fenians and the people of Ireland, & to make the people of Ireland indisposed to cross it'. Quoted in Matthew, *Gladstone 1809–1898*, 194.

ministries to 'kill Home Rule with kindness' which culminated in Wyndham's Land (Purchase) Act of 1903. Both major British parties, in quite distinct ways, regarded Irish policy as a counter-revolutionary project.[5] And they largely succeeded. Constitutional or Home Rule nationalism, bolstered after 1884 by the widened franchise, provided most Irish nationalists, particularly the Catholic bourgeoisie, with a political commitment that was emotionally satisfying, compatible with everyday life and politically plausible.

Radical nationalism did not lose all momentum. The complaint that the representative politics of Home Rule reduced the agency of 'the people', so central to the articulation of mid-Victorian Fenianism, to paying party dues, affirming resolutions and casting a vote on election day had some political traction, while the idea that armed insurrection was the only way the Irish people could exercise the political autonomy befitting a sovereign nation retained adherents and attracted young recruits.[6] This was particularly so in the first decade of the twentieth century, when a new generation of young Irish Republican Brotherhood (IRB) men revitalised the organisation from within and went on to plan and execute the 1916 Rebellion. After 1910, this radical nationalism found expression in the editorial columns of *Irish Freedom* and in the fervid eschatology of Patrick Pearse, but was not interchangeable with the more widespread talk of the male citizen's right to bear arms that shaped nationalist responses to the Ulster Crisis.[7] Volunteering destabilised the Liberal–Home Rule nexus, challenging the authority of the Home Rule leadership and the parliamentary process, but it did not mark a wholesale conversion to radical nationalism by the 'manhood of Ireland'. That Dublin Castle invested more resources in monitoring the activities of the Ulster Volunteer Force than the Irish Volunteers indicated where it thought the greatest threat to the authority of the state lay, and much can be inferred from the rush to join the Irish Volunteers following John Redmond's takeover of the organisation in June 1914.[8]

Fenianism was not the only radical challenge to the Liberal–Home Rule nexus. Feminism and the women's suffrage question; socialism, the

---

5 See A. Gailey, *The Death of Kindness: The Experience of Constructive Unionism, 1890–1905* (Cork: Cork University Press, 1987).

6 See M. Kelly, 'The *Irish People* and the Disciplining of Dissent', in J. McConnel and F. McGarry (eds.), *The Black Hand of Irish Republicanism* (Dublin: Irish Academic Press, 2009).

7 M. Kelly, 'The Irish Volunteers: A Machiavellian Moment?', in C. George Boyce and A. O'Day (eds.), *The Ulster Crisis 1885–1921* (Basingstoke: Palgrave Macmillan, 2006).

8 On Dublin Castle and volunteering, see the Colonial Office papers, CO 904, TNA, Kew.

co-operative movement and trade unionism; cultural and language revivalism; and what came to be known as Sinn Féin all challenged the working assumptions of the Home Rule Party. For some, radical commitments like these were integral to their separatism, whereas others defaulted to non-Home Rule nationalism as the Irish Parliamentary Party proved to be an ineffective vehicle for the promotion of their concerns. This was particularly the case for women's suffrage activists who put their faith in the parliamentary process and found during the Ulster Crisis that the Irish Parliamentary Party would not support women's suffrage if this risked jeopardising its primary objective of achieving Home Rule.[9] Incidentally, focusing on nationalism and women's suffrage should not obscure how the issue could generate feminist solidarity across the political and sectarian divide or the way Unionist political priorities could equally see the women's suffrage campaign marginalised or treated with outright hostility.[10]

By contrast, the struggle over the right to unionise exposed the class-based rather than gendered fissures that ran through nationalism. By British standards, class-based conflict in Ireland was inhibited by how the nationalist–unionist divide militated against the creation of strong cross-community class solidarity, particularly in industrialised Belfast, and the relatively non-industrial nature of the rest of the Irish economy. When the logics of this politics finally escalated into the Dublin Lockout of August 1913–January 1914, the 20,000 workers that came out under the charismatic leadership of Jim Larkin and the Irish Transport and General Workers Union attracted little sympathy from either established Irish politicians or the mainstream nationalist press.[11] One legacy of the struggle were the soured relations between Dublin workers and the Home Rule Party, which had political consequences in the years that followed, most obviously during the 1918 general election; another was the small group of socialists who formed the Irish Citizen Army under James Connolly and fought in the Easter Rising.

As the foregoing suggests, rather than seeking to define radical nationalism, identifying its stipulative or canonical features, it is best treated as relational and contingent. It should not be reduced to a neo-Fenianism and historians should be wary of defining as radical all nationalist hostility to the Irish Parliamentary Party; nor should histories of radical nationalism seek

---

9 S. Pašeta, *Irish Nationalist Women, 1900–1918* (Cambridge University Press, 2013), 63–91.
10 D. Urquhart, *Women in Ulster Politics 1890–1940* (Dublin: Irish Academic Press, 2000), 7–45.
11 J. McConnel, *The Irish Parliamentary Party and the Third Home Rule Bill Crisis* (Dublin: Four Courts Press, 2013), 164–81.

to evidence an edifying progressiveness that challenges the historical consensus with respect to the ascendancy of the conservative-minded Home Rule Party. Instead, an appreciation of the currents of radicalism at work within nationalism, whether feminist, socialist, democratic or revolutionary, complicates historical accounts of what constituted Irish nationalism in the pre-war period and how it was articulated, inviting questions about its transformative potential. In the following chronological treatment of radical nationalism between the end of the Land War and the Easter Rising, little indicates that radical nationalism posed a threat to the Liberal–Home Rule nexus, which ultimately failed on its own terms, but much suggests the short-term causes of the Irish revolution need to be related to longer-term developments in attitude and mentality.

Radical Nationalism and Home Rule

The Irishman newspaper, established in 1858, was Fenian in tone and revolutionary in intent but not a formal IRB enterprise. From 1865, it was effectively the personal vehicle of Richard Pigott, its notorious owner and editor. Pigott's core readership was broadly working class, opposed to the Act of Union, hostile to Dublin Castle, and little integrated into mainstream nationalist political culture. It included the Fenian-influenced membership of the Workingmen's Clubs, and it was from this milieu, particularly in its urban setting, that the early Gaelic Athletic Association (GAA) drew much of its energy. Prior to the establishment of the GAA in 1884, this political and social sub-culture was most visible during the annual Manchester Martyr parades that sustained the popular memory of Allen, Larkin and O'Brien, the IRB men executed for the murder of a policeman during the successful attempt to rescue two Fenian prisoners from a police van in Manchester in 1867.[12] Their public hanging outside Salford Gaol gave Fenianism its Calvary, allowing 1867 to be remembered as a heroic enterprise that ended in the ghastly spectacle of British judicial murder, a miniature of the brutal suppression provoked by the United Irish rebellion in 1798. Here vindicated was the view of the British as a fundamentally malign presence in Ireland, whose liberal principles were set at naught once confronted by Irish claims to national sovereignty. Home Rule, it followed, would prove a chimera, with liberty and justice only possible through complete separation.

---

12 E. McGee, ' "God Save Ireland": Manchester Martyrs Demonstrations in Dublin, 1867–1916', *Éire-Ireland*, 36, (Fall–Winter 2001), 39–66.

That, though, remained the minority view and Charles Stewart Parnell, the leader of the Irish Parliamentary Party, was determined it would remain so. Pigott sold his newspaper group to the Land League in 1881 and William O'Brien built *United Ireland*, the in-house journal of the Home Rule movement, on the foundations it provided. *The Irishman* eventually ceased publication in 1885. Sound financial reasons doubtlessly precipitated this decision, but the demise of *The Irishman* also reflected the progressive marginalisation of radical nationalism as a component of Home Rule politics in the months and years following the end of the Land War. The 'Kilmainham Treaty' of May 1882, agreed between Parnell and the Liberal government, which saw the release from prison of the Land League leadership, was predicated on Parnell's decisive rejection of the revolutionary or radical implications of the latter stages of the Land War. Parnell's re-positioning was reinforced by the murder of Lord Frederick Cavendish, the newly installed Irish Chief Secretary, and T. H. Burke, the Under-Secretary, in Dublin's Phoenix Park just a few days later.

The shock of the Phoenix Park murders transformed the discursive field, forcing conservative and radical nationalists to clarify what constituted legitimate political action. The Invincibles, the dissident IRB cell responsible, faced public condemnation by Home Ruler, Land Leaguer and Fenian alike, as well as the British political parties. Pigott's *Irishman* associated the crime with the 'soiling slough of Russian nihilism', regarding the attack as a foreign import alien to Fenian principle, whereas John O'Leary, prominent IRB activist of the 1860s generation, convicted treason-felon and conservative on the land question, characterised the murders as a degraded agrarianism, symptomatic of the demoralisation brought about by the Land War.[13] Parnell, it seems, thought the murders fundamentally undermined his authority and was ready to resign the leadership of the party, but Gladstone, recognising the opportunity the murders posed to reinforce the Kilmainham settlement, helped persuade him to stay on.[14] In a limited sense, Parnell was right, for although the Invincibles did not represent a distinct social or political group, they were an extreme symptom of the little attention mainstream nationalism paid to the needs of the urban working class and its failure to integrate it into the party's associational culture. A Home Rule MP like Dublin's William Field might try to represent the needs of labour, but in general the working class exercised

---

13 M. Kelly, *The Fenian Ideal and Irish Nationalism, 1882–1916* (Woodbridge: Boydell Press, 2006), 16.
14 F. S. L. Lyons, *Charles Stewart Parnell* (Glasgow: William Collins, 1977), 209; Matthew, *Gladstone*, 455–57.

little leverage over the party and could be safely ignored, allowing the party to sustain the fiction that it was an effective exercise in vertical class integration.

The unifying effect the Phoenix Park murders had on nationalist opinion should not obscure the degree to which the end of the Land War signalled a more marked retreat from radicalism with respect to agrarian ideas, particularly those popularised by Henry George. Agrarian radicals like Michael Davitt or Anna Parnell (Charles's sister) and the Ladies' Land League had taken up George's notion that the answer to the land question was nationalisation and it was no coincidence that the day Davitt began a lecture tour of the United States in June 1882 the *New York Herald* published an interview with Parnell which made clear he rejected nationalisation and favoured the creation of a 'peasant proprietorship'.[15] That autumn, Parnell's coterie further consolidated its hold over the movement by establishing the Irish National League (INL) and committing it to a reformist programme that sought to improve the condition of the Irish people without fundamentally disrupting existing property relations. Two years later, the Catholic hierarchy was persuaded that the Home Rule Party could be relied upon to protect its political interests, particularly with respect to denominational education. Parnell's coalition was in place.

Davitt later described the developments of autumn 1882 as a 'counter-revolution' that saw 'the overthrow of a movement and the enthronement of a man; the replacing of nationalism by Parnellism', generating a 'nominal dictatorship'.[16] A Parnell cult was certainly in the making, as evident in the idea of him as the 'uncrowned king of Ireland', but Davitt's perspective was distorted by ideological convictions that denied the Irish people their agency and exaggerated its credulity. Parnell's ascendancy over the Home Rule Party and the INL was rooted in popular acclaim and the ready acquiescence of the party, which in the final judgement of F. S. L. Lyons rested on how Parnell's leadership 'gave his people back their self-respect'.[17] Nationalist Ireland, however, was not a monolith unquestioningly falling into line behind party leaders. It thus made tactical sense to leave the ultimate object of the Home Rule movement uncertain, for this it could be presented as tolerably consistent with radical nationalist sentiment – dissecting Parnell's capacity for rhetorical dissimulation was once something of a cottage industry for historians. As such, Home Rule could be many things: a pragmatic response

---

15 L. Marley, *Michael Davitt: Freelance Radical and Frondeur* (Dublin: Four Courts Press, 2007), 61.

16 Marley, *Davitt*, 66–7.

17 Lyons, *Parnell*, 644.

to the reality of British power by nationalists wishing for greater independence or a sincere attempt to re-structure the United Kingdom of Great Britain and Ireland through a significant act of devolution to Ireland: it was at once the specific aim of a specific political party *and* the principal signifier of an ascendant, if flexible, language of nationalist assertion. If this malleability was most evident in the contrast between Parnell's restrained register after Gladstone's adoption of Home Rule in late 1885 – the period of the 'Union of Hearts' – and his so-called 'appeal to the hillside men' during the party split of 1890–1891, it was also seen in the way Home Rule MPs at public meetings, particularly in their constituencies or before the Irish-American audiences that helped bankroll the organisation, cultivated radical nationalist support. As Michael Wheatley has shown, the conciliatory language that tended to characterise parliamentary Home Rule was often at odds with the language of Home Rule in provincial Ireland, where the tone and content was persistently aggressive and Anglophobic.[18]

This left little scope for an alternative politics. Leftist organisations like the Irish Labour and Industrial Union, the Dublin Democratic Association or the Socialist League, among others, as well as organisations that sought to improve the security of tenure for urban tenants, cropped up over the course of the 1880s. Such organisations generally lasted only a few months, had tiny memberships and struggled to find places to meet.[19] Not even a visit from a luminary like William Morris, the celebrity socialist and artist, gave much of a boost.[20] Still, Dublin Castle kept an eye on their activities, filing reports on labour organisations among those mainly focused on IRB activity.[21] Trade union organisations like the Gasworkers' Union could have radical nationalist and socialist tendencies, but most trades councils were not socialist and were hostile to the new unskilled trade unions; and wary of Parnellism's centralising tendencies, resisted co-option by the party.[22]

Separatist nationalists of a more conventional bent sustained a lively if marginal associational culture, particularly through new initiatives like the

---

18 M. Wheatley, *Nationalism and the Irish Party. Provincial Ireland 1910–1916* (Oxford University Press, 2005), 74–94.
19 F. Lane, *The Origins of Modern Irish Socialism* (Cork: Cork University Press, 1997), 92–6, 120–36
20 Lane, *Origins*, 123
21 In general, see 'Intelligent Notes compiled for Chief Secretary Arthur Balfour 1887–91' PRO 30/60/1–4.
22 M. Cronin, 'Parnellism and Workers: The Experience of Cork and Limerick', in F. Lane and Donal Ó Drisceoil, *Politics and the Irish Working Class, 1830–1945* (Basingstoke: Palgrave Macmillan, 2005), 141–6.

Young Ireland Society (YIS). The YIS is best known for the influence it had on the young W. B. Yeats, who joined in 1885, but the society had in fact been established at the height of the Land War, had a loyal membership, kept detailed minute books, held weekly meetings, including socials open to women, and remained active until at least 1887. Little-noticed provincial branches could have a significant membership, and existed into the twentieth century – a police observer suggested County Kerry had as many as 300 members at its peak.[23] As an IRB front organisation, the Dublin branch had been the site of a minor power struggle that led to it coming under the control of the circle of young Fenians associated with Fred Allan in 1883, before they too were alienated when O'Leary returned from exile in 1885 and asserted his authority. As a monarchist and a landowner, O'Leary was never an orthodox Fenian and as president of the YIS he promoted a 'tolerant' gentlemanly politics that emphasised cultural uplift rather than revolutionary activism and judged the Home Rule opposition not by its beliefs but the sincerity with which it worked for Ireland.[24] O'Leary, now in middle age, his perspective doubtless shaped by his experience of exile, recognised the significance of Parnell's achievement and seemingly found the rejection of Parnellism by marginal young men preaching revolution a little foolish.

Despite O'Leary's lecturing, Parnell's dubious reputation among the most ideologically rigorous 'advanced' men was not improved by the Special Commission hearings of 1887–1888. This official investigation into the purported relationship between 'Parnellism and Crime' was prompted by the publication in *The Times* of letters sold to them by Pigott which directly implicated Parnell in the Phoenix Park murders. Although the letters were eventually revealed to be forgeries – Pigott broke down in the witness stand and fled to Spain where he committed suicide in a hotel room – the commission nonetheless exposed much about the progress of the Land War that the leadership would have preferred kept out of public view.[25] Parnell's performance in the witness stand, moreover, was evasive, laconic and deeply offensive to the separatists, who found his haughty contempt, usually reserved for his opponents in the House of Commons, turned on them. Parnell's exoneration was certainly a defeat for the Tory interest, and the theatrics of his consequent appearance in the House of Commons helped consolidate the Parnell myth, but obscured from view by Parnellite triumph were signs that the 'advanced'

---

23 See report dated 1–15 January 1890 (PRO 30/60/2).
24 Kelly, *Fenian Ideal*, 22–40.
25 See M. O'Callaghan, *British High Politics and a Nationalist Ireland. Criminality, Land and Law under Forster and Balfour* (Dublin: Irish Academic Press, 1994), 104ff.

men increasingly resented the assumed authority of the Home Rule leadership within nationalism. Scattered police intelligence suggested that Fenian activists felt increasingly alienated from Parnellism while Home Rule MPs appearing on Amnesty Association platforms urging the release of the handful of prisoners convicted on dynamite offences in the early 1880s could face hostile crowds.[26]

This resentment shaped the progress of the Home Rule Party split after Captain William O'Shea named Parnell as co-respondent in his divorce proceedings in late 1890. When the Catholic hierarchy in Ireland and the Liberal leadership demanded Parnell's resignation, most Home Rule MPs followed suit, but a minority insisted that they would not be 'dictated' to by the prime minister. Parnell's bid to regain the leadership of the party was predicated on his attempt to construct a new Home Rule platform based on 'independent opposition' at Westminster, an idea associated with the failed constitutional nationalism of the 1850s, but which in the new circumstances seemed suggestively radical. Recognising that the Catholic bourgeoisie that constituted the backbone of the party could no longer be relied upon, Parnell sought to transform his support base, vying for the support of nationalists who had been marginal to Home Rule politics, particularly the working classes of urban Ireland. His popularity could be taken for granted in few places outside of Dublin.[27]

Although the evidence suggests that the IRB did not take a formal position on the leadership question, the course of the split revived a residual Fenian anti-clericalism as well as an eagerness to defy established authority in some sections of the population. P. N. Fitzgerald, a prominent IRB organiser with links to Dublin Labour, played a significant role in the campaign, falling out with P. J. Hoctor, a longstanding Fenian associate and employee, over whether Parnell was worthy of IRB support.[28] As this suggests, the credulity of Parnell's Fenian support should not be exaggerated. Many recognised that the radical tone of Parnell's rhetoric was strictly delimited by the principle of 'independent opposition' and though few Fenians took Parnell's 'revolutionary hints' seriously, the opportunity to confront old enemies in the Catholic Church and at Westminster was hard to resist. O'Leary took Gladstone's intervention to be the key moment – it was not for 'an Englishman' to dictate the terms of Irish politics – and while some advanced nationalists were swept

---

26 Kelly, *Fenian Ideal*, 47–8.
27 For the subtlety of Parnell's rhetoric, see the unsurpassed analysis offered in F. Callanan, *The Parnell Split, 1890–91* (Cork: Cork University Press, 1992).
28 Kelly, *Fenian Ideal*, 49.

up in the excitement, others calculated that the longer the contest was drawn out, the more damage it would do the Home Rule movement.[29] Either way, the Parnell Leadership committees established that year were often dominated by IRB men, particularly in Dublin, where the National Club became Parnell's headquarters and welcomed as members Parnellite MPs who normally gave it a wide berth. Police observers were genuinely surprised by the prominence of Fenian 'suspects' in the campaign, while R. Barry O'Brien, Parnellite MP and Parnell's biographer, admitted in a letter to O'Leary – and later in print – that without the support of Fitzgerald and his IRB entourage 'we could not have carried on the war at all'.[30]

When seeking specifically working-class support, Parnell publically admitted that it had little to thank the Home Rule Party for.[31] The Dublin labour conference of March 1891 boasted representatives of 69 organisations from throughout Ireland, though they were mainly from Dublin and adjacent counties, and enjoyed a high profile thanks to Parnell's attendance and speeches. Of the conference's radical programme, which included land nationalisation, manhood suffrage, state control of Ireland's transport infrastructure, and measures intended to improve the living standards of the working class, Parnell argued with his characteristic ambivalence that political leaders needed to take account of this agenda, whether they wanted to or not. Admittedly, little momentum was achieved and the Irish Labour League constituted by the convention lasted just a few months, but again exceptional circumstances brought to prominence an otherwise marginal political agenda.[32]

That July, the important Parnellite convention held in Dublin exposed the tensions at work in this new politics. Although dominated by representatives of the Irish National League, the convention grappled with the question of whether other organisations could formally affiliate to what was effectively a new party predicated on the principle of independent opposition. The Parnellite leadership was divided. Tim Harrington, MP, resisted a more inclusive approach, while William Redmond, MP, was keen to formalise a new Parnellite coalition based on a range of organisations.[33] This division troubled Parnellite politics from Parnell's death until the party's reunification under John Redmond in 1900. In the intervening years, Parnellites would struggle in particular to accommodate their Fenian comrades, fully aware

---

29 Ibid., 50.
30 Ibid., 56.
31 Ibid., 52.
32 Lane, *Origins*, 173–4.
33 Kelly, *Fenian Ideal*, 58–60.

that they provided significant organisational ballast but were a constant social and ideological challenge to this constitutionalist and broadly middle-class party. Harrington, a Dublin MP with long experience of the city's political grassroots, found this particularly trying, while few insiders could have been ignorant of the fact that Fred Allan, now business manager of the Parnellite *Independent* newspaper group, employed IRB men and held meetings on its premises.[34]

The Parnellite leadership kept the Fenians on side by its close association with the Amnesty Association. Recent work on the 'dynamitards' has emphasised the transnational component of the campaign, emphasising its foundational status in the modern history of terrorism,[35] but it is striking how on the domestic political front it played out in conventional terms. Home Rule MPs emphasised problems with the judicial process and the treatment of the prisoners rather than the crimes themselves, although William Redmond was prone to suggest that the crimes were a foolhardy if understandable response to the 'intolerable tyranny put upon this country by successive British governments'.[36] Constitutional nationalists had said much the same of the Fenians in the 1860s and 1870s. Parnellite MPs in the 1890s, following where Parnell had led, were now much readier to describe constitutionalism in pragmatic rather than absolute terms, apparently reserving the right to resort to revolutionary means should the constitutional path be shown to fail. When John Daly, the most celebrated of the dynamite prisoners, was returned unopposed as MP for Limerick in 1895, his electors could not but be aware of the precedents set by the return of Jeremiah O'Donovan Rossa and John Mitchel in the Tipperary by-elections of 1870 and 1875 respectively, just as the electors of Bobby Sands in Fermanagh and South Tyrone in April 1981 knew returning a hunger striker carried powerful historical resonances. The government's decision to release the last of the dynamite prisoners in 1900 helped pave the way for the reunification of the party under the leadership of Redmond by neutralising an issue that had allowed Parnellite MPs to connect to its new support during the Split, but left them peculiarly beholden thereafter.[37]

Separatists had much else to keep them occupied in the years between 1898 and the end of the Second South African War, a period of activism long

---

34 Ibid., 71–95.
35 N. Whelehan, *The Dynamiters: Irish Nationalism and Political Violence in the Wider World, 1867–1900* (Cambridge University Press, 2012) and J. Gantt, *Irish Terrorism in the Atlantic Community, 1865–1922* (Basingstoke: Palgrave Macmillan, 2010).
36 Kelly, *Fenian Ideal*, 81.
37 On reunification, Fred Allan got the sack.

recognised by historians as bringing into being a 'new' nationalism.[38] The 1798 centenary, anti-recruitment and pro-Boer activism, including the mobilisation of the Irish Brigade that went to South Africa to fight alongside the Boers, was followed by organised opposition to the royal visits of 1900 and 1903, making for a hazy mix of republicanism and anti-imperialism which undoubtedly gave radical nationalism a vital fillip.[39] Police observers were also kept busy detailing for Dublin Castle and the Irish Chief Secretary the significant IRB presence on the numerous committees established throughout the country to prepare the 1798 centenary celebrations. The musters that summer were dominated by Home Rule politicians keen to defuse their radical potential, but few condemned revolutionary activity outright, offering instead strongly contingent justifications of the revolutionary attempt of the United Irish and their present constitutionalism. Separatists, by contrast, were quick to blame lacklustre proceedings on the Spanish-American War for preventing a large number of Irish-Americans from making the journey across the Atlantic.[40]

Reports left by police note-takers also suggest that the IRB was busy during council elections in 1899, the first to be conducted under the democratic reforms of the 1898 Local Government Act. More numerically significant, however, were candidates identified as 'labour', some of whom were linked to the Home Rule Party, some to the IRB, and all of whom were working class, though not necessarily men or women of pronounced left-wing political convictions. Either way, this evidence of IRB and/or labour activism revealed a subterranean politics of little revolutionary potential but which had not succumbed to the hegemonic drive of the Irish Parliamentary Party. As the social profile of the electorate changed, at least in local elections, so changed the social profile of the elected, and as the Grand Juries were replaced with local councils, so a new forum for the expression of nationalist sentiment came into being.[41]

The South Mayo by-election of February 1900 helped place this radical nationalist activism in perspective by marking the beginning of a new era

---

38 The canonical account is R. F. Foster, *Modern Ireland 1600–1972* (London: Allen Lane, 1988), 431–60.

39 Various essays by T. J. O'Keefe, including 'The 1898 Efforts to Celebrate the United Irishmen: The '98 Centennial', *Eire-Ireland*, 28 (1992); various works by D. P. McCracken including *The Irish pro-Boers, 1877–1902* (Johannesburg: Preskor, 1989); and S. Pašeta, 'Nationalist Responses to Two Royal Visits to Ireland, 1900 and 1903', *Irish Historical Studies*, xxxi (November 1999).

40 Kelly, *Fenian Ideal*, 108–16.

41 Ibid., 144–9 and V. Crossman, *Local Government in Nineteenth-Century Ireland* (Belfast: Institute of Irish Studies, 1994), 91–7.

of ideological retrenchment: the inclusive ambiguities of Parnellism were giving way to the strictly parliamentary and increasingly pro-imperial Home Rule politics of Redmondism. The contest could not have been more symbolic: Major John MacBride, commander of the Irish Brigade in South Africa, and later executed as a leader of the 1916 Rebellion, was defeated by John O'Donnell, nominee of the Irish Parliamentary Party and prominent agrarian activist. O'Donnell, the protégé of William O'Brien, the popular and charismatic Home Rule MP, had served two terms of imprisonment as a United Irish League activist, a record less glamorous than MacBride's South African adventure, but more meaningful to most nationalists.[42] MacBride's defeat signalled the emergence of a more purist separatist nationalism, a more disciplined Home Rule politics and the return of the agrarian question to the centre of Irish politics.

That said, the revived Home Rule Party could still accommodate a young man of radical inclinations keen to establish himself in politics. Arthur Lynch, leader of the second Irish Brigade, stood as the party's candidate in Galway City in 1901. Where MacBride was an uncompromising militant separatist, soon to achieve further notoriety as the husband of Maud Gonne, Lynch had followed a more ambiguous trajectory. The defeated Parnellite candidate in Galway in 1892, he then spent time in the US, attending the inaugural convention of the Amnesty Association of America, before returning to Ireland, where he became involved in the Amnesty Association before heading off to South Africa as war correspondent for the London-based *Daily Mail*. During the Galway City campaign, Lynch declared himself a Parnellite, exploiting the ambiguity this allowed, while a policeman observed that although the IRB leadership took no part in the campaign, the rank and file 'voted for candidates of their choice on no fixed principle whatever'.[43] The separatists were not impressed by the outcome, believing that the voters had been hoodwinked into thinking Lynch's return was a radical nationalist gesture.

Perhaps the voters had been duped, for Lynch was preferred to his opponent, Horace Plunkett, the unionist president of the Irish Agricultural Organisation Society and vice president of the Department of Agriculture and Technical Instruction. Plunkett's radicalism was rooted in the cooperative ethos and challenged the vested interests of the 'gombeen men' who dominated provincial life in Ireland. The separatists were less concerned

---

42 P. Bull, 'A Fatal Disjuncture, 1898–1905: Sinn Féin and the United Irish League', in R. Phelan (ed.), *Irish-Australian Studies: Papers of the Seventh Irish-Australian Conference* (Sydney, 1994), 37–51.
43 Kelly, *Fenian Ideal*, 159.

that a Catholic electorate choose an unremarkable Catholic candidate over a remarkable Protestant candidate than by the continuing capacity of the Home Rule Party to create the illusion, particularly when its opponent was a high-profile unionist, that it represented a radical nationalist choice. What was not yet clear in 1901 was how the rigidity, discipline and conservatism of the Redmondite party would create space for a new nationalist radicalism.

The New Nationalism

In 1896, Alice Milligan and Anna Johnson (pen name Eithna Carbery), both Protestant republicans from Belfast, established *Shan Van Vocht* (1896–1899), an avowedly republican periodical that gave several young political radicals an opportunity to write for publication.[44] Maud Gonne, Alice Furlong, Katharine Tynan, William Rooney, James Connolly, W. B. Yeats, George Russell and Arthur Griffith were all contributors.[45] Although much of the *raison d'être* of the *Shan Van Vocht* was provided by the centenary of the 1798 rebellion and the historical lessons to be learned from the stirring deeds of the United Irishmen, space was also given to a broader range of viewpoints. A pamphlet on the agrarian radical James Fintan Lalor (1807–1849) by James Connolly, himself recently arrived in Dublin from Edinburgh to run the new Dublin Socialist Society, was favourably noticed, while Milligan also published Connolly's essay 'Nationalism and Socialism', albeit with an editorial disclaimer. Connolly emphasised the need to break with the past, telling readers that 'the national movement of our own day ... must demonstrate to the people of Ireland that our nationalism is not merely a morbid idealising of the past, but is also capable of formulating a distinct and definite answer to the problems of the present and a political and economic creed capable of adjustment to the wants of the future'.[46] Connolly would go on to be the foremost Irish socialist thinker and revolutionary of his generation and one of the signatories of the 1916 Proclamation.

Arthur Griffith, a working-class Dubliner but a protectionist rather than a socialist, was similarly convinced of the need for new, practical thinking. He also had been in South Africa, witnessing the British Empire in its war

---

44 On the significance of the nationalist song 'Shan Van Vocht', see R. Parfitt, '"Oh, What Matter, When for Erin Dear We Fall?": Music and Irish Nationalism, 1848–1913', *Irish Studies Review*, 23 (2015), 480–94.

45 Pašeta, *Irish Nationalist Women*, 31 and K. Steele, *Women, Press and Politics during the Irish Revival* (Syracuse: Syracuse University Press, 2007), 30.

46 C. D. Greaves, *The Life and Times of James Connolly* (London: Lawrence and Wishart, 1961), 81, 84–5.

of colonial retention, and had returned to Dublin determined to challenge nationalist orthodoxy. His preferred means was journalism and Milligan and Johnston got things started by donating their list of subscribers. *United Irishman* (1899–1906) was the result. For Griffith, the newspaper's launch brought to an end a decade-long apprenticeship. He had been a member of the Leinster Literary Society (1888–1893) and the Celtic Literary Society (1893–1903), both organisations of little immediate consequence but which showed young lower-class Dubliners creating new radical nationalist networks and learning to think independently. Although the Leinster Literary Society was Parnellite during the Split, both societies rejected the politics of Home Rule and shared much of the Gaelic League agenda, albeit with an overtly separatist inflection. Neither, however, were IRB front organisations. Essays published in the *United Irishman* by William Rooney, another working-class Dubliner and Griffith's closest collaborator, embodied this combination better than anyone. Speaking to the Celtic Literary Society on 20 January 1899, more than twenty years before W. B. Yeats's Nobel address, Rooney identified the importance of Parnell's death to the new cultural nationalism:

> Some little semblance of interest in the tongue of the Gael marked every generation before ours; but we, with our backs to everything native, our eyes perpetually on the parliament of the foreigner, dazed by joyous anticipation of a 'Union of Hearts', forgot everything but the shibboleth of the hour, and were gradually degenerating into mere automata, until a crash came, and in the rending of the veil we saw for the first time what was before us and paused.[47]

Following his death from tuberculosis aged 27 in 1901, Rooney came to be seen as a herald for a new age.[48]

Although neither straightforwardly revolutionary nor republican, *United Irishman*'s relentless assault on Ireland's hereditary enemy and its contempt for the Home Rule agenda made it the principal organ of radical nationalism for the best part of a decade. Evidence suggests that the IRB were quick to recognise its significance, promoting it at separatist events like the annual pilgrimage to Tone's grave at Bodenstown, County Kildare.[49] Whether taking a strongly pro-Boer stance during the Second South African War (1899–1902) or supporting the anti-enlistment campaign, whether publicising advanced

---

47 W. Rooney, 'A Recent Irish Literature', *Prose Writings* (Dublin, 1909?), 14.
48 P. J. Mathews, *Revival. The Abbey Theatre, the Gaelic League and the Co-operative Movement* (Cork: Cork University Press, 2003), 94–103.
49 Kelly, *Fenian Ideal*, 150–2.

nationalist opposition to the royal visits of 1900 and 1903, particularly Maud Gonne's rival 'patriotic children's treat' of 1900, or promoting the protectionist ideas of the Austrian economic Friedrich List, *United Irishman* was probably the most dynamic journalistic enterprise of the period. It was rivalled only by D. P. Moran's excoriating *The Leader*, itself broadly supportive of Home Rule and scornful of Griffith's thinking.[50]

Griffith's unorthodox nationalism, neither devolutionist nor separatist, was inspired by two historical precedents: the Austro-Hungarian *Ausgleich*, or compromise, of 1867 and the establishment and achievements of Grattan's parliament. Griffith mythologised or simplified both for distinctly presentist purposes. The *Ausgleich* had established the Austro-Hungarian Dual Monarchy, giving Hungary equal standing to Austria within the Habsburg Empire. Griffith thought Irish MPs should ape the Hungarians by withdrawing from the Westminster parliament, setting up a representative assembly in Dublin, from which a new Irish government would be drawn, and thus challenge the British to re-conquer Ireland. Griffith's thinking, soon reduced to the simpler principle of abstentionism, was reinforced by the idea that the complex legislation passed in 1782–1783 had given constitutional independence to Ireland and affirmed that the British monarchy was equally the Irish monarchy, there being no precedence between the two. Crucially, in Griffith's view, Grattan had got his way because the Irish people had been formed into volunteer corps, seemingly ready to fight for their national rights. Keen to bolster his radical credentials, Griffith tended to align himself with Henry Flood rather than Henry Grattan, just as he did with the Hungarian radical nationalist Lajos Kossuth rather than the moderate Farenc Deák.[51] In essence, if Gladstone thought the *means* by which the Act of Union was passed were 'unspeakably criminal', Griffith argued that the Act itself was unconstitutional and, as such, not legally binding on the Irish people. Ireland and Britain, like Austria-Hungary, was properly a 'dual monarchy'.[52]

Many found Griffith's thinking obtuse, and Moran had fun mocking his 'Green Hungarian band', but a knowing reader could quickly see how his best-selling historical tract, *The Resurrection of Hungary* (1904), was both a political argument and a clever commentary on contemporary Irish politics. Moreover, despite the obfuscation, Griffith's thinking had a clear rationale. He

---

50 On Moran, see: Mathews, *op. cit.* and F. S. L. Lyons, *Culture and Anarchy in Ireland 1890–1939* (Oxford University Press, 1979), 58–62.

51 Griffith was consistent, having given a paper to the Leinster Literary Society on 'Grattan and Flood – a Contrast', which was noticed in the *Weekly Freeman*, 3 January 1891.

52 See Gladstone's *Special Aspects of the Irish Question* (London: J. Murray, 1892), 9.

did not believe that Home Rule would restore Ireland's constitutional rights but instead would leave it a subordinate of Britain, which was incompatible with Ireland's claims to national sovereignty. In the short term, Griffith hoped to attract the support of frustrated Fenians and disillusioned Home Rulers, but in time he sought the wholesale conversion of the Irish Parliamentary Party. By pitching his radicalism as restorative rather than revolutionary, Griffith sought to reconfigure the nationalist centre-ground, but this strategy should not obscure his radicalism. Griffith was a self-conscious moderniser, who laid great emphasis on Ireland's need to achieve economic independence. Shortly after the publication of *The Resurrection of Hungary*, *United Irishman* carried a series of articles under the heading 'Working of the Policy'. These implicitly rejected narrowly ruralist conceptions of Ireland and placed much emphasis on Ireland's need to develop state institutions, exploit its natural resources more efficiently, develop an export-driven industrial economy, and promote her interests through independent consular representation abroad.[53]

The organisation that most closely came to represent Griffith's thinking was, of course, Sinn Féin. Formed over the course of 1904–1906, it was an amalgam of several smaller organisations, each with a specific political identity and core membership, and this prevented Griffith's thinking from achieving an uncontested hegemony within the organisation. Of the four component organisations, the National Council had grown out of the pro-Boer agitation and was established to coordinate opposition to the royal visit of 1900; Cumann na nGaedhael ('Society of the Gaels') and Inghinidhe na hÉireann ('Daughters of Erin') were, respectively, male and female membership organisations inspired by the Gaelic revival, broadly separatist, strongly influenced by the *United Irishman* and successor organisations to the Celtic Literary Society; and the Dungannon Clubs were northern republican groups under the leadership of Bulmer Hobson and strongly influenced by the IRB. Hobson, a Belfast Quaker, was the author of 'Defensive Warfare' (1909),[54] a pioneering separatist tract that detailed how to fight an asymmetric war and, in a Griffithite mode, it considered how 'the modern state's complex administrative machinery relies on the habit of acquiescence'.[55] Hobson also edited *Republic*, the in-house journal of the Dungannon Clubs, and though shaped by the atmosphere of cooperation that characterised IRB dealings with Sinn

---

53 Kelly, *Fenian Ideal*, 162–175.
54 Bulmer Hobson, *'Defensive Warfare: A Handbook for Irish Nationalists'* (Belfast: The West Belfast Branch of Sinn Féin, 1909).
55 C. Townshend, *Easter 1916* (London: Allen Lane, 2005), 20–1.

Féin in 1906–1907, its unambiguous separatism was a harbinger of ideological conflicts to come.

If the quest is for an unambiguously revolutionary separatist newspaper with socialist leanings, then the best candidate was *Bean na hÉireann* (1908–1911), the newspaper of Inghinidhe na hÉireann. Many of the leading women activists of the period, like Helena Maloney, Maud Gonne, the Gifford sisters and the Gore-Booth sisters, wrote for it or helped run it, and its militant editorial line was a direct challenge to Griffith's relative moderation. Maloney later described it as a 'mixture of guns and chiffon', 'a funny hotch-potch of blood and thunder, high thinking, and home-made bread'; friendly newsagents described it as 'the women's paper all the young men read'.[56] *Bean na hÉireann* espoused women's suffrage, its historical writing inserted women into the heroic narrative of nationalist militancy, claiming the Ladies' Land League as Inghinidhe na hÉireann's most immediate forebear, and its republicanism was overtly separatist and implicitly secular – though Maloney was a Catholic, its women writers were largely Protestant and kept their religious politics and identities somewhat oblique.[57] Like the *Shan Van Vocht*, *Bean na hÉireann* also attracted a stellar line-up of male contributors: George Russell, Patrick Pearse, Joseph Plunkett, Thomas MacDonagh and James Stephens wrote alongside suffragist and nationalist luminaries like Maeve Cavanagh, Susan Mitchell and Maud ffrench-Mullen. Much of its content blended Irish-Ireland and separatist ideas, while the subversive gardening column of Constance Markievicz (née Gore-Booth) has attracted the particular attention of historians – in 1909, Markievicz established the Fianna Éireann, a paramilitary boy scout movement.[58] As Senia Pašeta observes, these women moved in a 'kind of cultural and political *demi-monde* where social mores were much less rigid than they were in polite society'.[59]

Dissatisfaction with Griffith among radical nationalists was intensified by *Sinn Féin* (1906–1914), successor newspaper to *United Irishman*. The surviving correspondence and diaries of Patrick McCartan, Terence MacSwiney, Bulmer Hobson, P. S. O'Hegarty and Liam de Róiste, as well as patrons like Roger Casement and Joseph McGarrity of the Clan na Gael, are saturated with resentment of Griffith. Respect for his tremendous ability was undermined, first, by his refusal to consult (he was often referred to as 'dictatorial'),

---

56 Pašeta, *Irish Nationalist Women*, 97–9.
57 Ibid., 100–1.
58 K. Steele, 'Constance Markievicz's Allegorical Garden: Feminism, Militancy, and the Press, 1909–1915', *Communication Abstracts*, 24 (2001), 195–296.
59 Pašeta, *Irish Nationalist Women*, 51.

then by his apparent assumption that *Sinn Féin*, *his* newspaper, was the official voice of Sinn Féin, *their* organisation, and, finally, by the growing perception that Griffith's actions and writings no longer embodied purist nationalism. *Sinn Féin*'s apparent preoccupation with Dublin Corporation politics – it now had an elected presence – and its readiness to engage in debate regarding the prospects of Home Rule was thought indicative of Griffith's lack of principle. Much of this was spiced by a burning provincial resentment of Dublin. MacSwiney, writing to O'Hegarty from his Cork City fastness, frequently threatened to leave Sinn Féin because he believed membership was no longer compatible with his personal integrity as a separatist. O'Hegarty conceded that Griffith had changed significantly since he had edited *United Irishman*, having allowed his 'mind to run to … minor points, materialistic bread and butter points', but pleaded with MacSwiney that the ideological integrity of the movement could only be restored if men like him stayed involved.[60]

Irish Freedom, 1910–1914

For many radical nationalists the break with Sinn Féin came in 1909 when Griffith flirted with William O'Brien's All-for-Ireland League, an attempt to build a radical but inclusive constitutional nationalist alternative to the Home Rule party. The possibility that Griffith might run candidates for election in cahoots with O'Brien unified his detractors and in September 1910, Patrick McCartan wrote to Joseph McGarrity saying the IRB hoped to start a newspaper that would emulate the uncompromising *Gaelic American*, pointedly noting that it would fill the gap left by the demise of *United Irishman*.[61] Tom Clarke made a similar point in a letter to John Daly, describing the new newspaper as 'a monthly, on the same lines as *United Irishman*, or rather on a higher level'.[62] In the first issue of *Irish Freedom*, dated November 1910, P. S. O'Hegarty pointedly memorialised William Rooney, recalling how *United Irishman* had first come with the 'heaviness and bewilderingness of wine'. It had told separatists, isolated from each other, of the 'dazzling certainty' that they were not alone in working away at 'the old ideal of Tone and Mitchel'. By providing separatists 'knowledge of each other's existence', O'Hegarty argued, *United Irishman* had coordinated and strengthened separatist opinion, giving it voice, reasons to feel hopeful and things to think about, all of which 'stirred up deep

60 Kelly, *Fenian Ideal*, 184–6.
61 McCartan to McGarrity, 4 September 1910, 6 January 1911: Ms 17457/8 and /9, McGarrity Papers, National Library of Ireland.
62 Clarke to Daly, 5 October 1910 in Daly Papers, University of Limerick.

currents everywhere'.[63] O'Hegarty's subtext was clear enough. Celebrating Rooney by locating his 'Work and Gospel' in a nationalist trajectory 'from Brian Boroimhe [Brian Boru] to William Rooney' was a calculated snub to Griffith. Despite this, the republicans recognised the political capital accrued by the Sinn Féin label and were not prepared to dissociate from it altogether. 'Under whatever name we propagate our ideas', one editorial ran, 'the Irish Nation must be built on Sinn Féin principles, or non-recognition of British authority, law, justice or legislation: that is our basis and the principles of the Sinn Féin policy are today as sound as ever they were'. Sinn Féin as a movement, however, was considered 'temporarily suspended' as a consequence of its attempts to 'collar the middle classes and drop the separatists' by adopting the 1782 paradigm: 'when the separatists were dropped, there was no movement left'.[64]

Hindsight allows *Irish Freedom* to be seen as the in-house journal of the progenitors of the Irish revolution. It was published each month until December 1914 when Dublin Castle shut it down under the Defence of the Realm Act. As the RIC (Royal Irish Constabulary) Inspector General commented at its inception, 'it will be run as the Organ of the most extreme section in this country'.[65] Managed by Sean MacDermott, the charismatic young IRB organiser, with support from Tom Clarke, the former Dynamitard, it was primarily edited by Hobson, though McCartan and O'Hegarty sometimes took on the role. Others involved in the newspaper's management included Eamonn Ceannt, Micheal O'Rahilly, Cathal Brugha, Pearse Beaslai and Liam Mellows. It published work by Pearse, Ernest Blythe, MacSwiney, John Devoy, O'Hegarty, Hobson, Paddy O'Horrigan, the Gaelic editor, and Markievicz.[66] The Fianna were used to sell it at public events and IRB circles sometimes bought copies to distribute for free.[67]

Irish Freedom published a number of republican texts, later re-published as books, which were written because the newspaper existed. MacSwiney's 'Principles of Separatism' graced its pages over the course of 1911 and the private correspondence of MacSwiney and O'Hegarty makes clear that the newspaper's existence prompted MacSwiney into thinking about what he might write.[68] This was followed by Tom Clarke's 'Glimpses of an Irish

---

63 *Irish Freedom*, November 1910.
64 *Irish Freedom*, December 1911.
65 CO 904/12, November 1910 TNA.
66 V. Glandon, *Arthur Griffith and the Advanced Nationalist Press, 1900–1922* (Bern: Peter Lang, 1985), 75.
67 CO 904/12, August 1912; CO 904/88 TNA.
68 Kelly, *Fenian Ideal*, 196–7.

Felon's Prison Life' and John Daly's 'Fenian Recollections' in 1912, Pearse's 'Notes from the Hermitage' from September 1913, and Markievicz's Fianna column over the life of the paper. O'Hegarty, a persuasive if partisan chronicler of this world, later insisted on the newspaper's importance in the creation of the new separatist vanguard.[69]

The significance of the age profile of these contributors should not be missed. The push for *Irish Freedom* came from a new generation of IRB men who were both frustrated by the organisation's cautious leadership and alienated by Griffith. They identified strongly with the mid-Victorian Fenian generation and Patrick Pearse's well-known rhetoric about the 'failure of the last generation' was repeated again and again in the pages of *Irish Freedom*. If, as Roy Foster has suggested, the Irish revolution was partly a rebellion against paternal and maternal authority,[70] this often meant an alignment with symbolic grandfathers, as represented by Clarke and Devoy, and evident in respectful references to John O'Leary and the many column inches dedicated to the doings of the 1860s.

The ebullience of the young men owed a great deal to their connections in Irish-America. McCartan was McGarrity's man in Ireland, Hobson was greatly admired by the Clan na Gael leadership, and when McGarrity holidayed in Ireland in the summer of 1911, it was the young men rather than the old guard the police observed him with. These divisions became more marked in June 1910, when McCartan and Clarke, against the IRB Supreme Council's opposition to 'open activity', collaborated with Sinn Féin, the Ancient Order of Hibernians and the United Irish League in a protest against the visit to Ireland of King Edward VII. The old guard finally moved that December. They seized the half-printed copy of *Irish Freedom* and issued their own. McGarrity, as McCartan put it, 'saved the day' by supplying £100 as security for new printers. Two copies thus appeared, one under the aegis of the Supreme Council, the other announcing on its masthead that its editor was Dr Patrick McCartan. McGarrity's decisive intervention clearly indicated whom the Clan backed. By the spring of 1912, Fred Allan, prominent in the Dublin IRB and radical politics since the 1880s, was off the Supreme Council and MacDermott was on. Early that autumn, MacDermott was the IRB's delegate to the Clan na Gael convention in America. Clarke might have offered a permissive atmosphere for the young men, providing an alternative source of

69 P. S. O'Hegarty, *The Victory of Sinn Féin* (Dublin: Talbot Press, 1924) 11; Keiron Curtis, *P. S. O'Hegarty (1879–1955): Sinn Féin Fenian* (London: Anthem Press, 2010), 20–3.

70 Foster, *Vivid Faces*, 1ff.

authority to the Supreme Council, but the palace coup was eventually carried off thanks to Irish-American support. 'By gum', Clarke is supposed to have said, 'now if we don't get something done it'll be our own fault.'[71]

Irish Freedom's pages were filled with references to Fenianism. Histories of Fenianism or articles with titles like 'The Faith of a Fenian' were particularly prominent and part of an evident ambition to revive the reputation of a political tradition long treated by the nationalist mainstream as either harmless or contemptuous. The practical role Fenians had played in recent Irish history was emphasised, without which, for instance, 'the Land League would never have put up the resistance that it showed, or obtained the result that which it won'. Fenianism was also identified as crucial to 'the stauncher and more uncompromising side of the later movements in language, pastimes' – a reference to the GAA – 'or politics'.[72] A hidden history was being exposed here, in which Fenianism, 'laughed at by the great noisy current of Parliamentarian boastfulness', was granted its proper place in Irish history.[73] References to Fenianism also reflected an understanding of Irish history that placed the United Irishmen and the Fenians within the same historical tradition and in the first editorial John O'Leary was grouped together with Wolfe Tone, Robert Emmet and John Mitchel; on other occasions, a purist nationalism was signified by the coupling '1798 and 1867', while striking class claims also surfaced: thanks to Fenianism, 'practically for the first time we find artisans being added to the national martyrology'.[74]

How Fenianism provided these separatists with their standard was particularly clear in the editorial response to the Howth landing and Bachelors Walk shootings in July 1914. Two central columns of the front page were framed like a certificate and the headline ran 'THE BAPTISM'. The Volunteer Movement, the newspaper proclaimed, had been 'effectively baptised, baptised in the blood of the Volunteers – blood also of British soldiery'. The editorial continued: 'for the first time since Fenianism, blows have been made in Ireland for the clear definite principle of a free and an armed Nation, for the first time since Fenianism victory in such a fight has been with the Nation'. The next claim couldn't have been more Fenian. The landing was located to Clontarf: 'The shame of O'Connell is wiped out.'[75]

---

71 Kelly, *Fenian Ideal*, 193–5.
72 *Irish Freedom*, December 1910.
73 *Irish Freedom*, November 1910.
74 *Irish Freedom*, December 1911.
75 *Irish Freedom*, August 1914.

More could be observed about this baptismal certificate, not least the emphasis it placed on the display of masculine virility and the 'joy of the consciousness of achievement', an observation that chimed with a Fenian contempt for Home Rule politics. It also emphasised the fact that the arms had been brought safely into Dublin City in broad daylight. The city itself, through this act of territorial reclamation, had been transfigured by this 'battle in the ancient cause'.[76] City and people were becoming as one, for as *Irish Freedom* had argued in July 1914, Volunteering had wrought on Irish nationalists a transformation that was 'organic' rather than 'functional', 'psychological' rather than 'experimental'.[77] New experiences were helping the Irish people discern truths obscured by the clever rhetorics of Home Rule and the apparent benevolence of the Liberal Party. As this epiphany occurred, *Irish Freedom* aimed to discipline dissent, its homilies helping to ensure that its readers maintained an inward and outward ideological vigilance, seeing through the present crisis to the opportunity beyond. And by rejecting a providential account of Ireland's history – independence was not inevitable – *Irish Freedom* attempted to make the future by imagining plausible scenarios that would give Irish people faith in a different kind of political action. Revolution would become probable when a critical mass of the Irish people believed in its possibility, to which end *Irish Freedom* preached a kind of revelation in which the Home Rule crisis would lead unionists and home rulers alike towards realising that their positions within the Union were false. A unified Irish nation, republican and separatist, would be the result, whether or not Home Rule was successfully implemented.

The IRB did not rely on epiphany alone. The most distinctive component of separatist discourse in the years before the Great War was the centrality of anti-imperialism to its articulation of Ireland's right to complete independence. Anti-imperialism was not new to Irish nationalism, mid-Victorian nationalists having made much of their sense of affinity for the Indians, the Maori, the Italians and the Poles, but this had faded in the racialised context of the 'new imperialism' of the late nineteenth century – during the South African war, even Davitt failed to identify it as a struggle between colonising peoples, fought at the expense of the indigenous population.[78] Radical

76 Ibid.
77 *Irish Freedom*, July 1914.
78 P. Townend, 'Between Two Worlds: Irish Nationalists and Imperial Crisis, 1878–1880', *Past & Present*, 194 (February 2007), 139–74, and M. Kelly, 'Irish Nationalist Opinion and the British Empire in the 1850s and 1860s', *Past & Present*, 204 (August 2009), 127–54. Home Rule MPs like the Quaker Alfred Webb and Frank Hugh O'Donnell were

nationalism's renewed anti-imperialism was stimulated by Redmond's enthusiasm for empire, which James McConnel argues became more marked after 1906 and was strongly shaped by ideas of 'Greater Britain' and nascent commonwealth thinking, all reinforced for Redmond by earlier visits to Australia and New Zealand.[79]

As a means of distinguishing the object of radical nationalists from that of the Home Rulers, the anti-imperial trope proved an important breakthrough, granting Irish nationalism a wider purpose in the new century. For example, an *Irish Freedom* report on the ' "Federal" Rumours' in its first issue noted how commonplace it had become to add 'the adjective "Imperial"' to Home Rule,[80] while Redmond's Norwich speech of 7 November 1911 was condemned as 'an orgy of Imperialism'. Redmond had claimed:

> We are only asking for a local Parliament, subject to the unimpaired supremacy of the Imperial Parliament for the transaction of purely Irish local affairs. We disclaim with ridicule the charge that we are Separatists. What we are asking for is the very antithesis of Separation. It leaves you as strong, Ah! far stronger than you are to-day to deal with any demand for Separation in the future.[81]

Speeches such as these prompted *Irish Freedom* to condemn Home Rule as intended to maintain 'Imperial Supremacy', 'Imperial Taxation', and the 'Imperial Parliament'.[82] Deriding the idea that Home Rule was 'for "restoring Ireland to the Empire"',[83] *Irish Freedom* argued that its purpose was to 'consolidate the English Empire' by purchasing 'Ireland's adhesion to the Empire at the cheapest price at which ever a nation was asked to sell itself body and soul'.[84] The idea that the Home Rule campaign at Westminster was transactional rather than principled was a well-established advanced nationalist trope, but anti-imperialism gave it renewed traction: not 'for a spoonfed local legislature' or 'for patronage and power' or 'the lust of Imperialism' was

---

the exceptions that proved the rule, the former generally taken more seriously than the latter. See J. Regan-Lefebvre, *Cosmopolitan Nationalism and the Victorian Empire. Ireland, India and the Politics of Alfred Webb* (Basingstoke: Palgrave Macmillan, 2009) and H. Brasted, 'Indian Nationalist Development and the Influence of Irish Home Rule, 1870–1886', *Modern Asian Studies*, xiv (1980), 37–63.

79 For Redmond's rhetoric, see *Irish Freedom*, November 1911, and, more generally, J. McConnel, 'John Redmond and Irish Catholic Loyalism', *English Historical Review*, CXXV (February 2010), 83–111.

80 *Irish Freedom*, November 1910.

81 *Irish Freedom*, November 1911.

82 *Irish Freedom*, January 1912.

83 *Irish Freedom*, February 1912.

84 *Irish Freedom*, April 1912.

Irish Freedom willing to 'sell' Ireland's 'heritage' and 'trust'.[85] An editorial commenting on the Home Rule parliamentary debates in August 1912 provided a sharp summary of their position:

> One of the English speakers asked, and asked in vain, where now was the Separatist element in the Irish Parliamentary Party. There is none; it has got corrupted into Imperialism, an Imperialism which not alone is Imperialism but is almost pro-English. The situation in Ireland in the past has been complicated by the fact that the Party which claimed to carry on the work of Emmet and Mitchel was actually an Imperialist Party, attending the Imperialist Parliament, swearing allegiance to the English Crown and Constitution, and helping England to govern this country. That, at least, will now disappear, and there will be a clear line of demarcation in the future between the Nationalist and the Imperialist, between the traditions of Tone and the traditions of Grattan.[86]

Consequently, when in July 1912 *Irish Freedom* went so far as to imagine the IRB organising as a conventional political party in a Home Rule Ireland and competing for votes with the Redmondites, they imagined their opponents as 'a kind of Nationalist Imperialist Party'.[87] As such, the separatists could not 'go to the Irish people with a vague or ill-defined political ideal' but, thanks to the psychological transformation in train, 'even at the beginning' it would have 'sufficient strength' to 'disregard the possible alienation' caused by its '"extreme" principles'. 'It must therefore be either an '82 Party [i.e. 1782] or a Republican Party, and as an '82 Party will have no justification now save as a Monarchical Party, we think that the only possible basis is a definite Republican basis'.[88] As this makes clear, anti-imperialism had wide implications. When separatists first contemplated Griffith's ideas, less than a decade earlier, many were ready to compromise their principles for the reason that Sinn Féin might bring the Irish people a step closer to republicanism. Now that the Home Rule Party was rejected not because it was insufficiently nationalist but because it was imperialist, so it was consistent to reject Sinn Féin on account of its dual monarchism. The new emphasis placed on Home Rule as an imperialist creed invalidated any alternative to full separation.

'Unionist', writing in the *Cork Constitution*, castigated *Irish Freedom* for its 'audacity and cheek'. There was something shocking about the way the separatists confronted Ireland's greatest political crisis for more than a generation

---

85 *Irish Freedom*, November 1911. O'Hegarty, incidentally, is notorious for his later misogyny.
86 *Irish Freedom*, August 1912.
87 *Irish Freedom*, July 1912.
88 Ibid.

with scorn for the very principles on which it was based. But 'Unionist' was wrong to describe the newspaper's agenda as 'obsolete'. In the past, the successful promotion of Home Rule as nationalism, maybe even Fenianism by other means, had made the Home Rulers slippery opponents, allowing the separatists to be labelled extremist. By clearly and unambiguously identifying Redmondism as a form of British imperialism, separatists finally had a political language that allowed them to clearly distinguish the 'Home Rulers' from the 'nationalists'. The imperial definition of Home Rule gave them a conceptual language that allowed them to identify the fundamental difference – rather than difference of degree – between themselves and the Home Rulers. *Irish Freedom* articulated this with a clarity and directness that gave separatist nationalism new powers of expression.

Not only was the consistency and evident satisfaction with which *Irish Freedom*'s editorialists denounced Home Rule as imperialism, it also brought into sharp focus thinking that had been gradually evolving over the previous generation. If mid-Victorian nationalists had regarded the imperial government of Ireland as an externally imposed despotism incompatible with democracy, the neo-Fenians grafted onto this Irish Ireland thinking. To remove the outward forms of this despotism before the processes of cultural imperialism were reversed would mean change of little significance. 'We, on our side of the question', the newspaper explained, 'have wakened up to the fact that the danger to the nation was mental rather than physical: that we were threatened far more effectively by the permanent forces of Anglicisation, the English language and English ideas and outlook, than by its temporary physical force.'[89] Thankfully, the 'Irish Ireland Movement' had already given the 'nation a firm basis to counteract the corruption of the Parliamentarian political movement into a reactionary Imperialism'.[90] As a consequence, when, as late as February 1914, the separatists envisaged settling 'down to the serious business of running the nation' within the confines of 'the very limited administrative and financial powers' allowed by the Home Rule Bill, they emphasised the need to maintain the language movement if the Irish people's desire for greater autonomy was to be sustained.[91]

Rebellion

The outbreak of war, the suspension of the Home Rule Act and Redmond's commitment of the Irish Volunteers to the war effort – and the consequent

89 *Irish Freedom*, October 1913.
90 *Irish Freedom*, September 1913.
91 *Irish Freedom*, February 1914.

split in the organisation – saw *Irish Freedom* claim that Ireland once again faced a 'psychological moment', only this time it had a 'determined, drilled, mass of men of proved courage to meet it'.[92] The seeming acceptance of these developments by most Irish people helped justify the decision by a small *elite* group within the breakaway Volunteer faction to begin secretive preparations for a rebellion before the end of the war. In some respects the Easter Rising of 1916 was an act of witness, a means of making meaningful Fenianism's longstanding commitments and assumptions, not least the old adage that 'England's difficulty is Ireland's opportunity'. However, in order to guarantee that the rebellion came about, the democratic, secular republicanism of the old Fenians, which in many respects had been reimagined by the broader currents of pre-war radical nationalism, had to be abandoned for an *elitist* vanguardism, buoyed up by a religiously inspired cultural revivalism for which Patrick Pearse became the principal avatar. Overruling MacNeill's countermanding order and some rough handling in Dublin saw the Rising commence with something akin to a palace coup, while the fact that it went ahead despite poor planning and in the knowledge of Casement's failed attempt to land German arms off the Kerry coast underpins explanations of the rebellion that play down its military intent and find it an exercise in martyrdom, a 'blood sacrifice' made on the altar of nationhood.[93]

How far the Easter Rising embodied the radical ideas that had animated separatist nationalism over the previous generation or so is hard to fathom. The Proclamation, the best indicator of the leadership's intentions, is a peculiar mix of traditional nationalist shibboleths and liberal or civic ideals.[94] Certainly, the Proclamation was remarkable in being addressed to 'Irishmen and Irishwomen' – women played important 'auxiliary' roles during the rebellion – and there is no question that many of the rebels were in favour of women's suffrage, though it is worth noting that *Irish Freedom* could refer to nationalist 'men and women' without becoming particularly exercised about the matter. The emphasis placed on the protection of civil and religious

---

92 *Irish Freedom*, October 1914. The phrase 'psychological moment' crops up in O'Hegarty's later writing and this, like other textual evidence, suggests he played a particularly influential role in developing *Irish Freedom*'s editorial line. See F. Flanagan, *Remembering the Revolution. Dissent, Culture and Nationalism in the Irish Free State* (Oxford University Press, 2015), 252–60.
93 On the effectiveness of the rebel plans, see C. Townshend, *Easter 1916,* 252–60.
94 The Proclamation is reproduced in full in Foster, *Modern Ireland,* 597–8.

liberties was incontrovertible;[95] socialist connotations were oblique but manifest in the reference to 'the right of the people of Ireland to the ownership of Ireland', which strongly echoed the 1914 constitution of the Irish Citizen Army (ICA); and the celebrated intention to cherish 'all the children of the nation equally' signalled a desire to overcome the sectarian 'differences carefully fostered by an alien government'. Much effort has been made to explain whether Connolly could reconcile the internationalist Red with the nationalist Green, the most recent attempt being Lauren Arrington's ingenious argument that the targeting of Jacob's Biscuit Factory and the South Dublin Union related to earlier leftist struggles led by Larkin's ITGWU (Irish Transport and General Workers' Union).[96]

Absent from the Proclamation was any explicit reference to empire. Claiming Ireland should enjoy its due 'exaltation among the nations' recalled the language of the 'struggling nations' rather than the politics of anti-colonialism, and while Ireland was 'supported by her exiled children in America and by gallant allies in Europe', she relied 'first on her own strength'. As such, despite *Irish Freedom*'s anti-imperialism and the anti-Home Rule and anti-Sinn Féin subtexts at work in the rebellion, the Proclamation was in many respects a traditional nationalist document: European rather than global in its orientation and historicist in its thinking. By claiming that the 'Irish republic is entitled to, and hereby claims, the allegiance of every Irishman and Irishwoman' it is also authoritarian, offering a singular definition of Irishness, at least as a political identity, denying the legitimacy of non-Republican nationalism or unionism *tout court*. Finally, to act in 'the name of God and of the dead generations' from which Ireland received 'her old tradition of nationhood' carried an almost uncanny echo of Marx's claim in *The Eighteenth Brumaire* that 'Tradition from all the dead generations weighs like a nightmare on the brain of the living.'[97] Was Connolly oblivious to this resonance? The authors of the proclamation augmented that tradition as they bravely faced the nightmare of a British firing squad. Those who choose to succeed them were left to ask how conviction could be reconciled to 'the living stream'.[98]

---

95 Fighting with the ICA, Lieutenant Constance Markievicz was second-in-command to Michael Mallin at St Stephen's Green; Kathleen Lynn took over Connolly's command when he was unable to continue.

96 L. Arrington, 'Socialist Republican Discourse and the 1916 Easter Rising: The Occupation of Jacob's Biscuit Factory and the South Dublin Union Explained', *Journal of British Studies*, 53 (2014), 992–1010.

97 Karl Marx, *Later Political Writings* (Cambridge University Press, 1996), 32.

98 W. B. Yeats, *The Poems* (London: Macmillan, 1994), 229.

2

Home Rulers at Westminster, 1880–1914

CONOR MULVAGH

Introduction

The period 1880 to 1914 witnessed profound social, economic, cultural and political change in Ireland. In broad terms, such change was not unique. Like Russia on the other extremity of the European continent, Ireland's social revolution predated the political. This revolution was agrarian in nature and witnessed not the emancipation of a semi-feudal agrarian labouring class as in Tsarist Russia, but rather the elevation of a relatively prosperous tenant farmer class to the status of owner-occupiers. This process simultaneously forced the decline of the Irish landlord. Religious and ethnic denominators can be unhelpful here. The process was class-based and financially driven.

The rise of Charles Stewart Parnell within the Irish Parliamentary Party (IPP) of the late 1870s ran parallel to a rapidly evolving agrarian crisis. In 1877, Parnell won the presidency of the Home Rule Confederation of Great Britain from his party chairman, Isaac Butt. This signalled the shift that would culminate in Parnell's ascent to the chairmanship of the Irish Parliamentary Party in May 1880. Global economic shocks and poor harvests in Ireland during 1878 led to a rise in evictions in 1879. By then, the problem had been politicised through the foundation of the Irish National Land League in Dublin on 21 October 1879. Here, the American dimension was critical. Less than a month after Butt's death in May 1879, Parnell joined forces with the former Fenian convict and agrarian socialist Michael Davitt in what became known as the New Departure. This unlikely alliance can be traced to New York, where the prominent Irish-American Fenian, John Devoy, facilitated meetings between the two. For the Fenians, the New Departure represented a renewed experiment in constitutionalism. For Parnell, the New Departure offered the alluring prospect of hitching the rather abstract concept of Home Rule and national self-government to the more emotive, popular, and established political cause of the land.

In the absence of extensive suffrage, the fight for tenant rights and the transfer of land from landlord to tenant were issues in which a wide section of the populace could participate. Agitation stretched from grassroots level up to parliament. In the same way as Catholic emancipation had first politicised a large swathe of the Irish populace, now the land question mobilised a new generation through the great unifying cause of their era.

Land War

With Davitt on one side and Parnell on the other, the New Departure initiated a quasi-revolutionary campaign of agrarian agitation which lasted from autumn 1879 until May 1882. It brought about the upheaval of life in rural Ireland, the committal of Irish constabulary resources in a way not seen since 1867, and it returned Irish affairs to the centre of political debate at Westminster. As the focus here is on the constitutional, the Land War is relevant in the way in which democratically elected members of parliament threw themselves into campaigns of extra-parliamentary agitation and were criminalised and eventually gaoled for so doing. It can sometimes be tempting to trace the 1885 alliance between Irish Home Rulers and Gladstonian Liberals backwards. The period of Liberal government beginning in April 1880 witnessed as much coercion as conciliation when it came to Ireland. Gladstone's mission, after all, had been to pacify rather than placate the United Kingdom's western island.

Since its inaugural meeting in October 1879, Parnell had held the presidency of the Irish National Land League. Following the general election of April 1880, he combined this role with the chairmanship of the Irish Parliamentary Party. Land, as opposed to Home Rule, would be the immediate priority of the party. Upon taking office, Gladstone appointed William Edward Forster to the Irish Office. The new Chief Secretary shared much of Gladstone's sympathy for the plight of the Irish tenant farmer. Forster worked in earnest to alleviate the distress which confronted him in his new portfolio. One of his biggest challenges was keeping the landed section of the British Liberal party on side. He needed to convince these members that no threat was being posed to the general laws of property. In legislating against the interests of landlords in an effort to alleviate tenant distress in Ireland, he made it clear that the measures proposed were both temporary and territorially confined.[1]

---

1 M. O'Callaghan, *British High Politics and a Nationalist Ireland: Criminality, Land and the Law under Forster and Balfour* (Cork: Cork University Press, 1994), 34–5.

Even as late as April 1880, the Land League was still 'basically a Connaught phenomenon'.[2] When Gladstone returned to the premiership at the end of that month, the new government was faced with 'suffering and confusion in Ireland, but not yet with systematised disorder'.[3] By the summer, the situation was deteriorating and evictions began to increase. The government's response was to establish the Bessborough Royal Commission to inquire into the working of Gladstone's first Irish Land Act of 1870. Appointed in July, the Commission did not report until the first days of January 1881. In the interim, agitation in Ireland intensified. Boycott, intimidation, public meetings and demonstrations were used effectively by the Land League.

The government had been reacting to the developing situation in Ireland throughout 1880. However, by 1881, Gladstone had begun to regain the initiative. Following the report of the Bessborough Commission, the government worked speedily to introduce new legislation for Ireland. The Protection of Persons and Property Bill was enacted by March. By April, a new land bill was before the House of Commons. Furthermore, the government engineered an effective solution to the obstructionism which had dogged parliament since the mid-1870s. In February 1881, Gladstone successfully passed a set of resolutions which put an end to filibustering in its traditional form.[4]

Gladstone's Second Land Act, 'though mutilated by the Lords', passed into law on 22 August 1881.[5] The continued campaign of the Land League during the autumn – fuelled by William O'Brien's inflammatory journalism – renewed the Cabinet's appetite to deal harshly with agitation in Ireland. Parnell's call to 'test the Act' in the newly established land courts was adopted by a convention of the Land League in September. This further exasperated Gladstone and his ministers. However, despite the Land League's efforts to deride the new Land Act, the government was pleasantly surprised to see that arbitration on rents was taken up enthusiastically by tenants. Over 11,000 applications for review were received within two months of the enactment.[6] As the Land League carried on its campaign of agitation, the government capitalised on the perception that the movement had been weakened. In mid-October, Parnell and his most prominent comrades in the League were arrested and imprisoned without trial under the Protection of Persons and Property Act.

---

2 H. C. G. Matthew, *Gladstone, 1875–1898* (Oxford University Press, 1995), 186.
3 Matthew, *Gladstone*, 187.
4 F. S. L. Lyons, *Charles Stewart Parnell* (London: Collins, 1977), 145.
5 Lyons, *Parnell*, 164.
6 J. V. O'Brien, *William O'Brien and the Course of Irish Politics, 1881–1918* (Berkeley, CA: University of California Press, 1976), 19.

The gaoling of Land Leaguers was nothing new. Indeed, the revocation of Michael Davitt's parole earlier that year had been deeply damaging to the League's organisation. However, the incarceration without trial of leading Land Leaguers, who were also MPs, was a turning point in the history of the Land League. On the hillsides, it would intensify the agitation and exacerbate relations between agitators and police. For the League's leader, however, arrest was greeted with mixed feelings. The arresting detective granted Parnell the favour of writing several letters which he posted before entering Kilmainham Gaol. One of these letters was to Katharine O'Shea, then carrying his child. The overall tone of this letter was fatalistic, but Parnell concluded with a note of optimism: 'Politically it is a fortunate thing for me that I have been arrested, as the movement is breaking fast, and all will be quiet in a few months, when I shall be released.'[7]

Parnell thus treated his arrest with a degree of stoicism. By contrast, an early biographer of Chief Secretary Forster noted how, when Gladstone announced the news of Parnell's arrest to a meeting at the City of London's Guildhall, '[i]t was hailed almost as though it had been the news of a signal victory gained by England over a hated and formidable enemy'.[8] The Land League's response came from within the walls of Kilmainham. Within five days, William O'Brien had penned the 'No Rent Manifesto'. This called for the mass witholding of rents until the imprisoned Leaguers were released. In Kilmainham, Parnell put his name to the manifesto alongside John Dillon, Andrew Kettle, Thomas Brennan and Thomas Sexton. Conor Cruise O'Brien notes that only O'Brien, Kettle and Brennan were enthusiastic about the manifesto. Parnell apparently only signed to satisfy Patrick Egan, the League's Treasurer, and Patrick Ford, editor of the New York-based *Irish World*.[9]

The manifesto resulted in the immediate suppression of the Land League. From a government perspective, the imprisonment of Parnell and his lieutenants in Kilmainham proved to be a resounding success. It took the wind out of the sails of the League and it demoralised its supporters. In Kilmainham, Parnell was increasingly keen to end his ongoing imprisonment and was willing to compromise. Moonlighting and agrarian outrage continued

---

7 P. Bew, *Enigma: A New Life of Charles Stewart Parnell* (Dublin: Gill & Macmillan, 2011), 86. The letter in question was first published in Katharine's 1914 two-volume biography of her second husband.

8 T. Wemyss Reid, *Life of the Right Honourable William Edward Forster, 2 vols.* (London: Chapman and Hall, 1888), ii, 356.

9 C. C. O'Brien, *Parnell and his Party, 1880–1890* (Oxford University Press, 1957), 73, citing R. Barry O'Brien.

throughout the winter of 1881–1882. However, the Land League was rudderless in the absence of its leadership. The gambit of the 'No Rent Manifesto' failed to pay off. Personal matters gave a new impetus to Parnell's next move.

Ending the Land War: the Kilmainham Treaty

Parnell's daughter, Claude-Sophie, born to Katharine O'Shea on 16 February 1882, was sick and dying. On 10 April, Parnell had been granted temporary release from Kilmainham to attend the funeral of his nephew in Paris. *En route*, he had visited the O'Sheas and saw his daughter.[10] His return coincided with her death. Parnell returned to Kilmainham, while Katharine grieved without him. Prior to the events of mid-April, attempts at a compromise between Parnell and Gladstone had progressed slowly. William O'Shea acted as the go-between, but Katharine O'Shea's own contact with the prime minister was also significant. Her correspondence with Gladstone, preserved in the latter's papers, demonstrates the level of agency women in high-political circles could exert in this era.[11] Returning to her husband, Captain O'Shea was not simply an emissary between the Nationalist and Liberal leaders. He was as much suggesting his own solutions to Gladstone as he was conveying the sentiments of Parnell. Crucially, O'Shea had put himself in the position of intermediary, having reached out to Gladstone in a letter dated 8 April to offer his services at working towards a solution.[12] Gladstone responded enthusiastically. In correspondence and, crucially, during a long discussion on the eve of Claude-Sophie's death at Eltham, O'Shea hammered out the deal that would finally be concluded as the 'Kilmainham Treaty' between Parnell and Gladstone on 2 May.[13] Under the accord, Gladstone would address the difficulties of leaseholders and tenants in arrears. For his part, Parnell agreed formally to abandon 'no rent' – something he was more than happy to do – and to accept the 1881 Act as the settlement of the Land War and discourage further agitation.[14]

---

10 K. O'Shea (Mrs Charles Stewart Parnell), *Charles Stewart Parnell: His Love Story and Political Life*, 2 vols. (New York: G. H. Doran, 1914), i, 230–1.

11 See Gladstone – Katharine O'Shea correspondence, 1882–1888 Add. MS 44,269, ff. 75–313: British Library (hereafter BL).

12 William O'Shea to W. E. Gladstone, 8 April 1882 Add. MS 44,269, ff 15–16: BL.

13 See Gladstone to O'Shea, 15 April 1882, Add. MS 44,269, f. 27; BL. On the Parnell–O'Shea negotiations on the night of 21–22 April, see O'Shea, *Parnell*, I, 232–3 and Lyons, *Parnell*, 196.

14 See Lyons, *Parnell*, 203–4.

Beyond Kilmainham, 1882–1886

Conor Cruise O'Brien viewed the Kilmainham Treaty as a watershed which 'marked the transmutation of Parnellism from a quasi-revolutionary movement into a completely constitutional one'.[15] The Land League was wound up and replaced by the Irish National League, a move that Davitt only agreed to following pressure from Parnell. Furthermore, the Ladies Land League, in which Parnell's sisters Anna and Fanny played a leading role, was disbanded. Anna Parnell fell out bitterly with her brother over this. Years later, following the publication of Michael Davitt's *Fall of Feudalism in Ireland* (1904) – a work with which she took great umbrage – she penned *The Tale of Great Sham*, her own unapologetic narrative of the Land War.[16]

By severing links with the radical elements of his movement, Parnell protected the parliamentary party. However, just days after Parnell finalised his accord with Gladstone, the assassination of the newly-appointed Chief Secretary, Lord Frederick Cavendish, and his Under Secretary, Thomas Burke, in Phoenix Park on 6 May 1882, threw Irish constitutional nationalism into crisis. The group responsible, 'the Invincibles', had Burke as the intended target. However, the death of Cavendish, whose wife was Gladstone's niece, provoked greater outrage both in Ireland and Britain. For Parnell and his lieutenants, the denunciation of extra-parliamentary agitation now became a matter of urgency rather than concession.

The Irish National League was established in October 1882. It replaced the Land League and re-orientated the movement away from agrarian radicalism. The new organisation facilitated the centralisation of power within the constitutional nationalist movement. A year later, the introduction of a party pledge further enhanced discipline within the parliamentary party. The power of the pledge was always 'moral rather than quasi-legal', but it was nonetheless effective.[17] This new machine party saw the more patrician wing of the old Home Rule movement give way to a new generation who had begun to populate the movement after Parnell acceded to the chairmanship in 1880.[18]

In 1884, the Representation of the People Act almost doubled the size of the United Kingdom electorate, bringing it to 5,708,030 electors. In Ireland, the electorate more than trebled, rising from 229,204 in the 1880 general election

---

15 Cruise O'Brien, *Parnell*, 119.

16 A. Parnell, *The Tale of Great Sham* (ed. Dana Hearne) (Dublin: Arlen House, 1986).

17 F. Callanan, *The Parnell Split, 1890–91* (Cork: Cork University Press, 1992), 3.

18 D. Thornley, *Isaac Butt and Home Rule* (London: MacKibbon and Kee, 1964), 330 *et seq.*

to 737,965 in the elections of 1885.[19] Although initially wary of franchise extension, the Irish party quickly saw its benefits in practical terms. The number of Home Rule MPs rose dramatically from 63 seats in 1880 to 85 of Ireland's 103 seats in 1885. Under the new franchise, Parnell's party received 67.8 per cent of the poll, up from 37.5 per cent across the whole island.[20]

1885 was a year of extraordinary brinkmanship in British and Irish politics. On 9 June 1885, Conservatives and the IPP combined their votes in a late-night sitting and defeated the government. Gladstone handed over the reins of power, allowing Lord Salisbury to form a caretaker government. General elections under the new franchise were duly held in November. Parnell encouraged the Irish in Britain to vote Tory. The impact of this exhortation is difficult to gauge, but Parnell found himself holding the balance between 335 Liberals and 249 Conservatives. This parliamentary arithmetic meant that Irish nationalist MPs now found themselves in a position of real power between the two British parties for the first time. Faced with parliamentary uncertainty, Gladstone contemplated an alliance with the Conservatives. However, events took a dramatic twist on 17 December. Using his son Herbert to distance himself from the potential backlash, Gladstone flew the 'Hawarden Kite', signalling the Grand Old Man's conversion to Home Rule.[21] With Irish support, the Liberals had their majority and formed a government.

On the first day of the new parliament, 12 January 1886, Parnell brought with him the United Kingdom's first ever pledge-bound party, one that also enjoyed a greatly expanded popular mandate and held all but eighteen of Ireland's parliamentary seats. Less than four years after the Kilmainham Treaty, Parnell had successfully re-constitutionalised his party after the Land War. Ireland would now be offered a constitutional settlement through constitutional channels following a constitutional campaign.

The First Home Rule Bill

When drafting the 1886 Home Rule Bill, Gladstone kept its contents a closely guarded secret, even from his Cabinet colleagues. However, it was not a solo project. Parnell had submitted a 'Rough Sketch of proposed Constitution for Ireland' to Gladstone in October 1885.[22] His provisions were similar to those

---

19 All figures above from F. W. S. Craig, *British Electoral Facts, 1832–1987* (5th edn., Aldershot: Palgrave Macmillan, 1989), 67.
20 All statistics generated from data in Craig, *British Electoral Facts*, 67–8.
21 R. Jenkins, *Gladstone: A Biography* (New York: Random House, 1995), 526–31.
22 Add. MS 44,771, ff 1–2: BL.

of the first Home Rule Bill in some respects. However, Gladstone's bill moderated some of Parnell's more ambitious elements. Interestingly, Parnell was wholly ambivalent on the question of retaining Irish MPs at Westminster. 'The representation of Ireland in the Imperial Parliament might be retained or might be given up. If it be retained, the Speaker might have power to decide what questions the Irish members might take part in as Imperial questions, if this limitation were thought desirable.'[23] This 'in and out' model of Irish representation at Westminster would resurface seven years later when Home Rule came before parliament for a second time. In 1886, opposition to the bill galvanised two sections in particular. In parliament, Joseph Chamberlain spearheaded Liberal opposition to the bill. Outside parliament, the bill roused Irish unionist opposition.

Returning to the land question

F. S. L. Lyons asserted that 'the home rule debates of 1886 were less the climax of, than a deviation from, the logical and predictable development of Irish politics in the Parnellite period'.[24] In May 1886, John Dillon had remarked to the House of Commons that a 'truce of God' existed in Ireland while the Home Rule Bill was before parliament, but warned opponents of the bill not to '[send] us back to the suffering people of Ireland with the winter before us and our hands empty'.[25] A general election followed the defeat of the bill and, with the Liberals now split, Salisbury returned to office with a comfortable majority.

The advent of a Unionist government signalled the beginning of tougher times for Irish nationalism. Parnell introduced a tenant relief bill only to have it flatly rejected in the House of Commons. In October, five years after it had published the 'No Rent Manifesto', the pages of *United Ireland* were used to launch a new agrarian crusade: the Plan of Campaign. The Plan saw parliamentarians resorting to extra-parliamentary and ultimately illegal actions. This was at a time when the collapse of the 1886 Home Rule Bill heralded the return of a strong Unionist government. For the agrarian wing of nationalism, stasis in parliament afforded an opportunity to reassert some of the radicalism lost after Kilmainham. The authors of the Plan were Dillon, O'Brien and Timothy Harrington. Parnell fell seriously ill during the winter of 1886–1887 with an illness which remains mysterious to this day, but was most likely

---

23 Add. MS 44,771, ff 1–2: BL.
24 F. S. L. Lyons, 'John Dillon and the Plan of Campaign, 1886–90', *Irish Historical Studies*, xiv, (September 1965), 313.
25 *Hansard 3*, cccv, 999.

Bright's disease: acute nephritis.[26] Whatever its nature, the illness rendered Parnell inaccessible and unable to exert control over events in Ireland. However, it also freed him from the necessity of immediately pronouncing his official stance on the Plan. With Parnell unwilling to curb the new agitation, the government and other forces acted swiftly. On 18 December, the Plan of Campaign was proclaimed 'an unlawful criminal conspiracy'. The relatively benign Michael Hicks Beach was replaced by the more authoritarian Arthur Balfour as Irish Chief Secretary in March 1887.[27]

Irish constitutional nationalism now took on two distinct faces. In Britain, Parnell became a regular guest at Hawarden, where Gladstone, now relieved of the burdens of office, was happy to welcome him as an ally. In Ireland, by contrast, Balfour's relentless crackdown provoked animosity. A new coercion bill was enacted and tensions reached a high point in September with the 'Mitchelstown massacre'. Among his detractors, the new Chief Secretary was quickly labelled 'Bloody Balfour'.[28]

1887 was the high point of the Plan of Campaign; thereafter the project suffered serious reversals. A Papal rescript condemning the agitation came in April. By May, Parnell gave a speech in which he 'virtually disown[ed]' the Plan.[29] Compounding these blows, Dillon, O'Brien, and many key organisers served terms of imprisonment that year. The Plan was costing the National League dearly, to the point of financial collapse. Unlike previous campaigns, the Plan did not provoke excitement or elicit significant funds from Ireland abroad.[30] With costs spiralling and diminishing receipts, Dillon was forced to go cap in hand to Parnell in January 1889. He calculated that £10,000 would be necessary just to keep the campaign afloat. Some funds were granted by Parnell. This money had an unusual provenance. It came from the colonialist and mining magnate Cecil Rhodes, who had offered funds to Parnell on the condition that the Irish leader defend the retention of MPs at Westminster in the event of Home Rule being granted.[31]

26 Lyons, *Parnell*, 361–2 and J. B. Lyons, 'Charles Stewart Parnell and his Doctors', in D. McCartney (ed.), *Parnell: The Politics of Power* (Dublin: Wolfhound Press, 1991), 173.

27 On the transition from Hicks-Beach to Balfour see O'Callaghan, *British High Politics*, 142–4.

28 T. P. O'Connor, *The Parnell Movement: Being a History of the Irish Question from the Death of O'Connell to the Suicide of Pigott* (London: K. Paul Trench and Co. 1889), 319–22. For the 'Mitchelstown massacre', see below p. 133.

29 Lyons, *Parnell*, 432.

30 M. Keyes, *Funding the Nation: Money and Nationalist Politics in Nineteenth Century Ireland* (Dublin: Gill & Macmillan, 2011), 176–9.

31 S. Marks and S. Trapido, 'Rhodes, Cecil John (1853–1902)', *Oxford Dictionary of National Biography* (Oxford University Press, 2004); online edn., September 2013: www.oxforddnb.com/view/article/35731 (accessed 2 October 2017).

By 1889, the Plan of Campaign was on the brink of financial collapse. Officially, the campaign folded with the split of the Irish party in December 1890. That it had managed not to bankrupt itself prior to this was nothing short of a miracle. To conclude on this phase of agrarian agitation, the Plan was seen to have 'peaked early and … suffered a protracted demise'.[32]

Parnellism and Crime: Conspiracy and Forgery

While the Plan of Campaign was ongoing, the political world of London was being drawn back to the earlier agitation of 1879–1882. Beginning on 7 March 1887, a series of articles began to appear in *The Times* of London, entitled 'Parnellism and Crime'. The articles relied on a series of letters allegedly written between Parnell and others. These articles rested on claims that had been made in a popular pamphlet the previous year. There, Parnell had been placed at the apex of a conspiracy of murder and moonlighting.[33] Most sensational of all, one of *The Times'* letters appeared to show Parnell apparently condoning the Phoenix Park murders of 1882.

Such was the gravity of the allegations made about Parnell in *The Times* that a Special Commission was established by parliament in August 1888 to investigate the claims. Sitting over the course of thirteen months, the Special Commission revealed much about the inner workings of the Land League. It reached its spectacular conclusion in November 1889, when Parnell's counsel, Sir Charles Russell, cross-examined Mr Richard Pigott. Pigott was exposed as a forger, fled to Madrid and there committed suicide. One view is that Parnell had been vindicated by Pigott's unmasking and subsequent suicide. A radically different interpretation of the entire episode argues that 'the minutiae of the tragedy have diverted attention from the real triumph of Conservatism'.[34] In this version, Parnellism was killed by a Conservative strategy of containment in which the role of the Special Commission was to '[dismantle] the nationalist alliance by publically examining its entrails'.[35]

From Triumph to Rejection: Parnell's Last Years

The traditional interpretation sees Parnell's dramatic exoneration at the Special Commission as marking the high point of his political career.

---

32 A. Jackson, *Ireland, 1798–1998: Politics and War* (Oxford: Blackwell, 1999), 135.

33 [Anon.], *The Repeal of the Union Conspiracy, or Mr Parnell, M.P., and the I.R.B.* (London: William Ridgway, 1886).

34 O'Callaghan, *British High Politics*, 121.

35 O'Callaghan, *British High Politics*, 120.

However, much of the old Land League's dirty laundry had been aired in public. Personally, Parnell had come out of the ordeal strengthened and with an air of invincibility about him. On Christmas Eve 1889, Captain William O'Shea filed for divorce, citing his party leader as co-respondent. The fallout from this action would take almost a year to reach its conclusion. However, the seeds of an ominous new challenge to Parnell's public reputation had been sown.

Captain O'Shea was granted his divorce by *decree nisi* on 17 November 1890. On 24 November, Gladstone communicated that he could not support Parnell's continued chairmanship of the Irish party. Ignorant of the contents of this letter, the following day, Parnell's colleagues re-elected him sessional chairman of the parliamentary party as they had done annually since 1880. When Gladstone's position became known, the party was plunged into chaos. Convening in Committee Room 15 of the Palace of Westminster, the party thrashed out the moral and political arguments for and against the retention of its chairman. Amid tears, fisticuffs, and the destruction of long friendships, the party split on 6 December. Justin McCarthy led a majority of 44 out in opposition, while Parnell remained with a rump of 29 MPs.

The split that had occurred at Westminster, and the arguments rehearsed there, were now brought to the nation. In a bitter campaign lasting ten months, lines of demarcation hardened and Parnell was forced to fight for his political and personal reputation, appealing to some unlikely quarters for assistance along the way.[36] There was both a moral and a political dimension to the split within the party. Better understood is the widespread distaste for Parnell's now very public relationship with Mrs O'Shea. This sentiment existed both among Gladstone's non-conformist Liberal supporters and in Catholic Ireland. From a constitutional perspective, the more important issue centred on the political autonomy of the Irish party. Gladstone's temerity in pronouncing upon the Irish party's choice of leader jeopardised the status of the party as an independent third force in the House of Commons. On 29 November 1890, Parnell issued his manifesto 'To the People of Ireland', his longest-ever political tract.[37] Naturally, he focussed on constitutional arguments in his defence. His opponents, notably Tim Healy, fixated upon details of Parnell's private life which had been aired during the O'Shea divorce hearings.

---

36 A. Jackson, *Home Rule: An Irish History, 1800–2000* (Oxford University Press, 2003), 76–7.
37 D. McCartney, 'Parnell's Manifesto "To the People of Ireland", 29 November 1890', in P. Travers and D. McCartney (eds.), *Parnell Reconsidered* (Dublin: UCD Press, 2013), 197–203.

Years of Drift? Post-Parnell Politics

If the abandonment of Parnell by the majority of his party colleagues on 6 December 1890 signalled a major change in Irish politics, then Parnell's death, at the age of 45, on 6 October 1891, confirmed that there would be no reinstatement, reconciliation or return to the politics of the 1880s. Parnell's failure to cultivate a clear successor meant, as the anti-Parnellite William O'Brien put it, 'one-man power was replaced for Ireland by eighty-man powerlessness'.[38] However, Parnell's power had been anything but absolute prior to the split. The Plan of Campaign exemplified this. The idea of Parnell's omnipotence has been seen as a 'skilfully cultivated nationalist myth'.[39] From this perspective, the split merely exposed issues within nationalism that went much deeper.[40] It is also misleading to say that Parnell's death created a political vacuum; the 1890s witnessed decisive advances both in Irish policy and in Irish legislation. Instead, it is more correct to state that Parnell's exit precipitated a new era of political flux.

Ireland's Home Rule MPs had only months to regroup between the death of Parnell in October 1891 and the general election of July 1892. Of the three by-elections held between the death of Parnell and the general election, two anti-Parnellite nationalists were elected uncontested. In the third, the anti-Parnellite candidate, Martin Flavin, won a decisive victory over John Redmond in Parnell's old Cork City seat. Redmond had been MP for Wexford North since 1885, but was forced to vacate this safe seat in order to contest Cork. In the subsequent general election, he secured a seat in Waterford City, the constituency he represented until his death in 1918. The only pre-1892 by-election to have been won by a Parnellite came a month later in December 1891, when John Redmond, seatless since renouncing North Wexford, beat Michael Davitt by 546 votes in Waterford City.

The 1892 general election saw 71 anti-Parnellites, 9 Parnellites, and 21 Unionists elected. In Cork county, not one Parnellite candidate risked contesting any of the county's seven seats. In Cork City, meanwhile, two leading anti-Parnellites – William O'Brien and T. M. Healy – trounced John Redmond's brother William and his running mate. At the other end of the island in Ulster, the situation tended to be characterised by three-way contests between Home Rulers of both persuasions and a unionist candidate. The nationalist

---

38 O'Brien, *O'Brien*, 100.
39 Callanan, *Parnell Split*, 3.
40 Callanan, *Parnell Split*, 3.

electorate there showed themselves to be overwhelmingly anti-Parnellite. In the case of mid-Tyrone, George Noble Plunkett, later Sinn Féin's first MP and father of the 1916 rebel leader, Joseph Mary, received only 123 votes whereas his anti-Parnellite rival topped the poll with 3,667 votes, over a thousand votes clear of his more credible Unionist contender. One notable feature of the intra-nationalist electoral contests of the 1890s is that the Parnellite vote increased steadily from a low base-point following the split.

Dublin emerged as the stronghold of Parnellism in 1892, electing four of the country's nine Parnellite MPs. In Britain, the 1892 election brought the Liberals back into government after six years of Conservative and Liberal Unionist rule. On their own, Gladstone's Liberals were 41 seats behind their Unionist opponents. However, by forming an alliance with the Home Rulers, the Liberals were 40 seats clear of their parliamentary opponents. As in 1885, Ireland held the balance.

When Gladstone introduced his second Home Rule Bill, it differed from the 1886 version on several key points. First, it proposed a bicameral legislature for Ireland. It envisaged the retention of Irish MPs at Westminster, initially in an awkward system whereby these members could only vote on Irish or imperial issues. This was amended to retain full Irish powers of representation at Westminster, albeit with a reduced number of MPs.[41] The Bill's chaotically arranged financial clauses, remodelled since 1886, came in for criticism. After the Bill's introduction, it was realised that the figures on Ireland's existing financial relationship with Britain had been badly miscalculated. Excise receipts were overestimated by over £200,000, necessitating radical overhaul of Gladstone's Bill at committee stage.[42] Even before the full extent of the chaotic nature of the Bill's financial provisions had been exposed, the City of London showed itself to be deeply hostile to the Bill. On 3 May, less than a fortnight after the second reading of the Bill had been carried by 347 votes to 304 in the House of Commons, members of the London Stock Exchange – not usually a visible contingent in street demonstrations – marched in formation to the city's Guildhall, where they ceremonially burnt copies of the Bill. The Liberal Unionist leader, Joseph Chamberlain, was the principal speaker at this assembly.[43]

The second Home Rule Bill was undoubtedly the central issue of the extended session, 1892–1893. In total, it was the subject of 82 sittings of the

---

41 F. S. L. Lyons, *John Dillon: A Biography* (London: Routledge and Kegan Paul, 1968), 158.
42 Matthew, *Gladstone*, 337–8.
43 J. L. Garvin, *The Life of Joseph Chamberlain, volume II, 1885–1895: Disruption and Combat* (London: Macmillan, 1933), 563.

Commons.[44] After protracted passages through both committee and debate stages, the Bill was finally sent to the House of Lords where it was rejected, as predicted, on 9 September 1893. The prime minister strongly considered dissolving parliament upon the Lords' rejection of Home Rule, but found his Cabinet hostile to this idea. With Liberal Imperialists gaining hold in the cabinet and both Gladstone's power and eyesight in decline, he finally retired on 1 March 1894 at the age of 84.[45] The passing of the premiership to Lord Rosebery meant that Ireland was now distant from the legislative priorities of British Liberalism.

Somewhat rudderless on policy and suffering from deep infighting in Cabinet, the new Rosebery government limped on following Gladstone's exit.[46] Ultimately defeated in a snap vote on army supply, the government resigned and the general election of July 1895 ushered in ten years of Unionist rule. This new era of government would bring with it major legislative and infrastructural developments for Ireland; albeit with the aim of softening rather than satisfying the ultimate Irish nationalist demand for Home Rule. Just as Otto Von Bismarck had embarked on his policy of killing socialism with kindness in the 1880s, now the governments of Salisbury and Balfour would carry a decade-long campaign of 'killing Home Rule with kindness', or 'constructive unionism' as it was officially dubbed.

Constitutional Politics under Unionist Government, 1895–1905

The Conservative Lord Salisbury took over from the Liberal Lord Rosebery in 1895 and a series of major Irish reforms began. Of these, the Local Government Act of 1898 was the most far-reaching. Not only did it educate a generation of Irish political hopefuls through experience of local government, it also took small but significant steps towards the involvement of women in Irish politics. Large capital investment projects also began, especially in light railways and harbour facilities. However, at the turn of the century, the land question remained unresolved.

---

44 H. C. G. Matthew, 'Gladstone, William Ewart (1809–1898)', *Oxford Dictionary of National Biography*, Oxford University Press, 2004; online edn., (May 2011): www.oxforddnb.com/view/article/10787 (accessed 29 June 2015).

45 Matthew, 'Gladstone'.

46 See R. R. James, *Rosebery: A Biography of Archibald Philip, fifth Earl of Rosebery* (London: Weidenfeld and Nicolson, 1963), ch. 9 and Lyons, *Dillon*, 161.

A Conservative Land Act for Ireland was passed in 1896 but proved to be a source of disappointment for Irish nationalists, with the exception of Tim Healy. Healy had been expelled from his various posts in the anti-Parnellite party during 1895, shattering any illusion of unity in that faction. By 1896, Justin McCarthy gladly stepped down from chairmanship of the anti-Parnellite wing. A reluctant John Dillon took over, more comfortable in his position since the ejection of Healy. To add to the patchwork of ineffective and disunited Irish nationalist organisations that populated the 1890s, Healy established the People's Rights Association in 1896. This new body was dedicated to creating a model of political organisation that would be the antithesis to the centralising tendencies of Dillon. In 1895, pioneering efforts had been made into what late-twentieth-century Irish politicians would call 'consensus politics', with the establishment of the Recess Committee, a cross-party meeting of both elected representatives and 'other eminent men' who met between January and August 1896 with a view to making progress on the Irish land question.[47] Their efforts culminated in the establishment of the Department of Agriculture and Technical Instruction in 1900.

Continuing the electoral battles of 1890–1891, the last decade of the nineteenth century also played host to some of the bitterest electoral contests. The revived spectre of Home Rule intensified nationalist–unionist animosity. On the other hand, the rivalries of erstwhile allies in the pro- and anti-Parnellite factions resulted in impassioned contests in constituencies that had never known such acute electoral controversy theretofore.[48]

New Politics in the New Century

The 1890s had been a decade both of division and of drift in Irish nationalism. Land agitation had increased at the turn of the twentieth century, due in part to worsening landlord–tenant relations and also owing to refreshed tenant organisation through the establishment of the United Irish League in 1898. The establishment of the League precipitated the reunification of the divided nationalist factions in the interest of enhancing parliamentary strength. Fear of usurpation by the United Irish League brought the bitterly divided pro- and anti-Parnellite wings, and their sub-fragments, back together. In the parliamentary session of 1901, of 1,064 questions sampled across all parties, Irish nationalist MPs asked 44 per cent of all questions in the House of

47 C. King, 'The Recess Committee, 1895–6', *Studia Hibernica*, 30 (1998/1999), 21–46.
48 Jackson, *Home Rule*, 76–7.

Commons. That such a large proportion of questions were put by a group of MPs amounting to less than an eighth of the membership of the assembly indicates just how dominant were the reunited Irish Parliamentary Party in the period directly after reunification. As to the level of engagement with Irish versus Imperial matters, the Boer War being the most prevalent in the case of the latter, just over half of Irish nationalist questions were directed to the Irish Office and a fifth were directed to either the War, Colonial, or India Offices. In the same period, the Liberal Party asked almost one-third of the questions in the House of Commons, with 28 per cent of these going to the War Office, indicating the level of Liberal interest and engagement with the Boer question. After 1901, Irish nationalist MPs never again asked such a high proportion of parliamentary questions. Despite having peaked, between 1901 and 1918, Irish nationalist MPs still managed to ask one-quarter of all questions asked in the House.[49] By 1900 the Irish Parliamentary Party was reunified. It brought together factions who were split between advocates of conciliation and those who favoured a combative approach to relations with the government. However, nationalists now divided into those who saw room for progress through constructive unionism and those who maintained their distrust for the Conservative and Liberal Unionist government. From the inception of the United Irish League, William O'Brien became synonymous with conciliation and joined forces with the reunited party's chairman, John Redmond, in progressing initiatives on the land question through compromise. The culmination of these initiatives was the Wyndham Land Act, which went a long way to solving the Irish land question. The Wyndham Land Act witnessed massive investment by the British Treasury and had the highest uptake of any land act among the Irish tenantry. As Terence Dooley argues elsewhere in this volume, in spite of the litany of land legislation stretching back to 1870, the Wyndham Land Act constituted 'the first serious attempt to provide the inducements for landlords to sell and tenants to purchase'. When combined with the re-financing of the Act in 1909, Dooley shows that in excess of 170,000 tenants availed themselves of the terms of this scheme.

John Dillon quickly emerged as the most formidable and vehement opponent of what he saw as the overly-generous terms offered to landlords by the Wyndham Land Act. Dillon soon set out on an ultimately successful plan to purge both William O'Brien and his policy of conciliation from the Irish party. Up to the passage of Wyndham's Land Bill, William O'Brien played

49 C. Mulvagh, *The Irish Parliamentary Party at Westminster, 1900–1918* (Manchester: Manchester University Press, 2015), 178–81.

a central role in steering the policies of the Irish party through his role in the United Irish League. Contending with Dillon and others, he managed to exert a certain degree of influence over John Redmond. O'Brien 'effectively bulldozed' a convention of the United Irish League into endorsing the findings of the land conference of 1902–1903 while John Dillon, his main nationalist opponent, was abroad for health reasons. Upon his return to Ireland, Dillon launched his public assault against O'Brien. Dillon asserted that he had 'no faith in the doctrine of conciliation'.[50] In this campaign, his chief supporters were Michael Davitt and the West Belfast MP, Thomas Sexton.

Dillon and O'Brien waged their conflict through the press, with Dillon harnessing the powerful *Freeman's Journal* to advance his views. O'Brien, meanwhile, was forced to rely on the dwindling influence and circulation of his weekly *Irish People*.[51] This struggle culminated in the resignation of O'Brien from his various positions within the movement. Thereafter, Dillon's faction held sway within the party, and policy shifted away from O'Brien's conciliation model.[52]

The End of Political Experimentation

Constructive unionism continued to be the mainstay of the government's Irish policy after Wyndham's Land Act. For Irish unionists across the island of Ireland, the next advances in the policy would prove intolerable. Beginning in 1904, a scheme for the devolution of certain functions of government to Ireland was promulgated. The concept originated among Liberal Irish landlords, centring on the earl of Dunraven. For progressive unionists, the benefit of the scheme was that it did not envisage the undoing of the Act of Union. Without keeping his Chief Secretary informed, the scheme was advanced by the then Under Secretary at Dublin Castle, Sir Antony Patrick MacDonnell. Nicknamed 'the Bengal Tiger', MacDonnell was a Mayo-born Catholic and a former Indian civil servant.[53]

The scheme caused sizable consternation among more traditional Irish unionists but ultimately never materialised. Culminating in 1905, the episode

---

50 *Freeman's Journal*, 26 August 1903, quoted in Lyons, *Dillon*, 236.
51 Joseph V. O'Brien has described the *Freeman's Journal* at this time as 'more than a match for the lesser voice of O'Brien's faltering weekly', see O'Brien, *O'Brien*, 151. In an acknowledgement of defeat by O'Brien the *Irish People* would eventually cease publication for two years, beginning in November 1903, O'Brien, *O'Brien*, 159.
52 F. S. L. Lyons, *The Irish Parliamentary Party, 1890–1910* (London: Faber, 1951), 198 and O'Brien, *O'Brien*, 184.
53 P. Maume, 'MacDonnell, Antony Patrick', in J. McGuire and J. Quinn (eds.), *Dictionary of Irish Biography*, 9 vols. (Cambridge University Press, 2009).

had two important outcomes. First, it mobilised opposition in unionist Ulster, signalling a shift away from island-wide Unionist solidarity. As a result of the devolution threat, the Ulster Unionist Council was established. This body would become the backbone of the Ulster Unionist campaign during the Home Rule crisis of 1912–1914 when it oversaw Ulster unionist paramilitaries as well as the provisional government-in-waiting. The devolution scare also resulted in the resignation of George Wyndham as Chief Secretary on 6 March 1905. Following the fall of Wyndham, moderate Irish unionists and landlords would never again experience the prominence they had enjoyed under the Salisbury and Balfour governments.

By-election failures and internal fractures over the question of tariff reform ultimately put an end to Balfour's government in December of that year. Henry Campbell-Bannerman formed a caretaker government and called a general election in January. The Liberals secured a landslide victory, gaining 216 seats and an outright majority of 64 in the House of Commons. For Irish nationalism, this was something of a double-edged sword. On the one hand, there had not been a premier so sympathetic to Home Rule since Gladstone's exit in 1894. On the other hand, the Liberals had won their 1906 victory on the promise of an extensive programme of social legislation in Britain. There was neither the appetite nor the need to waste valuable time wading into the Irish morass as the government turned its attention to industry and education in the first phase of its legislative programme.

Campbell-Bannerman appointed the rather reluctant James Bryce to the Irish Office. Even before taking up office, Bryce had secured verbal assurances from the new prime minister that he would be at liberty to resign at will and, if any higher office were to become vacant, he would be considered and appointed if possible.[54] Such was the sentiment among British politicians regarding the poisoned chalice of the Irish chief secretaryship having witnessed the fall of Wyndham. In January 1907, Bryce was duly liberated from the Irish Office through his appointment as ambassador to Washington. He was replaced by the outgoing President of the Board of Education, Augustine Birrell. Birrell was equally reluctant to take up the Irish portfolio. However, after some protest, he acceded to his prime minister's request and took on this unexpected new challenge.[55] In contrast to Bryce, Birrell was determined that consultation with the Irish party leadership would be a hallmark of his term in office.

54 James Bryce, memorandum of meeting with Henry Campbell-Bannerman, 9 December 1905, MS 11,011: NLI.
55 A. Birrell, *Things Past Redress* (London: Faber and Faber, 1937), 195.

Between the 1906 and January 1910 general elections, the Irish Parliamentary Party experienced a crisis of purpose and sparked a national debate over continued attendance at Westminster as a viable tactic for the achievement of Home Rule. Cordial relations with Augustine Birrell were just one element of a growing docility among the leadership of the Irish party, content to bide their time and await progress from a benevolent Liberal administration. When Birrell finally unveiled his gradualist solution to the Irish question in 1907, the leadership of the Irish party was disappointed by its limited scope.

The Irish Council Bill was introduced on 7 May 1907. It proposed the establishment of an 'Administrative Council' comprising of 100 members. Eighty-two of these were to be elected on the local government franchise. Certain legislative and executive functions were to be devolved to this body. For nationalists, the Bill was viewed as an insulting 'half measure' of Home Rule. It was rejected by a convention of the United Irish League, putting an end to the Liberals' preferred option of a gradualist solution to Home Rule. Whatever enthusiasm remained in the Liberal Cabinet for addressing the Irish question was extinguished upon the resignation and subsequent death of the prime minister in April 1908. Campbell-Bannerman was succeeded by Herbert Henry Asquith, an avowed Liberal Imperialist. Back in 1905, T. M. Healy had famously dubbed him 'a cold-blooded Yorkshireman, thoroughly selfish and without a genuine trait'.[56]

The Irish Council Bill controversy provoked an immediate crisis in Irish nationalism. Many now began to question the efficacy of continued attendance at Westminster and the earnestness of the Liberals on the Irish question. This crisis was seized upon by Arthur Griffith, a Dublin pamphleteer and propagandist of a Parnellite persuasion. The disaffection brought about by the rejection of the Council Bill appeared to justify Griffith's advocacy for establishing a rival legislature based on the Hungarian model. In the climate of national discontent that prevailed between 1907 and 1908, 'many currents flowed into Sinn Féin'. This new party aimed towards a dual monarchist policy where only the crown would link otherwise autonomous Irish and British legislatures. Unlike Sinn Féin's post-1916 swing to advocacy of republicanism and physical force, the party under Griffith advocated nothing more than

---

56 T. M. Healy to Maurice Healy, 12 December 1905, IE P6/A/24/45: UCD Archives. An edited version of this letter, in which the clause about Asquith's selfishness is omitted, is included in T. M. Healy, *Leaders and Letters of My Day* (2 vols., London: Frederick A. Stokes, 1928), ii, 475.

non-violent parliamentary abstention.[57] Crucially, Griffith managed to win a number of supporters within the Irish Parliamentary Party.

The Sinn Féin threat evaporated after the defeat of an abstentionist candidate, the former Irish party MP, C. J. Dolan in February 1908. Before this, however, an attempt was made to close ranks against the threat. This included the readmission into the IPP of previously ousted malcontents, including William O'Brien and T. M. Healy. Once back inside the IPP, O'Brien attempted to re-establish control over party policy. At the UIL convention of 1909, while attempting to speak on the land question, O'Brien was shouted down and his supporters were forcibly ejected from the convention. This action had been orchestrated by Joseph Devlin, who had stewarded the meeting with Belfast-based heavies from the Ancient Order of Hibernians (Board of Erin) of which he was president.[58] The episode came to be known as the 'baton convention'.

The violent suppression of O'Brien and his followers at this meeting displayed the authoritarian nature of Devlin and the centralising tendency of the Irish Parliamentary Party in this period. Devlin now confirmed his status as part of a small and un-appointed policy-making core within the IPP alongside Dillon, O'Connor, and the chairman. Now outside the party, an alliance soon formed between O'Brien and Tim Healy. O'Brien was a noted anticlericalist and Healy a devout Catholic who relied upon the archbishop of Armagh to retain his seat in North Louth. In 1909, O'Brien and Healy established a new political movement, the All-for-Ireland League, which stood in opposition to Redmondism. Events in Westminster began to benefit this emerging parliamentary grouping when David Lloyd George introduced his 1909 Budget. The Budget was not only unpopular with the House of Lords but also with rural Ireland. It proposed increases in liquor, tobacco, land and death duties, which were deeply resented in Ireland. The Lords' rejection of this Budget provoked a constitutional crisis. The year 1910 saw two general elections being called, one in January and a second in December. These elections played host to the most concerted intra-nationalist contests since the split. The All-for-Ireland League, largely confined to Munster, clashed with official IPP candidates. In January, the damage was limited to the loss of ten seats for the Irish party. This figure dropped to eight by December; it was the All-for-Ireland League, and not Sinn Féin, who now constituted the single

57 P. Bew, *Conflict and Conciliation in Ireland, 1890–1910: Parnellites and Radical Agrarians* (Oxford University Press, 1987), 215.
58 Lyons, *Dillon*, 303–4 and W. O'Brien, *An Olive Branch in Ireland and Its History* (London: Macmillan, 1910), 441–56.

greatest threat to the dominant position of Redmond's Irish party up until the 1916 Rising.

The outcome of the two general elections had the unintended consequence of catapulting Ireland centre stage at Westminster for the first time since the 1890s. The first election of 1910 was held in January. When all seats were filled, the two main British parties were evenly matched. Holding the balance, as in 1885 and 1892, were the Irish nationalists. This inconclusive result necessitated a second election which was eventually held in December. In the interim, Redmond and Asquith entered into a pact. The Irish party would support the 1909 budget and parliamentary reform. In exchange, Asquith pledged to introduce a new Home Rule Bill.

Parliamentary reform was mutually beneficial to both sides, as it would remove the House of Lords' veto which had sunk the 1893 Home Rule bill. Lloyd George's budget, meanwhile, was a harder pill to swallow for the Irish party. The proposed new taxes were deeply unpopular in nationalist Ireland. Prior to his pact with Asquith, Redmond exclaimed to Lloyd George in the House of Commons that, 'The right hon. Gentleman for his "Dreadnoughts" is going to tax the tobacco of … [t]he poor of Ireland.'[59] Now, Redmond's agreement forced him to make a *volte face* on his budget policy. In Ireland, O'Brien and his allies made much political capital out of this.

With the stalemate of January 1910 replicated in December, a new government was formed, propped up by Irish votes. The Parliament Act was duly passed. It removed the Lords' veto on money bills and reduced its powers over ordinary legislation to the ability to delay. Two years after it was introduced, Lloyd George's controversial budget also became law in 1911. With these matters resolved, Asquith made good on his promise. The entire attention of Westminster now turned to Ireland. On 11 April 1912, the third Home Rule Bill came before the Commons.

The Bill, as introduced, contained wholly different financial clauses in order to account for the changed realities of the new century. It also included a clearer commitment to the retention of a reduced number of Irish MPs at Westminster. Otherwise, the third Home Rule Bill drew heavily upon its 1893 predecessor. In introducing the Bill, the shadow of Gladstone hung over Asquith who informed the House that he would 'not attempt to-day to retraverse the ground which he [Gladstone] covered. I do not presume to be able to bend the bow of Ulysses'.[60] The powers of the Irish legislature were to

---

59 *Hansard 5 (Commons)*, iv, cols. 790–3.
60 *Hansard 5 (Commons)*, xxxvi, col. 1399.

be defined not so much by what it was permitted to do but rather by what it could not. Control over imperial matters such as defence, foreign affairs, the crown, and weights and measures were reserved by Westminster. Religious freedoms were explicitly guaranteed in the third clause of the Bill, but this did little to assuage confessional concerns, especially in Ulster.[61]

Debate on the third Home Rule Bill began in 1912, with the less emotive topics of finance and federalism, and climaxed in 1914 with the Ulster question almost bringing Ireland, as well as Britain, to the point of civil war by July 1914.[62] Ironically, the period 1880–1914 began with a massive increase in popular participation in constitutional and parliamentary democracy and concluded with the rejection of constitutionalism by large sections of both nationalists and unionists in Ireland and Britain. The case for the special treatment of Ulster was first made at Cabinet on 6 February 1912 by Lloyd George and Churchill.[63] Specifically, they advocated 'contracting out'; in other words, exclusion. Churchill acted with astonishing duplicity as, immediately after his appeal to Cabinet, he went to Belfast to address an 8,000 strong pro-Home Rule rally alongside Joseph Devlin and the Liberal Belfast shipping magnate, Lord Pirrie, who was in favour of Home Rule.

In parliament, 'special consideration' for Ulster quickly mutated from legal safeguards for minorities towards the call for Ulster exclusion. John Redmond vehemently opposed the 'Two Nations' theory then being used to justify Ulster's exclusion. Dismissing the idea that unionists had a claim to nationhood, Redmond saw himself as the leader of an 'Irish race'. Immediately before and during the First World War, Redmond worked towards the cultivation of an increasingly civic form of Irish identity. By this, he hoped to provide an alternative to sectarian distinctions on the island.[64]

From the middle of 1913 onwards, the 'Ulster crisis' deepened and exclusion became the watchword both in Britain and in Ireland. The Home Rule Bill was rejected by the House of Lords on 15 July 1913 and, by the autumn, information on the importation and stockpiling of arms and ammunition in Ulster prompted the government to redouble their efforts at seeking a compromise. On 27 September 1913, the eve of 'Ulster Day', the Ulster Unionist

---

61 A stance well summarised in Joseph Hocking's *Is Home Rule Rome Rule?* (London: Ward Lock and Co. 1912).

62 On the impact of the Home Rule Crisis in Britain, see D. M. Jackson, *Popular Opposition to Irish Home Rule in Edwardian Britain* (Liverpool: Liverpool University Press, 2009).

63 R. Fanning, *Fatal Path: British Government and Irish Revolution, 1910–1922* (London, Faber and Faber, 2013), 63.

64 See Redmond's foreword in Bryan Cooper, *The Tenth (Irish) Division in Gallipoli* (London, H. Jenkins, 1918), xii–xiii.

Council proclaimed a provisional government for the province. By the end of November, Lloyd George and Asquith managed to extract from John Redmond and John Dillon their acceptance of partition, at least in principle.[65]

Although it was a key issue in Dublin, the 1913 Lockout did not preoccupy the Irish party leadership at this time. Instead, Ulster and the threat of partition consumed the attention of the Irish party leadership in the autumn and winter of 1913. While the Lockout was seen as an unwelcome side issue, the formation of the Irish Volunteers in November 1913 was watched more closely by Redmond and Dillon. The new force was a direct answer to the Ulster Volunteer Force, established eleven months previously. The Irish Volunteers acted in the name of Home Rule but were wholly outside Redmond's control.[66] With growing numbers of unionists and nationalists now pledged to the physical defence of their mutually opposing positions, the drift away from constitutionalism became a flight.

In March 1914, British army officers at the Curragh Camp, County Kildare, threatened a mutiny if they were ordered into action against Ulster unionists. On the night of 24–25 April, an estimated 25,000 rifles and three million rounds of ammunition were clandestinely landed by unionists along the north Antrim coast. Combined, these two events constituted a major threat to the government's legitimacy and its claim to be in control of Ulster. The Curragh incident represented the gravest breakdown of governmental control over the British armed forces in the twentieth century. It was an event that was followed with great interest in Paris and Berlin, as well as in London, as war clouds gathered.

The fact that Ulster was arming and the fear that the military could not be counted on to protect either Home Rule or the nationalist community in Ireland led to a surge in recruitment for the Irish Volunteers. Now recruiting at a level of 1,000 per week, by July, membership stood at 160,000.[67] John Redmond finally asserted control of the Irish Volunteers' provisional committee between May and June 1914. The democratically elected leaders of Irish nationalism and Ulster unionism now both had under their control private paramilitary armies. Asquith greatly feared he would become the first premier since the 1640s to witness the kingdom's slide into civil war. At this

65 John Dillon to T. P. O'Connor, 27 November 1913, MS 6740/213: TCD.
66 R. F. Foster, *Vivid Faces: The Revolutionary Generation in Ireland, 1890–1923* (London: Allen Lane, 2014), 179.
67 A. O'Rahilly, *Winding the Clock: O'Rahilly and the 1916 Rising* (Dublin: Lilliput Press, 1991), 102 and Lyons, *Dillon*, 350.

point, the monarch was brought into the fray to act as peacemaker and host a conference between all sides in a last-ditch effort to avoid conflict over Ulster.

Between 21 and 24 July 1914, the Speaker of the House of Commons chaired deliberations between Asquith, Lloyd George, Redmond, Dillon, Carson, James Craig, Bonar Law and Lord Lansdowne. Redmond and Dillon faced an uphill battle. Asquith's enthusiasm for Home Rule was contractual rather than emotional. For his part, Lloyd George had been an early advocate of partition. Thus the nationalists lacked support in their attempts to cling to an all-island settlement. Despite professing his disappointment at the outcome, the conference had achieved exactly what Asquith hoped it would – it delayed the day of decision.[68] Churchill, watching from the sidelines, despaired at how the prospects of settlement became bogged down in 'the muddy byways of Fermanagh and Tyrone'.[69]

The Buckingham Palace conference is an appropriate place to end the present chapter. On paper, it represented a high point in constitutionalism, a grand, statesmanlike assembly under the eyes of the king, settling problems of nationhood and territory in an unconscious rehearsal, albeit on a small scale, of the grand deliberations of Versailles some five years later. However, in reality, Buckingham Palace witnessed a polite and mutually beneficial observance of conventions by both Redmond and Carson. Neither hoped or wished for a settlement there. Both clung to the view that each would ultimately be granted the parliament and special treatment he desired. Both were committed to securing their positions through force, or rather the threat of force, rather than through parliament, the latter having been rendered mechanical rather than emotive with the passage of the Parliament Act.

The Buckingham Palace conference ended on a Friday. That Sunday, 26 July, arms were landed by the Irish Volunteers at Howth, County Dublin. The gun running was organised by an advanced wing of physical force nationalists within the Volunteers. Redmond had been warned about this faction months previously. Simultaneous to their efforts, Redmond was directing his own mission to procure arms for the Volunteers. His agent in this, Tom Kettle, was in Belgium securing transport for purchased rifles as Erskine Childers and his crew unloaded their consignment in Dublin.[70]

---

68 Fanning, *Fatal Path: British Government and Irish Revolution, 1913–1923* (London: Profile Books), 126 and H. H. Asquith to Venetia Stanley, 22 July 1914 [102], in H. H. Asquith, *Letters to Venetia Stanley*, ed. Michael and Eleanor Brock (Oxford University Press, 1982), 109.

69 Winston S. Churchill, *The World Crisis, 1911–1918, Volume I* (London: Odhams, 1938), 155.

70 John Redmond to Tom Kettle, 25 August 1914, LA35/135: UCD Archives, and Kettle's correspondence with Redmond in the Redmond papers, MS 15,199/6, NLI.

Freshly armed and returning to the city, the Volunteers clashed with military and police at Clontarf. The military unit involved was harassed by onlookers on its return to barracks. On the quays of the Liffey at Bachelors' Walk, the provocation of the citizenry proved too much for the military and two ranks were ordered to about face. They opened fire on an unarmed crowd. Four were killed in the incident.[71] With blood spilt on the streets of Dublin and two private armies now armed, the prime minister faced the very real prospect of civil war.

Within a fortnight, Britain had declared war on Germany and a conflict of a very different nature was underway. As one historian has observed, '[t]he Great War then enabled Asquith to do what he had always wanted to do about Ireland: nothing'.[72] Diplomacy and constitutionalism were not ended by the events of late July and early August 1914, but they were altered fundamentally both in the British Isles and internationally. The conflict would give birth to a wholly different world with different norms and conventions. Only in this context of war in Europe and the slowly evaporating prospect of settlement through constitutional channels in Ireland can the shift towards the 1916 Rising and all that followed in its wake properly be interpreted.

Conclusion

If it is possible to divide the long history of the Irish Home Rule movement into phases, the period under consideration here might neatly be subdivided into three. Naturally, there are continuities in personnel and ideas. However, the 1880s, the 1890s, and the years 1900 to 1914 each constitute a distinct phase in the progress of the movement. The decade of the 1880s was characterised by the rise and fall of Parnellism. It began with the radical reorientation of constitutional nationalism under its new chairman. It concluded with the bitter collapse of an alliance unrivalled in its magnitude or achievement since the time of O'Connell. The old assumption that the 1890s were a 'political vacuum' into which cultural nationalist forces were drawn has undergone revision. It was a decade that saw major developments in the concept of Home Rule. Gladstone's second Home Rule Bill prompted fresh debate over centralism and regional autonomy among Irish nationalists. Under the Conservatives, from 1895 onwards, tangible advances occurred in

---

71 D. Ferriter, *A Nation and Not a Rabble: The Irish Revolution, 1913–1923* (London: Profile, 2015), 148–9.
72 Fanning, *Fatal Path*, 354.

Irish infrastructure. Likewise, structural changes to local government and state involvement in agriculture were among the fruits of constructive unionism. Finally, the 1890s witnessed the drawing of lines of demarcation among Irish nationalists of all hues. O'Brienites, Dillonites, Redmondites and Healyites emerged from the unstable monolith of the 1880s. These distinctions did not end in 1900 with the reunification of the party. In fact, these distinctions lay at the heart of many of the internal struggles which punctuated the ensuing two decades of Irish nationalist experience. The reunification of the party marked something of a détente among groups that had formerly been bitterly opposed to one another. The founder of the Irish Volunteers, and later Sinn Féin/Cumann na nGaedheal TD and minister, Eoin MacNeill described this feeling in his memoirs:

> The main feature of the Parnell crisis was its bitterness. This was imparted to it by the speeches and the journalism on both sides and strange as it may seem, my recollection about it is clear that the bitterness of that time was deeper and sharper; and more widespread than anything we experienced afterwards even at the height of the [Irish] Civil War in '22.[73]

The land question was likewise a defining issue in the period 1880–1914. Ireland's economy outside the modest amount of industry in the four counties of northeast Ulster was heavily dependent on agriculture. The Land War and the Plan of Campaign in the 1880s gave way to a persistent culture of agrarian crime and agitation, albeit at a less intense level. Cattle-driving – the unlawful, and usually nocturnal, release of cattle from their pastures or enclosures – reached a new peak between 1906 and 1909. Alongside boycott and intimidation, cattle-driving was an established method of resistance to the transformation of agricultural smallholdings towards larger, ranch-style farming. This activity tended to be directed or at least condoned by elected politicians. However, it was inherently extra-parliamentary and frequently illegal, emphasising the blurred lines between constitutionalism and extra-parliamentary action in the period. Ultimately, the solution for rural unrest was the generously funded government legislation for land purchase. To put the level of change that had been brought about by Ireland's social revolution into numbers, by 1914, an estimated two-thirds to three-quarters of farmers in Ireland owned their holdings. The vast majority of these had availed themselves of the 1903 Wyndham Act, under which almost 300,000 sales had been transacted.[74] Coupled with land purchase, the social legislation championed

---

73 'A memoir written by Eoin MacNeill, *c.*1932/3', 25, Eoin MacNeill papers, LA1/G/ 372: UCD Archives. I am grateful to Mairéad Carew for providing me with this reference.
74 O'Callaghan, *British High Politics*, 151.

by David Lloyd George from 1908 onwards was equally popular among the Irish populace. The Ancient Order of Hibernians and other affiliates of the constitutional nationalist movement scrambled to be incorporated under the 1911 National Insurance Act. Meanwhile, the 1908 Old Age Pensions Act was both popular and of tremendous economic benefit in rural Ireland.[75]

Established parties were either unable or unwilling to make constitutionalists out of Ireland's youth. Cultural nationalism and physical force organisations proved very popular among the generation coming of age after 1900. Combined, the Ulster and Irish Volunteers had a membership exceeding that of any initiative in Irish politics since the Famine. For some, paramilitary volunteering found its unlikely endpoint in the trenches of the Western Front or the beaches of Gallipoli during the First World War. However, in an era when the actions of small and unrepresentative minorities could prove decisive, the week-long seizure of Dublin by rebels at Easter 1916 and especially the government response to it, began a sea-change in Irish political life. The various political movements of 1880–1914 gave to Ireland, north and south, a political tradition that would find expression throughout the twentieth century and beyond. Ultimately it was members of Sinn Féin and not the followers of John Redmond who populated the new parliament in Dublin. However, Home Rulers nonetheless left an indelible mark on Irish political life.

---

75 M. Wheatley, *Nationalism and the Irish Party, Provincial Ireland 1910–1916* (Oxford University Press, 2005), 49.

The Origins, Politics and Culture of Irish Unionism, *c*.1880–1916*

ALVIN JACKSON

Introduction

The Union and unionism became central, inescapable (if also deeply contested) features of Irish politics and society in the nineteenth century. Ireland (like Scotland) was successfully infiltrated by the British state and British culture – and indeed, just as Scottish historians commonly link the development of Scots national institutions in the nineteenth century to the condition and intrusiveness of the Union, so no assessment of the revival or creation of Celtic political and cultural institutions in the late nineteenth century is possible without an appreciation of the challenge posed by the Union to Irish distinctiveness.

In the constricted electoral circumstances of the nineteenth century, where the practice of politics remained bound to the possession of property, unionism thrived. For much of the first three-quarters of the century, Irish electoral politics were dominated by parties, Conservative and Liberal, that were united by a shared commitment to Union. Each of these traditions, but in particular the Conservative, fed into the creation of an organised Unionist movement between 1884 and 1886. Drawing upon a formidable range of social, financial and cultural resources, this movement (though representing perhaps only 30 per cent of the Irish people) successfully delayed the implementation of any form of Home Rule until 1920–21; and it has so far prevented the attainment of the historic nationalist goal of a united and autonomous Irish state. It may well be that (following Gladstone's analysis) one key result

---

* An earlier version of this chapter dwelling at greater length on Scottish comparisons and on the condition of Irish unionism before 1886 may be found in Alvin Jackson, *Two Unions: Ireland, Scotland and the Survival of the United Kingdom, 1707–2007* (Oxford University Press, 2012), 281–333.

of Irish unionism has been to prevent the reconciliation of Irish nationalism within a redefined and loosened British polity.[1]

Faith, Faction and Party

Irish unionism was a confluence – it was a religious, geographical, economic and party political intermingling. Irish unionism brought together different traditions of Protestantism, drawing in particular upon unifying evangelical and loyalist sub-cultures from the eighteenth century; but it also appealed for a time to a small minority of propertied Catholics – those who had been enfolded by schooling or profession within the Union and Empire, or whose economic standing depended upon the stability of the British state. Irish unionism was also, originally, an all-Ireland phenomenon, with perhaps 250,000 adherents outside the six counties of what would become Northern Ireland in 1920: a scattered and (allowing for the Big House strain) predominantly urban, indeed metropolitan, and Anglican and propertied unionism characterised the south and west, while the north was simultaneously more industrial, more farming and more Presbyterian in character. Liberals and Conservatives, Presbyterians and Anglicans, once mutually antagonistic, came to cooperate in the context of the looming threat from Parnellite Home Rule. An Irish Unionist Parliamentary Party, a forum for loyalists of all party traditions, was created in 1885–6; unionist missionary organisations – the Irish Loyal and Patriotic Union, the Loyal Irish Union – were created in Dublin and Belfast at the same time and united enthusiasts of all party creeds. Electoral cooperation between the parties at the local, constituency, level slowly took shape, though (as in Scotland) tensions and jealousies survived until (and beyond) the formal merger of Conservatism and Liberal Unionism.[2]

However, the rapidity of this Unionist organisation and coalescence in the mid-1880s was not simply a consequence of the enormity of the external political threat, though it was certainly partly that. Unionism was created with

---

1 For the Irish and Scots backgrounds to the unions and unionism see, e.g. C. Kidd, *Union and Unionisms: Political Thought in Scotland, 1500–2000* (Cambridge University Press, 2008). A. Blackstock, *Loyalism in Ireland, 1789–1829* (London: Boydell Press, 2007); J.R. Hill, 'Ireland without Union: Molyneux and his Legacy' in J. Robertson (ed), *A Union for Empire: Political Thought and the Union of 1707* (Cambridge University Press, 1995); J. R. Hill, *From Patriots to Unionists: Dublin Civic Politics and Irish Protestant Patriotism, 1660–1840* (Oxford University Press, 1997); D. Kanter, *The Making of British Unionism, 1740–1848: Politics, Government and the Anglo-Irish Constitutional Relationship* (Dublin: Four Courts Press, 2009), 12.

2 A. Jackson, *The Ulster Party: Irish Unionists in the House of Commons, 1884–1911* (Oxford University Press, 1989), 214–16

speed and efficiency because it built upon existing institutions and ideologies and half-formed alliances. Much, therefore, of the groundwork for unionist mobilisation had been prefabricated in an earlier age.

The 1790s were critical years in terms of the formulation of the institutions and culture of Irish, as of Scots and English, loyalism. Similarly, the 1830s were critical in terms of the invention of modern conservatism and unionism in Ireland, as in Scotland and the rest of the United Kingdom. In part, this reflected the need for fresh institutions to address the practical challenges of the new, reformed, British politics. In Ireland the imminent threat of reform stimulated the creation of the Irish Protestant Conservative Society (1831), designed to bolster local electoral registration and to raise funds through a 'Protestant rent' (an obvious borrowing from the earlier Catholic Association). This was followed by the foundation of the Belfast Conservative Society in 1835 and, in 1836, of the Dublin Metropolitan Conservative Society, a body that had significant intellectual ballast in the form of Isaac Butt and other Trinity College Dublin heavyweights.[3] However, while the Metropolitan Society reflected some of the emphases and inclusivity of Robert Peel's new 'Conservatism' and of his Tamworth Manifesto, there were specifically Irish contexts and inflections. The perceived threat posed by Daniel O'Connell was critical, not just in terms of indirectly inspiring Conservative reorganisation, but also through precipitating some more fundamental movement within Irish Protestant politics.

The challenge of O'Connell, combined with the opportunities created by a buoyant Protestant evangelicalism, helped to shape other emerging features of the new Conservative politics of the 1830s. It was said that 'during the first quarter of the present [19th] century, nine-tenths of the Presbyterians of Ireland were Whigs'.[4] The foremost Presbyterian divine of the age was Henry Cooke, who (though a moderate emancipationist in the 1820s) had been an opponent of the legislation of 1829, and was rooted in the 'Old Light', or Calvinist and theologically conservative, traditions of his Church. He was also, perhaps, the leading Presbyterian evangelical of the mid-nineteenth century. In the new – emancipated and reformed – circumstances of the 1830s Cooke shifted from the traditional Whiggery of his communion, and aligned himself behind the new Conservatism and in sympathy with the Established

---

3 K. T. Hoppen, *Elections, Politics and Society in Ireland, 1832–1885* (Oxford University Press, 1984), 278, 280. Cf. I. D'Alton, Protestant Society and Politics in Cork, 1812–44 (Cork: Cork University Press, 1980), 226–27.

4 J. Porter, *Life and Times of Henry Cooke DD, LLD* (London: John Murray, 1875 edition), 224. See also F. Holmes, *Henry Cooke* (Belfast: Christian Journals Limited, 1981).

Church. Just as O'Connell looked to define a unified Catholic historical identity, Cooke sought (despite the historic denominational tensions between Presbyterianism and Anglicanism) to proclaim its Protestant equivalent.[5] His message was clear: the Established Church, its predecessors, agents and allies, had indeed done bloody deeds against non-conformists, but they were no longer the principal threat faced by Irish Presbyterians.

Evangelical religion (and religious revival, as in 1859) were not simply a useful cement through which Presbyterians would be bound to conservatism: they were also an essential component of the leadership and culture of mid-nineteenth century Irish conservatism (and ultimately thereby of Irish unionism). Belfast and Ulster, particularly the outer, or 'frontier' counties, were hotbeds of evangelical conviction; but even the south of Ireland, and, in particular, Dublin, was not immune to its attractions: the extended Guinness family combined brewing, conservatism and evangelical religion in the nineteenth century. Sir Arthur Guinness (1768–1855), for example, was a contributor to the Waldensian church in Italy in the 1850s.[6] Trinity College Dublin was a particular fulcrum of the evangelical faith in the second quarter of the nineteenth century; and this influence was transmitted to a generation of Irish conservative leaders. Setting aside great Victorian Tory clans such as the Abercorns, Downshires and Londonderrys, the dominant figures in mid-century Conservatism, certainly bourgeois conservatism, were a community of evangelical lawyers, including Sir Joseph Napier (1804–82), James Whiteside (Napier's brother-in-law) (1804–76) and Hugh McCalmont Cairns (later first Earl Cairns) (1809–85).[7]

While intellectual leadership was provided by these Trinity evangelicals and by other Tories, particularly lawyers, recent scholarship has also made

5 Porter, *Henry Cooke*, 224–25, 233.
6 D. Raponi, 'British Protestants, the Roman Question, and the Formation of Italian National Identity, 1861–75', PhD thesis (University of Cambridge, 2009), 92. For the wider literature on Irish Protestant evangelicalism see: D. Bowen, *The Protestant Crusade in Ireland, 1800–1870: A Study of Protestant–Catholic Relations between the Act of Union and Disestablishment* (Dublin: Gill & Macmillan, 1978); I. Whelan, *The Bible War in Ireland: The 'Second Reformation' and the Polarisation of Protestant-Catholic Relations, 1800–40* (Madison, WI: University of Wisconsin Press, 2005); D. Hempton and M. Hill, *Evangelical Protestantism in Ulster Society, 1740–1890* (London: Routledge, 1992).
7 See Anon [Catherine Marsh], *Brief Memories of Hugh McCalmont, First Earl Cairns* (London: James Nisbet, 1885); A. C. Ewald, *The Life of Sir Joseph Napier, Bart., Ex-Lord Chancellor of Ireland, From His Correspondence* (London: Longmans Green, 1887); J. Whiteside, *Essays and Lectures: Historical and Literary* (Dublin: Hodges, Smith and Foster, 1868); J. Whiteside, *Early Sketches of Eminent Persons* (Dublin: Hodges, Smith and Foster, 1870). See also A. Shields, *The Irish Conservative Party, 1852–1868: Land, Politics and Religion* (Dublin: Irish Academic Press, 2006).

the case for the contribution of a liberal-conservative mercantile and pro-fessional community within Belfast in the first half of the nineteenth cen-tury. The focuses of this included the wealthy Tennent and Emerson clans, with (for example) James Emerson Tennent, Conservative MP for Belfast and (later) Lisburn, a prolific author, who identified with a range of 'advanced' causes, such as Greek nationalism.[8] The wider significance of this literate and outward-looking conservatism may still be open to debate; but at the very least it represented a britannic and metropolitan strain within the party, which was carried over (certainly in a vestigial manner) into Irish and Ulster unionism.

If evangelicalism provided one form of internal binding agent within Irish Protestantism, then external stimuli came not just from the O'Connellite mobilisation – but also, later, from the question of the Church of Ireland establishment, which was coming to the fore in the 1860s, and which was a natural development of the tithe and church endowment questions of the 1830s. For both Ireland and Scotland, the rights and status of the national churches were effectively tied up with the Union establishment. In each coun-try the question of disestablishment was linked, therefore, to the politics of Union. Indeed, the ferocious battle over the Irish Church in 1868–69 has been seen as a precursor to the Home Rule crisis, because disestablishment was an amendment of the terms of Union; and also because disestablishment brought to the fore individuals, attitudes and alliances, which would soon be redeployed in 1885–6.[9] In a sense, therefore, the crisis of the Irish Union was first precipitated, not in 1885, but rather in 1868 (or indeed earlier) – not when Gladstone first proclaimed that the Act of 1801 stood in the way of a true British–Irish union, but rather when he first published his conclusion that 'the true interests of religion were in conflict with establishment'.[10]

Aside from (or connected with) evangelicalism, the Orange Order sup-plied an additional medium through which forms of Protestant association and solidarity could be built, and through which the different cultures of late eighteenth-century loyalism could be melded within nineteenth-century unionism: unionism ultimately drew strength from the forms of loyalism

---

8 J. Bew, *The Glory of being Britons: Civic Unionism in Nineteenth Century Belfast* (Dublin: Four Courts Press, 2008). For a different emphasis see J. J. Wright, ' "The Perverted Graduates of Oxford": Priestcraft, "Political Popery", and the Transnational Anti-Catholicism of Sir James Emerson Tennent', in N. Whelehan (ed.), *Transnational Perspectives on Modern Irish History* (London: Routledge, 2015), 127–48.

9 See D. C. Savage, 'The Irish Unionists, 1867–86', *Eire-Ireland*, 2 (1967); and also P. M. H. Bell, *Disestablishment in Ireland and Wales* (London: S.P.C.K., 1969).

10 Bell, *Disestablishment*, 79–80.

that were originally defined in the era of the Revolutionary and Napoleonic Wars, of which the most important in Ireland was Orangeism.[11] As is well known, Orangeism grew largely from Protestant combinations in south Ulster, with its nativity being dated to the fall-out from a sectarian clash in north Armagh, the Battle of the Diamond, in September 1795. From its beginnings, it is clear that the Order functioned as a binding agent within Irish Protestantism, amongst the Irish Protestant diaspora in Britain and North America, and between Irish Protestants and British sympathisers: as early as 1797 a militarised Orangeism had become the predominant (though certainly not the only) form of loyalist expression in Ireland.[12]

The Order's numbers (which soon reached 100,000) are one measure of its significance in this respect. Another measure was the extraordinarily diverse and complex popular culture that Orangeism generated, in particular, tracts, ballads and poetry – with works such as Robert Young's 'The Orange Minstrel' (1832), dedicated to the 'Orange and Conservative Societies of Ireland', enjoying frequent reprints and wide circulation.[13] Yet another measure was its social diversity: the Order had, for a time, royal patronage in the shape of the dukes of York and Cumberland, brothers to King George IV. From the beginning, Orangeism had varied forms of polite sanction, including the patronage of south Ulster gentry such as Colonel William Blacker; and in 1845, when the Order was reconstituted, a Fermanagh landowner, the third earl of Enniskillen, agreed to act as the Grand Master (Lord Enniskillen was also the patron of Robert Young). The Order attracted some middle-class and intellectual backing: Castle lawyers such as William Saurin (Attorney General of Ireland between 1807 and 1822) and Thomas Lefroy (beloved of Jane Austen, Prime Serjeant, and later – between 1852 and 1866 – Lord Chief Justice of Ireland) combined family roots in continental European Protestant refugee culture with an aggressive Orange Toryism.

However, perhaps the most significant electoral exponent of an evangelical Orange Toryism was the impecunious landowner, journalist and novelist, William Johnston of Ballykilbeg, County Down.[14] Johnston's eccentricity and epic improvidence are such that it is tempting to view him as an isolated, or even comedic, phenomenon. He gained national celebrity through

---

11 See the arguments of Blackstock, *Loyalism in Ireland*.

12 Blackstock, *Loyalism in Ireland*, 129.

13 Blackstock, *Loyalism in Ireland*, 270–71; R. Young, The 'Fermanagh True Blue', *The Orange Minstrel or Ulster Melodist: consisting of Historical Songs and Poems* (Londonderry, privately printed 1832). The subscribers' list to the first edition includes nearly 900 names, some of whom took multiple – in two cases 25 – copies.

14 See A. McClelland, *William Johnston of Ballykilbeg* (Belfast: Ulster Society 1990).

flouting the controversial Party Processions Act: in July 1867 he led an illegal Orange march between Newtownards and Bangor in north Down, an act of defiance which won him two months' detention in Downpatrick Gaol – and a subsequent beatification within Orangeism. Yet Johnston, quirkily distinctive in several respects, also epitomises much of nineteenth-century Irish Conservatism. He clearly embodied the landed tradition of Orange sponsorship, which had been so central to the foundation and restoration of the Order; but he also represented a type of Trinity-educated lawyer and evangelical, so that (whatever his intellectual confusion and gaucheness) he stood at one end of a spectrum that included Napier, Whiteside and Cairns. His enthusiasms and fads, fully documented within an extensive diary, illustrate much of the powerful interlocking components of Victorian Unionist popular culture: Orangeism and evangelical religion, certainly, but also other related forms of associational or political activism (such as temperance, educational self-improvement, and women's suffrage).[15] Moreover, Johnston's swift rehabilitation within mainstream Conservatism underlines the capacity of that very formidable tradition to address and absorb many types of dissent.

Like its Scottish counterpart, the Irish Conservative party responded to the challenge of electoral reform and populist challenge through reorganisation and relaunch, but the Irish were first in creating a national coordinating body: the Central Conservative Society of Ireland was originally founded in 1850, in the aftermath of the critical Irish Franchise Act, and antedated its Scottish equivalent by over thirty years.[16] The Central Conservative Society not only foreshadowed the creation of the Scottish National Union of Conservative Associations (in 1882), it also anticipated the emergence of a distinctive Irish unionism in the mid-1880s: one of the Society's patrons, Joseph Napier, stressed 'the importance of having our Irish Party kept together', and indeed this was its principal purpose and achievement.[17] The Society, like unionism at the end of the century, was also strongly infiltrated by members of the Orange Order.[18] Specifically northern satellite bodies were later created in the shape of the Ulster Constitutional Union (1880) and the Ulster Constitutional Club (1883).

Drawing on these different cultural strands, Irish Conservatism survived and indeed thrived. As with Scots Conservatism in Glasgow and the West,

---

15 His extensive, but under-utilised, diaries survive: see PRONI, William Johnston Diary, D.989.
16 I. G. C. Hutchison, *A Political History of Scotland* (Edinburgh: John Donald, 1986), 59.
17 Hoppen, *Elections, Politics and Society*, 284.
18 Hoppen, *Elections, Politics and Society*, 284–5.

so Irish Conservatism was well-placed to channel popular urban reactions to Catholic political growth and activism. However, Scots' Conservative success in rural constituencies was much less marked than that achieved by their Irish counterparts, who had relatively strong roots in the landscape of the north of Ireland: Irish landlordism, and by extension Conservatism, benefited from a mild consolidation in the aftermath of the Great Famine. Both Scots and Irish Conservatives benefited, too, from an accession of Orange strength; but this was proportionately more significant for the Irish, who were also drawing upon a coalescent Protestantism (as opposed to the Scots after the 'Great Disruption' of 1843). Where Scottish Conservatism was for long overshadowed by the dominant Liberal tradition, Irish Conservatives enjoyed consistent success, being the single largest party in Ireland at the general elections of 1835, 1841 and 1859; in 1859, boosted by Independent support, and possibly by evangelical religious revival, they peaked with a majority of Irish seats (55 out of the 105 available).[19] Only in the context of a wider franchise and a more coherent Home Rule and farmer challenge did the Irish Conservative standing falter: these factors reduced the number of Conservative seats by roughly one half from their average in the 1832–85 era to between 16 and 22 in the years between 1885 and 1918.

The political confluence that created Irish unionism in the mid-1880s also owed much to its Liberal tributary. Like its Scottish and wider British counterparts, Irish liberalism had both Whig and radical strains, and a variegated ancestry: all looked back to a history of support for the 'Glorious Revolution' of 1688, limited monarchy, cautious reform and parliamentary sovereignty. Irish Whiggery in the eighteenth century was Protestant and patriotic, enlightened, often aristocratic and loyal. Great Whig magnates such as James Caulfeild, first earl of Charlemont (1728–1799), corresponded with Montesquieu, upheld classical and enlightened ideals in art and architecture, and pursued a patriotic agenda in politics. Enlightenment also frequently implied hostility towards the Catholic Church, however; and Anglican Whigs such as Charlemont (no less than Presbyterian radicals) easily combined the historic religious presumptions of Irish Protestantism with ostensibly 'enlightened' political ideals: Charlemont, for example, in common with other Whig patriots, was an opponent of Catholic emancipation in the 1780s.

In addition to this type of aristocratic and landed heritage within Whiggery, an urban variant of the tradition also thrived in Belfast. The capitalist class within early nineteenth-century Belfast was largely Whig, and rooted

19 Hoppen, *Elections, Politics and Society*, 286.

disproportionately in the textile industries.[20] The identification of Home Rule with moderate protectionism emphatically did not chime with the interests of this class, who often combined (in a characteristic mid-Victorian formulation) non-conformist, liberal and free trade convictions. Of course, not all of these magnates were Presbyterian or liberal: some enormously wealthy linen clans such as the Ewarts or Mulhollands were already, by the 1870s, conservative, while Peter Gibbon has argued that the shipowners of the city were generally conservative from the 1850s onwards.[21] However, even allowing for this drift towards Conservatism, and for the Conservatives' electoral ascendancy (by the 1850s), there remained a significant tradition of free trade Liberalism within the Presbyterian (and dissenting) business community (sustained by a 'nexus of interrelated Whig families' such as the Andrews, Barbours, Duffins, Dunvilles, Herdmans, Richardsons and Sinclairs).[22] Taking their lead from John Bright, this business elite carried their free trade convictions, and the commercial clout of their industry into organised unionism.

If some landed Whigs were being swiftly compelled towards conservatism and Unionism by the perceived pressure of popular Catholic activism, then other, more bourgeois and radical, forms of Irish liberalism initially identified different sources of political challenge. In addition, the aftermath of the Famine was characterised by a resurgence of landlordism, aided by a new class of incoming landlord, the actions of the land courts, and the ending of the old semi-feudal relationships binding landlord and tenant. Government legislation on the land question encouraged landlords to take a more legalistic view of their social and economic obligations, and this contributed to a cooling of agrarian relations even before the dramatic downturn of the later 1870s. By the 1860s there was a widespread suspicion that landlords were determined to destroy the customary rights of tenant farmers (the 'Ulster Custom') in the north of Ireland.[23] This (in the event, temporary) landlord efflorescence fed into the electoral consolidation of Irish conservatism, the party tradition that identified most unequivocally with the rights of Irish property.

This landed and conservative growth provided a spur to Liberal party organisation in Ireland, and also created an opportunity for electoral gain.

20 P. Gibbon, *The Origins of Ulster Unionism: The Formation of Popular Protestant Politics and Ideology in Nineteenth Century Ireland* (Manchester: Manchester University Press, 1975), 105.
21 Gibbon, *Origins of Ulster Unionism*, 106.
22 Gibbon, *Origins of Ulster Unionism*, 106.
23 F. Thompson, *The End of Liberal Ulster: Land Agitation and Land Reform, 1868–86* (Belfast: Ulster Historical Society, 2001), 302.

On 4 August 1865 the Ulster Liberal Society was established (in the Royal Hotel, Belfast), to be followed by the Ulster Reform Club.[24] But, more important even than these organisational initiatives, was the realisation that the otherwise formidable edifice of landed and Protestant conservatism did not accommodate the needs of the influential farmer interest, particularly in Ulster. This permitted Irish Liberals to draw upon their traditions of radical agrarian reform – traditions most conspicuously represented by the radical landed MP for Dundalk (1835–7) and Rochdale (1842–52), William Sharman Crawford. The Liberals successfully underscored a commitment to tenant right at the general elections of 1868 (when they won 66 out of the 103 seats) and 1874 (when their successful appeal to Ulster farmers staved off electoral annihilation by the Home Rulers).[25] The particular success of this appeal to Ulster farmers was highlighted by the fact that, outside the northern province, their party performed abysmally at the elections of 1874 and 1880.[26]

And yet, while this strain within Irish Liberalism deserves emphasis, it is important not to exaggerate its importance, or to invest the era before the Home Rule crisis with the wishful thinking of a later ecumenism. While it is possible to read the history of the 1870s as evidence of the creative potential remaining within Ulster politics, and indeed as evidence for the enormity of the shifts that came in 1885–6, the last hurrah of Ulster Liberalism concealed some more mundane realities. It is true that, by appealing to the farmer interest, Liberals succeeded in uniting Catholics and Presbyterians behind a reform agenda, and that this, ostensibly ecumenical, alliance brought electoral success in 1874 and 1880, on the eve of the open sectarianisation of the early and mid-1880s.[27] But, as K.T. Hoppen has observed, 'the most obvious feature of Liberal activity in Ulster was its dependence upon Presbyterian leadership and Catholic numbers'; and Presbyterian enthusiasm for Gladstone in 1874 and 1880 owed as much to the Grand Old Man's choleric thoughts on the Vatican Decrees as to his determination to root out the crimes of Ascendancy.[28] Moreover, northern Catholic support for Liberalism in 1880 depended largely upon the fact that only two Home Rulers had sufficient temerity to stand for election in Ulster (both in County

---

24 Hoppen, *Elections, Politics and Society*, 270.
25 Thompson, *End of Liberal Ulster*, 5 and ch. 6; B. M. Walker, *Ulster Politics: The Formative Years, 1868–1886* (Belfast: Ulster Historical Foundation, 1989), 116.
26 Hoppen, *Elections, Politics and Society*, 274.
27 Compare with the argument in Walker, *Ulster Politics*.
28 Hoppen, *Elections, Politics and Society*, 265.

Cavan). Presbyterian Liberals were opponents of Anglican Ascendancy, but they were also often opponents of Rome; while Ulster Catholics had, as yet, nowhere else to go, save for Liberalism.

Little wonder, then, that the glorious, but thinly-rooted, flowers of Ulster Liberalism wilted so dramatically in the early and mid-1880s. In a sense, shifting analogies, Ulster Liberalism was an alliance founded, not upon any historic reconciliation or empathy, but rather upon pragmatism and the appeal of a single issue. When that issue, tenant right, was satisfactorily addressed (through Gladstone's Land Act of 1881), then the alliance faltered; and indeed there was a certain irony here, in so far as the legislation owed much to the effort expended by Ulster Liberal MPs, who were thereby in a sense undercutting their own electoral support.[29] The material needs of Presbyterian farmers were satisfied by this legislation; while the spiritual needs of their Catholic counterparts were satisfactorily addressed by the developing nationalist political assault on Ulster. In sum, Ulster Liberalism stalled when (after 1881) Presbyterians felt once again that the Catholic threat to their consciences was greater than the threat posed by the Ascendancy to their livelihood: it stalled when Catholics found alternative structures wherein they could lead themselves.

Most Irish Liberals were, accordingly, shocked by Gladstone's conversion to Home Rule, for (in the words of the editor of the *Northern Whig*), they looked upon 'any proposal to repeal the Act of Union, or to tamper with it, as not a Liberal policy at all, but retrogressive, dangerous, incredible and impossible'.[30] Gladstone, in other words, was challenging the fundamentals of Irish Liberal self-definition. On 30 April 1886, in the context of the introduction of the first Home Rule Bill, a large gathering of Liberals met in the Ulster Hall, Belfast, to declare their opposition; and shortly afterwards the Ulster Liberal Unionist Committee was formed, soon to be renamed the Ulster Liberal Unionist Association. From these developments it was abundantly clear that the 'vast majority of the leading Liberals in Ulster opposed the Home Rule Bill'.[31] There had already been quiet and preliminary cooperation in 1885; but the general election of July 1886 revealed a wholesale (and, in the event, lasting) electoral alliance between Irish Conservative and Liberal Unionists.

29 C. F. Smith, *James Nicholson Richardson of Bessbrook* (London: Longmans Green, 1925), 68–9.
30 T. MacKnight, *Ulster as it is* (London: Macmillan, 1896), I, 170.
31 Walker, *Ulster Politics*, 236.

Unionist Cultures

The elaborate organisational carapace of formal Unionism in the mid-1880s was supported not only by this diverse and complex party heritage, but also by a rich popular and high culture. In part, this was influenced by the ascendancy in parts of Ireland and of Irish society, particularly in the North, of British commercial and imperial culture. But there was certainly much more to Irish Unionism than the presence and direct influence of the Union state.

In a general sense, it was possible to grow up in the north of Ireland at the end of the nineteenth century in an environment where schooling and work, recreation and leisure, religious worship and environment were all influenced by the values upheld within the British state. Youth organisations such as the Boys' Brigade, imported from Scotland into Belfast by the evangelical William McVicker in 1890, or Baden-Powell's Scouting Movement, with its strong imperial resonances, which had arrived in Belfast by 1909, provided a training not merely for life, but also for Unionism. The Orange Order founded youth lodges from the 1880s onwards. Public schooling was conducted in the English language, using texts where the history and geography of the Empire featured largely, and where the classroom might be overshadowed by the ubiquitous pink-splattered map of the world.

The workplace might well be located within the expanding public service; alternatively in a city such as Belfast, the dependence of most businesses upon the British or imperial connection would be made clear by the political activity of owners and managers.[32] Trade union membership in Victorian and Edwardian Ulster generally connected workers to their comrades in Britain. Place names and public space were disproportionately unionist: in 1910 a Belfast worker might journey to the shipyards of the Queen's Island, traversing Victoria Square and the Albert Bridge, and passing the Spencer Dock (named after the eponymous Earl, and lord lieutenant): he might later spend his wages in the shops of the main thoroughfare, Royal Avenue, or take a drink in the Crown Bar, or (venturing a mile or so further), the Hatfield Arms, by Salisbury Street.[33]

Voluntary associations, such as the Young Men's Christian Association, were clearly conditioned by the impact of Union and Empire: their reading materials and entertainments reflected these two critical influences. Church life, equally, was often inseparable from these political influences: while some

32 Compare with Gibbon, *Origins of Ulster Unionism*.
33 MacKnight, *Ulster as it is*, i, 263.

Church of Ireland and Presbyterian ministers were either Home Rulers, or fought to keep the church community as a politically neutral space, in reality much of the spiritual life of Ulster Protestants was unionist, at least in undertone.[34] The liturgy of the Church of Ireland was sprinkled with loyal references to the monarchy, as were the pew Bibles, while funerary monuments, and aging military standards, in Anglican and other Protestant churches, testified to British imperial exploits on the battlefield and elsewhere.

The intense interlinkages of the aristocracy continued to bind the upper echelons of Irish society with Britain and to unionism, as recent work has affirmed. The formal political influence of Irish unionist peers and landed gentlemen within the United Kingdom parliament has long been recognised (not least through the pioneering scholarship of Patrick Buckland).[35] Equally, the consolidation of a pan-British aristocracy 'in the last quarter of the 18th century and the first quarter of the 19th century' has been traced through the work of Linda Colley.[36] The integration of an individual clan such as the Londonderrys has been observed through the research of Diane Urquhart. But only now has the full extent of the engagement by northern aristocratic clans such as the Abercorns, Annesleys, Belmores, Caledons, Enniskillens, Ernes, Londonderrys and Rossmores with metropolitan society been fully grasped thanks to the work of scholars like Devon McHugh.[37] These were families that, in the era of Home Rule, lived a life of privileged transhumance, shifting from Irish pastures to the ostensibly more elevated feeding grounds of the imperial capital. The marriage patterns, leisure activities, dress and social codes, and artistic tastes of these Irish clans meant that they were enfolded within a broadly homogeneous United Kingdom social and political elite. Judged whether by the shape and print of their calling cards, their choice of dress or schools, their military and racing enthusiasms, or their

---

34 See A. Jackson, 'Unionist Politics and Protestant Society in Edwardian Ireland', *Historical Journal*, xxxiii, 4 (1990). For clergy unimpressed by the allure of unionism see: W. S. Armour, *Armour of Ballymoney* (London: Duckworth, 1934); D. Fitzpatrick, *'Solitary and Wild': Frederick MacNeice and the Salvation of Ireland* (Dublin: Four Courts Press, 2011); J. R. B. McMinn, *Against the Tide: J. B. Armour, Irish Presbyterian Minister and Home Ruler* (Belfast: Ulster Historical Foundation, 1985). See also H. Waddell, *John Waddell* (Belfast: Belfast Newsletter, 1949), 43–4.

35 See P. Buckland, *Irish Unionism I: The Anglo-Irish and the New Ireland, 1885–1922* (Dublin: Gill & Macmillan, 1972); P. Buckland, *Irish Unionism II: Ulster Unionism and the Origins of Northern Ireland, 1886–1922* (Dublin: Gill & Macmillan,1973).

36 L. Colley, *Britons: Forging the Nation, 1707–1837* (New Haven, CT: Yale University Press, 1992), 193.

37 D. Urquhart, *The Ladies of Londonderry: Women and Political Patronage* (London: I. B. Tauris, 2007); D. McHugh, 'Family, Leisure and the Arts: Aspects of the Culture of the Aristocracy in Ulster, 1870–1925', PhD thesis (University of Edinburgh, 2011).

close observance of an agreed social calendar, these were British aristocrats. The corollary of this, of course, was that any weakening of their status in Ireland implied a weakening of the overall condition of the United Kingdom.

In addition, it might be said that the intellectual condition of unionism in the early twentieth century fed into the strength of the party and movement in Ireland. The success of Edwardian unionism in the north of Ireland was linked, not just to the diversity of its political heritage and cultural under-pinnings, but also to the strength of its command over intellectuals. As in Scotland, so in Ireland, unionism flourished within the press, literature and the academy (though the intellectual hegemony of unionism in Scotland was more obviously robust than in Ireland). Unionism was not yet wholly seen in terms of party or sectarian ascendancy: this perspective would gain focus after fifty years of one-party rule by the Unionist bourgeoisie and residual gentry in Northern Ireland. But in the second half of the nineteenth century, it was still possible to interpret Union in Burkean terms – that is, as a guarantee, rather than a negation, of individual freedom. Liberal Unionism was therefore a morally and politically less challenging option for (in particular) Protestant intellectuals and scholars than would subsequently be the case in the aftermath of the Stormont years.

The main conservative newspaper in the North was the *Belfast News Letter*, owned at the end of the century by Sir James Henderson (who also served as a president of the Belfast St Andrews' Society). The corresponding Liberal Unionist organ was the *Northern Whig*, whose editors demonstrated particular intellectual distinction, not just in their copy, but more widely: Thomas MacKnight (1866–1891), J. R. Fisher (1891–1913) and W. S. Armour all published distinguished books on historical and political themes (though Armour was eventually lost to the Union).[38] Irish unionist proprietors and editors featured prominently elsewhere: Alfred and Harold Harmsworth (Lord Northcliffe and Lord Rothermere), the greatest journalistic forces of the age, owed something of their British nationalism and imperialism to family roots in Protestant Ireland (although they were also unsettled by the potentially catastrophic nature of the Ulster Unionist campaign in 1912–1914).[39]

---

38 See MacKnight, *Ulster As It Is*; J. R. Fisher, *The End of the Irish Parliament* (London, E. Arnold, 1911); Armour, *Armour of Ballymoney*; W. S. Armour, *Facing the Irish Question* (London: Duckworth, 1935); W. S. Armour, *Ulster, Ireland, Britain: A Forgotten Trust* (London: Duckworth,1938). See also (for example) K. Hughes, *The Scots in Victorian and Edwardian Belfast: A Study in Elite Migration* (Edinburgh: Edinburgh University Press, 2013), 95.

39 D. G. Boyce, 'Alfred Harmsworth, First Viscount Northcliffe', *ODNB*, (Oxford University Press, 2004).

Lesser figures still made significant contributions: the Dungannon-born W. F. Monypenny, Disraeli's biographer, was a respected journalist on *The Times*, and used its columns (and his position as the paper's Special Correspondent in Ireland) to promote a 'two nations' view of the political conflict in Ulster (his reports were later, posthumously, collected in a volume, *The Two Irish Nations*).[40]

The unionist presence in other realms of literature was significant. In fiction, the novel and unionism were intertwined in the nineteenth century in ways that were appreciated by contemporary unionists, and sanctioned by them. As is well known, the conflict over Union in 1800 was fought using a fusillade of pamphlets, which in turn relied upon 'an armoury of fictional methods and techniques'.[41] Equally, it has been observed that the novel was 'a genre adopted by Irish authors under the very shadow of the Union'.[42] The work of Maria Edgeworth and Sydney Owenson, Lady Morgan, though often highly responsive towards its Irish Catholic subjects, and (in the case of Owenson) bleak in its assessment of the fall-out from Union, can nevertheless (or, perhaps, consequently) be read within what Seamus Deane has famously referred to as 'the pathology of literary unionism': both authors have been seen as offering a form of complement to political or statutory unionism, in so far as their work was seen as a means of 'relating one cultural tradition to another'.[43] The literary critic, Mary Jean Corbett, has suggested that 'marriage-and-family plots by Edgeworth and Owenson ... represent the narrative consequences of union as a matter of legitimating inequality in gendered terms'.[44] Certainly Edgeworth, who grew more conservative with age, was championed by the doyen of Scottish Toryism and literary unionism, Sir Walter Scott: as no less a literary critic than Stanley Baldwin observed, Scott 'regarded her as the interpreter of Ireland, and as one who by her writings

---

40 W. F. Monypenny, *The Two Irish Nations: An Essay on Irish Home Rule* (London: John Murray, 1913)
41 C. Connolly, 'Completing the Union: The Irish Novel and the Moment of Union', in M. Brown, P. Geoghegan and J. Kelly (eds.), *The Irish Act of Union, 1800: Bicentennial Essays* (Dublin: Four Courts Press, 2003), 162; see also C. Connolly, *A Cultural History of the Irish Novel, 1890–1829* (Cambridge University Press, 2011) and W. J. MacCormack, *The Pamphlet Debate on the Union between Great Britain and Ireland, 1797–1800* (Dublin: Four Courts Press, 1995).
42 J. Leersen, *Remembrance and Imagination: Patterns in the Literary and Historical Representation of Ireland in the Nineteenth Century* (Cork: Cork University Press, 1996), 38–9.
43 Connolly, 'Completing the Union', 160; W. J. MacCormack, 'Maria Edgeworth', *ODNB*, (Oxford University Press, 2004).
44 M. J. Corbett, *Allegories of Union in Irish and English Writing* (Cambridge University Press, 2000), 12.

had helped to make more easy the passage of Union'.[45] Owenson found supporters within the Abercorn household, a stronghold of Irish Toryism, and amongst the very architects of Union, Lord Castlereagh and William Pitt.[46]

Complementing the literature characterised by an implicit or subliminal unionism, was fiction produced by those who frankly embraced political loyalism or Unionism. Among the many careers of the Orange hero William Johnston was that of novelist: Johnston produced *Nightshade* in 1857, where a world peopled by Bible-burning Catholic priests, trimming Anglo-Catholics, oleaginous tractarians and covert and oppressive Jesuits was presented to its readers.[47] As with many other conservative unionists at this time, the Siege of Derry and the Battle of the Boyne were important cultural reference points; and indeed these supplied a central focus for Johnston's *Under which King?* (1873) (as well as for work by Charlotte Elizabeth Tonna, Cecil Frances Alexander, Lord Ernest Hamilton and others).[48] The plays and novels of St John Ervine (a cultural nationalist until *c*.1916) increasingly reflected his concern to capture the speech patterns and cadences of his fellow northerners, their personalities and environments; and a novel such as *Mrs Martin's Man* (1914) was part of a wider genre of 'Ulster' literature which echoed the partitionist thrusts of formal Unionism.[49]

But unionist politics also had a diverse scholarly grounding, particularly in Trinity College Dublin, which elected two (invariably Unionist) MPs, and Queen's University Belfast. Historians and classicists were particularly notable for their identification with Unionism, both in terms of their scholarly work and their political profession. By the Edwardian era a large number of (in particular Trinity) historians advanced Unionist claims and interpretations: Richard Bagwell, F. E. Ball, C. L. Falkiner, T. D. Ingram, W. E. H. Lecky, W. A. Phillips (Bagwell was active in the Irish Unionist Alliance, Ball was Irish Secretary of the Unionist Joint Committee in the 1890s, Falkiner was a Unionist parliamentary candidate, while Lecky sat as a Liberal Unionist MP for Trinity).[50] Other scholars with historical or antiquarian passions such

45 Stanley Baldwin, *This Torch of Freedom: Speeches and Addresses* (London: Hodder & Stoughton, 1935), 166.
46 Connolly, 'Completing the Union', 164.
47 W. Johnston, *Nightshade: A Novel* (London: Richard Bentley, 1857), 295.
48 For a discussion of the siege theme, see I. McBride, *The Siege of Derry in Ulster Protestant Mythology* (Dublin: Four Courts Press, 1997).
49 J. W. Foster, *Forces and Themes in Ulster Fiction* (Dublin: Gill & Macmillan, 1974), 130–9.
50 Ball to Middleton, 9 July 1891, Arthur Balfour Papers Add.Ms.49849, f.53: BL.

as Edward Dowden (Yeats' *bête-noire*, and a distinguished historian of English literature), Sir Samuel Ferguson or George Petrie combined scholarship with unionism (Dowden, again, was a stalwart of the Irish Unionist Alliance). Some of the most prominent scientists and medical doctors of the age professed the unionist faith: the Belfast-born William Thomson, Lord Kelvin, Professor of Natural Philosophy at Glasgow, was an active Liberal Unionist in the west of Scotland, while Sir William Whitla, author of the best-selling *Elements of Pharmacy* (1882) and *A Dictionary of Treatment* (1892), served as a Unionist member of the Irish Convention (1917–1918) and Unionist MP for Queen's University Belfast (1918–1923).

Classics and unionism tended to go hand-in-hand, though it certainly should not be supposed that there was any automatic complementarity.[51] Still, it was amongst the classicists that the one of the greatest concentrations of Irish unionist sympathy was to be found within the late Victorian and Edwardian academy: John Bagnell Bury (the Monaghan-born Regius Professor of Greek at Trinity College Dublin, and of Modern History at Cambridge), Samuel Henry Butcher (Professor of Greek at Edinburgh and Conservative MP for Cambridge University), Samuel Dill (Fellow of Corpus Christi, Oxford, and Professor of Greek at Queen's College Belfast, 'quietly unionist', and related by marriage to James Craig's Minister for Home Affairs, Dawson Bates), and John Pentland Mahaffy (Provost of Trinity College Dublin). Bury and Dill's abiding interest in late antiquity (the latter was the author of *Roman Society in the Last Century of the Western Empire* (1898) and *Roman Society in Gaul in the Merovingian Age* (1926)) was shared by other Irish Protestants, and perhaps reflected some subliminal sense that the experience of the Western Empire had – however tenuously – resonances with the decline of an embattled aristocratic, imperial, and 'pagan' culture in Ireland. Each of these men was from an Irish unionist and Protestant (indeed often a clergy) background.

Unionists

The organised unionism of the Home Rule era drew upon these various strains within popular and high culture, and within Irish Conservatism and Whiggery, and inherited many of their characteristics. Unionism combined the support of much of the industrial and landed capital on the island, and

---

51 The case of Eric Robertson (E. R.) Dodds, Banbridge Presbyterian, Irish republican and Oxford Regius Professor of Greek, highlights the fact that this argument cannot be pushed too far: see E. R. Dodds, *Missing Persons: An Autobiography* (Oxford University Press, 1977).

subsumed a popular Protestantism, bound by Orangeism, loyalism, and evangelical conviction. In addition unionism drew strength both from the consolidation and expansion of the British state, as well as from a tradition of Irish patriotism and anti-Catholicism. Unionism was simultaneously an expression of Enlightenment, economic ascendancy and sectarian defensiveness.

These, then, were some of the roots of the movement which flourished between 1885 and the First World War, and which (in a truncated form) has survived within Northern Ireland since the establishment of partition in 1920. These were the roots of the movement that successfully thwarted Home Rule, and the ideal of a unified, autonomous Ireland. The deeply-laid, party political origins of the movement help to explain this longevity; but many other aspects of its early organisation, development and appeal are also relevant in any effort to illuminate its traction and success.

Paradoxically, given the strength of the Conservative inheritance, and the formerly close relationship between British and Irish parties, a semi-autonomous Irish unionist organisation was precipitated in the context of British Tory betrayal in 1884–1885. The occasion of the apparent treachery was the parliamentary reform (1884) and constituency redistribution (1885) of those years; and, as Sir Stafford Northcote remarked (with some insouciance), the British Conservative leadership had 'forgotten Ulster' in the negotiations to establish the details of the third reform measure.[52] However, if British Tories 'forgot Ulster', then Ulster loyalists did not readily forget (what they saw as) Tory betrayal, particularly in the context of the developing electoral challenge from Parnellite Home Rule. By January 1885 a semi-independent Irish Unionist Parliamentary Party (or 'Ulster Party') had emerged at Westminster, to be followed by local organisational initiatives such as the Loyal Irish Union and the Irish Loyal and Patriotic Union (each formed in the summer of 1885).

This autonomy had its immediate roots in the politics of reform, but (as has been observed) there was also a longer history of Irish Conservative distinctiveness. In part this reflected the condition of other national Conservative parties within the United Kingdom; and there were certainly some broad parallels between the development of Irish and Scottish Conservatism (with shared bursts of activity in the 1830s, late 1860s and early 1880s, all in the context of reform). But one measure of the distance between the two, and of the paradoxical condition of Irish Unionist politics, was that, while Ireland and its Union conditioned some of the fundamental contours of British politics between 1885 and 1920, Irish Unionism remained distinct and

---

52 Jackson, *Ulster Party*, 25.

semi-detached – despite the ongoing exasperation of senior ministers on the issue.[53] Scotland certainly had its separate Conservative institutions; but those in Ireland and (eventually) in Ulster were more elaborate and independent, and were more often revisited and extended. For example, the challenge of Home Rule in 1886 and 1893 brought comprehensive Irish Unionist organisational activity, and the creation of (aside from the bodies already named) the Irish Unionist Alliance (1891), the Ulster Convention League (1892), the Ulster Defence Union (1893) and the Templetown Unionist Clubs movement (from 1893). The reality of internal, popular unionist, dissent, and the renewed threat of devolution and Home Rule, brought a root-and-branch and local reorganisation of Ulster unionism in 1904–5, in the shape of the Ulster Unionist Council. This in turn provided an essential platform for the highly distinctive and particularist Ulster Unionist reaction against the third Home Rule Bill, in 1912–14.

The drift within Irish unionist politics during the Home Rule era, unlike in Scotland, was towards a regional concentration and predominance. The explanations for this 'Ulsterisation' of Irish unionism are manifold. Home Rule (1886–1912) coincided with a major democratic thrust in British politics, with the achievement of the secret ballot (1872), the curtailment of corrupt electoral practices (1883) and the reform and redistribution measures of 1884–5: politics retained a vestigial aristocratic presence and exclusivity, but they were more than ever about popular mobilisation. In Ireland, given the sectarian and political demographics, popular unionist mobilisation could only be achieved in the North.

Moreover, while there were some urban concentrations, the fatal strength of southern unionism lay in its disproportionate command over the landed classes. A formal, urban unionism certainly survived in Dublin City, where an exiguous network of Anglican parishes and Orange lodges upheld the faith: work on working-class and lower middle-class Dublin Protestantism in the era of Home Rule and the Revolution unveils a largely forgotten world of railwaymen, brewery workers, and low-grade clerks and civil servants – the world from which Sean O'Casey (railwayman and then lowly employee of Eason's & Co) and his brother (a British soldier) were sprung.[54] In the prosperous, Protestant suburbs of South County Dublin, a more deeply entrenched unionism thrived into the era of the Revolution, as the records of Kingstown

53 Balfour to Chamberlain, 29 February 1896 (copy), Balfour Papers, Add.Ms.49773, f.99:BL.
54 M. Maguire, 'The Organisation and Activism of Dublin's Protestant Working Class, 1883–1935', *Irish Historical Studies*, xxix (1994) no. 113, 65–87.

Unionist Club, and the election of successive Unionist MPs for South Dublin and (in 1918) for Rathmines, demonstrate. Other pockets of unionism existed in the northern suburbs (in Clontarf, for example); and indeed as late as 1895 a Unionist parliamentary candidate for North County Dublin was able to scrape together a respectable 2,280 votes, just over half the total garnered by the Nationalist victor. But, in general, this was a financially and socially vulnerable unionism – a unionism precariously dependent upon the patronage of a handful of Protestant business magnates (such as Edward Cecil Guinness, Lord Iveagh, or Andrew Jameson, or the Dockrells). Also critical to its survival were both nationalist tolerance and the protection of the British state in Ireland. With the gradual exhaustion of the former, and the collapse of the latter, Dublin Unionism speedily dissolved, giving rise to a wider nationalist expectation that the 'false consciousness' of northern Unionists would be similarly transitory.

In fact, the strength of the southern unionists, even in the heyday of Union, rested with the landed classes and their financial and political influence over the island as a whole. They were not only wealthy, but were also comparatively well organised: they had their own, powerful, lobbying organisation, the Irish Landowners' Convention, dominated by old Ascendancy magnates such as the Beresfords, marquesses of Waterford.[55] The wealth of great landed clans fed into the representative organisations of southern unionism (the Irish Loyal and Patriotic Union, the Irish Unionist Alliance), and from thence (in the 1880s and 1890s) into Ulster Unionist election campaigns.[56] Southern landlords were disproportionately well represented in the House of Lords and indeed in the House of Commons.[57] However these landed foundations for the southern unionist edifice were almost as precarious as those supporting urban unionism outside Ulster. Land was, relatively, a declining asset in the late nineteenth century, and nowhere in Europe at this time was the decline more precipitate than in Ireland, where not just the economic standing, but rather the moral and legal title of the existing landlord class was subjected to a ferocious assault by the farming interest. Successive land legislation defined the tenants' legal title – their right to 'free sale', 'fair rent' and 'freedom from eviction' – and ultimately created the financial mechanisms by which they could buy their holdings outright. Land purchase, as it was called, was the principle underlying legislation in 1885, 1887 and – most famously – in

---

55 See A. Pole, 'Landlord Responses to the Irish Land War, 1879–82', PhD thesis (University of Dublin, 2006).
56 See Jackson, *Ulster Party*, 198–211.
57 Buckland, *Anglo-Irish and the New Ireland*; Jackson, *Ulster Party*.

1903, when the Chief Secretary, George Wyndham, created the most expensive and successful of the purchase measures. The incremental effect of this legislation was to consolidate farmers' legal rights at the expense of their landlords, to curtail landlord freedom to arbitrarily fix rent levels and, in the end, to encourage landlords to sell up (as Terence Dooley has discussed elsewhere in the volume). Complementing this economic retreat was a political and physical withdrawal. Selling landlords retired, both actually and imaginatively, behind the walls of their demesnes, or to Dublin or England. The Irish landed presence in the House of Commons retreated, to be replaced by a bourgeois, professional and commercial, caste, more completely rooted in the north of Ireland. This process touched Scotland, where the Irish purchase (and Congested Districts) legislation provided a template for measures affecting parts of the western Highlands and Islands; but its economic, geographical and social impact was comparatively slight.

Ulsterisation was also related to the fissiparous condition of southern unionism. Southern unionism numbered at most perhaps 250,000 adherents in the Home Rule era; but this relatively small community contained all conditions and classes. The remnants of the evangelical and Orange working-class and artisan conservatism, which had been championed in the 1840s by the likes of Tresham Gregg, existed alongside the metropolitan sophisticates of Trinity College and the law courts. There was evidence of a small-scale and propertied Catholic unionism.[58] There were also early symptoms of a politically suicidal bloody-mindedness, as in 1891, when Cork Unionists ran a parliamentary candidate against the urgent advice of Arthur Balfour in Dublin Castle ('as regards the Cork election, I am in despair at the stupidity of our people'; 'the loyalists are, in my opinion, making perfect idiots of themselves over the Cork election, and I am as nearly as possible in despair') – or in 1900 when the self-regarding Sir Horace Plunkett and the hungrily ambitious James Campbell were each defeated for Dublin constituencies through the abstention of dissident unionists from the poll.[59] These divisions multiplied with the pressures of radical separatism, so that the main representative body of southern unionism, the Irish Unionist Alliance, split in 1919, with the schismatics led by the earl of Midleton into a new organisation, the Anti-Partition League. Midleton, like Plunkett (and indeed many others within the culture of an embattled unionism) was blessed with an unshakeable confidence in

58 J. Biggs-Davison and G. Chowdharay-Best, *The Cross of Saint Patrick: The Catholic Unionist Tradition in Ireland* (Bourne End: Kensal Press, 1984).

59 Balfour to MacDonnell, 29 October 1891, Balfour to Goschen, n.d. [12 December 1891]. Arthur Balfour Papers, Add.Ms.49830, ff.321, 428: BL.

his own political intelligence; and he subsequently broke with the dissidents whom he had originally led. In this way, southern unionism, already socially and financially reduced through the retreat of landlordism, lost whatever residual punch it might have delivered during the crucial early years of the independent Irish state.

All of this cast into sharper relief the distinctiveness and influence of Ulster unionism. As the most gifted southern Protestant writers sought to express their political and cultural aspirations within the Irish literary revival, and indeed sometimes within advanced separatism, so many Northern Protestant writers and historians (building upon the regional economic success story) elaborated a literature and a history with particular Ulster thrusts and resonance. One strain within this apologetic literature (evident, for example, in the work of Lord Ernest Hamilton) presented a racialised analysis of the plantation tradition, linked by ethnicity to Britain: this chimed with contemporary Anglo-Saxonist readings of English history, as well as with a 'Teutonised' Scottish historiography that emphasised the shared racial heritage of the lowlands with England.[60] As southern landlordism and unionism retreated, so Belfast business and Ulster unionism blossomed: the social and political regression of southern landlordism gained pace in the Edwardian period, at precisely the moment when Belfast business and its Unionist captains reached their apogee – when the Harland and Wolff yards and the associated White Star Shipping Line achieved an ascendancy within their respective spheres: the launch and fate of the *Titanic* in 1911–1912, emblematic of a universal hubris, can also be held to represent the high-water mark of the vaulting ambition and self-confidence of the Belfast Unionist bourgeoisie (the designer of the vessel, Thomas Andrews, was the son of a wealthy Unionist mill-owner, and the brother of John Andrews, Unionist Prime Minister of Northern Ireland (1940–1943)).[61]

Complementing these cultural and economic developments in Ulster, was the elaboration of a separate party structure. As has been mentioned, Ulster Unionism was thoroughly reorganised in 1904–1905, with the creation of the Ulster Unionist Council and (as in contemporary Scotland) the revitalisation of local electoral machinery. By 1910–1911 this local organisational machine, allied with a more middle-class leadership, was pushing Ulster Unionism not only towards a more particularist strategy, but also towards greater militancy.

---

60 C. Kidd, *Union and Unionisms: Political Thought in Scotland, 1500–2000* (Cambridge University Press, 2008), 157–69.

61 See S. Bullock, *Thomas Andrews: Shipbuilder* (Dublin: Maunsell, 1912).

These thrusts were further encouraged by the condition of British politics, where a combination of Liberal electoral ascendancy and the cerebral but bloodless leadership supplied by Arthur Balfour to the Conservatives, meant that Ulster Unionists appeared to be increasingly dependent upon their own local political resources. This was confirmed by the passage of the Liberal's Parliament Act in 1911, when one of the key obstacles to Home Rule – the House of Lords' veto – was converted into a mere suspensory power. Already by 1910 Unionists were importing small quantities of weapons into Ulster and adopting military formations: after 1911 this militarisation accelerated towards civil conflagration.

The military capacity of Ulster Unionism delayed and subverted Home Rule, and (whatever the moral complexities) clearly must be regarded as a source of strength that had no parallel in Scotland (or, rather, since the Ulster militants had a presence in Glasgow, only the weakest of parallels).[62] The outlines of Ulster Unionist militancy in 1912–1914 are familiar enough, though the central interpretative problems posed by this militancy still remain contentious: were the Unionists serious in their apparent determination to go to war, and (in counter-factual terms) could they have been successful in resisting the might of a British state intent on enforcing Home Rule? The creation of the Ulster Volunteer Force (UVF) during the winter of 1912–1913 certainly created a strong military capacity, for (at its peak, in 1914) perhaps 90,000 to 100,000 oath-bound Ulster unionists were recruited within its ranks. The UVF was strongly influenced by the British army, both in terms of its regimental structure and its use of ex-servicemen: it was also equipped with a nursing corps, motor-cyclists, telegraphists and other advanced forms of communication, and, as well, boasted a special forces unit. It had organised support outside Ulster, in various areas of Irish Protestant settlement in Britain, including Glasgow, where there is evidence of a UVF unit in operation. Also, Leith, the port of Edinburgh, was used as one of the entrepôts through which weapons were smuggled into Britain for the use of the Volunteers. There were several (illegal) importations of weapons, undertaken with the knowledge and cooperation of leading Conservative politicians, and culminating in the Larne gun-running of 24–25 April 1914, when perhaps 25,000 rifles were landed: this was achieved with the foreknowledge of the Conservative front bencher and leadership candidate, Walter Long, and probably with that of the leader himself, Andrew Bonar Law.[63] The UVF also appears to have had good sources

---

62 For an authoritative recent treatment see T. Bowman, *Carson's Army: The Ulster Volunteer Force, 1910–22* (Manchester: Manchester University Press, 2008).
63 A. Jackson, *Home Rule: An Irish History, 1800–2000* (London: Phoenix Paperbacks, 2004), 154–5.

of intelligence emanating not just from within the leadership of the British Army (courtesy of Sir Henry Wilson), but also on occasion from sources close to the Asquith government itself.

The strength of Ulster unionist militancy lay, not only in its support within the Conservative elite, and in areas of traditional sympathy (such as the west of Scotland), but also more generally within popular British conservatism. British organisations such as the Union Defence League, founded by Walter Long in 1907, or the British League for the Support of Ulster, founded by Lord Willoughby de Broke, a redoubtable backwoods 'ditcher' peer, in March 1913, focused money and support for the Ulster militants: Long's UDL seems to have been the key conduit through which money for the gunrunners was channelled. The British League was the means by which the British Covenant of Support for Ulster was organised, in March 1914: this document, based upon the Ulster Solemn League and Covenant of September (1912), was launched by an array of British luminaries, including Scots such as Lord Balfour of Burleigh, the economist William Cunningham, Lord Lovat, and John Stirling-Maxwell. Dan Jackson's work on the Unionist campaign tours of 1912–1914, from Liverpool (September 1912), Gateshead, Glasgow, Inverness, to Hyde Park, has dissected the elaborate rhetoric and organisation of these events, with their skilful use of large public buildings, arc-light technology, scarcely concealed sectarian appeals, and manipulation of the press.[64] The most famous of these meetings was that held at Blenheim on 27 July 1912, when Bonar Law endorsed the most extreme forms of Ulster unionist resistance.

This threatened resistance was also expressed within, and bolstered by, popular and high culture. British supporters were useful in this respect, with (in particular) the laureate of empire, Kipling, versifying on behalf of his Ulster Unionist allies: his 'Ulster 1912' carried a superscription from the book of Isaiah, and concluded with the ominous line – 'If England drives us forth, We shall not fall alone.' Sir Edward Elgar, whose music was inflected with some of the prevailing anxiety of the late Edwardian climacteric, was one of the lead signatories of the British Covenant (and, as one of several prominent Catholic supporters – along with the likes of the 14th Lord Lovat, the 15th duke of Norfolk, Lord Edmund Talbot – particularly useful to those worried by the sectarian overtones of Ulster unionism). Another pillar of the Edwardian musical establishment in Britain, the Dublin-born Sir Charles Villiers Stanford, wrote unionist letters to *The Times*, signed the Covenant,

---

64 D. Jackson, *Popular Opposition to Irish Home Rule in Edwardian Britain* (Liverpool: Liverpool University Press, 2009).

questioned hapless candidates for the Royal College of Music about their stand on 'Home Rule' ('and what d'ye think of Home Rule, me bhoy?'), and banned productions of his opera, *Shamus O'Brien* (1895), during the crisis for fear that its romantic Irishness would inadvertently give succour to the enemy's cause.[65]

Stanford's breezy interrogations illustrate the ways in which the Home Rule fury percolated into every corner of the British cultural establishment. Indeed the experience of C. S. Lewis further illustrates that the third Home Rule crisis influenced the outlook even of an emergent elite: as a Belfast schoolboy Lewis was already writing essays on the threat of Home Rule. In fact, there is little real surprise in this, given the extent to which Home Rule and militant unionism were all-encompassing themes in Irish and British society. In Ireland the seriousness of unionist conviction was reflected in the hero cult surrounding the leader, Edward Carson, and in the ways in which Unionist popular opinion was mobilised in support of the militants' strategies. As in Britain, so in Ireland, mass demonstrations focused and intensified militant feeling (the most famous of these being the mass meetings which launched the Ulster Solemn League and Covenant on 28 September 1912). Those (just under half a million men and women) who signed the Covenant were presented with a parchment copy of the document, which in many instances was framed and displayed: just under half of the 237,000 men who signed the Covenant joined the Ulster Volunteer Force, and were given a lapel badge and armband, and subsequently more elaborate adornment and uniform. Carson, too, was energetically marketed: his lantern-jawed image adorned china ware (produced, for example, by the Paragon Company), and Staffordshire crockery. He featured in high culture – in the work of the artists of *Vanity Fair* (where, over the years, he was portrayed three times), or in the caricatures of Max Beerbohm.[66] He was represented on badges and buttons, fund-raising stamps, and (in huge numbers and variety) on postcards. He was endlessly photographed, and filmed by pressmen.[67]

Militant unionism, its leadership and symbolism were therefore all pervasive. It is clear that this propaganda was a critical element of the militants' campaign, and that leaders like Carson knew the importance of a persuasive

65 See for example J. Dibble, *Charles Villiers Stanford: Man and Musician* (Oxford University Press, 2002).
66 See for example M. Beerbohm, *Fifty Caricatures* (London: William Heinemann, 1913), 10.
67 A. Jackson, 'Unionist Myths, 1912–85', *Past & Present*, 136 (August 1992); R. F. Foster and A. Jackson, 'Parnell and Carson', *European History Quarterly*, 39, 3 (July 2009).

ferocity. It is also evident that while Carson and some others within the leadership (like the sixth marquess of Londonderry) might have talked the talk of insurgency, they held back from action, and counselled caution. The Ulster Volunteer Force has generally been seen as a brake upon militancy, in so far as it channelled the furies of demotic loyalism into a disciplined and hierarchical environment. On the other hand, the gamble implicit in the Ulster Unionist strategy was that Asquith and the Liberal government would acquiesce before the pent-up aggression of the Volunteers spewed into sectarian or other forms of outrage; and by the summer of 1914 the odds on this gamble appeared to be narrowing perilously as Asquith obfuscated and played for time. Damned for his indecision, it is just possible that there was strategic method in the apparent madness of Asquith's procrastination.[68]

Viewed dispassionately, the great achievement of Unionists in 1912–1914 was not so much that they created a paramilitary threat; it was rather that they succeeded in commodifying their political case, so that (by the summer of 1914) the images and messages of their militancy were virtually inescapable throughout British and Irish society. However, one measure of Asquith's success was that, despite this cultural spread, indeed hegemony, the Unionists did not wholly succeed in thwarting the passage of Home Rule onto the statute books of the British parliament: this was achieved in September 1914. Nor did these militants create the partition issue, since this had been privately mooted within British high politics almost from the moment that Home Rule was accepted by part of the British political elite. All that had been achieved, by the summer of 1914, was that Asquith's Liberal government, in company with reluctant Irish nationalists, had accepted that some form of exclusion from Home Rule might be granted to some of the counties of Ulster. It would take the real militancy and bloodshed of the Western Front, as opposed to the virtual wars of the Ulster countryside, to translate this acceptance into something approaching practical politics.

With both Scotland and Ireland, the First World War acted to reinforce national identities, though in the Scots' case national sentiment remained largely curtailed within the frameworks of Union and of cultural politics. In Ireland, the experience of war appears to have radicalised and trained a generation of separatists who subsequently served with the IRA in the War of Independence and Civil War. In the north of Ireland, mass participation in the Great War coincided with, and advanced, a stronger unionist sense of Ulster's distinctiveness. This was partly the point of the mythology surrounding the

68 Jackson, *Home Rule*, 152–3.

actions of the main unionist fighting force on the Western Front, the 36th Ulster Division: on 1 July 1916, at the start of the epically bloody Somme offensive (following the official narrative by Cyril Falls) the Division successfully stormed the German Front Line, where (with over 5,000 casualties sustained) they were stranded in a maelstrom of killing owing to the failure of other British units and of the high command.[69] In essence, the Somme offensive served as a metaphor for the wider Ulster unionist condition and self-perception: in this particular reading the Ulstermen had done their duty, but in the end had fought and died on their own. Moreover, the (in fact far from complete) overlap between the Ulster Division and the Ulster Volunteer Force meant that the Division's purpose and actions were equated with those of the pre-war unionist militants. The badges, uniforms, gallantry certificates and (after the war) commemorative histories all emphasised the 'Ulsterness' of the Division, which (however inexactly) was equated with its unionism. The Division's memorial at Thiepval further underlines this point: this was a copy of Helen's Tower, the gothic folly that overlooked the UVF's training ground at Clandeboye, the Dufferin estate in County Down, and it was inaugurated by Sir Henry Wilson, former Chief of the Imperial General Staff and Ulster Unionist MP for North Down. The narrative of the war was therefore woven into the wider history of Ulster Unionist struggle and political identity; and these were phenomena which were taking on an increasingly particularist hue.

The idea of separating out the counties of Ulster with the greatest concentrations of Protestant and unionist population had been privately raised in 1886 and 1893, and was publicly mooted from June 1912; and by 1914 the principle of exclusion had begun to achieve a form of consensus, although deep disagreements remained over the physical and temporal extent of any practical scheme. In March 1914 it was fleetingly proposed that the six northeastern counties of Ulster should be excluded temporarily but *en bloc*; and this idea was resurrected in the aftermath of the Easter Rising, in May 1916, when it briefly (but deceivingly) appeared to have won the agreement of both unionists and nationalists. However, the notion of six-county partition reappeared in 1919–20, when it was given a federalist inflection; and it was thus a two-parliament, two-polity Ireland which emerged in the legislative cladding supplied by the Government of Ireland Act. The celebrants of 'Ulster' had won a form of homeland, even if the newly minted 'Northern Ireland'

---

69 See Cyril Falls, *The History of the Thirty Sixth (Ulster) Division* (Belfast: McCaw, Stevenson and Orr, 1922), 57, 61–2.

did not do justice to the intensity of their historical and political vision. Moreover, 'Ulster' came at a cost: over half a million dissatisfied and vulnerable nationalists were trapped within the new unionist polity, while Ulster unionism had effectively cast off one-third of its provincial identity (three Ulster counties were excluded from 'Northern Ireland'), as well as the whole of 'southern' unionism.

The impact of this new polity on Irish unionism is (naturally enough) frequently overlooked, given the history of alienation and injustice experienced by northern nationalists. The strength of Edwardian unionism had rested in its standing as an opposition creed, backed by landed and industrial capital, and boasting a formidable geographical, cultural and intellectual diversity. In their apparent moment of victory, Unionists in fact demonstrated the extent to which they had dissipated these former assets. Unionism was now reduced to a north-eastern, and preeminently bourgeois, core, with the complex cultures of southern landed unionism now dismissed and isolated. Equally, the bastion of Trinity College, with its heritage of an academic unionism, was largely set aside, even though its lawyers (most obviously Carson himself) had hitherto been a mainstay of the Ulster Unionist leadership. The plantation creed – the celebration of the achievements and travails of the Ulster colonists in the seventeenth century – now became the wholly inadequate governing theme – or, rather, colonial nationalist ideology – of Northern Ireland, rather than a balancing counterpoint to the motifs of Catholic Gaeldom and Irish-Irelandism. In sum, just as it was once said of the Scottish National Party in government at Holyrood that they 'don't believe they're a government. They are a campaign', so Unionists had difficulty making the same leap in faith and belief in 1921.[70]

A more unified and homogeneous unionism looked out from its six-county bawn; but it was intellectually and culturally diminished. And the movement's very homogeneity – its more complete identification with the economic interests of the northern industrial and commercial elite – rendered it more vulnerable than ever.

70 *Scotland on Sunday*, 1 February 2009.

4

Irish Land Questions, 1879–1923

TERENCE DOOLEY

Introduction

In May 1950, Fianna Fáil senator, Frank Loughman (1892–1972), spoke in the Seanad on the issue of land redistribution:

> I am a townsman from Tipperary but the people of my generation were reared on questions of land settlement. When we were young we used to hear slogans such as 'The land for the people and the road for the bullock'; 'We built the homes of Tipperary'; 'Undo the clearances' and so on. Even the songs we were taught were all concerned with resettlement on the lands of Ireland. The books we read – Kickham's stories, and others – all concerned this question of land settlement and, consequently, even the people in the towns, who stood by the people of the countryside in the old days, when we were fighting against the tyranny of the landlord, had a great interest in this question of land settlement.[1]

Loughman had been born in 1892, a year after the Parnellite split and at the end of the first two phases of the Land War (1879–1881, 1885–1891). He, therefore, was not a witness to the events. His speech was really of no great historical significance, except that its well-worn rhetoric reflected the post-independence social memory of the Land War era (as very often articulated in Dáil and Seanad speeches after 1922) and it contained the major features of the nationalist interpretation that had become orthodoxy: the slogans of the various land movements had promised land for everyone; agitators had opposed the odious mass clearances from estates; their heroic deeds had been handed down in song and story; the countrymen had stood with the townsmen in alliance against 'the tyranny of the landlord'. Loughman's contribution encapsulated the fact that nationalists had constructed the memory of the land question in simple oppositional terms as a conflict between usurping and alien landlords and oppressed tenants.

---

1 *Seanad Debates*, vol. 37, 4 May 1950, 1762.

By the 1950s, the standard text book on the Irish land question remained John Pomfret's, *The struggle for land in Ireland, 1800–1923* (1930).[2] Written in the direct aftermath of independence, it might be considered an interpretation more in sympathy with the new nation than with the realities of the past. Pomfret's exposition, not a million miles removed from Loughman's, would probably have appealed to the myth builders of the new state, if any of them had read it. It certainly appealed to at least one of the Land League generation, T. M. Healy, who regarded it as 'a monument of research' and 'the best history of the Irish Land question ever compiled', from which 'no advocate of the landlord class can find comfort from the presentation which he [Pomfret] makes of the struggle for Irish land'.[3] (Revealingly, post-1922 it was a different history in the newly-established Northern Ireland where because of a different demography and culture, the old landed class continued to be shown a greater degree of respect and allowed to share in the running of the new state.[4])

It was not until the 1970s that a new generation of historians began to reappraise land issues and, by avoiding the pitfalls of nationalist populism, punctured many myths to present a more nuanced interpretation firmly grounded in a wider spread of primary sources than those used by Pomfret, most particularly estate papers. These works became the foundation upon which numerous scholars have since built and published important national and local studies (the latter very often revealing that national truisms do not hold up when land and local politics are forensically examined).[5]

The 'new orthodoxy' did not deny the existence of rapacious landlords – many did, of course, exist – or that the system which gave rise to landlord opulence and elitism was morally and socially flawed; instead it presented a more nuanced picture, revealing nineteenth-century rural Ireland in all its complexities. Much had been hidden in the previous historiography by the simple fact that landlords had been regarded as a homogenous class and tenants likewise. There had been little consideration given to other facts, for

2 J. E. Pomfret, *The Struggle for Land in Ireland, 1800–1923* (Princeton, NJ: Princeton University Press, 1930), 19–27.

3 T. M. Healy, 'Review' of Pomfret, *The Struggle for Land*, in *Studies*, vol. 19, no. 76 (December 1930), 694, 695.

4 O. Purdue, *The Big House in the North of Ireland: Land, Power and Social Elites, 1878–1960* (Dublin: UCD Press, 2009).

5 The literature here is extensive but includes: T. Dooley, *'The Land for the People': The Land Question in Independent Ireland* (Dublin: UCD Press, 2007); J. S. Donnelly, Jr., Land and People of Nineteenth-Century Cork (London: Routledge and Kegan Paul, 1975); W. E. Vaughan, *Landlords and Tenants in Mid-Victorian Ireland* (Oxford University Press, 1994).

example that large aristocratic estates were very differently managed to small, less viable estates.[6] Or that for every estate characterised by neglect there was another characterised by investment and improvement; for every dissolute and indifferent landlord, there was a frugal and benevolent one; for every landlord who cleared his estate without compassion, there was one prepared to put his finances on the line to protect his tenants during periods of severe economic crisis. Paternalistic ties between landlord and tenant had existed on many, especially aristocratic, estates, which often overrode economic considerations. The plight of the poor in rural Ireland could no longer be seen as the exclusive fault of predatory landlords. The evidence clearly showed that in pre-Famine Ireland, where a phalanx of strong and middling farmers, smallholders, cottiers and landless labourers had co-existed with landlords it was usually the relationship between the large farmers and the classes below which was the main source of agrarian agitation caused by modernisation, economic growth, economic decline, social catastrophe, political upheavals and so on.

Throughout much of the nineteenth century agrarian issues were inextricably entwined with the political struggle for independence and the other great national issue of identity. Since the 1970s historians have been examining the interaction of land, politics and violence, drawing attention to just how complex rural society was in an age of unprecedented political and social change, where nationalism became the nemesis of landlordism (which was conflated with colonial oppression) and the ideology that promoted land as the basis of the nation was consolidated. Thus, what has traditionally been referred to as 'the land question' in Ireland was in fact, 'a dense matrix of interlocking issues and questions relating to the story of land in Ireland'.[7] The aim of this chapter is to examine some of these issues and questions from the beginning of the Land War in 1879 to the passing of the first Free State Land Act in 1923.

Post-Famine Ireland

The late-nineteenth-century land wars need to be understood in the much longer historical context of agrarianism in Ireland and especially the social

---

6 For the management of a large aristocratic estate in pre-Famine Ireland, see W. A. Maguire, *The Downshire Estates in Ireland 1801–1845: The Management of Irish Landed Estates in the Nineteenth Century* (Oxford University Press, 1972); on land agents and estate management, see C. Reilly, *The Irish Land Agent 1830–1860: the Case of King's County* (Dublin: Four Courts Press, 2014).

7 G. Ó Tuathaigh, 'Irish Land Questions', in F. Campbell and T. Varley (eds.), *Land Questions in Modern Ireland* (Manchester: Manchester University Press, 2013), 16.

changes wrought by the Great Famine of 1845–51. The Famine acted as a catalyst, accelerating social, economic and demographic change in Ireland. There has been an understandable emphasis on the plight of the impoverished, those who died in their hundreds of thousands from starvation and disease, the tens of thousands who were evicted, and the million or so who emigrated. However, as in every economic crisis there were invariably winners as well as losers; it remains the case that in the historiography of the Famine there has been little systematic analysis of those who benefited, and, as of yet, historians have been slow to answer the difficult questions posed by Cormac Ó Gráda on such important issues as the role played by farmers, shopkeepers and, more generally, the middle classes, in preventing or exacerbating mortality and emigration.[8] At the most obvious level, the auction of bankrupt estates in the Encumbered Estates Court from 1849 allowed the less affected aristocratic and gentry families to augment their estates and opened the way for professionals, shopkeepers, publicans, merchants and clergymen to buy farms of land consolidated from the small units previously occupied by smallholders and cottiers. Between 1845 and 1851, there was a decrease of 213,000 holdings between 1 and 5 acres in size and an increase of 14,000 of those above 15 acres. The total of land in holdings of more than 200 and less than 500 acres increased by one million acres, or 45 per cent, while the number of holdings over 500 acres rose by 53 per cent, to an aggregate of 700,000 acres.[9] By the 1870s the prosperity of the larger farmers was clearly evident in their impressive farmhouses and the material culture of their homes.

Indeed, large farmers and landlords prospered together. It has been estimated that the latter extracted an economic surplus of £340 million from Irish agriculture between 1850 and 1879.[10] But, operating in a social system that was seriously flawed and outdated, they borrowed extravagantly from banks, assurance companies, the Representative Church Body of the Church of Ireland, and even, from each other, on the collateral strength of their estates, with detrimental long-term consequences. Some were simply consolidating all their accumulated debts into one convenient mortgage, while

8 C. Ó Gráda, *Ireland: A New Economic History, 1780–1939* (Oxford University Press, 1995); see, however, T. Dooley, *The Decline and Fall of the Dukes of Leinster, 1872–1948* (Dublin: Four Courts Press, 2014) and C. Reilly, *Strokestown and The Great Irish Famine* (Dublin: Four Courts Press, 2014), which look at these important issues at estate level.

9 Statistics are taken from P. Bew, *Ireland: The Politics of Enmity 1789–2006* (Oxford, 2007), 215.

10 Vaughan, *Landlords and Tenants*, 224.

others used the upturn to embellish their houses and demesnes, thereby add-ing another generation's distinctiveness to their evolution.

While they may have improved their homes and demesnes, landlords have been criticised for not investing as much as they might have done in the improvement of their estates or, indeed, in technological advancement that might have benefited Irish agriculture in the long term.[11] From a purely busi-ness perspective, they have even been criticised for not exploiting the improv-ing markets of post-Famine Ireland.[12] However, by not doing so, and by keeping rents affordable, there were fewer rural tensions, as well as a marked decline in evictions, and a diminution in levels of crime in a changing rural society where strong farmers, shopkeepers and the Catholic clergy – now the dominant rural triumvirate – worked with the landlord to maintain social stability and control.[13]

With increased wealth and social position came a desire from the Catholic middle classes for a commensurate share in the governance of the country. In the 1850s the political agenda of the strong farmers was not clearly defined but much centred around the agitation for tenant right – a somewhat nebulous concept, harking back to the moral economy of a previous era and project-ing forward to the day when fair rents and dual ownership would be realised after the 1881 Land Act. When the Tenant League movement died an inglori-ous death in the 1850s large tenants continued to press for reform through their socially exclusive farmers' clubs. There were tensions after the passing of Gladstone's Land Act in 1870 – a political gesture enacted at the height of agricultural prosperity – when landlords attempted to have their tenants sign leases to circumvent the compensation terms of the act. This led to the estab-lishment of tenant defence associations in comfortable farming areas in many parts of the country from Kildare to east Galway and from south Monaghan to Kilkenny. While widespread agitation was kept at bay by continued eco-nomic prosperity, strong farmers became politicised and empowered by a series of reforms beginning with the 1850 Franchise Reform Act and later the Secret Ballot Act of 1872, the Franchise and Redistribution Acts of the mid-1880s and, in particular, the Local Government (Ireland) Act of 1898. Within

---

11 C. Ó Gráda, 'The Investment Behaviour of Irish Landlords 1850–75: Some Preliminary Findings', *Agricultural History Review*, 23 (1975), 139–55; Vaughan, *Landlords and Tenants*, 124–30.

12 B. L. Solow, *The Land Question and the Irish Economy, 1870–1903* (Cambridge, MA: Harvard University Press, 1971).

13 R. V. Comerford, 'Ireland, 1870–1921', in W. E. Vaughan (ed.), *A New History of Ireland, vol. VI: Ireland under the Union 1870–1921* (paperback ed., Oxford, 2010), xliv.

two generations of the Famine the emergent Catholic middle-class elite had become the controlling power in Irish local and national politics, setting the scene for the inevitable clash of cultures that took place during the extended Land War.

Land War, 1879–1891

No level of agricultural prosperity in the post-Famine decades could alleviate the plight of the impoverished small farmers in the less modernised regions of the west of Ireland where technical advance, specialisation, capital investment, or the improvement in conditions of tenure, had all proved insufficient to enable the rural economy to withstand the effects of any future depression.[14] As will be discussed below, the causes of the Land War have been the subject of much interpretative difference of opinion and have given rise to considerable historiographical debate but, tellingly, it was in the poorest region of the country that the Land War had its origin.

The catalyst to crisis was a disastrous run of bad harvests in 1877–1879 brought about by adverse climatic conditions and the fact that Europe was now being flooded with more competitively priced agricultural produce from the Americas. Irish agricultural prices plummeted. But more frightening for the lower classes was the return of blight to many areas and with it the horrible fear of another famine. Rural tensions were heightened by the fact that emigration, the traditional safety valve for social unrest, slowed dramatically, from a two-year average of 90,000 per annum in 1875 to 37,000 in 1876, and 38,000 in 1877.[15] It might be said that Ireland had locked in its disaffected.

James S. Donnelly Jr has argued that the Land War was caused by a 'revolution of rising expectations'. Theory that conflated revolutionary action with the downturn in the economic fortunes of a class was not new. In an influential article in the *American Sociological Review* in 1962, J. C. Davies had argued that a period of growing prosperity that raises people's expectations for a better life, followed by a sharp economic downturn that dashes these hopes would yield sharp feelings of deprivation and aggression.[16] Donnelly's application of this theory to the Irish situation in the 1880s was novel in terms of offering an explanation for the Land War but, as W. E. Vaughan later remarked, this explanation in itself was not enough; it was, he argued, 'everything that

14 Gribbon, 'Economic and Social History, 1850–1921', 270.
15 Bew, *Politics of Enmity*, 296.
16 J. C. Davies, 'Towards a Theory of Revolution', *American Sociological Review*, 27 (1962), 5–19.

happened between the Famine and the late 1870s [that] caused the Land War'.[17] Over the previous two generations, the middle classes of country and town had been drawn into an intricate web of credit and kinship. Farmer and shopkeeper alike had benefited from advancements in education. As literacy spread amongst all classes, provincial newspaper offices had sprung up all over the country, disseminating new and often radical ideas, and bringing news of deteriorating conditions, and reactions to them, throughout the country. Transport was greatly improved, thus facilitating movement between towns and countryside, and in this way people also became agents of change. The growth of the Home Rule movement in the 1870s pitted Catholic nationalists (and a tiny minority of Protestants) against landlords who failed to be won over by nationalism or the prospects of a Dublin parliament. As avowed Unionists, landlords put themselves in opposition to the will of the majority and thereby gave Nationalists further ammunition to denounce them from political platforms as the pariahs of rural Ireland and to demonise them as responsible for all its social, economic and political problems.

But even in their opposition to Home Rule, it was abundantly clear that landlords did not just fear for their civil and political rights and religious liberties; they were conspicuously concerned for their economic position. Having become so encumbered in the 1860s and 1870s (see below), they could not contemplate being abandoned in a Home Rule Ireland that might expropriate their properties without generous compensation. While the middle classes may have been threatened by the loss of their economic gains and increasing social respectability, the rural lower classes were threatened with much more, the very ability to survive. It was the latter who were the first to contend that they could not afford their rents, and so, ultimately, it was economics that drove the Land War; as R. V. Comerford has argued: landlords, farmers and shopkeepers simply strove 'to maintain the lifestyle on which their socio-economic standing and their self-esteem depended'.[18]

On 16 August 1879, the National Land League of Mayo was established which questioned the moral obligation of tenants having to pay existing rents in a period of economic decline. Two months later, the Irish National Land League was founded, the first nationally coordinated mass movement established to challenge landlordism. Within months, the agrarian crisis had

---

17 Donnelly, *Land and People of Nineteenth-century Cork*, 249–50; Vaughan, *Landlords and Tenants*, 211.

18 'R. V. Comerford, 'The Land War and the Politics of Distress, 1877-82', in W. E. Vaughan (ed.), *A New History of Ireland VI: Ireland under the Union II, 1870–1921* (Oxford University Press, 1996), 26–52.

created a popular political movement which propelled activists from the periphery to centre stage of Irish affairs and brought Charles Stewart Parnell to leadership of both political and agrarian movements.

While the Land League soon spread to the more commercialised regions of the midlands and the east, it failed to ignite in Ulster where, historically, a different cultural and religious bond existed between landlords and tenants. This is not to say that it was not embraced by the Catholic farmers there but rather that the Protestant farmers' response to it was much more complex, influenced as their reaction was by Orange opposition to Home Rule, and thus united tenant opposition to landlord was not as it was on estates that lay outside Ulster. Total dependence on the land had been reduced by the north-east's experience of a modest industrial revolution and by high emigration rates from Ulster during the nineteenth century. More particularly, while in the recent past Presbyterian farmers had been especially strong advocates of the legitimisation of tenant right and had agitated for the amelioration of agrarian grievances alongside their Catholic neighbours against Anglican landlords, the political march of the new nation in the 1880s – Catholic, Nationalist and Gaelic – towards Home Rule alienated the vast majority of them.

Further south, the fact that large farmers were prepared to fight alongside smallholders and labourers and to make common cause with them represented a significant cultural shift with the former realising that they were better off inside the mass movement than outside it, for, in that way, they could better control events. The Fenians joined in the hope that the land movement could be used to further their revolutionary agenda. John Devoy, exiled Fenian and leader of Clan na Gael, the Irish republican organisation in America, clearly associated the overthrow of the landlord system with the political struggle for independence, recognising the role which agrarian agitation could play in the stimulation of revolutionary activity amongst the lower agrarian classes. The role of shopkeepers and merchants was more ambiguous. While they showed their solidarity with large farmers on Land League platforms, sight should not be lost of the fact that as recession got worse there was a very significant increase in the number of civil bill suits entered in Irish courts.[19] And, finally, the constitutional politicians under Charles Stewart Parnell offered the parliamentary wing to support and direct the agitation. By the winter of 1879, land agitators, constitutionalists and separatists had aligned themselves in a 'New Departure', a rather loose informal alliance

---

19 Vaughan, *Landlords and Tenants*, 215.

which demanded self-government and the vigorous agitation of the land question in favour of tenant proprietorship. The timing of the agreement was perfect as the crisis was just about to worsen and so all focus turned to the land question.

At first the Catholic hierarchy tried to remain aloof from the League, fearing a close connection between the new agrarian movement and Fenianism which they had so strenuously fought against in the 1860s. The bishops worried that the distasteful actions of the Land League would threaten moral and legal conventions and thus pose a threat to all private property, not just that of landlords. However, at grassroots level, the parish clergy had to be more discerning. As the League was organised on a Catholic parish structure, this provided the parish clergy with the ideal opportunity to take a leading role and so, as Comerford has astutely noted, the parish priest often became a genuinely 'keen league supporter'. Even if some priests were not totally persuaded by the League's ideals or reassured by its ideologies, they still became involved so as 'to keep some upstart off the parochial pedestal'.[20]

All ages were represented in the Land League; there was even a short-lived (and research-neglected) Children's Land League in 1881. Women had their own organisation, the Ladies' Land League. While its success was short-lived, the activities and actions of women on the 'front' line was more pronounced: they were prominent in anti-eviction campaigns, they supported boycotts (see below), they worked in fields to support the families of the imprisoned, and, of course, kept their own homes while their husbands were in jail.[21] One of the most colourful contemporary descriptions of women's involvement at local level (as well as a revealing insight into how the memory of the Land War was created) comes from Fr Thomas Conefrey in his *The land war in Drumlish* (1892) where he describes the opposition to the 'hideous process server': 'Young girls rush up against the protecting bayonets, and strive to get a lock of his hair. ... Several showers of stones are directed at his doomed head by women and girls.' Similarly, one sarcastically-labelled 'heroic policeman' was forced to take 'to his heels and made the best of his way to the barrack, amid showers of stones from women and little boys'. After a defiant stand against the police, the women, under the command of Mrs Rogers of the Mill in Drumlish (sister of James McDonnell, the local Land League secretary), were compared to 'their kindred sex who mounted

---

20 Comerford, 'The Politics of Distress', 42.
21 J. Tebrake, 'Irish Peasant Women in Revolt: The Land League Years', *Irish Historical Studies*, 28 (1992), 63–80.

the breach at Limerick in the days of the siege of that historic city'. One young girl, Mary Loughry of Drumlish, was said to have almost strangled to death a bailiff named Purcell.[22] A century later, a monument was erected in the village of Drumlish 'for all who come to see the pride of a community in its ancestors'. The power of Conefrey's prejudiced memoir was clearly evident in the centenary commemorative pamphlet produced to mark the event which proclaimed that the people of the 1880s had shown 'courage in face of real danger; forebearance in face of age-long provocation; and an invincible sense of humour in face of pitiless exploitation and degradation, which must surely have been the one factor, along with their religion, which enabled them to resist becoming brutalised by a system which was expressly designed to brutalize them'.[23] It provides ample evidence of how difficult it is to understand the Land War if one does not engage with the memory of it.

While there was at the top a cadre of charismatic leaders such as Parnell, Davitt and Devoy, all of whom have received a great deal of attention from historians, not enough has emerged on such local personalities as Father Conefrey.[24] Just as was the case during the Famine, the Land League era provided the opportunity for men with ambition to rise to local prominence and the more politically active they became, the more they found opportunities to improve their social and economic positions. A notable example was Thomas Toal in Monaghan whose family used the local sectarianism of the Land War to oust Protestant traders, create their own large business enterprise, and buy large tracts of land. By 1900 Toal was chairman of Monaghan County Council, a position he was to hold for over forty years. Toal considered his venture as an opportunity to 'do credit to myself, my wife and family and to my religion and country'.[25] The statement was unambiguous – he saw the fulfilment of his ambitions in terms of the successful transfer of power from the Protestant elite to a Catholic family and regarded his success as both a patriotic and religious victory at a time when the nation was being redefined in Catholic Nationalist terms to the exclusion of others.

In every local community there were constitutionalists, agrarian radicals, Fenians, pacifists, opportunists, manipulators, victims and winners. While the

---

22 An Irish Priest [Father Thomas Conefrey], *A Short History of the Land War in Drumlish in 1881* (Dublin: James Duffy and Co., 1892), 7, 12, 21–22.

23 *Drumlish Land War Centenary 1881–1981 Commemorative Booklet* (Drumlish: County Longford, 1991), 4.

24 See, for example, G. Moran, 'Matthew Harris, Fenianism and Land Agitation in the West of Ireland', Campbell and Varley (eds.), *Land Questions in Modern Ireland*, 218–37.

25 'A Short Sketch of the Life of Thomas Toal' (Unpublished MS, Monaghan County Museum).

Land War may have had its heroes, it undoubtedly also had some villains who wanted to use it for reasons of personal vendettas, some who simply relished being involved in violent activity, and some who used their new-found power to manipulate situations to meet their own cravings for power. Violence could be personal as well as class or ideologically based. In other words, as Maura Cronin writes, some agitators may have been no better than members of 'a modern-day protection racket designed to line the pockets of prominent members rather than ameliorate the conditions of the poor'.[26] While there were thousands who were evicted from their homesteads because they could not pay their rents or because they refused to do so in support of Land League principles, there were many more who paid them in direct contravention of Land League mandates, often a 'delator [=denouncer] of land-grabbers' who was 'himself transacting business clandestinely with his landlord'.[27]

During the first phase of the Land War, 1879–82, rural Ireland became a violent and dangerous place to live. W. E. Vaughan has estimated that during those years, 11,320 agrarian outrages were committed.[28] On average there were seventeen murders per year in the same period. Transgressors of the law of the League were vitriolically denounced from Land League platforms and sometimes from the church pulpit. They were liable to be punished by some of the newly-established Land League courts, to be intimidated at night by prowling gangs, or to be boycotted which meant being ostracised by people who were neighbours or even relatives. In areas of Ulster where there were mixed religious communities, people found themselves backing either the League or the Orange Order, according to their religious sympathies, thereby adding a sectarian dimension. Ultimately, the Land War reinforced confessional divisions, even if there were Protestant supporters of the Land League or unsupportive Catholics.

If families were prepared to put up with such mental and often physical abuse what did it say about the desperate desire to hold on to land? Memories of Land League transgressors lived long in rural Ireland. Sean McNamara, commandant of the Clare IRA recalled that during the War of Independence 'in the new situation which had arisen some of the Volunteers or their people were among those who saw an opportunity to address grievances, especially against the "grabbers"'.[29] Gemma Clark's study of everyday violence

---

26 M. Cronin, *Agrarian Protest in Ireland, 1750–1960* (Dublin: Studies in Irish Social and Economic History, 2011).

27 Comerford, 'The Politics of Distress', 44; see also Edward Kennedy, *The Land Movement in Tullaroan, County Kilkenny, 1879–1891* (Dublin: Four Courts Press, 2004).

28 Vaughan, *Landlords and Tenants*, 209.

29 Witness statement of Sean McNamara, WS 1072: www.bureauofmilitaryhistory.ie/reels/bmh/BMH.WS1072.pdf#page=8, (accessed 20 October 2014).

during the Civil War emphasises how pronounced boycotting remained as a rural weapon, often deployed by the dispossessed.[30] Similarly, Leigh Ann Coffey's study of the Protestant families ('emergency men') who took farms at Luggacurran in Queen's County in the mid-1880s is revealing of the backlash suffered by them during the later revolutionary period when gangs of 100 or more, many of whom were armed, attempted to evict about eighteen of these families from their homes in the spring of 1922.[31] The history of boycotted families, from the extended period of the Land Wars through the Irish Revolution and after, would make for a very interesting study.[32]

Decisive and coordinated landlord reaction to demands for rental reductions was not forthcoming: some procrastinated, waiting for the storm to abate as it had done in the early 1860s; some granted reductions immediately, either because they had a paternalistic concern for the plight of their tenants or else, fearing no rents at all, they wished to avoid disputes with their own creditors. Some took great offence at the demands being made publicly from Land League platforms, resenting the public nature of what had traditionally been a private affair, and some refused point blank to contemplate any interference or to reduce their rents.[33]

Those landlords who procrastinated or refused to meet tenants' demands very often found themselves the targets of rent strikes and the vicious cycle began in which rent strikes led to a dramatic increase in evictions which, in turn, spawned agrarian violence. From the 1880s the politicisation of evictions remained a powerful tool in the Nationalist armoury. During the revolutionary period 1916–1923, the evicted were exalted as 'the wounded soldiers of the Land War', the victims of 'capricious eviction' and 'of rackrents so unendurable that eviction only precipitated a catastrophe which was bound to come'.[34]

That the evicted were martyrised by nationalist Ireland was of little comfort to those who subsequently struggled to survive without a livelihood. It was not until the passing of the Wyndham Land Act in 1903 that legislative steps were taken to provide for their welfare. Tenants who had been evicted

---

30 G. Clark, *Everyday Violence in the Irish Civil War* (Cambridge University Press, 2014), 36–44.

31 L. A. Coffey, *The Planters of Luggacurran, Co. Laois: a Protestant Community, 1879–1927* (Dublin: Four Courts Press, 2006).

32 See, for example, D. S. Lucey, *Land, Popular Politics and Agrarian Violence in Ireland: The Case of County Kerry, 1872–86* (Dublin: UCD Press, 2011), 177–82.

33 L. P. Curtis, 'Landlord Responses to the Irish Land War, 1879–87', *Eire-Ireland*, Fall/Winter (2003), 134–88.

34 Labhras MacFhionnghail [Laurence Ginnell], *The Land Question* (Dublin: James Duffy and Co., n.d. [1917]), pp 4–5.

in the previous twenty-five-year period were entitled to purchase loans to buy back their original holdings, if available, or alternative ones from the estates commissioners if they were deemed 'fit and proper persons'. Demand for reinstatement or the provision of a compensatory holding was so fierce that in 1907, the government was forced to introduce the Evicted Tenants (Ireland) Act. This provided the estates commissioners with powers to compulsorily acquire certain lands (excluding tenanted lands, lands already subject to purchase annuities, or untenanted lands which formed parts of a demesne or home farm). By March 1919, almost 3,600 tenants had been reinstated as purchasers on their original holdings or alternative ones. But this would have represented only about a third of the families evicted between 1879 and 1882 alone. It is perhaps not surprising that during the chaos of the War of Independence evicted tenants' associations were established in many parts of the country and that some of these took the law into their own hands. From May 1920 to December 1921, it was estimated that of 491 agrarian crimes enumerated by the police, 21.5 per cent concerned evicted tenants who wanted to repossess their former holdings.[35] After independence, the question of the evicted tenants continued to divide opinion between those who demanded their restitution and those who were pragmatic enough to realise the difficulties that would involve. In the end, Patrick Hogan, the Minister for Agriculture, conceded it was necessary to make provision for them under the 1923 Land Act but many thousands remained disappointed, probably for the simple reason, as one TD (Teachta Dála, member of the Irish parliament) put it in 1929, that they had 'small voting power when a general election comes on'.[36]

The first phase of the Land War came to an end with the passing of Gladstone's second major Land Act in 1881. It established the principle of dual ownership, much to the chagrin of landlords, gave legal status to the Ulster Custom throughout the country and, perhaps most importantly from a tenant perspective, established the Irish Land Commission, bestowing upon it the powers to establish courts to adjudicate on fair rents. Government interference in the establishment of dual ownership and in the lowering of rents – an obvious political expedient in a disturbed society – was greatly resented by landlords, especially as both contributed significantly to the further diminution of confidence in the collateral value of Irish land, thereby putting increased pressure on creditors to call in their existing loans. When

---

35 Police reports, 1914–21, CO 904: TNA.
36 R. S. Anthony (Cork, Labour), *Dáil Debates*, vol. 29, 25 April 1929, 1043.

the Arrears of Rent (Ireland) Act of 1882 extinguished £1.76 million in arrears from rentals, landlords became further demoralised as they regarded this extinction as a form of confiscation.

The lowering of rents dampened the large farmers' enthusiasm for further agitation. Having achieved their goal, they began to desert the Land League even before it was proscribed by the government, showing little solidarity with the landless or the labourers who had backed them in the movement. The Labourers (Ireland) Act of 1883 was poor recompense for those who had expected more. Thus, labourers and other victims of the economic recession simply continued to emigrate in their tens of thousands (as, indeed, did some of the more extreme leaders such as Thomas Brennan, Patrick Egan and later John Dillon). The large farmers cared little for their plight or that of the uneconomic holders who predominated along the western seaboard either then or into the future.[37]

The Plan of Campaign

After a short period of recovery in 1883–1884 the agricultural economy slumped once again in 1885. By then, Home Rule politics had come to the fore and landlords had been pushed to the political periphery. W. E. Vaughan makes the telling point that 'the past was captured by their opponents … and used against them'.[38] The rhetoric of Land League and National League platforms stereotyped landlords as the cormorant vampires descended from alien colonisers of Irish land who sucked the very lifeblood from the soil through their rapacious rents and their ruthless attitude towards estate improvements. As far as agrarian nationalists were concerned, it was now time for the stake to be driven through the heart of landlordism. The existing relationship of deference and clientship between landlords and tenants did not break down entirely on all estates, especially aristocratic ones, but it was certainly reshaped as strong farmers and their supporters rose to local prominence.

As another economic depression took grip, a single report in the *Freeman's Journal* on 22 December 1885 encapsulated the different demands and responses

---

37 D. Jordan, *Land and Popular Politics in Ireland: County Mayo from the Plantation to the Land War* (Cambridge University Press, 1994), 312; F. Lane, 'Rural Labourers, Social Change and Politics in Late Nineteenth-century Ireland', in F. Lane and D. O Drisceoil (eds.), *Politics and the Irish Working Class, 1830–1945* (Basingstoke: Palgrave Macmillan, 2005), 113–39.
38 Vaughan, *Landlords and Tenants*, 223.

on individual estates, the regional variations in crisis levels, and even illustrated how tenants on well-managed estates were willing to chance their arm, so to speak, in the demand for abatements of rent: Lord Digby in King's County [County Offaly] refused to grant abatements to tenants whose rents had already been judicially fixed, and his other tenants refused to pay their rent in sympathy with them. Elsewhere, Lord Roden's tenants in Dundalk, County Louth were met with 'the curt reply that they could go into the land court if they had any grievance'; Thomas Esmonde MP was praised for granting an abatement before he was even asked; Earl FitzWilliam granted a 25 per cent reduction on part of his Wicklow estate; while the tenants of Sir John Robinson of Rokeby Hall in Louth 'without a single exception' paid their rents because, it was reported, they were 'not highly rented and he has always been looked on as a kind, liberal and generous landlord'. By contrast, the agent on the Conyngham estate in Slane was reported to have refused the tenants' rents, offered with a 30 per cent reduction, and dismissed, in 'a very contemptuous manner', a deputation led by the parish priest. The tenants withdrew to the parochial house where they drew up the following petition:

> That we the undersigned tenants on the Slane estate of Marquis Conyngham, having attended at the courthouse today to pay our rents at 30 per cent reduction, and having been met and treated in the most discourteous, offensive, and insulting way by the agent, respectfully solicit the Marquis Conyngham to give us an agent with whom we can treat.

They lodged the money they had tendered to the agent in a bank account to be drawn upon 'for costs in maintaining and defending the action of the tenants in proportion to rent for each'.[39] The petition was illustrative of the shift in the deferential dialectic and the estate balance of power. This was almost a year before some of the most encumbered landlords in the country found themselves the victims of the Plan of Campaign that was launched on 17 October 1886 by the National League, which had replaced the Land League, and which obviously drew its inspiration from events in places such as Slane. Despite Parnell's reservations about the Plan, it was adopted on around 200 estates (but with ramifications for many more) from the mid-1880s to the 1890s.[40] As happened on the Conyngham estate, tenants were organised to present what they considered a fair rent to landlords and, if this was not

---

39 Both quotations from *Freeman's Journal*, 22 December 1885.
40 L. M. Geary, *The Plan of Campaign* (Cork: Cork University Press, 1986), 145, 180; for Parnell's objections, see A. Jackson, *Home Rule: An Irish History 1800–2000* (Oxford University Press, 2003), 71.

accepted, they were to withdraw and withhold all payment. A fund was put in place to help them fight their cause.

Invariably, rent strikes led to an increase in levels of evictions with some notorious clearances carried out on Plan of Campaign estates at Bodyke in Clare and Luggacurran in Queen's County [County Laois]. The growth in agrarian crime and general social unrest was met by the government's introduction of the Criminal Law and Procedure (Ireland) Act in July 1887. Its enforcement gave rise to one of the most infamous incidents of the period at Mitchelstown in County Cork when the members of the RIC fired into a demonstration, killing two and injuring several more. Another high profile event occurred in Tipperary where landlord-organised opposition to the Plan under A. H. Smith-Barry led to his tenants in Tipperary town leaving their shops and other properties and removing themselves to a hastily constructed 'New Tipperary'. The move was doomed to disaster from the beginning, and it proved altogether too heavy a drain on the National League's resources. The Plan's potential was further weakened in 1888 with the passing of another Land Act which legislated for a review of all judicial rents fixed between 1881 and 1886 that were to last for three-year terms. In addition, leaseholders were finally admitted to the benefits of the 1881 Act.

By the end of the decade the Plan had petered out on most estates, but not before it had further damaged landlords' ability to survive as a distinct socio-economic class. The 1880s had been characterised by one crisis after another and marked the most difficult period of economic exigency for them since the Great Famine. The withholding of rents, the voluntary granting of reductions, the enforced lowering of agricultural rents by government legislation, the closing off of all sources of borrowing, the increase in rates (caused by the increased generosity of Boards of Guardians – who during the 1880s became more nationalist in outlook – in providing outdoor relief), police taxes in disturbed areas, and so on, cumulatively meant that by the 1890s most landlords, big and small, realised that their economic situation had become untenable. This realisation had ramifications for the material culture of the Big House. With the passing of the Settled Land Act (Ireland) in 1882, landlords were granted the right to sell contents which in the past had been restricted by the laws of settlement and, as a result, big house contents were now more likely to be sold than collected. The Land War, therefore, signalled not just the beginning of the end of landed estates but also the stripping of Irish country houses of their contents and their worldwide dispersal.

Land Acts

Under the Land Acts from 1881 to 1896 inclusive, the Irish Land Commission advanced in the region of £23 million to almost 73,000 tenants to purchase farms comprising almost 2.45 million acres.[41] However, for a number of reasons no revolutionary transfer of ownership had taken place. Under the 1881 Act, the advance to enable purchase was restricted to 75 per cent of the price of the holding. Tenants were unwilling to invest 25 per cent in cash at a time when the Land Commission was lowering rents, while landlords looked for higher prices than tenants were prepared to pay. Under the 1891 Act, the mechanics of sale were changed. Landlords were paid in specially-created land stock instead of cash. This was a retrograde step as far as landlords were concerned, since stocks were subject to market fluctuations. Both sides were generally agreed that much more pragmatic and generous terms were required.

Nor did the Acts do much, if anything, to improve the efficiency of Irish agriculture. Arguably, the struggle for the 'three Fs' – fair rents, free sale and fixity of tenure – had concealed the fact that farmers, without the necessary technical instruction, were quite simply at a loss as to how best to farm. The Department of Agriculture and Technical Instruction, which did try to provide instruction, was not established until 1899. In the meantime, in many localities it was left to individuals, sometimes rectors, curates and parish priests, to try to offer advice and assistance. There were also a few from a landed background who tried to improve agriculture (and perhaps secure a place for their class in the 'new Ireland'). While some such as Horace Plunkett and the earl of Dunraven have come to the fore in Irish historiography, there must have been many more in a class numbering thousands whose contributions in this respect at local level have long been forgotten. Plunkett looked to the development of the cooperative movement under the newly-formed Irish Agricultural Organisation Society as means of combating the effects of the global recession. By 1894 there were around thirty cooperatives in Ireland, but the number rose spectacularly to 876 within ten years.[42] Under the 1891 Land Act the government established the Congested Districts Board and empowered it to buy land from landlords for the relief of congestion in the poorer western counties. The Act also offered an advice service for small farmers and sought to incentivise the development of small local industries.

---

41 *Report of Estates Commissioners, 1920–21*, iv.
42 F. S. L. Lyons, 'The Aftermath of Parnell, 1891–1903', in Vaughan (ed.), *Ireland under the Union*, 87–9.

However, it was not until the passing of the Wyndham Land Act of 1903 that a far-reaching transfer of landownership took place. The Act came into being for a combination of reasons: the mobilisation of the United Irish League after 1898 with the aim to break up grazier lands; renewed agrarian agitation, including in Ulster, under the leadership of T. W. Russell; high politics and the Conservative government's desire to 'kill Home Rule by kindness'; landlord desire to rid themselves of their encumbered estates for a decent return; and George Wyndham's personal desire to make a significant contribution to solving the Irish question.[43] Under the 1903 Act, and an amending Act in 1909, £77.3 million was advanced to 124,000 tenants to purchase 7.3 million acres, as well as £7.5 million to the Congested District Board to purchase over 720 estates encompassing 46,700 holdings.[44]

It might be said that the Wyndham Act represented the first recorded bailout of an existing elite. The success of the Act was based on the fact that it was the first serious attempt to provide inducements to landlords to sell and for their tenants to purchase. Payment of the entire purchase money was to be advanced to landlords in cash and, as an extra inducement, they were paid an additional 12 per cent bonus on the sale of estates. Under the 1891 Act, land had sold for an average of 18.1 times the yearly existing rents in 1901; just two years later, under the 1903 Act, the average rose to 25.4 years. These inflated prices made landlords more confident that the capital they would receive would allow them to move profitably from a rental income to an income derived from investments. At the same time, the large farmers saw significant advantage in having annuities lower than annual rents and this made them all the more keen to achieve their social ambitions to become proprietors as quickly as possible. Not all of the smaller tenants were so enthusiastic; some were apprehensive of purchasing and thus becoming liable to a bureaucratic state body that during economic recession might not consider a petition for an abatement of rent. But their position was, as it always had been, at the mercy of the controlling large farmers.

Landlords resident in England, and elsewhere, used the Wyndham Act as an opportunity to sell their Irish lands and take the money out of Ireland to be invested elsewhere. As Olwen Purdue has shown, such landlords included

43 P. Bull, 'The Significance of the Nationalist Response to the Irish Land Act of 1903', *Irish Historical Studies*, 26, 111 (May, 1993), 283–305; *idem.*, 'The Formation of the United Irish League, 1898–1900: The Dynamics of Irish Agrarian Agitation', *Irish Historical Studies*, 33, (November 2003), 404–23; F. Campbell, 'Irish Politics and the Making of the Wyndham Land Act, 1901–03', *The Historical Journal*, 45, (December 2002), 755–73.
44 *Report of estates commissioners, 1920–21*, iv.

the likes of Lord Waveney of Flixton Hall in England who sold his entire Antrim estate, Richard Wallace of Sudbourne Hall in Suffolk who sold his Down estate – he had built Lisburn Castle as late as the 1880s; and the duke of Manchester who sold 12,000 acres in Armagh.[45] Their reasoning was straight-forward enough: an Irish estate no longer had any collateral value, its rents were falling and, in any case they were difficult, sometimes dangerous, to collect. It stood to reason that if the estate could be sold and the money received from the sale invested elsewhere, it would provide a less troublesome and, possibly, more profitable return. What better time to sell than when prices were at their best under the 1903 Act?

There remains work to be done on the impact the change of status, from tenant to owner-occupier, had on Irish farmers. Did it incentivise them to work harder in the management of their land? Did they invest rather than hoard? While landlordism had created obstacles to progress and improvement, owner-occupancy created another set relating to drainage schemes, income tax and rates, lack of technical advice that might once have been provided by the landlord's employees, and the firming up of existing land divisions, all of which H. D. Gribbon has argued, 'made rationalisation of occupation patterns more difficult than ever'.[46] By 1932–1933, the new proprietors were almost £3 million in arrears on a collectable annuity of £4.6 million. Undoubtedly, many had taken advantage of the revolutionary period not to pay their annuities but equally many were smallholders who had run into financial difficulties during the post-War economic downturn. The creation of a nation of smallholding proprietors was not to be the long-term solution to Irish agricultural problems, let alone the basis for a thriving Irish economy.

While tenants had to find a way to make farming work to pay their annuities, landlords had to find a way to invest their capital to provide a livelihood and safeguard their future. Initially there was a good deal of confidence because of the prices achieved. In 1905, the earl of Dunraven anticipated: 'As a class there can be no question that the financial circumstances of the landed gentry will be improved by sale.' He expected that by providing landlords with a large capital sum they would remain both solvent and resident and so continue 'farming their own land, retaining the amenities of their position

---

45 Purdue, *The Big House in the North of Ireland*, 87.
46 H. D. Gribbon, 'Economic and Social History, 1850–1921' in W. E. Vaughan (ed.), *A New History of Ireland, vol. VI, Ireland under the Union Part 2, 1870–1921* (Oxford University Press, 1996), 275.

and finding ... a larger scope for usefulness than they have hitherto enjoyed'.[47] However, while farming may have been familiar to many, few had any real experience of the City. Land had been the major constant in their lives but now they were dependent upon financial instruments they knew little about, and worse, over which they had no ultimate control.

John Shawe-Taylor, one of the landlords who had called for the land conference in 1902, the report of which provided the basis for the Wyndham Act, urged that 'it is of the greatest importance that income derived from the sale of property in Ireland should be expended in Ireland'.[48] However, with very few exceptions, this was not to be the case. The Leinster estate, for example, invested the vast bulk of the £800,000 received in mortgages in Britain. Alvin Jackson has found that in relation to the sale of the 10,000-acre Saunderson estate in Cavan, the owner converted the proceeds 'into an extensive colonial share portfolio' and that 'only in Ireland did Somerset [Saunderson] resist investment'.[49] The general reluctance of landlords to invest in Ireland said much about their confidence in the future prosperity of the country and may have been influenced by the fall-out from the Devolution Crisis of 1904–05 which forced Wyndham's resignation. More generally, anti-Home Rule resolutions showed how little faith landlords, amongst other Unionists, had in a Dublin parliament being able to run its financial affairs successfully. Those who remembered the Land War era could recollect the rhetoric espoused by agrarian radicals that threatened landlords with being run out of the country without ample compensation for their lands, when a Home Rule parliament was established in Dublin. Their fears were compounded when the Ranch War broke out in 1906 and agrarian agitators, this time led by the United Irish League, called for the breakup of large grazing farms in parts of the west and through the midlands. By 1907, Lord Ashtown was convinced that agitation was frightening landlords and scaring their capital out of Ireland. He told the Royal Commission on Congestion: 'As matters are going on now, the money they invest will leave the country. It will not be invested here'.[50]

---

47 Wyndham-Quin, W. T. 4th earl of Dunraven, *The Crisis in Ireland, An Account of the Present Condition of Ireland and Suggestions Towards reform* (Dublin: Hodges Figgis, 1905), 21, 35.

48 Quoted in W. O'Brien, *An Olive Branch in Ireland and its History* (London: Macmillan, 1910), 478.

49 A. Jackson, *Col. Edward Saunderson: Land and Loyalty in Victorian Ireland* (Oxford University Press, 1995), 208. Somerset was Saunderson's eldest son.

50 Quoted in P. Cosgrove, 'Irish landlords and the Wyndham Act', in T. Dooley and C. Ridgway (eds.), *The Irish Country House: Its Past, Present and Future* (Dublin: Four Courts Press, 2011), 101.

It is probably the case that many of the more insolvent landlords also sold their Irish houses and demesnes and moved to England, or further afield, after they sold their estates. Lord Ashtown of Woodlawn, who was determined to hold out against UIL pressure to force him to sell his estate, complained to Andrew Bonar Law in 1912: 'It is simply lamentable to see their empty demesnes, with their houses falling down', suggesting that at least a few had fled from Galway.[51] There were, of course, many insolvent estates that had very little left to invest after debts were paid. The earl of Enniskillen, for example, received £22,400 from the sale of 16,300 acres but this was gobbled up between the debts owed to the Alliance Assurance Company and the fact that various loans to individuals such as Lady Kathleen Villiers and Viscount Crichton could not be repaid.[52]

The Ranch War

Traditionally, historians have argued that the Wyndham Act removed the potential for revolution from Irish politics and society but such a view has been challenged in more recent years.[53] Constitutional agrarian reforms had certainly altered Irish rural society in terms of land tenure and ownership since the 1880s but they did very little to meet the demands of the lower agrarian classes or to change social structures which, by extension, meant political structures.

Philip Bull has claimed that there was potential for a much more conciliatory approach to be adopted by the Irish Parliamentary Party towards landlords after the passing of the Wyndham Act in 1903 principally because the issue of tenure had been taken out of agrarian politics.[54] Certainly this is what forward-looking members of the landed class such as the earl of Dunraven or Horace Plunkett had hoped for. But they were in the minority. Most landlords were simply concerned with, first, gaining as much as they possibly could from the sale of their estates and, second, protecting their future financial stability. It was a very individualistic approach; in the same way that the large farmers showed little concern for the smallholders, the aristocratic landowners showed little solidarity with the lesser gentry. Indeed, the payment of

---

51 L. P. Curtis, 'Ireland in 1914', in Vaughan (ed.), *Ireland under the Union*, 159.
52 Purdue, *The Big House in the North of Ireland*, 101.
53 T. Dooley, 'Land and Politics in Independent Ireland: The Case for Reappraisal', *Irish Historical Studies*, xxxiv (November 2004), 175–97.
54 Philip Bull, *Land, Politics and Nationalism: A Study of the Irish Land Question* (Dublin: Gill & Macmillan, 1996), 168–73.

excessive prices for estates to aristocrats such as the duke of Leinster quickly threatened to exhaust the funds set aside for the Act.

Trying to implement the 1903 Act proved to be a bureaucratic nightmare. And the subsequent delays became one in a conjuncture of factors which led to the aforementioned Ranch War that broke out in 1906. Other factors included the reluctance of some landlords, notably large ones, such as Lords Clonbrock and Ashtown in east Galway, to sell their estates, and their hesitancy led to much tenant frustration. The revived United Irish League exploited this frustration and renewed its demands for the redistribution of untenanted lands for the relief of congestion.

Instead of becoming more conciliatory towards landlords, individual members of the Irish Parliamentary Party became much more truculent, in particular the followers of John Dillon. However, the IPP did not involve itself in the Ranch War until the UIL had gathered such momentum that it would have been politically unwise not to, and in the summer of 1907 John Redmond eventually expressed his support. The rural discord was not primarily between landlord and tenant but rather in the more traditional manner of conflict between those who held too much land and those who had not enough, which brought the smallholders into conflict with the graziers.

According to a parliamentary return for 1906, there were at least two million acres of untenanted lands still in landlord possession. Lord Ashtown of Galway would later claim that the importance of untenanted land to a landlord lay 'not only in the income or annual profit he may be deriving from it, but also his proprietorial rights, which are often of great value'.[55] From the beginning of the Land War, many landlords had not re-let evicted holdings in the traditional way but instead used the eleven-month or conacre system. In this way, they did not have to abide by the legislative conditions set out in the 1881 Land Act with particular reference to fair rents and so they could exploit the market demand for access to land. Much of this land was taken by graziers, a class that inhabited a very anomalous world on extensive ranches which predominated in Roscommon, East Galway, south Mayo, and through the midlands belt of Westmeath, Meath and King's County (now Offaly). Some graziers were full-time farmers; others were businessmen with large farming interests. They comprised a rural social class in a state of constant flux, for shifting markets meant that men who were prosperous one year, and who found themselves over-extended the next, might simply disappear under an avalanche of debt. They were loathed by the labourers

---

55 *Royal Commission on Congestion in Ireland*, [Cd 4007], HC 1908, xliii, 178.

because they offered so little employment and equally, they were detested by the smallholders. Donald Jordan's *Land and popular politics in Ireland* shows that in County Mayo tensions were most acute in areas where large tracts of fertile land were contiguous with poorer lands teeming with smallholders. This was not just a western phenomenon; as late as 1921 an average of 65 per cent of all agricultural holdings in each of the counties outside the designated congested areas came under the definition of 'uneconomic' as set out by the Land Commission, that is below £10 valuation or roughly 20 acres of 'reasonable' land.[56] These marginal farmers were suffocating economically, unable to compete in a modernising agricultural economy, eking a living on farms too small to sustain a family. The general belief was that if grazier lands were to be redistributed, more families would have a better chance of succeeding as commercial farmers. Thus, the UIL firmly focused rural antipathy on the graziers and changed the focus of the land question and agitation from ownership to the redistribution of land.

However, the relationship between the UIL and graziers at local level was a complicated one. To take a more atypical geographical example, in the south Ulster county of Monaghan there were 6,600 UIL members in 1907. The nature of local politics and support for the Irish Parliamentary Party was, of course, a major reason for this high membership figure but so also was the fact that local nationalist politicians continued to play the agrarian card. As late as January 1917, the UIL-dominated County Council enthusiastically welcomed the compulsory tillage order because its members agreed it would provide the ideal pretext to break up the 300 or so holdings in the county that were in excess of 50 acres in size.[57] The debate that ensued amply encapsulated the anomalous position of graziers and, even more particularly, the blatant hypocrisy of rural politics. The chairman of the council, Thomas Toal, was a UIL man and the county's leading political power broker. He threw himself into the debate, raging against graziers, although he himself was one of the largest graziers in the north of the county. He fairly typified Maura Cronin's observation that '... the presence of graziers among the organisers of the United Irish League, the very organisation established in 1898 for the express purpose of challenging the grazing system, reminds us that the complexities of local life and relationship defy any simple class or economic explanation'.[58] Toal was merely holding the middle ground until such time

56 *Report of the Estates Commissioners for the Year from 1 April 1920 to 31 March 1921*, vi.
57 Minutes of Monaghan County Council, 7 January 1917: Monaghan County Museum.
58 Cronin, *Agrarian Protest*, 48.

as Home Rule would come out of cold storage, having been enacted in the summer of 1914 but suspended for the duration of the war. When that time came, he would be enshrined as part of the ruling elite.

The Monaghan County Council debate suggested the existence of an even more iniquitous but very subtly massaged local nationalist agenda. When a Unionist councillor, Michael Knight, acutely aware that the Protestant community owned a disproportionate share of the larger farms in the county, proposed that the council 'ought to make their position perfectly clear and not leave themselves open to any charge that they were utilising this cry for increased tillage for the purpose of injuring any particular class of people', he could not find a seconder for his resolution.[59]

In 1909, in response to the Ranch War and as an attempt to expedite the backlog of purchase agreements, the Liberal government introduced yet another Land Act. So far as landlords and tenants were concerned, its terms were retrograde: landlords were now to be paid in land stock instead of cash, and tenants' annuities were higher. However it did go some way towards easing rural tensions. In the years that followed, the third Home Rule crisis offered a diversion and with the outbreak of the Great War in 1914, the flagging agricultural economy was reinvigorated. However, prosperity for some, namely the class of large farmers (and this now included many former landlords), meant frustration and resentment for others, both the smallholders who wanted access to more land and the labourers – many of whom were the younger sons of farmers – who wanted better wages commensurate with the large farmers' increased profits. Graziers were prepared to pay outrageous prices for land let on conacre but they were unwilling to provide more land for tillage, even after the passing of the compulsory tillage order in 1917. To add to rural frustrations, land purchase came to a standstill as the government diverted its resources to the war effort; by 1921, there were 1,248 estates encompassing 46,600 holdings on 1.5 million acres that sales to the value of £10.7 million had been agreed upon, but for which advances had not yet been made.[60] As the war closed emigration channels, socially discomfited young men and women were again locked into the country and, as had happened on the eve of the Land War, rural Ireland became a prison of the malcontented.

---

59 Minutes of Monaghan County Council, 7 January 1917: Monaghan County Museum; *Dundalk Democrat*, 13 January 1917.

60 C. F. Kolbert and T. O'Brien, *Land Reform in Ireland: A Legal History of the Irish Land Problem and its Settlement* (Cambridge University Press, 1975), 46; *Report of the Estates Commissioners for the Year from 1 April 1919 to 31 March 1920*, 661.

Revolution and Land, 1917–1923

The Irish Parliamentary Party went into irreversible decline during the years of the Great War, and Sinn Féin emerged after 1916 to fill the vacuum. Its leader, Arthur Griffith, wrote that 'a mere agricultural state is infinitely less powerful than an agricultural-manufacturing state' but his economic principles were reshaped by party members and IRA leaders who saw the potential of using the land question as a catalyst in the drive for independence in the form of a republic.[61] By the end of 1918, with a post-War general election looming and the Representation of the People Act having given the vote to all men at 21 and women at 30, it was clear to Sinn Féin that much of its appeal, particularly to the smallholders and labourers, might lie in the promise of compulsory acquisition and redistribution of land contingent on a successful revolution. When Sinn Féiners encouraged agrarian agitation, they also emphasised the need 'to ignore British authority'.[62]

The potency of the appeal of farm grants in the encouragement of voluntary enlistment was also acknowledged by the British government. In June 1918, a proclamation issued by Lord Lieutenant French tried to encourage recruitment amongst young men in urban areas – 'mostly transplanted countrymen, the sons of small farmers' – in order to replenish the Irish divisions at the Front. They were promised 'as far as possible, that land shall be available for men who have fought for their country'.[63] In December 1919, the British government enacted the Irish Land (Provisions for Soldiers and Sailors) Act intended to provide land for the demobilised men returning to Ireland. Up to March 1921, 134 had been given possession of holdings comprising 2,700 acres. Theirs was an unenviable position: British ex-servicemen provided with farms by the Irish Land Commission, financed by the British government, just as the War of Independence broke out.[64]

Studies of IRA membership in rural areas have found that it was the small farmers, the labourers and the landless that were most likely to join or support the IRA, while the large farmers remained aloof.[65] How many became

---

61 Arthur Griffith, *Economic Salvation and the Means to Attain It* (Dublin: Whelan, n.d. 1923?), p. 20; Michael Hopkinson, *Green against Green: The Irish Civil War* (Dublin: Gill & Macmillan, 1988), 45.

62 Inspector General's monthly report, January 1918: CO 904: PRO.

63 *Irish Times*, 4 June 1918.

64 E. P. Tynan, 'War Veterans, Land Distribution and Revolution in Ireland 1919–1923' (unpublished PhD thesis, NUI Maynooth 2012).

65 See, for example, P. Hart, *The IRA and its Enemies: Violence and Community in Cork, 1916–23* (Oxford University Press, 1998), 143; J. Augusteijn, *From Public Defiance to Guerrilla*

members of the IRA in the hope of getting a farm of land or more land to augment what they already had may never be known; the witness statements of veterans in the Bureau of Military History files and the pension records do not shed light on the less patriotic motives for joining, and the Land Commission generated no statistics to confirm how much land IRA veterans received under the post-independence Land Acts. There is, however, plenty of anecdotal evidence that IRA members received farms under both the Cumann na nGaedheal and Fianna Fáil administrations between 1923 and c.1939.[66]

From the spring of 1920, when the RIC abandoned rural barracks and retreated into the larger urban areas, the level of agrarian crime rose dramatically in what was effectively the last phase of the Irish Land War. The statistics which are available are unreliable – many crimes undoubtedly went unreported – but they can be taken as a gauge. The total number of agrarian crimes reported for the period from 1 January to 19 May 1919 was 156. For the same period in 1920, the number rose to 712. No agrarian-related murder was recorded for 1919 but there were 4 recorded for the first five months of 1920 (and three more later that year). The number of cases of 'firing at the person' rose from 7 in the 1919 period to 28 for the 1920 period; the number of threatening letters from 72 to 254; the number of injuries to property from 25 to 205 and the number of cases of firing into dwellings from 9 to 91. Of a total of 491 crimes reported for the period May 1920 to December 1921, 287 (58.5 per cent) were put down to the fact that an estate, a demesne or a farm was wanted for division; 106 (21.5 per cent) were categorised as disputes concerning evicted tenants who wanted to repossess their former holdings.[67]

Agitation was by no means nationally coordinated. It was carried out along traditional battle lines: landlords who continued to hold substantial tracts of tenanted lands versus tenants; small farmers versus graziers; small farmers versus large farmers; labourers versus farmers. It involved individuals, gangs, landless associations and evicted tenants' associations. The crimes were traditional: cattle driving, threatening letters, destruction of property, boycotting and intimidation. It affected Catholic and Protestant landowners, those who had bought farms under the Land Purchase Acts, as well as those who had taken over farms from which families had been evicted during and after the Land War. The motivation for the arson attacks on a significant proportion of

Warfare: The Experience of Ordinary Volunteers in the Irish War of Independence, 1916–21 (Dublin: Irish Academic Press, 1996), 359.
66 See Dooley, 'The Land for the People'.
67 Police reports 1919–21, CO 904 series, part iv: PRO.

the 300 or so country houses burned during the years 1920 to 1923 was land hunger and the desire to have untenanted estates and demesnes redistributed amongst local uneconomic holders.[68] Looking back on the agrarian crisis, Erskine Childers, the Dáil's Minister for Propaganda in 1921, wrote: 'There was a moment when it seemed that nothing could prevent wholesale expropriation.' His fear was that 'the mind of the people was being diverted from the struggle for freedom by a class war'.[69] Arthur Griffith felt that if agitation were not dealt with, it would 'wreck the entire national movement'.[70]

The Dáil was forced to adopt a two-pronged approach to restoring the countryside to more peaceful ways. It established Sinn Féin arbitration courts to deal with land disputes (amongst other crimes) and ordered that the IRA be used to protect the victims of agrarianism and bring perpetrators to justice in the Sinn Féin courts. The approach had some success but when the Civil War broke out, and the countryside was denuded of law enforcement bodies, agrarian agitation simply thrived amidst the political violence. On 11 January 1923, when the government met with the Army Council, both Patrick Hogan, Minister for Agriculture, and Kevin O'Higgins, Minister for Home Affairs, put forward dramatic accounts of a countryside falling into anarchy. O'Higgins established a Special Infantry Corps, specifically to tackle agrarian disorder in the most disaffected areas, while Hogan planned for the introduction of a Land Bill that would defuse agitation as had happened under the British Land Acts between 1881 and 1909.[71]

The government threatened to deny access to land to anyone who continued to support rural violence but the Bill, passed into law on 9 August 1923, less than three weeks before the general election, promised enough to prevent the expanding electorate from looking for an alternative to Cumann na

---

68 Dooley, *The Decline of the Big House in Ireland*, 171–207; A. O'Riordan, *East Galway Agrarian Agitation and the Burning of Ballydugan house, 1922* (Dublin: Four Courts Press, 2015); Purdue, *The Big House in the North of Ireland*, 145–51; C. J. Reilly, 'The Burning of Country Houses in Co. Offaly during the Revolutionary Period, 1920–3', in Dooley and Ridgway, *The Irish Country House*, 110–33; J. S. Donnelly Jr, 'Big House Burnings in County Cork during the Irish revolution, 1920–21', *Éire-Ireland*, 47 (Fall/Winter 2012), 141–97; Clark, *Everyday Violence in the Irish Civil War*, esp. ch. 3; see also P. Bew, 'Sinn Féin, Agrarian Radicalism and the War of Independence', in D. G. Boyce (ed.), *The Revolution in Ireland, 1879–1923* (Dublin: Gill & Macmillan, 1988), 217–35.

69 E. Childers, *The Constructive Work of Dáil Éireann* (Dublin: Talbot Press, 1921), 10, 12.

70 According to Kevin O'Shiel, *Irish Times*, 11 November 1966.

71 P. Hogan, 'Report on the Land Purchase and Arrears Conference of 10–11 April 1923', 17 April 1923: Blythe papers, P24/174: UCD Archives; J. Regan, *The Irish Counter-revolution 1921–1936: Treatyite Politics and Settlement in Independent Ireland* (Dublin: Gill & Macmillan, 1999), 121.

nGaedheal – the completion of land purchase and the compulsory acquisition and redistribution of untenanted lands required for the relief of congestion – but at the same time, Hogan declared, it was conservative enough to protect 'the reasonable landlords' who were prepared to accept an offer 'approaching fair play'. Ultimately, they had to accept payment in land bonds, a much less enticing proposition than what had been available under the Wyndham Act in 1903. Both O'Higgins and Hogan understood that property owners had legal rights that could not be ignored without running the risk of diminishing the credit of the new state. The £25–30 million needed to implement the Act had in the end to be provided by Britain.[72] It has been contended that the introduction of this Act: 'was a clear signal by the Free State government of its determination to go down the route of parliamentary democracy. The willingness of the Provisional Government to negotiate with and, ultimately, receive financial support from the British government was a major triumph of pragmatism over ideology.'[73]

Meanwhile, in May 1923, a committee on land purchase under the chairmanship of Lord Eustace Perry reported to the newly established legislature of Northern Ireland. It formed the basis of the Northern Ireland Land Act that came into force on 28 May 1925. As with the Free State Act, the terms now on offer were much less generous than under the Wyndham Act, for example the purchase annuity was higher and the rate of interest was raised from 3.5 to 4.5 per cent. With few exceptions landlords were compulsorily obliged to sell. In total, 38,500 tenants purchased just over 800,000 acres and landlordism in Northern Ireland came to an end.[74]

In the Irish Free State, the 1923 Land Act served a purpose in bringing rural agitation to an end, but it left much more to be done in terms of land transfer and land redistribution. The ending of the land question in independent Ireland was a much longer process than in Northern Ireland; the last Land Act was not passed until 1965. Consequently, Irish society remained animated by the politics of land for decades after independence, arguably right up to Ireland's accession to the European Economic Community in 1973. It is a point not always given serious consideration by historians of twentieth-century Ireland.

---

72 Financial agreements between the Irish Free State government and the British government, 12 February 1923, Dept of Taoiseach files, S3459: NAI.
73 T. Dooley and T. McCarthy, 'The 1923 Land Act: Some New Perspectives', in M. Farrell, J. Knirck and C. Meehan (eds.), *The 1920s: Ireland's Formative Decade* (Dublin: Irish Academic Press, 2015), 150.
74 Purdue, *The Big House in the North of Ireland*, 99.

5

Social Conditions in Ireland 1880–1914

CAITRIONA CLEAR

Introduction

Spanning the front of the Tipperary-based newspaper, the *Nenagh Guardian* on 9 February 1881 was a large advertisement for W. & H. M. Goulding's Manures; slightly smaller was one for Cannock's furnishing establishment in nearby Limerick city. Further down the page readers were informed that Fred W. Day, Nenagh, sold everything from chilblain liniment to cigarettes; P. Grace, Dublin Road, Nenagh, used a smaller space to assure the public of his indispensability to 'everyone who keeps a horse'. Four other advertisements were for a Dublin-based tailor, two mineral water firms also based in Dublin, and a London-based jeweller. The Norwich Union Insurance Company announced its presence in Dublin, and a Ballinasloe, County Galway firm of solicitors advised readers that they had up to £20,000 to lend, on security of land. Two advertisements looked for agents for firms based in London. Volumes of parliamentary debates were offered at a discount, and shipbrokers Laing, Grey & Co. (London), announced vacancies for midshipmen and first-class apprentices. The remaining six notices were for products for which readers had to send away to Britain, to strengthen the blood, cure urinary problems, preserve hair, prevent cholera, improve health generally, and to 'destroy, entice and take alive' rats. *The Warning Voice*, a health booklet for men, with a smaller section for women, could be had from Dr Henry Smith, London; another London-based doctor, J. A. Barnes, promised a similar but less portentously titled publication: *How To Ensure Health*.

The 1880s and 1890s saw a flowering of the retail trade throughout the country, and in 1896, 16 of the 21 advertisements on the front of one issue of the *Kerry Sentinel* were for Tralee businesses, two for Cork businesses, one for a Dublin business and two for send-away-to-Britain products. The front page of the Waterford-based *Munster Express* on an issue in 1913, was even more locally-oriented. Waterford Gas Company assured potential customers of the safety of their product (used by medical professionals), and no less an authority than the 83-year-old Dr Charles A. Cameron, formerly Dublin's Medical Officer for Health, endorsed the locally made Powers' Cider. Among the other Waterford, Kilkenny and south Tipperary businesses featured, were several family grocers, a general store, a shipping company, a picture framer, a leather store, a ladies' and gents' tailor, a shoe shop, a seed merchant, a pawnbroker, a gunsmith and a poulterer. The increasingly important imperative of an attractive appearance was evident in the advertising of artificial hair from O'Grady Hairdressers, Kilkenny, and artifical teeth from W. J. Jones, Waterford. Five companies, three of which were based in Waterford city itself, one in Dublin and one in Manchester, offered loans on favourable terms.[1]

These 34 years – which could span in one lifetime, infancy to young middle age, young adulthood to vigorous middle age, middle age to old age – saw a far-reaching and permanent transformation of Ireland. The development of transport and communications, the acceleration of the retail trade and the growth of a consumer economy gave many people the hope, and sometimes the reality, of a safer, more comfortable and more interesting life. These were years of intense sociability and an increasing organisation of people in all kinds of endeavours – social, political, sporting, religious. In these years also, more and more Irish people were scrutinized than before, whether they were employed in new kinds of work, rehoused, schooled, isolated, vaccinated or cured, instructed in matters agricultural, vocational or hygienic, or simply, enumerated in new ways. Births and deaths had been registered since 1865, but from 1880 to 1914, government preoccupied itself with specific stages of the life cycle. Compulsory schooling, introduced in 1892 for all children from 6 to 14, focused official attention on the very young, as did the Children Act of 1908. The Old Age Pension, introduced in 1908–1909 for all people over the age of 70, shone a spotlight on the elderly. The collection and separate tabulation of statistics relating to infant and maternal mortality began in the closing years of the nineteenth century and that, along with the National Insurance Act in 1911, signalled that family survival was now an accepted concern of government. It would be some decades more before it became a priority, in either jurisdiction.

This chapter looks at how people made a living, what they wore and ate, and where they lived, and what they lived through, suffered from or died of, in these years.

---

1 *Nenagh Guardian* 9 February 1881; *Kerry Sentinel* 5 September 1896; *Munster Express* 10 May 1913.

Work

When 13-year-old Florrie Byrne from Prosperous, Co. Kildare, was offered a job in a grocery in Tipperary in 1914 she 'cried all Christmas that I wasn't going back to school with my pals'. She did not, however, consider going against her parents' wishes; they had a big farm, and nine children to rear. Florrie learned her trade in Tipperary and was never out of a job until her marriage. She was lucky and she knew it; men still made up the majority (76.4 per cent) of those gainfully occupied in Ireland, in all fields of employment, on the eve of the Great War. Agriculture remained the single biggest employer in 1911, as it had been 30 years earlier (18.2 per cent of the population were thus engaged in 1881, 17.7 per cent in 1911). Those working in industry made up 13.3 per cent of the population in 1881, and 13.9 per cent in 1911. Industrial workers, as one would expect, were most heavily concentrated in eight of the nine Ulster counties (Cavan was the exception) in Dublin County and City, and County Louth. Telecommunications had 16,502 new workers by 1911, over one-eighth (13 per cent) of them female. Financial, wholesale and retail businesses and the extension of the government's administrative arm in a variety of new enterprises meant that there were nearly 7,000 more clerical workers in Ireland in 1911 than there had been in 1881; at the later date, over a third of these (38 per cent) were women. The number of general shopkeepers, as one would expect, rose from 165,332 in 1891 (3.5 per cent of the population) to 197,943 (4.5 per cent) 20 years later.[2]

The professional sector increased by 10,000 in the first decade of the twentieth century, that number more or less evenly divided between males and females. Teachers accounted for between 10 and 12 per cent of all professionals over these 34 years. In only two counties in 1901 – Carlow and Fermanagh – did women, at 43 per cent and 46 per cent respectively, make up fewer than half of all teachers. In the cities and all other counties their percentage was always more than half, often two-thirds and occasionally three-quarters of

---

2 'All God's Children: Mrs Florrie Kelly', Joe O'Reilly with fifth class, Edenderry (ed.) *The Pauper's Graveyard* (Convent School, Edenderry 1993), 240–47; all information here and below on occupations taken from *Census of Ireland 1881*, General Report 19–25, and Table 18, 108–9; and county breakdown Vols I–IV, Table XVIII in each county (page numbers vary); *Census of Ireland* 1891 General Report, 22–27, and Table 18,112–3; and county breakdown Vol. I–IV, Table XVIII; *Census of Ireland* 1901, General Report, 22–28 and Table 19, 115–16; county breakdown, Vol. I–IV, Table XIX, (page numbers vary): *Census of Ireland* 1911 General Report, xxvii–xxxi and Table 19, 7–8; and county breakdown in volumes entitled Leinster, Munster, Ulster and Connaught, Table XIX in each one (page numbers vary). Accessed via www//histpop.org/ohpr/servlet.

the total. State elementary school teaching was the great nineteenth-century career opportunity for working-class, small farming and lower-middle-class people all over the western world, and it attracted marginally more women than men in early twentieth-century Ireland. The first female president of the Irish National Teachers Organization was elected in 1911, Catherine Mahon from Tipperary. Several of her siblings were also National teachers. Their father was a labourer, although both parents went on to work as domestic servants in their later years, their mother as a housekeeper/cook, their father as a gardener/coachman.[3]

The Mahons were atypical, because the usual domestic servant was the young, single female. Service was still the biggest single occupational category for women in 1911, accounting for 29.8 per cent of all gainfully-occupied women in Ireland. None the less, in Ireland as elsewhere, it was in decline. In 1881 there were 240,746 domestic servants, in 1901 174,631 and in 1911 131,788 – never less than 95.5 per cent of these were female. This was a decline of 45 per cent in the number of domestic servants over a 30-year period when population had declined by 15 per cent.

The number of servants might have fallen because of the possibility of alternative work in this period, as opportunities – however short-term – opened up in small, or large-scale, manufacturing. In the early 1880s in the daily newspapers such as the *Freeman's Journal*, *Belfast Newsletter* and *Cork Examiner* (which all had regional/national readerships) most 'situations vacant' advertisements were for men and nearly all of those that sought females wanted domestic servants. Moving to April 1897, however, 27 of 37 job advertisements for females in the *Freeman's Journal* were for vacancies in the dressmaking trade (about evenly divided between apprentices and others), 7 were for confectioners, 2 for drapers and 1 each for bookkeeping and grocery. (Advertisements for domestics were in a separate category and numbered 26). In 1905, in the same newspaper, there were 34 advertisements for women's trades (30 of them drapery, dressmaking and millinery) compared to 19 advertisements for domestic servants, and 58 advertisements for male jobs of all kinds. The *Cork Examiner* in April 1898 gives a sample of these male jobs; bakers, assistants to the wine and spirit trade, grocers, machine workers, farm labourers, a creamery manager, and a London firm which required agents for jewellery, pipes, clothing, toys, wringers, cycles and tea. Agents of all kinds were increasingly sought throughout this period, indicating the

---

3 S. Chuinneagáin, *Catherine Mahon: First Woman President of the INTO* (Dublin: INTO Publications, 1998).

growth of the retail trade and an over-abundance of British-based companies eager to take advantage of the new-found spending power of the Irish.
The ubiquity and enthusiasm of the advertisements suggests that this was a
thankless job. The abundant advertisements for 'boys' and 'girls' as apprentices to the millinery, drapery, grocery, dressmaking, bookbinding, stationery,
hardware, ironmongery, bakery, bootmaking, confectionery, coachmaking
and other trades might sometimes have been unscrupulous employers' short
cuts to free labour. It was probably because of this that a Mr Ferguson, in
Ballina, County Mayo, in 1910, used some of his costly front-page advertisement wordage to assure potential applicants for his tailoring apprenticeship
that they would be 'well-treated'. Miss O'Callaghan of Dundalk who sought
'a number of smart girls as apprentices and improvers to the dressmaking' in
1903 specified, probably for the same reason, that cutting and fitting would be
taught. Well-treated or not, an increasing number of 13- to 18-year-olds were
learning trades which would prove useful to them later, and demand for their
labour increased significantly over this period.[4]

In Ireland as elsewhere, there was a decline in some independent trades
(weaver, sawyer, nailer and cooper, for example), but some trades expanded.
The house-building trades rose from 51,000 in 1891 to 58,884 ten years later,
stabilising at 57,944 in 1911. Engine and machine makers doubled in number between 1881 and 1911, stone and clay workers increased also, and (on a
smaller scale) shipwrights, printers and papermakers, industrial railway workers, bicycle-makers, saddlers and coachmakers grew. Outside the industrial
north-east, there were small but significant clusters of non-agricultural workers. Historians usually focus on big numbers and sharp and dramatic spikes
and troughs, and steady maintenance can often be overlooked. It is tempting
to pass over the 435 miners in Kilkenny (in Castlecomer) in 1901, the 524 men
working in precious metals and stone in Galway in the same year, the 297
men in Cork working in wood and timber, and in 1911 the 630 men working
in iron and steel in Tipperary, 629 in the same field in Wexford, and 1,491 people, 76 per cent of them female, working in textiles in Louth. These numbers
were small compared to the thousands in the Belfast shipyards, spinning mills

---

4 Mr Ferguson, Ballina advertisement, *Western People* 21 May 1910; Miss O'Callaghan,
  Dundalk Democrat, January 10 1903. For comparative newspaper advertisements over
  time, see *Freeman's Journal* 'Appointments Vacant', 4 April 1881, 7 September 1881; *Belfast
  Newsletter* 'Wanted', 4 April 1883, 6 September 1883; *Cork Examiner* 'Situations Vacant', 7
  April 1885. *Freeman's Journal,* 4 April 1888 has far more varied 'appointments vacant'; *Cork
  Examiner,* likewise, 7 September 1892, 6 April 1898, 13 September 1898; *Belfast Newsletter,*
  2 April 1890; *Freeman's Journal,* 6 April 1893; 7 September 1893; 8 April 1897; 5 April 1905.
  Advertisements for agents are found throughout the provincial papers.

and shirt factories, but every one of these workers probably supported at least one dependent, and generated demand for goods and services – grocers, shoemakers, tailors, dressmakers, builders, teachers and nurses – over time. Established non-retail town trades like blacksmith, plumber and carpenter were rarely advertised, because they were usually passed on within families. This was also true of jobs in shirt factories in Derry and in spinning mills or shipyards in Belfast, and (tradition would suggest) of factory jobs in other cities and towns also – for example, the Dublin, Cork and Kilkenny breweries and the Cork woollen mills.[5]

Trained nurses and midwives were counted in the census for the first time as a separate occupational group in 1911. This profession attracted girls and women from a variety of backgrounds; Annie Smithson, from a middle-class Protestant Dublin family, went to England to train as a nurse when she was in her early twenties, and returned to Ireland in 1900 to undertake further training as a Jubilee (district) nurse. A Mrs McDonald, who returned to Toomevara, County Tipperary at the end of the nineteenth century as the district midwife, had sold her business on her husband's death and moved to Dublin with her five children to train in one of the hospitals there. A certain level of maturity was often required of district nurses – Mullingar Union in 1896 specified that the district nurse to whom they were offering a miserly £20 a year and 5s expenses, should be at least 40 years old. Registration was not standardised on a national (i.e. Britain and Ireland) basis until 1919, and before this, every employer had his or her own idea of what constituted training. For Ardee Union (County Louth) which in 1902 was offering £40 a year with apartments and rations to a 'trained nurse' for the workhouse infirmary, training meant having spent not less than two years in a hospital recognised by the Local Government Board and having obtained, after examination, a 'Certificate of Proficiency'. Many Poor Law Unions appointed district nurses from the 1880s onwards, and these together with the celebrated Jubilee and

---

5 Numbers of miners and other workers here are taken directly from the Censuses, see footnote 2. See also L. M. Cullen, *An Economic History of Ireland since 1660* (London: Batsford, 1972); C. Ó Gráda, *Ireland: A New Economic History 1780–1939* (Oxford University Press, 1994); A. Bielenberg, *Cork's Industrial Revolution 1780–1870: Development or Decline?* (Cork: Cork University Press, 1991); L. Kennedy and P. Ollerenshaw (eds.), *An Economic History of Ulster 1820–1939* (Manchester: Manchester University Press, 1985); B. Messenger, *Picking up the Linen Threads: A Study in Industrial Folklore* (Belfast: Blackstaff, 1980); J. C. Beckett et al. (ed.), *Belfast: The Making of the City* (Belfast: Appletree Press, 1983); B. Lacy, *Siege City: The Story of Derry and Londonderry* (Belfast: Blackstaff Press, 1990); D. Jacobs and D. Lee (eds.), *Made in Limerick: History of Industries, Trade and Commerce* (Limerick: Limerick Civic Trust, 2003).

Lady Dudley nurses, founded in 1897 and 1903 respectively, were apostles of public health in rural Ireland. The bicycle facilitated their work greatly.[6]

Shop assistant, as a job description in itself, was also coming into its own, though such workers are almost impossible to find in the census, collapsed as they were into the retail trades in which they were involved. Increasingly organised about pay and conditions in the 1890s, they had a well-developed identity. Even the smaller provincial towns – Ballyhaunis, County Mayo for example – had active shop assistant associations at this stage. Two hundred and seventy-one workers (21 of them female) were 'living in' on the night of the big fire in Arnotts department store in Dublin in 1894 (all escaped with their lives). The living-in system was deplored by trade unionists on both sides of the Irish Sea. Female shop assistants were more common from the 1880s, as lady customers preferred to be served by them. The 'shopgirl' was alternately romanticised by musical comedy and pathologised by 'social novelists', but work in a good respectable shop in any size of a town was a highly sought-after job for boys and girls, men and women, until well into the second half of the twentieth century.[7]

The nature and the pace of 'old' work also changed in these years. Agricultural work became less back-breaking as sales of the accessibly-priced 'tumbling paddy' rake, root-cutters, flails, sprayers, harrows and winnowing-trays doubled between 1885 and 1895. The rise in the number of horses and donkeys testifies to improvements in roads, tracks and boreens (country lanes). Very big tillage farmers hired threshing machines from the 1890s onwards. The overall shift from tillage to pasture farming throughout most of the country has been well-documented and debated. This shift did not of itself 'cause' the 'disappearance' of agricultural labourers for their numbers had been falling since the 1840s; anybody depending on tillage for his or her

---

6 On history of nurses in Ireland, P. Scanlan, *The Irish Nurse: A Study of Nursing in Ireland 1718–1981* (Leitrim: Drumlin Press, 1991); J. Robins, *Nursing and Midwifery in Ireland in the Twentieth Century* (Dublin: Institute of Public Administration, 2000); and G. Fealy (ed.), *Care to Remember: Nursing and Midwifery in Ireland* (Cork: Mercier Press, 2005). On Smithson, see her autobiography, *Myself and Others – and Others* (Dublin: Talbot Press, 1944) and on Mrs McDonald, see D. Grace, *Portrait of a Parish: Monsea and Killdiernan Co.Tipperary* (Monsea: Relay Press, 1996), 200.

7 On Dublin shop assistants, S. Rains, *Commodity Culture and Social Class in Dublin 1850–1916* (Dublin: Irish Academic Press, 2010), 173 and *passim*; J. Cunningham, *Labour in the West of Ireland:Working Life and Struggle 1890–1914* (Belfast: Athol Publications, 1995), 91–5; Emile Zola, *Au Bonheur des Dames / The Ladies' Paradise* (Paris, 1886) and George Gissing, *The Odd Women* (London, 1897) paint grim pictures of female shop assistant lives. On British shop assistants, P. Cox and A. Hobley, *Shopgirls: The True Story of Life Behind the Counter* (London: Hutchinson, 2014).

livelihood worked – and earned – only for short intensive periods through-out the year. Pasture-farming employed much fewer people, but there was some work all the year round. Labourer numbers declined countrywide, but those who remained were such an important part of the rural workforce in these decades in the big-farming regions of Leinster and Munster that they managed to make their voices heard in a number of ways – by successfully clamouring for housing, by inclusion in some parts of the Land Acts, and by joining labourers' unions and making up the rural backbone of the Irish Transport and General Workers' Union from 1908 on.[8]

Most farm work was done by farming families themselves; over two-thirds of all farms were 30 acres or under, throughout the period up to the Great War. Changing standards and practices in agriculture in the 1880s and 1890s were demanded by an expanding market at home and abroad, and encouraged by bodies like the Irish Agricultural Organisation Society (1894) and the Department of Agriculture and Technical Instruction (1899). The railway had been facilitating the export of livestock for several decades, now its extension to the westernmost parts of the country and to off-the-beaten-track midland towns gave a spur to dairying and poultry-rearing in those areas as well. The rise of creameries, especially in Munster and Leinster, testifies to the importance of Irish milk and butter, but this development did not necessarily encroach on women's economic power; great numbers of turkeys, geese and hens flapped in to take the place of butter and milk for the *bean a' tí* (woman of the house). Besides, throughout Connacht and Ulster in particular, up to the 1950s, many women continued to make but-ter that, along with eggs, often partially paid for their groceries at the shop. These were the responsibilities of farmers' womenfolk in general, but as far as those with the actual title of farmer were concerned, 16 per cent were female in 1891. By 1911 this had fallen to 14.7 per cent. Only 6.8 per cent of farmers had been women in 1861. The rise of the female farmer was a long-term development of post-Famine Ireland. Connacht's share of female farmers was roughly the national average at both dates while Leinster's was significantly above it, at 19 per cent in 1891 and 17 per cent in 1911. Rural marriage patterns of husbands up to ten years older than wives in Leinster,

---

8 J. Feehan, *Farming in Ireland: History, Heritage and Environment* (Dublin: University College Dublin Press, 2003), 93–120; on agriculture generally, there are so many works that only three can be given here, P. Lane, 'The Organization of Rural Labourers 1870–1890', *Cork Archaeological & Historical Society Journal* 10 (1995), 159–60; M. Turner, *After the Famine: Irish Agriculture 1850–1914* (Cambridge University Press, 1996); D. Bradley, *Farm Labourers: Irish Struggle 1900–1976* (Belfast: Athol Publications, 1996), 24–54.

Munster and the big-farming areas of Ulster in the 1850s and 1860s, automatically created widows some decades later who retained the title of farmer as long as they lived. The small but significant number of spinster farmers suggests that there were female heirs to farms who preferred to hire, rather than marry, the male labour they needed.[9]

The stepped-up pace of agricultural work reflected the faster pace of work everywhere, even for unpaid women workers in the house. Advertisements, even for domestic servants, specified 'smart' boys and girls. This meant intelligence, speed and only-having-to-be-told-a-thing-once, but it also referred to a neat and attractive appearance. Even where jobs required rough clothing (farming, some kinds of factory work), the extended leisure timetable of people of all classes – even if this only consisted of 'following' bands around towns on summer evening[10] – demanded decorative and fashionable clothes. Improved appearance could only be achieved through the constant making, buying and maintenance of clothes – hence the steady demand for workers in the clothing trades as outlined above.

Clothes

Everyday wear varied. A middle-aged Sligo farmer's wife photographed going to market in the 1880s with a donkey and creels wore a toque and a mantle. In a group of old age pensioners photographed in Clonown, County Roscommon in 1909, however, while the men were shirted, suited and bowler-hatted, the women were uncompromisingly 'traditional' – shawled, long-skirted and broad-aproned. This must have been how they wanted to present themselves, because they probably dressed up to be photographed. Towards the end of the century even in parts of the country where traditional wear was noticed and celebrated by cultural revivalists, modern fashionable clothes, whether made up from a pattern, copied from a sketch in a newspaper, or sent in a parcel from America, were being blended in with, or occasionally substituted for, traditional wear. Then as now, people wore different kinds of clothes for different occasions and settings, but the sewing machine (well in place by 1880), the developing retail trade, emigrant influence and

---

9 On women in late-nineteenth-century farming the classic work is J. Bourke, *Husbandry to Housewifery: Women, Housework and Economic Change 1890–1914* (Oxford: Clarendon, 1993). See also C. Clear, *Social Change and Everyday Life in Ireland 1850–1922* (Manchester: Manchester University Press, 2007), 11–13, and Appendix 2, 166, whence come the figures on female farmers.

10 F. Lane, 'Music and Violence in Nineteenth-century Cork: The "Band Nuisance" 1879–82' *Saothar: Journal of the Irish Labour History Society* 24 (1999), 17–31.

the advent of mass literacy all played a part in adapting clothes to something approaching fashion.[11]

Men's 'knee-britches and coat of emerald green' so often caricatured, but with a basis in real everyday wear in the early nineteenth century, had disappeared by the period under discussion. The small farmers of Mayo and the coastal dwellers of Connemara in the 1880s wore ankle-length pants, jackets, waistcoats, though these were likely to be báinín, or worsted, rather than serge or tweed, and oatmeal-coloured rather than black. In the towns and cities, tradesmen often wore collars and ties and bowler hats for every day, while labourers wore more hard-wearing fabrics (moleskin and corduroy) and cloth caps. Men's clothes, because they were of heavier fabric and tailored, were always more expensive than women's. Clothes, for both men and women, were layered for warmth. A Kildare farmer is described as follows getting ready for her bed in the early years of the twentieth century:

> First her black woollen waistcoat was taken off and left on the cane-bottomed chair beside the bed. Then her check apron, her serge blouse, and her heavy black skirt. A black sateen petticoat came next, and a red flannel bodice and underskirt. ... She would pull [her grey flannel nightdress] over her head and, screened by its ample folds, remove her stays, her chemise and long flannelette drawers.

This elderly widow was indeed modern to be wearing drawers; for most older women the chemise, or shift, was the garment worn next to the skin.[12] This farmer's last act of preparation for the night (after extensive prayers) was to take down her hair and twist it into two plaits. Before the 1920s, short hair on women meant religious vows, illness or disgrace while long hair, like a long skirt, was an adult female inevitability. Hair was 'put up' at 17 or 18, signalling the transition to young adulthood. Women who did not do this were scorned as trying to make themselves out to be younger than they were. Friends and female relatives were the only hairdressers most women ever had (except for very wealthy ladies of fashion who had ladies' maids), and every morning

---

11 Photograph in M. Jones, *The Other Ireland; Changing Times 1870–1920* (Dublin: Gill & Macmillan 2011), 93. The Clonown photograph is reproduced in R. Fallon, *A County Roscommon Wedding 1892: The Marriage of John Hughes and Mary Gavin* (Maynooth: Maynooth Local History Series 2004), 35; see also the photographs in K. Kearns, *Dublin Tenement Life: An Oral History* (Dublin: Gill & Macmillan, 1995). On the history of clothes in Ireland the classic is M. Dunlevy, *Dress in Ireland* (Cork: Cork University Press, 1999), but for the tradition/modernity interface, see S. de Cléir, 'Bhí bród as sin i gcónaí; cruthaitheacht agus cultúr na mban i dtraidisiún fheisteas Oileáin Árainn' *Béascna: iris béaloideasa agus eitneolaíochta* 1 (2002), 85–100.
12 M. Laverty, *Never No More: The Story of a Lost Village* (London: Longmans, 1942), 34–5.

demanded a long session before a mirror with hairpins that could bruise the scalp. The weight of the hair up and the tightness with which it was pinned often caused headaches.[13] No wonder that the first wave of women's emancipation during and after the Great War led not only to shorter skirts, but to the option of cropped hair. It was then that female hairdressing came into its own as a lucrative trade. But from 1880 to 1914 men's hair, on their faces or their heads, was (like their clothes) more labour intensive and expensive than women's, and the number of barbers multiplied by 3.5 between 1861 and 1911, in a falling population.[14]

The requirement for respectable and inexpensive everyday clothing in the new jobs opening up accelerated the demand for drapers' shops, where fabrics, or even ready-to-wear clothes, could be bought. In 1885 Hyams of Dublin and Belfast were advertising in provincial papers around the country, offering trousers ranging in price from 6s 8d to 21s, but by the early twentieth century, pride of advertising space in most local papers went to local drapery firms like Todds of Limerick, Pattesons of Dundalk, Hacketts of Enniskillen, Tarpeys of Kilkelly (County Mayo), Boyers of Longford, and many more. In 1909 Floods of Carrick-on-Shannon promised suits made to order in seven days.[15] Once bought, or made, clothes had to be stored and preserved, and this created a need for wardrobes, presses, hangers or just hooks on the backs of doors, even in one-roomed dwellings. And in homes big and small, with and without paid help, clothes had to be washed. In many dwellings up to and after 1914, every drop of water had to be carried in and carried out again to be disposed of. It is impossible, therefore, to overstate the advantage of even a tap and a sink in the scullery, as provided in some of the local authority-provided urban new-build houses in the bigger cities and towns. But even in these houses, the water still had to be heated, not only for washing, but for rinsing, and the only way of doing so was the fire – copper boilers in outhouses were rare. And because several basins were necessary (for rinsing clothes which required different temperatures), it could not all be confined to

13 S. Czira, née Gifford, describes this process in *The Years Flew By: Recollections of Sidney Gifford Czira* (Galway: Arlen House, 2000), 3: Smithson, *Myself*, describes the pain and the weight, p. 80. For Mary Colum, *Life and the Dream* (London: Macmillan, 1947), 86, short hair was a landmark event.

14 On changing appearance generally, see Clear, *Social Change*, 149–55.

15 Hyams advertisement, *Westmeath Examiner*, 10 March 1883, *Anglo-Celt*, 9 May 1885; other department stores in chronological order, Pattesons, *Dundalk Democrat*, 21 October 1901; Hacketts, *Fermanagh Herald*, 8 April 1905; Boyers, *Longford Leader*, 14 April 1906; Todds, *Limerick Leader*, 23 October 1908; Floods, Carrick-on-Shannon *Leitrim Observer*, 15 May 1909; Tarpeys of Kilkelly *Western People*, 21 May 1910.

the big sink (where one existed) – 'the wash' extended all over the living area. Once washed, clothes had to be dried, outdoors if there was space and if the weather was propitious, indoors if not. Can the increased susceptibility of many Irish people to some kinds of respiratory diseases in the early twentieth century (see health, below) be partly attributed to the more regular washing and drying of clothes? This task, even under optimal circumstances, was heavy and hard, and there was also the unhealthy humidity (lasting several days) of clothes being dried indoors.[16] Even improved housing did not solve this problem.

Housing

A finely-rendered drawing of a flush toilet with wall-mounted cistern and chain occupied a large space on the top left quarter of the front page of the *Westmeath Examiner* in 1895, drawing readers' attention to Mullally's Home Plumbing, Mullingar. Another 60 years, however, would pass before every rural household in Ireland had an indoor water closet to call its own. In Ireland as in most of rural Europe, up to the Second World War the chamber pot or bucket, regularly emptied outside the house (into an earth closet, a water closet or simply a dungheap), remained the norm. The desired basic qualities of a good dwelling in the late nineteenth and early twentieth centuries were dryness, ventilation, warmth, solid roofing and flooring, ability to be kept and swept clean, and lack of in-built vermin (bugs in walls, for example, common in houses built in the early nineteenth-century city). By the last quarter of the nineteenth century, added to this were ease of access to clean water, and at-hand facilities for the safe disposal of waste – usually a communal water or earth closet outside the house. In 1914 indoor flush toilets and bathrooms were only supplied in new-build middle-class houses in cities, and in institutions.[17]

---

16 See C. Kinmonth, *Irish Rural Interiors in Art* (Yale University Press, 2006), 79–126 for discussion on washday.

17 Mullallys, Mullingar, *Westmeath Examiner,* 21 September 1895; on Irish housing in the twentieth century, C. Clear, *Women of the House: Women's household work in Ireland 1922–1961* (Dublin: Irish Academic Press, 2000), 143–70. On nineteenth- and early-twentieth-century housing generally, A. Gailey, 'Changes in Rural Housing 1600–1900', in P. O'Flanagan (ed.), *Rural Ireland 1600–1900: Modernisation and Change* (Cork: Cork University Press, 1987), 86–103; M. Fraser, *John Bull's Other Homes: State Housing and British Policy in Ireland 1883–1922* (Liverpool: Liverpool University Press, 1996); E. McKay, 'The Housing of the Rural Labourer 1880–1916' *Saothar: Journal of the Irish Labour History Society* 17 (1992), 27–39; C. Kinmonth, *Irish Country Furniture 1700–1950* (New Haven, CT: Yale University Press, 1993); M. E. Daly (ed.), *Dublin's Victorian Houses*

Improvements in accommodation were not universal. One-third of Dublin city's population in 1900 lived in the former bedrooms and reception rooms of large houses in the inner city, the tenement houses. Taps or pumps for clean water, toilets or latrines for waste were at ground level, one for up to 100 people. Efforts were made to ameliorate this situation in the years under discussion but it was never fully dealt with as long as the tenements lasted. In all cities, towns and villages, the poor lived where and as they could, sometimes paying exorbitant rent for one or two rooms in multi-occupancy houses, or, in smaller towns, living in poorly-built cottages on the fringes. For a number of reasons the housing of the rural labouring class was better developed. Ninety-four of 161 Poor Law Unions were building 'cottages' from the early 1890s, many of which still stand. Slated roofs, glass windows, designated bedrooms, large fireplaces for cooking and sometimes parlours or 'good rooms' were features of these houses. The Congested Districts Board houses, built from the early 1890s in the west of the country, had three good-sized rooms and two fireplaces. The houses they replaced often had holes in the ceiling, no chimneys and no windows. But even in those inadequate old houses, rural living was better than urban; clean water was usually available from a spring or well, rain water was collected for washing, and waste was disposed of so that it did not contaminate either supply, although the presence of dungheaps outside front doors in parts of the west, shocked visitors. Still, the parts of the country with the least developed rural housing, had the lowest sickness and death-rates up to the early twentieth century (see health, below). Older and more prosperous farm houses in the countryside were sturdy and serviceable; thatch that could be replaced or refurbished every few years was warm and ergonomic, and as long as chimneys were properly constructed and windows correctly aligned, these houses (which have been painstakingly recreated in folk parks north and south) were snug and weatherproof, and many survived into the twentieth century.[18]

Urban district councils also began to build 'labourers' or 'artisans' cottages in the 1880s and, by the early twentieth century, housing had become a staple item on the agenda of local government meetings. Based on a variety of designs, these dwellings had all the features of the rural houses though they

---

(Dublin: A. & A. Farmer, 1998); J. V. O'Brien, *Dear, Dirty Dublin: A City in Distress 1890–1914* (Berkeley: University of California, 1982). See also Clear, *Social Change*, 142–45.

18 These can be seen in Bunratty Folk Park, Bunratty Castle, County Clare, the Ulster Folk and Transport Museum, Cultra, County Down and the Irish-American Folk Park, Omagh, County Tyrone. The Museum of Country Life, Castlebar, County Mayo, while it does not have houses as such, has artefacts, photographs and a lot of other rich information to offer on nineteenth and early- twentieth-century rural housing.

were sometimes two-storey. Back doors, for ventilation and the disposal of waste, were important. Depending on the town's level of aquafication, some had a tap and a sink in the kitchen or scullery; all had a wet or dry closet in the yard. From 1874 local authorities of towns of over 6,000 were obliged to have sanitary officers and to provide clean water and safe disposal of waste. The major cities had their clean water and sewerage systems in place by 1880, but developments in the rest of the country proceeded unevenly, and in small towns and villages the process took longest. 'The Eternal Question of the Drumsna Pump' was the facetious sub-heading about the proceedings of Carrick-on-Shannon District Council in 1909. A pump had been out of order in this village for a year, and inhabitants had to draw their drinking water from the river into which the sewerage of the town ran. The councillors treated this as a joke, but four years earlier in Dungloe, County Donegal, a similar problem was taken more seriously, probably because there had been 15 cases of typhoid in two years – 'And I only wonder that we have not had more', commented the local doctor.[19]

From the 1880s, Belfast had the best, and the most plentiful urban housing, with street after street of solid 'two-up, two-down' houses. There was a limited supply of houses like this in other Irish cities too – on King's Island and Thomondgate in Limerick, in Cork's Blackpool, and in Dublin's Oxmantown, Liberties and North Wall areas.[20] These comparatively good houses did not house all the urban working and labouring class. Like the rare company houses (railway cottages throughout the country or Guinness houses in Dublin for example) they were rented mainly by artisans and those who could afford them. The newly-built artisan's dwelling in which Mary Loughman grew up in Kilkenny city in the early twentieth century had a weekly rent of 3s 6d; her step-father was the asylum tailor. Housing shortages, however, meant that even comparatively well-paid artisans often ended up living in poor conditions especially in Dublin. Worst of all, in every town and city, were the 'lanes' and 'courts'; inadequate space, poor ventilation and, often, open sewers running in channels down the middle of the yard or street, made these dwellings dangerous to health. A fitter and a painter gave separate evidence to Mullingar Rural District Council in 1910 of paying over 2s rent weekly (in each case) for two such rooms, without any 'sanitary

---

19 Drumsna, *Leitrim Observer*, 25 May 1909; 'Dungloe Sanitation' *Derry People & Donegal News*, 10 June 1905.
20 M. Healy, *For the Poor and For the Gentry: Mary Healy Remembers her Life* (Dublin: Geography Publications, 1989), 3.

accommodation'.[21] Another advantage which purpose-built houses (however small and expensive, and whether urban and rural) had over tenements, lanes and the old mud cabins, were purpose-built cooking facilities.

Food

In the new dwellings all over the country – and in some older ones such as the O'Brien house in Lough Gur, County Limerick, where the fireplace took up an entire wall – some variety and even innovation in diet was possible, as it was in new urban artisans' dwellings where small ranges or big fireplaces were provided. The tenement or lane dweller had to coax cooking heat out of tiny fireplaces originally designed for bedrooms or stables, which explains the popularity of slow-simmered one-pot dishes like coddle (layered potato, bacon and onion) and oxtail stew in towns. Short-lived intense heat could also be used to fry the cheap by-products of pig processing – rashers, sausages, blood puddings and all kinds of offal (each town had its own preferences) – or to boil water for tea, but the longer-lasting intense heat needed to bake bread on the fire was usually not feasible. People's diet therefore depended not only on what was locally available, affordable and accessible, but on what could be cooked and stored. Before refrigeration, food could not be stored anywhere without attracting mice or worse. Flour and meal taken from bins in houses (mainly rural) that had room for them had to be sifted carefully for vermin. The urban woman of the house, particularly if she was in poor accommodation, provisioned her family from day to day on a 'just-in-time' basis. A nearby grocer who would sell small quantities of food was vital.[22]

Rural diet even among the very poor was not only more nutritious, it was also safer; cows' milk, if consumed, had a shorter distance to travel and was not subject to as much environmental contamination. The diet of rural people, based as it was around locally-grown and reared foodstuffs – potatoes, oatmeal, soda bread, eggs, cabbage, buttermilk and butter, with variations depending on locale (seafood, river fish) was better than it had ever been before, because it was more guaranteed and, at this period, more varied. Tea,

---

21 'Houses for the Artizans' *Westmeath Examiner*, 15 June 1910.

22 M. Carbery, *The Farm by Lough Gur* (London, 1937: new edition, Cork: Mercier Press, 1973), 20–1; on the history of Irish food generally, L. Clarkson and E. M. Crawford, *Feast and Famine: A History of Food and Nutrition in Ireland 1500–1920* (Oxford University Press, 2001), 88–110; R. Sexton, *A Little History of Irish Food* (Dublin: Gill & Macmillan, 1988); on food storage, C. Kinmonth, *Country Furniture*; K. Kearns, *Dublin Tenement Life*; Clear, *Social Change*, 145–49.

which had come into the diet of most people on the island by the 1890s, is now thought to contain valuable anti-oxidants, and the shop-bought white bread which alarmed contemporaries was usually bought only as a treat and could hardly have undermined this excellent diet.[23]

Retailing and advertising were not the only influences on dietary change; some very good counsel came from the Women's National Health Association, the Department of Agriculture and Technical Instruction and various other bodies who ran cookery classes and demonstrations, eagerly availed of by both country- and towns-women, in the early years of the twentieth century. The language of the reformers was respectful, practical and strongly rooted in the material culture of the people it addressed. Josephine Redington, Head Teacher in the Irish Training School of Domestic Economy in Dublin, drew praise from newspapers, bishops and domestic economy authorities from Belfast to Brooklyn for her very practical and widely-sold *Economic Cookery Book* which was published in 1905. All the recipes in it, and in Kathleen Ferguson's popular two-penny pamphlet published two years earlier, could be cooked or baked on the open fire; all foodstuffs were available locally.[24]

The emphasis in these books was not just on nutrition but also on hygiene; public health was now more than ever a burning social concern.

Health

People's health in Ireland between the Land War and the Great War got worse before it got better. The national rate of illness fell, from 13 per 1,000 in 1861 to 7 in 1911, but sickness became, first more, then less lethal; Ireland's overall death rate in 1885 was 18.4 per 1,000; it rose to 19.6 in 1900, before falling again to 17.1 in 1910 and to 16.3 in 1914.[25] Nineteenth-century improvements in

---

23 On tea, see Ó Gráda, *Ireland: Economic History*, 236–54; M. Kelly, 'Down Memory Lane: The Tea Travellers' *Cathair na Mart: Journal of the Westport Historical Society*, 15 (1995), 66–69.

24 J. Bourke, 'The Health Caravan: Domestic Education and Female Labor in Rural Ireland' *Eire-Ireland* 24 (1989), 21–38; J. Redington, *The Economic Cookery Book* (Dublin: M.H. Gill, 1905) 2nd edn.; K. Ferguson, *Lessons in Cookery and Housewifery* (Dublin: Leabhairíní na Seamróige, 1900).

25 All the ensuing information on death and sickness rates is taken from the following: *22nd detailed Annual Report of the Registrar-General for Ireland 1885* (Dublin, 1886), 9–15; *28th Detailed Annual Report of the Registrar-General for Ireland 1891* (Dublin, 1892), 9–11; *31st Detailed.......1894 (1895)*, 812, 169; *37th Detailed.....1900* (1901), 7–15; *47th Detailed......1910* (1911), xii–xxx; 142–4; *51st Annual Detailed....1914* (1915), xii–xxxix. Specific references will be given below for sickness rates, 1891 and 1911, and for maternal and infant mortality below.

the care of the sick – the Medical Charities Act of 1851 which established dispensaries, and the opening up of workhouse infirmaries to the general public ten years later – were reinforced by several pieces of preventative legislation including the Public Health Act of 1874. Registration of births and deaths from 1865 focused attention on patterns of death and disease. The take-up of smallpox vaccination from 1858 on was almost universal, cholera was in retreat, and typhoid and typhus (though transmission of the latter would not be understood till the early twentieth century) were more effectively identified and isolated than before, and killed fewer people.[26] However, whooping-cough remained dangerous right up to 1914; 1,735 people died of it in 1864, and 1,297 in 1910, in a much smaller population. Annual deaths from scarlatina only fell below the thousand in the late 1880s, and below 500 at the dawn of the twentieth century. On the other hand there were only 45 deaths from typhus in 1914. The big epidemic-like killers at this stage were pneumonia, bronchitis (it killed 6,009 in 1914 with an annual average of 7,329 for the years 1904–1913) and tuberculosis, which abated somewhat from 1910; there were 9,069 deaths from it in 1914, compared to a high point of over 12,000 at the end of the nineteenth century.

As a general rule, the less 'developed' and more 'rural' a place was, the lower its sickness and death-rate. In 1885, Leinster's death-rate was 20.2 per 1,000, compared to Munster's 17.7, Ulster's 17.6, and Connacht's far lower 13. Four of the five Connacht counties, Mayo, Galway, Leitrim and Sligo, had the lowest mortality rates in the country in this year of land agitation and periodic distress, as did Cavan. Connacht and Ulster (despite Belfast and Derry) were the two least urbanised provinces throughout this period, and if we turn from death-rates to the incidence of sickness, Ulster (rural) and Connacht, in 1891 and again in 1911, accounted for 17 out of the 20 Superintendent Registrars' Districts where sickness was lowest (between 3.4 and 4.8 per 1,000 in 1891, between 2.2 and 4 in 1911 – compared to an average of 13.4 (1891) and 10.7 per 1,000 (1911) in districts where it was highest).[27]

---

26 General works on the history of Irish health are E. Malcolm and G. Jones (eds) *Medicine, Disease and the State in Ireland 1650–1930* (Cork: Cork University Press, 1999); T. Farmar, *Patients, Potions and Physicians: A Social History of Medicine in Ireland* (Dublin: A & A Farmar, 2004); J. Robins, *The Miasma: Epidemic and Panic in Nineteenth-century Ireland* (Dublin: IPA, 1995); Clear, *Social Change*, 90–107; L. Carroll, *In the Fever King's Preserves: Sir Charles Cameron and the Dublin Slums* (Dublin: A & A Farmar, 2011) is useful for Dublin.

27 *Census of Ireland 1891: General Report, Tables of Sickness in Poor Law Superintendent Registrars' Districts 1891* (Dublin, 1892), 30; *Census of Ireland 1911 General Report*, xxiv, and Table 77, 136–7.

This association of rurality with health is confirmed by the death-rates of 1885: Dublin (city and county) and Antrim (including Belfast) had the highest (27.4 and 22.4 per 1,000 respectively) followed by Waterford (including the city) and Limerick (likewise) at just over 19 in both cases. In this year, Connacht had a consistently lower mortality rate for nearly every 'zymotic' (i.e. contagious) disease than the other three provinces – its death-rate from scarlatina, for example, stood at 3.5 per 1,000 compared to Leinster's and Ulster's 19.3 and 19.8 and Munster's 39.5. A notable exception for Connacht was 'fever' (most likely typhus), where the death rate at 30.1 exceeded that of Ulster at 23.4, but was lower than that for Leinster and Munster (both over 35). Jumping a decade to 1895, the national death-rate was 18.2 per 1,000; Leinster was highest at 20.1, Connacht lowest at 14.8. The situation in Connacht, it will be noted, had worsened somewhat over the intervening years, while Leinster had not improved. The counties (as opposed to provinces) with the lowest death-rates were Roscommon (13.8 per 1,000), Donegal (14), Kerry (14) and Cavan again (14.2). Dublin and Antrim still had the highest death-rate, though each was lower than they had been a decade earlier – Dublin's death-rate was now 23.4 and Antrim's (including Belfast) 21.8. Carlow and Wexford were hot on their heels. In 1914, however, when the national death-rate had fallen to 16.3 per 1,000, Connacht, while it still had the lowest mortality of all, was not that much lower than the national average at 13.6, and Leinster was not markedly higher at 17.7 – Ulster was 16.8, and Munster 15.4. In this year, Mayo and Kerry (12.8) and Roscommon and Clare (both 13.2) were the least lethal places, while Dublin, Belfast, Limerick (including the city) and Monaghan were the most – Dublin's death-rate was 23.7 per 1,000, Belfast's 18.3, while Limerick and Monaghan tied at 17.5. Dublin was indeed the most unhealthy city on the island, even compared to its closest rival, Belfast.

The story of tuberculosis and the efforts taken to defeat it has been well-told elsewhere, but throughout the period patterns of deaths from the disease bear out the national mortality patterns; first Leinster, then Munster, then Ulster – with the western province bringing up the rear, at about two-thirds Ulster's rate. Tuberculosis was most easily transmitted in dry and dusty urban environments. Connacht's overall rurality (and perhaps its chronic dampness) offered some protection, though numbers were by no means infinitesimal there.[28]

---

28 G. Jones, *Captain of All These Men of Death: The History of Tuberculosis in Nineteenth and Twentieth-century Ireland* (Amsterdam: Rodopi, 2001). Tuberculosis figures taken from *37th Registrar-General Report 1900*, 14–15.

From the 1880s and 1890s on, Irish people were brought together more regularly and more often than ever before in workplaces, for buying and selling, for worship, for education, in leisure and other organisations. Railways – both 'national' and 'light' – and the bicycle, shortened the distances between people and places. For germs and disease-causing bacteria, this was one extended bank holiday excursion. No part of the country was exempt, and the apparent 'levelling out' of the national death rate in 1914 – its slight rise in Connacht and its fall in Leinster – is one of the surest indications of the gradual economic and social integration of the entire country over this period.

However, the story of health versus sickness and survival versus death cannot be reduced to 'rural-primitive good' compared to 'urban-modern bad'. Some conditions were worse in less 'developed' areas. Typhus ceased to be a major killer, but was never wiped out in Connacht until the 1940s. In the early twentieth century the death of mothers in childbirth was connected to rurality. By 1900 the Irish Registrar-General, in common with public health administrators all over the western world, had begun to pay attention to maternal death, and in that year the overall Irish maternal mortality rate was calculated at 6.4 per 1,000 births, compared to an average of 6.6 per year for the five years 1895–99. Thereafter it fell (never to below 5.6) and rose, averaging 6.09 per 1,000 births per year for the decade 1904–1913. This made maternal mortality in Ireland worse than in England and Wales (where it stood at 4.8 in 1900 and 4.1 in 1914) but around the same as in Belgium. In all countries where records were kept, regardless of the extent of medical development, the big childbirth killer, puerperal sepsis, remained deadly and unpredictable up to the late 1930s.[29] However, in late nineteenth and early twentieth-century Ireland, between 65 per cent and 70 per cent of all maternal deaths were from causes other than puerperal sepsis: haemorrhage, placenta praevia and toxaemia of pregnancy were the major killers. Mayo, the county that had the second lowest death-rate in Ireland in 1910, had more mothers dying in childbirth per head of the population in 1914 than either dirty Dublin, busy Belfast or lethal Limerick.[30] Proximity to medical expertise and intervention, therefore, played some role in safeguarding mothers, and women readily availed of such services whenever they could. The Dublin and Belfast maternity hospitals were

---

29 1900 maternal mortality, *37th Registrar General Report 1900*, 14; international figures, I. Loudon, *Death in Childbirth: An International Study of Maternal Care and Maternal Treatment* (Oxford University Press, 1992), see especially appendices, 543 (UK) and 557–8 (Belgium).

30 *51st Registrar General Report 1914*, Table XIII, xxxv, xxxvi; table at 141, deaths from several causes in four provinces and counties of Ireland.

used by city women while their medical students and midwives helped with home deliveries. Women giving birth, wherever they lived, were increasingly anxious to prevent things going wrong; when Blasket Island dweller Peig Sayers was expecting her first child in the 1890s, she went home to her own mother on the mainland, so that a priest or doctor could be sent for if needed. Luckily all went well, and Peig's first-born was delivered by a local woman, Neill Pheig. She was a traditional attendant or 'handywoman' rather than a trained midwife, but she would have sent for a doctor had the need arisen. In the dispensary district of Finnea, County Longford in 1905–1906 only 35 out of 71 births were attended by a doctor or midwife – the others were managed by handywomen. The handywoman was barely legal, but she sometimes had some rudimentary medical knowledge; in any case, she was often the only birth attendant available.[31]

The patterns of the other preventable death, infant mortality, fit more with general regional trends, although it was only in the early twentieth century that separate statistics for these deaths were collected at all. Proximity of skilled medical attention seems to have made little difference to babies in their first year of life. The national rate of infant mortality was 87.3 per 1,000 births in 1914; Dublin, and Belfast and Antrim (the last two reckoned together) had the highest rates, at 143.2 and 128 respectively, followed by Waterford (county and city) at 100, Belfast and Down (together) at 98.4, Limerick county and city at 98.2. Roscommon was the safest place to spend one's first year, with an infant mortality rate of 37.7. Cavan was next best at 40.4, followed by Leitrim at 41.9. These were also the three counties in which the largest proportion of the population was engaged in agriculture, in 1911. (Could it be that it was not just rurality, but more specifically, agriculture, that protected babies? Neither of these three counties had a predominance of big farms, so wealth was not the decisive factor in infant survival.)[32] Then (as still, sadly, in some parts of the world), rapid dehydration brought on by diarrhoea and vomiting was the major baby-killer. Urban mothers who weaned their babies off the breast were at the mercy of milk suppliers – rural milk was closer at hand and less likely to be contaminated – but even the best-quality urban milk

31 Peig Sayers, *Peig* (An Daingean: Eagrán An Sagart, 1998), 143; on Finea, 'Finea Dispensary District' *Longford Leader*, 14 April 1906. On handywomen, Robins, *Nursing*, 14–15, takes rather a negative view.
32 *51st Registrar General 1914* report, xxxix–xl; on infant mortality in Britain but also containing valuable information on France, D. Dwork, *War is Good for Babies and Young Children: A History of the Infant and Child Welfare Movement in England 1891–1918* (London: Tavistock, 1987).

was hard to keep clean and to warm properly, and actually getting it into the baby via vessels that could not be boiled was beset with risks. Everywhere in Europe, summer brought a spike in the urban infant mortality rate as disease-bearing flies landed on milk and Ireland was no exception. The most careful mother was powerless under these circumstances. Flies were also plentiful in agricultural areas, but they were less likely to be carrying disease. The family and the family's animals, though they were usually by this stage not sharing accommodation, were probably immune to one another's germs.

Conclusion

Social change is uneven, and the preceding exploration has failed if it has portrayed Ireland between the Land War and the First World War as an ever-brightening landscape of opportunity and social amelioration. Even to suggest that every improvement came at a cost is a mis-statement, because not every change was necessarily beneficial – tuberculosis was no great improvement on smallpox (which still surfaced occasionally), jackets were no warmer than shawls, and even slate, all other things being equal (solid floors, walls and chimneys) is no better than thatch. Undoubted changes for the better were the gradual provision of clean water and sewerage facilities in towns, and the sound and practical dietary advice provided by various government and non-governmental agencies, but these were intended to counteract the disadvantages of modernisation – the urban clustering of population, and the availability of inferior bought foodstuffs. However, medical expertise played some part in combatting disease, raising awareness about it, and alleviating suffering, and maternal survival in childbirth was likeliest where medical facilities were close at hand.

Modern living, as well as being somewhat safer for women, was also perhaps a bit more interesting and, indeed, demanding for females of all ages and conditions. These years saw the beginning of what would become an irreversible emergence of girls and women from lifelong domesticity, even if this emergence was only for five or ten years. Girls as well as boys were compelled to attend school for their childhood years from 1892 on, but also, as we have seen, significant numbers of women were trickling into non-domestic occupations. Furthermore, a minority were beginning to participate in cultural, and nationalist and unionist organisations.[33] One group of women

---

33 A discussion of women in public life is beyond the scope of this chapter; comprehensive accounts of the Ladies Land League (1881–82), the Irish Women's Suffrage and Local Government Association (1876–1918), Inghinidhe na hEireann (Daughters of Ireland)

forsook domesticity entirely; nuns, or female religious. Their numbers grew by 63.5 per cent between 1881 and 1911, when the number of ordained and professed men rose by a comparatively low 7 per cent. Nearly all women who entered convents in these years worked energetically in the fields of education, health care and institution administration. These exemplars of female authority and expertise, who lived independently of everyday male dominance, were, of course, silent in the public arena – they neither lobbied nor campaigned. They were, however, acutely aware of the changing world they lived in, and their insistence, in all their institutions and projects, on cleanliness, discipline and strict adherence to timetables, was as modern as it was monastic.[34]

Lack of appropriate anxiety about timetables was becoming unacceptable to the point of being seen as hilarious in these years, which was why Percy French's ballad on the West Clare Railway in 1901 was successful to the point that the railway company sued him. The West Clare was one of the light railways set up by constructive unionism which opened up the west for tourism and commerce. In the song, however, all the humorous scenarios have to do with thwarted leisure or the frustration of those working in the leisure industry – tired town-workers are left sitting in the train for an hour in the station waiting for an excursion, a parcel for a shopkeeper or lodging-house keeper goes astray. There is even indignation in one verse because the excursionists are delayed in a siding, to give priority to a goods or cargo train.[35] Transport was for pleasure as well as business: 'Three and a half hours at the seaside

from 1900, and the participation of women in the Gaelic League, Sinn Féin and other organizations can be found in Margaret Ward, *Unmanageable Revolutionaries: Women and Irish Nationalism* (Dingle: Brandon Press, 1982), Rosemary Cullen Owens, *Smashing Times: A History of the Irish Women's Suffrage Movement 1889–1922* (Dublin: Attic Press, 1984), and Diane Urquhart, *Women in Ulster Politics 1890–1940* (Dublin: Irish Academic Press, 2000).

34 The main authorities on Irish nuns, or female religious, are T. Fahey, 'Nuns in the Catholic Church in Ireland in the Nineteenth Century', in M. Cullen (ed.) *Girls Don't Do Honours: Irish Women in Education in the 19th and 20th Centuries* (Dublin: Women's Education Bureau, 1987), 7–29; C. Clear, *Nuns in Nineteenth-century Ireland* (Dublin: Gill & Macmillan, 1987) and M. P. Magray, *The Transforming Power of the Nuns: Women, Religion and Cultural Change in Ireland 1750–1900* (Oxford University Press, 1998). The figures on the increase in the numbers of religious are taken from *Census of Ireland* 1881 General Report, Table 18, 108–9, and *Census of Ireland* 1911, General Report, Table 19, 7–8.

35 'Says the guard back her down in the siding / There's a goods from Kilrush coming in.'; P. French, *Prose, Poems and Parodies of Percy French* (Dublin: Talbot Press, 1973), 'Lay on the Wild West Clare'; also known as 'Are You Right There Michael'. William Percy French (1854–1920) was an Inspector of Drains, watercolorist and ballad-maker from Roscommon. James N. Healy, *Percy French and His Songs* (Cork: Mercier Press, 1966). On railways, J. J. Lee, 'Railways in the Irish Economy', in L. M. Cullen (ed.) *The Formation of the Irish Economy* (Cork: Mercier Press, 1976), 77–88.

for 8d!' promised the Tralee and Dingle Light Railway Company's Saturday afternoon excursion to Castlegregory in September 1896. New working patterns, and possibly universal schooling, promoted the idea of 'time off' for increasing numbers of people; wages in cash rather than kind facilitated this kind of leisure. The bicycle, so important for postmen, policemen and nurses in their daily work, was also used for pleasure; from the 1890s, cycling clubs everywhere from Tyrone to Tralee, from Sligo to Wexford, filled in the free time of people from all social classes. Although task-orientation did, of necessity, prevail on the farm, the town had some influence; when Foxford Woollen Mill was up and running in the 1890s, farm workers in the surrounding north Mayo countryside came to align their stopping and starting with the factory 'buzzer'.[36] The cantankerous Michael J. F. McCarthy in his travels around Ireland at the dawn of the twentieth century sneered at what he saw as the pretension of the 'Castlebar Commercial Quadrille Party' hosting a Christmas dance.[37] Towns like Castlebar had plenty such associations; even the smallest river towns in early-twentieth-century Ireland had rowing clubs for their 'commercials' (as shop assistants and white-collar office employees called themselves), and a plethora of other associations besides.[38] It is debatable whether shops and sugar, tea and trains made life in Ireland 'better' than it had been before, but they certainly made it more interesting and colourful, and brought a great variety of men and women, boys and girls, out of their homes and off their holdings, and into contact with each other.

36 Narration at Foxford Woollen Mills information, Interpretive Centre, Foxford, County Mayo; Tralee and Dingle excursion, *Kerry Sentinel,* September 5 1896; B. Griffin, *Cycling in Victorian Ireland* (Dublin: Nonsuch, 2006), 33–101 and *passim.*
37 M. J. F. McCarthy, *Priests and People in Ireland* (London: Hodder & Stoughton, 1902), 156–7.
38 On rowing clubs, I am indebted to information from Eamonn Colclough of the Irish Amateur Rowing Union.

6

The Irish Literary Revival

ROY FOSTER

Origins

The idea of a 'literary revival' in Ireland at the end of the nineteenth and beginning of the twentieth century gained currency very swiftly at the time, and has been intensively canvassed since. As early as 1894, W. P. Ryan published a book called *The Irish Literary Revival*,[1] marketing the idea before the appearance of most of the seminal works we now associate with the phenomenon. W. B. Yeats was still at the beginning of his career, Douglas Hyde had only just begun to publish, and J. M. Synge and Augusta Gregory were as yet unknown; while the Irish Literary Theatre (later the Abbey) was still five years in the future. In 1902 the still-unknown Synge analysed the 'new Irish intellectual movement' in a French journal, pinpointing 'a new literature' which had grown up in contradistinction to William Carleton and the writers of the mid-nineteenth century, and emphasizing the importance of Yeats's poetry and the productions of the new dramatic movement.[2] The Revival continued to be analysed, commented upon and historicised even as it developed, in books such as Ernest Boyd's *Ireland's Literary Renaissance* (1916).[3] But the most influential act of canonisation came when Yeats defined the idea of a literary renaissance that was a political as well as a cultural phenomenon in his speech accepting the Nobel Prize in 1923.

> The modern literature of Ireland, and indeed all that stir of thought which prepared for the Anglo-Irish War, began when Parnell fell from power in 1891.

1 W. P. Ryan, *The Irish Literary Revival: Its History, Pioneers and Possibilities* (privately printed, London, 1894; reprinted by Lemma Publishing, New York, 1976).
2 'Le Mouvement Intellectuel Irlandais', in *L'Européen*, 31 May 1902; reprinted (translated by Michael Egan) in D. Kiberd and P. J. Matthews (eds.), *Handbook of the Irish Revival: An Anthology of Irish Cultural and Political Writings 1891–1922* (Dublin: Abbey Theatre Press, 2015), 68–72.
3 References below are to the expanded version published in London and New York in 1922.

A disillusioned and embittered Ireland turned from parliamentary politics; an event was conceived; and the race began, as I think, to be troubled by that event's long gestation.[4]

This influential reading not only elides the record of Irish constitutional nationalism between 1891 and 1916, but begs a large question of chronology; much of the groundwork for the Irish Literary Revival was undertaken in the 1870s and 1880s. Yeats's interpretation was part of an enterprise of reclamation, whereby he was placing himself and his colleagues (particularly J. M. Synge and Augusta Gregory) firmly in the mainstream of the upheaval which had brought about a radicalised nationalism and then partial independence for Ireland a year or so before.[5]

And there were other carefully-promoted agendas too. Yeats's laying claim to the Revival took it for granted that the national literature which he and his generation pioneered was no less distinctively Irish for being written in the English language. This was not accepted by everyone, as the influential 'Irish-Irelander' journalist D. P. Moran made clear in 1905, when he announced that all recent 'Irish' literature in the English language, however widely acclaimed, was in no sense national. In Moran's reading of the Literary Revival, Irish nationality had been thoroughly debased by reading English literature and producing cheap imitations.

> A number of writers then arose, headed by Mr W.B. Yeats, who, for the purposes they set themselves to accomplish, lacked every attribute of genius but perseverance.... Practically no-one in Ireland understands Mr Yeats or his school; and one could not, I suggest, say anything harder of literary men. For if a literary man is not appreciated and cannot be understood, of what use is he? He has not served his purpose. The Irish mind, however, was wound down to such a low state that it was fit to be humbugged by such a school.[6]

Moran's contempt therefore stretched not only to Yeats and his associates, but to the corpus of nineteenth-century literature preceding them – which Yeats, as it happened, saw as the necessary seed bed for the innovations nurtured by his own generation.

---

4 W. B. Yeats, *Autobiographies* (London: Macmillan, 1955), 559.
5 See my 'Thinking from Hand to Mouth: Anglo-Irish Literature, Gaelic Nationalism and Irish Politics in the 1890s', in *Paddy and Mr Punch: Connections in Irish and English History* (London: Allen Lane, 1993), 262–80, and 'Yeats at War: Poetic Strategies and Political Reconstruction', in *The Irish Story: Telling Tales and Making it up in Ireland* (London: Allen Lane, 2001), 58–79.
6 'The Battle of Two Civilizations', in *The Philosophy of Irish Ireland* (1905), extracted in Seamus Deane, *The Field Day Anthology of Irish Writing* (Derry: Field Day, 1991), II, 554

Another issue which Yeats skated smoothly over in his Nobel speech was the fact that not only were his colleagues in the dramatic movement, Gregory and Synge, Protestants of the caste often called 'Anglo-Irish'; so were Samuel Ferguson, Standish James O'Grady, Douglas Hyde and several others avatars of the Revival. If the term were extended to include some highly talented Irish novelists working in this era, such as Violet Martin, Edith Somerville and Emily Lawless, the preponderance would be even more striking; but such people are usually placed in a different compartment, often with a brutal emphasis. Aodh de Blacam, an influential Sinn Féin publicist who produced a number of commentaries on Irish literature in the early twentieth century, delivered a judgment on 'Somerville and Ross' (the *nom de plume* of Martin and Somerville) which was, for its time, fairly typical:

> Their stories are popular in England, but are disliked in Ireland, where an image of reckless, empty, foolish ways offends national sentiment and offers nothing to gratify the national taste … In a word, the Somerville and Ross books are the writings of spiritual Nihilists, and it is fitting that the only book of the series which is not comic is a 'realistic' novel, in which a dreadful picture is drawn of a great house dying in madness and despair.[7]

This dismissal suggests that questions of identity and politics lie at the centre of the 'Revival', and that those writers associated with it are generally assumed to have been cultural nationalists, if not political nationalists as well; though with some inspirational figures of Samuel Ferguson and Standish James O'Grady, this raises some awkward questions, since both were firm Unionists. There is also the question, raised by J. W. Foster, of the profuse and lively corpus of fiction by Irish writers in this period, whose work is identified with the Revival in some respects, but not in others. This would apply to Katharine Tynan and Jane Barlow, who moved from writing Revivalist poetry to popular novels and romances.[8]

Nonetheless Yeats's influential historicisation of the Revival set the template for many historical treatments of Ireland's *fin-de-siècle*, and the ensuing period of revolution, though it has not gone uncontested. It owes much to Yeats's determination to inscribe himself, his colleagues, and the Abbey Theatre into the history of their times, as authors of the newly-founded Irish

---

7 *A First Book of Irish Literature, Hiberno-Latin, Gaelic, Anglo-Irish, From the Earliest Times to the Present Day* (Dublin: Talbot, n.d. [1935?]), 225. The novel referred to is *The Big House of Inver* (1925); de Blacam's generalization ignores Somerville and Ross's masterpiece, *The Real Charlotte* (1894).

8 See J. W. Foster, *Irish Novels 1890–1940: New Bearings in Culture and Fiction* (Oxford University Press, 2008).

Free State; but it also reflects the way that questions of political agendas and national identities were woven into Irish literature throughout the nineteenth century, from the era of highly prescriptive 'national tales' produced in the era of the Act of Union and Catholic Emancipation.[9] During the Revival, as in that earlier period, the politics of language, literature and identity lay close to the surface of an intensely articulated literary culture: and so too did sensitive and controversial questions of audience, intention and literary markets. If the label of 'Revival' was intended to imply a return to the glories of ancient Irish bardic literature, there were also other, and much more recent, literary themes being resuscitated as well, and (from Yeats and Synge at least) suggestions of other, exotic, influences from the wider world of 1890s Europe. In 1899, Yeats invoked the 'passionate influence' of *Peer Gynt* and Wagner's *Ring* (together with what Yeats conceived to be 'his mainly Celtic *Parsifal* and *Lohengrin* and *Tristan and Isolde*'), while insisting that the old Irish legends had the superior power of 'revealing the beauty and power of altogether new things'.[10] The currents that flowed into the literary revival of the late nineteenth century were varied, arose from different sources, and did not always mingle smoothly into one continuous stream.

This should not come as a surprise. Literary history does not proceed in a consistent, incremental course, nor by a linear progression; there are saltatory leaps, and developments obscured by anxieties of influence. In Richard Ellmann's words, 'writers move upon other writers not as genial successors, but as violent expropriators, knocking down established boundaries to seize by the force of youth, or of age, what they require; they do not borrow, they override'.[11] However, even while bearing these strictures in mind, it is clear

---

9 See K. Trumpener, *Bardic Nationalism: The Romantic Novel and the British Empire* (Princeton, NJ: Princeton University Press, 1997); I. Ferris, *The Romantic National Tale and the Question of Ireland* (Cambridge University Press, 2002); Claire Connolly, *A Cultural History of the Irish Novel, 1790–1829* (Cambridge University Press, 2011); and my *Words Alone: Yeats and his Inheritances* (Oxford University Press, 2011), ch. 1.

10 A note to his review of 'The Poetry and Stories of Miss Nora Hopper', reprinted in John Eglinton, W. B. Yeats, A. C. Larminie, *Literary Ideals in Ireland* (London: T. Fisher Unwin, 1899), 18–189. Eglinton's silky reply is worth quoting: 'I was not aware, I confess, of the fact which Mr Yeats mentions, that Wagner's dramas are becoming to Germany what the Greek tragedies were to Greece. The crowd of elect persons seated in curiously-devised seats at Bayreauth does not seem very like the whole Athenian democracy thronging into their places of a couple of obols supplied by the State, and witnessing in good faith the deeds of their ancestors... The Greeks were a poetical people, just as the Germans are a musical people, and as the Greek dramas have come down to us without music, so, one fancies, Wagner's music, or fragments of it, will go down to posterity without the words.' Ibid., 24–5.

11 R. Ellmann, *Eminent Domain: Yeats among Wilde, Joyce, Pound, Eliot and Auden* (Oxford University Press, 1967), 3.

that from about 1890 there was an astonishing 'upward curve' in Irish literary and dramatic achievement and influence, much as Isaiah Berlin has described in contemporary Russia.[12] The same image was used by Augustine Birrell, the literary-minded Chief Secretary who arrived at Dublin Castle in 1907:

> Irish literature and the drama, Messrs. Maunsell's list of new Irish publications, and the programme of the Abbey Theatre became to me of far more real significance than the monthly reports of the RIC. The plays of John Synge and Lady Gregory, the poems of Mr Yeats, AE and Dora Sigerson, the pictures of Orpen, Lavery and Henry, the provocative genius of Mr Bernard Shaw, the bewitching pen of Mr George Moore, the penetrative mind of Father Tyrell (the list could easily be prolonged) were by themselves indications of a veritable renaissance – a leap to the front rank of thought and feeling altogether novel.[13]

Part of the 'novelty' lay in the fact that Irish writers consciously chose material, and looked for sources, that would differentiate their themes and style from the metropolitan literary culture of Britain. It is also clear that this built upon scholarly research into medieval Irish poetry and saga literature, developing from the later eighteenth century and was closely related – as in other European countries – to romanticism and nationalism.[14] 'Bardic nationalism' affected the literature of Scotland as well as Ireland from the turn of the century, laying fertile ground for much that followed. From the 1830s, the politics of Irish literature were complicated by sensitive issues of translation, as Irish folk songs and sagas were utilised by anthologists such as James Hardiman and poets like Samuel Ferguson and James Clarence Mangan, as well as by the writers of the *Nation* circle in the 1840s; Yeats was particularly conscious of these predecessors, and worked hard to restore them to the highly politicised canon of Irish literature which he tried to define in the 1890s. But the material which he and his contemporaries plumbed for inspiration in the 1880s and 1890s came from the sagas and traditions first made available through publications such as the *Revue Celtique*, the *Transactions of the Ossianic Society*, the *Proceedings of the Royal Irish Academy*, and O'Curry's *Manners and Customs of the Ancient Irish*; these versions were popularised from the 1860s and 1870s by such works as P. W. Joyce's *Old Celtic Romances* (1875) and Eleanor Hull's editions of the Cuchulain legends. Much the same process had been pioneered

---

12 Isaiah Berlin, *Russian Thinkers* (London: Penguin, 1978).
13 Augustine Birrell, *Things Past Redress* (London: Faber, 1937), quoted in Kiberd and Matthews, *Handbook of the Irish Revival*, 416.
14 See C. O'Halloran, *Golden Ages and Barbarous Nations: Antiquarian Debate and Cultural Politics in Ireland c.1750–1806* (Cork: Cork University Press, 2004).

by nationalistic Finnish writers in the previous generation, exploiting the saga-tales of the *Kalevala* made available by the folklorist Elias Lonnrot – another European example often invoked by Yeats.

However, the real sense of a 'revival' in Ireland, underpinned by a distinctly national sense of an independent literature, is traditionally traced to Standish James O'Grady's popularisations from the 1870s, where the material of 'bardic literature' was re-packaged in the language of reactionary Carlylean romanticism. O'Grady's self-published *History of Ireland: The Heroic Period* in 1878 was followed by a stream of high-octane romantic histories, featuring knightly brotherhoods (the Red Branch, the Fianna), mythic romances like that of Deirdre, the runaway wife of King Conchobar, the tale of the Cattle Raid of Cooley, and above all the all-purpose hero Cuchulainn. This emblematic man of action was described by George Russell in 1899 as a Promethean heroic spirit who could act as 'the redeemer of man';[15] he would go on to inhabit Yeats's mythic play-cycle as an alter ego of the author. Later – courtesy of Patrick Pearse – who took him as the personification of nationalist resistance – the redeemer Cuchulainn would 'stalk through the Post Office' in 1916.

O'Grady's histories have been described as 'fictions',[16] and he would have agreed; in the texts he squarely faced the question of unreliable evidence, discussed different approaches from the annalistic to the anecdotal, and finally opted for his own poetic and visionary strategy. Bardic history, he maintained, was the imaginative record of a nation, before the corrupt and self-serving interpretation put upon it by monastic chroniclers, whom he mocked and derided. His versions operated by means of visionary epiphanies, etched in microscopic detail, and freely airing his own prejudices (against industrialisation, materialism, political trimmers, and above all the Roman Catholic Church). O'Grady's romances are quintessentially high-Victorian in their feudal trappings, deliberate archaism and poetic references. They were none the less crucial for writers such as Yeats, AE, Augusta Gregory, Ella Young, Alice Milligan, and even the sardonic modernist Synge, who while writing poems parodying his colleagues' liking for 'the plumed and skinny Shee [*Sidhe = fairy*]', produced his own version of the Deirdre legend.

O'Grady forecast in 1882 that Irish nationalism would end in 'anarchy and civil war … [and in] a shabby sordid Irish republic, ruled by corrupt politicians and the ignoble rich': his unabashed unionism and scornful anti-clericalism

---

15 Eglinton, Yeats, Larminie, *Literary Ideals*, 51.
16 J. W. Foster, *Fictions of the Irish Revival: A Changeling Art* (Syracuse, NY: Syracuse University Press, 1987), ch. 3.

could be something of an embarrassment to his nationalist acolytes, especially if they were devout Catholics. In his *Story of Ireland* (1893), intended for young readers, he preached that Irish Christianity was marked from the beginning by 'a lack of straightforward, bold and honest dealing, which afterwards became a national vice, so that many of our great saints were also great liars, and fell under the just scorn and contempt of those who had no religion at all but simply preserved the old Pagan abhorrence of falsehood and doubledealing'; monasteries 'perverted' the understanding of the monks and the Book of Kells was 'an appalling monument of misdirected labour'. Pagan Ireland was the repository of decent, manly values and virtues (though he had a weakness for the Normans, whose coming to Ireland O'Grady felt to be a good thing). O'Grady's own politics were thus utterly different from those of most of his acolytes, but his work provided a storehouse to be plundered by the Yeats generation; it is striking how many story-titles transmute directly into the names of Yeats's poems ('A Hosting of the Sidhe', 'The Death of Cuchulain'[17]). And the tradition of a dialogue between St Patrick and the miraculously long-lived Oisin, son of Finn Mac Cumhail of the Fianna, reiterated by P. W. Joyce and many others as well as O'Grady, would be reworked by Yeats into his first landmark volume, *The Wanderings of Oisin*. O'Grady's versions would also inspire Augusta Gregory's influential re-tellings of the sagas, *Cuchulain of Muirtheimne* and *Gods and Fighting Men*, as well as Ella Young's versions for young people, George Russell's visionary stories, and plays by Alice Milligan, Bulmer Hobson and other idealistic young nationalists.

And the message that such writers took from this material was 'national' in a way that O'Grady himself would neither have appreciated nor approved. Addressing the Irish Literary Society in 1893 on 'Nationality and Literature', Yeats insisted that the epic period of Irish pre-history held the secret of a distinct Irish identity. Unlike the anti-modernist O'Grady, his message was one of continuity. Ireland was:

> A young nation with unexhausted material lying within us in our still unexpressed national character, about us in our scenery, and in the clearly marked outlines of our life, and behind us in our multitude of legends. Look at our literature and you will see that we are still in our epic or ballad period. All that is greatest in our literature is based upon legend – upon those tales which are made by no one man, but by the nation itself through a slow process of modification and adaptation, to express its loves and its hates, its likes

---

17 See 'Irish Bardic History' in E. Boyd (ed.), *Standish O'Grady: Selected Essays and Passages* (Dublin: Talbot Press, n.d.), 23–148.

and its dislikes. Our best writers, De Vere, Ferguson, Allingham, Mangan, Davis, O'Grady, are all either ballad or epic writers, and all base their greatest work, if I except a song or two of Mangan's and Allingham's, upon legends and upon the fortunes of the nation. Alone, perhaps, among the nations of Europe we are in our ballad or epic age. The future will put some of our ballads with 'Percy's Reliques' and with the 'border' ballads, and at least one of our epic songs, the 'Conary' of Ferguson, among the simple, primitive poems of the world. Even the 'Spirit of the Nation' belongs to the epic age, for it deals with great National events.[18]

This last remark, invoking the collected writings of Thomas Davis and others of the *Nation* circle in the 1840s, was part of Yeats's deliberate attempt to co-opt nationalist writers of the earlier nineteenth century into a canon of Irish literature which he was determined to define; and to show that the work of the writers of the 'Revival' were bringing to maturity and completion elements of distinctive Irish tradition which had previously existed in potential form only, like an angel within a block of marble. To this end, he devoted much time in the 1880s and 1890s to anthologising the Irish fiction of the early nineteenth century, firmly placing William Carleton as a distinctively Irish writer of genuine national importance and 'rough-hewn power'. Yeats portrayed him as the real historian of peasant Ireland, but there were further attractions too, in the strong vein of Gothic and supernatural imagery which runs through Carleton, and is woven into the complex web of Revival literature. (There were also questions of contested Irish identity here, since Carleton had swerved away from his Catholic faith and been taken up by evangelical Protestants, a subject on which Yeats steered a very careful course indeed.)

Another major theme of 'recovery', inseparable from the notion of literary revival, concerned the literature of folk-tale. This too had its roots in the early nineteenth century, with the collections of Thomas Crofton Croker and William and Francesca Wilde, much exploited by Yeats for his landmark collection *The Celtic Twilight*, a key book for Revivalists. In a sense this was also part of Yeats's energetic attempt to create a canon of authentic Irish literature; folk-tales were part of an 'aristocracy of thought' by which a people might know itself, and define itself against modernity, materialism and cultural colonialism. The early nineteenth-century paths blazed by the Grimms in Germany, Lonnrot in Finland and Walter Scott in Scotland were built into the structure of literary revival in Ireland. In the Irish jurisdiction, however,

18 J. P. Frayne (ed.), *Uncollected Prose by W. B. Yeats*, vol. I (London: Macmillan, 1970), 273.

fairies, at least in Yeats's re-tellings, were very different from the pretty beings conjured up by Arthur Rackham's illustrations for children's books. Crofton Croker had seen fairy legends as receding into insubstantiality 'as knowledge advances'; Yeats and his colleagues were determined to present these supernatural beings as tougher and more resilient customers, engaged in horse-dealing, drinking, smoking, dancing, theft, and various acts of abduction and assassination. In the world of Irish fairies conjured up by Yeats, George Russell and other Revivalists, historical memories of dispossession, invocations of long-ago battles, and memories of invasion also featured large. By implication, the *Sidhe* were not only the distant descendants of ancient god-like beings who had once peopled Ireland (the Tuatha de Danaan); they also suggested the stratagems of an oppressed people, living without the law, and inhabiting a parallel universe to that of the daily world. (This conception has a particular appeal for those Irish Protestants inclined to the occult cosmogony of Emmanuel Swedenborg, such as Yeats and, earlier, Joseph Sheridan Le Fanu.)[19] Irish fairies are also adept at evading the police, and are notably opposed to clerical authority.

The purposes and functions of folk and fairy tales for writers of the Revival were many. Like the saga literature, folk tradition was, in a sense, pre-Christian, and certainly pre-Reformation: it thus provided a forum of Irishness in which those from Protestant backgrounds could affirm a fully national identity, as well as plumbing depths of cultural tradition which was primal, mysterious and thrillingly exotic. Mysticism and esotericism had a particular appeal for members of a declining Protestant Ascendancy, still affected by the afterglow of a different kind of Revival. The eclipsing power of the Protestant elite in Ireland is an important element in the sociology of the Literary Revival; interestingly, W. P. Ryan's early history of the literary movement stressed the self-realisation brought about by the Land War of 1879–81, dealt with elsewhere in this volume, but did not proceed to analysing what this meant for the people behind the now-crumbling demesne walls. Given their slightly *déclassé* Protestant backgrounds, joining (and commandeering) a new cultural movement was important for Gregory, Synge, Hyde and Yeats.[20] The first three could further attest their credentials by their ability to read, write and speak the Irish language. Yeats never mastered this, but in his *Celtic Twilight* essays

---

19 See my *Words Alone*, ch. 3, for a more detailed treatment.
20 For considerations of these issues see J. W. Foster, *Fictions of the Irish Literary Revival*, 59–61, and my 'Protestant Magic: W. B. Yeats and the Spell of Irish History', in *Paddy and Mr Punch*, 212–32.

and stories he did perfect a style which used intonations and phrasing heavily inflected by Irish-language structures. This was a stratagem also used to brilliant effect by Synge; in the hands of Augusta Gregory the creation of a 'Kiltartanese' patois was not universally successful, and in some more maladroit practitioners the results were disastrous. The style spread to embrace a cross-channel Celtic Revivalism, headed in Scotland by the lush verbosity of 'Fiona Macleod', the alter ego of the journalist William Sharp, who wrote highly-charged stories and poems with titles such as *The Winged Destiny* and *Green Fire*. Both Yeats and George Russell temporarily fell for Fiona's charms, before reacting sharply against her.

As the ripples of Revivalism spread further, the circles of weak imitativeness widened into blatantly derivative versifying from now-forgotten writers such as Jane Barlow and Nora Hopper, whose *Ballads in Prose* (1894) and *Under Quicken Boughs* (1896) not only drew heavily from popular legends and Gaelic folklore, but went so far in slavish imitation of Yeats as to begin a poem 'I will arise and go hence to the west / And dig me a grave where the hill-winds call.' The writings of the Revival appealed to an audience in France, assiduously mediated by Yeats's admirer, Henry Davray, in the *Mercure de France*. Revivalist writers had themselves been inspired by the Sorbonne lectures on Celtic mythology given by Henri d'Arbois de Jubainville from 1898, attended by Synge among others, and widely read in published form (*Le cycle mythologique irlandais*, translated into English by Richard Best in 1902).

Other writers of the Revival such as Katharine Tynan, widely read and reviewed at the time (though censured by W. P. Ryan as too much inclined towards 'an English art and standpoint'[21]), are now remembered mainly for their association with Yeats; as George Moore sarcastically remarked to Ernest Boyd when advising him about his history of the Revival, 'all begins in Yeats and all ends in Yeats'.[22] But this is not an adequate definition, for, while Yeats's genius was indubitably stamped onto the products of the Literary Revival, the phenomenon as a whole incorporated and energised spheres of writing, notably in drama and fiction, where the arch-poet's influence was less obvious. Perhaps because of this, Irish novels and plays of this era have been located less securely in the revivalist canon.

---

21 Ryan, *Irish Literary Revival*, 117.
22 George Moore to Ernest Boyd 17 August 1914, Healy Collection, Stanford University; quoted in my *W. B. Yeats, A Life: Volume I, The Apprentice Mage 1865–1914* (Oxford University Press, 1997), xxv.

Culture

If the Revival was about a good deal more than Yeats, however, his formidable gifts as publicist, reviewer and anthologist, none the less helped to package, market and direct the phenomenon. The fact that political controversy rapidly became part of the story, played out in public battles about what constituted a genuinely Irish canon of literature, similarly owed something to Yeats's confrontational style, and his struggles with Sir Charles Gavan Duffy over the direction of the Irish Literary Society and its publishing plans.[23] But it also reflected the fact that central to the Revival was the rediscovery of Irish history, and this was inevitably going to be a contested arena. O'Grady's determination to reinvent 'bardic history' was specifically driven by a desire to contest what he saw as the bigoted versions of Irish history put across by monkish chroniclers and their later interpreters; coming right up to date, it was also – more obscurely – intended to rouse the landlord class to a manly recognition of their duties as leaders of Irish society. This sat uneasily with the Parnellite, nationalist or armchair-Fenian politics subscribed to by several Revivalists. Yeats and other chroniclers of the Revival had to step gingerly around O'Grady's politics, taking refuge in Augusta Gregory's description of him as a 'Fenian Unionist': to be touched by Fenianism was seen as his saving grace.

A similar equivocation was necessary with Samuel Ferguson, who also held nationalism in contempt, while inspiring young nationalists to feats of literary emulation. Significantly, the young Yeats's first major critical essay in 1886 was a subtle attempt to claim Ferguson as a sort of proto-nationalist.[24] It would be followed by a campaign, pursued through anthologising, editing and reviewing, to claim the traditions of Ferguson's contemporaries and rivals, the writers of the Young Ireland generation. Ferguson's own connections to the *Nation* circle helped to make the case, and Yeats was determined to present the enterprise of the Revivalists in the late 1880s as a completion of the Young Ireland project of a half-century before. In this, he was not alone. The Literary Revival began, in a sense, with the establishment of literary circles and reading-groups in the 1880s that were consciously inspired by the Young Irelanders, and that took their name when they formed a 'Young Ireland

23 See my *Apprentice Mage*, ch. 5.
24 First published in *Irish Fireside*, 19 October 1886, and extended for the *Review* in November.

League' in 1891.[25] In his Introduction to *Representative Irish Tales*, written in 1891, Yeats anticipated Synge's 1902 analysis and the famous 'long gestation' trope of his own Nobel speech, by declaring 'We are preparing likely enough for a new Irish literary movement – like that of '48 – that will show itself at the first lull in this storm of politics.' But this sense was well-established long before the 'storm' of the Parnell split. Writing about Ferguson in 1886, and invoking the spirit of the early nineteenth century, the young Yeats decried 'the professorial classes' and 'the shoddy society of "West Britonism"', calling instead to 'those young men clustered here and there throughout our land, whom the emotion of patriotism has lifted into that world of selfless passion in which heroic deeds are possible and heroic poetry credible'.[26] If the poetry of the Revival was – as Matthew Campbell has suggested – trying to escape the 'law and order' of Victorian English verse, it often gestured towards opposing other forms of 'law and order' too.[27]

Poems and Ballads of Young Ireland (1888), an anthology largely masterminded by Yeats, was described by Ernest Boyd as 'the first offering of the Irish Literary Revival' and therefore 'a historical document'.[28] Most of the contributors (such as T. W. Rolleston and John Todhunter) are now forgotten but Yeats's four poems, headed by 'The Stolen Child' set the tone for Revivalist sensibility. Significantly, the book was dedicated to John O'Leary and the Young Ireland Societies. The circles of young men and women addressed by Yeats here, and in his Ferguson essay, included highly politicised figures such as Arthur Griffith and his friend William Rooney, whose poetry was firmly modelled on Thomas Davis lines; in literary terms, there was not much shock of the new about it. The same was true of the Southwark Literary Society in London, the progenitor of the much higher-profile Irish Literary Society. Ryan's 1894 study claimed the Southwark group as the germ and nucleus of the literary revival (though this was partly a vain attempt to keep Yeats in his place). The poetry and prose that came out of Southwark was uniformly derivative, and its active members have survived only as minor footnotes to the cultural and social history of Irish communities in Britain. Nonetheless, they included a striking number of influential journalists, and it is unlikely that the Revival would have taken root and flourished in the way it did without the power of the periodical press, and

---

25 See ch 4, 'Literary Fenianism and Fenian Faction', in M. J. Kelly, *The Fenian Ideal and Irish Nationalism 1882–1916* (Woodstock, 2006), 96–129. For the original Young Ireland movement see the chapter by Patrick Geoghegan in volume 3.
26 Frayne, *Uncollected Prose*, vol. I, 104.
27 M. Campbell, *Irish Poetry under the Union, 1801–1924* (Cambridge University Press, 2013), 22.
28 Ryan, *Ireland's Literary Renaissance*, 95.

the important influence wielded therein by people with Irish backgrounds, identifications and interests. (This was a syndrome established long before, as the novels of Thackeray bear witness.[29]) This is too easily forgotten. Maud Gonne's place in the Revival is generally identified as the inspiration for Yeats's most famous love poems of the era, consummately using tropes and inversions resonant of Gaelic literature and blending them with eighteen-ninetyish yearning: 'The White Birds', for instance, gestures towards astrology, twilight, sensual symbolism, the legendary Ireland of the Tuatha de Danaan, and the Irish folk tale of the Children of Lir, transformed into swans and condemned to wander the waters of Ireland.

> I would that we were, my beloved, white birds on the foam of the sea!
> We tire of the flame of the meteor, before it can fade and flee;
> And the flame of the blue star of twilight, hung low on the rim of the sky,
> Has awaked in our hearts, my beloved, a sadness that may not die.
>
> A weariness comes from those dreamers, dew-dabbled, the lily and rose;
> Ah, dream not of them, my beloved, the flame of the meteor that goes,
> Or the flame of the blue star that lingers hung low in the fall of the dew:
> For I would we were changed to white birds on the wandering foam: I and you!
>
> I am haunted by numberless islands, and many a Danaan shore,
> Where Time would surely forget us, and Sorrow come near us no more;
> Soon far from the rose and the lily and fret of the flames would we be,
> Were we only white birds, my beloved, buoyed out on the foam of the sea!

But Gonne was much more than a mystic muse. A committed nationalist and feminist, she played an equally important role as a journalist, editor and financial supporter of papers such as *L'Irlande Libre* and *United Irishman*.[30] And the products of the Revival were put on the British market by editors such as W. E. Henley of the *National Observer* and T. P. Gill of the Irish *Daily Express*, and useful publishing contacts such as Ernest Rhys and T. Fisher Unwin: often, inevitably, lined up by Yeats. Katharine Tynan's later belief that the Revival 'was a pure movement, in which money and worldly success were never dreamt of', should be taken with a large grain of salt.[31] It was in many ways a hard-headed enterprise.[32]

29 See F. Cullen and R. F. Foster (eds.), *Conquering England: Ireland in Victorian London* (London: National Portrait Gallery, 2005).
30 See K. Steele, *Women, Press and Politics during the Irish Revival* (Syracuse, NY: Syracuse University Press, 2007) and her edition of *Maud Gonne, Nationalist Writings 1895–1946* (Dublin: Irish Academic Press, 2004).
31 K. Tynan, *The Wandering Years* (London: Constable, 1922), 287.
32 J. M. Chaudhury, *Yeats, the Irish Literary Revival and the Politics of Print* (Cork: Cork University Press, 2001).

None the less, the use of myth, saga and fairytale for the purposes of Celtic Revivalism ran the dangers of invoking notions of the Celt, immortalised in Matthew Arnold's 'The Study of Celtic Literature'. Though intended as an argument for the importance of instituting chairs of Celtic literature in British universities, this essay is more influentially remembered as a characterisation of Celtic character as both necessary to a full British identity, and incapable of separate and independent development (in other words, self-government).

> Balance, measure and patience, these are the eternal conditions, even sup-
> posing the happiest temperament to start with, of high success; and balance,
> measure and patience are just what the Celt has never had. Even in the world
> of spiritual creation, he has never, in spite of his admirable gifts of quick
> perception and warm emotion, succeeded perfectly, because he never has
> had steadiness, patience, sanity enough to comply with the conditions under
> which alone can expression be perfectly given to the finest perceptions and
> emotions. The Greek has the same perceptive, emotional temperament as
> the Celt; but he adds to this temperament the sense of *measure*, hence his
> admirable success in the plastic arts, in which the Celtic genius, with its chaf-
> ing against the despotism of fact, its perpetual straining after mere emotion,
> has accomplished nothing.[33]

The writers of the Revival were anxious to dispute this, which is one rea-
son why they constantly compared the qualities and achievements of ancient Ireland to those of the Greeks, and asserted the manliness, independence, strength and economy of Irish style; Yeats liked to add, approvingly, the Irish propensity for strong 'hatred', while journalists such as D. P. Moran reversed Arnold's conclusion by declaring that the Gael must be 'the element that absorbs'. Literary revivalism was projected into national *révanchisme* in more ways than one. At the same time, many Revivalists unconsciously echoed Arnoldian tropes, while determined to politicise the Celtic aesthetic. The 1916 revolutionary leader, Thomas MacDonagh, a poet who owed much to Yeats, declared in *Literature in Ireland* (published after his execution) that there was a specifically 'Irish mode' of verse, stemming from 'a people to whom the ideal, the spiritual, the mystic are the true'.[34] When the issue of language revival was added in, this complicated matters further.

Lip service was paid to the desirability of writing in the Irish language as well as speaking it, but the Literary Revival (like much of the long-gestated

---

33 Matthew Arnold, *On The Study of Celtic Literature and Other Essays* (London: 1910), 82.
    The original essay was published in 1867.
34 See S. Deane's Introduction to 'Poetry 1890–1930' in Deane et al. (eds.), *The Field Day Anthology of Irish Writing*, II (Derry: Field Day Publications, 1991), 720–3.

Irish revolution) happened in English. The flexibility, originality and vigour of much Revivalist writing, none the less, came out of a complex world of language shift, characterising Irish writing in English since the late eighteenth century: 'an unsettlingly creative place', in Matthew Campbell's phrase.[35] The Revival generation both recognised the phenomenon, and made it new. Douglas Hyde's strikingly simple and resonant translations of Irish songs and stories, often printed with the Irish-language version on a facing page, became essential guidebooks for the Revival generation. Moreover, his 1892 lecture 'The Necessity for de-Anglicising Ireland', arguing for reviving the Irish language and adopting Gaelic modes of dress as well as address, carried a necessarily political implication whether he wanted it to or not. In Terence Brown's opinion, 'in the contradictions and confusion of its argument, this lecture suggests how problematic a thing it was for a member of the Protestant Anglo-Irish social caste to espouse the cause of Irish Ireland, since a key element of that movement's ideology was the Catholicism of the Irish people and the inauthenticity of the Protestant Irish'.[36]

Politics

The political dimensions of the revival were often implicit and metaphorical rather than explicitly polemical, but they lurked in the background; for instance, his/her political unionism was one of the factors that alienated Yeats and Russell from William Sharp/Fiona Macleod. Throughout the 1890s Yeats was involved in fringe Fenian activity, principally through Maud Gonne, and poems such as 'Red Hanrahan's Song About Ireland' (which remained her favourite among his works) openly reflect this. It is fair to say, none the less, that the cultural energy of this period also reflected expectations of the political future that were not necessarily separatist (as with Yeats) nor millennial (as with Russell); the idea of cultural independence, a distinctive Irish literature and even revival of the Irish language, were all compatible with expectations of a Home Rule future. The fiction of the period has been under-attended until recently.[37] However, novels such as Canon Sheehan's *My New Curate*, George Moore's *A Drama in Muslin*, Katharine Cecil Thurston's *The Fly on the Wheel*, and even Daniel Corkery's *The Threshold of Quiet* generally suggest a world where the Edwardian Irish Catholic bourgeoisie are expecting to come

---

35 Campbell, *Irish Poetry under the Union*, p. 13.

36 'Cultural Nationalism 1880–1930', in Deane et al. (eds.), *Field Day Anthology*, II, 517.

37 J. W. Foster, *Fictions of the Irish Literary Revival* and *Irish Novels 1890–1940*.

into their own, rather than intimations of a future revolution. (This would change after the paramilitary confrontations from 1912, a change reflected in Sheehan's final novel *The Graves of Kilnamorna* in 1915.) The concerns of the Revival as generally conceived were more closely attended to in George Moore's landmark short story collection, *The Untilled Field* (1903) and his novel about a recalcitrant Catholic priest, *The Lake* (1905); the influence of his fictionalised autobiographical writings on the young James Joyce was also notable. However, Moore would later abandon the Revival in a characteristic act of repudiation, and none of his other fictions of this era dealt with Irish themes. The George Moore who wrote *Esther Waters, A Mummer's Wife,* and *The Brook Kerith* is grouped with Francophile English realists and proto-modernists rather than the Irish Literary Revival. Logical or not, this indicates the political implications behind the concept.

Those implications would be more clearly played out in another forum, the theatrical stage. The transfer of idealistic energy from politics into culture, which Yeats described as beginning with Parnell's death in 1891, did not affect drama for another decade – beginning with a key conversation on a wet day in County Galway, described long afterwards by Augusta Gregory.

> On one of those days in Duras in 1898, Mr Edward Martyn, my neighbour, came to see the Count [de Basterot], bringing with him Mr Yeats, whom I did not know then very well, though I cared for his work very much and had already, through his directions, been gathering folklore. They had lunch with us, but it was a wet day, and we could not go out. After a while I thought the Count wanted to talk to Mr Martyn alone so I took Mr Yeats to the office … We sat there through that wet afternoon, and though I had never been at all interested in theatre, our talk turned on plays. Mr Martyn had written two, *The Heather Field* and *Maeve*. They had been offered to London managers and now he thought of trying to have them produced in Germany where there seemed to be more room for new drama than in England. I said it was a pity we had no Irish theatre where such plays could be given. Mr Yeats said that had always been a dream of his but he had of late thought it an impossible one, for it could not at first pay its way, and there was no money to be found for such a thing in Ireland. We went on talking about it, and things seemed to grow possible as we talked, and before the end of the afternoon we had made our plan.[38]

Like all canonical versions of foundational myths, this contains inaccuracies. The plan was made in the summer of 1897 (by 1898 Augusta Gregory knew Yeats very well indeed). Further recollections of the origins of the Irish

---

38 *Our Irish Theatre* (1913), quoted in Kiberd and Mathews, *Handbook of the Irish Revival*, 158.

theatre movement, by Yeats as well as Gregory, are skewed by the ruthless way in which both she and Yeats excised Martyn from the record. But the birth of the Irish dramatic movement was heavily dependent not only upon Martyn's money, but upon his wish to introduce an Ibsenite note into Irish culture, which was not part of Yeats's agenda. The first version of the manifesto, drawn up in Yeats's handwriting in the summer of 1897, described the theatrical project as 'The Celtic Theatre', and announced that the initial repertoire would include 'a play of modern Ireland and in prose by Mr Edward Martyn & a play of legendary Ireland & in verse by Mr W.B. Yeats'. Later dramas were expected from George Moore, Standish James O'Grady and Fiona Macleod. With the partial and unsuccessful exception of a play by Moore, these never appeared, but the menu clearly was steeped in Revivalist inspiration. Famously, the manifesto went on to decry the English stage as possessed by mere 'dramatic journalism', and to invoke an Irish audience as an uncorrupted and imaginative audience, proving that Ireland was 'not the home of buffoonery and easy sentiment, as it has been represented, but the home of an ancient idealism'.[39]

The project would also be 'outside all the political questions that divide us'; a nationalist slant would have frightened off the kind of people whom Gregory would shortly pursue for funding. This was also, perhaps, the reason for abandoning the name of 'Celtic'. Politics, however, inevitably broke in. A controversy was carefully fomented throughout 1898 via the *Daily Express*, starting with John Eglinton's combative piece 'What Should Be the Subjects of a National Drama?', pouring cold water on the exploitation of legends, which to Eglinton seemed a mere evasion of the proper concern of a national literature: 'a native interest in life and its problems and a strong capacity for life among the people'. This was replied to by Yeats and Russell, and the debate was published as a book the following year, entitled *Literary Ideals in Ireland*. The Irish Literary Theatre, quickly organised by subscription, caused a stir with productions such as Yeats's Wagnerian play about famine, soul-harvesting demons, and a self-sacrificing heroine, *The Countess Cathleen*, roundly denounced by several Catholic authorities, and Edward Maryn's Ibsenite treatment of modern Irish politics, *The Heather Field*. The first phase of this dramatic initiative would climax with *Cathleen ni Houlihan*, an advanced-nationalist allegory about the 1798 Rising, attributed to Yeats but mostly Gregory's work. Here, the politics of Fenian resistance for once coalesced with Revival literature. The first performances of the play, with Maud

---

39 For the original draft of the manifesto, see my *Apprentice Mage*, 184.

Gonne in the title role of an old woman who represents Ireland, electrified Dublin audiences, and was constantly revived. The closing line of the play, reporting the transfiguration of the poor old woman into a 'young girl with the walk of a queen', as she leads young men away to fight for Irish freedom, had a seismic effect. But it was anything but typical, and should be seen as a late flowering of the centenary celebrations of 1898, so important in the revival of Fenianism[40] rather than an earnest of agit-prop theatre to come.

The Abbey Theatre, which succeeded the Irish Literary Theatre, accordingly moved decisively away from political themes, whether treated allegorically or representationally. The theatre quickly established its own distinguished acting style, influenced by the production abilities of William and Frank Fay, and reliant on the talents of strikingly talented home-grown actors; they would have great success on tours of the UK and America. Yeats's plays, which with Gregory's rural comedies made up the theatre's staple fare, often chose Irish saga themes – notably in a cycle of plays about Cuchulainn, also the subject of Gregory's influential volume of sagas re-told for Anglophone readers, *Cuchulain of Muirthemhne*. (She did the same thing for the legends of the Fianna in *Gods and Fighting Men*.) But in Yeats's drama, Cuchulainn is an alter ego reflecting the struggles of his own life, rather than a martial hero who will liberate his country – reflecting the author's own incremental disillusionment with 'advanced nationalism' through the first decade and a half of the twentieth century. This would change – cautiously – after the 1916 Rising, but was reflected in bitter poems about public life in Ireland and the death of idealism such as the now-canonical 'September 1913'. In terms of style as well as content, the poems gathered together in the volume called *Responsibilities* (1914) spelt out a repudiation of the kind of subject matter and approach supposed to typify the Revival. They also indicated the kind of disagreements that drove young nationalist radicals away from the Abbey to start up their own, more obviously politicised, ventures – primarily in the intimate world of 'drama-mad' Dublin as remembered by Mary Colum.

> Dublin was a small city, the suburbs stretched out to a distance, but the centre, the old part of the city, was circumscribed and bristled with movements of various kinds – dramatic, artistic, educational; there were movements for the restoration of the Irish language, for reviving native arts and crafts, for preserving ancient ruins, for resurrecting native costume, an array of political movements; here, too, were the theatres and the tearooms and pubs which corresponded to the café life of the continental city. In the centre,

40 See Chapter 1 by Matthew Kelly in this volume.

too, were the headquarters of the clubs and societies, some at war with each other, but all exciting and, somehow, focused towards one end, a renaissance. Between Abbey Street and College Green, a five minutes' walk, one could meet every person of importance in the life of the city at a certain time in the afternoon. The city was then drama-mad and every actor with an ambition to play any drama, ancient or modern, tried it out in Dublin.[41]

Those who repudiated the aesthetics of the Abbey would include several writers who took leading roles in the 1916 Rising, including Patrick Pearse, Thomas MacDonagh and Joseph Mary Plunkett. Pearse had long been prominent in Gaelic League circles, editing its journal *An Claidheamh Soluis* and founding an experimental school where Irish was a central part of the curriculum; MacDonagh, who lectured at University College Dublin, wrote a searching critique of Irish literature as well as poetry and plays; Plunkett published fervent and semi-mystical religious poetry, and (with MacDonagh) founded and ran a small theatre in Dublin. They might seem to bear out Yeats's later theory that cultural excitement led to political revolution, but it is uncertain whether their literary work would have stood the test of time if they had not been executed as revolutionaries, and thus passed into martyrdom. What their extraordinary careers do illustrate is the central part played by theatrical involvement in the lives of nationalist revolutionaries: other instances include Constance Markiewicz, Liam de Róiste, Daniel Corkery, Terence MacSwiney and Piaras Béaslaí, who was influential in starting an Irish-speaking theatre movement, Na h-Aisteoirí.[42]

The work produced by young nationalists in this era tended to be politically didactic pieces such as Casimir and Constance Markiewicz's *The Memory of the Dead* (dealing with 1798), or MacSwiney's five-act *The Revolutionist*; but MacDonagh's plays *When the Dawn Is Come* and *Pagans* suggested that Ibsen's influence was still strongly at work, while his satirical *Metempsychosis* poked fun at the mysticism and occult ideas of Yeats and Russell. The Markiewiczs' Theatre of Ireland also produced the work of Padraic Colum, a gifted playwright and minor poet whose plays *Broken Soil* and *The Land* added the kind of realism too often lacking from the productions at the Abbey. Pearse's dramas were generally short morality plays, revolving around themes of redemption and sacrifice; the entertainments which he mounted at St Enda's owed much to the pageants and *tableaux vivants* constructed by Alice Milligan out of materials culled from Standish James O'Grady. Milligan's influence

41 M. Colum, *Life and the Dream* (Garden City, NY: Doubleday, 1947), 94–5.
42 See my *Vivid Faces: The Revolutionary Generation in Ireland 1890–1923* (London: Faber & Faber, 2014), ch. 3.

could also be discerned in the Ulster Literary Theatre, founded by the young Quaker republican, Bulmer Hobson and his friends after a rather bruising visit to the Yeats–Gregory enterprise in Dublin, where they felt themselves unwelcome. The Belfast experiment began with works inspired by the Ulster cycle and other Revivalist staples, but fairly quickly became the repository of locally-inspired dramas dealing with the everyday confrontations and prejudices of Ulster life – some of them, by Gerald McNamara, mordantly satirical about local pieties. The Ulster Literary Theatre became a regional phenomenon, whereas the relevance of much of the metropolitan dramatic output, over the last decade or so of the Revival period, is its contribution to a sense of national identity building: as Yeats liked to misquote Victor Hugo, 'in the theatre the mob becomes a people'. But much of the dramatic energy pulsing around Dublin, Belfast and Cork in the early twentieth century did little towards creating a distinctive break with English literary tradition, or pioneering the essential originality of a new Irish voice in dramatic art, as Yeats and Gregory had initially anticipated. That phenomenon arrived with the discovery of J. M. Synge.

Both Yeats and Gregory liked to write as if they had indeed 'discovered' the taciturn young Wicklow man whom Gregory had observed (though not accosted) on an early visit to Aran, and whom Yeats met in Paris in the late 1890s. The Parisian connection was important; much as Martyn had thought of Germany as a more advanced forum for his own drama, both Yeats and Synge had absorbed some idea of modern theatrical experiment at the Théâtre de l'œuvre and the Théâtre Libre in Paris. Yeats had attended the first production of Villiers de l'Isle-Adam's symbolist drama, *Axel*, and also of Alfred Jarry's genre-busting *Ubu Roi*. However, Yeats took credit for pressing Synge to find the subjects of his art in the west of Ireland rather than on the streets of Paris. As with his future Abbey colleagues, a certain flavour of primitivist anthropology adhered to Synge's interpretation of the pre-lapsarian world of the west. In 1907 he described the Aran Islands as a place where the people were in a 'strange archaic sympathy' with their surroundings and artefacts, and were innocent of modern notions of time.[43] But his idealisation was undercut by a sardonic realism. Yeats and Gregory enthusiastically encouraged Synge's first works: the tragic one-act play about death in a fishing community, *Riders to the Sea*, and the far more scandalous *Shadow of the Glen*, dealing with a loveless marriage and a discontented wife

---

43 See S. Garrigan Mattar, *Primitivism, Science and the Irish Revival* (Oxford University Press, 2004) for a broader treatment of this theme.

on a Wicklow farm, ending with an Ibsenite denouement, when the wife leaves for a life on the open road with a golden-tongued tramp. Synge was already a controversial figure, in the view of the conventionally pious, when he joined those other high-handed Protestants, Yeats and Gregory, as one of the three directors of the new Abbey Theatre after the company's reconstruction with the aid of the English tea heiress Annie Horniman. In 1907 he gave the Abbey both a new controversy, and its most enduring artistic success until the first plays of Sean O'Casey nearly twenty years later: *The Playboy of the Western World*.

To a later age, the power of the play resides in Synge's unique dramatic language, and the psychological force of a story where admiration and sexual success comes the hero's way for just as long as the local community thinks he has murdered his father. To many nationalist contemporaries the play was a cynical libel on the qualities of Irish country people, with an unpleasantly lascivious undercurrent about sexually rapacious women and opportunistic young men. The near-riots that accompanied the first performance, and the subsequent public debates orchestrated by Yeats and others, mark a key juncture in the politics of the Literary Revival, though it should be remembered how quickly the play entered the Abbey's repertoire and stayed there. They also focused an issue implicitly aired in the Eglinton-Yeats-Russell debate on 'Literary Ideals in Ireland', which was the uneasy concept of cosmopolitanism in Irish culture.

Neither Yeats nor Synge would have used the word about their own inspiration: in this era 'cosmopolitanism' generally implied a shallow dilution of national verities, acting as a stalking-horse for imperial values. Yeats, in fact, specifically attacked 'cosmopolitanism' – while enthusiastically pursuing Indian mysticism, Japanese drama, and French symbolism, and retaining a lifelong debt to Spenser, Shelley and Morris. However to D. P. Moran in *The Philosophy of Irish Ireland*, the now-alienated Arthur Griffith in the Sinn Féin paper *United Irishman*, and several other formidable polemicists, 'cosmopolitanism' was the corrupt crux of all that the Revival ought to replace, and Yeats and his friends exemplified it. Griffith's condemnation of Synge's plays came down to a clinching judgment: 'Cosmopolitanism never produced a great man nor a good artist yet, and never will.'[44] John Eglinton continued

---

44 Quoted in F. S. L. Lyons, *Ireland since the Famine* (London: Collins, 1973), 242. For a thoughtful and provocative discussion of the 'cosmopolitanism' issue see D. Kiberd, *Inventing Ireland: The Literature of the Modern Nation* (London: Jonathan Cape, 1995), ch. 9, 'Nationality or Cosmopolitanism?'

to counter this. In 1906 he queried Douglas Hyde's 'De-Anglicisation' thesis with an essay called 'The De-Davisisation of Irish Literature', calling on Irish writers to speak in their human rather than national capacity.

> Literature must be free as the elements; if that is to be cosmopolitan, it must be cosmopolitan. Literature, even when it is really national, is not a matter about which any nation, fortunately for its peace of mind, gives itself great concern. It proceeds quietly in the pursuit of truth and wisdom, and occasionally attracts attention to itself as an elemental force by an electric discharge of thought: whereupon follows, as a rule one of those regrettable movements already mentioned [religious, political, fundamental questions] and the relegation of the reigning system of thought to the status of a lost cause.[45]

In fact, especially after Synge's early death in 1909, and Yeats's shift of interest and style around that date, it was Eglinton's own approach that was relegated to a lost cause. He would, like Standish James O'Grady, George Russell, George Moore and several other luminaries of the early Revival, turn against the semi-independent Ireland that emerged from Yeats's 'long gestation' and end his days living in England.

A wider perspective

This raises the question of residence. How far was the Literary Revival a cross-channel enterprise? During the thirty-odd years of the Revival (loosely, 1890–1920), Yeats lived far more in England than in Ireland, and indeed his London residence was an important factor in publicising (and publishing) its writers and products. The same was true for several of his literary colleagues. In *Hail and Farewell*, his scabrously entertaining account of Revival times, George Moore announced that he gave up Paris and London for Dublin because the 'sceptre of intelligence' had passed to the Irish capital, with the birth of a new literature midwifed by Yeats. However, his memoir told a story of disillusionment and return; partly because he had seen his mission (reversing that of St Patrick) as coming from France to rescue the Irish from religion, and this was another lost cause. A thornier question concerns how far two brilliant Irish dramatists working in this era can be considered part of the Revival. Neither Oscar Wilde nor George Bernard Shaw saw himself as an 'exile', though the term has been retrospectively applied to

---

45 Quoted in Deane et al. (eds.), *Field Day Anthology*, II, 997.

them; cosmopolitanism comes into question once again. Wilde had little or no interest in contemporary Irish inspirations, and his taste for fairy tales was very different from Yeats's (though they both received inspiration from the collections put together by Wilde's mother). In contrast to most Revivalists, Shaw believed nationalism was a necessary illness that had to be suffered, survived and rejected in order to achieve a balanced view of the world; attempts to suppress it would only preserve an infantile disorder beyond its natural life. He also believed that the Revival was an invention of west London, brought into being by Yeats and his coterie. These ideas were proclaimed in the explosively funny play he wrote for the Abbey's first season, *John Bull's Other Island*; Yeats managed not to put it on, but the play – and particularly the brilliant 'Preface for Politicians' which Shaw later appended to it – stands as a coruscating challenge to the Irish propensity for 'dreaming', and the propensity of English people to misunderstand and idealise the Irish rather than to comprehend them. If Wilde and Shaw are indubitably Irish writers, producing extraordinary work between 1890 and 1920, this does not make them Revivalists; their concerns are too different.

With a third great Irish writer working outside the island in this period, the question is much more complex. James Joyce's relationship to the Literary Revival was intermittently engaged, rejectionist and quizzical. He shared with many Revivalists (from Edward Martyn to Terence MacSwiney) a passion for Ibsen, though the Abbey would reject his Ibsenite play *Exiles*. His early work was steeped in Yeatsian influences, notably from Yeats's occult short stories collected in *The Secret Rose*, one of which he knew by heart. (Significantly, it was called 'The Crucifixion of the Outcast'.) As a student at the National University he defended Synge's plays, but also excoriated Yeats's idea of national theatre in a scornful pamphlet, *The Day of the Rabblement*. He allowed Yeats to try and help his early career, but only to a certain extent. After Joyce 'flew by the nets' of nation, family and religion to settle on the Continent, their connections lapsed, though Yeats continued to admire his work, campaigned successfully to get him a Royal Literary Fund pension in 1915, and was a passionate advocate of *Ulysses* as a great European masterpiece, on a par with the work of Rabelais or Tolstoy. The fact that Yeats saw it in these terms suggests that he never saw Joyce as part of his own literary world, and their approaches were distinctly different, as beautifully defined by Richard Ellmann.

> Joyce said he preferred the footprint seen on the sand by Robinson Crusoe to the eternal city envisioned by John. The fallen world was his natural habitat.

Yeats's impulse toward order makes the myths which appear in his work, such as the annunciation of a new era, ritualized, heraldic, supernatural; for Joyce similar myths appear unrehearsed, casual, part of the order of things.[46]

But Joyce's greatest short story 'The Dead', written in 1907, has been seen convincingly as a key text of Revival literature,[47] and its concerns are central to the consciousness of the movement. The protagonist, Gabriel Conroy, is a quintessential figure of the National University world Joyce knew: at once self-questioning and pompous, a *littérateur*, intellectually inclined towards continental models, condescendingly fond of his elderly Dublin relations, and loving though uncomprehending towards his young Galway wife – whose revelation about a lost, dead western love provides the desolating epiphany at the end of the story. Linked with the confrontation between Gabriel and an assertive Gaelic Leaguer earlier in the evening, the story brings together themes of the west of Ireland, authenticity, the petty alienations of urban bourgeois life, and the (possibly delusive) need to reconnect with an older Irish world.

Themes of the Revival echo in the background of other stories in *Dubliners*, and in *A Portrait of the Artist as a Young Man*; but the publication of *Ulysses* in 1922 signalled that the Revival had definitively ended. Ernest Boyd's early history of the movement declared that in Ireland 'modernism is a problem which we have not yet faced'[48]; yet as early as 1899 John Eglinton had invited 'our poetic dreamers to apply their visionary facility and quaint rhythmic trick to a treatment of the mechanical triumphs of modern life', adding that 'the epics of the present are the steam-engine and the dynamo, its lyrics the kinematograph, phonograph etc., and these bear with them the hearts of men, as the Iliad and Odyssey of former days uplifted the youth of antiquity'.[49] Joyce, with his interest in the cinema, would not have disagreed. In the 1922 version of *Ireland's Literary Renaissance,* Boyd spent ten pages on Joyce. While declaring that there was no sign that Joyce exercised any influence in his native country, he placed him squarely in the tradition of Irish writing, in the light of what the Revival had brought about.

> Those who have with some difficulty weaned themselves from the notion that the harum-scarum sportsmen and serio-comic peasants of the [Charles]

46 R. Ellmann, *Eminent Domain: Yeats among Wilde, Joyce, Pound, Eliot and Auden* (Oxford University Press, 1967), 54–5.
47 J. W. Foster, *Fictions of the Irish Literary Revival*, ch. 8.
48 E. A. Boyd, *Ireland's Literary Renaissance* (Dublin: Maunsell, 1916), 111.
49 Eglinton, Yeats, Larminie, *Literary Ideals*, 43.

Lever school represent Ireland, only to adopt the more recent superstition of a land filled with leprechauns, heroes out of Gaelic legend, and Celtic twilight, naturally find James Joyce disconcerting. Accordingly they either repudiate him altogether, or attempt to explain him at the expense of all his Irish contemporaries. The syllogism seems to be: J.M. Synge and James Stephens and W.B. Yeats are Irish, therefore James Joyce is not. Whereas the simple truth is that *A Portrait of the Artist as a Young Man* is to the Irish novel what *The Wanderings of Oisin* was to Irish poetry and *The Playboy of the Western World* to Irish drama, the unique and significant work which lifts the genre out of the commonplace into the national literature.[50]

But significantly, Boyd did not attempt to work the just-published *Ulysses* into this scheme, describing it as 'simultaneously a masterpiece of realism, of documentation, and a most original dissection of the Irish mind in certain of its phases usually hitherto ignored, except for the hints of George Moore'; he related the great leviathan novel not to Irish tradition, but to the recent theories of German Expressionism.[51] Writing about the same time on 'Heredity in Literature', George Russell mischievously postulated that Joyce was the spiritual and artistic son of Yeats, driven by an Oedipal urge 'to balance in our national life an intense imagination of beauty, by an equally intense preoccupation with its dark and bitter opposites'.[52] He might have added that, in this reacting, Joyce was also detonating the whole structure built up by the Literary Revival.

And Yeats himself was already well embarked on a process of disassociation from the mood and themes of this early work, and of the Revival itself. Long before, in 'Ireland and the Arts', a key Revival text, he had reflected that by writing about Ireland he had found his style: 'I might have found more of Ireland if I had written in Irish, but I have found a little, and I have found all myself.' But by the time he published *Responsibilities* in 1914, he had determined to leave the Revival to others, and repudiated his own early models. If Synge had taught him that style was born 'out of the shock of new material', he would look for that new material outside Ireland. Romantic Ireland being dead and gone, the search for authenticity would be sought in a different and changing world.

> I made my song a coat
> Covered with embroideries

---

50 Ryan, *Ireland's Literary Renaissance*, 405.
51 *Ibid.*, 410.
52 Originally in the *Irish Statesman* no. 8, this was reprinted in Monk Gibbon's edition of Russell's writings, *The Living Torch* (London: Macmillan, 1937), 137–9.

> Out of old mythologies
> From heel to throat;
> But the fools caught it,
> Wore it in the world's eyes
> As though they'd wrought it.
> Song, let them take it,
> For there's more enterprise
> In walking naked.

When Yeats published 'A Coat' as the envoi to *Responsibilities* in 1914, his sense of an ending was not at fault, though he would be as astounded as many other people by the advent of the Irish revolution two years later; and Ireland would continue, as Auden put it, to hurt him into poetry. But the age of revivalism had passed. George Russell would later remember 1903 to 1913 as the golden period of the Revival, one that ended when paramilitarism raised its head with the creation of Volunteer militias, north and south[53]; elsewhere it was sardonically remarked that the 1916 Rising put an end to the rule of the fairies.[54] The process would be ended by the disillusionment brought about by the Civil War and the conservative culture of the Free State. Again as in Russia, a period of extraordinary cultural efflorescence was succeeded by an era of ruthless restabilisation in politics and arid conventionality in art.

The connections between radical politics and cultural revival remains uncertain. Russell and Yeats aligned themselves on the side of the workers against the masters in the 1913 Lock-out, dealt with elsewhere in this volume, but in Yeats's case this was impelled by his quarrel with William Martin Murphy and other 'wealthy men' over their refusal to support Hugh Lane's plan for a modern art gallery in Dublin, rather than by any sympathy with Labour politics. The relationship between the revolutionaries of 1916 and the literary revivalists remained ambiguous. With the exception of Thomas MacDonagh, who retained his early admiration of Yeats and knew him personally, most of the revolutionary generation disapproved of the general direction Yeats and his contemporaries had taken, identifying instead with the more political and less literary activities of the Gaelic League, and cheering on the brickbats hurled at the older Revivalists by journalists such as D. P. Moran and Arthur Griffith. The complex and often adversarial relationships between Yeats and the leaders of the Rising are sharply delineated in the first stanza of his poem of partial expiation 'Easter 1916', though that work is

---

53 See pp. 7, 113–14, 225–6 in this volume.
54 Quoted in Kiberd, *Inventing Ireland*, 1.

remembered mainly for its canonical refrain, 'a terrible beauty is born'. The poem makes clear that by 1916, Yeats and his circle were inhabiting a different sphere from the 'cellars and garrets' where revolution was planned by the IRB Military Council from 1914.[55]

There were also implicit tensions between several of the most influential Revivalists, with their Protestant, Theosophist, mystical or and occultist identifications, and the reborn religiosity of the revolutionary movement after 1916. As the Catholic Church moved decisively to support the nationalist revolution, and subsequently the Treaty of 1921, the path was prepared for a reassertion of traditional values in art as well as life. In 1925 Russell wrote privately that 'we in Ireland are reacting against the idealism that led us to war and civil war and I fear we are in for an era of materialism'.[56] It would also be an era of Catholicisation. Back in 1905, John Eglinton had gone so far as to cheerfully state that 'one of the most genuine signs of the new awakening in Irish life of late is the recrudescence among us of religious bigotry'; a year later he would argue that Catholicism was essentially alien to Irishness, instancing the hostility of bard to saint in Irish literature and the 'inartistic puritanism' of Catholicism as practised in Ireland.[57] But inartistic puritanism characterised the values proclaimed by the new Irish Free State from 1922, reducing the memory of Revivalism to an ersatz-Gaelic prettiness and pietistic didacticism. This was much to the discomfiture of Eglinton and many of the Revival generation, not least Yeats – though unlike Eglinton and others, he stayed in Ireland and tried to combat them. The values of the Revival would be queried by what has been called a 'counter-revival': not only the parodies of its high style in the fictions of Eimar O'Duffy, James Stephens and Flann O'Brien, but in the reactions of the next generation of modernist poets, such as Thomas MacGreevy and Austin Clarke. The process was sealed by Samuel Beckett's fictions and plays, infused with an Irish (even an Irish-Protestant) sensibility but determined, even more than his sometime mentor Joyce, to fly by the nets of identity politics and national agendas. It is none the less true that the lives and sensibilities of many of the state-builders had been inspired and formed by the extraordinary literary energies released in the Ireland of the *fin-de-siècle*, whether they acknowledged it or not. There

---

55 See the chapters by Matthew Kelly and Fearghal McGarry in this volume.
56 Quoted in Foster, *Fictions of the Irish Literary Revival*, xix.
57 See extract in Kiberd and Matthews, *Handbook of the Irish Revival*, 234, and also J. Eglinton, 'The Land of Saints', in *Bards and Saints* (1906), quoted in Boyd, *Ireland's Literary Renaissance*, 250.

remains more than a grain of truth in Yeats's claim that the 'long gestation' of revolution was mediated by the surge of energy that characterised Irish literature and drama over the preceding quarter-century. And if the revolution that transpired did not produce the kind of cultural effect prophesied by the brokers of Literary Revival, that should probably not surprise us.

7

The Culture War: The Gaelic League and Irish Ireland

BRIAN Ó CONCHUBHAIR

Between the Land War and the Anglo–Irish War, and straddling the Great War lies another, much less violent, but no less intense, conflict fought during a forty-year period over the definition of Irish identity. Culture, rather than politics, became ground zero where questions about the 'Irish nation' were vigorously debated. Labels used to define this era, such as Celtic Revival, Irish Renaissance or Irish Revival invariably conflate an eclectic variety of groups and their agendas. 'Irish-Ireland' serves as a convenient, if clumsy, generic umbrella term – it is the title of D. P. Moran's 1905 collection of essays *The Philosophy of Irish–Ireland* – to capture some of the cultural, literary, social and sporting movements that achieved popular political, cultural and literary success from 1876 to 1916. This chapter examines 'that broad anticolonial cultural, economic, political, and social movement that was the Irish Revival understood in its most expansive sense'[1] through the lens of Conradh na Gaeilge/The Gaelic League, 'the quintessential Irish-Ireland organization'.[2] To illuminate the concerns of Irish-Ireland it traces the Gaelic League's relationships with other Irish-Ireland organisations and interest groups, including the Gaelic Athletic Association (GAA), the Abbey Theatre (both critiqued by Paul Rouse and Roy Foster in their respective contributions to this volume), the cooperative movement, Sinn Féin, Cumann na nGaedhael and the Catholic hierarchy amongst others.[3] This hyphenated label – opposing an English-Ireland, Anglo-Irish Ireland, or indeed British-Ireland – condenses

---

1 G. Dobbins, 'Whenever Green Is Red: James Connolly and Postcolonial Theory', *Nepantla*. 1, (2000), 605.

2 T. G. McMahon, *Grand Opportunity: The Gaelic Revival and Irish Society, 1893–1910* (Syracuse: Syracuse University Press, 2008), 2.

3 See B. Ó Cuív, 'The Gaelic Cultural Movements and the New Nationalism', in K. B. Nowlan (ed.), *The Making of 1916: Studies in the History of the Rising* (Dublin: Stationery Office, 1969), 1–27. P. J. Mathews, *Revival: The Abbey Theatre, Sinn Féin, The Gaelic League and the Co-operative Movement* (Notre Dame: University of Notre Dame Press, 2003), 21.

internal differences, divisions and distinctions between a broad coalition of similarly-minded organisations. It simultaneously distinguishes them from those who, actively or passively, accommodated themselves to late Victorian and Edwardian provincial British imperial culture as well as those for whom political independence, devoid of cultural independence, simply meant a parliament in Dublin. The term, notes Terence Brown, served to 'define a community's awareness of itself as Irish in an indigenous autochthonous sense. And it adopted this apparent tautology in lively opposition to what was perceived to be the Anglicisation of Irish life.'[4] If 'Irish-Ireland' is less than satisfactory, we also lack any neutral label for those Irish groups and organisations directly opposed to the Irish-Ireland agenda other than the loaded terms – West Brits, Castle Catholics, shoneens and surfaces – mainly coined by *The Leader*'s irascible editor, D. P. Moran.

Irish civil society underwent not one, but several, transformations in the period 1890–1914, before the violent and political upheavals of 1916, 1919–1921 and 1921–1923. In 1896 Ireland boasted some 360 friendly societies – organisations composed of people who joined together for a common financial or social purpose – but by 1914 this number had increased by 243 per cent to 1,125.[5] Such proliferation not only increased the overall density of Irish civil society but marked 'an important shift in the way in which Irish civil society operated'.[6] This quickly expanding Irish associational life was organised, mobile, politicised and hostile to the British state. Irish-Ireland, as R. V. Comerford summarised, consisted of:

> a profusion of formal and informal campaigns – sometimes dependent on one another, sometimes independent, frequently antagonistic to one another, but considerably overlapping in support – on such issues as native manufactures, native games, rural reform, agricultural cooperation, national literature, national theatre, national self-reliance, anti-imperialism, dual monarchy, separatism, the curbing of clerical power, the organization of labor, de-Anglicization, and the revival of Irish.[7]

The main sites of differentiation were popular culture, language, literature and religious affiliation. The Irish-Ireland movement attempted to create and

---

4 Terence Brown, 'British Ireland,' in Edna Longley (ed.), *Culture in Ireland: Division or Diversity?* (Belfast: Institute of Irish Studies, The Queen's University of Belfast, 1991), 72.

5 J. Cormier and P. Couton, 'Civil Society, Mobilization, and Communal Violence: Quebec and Ireland, 1890–1920', *The Sociological Quarterly*, 45 (2004) 498.

6 Ibid., 498.

7 R. V. Comerford, 'Nation, Nationalism and the Irish Language', in T. Hachey and L. J. McCaffrey (ed.), *Perspectives on Irish Nationalism* (Lexington, KY: University of Kentucky Press, 1989), 29.

codify a distinct Irish culture through a rejection of British culture: sports (hurling and Gaelic football rather than rugby, soccer, cricket), a distinct form of speech (Irish, Hiberno-English, Kiltartanese rather than Received Pronunciation or dominant English accent) and ultimately, but controversially, a particular form of religion (Roman Catholicism rather than any form of Protestantism or atheism). 'Irishness' would be distinctive in literature, print (gaelic font rather than roman font),[8] dress,[9] music[10] art,[11] design,[12] word[13] and dance.[14] Such claims of ethnic distinctiveness abound across late nineteenth-century Europe and 'few rhetorics have been more repetitively general' writes Perry Anderson, 'than claims for the ethnically particular'.[15]

At one time the rise of cultural nationalism was attributed to the lull in constitutional politics following Parnell's 'fall', the acrimonious split in the Irish Parliamentary Party and the party's ensuing demise into impotent cliques. Under Parnell, the Home Rule Movement, hierarchical and autocratic in structure, had successfully united a tightly disciplined National League and an increasingly confident Catholic Church to move parliamentary constitutionalism to the fore in Ireland and had wielded considerable political clout without advocating a particular cultural or linguistic agenda. On the party's implosion, the energy invested in Parnell and the Home Rule campaigns, it has been argued, transferred to the realm of the arts and culture. One of the many flaws in this obstinately resilient, yet convenient myth is it cannot account for the failure of cultural nationalism prior to Parnell. Such readings all too frequently ignore the Gaelic League's predecessors: The Society for

---

8 See B. Ó Conchubhair, 'The Gaelic Font Controversy: The Gaelic League's (Post-Colonial) Crux', *Irish University Review*, 33 (2003) 46–63. See also B. M. French, 'Linguistic Science and Nationalist Revolution: Expert Knowledge and the Making of Sameness in Pre-Independence Ireland', *Language in Society*, 38, (November 2009), 607–25.

9 K. Steele, *Women, Press, and Politics During the Irish Revival* (Syracuse: Syracuse University Press, 2007); H. O'Kelly, 'Reconstructing Irishness: Dress in the Celtic Revival, 1880–1920', in J. Ash and E. Wilson (eds.), *Chic Thrills: A Fashion Reader* (London: Harper Collins, 1992); M. Dunlevy, *Dress in Ireland* (London: B. T. Batsford, 1989).

10 M. Dowling, *Traditional Music and Irish Society: Historical Perspectives* (Burlington, VT: Ashgate Publishing, 2014).

11 J. Helland, *British and Irish Home Arts and Industries 1880–1914* (Dublin: Irish Academic Press, 2007).

12 J. Sheehy, *The Rediscovery of Ireland's Past: The Celtic Revival 1830–1930* (London: Thames & Hudson, 1980).

13 Amongst others, see N. Gordon Bowe and E. Cumming, *The Arts and Crafts Movements in Dublin and Edinburgh 1885–1925* (Dublin: Irish Academic Press, 1998).

14 See C. E. Foley, *Step Dancing in Ireland: Culture and History* (Burlington, VT: Ashgate Publishing, 2013) and B. O'Connor, *The Irish Dancing: Cultural Politics and Identities, 1900–2000* (Cork: Cork University Press, 2013).

15 P. Anderson, *A Zone of Engagement* (London: Verso, 1992), 249.

the Preservation of the Irish Language (1876) and the Gaelic Union (1880).[16] Some historians posit the early revival as less a response to Parnell's fall but more 'politically Parnellite'[17] yet others see the literary activity as accompanying much non-traditional political activity outside the realm of constitutional politics.[18] Equally deserving of attention is the confidence Unionists felt in exploring cultural identities from 1893 to 1907 when, with the prospect of Home Rule apparently forlorn and the Liberals defeated, the threat of cultural exclusion seemed altogether less menacing.

By contrast, and in competition with the post-Parnell transference theory, the so-called 'blocked mobility' thesis sought to account for the rise of Irish-Ireland. It stressed the educational overproduction of young, upwardly mobile professionals who found their career trajectory inhibited by external, biased considerations and on experiencing collective social closure – based on language, social, religious or ethnic difference – became collectively disaffected. Catholic numbers in second-level education more than doubled between 1861 and 1911 while other denominations stagnated. Nevertheless, Catholics remained underrepresented in government positions, the professions and commercial businesses. The challenge facing Catholic women was even more acute. Teaching remained accessible, but offered lower pay, less security, and poorer status than that enjoyed by English counterparts. Ill-disposed towards the British state that, in their opinion, had betrayed them, young Irishmen and women mobilised. With social mobility blocked and professional ambitions thwarted, ambitious young Irish sought an alternative model.[19] Having embraced the British state's values, language and culture – and in the process rejected their local and traditional values – they still felt excluded. Now 'doubly isolated', neither one thing nor the other, they found purpose as the natural leaders of 'a unique community that is both historically rooted and continuously mobile'.[20] Thus, it may be argued, that it was less a love of language and a burgeoning of national pride that swelled the ranks of the Gaelic League and Irish-Ireland and more

16 M. Ó Murchú, *Cumann Buan-Choimeádta na Gaeilge: tús an athréimnithe* (Dublin: Cois Life Teo., 2001).
17 M. Kelly, *The Fenian Ideal and Irish Nationalism, 1882–1916* (Woodbridge: Boydell & Brewer Ltd, 2009).
18 P. J. Mathews, *Revival*, 6–12.
19 See McMahon, *Grand Opportunity*, 3–4 and 85–126.
20 Cormier, however, expressed a general scepticism about the overpopulation of graduates in Ireland and rejected grievance-based explanations as sufficient motivation for individual members of the intelligentsia risking their personal stake for the collective good. J. J. Cormier, 'Blocked Mobility and the Rise of Cultural Nationalism: A Reassessment', *International Journal of Politics, Culture, and Society*, 16 (2003), 525–49.

the discontent of a rising generation. D. P. Moran, through his newspaper, *The Leader*, fed their resentment by exposing discrimination in appointments to public service positions in the railways and in the awarding of contracts for public works. More recently, however, scholars have questioned the blocked mobility thesis's applicability and advanced the productive concept of notional nationalism, while others have framed it as an Irish response to the European *fin de siècle*.[21] Comerford observes that the decades before 1914 witnessed a similar proliferation of social, political, and cultural organisations across Europe. Nor should the role of language endeavours in the United States be ignored: in 1888 some 44 newspapers nationwide published articles in Irish;[22] the first feis ceoil [=Irish music festival], and the first staged Irish-language play occurred in that country, and many of the revival's leading figures lived in and visited there. Waters' examination of thirty-two early Gaelic Leaguers and Irish-Irelanders found 'at least seventeen had been emigrants and of these at least twelve had first become involved in the League while living outside of Ireland'.[23] Celtic columns existed in most large-circulation Irish-American newspapers by the 1880s. The United States also boasted *An Gaodhal*, a bilingual newspaper dedicated to Féin-Riaghla Cinidh na hÉireann – Self Rule of the Irish Race.

The dominant narrative of the Irish-language revival privileges the Gaelic League, founded by Douglas Hyde and Eoin Mac Néill in 1893. The League was a direct outcome of Hyde's 1892 public lecture 'On the Necessity for De-Anglicising Ireland'[24] which 'articulated the philosophy that inspired the formation of numerous cultural, social, and political movements in Ireland in the final decades of the nineteenth century'.[25] This version of language

---

21 See P. Murray, 'Irish Cultural Nationalism in the United Kingdom State: Politics and the Gaelic League 1900–18', *Irish Political Studies*, 8 (1993), 55–72. See P. J. Mathews, *Revival* and also McMahon, *Grand Opportunity* and B. Ó Conchubhair, *Fin de Siècle na Gaeilge: Darwin, an Athbheochan agus Smaointeoireacht na hEorpa* (Indreabhán: An Clóchomhar, 2009).

22 F. Uí Fhlannagáin, *Fíníní Mheiriceá agus an Ghaeilge* (Dublin: Coiscéim, 2008).

23 M. Waters, 'Peasants and Emigrants: Considerations of the Gaelic League as a Social Movement,' in D. Casey and R. Rhodes (ed.), *Views of the Irish Peasantry, 1800–1916* (Connecticut: Archon Books, 1977), 166–8.

24 The lecture was originally delivered in New York on 16 June 1891. For Hyde and Irish-Ireland, see D. McCartney, 'Hyde, D. P. Moran and Irish-Ireland', in F. X. Martin (ed.), *Leaders and Men of the Easter Rising, Dublin 1916* (Ithaca, NY: Cornell University Press, 1967). See also J. and G. Dunleavy, *Douglas Hyde – A Maker of Modern Ireland* (Berkeley, CA: University of California Press, 1991) and G. Grote, *Torn Between Politics and Culture: The Gaelic League, 1893–1993* (Münster: Waxman, 1994). See also M. Tierney, *Eoin MacNeill: Scholar and Man of Action, 1867–1945* (Oxford University Press, 1980).

25 M. L. O'Donnell, 'Owen Lloyd and the De-Anglicization of the Irish Harp', *Éire-Ireland*, 48 (2013), 155–75.

politics obscures the foundational and critical achievements of the Society for the Preservation of the Irish language (SPIL) founded in 1876, the Gaelic Union founded in 1880 and the Celtic Literary Society founded in 1893. SPIL, a successor of earlier archaeological societies such as the Ossianic Society (1853–1863),[26] was instrumental in securing a place for the language in the programme of the 'national' school system in 1878. In that year the national education commissioners acceded to a widely subscribed SPIL petition allowing Irish as an optional subject outside of school hours. The list of signatories, as Comerford notes, 'showed a strong weighting toward Catholic and Home Rule Ireland, but there was no question of the language being a Catholic or a Home Rule issue, as was signaled by the signatures of a Protestant bishop and three deans, fifty other Protestant or Presbyterian clergymen, and ten professors of Trinity College'.[27] However, the Gaelic League, unlike its antecedents, embraced vernacular Irish as a living, formal linguistic register rather than a barbaric, corrupted form of classical Irish. It also cultivated a contemporary literature composed in vernacular speech rather than merely editing classical and ancient texts for linguistic purposes.

Hyde framed his famous lecture in terms of Darwinian evolutionary theory and *fin de siècle* fears of racial decline and intermixing. In doing so he strategically merged the issue of language and culture with broader national and international concerns to argue that Ireland should follow her own traditions. Failure to do so, according to popular pseudo-scientific racial thinking, would result in the emergence of a hybrid race, neither Irish nor English, but one that was degenerate in language, physique, thought and behaviour. Race suicide and ultimate eradication would be the only outcomes. For a nation still trying to come to terms with the Famine, such theories were neither alarmist nor inconceivable. Hyde's lecture had a deep impact on Eoin MacNéill, the Antrim-born law clerk and future academic, who had recently published 'Why and How the Irish Language is to be Preserved' in 1891, and 'A Plea and a Plan for the Extension of the Movement to Preserve and Spread the Gaelic Language in Ireland' in 1893.[28] Together, they formed Conradh na Gaeilge[29]/ Gaelic League on 31 July 1893 as a non-sectarian, non-political popular language movement.

---

26 See D. Murray, *Romanticism, Nationalism and Irish Antiquarian Societies, 1840–80* (Maynooth: Maynooth Monographs, 2000).
27 R. V. Comerford, 'Nation, Nationalism and the Irish Language'.
28 D. McCartney, 'Eoin MacNeill and Irish Ireland', in F. X. Martin and F. J. Byrne (eds.), *The Scholar Revolutionary* (Shannon: Irish University Press, 1967), 75–97.
29 Hyde favoured 'Léug na Gaedhilge'.

The Gaelic League's aims were twofold: first, the preservation of the Irish language and its extension as a spoken language and second, the creation of a modern literature in Irish. These innovative aims clearly contrasted with those of their predecessors, the Gaelic Union, the Society for the Preservation of the Irish Language and the Irish Literary Society (London). In contrast to them, and influenced by emerging theories of comparative grammar, it embraced vernacular forms of Irish (the dialects previously despised as patois) as undeniable evidence of the strength and energy of Irish as a living, and in the Darwinian sense, evolving and developing, language that constantly adapted and modified over time. The Gaelic League presented Irish – and its dialects – as 'respectable' and pure, rather than as barbarous jargon and contrasted it with the 'mixed' English language.

Gaelic League membership grew slowly in the early years. Branches appeared in Galway (24 January 1894); Cork (22 April 1894); Derry (1894); New Ross, Wexford (May 1894); Aries, Cork (December 1894) – the first rural branch; London (October 1896). By 1896 the League numbered forty-three branches with eight overseas. The League's rapid growth in Dublin in 1899 is traceable to 'The Turning of the Tide', Father Peter Yorke's lecture delivered in the Antient Concert Rooms on 6 September 1899. By 1901, the League boasted thirty branches in Dublin and its suburbs.[30] The movement swelled from fifty-eight branches to some 120 after the lecture and reached 500 by 1903.[31] The Dublin-based leadership, however, had little control over the actions of branches at home or abroad. Forty-three pounds collected in membership fees in 1895 increased to £2,000 in 1900, permitting it to hire paid officials, including full-time *timirí* – community organisers to travel through their dedicated regions, establish branches, advise school teachers, initiate cultural and social events and proselytise.[32] By 1904 membership had increased to some 50,000 members in 600 branches and had grown to 100,000 members in 900 branches in 1905.[33] Nor was interest confined to Ireland: Branches registered in Scotland (1895 – Glasgow); England (London, Liverpool, Manchester, Portsmouth, Southampton, Rugby, Birmingham, Leicester, Wigan, Oldham,

---

30 *Annual Report of the Gaelic League*, 1901 (Dublin: Gaelic League, 1901), 10.
31 See P. Mac Aonghusa, *Ar Son na Gaeilge: Conradh na Gaeilge 1893–1993* (Baile Átha Cliath: Conradh na Gaeilge, 1993), 65, 82. See also P. Ó Fearáil. *The Story of Conradh na Gaeilge*, 30, 42.
32 See D. Ó Súilleabháin, *Na Timirí i Ré Tosaigh an Chonartha 1893–1927* (Dublin: Conradh na Gaeilge, 1990) and C. Ó Cearúil, *Aspail ar son na Gaeilge: Timirí Chonradh na Gaeilge 1899–1923* (Dublin: Conradh na Gaeilge, 1995).
33 See J. Augusteijn, *Patrick Pearse: The Making of a Revolutionary* (Houndsmills, Basingstoke: Palgrave Macmillan, 2010), 80–1.

Salford, Coventry, Bolton); Wales (Cardiff); Argentina (Piedad, Buenos Aires); USA (Chicago, New York, Rhode Island, Holyoke, New York); New Zealand (Miltown, Balclutha); South Africa (Capetown, Kimberley); and Bolivia. The branches' activities were seasonal: classes at night during the winter months, with public performances, *aonaigh, seilgí, aeraíochtaí* and *feiseanna* [=gatherings, fairs, festivals] in the spring. The League's membership benefited from crossovers with GAA clubs, athletic clubs and cycling clubs which were also committed to the improvement and invigoration of the Irish race and whose members enrolled in language classes. Women also bolstered membership considerably.

Despite receiving voting rights in the 1898 local elections, women were precluded from parliamentary elections. But unlike many of its peers, the Gaelic League accepted women as members.[34] It afforded them full rights, including holding office on local Branch Committees and the national executive. Mixed classes sometimes led to conflict with Catholic priests in places.[35] In focusing on cultural nationalism rather than political nationalism, the 'home and the hearth' rather than the ballot-box became the site of contestation. Consequently, the League and the wider Irish-Ireland movement tacitly acknowledged that 'even if limited to their traditional roles as homemakers and teachers, [women] had a crucial contribution to make in building the Irish nation'.[36] In 1906 the Gaelic League convention elected seven women (15.5 per cent) to the forty-five national executive positions.[37] D. P. Moran of *The Leader* viewed the suffragette movement as further evidence of anglicisation and de-nationalisation, but W. P. Ryan of the *Peasant* was more progressive and welcoming. The Gaelic League provided women with a public space in which to play significant administrative roles, a space less radical, less political and less controversial than that offered by Inghinidhe na hÉireann [=Daughters of Ireland].

The League's achievements were many and varied. It established a press and produced newspapers such as *Fáinne an Lae* [=Daybreak] and *An Claidheamh Soluis* [=The Sword of Light] later edited by P. H. Pearse (1903–1909) and Michael Joseph O'Rahilly (The O'Rahilly) (1913). *An Claidheamh Soluis* published Eoin Mac Néill's 'The North Began' and Pearse's 'The Coming Revolution', both

---

34 D. A. J. MacPherson, *Women and the Irish Nation: Gender, Culture and Irish Identity, 1890–1914* (Houndsmills, Basingstoke: Palgrave Macmillan, 2008).

35 For misogyny see Ó Conchubhair, *Fin de Siècle na Gaeilge*.

36 F. A. Biletz, 'Women and Irish-Ireland: The Domestic Nationalism of Mary Butler', *New Hibernia Review*, 6 (2002), 59.

37 Maire de Buitléir, Eibhlín Nic Neill, Bean Uí Choisdealbha (Miss Drury), Úna Ní Ghaircheallaigh, Máire Ní Aodáin, Máire Ní Chinnéide and Eibhlín Ní Dhonnabháin.

key tracts in the crisis years of 1912–1916.[38] It also issued Eugene O'Growney's highly successful series of Irish primers for adults and children. To demonstrate the vitality of popular *Gaeltacht* (=Irish speaking) culture, the League inaugurated *An tOireachtas*, a cultural festival, in 1897.[39] Public events and spectacles such as Irish-language weeks and language processions in Dublin were intended to proselytise and promote the League's aims. The League also published novels, short stories, histories, collections of poetry and folklore, and produced plays, pageants, and, on occasions, operas in Irish.[40] It organised lectures on Irish history, underscoring the point that the English language was a relatively new cultural and linguistic phenomenon in Ireland and that it not only coincided with but was directly connected with the decline in Irish fortunes politically, morally, industrially, racially and physically. The Gaelic League compelled the Postal Service to recognise and accept parcels and mail addressed in Irish; secured the bilingual naming of all Dublin streets and roads; established and codified what is now recognised as Irish dance; collected a considerable amount of folklore, song and music from native Irish-speakers; oversaw the codification of the language, and fostered the emergence of a modern literature in Irish. But its major achievements and lasting legacy were in the educational sector.

To mould the future generation the League agitated for an increased role for Irish, as a subject and as a means of instruction, at all levels of the educational system. The attempt in 1889 to downgrade Irish in the intermediate examination resulted not only in a significant victory over Trinity College, Dublin, a bastion of Anglicisation, but also led to the public humiliation of Trinity scholars, J. P. Mahaffy and Robert Atkinson who had, most unwisely, testified to the poor moral quality of literature in Irish and to the chaotic state of the language. It also brought the League to national and even international prominence. Hyde, drawing on the testimony of European scholars, rubbished their claims and exposed Atkinson's scholarly limitations. The

---

38 R. Uí Chollatáin, '*An Claidheamh Soluis*: A Journalistic Insight to Irish Literary Reviews in the Revival Period 1899–1932', *Proceedings of the Harvard Celtic Colloquium*, 23 (2003), 284–98; R Uí Chollatáin, *An Claidheamh Soluis agus Fáinne an Lae 1899–1932* (Dublin: Cois Life Teo, 2004); C. Nic Pháidín, *Fáinne an Lae agus an Athbheochan* (Dublin: Cois Life Teo, 1998).

39 P. Mac Aonghusa, *Oireachtas na Gaeilge, 1897–1997* (Dublin: Conradh na Gaeilge 1997). See also McMahon, *Grand Opportunity*, 155–86.

40 See P. O'Leary, *The Prose Literature of the Gaelic Revival, 1881–1921: Ideology and Innovation* (University Park: Penn State University Press, 2005).

episode became a *cause célèbre*, raising the League's status considerably and reinforcing Trinity's image as anti-Irish.

As a result of the League's aggressive campaigning, the number of schools that taught Irish as an additional subject increased: 105 (1899); 88 (1900); 1,198 (1901); 1,586 (1902); 2,018 (1903); and 1,983 (1904).[41] In 1904 the government authorised a Bilingual Programme for schools in Gaeltacht and bilingual areas where teachers were proficient in Irish. This initiative led to the setting up in 1904 of the first dedicated Irish-language teachers' colleges to train educators in second-language methodology. The National Board of Education officially recognised the Gaelic League's Teachers' Colleges from 1906. The *Morning Post*'s notorious attack on Irish MPs for their promotion of Irish ('Kitchen Kaffir') led Roger Casement, then British Consul in the Belgian Congo, to resign his London club membership and contribute the fee to Coláiste na Mumhan.[42] Other new colleges followed: in 1905 Coláiste Chonnacht (Tourmakeady, Mayo), The Munster University (Waterford), and Coláiste Comhghaill (Belfast's winter college), while 1906 brought Coláiste Cholmcille (Donegal), Leinster College (Dublin's winter college), Coláiste Thamhain (Galway), and Coláiste Chonnacht (Galway).

The Gaelic League agitated for Irish to be a required matriculation subject in the entry examination for the proposed National University of Ireland.[43] Matters came to a head in December 1908 when the Catholic bishops and the League issued opposing public statements on the language issue. This disagreement caused a permanent split between the League and the Catholic hierarchy.[44] Arguing that Irish should be required as a matriculation subject, the League found itself in opposition to distinguished public figures such as John Dillon, Isaac Butt, Liam Dillon, William Delany, S. J., as well as most of the Catholic bishops. A forthright letter by the Rev. Micheál O'Hickey, Professor of Irish at Maynooth, read to a December 1908 public meeting in the Rotunda, stated categorically that the language, literature and history of Ireland constituted the essence of all Irish education. Subsequently published

---

41 T. Walsh, 'The Revised Programme of Instruction, 1900–1922', *Irish Educational Studies*, 26 (2002), 127–43.

42 A similar Welsh-language educational project began in Aberystwyth in 1903. The London branch provided financial support.

43 See G. Ó Tuathaigh, 'The Position of the Irish Language', in T. Dunne (ed.), *The National University of Ireland, 1908–2008: Centenary Essays* (Dublin: UCD Press, 2008), 33–46.

44 See P. Mac Aonghusa, *Ar son na Gaeilge: Conradh na Gaeilge 1893–1993: stair sheanchais*, 90.

as *An Irish University or Else* in early 1909, it moved the hierarchy to discipline him. He was instructed to resign as Professor of Irish at Maynooth, and when he refused, he was fired on 29 July 1909.[45] Despite this setback, the League overcame both the Catholic hierarchy and the Irish Parliamentary Party when it allied with those county councillors, elected as a result of the Local Government (Ireland) Act (1898), who refused to fund scholarships from local rates to attend the third-level institutions until the language stipulation was conceded. Nor was this first occasion the League and Catholic hierarchy had clashed. With branches throughout the island, the League's involvement in social intercourse led, as noted, to conflict with the Catholic Church over mixed night-time classes, but also to controversy over religious rites carried out through Irish in Irish-speaking districts, as well as acceptance of 'Irish' names for baptism and even Irish as a subject in schools under the clergy's control.[46] Given the threat the League posed to the Catholic Church's social authority, it is hardly surprising that the clergy quickly made 'a concerted effort to graft their moral concerns onto the language project'.[47]

The Gaelic League sought to offer alternatives to anglicised forms of popular culture, sport, literature and entertainment, and to instill pride in these 'Irish' alternatives. They agreed with the GAA on the importance of fitness, and the need for energy and strength to counteract what they considered the debilitating, paralysing, impact of Anglicisation. They shared common ground with the Abbey Theatre, discussed by Roy Foster in this volume, on the importance of a distinct form of Irish theatre and a distinctive form of national literature, but disagreed on the language of that national literature. The wider concern with culture that supported and underpinned language usage and language maintenance brought the League into cultural realms beyond language and literature and into contact and conflict with other elements of 'Irish-Ireland'.

The Gaelic League and Irish-Ireland also recognised the importance of material wellbeing and economics – perhaps due to criticism by socialists such as James Connolly, Pádraic Ó Conaire and Sean O'Casey among others.[48] In advocating for Irish industries and Irish-made goods, and in establishing an Irish Industrial Committee, they found common ground with several other

45 Ibid., 90–95. See also L. McDiarmid, *The Irish Art of Controversy* (Ithaca and New York: Cornell University Press, 2005), 50–86.

46 McMahon, *Grand Opportunity*, 34–84.

47 Mathews, *Revival*, 26.

48 J. Connolly, 'The Language Movement', *The Workers' Republic*, 1 October 1898. For Griffith, see E. McGee, *Arthur Griffith* (Dublin: Irish Academic Press, 2015).

groups who sought to re-imagine Ireland's future as something other than as a provincial British backwater. Hyde, allegedly, described the League as 'an educational body tinged with an industrial strain'.[49] The *Tablet* explained in 1908:

> It was not sufficient for an Irishman to speak his own language, to write it and read it, to review the bygone customs, but he had also to further everything that was for the betterment of his country. With the increase of the League came an increase in such demands, till at last a considerable amount of public opinion was brought to bear on the question of Irish Industry, advertisements of Irish goods found their way into the papers, and the Irish Ireland publications gave long lists of all the things made in the country. Then at Gaelic gatherings such as the *Oireachtas* and *Feiseanna* there were industrial exhibitions, and *Aonacha* – fairs for the selling of Irish goods – were held in London, Paris, and America.[50]

The 'Déanta i nÉirinn' (made in Ireland) symbol[51] that appeared on the front page of Griffith's *Sinn Féin* newspaper from 1909 allowed manufacturers to brand themselves, and their products, as Irish-made. Ironically Sinn Féin (ourselves), as McMahon observes, connotes self-reliance, responsibility and resourcefulness – a very Victorian concept at the heart of Irish-Ireland.[52]

If the Gaelic League claimed a non-sectarian, non-political status, *The Leader* newspaper, edited by D. P. Moran, spoke for devout Catholic nationalists.[53] Moran had served his journalistic apprenticeship with *The Star* in London where he had joined the Irish Literary Society and the Gaelic League, while also serving as secretary of the Irish National League's London Branch.[54]

---

49 S. Brooks, 'The New Ireland: VI. The Gaelic League', *The North American Review*, 188 (1908), 268.

50 'The Irish Industrial and Social Revival', *The Tablet*, 31 October, 1908, 9.

51 Attributed to Austin Molloy. See B Ó Conchubhair, 'An Gúm and the Irish Language Dust-Jacket', in E. Sisson and L. King (eds.), *Negotiations: Modernity, Design and Visual Culture in Ireland, 1922–1992* (Cork: Cork University Press, 2011), 93–113.

52 See McMahon, *Grand Opportunity*, 7.

53 See P. Maume, *D. P. Moran* (Dundalk: Dundalgean Press, 1995).

54 P. Delaney, 'D. P. Moran and the Leader: Writing an Irish Ireland through Partition', *Éire-Ireland*, 383–4 (2003), 189–211.

On returning to Ireland, he denounced anglicisation in a series of articles in the *New Ireland Review* and went on to establish *The Leader* on 1 September 1900. With a large circulation, it soon spoke to and for the Catholic wing of Irish-Ireland and largely shaped popular Irish-Ireland philosophy, despite lacking an organisational structure or mass membership. Moran, a capitalist, also urged the regeneration of the Irish economy and the development of local industries. As with Hyde, he believed the revival of the Irish entrepreneurial spirit lay in rediscovering local and vernacular pride – but only in Catholic terms. Moran reserved his renowned opprobrium for 'humbug' and shoddy appointments. He despised what he considered 'West-Britishism' and 'Castle Catholicism'. It was not the British Empire that exploited the workers of the world, he maintained, but Irish Protestants and corrupt Catholics who prevented Irish Catholics from entering, and excelling, in the imperial system. Yet if Moran found common ground with the Gaelic League in the importance of the language, he never mastered it. For him liturgy rather than language was paramount for the Irish identity. For Moran and *The Leader*, the Irish nation was essentially Catholic and its cultural base was 'Gaelic'. Once strengthened, this base would absorb all 'extraneous' elements. His brilliant but bellicose style allied to his passion for controversy earned him numerous enemies. Mocked as being more Catholic than the Pope, he crossed swords with the novelist AE (George William Russell), leading businessman, William Murphy and, the founder of Sinn Féin, Arthur Griffith. Among his achievements we may list the removal of bookmaking facilities from GAA matches and, from 1903, the closing of public houses on St Patrick's Day.[55]

The issue of a 'national' literature was a vexed subject for Irish-Ireland. Moran held literature of the 'Celtic Note' in particular contempt and supported the Gaelic League on the impossibility of an Irish national literature in English. The League, despite Hyde's respectful relationship with Yeats and Lady Gregory, dismissed any notion that the Abbey's plays in English contributed in any way to 'Irish' literature. For Moran, propaganda was the only contribution literature written in English could make. An Irish national literature had to be written in Irish; English literature was written in English. Challenged to a debate in Irish by dramatist Sean O'Casey, he declined the invitation as he had never mastered the spoken language. In 1892 Yeats, along with the former Fenian John O'Leary, and in association with Douglas Hyde, established the National Literary Society in Dublin. Closely related to the London-based Irish Literary Society, also founded by Yeats with

---

55 See J. Augusteijn, *Patrick Pearse: The Making of a Revolutionary*, 80–81.

T. W. Rolleston, this Dublin-based society aimed at publicising ancient Irish literature, legends and folklore. With Lady Gregory and Edward Martyn, Yeats also established an Irish Literary Theatre in 1898 – the year Hyde, Norma Borthwick and Eleanor Hull established the Irish Texts Society.

In 1901 the Irish Literary Theatre staged Hyde's *Casadh an tSúgáin* [The Twisting of the Rope], the first Irish-language play to be given a professional production. In 1903, the Irish National Theatre Society put on Irish plays in English, considerably different in tone and tenor to the shows and music hall entertainment offered by touring British companies. Such heroic Irish material, gleaned from romantic versions of Irish history, emerged frequently and spectacularly in parades, popular pageants, *tableaux vivants* and plays produced by Cumann na mBan, the Ulster Literary Society, the Gaelic League and by Pearse's school, St Enda's, among other troupes.

J. M. Synge's 1903 *In the Shadow of the Glen* was met with dismay, with Griffith being particularly hostile.[56] The Gaelic League's P. H. Pearse also rebuked his 1904 *Riders to the Sea* for its depiction of western inhabitants[57] and Irish-Irelanders in general considered his 1907 *Playboy of the Western World: A Comedy in Three Acts*, an insult to Irish identity and a denigration of the western peasants they lionised as the epitome of their idealised Irish man and woman. What began as hisses quickly led to open fighting in the theatre. The subsequent court case ensured that the event lived long in the collective memory.[58] The Abbey, along with Trinity College, was therefore firmly in the sights of 'Irish-Ireland' as agents of the hated 'Anglicisation'. Further controversy ensued on 7 May 1910 when Lennox Robinson, the new director, kept the Abbey open despite other Dublin theatres closing on the death of King Edward VII. Not Irish enough for Irish-Ireland, and neither royal nor loyal enough for Unionists, this blatant disrespect for the monarch led Annie Horniman to withdraw her financial support, creating a crisis for the Abbey.

Seeking funds, and following in Hyde's footsteps when he had successfully raised £12,400 in the United States for the League, the Abbey crossed the Atlantic to tour America in 1911 with Synge's *Playboy*. If the Abbey managers had believed American audiences would prove more receptive than Dublin audiences to Synge's work they were quickly disabused of this idea. Philadelphia police officers arrested the entire cast and charged them

---

56 Mathews, *Revival*, 117–45.
57 Pearse would later revise his attitude. See McMahon, 6. See also O'Leary, 281–94.
58 J. Fitzpatrick Dean, *Riot and Great Anger: Stage Censorship in Twentieth-century Ireland* (Madison, WI: University of Wisconsin Press, 2004).

with producing an immoral play. Happily, the judge dismissed the case and, undaunted by this dramatic ordeal, the Abbey toured the United States again in 1912–1913 and 1914.

The Irish National Theatre Society was only one of several troupes that abounded in Dublin and Ireland in this period. Other rival groups that perished without achieving the Abbey's heights or longevity include the Theatre of Ireland, Irish Theatre Company, the Leinster Stage Society, Cumann na nGaedheal Theatre Company, Inghinidhe na hÉireann, Independent Theatre Company, National Players Society, Cumann na mBan, the Ulster Literary Theatre, the Cork Dramatic Society, Na hAisteoirí and Na Cluicheoirí. What linked these less glamorous, and less successful, theatrical companies to the Abbey is their shared commitment to theatre and their belief in performance's power to examine, inspire and advance ideas about nationalism and Irish culture.[59] In turning to Irish literature for inspiration, Lady Gregory, Synge and Yeats perceived an 'Irish' tradition more pagan than Christian. For conservative Catholics, whether members of the Gaelic League, the Catholic Truth Society, Cumann na mBan or loyal adherents of D. P. Moran's *The Leader*, such a culture, no matter how artistic or dramatic, was no better than loutish anglicisation. For many in the Gaelic League, Ireland's national literature had to be in Irish; for many readers of *The Leader* it had to be Catholic. Issues of literary merit were less a concern.

The Gaelic League as a non-political organization allowed Catholic and Protestants, males and females, to engage with social and national affairs without raising suspicions. As terms of employment forbade national teachers and civil servants from engaging in politics, the League, which theoretically sought to create harmony and accord between Catholics and Protestants on the shared issue of a common ancestral language, afforded a safe space. In 1895 Rev. Dr Richard Kane served as the Gaelic League's patron in Belfast while simultaneously serving as Belfast's Grand Master of the Orange Order. Historian Tom Garvin notes that the language movement offered clerics a 'means of escape from the localist pressures of the diocese', and the institutional Catholic Church, as noted, was to encounter trouble in dealing with Gaeilgeoir [=Irish-speaking] priests such as Micheál O'Hickey.[60] For

---

59 For theatre see: M. Trotter, *Ireland's National Theaters: Political Performance and the Origins of the Irish Dramatic Movement* (Syracuse: Syracuse University Press, 2001); P. Ó Siadhail, *Stair Dhrámaíocht na Gaeilge: 1900–1970* (Indreabhán: Cló Iar-Chonnacht, 1993); E. Ní Mhuircheartaigh and N. Mac Congáil, *Drámaí Thús Na hAthbheochana* (Dublin: Arlen House Press, 2009).

60 Tom Garvin, *Nationalist Revolutionaries in Ireland 1858–1928* (Dublin: Gill Books; New edition, 2005), 65.

Protestants, such as Hyde, their motivation in reviving the Irish language and joining the League might be seen as a concerted effort to create a common cultural and linguistic space. Protestants, uncomfortable about Home Rule but unconvinced by militant unionism viewed the League as an opportunity for 'moving away from the bitter politico-sectarian division that had afflicted Irish society for decades and even generations'.[61] The 1906 resignation of Gaelic League executive member Canon James Owen Hannay (whose pen-name was 'George A. Birmingham') complicated such matters, however.

The Gaelic League, in theory, allowed Protestants to claim an Irish identity without jettisoning or subordinating their religious beliefs and, as Garvin comments: '[A]fter all, an Irish-speaking Protestant could logically claim to be more Irish than a monoglot English-speaking Catholic; he might also irritate him.'[62] The prevalence of Catholic clerics in honorary positions in rural branches of the League was, however, striking but was probably inevitable, for Ireland 'was particularly dependent on its priesthood for organizational and ideological leadership'.[63] Lay ideologues like Moran and Mac Néill understood well that the endorsement of the priests was required if the object was to organise mass support for a neo-Gaelic nationalist project. *The Leader* consistently sought clerical approval and condemned anti-clericalism. None the less, the Gaelic League publicly challenged the Catholic hierarchy over its objections to mixed-sex classes and over its stance on the role of Irish in admission policies for the proposed new university.

In the 1880's, the Catholic Church committed itself to political nationalism through the agency of the Irish Parliamentary Party led by Parnell. The 'Irish-Ireland' movement, however, by challenging the primacy of constitutional politics also contested the role that the Catholic Church had assumed for itself in post-Home Rule Ireland and set down a new cultural agenda.[64] Admittedly, many clerics supported lay cultural nationalists, but there were also very significant differences over particular issues of control.[65] The Revival period also saw the emergence of 'closed Catholicism', described by Whyte as 'a development within the Catholic Church, by the Roman Catholic hierarchy and laity,

---

61 Comerford, *Nationalism and the Irish Language,* 29.
62 Garvin, 70–1.
63 Comerford, 36–7.
64 F. A. Biletz, 'The Irish Peasant and the Conflict between Irish-Ireland and the Catholic Bishops 1903–10', in S. J. Brown and D. W. Miller (eds.), *Piety and Power in Ireland 1760– 1960: Essays in Honour of Emmet Larkin* (Notre Dame, IN: University of Notre Dame Press, 2000), 108.
65 See K. Collins, *Catholic Churchmen and the Celtic Revival in Ireland, 1848–1916* (Dublin: Four Courts Press, 2002).

of specifically Catholic social and political organisations'.[66] The changing orientation within the Gaelic League would see some Protestant members leave in 1914 to form Cumann Gaelach na hEaglaise at St Ann's Parish Hall, Dawson Street and to set up a journal, *An tEaglaiseach Gaedhealach*, (= The Irish Churchman) in 1919.

If Irish-Ireland demanded distinct forms of national literature, the same held true for national culture and sport. A distinct Ireland required a distinctive sporting culture: a game that would separate it not only from British games, but in keeping with Darwinian thought and muscular Christianity, would provide manly exercise for Irish youth. Maurice Davin and Michael Cusack launched the GAA as a non–political, non-sectarian, recreational association aimed at regenerating Ireland through sport in 1884. Paul Rouse's chapter in this volume details the GAA's growth and role in this period. The GAA, as an integral part of Irish-Ireland, offered a native sporting alternative to anglicised games. The GAA's attitude towards the language changed with Cusack's departure from the organisation in 1886 and the emergence of a stronger Irish Republican Brotherhood (IRB) element at a senior level. A year later, the GAA faced an internal split: one faction favoured the IRB's physical force policy, the other the Irish Parliamentary Party. At the November 1887 Congress, an IRB-backed candidate defeated Maurice Davin for the position of President in what was part of a wider IRB-led electoral strategy of seizing the top administrative posts. In the event, following Archbishop Croke's mediation, a special Congress re-elected Davin in January 1888, but by 1889 the GAA's commitment to the Irish language had waned.[67] The January 1888 convention also excluded members of the Royal Irish Constabulary (RIC) and Dublin Metropolitan Police (DMP) from membership, but did not extend this ban to members of the British army or Royal Navy – indicating that the ban resulted from police [mis]behaviour during the Land War.[68] A definition of identity that was based on the politics of exclusion proved easier to manage than an embrace of culture. Rescinded in April 1893 as a 'reflection of the diminished political and agrarian agitation in the intervening period', the ban was reintroduced in 1906 for all counties and extended to British soldiers and

---

66 J. H. Whyte, *Catholics in Western Democracies: A Study in Political Behaviour* (Dublin: 1981), 48–9. See also P. Ó Baoighill, *Cardinal Patrick O'Donnell 1856–1927* (Baile na Finne, Foilseacháin Chró na mBothán, 2008).

67 C. Billings, 'First Minutes: An Analysis of the Irish language with in the Official Structures of the Gaelic Athletic Association, 1884–1934', *Éire-Ireland*, 48 (2013), 41.

68 See P. Rouse, 'The Politics of Culture and Sport in Ireland: A History of the GAA Ban on Foreign Games, 1884–1971, Part One: 1884–1921', *International Journal of the History of Sport*, 10 (1993), 342–3.

anyone participating at sports events organised by the RIC. However it was always applied more in the exception than as the rule.[69] Plans to reinstitute An tAonach Tailteann, the ancient Tailteann Games, in Dublin in 1889 led to a disastrous fund-raising tour of America in 1888.[70]

By 1916 the GAA was Ireland's largest nationalist organisation with a presence in almost every parish in Ireland.[71] The RIC reported that while its leaders held extreme views and its general tone was disloyal, at the local level the GAA mostly concerned itself with athletic pursuits.[72] The GAA and Gaelic League's interests and memberships overlapped as both endeavoured to shake the nation from its stupor: but they differed on how to achieve that common goal. The GAA emphasised athletic pursuits; the Gaelic League the Irish language. It was that which distinguished the GAA from the Gaelic League and led the latter to refer to the former as 'Feet Gaels'[73]: those who defined their identity by the games they watched and played, rather than the language they spoke. Admittedly the League supported the GAA financially, but it always deployed the language symbolically rather than functionally.[74]

In organising and energising communities – urban and rural – and instilling a sense of pride in localities through rivalries and competitions, the GAA and the Gaelic League overlapped with another key strand within 'Irish-Ireland' – the Irish Agricultural Organisation Society's efforts to improve the collective lot of farmers and rural communities.[75] The IAOS movement focused not on culture but on emerging technologies and scientific approaches with a view to stemming emigration and the resulting destruction of rural communities. New approaches in agriculture based on advances in science had spread across Europe in the late nineteenth century. The sudden emergence of low-salt creamery butter had posed a serious challenge to Irish dairy farmers in the 1880s coupled with a collapse in consumer demand for firkin butter. Horace Plunkett, an Eton-educated social

---

69 See the chapter by Paul Rouse in this volume.

70 See M. Cronin, 'Projecting the Nation through Sport and Culture: Ireland, Aonach Tailteann and the Irish Free State, 1924–32', *Journal of Contemporary History*, 38 (2003), 395–411.

71 R. McElligott, '1916 and the Radicalization of the Gaelic Athletic Association', *Éire-Ireland*, 48 (2003) 95.

72 M. Wheatley, *Nationalism and the Irish Party: Provincial Ireland 1910–1916* (Oxford University Press, 2005), 67.

73 See P. O'Leary, *Gaelic Prose in the Irish Free State, 1922–1939* (University Park: Penn State University Press, 2004), 47–51.

74 See Billings, 32–53, 33.

75 See Mathews, *Revival*, 5–34.

philosopher and pro-Union politician, recently returned from a ten-year stint in Wyoming, attempted to regenerate rural Ireland through a system of cooperatives and sought through the education of Irish farmers to apply scientific approaches to agriculture.[76] Two facts shaped Plunkett's thinking, writes Kennelly 'the importance of what is today called "social capital" – the reciprocal bonds and ties that link people together in a variety of networked connections – and second, that Irish commercial achievement would need to take place within the context of an international marketplace where competition was global'.[77] In 1893 Ireland had 39 cooperatives; by 1895, there were 56 cooperative societies and no fewer than 350 by 1905.[78] By 1920, the number had grown to 675, a 17-fold increase. In addition to joint-purchasing, cooperatives introduced quality control and established credit societies to combat indebtedness, a common feature of rural life.

Plunkett, however, alienated many segments of the Irish-Ireland movement as well as the landed gentry who had links to the merchant classes and who suffered financially from such developments. Consequently, the *Freeman's Journal* and the *Irish Daily Independent* displayed 'open hostility'.[79] Any hope that the Catholic hierarchy would embrace the cooperative movement disappeared with the publication of Plunkett's 1904 book, *Ireland in the New Century*. In this work he attributed the retarded nature of Irish agriculture and low productivity to Catholic teaching, and his thesis was widely perceived as anti-Catholic.

Regardless of all this cultural renewal, the energy and enthusiasm thereby generated produced very few tangible political results. Cumann na n Gaedheal attempted to offer an alternative agenda within the Irish-Ireland movement to the non-sectarian, non-political approach. Founded by Arthur Griffith, Denis Devereux and William Rooney in September 1900 as a cultural and educational association aiming to popularise Irish history, language, and music and combat anglicisation, it advocated Irish economic independence and worked to unite advanced nationalist groups for political advantage rather than for cultural objectives alone. Rooney and Griffith first met as members of the

---

76 See K. H. O'Rourke, 'Property Rights, Politics and Innovation: Creamery Diffusion in Pre-1914 Ireland', *European Review of Economic History*, 11 (2007), 395–417. See also J. Mokyr and C. Ó Gráda, 'Poor Getting Poorer? Living Standards in Ireland before the Famine', *Economic History Review*, 41 (1988), 209–35.

77 J. J. Kennelly, 'Horace Plunkett and the Cooperative Movement', *New Hibernia Review*, 12 (2008) 64.

78 C. King, 'The Early Development of Agricultural Cooperation: Some French and Irish Comparisons', *Proceedings of the Royal Irish Academy*, 96 (1996), 70.

79 Mathews, *Revival*, 9.

Irish Fireside Club in the late 1880s, before moving on to the Leinster Debating Society and the Leinster Literary Society. Rooney described by Mathews as embodying 'the voice of civic–minded republicanism [that was] very much at odds with the radical ideas of bourgeois cultural nationalism',[80] formed the Celtic Literary Society in February 1893, dedicated to the cultivation of Irish language, history, literature and music, and edited its journal, *An Seanachuidhe* [=The storyteller].[81] In March 1899, Rooney and Griffith co-founded the *United Irishman* to circulate Irish-Ireland ideas alongside Moran's *The Leader,* the League's *An Claidheamh Soluis* and W. P. Ryan's more radical and socialist leaning *The Peasant*. In literary terms, Rooney and Griffith acknowledged the Anglo-Irish literary tradition as part of Ireland's cultural inheritance and, more controversially, accepted a contemporary Irish literature written in English.[82] This even-handedness was anathema to most Gaelic Leaguers, as indeed it was to Moran. Rooney criticised the Gaelic League for its refusal to participate in the 1798 anniversary. The League had defended its stance on the grounds that the commemoration had political, even sectarian overtones. Rooney urged the League to abandon its non–political stance. Griffith, as a member of the Young Ireland Executive, had been active in the Irish Language Congress Committee in 1893 and, in 1902, had served on Gaelic League Industrial Committees established to promote native industries. For Rooney, cultural nationalism ultimately and unavoidably led to political activism, while for Griffith the emphasis on cultural definitions of the nation ignored economic dimensions. Such distinctions, as well as its call for the Irish Parliamentary Party to withdraw from Westminster, set Cumann na nGaedheal apart.

The announcement that Queen Victoria would visit Ireland in April 1900 afforded those who had opposed the Boer War in 1899 another opportunity to protest British actions. Here, Griffith and Maud Gonne, whose Transvaal Committee had coordinated anti-recruitment protests, found common cause with W. B. Yeats. Gonne organised a group of women in opposition to the Queen's visit. They subsequently became Inghinidhe na hÉireann and were socialist and feminist in outlook, were opposed to the Irish Parliamentary Party and Home Rule, but were committed to self-reliance and to the language revival.[83] Actor and socialist, Helena Molony,

---

80 P. J. Mathews, 'A Battle of Two Civilizations?' *Irish Review* 29 (2002), 29.

81 M. Kelly, '… and William Rooney Spoke in Irish', *History Ireland*, 15 (2007), 30–4. For Fireside Club, see R. Nic Congáil, ' "Fiction, Amusement, Instruction": The Irish Fireside Club and the Educational Ideology of the Gaelic League', *Éire-Ireland*, 44 (2009) 91–117.

82 See Mathews, *Revival*, 92–116.

83 Countess Markievicz founded Clan na nGaedheal as an Irish equivalent of the girl scouts in 1910.

edited its feminist-nationalist journal, *Bean na hÉireann* [= The Irish Woman], 'the women's paper that men buy'. The experience of coordinating protests over the Boer War and the 'Famine Queen's' visit persuaded Griffith of the need for a formal harmonised network to combat the influence of the Irish Parliamentary Party, Dublin Castle and Dublin Corporation. Despite the Gaelic League and the GAA's impressive growth as non-political organisations, no group channelled that cultural energy in an explicitly political direction. Consequently Griffith formed Cumann na nGaedheal [= The Irish Club], financed by Maud Gonne, in September 1900, with the Fenian John O'Leary as president. Its objective: to fuse politics and culture. However as Senia Pašeta has noted, 'its amorphous nature and changeable membership ensured that diverse cultural and political aims did not produce any sort of coherent policy'.[84] In association with Rooney, in 1899 Griffith established the *United Irishman* which he maintained until 1906 despite Rooney's death, aged 27, from tuberculosis, in 1901. Two years later, in conjunction with Maud Gonne, Griffith launched the National Council to campaign against King Edward VII's visit. Its emphasis on cultural policies attracted a broad alliance of cultural and sporting groups. In 1904 Griffith, over the protests of Michael Davitt and John Redmond, offered editorial support for the Limerick boycott of Jewish businesses organised by the Redemptorist priest John Creagh.[85] In 1906, after the *United Irishman* journal collapsed following a libel suit taken against it, Griffith re-founded it under the title *Sinn Féin* and set up a similar organisation, the Sinn Féin League, to give life to ideas previously articulated in the *United Irishman*. The title – derived from the early Gaelic League motto: 'Sinn féin, sinn féin amháin' [= ourselves, ourselves only] – was suggested by Máire de Bhuitléir, a leading Gaelic League member who in 1902–1903 had used the phrase as the title of her publication in Oldcastle, County Meath.[86] In 1907 the Sinn Féin League merged with the Dungannon Clubs and the National Council to form a new group, Sinn Féin. Its newspaper, the *Sinn Féin Daily*, founded in 1908 briefly became a daily in 1909 and survived until its suppression in November 1914, after which it was sporadically revived as the nationalist journal, under the title *Nationality*. The year 1912 also marked organised protests at George V's visit to Ireland. In November 1910, Tom Clarke, returned from New York, and Belfast Quaker Bulmer Hobson,

---

84 S. Pašeta, 'Nationalist Responses to Two Royal Visits to Ireland, 1900 and 1903', *Irish Historical Studies*, 31124 (1999), 503.

85 See D. Keogh, *Jews in Twentieth-century Ireland* (Cork: Cork University Press, 1998).

86 See Biletz, 'Women and Irish-Ireland: The Domestic Nationalism of Mary Butler', 59–72.

established *Irish Freedom*, an IRB monthly newspaper managed by Seán Mac Diarmada.

This proliferation of groups led to increased rivalry between them as they sought to distinguish themselves from one another and consequently brought a narrowing of aims and attitudes as Irish-Ireland became more confident and assertive. The second decade of the twentieth century saw the emergence of *An Fáinne* [=The Ring] – a radical Irish-language organisation founded in part by novelist and socialist, Pádraic Ó Conaire[87] and Liverpool-born Piaras Béaslaí[88] and committed to engaging with state officials only through Irish. Believing the League to be too soft in advancing its agenda at the state level, they advocated refusing to speak English with state officials regardless of the consequences – leading to Ó Conaire's arrest and trial in 1916 and also, on similar charges, to that of Lawrence Grinnell, John Dillon's private secretary and former Irish Parliamentary Party MP.

By 1913 Hyde, who had served as president for 20 years, had become increasingly agitated by attacks on his alleged cozy relationship with Dublin Castle, by allegations that he benefited professionally from his role as president, by false statements attributed to him, and by the petty attacks of the IRB-leaning Keating branch that demanded a more militant, political League. In 1913 he published essays in *Sinn Féin* and the *Freeman's Journal* denouncing his critics in advance of that year's Ard–Fheis [=Annual conference] in Galway. Éamonn Ceannt and the O'Rahilly persuaded him to stand unopposed as League President. Shortly afterwards, the 1913 Lock–out began, with Pearse supporting the strikers and, their leader, Jim Larkin, whose children attended Pearse's school St Enda's. The socialist leader, James Connolly, in his 1908 'Sinn Féin and Socialism' had earlier rejected the ideological incompatibility of socialism and the League arguing that any 'revaluation of the speech of the Gael, will in all probability also lead to a re-study and appreciation of the social system'.[89] Hyde for his part insisted that the League must refrain from involvement in social matters and urged the maintenance of its non-political, non-sectarian, stance throughout the strike and, later, during the Great War, despite the prominence of many leading Gaelic League members in the Irish Volunteers, including Eoin Mac Néill.

87 A. Ó Cathasaigh, *Réabhlóid Phádraic Uí Chonaire* (Dublin: Coiscéim, 2007) and *An tAthrú Mór: Scríbhinní Sóisialacha le Pádraic Ó Conaire* (Dublin: Coiscéim, 2007).
88 P. Ó Siadhail, *An Béaslaíoch: Beatha agus Saothar Phiarais Béaslaí (1881–1965)* (Dublin: Coiscéim, 2007).
89 See G. Dobbins, 'Whenever Green is Red: James Connolly and Postcolonial Theory', *Nepantla*, 1, 605–48.

On 1 November 1913, in response to the Ulster Volunteers, Mac Néill published 'The North Began' in *An Claidheamh Soluis*, an article that led to the foundation of Óglaigh na hÉireann/the Irish Volunteers. Availing of the League's extensive network of branches, the new movement spread quickly, often mirroring existing League branches. Membership estimates indicate that the majority of Gaelic League members joined. And prominent Gaelic Leaguers – P. H. Pearse, Roger Casement, Éamon de Valera, Richard Mulcahy, Cathal Brugha, S. T. Ó Ceallaigh, Seán Ó Muirthile, Maurice George Moore, Michael Collins, Thomas Ashe and Seán Mac Diarmada, were closely involved from the beginning. While Hyde praised the Volunteers, and in 1914 declared 'the way of the Volunteers has been made easier by the doctrines preached by the Gaelic League',[90] Garvin suggests that by 1914 many League leaders recognised the enormity of the task involved in undoing the linguistic shift and 'may have felt impelled to resort to insurrectionary political activity in part as a compensatory device'.[91] A week after Hyde's 1914 re-election at the Killarney Ard–Fheis, the Great War broke out. The League's non-political stance allowed it to act as a home for Irish-speaking Redmondites, and Irish-speaking 'Sinn Féiners', Irish-speaking recruiters and Irish-speaking objectors. William Gibson (Baron Ashbourne) and Tomás Ó Domhnaill MP, both acknowledged Gaelic Leaguers, encouraged young men to enlist, and Michael O'Leary, a native Irish-speaker from Cork, became the poster boy for recruitment after winning a Victoria Cross. On the other hand, Irish-speakers who spoke publicly against recruitment meetings risked being jailed for sedition. If *An Claidheamh Soluis* attempted to avoid commenting on the War, the Irish-language paper *Ná Bac Leis* [=Ignore It] ridiculed both Irish involvement in the war and those who promoted Irish recruitment.[92]

The IRB ultimately succeeded in undermining Hyde and the League's non-political stance. The 1916 Rising was plotted at a meeting chaired by Tom Clarke, a nominal member of the McHale Gaelic League Branch on 9 September 1914 in the Gaelic League's headquarters at 25 Parnell Square.[93] In 1915, in advance of that year's Ard-Fheis to be held in Dundalk, Clarke convened a meeting at the Foresters' Hall in Parnell Square to propose motions and orchestrate voting to ensure Seán T. Ó Ceallaigh would replace Pádraig Ó Dálaigh, who had accepted a position in the Educational

---

90 5 July 1914, Bray. Cited in Mac Aonghusa, 143.
91 Garvin, 55–6.
92 A. Ó Cathasaigh, *Ná Bac Leis: Rogha as nuachtán reibiliúnach* (Dublin: Coiscéim, 2015).
93 P. Mac Aonghusa, *Ar Son na Gaeilge*, 155.

Company, as Ard-Rúnaí [=Chief Secretary]. Consequently it was IRB members Piaras Béaslaí and Martin Conallan, on behalf of the McHale branch, of which both Clarke and Mac Diarmada were members, that proposed the two controversial motions to amend the League's constitution. Following the intervention of members of the Irish Parliamentary Party, the goal of an 'Independent Ireland' was replaced by a 'Free Ireland' but Hyde was not appeased. He left the congress and announced his resignation by mail the following day. With Hyde's resignation and the evident role of prominent IRB members, the Gaelic League came under increased RIC and Dublin Castle attention, though in fact it had been regarded as a subversive organisation since 1903.[94] Six of the seven signatories of the 1916 Rising were Gaelic League members as were many of the rank and file who participated in the Rising. The League's first post-Rising Congress met on 8 August 1916 in Parnell Square with Father Cathaoir Ó Braonáin in the chair. Its president (Eoin Mac Néill), chief secretary (S. T. Ó Ceallaigh), and chief clerk (Liam Ó Rinn) had all been jailed for their role in the Easter Rising. Seán P. Mac Enrí, the noted educationalist and former vice president of the London Gaelic League, advocated rescinding the controversial 1915 amendments and returning the League's constitution to its non-political state. If that failed, he urged the formation of a new body, closer in outlook to the original League. The IRB once again used the Ard-Fheis to their own advantage and in the course of the meeting, scheduled a meeting to restructure the IRB's command structure.[95]

Irish-Ireland saved neither traditional Ireland nor the Gaeltacht, but it moulded a new form of Irish identity. In 1922 the Irish Free State 'simply adopted the strategies for Gaelicisation already formulated by the Gaelic League in the first decade of the century'.[96] The dominant 'communal' values of Free State Ireland would be Catholic rather than Gaelic for the simple reason that the most powerful and widely shared 'sense of peoplehood' in early twentieth-century Ireland was religious rather than linguistic.[97] And in that regard, it was the Irish-Ireland of *The Leader* rather than that of the Gaelic League or Cumann na n Gaedheal that triumphed. Irish-Ireland's legacy however, was more than the preservation of the Irish language, the apotheosis of

---

94 Mathews, *Revival*, 25.
95 Mac Aonghusa, 160–1.
96 G. Ó Tuathaigh, 'The Irish-Ireland Idea: Rationale and Relevance', in Longley (ed.), *Culture in Ireland*, 63.
97 Ibid., 63.

vernacular dialects and the creation of modern fiction. Its legacy is evident in music, dance, sport and design, it is revealed in the bilingual signage and bilingual postal service, legal and banking services that exist in early-twenty-first century Ireland. Irish-Ireland set the cultural agenda for twentieth-century Ireland and it is impossible to discuss issues of culture, literature or ideology in Free State Ireland without recourse to Irish-Ireland, not least because it was the smithy in which almost all Irish leaders forged their intellectual and cultural souls whatever their attitude towards the project.

PART II

*

WAR, REVOLUTION AND THE
TWO IRELANDS, 1914–1945

8

Ireland and the Great War

DAVID FITZPATRICK

Mobilisation

As a more or less integral part of the United Kingdom, Ireland went to war in August 1914 on the same constitutional and legal footing as Great Britain. In both countries, King George V ordered general mobilisation, declared a state of war, and assented the Defence of the Realm Act (DORA), under which wide-ranging civil rights were subsequently curtailed by regulation. As in Britain up to 1916, military participation in Ireland was sought not through compulsion (as in most belligerent countries), but persuasion. Mass enlistment and communal support were secured not by demanding obedience to Asquith's Liberal government, but by invoking loyalty to the monarch as a figure-head (representing the history and values associated with Britain, Ireland, and the empire), and love of one's country (whether 'Britain', England, Wales, Scotland, or Ireland). The British empire and its European allies were portrayed as the defenders of representative democracy and liberal values against oppressive despotism.

On the eve of war, it was far from clear that Ireland would embrace the Entente's cause as an expression of Irish patriotism. The major unionist and nationalist parties were each supported by armed paramilitary forces formed in 1913, the Ulster Volunteer Force (UVF) and Irish (National) Volunteers (INV). Following the collapse of the Buckingham Palace conference in late July 1914, there seemed no imminent prospect of compromise over the vexed issue of Home Rule, which was due to receive royal assent without agreement on any specific provision for all or part of Ulster. Consequently, it seemed likely that Ireland would soon be engulfed in rebellion, or civil war, or both. If Home Rule were applied without amendment, Ulster's 'provisional government' was poised to seize power in the province, confident that the Royal Irish Constabulary (RIC) would prove ineffectual against the UVF, and that the government would not dare to deploy the army following the

'Curragh mutiny' of March 1914. If Asquith's government resigned, the most likely outcome was its replacement by Bonar Law's Unionists, the abandonment of Home Rule, widespread Nationalist rejection of 'constitutionalism', and separatist rebellion.

So great was the threat of conflagration in Ireland that influential German and Austrian observers believed the United Kingdom would not risk despatching the British Expeditionary Force (BEF) if Germany invaded Belgium and France. Ireland was universally regarded as an essential element in Britain's naval defences, and the formidable difficulty of securing the island and Irish waters against invasion and infiltration would be magnified by widespread Irish antipathy to Britain. Exaggerated expectations of Irish 'disloyalty' may indeed have been a significant factor in precipitating the war itself.[1]

In the event, Redmond's Irish Parliamentary Party and Carson's Ulster Unionists immediately threw their weight behind Britain and her allies, reassuring Sir Edward Grey that Ireland was the 'one bright spot' in Europe and confounding both British pessimists and German optimists. There was nothing aberrant about the fact that two parties of questionable 'loyalty' found it both right and expedient to sink their domestic differences in the common cause. The same applied to socialists and feminists throughout Europe, anxious to affirm their patriotism and allay popular mistrust with a view to post-war acceptance of their demands for full citizenship and equitable treatment.

Both Redmond and Carson have been accused of political opportunism in declaring support for the war effort at the outset, yet withholding concerted military mobilisation of their followers until mid September. By that time, the Government of Ireland Act had been simultaneously assented without amendment, suspended (eventually for the duration of the war), and qualified by Asquith's promise that Home Rule would not be implemented without special provision for Ulster. Though superficially favourable to nationalists and indignantly denounced by unionists, this compromise offered both parties ample opportunity for future political manoeuvring. Yet neither Redmond nor Carson viewed their wartime pursuit of political advantage as a 'zero-sum game'. Both sincerely hoped that the experience of common sacrifice, in the field and at home, would erode the mutual mistrust of the Catholic and Protestant communities, promote reconciliation, and so facilitate a workable compromise once the war had been won. Contrary to

---

1 J. aan de Wiel, 'The "Irish Factor" in the Outbreak of War in 1914', in *History Ireland*, 19, no. 4 (2011), 32–5; and *The Irish Factor, 1899–1919: Ireland's Strategic and Diplomatic Importance for Foreign Powers* (Dublin: Irish Academic Press, 2008), chs 2, 3.

popular belief, Redmond's appeal to the INV to serve 'wherever the firing line extends', first mooted in the House of Commons on 15 September, did not represent the second stage of a premeditated bargaining process. On 3 August, when Redmond vainly proposed deploying both volunteer armies for Home Defence in the absence of a Territorial force in Ireland, this was a far more pressing issue than enlistment for overseas service. Six weeks later, with the first BEF in tatters, the need to enlist millions for Kitchener's new armies had become an urgent priority.

Redmond and Carson had used the interval to secure the formation of new army divisions, subject to a measure of partisan control, through which they hoped to harness popular patriotism and facilitate military enlistment under 'Irish' and 'Ulster' banners respectively. In practice, the 10th (Irish) division was neither distinctively nationalist nor unionist, almost two-thirds of its remaining members in late 1915 being Protestants.[2] Its first commander was Sir Bryan Mahon from Belleville, County Galway, a broad-minded if prickly Protestant, who sank into a sulk at a vital point in the Gallipoli campaign but went on to command the forces in Ireland after the 1916 rebellion. The War Office was reluctant to allow nationalist politicians any major role in the recruitment, training, or selection of officers for the 16th (Irish) division, though Redmond was eventually allowed to present the division with Irish wolf-hounds as mascots. Its commander at home, Sir Lawrence Parsons of Parsonstown, King's County, was a Protestant of vaguely national sympathies who took a dim view of requests for commissions from candidates 'quite socially impossible as Officers – men who write their applications in red or green ink on a blank bill-head of a village shop. These are the class most successfully weeded out by the enlisting ordeal, as they think it beneath their dignity to enlist as "Common" Soldiers to be herded with "riff raff" '.[3] He was succeeded in the field by Sir William Hickie, a Tipperary-born landed gentleman who had the rare credential of being a Catholic. The structure of the 16th division owed little to that of the INV, though a few commissions were eventually given to MPs and Volunteer leaders such as John Redmond's brother Willie (a former militia officer).

---

2 In November 1915, 35.8 per cent of the division were returned as Roman Catholics, 53 per cent as Episcopalians, 8.2 per cent as Presbyterians, and 3 per cent as Methodists: Return by divisional chaplain, November 1915, abstracted in T. Hennessey, *Dividing Ireland: World War I and Partition* (London: Routledge, 1998), 117.

3 Parsons to Secretary, War Office, 29 November 1914: MS 21278 Parsons Papers: National Library of Ireland (NLI).

Only the 36th (Ulster) division set out with a pronounced political ethos, though even that was diluted by the enrolment of a few Catholics from the Young Citizen Volunteers (YCV), and subsequent intake of Welsh, English and Catholic Irish troops as the division fell below strength.[4] By spring 1918, according to a Jesuit chaplain whose battalion had been drafted into the division, it contained over 3,000 Catholics: 'When this division came from Ireland, their boast was that there was not a single RC in their ranks! [Now] the four RC Chaplains were SJs and the three interpreters French priests!'[5] Initially, Unionist leaders had used their influence at the War Office to remarkable effect, nominating a substantial part of the division's officer corps (though many served only during the prolonged period of training in Ulster and England). They also directed group enlistment of entire UVF units as companies and battalions in the 36th division, and pursued ideological education (as well as *esprit de corps*) through formation of Orange military lodges in Ulster, England and France. Command of the 36th division also changed when it finally reached France, in early 1916, under Sir Oliver Nugent of Mount Nugent, County Cavan, who had as little time for political placemen and the Orange Order as he had for nationalists.[6]

To a remarkable extent, Redmond and Carson managed to mobilise both Catholic nationalists and Protestant unionists in practical support for their conflicting political strategies. In order to win popular acceptance and participation, it was essential to persuade both communities that the deepest interests of Ireland (or Ulster) were best served by immersion in the imperial war effort. For Ulster Unionists, despite their pre-war admiration for 'Prussianism' and contempt for Asquith's 'radical' government, it was fairly easy to interpret war service as an expression of loyalty to the monarch (rather than the government), invoking an idealised British past untainted by modern reforms and betrayals.

For Redmondite nationalists, participation in the war gave Ireland the chance to assert its credentials as a future self-governing dominion in a

---

4 For the growing Catholic component in the 14th Royal Irish Rifles (YCV), see N. Perry, 'Nationality in the Irish Infantry Regiments in the First World War', in *War and Society*, 12 (1994), 83–4, 94 (n. 73). Only 2 per cent of those embarking for France in October 1915 were Catholics, but the Catholic component of reinforcements rose to 7 per cent (December 1915–May 1916) and then 18 per cent (July 1916).

5 Diary of Henry Gill, SJ, extracted in D. Burke (ed.), *Irish Jesuit Chaplains in the First World War* (Dublin: Messenger Publications, 2014), 65.

6 N. Perry (ed.), *Major General Oliver Nugent and the Ulster Division, 1915–1918* (Stroud: Sutton Publications, 2007). Nugent replaced Charles Herbert Powell, a former Indian army officer without close Ulster connections.

devolving 'commonwealth', and to persuade Britain that it should no longer be treated as an informal colony. The widespread belief that Britain could indeed be persuaded to treat Ireland like Canada or Australia had been fostered by the reformist programmes of both Liberal and Unionist governments since the 1880s, and the evident determination of Augustine Birrell's Dublin Castle administration to apply 'Irish ideas' to governing the country in preparation for Home Rule. Nationalists, and even some Ulster Unionists, were attracted by the avowed commitment of Britain and France to the defence against invasion of 'small nations' such as Belgium and Serbia, and to the principle of national self-determination. Official propaganda alone would never have won over Irish or Ulster 'hearts and minds' in the absence of self-mobilisation, encouraged by political leaders but ultimately sustained by the apparent benefits of engagement and collaboration with the empire.

Self-mobilisation, however, was reinforced by a wide array of public and private agencies. The recruiting campaign, initially conducted by the War Office and the Parliamentary Recruiting Committee, was reshaped in 1915 to take account of Irish conditions, enrolling prominent Irishmen as advocates. The Central Council for the Organisation of Recruiting in Ireland, launched under the viceroy (Lord Wimborne) in February 1915, presided over a wide range of local recruiting committees in almost every county. Colourful recruiting rallies, often addressed by prominent nationalists such as Tom Kettle, the brilliant but excessively alcoholic ex-MP, attracted huge crowds but few recruits. Six months later, the Department of Recruiting in Ireland was established to coordinate the civil and military authorities with assistance from nationalist as well as unionist politicians. An Irish Recruiting Council, dominated by nationalists such as Stephen Gwynn (an elderly Protestant MP who had with difficulty secured a commission), was established in mid 1918 without overt official participation, in a final attempt to counteract the rampant anti-war movement. All of these bodies were supported by massive propaganda, most strikingly in the form of posters of various formats designed for both indoor and outdoor display. By mid 1915, many posters had a distinctly Irish hue, with growing use of the colour green, Hibernian tokens such as round towers, harps, and shamrocks, appeals from John Redmond, and images of vulnerable colleens. Several hundred posters were printed in Ireland, in batches of up to 40,000 copies (the median print-run was 5,000).[7]

---

7 M. Tierney, P. Bowen, and D. Fitzpatrick, 'Recruiting Posters', in D. Fitzpatrick (ed.), *Ireland and the First World War* (Dublin: Trinity History Workshop, 1986), 47–58.

Appeals from state agencies and politicians to support the war effort were crucially reinforced by businessmen, the press, and the churches. The involvement of prominent Catholic and Protestant businessmen in local recruiting committees was accompanied by practical measures to ease the passage of employees into the forces. The chambers of commerce in Belfast and Dublin encouraged members to guarantee employment for their workers on demobilisation.[8] Trades unions, like fraternities and friendly societies, sometimes allowed their members to remain on the books without paying fees while serving the Crown. Very few newspapers questioned the cause of the Entente, though the initial response of the unionist as well as the nationalist press was notably more tepid than in Britain (even there the prevalence of 'war fever' has been widely exaggerated).[9] Caution was encouraged by fears about the domestic consequences of depleting the paramilitary forces, and by uncertainty about Ireland's constitutional future. Until 1916 at least, syndicated war news dominated the local weekly press (the main source of information for most people), casualty lists and letters from the front appeared regularly, and advertising was permeated by war themes and images from recruiting posters.

Likewise, few Irish clergy doubted the morality of the cause, deeming it a case of justified war according to Thomist doctrine and thus a matter for secular rather than spiritual determination. Only the Christadelphians and the Society of Friends, which encouraged Quakers to join its ambulance corps in place of military service, rejected taking up arms on theological grounds. Though some Protestant clergy and bishops used inflammatory language against the Hun or Johnny Turk, most concentrated on the spiritual functions of the churches in time of war rather than acting as recruiting sergeants. The churches became sites for prayers of intercession, commemorative ceremonies, and organisation of war funds and comforts for the troops. In Ulster, a feature of the war was the joint involvement of some Catholic and Protestant congregations in organising local war charities. Several hundred Irish clergy became military chaplains at home or at the front, and Catholic chaplains (assigned through the archdiocese of Westminster rather than Dublin or Armagh) were particularly admired for their courage and selflessness in braving the front line, comforting the dying, and administering

8 Belfast Chamber of Commerce (CC), Minutes of Council Meeting, 7 September 1914: Public Record Office of Northern Ireland, D1857/1/AB/8, p. 106; report of recruiting meeting, Dublin CC, *Freeman's Journal*, 5 March 1915, in Chief Secretary's Office (CSO), Newspaper Cuttings Books (NCB), vol. 48, NLI.
9 C. Pennell, *A Kingdom United: Popular Responses to the Outbreak of the First World War in Britain and Ireland* (Oxford University Press, 2012).

last rites. In 1914, the church vigorously denounced German atrocities against Catholics (especially nuns) in occupied Belgium, encouraging the faithful to take in Belgian refugees. Even so, the hierarchy and clergy in Ireland were notably reticent in support of the war by comparison with their British counterparts, who did their best to outdo the Protestant churches in proclaiming patriotism. A few 'Sinn Féin' priests and Bishop O'Dwyer of Limerick delivered 'seditious' or 'pro-German' addresses which were faithfully reported by the RIC, but until 1916 their influence was negligible.

To the bewilderment of separatists reared on the doctrine that England's war was 'Ireland's opportunity', Redmond's commitment to the war effort led to few defections from the constitutional strategy. Only a fifteenth of the INV followed Eoin MacNeill's lead into the secessionist Irish Volunteers (precursors of the IRA), and less than a tenth of that rump participated in the 1916 rebellion in Dublin. With the exception of the Irish Republican Brotherhood (IRB), which gained a few hundred members between 1914 and 1916, no 'advanced nationalist' organisation prospered. Arthur Griffith's Sinn Féin remained moribund; Douglas Hyde's ostensibly apolitical Gaelic League became increasingly divided, leading to his removal as president in 1915; James Larkin's Irish Transport and General Workers' Union, under James Connolly's wartime direction, had as many ex-members in the trenches by 1916 as active members in Ireland. The Gaelic Athletic Association, deeply infiltrated by the IRB, also lost members to the forces and held fewer matches, partly as a result of wartime restrictions on Sunday excursion trains.

Meanwhile, nominal membership of the major constitutionalist bodies scarcely declined, though most of their normal functions were redundant during the war. The United Irish League (UIL), the main electoral organisation, was immobilised by the 'party truce' at Westminster, with no general election or seriously contested by-elections before 1917 (the only Irish contests involved rival nationalist or unionist factions and, in one case, Labour). The suspension of state funds for land purchase led to further ossification of local branches normally engaged in prolonged negotiations with landlords. Only the Ancient Order of Hibernians (AOH) remained fully active in the economic field, having been designated as an 'approved society' for administering benefits under the National Insurance Act (1911). Reinforced by wartime extension of the categories of insured workers, the AOH still catered for 150,000 insurance members at the end of 1918.[10] In its less benign manifestation as a

---

10 D. Fitzpatrick, *Politics and Irish Life: Provincial Experience of War and Revolution, 1913–1921* (Dublin: Gill & Macmillan, 1977), 317 (n. 50).

sectarian fraternity, restricted to practising Catholics and deeply hostile to the Orange and Masonic orders, the AOH became dormant. This was mainly due to self-imposed restrictions on provocative Orange parades (fortified by the prohibition of processions throughout Ireland for six months after the Dublin rebellion), and the fact that most leading Catholic and Protestant churchmen were united in their support for the war effort. Given the pugnacity of rebellious rhetoric in pre-war Unionism and Orangeism, it is surely astonishing that no significant 'dissident' unionist movement emerged, in opposition to Carson's wartime strategy of affirming Ulster's imperial patriotism and discouraging anti-nationalist and anti-Catholic rhetoric.

The continuing unpopularity of radical nationalism created a strong sense of shared outrage and frustration among the marginalised coteries of separatist thinkers and organisers. Given the impracticability of a successful military rebellion in a country flooded with troops in training or on leave, easily accessible in emergency by reinforcements from Britain, Birrell's administration reasonably (but wrongly) concluded that no rebellion would be attempted – unless the government provoked it by a pre-emptive strike against the very vocal and visible separatist minority. Ridicule, for Birrell, was a more potent weapon than DORA. Though infuriating for Unionists, who had some success in subverting Birrell's non-interventionist strategy after the formation of a coalition government including Carson in May 1915, this policy should have prevailed – in a rational world.

The ultimate failure of Birrell's strategy was largely attributable to the ingenuity of a few heterodox dreamers such as Patrick Pearse, Thomas MacDonagh, Joseph Mary Plunkett, and James Connolly. Disappointed in their expectations of winning popular support on a wave of revulsion against the war, separatists like these contrived to awaken the supposedly dormant national spirit through a melodramatic act of ritualised sacrifice. While no serious plans were made for a coordinated national rising, a consortium of mavericks decided to occupy and defend a number of highly vulnerable public buildings in the capital, with the inevitable consequence of artillery bombardment, fearful destruction of commercial and residential property, and loss of civilian lives in the cross-fire. Though historians disagree about the extent of rebel culpability for civilian losses, and of rebel prescience in anticipating counter-productive coercion from the wartime government, the desire of senior separatists for an act of collective sacrifice is incontestable.

The outcome of the rebellion exceeded the most sanguine hopes of rebel strategists. Having been indirectly responsible for property losses amounting to several million pounds and the death of about 250 civilians (as well as 80 rebels and 132 police and soldiers), the rebels were initially subjected to widespread incredulity, disgust and abuse. Within weeks, the target of popular outrage had shifted to the government. This followed the execution of minor players such as Pearse's brother Willie, the internment of several thousand deviant nationalists and radicals throughout the country (most of whom had no part in either planning or performing the rebellion), and the haphazard campaign of raids and punitive measures conducted under martial law (from May to November 1916). The effect of indiscriminate coercion was indeed to reverse the hard-won progress of Anglo-Irish reconciliation since the 1880s, to persuade many nationalists that Ireland remained essentially a colony rather than a partner, and to confirm unionist fears that nationalist adherence to King and empire was superficial and reversible. In the aftermath of the rebellion, the pro-war consensus in Ireland was shattered, although (as shown below) Irish support for the war effort was never eradicated. Both the rebellion and coercion took forms unimaginable in the absence of external conflagration, implying that the subsequent revolution was itself a by-product of the Great War.

Motives for Enlistment

At first glance, the most obvious test of Irish 'loyalty' and 'patriotism' was the extent to which the various Irish communities 'answered the call'. By using a combination of police and military and returns, it may be shown that the Irish contribution to the wartime forces was about 206,000, excluding those who enlisted outside Ireland under very different conditions. About 58,000 Irish servicemen were mobilised at the outset, including 21,000 regular soldiers, 18,000 reservists (former regulars), 12,000 special reservists (incorporating former militiamen), 5,000 naval ratings, and perhaps 2,000 officers. In the course of the war, about 134,000 men enlisted in the army, 6,000 in the navy and naval reserve, and 4,000 in the airforce, while 3,700 wartime army commissions had been granted in Ireland by early 1916. The deployment of over 200,000 men in the 'British' wartime forces dwarfed all other military enterprises in Irish history (only 1,200 rebels 'rose' in 1916, while membership of the revolutionary IRA in July 1921 fell short of 70,000, of whom fewer than 4,000 had rifles).[11] In addition to military and naval personnel, Ireland supplied

---

11 Statistics and findings relating to enlistment are derived from D. Fitzpatrick, 'The Logic of Collective Sacrifice: Ireland and the British Army, 1914–1918', in *Historical Journal*, 38 (1995), 1,017–30; and 'Militarism in Ireland, 1900–22', in T. Bartlett and K. Jeffery (eds.), *A Military History of Ireland* (Cambridge University Press, 1996), 379–406, 498–502. See

thousands of nurses for military hospitals at home and field stations abroad, as well as ambulance workers under both official and private direction. Even so, Irish military participation fell proportionately far short of that elsewhere in Britain and in parts of the empire. Scotland and Australia, like Ireland, had populations of about 4.5 million in 1911. Yet Scotland delivered 321,000 army recruits (and 236,000 conscripts), while 330,000 volunteers embarked for overseas service with the Australian Imperial Force and other units.[12] Irish fatalities (excluding those enlisted outside Ireland) probably amounted to 32–35,000, compared with 60,000 Australians and 78,000 Scots (including conscripts).

The Irish shortfall was partly attributable to differences in pre-war military organisation, since Scotland had a thriving Territorial force while compulsory home service had recently been introduced in Australia. An even more important difference was the predominance of agriculture in the Irish economy, whereas Scotland and Australia were among the most urbanised countries on earth. In many countries, farmers and their sons were notoriously reluctant to enlist, an attitude intensified in Ireland by the predominance of family farming and the consequent domestic cost of releasing young adult males. If we assume that virtually no Irish agriculturists enlisted, as the police repeatedly affirmed, a more realistic comparison between Irish and British enlistment rates before 1916 may be calculated on the basis of the population of males with non-agricultural occupations in 1911. This indicates that the ratio of Irish recruits to the base population was 6.3 per cent in 1914, compared with 9.9 per cent in Britain. The corresponding figures for 1915 were 6.6 per cent in Ireland and 10.7 per cent in Britain. How should we explain the residual reluctance of Irishmen to join the forces?

Whereas no aggregate reports were compiled showing the religion or paramilitary experience of British recruits, Irish historians benefit from the elaborate monthly returns of enlistment from each county submitted by the RIC between 1914 and 1917. Though doubtless unreliable in detail, the aggregate police figures closely match those derived from military sources. The returns by religion indicate that Catholics accounted for 53 per cent of naval recruits, 68 per cent of army reservists, and 57 per cent of military recruits,

---

also P. Callan, 'Recruiting for the British Army in Ireland during the First World War', in *Irish Sword*, 17 (1987), 42–56.

12 Recorded aggregate voluntary enlistment in Scotland and Ireland was 320,589 and 134,302 respectively: *General Annual Reports of the British Army (including the Territorial Force from the Date of Embodiment) for the Period from 1st October, 1913, to 30th September, 1919, prepared by Command of the Army Council*, 9, in House of Commons Papers, 1921 (Cmd. 1193), xx, 469. For Australian statistics, see Colonel A. G. Butler, *The Australian Army Medical Services in the War of 1914–1918*, vol. iii (Canberra: Australian War Memorial, 1943).

the Catholic component in army recruiting being much higher in 1915 (61 per cent) and 1916 (63 per cent) than 1914 (46 per cent). Though falling short of the Catholic proportion of all men with non-agricultural occupations (66 per cent), these figures do not reveal any marked religious bias. It follows that the predominance of Catholic nationalism cannot adequately 'explain' Ireland's relatively low rate of voluntary enlistment.

Examination of county returns suggests that region was more important than religion in determining variations in enlistment. Military enlistment between 1914 and 1916 (16 per cent of the non-agricultural base population) was most intense in the province of Ulster (22 per cent), followed by Leinster (14 per cent), Munster (11 per cent), and Connaught (10 per cent). The region of heaviest enlistment was north-east Ulster embracing Belfast, Antrim and Down (25 per cent), but the Irish aggregate figure was also surpassed in Fermanagh (23 per cent), Carlow (22 per cent), Tipperary and Londonderry (20 per cent), Armagh (19 per cent), Longford (18 per cent), and Dublin (16 per cent). Though not closely correlated with Ireland's economic geography, the county rankings indicate heavier enlistment in Ulster and the midlands, with lighter enlistment in most coastal counties, especially those marked by poverty and 'congestion' along the Atlantic seaboard. Some of the richest counties had high enlistment rates, contradicting the superficially plausible assumption that military enlistment appealed most strongly to the poor and unemployed.

When account is taken of these regional variations, the residual under-representation of Catholic recruits almost disappears. Because Ireland's Protestant population was so heavily concentrated in Ulster and especially the north-east, where enlistment was heaviest, much of the Catholic short-fall is attributable to the concentration of Catholics in regions of relatively low enlistment. The provincial returns for 1914–1917 show that Catholics were consistently *more likely* than Protestants to enlist in both Leinster and Munster. In Ulster as a whole, the Protestant rate was higher, yet Ulster Catholics were markedly more likely to enlist than Catholics elsewhere. County returns by religion, available only for 1915, indicate that Catholics were actually more inclined than Protestants to join up in the Belfast region, belying the innuendo that Belfast Catholics 'shirked' while their Orange and Unionist adversaries answered the empire's call.[13] There was a pronounced positive correlation between Catholic and Protestant local enlistment rates

---

13 For county returns, see CSO, Dublin Castle, *Intelligence Notes, 1913–16, preserved in the State Paper Office*, ed. B. Mac Giolla Choille (Dublin: Stationery Office, 1966), 182.

across the 32 counties, confirming the limited impact of religious affiliation. No wonder that Redmond set such store in these enlistment returns, tirelessly requesting and manipulating the figures to refute Unionist slurs against nationalist Ireland.

Though credible as an explanation for pre-war recruitment patterns, the model of economic self-interest is nonsensical if applied to wartime service, when the risk of being killed, maimed, wounded or traumatised vastly outweighed any material benefits such as free travel, board and lodging in the trenches, pocket-money, and separation allowances for family members. Returns gathered in October 1914 from Irish firms, by the Board of Trade, reveal particularly heavy enlistment in sectors characterised by high wages, skilled employment, and enhanced wartime demand, especially shipbuilding, engineering, chemicals, and linen manufacture. The immediate loss of workers to the forces was much *lower* in the case of industries that became stagnant during the war, such as mining, building, or paper and printing. Returns for the entire United Kingdom (unavailable separately for Ireland for most occupational groups) also indicate high enlistment among clerical workers and professionals, confirming the perverse proposition that military service was most attractive to those with most to lose. 'Rational action' is a very poor model for explaining risk-taking in time of war.

The most persuasive explanation for making an irrational decision, such as translating patriotic sentiments into wartime enlistment, is the influence of 'peer-groups' such as kindred, neighbours, school-fellows, societies, fraternities, paramilitary forces, and more informal groups of 'pals' and friends. When peers and rôle-models set an example, the individual decision will be framed in terms not of self-interest, but of honour, duty and loyalty to the group. Such sentiments, also evident in sports where the individual player irrationally invites injury 'for the team's sake', were easily translated into the language of patriotism and national honour. Recruiting organisers and poster-designers – sometimes guided by advertising professionals well versed in the American science of using psychology to sell soap – made full use in propaganda of regimental traditions, sporting analogies, duty to women and dependants, and fear of losing face among peers and potential girl-friends.

The army's organisation into regimental districts was designed to exploit neighbourhood loyalties and military traditions within families. Thus recruits could translate local patriotism into enrolment in the Royal Irish Regiment (depot in Clonmel), Royal Irish Rifles (Belfast), Princess Victoria's Royal Irish Fusiliers (Armagh), Royal Inniskilling Fusiliers (Omagh), Connaught Rangers (Galway), Prince of Wales's Leinster Regiment (Birr), Royal Munster Fusiliers

(Tralee), or Royal Dublin Fusiliers (Naas). These regiments incorporated battalions derived from the disbanded county militia, based in barracks throughout the country. Other nominally 'Irish' units included the Irish Guards (London) as well as various cavalry regiments.

Local groups, often linked by shared occupations or schooling, were encouraged to form 'pals' battalions' or companies, though few were formed in Ireland apart from battalions of the 36th division directly linked with UVF county units. Notable exceptions were the 14th battalion, Royal Irish Regiment, and D company, 7th battalion, Royal Dublin Fusiliers. Unlike other units of the 36th division, the 14th emerged from an initially apolitical group of clerical and professional workers from the Belfast region who had joined the YCV. D company, initiated by the president of the Irish Rugby Football Union, brought together a loose network based on shared schools, universities, games and personal friendship. Celebrated as 'the Pals of Suvla Bay', D company was almost extinguished in its first engagement as part of the 10th division on the Gallipoli peninsular in August 1915.[14] Likewise, the YCV suffered disproportionately in the first Battle of the Somme in July 1916.

The success of political and social leaders in mobilising so many Irishmen demonstrates that powerful group loyalties were at work, even in a country where peer-groups (especially in the rural south and west) often *discouraged* enlistment. Police figures indicate the extraordinary contribution to the forces of the rival paramilitary forces: all told, the INV supplied 32,000 men between 1914 and 1917 compared with 31,000 from the UVF. Admittedly, most paramilitaries did not serve in the war: when compared with peak membership, enlistment represented 17 per cent of the INV and 36 per cent of the UVF. Yet ex-paramilitaries comprised a much higher proportion of recruits from each community: 34 per cent of Catholic recruits belonged to the INV (ignoring the small minority of Protestant members), and no less than 57 per cent of Protestant recruits belonged to the UVF. The paramilitary link was even stronger in the case of reservists, who had been largely responsible for training and drilling both forces. The ratio of INV members to Catholic reservists was 63 per cent, and the ratio of UVF members to Protestant reservists was even higher (82 per cent). Though many members doubtless joined up for reasons other than paramilitary solidarity, it is likely that Irish participation in the Great War would have been far smaller but for the existence and mobilisation of 'Carson's army' and Redmond's counter-army.

---

14 H. Hanna, *The Pals at Suvla Bay, being the Record of 'D' Company of the 7th Royal Dublin Fusiliers* (Dublin: E. Ponsonby, 1917).

Many other organisations and fraternities helped feed men into the war-time army. Protestant youth organisations such as the Boys' Brigade, the Church Lads' Brigade, and Baden Powell's Boy Scouts all provided train-ing in discipline and obedience, and encouraged members to join the forces with considerable effect, particularly in Dublin and Belfast. Nearly half of all Protestant recruits in Dublin were reportedly veterans of the Boys' Brigade alone. In rural areas, where fraternities played a central part in communal organisation for both Catholics and Protestants, these too acted as a conduit for military enlistment despite the general recalcitrance of farmers and their sons. The exceptionally high rate of enlistment in the Belfast region cannot be attributed to the influence of the UVF or any other Unionist organisation, as the UVF, the Orange Order, the Unionist Clubs, and support for the Ulster Covenant of 1912 were all notably weak in Belfast and Antrim. On the other hand, the high 'density' of each of these populist movements in mid and south Ulster, and their weakness in Donegal, is mir-rored in the regional pattern of Protestant enlistment in 1915. The associa-tion at county level between Catholic enlistment and support for the AOH is more tenuous; but both enlistment and Hibernianism were most intense in the province of Ulster. Alas, neither the AOH nor the Orange Order compiled a roll of honour, and that issued by the Freemasons is manifestly incomplete and marred by duplication. We can neither aggregate the con-tribution of fraternities to Irish military recruitment, nor prove that group loyalties were the *primary* factor in prompting individuals to enlist. Even so, the vigorous support for the war effort provided by local lodges and divi-sions, in an era when fraternities played a vital part in social life, must have acted as an important catalyst.

To what extent was participation encouraged by an Irish 'martial tradition', so often invoked by politicians and historians? Was Irish culture unusually vio-lent, militaristic, or regimented? Was a military career widely sought because of a scarcity of alternative livelihoods? Despite pre-war Ireland's reputation for violence and paramilitary activity conducted by 'secret societies' and 'fac-tions', it is difficult to demonstrate that either symptom of 'militarism' was widespread by 1914. Judicial statistics showed low rates of reported violent crime, particularly in rural areas, and secret societies such as the IRB had long since confined their militarism to commemorative rhetoric. It is true that the use of 'physical force' was exalted by both nationalists and unionists, being widely regarded as a more manly and honest option than 'constitutional' or 'political' activity. The popularity of disciplined youth movements and frater-nities using martial ceremonial confirms that many outwardly law-abiding and respectable people were romantically attracted to military life. But the same was true of Britain, as exhibited in youth organisations and national service movements, and likewise throughout pre-war Europe. Apart from the virtual absence of pacifists (even Frank Sheehy-Skeffington acted as an intermediary for the IRB in America), the prevalence of militarism in Ireland was unexceptional.

The thesis that poverty and lack of employment opportunities had driven generations of young Irishmen into the forces, so creating a 'martial tradition' not generated by disposition or ideology, is superficially more appealing. It is true that almost all of the 39,000 regular soldiers and reservists mobilised at the outbreak of war had been without occupation at the time of attestation aged about 18, and that most probably came from proletarian families for whom peace-time soldiering was an attractive economic option. In many Irish towns, especially in the vicinity of major barracks, generations of certain families had sent boys to the same regiment. The same applied to naval enlistment near the major ports and stations. For much of the nineteenth century, natives of Ireland had been notably over-represented in the British army. Yet by 1905–1913, when the economic gap between Ireland and Britain had greatly diminished, the Irish element (8.7 per cent) was slightly below Ireland's share in the population of the United Kingdom. The British army was no longer a force disproportionately manned by Irish 'corner-boys'.

The pre-war officer caste was another matter. The martial reputation of the Irish landed gentry is confirmed by the extraordinarily high Irish-born proportion of army officers in 1901 (14.4 per cent). By comparison, Irish Protestants comprised only 2.8 per cent of the population of the United Kingdom. Whereas the class composition of those enlisting in the ranks was transformed by the war, much greater continuity applied to the selection of officers.[15] Though many middle-class Catholics as well as Protestants secured wartime commissions, and promotion of 'rankers' became commonplace, sons of the Irish gentry remained conspicuous in the *Army List*, the *London Gazette*, and press reports of officer casualties. The stereotype of the Irish 'officer and gentleman' was, for once, faithful to fact.

---

15 Though the religious affiliation of officers was not enumerated, we may assume that very few pre-war Irish officers were Catholics. Perry's analysis indicates that the Catholic gentry (comprising perhaps 15 per cent of landed families with estates exceeding 1,000 acres in the 1870s) were 'slightly less' likely than Protestants to become officers, both before and during the Great War: N. Perry, 'The Irish Landed Class and the British Army, 1850–1950', 322, in *War in History*, 18 (2011), 304–32.

'The Irish' at War

Many recent publications on Ireland and the Great War have concentrated on personal testimony and individual experiences, reflecting a commendable desire to unveil the 'realities' of war hitherto obscured by celebratory propaganda and historicist interpretations. These narratives confirm the degrading conditions of life in billets and in the trenches, the endemic horrors of mud, excrement, lice, rats and flies (unbearable at Gallipoli), the monotony associated with long periods of inactivity between engagements, the infrequency of personal contact with the enemy, the moments of revelation in which those of other nationalities (even 'Huns') assumed human characteristics, the impotence of those ground down by military technology, the rudeness and inconsiderateness of many officers and NCOs, the solidarity of men exposed to common risks arising from disease and lack of training as well as from combat, the tactics used by 'shirkers' and 'malingerers' trying to minimise those risks, and the relief experienced by those who were merely wounded and those liberated after the armistice. These 'Irish' stories include accounts of cowardice as well as heroism, dogged survival as well as high ideals. Whereas stories of heroism were once predominant, current writers tend to picture their subjects as passive victims of a futile conflict, helpless in the face of an intractable war machine. Doubtless, as in recent British and Australian accounts of the Great War, tales of survivorship and resourcefulness will eventually outshine those of victimhood.

During the war, both nationalist and unionist writers took full advantage of anecdotes about 'the Irish' or 'Ulstermen' to depict the 'martial spirit', reckless courage, and devotion to duty of Irish servicemen. National pride was fostered by stories of the London Irish following a football into battle at Loos, or a Catholic chaplain blessing Irish troops before battle, or Sergeant Michael O'Leary capturing a machine gun and the Victoria Cross. Nationalist publications included *The Irish at the Front*, *What the Irish Regiments have done*, and *The Irish on the Somme*, each prefaced by John Redmond and circulated by the war propaganda office at Wellington House, London. Though obviously designed to promote enlistment by celebrating Irish achievements, these works included many candid interviews with participants and circumstantial accounts of horrific suffering.[16] The nationalist message was reinforced by

---

16 M. MacDonagh, *The Irish at the Front* (London: Hodder and Stoughton, 1916) and *The Irish on the Somme* (London: Hodder and Stoughton, 1917); S. Parnell Kerr, *What the Irish Regiments have done* (London: T. Fisher Unwin, 1916).

widely reproduced paintings depicting Irish troops, notably by non-Irish artists such as Fortunino Matania and James Prinsep Beadle. The most famous was Beadle's depiction of the charge of the Ulster division at the Somme, led by an officer with an orange handkerchief, modelled by an Englishman. Tales and images of Irish and Ulster heroism supplied the basis of subsequent commemoration as well as contemporary propaganda.

The belief that Irish soldiers were indeed a breed apart, particularly by comparison with the English, is also evident in personal testimony.[17] Writing in 1938, John F. Lucy, a Corkonian corporal and later an officer in the Belfast-based 2nd Royal Irish Rifles, recalled the bravado of Irish troops in between battles during the first winter of the war: 'The carelessness of the Irish, so useful in active operations, was accounted bad soldiering, in position warfare. The number of avoidable deaths in our battalion caused comment. The men flouted death by recklessly walking in the open and by taking dangerous short cuts. The Australians later showed the same characteristic.'[18] The piety of Catholic servicemen was confirmed by many witnesses, including a chaplain writing in January 1915: 'There were about a dozen of our men behind blazing away for all they were worth, and the bullets were coming whizzing across ... I remained there for about half-an-hour hearing confessions. I sat behind a couple of sandbags and the men came in turn and knelt in front of me. They came and knelt in mud and I sat in the mud. They were caked in mud, their faces grimy with smoke, their bandoliers tight with live cartridges.'[19] Rowland Feilding, English commander of the 6th Connaught Rangers at Wytschaete in October 1917, drily observed the humanity of his Irish troops in the 16th division: 'This morning one of my corporals killed a German and wounded another in No Man's Land. The latter crawled back towards his line and as he neared it, three of his friends came out after him. My men then acted in a manner which would perhaps nowadays be regarded as quixotic, so relaxed – thanks to our opponents – have the rules of this game of war become. They did not shoot.'[20]

Though sometimes riveting, such narratives may offer a distorted impression of the distinctive collective experience of *Irish* servicemen. Were the Irish more often heroic, less cowardly, more humane, more pious, chirpier,

---

17 See T. Denman, 'The Catholic Irish Soldier in the First World War: The "Racial Environment" ', in *Irish Historical Studies*, 27 (1991), 352–65.

18 J. F. Lucy, *There's a Devil in the Drum* (London: Faber, 1938), 312.

19 'From a Clongownian Chaplain', 15 January 1915, in the *Clongownian* (1915), extracted in Burke (ed.), *Irish Jesuit Chaplains*, 20.

20 Major Rowland Feilding to his wife Edith, 17 October 1917: J. Walker (ed.), *War Letters to a Wife* (Staplehurst, Kent: Spellount, 2001; 1st edn., 1929), 80.

or better disciplined than other combatants? Is it plausible that one nationality would stand out in a conflict where many nationalities faced much the same challenges and risks with much the same human and technical equipment? Is it possible to quantify such attributes? A crude measure of heroism is the frequency with which Irishmen were awarded the Victoria Cross, the highest military decoration. The most comprehensive study of 'Irish' VCs lists 44 names, amounting to 7.0 per cent of all 628 VCs awarded between 1914 and 1919 (less than 3.5 per cent of wartime British troops were raised in Ireland). On closer inspection, the evidence for excess Irish heroism dissolves. Of 32 VCs born in Ireland, only 17 served in Irish regiments, along with 6 in British regiments, 1 each in the Royal Navy and Royal Horse, and 7 in colonial forces. Of 12 VCs born elsewhere with an Irish parent, only 3 joined Irish regiments. If we include all Irish-born VCs apart from those in British and colonial regiments, the 'Irish' proportion of non-colonial VCs (4.0 per cent) scarcely exceeds the country's overall contribution to the forces.[21]

This exercise confirms the importance of distinguishing sharply between those who joined up voluntarily in Ireland, where loyalty to King and country was uniquely problematic, and those with Irish origins who enrolled in Britain or the dominions. As in so many 'Irish' rolls of honour, the laudable desire to enumerate and celebrate Ireland's 'contribution' leads to inflated figures which cannot be set against any base population, since the number of emigrants and their children who joined outside Ireland cannot be ascertained. By overstating the number of Irish fatalities, it is easy to generate startling statistics indicating that the Irish were more at risk of death than British or colonial forces, with the innuendo that they were regarded as dispensable cannon-fodder. Some journalists and politicians still cite the notoriously inflated figure of 49,435 in *Ireland's Memorial Records* (1923), replete with emigrants, their descendants, and Britons attached to Irish regiments. Various journalists and historians, contributing potted accounts for newspaper supplements arising from the interminable state-sponsored 'decade of commemorations', have recently suggested that the relentless resurrection of forgotten deaths by local historians may eventually inflate the currently accepted total (32–35,000) to 40,000 or more.[22] By comparison with the most

21 My categorisation of VCs is derived from individual entries in R. Doherty and D. Truesdale, *Irish Winners of the Victoria Cross* (Dublin: Four Courts Press, 2000) and M. Arthur, *Symbol of Courage: A History of the Victoria Cross* (London: Sidgwick and Jackson, 2004). Arthur's entries indicate that 412 of 628 VCs were awarded to men serving in the British army, 62 in the naval and air services, and 154 in colonial forces.

22 For detailed statistical analysis of Irish army fatalities officially listed in *Soldiers died in the Great War* and omitting officers and those in services other than the British army,

reliable estimate of Irish enlistment (206,000), this would imply an Irish fatality rate of almost 20 per cent, compared with 12.3 per cent for the entire British army and 18.0 per cent for Australians who embarked overseas. Admittedly, the British fatality ratio was depressed by the fact that, by contrast with the Irish and Australian volunteers who mainly enlisted in 1914–1915, so many British servicemen were conscripted in the second half of the war and therefore at risk for a shorter period. Even the currently accepted total implies an Irish rate of 15.5–17.0 per cent. It may be that the Registrar-General's return of 27,405 deaths overseas of Irish soldiers (13.1 per cent) is, after all, closer to the true figure for those normally resident in Ireland.[23]

Had the 'Irish' regiments and divisions been truly Irish, it might have been possible to draw convincing comparisons between Irish and British soldiers, and between Irish nationalists and unionists. Indiscipline is measurable through the frequency of courts martial, indicating similar levels overall in the 16th and 36th divisions, and wide variations within both divisions (battalions associated with Belfast and Dublin being unusually ill-disciplined).[24] Yet the only valid comparisons refer to the period of training, since all 'Irish' units were rapidly diluted with non-Irish reinforcements after taking the field. The one major mutiny involving an Irish regiment occurred in 1920, when members of the Connaught Rangers briefly revolted in the Punjab. Only 56 Irish prisoners of war at Limburg joined Sir Roger Casement's 'Irish brigade' in the winter of 1914–15, despite material inducements, and news of the Dublin rebellion was greeted with indignation in Irish regiments. Nor is there convincing evidence that Sinn Féin's growth after 1916 provoked widespread unrest among soldiers at the front, though some soldiers when home on leave surrendered weapons to the Irish Volunteers with varying degrees of reluctance.

Admittedly, divisions and battalions with Irish titles retained their Irish reputation even after 'Indianisation' of the 10th division in early 1918,[25] or the

---

see P. J. Casey, 'Irish Casualties in the First World War, in *Irish Sword*, 20 (1997), 193–206; Perry, 'Nationality', 65–95. Casey identified some 30,216 Irish-born fatalities in all units (including 437 not listed in *Soldiers died*); Perry analysed 30,716 fatalities in the 9 Irish infantry regiments, of which 9,055 were born outside Ireland.

23 This total, based on 'lists' held by the Registrar-General which cannot be located, excludes officers, servicemen dying in the United Kingdom, and evidently naval and air personnel: Saorstát Éireann, Department of Industry and Commerce, *Census of Population, 1926*, vol. X, *General Report* (Dublin: Stationery Office, 1934), 12.

24 T. Bowman, *The Irish Regiments in the Great War: Discipline and Morale* (Manchester: Manchester University Press, 2003); L. Speer Demisko, 'Morale in the 16th (Irish) Division, 1916–18', in *Irish Sword*, 20 (1997), 217–33.

25 J. E. Kitchen, *The British Imperial Army in the Middle East* (London: Bloomsbury, 2014), 200–13.

mass infusion of Welsh and English troops into the 36th division after the catastrophe at the Somme. Yet, increasingly, the companions who accompanied an Irishman into battle were unlikely to be Irish, not least because the troops deployed in each battle zone were drawn from various divisions and regiments without regard to nationality. Despite hopes that Irish Catholics and Ulster Protestants would fight shoulder to shoulder, this seldom occurred. A notable exception was the Battle of Messines in June 1917, when the 16th and 36th divisions were deployed in adjacent sectors, suffering similar casualties. When Major Willie Redmond, the oldest officer in the 16th division, was mortally wounded by a shell splinter, he was carried from the field by men of the Ulster division and tended by his unrelated namesake John Redmond (an Anglican army chaplain who became a leading Orangeman of unusually liberal outlook after his return to Belfast). Also at Messines, Catholic and Protestant servicemen from West Belfast, separated by invisible barriers at home, were involuntarily brought together.[26] In general, however, their comrades in action were more likely to be British, French, Canadian or Australian. The war generated a bewilderingly cosmopolitan environment, utterly at odds with the relatively homogeneous culture of the home parish or training camp. Irishness, if it had any impact on individual attitudes or experiences, was but one of many factors fostering solidarity or hostility in the field.

The extent to which Irishness was submerged in the wartime army is evident from two studies of fatalities revealing that 29 per cent of men killed while serving in 'Irish' regiments were not Irish-born, while 28 per cent of Irish-born fatalities were not serving in Irish regiments.[27] These facts call into question the concentration of military historians on avowedly 'Irish' units,[28] leading to the neglect of the significant minority of Irish servicemen who joined British regiments or specialist forces such as the Royal Engineers, Royal Artillery, Royal Army Medical Corps, and Royal Army Service Corps, along with the Royal Navy, Royal Flying Corps and Royal Air Force. Individual careers, especially of officers, often involved transfers to different

---

26 Tom Johnstone, *Orange, Green and Khaki: The Story of the Irish Regiments in the Great War, 1914–18* (Dublin: Gill & Macmillan, 1992), 269–81; T. Denman, *A Lonely Grave: The Life and Death of William Redmond* (London: Irish Academic Press, 1995), ch. 6; Denman, *Ireland's Unknown Soldiers: The 16th (Irish) Division in the Great War, 1914–1918* (Dublin: Irish Academic Press, 1992), 111–15; R. S. Grayson, *Belfast Boys: How Unionists and Nationalists fought and died Together in the First World War* (London: Continuum, 2009), 109–19.

27 See note 24 above.

28 H. Harris, *The Irish Regiments in the First World War* (Cork: Mercier Press, 1968); Johnstone, *Orange, Green and Khaki*.

units, regiments, or services, further diluting the Irish character of the military experience. It follows that the Irish case cannot be disentangled from the broader history of the British and imperial war effort.

'Dilution' in response to inadequate regional enlistment was not unique to the three Irish divisions, reflecting the predictable reduction in enlistment rates after abatement of the uncontrolled flood in 1914. As the war continued, the pool of young adults primed for enlistment was steadily emptied, leading to a downward trend in both Britain and Ireland and consequent pressure for conscription. Enlistment also fluctuated from month to month in response to ever changing criteria relating to age, height, fitness and occupational exemptions. In both Britain and Ireland, there were marked surges in military enlistment in spring and late autumn 1915, reflecting the success of sustained recruiting campaigns despite universal awareness of fearful casualties. These surges were particularly marked in Ireland, demonstrating the limited impact of the separatist anti-recruiting campaign and the fact that both nationalist and unionist public opinion remained, at least in principle, favourable to the war effort. After January 1916, the introduction of conscription in Britain ruled out any comparison with Irish enlistment patterns, while the ultimately successful Irish campaign against conscription suggests a reversal of public attitudes to the war following the rebellion. Yet this is difficult to reconcile with the fact that monthly army intake in Ireland rose markedly in the months after April 1916, and again at the height of the anti-conscription movement in spring 1918. Though Irish enlistment invariably fell short of War Office demands, it remained significant in defiance of the mass conversion of nationalists to anti-war republicanism.

In one important respect, the war experience of Irishmen in the British forces was distinctive. In the absence of conscription, Irish enlistment was heavily concentrated in the first year of the war, leading to relatively light Irish casualties in 1917–1918. Whereas British army fatalities overall were far greater in the second half of the war,[29] almost three-fifths of deaths in Irish units occurred before 1917.[30] The most conspicuous Irish blood-lettings

---

29 The number of recorded deaths from all causes in the British Regular army and Territorial force (for each year ending 30 September) was 6,161 (1914), 79,683 (1915), 125,041 (1916), 162,502 (1917), 159,113 (1918), and 41,007 (1919), implying that only 37 per cent of fatalities antedated September 1916. These figures exclude other services as well as colonial and Indian forces, and omit 254,176 men reported missing, of whom 100,068 were unaccounted for after the release of prisoners of war: *General Annual Reports of the British Army*, 62–70.

30 The number of recorded deaths (excluding officers) in each calendar year was 2,160 (1914), 7,021 (1915), 8,693 (1916), 6,495 (1917), 6,309 (1918), and 38 (1919), implying that 58 per cent died before the end of 1916: Perry, 'Nationality', 71.

occurred at Gallipoli in 1915 and at the first Battle of the Somme in the following summer. Almost 3,000 members of Irish regiments were killed in the Dardanelles campaign, accounting for 9.1 per cent of total wartime fatalities, compared with only 2.6 per cent for the British army as a whole. The Irish Gallipoli component rivalled those for the Ottoman empire (13.8 per cent), Australia (14.0 per cent), and New Zealand (16.7 per cent), countries (unlike Ireland) in which the Dardanelles or Çanakkale campaign became the major focus of war commemoration.[31]

The 10th (Irish) division alone suffered 1,773 fatalities at Suvla in August and September 1915, of whom two-thirds were born in Ireland. Its losses were only slightly exceeded on the Somme in July 1916, when the 36th (Ulster) division lost 1,866 men, 89 per cent of whom were natives of Ireland. Neither division had any experience of combat before the battles in which they suffered most, and each lost much of its national character as a result of that first blooding. The destruction of the 16th (Irish) division was drawn out over a longer period, with 601 fatalities in its first major engagement at Hulloch (April 1916), 1,079 at Guillemont and Ginchy, deathplace of Tom Kettle (September 1916), 201 at Messines (June 1917), 890 at 3rd Ypres (August 1917), and 753 in March 1918.[32] Episodes such as Verdun in 1917 and the German spring offensive of 1918, central to French and British war commemoration, had far less impact in Ireland. Though most Irish casualties nevertheless resulted from attritional trench warfare on the western front, the concentration of the 10th division on the eastern front, at Gallipoli and then Salonika, exposed it to an equally brutal but less impersonal form of warfare. This was marked by hand-to-hand combat and handball-like grenade exchanges, between forces initially unseparated by any no-man's-land and without defensible supply-lines.

Irish participation in the war effort was not limited to those enlisting in Ireland. As already noted, uncounted emigrants and their offspring enlisted outside Ireland, sometimes involuntarily through conscription in Britain, Canada and New Zealand, along with the American draft. In Britain, long before conscription was imposed on Irish residents in 1916, nationalist organisations reported massive enlistment of emigrants and

---

31 Perry, 'Nationality', 67, 79; *Statistics of the Military Effort of the British Empire during the Great War, 1914–1920* (London: War Office, 1922), 237–43, 284–7; E. J. Erickson, *Ordered to Die: A History of the Ottoman Army in the First World War* (Westport, CN: Greenwood Press, 2001), 237–43.

32 Perry, 'Nationality', 79–80. The Irish-born proportion of fatalities for the 16th division in each episode was 85 per cent, 76 per cent, 66 per cent, 52 per cent, and 64 per cent. Figures for the 10th and 16th divisions exclude the 10th and 11th Hampshires respectively.

their descendants, including over 100,000 'Irishmen in Great Britain' by February 1915.[33] Once again, Irish loyalty was proclaimed through the raising of units such as the 'Tyneside Irish' (in the Royal Northumberland Fusiliers), manned mostly by sons or descendants of emigrants. Few members of the Tyneside Irish emerged unscathed from the first day of the first Battle of the Somme.[34]

In Australia, where overseas conscription was twice rejected by referendum, the Irish-born component enlisting for overseas service (1.3 per cent) almost exactly matched the Irish-born proportion of young men enumerated in the Australian census for 1921. About a fifth of Australian servicemen were Catholics, mostly of Irish origin, only slightly below the expected proportion.[35] Even Archbishop Daniel Mannix of Melbourne, an inveterate opponent of conscription who expressed growing support for Irish republicanism, made a point of demonstrating the loyalty of his flock by parading thousands of Catholic ex-servicemen and a clutch of 'Irish' VCs (mostly Protestants) on St Patrick's Day, 1920.[36] The Canadian expeditionary forces contributed no less than five VCs of Irish birth, and included several units with Irish titles. In the United States, where the draft applied only to American citizens, propagandists claimed that Irish aliens were more likely than any other nationality to seek naturalisation during the war. Once again, supporters of the Irish anti-war movement lost no opportunity to flaunt Irish loyalty, especially after America finally entered the fray in 1917. The martial tradition of New York's 'Irish Brigade', formed by Thomas Francis Meagher from Irish émigrés during the American civil war, was invoked in the wartime resurrection of the 69th infantry regiment in France. The stereotype of the fighting Irish, dubious though it may seem to historians, proved to be a potent rallying call wherever the Irish settled.

33 According to incomplete returns collected by the UIL of Great Britain, 115,513 had enlisted by February 1915 including 40,786 in Lancashire and 25,260 in Scotland: *Freeman's Journal*, 25 February 1915, in CSO, NCB, vol. 48.

34 See F. Lavery (comp.), *Irish Heroes in the War* (London: Everett, 1917); J. Sheen, *Tyneside Irish: 24th, 25th and 26th and 27th (Service) Battalions of the Northumberland Fusiliers* (Barnsley: Pen and Sword Books, 1998).

35 According to the Australian census for 1921, 1.4 per cent of men aged 20–49 were Irish-born while 21.8 per cent were (Roman) Catholics. Census returns for ex-servicemen still in Australia in 1933 state that 1.3 per cent were Irish-born while 17.5 per cent were Catholics. Returns for members of the Australian Imperial Force who embarked for overseas service (reliable only for comparisons between the four major denominations) indicate a slightly higher Catholic component (20.6 per cent compared with 18.6 per cent for ex-servicemen excluding those of other denominations): Butler, *Australian Army Medical Services*, 890.

36 B. Niall, *Mannix* (Melbourne: Text Publishing, 2015), 146–9.

Economic Consequences

Despite dire predictions of mass unemployment and industrial melt-down in the early months of the Great War, its economic consequences were surprisingly positive in Ireland as in Britain.[37] Though traditionally key sectors such as retailing, building, and construction languished, the resulting unemployment was eventually offset by the expansion of war-related industries such as engineering, metals and chemicals, shipbuilding, and even linen manufacture (essential for the fabric of aeroplanes). Between July 1914 and July 1918, employment of insured workers in engineering rose by a quarter and in shipbuilding by 14 per cent, whereas employment in building and construction fell by a tenth. Many businesses reshaped their production to suit wartime demand and became 'controlled establishments', while the government established vast munitions factories relying heavily on women and other workers without recognised 'skills'. The state-regulated 'dilution' of labour permitted rapid expansion of the industrial workforce as qualified male workers left for the forces, providing jobs for many who had lost or never had paid employment. By January 1916, over four-fifths of Ireland's munition workers were located in Belfast and in the north Ireland, though substantial employment was provided by the national shell factory at Parkgate, Dublin, and the explosives factory in Arklow, County Wicklow. In addition, over 34,000 women and men were recruited from Irish labour exchanges by British munition factories in 1917–1918 alone.[38]

The outcome was a substantial reduction of unemployment in almost all recorded sectors of Irish industry, though in 'traditional' industries unemployment in Ireland (unlike Britain) was never entirely eliminated. Almost full employment was achieved in engineering and shipbuilding, giving the Belfast region a marked advantage over Dublin, where heavy industry was minimal. Between mid 1914 and mid 1918, Irish unemployment among insured workers fell from 4.5 per cent to 1.1 per cent in shipbuilding, 4.9 per cent to 2.5 per cent in engineering, and 7.0 per cent to 4.0 per cent in building and construction. In printing, however, unemployment remained relatively high and unstable, with no definite downward trend.[39]

37 For detailed analysis, see D. Fitzpatrick, 'Irish Consequences of the Great War', in *Irish Historical Studies*, 39, (2015), 643–58; also 'Home Front and Everyday Life', in J. Horne (ed.), *Our War: Ireland and the Great War* (Dublin: Royal Irish Academy, 2008), 131–42, 283.
38 Brennan Papers, National Library of Ireland, MS 26191; N. O'Flanagan, 'Dublin City in an Age of War and Revolution, 1914–1924' (MA Thesis, University College, Dublin, 1985), 47.
39 Statistics refer to the proportion of insured workers in each sector whose unemployment books were lodged compulsorily at labour exchanges on 30 June (for printing,

As in Britain, the departure of so many male workers opened up new employment sectors for women, especially as munition workers, temporary civil servants and clerks, though there were few Irish reports of female bus conductors or dockers to disturb gender stereotypes. Thousands of Irish women also served as nurses (working in Volunteer Aid Detachments at home and abroad, or with the more highly trained Red Cross and St John's Ambulance Brigade) and as uniformed members of military forces such as Queen Alexandra's Imperial Military Nursing Service.[40] Predictably, the voluntary workers were mainly drawn from the gentry and bourgeosie, whereas the women who joined the auxiliary services were more likely to be working-class Catholics. For women whose husbands, fathers, or brothers had joined the forces, these wartime employment opportunities seldom compensated for lost income from male breadwinners, though separation allowances provided some compensation.[41]

Another effect of the war throughout the United Kingdom was steady inflation, leading to the doubling of wholesale and retail prices between July 1914 and November 1918. This was an unavoidable consequence of the shortage of imported goods and the state's reliance on massive borrowing to fund war production. Inflation brought certain benefits, encouraging easier access to credit and leading to marked expansion of cooperative wholesaling, savings banks and pawnbroking. The negative impact of inflation and shortage of food was greatest in towns and cities such as Dublin, where consumers were reliant on shops and unemployment remained a problem.[42] For employed workers, particularly in war-related industries, the state and the major trades unions combined to protect the interests of marginal workers through guaranteed minimum wages in 'essential' sectors, reduction in the premiums paid to skilled workers and expansion of National Insurance coverage. In return, the unions accepted curtailment of strikes and curbs on labour mobility which amounted, in the view of radical critics, to 'industrial conscription'. Yet the net result was to ensure

statistics are based on returns from selected trades unions, not published separately for Ireland after 31 Dec. 1917): *Labour Gazette* and *Abstract of Labour Statistics, passim*.

40 C. Clear, 'Fewer Ladies, More Women', 161–2, in Horne (ed.), *Our War*, 157–70, 283–6; E. Reilly, 'Women and Voluntary War Work', in Gregory and Paseta (eds.), *Ireland and the Great War*, 49–72; M. Downes, 'The Civilian Voluntary Aid Effort', in Fitzpatrick (ed.), *Ireland and the First World War*, 27–37.

41 For systematic discussion of the war's demographic and economic consequences for women, see F. Walsh, 'Irish Women in the First World War', PhD Thesis (Trinity College, Dublin, 2015).

42 O'Flanagan, 'Dublin City'; P. Yeates, *A City in Wartime: Dublin, 1914–18* (Dublin: Gill & Macmillan, 2011).

that money wages in most sectors, in Ireland as in Britain, almost kept pace with inflation, and that inequalities of income within the proletariat were reduced. Though systematic official returns of wages were not published during the war years, most categories of Irish workers were paid between 170 per cent and 190 per cent more in December 1920 than in October 1913. Meanwhile, the most comprehensive index of wholesale prices recorded an increase of 195 per cent.

If real wages remained fairly stable, benefiting an expanded pool of workers, an apparently negative effect of the war was severe restriction of consumer choice. Imported commodities and many essential foods soon became scarce, in response to requisitioning of most of the merchant fleet and the risk of destruction by enemy warships, submarines, and mines. From late 1917, rationing ensured that even the Irish poor had access to sugar, though other scarce commodities rationed in Britain escaped control. The restriction of choice was offset by an energetic and imaginative programme of food control, designed to wean the Irish and British people from dependence on inferior processed products (such as white bread, cakes and jams), and to encourage use of nutritious substitutes such as oatmeal and carrot preserves. Farmers and gardeners were encouraged to grow fresh vegetables and fruit. Despite widespread ridicule of the sometimes disgusting nutritious alternatives, the Irish diet probably benefited from these enforced changes, even if consumers groaned.

Irish farmers gained more than any other group from the war, eventually making them almost as unpopular as the 'profiteers' and 'gombeen-men' who evaded reduction of their profit-margins and interest-rates while others practised self-denial. The same factors that reduced transoceanic imports to a trickle provided Ireland with a captive market of British consumers, whose food requirements far exceeded the capacity of Britain's small and shrinking agricultural sector. As a result, the volume of Irish farm exports soared and prices for farm produce greatly outstripped inflation. Between 1913 and 1918, the increase in average annual prices was 127 per cent for wheat, 130 per cent for white oats, and 140 per cent for fat pigs, with similar increments for beef, mature store cattle, and eggs. Flax prices rose even more sharply because of demand from the booming linen industry, whereas the price of potatoes, catering mainly for domestic consumers, increased by only 46 per cent. The relative cheapness of potatoes cushioned the impact of inflation on urban workers, except in periods of scarcity attributable to poor weather and disease, as in the winter of 1916–1917 when potatoes cost almost three times as much as in 1913.

The acute shortage of flour in Britain provoked a significant increase in Irish tillage, temporarily reversing a trend evident since the Great Famine. When the government introduced regulations compelling Irish farmers to increase the acreage under tillage after 1916, there was little resistance because the financial reward outweighed the usual outrage against British dictation. Since corn production was more labour-intensive than cattle-rearing, the paid labour force expanded and took advantage, for the first time, of minimum wage rates imposed by the state. The agricultural boom reverberated well beyond the farm workforce, enriching shopkeepers, middlemen, bankers, priests, and other beneficiaries of rising farm income.[43]

The contrast between agricultural enrichment and urban deprivation, outside the north-eastern industrial zone, led to working-class unrest during periods of acute food shortage such as the winter of 1916–1917. In Ireland as in Britain, the first half of the war was marked by very low incidence of strikes, but in both countries conflict intensified thereafter. The most active agent in fomenting unrest in 1916–1917 was not organised Labour but Sinn Féin, which performed as champion of the poor by opening cut-price food markets in towns and interfering with farm exports to Britain. These markets infuriated shopkeepers, the blockade of ports antagonised farmers, and after a few months Sinn Féin prudently declared the campaign a success and abandoned it. Like its constitutionalist rival, the evolving republican movement relied heavily on monetary and moral support from the 'substantial' classes of farmers, businessmen, and priests, whose conservative influence soon stifled its social radicalism. Even so, this episode revealed that the impact of war on class inequalities was not always positive, despite extensive state intervention designed to cushion the burden imposed on workers, women and the dependants of servicemen.

With the notable exception of agriculture, the economic impact of the war in Ireland resembled a less extreme version of the better documented British experience. The same applied to its demographic and social impact. Since lower enlistment entailed less shortage of adult manpower in Ireland, the additional demand for juvenile and female substitutes was much feebler. In the rural west, the effect of the war was actually to enlarge the supply of labour, both female and male, as a result of the virtual stoppage of transatlantic emigration from summer 1915. The western economy had long been shaped by the continuous depletion of at least a third of each cohort, mostly through chain-migration of unmarried farmers' children in their early

---

43 Fitzpatrick, *Politics and Irish Life*, esp. ch. 7; C. Cousins, *Armagh and the Great War* (Dublin: History Press, 2011), ch. 3.

twenties. Where wartime enlistment was heavy and pre-war emigration relatively low, as in urban regions and along the east coast, the war's effect on the labour market mirrored that in Britain. Where a tradition of heavy emigration coincided with low enlistment, as in Connaught, the effect of keeping prospective emigrants at home was to increase under-employment and foster inactivity and frustration. It is significant that the regions most affected by stoppage of emigration were also those with the highest concentration of Sinn Féin membership by January 1919. As in many other respects, the war helped to shape the gathering revolution.

Otherwise, the war's demographic impact was quite predictable. Registration statistics reveal a reduction of 11 per cent in births 1910–1913 and 1914–1918, though the decline was much steeper in England and Wales (17 per cent), France (42 per cent), and Germany (43 per cent). In Ireland, unlike Britain, there was no increase in reported illegitimacy. It is noteworthy that the number of marriages remained stable in both countries, apart from a brief surge in 1915. The loss of over 30,000 lives in the course of war service exceeded the predicted peacetime mortality among men aged 20–44 years, based on deaths registered between 1901 and 1910. War losses conferred added value on human life, inspiring investment by both government and the Carnegie Trust in Irish child and maternal welfare schemes. The state and philanthropic agencies joined forces to ensure that infants had access to uncontaminated cows' milk; baby clubs and welfare centres multiplied. In July 1917, Baby Week was officially launched to 'stem the torrent of death in babyland': 'Ireland's babyhood is being slaughtered in battalions owing to Ireland's neglect'.[44] The long-term decline in infant mortality continued during the war, despite fluctuations attributable to epidemics of infectious disease. Little is yet known about wartime morbidity in Ireland, though any general improvement (as reported for Britain) was overwhelmed by the catastrophic impact of influenza in 1918–1919.[45]

Though somewhat cushioned by enhanced welfare and insurance provision, family life was profoundly disrupted by the war. Even if there was no 'lost generation' in Ireland, the landed gentry in particular suffered fearful losses, hastening its social disintegration. If some working-class women

44 J. Dunwoody, 'Child Welfare', in Fitzpatrick (ed.), *Ireland and the First World War*, 69–75; Carnegie United Kingdom Trust, *Report on the Physical Welfare of Mothers and Children*, vol. iv, *Ireland* (Dublin: CUKT, 1917); article by Mrs Maud Walsh, head of women's section, Department of National Service (Ireland), in *Weekly Irish Times*, 17 July 1917: cutting with file on women's national service in CSO, Registered Papers (RP) 3950/1922, National Archives, Dublin.
45 See Walsh, 'Irish Women'.

perceived an economic advantage in exchanging a hungry husband or son for a separation allowance, such bloody-minded calculations were surely outweighed by the practical and psychological impact of prolonged separation and anxiety, often followed by death, debility or disfigurement. Though many households, particularly in rural Ireland, were not directly affected, almost all had close kindred or neighbours in the forces. The loss or the ruin of a father or son was felt long after the conflict ceased, leaving gaps in families that might never be healed. Yet widespread suffering had the positive effect of developing solidarity within communities as people shared each other's anxiety and grief. Reports of commemorative ceremonies and church services during the war suggest that in parts of Ireland, as in Britain, the awareness of collective sacrifice acted as a powerful social cement, despite the disruptive impact of political conflict after 1916.

Consequences of Political Radicalisation

The political convulsion following the rebellion of 1916 fundamentally changed Irish perceptions of the war, even if most Nationalists as well as Unionists still hoped for the defeat of Germany. The sense that there was no practical alternative to more or less active support for the war effort was eroded by Sinn Féin's alternative strategy of minimising Irish involvement, and relying on the expected peace conference rather than Westminster to deliver independence. The prospect of war-inspired reconciliation rapidly receded, apart from an unprecedented convergence of Redmondite and southern unionist proposals at the abortive Irish Convention of 1917–1918. The Irish Parliamentary Party and its local organisations (except for the AOH) declined sharply, despite three by-election victories over Sinn Féin in 1918. Only six of its MPs secured election for Irish constituencies in the post-armistice general election in December. The rising popularity of Sinn Féin, however superficial the 'conversion' of many of its supporters seemed, meant that the government had no useful political allies in Ireland except Carson's Unionists. This greatly impeded attempts to revive recruiting and prepare public opinion for further wartime interventions in the economy. Even so, about 15,000 recruits were raised in Ireland during 1918, partly through propagandist concentration on the Royal Air Force (with its romantic associations and need for technicians at one remove from the conflict) rather than the 'bloody infantry'.[46]

---

46 One of several variant abstracts of enlistment in Irish districts (1 January–9 November 1918) enumerated 10,522 recruits to the army, 1,085 to the Royal Navy, and 3,489 to the Royal Air Force: NS 1/84, TNA.

The issue of conscription provided a splendid opportunity for nationalists and Catholics to oppose British 'oppression' without unambiguously opposing the war effort and so alienating American allies. In 1916, the government had twice excluded Ireland from the military service acts for fear of fostering radical opposition to Redmond. The difficulty of gaining public acceptance for conscription in Ireland was intensified by the relatively low proportion of men of military age who had enlisted voluntarily, so weakening the argument for equality of burden. In Britain, where far fewer potential servicemen remained, the argument for a fairer system of assigning men to military and civilian employment was widely accepted even by Labour. In much of Ireland, however, conscription would have affected most of the cohort. It was therefore expedient from a military viewpoint to avoid provoking a crisis in Ireland in pursuit of a rather small additional intake under unfavourable conditions.

The German spring offensive in 1918 forced the government to further expand conscription in Britain, making it *politically* expedient to extend its scope to Ireland in order to restore the appearance of equity in its application. Though most senior administrators and commanders in Ireland deplored the proposal, which was expected to yield fewer soldiers than the number required to enforce it, the measure was enacted in April 1918 with provision for future implementation through an 'order in council' by the Irish executive. This provoked an impressively coordinated and wide-ranging resistance movement embracing all nationalist factions, organised Labour, and the Catholic hierarachy. The impression of a sectarian movement was mitigated by an auxiliary pledge taken by a few hundred Protestants, and even some unionists were thought to sympathise privately with the anti-conscriptionists despite Carson's ostentatious backing for the government.

Unlike the less popular and largely ineffectual movement against conscription in Britain, the Irish campaign had no pacifist and little socialist content. No reference was made to liberty of conscience, nor was the general illegitimacy of British government in Ireland unambiguously asserted in the skilfully worded pledge and episcopal declaration. Even though the organisers failed to compute the number of signatories, so missing an opportunity to emulate the propagandist impact of the Ulster Covenant of 1912, the effect of the campaign was sufficient to dissuade the administration from putting conscription into effect. Instead, appeals were made for accelerated voluntary recruiting, with promises that districts achieving an ever-diminishing 'quota' would be exempted. The armistice came just in time to avert the necessity for yet another embarrassing fudge.

Even after the end of European hostilities, the war continued to shape Irish politics through the subsequent peace conference. Sinn Féin's electoral success was predicated on the superficially plausible yet ludicrous belief, expounded by Arthur Griffith and Éamon de Valera, that President Wilson would be obliged by his wartime advocacy of self-determination for small nations to coerce Britain into granting Irish independence. This was based on the fact that the victorious European powers were hopelessly indebted to American buyers of war bonds, thus supposedly empowering Wilson to blackmail Britain into breaking up her own empire (on the premise that Ireland was a colony). Predictably, the Paris peace conference restricted its attention to the defeated empires, leaving those of Britain, France, Italy, and America herself undisturbed. Despite the fabled influence of the 'Irish' vote in America, the delegates of Dáil Éireann (the new assembly formed by Sinn Féin) failed to gain access to Wilson or to any session of the conference. This setback, though not terminating the republican campaign for international recognition of Ireland's claim, strengthened the drift towards armed conflict in Ireland itself. Yet again, the course of Irish politics had been diverted by the war.

Veterans and Commemoration

The most visible imprint of the war was its human residue, the returned servicemen (so often maimed or disabled, some requiring decades of treatment for physical and mental ailments). Throughout Europe and beyond, veterans comprised a large, restive, and influential element in the post-war population. In the United Kingdom, over four million men were demobilised from the army and RAF between the armistice and May 1920, more than a third of the male population aged 20–49 in 1921. Over a quarter-million servicemen were repatriated to Australia during and after the war, amounting to almost a quarter of the same age-group at home. The return of so many men naturally fostered friction with civilian trades unionists who resented the flooding of the labour market, with families whose pecking-order was threatened by the hard men back from the trenches, and with civilian society in general, often viewed by veterans as being governed by shirkers who had done well out of the war. Men released from harsh military discipline were naturally inclined to behave wildly on return to the tame world of home, leading to well-publicised prosecutions for fraud and theft as well as violence and disorderly behaviour. Throughout Europe, veterans became prominent in radical movements ranging from communism to fascism, in paramilitary activity, and in other challenges to the established order. Though never form-ing a cohesive political movement in Britain, veterans pursued their common interests through fraternities and social clubs, such as the British Legion of Ex-Servicemen and its precursors, which were strong enough to apply pres-sure to all major political parties.

In Ireland, the demographic impact of demobilisation was far smaller than in Britain. Almost 100,000 soldiers and airmen were demobilised through Irish dispersal stations between the armistice and May 1920, typi-cally receiving a 'protection certificate', a railway warrant for the journey home, and some cash upon surrendering their weapons.[47] Another 10,000 probably returned to Ireland after being discharged or demobilised without record being kept of their destination. Officers comprised 5.0 per cent of the demobilised Irish, akin to the Scottish proportion (5.2 per cent) but mark-edly above that for English veterans (3.8 per cent).[48] Tens of thousands more had been discharged through injury or illness in the course of the war (no Irish or British statistics are available, but a third of all repatriated Australians returned before the armistice).[49] They embodied its horrors more than its heroics, subsisting on modest pensions and charity. By comparison with the flood of men returning to Britain, Irish veterans formed a small minority of the working population, leaving them in a much weaker position when con-fronted with civilian competition (exacerbated by republican antipathy to Redmondism). Those demobilised after the armistice amounted to less than a tenth of the male population aged 20–49 in 1911. Yet the group was quite large enough to figure prominently in the courts and become embroiled in violent clashes with Sinn Féin and the IRA, particularly on commemora-tive occasions such as Peace Day (19 July 1919) and Remembrance Day (first marked on 11 November 1919).

Irish veterans returned to a mixed welcome and heavy unemployment, though some relief was provided by the out-of-work donation for uninsured workers, which was soon closed to Irish civilians but remained open to veterans for a year after dispersal (60,000 veterans had claimed the dole by November 1919). Only disabled men and war widows were entitled to war pensions. The

---

47 The authoritative studies are by J. Leonard, including 'Survivors', in Horne (ed.), *Our War*, 209–23, 288–9. See also P. Taylor, *Heroes or Traitors? Experiences of Southern Irish Soldiers returning from the Great War, 1919–1939* (Liverpool: Liverpool University Press, 2015).

48 *Statistics of the Military Effort*, 708.

49 Of 264,373 members of the Australian Imperial Force repatriated to Australia, 92,826 (35.1 per cent) were returned before 1919: Butler, *Australian Army Medical Services*, 891.

economic turmoil provoked by termination of war industries did not yet lead to sustained recession, which followed in late 1920. Over 20,000 unemployed veterans as well as 100,000 civilians were registered in labour bureaux by May 1921, at the height of the revolutionary conflict.[50] Thousands were employed on public works funded by various ministries and agencies, and some republican local councils cooperated with these schemes (especially if beneficiaries had joined the IRA or provided intelligence since demobilisation). The British government, through the Irish Sailors' and Soldiers' Land Trust which continued to operate in the two new Irish states, also built clusters of cottages for ex-servicemen with families and two substantial estates (Killester in northside Dublin and Cregagh in east Belfast). Such measures helped veterans to form distinct communities and to protect their common interests and heritage in a sometimes hostile and dismissive environment. A minority joined societies such as the Comrades of the Great War and the Federation of Discharged and Demobilised Sailors and Soldiers, amalgamated in southern Ireland as the Legion of Irish Ex-Servicemen in 1922. Three years later, this body became an affiliated section of the British Legion,[51] though the Irish Nationalist Veterans' Association remained apart. The British Legion had already formed a separate district for Northern Ireland in 1922, in competition with the Ulster Ex-Servicemen's Association. Between 1925 and 1939, the British Legion never had more than 9,000 members throughout Ireland, perhaps a tenth of its potential membership.[52]

Since making war was often their most marketable skill, many veterans contributed their expertise to whatever armed groups sought their services. A few hundred Irish ex-servicemen enrolled as temporary police constables ('Black and Tans') in early 1920, in addition to ex-officers who joined the RIC's notorious Auxiliary division. The Ulster Special Constabulary was composed largely of Protestant ex-servicemen, and the 'national' army established in 1922 to defend the nascent Irish Free State is thought to have enlisted tens of thousands of veterans, probably exceeding its intake from the IRA. More than 600 veterans became officers between 1922 and 1924, some serving as senior commandants.[53] During the revolutionary conflict, defection to the IRA was also an option for some who were prepared to sacrifice veteran solidarity for

50 On 6 May 1921, the live register contained 22,242 ex-servicemen, 64,858 civilian men and 37,408 civilian women, compared with 27,919 ex-servicemen, 29,971 civilian men and 25,941 civilian women on 28 January 1921: CSO, RP 2195/1921.
51 *Irish Times*, 19 January 1925.
52 Leonard, 'Survivors', 220.
53 Leonard, 'Survivors', 219.

a passport into the new Ireland. These included some of the most ruthless guerrilla leaders, most famously Tom Barry of Bandon and Mesopotamia, who had been active in the Bandon Comrades of the Great War in 1919.

Despite the substantial presence in the Irish Free State of ex-servicemen, many of whom had close communal and associational ties with other veterans, they exercised little political influence at national level (except briefly through the Irish National League formed by Major William Archer Redmond, John Redmond's son, in 1926). The mainly Catholic ex-service vote had more influence in local elections, often in support of independents or ratepayers' spokesmen. Though no direct statistics are available on the religion of ex-servicemen in the Irish Free State, the Catholic component was presumably similar to the proportion for recruits from the 26 counties (85–90 per cent). In Northern Ireland, even though a slight majority of all Irish servicemen were southerners, veterans constituted a much higher proportion of the population. Of roughly 50,000 who returned to the 'province', less than 30 per cent would have been Catholics.[54] The British Legion quickly became a significant lobby within unionism, but nationalist veterans were dependant on the rather ineffectual advocacy of Joe Devlin's usually abstentionist opposition.

Whereas the Unionist Party under Craigavon and his successors was deeply imbued with the legacy of the war and the value of Ulster's contribution, all major parties in the Irish Free State kept their distance from the veterans. They did not, however, interfere with welfare schemes funded by the former administration, or with the maintenance of plots in Irish cemeteries by the Imperial War Graves Commission. Many veterans therefore belonged to a marginalised yet cohesive sub-community, alien to the new order but seldom under immediate threat from its architects. In several material respects, indeed, veterans were better treated in the Irish Free State than in Northern Ireland or Britain. That had not been the case during the conflict of 1919–1924, when over 120 civilian veterans were murdered on the pretext that they had supplied 'information' to the enemies of Ireland.[55] Though compensation files contain rich documentation of attacks against veterans, their property, and their clubs, the extent to which these attacks were motivated *primarily* by resentment arising from their military service remains contentious.

---

54 Religious breakdowns are available by province for army reservists and recruits (1914–1916), but the only county breakdown is for 1915 (see note 13 above). Using Ulster figures adjusted from the 1915 returns, the best estimate for the Catholic proportion (1914–1916) is 27.5 per cent for the six counties and 87.2 per cent for the 26 counties.

55 Leonard, 'Survivors', 218; Leonard, 'Getting Them at Last: The I.R.A. and Ex-Servicemen', in *Revolution? Ireland 1917–1923*, ed. D. Fitzpatrick (Dublin: Trinity History Workshop, 1990), 118–29.

The vexed issue of how Ireland's war has been commemorated, appropriated and ignored lies beyond the scope of this chapter.[56]

Over the past three decades, in both Irish states, growing public awareness of the shared legacy of the Great War has led to more inclusive ceremonies and sentiments. Even in Sinn Féin, it has become fashionable and expedient to boast of a grandfather or great-uncle who served in the Great War. Among politicians and historians, the long-standing inability to speak or write about the war ('aphasia', never amnesia) has been superseded by a surfeit of worthy if often empty utterances and publications. But the change has come far too late to comfort any of those who actually lived through the war and experienced its direct consequences. We cannot know what passed through the minds of Irish veterans and their families each year during those two minutes of silence, so often disturbed by the indifference or hostility of passers-by. For those who wear the poppy in Ireland today, the core of remembrance is perhaps not so much the war itself, or the individuals who endured it, as a gesture of recompense.

56 See the chapter by Guy Beiner in this volume.

9

Revolution, 1916–1923

FEARGHAL McGARRY

Introduction

Few periods of Irish history have generated as much historiographical controversy as the revolutionary era. The key issues were identified as early as 1924
by P. S. O'Hegarty whose pessimistic pro-Treaty polemic, *The Victory of Sinn
Féin*, argued that the unnecessary use of political violence after the Easter
Rising had destroyed the spirit of the national movement and demoralised
the Irish people.[1] Reflecting a wider literature of disillusionment, articulated
primarily through fiction and drama (most notably Seán O'Casey's powerful Dublin trilogy), O'Hegarty's thesis did not elicit a response from professional historians for almost half a century. Consequently, the first draft of the
history of the revolution was written by republicans. Memoirs such as Dan
Breen's *My fight for Irish freedom* (1924), Tom Barry's *Guerrilla Days in Ireland*
(1949), and the *Fighting Series* accounts recorded by Irish Volunteers depicted a
conflict between the Irish people and the malign forces of the British Empire
(even if some of these accounts registered uncertainty about the extent of
popular commitment to republican ideology and armed struggle). The Civil
War was largely overlooked, as were the perspectives of those who had not
experienced the preceding 'four glorious years' as a period of liberation. The
First World War, the formative event of the decade, provided little more than
a backdrop to the conflict in Ireland. This narrative was reinforced by school
textbook, as well as by State commemoration that centred on the sacrificial
gesture of Easter 1916 rather than on the more divisive violence that followed. The emergence of a post-revolutionary Catholic nationalist consensus ensured that the significance of earlier radical impulses was marginalised.

---

1 P. S. O'Hegarty, *The Victory of Sinn Féin* (new edn., Dublin: University College Dublin
Press, 2015).

In the 1970s, when professional historians belatedly turned their attention to the period, more critical interpretations emerged. Emphasising the conflict's uneven geographical impact, local studies presented a more complex picture of the revolution at its grassroots.[2] These 'revisionist' accounts emphasised social and political divisions rather than nationalist unity, and explored how factors other than selfless patriotism, such as generational conflict, collective pressures and increasing social frustrations, motivated many activists. They identified continuities between the separatist and constitutional nationalist movements, such as their cross-class appeal and reluctance to adopt socially divisive policies. The emergence of a popular physical-force movement was presented more as a departure from Irish political tradition than, as nationalist interpretations had suggested, an inevitable outcome of centuries of resistance to British rule, the cultural revival of the late nineteenth century, and the Irish Party's compromises. The resilience of constitutional nationalism before the de-stabilising impact of the Ulster crisis, First World War and Easter Rising was emphasised, while the light grip of British rule appeared a more important causal factor than the grievances and sense of oppression articulated by the 'revolutionary generation'.

British shortcomings in administration, counter-insurgency, intelligence-gathering and propaganda were seen as more important to the outcome of the conflict than the heroism or ingenuity of republicans.[3] In recent decades, revolutionary violence has emerged as a central issue as the focus has shifted from fighting for freedom to killing for Ireland.[4] It was shown that civilians formed almost half of the revolution's victims, and that combatants more often died, unarmed, at the hands of hidden assailants rather than as a result of the daring ambushes at crossroads described in IRA memoirs. The nationalist conceptualisation of the conflict as an 'Anglo-Irish War' was challenged by the idea that the campaign for independence also encompassed a form of civil war between antagonistic religious and political groups within Ireland. The term 'revolution' was increasingly adopted, acknowledging not only the radical nature of the process by which a transfer of political sovereignty was brought about by violence, but also the

---

2 One of the earliest and most influential was D. Fitzpatrick's *Politics and Irish Life, 1913–1921: Provincial Experience of War and Revolution* (Dublin: Gill & Macmillan, 1977).

3 C. Townshend, *The British Campaign in Ireland 1919–1921. The Development of Political and Military Policies* (Oxford University Press, 1975).

4 Most notably in another influential local study, P. Hart's *The I.R.A. and its Enemies. Violence and Community in Cork 1916–1923* (Oxford University Press, 1998).

extent to which it was bound up with wider strands of sectarian, agrarian and intra-communal conflict.[5]

Against the backdrop of the Northern Irish 'Troubles' (1969–1997), the acrimonious debates prompted by these new interpretations revealed a gulf between popular assumptions and scholarly perspectives. For many of its critics, and some of its advocates, 'revisionism' represented a riposte, conscious or not, to the Provisional IRA's appropriation of Irish history as much as the outcome of new research or methodological and theoretical advances.[6] It was also criticised for replicating some of the limitations of the nationalist historiography it sought to revise, such as its Anglo-Irish focus and preoccupation with moral concerns. A key question, for example, remained that raised by O'Hegarty: 'whether the bloody catalogue of assassination and war from 1919–21 was necessary'.[7] The end of the Troubles saw much heat dissipate from these disputes, as is evident both from changing popular attitudes and 'post-revisionist' historiography. For example, despite being criticised for its nationalist bias, Ken Loach's influential film, *The Wind that Shakes the Barley* (2006), did not shy away from depicting republican brutality, or acknowledging how social factors shaped the conflict. Although contentious aspects of IRA violence, particularly in Cork, continue to provoke historiographical disputes and press coverage, these controversies are better understood as a 'metaphor for far wider disputes over Irish national history and identity' than the product of genuine disagreements over evidence, methods or interpretations.[8] By contrast, the transformation of public attitudes to Irish soldiers in the Great War provides a striking example of the extent to which a more pluralistic understanding of the past has gained ground. By incorporating the campaign for Home Rule and Ireland's experience of the First World War alongside the War of Independence, and by encompassing the experiences of previously marginalised groups such as labour and women, the Irish Government's 'Decade of Centenaries' programme similarly reflects a more nuanced approach than previous commemorations.

---

5 C. Townshend, 'Historiography: Telling the Irish Revolution', in J. Augusteijn (ed.), *The Irish Revolution 1913–1923* (Basingstoke: Palgrave, 2002). The 'realization that both social revolution and ethnic conflict were part of a broader concept, formerly known as rebellion and now defined as civil war' has also informed wider historiographical approaches in recent years (S. Kalyvas, *The Logic of Violence in Civil War* (Cambridge University Press, 2006), p. 417).

6 See, for example, the introduction to R. Fanning's *Fatal Path. British Government and Irish Revolution 1910–1922* (London: Faber and Faber, 2013).

7 R. F. Foster, *Modern Ireland 1600–1972* (London: Allen Lane, 1988), 506.

8 S. Howe, 'Killings in Cork and the Historians', *History Workshop Journal* (2014), 77, 178.

Popular and scholarly perspectives have also been shaped by the availability of new sources such as the Bureau of Military History and the Military Service Pensions collection. Recent historiographical developments include a greater focus on the experience of people from ordinary rather than elite backgrounds; the use of collective biography to explore the formation of the revolutionary generation; consideration of the conflict within the broader context of the enthusiasm of the 'pre-revolution' and disillusionment of independence; and more sophisticated research on the relationship between sources, historical narratives and memory of the revolution.[9] Complementing the detailed focus provided by an ever-expanding range of local studies, comparative and transnational approaches are providing broader perspectives on revolutionary violence, as well as demonstrating more clearly how political change in Ireland was shaped by global influences, including wider currents of modernity.[10]

Rather than offering a detailed account of the course of the revolution, this chapter focuses on the relationship between violence and political developments during these years, highlighting recent historiographical shifts where significant. Why did the period after the Easter Rising see the emergence of a formidable threat to British power rather than, as occurred after previous insurrections (1803, 1848, 1867), the collapse of republican resistance? How did the revolutionaries' popularity after 1916 shape their ideology? Was the relative success of the campaign for independence due more to the use of violence or to the political mobilisation that underpinned it? What role did external factors play? Why, given the militancy of the republican campaign, was its outcome so conservative?

Easter 1916

The revolution began in 1916. While a military failure, it was the Easter Rising that provided 'Ireland's 1789 or 1917', including 'a preliminary sketch of the

9 See, for example, R. F. Foster, *Vivid Faces. The Revolutionary Generation in Ireland 1890–1923* (London: Allen Lane, 2014); D. Ferriter, *A Nation and not a Rabble. The Irish Revolution 1913–1923* (London: Profile Books, 2015); R. S. Grayson and F. McGarry (eds.), *Remembering 1916: The Easter Rising, the Somme and the Politics of Memory in Ireland* (Cambridge University Press, 2016).
10 See, for example, N. Whelehan (ed.), *Transnational Perspectives on Modern Irish History* (London: Routledge, 2014); R. Gerwarth and J. Horne (eds,), *War in Peace: Paramilitary Violence in Europe after the Great War* (Oxford University Press, 2012); T. Wilson, *Frontiers of Violence. Conflict and Identity in Ulster and Upper Silesia 1918–1922* (Oxford University Press, 2010); M. Walsh, *Bitter Freedom. Ireland in a Revolutionary World 1918–1923* (London: Faber & Faber, 2015).

revolution to be, complete with a claim to exclusive sovereignty by the insurgent government and army'.[11] Despite years of planning by a determined revolutionary faction, the rebellion's impact owed more to the collapse of the political assumptions underpinning the alliance between the Irish Party and the Liberals (outlined by Matthew Kelly in an earlier chapter in this volume) than the inherent appeal of insurrectionary republicanism.

Three key factors had created this long-awaited opportunity. The most significant of the 'longer-term developments in attitude and mentality' identified by Kelly derived from the impact of the late nineteenth-century cultural revival on nationalist consciousness. Vigorously cultivated by organisations such as the Gaelic League and the Gaelic Athletic Association, particularly amongst the younger generation, the idea of an Irish national identity that was not only separate to that of Britain but was defined in opposition to English values implicitly challenged the underlying integrationist assumptions of John Redmond's political project. The Home Rule crisis of 1912–1914 presented a more immediate political challenge. The emergence of the Ulster Volunteer Force and Irish Volunteers, and the arming of both organisations in the spring of 1914, undermined popular nationalist faith (never unconditional, as even the rhetoric of Irish Party politicians made clear) in the ability of constitutional methods to secure fair play from Westminster. It also weakened British authority in Ireland, as was demonstrated by the Curragh mutiny and the increasingly anxious tone of police reports outlining the threat of civil war in Ulster.

The third, and most important, destabilising factor was the outbreak of the First World War. As in other imperial states with discontented nationalities, the pressures of total war created the conditions for revolution: 'As surely as Verdun or the Somme, Dublin in 1916 was a First World War battlefield.'[12] But notwithstanding the events that would follow, it is important to note the lack of popular support for militant nationalism in the summer of 1914. Despite the many difficulties the war would later present for the Irish Parliamentary Party, Redmond's prestige was affirmed, first, by the enactment of Home Rule at Westminster (albeit suspended for the war's duration) in September 1914, and second, by his ability to retain the support of over 90 per cent of the Irish Volunteers following the split triggered by his decision to fully commit his party to the British war effort.

---

11 P. Hart, *The I.R.A. at War, 1916–1923* (Oxford University Press, 2005), 12.

12 K. Jeffery, *1916. A Global History* (London: Bloomsbury, 2015), 104.

Consequently, the decision to mount an insurrection, taken by the IRB's supreme council shortly after the outbreak of the First World War, should be seen as a reflection of separatist weakness, as well as frustration at the moderate state of popular opinion demonstrated by nationalist goodwill for the war effort.[13] Both the IRB and Irish Volunteers were divided on the merits of an unprovoked rebellion, with only James Connolly's small socialist Irish Citizen Army fully committed to a policy of insurrection. The posthumous significance accorded to Patrick Pearse, the president of the Irish Republic proclaimed at the General Post Office, ensured that the Rising was subsequently widely seen as a 'blood sacrifice'. The rebellion's key organisers, veteran Fenian Thomas Clarke and Seán Mac Diarmada, were influenced by less mystical considerations. They intended a principled and heroic gesture to reawaken the spirit of militant nationalism amongst the apathetic masses, an aspiration that helps to explain their prioritisation of symbolic gestures, such as the proclamation of a republic, over military objectives during Easter week.[14]

The rationale for the Rising was essentially provided by the war: a distracted Britain, a powerful German ally, and the promise of weapons, military assistance and diplomatic support practically obliged Irish revolutionaries to rise. Even defeat, acknowledged by many leading rebels as the most likely outcome, held out the promise of subsequent success when – as most separatists assumed – Germany won the war. Emotional considerations were also vital, with leaders such as Clarke, Pearse and Mac Diarmada articulating to subordinates the shame and humiliation they would feel if the war ended without an attempt to assert Irish independence in arms. These motives were viewed as irrational by contemporaries such as Eoin MacNeill, the nominal commander of the Irish Volunteers, as well as by some later revisionist historians, but the insurrectionaries' belief that, in time of war, the advantages of an unsuccessful rebellion – the assertion of separatist credibility, the revival of the physical-force tradition of which they saw themselves as guardians, and the undermining of the Irish Party and its denationalising Home Rule project – were preferable to inaction, was borne out by subsequent events.

A dramatic string of mishaps led up to the Rising, among them the interception of the *Aud* with its cargo of arms by the British navy, the arrest of Roger Casement following his landing at Banna Strand, County Kerry, and the issuing of a countermanding order by the ostensible commander

---

13 Jeffery, *1916*, 105.
14 F. McGarry, *The Rising. Ireland: Easter 1916* (Oxford University Press, 2016 edn.).

1. Eoin MacNeill (1867–1945). Gaelic scholar and nationalist politician. Chief of Staff of the Irish Volunteers in 1916.

of the Volunteers, Eoin MacNeill, the effect of which was to largely con-fine the rebellion to Dublin. Yet the scale of the insurrection proved suf-ficient to achieve the military council's objectives. The occupation of the GPO and other prominent buildings throughout Dublin by around a thou-sand rebels (their numbers rising during the week) on Easter Monday, 24 April 1916, led to a week-long battle for the capital that gripped Irish and global attention. Confronted by some 20,000 British troops, many of Irish nationality, the rebels had no chance of military success. The insurrection was over within six days, leaving almost 500 people (the majority of them civilian) dead, and much of the centre of the city in ruins. The punitive British response to the rebellion, understandable in the context of what was regarded as a treacherous 'stab in the back' in a time of war, further ensured the success of the military council's aims. The decision to execute sixteen rebel leaders, arrest 3,000 suspects (many innocent of any involvement in the Rising), and intern two thousand men and six women in British prison camps ensured that public hostility to the rebels' actions began to give way to popular sympathy for the rebels and, subsequently, their political cause, such as it could be discerned.

The Rise of Sinn Féin

As the signatories of the Proclamation had intended, many Irish republicans would come to see the Rising 'as the starting point for all subsequent history'.[15] That the insurrection seemed to herald not only political but social and cultural transformation was clear from contemporary responses. Within days of the executions, critics of the 'childish madness' of the rebellion, such as the embroiderer Lily Yeats (sister of W. B.), were anticipating 'the beginning of Ireland'.[16] However, the Rising also marked the end of an era for some within the tiny revolutionary world that existed before Easter 1916 when an idealistic minority pursued republican and other radical aims. The execution of the signatories of the Proclamation – a document which epitomised the rebellion's inchoate radicalism – marked one rupture, but so too did the emergence of a popular mass movement led by Éamon de Valera, one of the most socially conservative of the Rising's surviving leaders, which recruited a younger, more rural, and more nationalistic cohort of activists radicalised after 1916. This development saw the eclipse of modern influences such as socialism and secularism that – alongside physical-force republicanism, cultural nationalism and a sense of victimhood – were espoused by marginal pre-revolutionary organisations.[17] The extent to which the meaning of the Rising came to be located in a narrower understanding of freedom is illustrated by the popular ballads and print culture that flourished after 1916. For example, the popularity of 'The Soldier's Song' which spread, alongside the new Sinn Féin movement, like wildfire demonstrated the appeal of martial values and the idea of a heroic struggle between 'the sons of the Gael' and the 'Saxon foe' which reflected the historical narratives absorbed by the revolutionary generation. The marginalisation of women's voices, previously a significant

15 Ferriter, *A Nation*, 168.
16 R. F. Foster, *W. B. Yeats: A Life. II: The Arch-Poet 1915–1939* (Oxford University Press, 2003), 45–50.
17 R. F. Foster, *Vivid Faces*; F. McGarry, *The Abbey Rebels of 1916. A Lost Revolution* (Dublin: Gill & Macmillan, 2015).

element within advanced nationalist circles, formed another aspect of this development.[18]

Despite its disorienting speed, the Irish Party's demise was far from inexplicable. The cumulative impact of the Ulster crisis, First World War, and Easter Rising exposed the contradictions between the moderate, conciliatory, imperialistic rhetoric of Redmondism and the popular nationalist sentiment expressed by grassroots Irish Party politicians: Irish interests, it became clear, were not so easily reconciled to those of Britain. Out-manoeuvred by his ostensible allies within the Liberal Government, as well as his opponents within Ulster unionism and the Tory Party, Redmond's currency was devalued by his repeated concessions, particularly on partition and support for Irish enlistment, in return for the same post-dated cheque for Home Rule. By placing implacable opponents of Home Rule, such as F. E. Smith, Andrew Bonar Law and Edward Carson, at the heart of the cabinet, the coalition government of 1915 had further damaged the Irish Party's credibility, as did growing anxiety about conscription.[19] There were also other, longer-term, factors at work: the party's aging leadership made it seem out of touch, and the perception that it was wholly embedded in a Westminster establishment, contributed to this malaise. And recent historiography has emphasised the importance of generational change in the party's demise.

The impact of the Rising accelerated these difficulties, as did the executions, and the failed attempt to introduce Home Rule in the immediate aftermath of Easter week. The inability of the Irish Convention, which met from July 1917 until March 1918, to achieve a consensus on implementing Home Rule may have represented the last chance for a peaceful settlement, as nationalist support for self-government within the United Kingdom was further eroded by a radical shift in post-war expectations. As the Hapsburg, Ottoman and Russian Empires crumbled, other subject nationalities threw up their 'own Redmonds and de Valeras debating the merits of cooperation or resistance', and it was not only in Ireland that the resisters 'were in the ascendant' by 1918.[20] However, there was nothing assured about the rise of separatism, nor prescriptive about the precise form it would come to take. The consensus that

---

18 For women before the revolution, see S. Pašeta, *Irish Nationalist Women, 1900–1918* (Cambridge University Press, 2013).

19 On decline and poor strategy, see respectively M. Wheatley, *Nationalism and the Irish Party: Provincial Ireland, 1910–1916* (Oxford University Press, 2005) and Fanning, *Fatal Path*. J. McConnel's *The Irish Parliamentary Party and the Third Home Rule Crisis* (Dublin: Four Courts Press, 2013) presents a more positive view of the party.

20 Walsh, *Bitter Freedom*, 37–8.

emerged around the goal of a republic masked the ideological incoherence of the marginalised coalition of republicans, cultural nationalist intellectuals, militant Catholic nationalists and socialists that had brought about the rebellion. The new nationalism was sustained, as Ernie O'Malley's revolutionary memoir suggests, more by the iconography and emotional appeal of the Rising's legacy:

> The people as a whole had not changed; but the new spirit was working slowly, half-afraid, yet determined. The leaders had been shot, the fighting men arrested, and the allied organizations disrupted. Without guidance or direction as if to clarify itself, nebulous, forming, reforming, the strange rebirth took shape. It was manifest in flags, badges, songs, speech, all seemingly superficial signs. It was as if the inarticulate attempted to express themselves in any way or by any method; later would come organization and cool-headed reason. Now was the lyrical stage, blood sang and pulsed, a strange love was born that for some was never to die till they lay stiff on the hillside or in the quicklime near a barrack wall.[21]

Notwithstanding the shifting sands of public opinion, no organisation could readily claim the Rising's legacy: Sinn Féin had not supported the Rising; the Irish Republican Brotherhood (IRB) was a secret fraternity; and the surviving 1916 leaders were obscure figures. Nor was it clear how the rebels' aspirations – even if popularly endorsed – could be achieved. Re-emerging in 1917, the executive of the Irish Volunteers affirmed its determination to renew the struggle for the Republic but prudently made clear that its members would not be called upon to repeat the tactics of Easter 1916.

Sinn Féin's October 1917 convention brought together advanced nationalists identified with Arthur Griffith's party, rival groupings such as Count Plunkett's Liberty League which had won considerable support, militaristic Irish Volunteers and the IRB's radical separatists. The evidence of growing support for this 'new nationalism' provided by a series of by-election victories strengthened the impetus towards unity. While Griffith's pragmatic argument that a republic could not be achieved without a British military defeat was outweighed by the emotional appeal of the legacy of Easter 1916, the convention fudged other key issues such as the party's stance on violence. Sinn Féin's strategy of passive resistance – exemplified by the policy of abstention from Westminster and advocacy of a revolutionary counter-state to undermine the British administration in Ireland – remained in place, albeit as much due to the

---

21 E. O'Malley, *On Another Man's Wound* (Boulder, Colorado: Roberts Rinehart, 1999 edn.), 47.

2. Police 'mugshot' of 'B. Stuart', aka Ernie O'Malley (1897–1957), revolutionary and writer, ND *c*.1920.

lack of any alternative as to widespread commitment to the ideas of Griffith whose former advocacy of a 'dual monarchy' rendered him suspect to both doctrinaire republicans and militarists. Two days after replacing Griffith as leader of Sinn Féin at the convention, Éamon de Valera was confirmed as the president of the Irish Volunteers, marking an uneasy convergence between the republican movement's political and military wings.

An 'attitude or an atmosphere rather than a strategy', Sinn Féin acquired popular support before it possessed an agreed leadership or political programme. Its appeal was based primarily on a rejection of the old (Redmondite) order. It was less evident what it stood for: 'Republicanism, for most of its adherents, was about achieving separation – sovereign independence – rather than implementing any concrete political programme.'[22] It also entailed an important moral dimension, rooted in the cultural forces that had moulded the revolutionary generation. Whereas constitutional nationalists usually emphasised pragmatic arguments for self-government, republicans agreed on

22 C. Townshend, *The Republic. The Fight for Irish Independence* (London: Allen Lane, 2013), 19–25, 52–7.

the spiritual basis for independence. For the committed, republicanism was less a political preference than a moral outlook, characterised by the cultivation of masculine values such as patriotism, virility, temperance and integrity.[23] Influenced by Young Ireland's romantic nationalism, this ideology drew strongly on the cultural revival and, increasingly, on Catholic nationalism. The restoration of Irish, for example, became a central aim, and ideas about Irish history and national identity were more influential than republican political theory. The chauvinistic dimension of cultural revivalism must be seen in the context of generations of discrimination and insecurity, but it is not difficult to discern the roots of post-revolutionary conservatism in this moralistic vision.

A party that thrived on agitation, Sinn Féin benefited from the indecisiveness of the British government whose policies oscillated between counterproductive coercion and ineffective conciliation. The government's inevitable prioritisation of the war effort over Irish political considerations also enhanced republican fortunes. The most striking example of this was the decision to extend conscription to Ireland in April 1918, a policy necessitated by the political cost of not doing so in the rest of the United Kingdom rather than the practical benefits of imposing the measure on Ireland. As H. E. Duke, the Irish Chief Secretary, observed: 'You might as well recruit Germans.'[24] The resulting crisis destroyed the Irish Party's credibility and facilitated a closer relationship between the Catholic hierarchy and Sinn Féin. Resistance to conscription which, quite predictably, was never imposed, 'was probably the most potent single motive for radicalisation throughout the war'.[25]

The Counter-state

Sinn Féin won 73 seats in the December 1918 general election, reducing the Irish Party – which had dominated nationalist politics since the 1880s – to six seats (four of which were the result of an electoral pact with republicans

23 M. Laffan, *The Resurrection of Ireland. The Sinn Féin Party 1916–1923* (Cambridge University Press, 1999), 214–65; T. Garvin, *Nationalist Revolutionaries in Ireland, 1858–1928* (Oxford University Press, 1987).

24 A. Gregory, ' "You Might as Well Recruit Germans": British Public Opinion and the Decision to Conscript the Irish in 1918', in A. Gregory and S. Pašeta (eds.), *Ireland and the Great War: 'A War to Unite Us All'?* (Manchester: Manchester University Press, 2002).

25 Townshend, 'The Irish War of Independence. Context and Meaning', in C. Crowe (ed.), *Guide to the Military Service Pensions Collection* (Dublin: Óglaigh na hÉireann, 2012), 111. See, for example, J. Borgonovo, *The Dynamics of War and Revolution: Cork City, 1916–1918* (Cork: Cork University Press, 2013).

brokered by Cardinal Logue). Republicans had benefited from the trebling of the electorate by the 1918 Representation of the People Act, and the UK's first-past-the-post electoral system, but the result marked a watershed. The sectarian electoral map remained unchanged, however, with Unionists dominant in the north-east. Designating themselves TDs (=Teachta Dála, or Deputy), Sinn Féin's representatives met at the Mansion House, Dublin, to establish an Irish parliament. They proclaimed independence on 21 January 1919, the same day that an ambush by Irish Volunteers at Soloheadbeg, County Tipperary, killed two policemen.

There was nothing inevitable about the drift to war that followed. Reserving the right to make 'use of any and every means', Sinn Féin's manifesto had emphasised the importance of securing a democratic mandate to allow it to mount an appeal for independence at the Paris Peace Conference. In documents such as the 'Message to the Free Nations' and 'Declaration of Independence', the party drew on a wide, if not necessarily consistent, range of justifications for independence. These included the right to self-determination, the cultural, historical and racial unity of the nation, international law, the 'principle of government by consent of the governed', as well as 'the old tradition of nationhood handed on from dead generations'. Depending on the intended audience, racial assumptions could displace anti-colonial rhetoric, as with de Valera's complaint that 'Ireland is now the last white nation that is deprived of its liberty'.[26] Predictably, given the ebbing of the Wilsonian tide, little subsequently came of the appeal to Paris that had formed such a central aspect of Sinn Féin's election manifesto: 'self-determination was a panacea to be introduced only in the defeated empires'.[27]

Local studies have provided a sophisticated anatomy of the Irish revolution on the ground but shed little light on the extent to which transnational factors determined its outcome. Regardless of the failure at Paris, republicans – as their propaganda made clear – were emboldened by a growing awareness of how imperialism was giving way to a new world order whose legitimacy stemmed from the growing acceptance of the principle of national self-determination: 'In 1914 Ireland's cause seemed a parochial dispute within the United Kingdom; now, in 1918, empires had collapsed and the world was being re-ordered according to the "national principle".' In the weeks preceding

---

26 Quoted in B. Nelson, *Irish Nationalists and the Making of the Irish Race* (Princeton, NJ: Princeton University Press, 2012), 234.

27 Walsh, *Bitter Freedom*, 39; E. Manela, *The Wilsonian Moment: Self-Determination and the International Origins of Anticolonial Nationalism* (New York: Oxford University Press, 2007).

the 1918 general election, republics were proclaimed in Germany, Austria, Czechoslovakia, and Hungary, while even Britain and France had deemed it necessary to affirm that national governments should derive 'their authority from the initiative and free choice of the indigenous population'.[28]

While much shaped by contingency, the republican campaign combined an impressive variety of strategies ranging from long-established techniques such as the use of arbitration courts, moral force, and electoral politics to more novel innovations such as guerrilla warfare and the establishment of a revolutionary government. Some Sinn Féin candidates emphasised the aim of a republic, but others spoke more vaguely of independence. The flexible nature of the campaign, particularly its potent combination of collective mobilisation, counter-state formation and violence, presented a far more formidable challenge to British power than previous insurrections. Irish Republicans, Peter Hart has suggested, 'invented modern revolutionary warfare, with its mass parties, popular fronts, guerrilla warfare, underground governments, and continuous propaganda campaigns'.[29]

Irish revolutionaries achieved more success in the sphere of propaganda than on the field of combat.[30] The republican campaign was underpinned by a sophisticated effort to mobilise international public opinion and diplomatic support. De Valera's presence in the US from June 1919 to December 1920 demonstrated the importance attached to global opinion, even if his presence there divided Irish-American opinion, failed to secure diplomatic recognition, and, while $5 million was raised by an external Dáil loan, little of this money reached Ireland. The republican government's Department of Foreign Affairs established representatives abroad, while the Department of Propaganda cultivated the international press. The publicity generated by such activities constrained Britain's military campaign in Ireland, and brought increasing pressure from Washington on London to reach an accommodation with Irish republicans.[31]

Republicans also benefited from the rapid development of modern communications which offered 'imperial administrators, unionists and nationalists alike a tangible connectedness with a larger, trans-national network'.[32] While illustrating how the republican campaign provided a model for other

28 Walsh, *Bitter Freedom*, 37–8.
29 P. Hart, *I.R.A. at War*, 3.
30 M. Walsh, *The News from Ireland: Foreign Correspondents and the Irish Revolution* (London: I. B. Tauris, 2011).
31 Townshend, *The Republic*, 70–2.
32 C. Morash, *A History of the Media in Ireland* (Cambridge University Press, 2010), 130.

anti-colonial movements, recent research has also provided more nuanced insights into how ideas about empire, race and self-determination shaped alliances between Irish republicans and other subject peoples.[33] Studies of international responses to the revolution similarly demonstrate how efforts to mobilise support were shaped by the shifting identities and aspirations of Irish emigrant communities, with striking differences between diasporic responses in the United States and Australia and New Zealand where the political and demographic context limited support for Irish republicans.[34]

Revolutionary efforts at home were similarly innovative. While not always resulting in practical outcomes, the attempt to establish a functioning Dáil administration strengthened the republican claim to legitimacy. The raising of a loan of half a million pounds from 150,000 Irish subscribers funded pilot schemes in housing, land purchase, fisheries and cooperative enterprises.[35] The establishment of arbitration and special land courts, and the takeover of local government, made the Dáil a tangible presence throughout much of the country, including areas that experienced little conflict. Not all initiatives were as successful. Policing, conducted by Irish Volunteers, relied on fines, beatings, and expulsions, while the suppression of republican courts made such rough justice even less accountable.

Ultimately, the significance of the Dáil government lay in its symbolism. Even the most successful practical manifestation of the republican admin-istration – its network of arbitration courts – had an important propaganda function, as the increasingly demoralised Royal Irish Constabulary com-plained. The establishment of a native legal system, the London-based *Daily Herald* noted, demonstrated both the credibility of the Dáil and the popular repudiation of the legitimacy of British rule: 'This invisible Republic with its hidden courts and its prohibited volunteer troops, exists in the hearts of the men and women of Ireland, and wields a moral authority which all the tanks and machine guns of King George cannot command.' While the will-ingness of Unionists to resort to republican courts was primarily motivated

33 See, for example, Walsh, *Bitter Freedom*; Kate O'Malley, *Ireland, India and Empire: Indo-Irish Radical Connections, 1919–64* (Manchester: Manchester University Press, 2008); M. Silvestri, *Ireland and India: Nationalism, Empire and Memory* (Basingstoke: Palgrave Macmillan, 2009); K. Kenny (ed.), *Ireland and the British Empire* (Oxford University Press, 2006).

34 Nelson, *Irish Nationalists*; T. J. Meagher, 'Irish America Without Ireland: Irish-American Relations with Ireland in the Twentieth Century' in Whelehan (ed.), *Transnational Perspectives*; R. Sweetman, 'Who Fears to Speak of Easter Week? Antipodean Irish Catholic Responses to the 1916 Rising', in R. O'Donnell (ed.), *The Impact of the 1916 Rising. Among the Nations* (Dublin: Irish Academic Press, 2008).

35 Ferriter, *A Nation*, 214–28.

by self-preservation, the widespread acceptance of Dáil institutions under-mined the efforts of British propagandists to associate republicanism with lawlessness and Bolshevism. The 'Irish Republic is very nearly in being', the unionist *Irish Times* reported in July 1920: the 'Sinn Féin flag flies already over the whole province of Munster, and soon will fly over the whole of Leinster and Connaught and over a large part of Ulster'.[36]

Arbitration and land courts (backed, when required, by IRA force) also diffused the potential for agrarian agitation which socially conservative politicians such as Griffith feared could 'wreck the entire national move-ment'.[37] Revolutionary violence stemmed not only from competing ideol-ogies but from the breakdown of state authority, socio-economic pressures and communal tensions. The collapse of law and order, suspension of land redistribution, curtailing of emigration, and increasing pressure on land due to rising food prices, had created a surge in agrarian agitation in the spring of 1920, resulting in cattle-drives, land seizures, and violent intimi-dation. This was most evident in the west of Ireland where landless labour-ers and small farmers on uneconomic holdings struggled for survival in the shadow of landed estates and large grassland farms. In an effort to prevent such unwelcome developments, the Dáil prohibited land agitation in June 1920 and, more constructively, established a bank to facilitate land purchase.

While politically astute, Sinn Féin's determination to alleviate rural class tensions, particularly in Connacht where there was a strong link between popular agrarianism and support for the new movement, demonstrated the limits of the republican challenge to the existing social order. While Sinn Féin could do little to alter the fact that some two-thirds of agricultural holdings were classified as 'uneconomic', agrarian radicals came to realise that repub-lican court rulings were oriented towards the status quo. David Fitzpatrick has attributed the movement's social conservatism to a thick strand of grass-roots continuity with the Irish Parliamentary Party, which resulted in the 'old wine' of Home Rule politics being 'decanted into new bottles'. This thesis has been challenged by local studies of other regions that have emphasised the lower socio-economic status of Sinn Féin activists.[38] Republican policy was

---

36 Quoted in A. Mitchell, 'Alternative Government: "Exit Britannia" – The Formation of the Irish National State, 1918–21', in Augusteijn (ed.), *Irish Revolution*, 76–7.
37 T. Dooley, *'The Land for the People'. The Land Question in Independent Ireland* (Dublin: University College Dublin Press, 2004), 46. And see above pp. 142–4.
38 Fitzpatrick, *Politics and Irish Life*, p. 107; F. Campbell, *Land and Revolution. Nationalist Politics in the West of Ireland 1891–1921* (Oxford University Press, 2005), 225, 262.

also shaped by the relatively middle-class background and social conservativism of Sinn Féin's national leadership.

Countess Markievicz's Department of Labour similarly strived to dampen labour agitation. Despite a sharp resurgence in the fortunes of general trades-unionism, driven by government-imposed wartime labour regulations and successful campaigns for pay increases by agricultural workers, there was little support for radical socialism within the leadership of the Irish Transport and General Workers' Union whose membership soared from 5,000 to 120,000. Following the execution of James Connolly, his successors such as William O'Brien – who has been criticised for failing to appreciate the strength of nationalist sentiment amongst Irish workers – prioritised labour interests over revolutionary politics. The Labour Party's pragmatic decision not to contest the 1918 general election could not but marginalise working-class political representation during a formative period, even if the party performed well in 1922. As with its response to other sectional groups, such as feminists, Sinn Féin sought to placate labour without committing itself to radical change. A Democratic Programme – substantially drafted by trade-unionist and Labour leader Thomas Johnson – which outlined a range of social democratic aspirations was endorsed but never implemented. Moreover, even with the dilution of its socialist rhetoric by Sean T. O'Kelly, this modest document was derided as 'mostly poetry' by Kevin O'Higgins whose subsequent prominence in the Irish Free State executive council demonstrated the ascendancy of right-wing impulses after the revolution.

Sinn Féin's cautious approach proved effective notwithstanding a surge in strikes and increased class conflict, trends attributed by one labour historian less to 'the exploits of the IRA and the achievements of Sinn Féin' and more to the 'real inspiration provided by events in Europe; the Russian revolution, the factory occupations in Italy, the industrial unrest in Britain and Germany, and, most of all, by the way the victorious allies turned the old world upside down in 1919'.[39] Revealingly, each of the major strikes between 1919 and 1921 – an anti-conscription general strike in April 1918, a protest in Limerick provoked by its proclamation as a special military area in April 1919, a two-day strike in support of hunger-striking prisoners in April 1920, and a protest by railway workers who refused to transport munitions between May and December 1920 (leading to the dismissal of a thousand workers) – were motivated by

---

39 E. O'Connor, 'Agrarian Unrest and the Labour Movement in County Waterford, 1917–1923', *Saothar. Journal of the Irish Labour History Society*, 6 (1980), 54–5.

national rather than class politics.[40] Such civil resistance, Charles Townshend suggests, was more effective in terms of its impact on morale than on the British military campaign: 'Ireland's struggle for independence was, fundamentally, a struggle not for military victory but to impress upon Britain the seriousness of Ireland's claim. What was really under attack was the legitimacy of British rule.'[41]

Other aspects of the Dáil experiment were less successful. Its institutions had no authority in north-east Ulster, nor did Sinn Féin formulate a constructive policy to address Unionist concerns. The implementation of the 'Belfast Boycott' of northern goods in response to the intimidation of Catholic workers by Belfast loyalists merely heightened sectarian tensions. The takeover of local government in the South after the 1920 local elections exposed the British claim that republicans lacked popular support, but the Local Government Board's docking of funds to councils that declared their allegiance to the Irish Republic blunted the impact of this development. Efforts to build Griffith's counter-state also attracted the contempt of some within the IRA including Liam Lynch who described Sinn Féin branches and Dáil bodies as 'a burden on the Army'.[42] Such hardliners may have welcomed the authorities' decision to ban Sinn Féin and suppress the Dáil in September 1919, which ensured that violence, rather than politics, increasingly determined the pace of events.

The War of Independence

The military conflict can be divided into three phases. The period from 1918 to 1919 saw the formation of Irish Volunteer companies, and a gradual shift, driven by militants within the movement, from public defiance to guerrilla warfare.[43] The first sustained violence in Dublin came with the targeting of policemen and Dublin Castle officials by Michael Collins's 'Squad' of assassins. There was initially little public support for such ruthless methods and

---

40 F. Costello, *The Irish Revolution and its Aftermath 1916–1923. Years of Revolt* (Dublin: Irish Academic Press, 2003), 151–85.

41 C. Townshend, 'The Irish Railway Strike of 1920: Industrial Action and Civil Resistance in the Struggle for Independence', *Irish Historical Studies*, 22 (1979), 282. For a contrary view, emphasising class consciousness, see C. Kostick, *Revolution in Ireland: Popular Militancy 1917–1923* (Cork: Cork University Press, 2009).

42 Hart, *The I.R.A. and its Enemies*, 229.

43 C. Townshend, *Political Violence in Ireland. Government and Resistance since 1848* (Oxford University Press, 1983); J. Augusteijn, *From Public Defiance to Guerrilla Warfare. The Experience of Ordinary Volunteers in the Irish War of Independence 1916–1921* (Dublin: Irish Academic Press, 1996).

they were often condemned by Catholic clergymen.[44] Although the campaign had been preceded by a Dáil-led effort to sever links between the local community and the RIC, branded as 'spies in our midst',[45] many republican politicians were also shocked by such killings which contributed to tensions between the political and military wings of republicanism.

The second phase, from early 1920 (when assassinations were retrospectively endorsed by the IRA leadership at GHQ) to the summer of 1920, saw greater coordination between IRA units to attack barracks and the consequent withdrawal of the RIC from much of rural Ireland. Technically the responsibility of the Dáil's Minister for Defence, Cathal Brugha, the IRA campaign was conducted by the 'band of brothers' at GHQ with little regard for political oversight. The influence of Collins's Irish Republican Brotherhood, a rival power structure within the Irish Volunteers, further complicated relations between the government and army.

The final phase witnessed a professionalisation of the IRA campaign through the formation of flying columns of 'on the run' men, a local initiative endorsed by GHQ. By early 1921, increasing British military pressure saw a return to smaller-scale operations, with occasional exceptions such as the disastrous burning of the Custom House (which resulted in the death of three Volunteers and the arrest of 80 more). It was not until this period that the Dáil formally endorsed the IRA campaign, but tensions still remained, not least between followers of de Valera, president of Dáil Éireann, and the versatile Michael Collins whose offices included that of Minister of Finance, IRB president, and GHQ director of intelligence.

Volunteer companies often emerged from pre-existing youth networks such as GAA clubs.[46] With a median age of 23, IRA men were younger than Sinn Féin members, with many viewing themselves as more committed to the struggle. A radical minority, often from Fenian backgrounds, played an important role in establishing companies but the decision to join the IRA was for many a collective one. Shaped more by peer pressure than ideology, companies sprang up overnight as influential community leaders recruited

---

44 For the wide range of clerical attitudes to republican violence, see B. Heffernan, *Freedom and the Fifth Commandment: Catholic Priests and Political Violence in Ireland, 1919–21* (Manchester: Manchester University Press, 2015).

45 *Dáil Éireann*, Minutes of Proceedings, 1919–1921 (Dublin: Stationery Office, n.d.), vol. 1, 10 April 1919, p. 67.

46 For the IRA's composition, see Hart, *The I.R.A. at War*, and local studies such as Augusteijn's *From Public Defiance* and J. O'Callaghan's *Revolutionary Limerick. The Republican Campaign for Independence in Limerick, 1913–1921* (Dublin: Irish Academic Press, 2010).

'friends, neighbours, cousins, work- and teammates'.[47] This suggests that radicalisation was often more a consequence than a cause of IRA membership, even if countless Volunteers subsequently testified to the motivation provided by the impact of the Easter Rising and the cultural revival. Described by the police as unskilled, unemployed, or otherwise lacking in social status, the composition of the IRA broadly reflected Irish society. The rich and poor tended not to join, while lower middle-class shop assistants, clerks, and skilled workers were overrepresented. Most IRA men were single, literate, employed, and, disproportionately, Catholic. A strong identification with moral values and ideas of respectability was common, particularly among officers.

A volunteer rather than professional army, which drew its support from urban as well as rural Ireland (despite a tendency in revolutionary memoirs to romanticise the latter), the IRA was defined by a strong localism. Regional leaders often resented the efforts of Richard Mulcahy's GHQ – which was unable to supply weapons in the quantity desired or to meaningfully direct operations – to impose its authority through a combination of bureaucracy and exhortation. GHQ ultimately failed to mesh a campaign of local struggles into a nationwide campaign. 'Each county was different', recalled Ernie O'Malley: 'the very map boundaries in many places seemed to make a distinction.... Sometimes I came to a townland where there was a company of twenty or thirty men and boys. Tall, well set-up or lanky, eager, lithe, willing to learn and anxious to take risks. Six miles away across the barony the people were cowed; the men had no initiative'.[48] Varying levels of local initiative contributed to the unevenness of the campaign, with determined leadership and levels of communal support often proving more important than the availability of weapons or social or geographical factors.[49]

Women played a significant role in revolutionary mobilisation although Cumann na mBan's activities – centring on first aid, catering, fund-raising, propaganda, attendance at funerals and rallies, and carrying despatches and arms – were firmly gendered.[50] Few would have expected otherwise, as Eithne Coyle recalled: 'We were more or less auxiliaries to the men, to the fighting men of the country. It wasn't a case of taking orders because we had our own executive and we made our own decisions, but if there were any jobs

---

47 Hart, *The I.R.A. and its Enemies*, 188.
48 O'Malley, *Another Man's Wound*, 140.
49 O'Callaghan, *Revolutionary Limerick*, 209–15.
50 M. Coleman, *County Longford and the Irish Revolution, 1910–1923* (Dublin: Irish Academic Press, 2003), 179–90.

or anything to be done, the men – they didn't order us – but they asked us to help them, which we did.' Women were also marginalised within Sinn Féin. Countess Markievicz made headlines as the first woman elected to Westminster, but she had been only one of two female republican candidates in 1918. Six women were elected to the Dáil in the 1921 election but four were widows or mothers of republican martyrs. At the grassroots, where attitudes were more conservative, women played little role in the party.[51]

Women who performed more dangerous roles, such as spying, were often overlooked in subsequent accounts such as the *Fighting Stories* that relegated their role to short features such as 'How the Women Helped'.[52] They were also denied military pensions in the early years of the Irish Free State. Margaret Skinnider, who had been shot three times as she led men in battle in 1916, was refused on the grounds that 'the definition of "wound" … only contemplates the masculine gender'. Women were subsequently permitted to apply for pensions but the criteria emphasised auxiliary 'service of a military nature' rather than political activism.[53] The reluctance to acknowledge the active role of women formed part of a wider post-revolutionary dispensation that valued women as mothers rather than citizens. While yet to be integrated into the wider historiography, new sources such as the Military Service Pensions collection are providing greater insight into women's roles but there remains a need for further gendered analysis of the revolution, including how ideas about masculinity shaped the exclusively male organisations which dominated the republican movement.[54]

By 1920 it was clear that the demoralised police could no longer cope with the republican challenge. With the exception of the political policemen in G Division, who were targeted for assassination, the Dublin Metropolitan Police, which refused to carry weapons on patrol, played little role in the conflict. Within the RIC, an armed force that operated outside Dublin, many resigned, kept their heads down, or (as within the wider British administration) provided the IRA with information. The effectiveness of the IRA's intelligence network partly accounted for Dublin Castle's failure to suppress republicanism, as did weaknesses within the British administration including

---

51 Quoted in M. Hopkinson, *The Irish War of Independence* (Dublin: Gill & Macmillan, 2000), 199; Laffan, *The Resurrection of Ireland. The Sinn Féin Party 1916–1923* (Cambridge University Press, 1999), 201–4.
52 Coleman, *County Longford*, 190.
53 Ferriter, *A Nation*, 340.
54 For unionist masculinities, see J. McGaughey, *Ulster's Men. Protestant Unionist Masculinities and Militarization in the North of Ireland, 1912–1923* (Montreal: McGill-Queen's University Press, 2012).

its 'inexperienced officers, amateur techniques, poor security, [and] lack of co-ordination' between the seven or so organisations tasked with intelligence-gathering. The resulting intelligence failures allowed influential reactionaries in the British establishment to depict Sinn Féin as 'a minor, temporary, unrepresentative phenomenon that could be eradicated', contributing to the cabinet's reluctance to pursue peace initiatives during the final 12 months of the conflict. Intelligence failures though were as much a consequence as a cause of inept government policy.[55]

Throughout early and mid-1920 British security forces in Ireland were restructured to cope with the growing IRA threat. Pay was increased and the RIC was stiffened by three new forces. These included 10,000, primarily British-recruited 'temporary constables' (dubbed 'Black and Tans' because of their improvised uniforms), and a 2,300-strong 'Auxiliary Division' that was recruited from former army officers who 'neither looked like police nor behaved like them'.[56] The appointment of General Sir Nevil Macready as commander-in-chief in Ireland improved the morale and effectiveness of the army but Major General Hugh Tudor struggled to coordinate the five police forces he inherited under a poorly defined role as 'police advisor'. The central flaws of Britain's 'hopelessly uncoordinated' counter-insurrectionary campaign remained: the lack of a unified command over security forces, and the government's inability, despite Macready's pleas, to commit itself to a clear military or political strategy.[57]

The Black and Tans earned their reputation for unruly behaviour but recent research offers more nuanced insights into this hastily recruited and poorly trained force. Predominantly urban, working-class, British, and Protestant, these 'rough' men did not conform to the more disciplined, respectable ethos of the mainly Catholic, rural RIC, but it has been argued that they were not necessarily more likely to be involved in reprisals than the Irish-born policemen they worked alongside. Less prominent in collective memory, the Auxiliaries – who operated independently of the restraining influence of the RIC – behaved more egregiously. Rather than comprising the dregs of society or brutalised First World War veterans, D. M. Leeson suggests, both forces were composed of ordinary men acting under extraordinary pressures. Republicans were conscious of the overwhelming military superiority of the Crown forces, but the

---

55 P. McMahon, *British Spies and Irish Rebels. British Intelligence and Ireland 1916–1945* (Suffolk: Boydell Press, 2008), 427, 429.
56 Townshend, *The Republic*, 158.
57 D. Fitzpatrick, *The Two Irelands 1912–1939* (Oxford University Press, 1998), 92; McMahon, *British Spies*, 49–54.

view from inside the police barracks looked rather different: 'From the police perspective, the Irish insurgency was a one-sided war. The guerrillas did most of the killing, and the police did most of the dying.'[58] The RIC, which regarded itself as a civil police force, endured casualties of 10 per cent (rising to 24 per cent killed and 42 per cent wounded for those involved in combat).[59]

The new paramilitary forces were allowed a loose rein, particularly in comparison to the army which took discipline more seriously. Accountability was further diminished by the Restoration of Order in Ireland Act which replaced trial by jury and coroners' inquests with courts martial and military courts of inquiry. These measures reflected the authorities' remarkable failure to convict a single republican for murder by the summer of 1920. The controversial policy of reprisals – the use of collective punishment including the burning of houses and economic targets such as shops and creameries in areas where IRA attacks occurred – further encouraged outright lawlessness. There is disagreement among historians regarding how much reprisals such as the burning of Balbriggan on 20 September 1920 or the destruction of much of the centre of Cork in December 1920 were officially sanctioned, but influential figures from Winston Churchill and General Macready down to divisional police commissioners were certainly implicated in reprisals which, at different stages of the conflict, were connived at, denied, condoned, punished and eventually authorised.[60]

Almost half of the 2,141 fatalities recorded between January 1917 and December 1921 occurred within three counties (Cork, Dublin and Antrim), with the ten least violent counties accounting for less than 5 per cent of fatalities.[61] The IRA was responsible for inflicting around 46 per cent of fatalities, while the Crown forces accounted for at least 42 per cent. The IRA and police each made up around two-fifths of combatant fatalities with the army (20 per cent) accounting for the remainder. On both sides only a small proportion of combatants killed people but the brutalisation of some of those who did so contributed to the cyclical patterns of violence that emerged. While the IRA depicted itself as a defensive force, its violence was often intended to force the pace of events. This was a rational and effective strategy, as the frequently indiscriminate response of the Crown forces, which were usually

---

58 D. M. Leeson, *The Black and Tans. British Police and Auxiliaries in the Irish War of Independence* (Oxford University Press, 2011), 191, 130.

59 Townshend, *The Republic*, 159–60.

60 Fitzpatrick, *Two Irelands*, 91; Leeson, *Black and Tans*, 223.

61 E. O'Halpin, 'Counting Terror: Bloody Sunday and The Dead of the Irish Revolution', in D. Fitzpatrick (ed.), *Terror in Ireland 1916–1923* (Dublin: The Lilliput Press, 2012), 152. The following statistics derive from the same source.

unable to identify their assailants, alienated moderate opinion, further under-mining British legitimacy. Describing the 'thrilling' course of events in mid-1920, Collins eagerly anticipated how 'Ireland is in for the greatest crucifixion she has ever yet been subjected to'.[62] The level of violence was low compared to other contemporaneous conflicts but it escalated sharply. Crown force cas-ualties, for example, doubled every six months in the final 18 months of the conflict, while over three-fifths of fatalities between 1917 and 1921 occurred in 1921.[63] While fatalities provide a concrete measure of violence, like any other statistic, they can distort the picture. The increase in the proportion of non-combatant fatalities in the final months of the conflict may have reflected the difficulty of killing 'hard targets' such as soldiers (despite increasing numbers of IRA attacks) rather than greater brutality.[64]

Crown forces killed more civilians (42 per cent) than the IRA (31 per cent) but historiographical controversy has tended to focus on IRA violence. A dis-proportionate number of the IRA's civilian victims were Protestant, particu-larly in Cork where 70 of the IRA's 200 civilian fatalities were Protestant (five times their percentage within the population).[65] Given that Protestants were overwhelmingly Unionist, some of these were killed for allegedly passing information to the authorities but Protestants were also targeted because their status as 'other' aroused suspicion or resentment. In many areas of the country, however, IRA discipline prevented or constrained sectarian vio-lence. Peter Hart's contention that many of the IRA's civilian victims were shot because of who they were rather than what they did has been robustly challenged. In particular, the extent to which the execution of 'spies' and 'informers' was justified by security concerns rather than religious affiliation has produced extensive debate. IRA intelligence in Cork city, for example, has been shown to be more effective than Hart suggested.[66] Hart also overstated the extent to which revolutionary violence was responsible for the decline of the Protestant minority in Southern Ireland by 33 per cent between 1911 and 1926, while his claim that ex-servicemen were systematically persecuted by the IRA has also been persuasively challenged.[67]

62 Quoted in Ferriter, *A Nation*, 204.
63 Townshend, 'The Irish War of Independence', 113.
64 P. Óg Ó Ruairc, *Truce: Murder, Myth and the Last Days of the Irish War of Independence* (Cork: Mercier Press, 2016).
65 Hart, *The I.R.A. at War*, 234.
66 J. Borgonovo, *Spies, Informer, and the 'Anti-Sinn Féin Society': the Intelligence War in Cork City, 1920–1921* (Dublin: Irish Academic Press, 2007).
67 D. Fitzpatrick, 'Protestant Depopulation and the Irish Revolution', *Irish Historical Studies*, 38 (2013), 643–70; P. Taylor, *Heroes or Traitors? Experiences of Southern Irish Soldiers returning from the Great War 1919–1939* (Liverpool University Press, 2015), 244.

None the less, as Hart's ground-breaking work so compellingly demonstrated, much revolutionary violence was intimate, brutal and shaped by a complex range of social forces. Individuals of low social status, for example, were disproportionately targeted. In the revolutionary backwater of County Monaghan, around half of the 20 or so individuals killed by the IRA during the 'Tan War' (as the conflict was termed by some republicans) were civilians. Labelled as spies or informers, they included Hibernian supporters of the Irish Party, Protestants, ex-soldiers, pedlars, the 'weak-minded' and others on the margins whose perceived lack of respectability increased their vulnerability in a climate of terror. Although the likelihood that 'private vengeance exacted its toll under cover of civil turmoil' was acknowledged publicly at the time, such killings were rarely mentioned after independence.[68] One reason why controversies such as the shooting of the Pearson brothers in Coolacrease, County Offaly, or of suspected Protestant informers in Dunmanway, County Cork, generate more heat than light is the difficulty of disentangling fact from rumour, or communal enmities from ideological motivations.[69] Given the importance of security concerns in guerrilla warfare, moreover, such killings – regardless of their justification – served a purpose; as one IRA man explained, they 'had the effect of keeping "our own weak ones right" '.[70]

Ten per cent of civilian fatalities were female. These were mostly accidental deaths, often the result of trigger-happy police patrols. The IRA killed three women notwithstanding GHQ's ban on such executions. In Monaghan republicans killed Kate Carroll (described by one IRA man as 'a half-wit') because her involvement in poitín-making gave rise to concerns about spying, but her marginal status and more intimate factors may have contributed to her death.[71] Recent research has shed light on gendered violence ranging from intimidation or the cutting of hair (a punishment commonly inflicted by both sides on women suspected of fraternising with the enemy) to rape (which the republican *Irish Bulletin* devoted an issue to publicising). While the sources are problematic, sexual (as opposed to gendered) violence appears to have been comparatively rare.[72]

---

68 *Dundalk Democrat*, 31 December 1921, quoted in F. McGarry, *Eoin O'Duffy. A Self-Made Hero* (Oxford University Press, 2005), 72.

69 J. Augusteijn 'Coolacrease', *History Ireland*, 17 (2009), 56–7; Howe, 'Killing in Cork'.

70 McGarry, *O'Duffy*, 47–73.

71 Ibid., 65–6; Ferriter, *A Nation*, 209.

72 Ferriter, *A Nation*, 210; L. Ryan, ' "Drunken Tans": Representation of Sex and Violence in the Anglo-Irish War, 1919–21', *Feminist Review*, 66 (2000), 73–95; M. Coleman, 'Violence against Women in the Irish War of Independence, 1919–1921', in D. Ferriter and S. Riordan (eds.), *Years of Turbulence: The Irish Revolution and its Aftermath* (Dublin: University College Dublin Press, 2015).

As with other aspects of the conflict, Ulster was a place apart. The IRA campaign there was restricted to areas with substantial Catholic populations, such as Monaghan and south Armagh. Belfast (where over 500 people were killed between 1920 and 1922) was, in per capita terms, the most violent place in Ireland. The conflict in Ulster has received relatively little historiographical attention. Debates about sectarian violence, for example, have focused on Cork, despite the much greater role played by religious identity in structuring violence in the North.[73] Many of Belfast's fatalities died as a result of communal rioting and sectarian reprisals. Sparked by rumours of republican infiltration fanned by 12 July celebrations, as well as the assassination of a Banbridge-born RIC officer in Cork five days later, riots spread throughout the north-east in 1920. These culminated in the expulsion of 5,500 Catholics and 1,900 'rotten Prods' from the shipyards, a phenomenon that also reflected economic competition between insecure workers in a declining industry. The killing of D. I. Swanzy in Lisburn, again by the Cork IRA, resulted in a further wave of violence the following summer: 'Long-standing communal rivalries, inflamed by armed gangs in various uniforms and disguises, ensured that in Ulster the "Anglo-Irish" conflict began to take the shape of a sectarian civil war.' Catholics, outnumbered and confined to vulnerable enclaves, inevitably bore the brunt. Only 23 per cent of the population in Belfast, they accounted for 56 per cent of deaths, 75 per cent of workplace expulsions, and 80 per cent of those displaced. Violence was, none the less, two-sided rather than a pogrom, with combatants from both communities justifying their murderous actions as defensive.[74]

Violence in Ulster peaked after the Truce of July 1921, demonstrating the limitations of applying conventional (i.e. Southern Irish) periodisation to the conflict as a whole. The pattern of violence in Ulster was shaped by preparations to establish a Northern Irish State following the introduction of the Government of Ireland Act in 1920. Under pressure from James Craig, the Northern prime minister in waiting, the British cabinet approved the formation of the Ulster Special Constabulary, ignoring warnings from senior officials about the likely consequence of arming one side in a sectarian conflict. Control over this force was ceded to Ulster Unionists, ensuring that security concerns were prioritised over the admittedly slim possibility of reconciling northern Catholics to the new state. Levels of violence in Belfast matched the

73 R. Lynch, *The Northern IRA and the Early Years of Partition, 1920–1922* (Dublin: Irish Academic Press, 2006); idem., 'Explaining the Altnaveigh Massacre', *Éire-Ireland*, 45 (2010), 186–7.
74 Fitzpatrick, *Two Irelands*, 96–9; Peter Hart, *The I.R.A. at War*, 241–58.

worst years of the recent Troubles but Ulster did not experience anything like the scale of violence that marked other contemporaneous ethnic border conflicts. The killing of a Catholic publican, Owen McMahon, along with four of his sons and an employee, by a squad of RIC and B Specials in North Belfast in March 1922, and the killing of six Protestant civilians in rural Armagh by Frank Aiken's Fourth Northern Division, were shocking precisely because they were exceptional.[75] Tim Wilson's comparative research on conflict in Ulster and Upper Silesia (a disputed frontier zone between Germany and Poland) suggests that ethno-nationalist violence was qualitatively and quantitatively greater in areas where boundary markers were ambiguous. Ulster's conflict, structured by the 'hard boundaries' of its religious divide, was less violent than in Silesia where language and religion transcended national affiliation, rendering communal blocs more permeable. As in all civil wars, violence – whether intended to polarise identities, reinforce boundaries or assert control over territory – was far from irrational.[76]

The importance of the social mechanisms that limited violence require further research, as do the experiences of the many parts of the country that witnessed little conflict. Important constraints included parental and clerical authority, morality, compassion and the fear of punishment (criminal or divine). There has perhaps been too much focus on violence given the importance of other factors in determining the outcome of the conflict. Like the activities of the Dáil, the IRA's role was essentially propagandistic. Levels of republican violence are not necessarily the most reliable means of gauging revolutionary support, while other forms of agitation, such as the struggle in the prisons, did much to shape the campaign. The confinement of almost 6,000 men by June 1921 ensured that imprisonment 'was one of the most common experiences shared by activists'. By turning 'sites that were supposed to "quell political dissent" into places where resistance, even revolution was nurtured', prison protests were arguably more effective, both in terms of raising public consciousness and exposing the limitations of the British State, than the killing of small numbers of Crown forces.[77] Even unsuccessful protests, such as those of Thomas Ashe, who died in 1917 following force-feeding, and Terence MacSwiney, who died in Brixton Prison on 25 October 1920 after

---

75 T. Wilson, '"The Most Terrible Assassination that Has Yet Stained the Name of Belfast": The McMahon Murders in Context', *Irish Historical Studies*, 37 (2010), 83–106; R. Lynch, 'Altnaveigh Massacre', 184–210.

76 T. K. Wilson, *Frontiers of Violence*; Kalyvas, *The Logic of Violence*.

77 W. Murphy, *Political Imprisonment and the Irish, 1912–1921* (Oxford University Press, 2014), 1, 10.

a 74-day hunger-strike, generated enormous publicity and sympathy, focusing global and British opinion on Ireland.

One reason for the British government's continued reliance on coercion by late 1920 was the grip over Irish policy exercised by its partisan administrators. Supported by well-placed figures in Britain, including the chair of the cabinet's Irish committee Walter Long, and Field Marshal Sir Henry Wilson, the Chief of the Imperial General Staff, the alarmist reports of Dublin Castle officials to Downing Street depicted republicans as an unrepresentative 'murder gang' and, more outlandishly, as part of a global Bolshevist threat. The Unionist stranglehold over policy was weakened by the appointment of Sir Warren Fisher, the head of the British civil service, to investigate the British administration in Ireland. His damning report – 'the Castle administration does not administer' – saw hardliners marginalised in favour of more pragmatic administrators such as the reforming undersecretary Sir John Anderson and the Dublin Castle 'fixers' Mark Sturgis and Alfred Cope.[78] Publicly, however, as the rhetoric of the new chief secretary, Sir Hamar Greenwood, made clear, Britain's aim remained the effective prosecution of the war. Continued reliance on repression also reflected the belief of the Prime Minister, David Lloyd George, widely shared throughout Britain, that Irish independence would be 'fatal to the security of the Empire'.[79] This helps to explain the failure to exploit tensions between republican moderates and militarists, as well as the lengthy delay in closing the gap between the offer of Home Rule and a more realistic settlement. Lloyd George, while instinctively a pragmatist, was further constrained by the Liberals' reliance on the Tory majority in government. Studies of the wider British world suggest, however, that the principal reason for inaction in Ireland was the more urgent demands placed on overstretched military, intellectual and political resources by anti-colonial violence across India, Egypt and the Middle East.[80]

November 1920, the bloodiest month of the conflict, might be seen as a turning point. Bloody Sunday, when 35 people (including British agents and spectators at a GAA match) were killed in Dublin, and the IRA ambush at Kilmichael, in which 17 Auxiliaries were killed, shocked British public opinion. By demonstrating the credibility of the IRA's campaign, such violence increased the impetus for a decisive policy response. As at the beginning of the revolutionary decade, Ulster – or six counties of it – played an important

---

78 Townshend, *The Republic*, 138.
79 Leeson, *Black and Tans*, 225.
80 K. Jeffery, *The British Army and the Crisis of Empire, 1918–22* (Manchester: Manchester University Press, 1984).

role in the final stage of the conflict. The real purpose of the 1920 Government of Ireland Act, which established parliaments in Dublin and Belfast, was to secure Northern Ireland's existence prior to British negotiations with republicans. Although the origins of the Irish revolution lay in Ulster's campaign against Home Rule, Belfast and London now perceived the advantages of a measure that 'offered Unionists power over a restricted territory, while absolving the British government of direct responsibility for the application of that power'.[81] Demographic realities ensured that Unionists in Cavan, Monaghan and Donegal had now to be abandoned by their Ulster Unionist brethren in order to secure a more manageable six-county settlement. For Northern Catholics, reduced to a permanent minority without the safeguards previously provided by 'direct rule' and an Irish nationalist majority, it was the worst possible outcome. Lloyd George's decision to partition Ireland before negotiating with republicans may have been a 'short-term fix' with 'dire long-term consequences',[82] but it is difficult to envisage other means by which Conservative support could have been won for the more generous settlement necessary to bring peace to Southern Ireland.

Treaty and Civil War

Hawks on both sides of the War of Independence depicted the Truce of July 1921 as a missed opportunity but this often reflected disillusionment about the compromises that followed. Conversely, Treaty supporters such as Richard Mulcahy, who lamented the IRA's inability 'to drive the enemy from anything but a fairly good-sized police barracks', stressed republican weaknesses. While inflicting more casualties than ever, the IRA was also sustaining higher losses due to improvements in British intelligence and counter-insurgency methods. The internment of 4,500 men and incarceration of a further 1,000 convicted prisoners intensified the pressure on the IRA to reach a settlement.[83] While in a position to bring ever greater resources to bear, British officers such as Macready – who warned the cabinet of the need 'to go "all out" or "get out"' – painted a disturbing picture of the methods required to secure victory. As in the late twentieth century, the belated acceptance by British politicians of the need for a more far-reaching political settlement pointed to the effectiveness of republican violence.

81 Fitzpatrick, *Two Irelands*, 101.
82 Hopkinson, *War of Independence*, 203. For British policy, see Fanning's *Fatal Path*.
83 M. Hopkinson, *Green against Green: The Irish Civil War* (Dublin: Gill & Macmillan, 1988), 9.

Despite sparring between de Valera and Lloyd George through July 1921, it was clear that any likely deal would centre on dominion status. De Valera had pointedly informed the Dáil that 'we are not doctrinaire republicans'. On the other hand, on her return from the United States after the Truce, the militant republican, Mary MacSwiney, had been alarmed by the 'atmosphere of what I can only call compromise' that she found in Dublin. 'I was told to the right and left of me that we could not possibly get a Republic.'[84] Tensions between and within the IRA and Sinn Féin increased as the talks dragged on through the autumn. To the irritation of Collins and Griffith, who led the negotiations in London, de Valera – who controversially chose to remain in Dublin rather than tarnish the status of his presidential office as a symbol of sovereignty – continued to insist on external association, an ambiguous concept based on voluntary association with the Commonwealth. This subtle attempt to bridge the gap between independence and a humiliating subordination to empire held as little appeal for militant republicans as their Tory counterparts.

Following two months of negotiations the Treaty was concluded on 6 December after Lloyd George melodramatically threatened the Irish plenipotentiaries with 'terrible and immediate war'. Clearly under immense pressure, their willingness to sign the agreement without referring the final version back to Dublin (later the subject of much recrimination) reflected their belief that it represented the best attainable settlement, as well as the virtual breakdown of relations between Collins and Griffith on the one hand and their less pragmatic cabinet colleagues at home on the other. De Valera's surprising inability to persuade a cabinet majority to reject what he saw as an attempt to impose the Treaty as a *fait accompli* ensured that it was left to the Dáil to determine the Treaty's fate. That institution, it would soon become clear, lacked the authority to contain differences over the Treaty within constitutional parameters.

The Treaty debates divided those who advocated the settlement as a stepping-stone to full independence from those who rejected the Dáil's right to dis-establish the republic. Doctrinaire TDs such as MacSwiney dismissed the influential pro-Treaty argument, reiterated by GHQ figures, that the only alternative was a return to a conflict that the IRA could not win by asserting that 'the issue is not between peace and war, it is between right and wrong'.[85] Concepts such as loyalty, honour, deceit and hypocrisy featured more than

---

84 Laffan, *The Resurrection*, 346; T. P. O'Neill (ed.), *Private Sessions of the Second Dáil* (Dublin Stationery Office, 1972), 17 December 1921, 247.
85 Laffan, *The Resurrection*, 356.

ideology, indicating the continuing importance of a republican discourse of virtue rather than ideology.[86] Backed by public opinion, pro-Treatyites could afford to distance themselves from extreme expressions of such attitudes, whereas even relative moderates such as de Valera resorted to legitimist assertions such as 'the people have no right to do wrong'. Partition seldom featured in the debates. For Irish republicans, as for imperialists like Churchill, symbolic issues centring on sovereignty, such as the oath of fealty to the monarch and membership of the British Empire, were paramount.

The occasion as much as the cause of the Civil War,[87] the Treaty brought to a head tensions within a party that encompassed dual monarchists, pragmatic nationalists, and republican separatists who rejected any link with Britain. Many anti-Treatyites depicted the split as one between those who remained loyal to the Republic and those they cast as apostates but tensions between rival personalities melded with ideological and political differences. Encompassing social issues as well as local rivalries, the factors that determined the stance of ordinary IRA men across the country were not restricted to attitudes to the Treaty: as one IRA veteran recalled, 'it all depended on which crowd you got into'.[88] The repudiation of de Valera's proposed alternative to the Treaty by some anti-Treaty IRA leaders also suggested that some form of conflict was likely whatever compromise was struck in London. In contrast to the Provisional Republican leadership of the 1990s, little effort had been made to prepare the way for compromise before the 1921 ceasefire.

Like the War of Independence itself, the split can also be seen as a consequence of the Rising's 'politics of exaltation' which narrowed the potential for political compromise. 'You are all abstract fanatics', complained Eileen Gould to her future husband, the writer and anti-Treaty IRA volunteer, Sean O'Faolain, 'suffering, not out of love for your fellow man but out of love for your own ruthless selves'.[89] Reflecting on the elitist impulses within republicanism, Ernie O'Malley also conceded 'a certain hardness in our idealism. It made us aloof from ordinary living, as if we were above it'. This suspicion of the masses – who had only been shaken from their complacency by the violence of 1916 – was demonstrated by Liam Lynch's injudicious observation

---

86 J. Knirck, *Imagining Ireland's Independence. The Debates over the Anglo-Irish Treaty of 1921* (Lanham, MD: Rowman & Littlefield, 2006), 175–6.

87 Joe Lee, *Ireland, 1912–1985: Politics and Society* (Cambridge University Press, 1989), 105.

88 Sean Harling, quoted in K. Griffith and T. O'Grady, *Curious Journey. An Oral History of Ireland's Unfinished Revolution* (Cork: Mercier Press, 1988), 285.

89 S. O'Faolain, *Vive Moi! An Autobiography* (London: Sinclair-Stevenson, 1993 edn.), 165. E. O'Malley, *The Singing Flame* (Dublin: Anvil, 1978), 285.

that the people 'were merely sheep to be driven anywhere at will'.[90] Some political scientists have identified a clash between romantic idealists and pragmatic realists as central to this split but historians place more emphasis on contingent factors. Charles Townshend has suggested, however, that those who most vehemently opposed the Treaty 'had mostly been less committed to the task of turning the Republic from an abstract concept into a functioning machine of representative government'.[91]

Accounts of the split often reflect the terms of the original rupture. Interpreting the pro-Treaty victory as the 'birth of Irish democracy', Tom Garvin's analysis echoed many of the arguments articulated by P. S. O'Hegarty's 1924 polemic, while Brian P. Murphy's republican account conveys sympathetically the legitimist ideals that framed the anti-Treaty outlook.[92] Emphasising the often overlooked role of the threat of British violence should the Treaty be rejected, some political scientists now interpret the conflict as one between the conflicting rights of self-determination and majority rule rather than, as previous accounts had suggested, between anti-democratic 'Gaelic Romantic' and more modern 'Irish-enlightenment' values.[93] Inevitably, the evolution of the Irish Free State to full independence, a development predicted by Collins and, ironically, achieved by de Valera, has diminished understanding of the anti-Treaty rationale. However, notwithstanding popular support for the Provisional Government, the idea of the Irish Civil War as a vindication of democracy and the rule of law is complicated by Treatyite authoritarianism and the new state's execution without trial of scores of prisoners.[94]

The postponement of violence until the summer – despite the provocative occupation of garrisons by anti-Treaty IRA forces, and the intemperate rhetoric of de Valera who warned that republicans may need 'to wade through Irish blood' – made clear the reluctance of both sides to resort to arms. Given that a majority within the IRA opposed the Treaty, Collins's conciliatory initiatives also allowed the Provisional Government and its fledgling army an opportunity to establish their authority. Efforts to avert conflict included

90 Quoted in T. Garvin, *1922. The Birth of Irish Democracy* (Dublin: Gill & Macmillan, 1996), 43.
91 Townshend, *The Republic*, 449.
92 Garvin, *1922*; B. P. Murphy, *Patrick Pearse and the Lost Republican Ideal* (Dublin: James Duffy, 1990).
93 B. Kissane, *The Politics of the Irish Civil War* (Oxford University Press, 2005); J. Prager, *Building Democracy in Ireland. Political Order and Cultural Integration in a Newly Independent Nation* (Cambridge University Press, 1986).
94 J. Regan, *Myth and the Irish State* (Dublin: Irish Academic Press, 2014).

3. The Four Courts, Dublin, on fire at the beginning of the Irish Civil War, 1922.

cooperation on attempts to destabilise the North (which resulted in renewed communal violence, and the collapse of the northern IRA), an attempt to devise a republican constitution (scotched by London), an abortive pact election, and repeated efforts by IRB leaders to reach a compromise. Beginning with the shelling of the Four Courts by the Provisional Government army on 28 June 1922, the Civil War was fought in two phases: a brief period of relatively large-scale fighting which saw the anti-Treatyites pushed out of urban strongholds, and a longer period of more familiar low-intensity rural conflict. Although the anti-Treaty IRA outnumbered Provisional Government forces at the outset of the conflict, its initial adoption of a 1916-style defensive strategy prevented it from exploiting this advantage. This may have reflected a commendable lack of ruthlessness – 'the truth is, our hearts were not in it, and this alone contributed a good deal to our military defeat' – but it also stemmed from deep divisions among the anti-Treaty leaders.[95]

In contrast, the Provisional Government – if not necessarily its inexperienced and less ideologically committed soldiers – demonstrated a greater

95 M. Harnett, *Victory and Woe* (Dublin: University College Dublin Press, 2002), xii.

sense of purpose notwithstanding cabinet divisions between conciliatory militarists (such as Collins and Mulcahy) and hawkish civilians (like O'Higgins). Following the collapse of large-scale resistance by the autumn of 1922, the IRA could do little more than prolong a destructive campaign of sabotage and guerrilla warfare. By the final stages of the conflict, the government forces – drawing on British resources – numbered 55,000, while some 10,000 republicans (including 500 women) had been interned. The death of Collins in an ambush in rural Cork on 22 August 1922 prompted a harder line from the Provisional Government. A Public Safety Act in September permitted the execution of those caught bearing arms. As with the earlier conflict, legitimacy proved crucial. Dependent on commandeered resources, the presence of the IRA was often resented by civilians, while the republican government established by de Valera commanded little allegiance. Similarly, republican hunger-strikes led to demoralisation rather than public sympathy. Regardless of anti-Treaty condemnation of the 'Green and Tans', the 77 (or more) executions carried out by the Free State army provoked less disquiet than the 24 carried out by the British during the War of Independence notwithstanding the fact that some of these – such as the shooting of four IRA leaders on 8 December in reprisal for the assassination of a TD after their imprisonment – were conducted without much pretence of legality. The public appeared to accept Kevin O'Higgins's crude assertion that 'the safety and preservation of the people is the highest law'.[96] Despite private misgivings about these draconian measures, the Catholic hierarchy also provided important moral support to the Provisional Government by issuing a joint pastoral condemning the anti-Treaty campaign.

The violence of the Civil War requires further research, as is clear from the uncertainty around its level of fatalities, estimated at around 1,500 deaths. From Pearse's sacrificial gesture in 1916, republican violence had come full circle, with combatants ruthlessly inflicting atrocities on former comrades. Operating as the Criminal Intelligence Department, and within the Dublin Guard, former members of Collins's Squad were involved in the worst excesses such as the murder of 17 anti-Treaty combatants who were tied to mines in three separate incidents in Kerry on 6–7 March 1923. In Dublin the corpses, in some cases mutilated, of around 25 abducted republicans were dumped on the streets.[97] The psychological impact of such harrowing incidents on a tightly-knit movement probably contributed more than the relatively low levels of violence (around 25,000 deaths and 8,000 executions occurred in the roughly contemporaneous

96 Ferriter, *A Nation*, 281.
97 Ibid., 287; Townshend, *The Republic*, 441–3.

Finnish Civil War) to the Civil War's bitter legacy. In contrast to the aftermath of the recent Troubles, a general amnesty ensured that these killings were never investigated. Civil War enmities were central to Free State politics but a veil of silence was drawn over much of the violence of the conflict. This was particularly the case on the pro-Treaty side where the duty to remember their dead took second place to the need to secure support for the new state.[98]

As with the preceding conflict, wider social tensions had shaped revolutionary violence. Some parts of the west of Ireland, relatively quiet during the previous conflict, were more active in the Civil War. The discontented – including landless labourers, small farmers, and striking workers – often perceived their interests as lying with the unfulfilled aims of the republic rather than the Free State whose politicians identified themselves with the restoration of law and order and the return of the bailiff.[99] A counter-revolution of sorts could be discerned in the Provisional Government's use of a Special Infantry Corps to break strikes and restore land to its owners. The changing economic context provided an important, if widely overlooked, factor in shaping social conflict during the revolutionary period. The collapse of the wartime agricultural boom triggered by the resumption of international trade in late 1920 simultaneously increased rural grievances while undermining labour's bargaining power, thereby 'making class a less significant factor in the later phases of unrest despite the dreams of Liam Mellows and Roddy Connolly'.[100]

Those in favour of the Treaty drew support from the press, business interests and the propertied, but, equally, the Labour Party and trade-union movement were also broadly pro-Treaty. While reactionary Free State generals such as O'Duffy denounced anti-Treatyites as Bolsheviks and criminals, a contested discourse centring on status and respectability provides more insight into the Civil War's divisions than clear-cut class distinctions.[101] As during the earlier conflict, Protestants were disproportionately targeted. Around 200 properties, mainly 'big houses', were burned between December 1921 and the end of the Irish Civil War. Arson, often carried out by non-combatants, formed part of a wider campaign of intimidation, cattle-maiming, personal

98 A. Dolan, *Commemorating the Irish Civil War. History and Memory, 1923–2000* (Cambridge University Press, 2003).
99 See, for example, M. Farry, *The Aftermath of Revolution. Sligo 1921–23* (Dublin: University College Dublin Press, 2000).
100 D. Fitzpatrick, 'Irish Consequences of the Great War', *Irish Historical Studies*, 39 (2015), 650.
101 G. Foster, *The Irish Civil War and Society. Politics, Class and Conflict* (Basingstoke: Palgrave Macmillan, 2015).

violence and economic sabotage, illustrating how revolutionary violence overlapped with communal enmities and conflicts over land, property and authority.[102]

Aside from its demoralising legacy – 'a kind of rot proceeded in the country', one government minister recorded – the Civil War proved damaging in several respects. It was ruinously expensive: £10m of £26.5m spent on public services in 1922–1923 was devoted to security and reconstruction, while Treatyite concern about the threat to the state saw, as in other interwar 'successor' states, the erosion of liberal democratic principles. The coincidence of state formation and military crisis stymied administrative change, ensuring reliance on existing British administrative structures in Ireland rather than the divided republican institutions that had emerged during the revolution. Revealingly, the republican courts, the Dáil government's most successful innovation, were scrapped in favour of a return to the *status quo ante*. The conflict left little scope for initiative: one of few such successful developments, the formation of an unarmed police force, was the product of necessity (following a mutiny), and owed more to the British (rather than colonial) model of policing than innovation. The resulting continuity was partially masked by the adoption of Gaelic names and symbols. Such continuity did, however, reinforce the stability of the new regime, one of few successor states to remain a functioning democracy by 1939.

The Civil War also contributed to 'the sharply conservative aftermath of the revolution, when nascent ideas of certain kinds of liberation were aggressively subordinated to the national project of restabilization (and clericalization)'.[103] This was particularly evident from the experiences of women. Although the opposition of many prominent republican women (including all six female TDs) to the Treaty was often a product of their personal ties to martyred republicans, their stance was presented as evidence of the hysterical nature of women and their unsuitability for political life. By empowering the more moderate section within Sinn Féin, the split ensured that the Treaty became an end in itself rather than a stepping-stone to unity (although the limits of Michael Collins's more expansive interpretation of the Treaty settlement were evident by the time of his death). The endurance of Civil War hatreds also reinforced the marginal role of ideology in a party political system which, unlike most European countries (but like most former colonies),

---

102 G. Clark, *Everyday Violence in the Irish Civil War* (Cambridge University Press, 2014).
103 Foster, *Vivid Faces*, 117.

4. Irish Free State soldiers in jubilant mood, 1923, possibly at announcement of an end to the Civil War.

was structured more by divisions over the national question than by social or class issues.

Conclusion

The revolutionary period can be seen as a decade-long negotiation over the terms of British withdrawal. Although much the weaker side, republicans benefited from the rapidly changing international context between 1912 and 1923, as well as from their skilful mobilisation of revolutionary politics, propaganda and armed struggle. Around 7,500 people were killed or wounded as a result of political violence during the revolution.[104] Although comparatively low, these statistics represented 'the culmination of a process in which, over three years of guerrilla conflict, violence permeated society'.[105] Violence accelerated the pace of change, resulting in a level of independence that few

104 Hart, *The I.R.A. at War*, 30.
105 Townshend, *The Republic*, 452.

could have anticipated before 1914, but it also narrowed the potential for accommodation between the two Irelands and between Ireland and Britain.

Notwithstanding the relative success of the republican campaign, which influenced anti-imperial movements elsewhere, Irish revolutionaries did not achieve their central aims: the restoration of the Gaelic language, complete separation from Britain (for many, the essence of republicanism) and territorial unity. Nor did they fully comprehend the tensions between the last and first two of these aims. Independence rarely lived up to expectations. The enthusiasm of the revival gave way to a more insular ethos, and it became clear that political independence would not automatically lead to greater prosperity, improved standards of welfare or an end to emigration. The revolution produced losers as well as winners, including liberals, feminists, and labour; religious minorities on both sides of the border were left, in Churchill's caustic words, 'to stew in their own juice'.[106] Among the losers can also be counted the many revolutionary veterans who endured lives of hardship and disappointment after, as well as during, the conflict. For all the achievements of independence, the radical impulses that brought about the Irish revolution failed to prevent the dawning of a conservative settlement across the island.

106 Fanning, *Fatal Path*, 360.

10

Politics, Economy, Society: Northern Ireland, 1920–1939

SUSANNAH RIORDAN

Introduction

Few topics in modern Irish history have reduced their historians to such evident frustration as the first two decades of Unionist rule in Northern Ireland. In the preface to a 1979 study, the first to draw on previously unavailable cabinet and departmental papers, Patrick Buckland declared that when he had begun his research he had been 'favourably disposed both to partition ... and to regional government'. By the time he had finished writing his book, although he remained convinced that partition had been necessary, 'the preference for regional government had turned to distaste and despair'.[1] An elegant writer, Buckland would become one of Northern Ireland's most prolific and influential historians and the title of his first full-length study – *The Factory of Grievances* – set the tone for much subsequent work. Though few achieved the level of rage of Michael Farrell's earlier *Northern Ireland: The Orange State* (1976), written from an unapologetically 'anti-imperialist and socialist standpoint',[2] most survey histories followed Farrell and Buckland in approaching self-government in Northern Ireland almost exclusively in terms of a history of the discrimination by the Protestant majority against the Catholic minority, the alienation and political disengagement of that minority, and the ways in which governance was subordinated to the retention of power. With the exception of Bryan Follis's detailed study of the process of devolution, *A State Under Siege: The Establishment of Northern Ireland, 1920–1925* (1995), Ulster Unionism in this period has had few sympathetic historians.

Despite the carefully-chosen titles, the wide variety of ideological perspectives (nationalist or unionist, marxist or otherwise), and the greater-than-usual

---

1 P. Buckland, *The Factory of Grievances: Devolved Government in Northern Ireland 1921–39* (Dublin: Gill & Macmillan, 1979), ix.

2 M. Farrell, *Northern Ireland: The Orange State*, 2nd edn. (London: Pluto Press, 1980), 12.

willingness to state these, there has been a remarkable consensus among the historians writing about inter-war Northern Ireland during the 'Troubles' of the 1960s to 1990s. They might differ as to the causes of partition or the best solution to the contemporary conflict but they were united in identifying the roots of the Troubles in the 1920s and 1930s and embraced a common chronology of significant events. The partition of the island in 1920 had been accompanied by the establishment of a parliament in Northern Ireland with powers that were too great in some respects and too limited in others; partition had resulted in government by a permanent Ulster Unionist majority that would last for half a century; and this government had indulged in forms of discrimination – particularly in the areas of representation, law and order, employment, and education – which might be explained if not justified by the violence and insecurity of the years directly following partition but which actually became more blatant as the immediate threats faded.

Historians did not have to dig very hard to find their evidence. Institutionalised sectarianism in Northern Ireland had no hidden history. It was overt and accompanied by a political rhetoric that did not so much defend discrimination as celebrate it. Indeed, one of the few points of difference between historians of Northern Ireland who have studied this period is whether actual discrimination was capable of reaching the heights of the rhetoric. It is certainly important to note that when, in 1934, Northern Ireland's first Prime Minister, Sir James Craig, famously stated that 'all I boast of is that we are a Protestant Parliament for a Protestant People', he was commenting on the Irish Free State's portrayal of itself as a Catholic state.[3] However, it is also necessary to bear in mind that Craig's language was habitually mild by comparison with that of some of his supporters.

Buckland has cautioned against 'facile' interpretations in which responsibility for discrimination 'is laid at the door of bigoted Ulster unionists and Protestants, particularly the people of property, exploiting religion and playing on the baser instincts of the Protestant working class to maintain their own position or to carry out the dirty work of British imperialism'. Rather, he suggests, it is essential to understand the history of unionism and nationalism and the difficult position of the former in the conflict of the latter with British imperialism.[4] However, Joseph Ruane and Jennifer Todd have argued that while the threat from nationalism was real, the means taken to combat

---

3 T. Wilson, *Ulster: Conflict and Consent* (Oxford: Basil Blackwell, 1989), 73.
4 P. Buckland, 'A Protestant State: Unionists in Government, 1921–39', in D. G. Boyce and A. O'Day (eds.), *Defenders of the Union: A Survey of British and Irish Unionism Since 1801* (London: Routledge, 2001), 211.

it were counter-productive: 'Some effort might have been made to win the allegiance, or at least the toleration of the minority for the Northern state. The failure even to attempt this … the evident satisfaction which many unionists took in disadvantaging Catholics and the scant respect they paid to their sensibilities, suggest that the motivation went much deeper than simply countering nationalism.'[5]

Much of the energy of historians and other scholars since the 1970s has been devoted to exploring the motivations of unionists and the bonds between the Protestant middle and working classes, while others were more concerned with teasing out the relationships between Belfast and London and Belfast and Dublin. The emphasis was overwhelmingly on political history and largely on the politics of unionism, whether at governmental or at street level. Notable exceptions were the relevant chapters of Jonathan Bardon's dazzling *History of Ulster* (1993), which attempted to humanise and diversify what had by now become a familiar story, and Mary Harris's, *The Catholic Church and the Foundation of the Northern Irish State* (1993) and Eamon Phoenix's *Northern Nationalism: Nationalist Politics, Partition and the Catholic Minority in Northern Ireland 1890–1940* (1994) which, *inter alia*, drew attention to the extent of sectarian rhetoric and practice among Catholics. Studies of Northern Ireland's Labour Party from Graham Walker's *The Politics of Frustration: Harry Midgley and the Failure of Labour in Northern Ireland* (1985) to Aaron Edwards's *History of the Northern Ireland Labour Party: Democratic Socialism and Sectarianism* (2009) have also contributed to the development of a more nuanced history, though, as their titles suggest, without challenging the prevailing narrative.

The historiography of Northern Ireland in the 1920s and 1930s, then, remains dominated by the politics of Protestant sectarianism, the ghettoisation of Catholics and the failure of cross-community alternatives. This historiography is characterised first, by a tendency to speculate on missed opportunities and what-might-have-been, asking whether this event or that was the moment when the future became inevitable, and second, by a sense of wonder at the fact that Northern Ireland survived as a political entity and a degree of admiration, however grudging, for the achievement of the first Prime Minister, Sir James Craig, and his government in ensuring that it did so.

---

5 J. Ruane and J. Todd, 'Irish Nationalism and the Conflict in Northern Ireland', in D. Miller (ed.), *Rethinking Northern Ireland* (Harlow: Addison Wesley Longman, 1998), 59.

Preparation for Government

Northern Ireland was neither intended nor designed to survive as a self-governing state. The Government of Ireland Act, 1920 established the parliaments of Northern and Southern Ireland, and the institutions through which Northern Ireland was to be governed. It was a compromise solution to the Irish problem which, by establishing two parliaments with identical limited powers, each subordinate to Westminster, emphasised to international public opinion that partition was an attempt to reconcile, not to deny, the aspirations of both nationalists and unionists to self-determination. It also allowed Britain to extricate herself from Ireland to the greatest extent compatible with her imperial and security priorities. But no one was enthusiastic about this solution: it appalled nationalists and represented a least worst option for both British and Irish unionists. The argument that both partition and self-government had been imposed on Northern Ireland contrary to the will of the unionist people, who had, in Craig's words, made 'the supreme sacrifice' in accepting them,[6] would subsequently be used by the government to considerable effect in squeezing concessions from London.

The Government of Ireland Act was drafted with a number of considerations in mind, none of which was the creation of sustainable constitutional arrangements that were well-suited to the political, economic, social, cultural or even historical circumstances of the six north-eastern counties. Rather, the Act simply – and rather carelessly – extended to Belfast arrangements for limited self-government which had been designed with Dublin and the need to restrain some of the feared impulses of a nationalist Irish government in mind. Second, the drafters anticipated that partition would last no more than three years. Unionists' fears of the potential religious, agrarian and separatist excesses of a Dublin government were exaggerated, it was believed, and soon the benefits of north–south cooperation, and ultimately of reunification, would appeal to the Unionists' good sense and economic self-interest.

The Act created northern and southern institutions which would not jeopardise imperial concerns; would restrain any urges towards economic or religious extremism; would encourage and facilitate cooperation and eventual reunification; and which mirrored, balanced and were symbiotic with each other. Indeed, the Act reads more as an exercise in creating a pleasing

---

6 A. T. Q. Stewart, *The Narrow Ground: The Roots of Conflict in Ulster*, 2nd edn. (London: Faber & Faber, 1989), 170.

and elegant constitutional harmony on paper than an attempt to create a realistic instrument of government. Its intrinsic shortcomings would soon be exacerbated by the violence which marked the early years of Northern Ireland's existence and the unionist response to that violence, by economic crises, and ultimately by the Anglo-Irish Treaty of 1921. This tore up the Government of Ireland Act insofar as it applied to 'Southern Ireland' but left it in place in Northern Ireland despite the fact that the entire edifice had been founded on balance and unity. That the consequence was that the part of Ireland that had most ardently resisted Home Rule became the only part to get it is an irony that has appealed to historians. Nor was not it lost on contemporaries. As the Reverend James B. Armour observed, 'Because they had yelled about "No Home Rule" for a generation, Ulster Unionists were compelled to take a form of Home Rule that the Devil himself could never have imagined.'[7]

British Prime Minister David Lloyd George revealed his plans for the two Irish parliaments in December 1919 and the Government of Ireland Act passed into law a year later. Throughout 1920 preparations were made for the establishment of the parliaments and the transfer of powers. As Edward Carson began to withdraw from Ulster unionist politics, Craig played a vital role in these arrangements, effectively being treated by London as Northern Ireland's prime minister in waiting. The region which Craig was preparing to govern was defined by the Act as consisting of the parliamentary counties of Antrim, Armagh, Down, Fermanagh, Londonderry and Tyrone, and the parliamentary boroughs of Belfast and Londonderry. Its composition had been determined by religious demography: with the other three counties of the province of Ulster – Donegal, Cavan and Monaghan – excluded, Protestants would enjoy a majority of 66 per cent or 820,370 to 430,161 Catholics, based on the 1911 Census. However, the population was unevenly distributed, with the Protestant majority being strongest in the east and the Catholic population strongest in the south and west. Of the cities, Belfast had a Protestant majority but contained a large Catholic community, roughly a quarter of the city's population. Derry had a Catholic majority but a largely Protestant hinterland.[8] Religion was the most obvious, but not the only, source of social division (and the 'Protestant' majority was itself made up of Presbyterian, Church of Ireland, Methodist and other communities). Urban/rural, regional and class differences sometimes cut across, and sometimes reinforced, the

---

7 Cited in J. Bardon, *A History of Ulster* (Belfast: Blackstaff Press, 1992), 514.
8 P. Buckland, *A History of Northern Ireland* (Dublin: Gill & Macmillan, 1981), 24–5.

sectarian divide and such considerations had profound implications for local and, as it would emerge, parliamentary politics.

In addition, David Harkness paints a grim picture of the social and economic problems which plagued the region: 'The area to which the Government of Ireland Act was in fact to apply was recognised to be backward in almost every public service' with 'levels of tuberculosis, infant mortality, disease, malnutrition and poverty [that] were themselves eloquent testimony to existing deficiencies.' The road infrastructure and housing stock were poor and the economy, precariously dependent on outdated agricultural and industrial practices, was 'in trouble'.[9]

Northern Ireland was to have a parliament modelled on, and subordinate to, that of the imperial parliament in Westminster and consisting of the King; a House of Commons of 52 MPs, elected for five years by proportional representation; and a Senate of 26 members. Thirteen MPs would also represent Northern Ireland in Westminster. The Northern Ireland parliament would have no legislative power over matters such as the Crown, war and peace, the armed forces, and external trade. Complicated financial arrangements would also limit the ability of the Belfast government to raise revenue. The most important forms of taxation, including customs and excise duties and income tax would continue to be set and collected by London and levied in Northern Ireland at the same rate as elsewhere in the United Kingdom. A share of this revenue would be returned to Belfast once an 'imperial contribution' had been deducted.

The main mechanism for cooperation with Southern Ireland was to be a Council of Ireland, consisting of twenty members elected by each of the two parliaments. The Council of Ireland was initially to have responsibility for railways, fisheries and the contagious diseases of animals but it would be possible for the two parliaments to transfer further powers to it. It was anticipated that they would quickly do so and that the Council of Ireland would form the basis of a unified Irish parliament. Some services, such as the postal service, were described in the Act as being 'reserved', meaning that they would be administered by Westminster until transferred to a united Irish parliament. The two police services – the Royal Irish Constabulary and the Dublin Metropolitan Police – were, crucially, to be 'reserved' for up to three years, though responsibility for policing might be transferred to a united parliament should one exist before this period expired. The implications were clear: it was assumed that Irish reunification would quickly take place through

---

9 D. Harkness, *Northern Ireland since 1920* (Dublin: Helicon, 1983), 7.

the voluntary actions of the two parliaments. Should this not happen, further arrangements would require to be made but there is little evidence that much thought was given to this possibility.

Both jurisdictions were prohibited from endowing any religion and from passing legislation which discriminated on the basis of religion and both were obliged to retain the system of proportional representation in parliamentary elections for three years. However, as Buckland points out, these provisions were intended to give protection to the small and geographically-scattered Protestant and Unionist minority in Southern Ireland and did not address the different problems which would arise from the existence of a large, concentrated and disaffected religious minority in Northern Ireland.[10] Recognition of the differing religious profiles of Northern and Southern Ireland can be found only in the separate constitutions of their respective senates. Unlike the Senate of Southern Ireland which was designed to encourage political participation by the religious minority, the Senate of Northern Ireland was to be elected by the House of Commons, in which, it was assumed, the minority would be adequately represented. The Northern Ireland which was envisaged by the drafters of the Government of Ireland Bill was, therefore, a state in which religious divisions would influence, but be expressed largely through, the operation of parliamentary democracy. The historiography of Northern Ireland since 1979 suggests that this assumption was unduly optimistic in the spring of 1920: by the end of the year, it bore little relation to reality.

The six north-eastern counties were relatively unaffected by the early stages of the Anglo-Irish War, highlighting the fact that the north-east was different from the rest of the country and, possibly, amounting to an argument in favour of partition. This was one reason why a series of IRA attacks began in the summer of 1920. These were accompanied by severe outbreaks of communal sectarian violence in Belfast and Derry, culminating in the expulsion of thousands of Catholic workers from the Belfast shipyards and other industries. In retaliation, a number of southern local authorities began to implement a boycott of Ulster banks and businesses. Later endorsed by the Dáil, the 'Belfast boycott' was widely supported in independent Ireland, as well as by northern nationalists and the Catholic church, causing significant economic damage and offering evidence to those who wanted it that nationalists and Catholics of all shades were intrinsically hostile to Northern Ireland in general and to northern business interests in particular. Craig and his Ulster Unionist colleagues were also becoming concerned that the authorities in

10 Buckland, *History of Northern Ireland*, 23.

both Dublin Castle and London had decided to prioritise achieving peace in the island as a whole over establishing a government in Northern Ireland. For example, neither Dublin nor London was cooperative over the transfer of civil service personnel to Belfast. In time it would become clear that both were willing to recognise and, ultimately, to negotiate with, Sinn Féin.

With the Ulster Volunteer Force (UVF) beginning to reform, Craig pressed the British to establish a 'special constabulary' for Northern Ireland, intended both to police public order and to act, if necessary, as a defence against IRA offensives. It would be independent of Dublin Castle's control and recruited from the UVF. Both London and Dublin Castle had serious reservations about doing so but, concluding that it would be preferable to the re-emergence of Unionist paramilitarism, agreed in September 1920. The Ulster Special Constabulary (USC) was to consist of a full-time paid and armed force; a part-time, unpaid force; and a reserve, to be known respectively as the 'A', 'B' and 'C' Specials. Although there were some, partially successful, early attempts to encourage Catholic recruitment, the great majority of 'Specials' were drawn from the ranks of the old UVF, with the Orange Order playing a significant role in recruitment.[11] Nationalists were apprehensive and, according to Follis, unionists hopeful, that the USC would act as a standing army placed at the disposal of the Ulster Unionist Party to guarantee that the partition settlement was not interfered with.[12]

By December 1920, then, when the Government of Ireland Act came into effect, the political landscape was very different to what it had been when the terms of the Act were unveiled. The deterioration of conditions throughout the island meant that, had there been any possibility of nationalist acceptance of the Act, this had now 'evaporated'.[13] The formation and activities of the Special Constabulary had added to Catholic fears and conflict continued throughout 1921. On the other hand, Ulster unionists felt isolated and besieged and had developed a pronounced hostility to anything emerging from Dublin or conceived of as being on an all-Ireland basis. Craig was convinced that a rapid transfer of services, including reserved services, was essential and, to this end had, also in September 1920, successfully requested the appointment of an Undersecretary in Belfast. Once appointed, Sir Ernest Clark became the main architect of the government of Northern Ireland, working with Craig, who became leader of the Ulster Unionist Council on 4 February 1921. In a letter to

---

11 Ibid., p. 41.
12 B. A. Follis, *A State Under Siege: The Establishment of Northern Ireland 1920–1925* (Oxford: Clarendon Press, 1995), 16.
13 Harkness, *Northern Ireland*, 3.

a friend in April, Clark described himself as being 'more like John the Baptist than any person I can think of, with an unknown saviour, who has only one chance in a hundred of bringing peace and goodwill on the earth (or this portion of it), whoever he may be'.[14]

War and peace

Elections to the Parliament of Northern Ireland took place on Empire Day, 24 May 1921, after a campaign which revolved solely around the question, as Craig put it, 'Who is for Empire and who is for a Republic?'[15] The Ulster Unionist Party's victory was even greater than expected, with all forty candidates returned, while, despite an electoral pact intended to avoid splitting the nationalist vote, Sinn Féin and the Nationalist Party – the remnant of the Irish Parliamentary Party, led by Joe Devlin until his death in 1934 – won six seats each rather than an anticipated total of twenty. Nationalists claimed that the Unionist victory had been assisted by violence and voter intimidation, but in reality, their triumph also reflected the divisions among the anti-partition parties. Both intended to abstain from taking their seats in parliament and the campaign was marred by sometimes violent encounters between their supporters. The Labour Party did not contest the election; four Independent Labour candidates in Belfast all lost their deposits.

Craig formed a government and a cabinet consisting of Hugh McDowell Pollock (Minister of Finance), John Miller Andrews (Minister of Labour), Sir Richard Dawson Bates (Minister of Home Affairs), the marquess of Londonderry (Minister of Education) and Edward Mervyn Archdale (Minister of Agriculture and Commerce). Craig, Bates and Andrews would still be members of the cabinet in 1939; death in office was more usual than resignation or retirement. These were not, perhaps, men of vision but were appointed largely in recognition of their past services to unionism and to achieve a regional and sectional balance in the cabinet. Nonetheless Buckland, who is in general scathing of the calibre of Ulster politicians of this generation, regards them as men of some talent, with the exception of Bates; a view shared by most historians who have deplored the decision to appoint to the vital Home Affairs Ministry, with responsibility for law and order, justice and policing, a man of modest intellectual abilities who 'looked upon all

14 Follis, *State Under Siege*, 31.
15 T. Hennessey, *A History of Northern Ireland 1920–1996* (Houndmills: Palgrave, 1997), 15.

Catholics as nationalists and all nationalists not just as political enemies but as traitors'.[16]

On 22 June 1921, the Northern Ireland parliament was formally opened by King George V, whose speech had been carefully drafted with a view to suggesting to Sinn Féin that the British government was ready to open negotiations. A truce between the Crown Forces and the IRA was negotiated in July and preliminary negotiations began. Craig now discovered that the Ulster Unionists' suspicions had been proved correct and that Lloyd George had come to favour some sort of all-Ireland solution which would overturn the Government of Ireland Act. Craig resisted pressure either to meet Éamon de Valera or to consider an agreement that would make the Northern Ireland parliament subordinate to Dublin rather than Westminster, pressure that increased as formal negotiations with Sinn Féin began in October. However, Craig's discussions with the British Prime Minister undermined Unionist confidence in Craig's administration and this dissatisfaction was exacerbated by the violence which marked the second half of 1921. During the truce, the IRA built up its strength in the north and there were frequent breaches of the ceasefire, often followed by rioting. The new government seemed, and effectively was, powerless to react. Responsibility for policing remained in the hands of Westminster, and under the terms of the truce, the London government had rolled back the powers and operational capacity of the Crown Forces.

Lloyd George began a dangerous balancing act. He continued to assure Sinn Féin representatives that he was sincere about pursuing an all-Ireland solution. However, he was aware that he did not have the support of his Conservative colleagues in government on this point and was troubled by rumours that preparations were being made in Northern Ireland to mount an armed resistance to any attempt to undermine Northern Ireland's constitutional status. In November, Craig extracted a promise from Lloyd George that 'Northern Ireland's rights would not be compromised against her will' which he successfully portrayed to his wavering Unionist followers as having 'secured the existence of Northern Ireland'.[17] In addition, Lloyd George agreed with Craig that it was necessary to demonstrate the reality of self-rule in Northern Ireland by expediting the transfer of powers. Most of this was accomplished by 22 November, meaning that by the time the Articles of Agreement for a Treaty between Great Britain and Ireland were signed on 6

---

16 Buckland, *History of Northern Ireland*, 33.
17 Follis, *State Under Siege*, 67.

December 1921, the government of Northern Ireland had moved from being a paper creation to a functioning entity.

The Treaty was, to ulster Unionists, a betrayal of the assurances which Lloyd George had given previously and a surrender to what Carson described as a 'murder gang'.[18] It proposed to transfer immediate sovereignty over the parliament of Northern Ireland from Westminster to Dublin, though the government of Northern Ireland was empowered to opt out of this arrangement. Should it do so – and it promptly did – the Government of Ireland Act would remain intact so far as Northern Ireland was concerned, despite being fundamentally revised in the case of the new Irish Free State. This would have unknown and potentially catastrophic consequences. Additionally, under the terms of Treaty, the inevitable opt-out meant that a Boundary Commission would be established to review the border between the two jurisdictions, 'to determine, in accordance with the wishes of the inhabitants, so far as may be compatible with economic and geographic conditions, the boundaries between Northern Ireland and the rest of Ireland'. This was 'an ambiguous and cryptic brief, which could either bolster or undermine the nascent regimes in Northern Ireland and the Irish Free State and, by implication, the entire Treaty settlement'.[19]

The prospect of this Boundary Commission would have a significant impact on the early development of Northern Ireland. Unionists feared, and nationalists hoped, that it would transfer sufficiently large an area and population to the Irish Free State as to make Northern Ireland unviable. In Craig's view, the best means to avert the impending disaster was quietly to insist on the transfer of the remaining powers, which was achieved by February 1922, and to ensure that these were used for, and not against, the interests of unionists. On the other side, northern, like southern, nationalists appear to have regarded the Boundary Commission with undue optimism, as meaning that the period of unionist rule in northern Ireland was limited and that it was therefore unnecessary to come to terms with it. Delays in the establishment of the Boundary Commission, together with the outbreak of Civil War on the island, served to further entrench these attitudes.

In the early months of 1922, Craig held meetings with Michael Collins. Both emphasised their enthusiasm to establish peace and good relations,

18 Harkness, *Northern Ireland*, 13.
19 K. J. Rankin, 'The Provenance and Dissolution of the Irish Boundary Commission', Working Papers in British-Irish Studies, 79 (Dublin: Institute for British-Irish Studies, University College Dublin, 2006), 1.

Collins undertaking to end the Belfast boycott and Craig to use his influence to facilitate the return to work of expelled Catholics, insofar as economic conditions allowed. Both were also keen to make the proposed readjustment of the boundary a matter for mutual agreement rather than a commission. However, their initial agreement appears to have been based on a fundamental misunderstanding created not least by Lloyd George's tendency to be all things to all Irishmen. He had led Craig to believe that any land transfer would be minor and Collins that it would be considerable.[20] Following the breakdown of a meeting in Dublin on 2 February, Collins sanctioned IRA operations in Northern Ireland.[21]

Extraordinary measures were adopted to deal with both IRA violence and civil disorder, including the Civil Authorities (Special Powers) Act (NI), 1922. Intended to be in force for one year only, the Act authorised the Minister for Home Affairs, or a police officer acting on his behalf, to 'take all such steps and issue all such orders as may be necessary for preserving the peace and maintaining order'. A Unionist backbencher, G. B. Hanna, characterised the Act as needing only one section: 'The Home Secretary shall have power to do what he likes, or else let somebody else do what he likes for him.' Though Buckland describes these powers as 'frankly despotic',[22] he notes that it was, in some regards less draconian than the Restoration of Order in Ireland Act, 1920 on which it was based. For example, it did not implement any kind of military court. This was an example of the government's fear of appearing provocative in British eyes – not least because of the necessity of negotiating the payment of the Special Constabulary from increasingly wary British officials. Though responsibility for policing had by now been transferred, the Northern Ireland government argued that it was unreasonable to expect it to bear the full cost given that the security emergency was largely attributable to Britain's Irish policy. The British government agreed to continue payment in the short term, though only on an *ad-hoc*, grant-in-aid basis.[23] It did so reluctantly, aware that the Special Constabulary was becoming the main force charged with defending against IRA operations and concerned that support for what was effectively a military, rather than a police, force might endanger relations with what would shortly become the Irish Free State. The

20 M. Hopkinson, 'The Craig-Collins pacts of 1922: Two attempted reforms of the Northern Ireland government', *Irish Historical Studies*, 27 (1990), 147–9.
21 M. Lewis, 'The Fourth Northern Division and the Joint-IRA Offensive, April–July 1922', *War in History* 21 (2014), 307.
22 Buckland, *History of Northern Ireland*, 40.
23 Follis, *State Under Siege*, 121.

distaste was more than shared in nationalist Belfast where the B Specials were regarded as the vanguard and arms-suppliers of loyalist mobs.

In March, representatives of the Northern and Provisional governments held another meeting in London under the auspices of the British government and concluded a second 'Craig-Collins pact'. Under the terms of this agreement, the IRA would cease operations in Northern Ireland while Craig once again undertook to have expelled Catholics returned to their workplaces, to establish mechanisms for recruiting Catholics into the Special Constabulary, and to set up a conciliation committee with alternating Protestant and Catholic chairmen to investigate outrages and complaints of intimidation.[24] Again, the question of the border was raised and again the two leaders agreed to see whether the two governments could settle the matter without recourse to a Boundary Commission. Once more, however, the agreement was stillborn. Not for the first time, Craig found his negotiations with southern leaders deeply unpopular with unionist opinion in general and with his cabinet colleagues in particular. Nor could he point to positive results: the pact was repudiated by many IRA commanders, who were ultimately encouraged to do so by Collins himself – partially in the largely counter-productive interest of protecting the Catholic minority and partially with a view to holding the IRA together in pursuit of a common agenda. By early May, both IRA operations and deadly inter-communal violence had resumed.

The government's reluctance to appear provocative did not survive the IRA's May 1922 offensive. Dawson Bates invoked his powers under the Civil Authorities (Special Powers) Act (NI), 1922, proscribing the IRA and introducing internment. Within 24 hours, 500 people had been arrested and interned on a prison ship, the *Argenta*. Internments, almost exclusively of Catholics and nationalists, continued until December 1924. Flogging, permitted under the Act as a 'special punishment' was now increasingly used and special non-jury courts were established. In June 1922, a curfew was imposed over the entire six counties and an exclusion regulation was introduced to control the movement of people.[25] Meanwhile, the lives of Catholic citizens were frequently disrupted by the unannounced closing of roads and by increased searches, all facilitated by the mass mobilisation of the B Specials, now attached to the Royal Ulster Constabulary the (largely but not exclusively Protestant) regular police force which had replaced the Royal Irish Constabulary in Northern Ireland. On the other hand, both government and police authorities regarded

---

24 Hopkinson, 'Craig-Collins Pacts', 151.
25 Buckland, *History of Northern Ireland*, 46–7.

the policing of loyalist violence to be a matter that required delicacy and a light hand so that 'it was not that there was one law for Catholics and another for Protestants. Rather, there was one law, but it was enforced more stringently against Catholics'.[26]

It is open to question whether these measures were successful in reducing the number of IRA operations or whether this was due to the outbreak of Civil War in June which ended cooperation between the pro- and anti-Treaty IRA factions and opened up new theatres in the south. However, by the late summer of 1922, Northern Ireland had become relatively peaceful. But, as Eamon Phoenix points out, 'the northern Catholic population, including even moderate Devlinites, were convinced that the events of 1920–22' – the deaths from loyalist violence, the mass expulsions from employment, the creation of the USC – 'constituted a pogrom which had been carefully planned with the objective of driving the minority out of the new state'. In consequence, that state 'would find the minority difficult to govern, let alone assimilate'.[27]

Securing Unionist Rule

In addition to discrimination in the area of law and order during these crucial early months, historians have highlighted the areas of education and representation, though responsibility for some of the discrimination in education has often been laid at the feet of the minority community itself. With the Catholic hierarchy supporting the nationalist refusal to recognise the government, it refused to nominate representatives to the Lynn Committee which was established in September 1921 to examine and propose reforms for the ramshackle system of education which Northern Ireland had inherited. The members of the Lynn Committee claimed to have borne Catholic interests in mind when making their recommendations, and can hardly be held responsible if their understanding of these was limited.

The discrimination which came to characterise the system of representation was far more overtly intended to safeguard unionist interests. The 1920 local elections had shown how effectively proportional representation

---

26 P. Buckland, 'A Protestant Parliament and a Protestant State: Regional Government and Religious Discrimination in Northern Ireland, 1920–1939', in A. C. Duke and C. A. Tamse (eds.), *Britain and The Netherlands: Volume VII Church and State Since the Reformation: Papers Delivered to the Seventh Anglo-Dutch Historical Conference* (The Hague: Martinus Nijhoff, 1981), 233.

27 E. Phoenix, *Northern Nationalism: Nationalist Politics, Partition and the Catholic Minority in Northern Ireland 1890–1940* (Belfast: Ulster Historical Foundation, 1994), 394.

achieved its intended purpose, that of boosting minority representation. It had resulted in nationalist majorities in some traditionally marginal constituencies, including Londonderry Corporation. For many unionists, the imposition of an electoral system that could be characterised as neither British nor democratic and which gave electoral advantages to the disloyal at the expense of ratepayers was an outrage. In July 1922 the government responded to this pressure by passing a bill to abolish proportional representation for local elections, apparently completely oblivious to the possibility that such a move might be regarded as a form of religious discrimination and so prohibited under the Government of Ireland Act.

Collins protested to the British government and the royal assent was withheld for more than two months. London caved in, however, when Craig threatened to resign. Despite Westminster's sovereignty over Northern Ireland, despite the British government's responsibility for the millions of British taxpayers' money which, as will be discussed, was subsidising the transferred services, and despite an awareness that the governance of Northern Ireland could have negative implications for Anglo-Irish relations, the options were perceived to be limited by the lack of a palatable alternative to Ulster Unionist government.

This reality would also have an important impact on the financial relationship between Belfast and London. With the most important forms of taxation 'reserved' under the Government of Ireland Act, the Belfast government had little control over the raising of revenue and there were serious doubts concerning its ability to fund the transferred services from existing resources. The situation was exacerbated by the post-war depression which impacted significantly on the province's agriculture and industries in the years following partition, reducing tax income and adding to the number unemployed. Indeed, it was the prospect of bankruptcy as much as that of the Boundary Commission which persuaded many northern and southern nationalists that Northern Ireland was not a viable entity.

From the Unionist government's perspective, the financial provisions of the Government of Ireland Act were unduly onerous, imposing as they did an annual 'imperial contribution' of £8,000,000. This sum, Craig's government argued, was based on a miscalculation of both the Northern Irish tax base and its liabilities for domestic expenditure. Moreover, it took no account of either the economic damage resulting from partition or of the fact that the financial obligations imposed on Southern Ireland by the Government of Ireland Act had been lessened under the terms of the Anglo-Irish Treaty. Over the course of 1923, the numbers of the Special Constabulary were scaled back and further government economies made but, as the financial situation in Northern Ireland became increasingly precarious, the new state not only remained dependent on British subventions but also on the fluctuating good-will of rapidly-changing British governments.

Andrew Bonar Law's Conservative government, which came to power in October 1923, agreed to refer the question of Northern Ireland's imperial contribution to arbitration by what became known as the Colwyn Committee. The Committee made its final report in December 1924 and its most significant recommendation was that Northern Ireland's imperial contribution would henceforth be determined on the basis of the excess of income over 'actual and necessary' expenditure. This was not meant to be a profligate's charter: 'actual and necessary' expenditure was defined in a manner which meant that *per capita* social services expenditure would increase only at the same rate as in Britain. In practice, bringing the social services up to and maintaining them at British levels (at the expense of the imperial contribution and thus of the British exchequer) became an objective of and not a limitation to Ulster Unionist policy. The Northern Ireland government argued successfully that as its citizens paid the same rates of tax as other UK citizens they had a right to the same social standards and the same rates of unemployment and sickness benefits and old age pensions. As this would negatively affect the imperial contribution, it meant that the British exchequer would henceforth undertake the cost of bringing Northern Ireland's social services to, and maintaining them at, British levels.

In January 1924 a short-lived Labour government came to power in Britain under Ramsay MacDonald, putting grant-in-aid arrangements in jeopardy. Though the government fell from power in October 1924 without having repudiated its predecessor's financial commitments to Northern Ireland, it attempted to use the threat of doing so as leverage to oblige Craig's government to cooperate in reaching an agreement with the Irish Free State government over the solution to the boundary question. Following the failure of a tripartite conference held in London in April 1924 to reach an agreement, the Irish Free State formally requested the establishment of a Boundary Commission. MacDonald's government acceded to this but could not persuade Craig to nominate a representative from Northern Ireland to sit on the Commission.[28]

The Commission, as finally constituted, consisted of a South African Supreme Court Judge, Richard Feetham, as chairman, Minister for Education Eoin MacNeill representing the Irish Free State, and Belfast barrister and

28 Follis, *State Under Siege*, 159–61.

journalist J. R. Fisher, nominated by the British government to represent the interests of Northern Ireland. The hopes of Ulster unionists that the return of a Conservative government would result in the abandonment of the Commission were quickly dashed and the Commission began its work in November, hearing legal submissions, touring the border area and considering written and oral evidence. In the event, unionist fears were to prove unfounded: the Commission determined on a resolution of the border issue which would transfer a mere 282 square miles and 31,319 souls to the Irish Free State and 78 square miles and 7,594 souls in the opposite direction.[29] The leaking of this information, which was guaranteed to be a major embarrassment to the Irish Free State's government, turned potential trilateral crisis into farce: after some shuttle diplomacy, all three jurisdictions agreed to shelve the report of the Boundary Commission and confirm the existing border.[30]

As part of the same agreement, some outstanding administrative and financial matters were settled and issues relating to compensation and the release of prisoners were addressed generously on all sides. More significantly, the Council of Ireland envisaged by the Government of Ireland Act was transmuted into an agreement that the Dublin and Belfast parliaments might meet, as they thought fit, to discuss matters of common interest. In the opinion of Follis, 'The Boundary Agreement entered into on 3 December 1925 by the governments of Northern Ireland, the Irish Free State, and the United Kingdom heralded a new era of peaceful co-existence.'[31]

Political Culture

Between 1920 and 1925 Northern Ireland's politics had been dominated by the issues of security and status but not exclusively so. Even in the Ministry of Home Affairs, there had been time to pass legislation improving provision for the development of housing and roads and restricting the opening hours of licenced premises in 1923.[32] In the same year, Lord Londonderry, the Minister for Education, had introduced an Education Bill which aimed to establish a system of non-denominational primary schools under public control. With the establishment of relative peace and the waning of the threat posed by the Boundary Commission, there were signs that the political climate was

---

29 Rankin, 'Provenance and Dissolution', 20.
30 M. Kennedy, *Division and Consensus: The Politics of Cross-Border Relations in Ireland, 1925–1969* (Dublin: Institute of Public Administration, 2000), 9–15.
31 Follis, *State Under Siege*, 131.
32 Harkness, *Northern Ireland*, 31.

evolving and alternatives to the sterile politics of partition beginning, tentatively, to emerge.

Although the three-year moratorium on abolishing proportional representation had passed, it had been retained for the 1925 general election. The deliberations of the Boundary Commission had an impact in border constituencies where the unionist vote was slightly increased, allowing Craig to portray the result as a mandate to defend the *status quo*. However, Independent Unionists and the recently-formed Labour Party of Northern Ireland won four and three seats respectively in Belfast, at the expense of the Ulster Unionists and in northeast Antrim a farmers' candidate unseated the Junior Minister of Home Affairs.[33] Most significantly, encouraged by the Catholic church which felt its interests were being inadequately represented in the reform of education, Nationalist candidates indicated that they would consider taking their seats.[34] The result was a considerable swing away from abstentionist Republicans and the return of ten out of the eleven Nationalists nominated. It would take until 1927 for all the Nationalist MPs to enter parliament and they refused to accept the role of official opposition. However, during the second part of the decade the party began to develop some of the characteristics of a functioning political party, including grassroots organisation and a programme. The party stood first, for a united Ireland and second for the defence of Catholic interests, but its third objective was social and economic reform, and by the general election in 1929, it had developed a 'strongly radical' manifesto which included a public works programme to alleviate unemployment, an increase in the school leaving age and a reduction in the age of qualification for old age pensions.[35]

However, these early signs of a more vibrant politics were largely superficial, and if the settlement of the boundary question had created greater possibilities for normalising both internal and external relations no advantage was taken of it. There was no obvious improvement in Northern Ireland's relationship with the Irish Free State – neither government regarded this as a priority and each was wary of appearing to engage too closely with the other. The inter-governmental communication envisaged by the Boundary Agreement was not utilised and, although there was some movement towards north–south cooperation on matters such as electrification, this did not immediately materialise and contact took place at official and junior departmental levels.[36]

33 Follis, *State Under Siege*, 176.
34 M. Harris, *The Catholic Church and the Foundation of the Northern Irish State* (Cork: Cork University Press, 1993), 144–5, 170.
35 Phoenix, *Northern Nationalism*, 364.
36 Kennedy, *Division and Consensus*, 42.

With the change of government from Cumann na nGaedheal to Fianna Fáil in the Irish Free State in 1932 Unionist attitudes were further hardened. De Valera's approaches to the London government with a view to ending partition and, in particular, the drafting of the 1937 Constitution with its claim to sovereignty over the entire island, were closely watched and turned to advantage at home. The election which Craig called for 1938, overtly as a response to de Valera's new Constitution, was primarily intended to dispose of the threat to the Ulster Unionist party posed by the recently formed Progressive Unionist Party which espoused a more interventionist approach to the economy and advocated programmes of house-building and public works.[37] None of the smaller party's ten candidates was returned.

Internally also, Harkness suggests, rather than creating the conditions for developing a more just society, the relative peace of the years after 1925 combined with economic depression to exacerbate factors such as the economic shortcomings of the Government of Ireland Act, the divisions within unionism, the irreconcilable opposition of nationalists to the state's existence and the absence of vision in government. There were 'no landmarks of political change, few debates, even at election time about the desired social order, merely the evidence of a dull government surviving, admittedly in difficult times'.[38]

The unionist majority in Northern Ireland was not sufficiently large to be entirely confident. Indeed, A. T. Q. Stewart has suggested that 'the Ulster unionists have the worst of both worlds: the ratio of two to one in population is undoubtedly the most difficult, for it means that while the Protestants have always been absolutely sure of a safe majority in political matters, the Catholics know perfectly well that they are numerically strong enough to disrupt the state at any time if the price is worth paying'.[39] Particularly in border areas and in Protestant enclaves surrounded by Catholic populations, Protestants felt vulnerable. In addition, Ulster Unionist hegemony depended on preventing the fracturing of a party which was based on a precarious alliance of sectional interest groups, divided by geography, class and religion. Measures which were openly, and unapologetically, taken to give electoral advantages to unionists had the added benefits of keeping minds focused on the necessity for doing so – the fundamental disloyalty of the nationalist population and the threat this posed to the state, the Union and the Protestant faith – and

---

37 G. Walker, *A History of the Ulster Unionist Party: Protest, Pragmatism and Pessimism* (Manchester: Manchester University Press, 2004), 74.
38 Harkness, *Northern Ireland*, 44.
39 Stewart, *Narrow Ground*, 159.

of discouraging competition for Protestant votes. The return to single seater constituencies following the abolition of proportional representation in 1922 permitted the redrawing of constituencies to Unionist advantage. Early reluctance to gerrymander too brazenly gave way to local pressures so that in 1936 a scheme was devised which ensured a Unionist majority on Londonderry Corporation despite a two-thirds Catholic majority population – a process described by Craig as 'maintain[ing] the integrity of the maiden city'.[40]

In 1923 also a higher property qualification than in the rest of the United Kingdom was introduced for local elections and, in 1928, when the extension of the franchise to all adult women prompted concerns that female migrant workers from the south would unduly increase the nationalist vote in border areas, long residence requirements and a limited company franchise were introduced. Local politics were deeply conservative, dominated by the protection of business interests, obsessed with avoiding increases in the rates, and otherwise primarily engaged in cultivating and retaining the support of electors of one's own religious persuasion. Nationalist-dominated local authorities discriminated in favour of their own community in employment and housing, Unionist-dominated authorities did the same. However, 'there were not only more unionist authorities but more than there ought to have been'.[41]

Additionally, the Parliament of Northern Ireland never rose above the same amateurish and localist approach to politics to develop any degree of statesmanship or even of civic responsibility. Politicians were expected to be available to discuss and respond to the concerns of individual constituents and interest groups, in a manner that encouraged the development of policy outside of parliament and that by-passed democratic procedure. And, parliamentary, no less than local, politics frequently amounted to satisfying the interests of one's own supporters. Bew, Gibbon and Patterson have argued that 'the "Protestantism" of Craig's "Protestant state" ... amounted to a combination of clientalism, "responsiveness" and a practical "Keynesianism". It was modified by liberal democratic practices, rather than the other way around'.[42] For the Ulster Unionist Party, its monopoly of political power became a means of satisfying Protestant demands so that 'discrimination became built into the processes of government and administration, as the government pandered to Protestant and unionist whims large and small'.[43]

---

40 Buckland, 'Protestant parliament', 235.
41 Harkness, *Northern Ireland*, 29.
42 P. Bew, P. Gibbon and H. Patterson, *Northern Ireland 1921–2001: Political Forces and Social Classes* (London: Serif, 2002), 55.
43 Buckland, *History of Northern Ireland*, 61.

In the case of some forms of discrimination, such as the allocation of jobs in the public service, historians are divided as to the degree of preference given to Protestants and to supporters of the Ulster Unionist Party. However, discrimination in representation, law and order, and education, not only continued but became ever more obvious. Proportional representation was abolished for general elections in 1929, largely to prevent the dissipation of Protestant votes which had occurred in 1925. This had the desired result, reducing Independent Unionist seats by one and Labour seats to one. The party would never repeat its short-lived success. Vulnerable to criticism from a Protestant and unionist perspective for its 'equivocation on the question of Northern Ireland's constitutional position',[44] Labour candidates standing in traditionally Catholic wards and constituencies would also face 'dirty', sectarian, campaigning from nationalists and Catholic clergymen.[45] The re-introduction of a first-past-the-post electoral system had little impact on the overall representation of Catholics – nor was it intended to – but the abolition of proportional representation took on enormous symbolic importance for the minority. It added not only to the polarisation but to the stagnation of politics: at the next general election, in 1933, thirty-three out of fifty-two MPs were returned unopposed.[46] Discrimination in the administration of law and order remained conspicuous long after the levels of political violence declined. The Special Powers Act was renewed every year until 1928, by which time the presence of Nationalists in Parliament had turned the annual debate on the measure into 'an occasion for unedifying mutual recrimination'.[47] The government's solution was to renew the Act for five years and then, in 1933, to make it permanent.

In keeping with the Government of Ireland Act's prohibition on the endowment of religion and with his own enthusiasm for non-denominational education, Lord Londonderry's 1923 Education Act had introduced a graduated scale of state grants to schools. Only schools which were non-denominational and provided religious instruction outside the hours of compulsory attendance were entitled to a full grant; those who wished to retain their vocational status and control over religious education got the smallest amount, losing the 60 per cent building and reconstruction grants they had received

---

44 A. Edwards, *A History of the Northern Ireland Labour Party: Democratic Socialism and Sectarianism* (Manchester: Manchester University Press, 2009), 19.

45 Harris, *Catholic Church*, 182.

46 M. Laffan, *The Partition of Ireland 1911–1925* (Dublin Historical Association, 1983), 108.

47 Buckland, *History of Northern Ireland*, 65.

before partition. None of the churches was happy with the Act and protests by the Orange Order and the United Education Committee of the Protestant Churches, as well as the Catholic Church, played a significant role in the 1925 and 1929 general elections. In 1930 the government produced an Education Act which, by altering the procedures for appointing teachers, meant that 'Protestant interests were able to ensure that only Protestant teachers were appointed' to fully state-funded schools.[48] Additionally, such schools would be permitted to introduce Bible study during the hours of compulsory attendance. This 'virtually turned public elementary schools into Protestant establishments'.[49]

The British Home Office expressed concern that the Act amounted to the endowment of religion, contrary to the Government of Ireland Act and threatened to refer it to the Privy Council but was reassured when concessions were made to Catholic voluntary schools that restored much of the grant entitlements lost in 1923. The impact of the Act was the establishment of a dual system of denominational education taking place in Protestant state schools and Catholic voluntary ones. The abandonment of the principle of non-denominational education would ultimately come to be regarded as one of the greatest lost opportunities of the early decades of Unionist rule in terms of its social consequences, and perhaps the most studied aspect of Northern Irish society before and during the Troubles;[50] but few contemporaries shared Lord Londonderry's initial enthusiasm for the project.

Economic Crisis

In some crucial areas of economic and social policy, however, the government was no better equipped to respond to Protestant, than to Catholic, needs. During the 1920s, and to an even greater extent the 1930s, Northern Ireland was blighted by economic depression and severe deprivation. Ulster's boasted prosperity, which had been featured so prominently in the campaign against Home Rule, was destroyed by the global economic downturn which coincided with partition and by a changing economic and technological environment that undermined agriculture and the shipbuilding and linen industries upon which the livelihood of so many depended.

---

48 D. H. Akenson, *Education and Enmity: The Control of Schooling in Northern Ireland 1920–50* (Newton Abbot: David and Charles, 1973), 112.
49 Buckland, *History of Northern Ireland*, 77.
50 J. Whyte, *Interpreting Northern Ireland* (Oxford University Press, 1990), 42.

Although unemployment figures fell between 1921 and 1925 as conditions became more settled, they then began to rise again – the election of three Labour MPs in the general election held in April 1925 undoubtedly owed something to the 48,000 people who were out of work that month.[51] By 1932, despite high levels of emigration, the number unemployed had risen to 72,000. Inevitably, policies developed either to create jobs or to regulate unemployment benefits were both devised and criticised from the perspective of their relative impact on the two communities. Unemployment was also a gendered problem, often higher among males than females and giving rise to a society notable for the number of married women whose low-paid jobs were their family's main source of income.

It was generally accepted that Northern Ireland's economic difficulties were structural, with agriculture and linen production organised around small family farms and businesses that were inefficient and uncompetitive. However, it was also recognised that attempts to rationalise production would increase unemployment in the short- to medium-term and would be politically inadvisable in addition to increasing the sum of misery. Northern Ireland's first Minister for Agriculture, Edward Archdale, and his successor from 1933, Sir Basil Brooke, are among the few Ulster Unionist politicians who have elicited genuine praise from historians for handling their briefs with some imagination and verve. Their department enjoyed considerable success in promoting the modernisation of farming, improvement of standards and development of marketing schemes, so that many of Northern Ireland's agricultural products came to enjoy an excellent reputation for quality and the region was well placed to take advantage of Britain's move from free trade to protection. Indeed, Buckland went so far as to suggest that 'the particular type of help given to agriculture in Northern Ireland, the way in which its particular needs were identified and catered for, does provide a cogent argument in favour of the devolution of government'.[52]

Efforts to improve industrial employment were more difficult to devise and less successful. In addition to concerns about temporary additions to the number of those unemployed in the linen industry, Belfast's powers to make trade agreements were limited and it was difficult to persuade the British government to divert naval contracts from other hard-pressed shipyards. The unemployment figures for linen workers fluctuated considerably, and there were some signs of recovery by the end of the 1930s, largely the result of

51 Farrell, *Orange State*, 12.
52 Buckland, *Factory of Grievances*, 130.

keeping wages low and hours long.[53] In shipbuilding, the job losses were dramatic. In 1933 the workforce stood at a tenth of its 1924 total of 20,000.[54] While government support and entrepreneurial skill kept shipyards open, it was the threat of European war that ensured survival at least for a time: by the end of the 1930s Northern Ireland's peripherality had become an advantage not only for shipbuilding but also for aircraft manufacture. Prior to this, government incentives to attract new industries had enjoyed little success. Such new industries as were established tended to locate in the existing industrial centres and had little impact on the areas of greatest unemployment in the rural and Catholic areas. The belief that this reflected government strategy became another source of minority grievance.

Unemployment was accompanied by serious levels of distress. Northern Ireland was the poorest part of the United Kingdom. In 1939, the average income was only 58.3 per cent of the United Kingdom average.[55] When, in 1921, the government took responsibility for the Unemployment Insurance Fund, it was already running at a deficit. Even before the British government had conceded the principle, John Andrews, the Minister for Labour had been convinced, on both humanitarian and political grounds, of the need to continue and increase the rate of benefits in line with their British equivalents. This brought him into conflict with Minister for Finance Hugh MacDowell Pollock on the grounds not only of the latter's responsibility for attempting to balance the budget but also of his distaste for what he regarded as socialistic policies that prioritised labour over employers.[56] Craig sided with Andrews and by 1926 succeeded in negotiating a new agreement with London which would make considerable sums available to support Northern Ireland's unemployment payments. This meant that the relief of distress through income-maintenance services would run at the same rate and under the same conditions as in Britain.

Relief of the uninsured, including those who had exhausted their entitlement to benefits after two years' unemployment, however, was in the hands of the Poor Law Guardians who were, especially in Belfast, notoriously reluctant to provide outdoor relief. There were widespread protests against the Belfast Guardians in 1925 and 1926 but confrontation was prevented by a temporary upturn in trade and by the Guardians' agreeing to give outdoor relief to the heads of families. However, the payments were considerably lower than

---

53 Bardon, *History of Ulster*, 547.
54 Harkness, *Northern Ireland*, 50.
55 Buckland, *History of Northern Ireland*, 74.
56 Follis, *State Under Siege*, 147–8.

anywhere else in the United Kingdom and those who qualified were obliged to undertake two and a half days' 'task work' per week – public work such as road repair – if this was available. If it was not, they would be paid in kind, not cash.[57] As Bew and Norton emphasise, Belfast relief levels were lower because Belfast rates were lower; the government's reluctance to put pressure on the Belfast Guardians suggests that, forced to make a choice between privileging the Protestant working class or the Protestant middle class, the populists who dominated the cabinet had chosen the latter.[58]

In 1932 an Outdoor Relief Workers' Committee was established, holding a series of mass meetings and eventually declaring a strike. A massive demonstration planned for 11 October was banned but went ahead. This led to confrontations between the RUC and the protestors and ultimately to rioting that claimed two deaths and considerable loss of property. These disturbances were remarkable for the fact that they were not sectarian and have often been held up as evidence that a basis existed for the growth of a class identity and politics which could overcome class identities and prejudice. Inter-communal violence was, however, a far more usual response to economic distress and limited employment opportunities. In 1931 an Ulster Protestant League had been formed to protect Protestant jobs and in July 1935 the tensions surrounding the organisation resulted in three weeks of rioting, 11 dead, and 300 (mainly Catholic) families driven from their homes.[59]

Nonetheless, the political danger posed by a dissatisfied Protestant working class had long haunted the government and in consequence determined the financing and development of social services which therefore reflected a number of sometimes conflicting practical, political and ideological considerations. Social policy was often developed with more regard to what would be acceptable to London than to what was required or desirable in Northern Ireland. Negotiations took place in private between officials, further undermining democratic processes. There was little debate over the social needs of the region or of the proper allocation of resources, and no regional planning. The levels of cash benefits were maintained without discussion as to whether they were either necessary or the best means of addressing the region's chronic social, economic and health problems. Services such as education, health and housing were severely neglected.[60]

---

57 Farrell, *Orange State*, 124–5.
58 P. Bew and C. Norton, 'The Unionist State and the Outdoor Relief Riots of 1932', *Economic and Social Review*, 10 (1979), 259.
59 Buckland, 'A Protestant State: Unionists in Government', 223.
60 Buckland, *History of Northern Ireland*, 72–8.

The 1926 agreement concluded the process under which London undertook, through a variety of means, financially to support the government of Northern Ireland. However, it broke down in the early 1930s as unemployment increased in Britain and was only renegotiated in 1936. In the meantime, the Northern Ireland government attempted to get London's agreement to the concept of Northern Ireland making a 'negative' imperial contribution under which Britain would simply make up the shortfall in Northern Ireland revenue in order to keep social services up to British levels. This was agreed in 1938 as an off-shoot of the financial arrangements that ended the Anglo-Irish 'Economic War' – a war which had a more adverse impact on Northern Ireland than on any other part of the United Kingdom.[61] Thus, in the 1930s, according to a senior British treasury official, the Northern Ireland budget was balanced only by ' "fudges" and "wangles" and "dodges and devices" giving "gifts and subventions within the ambit of the Government of Ireland Act so as to save the Northern Ireland Government from coming openly on the dole" '.[62]

Conclusion

By the end of the 1930s there was little to suggest even the forms of democratic government. Nationalist participation in parliamentary politics, never enthusiastic, had proved short-lived as the frustrating reality of the party's inability to influence policy became increasingly apparent. The party failed in its ambitions to build up a functioning party machine and never gave social or economic policies anything like the priority accorded to ending partition and defending Catholic interests. Nationalist candidates stood only in constituencies with identifiable Catholic majorities.[63] For eighteen months beginning in 1932, the party abstained from parliament in protest at its limited powers and thereafter individual MPs continued to abstain periodically until by 1937 only two remained sitting in the new Parliament Buildings, which had opened at Stormont on 16 November 1932.

The withdrawal of the Nationalist politicians from Stormont was only one of the most obvious indicators of the absence of Catholics from public life, partly enforced and partly self-imposed. The Catholic Church, not the Nationalist Party – which often looked suspiciously like the political wing of

---

61 Harkness, *Northern Ireland*, 54.
62 Buckland, *Factory of Grievances*, 102.
63 Phoenix, *Northern Nationalism*, 364.

the Catholic Church – was the main guardian of the minority's interests but, due to its opposition to the state, the church's hierarchy did not engage with government and a 'distinctly Catholic viewpoint' on political and social matters could only be observed in the field of education.[64] Rather, the Catholic Church had become a 'state within a state', the focus of civic and social energies and the main provider of social support for its faithful.[65] Though this resulted largely from political alienation, the widespread exclusion of Catholics from the public service, and the practice of discrimination in the social services, it also reflected a common Northern Irish politico-religious culture in which all churches – and the Orange Order – combined essential social and cultural functions with political lobbying. Throughout the 1930s, parliament became increasingly irrelevant as policies were decided by negotiation either with Protestant interest groups, or with the British Treasury. By the end of the decade, cabinet government had also largely ceased to function. Craig was 'old in office, remote and ill and ever more inclined to personal rule'[66] and, with most of his colleagues 'absent, ill or dying', cabinet meetings seldom took place and ministers were often only dimly aware of policy decisions for which they were nominally responsible.[67]

However remarkable Craig and his government's success in keeping Northern Ireland in existence, self-governing and not bankrupt, over the previous nineteen years the price that had been paid for that survival was very great and the tangible rewards very slight. As Buckland concludes: 'In the inter-war years Northern Ireland developed … [into] … a "factory of grievances", containing the most divided and disadvantaged people in the United Kingdom. Natural economic disadvantages, British indifference and the irredentism of the South all contributed, but the fundamental causes of this dismal performance were the provisions of the 1920 Act and the political immaturity of Ulstermen'.[68]

---

64 Buckland, *Factory of Grievances*, 60.
65 Fionnuala O'Connor, *In Search of a State: Catholics in Northern Ireland* (Belfast: Blackstaff Press, 1993), 174.
66 Harkness, *Northern Ireland*, 63.
67 Buckland, *History of Northern Ireland*, 81.
68 Ibid., 79.

11

Politics, Economy and Society in the Irish Free State, 1922–1939

ANNE DOLAN

Introduction

This is the history of a disappointment. At least that is the impression most of the historiography of Ireland in the 1920s and 1930s seems to leave. Book after book describes a flat, narrow place that lost the courage of its own revolution's convictions, a cruel, timid place that was hard on its weakest and too much in thrall to those who preached right from wrong. It is written as stubborn and wrong-headed, too accepting of its failures, too proud of its own parsimony, too quick to sacrifice another generation just to get by. Above all, it is written in anger, anger at those who seemed content to shut out the world and to let paralysis thrive. Though praise still comes for the feat of state-building, for establishing a state in civil war, for consolidating it through the uneasy times beyond, the compliment is wearing thin. It has become harder just to admire the bricks and mortar the more that becomes known about the kinds of threadbare life inside.

Disillusion

For all sorts of reasons disappointment might seem a natural response. Civil war made for a sorry start. For P. S. O'Hegarty, an advocate of the Anglo-Irish Treaty, it was lapsarian, a 'plunge from the heights to the depths'; it was an Eden smashed into the tiniest bits with the bitter knowledge that we had done it to ourselves. While independence demanded more than the illusions of a revolutionary's expectations, knowing that 'we were really an uncivilised people with savage instincts' was a cold place to start.[1] Some who had fought for independence found themselves with no 'wish to sacrifice myself in any

---

1 P. S. O'Hegarty, *The Victory of Sinn Féin* (2nd edn., Dublin: UCD Press, 1998), 91.

way whatsoever for this benighted country' even before civil war had begun.[2] While the methods chosen to put down opposition once it had emerged, executions and imprisonment on a scale never conceived by the British during 1919–1921, marked it out as an increasingly vindictive war where the point was to crush the enemy not fight towards victory or peace. For a generation that had cut its political teeth on the consequences of Easter 1916's executions, and on waging campaigns from cells in British jails, independence was never meant to start like this. The extra-judicial execution of four anti-Treatyite prisoners on 8 December 1922 in reprisal for the murder of the pro-Treatyite TD and Brigadier-General, Seán Hales, the day before, prompted Labour Party leader, Thomas Johnson, to declare 'I am almost forced to say you have killed the new State at its birth.' The Minister for Home Affairs, Kevin O'Higgins, defended the Act with 'we have no talisman except force'.[3] The Irish Free State was just two days old.

With time it grew into a particularly unpromising youth. It went awkwardly through its 'tedious years of adjustment' and maybe fearful of the chaos from which it had come, it was firm with its opponents, careful with its money and hard on those who needed its kindness most.[4] The Free State gave itself over to a frenzy of respectability; it worried about the moral welfare of its citizens, censored what they watched, what they read, fretted about how they danced, even how they loved. It made it harder to be virtuous when so many only seemed keen to see the sin. With a leader likened to 'the general manager of a railway company' in President W. T. Cosgrave, the Free State would aspire to be economically respectable as well.[5] The books should balance, and those deemed to be leading 'a parasitic existence' by J. A. Burke, the Minister for Local Government, counted fewer and fewer blessings in an Irish Free State.[6] 'The poor, the aged, and the unemployed must all feel the lash of the liberators.'[7] Reducing the old age pension by 10 per cent in 1924, admitting that 'people may have to die in this country and may have to die through starvation', believing that 'it is no function of government to provide work for anybody', independence only helped those who helped themselves.[8] While the cost of civil war had been high, spending was cut from £42 million

2 Joseph Dunne to James L. O'Donovan, 28 March 1922, MS 22,301: NLI.
3 *Dáil Debates, Official Report*, 2, col. 49 & 71 (8 December 1922).
4 V. S. Pritchett, *Dublin* (London: Bodley Head, 1967), 89.
5 *Irish Times*, 9 September 1922.
6 *Dáil Debates, Official Report*, 7, col. 3055 (25 June 1924).
7 J. J. Lee, *Ireland 1912–1985: Politics and Society* (Cambridge University Press, 1989), 124.
8 *Dáil Debates, Official Report*, 9, col. 562–3 (30 October 1924).

in 1923–1924 to £24 million within three years, but income tax was cut from five shillings in the pound in 1924 to just three in 1927–1928. The Free State settled for an economy built on agriculture. It settled even though Gordon Campbell, secretary of the Department of Industry and Commerce, warned the government to be mindful of the risks: 'if a nation is to depend on agriculture it must produce mainly a population of farmers: men of patience, endurance, thrift and modest intellectual aspirations. If it produces other types it must export them at an early age if it is not to risk the continual ferment of disappointed and distorted minds denied by circumstances their exercise.'[9] Campbell was right. Many did leave, and not just the restless 'other types'. As many as 150,000 agricultural labourers left the land in the 1920s, squeezed out of an agriculture that no longer needed them, and passed over by the Free State's first Land Act in 1923.[10] There was to be no 'land for the people' as the revolution once promised, and with bad harvests, falling prices and near famine conditions in the west, the memory of the wartime agricultural boom mocked this independence all the more.

For some pro-Treatyites the pace of independence itself was just too slow. A government of Treaty supporters before it officially launched itself as a political party in April 1923, Cumann na nGaedheal squabbled within its own ranks before it settled on what independence would mean. Michael Collins proved an awkward ghost; his freedom to achieve freedom view of the Treaty was an easy taunt and Cumann na nGaedheal bore the crippling legacy of what he might have done. When that kind of talk was heard within the army, however, it presented a much more serious problem for the state. A bungled mutiny in March 1924 revealed the unresolved tensions between the state and the men whose blunt methods it had used to defend it. No longer needed in peacetime, demobilisation threatened the position of many who had power and position because of their revolutionary reputations and their capacity for violence. Some wanted more to be made of this Treaty; some just found peace an uneasy place. It came down to establishing the monopoly on the use of force, and the state seized it even if the price was the resignations of its Ministers for Industry and Commerce, and Defence.

The anti-Treatyites, broken by prison and executions and disheartened by their disastrous hunger strike in 1923, tried to make their way in an often inhospitable civilian life. With state posts denied them, with employers often fearful of attracting the authorities' displeasure by taking on these 'irregular' types, many

---

9 Quoted in Lee, *Ireland 1912–1985*, 123.
10 Lee, *Ireland 1912–1985*, 159.

left for Britain and the United States. Refusing to take part in the state, which to them was an illegitimate expression of the abhorrent Treaty settlement, they abstained from the Dáil, leaving a Cumann na nGaedheal government, which never attained even two-fifths of the popular vote, to rule in artificial comfort.[11] Labour, independents, Farmers' Party deputies could oppose and vote against the government, but parliament was a lop-sided, awkward thing. When the Boundary Commission, the Treaty's promise to reconsider the border between north and south, collapsed in November 1925, the anti-Treatyite Sinn Féin party was not even in a position to add to the government's woes, to point out how much the Treaty had disappointed southern hopes. Those who wanted to do more than watch 'in impotent purity while history was made by its enemies', followed Éamon de Valera into a new party, Fianna Fáil, in May 1926, leaving a Sinn Féin rump on, what its president J. J. O'Kelly later called, 'a plane too exalted for the corrupt to thrive in'. Offering nothing 'but the old unrequited service to a deathless cause', Sinn Féin was not even banned when the government moved against other republican organisations in 1931.[12]

Unlike Sinn Féin, Fianna Fáil quickly thrived. It built a party machine, based around old IRA connections and kept lines blurred enough in the republican movement to build an accommodating church. It was only a 'slightly constitutional party' after all. Kevin O'Higgins's assassination by the IRA in July 1927 shook the state to its core, and part of the government's response was to compel all candidates running for election to pledge to take their seats in parliament if they won. The dreaded oath to the British King, abhorrent in 1922, became an 'empty formula', and Fianna Fáil entered the Dáil. Seemingly caught in the politics of 1923, Cumann na nGaedheal raised the shadow of the gunman, cast Fianna Fáil as an IRA front with de Valera as a Kerensky figure, a dupe for the gunmen to destroy the state. In Cumann na nGaedheal mouths, de Valera was to be the harbinger of a godless communism, and the politics of 'Red scare' went hand in hand with repressive measures to curtail the IRA and to dampen the ardour of the new Fianna Fáil mouthpiece, the *Irish Press*. Tension mounted as the general election approached in February 1932.

Sinn Féin in Power

After an ugly campaign, power passed peacefully to Fianna Fáil. While mutterings of a coup to keep Cumann na nGaedheal in government had subsided

11 D. Fitzpatrick, *The Two Irelands 1912–1939* (Oxford University Press, 1998), 188.
12 M. Laffan, *The Resurrection of Ireland* (Cambridge University Press, 1999), 441, 446.

by late 1931, and although some Fianna Fáil TDs brought guns in their pockets in case their opponents would not yield power, Irish democracy was healthier than that. When one of de Valera's first acts in government was to release ninety-seven IRA prisoners, many of their adversaries began to doubt its future prognosis, particularly when some, jubilant on release, promised 'no free speech for traitors' from now on. The perception that Fianna Fáil had its own private army led some within Cumann na nGaedheal to ally themselves more closely with the Army Comrades Association, a group of predominantly ex-soldiers who had banded together to protect free speech for opponents of Fianna Fáil. The party, which had in government in 1924 insisted on the state's monopoly on the use of violence, joined with a movement that took on a fascist bearing and a fascist salute. It is instructive of how much it feared Fianna Fáil's link with the IRA, of how desperate politically it had become. As clashes increased between Fianna Fáil supporters, many of them IRA members, and the Blueshirts, as this organisation became popularly known after its adoption of the eponymous shirt as a uniform, de Valera moved against the use of force by both Blueshirts and the IRA. Just as Cumann na nGaedheal had to cope with the use and threat of force that had helped to establish the state, de Valera confronted the forces he had used to win power. A sequence of murders by the IRA in the mid-1930s certainly contributed to his declaration in June 1936 that the IRA was now an illegal organisation in the state. Using the tools of his old enemies, de Valera expressed regret if his earlier indulgence of the IRA had 'led in any way to the murder of individuals in this state'.[13] It was no time to be 'slightly constitutional' anymore.

Throughout these years de Valera assailed the Treaty he despised, and jeopardised the relationship Cumann na nGaedheal had built up with London even as they pushed out the boundaries of what dominion status might mean. He legislated to remove the dreaded oath, undermined the office of the King's representative in Ireland, the Governor General, and took his chance in December 1936 while Britain was entangled in the King's passion for Wallis Simpson to remove the monarch from the Irish constitution altogether. And all of this while he was still head of His Majesty's government in the Irish Free State. The tattered constitution of 1922 was replaced by a new conception of the state. This new Éire, this republic in all but name, saw the aspirational and the actual inscribed. Staking a claim to Northern Ireland, it was ambitious or irredentist depending on which side of the border one stood on. For some it was too Catholic, for others not Catholic enough; it guaranteed fundamental

13 *Dáil Debates, Official Report*, 63, col. 112 (23 June 1936).

liberties, but was seen to inscribe paternalism at its core. The 'special position' of the Catholic Church, its view of 'woman', that it is woman rather than women, these elements have prompted most debate, most ire. But in chipping away at the trees we have sometimes missed the value of the wood.

Constitutional status aside, the quality of many lives did not improve quickly enough to satisfy the hopes placed in independence, never mind in Fianna Fáil. The party came to power in a small, still relatively open, economy in the midst of a world depression. It spent more money than Cumann na nGaedheal certainly: there was more aid, more houses built, better conditions for workers, and a greater sense that the state had a responsibility for the welfare of its citizens' lives. But need continued to grow, even though the move to increase production and the protection of Irish-made produce initially led to an unprecedented boom in Irish industry and industrial employment. An Irish market could take only so much of its own produce before it reached saturation point. The government refused to hand over the annuities due for the Land Purchase Acts, and Irish agricultural produce was hit by British tariffs and quotas in response. This economic war lasted from 1932 to 1938. While this allowed Fianna Fáil to intensify its self-sufficiency drive under the guise of a new kind of war with the old enemy, Irish farmers paid the price. Global depression had already hit them hard, but economic war added another considerable burden for the already laden down to bear. This might explain all of the extra government provisions for the unemployed, why there had to be a 'farmers' dole' in 1933. The Great Depression meant emigration no longer relieved the pressures of too many people living off too little land, and while there were some attempts to acclaim their retention as the fruits of Irish independence, Minister for Industry and Commerce, Seán Lemass, admitted a different response: 'Those 25,000 or 30,000 people who, in other years, found an outlet through the emigrant ship are remaining at home and have to be provided for at home.'[14] When emigration was that ingrained it was not an economy built to go to war.

By that war's end in 1938, the Minister for Finance, Seán MacEntee conceded as much: 'In an effort to cope with this problem of unemployment, we have increased tariffs, ... we have shortened the working hours of the employed and given them holidays with pay, we have introduced quota restrictions, and we have established virtual monopolies. We have more regimentation, more regulation, more control everywhere. And more unemployed!'[15] It was

14 Ibid., 41, col. 1673 (12 May 1932).
15 S. MacEntee quoted in T. Garvin, *Preventing the Future: Why was Ireland so Poor for so Long?* (Dublin: Gill & Macmillan, 2004), 33.

a far cry from Todd Andrews's 'great leap forward' of 1932.[16] Nonetheless, in 1938 Fianna Fáil received its largest vote to date: 52 per cent of the electorate returned the party to government, where it remained for another ten years. Even though the economic war had bolstered the ranks of the Blueshirt movement, the new Fine Gael party that came out of the alliance of Blueshirtism, Cumann na nGaedheal and the Centre Party in September 1933, offered little but the very cuts to the public spending that so many voters had come to depend upon. Indeed, for historian Richard Dunphy, Fianna Fáil's victory in 1938 had less to do with the Anglo-Irish Agreement that ended the economic war, that returned the treaty ports and removed the final British presence in the state, but more to the dependence the party had cynically effected between itself and a growing proportion of what he sees as an infantilised electorate with little option but to keep its kind and progressively conservative master in place.[17] With a populist Fianna Fáil machine ruthless for power, Dunphy takes a grim vista and paints it black.

This whistle-stop tour of the inter-war years in independent Ireland has called at many of the familiar political sites. They are recognisable from the political histories of independent Ireland that have dominated its study for so long. However, the flowering of social and cultural history for this period has added many of the harsh narrownesses of Irish life to the itinerary for this trip. The censored, isolated culture of independence left its citizens a limited diet of westerns and romances, and chopped up films that a paternalistic state thought them fit to digest. A buoyant and increasingly confident Catholic Church may have begun worried by the irreverence of the revolutionary years, but soon became certain that 'the old restraints would be again observed'.[18] In dance halls, and in the length of women's skirts, it saw and decried the devil at every turn. Religious minorities in a state of more than 93 per cent Catholics looked carefully and quietly on; it could be a daunting place for those outside that muscular Catholic embrace. Magdalene laundries, industrial schools, institutions of all sorts kept those who transgressed largely out of sight. A child born outside of marriage was four times less likely than the progeny of its parents' married peers to reach the end of its first year; in the valley of the squinting windows respectability was a cruel and exacting king.[19]

---

16 C. S. Andrews, *Man of No Property* (2nd edn., Dublin: Lilliput Press, 2001), 113.
17 R. Dunphy, *The Making of Fianna Fáil Power in Ireland 1923–1948* (Oxford University Press, 1995), ch. 4.
18 P. Colum, *The Road Round Ireland* (New York: Macmillan, 1927), 39.
19 F. Kennedy, *Cottage to Crèche: Family Change in Ireland* (Dublin: Institute of Public Administration, 2001), 37.

While brevity has lent itself to generalisation, maybe exaggeration, even caricature, this is the kind of independent Ireland that tends to come from the pages of the historiography almost book after book. It is an historiography that is angry and disappointed with this past and perhaps Ireland's problems throughout the twentieth century and into the twenty-first have made it hard to absolve the 1920s and the 1930s of at least some of the blame. It is easy to find reasons to be angry. Read back through the 1950s, how could it be otherwise? The 'vanishing Irish' are a bitter indictment of independence. 'No longer shall our children, like our cattle, be brought up for export.'[20] Too many of those children to whom de Valera had promised better in 1934 were gone by 1954 for us to see him or the 1920s and 1930s straight. Read back through the 1980s, again, how could it be otherwise? As more and more of the state's earliest records were released in that decade they were fathomed and framed as dole queues and as queues for American visas grew and grew, as Northern Ireland tore itself more furiously apart. Anthropologist Clifford Geertz gave a theoretical turn to the frustration of another generation of Irish historians with this past. The 'deflating experience' of living in, rather than imagining independence, strongly influenced J. J. Lee's seminal interpretation of the 1920s and 1930s.[21] It worked well with the anger of many of his conclusions, written through the 1980s, and first published in 1989. Lee presented the Irish Free State as a disappointment 'in the context of historical expectations'.[22] It is a view that has been broadly perpetuated since. More recent research has focused on how the most vulnerable were treated. A generation of historians shaped by the venomous referenda on abortion and divorce, shaped by a society still battling with its own sense of what secular means, had to speak up, if nothing else, to show how far Irish society had since come. As religious and institutional scandals made headlines this was also a history that an Irish public was willing at last to hear. Nothing was as we would have liked it to have been, and as research has developed, the 1920s and 1930s have found more and more ways to let us down.

A Conservative State

Even though it takes in the political, social, cultural and economic, there is a striking sameness to how this disappointment was expressed. And it was

---

20 Quoted in T. P. O'Neill and Lord Longford, *Éamon de Valera* (London: Hutchinson, 1970), 334.

21 C. Geertz, *The Interpretation of Cultures* (New York: Basic Books, 1973), 235.

22 Lee, *Ireland 1912–1985*, 173.

there long before Lee. F. S. L. Lyons's discussion of 'the partitioned island', begins: 'That the revolutionary of today is the conservative of tomorrow is a truism of politics in no way contradicted by the recent history of modern Ireland.'[23] Within a few pages the state slinks away to the flickering shadows of Plato's cave. By the time of the publication of Roy Foster's *Modern Ireland* conservatism was a given. A chapter on the Irish Free State could begin with 'the rigorous conservatism of the Irish Free State has become a cliché', and like most clichés it was found to have more than its share of truth.[24] Theo Hoppen went further. Independent Ireland was not just conservative. It had a 'singular capacity . . . for standing still'.[25] An Ireland going nowhere was his last word. Hoppen's 'definitive' evidence for this was Kevin O'Higgins's pronouncements on the 'conservative-minded' nature of Ireland's revolutionaries.[26] O'Higgins's verdict crops up with monotonous regularity in assessments of 1920s Ireland, not least because as the first Vice-President of the Irish Free State, he is an ideal witness for the prosecution's case. Indeed, O'Higgins himself, became a fundamental part of historian John Regan's thesis that not only was this a conservative state, but it had become a counter-revolutionary one, aggressively undoing the remnants of that which might have been revolutionary in the revolution in the first place. Regan concludes: 'it is the non-events, the absence of real extremes . . . ultimately the monotony of Irish nationalist politics which remain most compelling'.[27] Compelling they may be, but they are non-events, absences and monotony just the same. Diarmaid Ferriter's *The Transformation of Ireland* demonstrates how much this sense of conservatism has shaped the emerging social history as well. Ferriter ends by asking 'what was it all for', using Michael Moran, John McGahern's fictional veteran of the Irish revolution, to sum up the 'failures of Irish independence' itself: '. . . "some of our own Johnnies in the top jobs instead of a few Englishmen . . . The whole thing was a cod". . .'.[28] The kinds of personal costs Ferriter saw many people paying may have prompted this view. And backed up by research since on the cruelties at the heart of many Irish lives it is a view that has taken root. Thomas Bartlett's *Ireland* records 'plenty of fear

---

23 F. S. L. Lyons, *Ireland since the Famine* (2nd edn., London: Weidenfeld and Nicolson, 1973), 471.
24 R. F. Foster, *Modern Ireland 1600–1972* (2nd edn., London: Penguin, 1989), 516.
25 K. T. Hoppen, *Ireland since 1800: Conflict and Conformity* (London: Routledge, 1989), 256.
26 Ibid.; *DE Official Report*, 2, col. 1909 (1 March 1923).
27 J. M. Regan, *The Irish Counter-revolution 1921–1936* (Dublin: Gill & Macmillan, 1999), 383.
28 Quoted in D. Ferriter, *The Transformation of Ireland 1900–2000* (London: Profile Books, 2004), 758–9.

and loathing', with a 'stifling consensus at the heart of Irish life'.[29] It seems the vocabulary has been settled; the severity of the adjectives is all that is left to disagree on.

But does the conservative, inward-looking Ireland of much of the historiography stand up to a simple test? One day, one random day of a national newspaper reaching approximately 150,000 homes, does it reflect this narrow place? On 31 May 1935 the *Irish Independent* noted the stuff of another day gone by. Readers read of the 'bustle' of a coming by-election, of a police raid in Dublin, of republican offices temporarily closed down.[30] They read about Eamon Ceannt's last letter going on display at the National Museum, about 1916's rebels feted just as Cumann na mBan's typewriters were seized and went still. They read of things changing: about Limerick's new TB hospital, about the city's 380 new homes. They read about nothing changing, about poverty and relief grants, about the things that stayed stubbornly the same as well. London made a statement about the Commonwealth and Dublin retorted with a predictably pugnacious reply. A bomb was thrown in Belfast, and the journalist's brevity maybe said there was little new in that. In announcements of births, marriages and deaths, life went its own way on.

The 31 May 1935 edition gives us the historiography's familiar Ireland. There are traces of its predictable politics, its wayward economics; there is plenty to confirm the kinds of life we have been told were there to find. This national newspaper, and it could have been any newspaper, this day, and it might have been many other days, gives its own clear hints of the society the state had built itself upon. But in this one newspaper, on this one day, in all that lived cheek by jowl with the new houses and the old politics, there is the challenge of far more than we have come to expect to find. Noticing that this newspaper carried a considerable amount of foreign news is not enough, even if its extent and its reach crudely question any easy assumptions that the Free State was a closed-off place. Of course, readers on 31 May 1935 read of the fall of the French government, of Roosevelt's meeting with the Industrial Recovery Board. But Japan is there issuing warnings to China; shots are fired at strikers at Rhodesia's mines, and peace is hoped for between faraway Bolivia and Paraguay. Yet, far more than this, the wider world is rushing in, revealing in a quiet and taken-for-granted fashion that lives were being lived in ways that an historiography convinced of homogeneity and isolation has not really sought

29 T. Bartlett, *Ireland: A History* (Cambridge University Press, 2010), 445.
30 *Irish Independent*, 31 May 1935.

to uncover. Front-page advertisements vied with one another to whisk read-ers off to Naples, Madeira and Cadiz. Cruise ships promised Egypt, Ceylon and the Straits. With facilities on board 'for holy mass', Lamport and Holt Cruises knew their Irish market or perhaps assumed they did. A 300-page brochure of Cook's tours is unsettling reading for an Ireland apparently at its wits' end in economic war. 'Seeing Soviet Russia' is a puzzling invitation if this is the Free State of 'Red scares', of so many prayers offered up to save the world from socialism and communism and to bring about the conversion of Russia most of all. The *Irish Independent* of 31 May 1935 captures a place that seems hungry for the newest, the most modern of everything: 'Brownie crystal sets', 'every Decca record in stock', Hillmans or Hupmobiles. For all that has been assumed about inwardness and isolation, it is clear even in the columns of easily passed over classifieds that this Free State thought itself, or was cajoled by the advertisements to think itself, an up-to-the-minute type of place. No frugal, homespun Ireland here.

From the second-hand wedding rings to the 'strictly private . . . loans by post' for the middle-class spendthrift, the Irish Free State was keeping up appear-ances and there were appearances to keep. Mr Morosini-Whelan offered private lessons claiming dancing is now 'a social necessity'. As a 'teacher of dancing to Castleknock, Clongowes Wood, Blackrock, and Terenure Colleges' he taught the coming men of an aspiring Catholic elite: however, quick-steps and foxtrots on the curriculum of the best Catholic schools strike a jarring cord with the chorus of clerics who currently populate the historiography railing against dancing as the source of most sin. On 31 May 1935, regardless of censored scenes, Dublin cinema audiences enjoyed Dashiell Hammett's '*The Thin Man*' starring William Powell, Myrna Loy, and Asta, their fox terrier. On the same night, the Bohemian Cinema offered '*Jew Süss*'. Having played to packed houses for several weeks, there was clearly a popular audience for this critique of the anti-Semitism of the Nazi regime. Other days' examples suggest a greater openness still. In October 1934 the *Irish Press* promised forth-coming concerts featuring Paul Robeson, Beniamino Gigli, and Vladimir Horowitz.[31] Conservative, isolated, censored, repressed – they do not sit so easily with the experience or at least the opportunity for dancing and Russian holidays, with all the interest taken in a wider world, or with sitting in the dark and lusting after Myrna Loy. We package a period and a people neatly up at our peril, particularly when just some of one day's newspaper can turn it all awry.

31 *Irish Press*, 11 October 1934.

Of course, the experience of Dublin cannot speak for the rest of the state. But one day, one random regional newspaper, on 26 September 1925, stands up to the same scrutiny.[32] The weekly *Anglo-Celt*, serving the readers of Fermanagh, Westmeath, Meath, Leitrim, Monaghan, Cavan, Longford and Louth, presents all of the same prospects almost a decade before. The stuff of the familiar narrative is there: news of disgruntled ex-IRA men meeting in Longford, reports of local councils, the detailed record of the most local of local news. 'Emigrating – a number from Carrigallen and other parts of Leitrim have left for the USA' came just as a statement of accepted fact. It was a commonplace thing like the death of a 'respected resident' or the poisoning of a dog. There is all of the disappointing Ireland we have come to know. A column on religion, 'The Church', comes with all the certainty of that definite article; there was only one faith worth writing about. But even this does not sit easily. It is not a sanctimonious listing of local piety and prayer; instead it records the Pope's concern for the Czechoslovakian church, and notices a new basilica in Quebec. It crows certainly about the ordination of a Jewish convert in Oregon, but though the terms and the tone may sit uneasily with us, this is still one day of a wider Catholic world than we have come to expect. Equally 'news for the week' ranged far and eclectically wide. While a Mrs McCarthy was 'badly injured by a freshly-calved cow', and there were arrests and fines and other run-of-the-mill local and national things, readers also got '500 Druces' [sic] killed in Syria and they got Lady Cynthia Mosley declaring herself 'an out-and-out Socialist' into the bargain. Cavan and Meath and Leitrim and Louth were even offered the latest gossip on the King of Spain. He had arrived in Paris for 'the monkey gland treatment', and Cavan and Meath and Leitrim and Louth did not need an explanation of what that meant. What maybe matters more is what passed as a given: 'A party of Irish farmers arrived in Denmark' to learn new methods and to bring that knowledge home. While it is one thing to accept that the Department of Agriculture hoped to encourage Irish farmers to follow Danish ways, that simple passing sentence in a local paper shows the message was hitting home. An advertisement just two pages before for 'Denmark's Pig Powder', with its claim that it 'is now used throughout Ireland by all far-seeing Pig Feeders', may just have been brash and topical advertising, but it took the attraction of foreign, modern methods as a given, and behind it lay the assumption that Cavan and Meath and Leitrim and Louth wanted to be 'far-seeing' most of all. The *Anglo-Celt* told its female readers about new trends in furs, that 'Paris

32 *Anglo-Celt*, 26 September 1925.

has gone in strong for lace gowns'. While the farmers' wives of Shercock and Killashandra might well have scoffed, they kept an eye to Paris all the same. Like the dancers of a decade later *Anglo-Celt* expressed no anxieties about any possible occasions of sin. With 'proceeds in aid of a parochial object', with another dance 'in aid of funds for repairs of curate's house', the Catholic Church's view of dancing was not so straightforward after all. It is not only the sophisticated metropolitans who pass the test.

This is not a plea for a swing to the other extreme, for the kind of revisionist debate that has shaped the history of inter-war Britain. Some have strayed from *The road to Wigan Pier*, because for them too many spent too much on cars and golf clubs and bungalows for Orwell to have it all his own way. But it is not about replacing the disappointed version of Irish independence with some blindly buoyant view, trading in the 'worst of times' for the 'best of times' because a few advertisements said 'we had everything before us' after all. It is more of a plea for context in all its forms: the context of the local and the particular, the kind of disruption that just one copy of the *Anglo-Celt* brings, but also the context of what people at the time defined as their own expectations and norms. We can, for example, rail against the nature of poverty in the Irish Free State, but poverty is relative to its own times, abject according to each period's ways of making ends meet. In 1923 Frank O'Connor got a job as a trainee librarian in Sligo's Carnegie Library on thirty shillings a week.

> I found lodgings near Sligo Cathedral at twenty-seven and sixpence a week and had a whole half-crown for laundry, cigarettes and drink. Mother had worked it out that it would be cheaper to post my laundry home than to get it done locally, and every week I posted home my shirt, my underpants, a pair of stockings and some handkerchiefs.

While this tells us something of his priorities, about the expectations that a man should have money for cigarettes and drink, while it may tell us more about his mother who borrowed to buy him a cardboard suitcase, who agreed to add half-a-crown to his weekly wage which she had to go out and earn, it gives us a scale, not thriving, not sinking either, but a sense of what it took to get by. And if that was getting by, one shirt on, one shirt off, in what many would have thought a respectable job where the day ended with no dirt, with no calluses on O'Connor's hands, we have a far better sense of what poverty meant in 1923. His pity for the 'poor country girl' found sleeping in the garden of his lodgings because she had been 'thrown out by her parents and had nowhere in the world to go' said what he thought poverty was.[33] We cannot

---

33 F. O'Connor, *My Father's Son* (3rd edn., Belfast: Blackstaff Press, 1994), 13–14.

chart the course of the haves and the have-nots without the struggle of the strivers in between.

What did Irish People Actually do?

While our understanding of the lived experience has broadened, we have been quickest to find the cruelties that court records allow us to find; infanticide, abortion, rape and child abuse have all been explored to quite striking effect. Indeed, much of this work has informed the acknowledgement that past wrongs have to be put right. Happiness, or what passes for it, has been harder to find; it leaves fewer traces, and not as many pressing reasons to search. Yet, it is needed, if nothing else to set the awfulness against; even a glimpse of happiness makes misery hurt the more. For Frank McCourt 'the happy childhood is hardly worth your while', but Alice Taylor's *To school through the fields* makes *Angela's ashes* hit harder home.[34] However, happiness is also needed on its own terms. So much of the history of Irish sexuality centres on its repression and control, but is there any sense of love, even love aspired to or sentimentalised, even love reduced to the practical demands of the matrimonial classifieds? Two individuals, perhaps stirred by spring to find a mate, set out their terms in March 1930: 'Gentleman, 30, strict T[ee] T[otal], with a nice capital [sum] would wish to meet a Young Respectable Lady, with a business or farm of her own'; 'Young Lady Protestant, good family, some capital, wishes correspond [*sic*] varsity man or banker, age 40, view matrimony; genuine.'[35] In both, there is a sense of what was meant to impress; in both there is the tangle of respectability and class and, maybe eventually, love. There are enough marriages captured on newsreels, smiling at their outset in wedding photographs, enough idealised romances in cheap novelettes, enough concern about the nature of courtship in darkened cinemas, in ditches, in the back of cars to suggest that there was at least some pleasure taken, some happiness glimpsed, even if only for a short while.

Writing in the context of censorship, Ferriter has argued that 'perhaps historians have fallen into the trap of becoming consumed with what Irish people were supposedly not permitted to do as opposed to what they actually did'.[36] While the extent of the exhortations to stop might suggest that widespread moral laxity was the norm, Ferriter's principle could be extended

---

34 F. McCourt, *Angela's Ashes* (London: HarperCollins, 1996), 1; A. Taylor, *To School through the Fields: An Irish Country Childhood* (Dingle, County Kerry: Brandon, 1988).

35 *Irish Independent*, 7 and 14 March 1930.

36 Ferriter, *The Transformation of Ireland*, 10.

far beyond that which was prohibited in cultural or sexual terms; it could be a broader plea for experience in all sorts of contexts. While we know that people danced on despite the bishops' urgings, that they watched on despite the film censor's propensity to snip, the scope for the experience of 'what they actually did' could be broadened in all kinds of ways: how they worked, how they spent the money they did or even did not have, how they lived and died according to their own lights. In a period of new political parties, new movements, new religious organisations, what was it, not just to be counted as, but to be, a member, to participate, to play a part? The whist drives and dances, the outings and excursions, the strong social dimension built into every group whether Fianna Fáil, the Blueshirts or the Irish Countrywomen's Association, suggests room to understand any and all of these groups as more than the sum of their manifestos or their well-meaning aims. The same *Anglo-Celt* carries notice of the first annual dance of the Mountnugent branch of Cumann na nGaedheal: 'Gents' two shillings in, 'ladies' only 1s 6d, both significant sums when the likes of Frank O'Connor were expected to live on the little left of his 30 shillings a week.[37] A social history of politics makes sense when tens of thousands joined Fianna Fáil's 1,300 cumainn by late 1927, when some 50,000 joined the Blueshirts, and danced and cycled and picnicked their way around their heartlands, socialising with those of the same class, of the same political mind. The back pages of party newspapers hum with the life of movements that have only been looked at in political terms. That much of the tension between Fianna Fáil supporters and Blueshirts expressed itself, according to Department of Justice files, at rival dances is suggestive in itself. The same case might be made for religion. The sociability before and after religious practice in rural Ireland, where the week might not have brought a single face, or in urban Ireland, where the week might have brought none friendly or none known, cannot be underestimated. While it may have served to reassert a social order, a hierarchy of the holier-than-thou over those who stood at the back and held their own court, none the less, the increase, particularly in Catholic lay organisations in this period, suggests the appeal of filling evenings with all sorts of sodalities and companionable good works. That the coming of BBC television to Dublin in the 1950s coincided with a fall in attendance at evening devotions says something of this social role, a role that possibly played a far greater part in married women's and older women's lives, regardless of creed or church.[38] None of this is to undermine faith, or to

37 *Anglo-Celt*, 26 September 1925.
38 L. Fuller, *Irish Catholicism since 1950* (Dublin: Gill & Macmillan, 2002), 226.

question the sincerity of party allegiance; it is just to suggest that politics and religion meant more than party and church.

Religion

Majorities pose a problem no matter what they are made of. Convenience assumes homogeneity as a given, partly because the leaders leave more records than the followers, and it is easier to assume most dissidents left, and that most adherents did as they were told. Catholicism in Ireland poses a considerable problem in this regard. The experiences of religious minorities have been more sensitively and more extensively explored. Ian d'Alton has carefully teased out the type of 'parallel Irish Free State' created by much of a 7 per cent Protestant population of 1926 that had been 10 per cent in 1911. While that decline continued an already existing trend, outbreaks of sectarianism in the south during the revolutionary period had encouraged many Protestants not to rise above the parapet thereafter. Nonetheless d'Alton has mapped out the survival of a strong economic position for that 7 per cent, which still accounted for over 50 per cent of the bankers, over 20 per cent of the doctors, 40 per cent of the lawyers and more than 25 per cent of the large farms in the state in 1926.[39] Ignorance and bigotry certainly expressed themselves, particularly when even attending a Protestant service was a sin for a Catholic which could only be expunged by a bishop, but the expression of faith was guaranteed, even if the sheer force of Catholic numbers made any minority feel uneasy in this place. While the diversity of Protestant experience has been thoughtfully considered, curiosity about Irish Catholicism has largely concentrated on the hierarchy's grip on the new state. Inquiries into clerical and institutional abuse, the often painful progress to a more secular conception of personal morality, have made it even more problematic to understand the experience of the 93 per cent who ticked the box for Catholic on 1926 and 1936 census forms. The sense of an authoritarian church leading a pliant state by the nose is still a strong one; the role of the laity is harder to find never mind the range of complex negotiations any individual made with their own faith. The comfort of faith is easily diminished, and the fear of sin, or its consequences, is probably unfathomable now as Vatican II brought a far more merciful God. The rise of indulgences in this period to offset time in purgatory is easily mocked for the shallowness of its own obsessions. The

---

39 I. d'Alton, ' "A Vestigial Population"? Perspectives on Southern Irish Protestants in the Twentieth Century', *Éire-Ireland*, 44 (Fall–Winter, 2009), 14.

challenge is to allow for the meaning people took from this, from their own piety, whatever form it took. Equally, there is a glorious disparity to upset any easy summation of Irish Catholic life. On *The road round Ireland* Padraic Colum noted the diversity even from parish to parish: 'In Father Michael's parish, for instance, people are terrified of having a dance at their house, and young men and women can meet only in the most furtive way. In the next parish, however, there is absolute freedom.' He found that being seen to be pious was as much about the tyranny of neighbours' expectations as any priest's. He noted that women in rural Kerry 'put on their boots coming into the town, so that they will be respectable-looking at Mass'; respectful of their religion, perhaps, but not giving their 'betters' the satisfaction of sneering at their bare and dirty feet.[40] For all sorts of reasons Catholicism in this period has been easy to caricature, but there is far more to fathom in the nature of faith between the good intentions of a Sunday morning and the temptations of a Saturday night.

The Catholic Church has been key to the disappointment the historiography has expressed for so long. Gerard Hogan, a constitutional lawyer, has taken historians' interpretations of the 'special position' of the Catholic Church in the 1937 Constitution vigorously to task: he argues that it was meaningless in law, was overpowered by the freedom of expression of faith safeguarded by the same article, and in any case was liberal by comparison to many contemporary European states, such as Britain and Norway, where law enshrined an established church. The Constitution's explicit recognition of the Jewish faith, given the wider European context of 1937, has been largely overshadowed by the obsession with predictable concerns. Hogan has identified a range of international influences on the Constitution, including the American Constitution, the Weimar Constitution, and admits that while aspects of Catholic social teaching are also evident, he asks whether we should default so readily to criticism of the source if the articles had a positive practice in law. While some historians' sense of the Constitution as a document drafted by de Valera along with 'Jesuits and other clerical advisers' has subsided to something more nuanced, the issue of influence Hogan raises presents a challenge to the broader historiography.[41] The sense of an Irish state shutting out the world under the sway of a narrow Catholicism is undermined by the kinds of Catholicism that were growing in prominence. The rise

40 Colum, *The Road*, 31, 474.
41 G. Hogan, 'De Valera, the Constitution and the Historians', *Irish Jurist*, 40 (2005), 293–320; Fitzpatrick, *The Two Irelands*, 230.

of lay organisations such as the Legion of Mary, the growth of groups such as Muintir na Tíre inspired directly by the 1931 Papal Encyclical, *Quadragesimo Anno*, present a Catholic firmament bristling with all sorts of international influences. Catholic social teaching expressed itself in a multiplicity of ways, just as it did across Europe, from the Muintir na Tíre approach of local people working together to address local need, to the more extreme expressions of people like Fr Denis Fahey, Professor of Theology at the Holy Ghost Fathers' seminary, who was enthused by strains of continental Catholicism that saw Jews, Communists and Freemasons plotting world conspiracy at every turn. Catholic social teaching's amorphous capacity for best and worst was part of a wider ferment of discussion about how society might be structured, how the state might emerge. That much of this talk came to nothing should not underestimate the energy expended in the debate. The legacies of Catholicism from this time may well be the very things that underline the narrowness and the inwardness that disappoint so many with this period, but this was part of the wider world rushing in. Looking back, it may seem to be the essence of conservatism, but we cannot say it was not international and modern just because we do not like the parts that stuck.

The International Context

All the prayers in favour of faith and fatherland in Spain, all the novenas to save the world from communism, even the fear that prompted James Hogan to ask *Could Ireland become Communist?* in 1935, are part of this same engagement with a wider world.[42] That the majority sided with Franco's cause in Spain, may not endear its instincts to us now, but those instincts were utterly modern and international for all that. When Patrick McGlinchy died in April 1933, the Donegal publican bequeathed a hall for public use in his parish. He left a clear stipulation in his will: 'No communist or anti-God organisation is ever to have the use of the Hall, and no Communist shall ever be elected a member of the Committee of Management.'[43] With his dying breath he was fighting communism on his own front; Raphoe was his Guadalajara, his Guernica. Fear, particularly fear of something that never comes to pass, is easily, often mockingly dismissed. The fear of the modern, the outrageous forecasts of doom should a dance be danced, or a book read, may seem ludicrous once the first step is taken and the world does not end, but in both the raging

---

42 J. Hogan, *Could Ireland become communist? The facts of the case* (Dublin: Cahill, 1935).
43 *Leitrim Observer*, 8 December 1934.

of all the King Canutes, and in the force and the frequency of all the waves, Ireland was thoroughly transnational in its instincts, its fears, and its appetites. The difference may well be in degree, but the perspective is where the challenge begins. France, Belgium, Italy, prohibited the sale of contraceptives in 1920, 1923, 1926 respectively; it took the Irish Free State until 1935.[44] Emigration of Irish citizens beyond Europe, admittedly curtailed to America by quotas after 1924, saw 1,031 Irish leave in 1935. That same year, Italy lost 26,829, Poland 34,623 and Greece 11,652: rates two, three and five times higher per capita than independent Ireland. How many of England and Wales's 25,036 migrants were Irish the *Statistical Abstracts* are shy to say, but even the envied Denmark lost 2,214, again twice the Irish rate.[45] That the state saw itself, recorded itself, noted its problems, its achievements, in the context of the international information it could get suggests a sense of a place in the world we sometimes underestimate, a sense of comparison that ranges far beyond the historiography's obsession with the Anglo–Irish relationship. In 1939, birth and death rates for independent Ireland nestle between those of Hungary and Italy, and the list ranges from Austria to the Federated Malay Straits, taking in Costa Rica, New Zealand and the Argentine along the way. Independent Ireland was one of forty-eight states noted, including three separate categories to cover the complexity of birth and death in the USSR. Certainly the disappointments of independence clearly come through in the *Statistical Abstracts* of that same year. While independent Ireland's population could boast a comfortable 27.6 per cent of 0–14 year olds against a Swedish low of 22.2 per cent and a Portuguese high of 31.9 per cent, too many had left for the state to rank so well in the category of 15–34-year-olds. Only France had more citizens over 60 years of age than independent Ireland; one of Europe's older populations certainly, but this place clearly brought the expectation of a longer life.[46] The state thrives or fails on a variety of scales, depending on how one chooses to judge. The same comparisons could be made for rates of unemployment, and for every other tabulated experience between birth and death. What is striking, however, is the attempt made to understand the state in comparative terms, an instinct expressed in the Statistical and Social Inquiry Society of Ireland (SSISI) and its journal long before and after independence, by journals such as *Studies*, even in the daily newspapers, and in the cut and thrust of Dáil and Senate debates. The range of countries referenced by contemporaries on

44 Kennedy, *Cottage to Crèche*, 19.
45 *Statistical Abstract 1938* (Dublin, 1938), 205.
46 *Statistical Abstract 1939* (Dublin, 1939), 212–13.

topics as diverse as rates of illness or penal policy, the instinct to see the state beyond isolated Irish terms, undermines the easy assumption that this was an insular and, most of all, an exceptional place. Any single year of papers read to the SSISI through this period suggests a will to compete and to be bettered by the comparative experience of the wider world. Indeed, choosing to see the protectionist policies of the 1930s as emblematic of de Valera's conception of an isolated, self-supporting economy says more about the lure of hindsight than it does about Irish policy in the wake of the Wall Street Crash. Protectionism could not have been more international in the 1930s; John Maynard Keynes told his audience in Dublin this when he lectured on 'National self-sufficiency' in April 1933.

The reluctance to undermine Irish exceptionalism is perhaps expressive of a fear that, without it, the state simply fades into a kind of also-ran. Comparatively, the Free State had a small civil war: its dead came to between one and two thousand. By contrast 36,000 people, over 1 per cent of Finland's population, died within six months in its civil war. The state returned to stability at a quite striking pace compared to Europe east of the Rhine. However much Kevin O'Higgins saw the threat of 'Irregularism' at every turn, this was no Hungary and no Poland. Indeed, part of the shock of O'Higgins's assassination was it seemed like an intrusion of the methods of previous years. Economic fortunes, when viewed in isolation, were poor; more might certainly have been done, but for all the subsistence, even for the tragedy of starvation in Adrigole, County Cork, where a family died of hunger in March 1927, this was not the poverty Richard Titmuss described in the North of England and Wales, where he estimated that between 1928 and 1938, 150 Britons died from malnutrition every day.[47] The Great Depression saw exports fall by 65–70 per cent in the Free State between 1928 and 1929 and 1932 to 1933, but the fall was precisely the same in Argentina, Canada, Holland, Estonia, India, and Spain; it was 75–80 per cent in China, over 50 per cent in twenty-two other key exporters at the same time. Even the economic war has to be reassessed as more than de Valera's private battle against Britain: Britain's new National Government of August 1931 was committed to the protection of British agriculture before de Valera even came to power.[48] How can we write of the 'failures of Irish independence' without a sense of what we mean by, what anyone at the time could have conceived, as success?[49]

---

47 R. Titmuss, *Poverty and Population* (2nd edn., Basingstoke: Palgrave Macmillan, 2002), 301.
48 K. O'Rourke, 'Ireland and the Bigger Picture', in D. Dickson and C. Ó Gráda (eds.), *Refiguring Ireland* (Dublin: Lilliput Press, 2003), 347–8.
49 Ferriter, *The Transformation of Ireland*, 759.

The sense of the state as a conservative place is striking in the historiography. Conservative is a relative term, but in much of the analysis it is not clear who calibrated where 'radical' begins and 'conservative' ends. There is an acceptance that what passed for a political divide in Irish politics was simply a continuation of the civil war, that there was not the kind of natural division between right and left common to the rest of Europe, that there was a persistence of the 'national question' to the detriment of a genuinely left-wing outlook in the state. The natural corollary of this is the fascination with the type of political cultures that found themselves more and more likely through the inter-war period to take their rhythm from the beat of a fascist or a communist jackboot. The value of stability was not lost on Kevin O'Higgins who, when speaking two days after an election in Britain in October 1924, pointed out to his audience in Oxford University that since becoming a member of the Irish government, 'I have shaken hands with four English Prime Ministers, and may be meeting the fifth any time now.'[50] While he was hammering home that the Irish were capable of ruling themselves, the comparative stability of the Free State is none the less clear. And there were far more unstable places beyond the British Isles. Fourteen parties won seats in Czechoslovakia's elections in 1920; thirty-one featured in the Polish result in 1926. Neither state existed by the end of 1939. Indeed, of the twenty-two democratic constitutions Mirkine-Guetzevitch enumerated in 1920s Europe, the Free State's was one of the few that survived.[51] Eric Hobsbawm counted only five states in inter-war Europe where 'adequately democratic political institutions' continued to function without interruption, and the Free State was one.[52] Stability was a valuable commodity in inter-war Europe, however much it seemed to look like stasis after 1945.

The Shadow of the Revolution

The sense that the state lived in the shadow of its revolution, that its political life was defined by the civil war divide, underestimates the intensity of bread and butter politics from the very outset. It is there to be found in the extent and the range of legislation passed, while the frequency with which questions of land arose in the Dáil in this period is suggestive of a polity moving

---

50 K. O'Higgins, *Three Years Hard Labour* (Dublin: Cahill, 1924), 12.
51 Lee, *Ireland 1912–1985*, 80; M. Mazower, *Dark Continent: Europe's Twentieth Century* (London: Allen Lane, 1998), 5.
52 E. Hobsbawm, *Age of Extremes: The Short Twentieth Century 1914–1991* (London: Michael Joseph, 1995), 111.

naturally and ploddingly on.[53] The election literature of all parties, across the period, shows that pounds, shillings and pence mattered when it came to the ballot box. A Cumann na nGaedheal supporter saw his party's defeat in 1932 in very plain terms:

> I met some hard-headed wealthy middle-aged large-familied Mayo shopkeep-ers that I know in the train. Their enthusiasm and determination for the FF policy of high protection and development of the country's resources by strong measures was astonishing and the most curious thing was that they had no delusions about DeV's own personality and culpability in '22. 'But what matter now, he has the right policy and we'll see it through and make it succeed.' Voilà![54]

This questions David Fitzpatrick's view that 'affiliation to de Valera's Fianna Fáil was primarily determined by the legacy of the civil war rather than by the appeal of specific policies'.[55] One party certainly presented itself as the 'men of no property', aimed to 'speed the wheels' and 'speed the plough', and even had the arrogance to promise to 'abolish unemployment' in 1933. For econo-mist Kevin O'Rourke 'the claim that Irish party politics have been informed not by economic differences but rather by idiosyncratic quasi-tribal factors is not supported by the evidence'.[56] The civil war mattered; it remained a handy register of abuse, but we take too readily for granted that politics in the state was bound to 'be disfigured by the hatreds, betrayals, and disillusionment of the civil war'.[57] In the 1920s and 1930s Military Service Pension applicants from both sides requested supporting references from old civil war enemies; it seems to have taken the historiography longer to get over the divide. It is still looking for the divisions, not what put this place back together again.

In March 1923 George Russell lamented that 'the mass of people in the country continue to think as they did before the revolution', revolution 'tri-umphed solely in externals'; the fundamental fabric was not expected to change.[58] For Patrick Lynch, writing in 1966, independence amounted to the 'social revolution that never was', and most historians have accepted his tra-ditional sense of what that revolution should have been. Lynch blamed the dead hand of the civil service in the new state; the continuation of nigh on 98

---

53 T. Dooley, 'The Land for the People': The Land Question in Independent Ireland (Dublin: UCD Press, 2004), 3. See also the chapter by Dooley on the Land Question in this volume.
54 Quoted in Regan, The Irish Counter-revolution, 305.
55 Fitzpatrick, The Two Irelands, 197.
56 O'Rourke, 'Ireland and the Bigger Picture', 350.
57 F. McGarry, Eoin O'Duffy: A Self-made Hero (Oxford University Press, 2005), 114.
58 G. Russell (AE), 'Lessons of Revolution', Studies, 12 (March 1923), 2.

per cent into independence meant the 'conventional wisdom of Whitehall' far outweighed that of Connolly or Pearse.[59] That same continuity of service could also be the reason why the state survived. There were relatively robust institutions functioning relatively quickly, and Lynch's assumptions fail to take account of that or to recognise the fundamental rights and liberties enshrined in the state from the outset. The sense of an absent social revolution may instead reflect a will to impose a chronology that simply does not fit: social revolution possibly predated the political one. We may need to look to the changes of the late nineteenth and early twentieth centuries in terms of land ownership and local government, and in terms of the changing expectations of more relief that came with the old age pension in 1908. A small farmer was able to speak in the mid-1920s of 'what had been gained by the land-revolution – what had been gained by the political revolution had not yet come into his consciousness'.[60] Whatever either revolution meant to him they were distinctly separate things.

While the Irish welfare system lagged far behind its British equivalent, improvements were made none the less. Changes came, whether with more pensions, more allowances, or more reforms of the conditions of work; that there was still so much to do maybe emphasises the value of the little that was achieved. Because the source of much of the change was Fianna Fáil, because, as Seán MacEntee has already admitted, in spite of it all there was still 'more unemployed', many have refused to accept that if there was a social revolution, MacEntee's party might well have been its only source. When Minister for Local Government and Public Health, Seán T. O'Kelly bragged in 1937 that the 'Labour Party had no more responsibility for the passing of the Widows and Orphans' Pensions Act than the King of Bulgaria', he had a point.[61] Hindsight might hope to find a different kind of social revolution, but if electoral results are any measure then independent Ireland showed little appetite for more than what it got.

If independence was a far cry from the Limerick Soviet of 1921 where V. S. Pritchett was told to leave his hat on because 'they had finished ... with bourgeois manners', indeed, if bourgeois manners were the very thing that triumphed in the Free State, maybe there were other kinds of social revolutions to look for.[62] They may have come in the shape of a crystal radio set;

---

59 P. Lynch, 'The Social Revolution that Never Was', in D. Williams (ed.), *The Irish Struggle 1916–1926* (London: Routledge and Kegan Paul, 1966), 53.
60 Colum, *The Road*, p. 25.
61 *Irish Press*, 23 June 1937.
62 V. S. Pritchett, *Midnight Oil* (London, 1973 edn.), p. 117.

for George Bernard Shaw, one radio in a small place meant 'overnight the village was in the twentieth century'.[63] They may have come with the crackling of gramophones breaking the silence, in the records that brought jazz to Belmullet and Caruso to the tenements. They may have come with access to running water, to electricity, to more shop-bought goods, with more sociability, more houses, more bicycles, and more cars. The Shannon Scheme was not just a symbol of the modern in the state; it was a means of social change. Perhaps above all, they came for Miss Newton of the 'Big House' who told Padraic Colum 'we have had a great come down; we were once everything in the country, and now we count for hardly anything at all'. For her 'the real signs of an accomplished revolution' came in who administered local power. The head of the Civic Guard in her area was the 'son of the smith who used to shoe Miss Newton's horse'. Colum saw it in a trader's widow who could put up an altar in the chapel 'at the cost of a thousand pounds'; he saw it in the grandson of a labourer who was now the 'richest man in the place'.[64] It was perhaps born of narrow ambition, but it was a social revolution none the less.

There is much work to be done in order to understand the nature of social mobility in the new state, to grasp the gradations of class, particularly in rural Ireland, and to measure the power that tuppence ha'penny exerted over tuppence. Even Frank McCourt had someone to look down on in Limerick's lanes. There may have been no social revolution of the sort expected, but respectability ran rampant and, in fathoming that, we will begin to see why some prospered and some failed, why some daughters were kept at home, why others were put away out of sight. Its history is in the steady slights. A tender for the construction of fourteen houses by Birr Urban District Council was advertised in October 1934 in the *Irish Press*. They were fourteen of the government's tally of more than 82,000 homes constructed between 1932 and 1942.[65] Building on the approximately 25,000 houses funded by Cumann na nGaedheal governments from 1922, each one can be acknowledged as a key part of what little amounted to social change. But the tender called them '14 working-classes [sic] houses'.[66] Even in that misspelt word we begin to see why some were never allowed to forget the help they got. The power of local charity over local need, of local credit over local debt, the power of parents

---

63 S. O'Faolain, *The Irish* (3rd edn., London: Vintage Books, 1980), 147.

64 Colum, *The Road*, 15–16, 34–5.

65 C. Ó Gráda, *Ireland: A New Economic History 1780–1939* (Oxford University Press, 1994), 440.

66 *Irish Press*, 11 October 1934.

over daughters and sons, spouse over spouse, the tyrannies of propriety in a small place need to be understood. The concentration of power in central government in the new state has been noted, but who ordered out the everyday in society as a whole?

Conclusion

Sean O'Faolain, reflecting on three decades of independence, noted 'we have had our protesters, sometimes violent, rarely articulate or creative, but they have been all too few', so that if a politician asked 'what exactly do they want' then ' "they" rarely do know'. For Diarmaid Ferriter, writing nearly sixty years after O'Faolain, 'the real surprise is that more unrest was not shown by those most distressed'.[67] It is as if George Bernard Shaw's view still holds. Voicing his disappointment with the prospect of censorship in 1928, he complained 'the average man is a coward', and so much of the disappointment with this period of Irish history seems to echo this sentiment.[68] And yet, so much that is now perceived as conservatism in the state often had overwhelming popular support, even had advocates prepared to push for what seems even greater repression. The voices that spoke up for women's rights were largely ignored, the concern some fathers had that the farmer's dole might undermine their control of their sons, the failure to raise the school-leaving age because the need for a child's labour was too pressing for too long, these and so many other examples suggest people were not always thwarted: they just were not prepared to do as we hoped they should have done. The number and extent of inquiries instituted by the state in these two decades suggests that curiosity was there to see and perhaps improve people's lives, but most investigations were shelved and not acted upon. That tussle between the instinct to know and the inability to act has more to give us than just the disappointment that nothing was done. There were eloquent contemporary critics of independence, and much eloquent criticism since, but the experience of the 1920s and 1930s is too diverse to settle for criticism alone. Colum leaves us with the home of Pierce Moynihan in the midlands, a four-roomed house, a 12-acre farm. Moynihan had several children in America, two sons and one daughter still at home. With pictures of America on the wall, his daughter was in a hurry to be on her way: 'she had no need to leave ... still she had no wish to settle here'. The youngest son 'was very

---

67 O'Faolain, *The Irish*, 160–1; Ferriter, *The Transformation of Ireland*, 318.
68 G. B. Shaw, *The Irish Statesman*, 17 November 1928, 207.

hostile to the government – they were spending the people's money on themselves; the people were better off under the British, and all that sort of thing'. The eldest son, who had fought in some way for this freedom, had a different view: 'he is interested in agricultural organization abroad, and had heard of conditions in Denmark. All that he said about the conditions and problems of the countryside was thoughtful'.[69] He was looking outward, hopeful for the future, for change. In these four rooms, 12 acres, and three siblings there is more than the sum of our disappointment; the lives that were lived were more vivid than that.

69 Colum, *The Road*, 24–7.

12

Neutrality and Belligerence: Ireland, 1939–1945[1]

PHILIP OLLERENSHAW

Introduction: Neutrality and Belligerence

Wartime Northern Ireland and independent Ireland during the 'Emergency' exhibited some features in common and some stark contrasts. As part of the United Kingdom, the six-county region of Northern Ireland was at war from 3 September 1939 when the government in London declared war on Germany. The UK remained at war until victory over Japan on 2 September 1945. The twenty-six county area officially known until 1937 as the Irish Free State and, after the new constitution of that year as 'Ireland', remained officially neutral throughout this period. Éamon de Valera, President of the Executive Council (renamed Taoiseach from 1937) and also Minister for External Affairs between 1932 and 1948, never wavered in his determination to preserve Irish neutrality, in spite of periodic pressure from Britain, the United States and some Commonwealth countries to abandon this policy. He remained unmoved on the two occasions (June 1940 and December 1941) when the British government appeared to offer an eventual end to partition in exchange for participation in the war.[2] Neutrality had enormous public support and was even more popular than appeasement in 1930s Britain. It was also seen by many as a morally superior policy to adopt.

Under the 1920 Government of Ireland Act, the Belfast government had no power to make war or peace, no control over the army, navy or air force, foreign policy or Empire–Commonwealth relations. Decisions in these areas were taken in London on behalf of the UK as a whole. Although Northern Ireland was a belligerent throughout the war, it had no military conscription and no general industrial conscription. This distinguished it from the rest

---

1 I am very grateful to Tom Bartlett, Bryce Evans, Brian Girvin and Hilary Ollerenshaw for their constructive criticism of an earlier draft of this chapter.
2 See for example, G. Roberts, 'The British Offer to End Partition, June 1940', *History Ireland*, 9 (2001), 5–6.

of the UK and meant that the region never fully mobilised its resources to experience total war. One consequence of this was that unemployment was higher than for any other UK region and that the contribution of women to the industrial war effort was less than that in Britain.

At the start of 1939, Ireland was practically defenceless with virtually no airpower or navy; there were fewer than 7,000 regular troops with a reserve force of some 12,000, many of whom had poor training and equipment. The army expanded during the Emergency and the largest exercises in the period, involving two complete divisions, took place in the autumn of 1942.[3] While de Valera habitually referred to partition as a key reason for refusing to consider entering the war on the Allied side, such participation would have brought large-scale social and political conflict, as well as aerial bombardment and the destruction of Irish cities and infrastructure, with all the associated problems that became plain to see elsewhere. The fact was that any policy other than neutrality made no sense to the great majority of voters, politicians and clergy. Partition gave de Valera a reason for non-participation in the war and enabled the country to remain neutral throughout. At the same time, he was consistent in his position that he would not allow any foreign power to use Ireland as a base from which to attack Britain. His personal contribution to promoting security liaison with Britain from 1938 was significant.[4]

In order to reinforce the policy of neutrality and to enable the government to defend the state, widespread censorship – postal, telegraphic, literary and media – was enforced. Planning for this policy, in fact, had been underway since October 1935 when Frank Aiken, then Minister of Defence, appointed an interdepartmental committee 'to consider the question of censorship in a future war'. The subsequent report followed British examples and practice to a considerable extent but was modified to meet Irish circumstances. When war broke out, the new Emergency Powers Act provided the government with the legal basis 'for securing public safety and preservation of the State' in wartime. Most importantly, included in the Act was the right of government to issue emergency orders to censor communications. These orders would provide essential building blocks for the elaborate structure of censorship that quickly evolved. Within a week of the Act becoming law, the 'dogged, rigid

3 G. A. Hayes-McCoy, 'Irish Defence Policy, 1938–51', in K. Nowlan and T. D. Williams (eds.), *Ireland in the War Years and After, 1939–51* (Dublin: Gill & Macmillan, 1969), 40, 50.

4 E. O'Halpin, 'MI5's Irish Memories: Fresh Light on the Origins and Rationale of Anglo-Irish Security Liaison in the Second World War', in B. Girvin and G. Roberts (eds.), *Ireland and the Second World War: Politics, Society and Remembrance* (Dublin: Four Courts Press, 2000), 141–3.

and unyielding' Aiken had become Minister for the Coordination of Defensive Measures with overall responsibility for censorship, and he remained in this position until the end of the war.[5] Censorship was much more stringent in independent Ireland than in other neutral countries and would only be lifted in May 1945, three days after the end of the war in Europe.[6]

A further aspect of contingency planning in 1935 was the establishment of an interdepartmental committee to consider the supply of essential materials should a conflict break out. The committee included two representatives each from the Departments of Defence and from Industry and Commerce, and one each from Finance, External Affairs and Agriculture.[7] One outcome was the establishment in September 1938 within Industry and Commerce of the Emergency Supplies Branch which a year later was upgraded to a full Department with Seán Lemass as Minister. In the Dáil in September 1939, de Valera stressed the importance of this innovation: 'on the success of that Department will largely depend how far we shall be able to escape the larger evils which are consequent on the general disruption caused by this war. … It will be, in fact, the central planning department for our economic life'.[8] Following a reshuffle in August 1941 Lemass became Minister for both Supplies and for Industry and Commerce. This not only widened his governmental powerbase, it was also conducive to a reconsideration of his approaches to economic management, the role of the state and postwar planning within a capitalist framework. Lemass was much influenced by the ideas of the British liberal economists William Beveridge and John Maynard Keynes. Even if conservative forces proved far stronger than he anticipated, Lemass at least demonstrated a willingness to contemplate a range of imaginative state-led policies to expand industrial and agricultural output to a greater extent than other ministers.[9]

In the later 1930s, connections between Ireland and the Commonwealth had been weakened, and de facto independence achieved, by a series of measures

5 D. Ó Drisceoil, *Censorship in Ireland, 1939–1945: Neutrality, Politics and Society* (Cork: Cork University Press, 1996), 10–14.

6 E. O'Halpin, 'Irish Neutrality in the Second World War', in N. Wylie (ed.), *European Neutrals and Non-Belligerents during the Second World War* (Cambridge University Press, 2002), 290.

7 R. Fanning, *The Irish Department of Finance, 1922–58* (Dublin: Institute of Public Administration, 1978), 311–12. This committee produced three reports between 1935 and 1937 and was dissolved in February 1939.

8 *Dáil Debates*, 27 September 1939, vol. 77, cols. 262–3.

9 B. Girvin, *Between Two Worlds: Politics and Economy in Independent Ireland* (Dublin: Gill & Macmillan, 1989), 134–5.

including the External Relations Act of 1936 and the 1937 Constitution (which had created the office of president), while the Economic War between 1932 and 1938 had done considerable short-term damage to British–Irish relations. However, those relations had improved following three agreements concluded in April 1938, while Neville Chamberlain was British prime minister, and these in turn would have a significant impact during the war. The first agreement transferred the three Treaty Ports of Berehaven, Cobh and Lough Swilly from Britain; the second settled, to Ireland's great financial advantage, the long-running dispute over land annuities that had triggered the Economic War, while the third went a long way to normalise trade relations, facilitate access to each other's markets and recognise the close commercial and financial links between the UK and Ireland.[10] The dependence of Ireland on the UK was greater than that of any other European country on one market.[11]

The restoration of the Treaty Ports made neutrality in any future war far more feasible than at any time since the formation of the state, but at the same time it raised the importance of defence as an issue for all political parties. While there would be significant tensions, the agreements of 1938 permitted the evolution of a much more constructive wartime framework for British–Irish relations than would otherwise have been possible. Had Winston Churchill been British Prime Minister in the later 1930s, this would not have been the case. In seeking a more positive relationship with the Dublin government, Chamberlain had the strong support of Dominions Secretary Malcolm MacDonald as well as Sir Warren Fisher, Head of the Civil Service. As Fisher noted early in 1938, the Irish were 'historically on incontestable ground in their view of England as an aggressor. … Obviously, an Ireland gradually becoming less hostile to England would be to us of great value, positive and negative, alike militarily and agriculturally'.[12] Since 1923, the defence of Ireland had been neglected by all Irish governments not only on financial grounds but also because of an understandable fear of maintaining a large standing military force in a country so recently engaged in civil war.[13] Between 1939 and 1945, by keeping defence expenditure low, the

---

10 J. Meenan, *The Irish Economy since 1922* (Liverpool: Liverpool University Press, 1970), 78–9.
11 K. Kennedy, 'The Roots of Contemporary Irish Economic Development', in D. Dickson and C. Ó Gráda (eds.), *Refiguring Ireland: Essays in Honour of L. M. Cullen* (Dublin: Lilliput Press, 2003), 373.
12 Sir Warren Fisher quoted in P. Canning, 'Another Failure for Appeasement? The Case of the Irish Ports', *International History Review*, 4 (1982), 389.
13 B. Girvin, *The Emergency: Neutral Ireland, 1939–45* (London: Macmillan, 2006), 75.

Dublin government was able to ease the financial burden on its citizens. In a macroeconomic context this led to the remarkable result that, during the Emergency, government expenditure as a proportion of GDP actually fell.[14]

In terms of historiography, one of the best-known images of neutral Ireland during the Emergency is that of F. S. L. Lyons who, in *Ireland Since the Famine*, wrote of the country's 'almost total isolation from the rest of mankind . . . The tensions – and the liberations – of war, the shared experience, the comradeship in suffering, the new thinking about the future, all these things had passed her by. It was as if an entire people had been condemned to live in Plato's cave . . .'[15] Lyons's discussion of the Emergency is inexplicably brief and is concentrated in half a dozen pages. Moreover, his image of Plato's cave has been repeatedly criticised as a distortion of the nation's experience between 1939 and 1945. John A. Murphy, for whom neutrality was '*the* formative experience in the history of the State', judged it to be 'mistaken and misleading' since, far from isolation, the country mobilised economic as well as military resources in order to sustain its policy of neutrality and address problems of widespread shortages. Murphy identified a 'sense of national purpose [which] transcended party political differences'. Former civil war adversaries were members of an all-party defence council and also shared recruiting platforms for the Irish army. In his view, this helped to heal the wounds left by the civil war.[16]

In a sustained critique of Lyons, subtitled *Farewell to Plato's Cave*, Bryce Evans has emphasised the social and economic impact of war on ordinary men and women.[17] One of the results of this research has been to show how the Emergency led to widespread problems and shortages from 1940 and, still more so, from early in 1941 when Britain curtailed supplies in a futile attempt to pressure de Valera to abandon neutrality. This also caused factory closures and short-time working.[18] Desmond Williams's verdict that only in 1942 did the war 'hit Ireland, economically speaking' is therefore untenable.[19]

---

14 D. Ó Drisceoil, '"Keeping the Temperature Down"; Domestic Politics in Emergency Ireland', in D. Keogh and M. O'Driscoll (eds.), *Ireland in World War 2: Neutrality and Survival* (Cork: Mercier Press, 2004), 175.

15 F. S. L. Lyons, *Ireland Since the Famine* (London: Fontana edition, 1973), 557–8.

16 J. A. Murphy, 'Irish Neutrality in Historical Perspective', in Girvin and Roberts (eds.), *Ireland and the Second World War*, 16. See also the chapter by Eunan O'Halpin in this volume.

17 B. Evans, *Ireland during the Second World War: Farewell to Plato's Cave* (Manchester: Manchester University Press, 2014).

18 M. E. Daly, *The Slow Failure: Population Decline and Independent Ireland, 1920–1973* (Madison, WI: University of Wisconsin Press, 2006), 145.

19 T. D. Williams, 'Ireland and the War', in Nowlan and Williams (eds.), *Ireland in the War Years and After*, 23.

In everyday life throughout Ireland, the war period brought about widespread shortages and rationing, leading to black markets and smuggling and eliciting robust responses by the state to limit these, not least through recourse to the law. By 1943, neutral Ireland had only 25 per cent of its normal tea supplies. The respective percentages for other products were petrol 20 per cent, paraffin less than 15 per cent, gas coal 16 per cent and textiles 22 per cent. There was virtually no coal available.[20] Given these shortages, the temptation to black marketeers was very great indeed and the need for state intervention correspondingly urgent. Some of the shortages would continue into the postwar years.

Wartime shortages and black marketeering led to the expansion of women's groups in independent Ireland. These included The Irish Countrywomen's Association (established in 1910 and known until 1935 as the United Irishwomen), and the Irish Housewives' Association (IHA), formed in 1942 by Hilda Tweedy, a Protestant from County Monaghan. The latter was largely middle class and Protestant in origin and its members were mainly married women. Although its denominational base quickly broadened, the IHA remained mainly a middle-class organisation. It was viewed with some suspicion by the Archbishop of Dublin, John Charles McQuaid who distrusted multi-denominational organisations in general. Tweedy was a key activist in the campaign against black market profiteering and was co-organiser of the so-called 'Housewives Petition' of May 1941 to lobby for rationing of essential foods. From 1942, IHA members were actively encouraged to inform on any trader considered to be engaging in profiteering.[21] One of the most significant of its early campaigns was to highlight the poverty of Dublin's poorest families and the failure of partial and voluntary rationing. The IHA was influential in persuading an initially reluctant Lemass to adopt general rationing, and to increase the fines for black marketeering, in June 1942.[22] Rationing came earlier to Northern Ireland and was widespread by December 1939.

From a cultural perspective, there is no doubt that the Emergency brought a sense of enforced isolation, but it also fostered initiatives to palliate that isolation, even if several of these did not survive long into the postwar period.

---

20 J. Meenan, 'The Irish Economy during the War', ibid., 36.
21 M. Cullen, 'Women, Emancipation and Politics, 1860–1984', in J. R. Hill (ed.), *A New History of Ireland, Vol. VII: Ireland 1921–84* (Oxford University Press, 2003), 877–9; A. Hayes (ed.), *Hilda Tweedy and the Irish Housewives' Association: Links in the Chain...*, (Dublin: Arlen House, 2011), *passim.*
22 B. Evans, *Seán Lemass: Democratic Dictator* (Cork: The Collins Press, 2011), 136–7.

The significance of refugees, conscientious objectors, tourists, artists, musicians and others who contributed to a cosmopolitan atmosphere during the Emergency is now widely appreciated. The emergence in 1940 of *The Bell* (edited throughout the Emergency by Seán Ó Faoláin), a monthly magazine of social and literary comment, enhanced the coverage of everyday Irish life and extended its readership into provincial Ireland.[23] By discussing Irish issues in a European context *The Bell* served as an antidote to intellectual introversion. It also published articles from many European countries.[24] Despite its short life (1940–1954), which was not unusual for a literary magazine, the influence of this monthly publication was profound.

North of the border, a similarly positive view of art and literature during this period has emerged. Edna Longley suggested that a body of writing from the region 'overspills borders and manifests a web of affiliation that stretches beyond any heartland – to the rest of Ireland, Britain, Europe'.[25] While the quality of Northern Irish poetry from the war period (as distinct from retrospectives by poets such as Seamus Heaney who was born in 1939) has been increasingly recognised, it is also the case that in visual arts the arrival of large numbers of foreign troops and significant numbers of European refugees brought new influences and encouraged greater adventurousness than had been the case before the war.[26]

During the war period, the image of a neutral Ireland free from the difficulties faced by belligerents was a common one in the UK and formed the basis for many negative comments by politicians and the press who tended to overlook the privations increasingly suffered by the Irish population as the war progressed. The image was established at an early stage by the Irish Tourist Association's Christmas campaign in 1939 designed to attract visitors from Northern Ireland. Its adverts declared 'Dublin has no BLACK-OUT! Dublin is the gayest city in Ireland this Christmas – no black-out, a carefree atmosphere, and all entertainments in full swing ... why not make this a Christmas of fun and merriment, instead of black-out boredom and irksome restrictions?'[27]

---

23 C. Wills, *That Neutral Island: A Cultural History of Ireland during the Second World War* (London: Faber & Faber, 2007), 282, 291–2, 298, 425.

24 B. Fallon, *An Age of Innocence: Irish Culture, 1930–1960* (Dublin: Four Courts Press, 1998), 233.

25 E. Longley, 'From Cathleen To Anorexia: The Breakdown of Irelands', in *The Living Stream: Literature and Revisionism in Ireland* (Newcastle-upon-Tyne: Bloodaxe Books, 1994), 195, quoted in G. Woodward, *Culture, Northern Ireland and the Second World War* (Oxford University Press, 2015), 11.

26 Woodward, *Culture, Northern Ireland and the Second World War*, 82–3, 131.

27 *Belfast Telegraph*, 19 December 1939.

The Great Northern Railway offered special trains with cheap return tickets between many Northern Irish towns and cities and Dublin, valid for travel up to New Year's Day 1940.

In both parts of Ireland, dominant political parties remained in government throughout the period 1939–1945, though both faced different challenges from other parties usually prompted by dissatisfaction with official policies relating to labour, land or social welfare. Unlike in Britain, neither in Belfast nor Dublin was there a national coalition government, despite some demands for such governments. The general election of June 1938 delivered Fianna Fáil a majority of sixteen, mainly at the expense of Labour and of Fine Gael, and strengthened de Valera's hand in the final period of peace and early years of war. There were general elections in 1943 and again in 1944. The former saw Fianna Fáil lose its overall majority, but this was regained the following year. Fine Gael, first under William Cosgrave and, from 1944, Richard Mulcahy, struggled to find a distinctively attractive programme and suffered a decline in terms of first preference votes and in the number of TDs over four consecutive general elections between 1937 and 1944. There was no substantial recovery for it until 1951. Despite its dominance during the Emergency, in the election of 1948 Fianna Fáil lost power for the first time in sixteen years, defeated by a shaky, fissiparous and short-lived five-party coalition of Labour, the National Labour Party, Fine Gael, Clann na Poblachta and Clann na Talmhan.[28]

While de Valera remained Taoiseach throughout the Emergency, in Northern Ireland there were two changes of prime minister. John Andrews replaced Viscount Craigavon following the latter's death in November 1940 and Andrews was himself succeeded by Sir Basil Brooke after a Unionist Party rebellion in 1943. That rebellion reflected wartime tensions different in scale and type from those south of the border. Factors contributing to Andrews' unpopularity included the continued presence of elderly and stale government ministers, several of whom had been in office since 1921, a palpable inability fully to mobilise the economy, and the embarrassment of widespread strike action, especially in the shipyards and aircraft factories. The trauma of the 1941 blitz on a virtually undefended and unprepared Belfast, and the Andrews' government's failure to address the social problems associated with evacuation, health and housing further increased the opposition to him within the Unionist Party. These problems encouraged women and young unionists to

---

28 R. Dunphy, *The Making of Fianna Fáil Power in Ireland, 1923–48* (Oxford University Press, 1995), 215, 304–7.

take a more significant role in politics than previously. There were no general elections for either the Belfast or Westminster parliaments between 1938 and 1945, although there were some by-elections that provided tests of public opinion. A number of them brought defeat for the Unionist Party and corresponding gains for Independents and for Labour. The 1945 election for the Stormont parliament saw a strong anti-unionist vote and the Unionist Party with fewer MPs than at any time since 1925.

In the period 1939 to 1945, both the Belfast and Dublin governments faced the same republican enemy from within and had comprehensive special powers to address this and other threats. Both experienced fears of invasion at different times: Ireland from Britain, Germany and even the United States; Northern Ireland from Germany. The extent to which neutral status would provide protection from invasion was always doubtful, especially after the German occupation of neutral Belgium and the Netherlands in May 1940, and this in turn would help to sustain a sense of insecurity no less persistent than that experienced by belligerent nations. From both parts of Ireland, emigration for civilian work or military service was significant and contributed in important ways to the British war effort. In social welfare policy, the publication of the Beveridge Report at the end of 1942 was instrumental in encouraging a debate about the role of the state throughout Ireland, a debate that drew in politicians, all the churches, the labour movement, women's groups and the general public to an unprecedented extent.

Special Powers and Security

In order to protect the state between 1939 and 1945, governments in Belfast and Dublin were equipped with wide-ranging special powers. In both parts of Ireland, special powers were directed against the IRA and in Northern Ireland against nationalist and republican activity broadly defined. South of the border, these powers also aimed to prevent the country being used as a base for either espionage or sabotage against Britain, to enable the state effectively to deal with covert activity by any foreign power within its borders, as well as to stop the leakage of all types of classified information. New measures included the Treason Act, the Offences Against the State Act and the Emergency Powers Act, all passed in 1939.[29] In Northern Ireland, a series of Special Powers Acts, the first of which was introduced in 1922 and intended

29 E. O'Halpin, *Defending Ireland: The Irish State and its Enemies Since 1922* (Oxford University Press, 1999), 200–3.

to be temporary but made permanent in 1933, gave the Minister of Home Affairs or his nominee extraordinarily wide-ranging powers that were primarily aimed at nationalists and republicans. The 1922 Act included (but was not limited to) the imposition of curfews, and the prohibition of meetings, processions and military drilling. It also allowed entry for the security forces into homes and premises and gave them the power to stop, search and seize vehicles, as well as to detain suspects and intern them. Publications deemed inflammatory or disloyal, as well as their distribution, fell under the remit of the Act.[30] Introduced to address the widespread violence and disorder of the early 1920s, the continuation of these powers once relative calm had been restored was questioned by nationalists and by civil rights groups such as the London-based National Council for Civil Liberties, established in 1934. The retention of these powers also attracted unfavourable international attention for the Belfast government. What had been intended as emergency and temporary powers had become the norm by the 1930s.

The Belfast government defended these Special Powers on the grounds that they were necessary to deal with an ever-present republican threat to the existence of the state. The IRA campaign in Northern Ireland from 1938, and in Britain from January 1939, and the outbreak of war itself, provided the government with sufficient pretext to exercise these powers rigorously through to 1945. Amongst the powers most frequently deployed were internment, the banning of meetings and processions, and the prohibition of particular publications. In the case of the latter, bans lasted typically for a year but were subject to renewal. For some publications, such as *An Phoblacht* [*The Republic*, an IRA publication] or the *Wolfe Tone Weekly* this meant a permanent ban for the duration of the war. Bans on meetings typically targeted commemorative activity such as those relating to the 1916 Easter Rising or to gatherings to protest against partition. In some cases the ban related to specific meetings in particular places, in others the ban applied throughout Northern Ireland.

Easter Week demonstrations to commemorate the 1916 Rising were both regular and geographically widespread, and during the war all such were officially banned.[31] The RUC also often did what it could to prevent the wearing of Easter lilies, especially in loyalist/nationalist interface areas such as those in West Belfast where sectarian disturbance was likely to result. This might

---

30 L. K. Donohue, *Counter-Terrorist Law and Emergency Powers in the United Kingdom, 1922–2000* (Dublin: Irish Academic Press, 2001), 356–7.

31 Ibid., 76, 89–90.

involve the RUC arresting women who were then prosecuted and imprisoned.[32] It was also sometimes the case that official bans were flouted and, in
other cases, prohibited meetings took place just over the border. There were
many instances of this before and during the war. For example, the republican meeting that took place on 10 April 1939 in Bridgend, County Donegal
was organised by Derry nationalists, but it had been banned earlier by the
authorities in Northern Ireland. Speakers included republican Maud Gonne
MacBride, who equated the persecution of northern Catholics with that of
the Jews in Germany, Patrick Maxwell (Nationalist MP for Foyle in the Belfast
Parliament) and Frank Pakenham (Lord Longford), then prospective Labour
Party candidate for Oxford City, who emphasised his determination, and that
of other Irishmen like himself resident in England, to continue to raise partition as a political issue.[33]

With regard to internment, the IRA campaign of late 1938, which included
attacks on a number of customs posts, was interpreted as the first stage of a
campaign to subvert the state. An IRA Army Council Statement of December
along with a proclamation of January 1939, were used by both the Belfast and
Dublin governments to strengthen emergency powers and accelerate internment. Sir Richard Dawson Bates, the Minister of Home Affairs, quoted the
recent 'egregious proclamation by the so-called Irish Republican Government
and the Irish Republican Army' as sufficient justification for internment. In an
interview, Bates referred to the proclamation which

> after reiterating at great length the claim that a Republic of Ireland is in exist-
> ence and that the present Governments of Éire [=Ireland] and Northern
> Ireland are in fact usurping authorities, calls for the assistance of all Irishmen
> in the effort about to be made to compel the evacuation of the armed forces,
> civilian officials, institutions, and representatives of England from Ireland
> and to enthrone a Republic of Ireland.[34]

Just a few weeks later, the same Army Council Statement and proclamation
were used in the Dáil by Patrick Ruttledge, the Minister for Justice, as a reason for the introduction of emergency legislation.[35] If there was one single
incident that persuaded the Irish government of the reality of the IRA threat,

---

32 P. Ollerenshaw, *Northern Ireland in the Second World War: Politics, Economic Mobilisation
and Society, 1939–45* (Manchester: Manchester University Press, 2013), 36–7.
33 *Manchester Guardian*, 11 April 1939.
34 Ibid., 17 January 1939.
35 Ibid., 8 February 1939. For a longer-term perspective, see in general D. Ó Beacháin,
Destiny of the Soldiers: Fianna Fáil, Irish Republicans and the IRA, 1926–73 (Dublin: Gill &
Macmillan, 2010).

it was the large-scale, successful IRA raid on the Magazine Fort in Dublin's Phoenix Park in December 1939. As a result of this, the government mobilised all the resources at its disposal to confront the challenge the IRA had laid down. Within a matter of weeks the ammunition (and more besides) had been recovered and discoveries of guns and ammunition secreted in IRA arms dumps had also been made. Internment began in early January 1940 and during the Emergency some 1130 individuals were interned. 1013 of these were tried by the Special Criminal Court and 914 convicted.[36] As the state became increasingly effective in neutralising the IRA, the Special Criminal Court was able to spend more of its time hearing allegations of black marketeering as well as rationing offences.[37]

The speed of the German victories in 1939 and 1940, and the high probability of German invasion of the British Isles until the summer of 1941, exercised a profound influence on British–Irish relations, and also on governments in Belfast and Dublin. The German invasion of neutral Belgium and the Netherlands elicited a protest from de Valera, but the unexpected fall of France in June 1940 seemed to raise the prospect of German victory to a near certainty. Responses to this varied from the apocalyptic (Englishman Charlie Almond in the Irish Department of Finance thought it was 'the effin end'),[38] to calls for a negotiated peace. Prominent in the latter category were Cardinal Joseph MacRory and Joseph Walshe at External Affairs. For Walshe, even in April 1940, the war was unwinnable since the British were 'too soft, too class-prejudiced (they are almost all of the wealthy Tory family type) to be able to win a war against men of steel like Hitler [and] Stalin'.[39] Despite Walshe's pessimism, it remains the case that he maintained a positive relationship with the British in security matters during the war. In May 1940 Walshe, together with Colonel Liam Archer (until 1942 Director of Military Intelligence, or G2) met with the British with a view to developing closer cooperation. Although this has been seen as a clear breach of neutrality, close cooperation would characterise the period to the end of the war. Walshe's regular contacts with David Gray, Sir John Maffey and Edouard Hempel, respectively representatives in Dublin of the USA, UK and Germany, enabled him to navigate a course through some very difficult moments with all

36 Girvin, *The Emergency*, 83–4.
37 S. Ó Longaigh, 'Emergency Law in Action, 1939–45', in Keogh and O'Driscoll (eds.), *Ireland in World War Two*, 76.
38 Quoted in Dermot Keogh, *Twentieth Century Ireland: Nation and State* (Dublin: Gill & Macmillan, 1994), 114.
39 Quoted in Evans, *Seán Lemass*, 120.

three.[40] British–Irish relations could easily have been disastrous during the war period, and especially after Churchill became prime minister in May 1940, but Walshe and Maffey were central to a much more constructive outcome.

Migration, Civil and Military Recruitment

One of the most remarkable contributions Ireland made to the UK war effort was through the migration of men and women to work in war-related manufacturing, agriculture and nursing as well as to join the armed forces in the fight against Nazi Germany. The scale of this migration (*c*.200,000 people) was impressive, and it was driven at least in part by high levels of unemployment (female unemployment in Ireland doubled between 1939 and 1943). Wartime emigration was about twice as high as it had been in the 1930s although it was not so great as to cause a decline in a population that, in 1946, was still slightly higher than in 1939.[41] Most emigration to Britain in the 1940s was from western seaboard counties, and from Dublin. During the 1941 to 1945 period, male emigration exceeded female by a ratio of 2.68: 1 and the men who left tended to be less skilled than the women.[42] For nine months after the start of the war there were no restrictions on ordinary travel between Britain and Ireland. The later part of this period coincided with the onset of labour shortages in the British economy.

With the fall of France in June 1940, and the accompanying fear of invasion in Britain and Ireland, restrictions on travel began to be imposed in order to try to prevent the 'leakage' of security information. The Passenger Traffic (No.4) Order of June 1940, issued by Dublin under the 1939 Defence Regulations was the first manifestation of this. Passports and permits were issued only on condition that the proposed journey was 'on business of national importance'. However, given the demand for labour in Britain, the high levels of unemployment in Ireland, and the well-established patterns of travel, it was neither desirable nor possible to enforce such harsh travel restrictions. A new

---

40 A. Nolan, ' "A most Heavy and Grievous Burden", Joseph Walshe and the Establishment of Sustainable Neutrality, 1940', in Keogh and O'Driscoll (eds.), *Ireland in World War Two*, 129, 143. One of the best-known examples was Frank Aiken's diplomatically disastrous meeting with Roosevelt in 1941: see B. Evans, 'The iron man with the wooden head? Frank Aiken and the Second World War', in B. Evans and S. Kelly (eds.), *Frank Aiken: Nationalist and Internationalist* (Dublin: Irish Academic Press, 2014), 133–57.

41 K. Kennedy, T. Giblin and D. McHugh, *The Economic Development of Ireland in the Twentieth Century* (London: Routledge, 1988), 51.

42 T. Connolly, 'Irish Workers in Britain during World War II', in Girvin and Roberts (eds.), *Ireland and the Second World War*, 124–9.

agreement in July 1941, however, proved complicated. Neutrality had to be preserved, and hence the Dublin government needed assurances that its citizens resident in Britain had the option to return home before being called up for military service. Further, it insisted that men who went to Britain specifically for war work would not be conscripted into the British forces nor would women who left for war work in Britain be liable to industrial conscription. Between 1941 and 1944 there was a tendency for the recruitment of Irish labour to be undertaken on a more centralised basis by agents working for government departments rather than through individual firms. In general, the recruitment of women had always been more centralised.[43] In the period before the Normandy landings in June 1944, severe restrictions were again imposed upon travel between Britain and Ireland, this time at the insistence of General Dwight D. Eisenhower, Supreme Commander of the Allied Expeditionary Force, in order to minimise the possibility of information about Operation Overlord being passed to Germany via Ireland. Begun on 10 March, the travel ban began to be relaxed to some extent once the invasion started on 6 June.[44]

Despite all the various difficulties and restrictions, the contribution of Irish men and women to the British war economy was very considerable, not merely in terms of numbers or the significance of the work they did (especially heavy unskilled labour which was virtually non-existent from British sources from 1940) but also because much of it was mobile and thus had a potential importance beyond its numbers. Apart from a minority of Irish men and women who expressed a preference to work for a specific firm or in a particular area, Irish labour was 'mobile and not subject to the preference rulings under which British labour was allocated. Recruitment in Ireland therefore gave the British Ministry of Supply a margin of labour to use at its discretion for urgent and difficult demands'.[45] In Ireland, the impact of extensive emigration made itself felt at many levels. Politically, it probably served as a safety valve for those unemployed, underemployed or simply low-paid young men and women who may have blamed Fianna Fáil for their situation and voted against the party in local and general elections, or even taken more radical non-parliamentary action. At the same time, emigrant remittances assumed increasingly large proportions in household budgets and helped to support

43 H. M. D. Parker, *Manpower: A Study of War-time Policy and Administration* (London: HMSO and Longmans, 1957) esp. 334–41.

44 O'Halpin, *Defending Ireland*, 233.

45 P. Inman, *Labour in the Munitions Industries* (London: HMSO and Longmans, Green & Co, 1957), 174; 167–75 of this volume deals with labour from neutral Ireland.

incomes during the Emergency. As early as 1939, postal and money orders from Britain totalled £1 million. This figure had doubled by 1941 and would continue to grow.[46]

While remittances were welcomed by tens of thousands of families, the scale of emigration also led to concern about the political and social implications of a mass return of migrants once the war was over. This concern climbed up the political agenda in 1942–1943 to such an extent that it played a crucial role in stimulating a debate on economic policy within the Cabinet. One result of this was the establishment in November 1942 of the Cabinet Committee on Economic Planning. This met no fewer than fifty-eight times between then and the end of the war in Europe, and became the forum for serious debate about national economic policy.[47] In the event, the feared mass return of migrants did not materialise.

The regular movement of migrant labour to and from Britain had the effect of introducing more modern, 'urban' ideas about work, such as independent wages and specified leisure time, to rural Ireland. This in turn served as a partial solvent of parental authority. Writing to de Valera in 1943, the Rev. Thomas McFall, a Church of Ireland clergyman from Fiddown in County Waterford, emphasised that very few people were aware of 'the hold which many farming parents keep on their grown-up children. I know of more than one instance where young men of 25 years still go to their father (or in one case their mother) to ask for the price of a smoke or the cost of a ticket to a dance or cinema'.[48] The experience of emigration, whether for civilian work or military service, or wartime work on Irish government schemes such as turf-cutting, increased the frequency of regular pay days and wages paid to the individual, and thus contributed to a sense of independence from parental authority. This was of immediate and enduring appeal to young people in an evolving consumer society.[49]

While the war emphasised the drift from the land, it also focused attention throughout Ireland on rural poverty and the bleak existence that so many families faced, especially on small farms. The background to Patrick Kavanagh's classic poem 'The Great Hunger', published in 1942 in the London-based *Horizon* magazine, almost a century after the start of the Great Famine,

---

46 Connolly, 'Irish Workers during World War II', in Girvin and Roberts (eds.), *Ireland and the Second World War*, 130; Wills, *That Neutral Island*, 332.

47 Dunphy, *The Making of Fianna Fáil Power in Ireland,* 227, 230.

48 Quoted in M. Daly, 'The Modernization of Rural Ireland, *c.*1920–*c.*1960', in Dickson and Ó Gráda (eds.), *Refiguring Ireland*, 359.

49 Ibid., 358–9, 361.

was his own upbringing on a smallholding in Inniskeen, County Monaghan. The poem points up the 'spiritual, sexual, and emotional poverty' especially in small farm Ireland and the perpetually narrow margin between life and death.[50] This bleakness, and the rural depopulation characteristic of so much of Ireland, was lamented by de Valera in a tacit acknowledgement that his government was unable to transform the economy in order to prevent it. The small farm worked by family labour remained his ideal, and formed part of his generally idealised picture of rural life in the most often-quoted part of his St Patrick's Day speech in 1943. That speech, entitled 'On language and the Irish nation' or, more commonly, 'The Ireland we dreamed of', in part echoed the original Fianna Fáil manifesto of 1926. However, it was an image to which de Valera remained convinced that Ireland should aspire, even though he realised and regretted that it would not be possible to turn back the clock to prevent the flight from the land with its attendant implications for rural Ireland.[51]

The increased awareness of the rural social problems occasioned by the war was also evident in Northern Ireland where pressure on housing was exacerbated by the large American military presence, as well as by the evacuation from Belfast of many thousand of its citizens. In addition, the low status, poor health and lack of education opportunities for rural women were highlighted in a BBC documentary in 1945, entitled 'Women on the Land in Ulster'. This programme provoked much indignation from the Ulster Farmers' Union and led to a widespread discussion of the issues involved both in the press and at Stormont. Critics of the programme's allegedly 'unfounded and scandalous statements' were led by Hugh Minford, Unionist MP for Antrim. However, a number of MPs welcomed the documentary's focus on real problems in the countryside.[52] Without the war, it is hard to see how such concerns could have been so widely publicised, and then debated.

Northern Ireland experienced high levels of unemployment compared to Britain during the years before the war, and during the war itself. Despite strong lobbying from the Belfast government after 1935, rearmament did not bring the orders that unionists thought they had a right to expect. The government preferred that work should be brought to workers in Northern Ireland rather than see them migrate to Britain to find employment. This became a political issue especially when Catholics, who were more likely to

---

50 C. Wills, *That Neutral Island*, 253.
51 P. Bew and H. Patterson, *Seán Lemass and the Making of Modern Ireland* (Dublin: Gill & Macmillan, 1982), 4–5.
52 Northern Ireland House of Commons Debates, Vol. 27, 25 January 1945, 2836–8, 3050–78.

be unemployed, saw themselves as coming under disproportionate pressure to migrate. In an official wartime history, migrant workers from Northern Ireland, many of whom worked in war-related industry in north-west England and the Midlands, were described as 'more difficult to handle than those from the South'.[53]

With regard to recruitment to the British armed services from both parts of Ireland, the problems of calculating the numbers involved have long been recognised, as has the question of identifying the motives of those who enlisted. The most recent estimates suggest that during the war 49,302 volunteers from Northern Ireland, and 50,644 from Ireland, enlisted in the British army. In addition, recruitment into the Royal Navy and Royal Air Force brought the probable total for the latter to between 60,000 and 70,000. Although the political context of enlistment in the British army was very different in the Second World War from the First, there were still a number of high-profile critics of the volunteers' actions. Perhaps the most predictable and consistent was *The Leader* which in April 1939 scathingly referred to the volunteer recruits as 'paid cut-throats' and, in June 1945, denounced them as perpetrators of treason. While some believed enlistment was the result of economic necessity, it is clear that several other motives were involved, including a family tradition of military service, an appetite for adventure and a simple desire to fight Nazism. Many of the volunteers actively supported their country's neutral stance and saw no conflict between this and voluntary enlistment in the British army, a force that itself was both multinational and multiethnic. It has been suggested that the British army was a welcoming, pluralist, organisation where volunteers from both parts of Ireland could form friendships, if not a shared identity.[54]

While the demands of neutrality and strict censorship meant little public comment on migration for military or civil purposes, reports on its scale, some of them exaggerated, did appear in the British press. For example, in April 1943, the *Bristol Evening Post* carried a *New York Times* piece from Henry Steele Commager, Professor of History at Columbia University in New York, to the effect that perhaps 100,000 people from neutral Ireland had volunteered for military service in Britain with another 50,000–60,000 in industry and agriculture. Some in the British press misinterpreted this as a sign of opposition to neutrality, but Commager himself noted that the great majority of

---

53 Inman, *Labour in the Munitions Industries*, 174.
54 These observations draw heavily on S. O'Connor, 'Irish Identity and Integration within the British Armed Forces, 1939–45', *Irish Historical Studies,* 39, (2015), esp. 418–19, 438.

the Irish population supported neutrality which was 'not even a debatable issue'.[55] In addition to the numbers, another impressive characteristic of military recruitment was the extensive range of ranks and duties involved: 'from high commanders to lowly private soldiers, from chaplains to commandos, from doctors to dispatch riders, from vets to gunners'.[56] Moreover, volunteers from neutral Ireland were awarded a total of 780 decorations, including eight Victoria Crosses.[57] Among the volunteers were many deserters from the Irish army who were court martialled or dismissed from the service on their return. Almost 5,000 had deserted during the war and not until 2013 would they receive official acknowledgement for their contribution to the war effort as well as a full pardon and amnesty.[58]

In Northern Ireland, publicly there was great support for military conscription from the unionist community – not only in the press but amongst Unionist MPs at Stormont and at Westminster. However, in private there were always misgivings about the impact that conscription would have. Memories of the anti-conscription campaign waged in 1918 by Sinn Féin, in association with the Catholic Church and some Home Rule MPs including Joe Devlin of West Belfast, who also served on the nine-strong nationwide Anti-Conscription Committee, were still relatively fresh. There was every reason to believe that nationalist and clerical opposition would be renewed in earnest should the threat be repeated. Cardinal MacRory had opposed conscription in an open letter to Irish bishops in May 1939 and his opposition would be reiterated on numerous subsequent occasions. The decision was taken in 1939 by Chamberlain, and confirmed later in the war by Churchill, that conscription would not apply to Northern Ireland. Within unionist circles, this decision was widely interpreted as appeasement of de Valera and of northern nationalists,[59] but it was based on a sober assessment of the backlash that conscription would be certain to provoke, as well as the police and troop numbers that would be required to deal with widespread disorder. It remains debatable whether the Belfast government would have introduced conscription at any time during the war had it been within its power to do so.

---

55 *Bristol Evening Post*, 27 April 1943. I am grateful to Nick Conway for this reference.
56 R. Doherty, 'Irish Heroes of the Second World War', in Girvin and Roberts (eds.), *Ireland and the Second World War*, 94.
57 Cormac Kavanagh, 'Irish and British Government Policy towards the Volunteers', ibid., 87.
58 *Irish Independent*, 7 May 2013; *The Times*, 8 May 2013.
59 D1327/20/2/24, Report of the Ulster Unionist Council for 1941, 3: PRONI.

In addition to opposition to conscription, there was considerable difficulty in many areas persuading people to become volunteers in a range of defence services such as Air Raid Precautions and firefighting. The UK National Volunteer register was launched in December 1938 and reflected the concern generated by the Czech crisis in September. National Service Committees, comprising local civic leaders, employers, trade unionists, representatives from the armed forces, the St John Ambulance and the nursing profession, raised the profile of the scheme, but sometimes found it difficult to overcome apathy or the suspicion (including amongst the unemployed) that it would lead to some kind of compulsory government service. In Derry for example, ex-servicemen were said to be 'apathetic' about the scheme, and apparently wanted something more active. As late as May 1940, in a number of areas, there were shortages of volunteers for many of the tasks that the government had identified.[60]

Outside Northern Ireland, the Dublin-based *Irish Times* in the spring of 1939 judged that conscription would bring 'all sorts of trouble north and south of the border', while the *Manchester Guardian* recalled the 'bitter experience' of 1918 and considered that nothing should be done to give a 'holy cause' to the republican movement, or to damage Dublin–London relations. For example, around the time war broke out, there were attacks on soldiers in uniform, along with burnings of gasmasks and the daubing of anti-British graffiti in nationalist areas of West Belfast.[61] Less than a year after the outbreak of war, Sir Basil Brooke was warned by unionists in Derry of the serious dangers that conscription would bring and that 'Derry would go up in flames' if it were introduced.[62] There was much private relief when the British government decided against the introduction of conscription. Churchill's comment in May 1941 that it was 'more trouble than it was worth' reflected the views of many. In his diary, Brooke considered this as 'probably a wise decision'.[63] If this was so, then it placed the onus on civilians to demonstrate their loyalty by strong voluntary recruitment. While the unionist press did much to talk up the initial enlistment figures by writing of a 'recruitment boom',[64] it quickly became apparent, in fact, that the numbers signing up were disappointing, and this shortfall in turn was the source of many nationalist jibes during the war. The figures were especially poor given the high levels of

---

60 Ollerenshaw, *Northern Ireland in the Second World War*, 34.
61 Ibid., 45–6.
62 Diary of Sir Basil Brooke, 12 August 1940, D/3001/D/31, PRONI.
63 Diary of Sir Basil Brooke, May 1941, 15–16, 20–27 D/3001/D/32: PRONI.
64 See, for example, *Belfast Telegraph*, 6 September 1939.

unemployment. For A. V. Judges, a London-based academic attached to the Ministry of Labour and National Service who surveyed the topic in an unpublished report of 1948, there was irritation on the part of the British public at the inequality of sacrifice and at

> the sight of young Ulstermen in possession of jobs which their own menfolk had left to go to war, but it was clear that with the modest total of 25,000 from the declaration of war to March 1941, voluntary recruitment for the forces had made a poor start in Northern Ireland ... and that without compulsory military recruitment there was little to be hoped for in the future from this source.[65]

While many opposed conscription on principle, the particular conditions of employment in the region meant that others feared it would be applied disproportionately to the Catholic and nationalist population. This was because most of the important 'reserved' occupations, such as membership of the RUC or the Special Constabulary, were dominated by Protestants who would therefore be exempted from conscription. In the absence of conscription, another consideration for unionists was that, if they volunteered, their jobs might be taken by nationalists from within the region or by migrants from south of the border. The concerns about immigration, should conscription be introduced, were raised by Dawson Bates at a Cabinet meeting in May 1941.[66] In Omagh, County Tyrone, where the balance of unionists and nationalists in the population was quite fine, a number of young Protestant men in 1941 were said to be 'unanimously in favour of conscription because under it their positions would be guaranteed'. However, several of them also claimed that they would have volunteered long before 'but for the fact that their positions would have been taken by republicans'.[67] During and after the war, this was a question that heightened the significance of the border for nervous unionists always worried about electoral arithmetic, especially in the south and west of Northern Ireland.

In both parts of Ireland, large-scale migration, and the range of rural and urban social problems that the war had revealed, provided fertile ground for discussion of the Beveridge Report on Social Insurance and Allied Services published in December 1942. While it had a British focus, the Beveridge

65 A. V. Judges, 'Irish Labour in Great Britain, 1939–45', excerpted in E. Delaney, 'Irish Migration to Britain, 1939–1945', *Irish Economic and Social History*, 28 (2001), 53.
66 Final Conclusion of a Meeting of the Northern Ireland Cabinet, 21 May 1941: CAB/4/475, PRONI.
67 *Londonderry Sentinel*, 27 May 1941.

Report had immediate implications for Ireland, not only because of the principles of state intervention on which it was based but also for welfare provision in both parts of Ireland in relation to each other and in relation to Britain. South of the border, two Maynooth professors, Cornelius Lucey and Peter McKevitt, were leading commentators on Beveridge and both gave the Report a guarded welcome. Others were more critical. Appreciation of social problems and the justice of universal benefits had to be balanced against the threat posed by a centralised state bureaucracy, and by fears of socialism and totalitarianism which ran counter to the Catholic emphasis on Christian charity and vocationalism, as emphasised in the papal encyclical *Quadragesimo Anno* of May 1931.[68] The latter had emphasised that socialism was based upon 'a theory of human society peculiar to itself and irreconcilable with true Christianity'.[69] The Commission on Vocational Organisation, established by a reluctant de Valera in 1939, was one response to this. However, in the event, its report of 1944 was quietly shelved.

Lucey was careful to emphasise that Ireland was not Britain and that regular financial contributions to support a welfare programme would have serious consequences for small property owners such as shopkeepers and farmers. However, he was also alive to the challenges to be faced, especially with regard to the perpetuation of partition and emigration, if the UK adopted the Beveridge scheme and Ireland did not: 'There is no closing our eyes to the facts. We cannot afford, either from the national or social point of view, to have a social security system that compares unfavourably with that of our nearest neighbours.'[70] Much of the post-Beveridge welfare reform would follow, with children's allowances in 1944, the establishment of Departments of Health and Social Welfare three years later, and the passing of Social Welfare Acts of 1948 and 1952.

In Northern Ireland, there was a similar range of responses to the Beveridge Report. Chronically poor health indicators, reflecting, in part, government indifference since partition, as well as wartime pressures on housing exacerbated by the blitz and the growing strength of organised labour, meant that the debate on Beveridge started immediately. This was reflected in West Belfast, at the by-election held in January 1943, the first in the UK since the

---

68 A. Kelly, 'Catholic Action and the Development of the Irish Welfare State in the 1930s and 1940s', *Archivium Hibernicum*, 53 (1999), 110–12.

69 *Quadragesimo Anno: On Reconstruction of the Social Order*, 15 May 1931, para. 120: http://w2.vatican.va/content/pius-xi/en/encyclicals/documents/hf_p-xi_enc_19310515_quadragesimo-anno.html (accessed 2 October 2017).

70 C. Lucey, 'The Beveridge Report and Éire', *Studies*, 32 (1943), 37.

publication of the Report. The Unionist Party candidate, Sir Samuel Knox Cunningham, spoke for many in the party when he declared in favour of putting welfare reform on hold until after the war had been won. Others in the party and within the civil service were concerned about the cost of Beveridge-style welfare reforms and the high level of employment needed to finance them. By contrast, the Labour candidate in West Belfast, Jack Beattie, was fully in favour of such reforms, and this was a factor in his election victory. Some Protestant clergy such as John Gregg, Archbishop of Armagh, expressed reservations about the threat Beveridge posed to individual independence and initiative, and the dangers of 'feeding out of the hand of the state'.[71] However, shortly after the war, and with additional financial assistance from Britain, the Belfast government had little choice but to embrace the welfare state.[72]

The Economies in Wartime

In Ireland in the five years after 1938, the dearth of raw materials as well as the acute shortage of shipping capacity led to a 50 per cent decline in exports, and an even greater fall in imports. That industrial production was subject to forces outside the government's control was a timely reminder of the limits to self-sufficiency, although one result of the shortage of imports was the increase in foreign reserves. By 1946, Irish residents had accumulated £260 million in external assets, roughly similar to Gross National Product in that year.[73] At an early stage, the government moved to control wages and to limit trade union action. A Dublin Corporation strike that began in February 1940 and lasted two months was instrumental to the introduction of the Wages Standstill Order and the Trade Union Act in 1941. While the former led to a 30 per cent decline in real wages by 1945 (business profits were not formally controlled), the latter exacerbated differences between larger and smaller unions, as well as between those which were Irish-based and those based in Britain. These conflicts, together with the 'red-scare' tactics that enjoyed strong clerical support, led in spring 1945 to a split in the labour movement between the Congress of Irish Trade Unions and the Irish Trades Union Congress. This

---

71 *Irish Times*, 27 October 1943.
72 See J. Privilege, 'The Northern Ireland Government and the Welfare State, 1942–8: The Case of Health Provision', *Irish Historical Studies*, 39, (2015), 439–59.
73 J. Haughton, 'The Historical Background', in J. W. O'Hagan (ed.), *The Economy of Ireland: Policy and Performance of a European Region* (Dublin: Gill & Macmillan, 2000), 32–3.

was preceded by a split in the Labour Party leading to the emergence of the National Labour Party in 1944. The net result was that in 1945 the Irish labour movement was 'weakened, divided and stultified'.[74] Employers' organisations, by contrast, especially the Federation of Irish Manufacturers and the Federated Union of Employers, were not subjected to the same governmental and clerical pressures, and grew stronger during the Emergency.

Ownership and control of shipping, which had long been ignored by government, became a key priority as the dependence on Britain and therefore susceptibility to economic sanctions demonstrated a vulnerability that was damaging both economically and politically. The result was the formation of Irish Shipping in 1941. This was a government-supported company whose bank loans of up to £2 million were guaranteed by the Ministry of Finance, though the success of the enterprise meant that loans were not needed for the long term. The founding of Irish Shipping was one of a number of examples that revealed the Department of Finance's participation in state and state-supported enterprises, and its success meant that it survived into the postwar years.[75]

Agriculture was central to the economies of both parts of Ireland, but was even more important south of the border where during the 1940s it accounted for one in every two jobs.[76] Both the Belfast and Dublin governments introduced a compulsory expansion of tillage acreage primarily to improve the supply of bread at reasonable prices, accompanied by a major publicity effort and threats of penalties for those who refused to comply. The threats of action from the Dublin government became more strident as the war went on and as the consequences of shortfalls in food production became correspondingly more acute. As a slogan, the mildly exhortatory 'Grow more wheat' was replaced by the threatening ultimatum 'Till, or Go to Jail'.[77] The government also went to considerable lengths to ensure the Catholic hierarchy would publicly support the campaign. However, as in Northern Ireland, the Dublin government had to revise its original policies in the light of local circumstances, especially having to pay attention to the quality of land and its capacity for alternative uses. The captive British market no doubt helped

---

74 Dunphy, *Making of Fianna Fáil Power in Ireland*, 268.

75 Fanning, *Department of Finance*, 349–52.

76 C. Ó Gráda and K. H. O'Rourke, 'Living Standards and Growth', in O'Hagan (ed.), *The Economy of Ireland*, 189.

77 See especially B. Evans, 'Coercion in the Irish Countryside: The Irish Smallholder, the State, and Compulsory Tillage 1939–45', *Irish Economic and Social History*, 38 (2011), 1–17; and Evans, *Ireland in the Second World War*, ch. 7.

to sustain agricultural incomes during the Emergency, although problems for farmers remained. These included the severe outbreak of Foot and Mouth disease in 1941, lower British government prices for Irish agricultural produce than before the war, and the dilapidated state of many farms as a result of the depression and Economic War.[78]

Non-compliance by farmers with government directives was penalised, although the ultimate state weapon, dispossession of a farm, was highly contentious in both parts of Ireland and was deployed only as a last resort. In the south, cases of dispossession or fines for non-compliance were publicised, and between 1941 and 1945 farmers were dispossessed of 7,365 acres of land. This compared with only four cases of dispossession in Northern Ireland, where state subsidies raised the level of compliance.[79] The drive to increase tillage proved successful, with acreage expanding from 1.49 million in 1939 to 2.57 million in 1944, the latter being the highest tillage acreage since 1872. The increase was especially significant for cereal crops (wheat, barley and oats). Pasture acreage declined by just over a million between 1939 and 1945 while the total acreage under crops and pasture remained almost the same.[80] The agricultural sector faced shortages of fuel, fertilisers, feedstuffs and machinery, and productivity also suffered as tillage expanded. Despite all these obstacles, in overall terms, gross output of the sector was maintained throughout the Emergency at roughly pre-war levels. By contrast, by 1942 the volume of manufacturing output was just over 75 per cent of the 1939 figure and this figure would not be exceeded until 1946.[81]

During the war, much of the agricultural policy was UK-wide and the government there had learned much from the experience of the First World War. Planning a national agricultural policy had accelerated from 1936 following the Abyssinian crisis and the remilitarisation of the Rhineland. In terms of value, the UK imported some 70 per cent of its food supplies in the last full year of peace (1938), and a significant proportion of animal feedstuffs and fertilisers also came from abroad. The aims of the policy were not only to avoid shortages of essential foods, but also to see how best to control food prices in order to avoid the social unrest and loss of morale which might well accompany shortages and high prices. All of this implied massive and sustained

---

78 J. Meenan, 'The Irish Economy during the War', in Nowlan and Williams (eds.), *Ireland in the War Years and After*, 32–3.

79 Evans, *Ireland in the Second World War*, 140.

80 Meenan, *The Irish Economy since 1922*, 117.

81 Kennedy, Giblin and McHugh, *Economic Development of Ireland in the Twentieth Century*, 50.

state intervention in food production, distribution and sale, with correspondingly difficult negotiations with farmers and their representatives. The most important of the latter was the Ulster Farmers' Union (UFU), formed in 1917 as a wartime innovation to negotiate between farmers and government. The effectiveness or otherwise of agricultural policy was a central part of the war effort as a whole between 1939 and 1945, as it had been between 1914 and 1918.

The Second World War brought significant changes in the production, marketing and control of agriculture as well as in the extent of mechanisation. On the eve of war, almost two-thirds of farms in the region were small (under 30 acres) and during the war the farming sector came under great strain. The centrepiece of wartime agriculture was the expansion of tillage. The Ministry of Agriculture, headed between 1933 and 1941 by Sir Basil Brooke, himself a landowner and accomplished farmer, conducted a campaign via newspapers, radio and public lectures and meetings to drive home the message about increased production. While there were some difficult negotiations between government and farmers, and some initial resistance to Sunday working organised by Presbyterian groups and the Orange Order, in general the response to demands for increased production was positive. In only a few cases did the government meet with such persistent refusal to increase tillage acreage that legal proceedings had to be taken.

The success of the tillage campaign owed much to increased mechanisation. The extent to which lack of knowledge and technology might have seriously held back the campaign is illustrated by the fact that in some areas (e.g. County Fermanagh, Sir Basil Brooke's home county) tillage quotas per farm had to be reduced in 1943 because farmers were 'without implements or knowledge of tillage other than spade work'.[82] At the start of the war there were only 550 tractors at work on farms in the region, compared with 75,000 horses. Aided by a financially advantageous purchase scheme, as well as government-organised training programmes, the number of tractors had risen to 7,301 by 1945, and there had been big increases in the number of tractor-drawn ploughs, disc harrows, self-binders and portable threshing machines. In 1944, the last full year of the war, some 91 per cent of the total ploughed area was devoted to three crops: oats, potatoes and flax. Flax acreage had long been in decline and the linen industry was more dependent on supplies of raw material than almost any other UK industry. Persuading farmers to grow flax was not easy, nor was it a simple crop to grow and harvest. None the less, the region registered an almost fourfold increase in flax acreage

---

82 J. M. Mogey, *Rural Life in Northern Ireland* (Oxford University Press, 1947), 27.

during the war, though it resumed its decline thereafter. As labour became scarcer, some help with gathering in the harvest, especially in the countryside around Belfast and other towns, came from volunteers under the Volunteer Land Scheme, established in 1942. On other occasions, for example the harvest of 1941, help came from the military. As part of the drive to increase the production of fruit and vegetables, the number of allotments rose from 1,500 in 1939 to 8,500 by 1944 and most of these were in the Belfast area.

If agriculture in Northern Ireland benefited from UK-wide policies, the region's manufacturing industries faced many difficulties during the war. Geographical distance from Britain increased business costs and reduced competitiveness in tendering for government contracts. The region's reputation for community conflict was also a disadvantage in this respect. Remoteness from decision-making in London was a problem for Northern Ireland (as it was for Scotland), while devolved government and lack of full political integration were obstacles too. The leading manufacturing industry, linen, was more dependent on raw material supplies from Europe than virtually any other UK industry, and the curtailment of these from an early stage in the war contributed to a level of unemployment which reached 37 per cent in the spring of 1941, with especially serious consequences for women. The linen industry would suffer from excess capacity throughout the war. Textile engineering firms such as James Mackie & Sons Ltd and Combe Barbour saw demand for their products evaporate early in the war but they diversified into new lines, such as shell production and aircraft components. In Derry, even more remote from Britain than Belfast, the city's shirt and collar industry was very slow to receive government orders but these became more frequent during and after 1940.

Harland and Wolff expanded its workforce to more than 30,000 during the war, and a similar number were employed by Short and Harland, aircraft manufacturers. The latter, established only in 1935, was a rare example of a new industry in Belfast and its rate of expansion presented management with almost insurmountable problems of industrial relations that led to the firm becoming probably the most strike-prone of any in the region. This in turn contributed to the move to nationalise the parent company Short Brothers in 1943. Harland and Wolff was a relatively self-contained enterprise that took some time to develop links to sub-contractors. Further, its relations with the Admiralty and with the British government were sometimes severely strained. High costs were one problem, high rates of absenteeism among the workforce, failure to meet production deadlines, and poor facilities for its employees, were others. These culminated with a government- and bank-led move to replace top management in 1943.

War-related orders generated employment levels in manufacturing not seen for a generation, but as labour markets tightened and trade unions gained a rare (if brief) advantage, industrial relations deteriorated to such an extent that Northern Ireland moved from its pre-war position as the least strike-prone UK region to the most strike-prone. In the absence of conscription this led to much criticism of the region's contribution to the UK war effort by leading British politicians including Churchill and Ernest Bevin.[83] The failure to mobilise industry more effectively also contributed to the downfall of John Andrews as prime minister in 1943. The war economy began to contract well before the end of the conflict, and unemployment, especially amongst men, began to rise again and, with it, well-founded anxiety about the future of manufacturing in the region.

Conclusion

In economic terms, the impact of the war on the relative prosperity of the two parts of Ireland was considerable. Incomes in both were comparable before the war, but in the period 1938 to 1947 national income in independent Ireland increased by 14 per cent compared to 84 per cent in Northern Ireland. By the latter date, per capita incomes in the former were about 40 per cent, and those in the latter 70 per cent, of the British level.[84] During the Emergency, the 'balance of power' in Ireland moved increasingly towards the protected business sector and away from the ordinary worker and consumer and, apart from the much-contested introduction of children's allowances in 1944, there was little discernible improvement in social conditions although there would be important welfare reforms between 1947 and 1952.[85] At the end of the war, however, there was little appetite for radical economic change within the government as a whole. Buoyed by the 1944 election victory and the success of neutrality, it faced no serious internal political threats from either armed republicans, or the rival political parties of Labour and Fine Gael. Brian Girvin has suggested that the forces of conservatism were perhaps stronger in 1945 than they had been just before the Emergency.[86]

Widespread consensus on nationalism and self-sufficiency would survive well into the postwar years, while the dependence on a large and, in some respects, inefficient agricultural sector continued to pose challenges for

83 See in general Ollerenshaw, *Northern Ireland in the Second World War*, chs. 2 and 3.
84 Haughton, 'Historical Background', 32.
85 Dunphy, *Making of Fianna Fáil Power*, 221, 257.
86 Girvin, *Between Two Worlds*, 159–60, 167.

development strategists.[87] The country's position as a 'long-haul neutral' was never easy and led to serious tensions with the United States and the UK, but there were no feasible alternatives, and there is now much evidence that the Dublin government went as far as it was possible to go to support the Allies without jeopardising its neutral status.

Despite the many criticisms of its failure to mobilise fully, the role Northern Ireland played in the Battle of the Atlantic, and as a temporary base for US troops between 1942 and 1944, improved the status of the region with the new British Labour government elected in 1945. This was reflected in a number of ways, not least the Ireland Act of 1949 which strengthened Northern Ireland's place in the UK and was introduced after the declaration of the republic by Dublin. With unemployment relatively low, the Belfast parliament pursued an energetic regional economic policy after 1945 in order to attract new industries to offset the decline of the old staples, and the new National Health Service introduced in 1948 constituted a huge change in welfare provision. From the later 1940s to later 1950s the welfare state in Northern Ireland, together with relatively poor economic performance south of the border, 'strengthened the material argument for partition'.[88] At the same time, nationalist critics would find it relatively easy to criticise the Northern Ireland state and its policies. In the United States, the Belfast government would find it difficult to capitalise on the region's wartime role because of the dollar shortage and the highly effective Irish-American lobby. The new Irish Anti-Partition League established in 1945 would publicise the border question and raise other long-standing grievances of the northern nationalist minority nationally and internationally. While there was some effort made to embrace a more inclusive, forward-thinking unionism that might appeal to some members of the Catholic community, it was to founder on the implacable opposition of elements in the Unionist Party. Leading the argument for a more broadly-based unionism was Brian Maginess, then Attorney General, who in a speech to Young Unionists in 1959 suggested that 'We must look on those who do not agree with us, not as enemies but as fellow members of the community' and went on to criticise those who supported a 'policy of apartheid' and exhibited a 'paleolithic mentality'.[89] In the event, Maginess's brand of liberal unionism provoked a backlash in the party and so the opportunity to widen the appeal

87 B. Girvin, 'Economic Policy, Continuity and Crisis in de Valera's Ireland, 1945–61', *Irish Economic and Social History*, 38 (2011), 41–4.

88 H. Patterson, 'Brian Maginess and the Limits of Liberal Unionism', *Irish Studies Review*, 25 (2000), 109.

89 Ibid., 96–7.

of the Unionist Party was lost. The Unionist Party's inability to effect reforms was to a significant extent the result of the financial and vocal importance of hard-line border unionists within the party. Looking back in 1969 when violence in Northern Ireland had become commonplace, North Antrim Unionist MP and Minister of Agriculture Phelim O'Neill lamented that the war had not brought political change: 'The basic problem was that the Unionist Party had always done too little too late. … From 1920 to 1945 one could not have expected much change but since the War was over and change was abroad all over the world, that was the time change should have begun. But the plain fact was that the Unionist Party, unfortunately, did not do so.'[90]

---

90 H. Patterson, 'In the Land of King Canute: The Influence of Border Unionism on Ulster Unionist Politics, 1945–63', *Contemporary British History*, 20 (2006), 511.

PART III

*

CONTEMPORARY IRELAND,
1945–2016

13

Stability, Crisis and Change in Post-war Ireland 1945–1973

BRIAN GIRVIN

De Valera's Achievement and Ireland's Post-war Challenges

This chapter focuses on Ireland from 1945 to 1973, a time of continuity and change. Continuity in policy priorities was established around an agrarian, socially conservative society with Ireland lagging far behind small European states like Denmark that had embraced industrialisation and modernisation. Crucially, this period is also one of change, and possibilities, with the advent of more open industrial policies, the ending of protectionism, the emergence of a liberal minority and the opening of foreign and economic policy to membership of the European Economic Community.[1]

By 1945, Irish politics and society had been transformed after nearly four decades of upheaval. This Ireland is independent, nationalist and Catholic: its democracy is reinforced by a stable constitutional order. Post-war Ireland bears the political and institutional hallmark of what Éamon de Valera and Fianna Fáil had achieved since 1932. This achievement was considerable and established the parameters within which politics and social life would operate for the next thirty years. While not all of post-Emergency, Ireland reflected de Valera's achievement, his influence and that of Fianna Fáil was such that it affects how the period is understood and interpreted.[2] De Valera was still at the height of his powers and influence and his government was considering ambitious post-war plans for Ireland. In 1944, Fianna Fáil had returned to office with a clear majority, confirming its position as the dominant party. The

1 I would like to thank Rona Fitzgerald for her incisive comments on an earlier version of this chapter. The Arts and Humanities Research Council (AH/H0050/1) provided funding that facilitated the research for this work. I am responsible for the content and the views expressed.
2 B. Girvin, *From Union to Union: Nationalism, Democracy and Religion in Ireland* (Dublin: Gill & Macmillan, 2002), 106–200.

opposition was in disarray and every shade of nationalist opinion applauded de Valera's measured and dignified reply to Winston Churchill's criticism of Irish wartime neutrality in May 1945.[3]

Nor was there a backlash against the government with the ending of the Emergency. De Valera's candidate Seán T. O'Kelly won the presidential election in June and Fianna Fáil maintained its grip on local government on the same occasion. Even more remarkable, Fianna Fáil won three of the five by-elections in December 1945 and convincingly won the Cork Borough by-election in June 1946. In contrast, the Labour Party had split into two parties while Fine Gael lacked all direction and seemed unable to find suitable candidates to run in by-elections.[4] De Valera and Fianna Fáil could be forgiven for believing that their place in government was secure and that their task was to continue the policies and strategies that had proved successful since 1932.

Moreover, after thirteen years in office, the political success of Fianna Fáil had transformed Ireland's political culture, its institutional framework and its relationship to the United Kingdom. Ireland was, as de Valera asserted in 1945, a republic in all but name and its relationship to the Commonwealth was ambiguous.[5] In a comparative context, Irish democracy was consolidated and potential threats from the Blueshirts, the IRA and authoritarian Catholic movements had been defeated.[6] Few democracies had survived the inter-war period intact. This consolidation was secured by the introduction of a new constitution in 1937 that underpinned a notable compromise between democracy, nationalism, Catholicism and liberalism. While Irish democracy could be majoritarian, the Constitution provided a Supreme Court with the potential to constrain parliamentary majorities; a potential that was quickly realised.[7]

---

3 Elizabeth Bowen, 'Notes on Ireland', June 1945 for a contemporary view, DO/130/65: TNA. There is no satisfactory study of de Valera or Fianna Fáil during the period from 1945 to 1959; See Girvin, *From Union to Union*, 106–200 for a preliminary assessment; T. P. Coogan's *De Valera: Long Fellow, Long Shadow* (London: Hutchinson, 1993) is particularly deficient for this period and is one-sided generally; D. Ferriter, *Judging Dev: A Reassessment of the Life and Legacy of Éamon de Valera* (Dublin: Royal Irish Academy, 2007) is even-handed but not comprehensive.
4 N. Puirséil, *The Irish Labour Party 1922–73* (Dublin: University College Dublin Press, 2007), 110–32;' Cumann na nGaedheal/ Fine Gael General Purposes Committee, 14 November 1945 Fine Gael Papers 39/1/2; P39/MIN/4 and Fine Gael Party Meetings 5 December 1945: UCDA.
5 *Debates* Dáil Éireann, 17 July 1945, Vol. 97, cc. 2568–75; Maffey memorandum on meeting with de Valera 26 July 1947, 3 August 1946, DO35/2096: TNA.
6 P. Mair, 'De Valera and Democracy', in T. Garvin, M. Manning and R. Sinnott (eds.), *Dissecting Irish Politics: Essays in Honour of Brian Farrell* (UCD Press, 2004), 31–47; Department of the Taoiseach S.13552, NAI, contains extensive criticism of the Report of the Committee on Vocational Organisation.
7 Government legislation was declared unconstitutional in 1943 and 1946, thus establishing this principle.

Moreover, Fianna Fáil demonstrated that significant change could be promoted through democratic means, even in the face of sustained opposition from Fine Gael and the British government.

Fianna Fáil's ascendancy also had a significant impact on socio-economic policy. Protection was introduced for native Irish industry and a significant expansion followed. Major changes in agriculture altered the balance of production towards tillage and small farms, thus weakening the export-based producers who mostly supported Fine Gael. New social policies were promoted and the state, for the first time, took responsibility for the welfare of significant sections of its citizens. New institutions were established, such as the Central Bank in 1944 and the Industrial Relations Act 1946. The government was now in a better position to influence banking, welfare and labour policy. While Ireland ceased to be a minimalist state it never became a welfare state in the comprehensive fashion that emerged after 1945 in western Europe. Less successful were reforms in health and education which remained under denominational control. Despite this, the ambitious proposals in the Health Act 1947 suggest a willingness to explore new policy avenues even in the face of potential opposition from church authorities and vested interests.[8]

Understandably, de Valera would claim that Fianna Fáil 'had always been a progressive party with a long record of political, economic and social achievements', an emphasis reinforced by party publicity and public speakers.[9] However, it was never a left-wing party and might be compared to the broad coalition reformist parties such as the Roosevelt New Deal Democrats in the United States or to Christian Democratic parties in western Europe after 1945. These parties were 'catch-all' parties with progressive and conservative sections, while appealing to a national electorate. In the Irish case, Fianna Fáil's radicalism was constrained by the proprietorial nature of the society, the dominance of farming in the economy and the influence of conservative vested interests. Consequently, radical interventionist economic policies or expansionist fiscal policies were unlikely to be politically successful, as Seán Lemass discovered in 1945.[10] Notwithstanding this, Fianna Fáil had achieved a

---

8 S. Carey, *Social Security in Ireland, 1939–1952: The Limits to Solidarity* (Dublin: Irish Academic Press, 2007); B. Girvin, 'The State and Vocational Education 1922–1960', in J. Logan (ed.), *Teachers' Union: The TUI and its Forerunners* (Dublin, 1999), 62–92; E. McKee, 'Church–State Relations and the Development of Irish Health Policy: The Mother-and-Child Scheme, 1943–53', *Irish Historical Studies* 25 (1986), 159–94.

9 De Valera interview with Len Probich, 1952, P150/3060; UCDA: Frank Aiken speech 11 June 1946, P104/1463: UCDA.

10 B. Girvin, *Between Two Worlds: Politics and Economy in Independent Ireland* (Dublin: Gill & Macmillan, 1989), 131–68.

wide-ranging consensus due to its political success. Fine Gael recognised that continuity had to be maintained in policy terms and its support for neutrality removed one of the main points of disagreement between the two largest parties. Anti-partitionism remained an unchallenged dogma for nationalists; not only was it pervasive but it provided the emotive content to Irish nationalism's sense of superiority and grievance.[11] By the end of the Emergency, most republicans accepted this consensus and acknowledged the legitimacy of the Irish state. When Clann na Poblachta was established as a radical republican alternative to Fianna Fáil, its leaders insisted that they accepted the existing political system and the constitution.[12] Only the IRA stood outside this consensus and the Department of Justice reported in 1947 that the organisation had all but disintegrated.[13]

However, there were also substantial challenges. Within government, fears were voiced that the state would not be able to absorb the estimated 250,000 Irish citizens who were expected to return from war work in Britain or service in the British armed forces. In the event, these fears were not to be realised. The post-war period was characterised instead by accelerated emigration, especially by young women. Despite various initiatives by successive governments after 1945, policy had no discernible impact on the rate of emigration. Fianna Fáil reintroduced the policy mix that had been successful during the 1930s. However, the relatively low level of growth experienced by the Irish economy during the post-war period was never enough to generate the employment necessary to offset the attraction of emigration. The stable nature of the consensus prevented the introduction of policies or indeed innovative thinking to address these problems. In addition, those who remained in Ireland benefitted from the stability and were usually conservative in the face of change. Nor were the majority sympathetic to the many social problems experienced by the less well-off sections of the society. Those on lower incomes were more likely to die from TB than those on middle or higher incomes. Similarly, research demonstrated that lower-income families were much less likely to include meat, milk or fruit in their diet than middle-income families.[14]

---

11 Department of External Affairs memorandum for cabinet 26 October 1947 S. 14002A: NAI. Minutes of cabinet meeting 22 January 1947; Bowen, Notes on Ireland, June 1945: TNA.
12 E. MacDermott, *Clann na Poblachta* (Cork: Cork University Press, 1998), 11–12, 19–43; notes by MacEntee for by-elections 20 October 1947 MacEntee Papers, P67/372, P67/374 for Clann na Poblachta correspondence with MacEntee: UCDA.
13 Justice to Taoiseach's office, 15 May 1947, S.137101: NAI.
14 Department of Health memorandum 17 July 1948 S. 12064A: NAI.

This darker side to Ireland is also apparent in the treatment of less advantaged and marginal groups. The fate of unmarried mothers was especially severe in a society that condemned the 'moral failings' of these women, but did little to help them. Many women emigrated rather than give birth in Ireland. Those who remained were treated as second-class citizens whose children could be adopted by American Catholics. There is also evidence of serious neglect. In one case over 50 per cent of the babies born in a state-supported home died in one year. Other cases of neglect include the industrial homes for boys and the Magdalen laundries for young women.[15] Irish society at this time was not inclusive of Jews and Protestants. Indeed, anti-Semitism was popular and found expression in judicial and state policy. Support for denominationalism in health and education exacerbated the distance between Catholics and Protestants, establishing separate social spheres for the different communities. Fianna Fáil TD Erskine Childers expressed his concerns to his colleagues on a number of occasions. He was critical of Archbishop McQuaid's hostility to Trinity College Dublin and to organisations where Catholics and Protestants collaborated. He believed that Catholic teaching was privileged in the state and in the courts, and he feared that Protestants might be discriminated against in public appointments.[16]

By 1948 the implied promise made by Fianna Fáil in 1945 had not been realised. Though the circumstances that affected Ireland between 1945 and 1948 were not always under the government's control, they were held responsible for the consequences. A strike by teachers weakened morale within the party and the severe weather conditions in late 1946 and early 1947 led to the reintroduction of rationing. The Tánaiste Seán Lemass acknowledged that conditions in January 1947 were 'much more serious now than it was at any time during the war'. A supplementary budget in 1947 was poorly received and the devaluation crisis of the same year undermined the electorate's confidence in government. By this time, there was also a challenge to Fianna Fáil. After Clann na Poblachta won two by-elections in October 1947, de Valera called a general election. Despite Fianna Fáil's many accomplishments, as James

---

15 Report by Stanley Lyons on visit to Britain 4 November 1948 March Papers, MS 8306/ 8/1: TCD; D. Whelan (ed), *Founded on Fear* (Dublin: Irish Academic Press, 2006); 'Home for Unmarried Mothers at Bessboro', Department of External Affairs, P. 99NAI; E. O'Sullivan and I. O'Donnell, *Coercive Confinement in Post-Independence Ireland: Patients, Prisoners and Penitents* (Manchester: Manchester University Press, 2012). And see also the chapters by Earner-Byrne, Cox and Daly in this volume.

16 Childers to MacEntee (no date but from context 1945) P67/269, and Childers to MacEntee 11 February 1948, P67/298 MacEntee Papers; UCDA.

Hogan observed, 'the gratitude of a democratic electorate is notoriously short lived'. This proved to be the case in 1948.[17]

All Change or No Change: The First Inter-party Government 1948–1951

One of the consequences of stability and consensus was that a powerful anti-Fianna Fáil voting block emerged. As differences between all the parties narrowed, the prospect of an alternative government began to emerge. In particular, Fianna Fáil was less likely to receive lower-order vote transfers from other parties and other parties were more inclined to transfer among themselves. This pattern was in evidence at the presidential election in 1945 and again at the by-elections in 1947: it was crucial at the 1948 general election.[18] If de Valera called the 1948 general election as a preventative strike against the rise of Clann na Poblachta, he was only partly successful in stemming the anti-government tide. While it was a close-run election, Fianna Fáil lost. De Valera might have formed a government with support from the National Labour Party, but their TDs recognised that an alternative government was possible and supported the formation of the Inter-Party government, drawing together all five opposition parties and some independents. This outcome was possible because all parties were hostile to Fianna Fáil, and were concerned at the consequences of it remaining in power. It also marked the realignment in Irish politics between Fianna Fáil on one side and everyone else on the other; a pattern that was to continue for the next fifty years. Most remarkably, the gap between the parties on policy issues had narrowed appreciably. It became possible for a conservative party such as Fine Gael to join a government with the republican Clann na Poblachta and agree to a reformist programme. Statesmanship also contributed to this outcome as the Fine Gael leader Richard Mulcahy declined to become Taoiseach due to opposition from Clann na Poblachta. John A. Costello became the consensus candidate for the post when he was sworn in on 18 February 1948.[19]

---

17 Lemass note for Taoiseach, 1 January 1947, Dept of Trade, 97/9/720: NAI; J. Hogan, *Elections and Representation* (Cork: Cork University Press, 1945), 32: K. C. Kearns, *Ireland's Actic Siege: The Big Freeze of 1947* (Dublin: Gill & Macmillan, 2011).

18 M. Gallagher, *Irish Elections 1948–77: Results and Analysis* (London: Routledge, 2009), 31–5, 42.

19 D. McCullagh, *The Reluctant Taoiseach: A Biography of John A. Costello* (Dublin: Gill & Macmillan, 2010); D. McCullagh, *A Makeshift Majority: The First Inter-Party Government, 1948–51* (Dublin: Institute of Public Administration, 1998); McDermott, *Clann na Poblachta* for background to the election and formation of the government.

Fianna Fáil did not adapt well to opposition, believing that the party had been 'cheated' of office. Yet the relative ease with which the Inter-Party government replaced Fianna Fáil reflected the strength of the political system and the robustness of Irish democracy. Costello proved to be an ideal chairman in managing the complex challenges of a coalition government. The new Taoiseach accepted that each cabinet minister would exercise considerable autonomy within the context of the government's overall programme. This worked surprisingly well at first but would bring considerable difficulties later in the life of the government. The new cabinet appeared dynamic when compared to the previous Fianna Fáil government, which seemed tired and out of touch to even its own members.[20] That the government lasted over three years is testament to its success in providing the first real alternative to Fianna Fáil.

The star of the new government was the politically untested Minister for Health Noël Browne. With determination, skill and enthusiasm Browne pushed through an ambitious and comprehensive programme to eradicate TB which remained the major health threat to Irish families, especially those on lower incomes. James Dillon proved to be an energetic, if conservative, Minister for Agriculture, effectively representing the farming sector in government and in successful negotiations with the UK in 1948. Patrick McGilligan had served in the Cumann na nGaedheal government of the 1920s and brought his administrative experience to the Department of Finance. He remained cautious, continuing policies from the previous administration. He proved a foil for the more radical interventions by the Minister for External Affairs, Seán MacBride. MacBride had been IRA Chief of Staff and his emergence as a democratic politician demonstrates the strength of Irish democracy and its constitutional framework. He was ambitious to overhaul what he and his party deemed to be the failures of successive Fianna Fáil governments, especially in the areas of economic development and Irish unity.[21]

The new government was also more overtly clerical than its predecessor. At least four members of the Cabinet were members of the Knights of St Columbanus (a secretive Catholic lay organisation). At its first meeting the government promised 'filial loyalty and devotion' to the Pope and one of its parliamentary secretaries subsequently asserted he was a Catholic first and an

---

20 Childers to MacEntee 11 November 1947 P67/292, MacEntee Papers: UCDA.
21 J. Horgan, *Noël Browne: Passionate Outsider* (Dublin: Gill & Macmillan, 2000); M. Manning, *James Dillon: A Biography* (Dublin: Wolfhound Press, 1999); E. Keane, *Seán MacBride: A Life* (Dublin: Gill & Macmillan, 2007).

Irishman second.[22] Policy was generally cautious and continuity was the main feature of the government. However, the decision to establish the Industrial Development Authority in 1949 had far-reaching impacts. The introduction of a separate capital budget, which distinguished between regular budgetary demands and those for investment, was innovative if short-lived.

The decision to repeal the External Relations Act was the most dramatic action taken by the new government, declaring Ireland a republic and taking the state out of the Commonwealth. That was remarkable for a government led by a Fine Gael Taoiseach, but the decision itself was not unexpected: the British Representative (Ambassador) Lord Rugby had already informed London that repeal was likely. The government cast aside de Valera's ambiguity on the question, agreeing that an independent Ireland should be a republic.[23] This decision is persuasive evidence for the consensus in Irish politics. Unlike the changes introduced by Fianna Fáil during the 1930s, it caused little controversy. This was recognised rather grudgingly by Seán MacEntee in the Dáil but was widely welcomed in the nationalist community. The unintended consequence of this action was to bring partition back to the centre of Irish politics. The British government introduced the Ireland Bill, 1949 which provided that the status of Northern Ireland could not be changed 'without the consent of the parliament of Northern Ireland'. The result was consternation within the nationalist community and led to sustained protests to the British government by MacBride. What the government had failed to appreciate was that Irish neutrality, the declaration of the Republic and its decision not to join NATO had distanced the independent state from the United Kingdom and European opinion.[24] The declaration of the Republic copper-fastened partition and in effect confirmed Unionist hegemony in Northern Ireland. British politicians who had at one time voiced sympathy for Irish unification, such as Ernest Bevin, now refused to consider Irish pleas. Sir Basil Brooke, the Prime Minister of Northern Ireland, called a snap election in 1949, winning thirty-nine out of the fifty seats. The extension of the welfare state to Northern

---

22 C. Crowe, R. Fanning, M. Kennedy, D. Keogh, E. O'Halpin and K. O'Malley (eds.), *Documents on Irish Foreign Policy: Volume IX 1948–1951* (Dublin: Royal Irish Academy, 2014), 1; Brendan Corish is cited in M. Gallagher, *The Irish Labour Party in Transition 1957–82* (Dublin: Gill & Macmillan, 1982), 42.

23 Memorandum by John J. Hearne 'The Kingsmere Conversation' '(The Taoiseach and Prime Minister Mackenzie King)' 9 September 1948, DFA/10/P12/5: NAI. In this conversation Costello explicitly precluded any constitutional connection with the Commonwealth in the future, in *Documents on Irish Foreign Policy* IX, 142–4.

24 The Irish diplomatic record for this controversy is conveniently brought together in *Documents on Irish Foreign Policy Volume IX*, 366–91.

5. Basil Brooke, first Viscount Brookeborough (1888–1973), prime minister of Northern Ireland (1943–63), at home on his country estate, Colebrooke Park, County Fermanagh, ND *c*.1970.

Ireland confirmed Britain's continuing commitment to the province. The income and welfare gap between Northern Ireland and the Republic widened during the 1950s and some Unionists believed that their future had been secured. However, the conflict between nationalists and unionists had not been resolved and stability was short-lived.[25]

By 1950 Ireland was more independent in a formal sense than at any time since 1922 but the cost of that was isolation from developments in Europe and a decline in capacity to influence the British government in diplomatic terms. Britain acknowledged that Ireland had the right to leave the Commonwealth but officials were impervious to Irish demands to change the status quo in Northern Ireland, dismissing Irish complaints as self-inflicted damage to their cause.[26] In addition, delegates to the Council of Europe were dismissive of Irish attempts to use the forum to promote its

25 B. Barton, 'Relations between Westminster and Stormont during the Attlee Premiership', *Irish Political Studies* 7 (1992), 1–20; P. Bew, *Ireland: The Politics of Enmity 1789–2006* (Oxford University Press, 2007), 478–85.
26 'Sir Gilbert Laithwaite to Sir Percival Liesching 16 May 1950, Prem 8/1222 pt 2: TNA.

anti-partitionist position, maintaining that the Council existed to move beyond such narrow concerns.[27]

By the early 1950s independent Ireland was out of step with developments in Europe and uneasy with the changing nature of power that the Cold War had brought. The focus on partition prevented both Fianna Fáil and the Inter-Party government from appreciating the changing balance of global power that US intervention in Europe signalled. This was evident when Ireland addressed American plans for a new strategic and economic order in Europe. The United States remained unsympathetic to Ireland due to its wartime neutrality, and was irritated by persistent attempts to introduce the partition issue into negotiations on the Marshall Plan and NATO. The Taoiseach asserted that Ireland 'wields an influence in the world far in excess of what its mere physical size and the smallness of its population might warrant'.[28] Yet the reality was very different. Not only did Irish politicians and diplomats over-estimate their influence in the United States, Costello and MacBride further annoyed the United States government when they supported a campaign by Irish sympathisers in Congress to amend the Economic Cooperation Act to exclude Britain from further funding as long as partition was continued.[29]

In a comparative context, Ireland was the western European state that was least integrated into the new global order established by the United States. In contrast to Denmark, Ireland was not a member of NATO and did not join any of the multilateral organisations established after 1945.[30] Its relationship with the Organisation for European Economic Cooperation was distant and constrained by the continuing commitment to protectionism. Irish neutrality reinforced this isolationism and its diplomacy concentrated on maintaining the bi-lateral relationship with the United Kingdom. This position was maintained when Fianna Fáil returned to office in 1951, when it refused to ratify the Mutual Security Act with the United States because of Irish neutrality.[31]

27 M. Kennedy and E. O'Halpin, *Ireland and the Council of Europe: From Isolation Towards Integration* (Strasbourg: Council of Europe, 2000), 41–2; 45.

28 Cited in D. Keogh, *Ireland and Europe: 1919–1989* (Cork: Hibernian University Press, 1980), 214; Dáil Debates, 23 July 1948, vol. 112, cc. 1520–21.

29 For a recent detailed assessment of Ireland's involvement in the Marshall Plan, see B. Whelan, 'Ireland, the Marshall Plan and the United States: Cold War Concerns', *Journal of Cold War Studies* 8 (Winter 2006), 63–94.

30 I am grateful to Thorsten B. Olesen, University of Aarhus for identifying the contrasts between Ireland and Denmark during this period.

31 B. Girvin, 'Ireland and the Marshall Plan: A Cargo Cult in the North Atlantic?', in R. T. Griffiths (ed.), *Explorations in OEEC History* (Paris: OECD, 1997), 61–72.

Church, State and the Birth of Liberal Ireland

The Inter-Party government is best remembered for the controversy over the 'Mother and Child' scheme that led to Noël Browne's resignation from the Cabinet in 1951. The scheme would have provided free medical care for a mother and her child without a means test until the child reached the age of 16. Browne then published his correspondence with the Catholic hierarchy, providing for the first time an insight into the complex and opaque relationship between church and state in Ireland. Seán O'Faolain's pithy comment 'The Dáil proposes; Maynooth disposes' may have exaggerated the position, but the *Irish Times* in an editorial made a similar claim. The American writer, Paul Blanshard, acknowledged after a visit to Ireland that while Irish 'political democracy is genuine' it is also 'a clerical state' where an unofficial church–state alliance existed leading to 'ecclesiastical dictatorship and political democracy' living side by side.[32] Blanshard's assessment may seem one-dimensional but he also identified important features of church–state relations. Conflict was never the main feature of the relationship between church and state, as was the case in other Catholic states. A more realistic case can be made for a high degree of consensus among these actors, considerable collusion between them and occasional conflict. Most of the conflicts were managed within the collusive/cooperative sphere, but occasionally came into the open as with the 'Mother and Child' crisis. Even then the Taoiseach John A. Costello complained:

> All these matters should have been, and ought to have been, dealt with calmly, in quiet and in council, without the public becoming aware of the matter. The public never ought to have become aware of the matter.

At times too, there were demarcation disputes over dominance in specific spheres, as demonstrated in the continuing unease over the vocational education sector.[33] More specifically, it was considered appropriate to ask Archbishop McQuaid seek a settlement in a transport strike in 1951. Likewise when legal adoption was introduced, despite their misgivings the hierarchy was deeply involved in the details of the proposed legislation.[34]

---

32 The editorial appeared in *Irish Times* 12 April 1951; P. Blanshard, *Catholic Power in Ireland* (London: Derek Verschoyle, 1954), 27–35, 289–319; S. O'Faolain, 'The Dáil and the Bishops', *The Bell*, 17 (June 1951), 6–7.

33 *Dáil Debates*, Vol. 125, no. 5, c.784; Girvin, 'The State and Vocational Education 1922–1960', 62–92.

34 The standard study of these issues remains J. H. Whyte, *Church and State in Modern Ireland 1923–1979*, 2nd edn., 1980; D. Ó Corráin, *Rendering to God and Caesar: The Irish*

In fact, the Catholic Church was not simply another interest group. During the 1950s it retained its position as the most important institution in civil society. It reached deep into the social fabric of urban and rural society with a direct and daily connection to the lives of most Irish people.[35] During a visit to Ireland in 1945 Elizabeth Bowen observed that:

> The parish priest has complete control of the civic life of any village or small town. Any entertainment must be organised with his approval and, if well seen, generally receives his help.

Just over fifteen years later an American Jesuit concluded his research on Catholicism in Dublin by observing how pervasive the social influence of the Catholic Church was. Other sources both friendly and hostile share these views.[36] Additionally, there is little or no evidence for organised anti-clericalism of the kind found in other predominantly Catholic states in Europe at the same time. Furthermore, public expressions of religious faith were widespread and non-coercive. Questions need to be asked about church power; how and in what way did the Catholic Church influence the legislative programme of successive governments during this period. Did the hierarchy have undue influence over legislation in certain matters and what were the consequences?

The 'Mother and Child' controversy provides an insight into a question that the hierarchy insisted was a matter of faith and morals. The Taoiseach told Browne that it was for the hierarchy and not the minister 'to say whether or not the scheme contained anything contrary to Catholic moral teaching'.[37] However the question cannot simply be reduced to a clash between church and state. A majority of the cabinet was uneasy with the direction of policy. James Dillon had already gone to court to object to Fianna Fáil's legislation. The Taoiseach and Fine Gael were closer to the medical profession than to Browne. They also provided support for the Irish Medical Association in its

---

Churches and the Two States in Ireland, 1949–73 (Manchester: Manchester University Press, 2006).

35 Over 21,000 priests and nuns were registered by the census in 1961.

36 Bowen, 'Notes on Ireland', 18 June 1945; Bruce Francis Biever, *Religion, Culture, and Values: A Cross-Cultural Analysis of Motivational Factors in Native Irish and American Irish Catholicism* (New York: Arno Press, 1976); the book is based on Biever's 1965 PhD dissertation; J. Blanchard, *The Church in Contemporary Ireland* (Dublin: Clonmore & Reynolds, 1963).

37 Costello to Browne 22 March 1951; this and other correspondence are collected in C. Cullen and M. Ó hÓgartaigh (eds.), *His Grace is Displeased: Selected Correspondence of John Charles McQuaid* (Dublin: Merrion, 2013), 92–3.

opposition to Browne's plans. Moreover, Browne acted ineptly at times in his dealings with the hierarchy, his colleagues and the IMA.[38]

It is important not to underestimate the clash between church and state; the hierarchy objected on theological grounds to the extension of state responsibility into an area of policy deemed inappropriate.[39] Its intervention undermined the policy objectives established by the Department of Health, which Browne hoped to implement. That the stance of the hierarchy was crucial can be appreciated by the alacrity with which the cabinet acknowledged its right to adjudicate. Seán MacBride told his colleagues that 'we must therefore accept the views of the Hierarchy in this matter'. He added:

> It is, of course, impossible for us to ignore the views of the Hierarchy. Even if, as Catholics, we were prepared to take the responsibility of disregarding their views, which I do not think we can do, it would be politically impossible to do so.[40]

Nor did the issue end there. Fianna Fáil reintroduced a modified version of Browne's scheme when it returned to office in 1951. This led to acrimonious exchanges between the government and the hierarchy. The eventual compromise was reached with considerable difficulty. While the controversy did not become public knowledge, the hierarchy advised the government that 'it be understood that their acceptance of the amendments is not to be construed as a positive approval of the bill' as the legislation was not in accordance with the Catholic ideal.[41] McQuaid subsequently told the Papal Nuncio that the government had accepted some changes, 'but the Hierarchy has never approved the Act. It may be said that the crookedness of the measure was made sufficiently straight to avoid further condemnation'. McQuaid criticised Lemass and James Ryan who negotiated with the hierarchy on de Valera's behalf, as they maintained the autonomy of the state in the face of this pressure. He complained that the two Ministers were 'mentally incapable of grasping the principles, and the application of the principles, in this Health measure', adding that Lemass 'has been chiefly responsible for the very noteworthy socialisation of our country'. McQuaid linked his criticism of the Health Act with a more general view that this and other measures introduced by de Valera's government 'have tended to emphasise the trend

---

38 Horgan, *Noël Browne*, 59–159.
39 Staunton to Costello 10 October 1950 in Cullen and Ó hÓgartaigh, *His Grace is Displeased*, 88–90.
40 Note by MacBride for cabinet 6 April 1951. S. 14997D, NAI.
41 Archbishop of Cashel to de Valera May 1953. AB8/8/Gov. Box 4. McQuaid Papers, DDA.

6. Éamon de Valera (1882–1975), revolutionary, politician and president of Ireland in jovial mood with the Catholic archbishop of Dublin, John Charles McQuaid (1895–1973). ND c. 1960.

towards excessive State intervention, and, I would add, a latent anticlericalism that fears the influence of the Church and will always seek to eliminate that influence from public life'.[42]

Fianna Fáil proved to be successful in defending the state in the face of clerical criticism without becoming overtly anti-clerical, while Fine Gael was more sympathetic to the hierarchy's position. Yet there were limits here as well. When the rule of law was challenged by the Bishop of Killaloe in a case where a priest and some lay men assaulted two Jehovah's Witnesses, Costello quickly reminded the Bishop that if people took the law into their own hands 'not only would the public peace be threatened but the true interest of religion and morality would inevitably suffer'.[43] Ireland in the 1950s could be illiberal and majoritarian, but it was never theocratic. The Catholic Church was

---

42 McQuaid to Albert Levame, Papal Nuncio, 14 April 1956: AB8/B/XVII/678, McQuaid Papers: DDA.
43 Rodgers to Costello 27 July 1956; Costello to Rodgers, 14 August 1956; Costello to McQuaid 14 August 1956 with McQuaid note dated 16 August 1956. AB8/B/XVIII Government Box 1. McQuaid Papers: DDA.

powerful but not invincible. At a mass level, public opinion by the early 1960s had not changed much; it was intolerant towards other religions and conformist in respect of church teaching. In political terms a significant majority refused to acknowledge that there could be a conflict between church and state. However, if such a conflict occurred over 80 per cent agreed that the church was to be preferred over the state because the former was divinely inspired whereas the state was a man-made institution and therefore fallible.[44]

Notwithstanding this, the 1950s is also the decade when Irish liberalism appears as a coherent movement. Its origins lie in *The Bell* edited by Seán O'Faolain and the foundation of the Irish Association for Civil Liberties in 1948. The campaign against censorship was a key focus for many of these activists but so too was involvement in *Tuairim* established in 1954 by graduates of UCD. Senator Owen Sheehy Skeffington provided continuous public opposition to tyrannies big and small throughout this period.[45] The mobilisation in support of Noël Browne at the 1951 general election was another expression of this, as was liberal Catholic and Protestant opposition to the 1957 boycott of the Protestant community by their Catholic neighbours in Fethard-on-Sea. This case clearly distinguished an intolerant strain in Catholicism from a more moderate one, best expressed by Donal Barrington, a Fianna Fáil supporter and founding member of *Tuairim*, who unequivocally condemned the boycott before a large Catholic audience.[46] By the early 1960s the climate of opinion in Ireland was beginning to change in subtle ways. A new and better-educated generation was exploring possibilities in a world then just emerging.

A Crisis at the Heart of Traditional Ireland: the 1950s

Seán Lemass warned in 1947 that 'we must not approach these post-war problems with a pre-war mentality'.[47] However, successive post-war governments failed to adequately address Ireland's developmental challenges. While

---

44 These data are a summary of Biever, *Religion, Culture and Values*, Table 7, 311
45 'Irish Association for Civil Liberties' contains correspondence with Costello who originally agreed to be a sponsor but withdrew this when he became Taoiseach 97/9/48: Dept. of the Taoiseach: NAI; Archbishop McQuaid kept a close watch on the association – see XXI/59A/1–5: McQuaid papers, DDA. T. Finn, *Tuairim, Intellectual Debate and Policy Formulation: Rethinking Ireland, 1954–1975* (Manchester: Manchester University Press, 2012).
46 Owen Sheehy Skeffington Papers, Fethard-on-Sea file Ms 40,515/8: NLI.
47 Note by Lemass for de Valera 10 January 1947 with additional material prepared by Industry and Commerce, DT: 97/9/720; NAI: Lemass speech to Federation of Irish Manufacturers 11 February 1947, P150/2736: UCDA; Girvin, *From Union to Union*, 147–67.

industry continued to generate employment throughout the 1950s, there was a decline of 100,000 employed by 1960, mostly in agriculture. The economy had received a short-term stimulus between 1949 and 1951 but this was not sustained. Balance of payments difficulties led to deflationary budgets and for most of the 1950s growth and productivity were unimpressive. Elsewhere in Europe, Marshall Plan funding provided a welcome stimulus and was accompanied by the elaboration and implementation of comprehensive long-term policies to meet the new economic challenges that states faced. This is the decade when Ireland fell well behind northern Europe. Per capita income fell from 80 per cent of the western European average in 1950 to 63 per cent by 1960, a ratio that was to be maintained into the 1990s. Emigration soared, the population declined to its lowest level since independence and income and living standards were now far behind European levels. Moreover, while most of western Europe experienced full employment, spectacular growth and unprecedented income and consumption, Ireland experienced a recession by mid-decade that lasted into the 1960s.[48]

The origins of this crisis are complex but three factors can be identified. The first is the failure of agriculture to sustain growth, output and productivity. The land could no longer provide the means to employ those born in rural Ireland and without jobs elsewhere they emigrated. The second was policy continuity. Successive Irish governments maintained existing policies in place fearing that any change would lead to an even greater loss of employment. Finally, Ireland remained aloof from Europe, free trade and the innovative institutional arrangements associated with multilateralism and interdependency. In sharp contrast to other small European states such as Norway, Denmark or Austria, Ireland did not benefit from participation in the European Recovery Programme or the stimulus provided by American funding. Agriculture received most of what investment there was, yet there was no discernible impact on agricultural productivity or output. There was a short-lived construction boom and increased consumption during this period but this was followed by a decade of stagnancy.[49]

The political and social consequences were considerable. Ireland was now more often compared to peripheral European states rather than to the northern core. The secretary of the Department of Finance, T. K. Whitaker

---

48 B. Girvin, 'Did Ireland Benefit from the Marshall Plan?: Choice, Strategy and the National Interest in Comparative Context', in T. Geiger and M. Kennedy (eds.), *Ireland, Europe and the Marshall Plan* (Dublin: Four Courts Press, 2004), 182–220.

49 B. Girvin, 'Economic Policy, Continuity and Crisis in de Valera's Ireland 1945–61', *Irish Economic and Social History* XXXVIII (2011), 36–53.

emphasised the threat to Irish sovereignty: 'after 35 years of native government can it be, they are asking, that economic independence achieved with
such sacrifice must wither away?' The German writer Heinrich Böll recounts
entire families simply deserting their homes, leaving the electricity on and the
milk on the door step. By 1959 in Dublin, nearly 1,500 council tenancies had
been surrendered to the corporation, four times the number from earlier in
the decade. The sense of desperation is also reflected in the view offered by
James Dillon in 1957:

> I think we have to face the fact that we will never be rich in this country ...
> we are primarily an agricultural economy whose material resources consist
> of 12 million acres of arable land and the people who live in it. That will never
> provide in terms of money and goods the same standard of living as is avail-
> able in the great industrial economies.[50]

It is arguable that Ireland was left behind by its conservatism, its isolationism
and its failure to challenge existing vested interests in industry and agriculture.
These were influential but there was a deeper problem. Irish policy makers
could not design policies that would simultaneously integrate Ireland into the
global market while protecting existing employment. Most European states
achieved this by the mid-1950s, but Ireland was still searching for a means to
do so in 1960.

Throughout the 1950s Irish policy makers resisted free trade and did not
welcome the emergence of the European Economic Community or the
European Free Trade Agreement. When the British actively promoted EFTA
there was a real fear that Irish interests would be seriously undermined. The
Irish government appealed to both organisations for special treatment, wishing to benefit from any future arrangements without incurring any 'obligations or responsibilities'. Not surprisingly, neither organisation was prepared
to consider this nor was the UK prepared to support the Irish case.[51] Ireland
remained outside the active centre of European trade, unwilling to see opportunity for the state in becoming involved in any of these ambitious schemes.
Irish reluctance to engage with European integration and free trade dominated government concerns right up to July 1961 when the UK decision to

---

50 Manning, *James Dillon*, 315; H. Böll, *Irish Journal* (Evanston, Illinois: Marlboro Press/
Northwestern, 1998) original German edn. 1957, 52.
51 'Note on the proposal for a "Free Trade Area" embracing the countries of the OEEC
which may wish to join' October 1965; Meeting in Taoiseach's office 11 November
1956: DT S. 15281/A; NAI; 'Aide Mémoire for governments of the Six and Seven' 26 June
1959, S. 15281R; Aide mémoire for Commonwealth Relations Office, 19 September 1959
S. 15281S: NAI

apply for membership of the EEC forced the Irish government to do the same.[52]

Though successive governments were cautious in respect of free trade and Europe, there were some important changes in policy and attitude in response to the crisis. A more open attitude to foreign capital emerged by mid-decade. In 1958 Lemass introduced the Industrial Development (Encouragement of External Investment) Act as a conscious attempt to attract foreign capital to Ireland. Export Tax relief had been introduced in 1956 and the IDA was actively promoting Ireland as a destination for export industry.[53] Despite this, Ireland did not attract significant foreign direct investment until the 1960s, when the domestic policy environment proved more attractive. The secretary of the Department of Finance, T. K. Whitaker, played a decisive role in promoting free trade within the civil service and his influence is detectable when the government decided to publish his study *Economic Development* as an official document, an unprecedented departure from traditional practice. While there is some dispute about the economic impact of *Economic Development* it is rightly seen as promoting a decisive shift in policy direction. This was followed by *The First Programme for Economic Development* which for the first time sought to provide an element of planning to the developmental process.

Lemass and the Management of Change 1959–1966

Ireland remained in crisis when Lemass succeeded de Valera in July 1959. While change was limited, the educated public, sections of the civil service and some politicians recognised that if Ireland was to survive as a sovereign state decisive action was required.[54] Lemass has been described as 'pragmatic', 'idealistic' and 'business like' in his approach to politics. He quickly adopted a more conciliatory attitude to Britain in respect of Northern Ireland, recognising that the empty rhetoric of anti-partitionism had little appeal outside his own party. Lemass was anxious to engage with Unionism and unionists in ways that would have been unthinkable for de Valera. His openness is much in evidence when he made a conciliatory first move by

---

52 B. Girvin, 'The Treaty of Rome and Ireland's Developmental Dilemma', in M. Gehler (ed.), *From Common Market to European Union Building. 50 Years of the Rome Treaties 1957–2007* (Wien: Böhlau Verlag, 2009), 573–95.

53 F. Barry, 'Foreign Investment and the Politics of Export Profits Relief 1956', *Irish Economic and Social History* XXXVIII (2011), 54–72.

54 G. Murphy, *In Search of the Promised Land: The Politics of Post-War Ireland* (Cork: Mercier, 2009).

7. Terence O'Neill (1914–90), prime minister of Northern Ireland, 1963–69.

travelling to Northern Ireland in January 1965 to meet the Unionist Prime Minister Captain Terence O'Neill. While never an iconoclast, Lemass was often sceptical about received opinion, allowing him the political opportunity to modify, but not transform, de Valera's legacy. He remained a nationalist and a partisan politician.[55]

The major challenge remained the economy. By 1961 Ireland's population had fallen to 2.8 million and a significant gap had opened up between Ireland and Europe in income and living standards. Lemass conceded as much: 'it was only after the war, when the rest of Europe went so rapidly ahead in economic expansion and we began to fall behind – and we have not yet succeeded in catching up'.[56] However, he also recognised that the solution to Ireland's

55 J. Horgan, *Seán Lemass: The Enigmatic Patriot* (Dublin: Gill & Macmillan, 1997), 189–326 provides a positive evaluation of Lemass's period as Taoiseach; B. Evans, *Seán Lemass: Democratic Dictator* (Cork: The Collins Press, 2011), 207–65 is more critical but adds little to Lemass as Taoiseach.
56 Speech published in *Gleas: A Monthly Bulletin Issued by Fianna Fáil* 47 (Nollaig, 1959); *Dáil Debates*, 15 April 1964, Vol. 208, cc. 1768–1791.

difficulties was not deflation or lower living standards but sustained growth and expansion. The record for the period 1959 to 1966 suggests some success, but considerable obstacles remained. The economy performed better during the early 1960s than at any time during the 1950s. The *First Programme for Economic Expansion* was not the main contributor to this. The most likely explanations are increased expenditure by the Irish state and favourable conditions in the United Kingdom and Europe.[57] Lemass actively supported policies that would expand the economy, even when these were criticised as inefficient by the Department of Finance officials and fiscal conservatives. Increased public expenditure played a decisive role in this process along with the acceptance of a Keynesian perspective on economic policy. Lemass may have exaggerated the extent to which 'national policy should take a shift to the left' but he could claim by 1964 that confidence had been restored with more dynamism in the economy. He rejected the traditional view 'that governments should stand aside and allow economic and social forces to have free play and to work themselves out' arguing that coordination and planning were necessary ingredients of a modern economy.[58]

This change is evident during the downturn of 1965 to 1966. Unemployment was at its highest level since the 1950s. To prevent recession, the government applied active counter-cyclical measures to promote growth and stimulate the economy. In addition, the outline of a new economic policy was formulated. Ireland was becoming an industrial economy: employment creation, productivity and exports were now dependent on this sector. Foreign companies attracted to Ireland by generous incentives contributed most to this expansion. Consequently the IDA was reorganised and given additional authority to promote Ireland as an attractive location for foreign investment. The state however continued to play an important role in stimulating the economy through its budgetary strategy, promoting the coordination of interest groups and establishing new corporatist agencies such as the National Industrial Economic Council.

The most decisive policy change made by Lemass in this period was the decision to apply for membership of the EEC in 1961. He had been reluctant to act independently of the United Kingdom, but once the UK applied, the Irish became enthusiastic Europeans. This was crucial as the European Commission was sceptical about the Irish application because of the less

57 A. Bielenberg and R. Ryan, *An Economic History of Ireland since Independence* (London: Routledge, 2013), 19–22.
58 *Dáil Debates* Eireann, 15 April 1964, 208, cc.1769–71; 24 April 1963 202, c.305.

developed nature of the Irish economy when compared to the other applicants. De Gaulle's veto over Britain's application and, by extension, over Ireland's provided an opportunity to demonstrate both Ireland's commitment to Europe and its capacity for membership. Foreign policy was now redirected and given a strong European focus. Ireland joined a number of multilateral organisations and successfully negotiated a free trade agreement with the UK in 1965. This agreement was a public expression of Ireland's willingness to dismantle the protectionist system that had been in place since 1932.[59]

Compared to de Valera, Lemass was a moderniser. The economy, employment and emigration were the main focus of government attention between 1959 and 1966. Educational change was driven by the recognition that Ireland had fallen well behind European norms. The introduction of 'free' education and other reforms maintained Fianna Fáil's claim to be progressive, though the changes rarely challenged established interests. More radical was the decision to establish the Commission on Higher Education in 1960 whose report in 1967 contributed to the overhaul of third level education.[60] This in turn had long-term social and economic consequences. There is also a notable shift of emphasis among the political and educational elite. Ireland was no longer isolationist. The state actively engaged with Europe and with the United Nations. Furthermore, the trade union movement, the business sector and the civil service were professionalised and proved open to the influence of modernisation in other European states and in the UK. The Irish public also engaged with developments in other parts of the world largely through the advent of an Irish television service. A new generation of Catholic clergy was influenced by the decolonisation of the 1950s and by the new thinking coming from the Vatican Council. During this time the Irish anti-apartheid movement drew considerable support, determining the nature of the debate over the South African regime. Barriers to new ideas were weakened by the availability of British television in part of the state and through British newspapers. The reform of the censorship system in 1967 contributed to this growing openness.[61]

Lemass was pivotal to this process, though he also sought to secure Fianna Fáil's political dominance and manage the emergence of a new generation of

---

59 M. J. Geary, *An Inconvenient Wait: Ireland's Quest for Membership of the EEC, 1957–73* (Dublin: Institute for Public Administration, 2009), 53–80.

60 J. Walsh, *The Politics of Expansion: The Transformation of Educational Policy in the Republic of Ireland, 1957–72* (Manchester: Manchester University Press, 2009), 62–168.

61 See the essays in B. Girvin and G. Murphy (eds.), *The Lemass Era* (Dublin: University College Dublin Press, 2005); K. O'Sullivan, *Ireland, Africa and the End of Empire* (Manchester: Manchester University Press, 2012), 35–82.

politicians, many of whom he promoted. Always the partisan politician, he wanted to maintain Fianna Fáil's dominance in the party system. Fianna Fáil lost seats at the 1961 election but returned to power by default as there was no real alternative. The 1965 election was probably the last of Ireland's traditional elections but Lemass's success here was more decisive in the absence of a possible coalition.[62] He did more than this, however: he also encouraged civil servants, politicians and the public to think creatively about the future of Ireland. He advised Supreme Court judges to learn from the activism of the Supreme Court in the United States. The German novelist Heinrich Böll noted with some disquiet the considerable change that had occurred since his previous trips in the 1950s. By 1964, Archbishop McQuaid was expressing concern about the changing mood of Ireland, even telling fellow clerics that 'anti-clericalism is evident in the Irish character'. He considered it to be similar to the French variety 'in hardness of intelligence and in irony of criticism of authority'.[63]

Lemass had also begun to re-appraise his position on church and state. He moved cautiously at first, withdrawing support for locating the National Library in the grounds of Trinity College following objections by McQuaid. Lemass was also deeply influenced by the discussions and documents at the Vatican Council, as were Brendan Corish and Declan Costello. In 1964 he effectively criticised the conservative nature of the Catholic Church in Ireland, and in 1965 asked the Minister for Justice to explore the possibility that the Council's Decree on Religious Liberty would permit changes in the constitutional position on divorce (though these would only be applied to non-Catholics). Brian Lenihan initiated discussions with the Chancellor of the Dublin Dioceses who, speaking for the archbishop, rejected any moves in a more liberal direction. Lemass's response to this was significant. During a major speech in 1966 he announced the formation of an informal Oireachtas Committee on the Constitution which he tasked with reviewing its operation and offering recommendations for change. When Lemass retired in November 1966, he joined the committee and played a central role in its subsequent deliberations. The *Report*, published in 1967, reflected Lemass's input on a number of controversial issues including suggested revisions to articles 2 and 3 of the Constitution laying claim to Northern

---

62 Vivion de Valera to Lemass 22 November 1961, Fianna Fáil Papers, P176FF/79: UCDA forwarding details of an opinion poll on the election; Horgan, *Seán Lemass*, 206–10.
63 Committee on the Public Image of the Church, meeting in Archbishop's House, 24 January 1964, McQuaid Papers: DDA.

Ireland, and an amendment to permit non-Catholics to remarry if their religion permitted this.[64]

Change, Controversy and Crisis 1966–1973

Jack Lynch became leader of Fianna Fáil at a time of accelerating social change. His position in the party was never secure.[65] Prominent republicans like Charles J. Haughey and Neil Blaney were never reconciled to his leadership. Cautious and conservative, he was impervious to pressure for reform. For example he was dismissive of efforts to change the status of women and ignored the growing demands for reform of the law on contraception. The Commission on the Status of Women, established in 1970, was a result of feminist mobilisation and support from Charles Haughey and Patrick Hillery rather than any change of view on Lynch's part.[66] He was also faced with rising expectations within Irish society: farmers, trade unionists and the middle classes insisted that they should share in the benefits of expansion and growth. Radical left-wing politics made its presence felt and Marxist and leftist republicanism had a public presence for the first time in a generation. Furthermore the Labour Party moved to the left and adopted a party programme that was both radical and independent. Though much less radical, Fine Gael was also attempting to widen its appeal to the new middle class on a reformist agenda. Lynch's conservatism was in evidence when the Oireachtas Committee published its report on the Constitution. He ignored all the recommendations and instead called a referendum to abolish proportional representation, which the Committee had expressly not offered an opinion on. The government's decision was a humiliation for Lemass and it undermined any possibility of consensus on change which had also been Lemass's aim. Lynch adopted a partisan approach that suited his party and united the opposition against the proposed change. The referendum campaign was acrimonious and the government's proposal was decisively rejected in October 1968.

In contrast to other societies in the late 1960s and early 1970s, Ireland remained conservative at a mass level. The Pope's condemnation of

---

64 B. Girvin, 'Lemass's Brainchild: The 1966 Informal Committee on the Constitution and Change in Ireland, 1966–1973', *Irish Historical Studies* 38 (2013), 406–21.

65 D. Keogh, *Jack Lynch: A Biography* (Dublin: Gill & Macmillan, 2008); J. Walsh, *Patrick Hillery: The Official Biography* (Dublin: New Island, 2008) provide extensive discussion of the period from the perspective of two key figures.

66 For Lynch's correspondence with women's groups see, DT. S.7985B: NAI; B. Girvin, 'Contraception, Moral Panic and Social Change in Ireland, 1969–79', *Irish Political Studies* 23 (2008), 555–76.

contraception in Humanae Vitae was welcomed by many but in unprecedented fashion openly criticised by others. The Labour Party adopted a policy of reform in the area and the first family planning clinic was opened in Dublin in 1969. Support for change had its limits. A majority of those interviewed in the early 1970s continued to support prohibition on contraception. The forces of conservatism clashed openly with those seeking reform at the 1969 general election. The conservatives won decisively. Fine Gael and Fianna Fáil increased their seats in the Dáil, but while their vote increased Labour had a net loss of four seats. Fianna Fáil mounted a defensive campaign, stressing their achievements while criticising the Labour Party's socialism. The implication in some speeches was that socialism was anti-national and un-Irish. It is difficult to assess the impact of this 'red-scare' but what is clear is that Fianna Fáil benefitted from the divisions between Labour and Fine Gael over coalition. The incumbents also benefitted from its partisan re-configuration of the electoral constituencies, which were re-drawn to its advantage. As a consequence, Fianna Fáil maintained its dominance in the political system, extending its electoral appeal throughout the country. It now attracted the most support from every social category and from every region. It also attracted a higher percentage of working-class trade union support than the socialist Labour Party.[67]

This election consolidated Lynch's position as leader but it did not address the divisions within the party. The collapse of order in Northern Ireland in August 1969 provided the opportunity for critics to challenge Lynch's authority and leadership. Lynch along with his moderate colleagues attempted to manage the crisis without aggravating it, but this proved impossible. Lynch proved to be indecisive, losing control of his cabinet and policy towards Northern Ireland as a result. During 1969 and 1970 the actions of Haughey and Blaney challenged not only Lynch's leadership but the security of the state by negotiating with members of the IRA and seeking to import arms to be used in Northern Ireland. More generally, some members of Fianna Fáil considered the crisis an opportunity to secure the unity of Ireland, a key party doctrine. Lynch's hesitance exacerbated the crisis and he remained reluctant to act against Haughey and Blaney.[68] However, he was forced to dismiss them when Liam Cosgrave, the leader of the opposition threatened to reveal

67 J. H. Whyte, 'Ireland: Politics Without Social Bases', in R. Rose (ed.), *Electoral Behaviour: A Comparative Handbook* (New York: Free Press, 1974), 619–52.
68 Keogh, *Jack Lynch*, 163–287; Walsh, *Patrick Hillery*, 203–90; E. O'Halpin, ' "A Greek Authoritarian Phase"? The Irish Army and the Irish Crisis, 1969–70', *Irish Political Studies* 23 (2008) 475–90.

8. Election poster urging support for Jack Lynch (1917–99), Taoiseach 1966–79.

information he had obtained in relation to the importation of arms. This led to a crisis in the party exacerbated by the decision to prosecute Haughey and others involved in the importation of arms. Lynch was further challenged when the prosecution collapsed but he successfully reasserted his authority at a subsequent party meeting. Despite this he also weakened his own position by agreeing to endorse Haughey as a candidate at a future election.[69]

As the security situation deteriorated in Northern Ireland, opinion in the Republic divided on how to respond. Fine Gael and the Labour Party pursued a conciliatory policy while remaining critical of Unionism and the British government. Fianna Fáil did not endorse violence in the north, but attitudes within the party tended to remain militant even while the government was pursuing an anti-IRA security policy. The crisis also had an unintended consequence in that it provided a focus for cooperation between Fine Gael and the Labour Party. Labour had reversed its anti-coalition position in October 1970. Members were concerned at the revelations about the importation of arms and the breakdown of Cabinet responsibility in 1969 and 1970. However, this did not guarantee an agreement between the two parties and Lynch seized the opportunity in February 1973 to call a general election. To Fianna Fáil's surprise, Fine Gael and Labour agreed a programme of government that they presented to the electorate, providing for the first time in nearly twenty years a realistic alternative to Fianna Fáil in government.[70]

By this time Ireland had successfully negotiated membership of the EEC, assuming membership on 1 January 1973. This dramatic change also prompted changes in the constitution for the first time. The third amendment provided the constitutional basis for EEC membership, a requirement because of the implications of membership for Irish sovereignty. A further amendment was required to lower the voting age to 18. Under pressure from the opposition, Lynch agreed to include a constitutional referendum on the special position of the Catholic Church. Article 44 was removed in December 1972. A more subtle change was apparent by 1973. This involved a reconfiguration of political alignment within the party system. By 1973 Fianna Fáil had become the conservative party in Ireland, increasingly reluctant to support change in the Constitution, in respect of Northern Ireland or on moral issues. By this time Fine Gael and the Labour Party had adopted a progressive programme, involving reconciliation in Northern Ireland, changes to the constitution and some social reform. As yet the differences between the two sides were not wide but as new issues appeared the confrontation between conservative and progressive became a defining feature of Irish politics and public life.

---

69 Frank Aiken was a fierce critic of this decision and reluctantly agreed not to publicly criticise it, F. Aiken Jnr, 'Preface', in B. Evans and S. Kelly (eds.), *Frank Aiken: Nationalist and Internationalist* (Dublin: Irish Academic Press, 2014), xv–xx; B. Rice, ' "Hawks Turn to Doves": The Response of the Post-Revolutionary Generation to the "New" Troubles in Ireland, 1969–1971', *Irish Political Studies* 30 (2015), 238–54.

70 C. Meehan, *A Just Society for Ireland: 1964–1987* (London: Palgrave Macmillan, 2013), 83–99.

14

Ireland Transformed? Modernisation, Secularisation and Conservatism since 1973[1]

BRIAN GIRVIN

Introduction

In 1973 Ireland was still a poor predominantly Catholic country on the periphery of Europe with a conservative-nationalist political culture. Notwithstanding this, the country had begun to change and a more liberal and modern outlook was apparent in politics and society. Ireland is now a wealthy, multi-ethnic country deeply embedded in Europe and the global economic system. It is a society that has liberalised in its attitudes and behaviour, highlighted by the passing of a referendum on marriage equality in 2015. Ireland has experienced a process of modernisation and secularisation during this time and converged with the advanced liberal democratic states in Europe. Modernisation and secularisation took time. The period can be divided between a traditional conservative phase from 1973 to the early 1990s and a liberal pluralistic era from then until the twenty-first century. This chapter will focus on the ambiguities within the modernisation process and the impact of secularisation on church–state relations and religious identity. One notable feature was the continuing influence of traditional values that obstructed liberal and progressive initiatives. This provided the basis for successful conservative mobilisation against change. Thus, continuity is as important as change for explaining the nature of Irish politics and society at the end of this process. Furthermore, adaptation and flexibility rather than transformation have been the characteristic features of contemporary Irish history, though the cumulative impact may be transformative.[2]

1 I would like to thank Rona FitzGerald for her assistance, advice and encouragement when writing this chapter. I wish to acknowledge financial support from the Arts and Humanities Research Council, AH/H005013/1.
2 B. Girvin and G. Murphy (eds.), *Continuity, Change and Crisis in Contemporary Ireland* (London: Routledge, 2010), 1–18.

A Point of Departure?

Ireland joined the European Economic Community (EEC) on 1 January 1973 in what proved to be the most significant economic and foreign policy decision made by the Irish state since independence. Since the early 1960s, as noted earlier, membership of the EEC had been a central objective of successive governments' modernisation strategy, with the goal of bringing Ireland up to the socio-economic levels of other Western European states. It was recognised that as a poor region of the EEC, Ireland would benefit from generous transfers under existing programmes. The 1937 Constitution was amended by popular referendum for the first time, representing the first open break with de Valera's Ireland. The amendment was endorsed by 83 per cent of those who voted (on a 71 per cent turnout). The transfer of sovereignty involved in this process dismayed some nationalists. It is likely that de Valera himself voted against the change.[3]

Neither the nature of this change nor its implications were discussed in detail at this time or later; instead priority was given to the economic reasons for joining the EEC. In so far as political considerations entered the discussion, the positive goal of breaking trading links with the United Kingdom (UK) was emphasised. The question of sovereignty remained, and the Attorney General's Office warned in 1975 that European conventions entered into subsequent to joining might not be covered by the 1972 amendment.[4] The Supreme Court clarified the position in *Crotty v An Taoiseach and others* (1986), and subsequent changes to the EEC (and later the European Communities (EC) and European Union (EU)) were placed before the electorate in referendums.

Support among the general public for membership remained high (see Chart 1). By the late 1980s, approximately seventy per cent considered membership to be a good thing, with only 10 per cent considering it to be bad. Tellingly, political and institutional changes in Europe also received considerable support at each of the referendums held to expand the EEC/EC (see Table 1).

---

3 A. D. Devenney, '"A Unique and Unparalleled Surrender of Sovereignty": Early Opposition to European Integration in Ireland, 1961–72', *New Hibernia Review/Iris Éireannach Nua* 12 (2008), 15–32; D. Ferriter, *Judging Dev* (Dublin: Royal Irish Academy, 2007), 353–4.

4 Memorandum on Ireland's Constitutional difficulties in implementing certain proposed conventions between Member States of the European Community' prepared by the Attorney General's Office, February 1975. 2006/40/366 Dept. of the Taoiseach: NAI.

Table 1 *Referendums on Europe 1973–1998*

Date	Topic	Yes	No	Turnout
10 May 1972	Membership	83.1	16.9	70.9
26 May 1987	Single European Act	69.9	30.1	44.1
18 June 1992	Treaty on European Union (Maastricht)	69.1	30.9	57.3
22 May 1998	Treaty of Amsterdam	61.7	38.3	56.2

(*Source*: Department of the Environment, Heritage and Local Government, 2015)

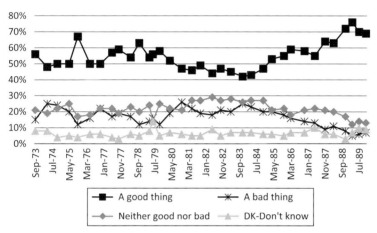

CHART 1. Generally speaking, do you think that (Ireland's) membership of the European Community (Common Market) is …?
(*Source*: Eurobarometer)

One consequence of the referendum process has been a greater public engagement with Europeanisation. Referendums have provided political legitimacy for each change and weakened the type of Euroscepticism that exists in a number of other European states. Europeanisation was often synonymous with modernisation in Ireland and critics found it difficult to counter the charge that their position was conservative or backward-looking. This representation of modernisation was very successful and by the 1980s former critics such as the Labour Party and the trade union movement had abandoned their scepticism and embraced Europe as a positive political objective.

Irish involvement in Europe has been managed by the Taoiseach and the Department of Foreign Affairs. While never simply an elite enterprise, the terms of engagement reflect a wide-ranging consensus among the political parties, the civil service and informed opinion. The policy framework was essentially established during the period 1973–1977 by Garret FitzGerald when, as Minister for Foreign Affairs, he sought to develop a 'distinctive Irish viewpoint' in respect of the EEC. His intention was to distinguish Ireland from the UK on the grounds that failure to do so would 'confirm the impression already existing that we are only a British satellite, without a mind of our own'.[5] Departmental officials shared this view, emphasising that Ireland should 'never seem to be a client state of Great Britain in the Community and we must not allow the British to put us in such a position'. It was also acknowledged that Ireland had acquired commitments:

> No matter how community-minded our partners may be, they still remain nation states and we can hardly expect to take from them all the time and give nothing in return. If this were to be the case, then in the long term we will run the risk that our interests will receive less than due consideration. A member of a club who takes everything going and gives nothing in return rapidly loses the esteem of his fellow members.[6]

FitzGerald made this explicit, arguing that limiting sovereignty was in the interests of small states such as Ireland. He believed it would be judicious to give up the veto exercised by each state, as this was not in Ireland's interest. He also enthusiastically endorsed moves towards economic and monetary union.[7]

In 1972, Taoiseach Jack Lynch claimed that 'In the EEC we can, by becoming better Europeans, become better Irishmen' though it is not entirely clear what he meant by this.[8] Ireland did become European in the sense that it chose the European option over alternatives, even when the benefits were in doubt. The first test came when the UK decided to re-negotiate the terms of membership and hold an in–out referendum. Despite the fact that two-thirds of Irish exports still went to the UK, FitzGerald and his officials agreed that Ireland should remain a member whatever the UK decided. To do otherwise and leave the EEC would 'confirm and even deepen the view that Ireland should be regarded and even regard herself as a United Kingdom appendage'. The government shared this view even if the short-term consequences created difficulties for the economy.[9]

5 'Basis of Irish Foreign Policy', 30 April 1973. DFA, 2005/145/2349: NAI.
6 Conference of Heads of Missions, Policy Issues – EEC Aspects, 16–19 April 1973, DFA 2005/145/2349: NAI.
7 Op. cit., 'Basis of Irish Foreign Policy'.
8 'EEC' contains a transcript of a radio interview with the BBC, 20 December 1972. DT S. 18523T EEC: NAI.
9 'Consequences of British Withdrawal from the Community' 24 February 1975, DT DFA 2006/130/8: NAI; NAIDT 2006/133/296 for detailed background to these discussions;

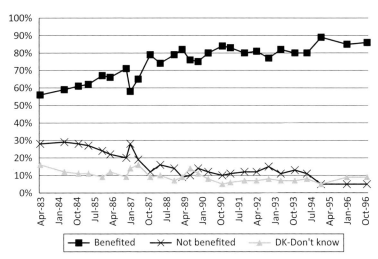

CHART 2. Question: Taking everything into consideration, would you say that (your country) has on balance benefited or not from being a member of the European Community (Common Market)?

(*Source*: Eurobarometer)

While Ireland did not have to make this choice in 1975, a political decision had been made to integrate Ireland into the European 'project'. This was reinforced in 1979 when Ireland broke its long-standing monetary link with sterling to join the European Monetary System.[10] While support for European integration could not be taken for granted, it remained strong until the twenty-first century (see Chart 2).

Nor was this an unrealistic view: by the late 1980s transfers from the EC had risen to the equivalent of 6 per cent of GNP. Ireland remained a net beneficiary until the twenty-first century. It is not surprising that a White Paper on Irish foreign policy in 1996 could assert that 'Irish people increasingly see the European Union not simply as an organisation to which Ireland belongs, but as an integral part of our future. We see ourselves increasingly, as Europeans'. If exaggerated, the claim contains an important truth for the Irish elite even

FitzGerald to Cosgrave 24 January 1975; 'Report of Inter-Departmental Group on Economic Consequences for Ireland of Withdrawal from the European Communities' 23 January 1975. DFA 2006/130/6, NAI.

10 European Monetary System: Dept. of Taoiseach, 2009/135/427–8: NAI; M. Wall, 'Ireland and the European Economic Community, 1973–1977', unpublished PhD thesis, National University of Ireland, Cork (2011).

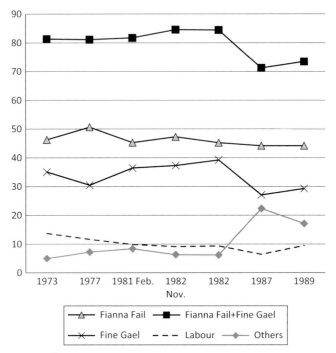

CHART 3. First Preference Vote: 1973–1989

(*Source*: Personal data collection, supplemented by Irish political data section, *Irish Political Studies* various years)

if not for mass opinion.[11] Nor was Irish opinion stable subsequently. The Nice and Lisbon referendums were rejected at first and had to be rerun. Moreover the experience of recession and austerity after 2008 promoted a more sceptical attitude on the part of the electorate.

Continuity in the Political System

If Europe represented change, continuity was the main feature of politics. The political system may have been adapting to new challenges in the early 1970s but Fianna Fáil and Fine Gael dominated elections as they had done since the 1930s. The combined vote for the two parties rarely dropped below 80 per cent during this time (see Chart 3).

11 Government of Ireland, *Challenges and Opportunities Abroad: White Paper on Foreign Policy* (Dublin: Government Publications, 1996), 59; J. Dooge and R. Barrington (eds.), *A Vital National Interest: Ireland in Europe 1973–1998* (Dublin: Institute for Public Administration, 1999).

These continuities in the political system lasted well beyond the 1970s and the 1980s. Fianna Fáil and Fine Gael remained nationalist parties with nation-wide support, reinforced by the 'catch-all' nature of their appeal, the need to compete in every constituency in the state and to attract support from every social category. In 1973, both parties won a seat in every constituency, with Fianna Fáil winning two seats in many constituencies. This pattern continued in 1982, with, however, Fine Gael coming close to Fianna Fáil when winning second seats. Fine Gael was affected by the arrival on the political scene of the Progressive Democrats in 1987 and 1989, but the long-term pattern was resumed in the 1990s. This continuity remained one of the hallmarks of the Irish political process and established the framework for both government formation and policy making.[12]

The 1973 election demonstrated how even a change in government reflected this continuity. The division between Fianna Fáil versus The Rest established during the late 1940s was maintained, but after sixteen years of Fianna Fáil government, Fine Gael and Labour were in a position to offer an alternative government. Jack Lynch had called a snap election in the hope of benefiting from joining the EEC, gambling that the opposition would not reach agreement. Yet this proved not to be the case. He also effectively excluded 140,000 new voters who would not be registered by the time of the election. One of Fianna Fáil's slogans at the election was 'Progress with Stability', yet after four years of turmoil the electorate seemed sceptical that Lynch could deliver either. It was Liam Cosgrave rather than Lynch who was elected Taoiseach on 14 March, forming the National Coalition government with the Labour Party. Cosgrave was personally conservative, but subtle shifts within both parties facilitated an agreement. In 1973, Fine Gael was less conservative on social change, welfare and education and there was considerable support for moderate reform within the party. Labour recognised the limited appeal of its socialism, acknowledging that a coalition was the only alternative to Fianna Fáil in a conservative society. The conflict in Northern Ireland and the arms crisis reinforced fears in both parties that continued Fianna Fáil rule threatened Irish democracy.[13] Fianna Fáil increased its share of the vote at the election but effective transfers between Fine Gael and Labour gave the

12 S. D. McGraw, *How Parties Win: Shaping the Irish Political Arena* (Ann Arbor: Michigan University Press, 2015).
13 C. Meehan, *A Just Society for Ireland? 1964–1987* (London: Palgrave Macmillan, 2013), 83–147; Brendan Corish Papers Box 2 provides considerable insight into labour thinking on the prospects of a coalition in 1973; N. Puirséil, *The Irish Labour Party 1922–73* (University College Dublin Press, 2007), 272–307.

prospective coalition a majority in the Dáil. Despite the change of government, there was no mandate for radicalism. The incoming government offered a cautious reform programme to the public.

The National Coalition seemed more modern after sixteen years of Fianna Fáil government. Some of its members were radical and iconoclastic (none more so than Conor Cruise O'Brien), additionally the agreed programme of government promised much. Increased benefits for welfare recipients and pensioners were well overdue and were welcomed, as were the public support provided for unmarried mothers and deserted wives. An Equal Pay Bill was introduced despite unease at the financial consequences of such a change for some businesses that depended on cheap female labour. The coalition government promoted an active housing policy, building approximately 100,000 new houses during its four years in office. Cosgrave could commend the first government budget to the Fine Gael ardfheis (the annual party conference) with some exaggeration:

> These measures collectively represent the most revolutionary and progressive single step towards a society of justice and compassion that has ever been taken in the history of this State.[14]

While this was an innovative government in some respects, there were limits to what it could achieve. Brendan Corish's ambitious proposals to reform medical and hospital services were thwarted by sustained opposition from the medical profession with support from some Fine Gael members. Minister for Finance Richie Ryan's attempt to introduce a wealth tax foundered on widespread opposition from farmers and those with property and wealth. The wealth tax exposed the real limits to Fine Gael's radicalism and Ryan effectively lost the support of his colleagues and crucial sections of its electorate. The National Coalition's achievements were considerable but these did not benefit it electorally. The government was blamed for the serious economic downturn that occurred as a result of oil price increases and the subsequent inflation and slow down. One of the alarming features of Irish policy making was that at no time between 1973 and 1994 was it possible to guarantee rising living standards, put an end to involuntary emigration and provide employment for all those who wanted it. Successive governments promised much, but electoral behaviour suggested a deep scepticism of how these goals might be achieved.[15]

14 Cited in Meehan, *A Just Society for Ireland?*, 106.
15 R. FitzGerald and B. Girvin, 'Political Culture, Growth and the Conditions for Success in the Irish Economy', in B. Nolan, P. J. O'Connor and C. T. Whelan (eds.), *Bust to Boom?*

In the run up to the 1977 general election, Fianna Fáil challenged the legacy of the outgoing government and published a manifesto outlining an ambitious developmental programme to create the conditions necessary for full employment. Not only did Fianna Fáil promise to abolish the wealth tax, it offered benefits to virtually every section of the electorate. These included the abolition of rates, a £1,000 grant to every first-time house buyer and the removal of road tax on most motor cars. These promises enabled Fianna Fáil to achieve a landslide victory. The Labour Party vote collapsed and Fine Gael lost significantly among large farmers and the professional middle classes. Support for Fianna Fáil was particularly strong among younger groups and those most exposed to the recessionary climate. It was claimed at the time and later that Fianna Fáil 'bought' the general election by 'bribing' the electorate. Certainly, the promises made created serious problems subsequently for the government. Yet the political system cultivated such politics and the electoral cycle prompted a bidding war. Martin O'Donoghue, the architect of the economic programme, defended the policies on Keynesian grounds arguing that sustained economic growth would pay for the Fianna Fáil government's largesse. Fianna Fáil may also have benefitted from the recognition that it had been the party of progress in the past, that in the 1930s and again in the 1960s it had rescued the state from economic uncertainty. Consequently, it could be argued that the 1977 election did not constitute a break with the past for the parties or the political system.[16]

One consequence of the election was that the leadership of all three parties changed. Garret FitzGerald succeeded Cosgrave in Fine Gael and Frank Cluskey became the new leader of the Labour Party. In the case of Fianna Fáil, Jack Lynch's leadership was challenged because of his moderate position on Northern Ireland, the failure of the economic programme and poor electoral results in 1979. The biggest surprise was that Lynch's support for George Colley as his successor was not endorsed by the party, which instead elected Charles Haughey, long-time critic of Lynch as the new leader in December 1979. Haughey had carefully cultivated the conservative and traditional sections of the party who were suspicious of the modernising group associated

The Irish Experience of Growth and Inequality (Dublin: Institute of Public Administration, 2000), 268–85.

16 H. R. Penniman (ed.), *Ireland at the Polls: The Dáil Elections of 1977* (Washington, DC: American Enterprise Institute, 1978); M. Gallagher, 'Societal Change and Party Adaptation in the Republic of Ireland, 1960–1981', *European Journal of Political Research* 9 (1981), 269–85.

9. Charles J. Haughey (1925–2006), three times Fianna Fáil Taoiseach, 1979–92: the dominant and most controversial politician of his generation.

with Lynch and the new liberalism evident in other parties. Haughey, while dynamic in some respects, was conservative on constitutional and moral issues and under his leadership the party moved further to the right (see Illustration 9).

If Fianna Fáil could no longer claim to be a progressive party this was because the nature of progressive politics had changed. There was a subtle change in the position of the parties by the beginning of the 1980s. Progress had been associated with economic growth, welfare benefits and the prospect of full employment, but what now divided the parties was something new: the Constitution, Northern Ireland and the balance to be achieved between church and state. Fine Gael and Labour shared a moderate liberal view on these issues, seeking reforms in each area. Fianna Fáil adopted a defensive attitude on reform, understandably as it had been responsible for introducing the Constitution which enshrined Fianna Fáil's political values in these areas.

Table 2 *Liberal-Conservative Scale on some attitudes in Dublin 1972–73*

Question	Agree	Disagree
There should be very strict control of RTE	28.8	67.7
Catholic Priests should be free to marry	46.7	44.5
Obedience to the directives of the clergy is the hallmark of the true Catholic	44.7	49.1
Homosexual behaviour between consenting adults should not be a crime	45.2	39.9
A thing is either right or wrong and none of this ambiguous woolly thinking	48.4	49.4
Premarital sex is always wrong	57.6	38.5
It is always wrong to use artificial contraceptives	31.3	63.0

Source: MacGréil, *Prejudice and Tolerance in Ireland*, Table 149, 411

The Politics of Morality

Ireland may have remained a conservative society during the 1970s, but in contrast with the early 1960s, change was in the air in Dublin. The city was no longer homogeneous or conformist: opinion was divided on a number of controversial issues on which the Catholic Church had taken a clear public stance (see Table 2).

Public opinion was also divided on Northern Ireland, now a major concern after years of violence. While some 57 per cent endorsed the traditional view that 'national unity' was essential to a 'just solution' to partition, there were also some unorthodox views articulated. Forty-two per cent considered that Northern Ireland and the Republic were 'two separate nations' (55 per cent disagreed). 40 per cent agreed with the statement that 'the position and influence of the Catholic Church in the Republic is a real obstacle to Irish unity' (53 per cent disagreed). When asked if Protestants in Northern Ireland 'have more in common with the rest of the Irish people than they have with the British' over 53 per cent disagreed (37 per cent agreed).[17] Dublin was not representative of the rest of Ireland in 1973, but the attitudinal changes identified here gradually if unevenly spread throughout the country over the following twenty years.[18]

17 M. MacGréil, *Prejudice and Tolerance in Ireland* (Dublin: College of Industrial Relations, 1977) Table 137, 377, 420.
18 M. MacGréil, *Prejudice in Ireland Revisited* (Maynooth: Survey and Research Unit, 1996) which reports a national survey undertaken in 1988–9.

Despite this creeping liberalism, Ireland remained an overwhelmingly Catholic country. In 1971, 94 per cent of the population identified themselves as Catholic. Moreover, the vast majority continued to practise their religion: regular church-going in the early 1970s was in the region of 90 per cent and twenty years later it was still over 80 per cent. If a decline in church-going is one of the hallmarks of secularisation and the weakening of the political influence of organised religion, then the evidence for this in Ireland is quite weak. In a comparative context, Ireland stood apart as the least secularised country in western Europe. What had changed was that issues concerned with morality had become matters of public controversy and the public had divided politically in response to this.[19]

Surveys and opinion polls suggest that an important division appeared in Ireland during the 1970s between liberals and conservatives. The controversy over contraception highlighted these divisions. Contraceptives for women had become easily available during the second half of the 1960s and about 16 per cent of Irish women were using them by the early 1970s (see Chapter by Earner-Byrne). There was also a very high-profile campaign in favour of legalisation. However the Catholic Church remained implacably opposed and traditional members of the Church voiced considerable unease at their availability under any circumstances. A majority opposed legalisation in 1971, but by 1974 there was a majority in favour of limited reform.[20] There was also widespread opposition within Fianna Fáil to the prospect of legalisation, especially after the Catholic hierarchy reasserted its opposition. The Minister for Justice, Desmond O'Malley, wrestled with the question, but failed to draft legislation that would be acceptable to the party or to the majority of Catholics. O'Malley warned his colleagues that appeals to individual conscience would set a precedent that could lead to the introduction of divorce and the legalisation of homosexuality. The National Coalition also remained cautious but was forced to act when the Supreme Court concluded that Mrs Mary McGee's privacy had been infringed when contraceptives intended for

---

19 Mark Franklin, Tom Mackie and Henry Valen et al., *Electoral Change: Responses to Evolving Social and Attitudinal Structures in Western Countries* (Cambridge University Press, 1992, 49); C. T. Whelan (ed.), *Values and Social Change in Ireland* (Dublin: Gill & Macmillan, 1994); T. Fahey, B. C. Hayes and R. Sinnott (eds.), *Conflict and Consensus: A Survey of Values and Attitudes in the Republic of Ireland and Northern Ireland* (Dublin: Institute of Public Administration, 2005).

20 K. Wilson-Davis, 'Irish Attitudes to Family Planning' *Social Studies* 3 (1974), 262–75; Keery Papers, Box 54 'Annual Report of Fertility Guidance Company Ltd., 1970/71', University College Cork Archives (UCCA); *This Week* 25 June 1971; Market Research Bureau of Ireland, 'Religious Practice and Attitudes Towards Divorce and Contraception among Irish Adults' *Social Studies* 3 (1974), 276–85.

her personal use were confiscated. The resultant legislation providing for the legalisation of contraceptives was extremely cautious but even so it was defeated by the combined opposition of Fianna Fáil assisted by a number of government deputies, including, remarkably, Taoiseach Liam Cosgrave, who saw no incongruity in voting against their own government measure.[21]

The incoming Fianna Fáil government in 1977 set about resolving the issue. The Minister for Health Charles Haughey recognised that there was support for a conservative reform which would limit availability to married couples. The legislation was restrictive and conservative, reflecting the extensive dis-cussions Haughey had with representatives of the Catholic hierarchy. Despite this, a number of Haughey's colleagues refused to support the modest reform involved. In an unprecedented move for Fianna Fáil, Lynch resolved this challenge by permitting individuals to abstain from voting on conscientious grounds, possibly weakening his own authority as a result.[22]

Divisions within Nationalism

The other major focus for division and conflict was Northern Ireland. Fear that the violence would spill over into the Republic reinforced a consensus among constitutional nationalist parties to defend the state and apply special counter-terrorist measures against republican militants. Despite this, there emerged serious differences in respect of how the conflict could be resolved. Fianna Fáil adopted the traditional nationalist view that Britain should with-draw from Ireland, and positively encourage the political unification of the island. By contrast, Fine Gael and a majority within Labour emphasised the need for reconciliation with Unionists in Northern Ireland before there could be any move to unity. The tensions between these views were evident dur-ing discussions in the All-Party Committee on the Implications of Irish Unity established by Lynch in January 1972. Most of the eighteen meetings con-cerned the Irish Constitution and how, or if, it should be amended to take account of concerns among Unionists. The most controversial issue con-cerned articles 2 and 3 of the Constitution, which made a territorial claim over Northern Ireland. The main critic of these articles was Conor Cruise

---

21 Fianna Fáil Parliamentary Party minutes, 31 March 1971, P176/448: UCDA; B. Girvin, 'Contraception, Moral Panic and Social Change in Ireland, 1969–79' *Irish Political Studies* 23 (2008), 555–76.

22 NAIDT: 2008/148/217 'Family Planning and Contraception' 13 December 1977 Dept. of Taoiseach, 2008/148/217: NAI; *Magill* (1, 3) December 1977, 27 for poll; NAIDT: 2008/148/217 Note by Lynch 4 May 1979 Dept. of Taoiseach, 2008/148/217: NAI; Fianna Fáil Parliamentary Party minutes 9 May 1979. P176: UCDA.

O'Brien, though he was in a minority in the committee on this question. Cosgrave reconvened the committee in 1973 as the All-Party Committee on Irish Relations which in a subtle shift emphasised reconciliation rather than unity. Fianna Fáil proved to be intransigent and disruptive in opposition and opposed any amendment to the Constitution. One Fianna Fáil committee member justified this on the grounds that article 44 (recognising the 'special position' of the Catholic Church in Ireland) had been amended as a goodwill gesture, but had had no impact on Unionist attitudes.[23]

Irish public opinion was deeply troubled by the violence in Northern Ireland, especially when it spilt over to the Republic. There was considerable ambiguity in southern attitudes towards the north and especially as regards Northern nationalists. While Haughey focused on British responsibility and the 'artificial' nature of Northern Ireland, FitzGerald and other moderates sought alternative policies to promote reconciliation. When he became Taoiseach, FitzGerald promoted the idea of a 'constitutional crusade' to make the Republic more attractive to Unionists, a campaign that was vigorously opposed by Haughey. Mass opinion was divided on a number of issues central to Irish nationalism: in 1983 a third of those polled considered the Irish nation to be limited to the twenty-six counties of the Irish state, while two-thirds believed that it included the whole island. In 1987, 49 per cent believed that Ireland would never be united, while a further 11 per cent thought it might occur in 100 years. In that year also 42 per cent of those polled believed that those who lived in Northern Ireland were both British and Irish, with 33 per cent considering them Irish and 15 per cent British. The Irish public remained nationalistic in the 1980s but were also prepared to consider new initiatives short of unification. There was support for revising articles 2 and 3 of the Constitution, but only as part of a political settlement.[24]

Conservatism and Consensus in the 1980s

By the early 1980s it was possible to measure the strength of conservatism and liberalism amongst the Irish population. Before this, issues concerning church and state, moral values and religion had had little impact on politics.

---

23 Minutes of the All-Party Committee on the implications of Irish unity. Lynch to Cosgrave 8 December 1971: Dept. of Taoiseach, 2004/21/506: NAI.
24 Market Research Bureau of Ireland, *Éire Inniu: An MRBI Perspective on Irish Society* (MRBI, 1987), 47–53; B. Girvin, 'Nationalism and the Continuation of Political Violence in Ireland', in A. F. Heath, R. Breen and C. T. Whelan (eds.), *Ireland: North and South* (Oxford University Press, 1999), 369–400.

The decision to legalise contraception mobilised Catholic traditionalists to protect what were envisaged to be core Catholic and Irish values.[25] This determination was reinforced by the visit of Pope John Paul II and his restatement of conservative Catholic doctrine. There was an air of religious revivalism in response to the Pope's visit and this was taken advantage of by the Pro-Life Amendment Campaign (PLAC) into securing the insertion of a right to life, anti-abortion, amendment into the constitution. This proved to be the most successful populist campaign ever organised in Ireland, until the marriage equality referendum, and attracted support from large numbers of people anxious about the changes occurring in the country. It also generated a less successful liberal counter-mobilisation, which in time persuaded both the Labour Party and Fine Gael to oppose the specific wording of the amendment. The Attorney General Peter Sutherland offered a highly critical assessment of the proposed amendment and Young Fine Gael openly opposed it, to the consternation of conservative Fine Gael members. Fianna Fáil actively promoted the PLAC position and in many parts of the country its members were central to that organisation. The referendum in 1983 was ratified by two-thirds of those who voted after a highly contentious and hugely divisive campaign.[26]

The campaign for the 8th Amendment split Ireland. The conservative majority drew its support from Fianna Fáil, from rural Ireland and from working-class communities within urban Ireland. The liberal minority drew its support from urban Ireland, especially Dublin, from the middle classes and from younger age groups. During the 1980s the conservative majority successfully imposed its position on the country. This group were critical of FitzGerald's constitutional crusade and decisively defeated a proposal to remove the constitutional ban on divorce in 1986. The anti-abortion movement also pursued through the courts family planning clinics that referred patients to Britain for abortions. In addition, the courts upheld various restrictions on information and travel for the purpose of obtaining an abortion. This culminated in the High Court decision in the 'X' case in 1992 when a 14-year-old girl was prohibited from travelling to Britain for a termination. The decision sent shockwaves around the world and Martyn Turner's cartoon in the Irish Times, representing the Irish republic as a prison camp for

25 T. Hesketh, *The Second Partitioning of Ireland: The Abortion Referendum of 1983* (Dun Laoghaire, Co. Dublin: Brandsma Books, 1990); B. Girvin, 'Church, State and Society since 1960', *Éire-Ireland* 43 (2008), 179–204.

26 See 'Eighth Amendment of the Constitution', which contains detailed inter-departmental correspondence and the Attorney General's brief for government 2013/98/28: NAI.

10. The X case divided Ireland and shocked the world. It also provided the opportunity for the first successful challenge to the 8th Amendment in the Supreme Court.

young girls, reflected the anger and dismay of many in Ireland. After a decade of moral politics, the conservative majority had reframed the moral debate within Ireland and there seemed to be little room for compromise between the two Irelands that confronted one another (see Illustration 10).[27]

27 Girvin, 'Church, State and Society', 84–8; Hesketh, *The Second Partitioning of Ireland*.

The divisions that accompanied moral politics did not necessarily extend to other aspects of public life. Fine Gael secured a new political consensus on Northern Ireland and on the economy during this decade. By 1981 it was clear that Lemass's optimistic view that a 'rising tide lifts all boats' was without foundation. The economy was in freefall and though the population was rising, job creation failed to meet the increased demands for employment. By 1981 only 36,316 additional people were in work when compared to 1971.[28] 1981 marked the end of so-called Keynesian demand management as a tool for economic development along with the application of neo-liberal policies to reduce public expenditure, debt and inflation. The Fine Gael–Labour coalition government also abandoned the policy of national wage agreements and excluded trade unions from influence over policy, reflecting the influence of the Irish Farmers Association.[29] Though the coalition government was unpopular, it successfully persuaded the public that austerity was required to secure Ireland's economic and fiscal sovereignty. Alan Dukes, the Minister for Finance, and Taoiseach FitzGerald provided a nationalist case for retrenchment, which proved to be particularly attractive to the middle classes and farmers. Haughey resisted this turn to austerity but Fianna Fáil supporters did not. Fianna Fáil middle-class and farming voters were as likely to support deflation as Fine Gael.[30]

Moreover, though Fianna Fáil won the 1987 election, Haughey had to reverse his opposition to deflation. He applied austerity more vigorously than the outgoing government. A new consensus on economic and fiscal policy emerged out of this election. It was facilitated by the political success of the Progressive Democrats (PDs) led by former Fianna Fáil Minister Desmond O'Malley, which adopted socially liberal moral policies and neo-liberal economic ones. The consensus was reinforced by Fine Gael's new leader Alan Dukes who agreed in the 'Tallaght strategy' to provide external support for the government's deflationary policies. The move to the right was widespread in western Europe but in the Irish case there were limits. Haughey brokered another consensus based on a return to national wage bargaining and an increasingly sophisticated and inclusive form of social partnership, first expressed in *The Programme for National Recovery* in 1987.[31]

28 B. Girvin, 'Before the Celtic Tiger: Change Without Modernisation in Ireland 1959–1989', *The Economic and Social Review* 41 (2010), 349–65.

29 B. Girvin, *The Right in the Twentieth Century* (London: Pinter, 1994), 206–15; G. FitzGerald, *All in a Life: An Autobiography* (Dublin: Gill & Macmillan, 1991), 454.

30 FitzGerald and Girvin, 'Political Culture', 275–81.

31 B. Girvin, 'The Campaign', in M. Laver, P. Mair and R. Sinnott (eds.), *How Ireland Voted: The Irish General Election 1987* (Swords, Co. Dublin: Poolbeg, 1987), 9–29.

This type of neo-corporatism would have been impossible in a government led by Fine Gael, and it took the PDs some time to accept it. The approach reflects Haughey's personal commitment to cooperation in the national interest, acknowledging the need to maintain Fianna Fáil's substantial working class and trade union electoral base. Social partnership became a key element in the transformation of the Irish economy in the late 1980s and early 1990s. It sustained industrial peace, wage restraint and deflation, underpinned by government commitments to weaker sectors of the community and welfare recipients. A significant achievement was the agreement among the social partners that membership of European Monetary Union was both a priority and a national interest and policies were agreed to achieve this.

A new consensus emerged on Northern Ireland. FitzGerald was in favour of a united Ireland but realised that this could not be achieved without addressing Unionist concerns and changing some aspects of politics in the Republic. His constitutional crusade failed to convince either nationalists or Unionists, a failure reinforced by the conservative moral politics of the period. The New Ireland Forum was established in 1983 to provide a constitutional and peaceful solution to the conflict in Northern Ireland. Its report in 1984 was dismissed out of hand by British Prime Minister Margaret Thatcher. Yet it also failed to reformulate nationalist objectives or to move beyond the narrow certainties of traditional nationalism expressed by Haughey. However, the Anglo-Irish Agreement in 1985 changed the nature of the debate, placing Haughey and Fianna Fáil on the defensive (See Chapter 15 by Paul Bew and John Bew). While Dublin acknowledged British sovereignty, the Agreement provided an enhanced role for the Irish state in Northern Ireland. FitzGerald emphasised that the Agreement changed the balance of power in Northern Ireland and provided the basis for change. Haughey concentrated on sovereignty, criticising the Agreement for weakening the Irish claim to the entire island of Ireland.

The detail was much debated but opinion in the Republic by and large welcomed the Agreement as a positive step forward. Fifty-nine per cent supported the Agreement and only 32 per cent agreed with Haughey's position (mainly Fianna Fáil supporters). Some 40 per cent of Fianna Fáil voters approved of the Agreement in 1985 and this increased to 50 per cent over the next year. Once again, Haughey was placed on the defensive and during the election had to shift his position. The PDs provided support for the Agreement in the Dáil and when they were in government after 1989. The Anglo-Irish Agreement undermined Fianna Fáil's dominant position on the national question and laid the foundations for an alternative and moderate policy that emphasised reconciliation over unification.[32] These are significant changes and they challenged Fianna Fáil's dominance in the political system. The party had to respond to this. One of the outcomes is that for the first time Fianna Fáil formed a coalition government with the PDs in 1989, abandoning a long-standing core principle that it would not make such arrangements when forming a government (especially with former Fianna Fáil dissidents). At first, coalition was considered a short-term strategy to remain in government, but in time this too became a stable feature of the political system.[33]

A Turning Point? Ireland in the 1990s

On the surface little seemed to have changed by the beginning of the 1990s.[34] The presidential election in 1990 was the first major challenge to the conservative majority. Mary Robinson was closely identified with progressive politics. A liberal, feminist and human rights activist, she was a hate figure among Irish conservatives (see Illustration 11). However, Labour leader Dick Spring recognised that she could generate support well outside the Labour left. Though nominated by the Labour Party, Robinson retained her independence and refused to re-join the party she had left due to disagreements over the Anglo-Irish Agreement in 1985.[35] Fianna Fáil nominated Brian Lenihan, a long-standing favourite among the party faithful, who was expected to win, while, in the absence of an alternative, Fine Gael nominated Austin Currie, a Northern civil rights activist who had entered southern politics. Lenihan's campaign was undermined by controversy over attempts he had made to pressurise the President not to dissolve the Dáil in 1982. The PDs put pressure on Haughey to dismiss Lenihan thus weakening the party's presidential campaign. Fianna Fáil engaged in muck-raking attacks against Robinson, criticising her radical views and questioning her status as wife and mother. Robinson met these challenges with dignity, demonstrating a stature that had wide appeal. Although Lenihan was ahead on the first count, Robinson won the election with significant transfers from Fine Gael's Currie. Robinson's core vote was located in Dublin and other urban centres but she also attracted a majority of Fine Gael supporters and 72 per cent of PD voters. The presidential election followed the broad patterns of the abortion and divorce referendums, but on this occasion liberals outnumbered conservatives.

32 Girvin, 'Nationalism and the Continuation of Political Violence', 379–83.
33 M. Gallagher and R. Sinnott (eds.), *How Ireland Voted 1989* (Galway: Centre for the Study of Irish Elections, 1990).
34 Whelan, *Values and Social Change in Ireland*, 7–44, 136–86.
35 J. Horgan, *Mary Robinson: An Independent Voice* (Dublin: O'Brien Press, 1997), 124–63.

11. Mary Robinson, first female President of Ireland, 1990–97.

This pattern was maintained at the 1992 general election when Fianna Fáil's vote dropped below 40 per cent for the first time since 1927. This seemed to confirm Spring's view that a new era in Irish politics had begun. More remarkably, Labour eschewed a coalition with Fine Gael, after John Bruton's unsatisfactory handling of the negotiations, and agreed an unprecedented coalition with Fianna Fáil. Even more surprising the programme for government was broadly progressive and included a commitment to hold another referendum on divorce. Although the Fianna Fáil/Labour coalition

426

encountered many difficulties and eventually collapsed in 1994, this progressive turn in Irish politics was maintained. The Supreme Court reversed the High Court's travel ban in the 'X' case and ruled that a pregnant woman who was suicidal had the right to an abortion under the 8th Amendment. This outraged the Catholic hierarchy and the anti-abortion lobby, and three referendums took place on the same day to take account of the Supreme Court's decision. The most controversial was a 'right to life' referendum that would have seriously circumscribed the decision on threatened suicide as a justification for abortion. This proposal was defeated as a result of liberal *and* conservative opposition, if for radically different reasons. The referendums on the right to travel and the right to information were comfortably ratified.[36]

These referendums suggested that on certain issues a liberal majority was available, a pattern confirmed in the divorce referendum that narrowly removed the prohibition on the right to remarry in November 1995. In 1992, Fianna Fáil's Máire Geoghegan-Quinn de-criminalised homosexuality, despite the Catholic hierarchy's explicit condemnation. In the same year the sale of condoms was liberalised without serious controversy. More controversial was the decision to introduce legislation to regulate the circumstances where information could be supplied to individuals wishing to have an abortion in Britain. Strong opposition came, as previously, from the hierarchy, Fianna Fáil and the anti-abortion lobby, yet the legislation was passed after an acrimonious debate. The electorate remained cautious on abortion and it was unlikely that it would be legalised in Ireland. Despite this, the divorce referendum suggested that a majority could be generated for reform in other areas. Moreover, the state and the political parties had reasserted their independence in respect of the hierarchy and the Catholic right and increasingly controlled the legislative process in these sensitive areas.

In 1994 a new government was formed comprising Fine Gael, Labour and the Democratic Left, the so-called Rainbow Coalition. The previous government had collapsed due to lack of trust between Spring and Reynolds, but also because of serious issues to do with possible corruption and sex abuse. Reynolds (see Illustration 12) was forced to resign and Bertie Ahern was elected Fianna Fáil leader, with a commitment to restore the coalition with Labour. While this did not happen, the experience of the 1992 election and the Rainbow Coalition confirmed that for Fianna Fáil coalition was no longer a temporary inconvenience but was now central to future electoral

---

36 Girvin, 'Church, State and Society', 88–92; B. Kennelly and E. Ward, 'The Abortion Referendums', in M. Gallagher and M. Laver (eds.), *How Ireland Voted 1992* (Dublin: Folens/PSAI Press, 1993), 115–34.

12. Albert Reynolds (1932–2014), Taoiseach, 1992–94. With John Hume and Gerry Adams, he played an important role in bringing about the IRA ceasefire of 1994.

and political considerations. Ahern was the main proponent of this position and Fianna Fáil was consequently in a position to offer either a centre-right or a centre-left coalition option to the electorate. This gave the party considerable flexibility in forming governments but seriously restricted its ability to impose its policy priorities on controversial issues such as abortion, divorce or Northern Ireland.

The Politics of the Celtic Tiger 1994–2011

Between 1994 and 2008 change accelerated and seismic shifts appeared in attitudes, behaviour and values. The 'Celtic Tiger' lasted approximately fourteen years, but its impact has continued to affect Irish politics and society. As an economic phenomenon it can be traced back to decisions taken between 1987 and 1994. However, real change was not evident until the second half of the 1990s nor was there agreement that change had indeed occurred. The

Rainbow Coalition did not benefit from these changes and was replaced by a Fianna Fáil-led coalition in 1997. Indeed, at that election a majority remained somewhat sceptical about the state of the economy: just 32 per cent believed that they or their family were better off as a result of the economic boom. The strongest support for this view came from the farming sector and the professional classes. Unemployment remained the most important single issue for nearly two-thirds of those polled in January 1997. By March, crime was also a major concern.[37] On balance the electorate remained cautious if not sceptical about the benefits of economic expansion in 1997.[38]

As a political and social phenomenon the Celtic Tiger had its greatest impact after 1997 and continued on through to 2008. The main beneficiary politically was Fianna Fáil and its new leader Bertie Ahern. The party remained in government from 1997 through to 2011, though always in coalition. The electorate welcomed coalitions and the PD's Michael McDowell played on unease about the prospect of a majority Fianna Fáil government at the 2002 election with the slogan 'One party Government? *No* thanks'.

That Fianna Fáil remained the 'pivot' party at the centre of the political system can be appreciated by its continuing flexibility (or opportunism) in its choice of coalition partners: the Progressive Democrats throughout the period, and the Green Party after 2007 (external support was provided by Independents). If the Haughey and Reynolds factor had weakened Fianna Fáil's appeal in the past, the 'Bertie' factor cemented Fianna Fáil's dominance and seemed to assure them a permanent position in government. For most of his tenure as Taoiseach, Ahern's satisfaction rating remained high: in February 1999 it rose to 70 per cent. The opposition parties remained weak and Fine Gael and Labour struggled to convince the electorate that they could maintain growth and enhance living standards through three successive elections (see Chart 4).[39]

Ireland changed more rapidly during this time than at any period since independence. If continuity and adaptability are the main features of Irish history since 1945, the period after 1997 constitutes a major departure for the society. Ireland becomes an affluent country for the first time, converging with wealthy European neighbours. Its per capita income rose to 141 per cent

---

37 S. King and G. Gillespie, 'Irish Political Data, 1997', in *Irish Political Studies* 13 (1998), 254, 239–40.

38 M. Marsh and P. Mitchell (eds.), *How Ireland Voted 1997* (Boulder, Colorado: Westview Press, 1999).

39 P. Leahy, *Showtime: The Inside Story of Fianna Fáil in Power* (Dublin: Penguin, 2009); G. Murphy, *Electoral Competition in Ireland since 1987: The Politics of Triumph and Despair* (Manchester: Manchester University Press, 2016).

of the EU average by 2003 and Ireland became one of the most expensive countries in Europe to live in. This was reflected in a consumption boom and an inflation in house prices, borrowing and debt. For the first time the country experienced near full employment. Furthermore, unemployment and involuntary emigration ceased to be election issues. The electorate was primarily concerned with health, education and crime at the 2002 and 2007 elections. The population reached four million by 2006 of which 10 per cent were foreign-born. Ireland became a complex multi-ethnic society, reflected in the estimated 167 languages reported in use at the 2006 census. For the most part these migrants were welcome during times of expansion though there is evidence of prejudice and intolerance. The female labour market participation rate increased dramatically from 38.5 to 56.5 per cent by 2004, as demand for labour grew. Attitudes to women in work and to gender equality also changed, reflecting both the stronger presence of women in the workforce and more female-friendly legislation, often driven by EU directives. For example, the Electoral (Amendment) (Political Funding) Bill 2011 included a condition that funding would be reduced if political parties did not nominate at least 30 per cent of women for elections.[40]

Irish society also became more tolerant and pluralistic during this time. Studies on levels of prejudice among the Irish population show a consistent liberalisation in attitude towards specific groups. The changing character of relations between Ireland and the United Kingdom improved attitudes towards the British government due to the active role played by Prime Minister Tony Blair in the peace process that led to the Good Friday Agreement. Attitudes towards Unionists, historically hostile, mellowed dramatically. In 1988–1989 only 30 per cent of respondents would admit Unionists to their family and 18 per cent would deny them citizenship. By 2007–2008, 66 per cent would accept them into the family while only 8 per cent would deny them citizenship.[41] This change is reflected in the overwhelming support for the constitutional referendum that amended articles 2 and 3 of the Irish Constitution and which endorsed the Good Friday Agreement. This does not mean that prejudice or intolerance is absent; however, it does suggest that the overall trend

---

40 T. Fahey, H. Russell and C. T. Whelan (eds.), *Best of Times? The Social Impact of the Celtic Tiger* (Dublin: Institute of Public Administration, 2007).
41 Compare the data in *Irish Times/MRBI Poll* 'Satisfaction Ratings and Party Support Divorce and Northern Ireland' (Market Research Bureau of Ireland/4320/95) September 1995, Table K; and *Irish Times/MRBI Poll* 'Northern Ireland Agreement & Amsterdam Treaty' (Market Research Bureau of Ireland/4704/98) May 1998, Table 12, copies in author's possession; M. MacGréil, *Pluralism & Diversity in Ireland: Prejudice and Related Issues in Early 21st Century Ireland* (Dublin: Columba Press, 2011), 221–26.

is towards more inclusiveness within the society. A good example is the Irish public's attitude to Muslims. In 1988–89 only one in five of the sample would admit Muslims to their family while 24 per cent would deny them citizenship. In 2007–2008, 23 per cent would still deny them citizenship but over 40 per cent would accept them as family members.[42] In political attitudes too, the public was more liberal and majorities endorse non-authoritarian views on a wide range of issues such as gender equality, divorce and contraception.[43]

If modernisation and secularisation are closely associated with liberal attitudes, then this period is clearly a liberal one in comparison to the conservatism of the 1980s or the mixed outcome for the 1990s. Some of this is generational but unexpected factors also contributed to the process. A series of tribunals and reports revealed extensive corruption in public life. Trust in politicians seriously declined, though this may also have reduced traditional deference to them.[44] Confidence in the Catholic Church was undermined by evidence of widespread sex abuse, as well as the unwillingness of church authorities to acknowledge these crimes.[45] These revelations of abuse and cover-ups accelerated patterns of inter-generational change that seriously challenged the church's legitimacy and its authority. Regular church-going had been a major feature of Irish religious life but this fell off rapidly during the Celtic Tiger period. In 1981, 82 per cent of Catholics attended church once a week or more. By 1990 weekly attendance dropped below 60 per cent for the first time. Church attendance fell to 42 per cent by the beginning of the twenty-first century. There has also been a significant growth of those who do not practise a religion or are without religious affiliation. By this time some 65 per cent of those polled expressed little or no confidence in the Catholic Church, further weakening its influence. When President Mary McAleese took communion in a Protestant ceremony she was roundly condemned by the Irish hierarchy. However, the public strongly supported her in this ecumenical act and fully 73 per cent thought her right to do so.[46] Though elected

---

42 MacGréil, *Pluralism and Diversity in Ireland*, 467–78.

43 Fahey, et. al., *Conflict and Consensus*, 114–61.

44 A. P. Mahon (Chair) *The Final Report of the Tribunal of Inquiry into Certain Planning Matters and Payments* (2012): www.oireachtas.ie/parliament/media/committees/ archivedcommittees/cnranda/The-Final-Report-Mahon.pdf; See also details of the Moriarty Tribunal at: www.moriarty-tribunal.ie/asp/detail.asp?objectid=310&Mode= 0&RecordID=545.

45 www.childabusecommission.ie/ Commission of Investigation, *Report into the Catholic Archdiocese of Dublin* (July, 2009).

46 M. MacCárthaigh and K. Totten, 'Irish Political Data', *Irish Political Studies*, 2001, 287– 352, at 319; for a comprehensive discussion of this question Fahey, et al., *Conflict and Consensus*, 30–56.

with the support of Fianna Fáil, McAleese consciously maintained Mary Robinson's commitment to pluralism and inclusiveness during her term of office. This reflects a growing disjuncture between what the general public believes, accepts or tolerates and what the Catholic Church considers what a faithful Catholic should believe.[47]

Despite these significant changes in attitudes and behaviour, most Irish people remain connected with the Church, if much less enthusiastically than before. In 2011, 84 per cent of the Irish population identify themselves as Catholic in the census, and the Catholic Church retains a strong cultural influence in the social sphere. The nature of this relationship with the church is weak however, reflecting the growth and acceptance of secular values in politics and in civic society. This is highlighted in the formulation of policy and legislation which increasingly reflects liberal values rather than religious ones. One example of this is the decline in natural law, a key Catholic construct, as an influence on Supreme Court decision-making in respect of constitutional issues.[48] Another is the extent to which the state now insists on oversight in areas once the preserve of the Catholic Church. Programmes such as the Child Safety Audit and Children First National Guidance 2011 underline this new-found independence on the part of the state as does the public criticism of the Catholic Church by politicians. This can be observed in legislation such as the Criminal Justice (Withholding Information against Children and Vulnerable Adults) Bill 2011. In an unprecedented statement after the publication of the investigation into the Catholic Diocese of Cloyne, the Taoiseach Enda Kenny moved that Dáil Éireann:

> Expresses its dismay at the disturbing findings of the report and at the inadequate and inappropriate response, particularly of the Church authorities in Cloyne, to complaints and allegations of child sexual abuse;
>
> Deplores the Vatican's intervention which contributed to the undermining of the child protection frameworks and guidelines of the Irish State and the Irish Bishops.[49]

---

47 R. Foster, *Luck and the Irish: A Brief History of Change 1970–2000* (London: Allen Lane, 2007), 37–66.

48 P. Hanafin, 'Same Text, Different Story: Reinterpreting Irish Constitutional Identity', *Bullán: An Irish Studies Journal* 4 (1998), 103–19; A. M. Buckley, 'The Primacy of Democracy over Natural Law in Irish Abortion Law: An Examination of the C Case', *Duke Journal of Comparative & International Law* 9 (1998), 275–309.

49 Dáil Debates, Commission of Investigation Report in the Catholic Diocese of Cloyne: Motion, 20 July 2011, cc. 519–32: http://beta.oireachtas.ie/en/debates/debate/dail/2011-07-20/32/ (accessed 4 September 2017).

The most significant aspect of the subsequent debate was the absence of dissent and general approval offered to Kenny for this, the unprecedented critical interrogation of the role of the Catholic Church in the Irish state.

This changing environment has also had an impact on other contentious areas such as abortion and the question of marriage equality and what constitutes a family. The Irish public continues to take a highly restrictive view of the issue of the provision of abortion. By the end of the twentieth century, while 38 per cent considered that homosexuality could never be justified, the comparable figure for abortion was still 60 per cent. However, the absolutist position on abortion was moderated by significant increases in those who considered that there were certain situations when an abortion could be justified. In 2002, 44 per cent considered an abortion should be available if a mother's life was in danger and 34 per cent thought so if the pregnancy was a result of rape.[50] In 2002 Taoiseach Bertie Ahern attempted to reverse the Supreme Court decision in the X case and to exclude threatened suicide by the pregnant woman as a cause for abortion. This constitutional amendment was narrowly defeated, despite active support from the Catholic hierarchy, the Fianna Fáil party and most of the anti-abortion groups. This defeat suggested that liberals and conservatives were fairly evenly divided by this stage. Even more dramatic changes in attitude followed: by 2013, 85 per cent of those questioned were in favour of abortion in certain circumstances and only 12 per cent thought it unacceptable under any circumstances. Over a third considered that abortion should be available 'if in the interest of the woman'.[51]

Abortion legislation has been slow in coming and it took pressure from the European Court of Human Rights and the outcry over the death of Savita Halappanavar, refused an abortion to save her life, to force the government's hand. The introduction of the Protection of Life During Pregnancy Bill, though conservative in intent, dramatically confirmed the significant changes taking place. Introduced by a Fine Gael/Labour coalition government it received overwhelming support from the Dáil. Criticism from the Church and anti-abortion mobilisation failed to weaken the government's resolve. Fine Gael deputies who voted against the Bill lost the party whip. The Taoiseach Enda Kenny insisted in the Dáil on the priority of the state and the constitution over other interests, making a distinction of some importance: 'Therefore, I am proud to stand here as a public representative, as a

---

50 Fahey, et al., *Conflict and Consensus*, 125–33; K. Gilland and F. Kennedy, 'DataYearbook 2002', A supplement to *Irish Political Studies* 17 (2002), Table 9.3 Abortion, 58.
51 P. Murphy and N. Matthews (eds.), 'Data Yearbook 2014', *Irish Political Studies* 29 (2014), 366–7.

Taoiseach who happens to be a Catholic but not a Catholic Taoiseach. I am a Taoiseach for all the people.'[52] Moreover, there was now significant support for a campaign to repeal the 8th Amendment. A further sign of change was the strong support generated for the marriage equality referendum in 2015. Nine years earlier, Bertie Ahern dismissed calls for a referendum on this issue on the grounds that it would be defeated, yet the proposal received the support of 62 per cent in May 2015.

A New Beginning?

Ireland had ceased to be a peripheral state in Europe, except in the geographical sense. Its success provided an example to the new democracies in central and eastern Europe of how convergence with the EU could be managed successfully. Ironically, success also generated considerable tensions between Ireland and the EU when Irish economic policy was criticised in the early 2000s. The Irish government rejected this, arguing that other states might benefit from following the Irish example. Growing scepticism about the future of Europe was in evidence for the first time, contributing to the defeat of the Nice referendum in 2001, albeit on a very low turnout. The government convened a National Forum on Europe in an imaginative attempt to defuse criticism. A second vote in 2003 endorsed the Treaty but only after the government included a section that provided a 'triple-lock' on the state's involvement in military and security matters. When the Lisbon Treaty was emphatically rejected in 2008, the government had to persuade the EU to make concessions before a second vote was taken. These issues were handled with some skill by the government but for the first time there were serious divisions within the elite in respect of the EU and the future of integration. Indeed, the impact of austerity and the role of the EU in the economic crisis have generated scope for even more scepticism about European integration. These concerns reappeared again in 2012 when the electorate endorsed the Treaty on Stability quite convincingly. Fianna Fáil's deputy leader Éamon Ó Cuív resigned his position because he was not prepared to support the party's decision to endorse the Treaty, though he drew back from actively opposing it. However, in the face of serious economic crisis a rejection was unlikely as this might have led to Ireland's exit from the Eurozone Monetary Union.

---

52 *Dáil Debates* Vol. 806, 12 June 2013, cc. 642–52: http://oireachtasdebates.oireachtas.ie/ Debates%20Authoring/DebatesWebPack.nsf/takes/dail2013061200006?opendocument (accessed 4 September 2017).

Despite this, Irish support for further European integration is no longer predictable and concerns about sovereignty in particular remain widespread.[53]

Ireland had been transformed in various ways by the early twenty-first century. Notwithstanding this, the political system and party competition appear impervious to change. Fianna Fáil remains the largest party, a position sustained since 1932. The success of the Celtic Tiger provided it with the opportunity to cement this dominance in government. Continuity was clearly in evidence at the 2007 general election. Bertie Ahern led Fianna Fáil to its third successive election success. Both Fianna Fáil and the Progressive Democrats emphasised stability and continuity, persuading the electorate that their policies would maintain affluence and economic growth. The election campaign was lively, yet the outcome has been described as 'the earthquake that never happened'. Sinn Féin had been expected to do well, yet lost a seat. Fine Gael won an extra twenty seats, without having any material impact on government formation. Continuity is expressed in the combined vote for Fianna Fáil and Fine Gael, which reached its highest level since the 1980s (see Chart 4).[54] The results strongly support the view that the larger parties in the political system were very successful in occupying the centre ground and marginalising smaller or insurgent parties to the left or right.[55]

Notwithstanding this, Fianna Fáil's dominance was quickly challenged. Ahern was forced to resign in 2008 due to unresolved questions concerning his finances. His successor, Brian Cowen promised continuity but under his leadership Fianna Fáil faced a challenge to its very existence. Concerns about the economy were dismissed by the government and there was general agreement that Ireland could expect a 'soft-landing' in the event of a downturn. Dramatically, Ahern had advised critics to commit suicide and he was not alone in ignoring the weaknesses in the economy. The other political parties were complicit. As late as July 2008 Brian Lenihan, Minister for Finance, expressed confidence in the underlying stability of the economy and the policies being pursued by the government.

The recession that followed was unprecedented in independent Ireland. It was also a crisis that was made in Ireland by a combination of government

---

53 B. Girvin, 'Ireland: More Referendums Anyone?', in M. Carbone (ed.), *National Politics and European Integration: From the Constitution to the Lisbon Treaty* (London: Edward Elgar, 2010), 126–43; M. Holmes (ed.), *Ireland and the European Union: Nice, Enlargement and the future of Europe* (Manchester: Manchester University Press, 2005).

54 M. Gallagher, 'The Earthquake that Never Happened: Analysis of the Results', in M. Gallagher and M. Marsh (eds.), *How Ireland Voted 2007* (Houndmills, Basingstoke: Palgrave Macmillan, 2008), 78–104.

55 McGraw, *How Parties Win*, 23–68.

failures and inept policy decisions. It is likely that there would have been a recession in Ireland even if there had not been a Eurozone crisis and a global downturn.[56] The Joint Committee of Inquiry into the Banking Crisis identified a large number of factors that contributed to the crisis, including failures in the banking sector, the irrationality of property developers, oversight weaknesses in state institutions and taxation policy. However, the main failure was in political leadership that focused on short-term considerations and the electoral cycle. This was compounded by the policy model adopted by successive Fianna Fáil-led governments, which was based on an unwarranted optimism in respect of the economy.[57]

Fianna Fáil had benefitted from economic success but it was blamed when the economy collapsed after 2008. The ill-judged guarantee to the banking system led to a collapse in Fianna Fáil's support. This became a rout in 2010 when Ireland effectively lost its economic sovereignty by agreeing a bail out from the major international institutions (the Troika).[58] In 2009 more people left the country than entered it for the first time since 1995. These events provided Fine Gael with the opportunity to project itself as a responsible alternative to Fianna Fáil, particularly to the middle classes. More significantly it afforded Sinn Féin the opportunity to present itself as a nationalist alternative to Fianna Fáil, emphasising strong anti-austerity positions. The 2011 general election shattered Fianna Fáil's dominance in the party system after nearly eighty years as the largest party, winning just twenty seats (see Chart 4).

However, the Irish electorate did not opt for an anti-austerity government but replaced one conservative government with a Fine Gael–Labour coalition that maintained the austerity policies prescribed by the Troika in 2010. Ireland effectively lost its economic and fiscal sovereignty; the stark reality for government was that decisions on the future of the state and its citizens were taken elsewhere. In particular the European Central Bank threatened the Irish government when it sought to have bond-holders share in the cost of the crisis and bail-out. The Joint Committee concluded that 'The ECB position in 2010 and March 2011 on imposing losses on senior bondholders, contributed to the inappropriate placing of significant banking debts on the Irish citizen.'[59]

56 K. Whelan, 'Policy Lessons from Ireland's Latest Depression', *The Economic and Social Review* 41 (2010), 225–54.

57 Houses of the Oireachtas, *Report of the Joint Committee of Inquiry into the Banking Crisis, Volume 1: Report Findings and Recommendations* (Dublin: Houses of the Oireachtas, 2016).

58 M. Marsh and K. Cunningham, 'A Positive Choice, or Anyone But Fianna Fáil?', in M. Gallagher and M. Marsh (eds.), *How Ireland Voted 2011: The Full Story of Ireland's Earthquake Election* (London: Palgrave Macmillan, 2011), 172–204.

59 Joint Committee of Inquiry into the Banking Crisis, *Report*, 17.

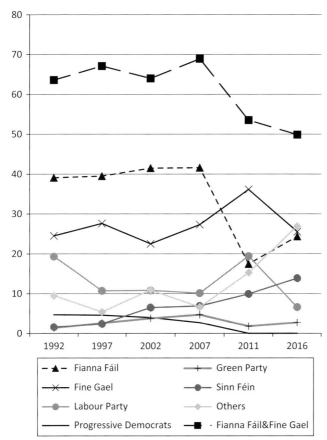

CHART 4. First Preference Vote at General Elections 1992–2016
(*Source*: Personal data collection, supplemented by Irish political data section and Data yearbook, *Irish Political Studies* various years. For 2016 *Irish Times*)

The 2011 Fine Gael–Labour coalition government has managed the economy positively and exited the bailout at the end of 2013. However a majority continued to believe that full sovereignty had not been restored. The Irish austerity programme has been cited by the European Union as a positive example for the politics of retrenchment; however, others consider it exceptional or misleading. Yet Ireland's recovery is real: unemployment dropped from 13 per cent in 2013 to 8.7 per cent in 2016. Exports are up substantially and the country continues to create new jobs and attract impressive inward investment. There are also signs of house price inflation in Dublin and personal debt remains high. In recognition of this, Enda Kenny appeared on the front page

13. Micheál Martin, leader of Fianna Fáil in the general election campaign of 2016. A poster of Enda Kenny, leader of Fine Gael looks on. Following the inconclusive election Fianna Fáil agreed to support a Fine Gael government on a 'supply and confidence' basis in 2016.

of *Time* magazine under the byline 'The Celtic Comeback'. However, his government did not receive much credit for its achievements. The crisis has undermined trust in political parties, the government and in the Dáil. Economic recovery has not changed this negative perception.[60]

The 2016 general election confirmed that there is little relationship between economic recovery and re-election. Fine Gael lost twenty-six seats; its share of

60 Behaviour and Attitudes, *Eurobarometer 84* (European Commission: Brussels, 2015).

14. Populist revolt: large demonstrations were held protesting against water charges, 2015. Steve Humphreys 10th December 2014.

the vote was only three points above its 2002 low. The election was disastrous for Labour, losing thirty seats with its share of the vote at its lowest since 1987. In effect the government lost the election, but no party actually won it. Two factors contributed to this. A majority of the electorate believed they had not benefitted from economic recovery and water charges were widely resented (see Illustration 14). Government formation was the most problematic for decades. In May 2016, Enda Kenny was once again elected Taoiseach, leading a minority government that included a number of independents. Crucially the government was only formed after Fianna Fáil agreed to provide limited external support under strict conditions (See Illustration 13). Fianna Fáil recovered some of the vote lost in 2011 and moved to second position not far behind Fine Gael. However the two parties have a combined vote that is just under 50 per cent, the lowest on record (see Chart 4). Sinn Fein has made considerable advances electorally, receiving 9.9 per cent of the vote in 2011 and 13.85 per cent in 2016. The party now has twenty-three seats in the Dáil and has polled well in local elections and at the 2014 European elections. Support for Sinn Féin is heavily concentrated among the losers in the Great Recession and it is too early to judge if it can make the breakthrough to compete with Fine Gael and Fianna Fáil. There is considerable uncertainty among the electorate: one in four voters now supports independent deputies or smaller parties. The larger parties will be attempting to attract these voters in future elections, but for the moment uncertainty is the main feature of the political system. Moreover, the system remains fragmented; no dominant party has appeared to replace Fianna Fáil at the centre of government formation. The new government and the mainstream parties will have their work cut out to restore confidence in the political system and to secure legitimacy from a sceptical electorate.

15

War and Peace in Northern Ireland: 1965–2016

PAUL BEW AND JOHN BEW

Introduction

Northern Ireland's 'Troubles', the era of violence and political crisis that defined more than three decades of its history (from the late 1960s through to the first decade of the twentieth century), presents a forbidding task for the historian. The recent past remains contested terrain in Northern Ireland, despite the largely successful peace process there. What have become known as 'legacy issues' about the Troubles era continue to cause controversy, with thousands of crimes still unresolved and with varying interpretations advanced of ugly events in Northern Ireland's past. There has yet to be a comprehensive political agreement on the treatment of 'the past'. The fruitless search for such a formula was elegantly captured in David Park's 2009 novel, *The Truth Commissioner*, made into a television drama in 2016. It tells the story of a career diplomat who fails in his efforts to establish a South African-style Truth and Reconciliation Commission because of the vested interests of those in power to prevent full and honest exploration of the past. The picture is further complicated by periodic revelations about the use of agents and informers, the 'origins' of the peace process, material which has come to light through official inquiries, releases of official State Papers in Ireland and Dublin, and even 'unofficial' releases through Wikileaks and other sources such as the leaked transcripts of conversations between former Prime Minister Tony Blair and American President Bill Clinton. Therefore any interpretation of the 'Troubles' has to be conducted on the basis of only partial information, and must also be subject to readjustment because of the rapidly changing evidential environment. The aim of this chapter is not to provide a definitive assessment of the years of 'the Troubles' but to bring a fresh perspective to it, by pulling together a number of these disparate strands. One author, Paul Bew, was closely involved in many of these events from the civil rights marches of 1968 up to the political struggle in and around the Good Friday Agreement of 1998. The other author, John Bew, has covered the release of the State Papers that deal with this epoch for the *Irish Times* for the last decade. The goal here is to offer a synthesis of personal knowledge, a survey of the most important academic literature, and the most recent documentary revelations.

Any serious analysis of the Northern Ireland conflict must begin with an appreciation of the respective roles of the two main state actors, the United Kingdom and the Republic of Ireland, in setting the context for the intercommunal conflict. This is doubly important because the roles of both the British and Irish governments have been the subject of persistent misunderstanding. Successive British governments have publicly asserted since 1990 that they had no selfish strategic or economic interest in Northern Ireland. On the contrary, the province has been something of a strain on its patience and a drain on its purse. Public expenditure in Northern Ireland has risen steadily throughout the Troubles to the point where it is now 23 per cent per head above the UK average. In truth, London has ended up paying for the upkeep of both sides in a sectarian war. For the most part, British cabinets have not considered it possible to leave Northern Ireland, though quitting has been periodically discussed. Some of Prime Minister Edward Heath's bright young men in the Central Policy Review staff believed that this was feasible in 1972. The Labour Prime Minister Harold Wilson was certainly inclined towards withdrawal but was generally dissuaded from going further down this route by his ministers and most of his officials. In the main, most British premiers believed they were stuck with Northern Ireland and that it was certainly unthinkable to have one's hand forced by a terrorist group like the IRA. They have, albeit rather wearily, supported the idea that Northern Ireland should not be forced to leave the UK in defiance of the majority will of its people – the principle of consent.

One reason why withdrawal from Northern Ireland was rejected as a serious option by the British government was the marked hostility of the government of the Irish Republic to any such prospect. British flirtations with withdrawal were normally accompanied by tentative negotiations with the leadership of the Provisional IRA (PIRA) in a way that threatened to undercut the authority of the Irish government. When Harold Wilson authorised a top-level official dialogue with the leadership of the Provisional IRA in 1974/ 5, Irish officials told London that they were both alarmed and indignant at this development. Where was the democratic voice of the Irish people in such a matter, they asked: was it the elected government of Ireland or the leadership of a military conspiracy? More fundamentally, the Irish government well knew that it had neither the army nor the funds to stabilise the North, in the event of a British 'scuttle'. The Troubles allowed plenty of opportunity for rhetorical grandstanding by the leadership of Ireland's main political parties; the Irish national question continued to play a significant part as an organis-ing dynamic in Irish politics (if, decreasingly so, in voters' considerations). However, there was always an underlying reality: Britain simply had to stay in the North, and Irish unity, while apparently desirable in the long term, was to be avoided at all costs in the short- to medium term. Without a sense of the mentality of the London and Dublin governments, the intense inter-communal conflict is inexplicable. The 'war' was more rather than less tragic because it was so inherently futile.

Irish academic researchers are not blessed with the power of prediction. Indeed, it might be argued that precisely the skills that are necessary to con-vey an understanding of a particular past epoch, even one in the recent past, are disabling when it comes to the anticipation of future change or collapse. In the early 1990s, it was common for scholars of Irish republican terrorism in Northern Ireland to stress the potency of the threat posed by the IRA, and its unwavering commitment to the armed struggle, just at the moment when, increasingly infiltrated by British informers and agents, it was taking its first steps towards what became the peace process.[1] There is no reason to be surprised, therefore, by the fact that there is nothing in the academic lit-erature on Northern Ireland that anticipated 'The Troubles' of 1969 to 1997. In 1962, two Quaker liberals, Professor Charles Carter and Dennis Barret published the *Northern Ireland Problem* (Belfast, 1962) in which, while there were some criticisms of government policy, the authors were in the main optimistic about the future. In 1965 Professor Reg Lawrence published his *Government and Politics of Northern Ireland* with its (then) authoritative account of Northern Irish governance and the evolution of its highly beneficial finan-cial arrangements with the British Treasury. These helped to create, by Irish standards, a significant improvement in the standard of living for 'ordinary' people in Northern Ireland. Moreover, Lawrence wrote that the 'student of comparative administration might learn something from the Royal Ulster Constabulary which appears to be an outstanding example of efficient policy organisation on a regional basis'.[2] None of these authors could be described

---

1 See, for example, J. Smyth, 'A Discredited Cause? The IRA and Support for Political Violence', in A. O'Day and Y. Alexander (eds.), *Ireland's Terrorist Trauma: Interdisciplinary Perspectives* (Basingstoke: Palgrave Macmillan, 1989), 101–23.
2 C. Carter and D. Barrett, *Northern Ireland Problem* (Oxford University Press, 1962); R. Lawrence, *The Government and Politics of Northern Ireland: Public Finance and Public Services, 1921–64* (Oxford University Press, 1965).

as Unionist diehards or reactionaries. Professor Carter had been a key figure in the transformation of Irish government economic policy under Seán Lemass and he was widely respected in Dublin. Professor Lawrence, a working-class boy from Hackney, London, had joined the Communist Party in the 1930s, rose from private to captain in the Second World War, got a First in Politics at the London School of Economics and then worked in the cabinet office of Labour Prime Minister Clement Attlee before taking up a lecturing job in Belfast.

In the 1960s, partly as a result of the implementation of Charles Carter's advice – to move away from nationalist economic policy – the Republic's economy began to improve.[3] Few in the north paid much attention. Nor should this academic verdict surprise. In the 1950s and 1960s, all facts of life seemed to favour the Union. The population in the Irish Republic, far from reaching the twenty million predicted by Padraig Pearse in 1916, was falling dramatically. Meanwhile, in 'Ireland unfree', as nationalists decried Northern Ireland, thanks in significant measure to the British welfare state, there had been a substantial rise. G. C. Duggan, the Comptroller and Auditor-General of the Northern Irish government was, in his own quiet way, a believer in Irish unity, who made a point of retiring to Dublin. But Duggan, in his 1954 pamphlet, *A United Ireland* felt it was his duty to point out the economic facts that stood in the way of unity, drawing attention to the relative social services budgets, north and south:

> The [public] assistance bill in the six counties is £4,500,000. In Eire, where external public assistance is drawn on much more austere lines, it is under £2,000,000. If the Northern Ireland model were followed in the South, the latter figure would have been multiplied by above five. In a welfare state, the taxpayers' purse is bottomless, especially if a wealthier neighbour is prepared to guide and help to finance parity of treatment.

The fact that the Catholic community was denied economic and social equality, seemed to be subordinate to this broader fact. The most obvious potential weakness of the Unionist regime – political sclerosis – had been rectified by the retirement of Lord Brookeborough in 1963 and his replacement by Terence O'Neill, who was younger and more open-minded.

As his diaries were to reveal, the new Prime Minister, Terence O'Neill, had liberal convictions, and was inclined towards modernising from the early 1960s.[4]

---

3 P. Bew and H. Patterson, *Seán Lemass and the Making of Modern Ireland* (Dublin: Gill & Macmillan, 1982), 105.

4 M. Mulholland, 'Assimilation versus Segregation: Unionist Strategy in the 1960s', *Twentieth-Century British History*, 11 (2000), 284–307.

He was appalled by the sectarian murder of a Catholic barman in 1966, and hated the 'simmering nastiness' he saw in extremist Protestant politics. He was also determined to reverse the electoral gains made by the Northern Ireland Labour Party (NILP) in Belfast between 1958 and 1962, partly at the expense of his Official Unionist Party. To this end he embraced a rhetoric and practice of planning and modernisation, though he was reluctant to confront the structural political elements of anti-Catholic discrimination (such as the demand for 'one man-one vote' against the old propertied franchise). Overall, O'Neill's view was that economic plenty would dissolve the old antagonisms over local government. It was a view that disturbed some Protestants who listened to the militant preacher, the Reverend Ian Paisley, but did not feel themselves particularly privileged under the existing system. Many traditionalist Irish nationalists also felt patronised by O'Neill's new departure. In the short term, his modernisation project proved popular enough to roll back the NILP's gains. This had the effect of undercutting more radical members of the NILP who had viewed it as the best vehicle for socialist political advancement, such as Eamonn McCann and Michael Farrell. At the same time, O'Neill's failure to address civil rights issues directly gave McCann and Farrell an alternative issue on which to exert their energies, in the form of the growing civil rights movement. It was this group of young radicals who gave the civil rights movement its tactical (though not strategic) *élan* which helped to destroy the 'moderation' of so-called 'O'Neillism'. When the civil rights crisis erupted after the police assault on the Derry March of 5 October 1968, O'Neill also sought to offer moderate reform on civil rights movement demands such as the continued gerrymander of Derry. Ironically, perhaps, ham-fisted efforts at moderate reform invigorated those with radical political energy.

The British State and the Ulster Crisis

Northern Ireland had never been given sustained attention by the British government in the decades preceding O'Neill's turn to moderate reform, and the reaction to it. They were not prepared for the civil rights crisis of the late 1960s, with marching and countermarching on the streets, televised scenes of disorder, and American coverage of Great Britain's 'deep south' problem which compared the problems to those of the American civil rights movement. Nonetheless, acquaintance with Ireland was more widespread among the British political elite than is widely known. Some of this was maintained because of the presence of those with a personal or familial connection with Ireland. For example, the grandfather of Denis Healey, a senior minister in various Labour governments had been born in Enniskillen, County Fermanagh. Healey's father retained a strong enough sense of Irishness to heckle 'What about Ireland, Major Healey?' at one of his son's electoral rallies in 1945.[5] The first three prime ministers to deal with the Irish question after 1968 – Harold Wilson, Edward Heath and James Callaghan – had all visited Northern Ireland before the Troubles. Heath stayed a number of times at the home of Robin Chichester-Clark (MP for Londonderry 1955–1974), while James Callaghan had visited the province in 1955, and Harold Wilson had been a young Whitehall mandarin tasked with attempting to improve Northern Ireland's wartime productivity. Wilson's Huyton constituency in Liverpool had a very large Irish Catholic element, leading him to make the rather tactless boast to a visiting Irish Taoiseach that he had more Irish constituents than the Taoiseach.[6]

There were significant blind spots in British political knowledge, of course. The Labour minister Richard Crossman commented in his diaries that nobody understood the finances of Northern Ireland.[7] Yet even here there is an element of overstatement. After each budget the chancellor of the day met with the Northern Ireland minister for finance to discuss its implications for the province. In some respects, this was a sign of the ambiguities that still surrounded the governance of Northern Ireland. The financial arrangements behind the Stormont government had evolved in an ad hoc way since 1921 – a messy system of 'fudges, dodges and wangles', according to Sir Richard Hopkins, treasury controller in 1939.[8] In part, this growing subvention from London reflected the need to preserve something close to parity with the rest of the United Kingdom in economic and social conditions, despite the rapid decline of the local economy since its pre-First World War heyday. The fact that the Northern Irish state was so propped up by the new welfare regime instituted by the Attlee government after the Second World War was not lost on contemporaries. In particular, Harold Wilson realised that Northern Ireland's financial dependence gave him a weapon with which

---

5 G. Bell, *Troublesome Business, the Labour Party and Ireland* (London: Pluto Press, 1982). Healey may not have been impressed: he regarded his father as a 'bodger'.

6 P. Bew, ' "The Blind Leading the Blind"? London's Response to the 1969 Crisis', *History Ireland*, 4 (Jul / Aug 2009), 49.

7 'Neither Jack Diamond (Chief Secretary to the Treasury 1964–70) nor the Chancellor knew the formula by which Northern Ireland gets its money. In all these years it has never been revealed to the politicians. I am eager to see whether we shall now get to the bottom of this very large and expensive secret.' R. H. S. Crossman, *Diaries of a Cabinet Minister*, iii, 1968–70 (London: Hamish Hamilton, 1977), 187.

8 Hopkins to the Chancellor, T 160 / 550 / 6563 / 021 / 1: TNA.

to help its moderate reformist prime minister, Terence O'Neill, against the hard-liners in the Ulster Unionist Party. In his memoirs, Wilson later claimed to have admired O'Neill's 'programme of easement' of Catholic–Protestant tension in Northern Ireland, and indeed, at the end of 1968, it looked as if O'Neill's British-government-sponsored reformism would succeed in calming tensions.[9]

That O'Neill's project soon went awry came about through a combination of accident and the force of events but also, to an extent which is sometimes underestimated, human agency. These were the sparks that helped cause the outbreak of violence in 1969. On 1 January 1969 the ultra-left People's Democracy march left Belfast for Derry, with only about 40 student marchers in attendance. The march was criticised by the Northern Ireland Civil Rights Association as needlessly provocative; and when it left the city the main nationalist newspaper the *Irish News* was still firmly in the O'Neill camp. On 4 January the march was attacked by loyalists at Burntollet bridge, outside Derry. According to Bernadette Devlin, one of the march leaders: 'A few policemen were, at least, trying to stop us from being killed, but some were quite delighted that we were getting what, in their terms, we deserved.'[10] One of the current writers, who was also present, did not see any delighted policemen (though it is a fact that one County Antrim Orange march in the 1990s listed 'Burntollet' as a victory, along with Aughrim (1691) and the Boyne (1690)). Nonetheless, the importance of this event, and the symbolism of it, cannot be overstated. The editorial tone of the main nationalist newspaper *Irish News* immediately turned hostile to O'Neill; it soon became clear that the prime minister had lost the Catholic middle class. The marchers – somewhat to their own surprise – moved from being regarded as hard-core Trotskyite extremists, to the darling of the Catholic middle classes almost overnight.

Those who were watching in London retained a suspicious attitude to the student radicals, whom they believed were motivated by the broader international student revolts of 1968. James Callaghan accepted that there were real civil rights issues in play but felt that the internationally inspired fervour was an additional complicating factor – 'a spark that enabled them to believe that they could really conquer'.[11] One thing about the strategy of this radical subset of the civil rights movement was its rejectionism. The notion that

---

9 H. Wilson, *The Labour Government 1904–70* (London: Penguin Harmondsworth, 1974), 140.

10 P. Bew, 'The Blind Leading the Blind', 47.

11 For this view, see his memoir, *A House Divided: The Dilemma of Northern Ireland* (London: Collins, 1973), 14.

liberal Unionism, in the O'Neill mould, was somehow the 'real enemy' was at the core of their strategy, a view found in Owen Dudley Edwards's book *The Sins of our Fathers*, published in Dublin in 1970. In an article in the pro-O'Neill *Belfast Telegraph* (titled 'What is the future for civil rights?'), the influential journalist Barry White noted that the slogan 'O'Neill must go' was just as popular in civil rights circles as among the followers of Ian Paisley.[12] While the People's Democracy admitted that O'Neill's departure might lead to an increase in state repression, this was deemed to be preferable to the stabilisation of the existing system. Such was the determination to see O'Neillism fail, that there were even fantasies of possible collaboration with Paisley, which saw Bernadette Devlin visit his house for a secret tea party.[13]

It was certainly not the case that the People's Democracy as a group wanted to open up Northern Ireland to a quarter-century of sectarian conflict. Nor did they revert to the old tropes of nationalist diagnosis of the fundamental problems facing Northern Ireland. On the contrary, in an interview with *New Left Review* on 9 April 1969, Eamonn McCann insisted that the Northern Ireland conflict was not a colonial one, and Bernadette Devlin almost seemed to apologise for relying on Catholic support to revolutionise the situation. 'Everyone applauds loudly when one says in a speech that we are not sectarian, we are fighting for the rights of all Irish workers, but really that is because they see this as a new way of getting at the Protestants', remarked McCann.[14] But why then carry on with such a strategy? McCann spoke of being 'in a pre-revolutionary situation'. It is hard to avoid the view that the sheer excitement of crisis suppressed rational calculation about possible outcomes. McCann himself appears to have believed that all the conventional metropolitan left-liberal views of Ulster were nonsense, but that the ongoing crisis would split the Protestant bloc in a way that would give control to the progressives. While this leftist fringe brought new thinking about the Northern Irish question into local politics, their legacy was not to be in the realm of ideas. Instead, they were to leave their mark in the history of 'the Troubles' through strategies of radical change, learned elsewhere, but which were to have explosive consequences when applied in Northern Ireland.

Bereft of moderate Catholic support, in good measure owing to the activity of the student radicals, O'Neill stumbled on to defeat: he was run close

---

12 O. Dudley Edwards, *The Sins of our Fathers: Roots of Conflict in Northern Ireland* (Dublin: Gill & Macmillan, 1970), 27.

13 Lord Bannside [Revd Ian Paisley] – obituary, *Daily Telegraph*, 13 September 2014.

14 L. Baxter, B. Devlin, M. Farrell, E. McCann and C.Toman, 'People's Democracy: A Discussion Strategy', in *New Left Review* 55, May/June 1969, 6.

by Paisley in the election in his own rural constituency, before stepping aside against the backdrop of growing disorder. Urban areas displayed significant popular O'Neillist support, but this was not enough. The *Belfast Telegraph* regretfully announced O'Neill's resignation on 28 April 1969. Acknowledging his lack of political dexterity, it took comfort from the fact that O'Neill had established (in his own words) that 'no solution based on the ascendancy of any section of the community can hope to endure'. O'Neill was replaced by a cousin, James Chichester-Clark, a brave soldier but handicapped with a stutter that left him a poor match rhetorically for the rising Protestant populist Ian Paisley. With a loss of authority on behalf of moderates, Northern Ireland veered further towards inter-communal violence, with growing numbers of Catholics and Protestants on the streets in the summer of 1969. Again, both sins of commission and omission played a part in the lurch towards violence. The prolonged rioting in Derry in August 1969 was provoked by a loyalist parade by the Apprentice Boys which Harold Wilson later said he had personally favoured banning.

The sheer theatrical force of the violence caused other actors to reassert themselves. Again, opportunities to stabilise the situation were missed. During this 'Battle of the Bogside', on 13 August, a troubled Taoiseach, Jack Lynch, broadcast that the Irish government 'can no longer stand by and see innocent people injured and perhaps worse'; he even asked the British government to request the immediate dispatch of a UN peace-keeping force to Northern Ireland, and announced that field hospitals were being prepared in County Donegal and other border areas. James Callaghan, who knew Lynch well, regarded his rhetoric as a departure from his usual good sense. It certainly helped to inflame the loyalists in Belfast.[15] On 14 August rioting in Derry continued and spread to Belfast, involving Catholic and Protestant crowds. On 15 August the rioting continued in Belfast, and many homes were burned in Bombay Street, in the Catholic Clonard area; Catholic refugees fled to the Republic. In the afternoon British troops took up their positions and established a peace-line between Catholic and Protestant areas in Belfast.

It is worth noting that in the days before this decisive move, lobby correspondents in London were urged by the government to leak the 'fact' that any call for British troops to control public order in Northern Ireland would lead to the abolition of Stormont and the introduction of direct rule, which, indeed,

---

15 See 'Callaghan on Lynch', in *History Ireland*, 4 (July/August 2009). This is an extract from the former Prime Minister's testimony to the Centre for Contemporary British History.

British officials at Whitehall had been considering formally since February 1969. Many shrewd observers were later to conclude that the Stormont government's (incorrect) assumption that a request for British troops would lead to the immediate abolition of Stormont had created a context in which an overstretched and badly organised police force was given responsibility for massive public-order problems, which the earlier utilisation of British troops would have averted.

Now more heavily involved, the key element in London's strategy was to replace the discredited B-Specials (a paramilitary force allied closely to the Unionist Party) with a new non-sectarian force, the Ulster Defence Regiment (UDR), under British army control. This change aroused many Unionists to fury, as an undercutting of the authority of the Stormont government. November 1969 was, however, to see a dramatic change in public perceptions of the UDR, which, crucially, was to be under British, not local, command like the B-men. At first, James Chichester-Clark continued to feel the tide of popular anger: on 12 November the prime minister was voted out of his place as vice-chairman of his local Unionist branch and was replaced by a 53-year-old bus driver, Fred Taylor. Two rising stars in the civil rights movement, John Hume and Austin Currie, urged Catholics to join the UDR, seen as a fresh start for security policy in the province. They were denounced by Eamonn McCann for acting as 'recruiting sergeants' for the British army. It is easy enough to see why James Callaghan's memoir is so careful to note the effects of what he saw as destabilising ultra-leftism working alongside the local sectarian dynamic. Over the following week, however, the Prime Minister, James Chichester-Clark, successfully persuaded the Unionist political class to back the new force, stressing, amongst other things, its attractive terms and conditions. By 21 November John Wallace, the chief political reporter of the *Belfast Telegraph*, recorded what was to him an 'astonishing turn of events'.[16] Nationalists were beginning to back away from the new force, as Unionists began to back it in growing numbers. One might say that this was a harbinger of future developments throughout the Troubles: the tendency of Protestants and Unionists to react with great hostility to change – the end of the B-Specials, the establishment of direct rule, and then the Good Friday Agreement – only to end up embracing the new dispensation. In the short term, this seemed to be a triumph for the new prime minister, who momentarily grew in authority. On the other hand, though this was unforeseen, the establishment of the UDR was to play a part in the rise of the Provisional IRA.

16 *Belfast Telegraph*, 21 November 1969.

Long-term structural inequalities created the context for resentment and suspicion between communities. Ultimately, the fact that violence became an engrained part in the fabric of everyday life in Northern Ireland was due to the fact that those who used it were pursuing an ideological agenda. As civil disorder spread across the year 1969, the leadership of a newly constituted IRA was preparing for war. It was its decision to attack the British army that transformed relations between the army and the Catholic community. In early 1969 the IRA had been relatively weak – though not so weak as is often claimed – but undoubtedly it was given a new legitimacy as the defender of Catholic rights and as a consequence of the loyalist attacks.[17] The question was – what would the movement do with that sense of legitimacy?

In December 1969 the IRA's Army Council met in Dublin to review strategy. The leftists in the IRA attempted to retain some sort of political focus. Others believed that the left-wing leadership was undermining the IRA's more traditional military role as defenders of the Catholic population. They broke away to form the Provisional IRA. This new group soon established dominance in the Catholic areas of Belfast and Derry. Later key figures like Gerry Adams and Martin McGuinness for a time oscillated between the 'Official' and the Provisional IRA, before casting their lot in with the 'Provos'.[18] The new movement was no longer defensive or reactive: it was proactive and based on a political calculation that was ultimately to prove to be a fantasy. Brendan Hughes, a leading Provo recalled: 'We wanted open confrontation with the army. Get the Brits out through armed resistance, engage them in armed conflict and send them back across the water with their tanks and guns. That was the Republican objective.'[19] The 'Provos' had some elite support in the Irish Republic. On 28 May the former Irish Finance Minister, Charles Haughey and former Agriculture Minister, Neil Blaney, appeared in court in connection with a plot to smuggle arms to the IRA. There is no doubt that the militant IRA in the north seemed to have come very rapidly into the possession of weaponry, some of it with Irish army links. More serious still was the emergence of large subsidies for the IRA from Provisional IRA sympathisers in America.[20] Moreover, for every senior Irish politician intoxicated by the romance of the Northern Ireland Troubles, as evocative of previous eras of

---

17 T. Hennessey, *The Origins of the Troubles* (Dublin: Gill & Macmillan, 2005).

18 For the story of the 'Officials', see B. Hanley, *The Lost Revolution: The Story of the Official IRA and the Workers' Party* (London: Penguin Harmondsworth, 2010).

19 Hennessey, *The Origins of the Troubles*, 375.

20 As an example of such sentiments, see the *Irish Edition*, a monthly newspaper published in Philadelphia, PA.

nationalist struggle, there were any number worried and frightened by the level of uncontrolled ethnic rage.

The surge of sectarianism was seized upon and put to use by those with long-term ideological objectives and radical strategies, entangling these forces for the duration of the conflict. Early in January 1970 the Provisional Army Council formally confirmed an all-out offensive against the 'British occupation system'. As Thomas Hennessey has put it bluntly, this, more than anything, explains how the rioting and disorder of 1969 turned into the sustained violent conflict which began in 1970: 'It was simple as that: on the sectarian embers of the 1969 violence was poured the inflammable liquid that was violent Republicanism.'[21] These two historical forces fused themselves with the most gruesome of consequences. On 26 June 1970 an IRA man in Derry, Thomas McCool, blew himself and his two young daughters up in his house in Derry while preparing an incendiary device. Carol McCool (4) and Bernadette McCool (9) were the first young girls to die in the Troubles, though not the last. On 27 June, clashes broke out around St Matthew's Church in the markets area of central Belfast. Two Protestants and one Catholic were killed by the well-armed 'defenders'. The one Catholic to die was actually killed by accident by Dennis Donaldson, later to be Stormont Chief of Staff to Gerry Adams and, from the mid-1980s, a paid British informant.

In June 1970, an evocative and neglected piece of journalism by Nell McCafferty captured the rancid sectarian world that the Provisionals sought to dominate and harness. It is worth pausing to reflect that the piece was written by one of the most admired radical feminist journalists of her generation. One of the present writers can vividly recall her leading role alongside Eamonn McCann on the Burntollet March. The piece entitled 'Anarchy amok in political impotence of Bogside' should be placed alongside Eamonn McCann's creditably honest interview in *New Left Review*. At its best the '68 generation looked for something better than the sectarianism which engulfed the North: but, of course, they ignored the fact that partisan outsiders in Dublin, London and the USA were unconcerned about local emotional realities and happily encouraged the tribalism of the locals:

> Who lost the World Cup? is this year's Bogside taunt to British soldiers, engaged in an exercise of containment, while within Bogside itself anarchy runs remorselessly amok. There are no demands for jobs or houses, no

---

21 Hennessey, *Origins of the Troubles*, 375.

mention of reforms. If it's dry, burn it; if it's wet, drink it; if it moves, hit it; and every man for himself. A lunatic carnival, with free booze and fireworks, to the chant of 'Easy, easy', as the breeze blows the CS gas back into the forces of law and order.

At 6am on Saturday I sat in the early morning light on empty wooden crates at Free Derry corner among a crowd of 30 men. They were drinking looted beer, and having a wake for the man who had been roasted alive in a fiery holocaust in a council house in Creggan the previous night. A man raised his beer can. 'He died for Ireland, boys.' They agreed. Then his face crumpled into tears.

'Come off it,' he said, 'he's just dead, and for what?'

An open lorry careens crazily towards us, loaded with drunken youths, piled high with crates of beer. They were singing Jailhouse Rock. Someone drove a small earth-mover round and round a building site, crashed it finally, and staggered off, a coil of copper wire around his shoulders. Two children came out of a builder's wooden hut. Minutes later it went up in flames.

Efforts were made to engage the British army. 'Hey, Sambo; hit this' called a young rioter pointing to his nose. But the soldiers withdrew. 'Send back the R.U.C., at least they'll fight,' the boys shouted furiously.[22]

There is an important political comment in McCafferty's article. She describes a key moment. There was only one way forward; galvanising violence launched by the republicans. Sean Keenan, a veteran republican leader, was confronted by an apparent stalemate. The Derry Defence Committee 'met late into the night in an atmosphere of political impotence. Trapped by their Civil Rights clarion call for freedom to march, there is little they can say about Orange parades. Calling for British standards, they can not manipulate anti-British feeling. There has been no military rape of Bogside, and they can not pose in self-defence'.[23] But it did not really matter. For Keenan's generation of old-school republicans, including similar men like Billy McKee in Belfast, the moment had come: a new opportunity now presented for a traditional IRA campaign to get the 'Brits Out'.[24]

Another feature of McCafferty's piece is that it cuts through all the conventional explanations that so dominated later analyses of the origins of the 'Troubles'. British Army overreaction? There is none here. She describes the British officer, Major Oulten, talking calmly to the rioters and then moving

---

22 *Irish Times*, 29 June 1970.
23 W. B. Smith, *The British State and the Northern Ireland Crisis, 1969–73* (Washington, DC: The United States Institute of Peace Press, 2011), 116.
24 For Keenan, see N. Ó Dochartaigh, *From Civil Rights to Armalites: Derry and the Birth of the Troubles* (Cork: Cork University Press, 1997), 41.

his soldiers out. Aggressive Orange marching in sensitive areas? Don't forget the civil rights demanded to be able to do the same. Denial of 'British standards'? In her interpretation, what becomes clear is the conflict between that objective and a specifically nationalist agenda. It reveals clearly that the Provisional IRA strategy from 1970 onwards is, in part, a response to the aggressive actions of loyalists in 1969; but, also, very decidedly a product of the local nationalist political culture the contours of which are adequately displayed also in her essay. British army overreaction, Orange provocation, and long-term mishandling of civil rights issues were all important ingredients in the outbreak of violence. But as McCafferty's description of the dynamics at work in Derry in the summer of 1970 demonstrates so effectively, they do not explain the strategy of the Provisional IRA. There is another particularly evocative moment in McCafferty's article that reflects the difficulties faced by constitutional nationalists and representatives of the Catholic community in trying to stem the tide. The arguments bounded futilely back and forth. 'I want a better life for my children', a woman screamed at John Hume. Hume, replied by referring to the immolation of the McCool family in the Creggan: 'Two children were burned to death in Creggan last night. If this keeps up your children may not be here to have a future. She would not listen.'[25] It showed that Hume, too, understood the forces that were being unleashed and the agendas behind them.

While the situation deteriorated rapidly, human agency continued to play a part, as inter-communal violence took a sinister turn. On 27 June 1970, the night after the death of the McCool family, drunken loyalists were lured into a conflict at St Matthew's church in the markets area of Belfast. Three died – two Protestant and one Catholic.[26] The next day 500 Catholics were expelled from the shipyards where even IRA veterans like Joe Cahill had been able to work in the pre-Troubles era. The same day, Gerry Adams has recalled, 'Riots broke out in Ardoyne on 27th June. In this instance, the IRA were ready and waiting and in the ensuing gun battle, three loyalists were killed.'[27] Not surprisingly, British sources concluded that the IRA was on the offensive and responded rapidly with the army curfew of the Falls Road that further alienated the Catholic community.[28] By making much of these orchestrated 'defences', the Provos began to dominate local communities, and squeezed

---

25 *Irish Times*, 29 June 1970.
26 See P. Maume's entry on Donaldson in the *Dictionary of Irish Biography (DIB online)*: dib. cambridge.org (accessed 2 October 2017).
27 See Adams's memoir, *Before the Dawn: An Autobiography* (Dingle: Brandon Press, 2001).
28 G. Warner, 'The Falls Road Curfew Revisited', *Irish Studies Review*, 4 (August, 2006).

out other voices.[29] These gave them the opportunity to escalate their campaign further. On 12 August, two RUC constables were killed by a booby-trap bomb in a car in Crossmaglen, County Armagh. The war against the state had begun, even if the servants of the state were slow to grasp it. On 18 September 1970, RUC officers voted, narrowly, to remain an unarmed police force. It was to look like a curious act before long, and reflected a desire to cling to the certainties of an era which had already passed. The death toll for 1970 had been 28. By the end of 1971, it had risen to 180.

Against the backdrop of these ugly scenes came the clunky and misbegotten response of the British state. In August 1971, the British government launched Operation Demetrius and internment was introduced into Northern Ireland. Internment without trial had full British government as well as Northern Irish government support, but as it failed to stabilise the province – violence rose markedly – the British began to blame Stormont for the mess.[30] The disaster of Bloody Sunday in Derry – in which 13 innocent civilians were killed by the British army[31] – was again by an act of 'displacement' blamed on Stormont which was now doomed. Indeed, the fact that the Provisionals so obviously were aiming for direct rule was the major factor in delaying its implementation. Towards the end of March 1972, Prime Minister Heath moved to strip away security powers from Stormont and then to prorogue it. The parliament in Northern Ireland met for the last time on 28 March 1972. There is no doubt that when the end came for Stormont it was due to a British perception that the United Kingdom could not continue to suffer the damaging international perception that it was linked to militarism in the North. There was not, however, any deep or profound consensus about future policy beyond that point.

For the Provisionals, direct rule was a triumph, and was perceived as a stepping-stone to victory. They declared that it 'places us in a somewhat similar position to that prior to the setting up of partition and the two statelets (i.e. the setting up of Northern Ireland and the Irish Free State in 1920 and 1922 respectively). It puts the "Irish Question" in its true perspective – an alien power seeking to lay claim to a country to which it has no legal right'. The Provos deceived themselves and claimed that 1972, and then 1974, would be the year of victory. In fact direct rule's greater significance lay elsewhere: its

---

29 To see how far this went, one neglected account is F. Burton, *The Politics of Legitimacy: Struggles in a Belfast Community* (London: Routledge and Kegan Paul, 1978). This survey was carried out in 1972/3.
30 See M. McCleery, *Operation Demetrius* (Manchester: Manchester University Press, 2015).
31 See P. Bew, 'The Role of the Historical Adviser and the Bloody Sunday Tribunal', *Historical Research*, 178 (February 2005), 120.

introduction represented the definitive end of the 'Orange state', which had, of course, also been the welfare state. But now the welfare benefits of the Union remained without Orange political hegemony. It allowed government the space to introduce a strategy of reform 'from above'. Loss of control of the local state also helped to generate a decade and more of disarray and confusion in Unionist politics. Indeed, these years were marked by the apparently inexorable rise of Ian Paisley and his populist Democratic Unionist Party and, alongside it, the growing weakness of the more 'respectable' Ulster Unionist Party. It was to take almost two decades for the Unionist Party to re-establish itself as the dominant force in Protestant politics, before losing that position again in the twenty-first century. The introduction of direct rule was the single most decisive moment of the crisis; it is the *sine qua non* for all later developments, including the 1985 Anglo-Irish Agreement that was, in effect, merely a green appendage to the direct rule machine.

In 1973, 250 people died as a direct result of the Troubles. The growing death toll increased the pressure on all politicians of good will to negotiate a power-sharing compromise; this they duly did at the end of this year at Sunningdale, Berkshire. The flaw in the Sunningdale Agreement was that those involved in it had completely different views as to what it entailed. The new Unionist leader, Brian Faulkner saw the projected Council of Ireland as an advisory body and raised few objections to it dealing with the 'harmonisation' of cross-border issues such as tourism, transport, agriculture and electricity which he believed was 'necessary nonsense'.[32] However, some members of the nationalist Social Democratic and Labour Party had a different opinion of what the Council of Ireland would mean: 'The general approach of the SDLP to the talks was to get all-Ireland institutions established which, with adequate safeguards, would produce the dynamic that would lead ultimately to an agreed single state for Ireland' recalled Paddy Devlin. That meant that SDLP representatives 'would concentrate their entire efforts on building up a set of tangible executive powers for the Council which in the fullness of time would create and sustain an evolutionary process'.[33]

The British government was also partly responsible for contributing to this confusion and uncertainty. By failing to define clearly the areas which the Council of Ireland would control and those which it would not, they succeeded in inflating nationalist expectations while at the same time raising

---

32 B. Faulkner, *Memoirs of a Statesman* (London: Weidenfeld and Nicolson, 1978), 32.
33 P. Devlin, *The Fall of the Northern Ireland Executive* (Belfast: P. Devlin, 1975), 32.

loyalist fears that the Council would be the means of forcing them into a united Ireland. In truth, the problem was to be a persistent one. For a settlement to work, mainstream unionists had to believe the 'necessary nonsense' thesis of Faulkner. However, British officials, anxious to take the steam out of the nationalist advance were reluctant to support such a message. It was only in the 1990s – the era when David Trimble was leader of the Unionist party – that this balancing trick was finally achieved; indeed, with such success that it is remarkable to note how uncontroversial new North–South arrangements have been since 1998.

In the immediate aftermath, the Sunningdale conference seemed a triumph for consensus politics. It is evident, however, that the parties involved, buoyed by their success in achieving agreement, missed some serious difficulties that lay ahead. They failed to recognise the strength of opposition building up within a Unionist community that was increasingly feeling that it was being railroaded into a united Ireland. The British government and Edward Heath in particular seemed insensitive to Brian Faulkner's weakening position. (Faulkner had succeeded Chichester-Clark as Prime Minister.) It is here that the British Home Secretary, William Whitelaw's experience might have made a difference for he would surely have been aware of the difficulties Faulkner would face in selling the deal on his return to Northern Ireland. At the same time, a promise by Heath to the SDLP that he would phase out internment and begin releasing detainees as soon as possible also failed to materialise. This left the SDLP to concentrate on the apparent benefits of the Council of Ireland, a policy which only served to heighten Unionist fears of the Sunningdale deal further. The Irish government also promised more than it was eventually able to deliver, and of the Irish delegation only Conor Cruise O'Brien seemed aware of the likely barriers to progress that had been erected at Sunningdale. The general election of February 1974 showed a majority of Northern Ireland's electorate – the entire electorate, not just the Unionist electorate – willing to vote for anti-Unionist Sunningdale candidates. This loss of credibility had a decisive effect on the newly-elected Prime Minister in London, Harold Wilson, who resolved not to defend an irreparably doomed executive when a loyalist general strike was called in May 1974.

The triumphant strikers brought down the Sunningdale Agreement but they had little time to celebrate their 'victory'. The law of unintended consequences which governed events so decisively during the 'Ulster Troubles' came into play again. The 'victory' of the strikers allowed Wilson, the one British prime minister of the epoch with a serious leaning towards 'withdrawal', to explore its consequences. He welcomed the fall of the executive because it opened the way for a sanctioned negotiation with the Provisional IRA leadership during the truce of 1974/5. This truce allowed the phasing out of internment, but Wilson's more ambitious ideas were thwarted by an angry Irish government which did not concede the right of the Provisional leaders to negotiate Irish unity. Fearful in particular of the financial consequences, the Irish government did everything in its power to stop a Provo-Wilson deal – both domestically (arresting the Southern IRA leadership team) and internationally via alarmed messages to Henry Kissinger, US Secretary of State. Loyalist violence and cruelty also increased dramatically as fears of a sell-out mounted in that community. The moment of danger for Dublin passed; by March 1976, James Callaghan, known to the Irish political leadership on account of his holiday home in Cork, was in charge of British policy.

The UK government in 1977 faced another loyalist general strike. While the main reason for the failure of this strike was the general lack of support from the Unionist community the British government's reaction was more planned and much more decisive than it had been in 1974. Secretary of State Roy Mason was excused from cabinet duties and stayed in Northern Ireland throughout the strike. A daily briefing was held in an operations room in Stormont every morning involving the Secretary of State, the army's General Officer Commanding and the Chief Constable of the RUC while the Northern Ireland Office (NIO) also successfully played a delaying game with the electricity workers whose support was crucial to the success or failure of the stoppage. The 1977 strike, even more than the 1974 strike, relied on violent intimidation.

The strike was a failed coup but saw the further degeneration of the conflict, in which the language of contractarian politics was grafted onto an ugly sectarian dynamic. The qualitative nature of the violence was more reflective of the latter. On 10 May 1977, Harry Bradshaw, a Belfast Citybus driver, was shot by the loyalist paramilitary organisation, the Ulster Defence Association on the Crumlin Road. Mrs Bradshaw said of her husband: 'He was loyal not only to Queen and Country but to his family as well. He had to support his family. I can't blame Mr Paisley for what has happened, but I can't say he's free from blame either.' In January 1979, UDA member Kenny McClinton was convicted both of the Bradshaw murder and the earlier murder of a Catholic man, Daniel Carville. Kenny McClinton – later Pastor McClinton – became a born-again Christian. 'Pastor' Kenny McClinton insisted that he did not murder because he was that 'type of person' but because of the influence of Ian Paisley.[34] McClinton's controversial remark appeared in a 2006 public exchange of letters with Ian Paisley Jr MP. At that time, the younger Paisley was making the case for a historic compromise in Northern Ireland.[35]

Senior Stormont officials discussed Paisley's 'association with paramilitaries' on the same day as Mr Bradshaw's murder. Sir Brian Cubbon, the Northern Ireland Office's permanent undersecretary, led a discussion that insisted on the importance of smashing all attempts at intimidation though he was alert to the need to respect the right of 'peaceful persuasion'. The minutes continue: 'It was posited, however, that the person responsible [Paisley] was associated with and had the support of the Protestant paramilitaries and it was queried whether he ought not to be held for conspiracy.'[36] Paisley 'lost' the strike of 1977 despite staking his political future on it. Remarkably, his electoral fortunes, far from fading, began to strengthen. Confronted by the violence of the IRA, a growing number of Unionists elected him – in particular in European elections where he always topped the poll. Even now, British officials speculated that Paisley could, at some point, be a kingmaker in any potential settlement, provided, of course, he was king. As early as 1975, for example, the outgoing Secretary of State for Northern Ireland Merlyn Rees suggested that Paisley was 'quite capable of doing a tactical turnabout if it would strengthen his position, as his ultimate aim is to lead a larger party at Westminster'.[37] Rees continued to maintain this conviction through the strike of 1977, Paisley's protests against the Anglo-Irish and Belfast Agreements of 1985 and 1998, through to his death in 2006.[38]

With internment and withdrawal both ruled out, what policy options did the British government retain for dealing with the IRA? The only possible answer was the one of 'criminalisation' pursued in the period when Roy Mason was Secretary of State. This policy, which involved, for example, the utilisation of informers to ensure multiple convictions demoralised the Provos. There was an obvious response to this, one deeply rooted in the republican tradition. As early as October 1979, the journalist Ed Moloney reporting on a Sinn Féin conference, noted the leadership's concern at 'the decline in public interest' in its activities and he concluded that there was one

34 *Sunday Tribune* [Dublin] 10 December 2006.
35 C. Donnelly, 'Brothers in the Lord: The DUP MP and LVF frontman', *Slugger O'Toole. com*, 11 December 2006.
36 E. Phoenix, 'Paisley's Paramilitary links', *Irish Times*, 20 December 2007.
37 Memorandum by Merlyn Rees, 12 December 1975, CAB 134/3921: TNA.
38 See J. Bew, 'Introduction', to D. W. Miller, *Queen's Rebels: Ulster Loyalism in Historical Perspective* (Dublin: Gill & Macmillan, 2007 edn.), xxi.

last card available: 'The never quite articulated threat of a hunger strike to achieve formal political status was in the smoky air last Sunday in speeches from Sinn Féin leaders Gerry Adams and Gerry Brannigan as well as in a letter from the prisoners themselves.'[39] In the end the death of ten hunger strikers in 1981 revived Sinn Féin's political fortunes. Catholics recognised the prisoners as local boys – the neighbour's child – rather than common criminals. Murals portrayed the hunger strikers as Christ-like martyrs not terrorist killers.

The hunger strikes became one of the turning points of the Troubles, though its effects were not immediately obvious. Ironically, given that they had little involvement in the dispute between the British government and the strikers, it was a turning point that eventually had deep implications for the local Protestant community. As slightly mystified onlookers, few Unionists realised that these events would cause the ground to move from beneath their feet. Sinn Féin reaped an electoral advantage. In the 1983 general election, the party obtained 13.4 per cent of the vote as against the SDLP vote of 17.9 per cent. Both the British and more especially the Irish government became alarmed lest Sinn Féin become the leading nationalist party in the North. A long and tortuous progress of negotiation began which led to the Anglo-Irish Agreement of 1985. But first it was necessary to improve relations between the British and Irish governments. When Douglas Hurd, Margaret Thatcher's Secretary of State for Northern Ireland, travelled to Dublin in late November 1981, the prime minister commented that the visit was 'of doubtful wisdom'.[40] Taoiseach Charles Haughey's, criticism of Britain during the Falklands War in 1982 further infuriated her. British officials at the Embassy in Dublin concluded that 'Anglo-Irish relations are in crisis even if Ministers have not . . . formally declared them to be so.'[41] Yet the next Taoiseach, Garret FitzGerald, who had been careful with his words during the election campaign at the end of 1982, was to prove rather more palatable to London.

The Road to Hillsborough

The first move towards rapprochement came from the Irish Ambassador in London, Dr Eamon Kennedy, in January 1983, when he told British officials about the new Irish government's 'desire to restore Anglo-Irish relations to

---

39 *Hibernia*, October 1979.
40 Thatcher's comment on visit, 3 November 1981, PREM 19/816: TNA.
41 Sir R. Armstrong, CAB 164/615:TNA.

normal', while acknowledging that 'rush would be counterproductive and that confidence must be rebuilt gradually'. The following day, on 15 January 1983, the British cabinet secretary, Sir Robert Armstrong, made clear his view that the responsibility for the deterioration in Anglo-Irish relations 'lay with the Irish', stating that the British government had 'no interest in seeking to force the pace, still less in appearing to woo or pursue the Irish'. Officials were given a personal directive from Thatcher herself that it was to be left to the Irish 'to do the running'.[42]

Although substantive discussions were postponed until after the British general election in June, Thatcher did agree to see the Taoiseach on the margins of the European Council in Brussels on 22 March. Privately she was insistent that this 'must not be a formal meeting' and said that she could only spare 20–30 minutes. She was eventually negotiated up to 40 minutes by Sir Leonard Figg, her ambassador in Dublin. At the meeting, Thatcher's tone was curt and abrupt with her Irish counterpart. When FitzGerald said that 'the aim of re-establishing contact should be to lay foundation for the future relationship', Thatcher replied that 'it was more a matter of keeping in touch'. When FitzGerald mentioned the need to bolster the SDLP against the growing electoral threat from Sinn Féin, Thatcher observed that it was difficult to give support to a party that was 'anti-Unionist'. In his first sign of frustration, FitzGerald retorted that the SDLP was 'also anti-IRA'.

When the two leaders met again on European Council business in Stuttgart on 19 June, Thatcher agreed to resume official contact again through Sir Robert Armstrong and Dermot Nally, the top British and Irish civil servants respectively. When her civil servants pressured her to agree to an official Anglo-Irish summit before the end of the year, she expressed her irritation, scribbling with her trademark blue fountain pen: 'I don't like this at all. The truth is that we haven't anything to talk about save security and EEC matters.' This was precisely the kind of activity that got the government 'into difficult situations with the Unionists'. Thatcher nonetheless relented and agreed to host Garret FitzGerald at Chequers, the Prime Ministerial residence, in November. This prompted a flurry of activity between British and Irish officials, in which the latter indicated their desire to adopt a new approach to the Northern Ireland problem. In September, the Secretary of State for Northern

---

42 J. Bew, 'State Papers', *Irish Times*, 30 December 2014. See also, C. Moore, *Margaret Thatcher: The Authorised Biography, vol 2 Everything She Wants* (London: Allen Lane, 2015), 298–342. For the conventional wisdom on the Agreement, see P. Smyth and M. Hennessey (eds.), 'Anglo-Irish Agreement', *Irish Times*, November 14 2015: http://irishtimes.com/news/politics/anglo_irish_agreement.

Ireland told the cabinet that there 'were signs that the implications of a united Ireland were being more seriously and realistically considered in both parts of Ireland than for many years'.

Much of the running was made by Michael Lillis, a close associate of FitzGerald, and the Head of the Anglo-Irish division in the Irish Department of Foreign Affairs, who remained in contact with the senior British diplomat David Goodall. Both Lillis and Goodall were later involved in the discussions which led to the Anglo-Irish Agreement. In a brief exchange of views in Dublin and a follow-up discussion at the British-Irish Association conference in Oxford in September 1983, Lillis told Goodall that the outcome of the recent abortion referendum in Ireland – in which there was a two-thirds majority in favour of a 'pro-life' amendment being added to the constitution – would put paid, at least for the time being, to any prospect of early success for the Irish government's policy of seeking to remove Protestant and liberal concerns about the Republic's Catholic ethos. While this was regrettable, Lillis believed it would also have the merit of clarifying the situation and forcing nationalist opinion to face up to the reality of partition and the fact that unification 'was at best a long term aspiration, not a political objective'.[43]

A memo from the cabinet secretary, Robert Armstrong, to Thatcher on 3 October laid out some of the proposals which Lillis was floating, including a commitment to accept Northern Ireland as part of the United Kingdom, and perhaps even an amendment to articles 2 and 3 of the Irish Constitution, in return for allowing members of An Garda Síochána (the Republic's police force) and Irish judges to be involved in the policing and judicial processes in the North. When British officials discovered that John Hume was not aware of the new proposals, as Lillis had claimed, it was agreed that it 'would be wise to stand off from Mr Lillis' in case he was overstating the Irish position. Nonetheless, in the forthcoming summit with FitzGerald, Thatcher was advised to 'listen sympathetically to what he has to say: probe him as to the realism of his approach: and, while striking a strongly sceptical note, make it clear that you would be prepared to look at any practical and realistic ideas which might help to reduce the level of violence in Northern Ireland'. The year ended on a sour note, when the IRA bombed Harrod's department store in London on 17 December, killing six people and injuring more than 90 others. At a cabinet meeting on 22 December, however, Thatcher observed that despite some high-profile incidents in recent weeks, the overall situation

43 See M. Lillis and D. Goodall, 'Edging Towards Peace', *Dublin Review of Books,* 13 (Spring, 2010), 1–20.

was calm and casualty figures for 1983 were the lowest for any year since the Troubles began. In the first indication that she was willing to respond to the Irish government's renewed efforts, she told the cabinet that 'consideration would need to be given to the wider aspects of the Irish question and the possibility of finding new approaches to it' in the new year.

In 1984, however, discussions were still very difficult. Margaret Thatcher believed that giving Dublin an official role in the running of Northern Ireland would put the province 'well on the way to civil war'.[44] During robust, rapid-fire exchanges at a critical summit in the run-up to the Anglo-Irish Agreement, she told FitzGerald that resolving the crisis could mean 'simply' moving the border. But the Taoiseach immediately rejected the apparent offer, warning it would be a 'fatal mistake'. During the two-hour meeting at Chequers, the Prime Minister said there were worries about a threat of more violence as a result of the Anglo-Irish talks. 'There was a real danger that a Marxist society could develop', she said.

FitzGerald said there had been agreement regarding an Irish government role in running the region, adding that he could not ask Dublin to give up its territorial claim over Northern Ireland without such a deal. But Mrs Thatcher insisted: 'It smacks too much of joint authority. That was definitely out.' She added: 'The Unionists would say you are giving up your constitutional claims but you are coming across the border and don't really need the claim. That would put us well on the way to civil war.' Later that day, in a press conference, Mrs Thatcher gave her infamous 'out, out, out' declaration, when she rejected three options put forward from the Irish for a solution to Northern Ireland – Irish unity, a two-state federation, or joint authority. The actual signing of the Anglo-Irish Agreement at Hillsborough in November 1985 was a triumph of persistence and backdoor diplomacy for the Dublin government, which was confronted with a divided British cabinet and an increasingly sceptical prime minister in Margaret Thatcher. The state papers for 1985 demonstrate how Irish officials and Taoiseach Garret FitzGerald kept up the pressure on the British throughout the year and when Thatcher reluctantly conceded – at a meeting with the Taoiseach in Milan in late June – it was too late to pull out of a deal.[45] On the British side, the driving force behind the agreement was Sir Robert Armstrong, the cabinet secretary, who built a particularly strong relationship with Dermot Nally, his Irish counterpart.

---

44 *Daily Telegraph*, 27 December 2014.
45 See J. Bew's analysis based on newly released state papers for 1984 in *Irish Times*, 30 December 2014.

Armstrong received strong support from the Foreign Office, headed by Geoffrey Howe, who was to play a central part in Thatcher's downfall five years later. Another influential voice in favour of the deal was Douglas Hurd, the Northern Ireland Secretary for the first part of the year. He became Home Secretary after a reshuffle in early September 1985. Opposition to the deal was strongest in the Northern Ireland Office and crystallised around the figure of Tom King, who replaced Hurd as Northern Secretary of State on 3 September just as negotiations reached a critical point. Other sceptics included Charles Powell, Thatcher's private secretary, and the prime minister herself, who regularly demanded that her officials push back against the Irish negotiators.

Thatcher later claimed in her memoirs that she regretted signing the Anglo-Irish Agreement as it failed to deliver on improved security cooperation. Initially, Irish officials seem to have engaged British attention by offering to make serious concessions. On 11 January, Armstrong informed Thatcher there was a serious prospect of the removal of articles 2 and 3 of the Irish Constitution, in return for a 'consultative' role in Northern Ireland. It soon became clear, however, that the FitzGerald government was not strong enough to risk a referendum on the Constitution and it was preferable to keep him in place, rather than risk the return of Charles Haughey. On 7 March, Howe informed Thatcher of his view that an agreement was a 'prize worth having'. Hurd agreed, although he warned that 'an agreement cannot be an end in itself'. There was 'still a significant gap to be bridged' and the British wanted something on the 'constitutional front'.

The language used in any agreement remained a sticking point. The Irish hoped for something more substantive and formalised than a 'consultative' role, whereas the British objected to use of the word 'joint' as it had connotations of 'joint authority'. While the Irish government wanted to give an electoral boost to the SDLP, the British were apparently less concerned about the rise of Sinn Féin. A report on the local elections in Northern Ireland in May noted that the SDLP had 'held its ground' and Sinn Féin's share of the vote had not increased. Meanwhile, the Irish asked the British to keep the Unionist parties in the dark about the talks, because of fears that they would attempt to derail the deal. After the elections, the Irish negotiators grew bolder. In addition to the agreement itself, they sought to tack on a series of 'confidence-building measures' to their demands. These included reforms to the Royal Ulster Constabulary and the Ulster Defence Regiment – such as a new code of conduct – with the professed aim of reassuring the minority community in Northern Ireland. Another was that of joint courts, made up of judges from both countries, to officiate in terrorism trials. Thatcher saw this as a tactical move. 'They are asking too much. Possibly this is deliberate', she wrote in May.

One consideration here was the attitude of the Americans if talks collapsed. In July, the British Foreign Office informed the Reagan administration that a deal was 'by no means a foregone conclusion, but that, if an agreement was not achieved it would not be because of any lack of seriousness on the British government's part'. Despite feeling that she had become locked into a negotiating process, Thatcher retained a tight rein on her officials and pored over every detail they presented to her. She was particularly upset by a suggestion that, if an Anglo-Irish Agreement led to 'a real and sustained reduction in the level of violence, that will be among the factors to be taken into account by the Secretary of State for Northern Ireland in reviewing the release of prisoners in Northern Ireland who have been convicted of terrorist crimes'.[46]

Jim Molyneaux, leader of the Ulster Unionist Party, and Ian Paisley of the Democratic Unionist Party both visited Thatcher to seek reassurance. At the start of September, Hurd impressed upon Peter Barry, the Irish Minister for Foreign Affairs, the need for a 'low-key measured approach to presentation which would achieve a period of reassurance' for unionists. The proposed Anglo-Irish secretariat could not be 'too high powered and interventionist'. Unionists had to see Irish assurances on 'the constitution and on security measures'. Peter Barry, Irish Foreign Minister, reiterated the need to reassure the nationalist community in Northern Ireland too. He said the 'most difficult nut to crack' was west Belfast and suggested that it would be a good thing for an Irish minister like himself to be seen having a drink in a local pub, in order to demonstrate things had changed. Hurd disagreed strongly. Serious tensions remained. The British refused to agree to establish mixed courts or to introduce reform of the Ulster Defence Regiment. Meanwhile, the Irish began to equivocate on their promise to accede to the European Convention on the Suppression of Terrorism. Charles Powell reported this to Thatcher on 26 September, saying this was 'one of the main attractions for us in the agreement, which has been an incentive to continuing the negotiations. Their sudden and belated change of direction calls into question their good faith.' The following day, Thatcher warned that this was a 'serious retrograde step'. The growing concern about the deal was articulated by Tom King. In his view, it seemed to offer 'considerably more to the Irish than it does to us'. 'The Irish have not been able to surrender their constitutional

---

46 Thatcher's comments on negotiations were extremely hostile as late as 3 July 1985, PREM 19/1550: TNA.

claim on the North', he complained. 'The most direct advantage for us will be in better security cooperation, but so far we have only a rather vague indication that the Republic will redeploy their task force to Border areas to combat terrorism.'[47]

Hurd, who remained involved, still believed it was right to pursue an agreement but admitted the 'balance of margin is a fine one'. Howe was firmer in pushing back strongly against King. 'We must judge the points made in Tom King's latest minute against that background of continuing Irish good faith in our determination to strike, if possible, a bargain that will stand the test of time', he wrote at the end of September. It would be wrong to postpone the deal any further, he warned. The Irish government was already having difficulty holding its position 'against the leaks and accompanying speculation, not all of which have come from their side of the Irish Sea', he added. In a note to Powell on 10 October, Thatcher wrote: 'I think we must fight for our viewpoint. The Irish are still trying to convey the impression that they are going to get some kind of authority in Northern Ireland.' The consultative status would 'give enough trouble as it is – the limitations of their role must be made clear', she countered.[48]

Despite these concerns of the prime minister, it was only at the last minute that the British government decided that the proposed Anglo-Irish Secretariat should not be housed in Stormont Castle or Stormont House.[49] At the end of October, the crucial breakthrough was made when King and Howe were able to agree on a joint communiqué to the cabinet, recommending that it support the agreement. 'From our own point of view, the balance of advantage is a fine one', the document read. That the deal was likely to provoke a bad reaction from Unionists would 'hinder rather than assist the process of reconciliation'. Long term, it was felt that it 'does offer considerable prizes': a better relationship with Dublin, taking away the SDLP's excuse for opposing power-sharing, and 'international benefits' for the UK's reputation, particularly in the US. After a fierce debate, the British cabinet agreed to support the deal, on the condition that King continue to lobby for 'the maximum possible improvements' in the text of the agreement, particularly on security cooperation, to the last minute.

47 For accounts of these meetings, and Anglo-Irish relations in 1985, see PREM 19/1548, PREM 19/1549, PREM 19/1550, and PREM 1551: TNA.
48 For all the internal British discussions in the final phase leading to the agreement, see PREM 19/1550 and PREM 19/1551: TNA.
49 B. Mawhinney, *Just a Simple Belfast Boy* (London: Biteback Publishing, 2013), 67.

Eventually however, the negotiators limped over the finishing line and the deal was signed on 15 November at Hillsborough Castle, County Down. It is true that Thatcher was, in part, influenced by American pressure and appears to have felt that Reagan would approve the deal.[50] She soon came to regret her decision. In 1985 there had been 54 deaths: 5 were loyalist killings, 47 were republican. By 1988, the impact of the Agreement, which had promised so much on security, seemed to be negative: there were 105 deaths. A distinctive feature of this was the rising loyalist share. From the very low base of 5 against 47 republican murders in 1985, loyalists actually took the lead from republicans in 1993, 48 to 39. Loyalist paramilitaries reassured by Roy Mason and Margaret Thatcher – before she signed the Anglo-Irish Agreement – were now much more aggressive. Their violence was a response not just to IRA activity but to uncertainty about British policy.

Towards a Settlement: New Thinking in Whitehall

There is a conventional wisdom in the Dublin political establishment but, rather less so in the London establishment, that the Agreement of 1985 pointed towards the Good Friday Agreement of 1998. In fact, the 1985 Agreement did play a role in preparing the ground for the Agreement of 1998. It brought home to the political leaders of the Unionist majority the limits of their power if confronted by a determined London government. In this respect, it built on the experience of the defeated strike of 1977. Also, once the Unionist leadership skipped a generation as when it passed from James Molyneaux to David Trimble in the mid-1990s, it passed into the hands of those who were determined to try their hand at negotiating. They felt that Molyneaux's passivity and fear of 'high wire' acts had led to the great humiliation of 1985. It is perhaps also the case that the Agreement of 1985 enhanced the Irish government's status in the eyes of the Provo leadership.

On the other hand, Britain gained little from the Agreement. Northern Ireland became more expensive and more violent. Megaphone diplomacy continued and the British Embassy in Washington DC continued to have a hard time on the Irish issue. In short, with the Unionists choosing to go into a kind of internal exile, the problem of Northern Ireland became even worse from a London point of view. In particular, the failure of the 1985 Agreement to endorse fully the principle of consent alarmed many Unionists and

50 C. Matthews, *Tip and the Gipper: When politics worked* (New York: Simon and Schuster, 2013), 134/5.

inflated nationalist expectations. The decision to leave articles 2 and 3 – which expressed a territorial claim over Northern Ireland – led to cases in the Dublin Supreme Court which, if anything, strengthened that claim – and provoked British exasperation. The claim that the Hillsborough Agreement embodied some new recognition of Northern Ireland's legitimacy within the UK had evaporated by 1990. There was, instead, an entirely new labour of negotiation required to achieve this effect in 1998 with the Good Friday Agreement. It is little wonder that ten years later, an official in the press office of John Major, Thatcher's successor as prime minister, was widely quoted as describing the Agreement of 1985 as that 'f.....g awful Agreement'.

The Anglo-Irish Agreement of 1985 did not, therefore, achieve its stated objective of reconciliation and better security. The succeeding years saw an increase, not a drop, in violence. An angry Mrs Thatcher declared later that she had received worse security cooperation from the Republic of Ireland than any other European country. It was the only major policy initiative of her premiership which she renounced.[51] The obvious question is clear: had she any right to be surprised given the Republic's failure to sign the European treaty on the suppression of terrorism as part of the deal? This was surely a sign of how things would work out. Electorally also the Agreement had little impact on the popular support for Sinn Féin: it stood at 13.4 per cent of the vote in the North in 1983. The Sinn Féin share fell to 11.8 per cent in the local government elections in the summer before the Agreement and then to 11.4 per cent in the general election after the Agreement. But a less obvious effect requires noting: in 1985, two-thirds of SDLP voters gave their second prefer- ence vote in the local government elections to the moderate Alliance, only one-third gave it to Sinn Féin. However, increasingly, the language of politics was dominated by the concept of a 'pan-nationalist pact', beginning with the Hume / Adams dialogue of 1988. These discussions in which John Hume, for example, drew the attention of Gerry Adams, the long-time leader of Sinn Féin, to Parnell's conciliatory speech in Belfast in May 1891 – may have helped pave the way for peace but at the price of an even deeper sectarianisation of Northern Irish politics. Senior members of the SDLP, including its deputy leader under John Hume, Seamus Mallon, have decried the way in which this dialogue legitimised Sinn Féin and helped it triumph over the SDLP. Adams 'played John Hume like 3lb trout', Mallon later commented. 'I think he was so immersed in the whole business of getting peace that he didn't, or couldn't, come to grips with the fact that his presence with them gave them, especially

---

51 'Enoch was Right on Ireland, says Thatcher', *BBC News*, 23 November 1998.

in the United States and in Ireland, a status that almost bordered on validating their actions of the past 30 years.'[52]

All these developments combined to create a space for new thinking in the British elite. John Chilcot and Quentin Thomas who took the lead at the Northern Ireland Office were Whitehall pragmatists who were unconvinced at the sagacity of the Anglo-Irish Agreement as an effort to stabilise the province. They wanted to re-engage with the Unionist political leadership. They were open to a new departure and in no way hostile to Hume's attempt to engage the Provos. It is now clear – in a way that it was not then – that they had vital political intelligence on the Provisional leadership from people like Denis Donaldson and Freddie Scapaticci, both highly placed informers within republican ranks. The brutal fact is that republican war weariness was enhanced by the increased level of loyalist killings. It is from this period that many of the most significant IRA claims of state collusion with loyalists date. The Provos were effectively treated like Michael Collins – take the carrot i.e. substantive negotiations about the future, or continue the dirty war with ever increasing personal risks. After some false starts, the two governments achieved their objective with the Good Friday Agreement of 1998.

The policy of 'including the extremes' whilst at the same time always believing that any new deal had to pass a referendum of the people of Northern Ireland was a brave one. The Northern Ireland Office embraced it in the early 1990s but in this respect it was well ahead of the entire local political class. One of the present authors recalls a dinner in Hillsborough Castle in 1993 when Sir Patrick Mayhew, then Northern Ireland Secretary, and his two leading officials, Sir John Chilcot, the permanent undersecretary and Quinton Thomas, the political director, outlined the new strategy. He recalls trying out these ideas on local leaders of all different shades – none showed any real interest – but in the end the N.I.O. prospectus won out.

The Downing Street Declaration of December 1993 was conceptually original.[53] It conceded the principle of self-determination to *one* Irish people on the island of Ireland but included the Irish government position that this could not be achieved without the consent of a majority in Northern Ireland. It advocated an 'agreed Ireland' – a common John Hume phrase – but this

---

52 Interview on BBC Talkback, reported as 'Seamus Mallon: Sinn Féin "played John Hume like 3lb trout", 28 December 2015: www.bbc.co.uk/news/uk-northern-ireland-35115892.

53 During the negotiation, the British took care not to exclude unionist opinion as in 1985. Archbishop Eames, for example, arranged a meeting in London between James Molyneaux and Albert Reynolds, which passed off in complete secrecy. For this epoch in British policy, see above all G. Spencer (ed.), *The British and Peace in Northern Ireland: The Process and Practice of Reaching Agreement* (Cambridge University Press, 2015).

now meant a power-sharing plus Irish dimension settlement underpinned by the principle of consent. It was said by insiders that the Downing Street Declaration – signed by premiers John Major and Albert Reynolds – was green on the outside but Orange on the inside.

The Downing Street Declaration of 15 December 1993 invited the Provisional IRA to enter into talks about the future of Northern Ireland if that organisation made a 'permanent' renunciation of violence. In the same day in the Irish parliament, the Foreign Minister, Dick Spring, declared that 'permanence' was to be proven by the handing over of weapons. Given this agenda, the IRA hesitated but by the end of August 1994 its leadership had decided to proclaim an IRA ceasefire. It did not prove permanent as was shown by its breakdown at the time of the Canary Wharf bomb of early 1996, but it was nonetheless a key moment in the peace process.

After the Downing Street Declaration of 1993, the main political question concerned the nature of the next British government initiative. John Major had resisted pressure from some in the Irish Department of Affairs to make Britain a persuader for Irish unity – but how to maintain a shaky IRA ceasefire? The answer was the inter-governmental decision to issue the Framework Document in early 1995. This document saw the return of cloudy green rhetoric attached to a description of cross-border institutions that Unionists found decidedly threatening. They were described as 'executive', 'dynamic' and 'harmonising' – few Unionists bother to look at the small print in paragraph 33 where the very narrow focus of the project of these bodies is made very clear. At first, the Unionist political leadership erupted in a fit of rage which allowed the IRA to sustain its ceasefire for another few months. But confronted by a weak Major government which – it began to believe was increasingly dependent on Unionist votes at Westminster – 'unruly elements', a phrase used to one of the authors by a senior republican at the time, regained control and bombing resumed in 1996. The weak response of the Major government – disappointment rather than anger – can only have been encouraging. It was no surprise when the IRA reinstated its ceasefire shortly after Tony Blair's Labour landslide victory in the summer of 1997.

Tony Blair, the first British prime minister since Bonar Law to have an Ulster Protestant parent, knew, however, that Labour's traditional leaning towards Irish nationalism might make it harder to work with the Unionists. One of the present authors saw at first hand in Downing Street the enormous efforts that Blair, and, in particular, his chief of staff, Jonathan Powell, made to achieve balance. Unionists had to accept a negotiating process in which the IRA always maintained a level of threat; on the other hand, the consent principle was never challenged. Indeed, when the Good Friday Agreement was published, words like executive, harmonising and dynamic were also absent in their description of cross-border institutions. On Good Friday 1998, a power-sharing plus Irish dimension agreement based on the principle of consent was negotiated successfully. It is worth noting that beneath frequent outbursts of green rhetoric, the Irish government's principal objective had always been stability on the island of Ireland and this proved decisive. It has to be acknowledged, however, that the high optimism – which one of the present authors recalls well on the morning of Good Friday 1998 – that the Ulster Unionists and SDLP would be rewarded for driving the peace process, was to be disappointed. It was as though the people confronted by the structure of a negotiated compromise could only tolerate it if their own rhetorical 'hard-liners' were in control. There was also an inclination on the part of the British government, in particular, to wrap the conflict in a bow, by bringing in those on the extreme flanks of the spectrum. That those on the so-called extremes were quick to name their price – Paisley's DUP, in particular, demonstrating its long-held desire to be the Unionist 'top-dog', whatever the dispensation, made this temptation too much to ignore. As an act of stabilisation and realpolitik, one can see the logic. A more comprehensive settlement was achieved; that said, it was one that in some ways rewarded those who bore much of the responsibility for the ugliness of life in Northern Ireland over the previous decades. In Seamus Mallon's memorable description of that process of bow tying: 'Stitch-up is a word that can be used in a very loose way. Let's say it was not the furthest thing from the minds of the governments that, in effect, the two greatest bullies would be best suited to govern the people of the north of Ireland.'[54] Ultimately, however, the peace process is best understood as a highly choreographed, painfully slow, and pre-condition-laden architectural achievement built on the foundations of a previously elusive 'sufficient consensus', namely the acquiescence of a moderate majority from both communities in an atmosphere slightly improved by the gradual asphyxiation of those responsible for violence.[55]

Was the IRA Defeated?

There is an intense academic debate on the subject of whether the Provisional IRA actually lost 'the war'. The problem with some academic assessments

---

54 Mallon interview on BBC Talkback: www.bbc.co.uk/news/uk-northern-ireland-35115892.
55 J. Bew, M. Frampton and I. Gurruchage, *Talking To Terrorists: Making Peace in Northern Ireland and the Basque Country* (New York: Columbia University Press, 2009).

is that they fail to appreciate the deliberate ambiguity in loaded terms such as 'stalemate', or the way in which defeat and victory are very difficult to define.[56] What we do know is that the security campaign against the IRA – particularly the often murky use of agents and informers – did have a significant impact on its strategy, coupled with the keeping open of an alternative route to the armed struggle (something which was on offer from 1970). Yet, optics and semantics play a crucial part in how these contending variables are assessed. On the tenth anniversary of the end of the campaign against Britain, in late July 2015, Gerry Adams insisted that the IRA was never defeated. He was responding to a claim by Prime Minister David Cameron that 'British resolve saw off the IRA's assaults on our way of life.' Adams has a point: there was no piece of paper on which P. O'Neill, the mythical IRA spokesperson, conceded with his or her signature the IRA's defeat. While the IRA was heavily penetrated by British agents and informers it still retained the capacity for secret operations such as the Canary Wharf bomb of 1996.[57] The IRA believed until at least 2005 that it retained the wherewithal for a significant renewed bout of violence. But, while conceding this, it is worth quoting Ed Moloney's persuasive counterpoint: 'Defeat or victory at the end of a conflict is also measured in other ways. For example, if one party to a conflict surrenders its weapons, that is, disarms itself at the insistence of its opponent, where that opponent holds on to their weapons then there is no doubt that the former lost and the latter won.'[58]

The IRA resisted the Downing Street Declaration message of 1993 that permanent renunciation of violence should be proven by the decommissioning of weapons but 12 years later they eventually capitulated. The IRA declared itself to be at war with the principle of 'consent' – that Northern Ireland had a democratic right to exist as part of the United Kingdom – but eventually accepted that principle. On these terms, it is hard to avoid the conclusion that the IRA was defeated. But what if we regard the IRA campaign, in Eamonn McCann's celebrated phrase as the continuation of the civil rights campaign by 'inappropriate means'? What if we suggest that its rationale was to give Northern Catholics a place of equality and prestige within their

56 J. Bew and M. Frampton, 'Debating the "Stalemate": A Response to Dr Dixon', *The Political Quarterly*, 83 (Apr.-June 2012), 277–82.

57 M. Ingram, G. Harkin, *Stakeknife: Britain's Secret Agents in Ireland* (Dublin: O'Brien Press, 2004). See also S. Grey, *The New Spymasters* (London: St Martins Press, 2015), which discusses British intelligence's exploration of paedophilia within the family of Gerry Adams.

58 E. Moloney, 'So, Was The IRA Defeated, Or Not?' *The Broken Elbow*: https://thebrokenelbow.com/2015/07/29/so-was-the-ira-defeated-or-not/.

society? This is something that Gerry Adams has tried to write back into the history of the Provisional IRA in recent years, most obviously in an interview with *The Guardian* in 2009. It was in this interview that Adams made what was an otherwise remarkable statement – presaged with the careful caveat 'I'm not speaking for the IRA' – that 'armed actions [by the IRA] were never about building the united Ireland, they were always about protesting or standing up to British policy, or British strategy.'[59] The difficulty with the Adams's reinterpretation of the nature of the struggle – and his notion that it had now evolved from an armed to a peaceful phase – was that it depended upon Sinn Féin successfully portraying itself as an all-Ireland movement rather than a party stuck within the structures of two states. This, in turn, depends on retaining the sort of trajectory and sense of momentum which has proved increasingly difficult to maintain. So what if we suggest a new political strategy exists involving mobilising large swathes of public opinion in the Irish Republic on an anti-austerity ticket, like that of the Greek political party Syriza? Even here the possibilities are not particularly exciting, as the Irish electorate views closely the vicissitudes of the Greek experiment. Nevertheless, electoral success in the Republic, if it came, might rejuvenate the Sinn Féin vote in the North, which has seen in recent years a dip in the total nationalist vote share.

Yet beneath the squalid surface reality of Northern Irish politics in 2015 there lurked an unacknowledged reality. The new 'normal', an ineffective Stormont power-sharing parliament, was widely supported because it delivered peace. In 1995, the two protagonists of Direct Action Against Drugs, Jock Davison and Kevin McGuigan, signalled by their murder of several drug dealers the end of the first ceasefire, 'a changing balance of force'[60] within the IRA. They were sending a message to the British that the first ceasefire was going to break down. Twenty years on, the two men, now enemies, were both murdered, one in retaliation, apparently, for the murder of the other. These murders provoked much public debate as it became clear that the IRA still existed, at least, for criminal purposes. What is truly remarkable is that there was no real enthusiasm within Unionism to walk away from power-sharing even though a perfect excuse had been provided: rather there is hope that Sinn Féin's embarrassment at these murders will make a deal on welfare reform more likely and lead to greater stability in the institutions. The nationalist community supported the new Agreement in the 1998

---

59 Gerry Adams interview with Nick Stadlen, *The Guardian*, 12 September 2009.
60 As one of present authors wrote in *Sunday Telegraph*, 20 December 1995.

referendum by over 90 per cent and the Unionists by just over 50 per cent. By 2015, however, the underlying solidity of support within unionism for the deal was, at least, as high if not higher than that of nationalism. It was not an outcome that anyone had predicted. As the year drew to a close, Sinn Féin and the DUP struck a deal which allowed for the full resurrection of the institutions and confirmed stability until a sudden destabilising blow in June 2016 – the decision by the British electorate to leave the European Union. Brexit intensified anti-UK sentiment – which had been largely dormant – in every segment of Irish nationalist opinion. It interacted with local antagonisms and disputes in Northern Ireland to strengthen Sinn Féin and polarise opinion. The institutions again collapsed. But it is worth noting that Gerry Adams, while insisting there was a crisis of the institutions, declared that there was no crisis of the peace process.

The Troubles cost almost three and a half thousand lives. Sixty per cent of those who died were killed by the IRA or its allies. Thirty per cent were killed by loyalist paramilitaries. Ten per cent were killed by the forces of the state.[61] There is today a debate about the role of state collusion, both that of the British and Irish state, but it is obvious that the main drivers of violence were the people in Northern Ireland themselves.[62] In the immediate aftermath of the Good Friday Agreement of 1998, Sir Kenneth Stowe, private secretary to Harold Wilson, James Callaghan and Margaret Thatcher – and then, from 1979–1981 permanent undersecretary at the Northern Ireland Office – was invited back to Belfast to discuss the bureaucratic consequences of the Good Friday Agreement. Slightly puzzled by their banality, Sir Kenneth asked 'What would Gerry Adams think if he was a fly on the wall?' It was an understandable question from a British official who had experienced the moment when a prime minister had wanted to withdraw from Northern Ireland, through the hunger strikes, but the truth is that the Troubles just fizzled out.

A little wistfully, the inhabitants of Northern Ireland have returned to a quieter world of provincial self-regard, or competing provincial self-regards. The era – from the collapse of communism in 1989 to the terrorists attacks of 11 September 2001 – when the politics of this small region of the UK might dominate the table talk of the president of the United States more than the crazed leadership of a North Korea armed for a nuclear war was

---

61 For the IRA's campaign in the border counties, see H. Patterson, *Ireland's Violent Frontier: The Border and Anglo-Irish Relations* (Houndsmills: Palgrave Macmillan, 2013).
62 J. Ware, 'Collusion cuts both ways', *Standpoint* (November 2015).

definitely over, though it has to be admitted that Tony Blair made a serious effort at Hillsborough Castle, on the eve of the invasion of Iraq, to explain the subtleties of Ulster politics to President George W. Bush.[63] The people of Northern Ireland had seen it all. Ian Paisley, whose anti-Catholicism had terrified Terence O'Neill co-operated warmly at the top of the new devolved administration with Martin McGuinness – two of the pre-eminent bogeymen for their respective communities. The Provisionals, who had fought a bitter and murderous internecine civil war with the Official IRA in the 1970s ended up embracing the 'Official' memes – devolution and peaceful 'non-sectarian' republicanism in particular. The large British financial subsidy continued to flow in, against all academic predictions and the desires of many British policymakers. The people of Northern Ireland absorbed it all during the years of 'the Troubles' – described, more aptly by the poet Michael Longley, as 'the Disgrace'.

63 T. Branch, *The Clinton Tapes: A President's Secret Diary* (New York: Simon and Schuster, 2009); Peter Stothard, *30 Days: A Month at the Heart of Blair's War* (London: Element Press, 2009).

The Troubles: A Photographic Essay

THOMAS BARTLETT

1. Burntollet, January 1969. In January 1969 a student-led People's Democracy march was ambushed at Burntollet Bridge outside Derry. About 200 loyalists, many of whom were off-duty members of the RUC, attacked them. The incident led to rioting in Derry and was instrumental in forcing Terence O'Neill's resignation some months later.

2. 'What about Ireland, Major Healey?' British defence secretary Dennis Healey (1917–2015) on a walkabout in Belfast in 1969.

3. Bernadatte Devlin and Eamonn McCann, both prominent members of People's Democracy entering Belfast Court House in 1970.

4. Nell McCafferty, acclaimed Derry-born journalist for the Irish Times during the early years of the 'Troubles'.

5. Gerry Fitt (1926–2005), nationalist MP for west Belfast (1966), founder and first leader of the SDLP. Famously beaten and drenched with water, along with some Westminster colleagues, by RUC officers in Derry in October 1968.

6. British soldiers on patrol in Belfast. Incurious children play on regardless (1970s).

7. Bombs were a daily occurrence in Belfast in the early 1970s. Here a man smoking a cigarette walks nonchalantly away from a bomb blast in central Belfast, early 1970s.

8. Brian Faulkner (1921–77), Prime Minister of Northern Ireland, 1971–2.

9. The newly formed loyalist Ulster Defence Association parade in Belfast in 1972.

10. Members of the UDA at a bonfire-barricade *c.* 1972. This organisation, under various titles, was responsible for over 400 deaths, mostly of Catholics during the Troubles.

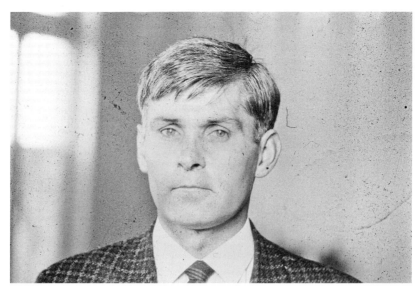

11. John McKeague (1930–82), one-time associate of Ian Paisley, prominent loyalist para-military, alleged child molester and RUC informer. He was murdered in mysterious circumstances in 1982.

12. RUC Detective Inspector Jimmy Nesbitt, widely credited with apprehending the loyalist murder gang, the 'Shankill Butchers', here pictured in an 'entry' or back lane off Tennent Street in the Shankill area, where the gang's mutilated Catholic victims were usually dumped.

13. Demonstration against the Parachute regiment, Ballymurphy estate, Belfast, 1972.

14. Lt Col. Derek Wilford, commander of the Parachute Regiment in Derry on 'Bloody Sunday', January 1972.

15. Anti-Internment marches in Belfast and Armagh, 1972.

16. Glenn Barr (1942–2017), loyalist politician, a prominent leader in the UWC strike of 1974, later active in cross community initiatives in Derry.

17. John Hume (b. 1937) founding member of the Social Democratic and Labour Party, architect of the peace process in the 1990s and (with David Trimble) a recipient of the Nobel Peace Prize in 1998.

18. Sean MacStiofáin (1928–2001), Chief of Staff of the Provisional IRA 1969–72. Despite having no Irish connections at all, he was active in the IRA since the 1950s but was later discredited because of his failure to carry through on a hunger strike.

19. David Irvine (1953–2007) joined the UVF in his youth and was sentenced to eleven years imprisonment for possession of explosives. In prison in the 1970s, he came under the influence of Augustus 'Gusty' Spence and on his release he became a strong advocate for loyalism to pursue a political path. He was widely regarded as being instrumental in bringing about the loyalist ceasefire in 1994.

20. Joe Cahill (1920–2004), IRA member since the 1930s, sentenced to death in 1941 for the murder of an RUC officer in Belfast, very prominent in the Provisional IRA in the 1970s and 1980s, and a convicted gun-runner on its behalf.

21. Reverend Ian Paisley (1926–2014), at a loyalist protest in front of Belfast City Hall in 1973. Reverend Martin Smyth (b.1931), Grand Master of the Orange Order is seated below him.

22. A heavily tattooed Alexander 'Buck Alec' Robinson (c1901–1995), loyalist gunman from the 1920s and 1930s, posing for a studio portrait with Augustus 'Gusty' Spence (1933–2011). Spence was a founding member of the reconstituted Ulster Volunteer Force in the early 1960s and was convicted with others of the murder of a Catholic barman, Peter Ward, in Malvern Street, off the Shankill Road in 1966. He later renounced violence while remaining influential in loyalist circles.

23. A television screen 'grab' of Seamus Twomey (1919–89), veteran member of the IRA and Officer Commanding the Belfast Brigade of the IRA in 1972.

24. Leading members of the 'Official IRA' c. 1980: Cathal Goulding (1923–98), Sean Garland, Dessie O'Hagan (1934–2015) and Tomás MacGiolla (1924–2010).

25. Man and child at Divis Flats, off the Falls Road, Belfast. The dismal flats complex was a stronghold of republican paramilitaries.

26. Jim Craig (1941?-1988), 'fund-raiser' for the UDA, with Andy Tyrie, Supreme Commander of the UDA. Craig was murdered by the UDA on suspicion of helping the IRA assassinate John McMichael, a rival UDA leader.

27. Alex Maskey (b.1952), first Sinn Féin lord mayor of Belfast, in a significant symbolic act, laying a wreath at the Centotaph in the grounds of Belfast City Hall commemorating the Irish dead at the battle of the Somme (2002).

28. Martin Meehan (1945–2007). Provisional IRA commander in the Ardoyne area of Belfast. Here posing with a photograph of himself on active service with PIRA.

29. Martin McGuinness (1950–2017). IRA commander in Derry in the 1970s and Deputy First Minister in Northern Ireland, 2007 to 2017.

30. Gerry Adams (b.1948), IRA activist and President of Sinn Féin (1983–2018) argues with Mairead Corrigan (b.1944) (Nobel peace prize recipient, along with Betty Williams, in 1976) about the justification for the IRA campaign (late-1970s).

31. Billy Hutchinson (b. 1955). Member of the Ulster Volunteer Force, convicted murderer, and later supporter of the 'Peace process'.

32. Hugh Smyth (1941–2014). Loyalist politician from the Shankill area of Belfast, and spokesman for the UVF.

33. Low intensity propaganda. A young loyalist on Belfast's Newtownards Road, 1980s.

34. Harry Murray, shipyard worker in Belfast and leader of the Ulster Workers' Council strike in 1974 that brought down the power-sharing executive set up under the Sunningdale Agreement.

35. RUC officer with machine gun ND 1970s.

36. RUC officers offer protection to an elderly country woman ND 1970s.

37. A heavily fortified and paint-splattered RUC barracks during the Troubles. RUC stations were frequently attacked by the Provisional IRA.

38. Hoarding erected on the border between the Republic and Northern Ireland in 2006 commemorating the republican hunger strikers of 1981.

39. IRA graffiti in Belfast, 1980s.

40. Revd. Ian Paisley lifted into position for a pose modelled on that of the statue of Sir Edward Carson at the entrance to Stormont, ND early 1980s.

41. Robust policing: an RUC officer deals with a protester complaining about a march by Rev Ian Paisley in Downpatrick, County Down, 1981.

42. The signing of the Anglo-Irish agreement in 1985 by Garret Fitzgerald, Irish Taoiseach and Margaret Thatcher, British Prime Minister, witnessed by the world's media.

43. 'Belfast says No': The banner signalled the beginning of what was to be a long-standing protest against the Anglo-Irish agreement, c. 1985.

44. James Molyneux (1920–2015), the largely ineffective leader of the Ulster Unionist Party, 1979–2005.

45. David Trimble, leader of the Ulster Unionist party (1995–2005), Nobel prize-winner (jointly with John Hume) in 1998, and First Minister in the Northern Ireland Assembly, 1998–2002. Here posing beneath a portrait of Sir James Craig, leader of Ulster's opposition to Home Rule in 1912 and later Prime Minister of Northern Ireland.

46. Republican poster calling attention to the plight of women in prison for IRA activities.

47. Scarcely a town in Northern Ireland escaped at least one IRA bombing during the Troubles. This is the aftermath of a bombing in Ballynahinch, County Down.

48. The aftermath of an SAS ambush that resulted in the death of eight members of the East Tyrone Brigade of the Provisional IRA, at Loughgall, County Tyrone, 1987. The wooden rods through the side of the IRA vehicle reveal the trajectory of the bullets fired.

49. The aftermath of the 1988 Ballygawley, County Tyrone, bus bomb in which eight soldiers were killed by the Provisional IRA.

50. The aftermath of the explosion of a 1000 lb culvert bomb by the Provisional IRA that killed four members of the Ulster Defence Regiment, near Downpatrick, County Down, in 1990.

16

The Irish Economy 1973 to 2016

JOHN O'HAGAN

Introduction[1]

In terms of simple geography, Ireland is a tiny country, an island to
the west of Britain, which in turn is a somewhat larger but much more
densely populated island to the west of mainland Europe: its population is
today (2016) over 15 times that of Ireland. Ireland and the United Kingdom
have a common labour market, a common language, and huge trade and
tourism flows in both directions; by and large people in both jurisdictions watch the same TV programmes and follow similar key sports and
cultural events. These are inescapable facts, which are important to an
understanding of the Irish economy, past and present. Ireland's relationship with its closest neighbour is crucial not just to its economic success
but also to continued peace on the island. This is because the island of
Ireland consists of two political units, the larger portion of which forms
the Republic of Ireland and the smaller portion Northern Ireland, which
is part of the UK. This too has had an impact on economic, social, and
political life in the Republic.

This chapter, though, is overwhelmingly about the economy of the
Republic of Ireland, and henceforth the terms economy of Ireland and Irish
economy refer to this economy, unless otherwise stated. Some reference
is made to the Northern Ireland economy, but because economic policy is
largely determined in London, it is difficult to devote much attention to policy there without also reviewing British economic policy in general. There
has been, though, increased cross-border cooperation on the economic front
since the Good Friday Agreement of 1998.

---

1 This section draws heavily on the Preface to J. O'Hagan and C. Newman (eds.), *The
  Economy of Ireland: National and Sectoral Policy Issues* (12th Edition) (Dublin: Gill &
  Macmillan, 2014).

Irish links, economic and cultural, to continental Europe are strengthening, something that low-cost air travel and the use of the euro has facilitated. Irish people are now much more familiar than they were even 25 years ago with political developments in Europe, and with European sporting and cultural events. Indeed, as a result of the previous boom in incomes, many own second homes there. Ireland joined the European Union in 1973 and adopted the euro in the late 1990s, with the euro replacing Irish notes and coins in January 2002. As such, there is no discussion in this chapter on monetary policy or on balance of payments and exchange rate policy in Ireland. These issues are now decided collectively at the eurozone level.

The policy emphasis now at an Irish level is almost exclusively on the competitiveness of the EU region, 'Ireland Inc'. Even in relation to this, Ireland must operate within an agreed competition and regulatory environment, determined, with Ireland as a voting member, at an EU level. Competitiveness is a key determinant of our attractiveness to foreign direct investment: the scale of US investment has been such that Ireland might be viewed in an industrial sense as a region of the American economy, despite the fact that in a monetary sense the country is an integral part of the eurozone. International benchmarking in terms of competitiveness is now commonplace and the *Annual Competitiveness Reports* produced by the National Competitiveness Council each year since 1997 are some of the most talked-about reports produced. Despite Ireland's industrial connection with the USA and the economic, monetary and political links with the EU, the eurozone in particular, the relationship with the UK for Ireland is still very important, for a variety of reasons. Not least, as mentioned already, is that part of the UK economy is on the island of Ireland with extensive common land borders with the Republic of Ireland. While the nature of this relationship may have altered significantly, its substance has remained the same.

The second section of the chapter will provide a broad overview of the development of the Irish economy from 1973. The third section will examine the overall population and labour force make-up in Ireland and the fourth section will then examine performance in terms of the crucial indicator for any economy, namely employment and unemployment. The fifth section will review Ireland's experience with living standards, paying particular attention to some unusual features of them. The sixth section will provide a brief overview of the Northern Ireland economy in terms of its main features: at once an integral part of the UK economy, and hence subject to economic policy decisions made in London, and yet with special ties to its immediate neigh-bour and the only economy with which it has a common (extensive) land border. The seventh section will conclude the chapter.

Into Europe: Trade, Investment, and Agricultural Supports 1973–2016[2]

In 1973 Ireland, along with Britain and Denmark, joined the European Economic Community (EEC, or the EU as it is known today). By joining, Ireland was committed to trading freely with the other member states, and by 1977 all tariff barriers had been removed. Many of the remaining restraints on trade within the European Union were dismantled as part of the effort to create a Single European Market. Officially these changes came into effect in 1992, although the full elimination of barriers in the EU is still not yet complete.

With lower trade barriers, it was recognised that some of Ireland's industry would not survive the competition from other member states, but it was also thought that Ireland would become a good platform from which companies from outside the European Community, particularly the United States, could serve the European market, and hence provide an alternative and hopefully greater source of employment. These expectations were largely met. While Irish exports amounted to 38 per cent of output in 1973, the proportion had risen to 94 per cent by 2002, one of the highest in the world. Membership of the EU also led to a net inflow under the Common Agricultural Policy (CAP), which subsidised farm prices. Higher farm prices helped farmers at the expense of consumers, but, as a net exporter of farm produce, Ireland was a net beneficiary. About two-thirds of EU transfers to Ireland were farm-related, with the remaining one-third consisting mainly of transfers from the 'structural funds', including the Regional Development, Social, and Cohesion funds. In principle, these funds might have added to investment and thereby boosted economic growth, but in practice they mainly appeared to have substituted for projects that the government would otherwise have had to finance. They thus made a more important contribution to living standards than to growth. Net receipts from the EU peaked at 6.5 per cent of Gross Domestic Product (GDP) in 1991, but had fallen to 0.3 per cent of GDP by 2011. By 2015, further reductions in the support of agricultural output and prices were effected so that reliance on EU funding from this source is now minimal. The much bigger benefit is free access to the EU market for food.

---

2 This section draws very heavily on J. Haughton, 'Historical Background', in O'Hagan and Newman, *Economy of Ireland*.

The Irish economy though could not escape the worldwide recession in 1974 and 1975, and GDP in these years stagnated. An over-heated economy in the developed world would have brought about anyway a major slowdown in growth, but few could have expected the oil price shock in this period. Overnight the price of oil was quadrupled. Allied to this was the realisation that the price could be increased much further and in fact all oil supplies cut off completely, given the almost total dependence on Middle Eastern oil.

As such, an air of deep pessimism engulfed the developed world with predictions of sustained recession and a looming energy crisis. Remarkably though, the Irish economy bounced back in the period 1976 to 1979 and, as with later in the period 1996 to 2007, became the focus of international attention for its remarkable growth in employment and living standards. A reflection of this was net inward migration in the 1970s, with one government minister even predicting zero unemployment by 1982. A sense of hubris gripped the country and, as a result, no one was prepared for the economic debacle of the the the 1980s.

Between 1979 and 1986, per capita consumption in Ireland actually fell slightly and GDP rose very slowly. Unemployment reached 18 per cent and remained at over 13 per cent for a decade. This indeed was a dark period for the economy. What were the causes of this stagnation? The higher price of oil meant that spending was diverted towards imports, thereby depressing aggregate demand for Irish goods and services. The solution adopted was to boost government current spending, and as a consequence the current budget deficit rose from 0.4 per cent of GDP in 1973 to 6.8 per cent by 1975. Thus the growth in the period 1976 to 1979, like in the period 2001 to 2007, was based largely on unsustainable public finances. The problem was that successive governments were unwilling to reduce the budget deficit during the growth years, and continued to borrow heavily, so that the ratio of government debt to GDP rose from 52 per cent in 1973 to 129 per cent by 1987, by then easily the highest in the European Union. By 1986 the cost of servicing this debt took up 94 per cent of all revenue from personal income tax. Much of the additional spending went to buy imports, and the current account deficit widened to an untenable 15 per cent by 1981. Partly as a result, the Irish pound was devalued four times within the European Monetary System in the early 1980s. In 1986 private capital fled the country on a large scale, anticipating a devaluation; the Irish pound was devalued in fact by 8 per cent in August. After eight years the country was in dire straits, with sustained recession, a huge rise in unemployment (see later) and the resumption of large-scale emigration. The experience of the 1950s had come back to haunt Ireland.

In 1987, though, the Fianna Fáil government introduced a very tight budget, cutting the current budget deficit to 1.7 per cent of GDP through reductions in real government spending. Capital spending was also sharply cut, especially on housing, and by 1992 the ratio of debt to GDP had fallen below 100 per cent, even though there had been no substantial increase in GDP. Economic growth resumed, as confidence (and investors) returned, and exports boomed, thanks in part to the devaluation of 1986 and to continued wage restraint. The lessons of allowing borrowing to rise to unsustainable levels was now understood: fiscal rectitude was vital for credibility and long-term growth. However, this was a lesson that was soon forgotten, as shall be seen later.

In 1979, in a move that was hailed at the time as far-sighted, Ireland broke the link with sterling (which dated back to 1826) and joined the European Monetary System (EMS). The reasoning was straightforward: Ireland had experienced inflation averaging 15 per cent between 1973 and 1979, much the same rate as in Britain, and it was believed that the key to reducing the inflation rate was to decouple the Irish pound from the high inflation sterling area and attach it to the low inflation EMS, which was dominated by the Deutschmark. Some also argued that sterling would appreciate with the development of North Sea oil, and that this would hurt Irish exports. While over 40 per cent of Irish exports still went to the UK in 1979, about a quarter went to the other EU countries, and so a change in the exchange regime was considered feasible. There was also a belief that Ireland, as part of the eurozone, would have some say with regard to monetary policy in Frankfurt, with the Governor of the Irish Central Bank a voting member of the Council of the European Central Bank, in contrast to the situation where monetary policy for Ireland was entirely determined in London.

By about 1990, Ireland could boast of low inflation, a tight budget, and a falling ratio of government debt to GDP, and it looked as if, after a decade of relative economic stagnation, the decision to join the EMS was finally paying off. Then in late 1992 the EMS collapsed. High interest rates in Germany, resulting from that country's need to finance reunification, caused the Deutschmark to appreciate. Sterling devalued, and the Irish pound ultimately followed, because 32 per cent of Irish exports still went to the UK, and in the absence of a devaluation, Irish competitiveness in the important British market would be too severely compromised.

After the collapse of the EMS, it became clear that a regime of 'fixed but flexible' exchange rates had to be replaced by a single currency. The schedule was set out in the Treaty of Maastricht, signed in 1992 and ratified the following year. As the decade progressed, it became increasingly clear that Ireland would qualify to join the euro. At the same time, the Single European Act came into effect in 1992, breaking down many of the remaining barriers to the movement of goods and people among the countries of the EU. To commit to entering the eurozone was as much a political as an economic decision, as mentioned above. The alternative for Ireland was to tie herself fully once again to sterling, with monetary and exchange rate policy for Ireland effectively being determined in London. Some claimed that having two separate currencies on the island of Ireland would constitute the biggest division in Ireland since Partition. The government though held its nerve and decided to commit to the single currency without Britain. This was one of the boldest independent economic statements ever made by the State.

The more open common market, and the prospect of a single currency, made Ireland a viable, even attractive, destination for US investors aiming to serve the EU as a whole. By then, Ireland's public finances were under control, there was a substantial pool of available, well-educated English-speaking workers, and a regime of low corporate taxation and industrial subsidies was firmly in place. The inflow of highly-productive, export-oriented labour-using investment, particularly in pharmaceuticals and information technology, had surprisingly large knock-on effects, boosting the large services sector, and raising employment substantially for the first time in a generation. By 2000, Ireland had caught up economically with its peers in the EU.

Ireland easily met the criteria for graduating to the euro, and the exchange rate was locked at €0.787564 per Irish pound on 1 January 1999. Ireland, like the states of the USA, no longer has the option of an independent monetary policy. This is not a radical break from the past; an independent monetary policy was not possible when the Irish pound was linked to sterling (1826–1979), and was severely circumscribed during the period of the European Monetary System. The main advantage of a common currency is much lower transaction costs, exchange rate and, hence, price certainty for exporters and importers, visibility of prices across national boundaries thereby increasing competition, and an increased incentive to cross-national mergers and acquisitions. The cost lies in a reduced ability to respond when faced by an external shock or domestic rigidity – for instance, if export prices fall or wages fail to adjust.

By 2000, the unemployment rate in Ireland had fallen to 4 per cent, the wave of American foreign direct investment had subsided, and one might have expected the boom to end – but it did not. The explanation partly follows from Ireland's accession to the euro. Prior to the single currency, credit was more expensive in Ireland than in Germany or France, in part because of currency risk. However, with the advent of the euro, interest rates were essentially equalised across the eurozone, as money flowed from (low-interest) Germany to (high-interest) Ireland. Irish banks, flush with funds, lent freely; households, increasingly accustomed to higher wages and lower unemployment, took on more loans; the government expanded tax incentives for housing; and inexperienced Irish financial regulators revealed their inexperience by believing that this time it was different. The result was a housing boom, sustained by a large inflow of construction workers from Eastern Europe (mainly Poland and Lithuania).

As early as 2000 the International Monetary Fund (IMF) had warned that property prices in Ireland were too high and that a housing bubble was in the making; but the growing chorus of warnings went unheeded, and house prices doubled between 2000 and 2006, before stabilising in 2007. The bubble finally burst in 2008, and by 2010 prices in Dublin were less than half their peak level. By the end of 2012, a fifth of commercial loans and more than a quarter of all mortgages were in arrears. By 2009, the major banks were insolvent, and could only survive because of a government guarantee to creditors, which in turn required the government to borrow heavily in order to foot the bill.

The recession cannot entirely be explained by a property crash. Since 2000, Ireland had steadily lost competitiveness vis-à-vis its eurozone partners, and it was inevitable on this score alone that a crash/collapse of some extent would happen. Workers had been paid unsustainable wages, with this applying in particular in the public sector. Ireland may have joined the eurozone but few fully understood that to stay competitive in that situation meant keeping costs in line with, or below, our competitors. The wages being paid, and hence the taxes raised, were at totally unsustainable levels.

The collapse of the housing bubble and the severe loss of competiveness coincided with a serious recession – world GDP fell by 0.6 per cent in 2009, the first decline since the end of the Second World War, and this ended any prospects of a rapid recovery for the Irish economy. By late 2010 the government was obliged to accept an €85 billion rescue package from the IMF and the EU, along with its accompanying strictures on taxation and spending. With little or no economic growth, unemployment rose sharply, as did emigration. The process of recovery was slow, in part because fiscal transfers among the states of the eurozone are unresponsive to economic shocks.

A mixture of fiscal restraint, falling house prices, and wage reductions have helped restore Ireland's competitiveness, the US economy has largely recovered, exports have rebounded, and job creation was strong enough from 2013 to 2016 to reduce the unemployment rate markedly. At first, most people were cautious about confirming a turnaround in the economy but, by early 2016, there can be little doubt that such a turnaround is under way, the main indicator of this being the quite dramatic lowering of the unemployment rate in just two years, albeit that it remains well above the historic lows of the period 1996 to 2007.

Some explanations for the roller-coaster performance of the Irish economy will be returned to again. For now, though, we are going to look at this performance through the prism of two of the fundamental indicators of such performance, namely, employment and living standards. Statistics on these probably better capture the narrative outlined above than any other measures.

Population and Labour Supply[3]

What happens in the labour market is probably the most important indicator of the success or otherwise of any economy, Ireland being no exception. In this regard, this section will examine what has happened in employment and unemployment in Ireland over the last 40 years, as the key story of the Irish economy, as seen above, relates to this. It is important also in this context to consider the population of the country and its components, especially migration. As shall be seen, it is migration that drives population more than any other factor in Ireland. Migration flows in turn respond to the performance of the labour market. As such, this section will begin with a discussion of Irish population. (For more on Migration see the chapter by M. E. Daly, p. 527.)

The size of the population has great emotive significance in Ireland, not surprisingly, given the huge reduction in population in Ireland following the Famine. As a result, the size of the population has in a sense become a policy objective in and of itself. Table 3 outlines the trends in population dating back to 1841. The population of the Republic of Ireland in pre-Famine days was over 6.5 million. The decline in Irish population numbers in the post-Famine period is all too obvious: a fall of over two million in 20 years. Given the high birth rate at the time, the population should in fact have increased substantially, were it not for death and emigration.

---

3 This section draws very heavily on J. O'Hagan and T. McIndoe-Calder, 'Population, Employment and Unemployment', ch 6 in O'Hagan and Newman, *op cit.*

Table 3 *Population, Republic of Ireland, 1841 to 2016 (millions)*

Years	Population	Years	Population
1841	6.529	1961	2.818
1851	5.112	1971	2.978
1861	4.402	1981	3.443
1871	4.053	1991	3.526
1881	3.870	2002	3.917
1891	3.469	2006	4.323
1901	3.222	2011	4.575
1911	3.140	2013[1]	4.593
1926	2.972	2016[2]	4.681
1951	2.961		

Source: O'Hagan and McIndoe-Calder, *op cit.*, Table 6.2.

[1] Preliminary.
[2] Forecast.

Population continued to decline up to 1926; almost 50 years later there was no increase on the 1926 level, when the population in 1971 still stood at only 2.978 million. Since then population size has increased by almost 1.7 million with most of this increase occurring between 1991 and 2014; the population in 2008 in fact exceeded its level in 1861 for the first time. Many see this sharp increase as a very positive development, one that reflects a reversal of a demoralising decline that had persisted for almost a century and a half. It is noteworthy that, even during the recession years, population continued to increase, up by almost 300,000 between 2006 and 2014.

The total population of a country depends on three factors: the number of births, the number of deaths and the level of net migration (i.e. the gap between those leaving and those arriving). The difference between the number of births and deaths is known as the natural increase and in most countries the natural increase translates directly into a population increase. This has not been the case in Ireland, where historically the change in population has 'tracked' much more closely the trend in migration than that of the natural increase. As seen in Table 4, the number of births per annum reached a peak in the 1970s and declined significantly after that. It increased again in the 2002–2006 period, and reached a new peak in the period 2006–2011, but this was more a reflection of the increase in the size of the child-bearing female population than of any large increase in the birth rate. This means that the natural increase in the population is now averaging around 44,000 per annum.

Table 4 *Components of Population Change, Selected Intervals (annual average in '000s)*

	Total births	Total deaths	Natural increase	Population change	Estimated net migration
1926–36	58	42	16	0	−17
1951–56	63	36	27	−12	−39
1956–61	61	34	26	−16	−42
1961–66	63	33	29	13	−16
1966–71	63	33	30	19	−11
1971–79	69	33	35	49	14
1981–86	67	33	34	19	−14
1986–91	56	32	24	−3	−27
1991–96	50	31	18	20	2
1996–02	54	31	23	49	26
2002–06	61	28	33	81	48
2006–11	73	29	45	70	25
2011–13[1]	73	29	44	13	−32

Source: O'Hagan and McIndoe-Calder, *op cit.*, Table 6.3.
[1] Preliminary.

While there have been significant changes in the natural increase, they are slight compared to the huge swings in net migration that can occur: 40,000 per annum leaving throughout the whole of the 1950s, and a similar number in some years in the 1980s, compared to a net annual immigration of 2,000 in the early 1990s, around 26,000 in the late 1990s, and 48,000 in the 2000s. Net out-migration again in recent years has run at 30,000 per annum or more, and as the Irish economy recovers possibly net in-migration will resume in the years ahead, perhaps even in the current year of 2016.

Labour supply in any country depends on three factors: the total size of the population, the proportion of that population of working age, and the proportion of the working-age population seeking or in work. This is illustrated by the identity:

(1) $L = (P).(Pa\,/P).(L/Pa)$

where L is the size of the labour force, P the size of the population, and Pa the size of the population of working age. The labour force, in turn, consists of those in employment (E) and those unemployed (UE). Hence:

(2) $L = E + UE$

Two further identities of interest to this discussion are the following:

(3) $Q/P = (Q/E) . (E/P)$

(4)   where $E/P = (E/L) . (L/Pa) . (Pa/P)$

Equation (3) links the demographic factors back to (1). It states that output per person employed and the proportion of the population employed determine output per head of population. We saw that increases in E were the most important factor accounting for record increases in Q in Ireland in the ten years after 1990; E/P also increased at a record rate in this decade, thereby pushing up Q/P to record levels. E/P (the proportion of the population in employment), as can be seen from Equation (4), is influenced by three factors, all of which increased in the fifteen years up to 2007: E/L (the proportion of the labour force in employment) increased as unemployment decreased; Pa/P (the proportion of the population of working age), as will be seen later, increased because of demographic factors; and finally, L/Pa (the proportion of the working population in the labour force) increased principally because of growing participation by married females in the labour force. These very favourable demographic trends, in terms of their impact on living standards, became known as Ireland's 'demographic dividend' in the 1990s and early 2000s. Since 2008 though there has been a decline in E/P, largely due to a decline in E/L, but also perhaps Pa/P.

As a result of the fall in the birth rate in the 1980s and 1990s, there was a later fall in the population aged 15 and under. However, because of the high birth rate prior to this, and more important the trends in migration observed above, there was a large increase in the population aged 15–64, and especially in the prime working-age population, 25–64. In any case, a large proportion of the immigrants fell into this latter category, thereby pushing up the population in this age group disproportionately. The number of people aged 25–64 rose from 2.18 million in 1991 to over 2.91 million by the year 2006. This represented a very large increase over such a short period and had a marked effect on Ireland's age dependency ratios. Table 5 highlights these changes in the composition of the population. In 1981, those aged under 15 years accounted for 51.4 per cent of those aged 15–64, but in just over 20 years this had dropped by almost 21 percentage points. At the same time, the population aged 65 and over, expressed as a proportion of the 15–64 population, also declined, albeit slightly.

Table 5 *Percentage Age Dependency Ratios,[1] 1981 to 2013*

	Young	Old	Total
1981	51.4	18.2	69.6
1991	43.4	18.5	61.9
2001	30.4	15.8	46.2
2011	31.8	17.3	49.2
2013	33.4	18.8	52.2

Sources: O'Hagan and McIndoe-Calder, *op cit.*, Table 6.6.
[1] The ratios in the first two columns are obtained by dividing the population aged 0–14 and 65 years and over by the population aged 15–64. The final column is the sum of these two.

As Table 5 illustrates, these favourable demographic trends have now run their course. However, there will be no worsening of the demographic situation until after 2021 when the percentage of the population classified as 'old' begins to rise significantly. These projections depend very much on what happens with regard to migration over the next decade or so. The 'young' ratio has crept up a little in recent years but is still well below the levels of 20 years ago.

An important factor when examining the employment situation in any country is the proportion of the working-age population that actually seeks work. This is known as the labour force participation rate. Table 6 provides data for Ireland, a number of other small EU countries, two countries of particular interest to Ireland (namely the UK and the USA) and the OECD average. As can be seen in Table 6, the labour force participation rate for males in Ireland in 2012 was below the OECD average but that for females, while considerably lower than for males, was at the OECD average. At the same time, the variation across countries is marked: for example, the figure for females for Ireland was 62.2 per cent, compared to a figure of 58.4 per cent in Greece (the lowest rate), 71.0 per cent in the UK, and 75.9 per cent in Norway (the highest rate).

A noteworthy feature is that female participation rates are rising in most countries, with Ireland being no exception. Following a substantial increase up to 1994, the rate grew further in Ireland, up from 45.8 to 62.2 per cent, a large rise in such a short period. By 2012 the rate for Ireland exceeded the OECD average but, as discussed above, still fell well below that in some key comparator countries, notably the UK. It is difficult to predict how much

Table 6 *Percentage Labour Force Participation Rates[1] in Selected OECD Countries, 1994 and 2012*

	Males		Females	
	1994	2012	1994	2012
Belgium	72.0	72.5	51.2	61.3
Denmark	83.7	81.4	73.8	75.8
Greece	77.0	77.4	43.2	58.4
Ireland	*76.2*	*76.7*	*45.8*	*62.2*
Netherlands	79.6	84.2	57.3	74.3
Norway	81.6	80.7	70.9	75.9
OECD	81.4	79.7	57.8	62.3
UK	85.1	83.2	67.1	71.0
USA	84.3	78.8	69.4	67.6

Source: O'Hagan and McIndoe-Calder, *op cit.*, Table 6.7.

[1] Ratios refer to persons aged 15–64 years who are in the labour force divided by the total population aged 15–64.

further this participation rate will grow in Ireland, but with the lower birth rate and if employment prospects continue to improve, it could rise to British levels if not to the heights attained in Denmark and Norway. If, as predicted, female participation rates continue to rise in Ireland, this would lead to a large increase in the labour force arising from this factor alone.

Employment and unemployment

The experience with regard to employment and unemployment has been the truly remarkable 'story' of the Irish economy over the last 40 years or so. Table 7 illustrates clearly the dramatic changes that have taken place since 1971. Who could have predicted the scale of the change from the early 1970s to the first decade of new millennium? Note that the employment figure in 1990 was just 111,000 higher than that for 1971 and that the only period during which there was a significant increase in employment up to this was during the 1970s, when over 100,000 net new jobs were created. Between 1990 and 2000, however, 525,000 net new jobs were created, a phenomenal increase in employment in such a short period. It did not stop there though as a further 462,000 jobs were created between 2000 and 2008, bringing to almost one million the total number of net new jobs created between 1990 and 2008. The decrease in unemployment during the same period, as seen in Table 7, was equally remarkable.

Table 7 *Employment and Unemployment: Ireland's Changing Fortunes*

	Employment (millions)	Unemployment rate (%)
1971	1.049	5.5
1980	1.156	7.3
1986	1.095	17.1
1990	1.160	12.9
1995	1.282	12.2
2000	1.685	4.6
2005	1.945	4.7
2008	2.147	5.7
2010	1.894	13.9
2012	1.836	15.0
2016[1]	2.000	8.5

Source: O'Hagan and McIndoe-Calder, *op cit.*, Table 6.1.
[1] Forecast.

At the same time and equally dramatic, there was the decline in employment between 2008 and 2012. Over 310,000 net jobs were lost in this short period with the unemployment rate rising from 5.7 per cent in 2008 to 15.0 per cent in 2012. And yet, the level of employment in 2012 remained way above that applying in 1995 and its level by early 2014 was similar to that in 2005: as such the huge gains between 1995 and 2005 have not been lost. The increase in employment was the main force behind the extraordinary increase in output in the economy in the period 1990–2008. By definition the following applies:

(5) $Q = (Q/E). E$

That is, the output of an economy (Q) can be expressed as the product of the average productivity of those in employment (Q/E) and the level of employment (E). The level of employment in Ireland in some years increased by over 6 per cent; this alone would have pushed up Q by 6 per cent assuming no change in productivity. Thus, increases in E were the main factor explaining the exceptional growth in Q in the period 1993 to 2008. Productivity was also increasing during this period, hence ensuring a much faster increase in Q than in E. The growth in productivity however in the 1990s and 2000s was not much higher than that seen in the 1970s and 1980s. The remarkable thing is that the huge increase in employment was not accompanied by any decrease in the growth of productivity. Just as the growth in employment drove the increase in output in the boom years, decreases in employment explain the huge decline in output between 2008 and 2012. Similarly the large rise in employment 2013–2016 in turn lay behind the increase in national output in those years. Thus swings in employment, and not productivity, are the driving forces behind the huge fluctuations in output in Ireland over the last 25 years.

Apart from the level of unemployment, its make-up is also of considerable interest to economists. The most important consideration in this regard, perhaps, relates to its composition, between those unemployed in the short term (under 12 months) and those experiencing long term (12 months or more) joblessness. Long-term unemployment (LTU) in Ireland rose significantly between 1980 and 1990. The long-term unemployment rate was only 2.8 per cent of the labour force in 1980, rising to 8.3 per cent in 1990. As Table 8 shows, a marked decline took place in LTU between 1990 and 2000. The fall was remarkable; the numbers in absolute terms were down to just over a quarter of their level in 1990, the drop in the LTU rate was even more dramatic, falling from 8.3 to 1.6 per cent, below the level pertaining in 1980. This picture remained largely unchanged up to 2008, when the first rise in LTU on all counts was recorded. Between 2008 and 2012 there was a dramatic worsening of the situation, with the LTU rate rising from 1.5 per cent to 9.2 per cent in four years, and the numbers in LTU increasing over six-fold. The LTU problem of the 1980s and early 1990s had returned to Ireland in a few short years. However, a considerable decline in LTU again did take place in the period 2013 to 2016.

Another major worry with regard to the composition of unemployment relates to youth unemployment (see Table 9). These data relate the numbers not in employment, education or training to the total population in the age groups 15–19 and 20–24. Thus, they include not just numbers unemployed but also those on disability benefit, those doing domestic unpaid work and discouraged workers. What is shown are not unemployment rates but, rather, 'inactivity rates'. These are more meaningful though than unemployment rates, which merely relate the numbers unemployed to the sum of those unemployed and to those in employment, and not to the total population in that age group. As such, one can get youth unemployment rates for, say, Greece, of over 55 per cent, when, as shown in Table 9 there are fewer than 25 per cent of that age group not in employment, education or training. In fact, the numbers unemployed, aged 20 to 24 years, in Greece probably account for not much more than 12 per cent of the population in that age group.

The data presented in Table 9 are quite striking. Over a quarter of all those aged 20–24 in Ireland are not in education, training or employment – a higher figure than that for Greece. The figure for Ireland increased dramatically, from 9.7 per cent in 2000 to 26.4 per cent in 2011. In the Netherlands the figure is as low as 6.9 per cent, but the figures for the UK and the US are also high, with

Table 8 *Long-Term Unemployment in Ireland, 1990–2013*

	Number ('000s)	Unemployment rate (%)	Long-term unemployment rate (%)
1990	110.2	12.9	8.3
2000	28.6	4.6	1.6
2005	31.6	4.7	1.5
2010	140.2	13.9	6.4
2011	178.1	14.6	8.2
2012	199.6	15.0	9.2
2013	175.0	13.9	8.1

Source: O'Hagan and McIndoe-Calder, *op cit.*, Table 6.12.

increases in inactivity in the 20–24 year-old group in the USA between 2000 and 2011. The great worry of course is that some of these people have been out of the labour market for more than one year and hence already could be categorised as belonging to the long-term unemployed or disabled.

Table 10 outlines the composition of employment in Ireland from 1994 to 2013. While the data are not strictly comparable, the table does show some broad trends over these years.

The once-central position of the agriculture sector has truly diminished and now accounts for just 5.5 per cent of total employment (down from over 12.0 per cent only 19 years ago). There are now more people employed in accommodation and food services than in the total agricultural sector, reflecting the increased importance of tourism to the Irish economy and the marked trend towards eating out by Irish people. The numbers employed in the health sector are more than the total for manufacturing and the numbers employed in education are almost 50 per cent higher than in agriculture.

The services sector as a whole is over four times the size of the industrial sector, and six times that of the manufacturing sector (other production services). As can be seen in the final column in Table 10, employment in all of the service sub-sectors grew between 1994 and 2008, but especially in transport, storage and communication, and in health. Between 2008 and 2013 there were further increases in employment in some service sectors but in particular in health, whereas there were declines in most other sub-sectors.

The figures in relation to employment in construction, however, tell the story of the overall economy: 91.5 thousand in 1994, 197.7 thousand in 2004, 246.1 thousand in 2008 with a sharp falling back to 102.7 thousand in 2013. This was truly a roller coaster in employment terms which in turn was reflected in the overall employment situation.

Table 9 *Percentage Youth Inactivity (neither employed nor in education or training)*

	15–19 year olds		20–24 year olds	
	2000	2011	2000	2011
Belgium	6.5	6.1	16.0	17.1
Denmark	2.7	5.3	6.6	11.9
Greece	9.3	8.3	25.9	24.3
Ireland	4.4	9.4	9.7	26.4
Netherlands	3.7	3.4	8.2	6.9
Norway	–	3.2	8.0	10.4
OECD	9.4	8.2	17.7	18.5
UK	8.0	9.5	15.4	19.1
USA	7.0	7.1	14.4	18.5

Source: O'Hagan and McIndoe-Calder, *op cit.*, Table 6.14.

Living Standards[4]

Apart from employment, the other important factor for most people is the standard of living they can enjoy arising from this employment. The ideal is low unemployment accompanied by high standards of living. Perhaps surprisingly, it is possible to have one without the other. It is quite possible to have increasing employment but without a rise, or even a decline, in living standards. Two decades ago, Ireland was one of the poorer countries of Western Europe, a small peripheral island with a dismal record of economic growth. Employment as seen earlier, at 1.2 million, had hardly risen in 50 years. Then, quite unexpectedly, the Irish economy grew rapidly, and the so-called Celtic Tiger years began. In the subsequent decade and a half real GDP rose two and a half-fold, employment grew to 2.1 million, and Ireland's economic and social indicators caught up with and, in some cases, surpassed, those of its Western European peers. By the standards of its European neighbours, this growth was truly exceptional. The second half of the boom (2000–2007), though, was largely built on an unsustainable basis, and could not be maintained. This section begins by looking at the basic statistics underlying the Irish 'story' in relation to living standards. How rich was Ireland, and how have other measures of wellbeing evolved over time?

4 This section draws very heavily on J. Haughton, 'Growth in Living Standards and Output', in O'Hagan and Newman, *op cit.*

Table 10 *Employment by Sector, Ireland*

	('000s)			
	1994	2004	2008	2013
Agriculture, Forestry and Fishing	147.0	113.8	116.0	103.4
Industry	343.3	492.0	537.5	341.1
of which:				
Other production services	251.8	294.3	291.4	238.4
Construction	91.5	197.7	246.1	102.7
Services	730.2	1,394.4	1,486.3	1,424.2
of which:				
Wholesale and retail trade	169.2	259.5	314.8	271.5
Accommodation and food services	68.4	107.2	128.7	129.6
Transport, storage and communication	55.9	152.1	166.3	166.4
Financial and other business services	114.3	148.0	184.9	156.9
Public administration and defence	66.4	90.1	103.5	95.1
Education	80.5	121.4	147.4	150.3
Health	101.0	177.4	222.8	244.6
Other	74.5	190.7	225.3	209.8
Total	1,220.6	1,902.3	2,147.3	1,869.9

Source: O'Hagan and McIndoe-Calder, *op cit.*, Table 6.10.

By most economic and social measures, Ireland has caught up with its peers in Western Europe. This shows clearly in Chart 5, which compares the evolution of Irish per capita output since 1980 with those of the USA, Denmark, and the UK. Denmark is included because it is, like Ireland, a small open economy, and has often been held up as a role model for Ireland to emulate. Two measures of Irish affluence are shown in Chart 5. The first is GDP per capita, which measures the money value of goods and services produced and marketed in the economy in a year. There was a clear acceleration in the growth of Irish GDP per capita starting in about 1994, with slower but still robust increases after 2000, and a sharp downturn after 2007. As can be seen, GDP per capita in Ireland in 2007 approached the USA level, and was well above the levels of the UK or Denmark. However, in the Irish case, GDP is not a particularly good indicator of affluence. Not all of the goods and services produced in Ireland accrue to Irish citizens or residents; for instance, profit that is repatriated does not contribute to local incomes. A more satisfactory measure of the output that stays in Ireland is Gross National Product (GNP): it starts with GDP and then adds net factor income from the rest of the world.

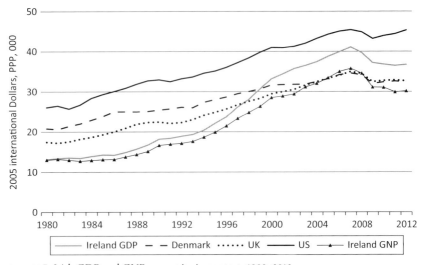

CHART 5 Irish GDP and GNP per capita in context, 1980–2012.

Source: Haughton, 'Growth in Living Standards and Output', in O'Hagan and Newman, *op cit.*

The most striking feature of these numbers is the uncommonly large value of net transfer payments out of Ireland, mainly the repatriation of profits by foreign firms operating in Ireland. Much of this is attributable to the pharmaceutical industry, which accounted for a remarkable 48 per cent of exports and 12 per cent of GDP in 2012, but just 2 per cent of employment. The expiration of patents, and hence the lower export price for drugs, is believed to have contributed to almost all of the 5 per cent drop in Irish exports seen in 2013. This also helps us understand the contradictory growth signals in, for example, 2013: GDP fell by 0.3 per cent, signifying recession, while GNP rose by 3.4 per cent, reflecting robust growth, and was consistent with the expansion of employment in 2013. An unknown part of factor income flows may be attributable to profit outflows that reflect transfer pricing, as some corporations overstate their exports and understate their imports in order to book their profits in low-tax Ireland – the corporation income tax is just 12.5 per cent, compared to 35 per cent in the USA. As a result of this measurement error, reported GDP may over-state 'true' GDP by as much as 10 per cent. However, this favourable cor-poration tax regime in Ireland has come under considerable pressure for change from other members of the EU in the last few years. This makes a difference: using GNP rather than GDP per capita, Ireland just caught up with the UK and Danish levels a decade ago, but has since slipped back, as Chart 5 shows clearly.

It is sometimes argued that the focus on per capita incomes is misguided, a reflection, perhaps, of the materialist emphasis of economists. In a much-quoted speech, Robert Kennedy in 1968 said, 'we will find neither national purpose nor personal satisfaction in an endless amassing of worldly goods ... the gross national product measures neither our wit nor our courage, neither our wisdom nor our learning, neither our compassion nor our devotion to country. It measures everything, in short, except that which makes life worthwhile.'[5] One might respond to Kennedy's critique by looking at other measures that presumably contribute to making life worthwhile. A selection of such variables is shown in Table 11 for Ireland and, to provide more context, for the EU and US, plus the best performer in the EU-27.

As can be seen, Ireland's life expectancy continues to rise, and surpasses the EU average for both men and women. The infant mortality rate – defined as the number of deaths of infants up to six months old per 1,000 population – is very low by historical standards, and is now well below the EU average. These measures, considered to be good indicators of health outcomes in general, show that Ireland has now caught up with the standards that prevail in Western Europe.

GNP represents an annual flow of final goods and services. Even when GNP rises, it can take time to build up a good stock of assets, such as houses, roads and general public infrastructure. This helps explain why Irish visitors to France, for instance, are often struck by the high quality of the infrastructure, in a country whose consumption per capita is now appreciably lower than that of Ireland. However, Table 11 shows evidence of catch-up: car ownership per capita almost doubled between 1990 and 2011, with a hugely improved infrastructure in place now to match. For years though, as incomes per capita increased rapidly there was huge congestion and disruption as the roads and other transport networks were upgraded, a process that can take many years.

House building rose above the long-term sustainable level after 2001; where Ireland had 330 houses per thousand people in 1990, this figure had risen to 440 by 2007, despite a 22 per cent increase in the population over the same period, bringing Ireland close to the EU average of 450 houses per thousand people. According to the OECD's 'better life' project, housing is now better in Ireland than anywhere else in Europe, and ranks behind only the USA and Canada in international comparisons. Ireland is also well connected to the web. Almost

---

5 Haughton, 'Growth in Living Standards'.

Table 11 *Indicators of the Quality of Life*

	Ireland			EU	USA	EU-27 best
	1970	1990	2012	2012	2012	2011
Health						
Infant mortality rate	20	8	3.8	4.5	5.2	2.6
Life expectancy, F	74	77	83.2	83.1	82.2	85.5
Life expectancy, M	69	72	78.7	77.5	77.4	79.9
Crime						
Prisoners/100,000	..	..	94	135	716	60
Homicides/millions	..	6	12	16	48	6
Environment						
CO_2/capita, tonnes	6	9	7.8	8.7	17.6	3.8
Municip. waste, kg/cap	..	..	660	540*	720	310
Particulate matter (10)	..	..	12.6	28.1	..	12.6
Connectivity						
% hh, Internet	..		79	75	81	94
Airline pass, millions	1.5	4.8	24	832	646	..
Mobile phones/100	0	0.7	107	126	98	173
Human resources						
Third level education			52	37	36	52
Total fertility rate			2.0	1.6	2.0	1.3
Assets						
Houses/1000	280	330	420	450	428	..
Cars/1000	..	227	434	446	423	665

Sources: World Bank, *World Development Indicators*, www.worldbank.org; Eurostat.

four out of five households have access to the internet, similar to the proportion found in the USA; and there are more mobile phones per head than in many other countries. Five times as many people flew into Ireland in 2011 as in 1990. Again, by American, but not European, standards Ireland has a low level of reported crime, despite the huge publicity that some crimes receive. The imprisonment rate is in line with European norms.

Tourism operators boast of Ireland's wild and open beauty and its clean air and water. While water is relatively clean, and the levels of particulates in Irish urban areas are lower than in any other EU country, emissions of CO_2, the main 'greenhouse gas', exceed the EU average. Besides, Irish firms and households generate 660kg of municipal waste per person per year, the highest in the EU, and close to the 720kg level of the USA. A particular problem in Ireland in this regard is the high numbers of cattle and sheep that, contrary

Table 12 *Human Development Index for Ireland*

1980	1985	1990	1995	2000	2005	2010	2012
0.720	0.739	0.768	0.799	0.855	0.886	0.895	0.916

Source: Haughton, 'Growth in Living Standards', Table 7.2.

to what one might expect, contribute significantly to the high greenhouse gas emission levels here.

There is another interesting way to evaluate Irish levels of affluence. The United Nations Development Program annually constructs its *Human Development Index*, which combines measures of life expectancy, educational achievement ('mean' years of schooling of adults aged 25 and over; and expected years of schooling for those of school-going age), and the log of GDP per capita (in Purchasing Power Parity terms) into a single index. The most recent figures refer to 2012, and rank Ireland seventh in the world with a score of 0.916 (out of a maximum possible 1.000). Ireland's Human Development Index has risen rapidly since 1980, as Table 12 shows.

An unsurprising consequence of the increase in real incomes and consumption has been a drop in absolute poverty, particularly since the late 1980s. Using a poverty line set at 60 per cent of average income in 1987, the proportion of the population in poverty was then 16 per cent, falling to 15 per cent by 1994, 8 per cent by 1998 and 5 per cent by 2001. The stagnation in wages, and the rise in the unemployment rate since 2007 have contributed to a recent rise in poverty: six-sevenths of the poor do not have employment. Social welfare payments have helped keep as much as a third of the population from falling into poverty (as measured by the EU norms).

Northern Ireland's Economy

As mentioned previously, it is difficult to consider the economic situation in Northern Ireland in isolation from that of the rest of the UK. The key economic decisions in relation to the North are made in London, not Belfast, and certainly not Dublin. Nonetheless it might be instructive to provide a brief overview of the regional economy there, using as a reference point the discussion on the economy of the Republic as outlined above.

Let us start with some comparative statistics. In 1971 the Republic accounted for around 66 per cent of the population of the island: by 2011 that had increased to almost 72 per cent. The absolute size of the population in the state had reached 4.6 million in 2011 compared to 1.8 million in the North. In 2011 agriculture accounted for 4.9 per cent of the workforce in the Republic but just 2.2 per cent in the North. In relation to the composition of employment by sector the other contrasts were as follows: public administration, defence, health, and social work accounted for 17.3 per cent of employment in the Republic, but 22.2 per cent in Northern Ireland. By contrast financial services, communication and so on, ran at 9.0 per cent in the Republic and 7.9 per cent in Northern Ireland. Thus there are significant differences between the two jurisdictions, but probably fewer than between regions in the Republic. There would, for example, be huge differences between, say, Connacht and Leinster. The major difference, though, between the Republic and Northern Ireland in this period was that gross value added per person outstripped that further north for much of the period, especially between 1991 and 2001. Living standards in the Republic are now considerably higher than in the North as a result. This is in marked contrast to the first 50 years of the Free State, when living standards lagged behind those enjoyed in Northern Ireland, and by some margin.

After partition in 1920, the island of Ireland as Bradley points out[6] offered a striking case of highly uneven industrial development, with the South poor and highly dependent on agriculture while the North, especially around Belfast, was heavily industrialised and prosperous. The following quotation captures some of the change since then.

> On the waterfront in Belfast stand two giant gantry cranes, silent reminders that the city was once home to one of the world's biggest shipbuilders. At its peak, Harland and Wolff employed 35,000 people to make the ships that linked Britain to its empire and defended it in wartime (as well as the doomed *Titanic*). In 2003, with just 135 workers, the firm officially registered as a small business. Shipbuilding had moved on, leaving the skeletons of bygone prosperity in its wake.[7]

The same article goes on to argue that, as with other former manufacturing strongholds in the UK, Northern Ireland is having today to reinvent its

---

6 John Bradley has written many recent papers on the situation in the North, especially in relation to the manufacturing sector. See J. Bradley, 'Economic Development: The Textile and Information Technology Sectors', in J. Coakley and L. O'Dowd (eds.), *Crossing the Border: New Relationships between Northern Ireland and the Republic of Ireland*, (Dublin: Irish Academic Press, 2006). And J. Bradley and M. Best, *Cross Border Economic Renewal: Rethinking Irish Regional Policy* (Centre for Cross Border Studies, March 2012): www.crossborder.ie/pubs/2012-economic-report.pdf.

7 www.economist.com/blogs/economist-explains/2013/11/economist-explains-4.

economy. From the late 1960s until the peace deal of 1998 took hold, the Troubles limited high-quality inward investment, retarded indigenous entrepreneurs and prompted many of Ulster's ablest offspring to emigrate. In the meantime a large public administration had emerged, with almost one in three workers employed in the public sector. State spending per head was even higher than in England's hard-hit north-east. As Bradley states: 'The size and persistence of the British Exchequer financing (the so-called subvention) serves to influence and colour every aspect of the northern economy.' He then claims that:

> Industry in Northern Ireland has yet to develop dynamic, self-sustaining characteristics, especially in terms of clusters of related and supporting industries. It remains heavily subsidized by public funding and is mainly concentrated in the low technology sectors of traditional industries such as food processing, textiles and clothing.[8]

How might this situation be improved he asks? Northern Ireland is not only separated geographically from Britain, but importantly, he argues, also appears to be very weakly integrated into the supply side of the British economy, even where demand for northern output is driven by the British market. Northern Ireland risks becoming both geographically and economically peripheral to Britain. However, recent improvements in access transport and a more positive political situation could help to alleviate this over time. But Northern Ireland he argues is unlikely ever to be placed on a par with the rest of the UK and is likely to remain economically peripheral to Britain. Bradley is also quite pessimistic concerning economic prospects following the Belfast Agreement, pointing out that there was little if any recognition of the concept of the island constituting a whole economy. In addition, he finds it 'impossible to envisage any politically acceptable process through which the economy of Northern Ireland can break free of the constraints of being a peripheral region of the United Kingdom. Remaining as part of the UK under direct rule will very likely doom Northern Ireland to play out the process of continued industrial decline, stagnation and dependency'.

This is perhaps an overly pessimistic assessment, but yet a salutary reminder of the problems of bringing the economy of the North up to the present-day standards in the adjoining Republic. One recent initiative is to try to introduce into Northern Ireland a corporate tax regime similar to that in the South. A future potential major impact on the economy of the North might come

---

8 Bradley, 'Economic Development', in *Crossing the Border*.

in the form of a British exit from the EU. If this were followed by a Scottish exit from the UK then the implications for the North could be immense, both politically and economically. This though illustrates again the fact that the economy of Northern Ireland is inextricably linked to economic policy in London and not Dublin. What happens in Northern Ireland on the political front, however, could have huge implications for the Republic, both in a political and hence economic sense.

Conclusion

What brought about the extraordinary changes in economic performance, especially in relation to employment and the growth of living standards in the Republic, over the last 20 years? Haughton posits a number of factors.[9]

Although hard to quantify, he argues that there appears to have been a change in attitudes over the past three decades, a change that favoured economic growth. In the 1970s, college students tended to aspire to jobs in the Department of External Affairs, later Foreign Affairs, the Civil Service more generally, or they sought positions as employees in well-established firms, such as Guinness. Now they are more likely to want to be entrepreneurs. According to the Global Entrepreneurship Monitor, in 2013, 9.3 per cent of Irish adults were either nascent entrepreneurs or managers of new companies, a rate higher than in France (4.6 per cent) and Italy (3.4 per cent) but lower than in the USA (12.7 per cent) or in the Baltic republics.

It is difficult to account for the change in attitudes, but a case can be made that high unemployment in the UK and the USA made emigration less attractive in the early 1990s. Forced to stay at home, but unable to find wage-paying work, many young, increasingly well-educated people started to improvise, learned to embrace change, and began to succeed. With greater opportunities for success, attitudinal change was strengthened. At the same time Ireland became better informed about, and more closely attuned to, attitudes prevalent in continental Europe. This in turn may have led to a sharp decline in the influence of the Catholic Church, assisted by various sex scandals in the church, thereby freeing Irish people to be even more innovative and entrepreneurial.

Another factor Haughton identifies is that if the USA did not exist, Ireland would not have experienced a growth spurt in the 1990s, although

9 Haughton, 'Economic Development'.

since 2000 most of the economic growth has been home-grown, and much of the most recent wave of foreign direct investment has come from Europe. In the 1990s, four-fifths of foreign direct investment originated in the USA, and US firms now account for a quarter of manufacturing employment and about a half of manufacturing output and exports. The high-tech wave that lifted the US economy in the 1990s and 2000s impacted on Ireland too, but failed to have much impact on the rest of Europe. The point is not that US investors raised the Irish investment rate, but rather that the investments that they made, and the associated learning and external economies of scale, had a large and immediate effect on output, and employment.

We still need to ask why US investors steered so much of their investment to Ireland rather than, say, Scotland or Greece or Portugal. In part the answer is because Ireland made them welcome, with low taxes and other benefits. As well, Ireland has historically had close links with the USA dating back to Famine days and before. There are strong cultural similarities between the two countries, and they share a common language. The Single Market Act of 1992 confirmed the position of Ireland as a platform for serving the EU, and the promise of its adhesion to the euro also worked in its favour, by lowering transaction costs. Haughton summarises the situation as follows.

> In a nutshell, the Irish growth spurt occurred perhaps because all the economic planets came into alignment at the same time. The key elements: a booming US economy providing firms there with the profits to invest abroad; a 10 per cent tax on manufacturing profits to attract them to Ireland, coupled with relatively light regulation of labour and product markets; the lure of a pool of well-educated and English-speaking workers; the creation of a Single European Market that could be served efficiently from Ireland; a credible and conservative macroeconomic stance; wage restraint due to the inertia built into early rounds of National Agreements; and a new-found attitude favourable to entrepreneurial activity. Once the boom began, it led to a virtuous circle, raising the demand for housing and other construction, as well as for a wide array of services such as restaurants, banks and accountants.

This good news story though was rudely interrupted between 2008 and 2013 and many people began to question the whole basis of the Irish economic success. Performance since then has countered some of this questioning, and the economy is once again used as an example of how best to cope with a devastating banking shock and a huge misalignment of pay rates within a currency union. Only with the hindsight that history offers will the true story of the Irish economy between 2000 and 2008 be fully understood, as time is needed to let the heated and often populist debates of the 2008 to 2013 period be placed in the context of what actually happened, what the causes of the recession were, and indeed the extent to which the recession is fully over and Ireland back on the remarkable growth trajectory that started around 1995.

17

Migration since 1914

MARY E. DALY

Introduction

Irish migration in the twentieth century is characterised by continuities and discontinuities with the past. During the nineteenth century, Ireland was the only European country where net emigration resulted in a falling population and this continued until the 1960s. Between 1921 and 2001, 1.5 million people left Ireland; an additional 500,000 left Northern Ireland. A further distinguishing feature is that internal migration has been much less significant than transnational migration; unskilled workers from rural Ireland were more likely to seek work in Britain or the United States than elsewhere in Ireland. Yet while Irish migration was in many ways exceptional, the Irish experience also reflected broad patterns in transnational migration.

The Irish were pioneers in mass emigration in the nineteenth century; would-be immigrants wishing to travel to North America, Australia or elsewhere, faced minimal restrictions, other than the cost of their fare. Although some migrants left Ireland for political or personal reasons, the overwhelming majority moved to secure a more prosperous future. By the end of the nineteenth century, however, the era of unrestricted transnational migration was coming to an end as governments sought to regulate immigration. In the twentieth, as in the nineteenth century, migrants moved from poorer to richer countries/regions, from agricultural and rural areas to industrial and service jobs in cities and towns. The flow of migrants waxed and waned depending on economic circumstances. Migration fell sharply during the depressed 1930s, was seriously disrupted during the Second World War, and rose sharply as developed economies boomed during the 1950s and 1960s. From the 1960s, the major migration flows originated outside Europe, though this changed somewhat with the end of communist regimes in Eastern Europe.[1]

Irish migration reflects these international patterns. The immediate aftermath of the Second World War, and the consequent boundary changes, resulted in significant migration by ethnic minorities throughout Europe. The Protestant population in the Irish Free State fell by almost one-third, from 327,129 in 1911, to 220, 719 in 1926, with most of the decline occurring between 1920 and 1923. The reduction was greatest in counties where the Protestant population was low. In Dublin or counties bordering Northern Ireland, the numbers held up better. The reasons for the fall in the Protestant population have been widely debated, especially the extent to which their migration constituted 'ethnic cleansing'. Casualties incurred amongst Protestant males during the First World War were at best a minor factor and the withdrawal of British troops after independence was much more significant. Landed families resettled in Britain following the destruction of their 'big house', as did former senior civil servants and RIC men (many of them Catholics). Bielenberg concluded that at least half of the fall in the Protestant population could be explained by economic and voluntary migration,[2] though not everybody would agree with this assertion. Protestant emigration from independent Ireland continued in the 1930s reflecting changing economic circumstances – especially the decline of landed estates – and a discomfort with the Gaelic/Catholic ethos of the new state. Britain and Northern Ireland were the most common destinations for Protestant emigrants. A smaller number of Northern Catholics migrated to the Irish Free State, having been displaced from their homes or businesses during the early 1920s.

Migration 1920–2000: An Overview

Political independence did not transform the Irish economy; indeed the gap in incomes between Britain and independent Ireland grew until the 1960s, when average incomes in the Republic were less than 60 per cent of those in Britain. Economically motivated migration was lower in the 1920s and 1930s

---

1 B. R. Chiswick, T. J. Hatton, 'International Migration and the Integration of Labor Markets', in M. Bordo, A. Taylor and J. Williamson, (eds.), *Globalization in Historical Perspective* (Chicago: University Chicago Press, 2003), 65–120.
2 P. Hart, 'The Protestant Experience of War and Revolution in Southern Ireland', in R. English and G. Walker (eds.), *Unionism in Modern Ireland* (London: Macmillan, 1996), 81; A. Bielenberg, 'Exodus: The Emigration of Southern Irish Protestants during the War of Independence and the Civil War' *Past and Present*, 218 (2013), 223; Protestant deaths exceeded births between 1911 and 1926.

than in earlier decades, due to adverse economic conditions in Britain and in 1930s America. The contrasting fortunes of Britain and Ireland were most pronounced in the aftermath of the Second World War, when Britain enjoyed near-full employment and steadily rising wages – hence the high rate of emigration in the 1950s. Northern Ireland was both more prosperous and more industrial, so the rate of emigration was lower than in independent Ireland. During the 1960s the Irish economy began to grow, and there was a slight narrowing of the income gap between Ireland and Britain and Northern Ireland. Emigration fell steadily during the 1960s, and it was widely believed/ hoped that Ireland's long history of emigration was coming to an end. This seemed to be confirmed in the 1970s when more people entered Ireland than left. The influx reflected expectations of greater prosperity when Ireland became a member of the EEC in 1973. There is anecdotal evidence that some of the returning emigrants may have fled Britain because of the impact of the Northern Ireland 'Troubles' on the Irish in Britain. What is clear is that emigration from Northern Ireland increased during the 1970s because of the economic consequences of the 'Troubles'. Some people may have emigrated to escape the violence and disruption to everyday lives.

A stagnant economy and high unemployment in the 1980s – a time when both the US and British economies were prospering – brought an unwelcome resurgence of emigration in Ireland. In 1985, net emigration was 28,000 and the population fell for the first time since the early 1960s. The gap between average British and Irish wages and unemployment rates rose significantly during that decade. Net emigration between 1986 and 1991 was exceeded only in the 1950s. By the early 1990s, however, the economy was recovering, and the numbers leaving Ireland more or less equalled those arriving. From the mid-1990s, with a booming economy, net immigration soared, and this continued until the global recession in 2007/8. The 1970s immigrants consisted almost entirely of returning emigrants, often accompanied by English-born children, and an English spouse. Many of those who had left in the 1980s returned home in the 1990s, and for the first time in almost 300 years, Ireland attracted significant immigration. In the mid-1990s Irish living standards began to match those in Britain and other western EU countries, and, with near-full employment, migrants from EU accession states in Eastern Europe, and Africa, Asia and South America began to seek work in Ireland. Between 2002 and 2006 the number of non-nationals living in Ireland rose from 224,000 to 420,000. Although many Irish people emigrated during the recession after 2008, immigration has continued to outstrip emigration; the 2011 Census recorded 544,000 non-nationals resident in Ireland. The 120,000 natives of Poland were the largest contingent, with 112,000 UK citizens in second place. Northern Ireland also became a country of net immigration after 2000, as the economic dividends of the Good Friday Agreement emerged, but net immigration was lower than in the Republic, because the economy was less dynamic, and because of incidences of hostility towards the new arrivals. More than one-third of those who came to Northern Ireland were from the UK. Immigration from EU accession countries will continue until their living standards approximate more closely to Irish incomes, or another EU country becomes a more attractive destination. Immigration from outside the EU is, in theory, under government control, but the growing numbers of migrants from war-torn countries suggest that the numbers of migrants will continue to rise. However in Ireland, births comfortably exceed deaths, in contrast to Germany and Italy, so there is no immediate requirement to rely on immigrants to provide those workers needed to sustain an increasingly ageing population.

Until the 1990s, Irish migration tended to consolidate ethnic and religious majorities. Protestant migration from the Republic reduced its share of the population, though a lower Protestant birth rate was also a factor. In Northern Ireland, Barritt and Carter estimated that between 1937 and 1951 emigration reduced the Catholic population by 9 per cent and the Protestant population by 3 per cent. Between 1926 and 1981, Catholics, who constituted roughly 33 per cent of the population, accounted for 60 per cent of net emigrants. Emigration offset the higher Catholic birth rate and served to maintain the denominational balance of the population.[3] The industrial drive of the 1930s brought a number of Jewish businesses to Ireland augmenting the resident Jewish population, but Ireland, north and south, proved an inhospitable destination for Jewish immigrants in the 1930s, and again for would-be immigrants after the Second World War. In 1911 there were 3,805 Jews in what became independent Ireland and 3,907 in 1946, but by 1991 the numbers had more than halved to 1,581, as Europe's Jews clustered in places with larger communities.[4] Recent immigration has resulted in significant increases (admittedly from a very low base) in the numbers of Muslims, Hindus, and minority Christian churches.

---

3 D. Barritt and C. Carter, *The Northern Ireland Problem. A study in Group Relations* (Oxford University Press, 1962), 107–8; J. Trew, *Leaving the North. Migration and Memory, Northern Ireland 1921–2011*, (Liverpool: Liverpool University Press, 2013), 95.

4 D. Keogh, *Jews in Twentieth-century Ireland: Refugees, Anti-semitism and the Holocaust*, (Cork: Cork University Press, 1998), 9, 224. B. Wasserstein, *Vanishing Diaspora: The Jews in Europe since 1945* (London: Hamish Hamilton, 2006).

Destination

In the nineteenth century roughly twice as many Irish emigrated to the USA as to Britain. Britain became the main destination after 1914. This change, which ironically coincided with the ending of the Anglo-Irish Union, reflected the impact of external economic and political forces. US immigrant quotas introduced in 1924 had only a marginal impact, because they reflected historic immigration patterns, and were relatively generous to Ireland. However, a growing number of Irish immigrants were rejected following medical checks at Ellis Island. It was the onset of the Great Depression, not quotas that effectively ended mass Irish emigration to the United States. 211,000 Irish emigrated to the USA in the 1920s, but only 11,000 in the 1930s. Would-be emigrants had to present evidence that they would not become a charge on public funds, mostly by securing a personal sponsor. Irish-Americans were among the worst-hit communities during the Depression because they were heavily concentrated in the cities. The Second World War acted as a further break on emigration to the USA. When normal communications resumed in the late 1940s, numbers increased, though Ireland never filled its annual quota in the 1950s. Of the 3.5 million who immigrated to the USA between 1941 and 1960; fewer than 100,000 were Irish.[5] By 1951 the number of the Irish-born in Britain was greater than in the USA. Only 62,400 of the 400,000 who left Ireland between 1951 and 1961 went to the United States; and Irish immigrants to the US filled less than half of Ireland's annual quota of 18,000, except in 1957 and 1958 when Britain was in recession.[6] A reform of US immigration law, which abolished ethnic quotas and gave priority to family reunification and emigrants' skills and qualifications came into effect in 1968. (Canada had made similar changes in 1962.) During the first six months of the revised system only 227 emigrant visas were awarded to Irish citizens.[7] When Irish emigration to the USA resumed in the 1980s, the Irish arrived as 'illegal', 'undocumented' migrants.

The shift towards Britain as the main destination reflects the importance of networks and communications on emigrant behaviour. Once mass emigration to

---

5 L. A. Dowling, 'Irish-America, 1940–2000', in J. J. Lee and M. Casey (eds.), *Making the Irish American. History and Heritage of the Irish in the United States,* (New York: New York University Press, 2006), 549. M. O'Brien, 'Transatlantic Connections and the Great Depression', in K. Kenny (ed.), *New Directions in Irish-American History* (Madison, WI: University of Wisconsin Press, 2003), 78–97.

6 M. E. Daly, 'Nationalism, Sentiment and Economics: Relations between Ireland and Irish America in the Postwar Years', in Kenny (ed.), *Making the Irish American*, 264. Trew, *Leaving the North*, 166.

7 Daly, 'Nationalism, Sentiment and Economics', 276.

the USA ceased, informal knowledge and networks were dissipated. Emigration to Britain had further advantages in that it was not subject to legal or medical controls. As well, the cost of travel was low and, in contrast to the United States, moving there was not seen as marking a permanent break with Ireland. Emigration to Britain continued, though at a reduced rate, during the economic recession of the 1930s, despite calls in Britain for restrictions on Irish workers. These went unheeded, perhaps because Irish immigrants were seen as mobile, dispensable and prepared to take jobs declined by Scottish or English workers – such as potato pickers or mobile construction workers.

Emigrant Profile

Nineteenth-century emigrants included significant cohorts of clergy, both Catholic and Protestant. Doctors, lawyers, engineers and other professionals were also prominent as were men holding military and civilian positions in the British Empire. This diversity continued after 1914. For the most part, however, the overwhelming majority of emigrants were young, poor and unskilled, and this remained the dominant profile until the late twentieth century. While emigrants from Dublin were not unknown – especially during the Second World War when many construction and factory jobs in the city disappeared – rural areas predominated, especially western counties with small farms and limited off-farm employment. During the Second World War, Irishmen built Britain's airfields, runways, and munitions factories, and provided a significant number of military recruits. After the war, they reconstructed Britain's war-damaged cities, and built the new power stations and motorways. Scotland, Lancashire and north-east England – major destinations pre-1914 – were replaced by London, the south-east and the midlands, reflecting the changing dynamic of the British economy. A willingness to work in remote areas, or to move as a motorway progressed, made Irish workers attractive. This transience may have suited those who were accustomed to the rhythms of the farming calendar because it enabled them to return to Ireland when a contract ended, and find work, perhaps elsewhere, on their return. Many wartime factories relied on Irish women, but service – either in private homes, or increasingly in hotels, hospitals and other institutions – was the dominant occupation, both in the United States and Britain, as it was in the nineteenth century.[8] Hynes Domestic Agency was still advertising for domestic staff in Irish local newspapers in 1969. Despite rising

8 E. Delaney, *The Irish in Post-war Britain*, (Oxford University Press, 2007).

numbers with secondary and third-level qualifications, in 1991 a significant number of Irish-born women in Britain continued to be employed in personal service – including domestic service and catering – and they continued to be under-represented in clerical, secretarial and sales jobs. Irishmen held a dis-proportionate number of jobs as labourers, skilled construction workers and heavy machinery operators.[9] These trends did not vary significantly between younger and older emigrants. In the 1980s, those Irish-born who had settled in Britain and who would have arrived over several decades, had less educa-tion than the British-born population, though the gap was widest among the older population. Emigrants from Northern Ireland had an occupational pro-file more similar to those born in Britain, and were more likely to hold jobs in management and administration. In the late 1950s the Irish consul-general in New York described recent Irish immigrants as having a somewhat higher sta-tus than earlier emigrants, but lower than native-born Americans, 'although by no means poor by Irish or, for that matter, British standards'.[10]

Irish emigrants were heavily represented in Britain's health services. Britain experienced a shortage of nurses from the 1920s on, and Irish women increasingly filled that gap, and would do so until the end of the century. In Ireland, nursing was regarded as a high-status career, especially for women from farming families, and Britain accepted trainees from more diverse social backgrounds, with lower educational standards and, importantly, without demanding a training fee. Nursing is one instance where emigrants could aspire to careers that were closed to them in Ireland. Qualified social work-ers and university graduates wishing to become teachers, emigrated in large numbers in the 1960s, because of the absence of satisfactory career paths in Ireland: secondary school teaching was dominated by religious orders, as was social work.

The 1980s: Transition and Continuity

Between 1983 and 1993, 472,000 left Ireland; 70,600 went in a twelve-month period – 1988–1989.[11] These figures were eerily similar to the 1950s. By the 1980s however, Ireland was the only EU country experiencing net emigra-tion. Former emigrant countries such as Spain, Greece and Portugal no

9 M. Hickman and B. Walters, *Discrimination and the Irish Community in Britain* (London: Commission for Racial Equality, 1997), 37.

10 Daly, 'Nationalism, Sentiment and Economics', in Kenny (ed.), *New Directions*, 272.

11 D. Courtney, 'A Quantification of Irish Migration with Particular Emphasis on the 1980s and 1990s', in A. Bielenberg (ed.), *The Irish Diaspora*, (Harlow: Longman: 2000), 300–3.

longer featured on that list.[12] A 1991 report of the National Economic and Social Council (NESC) suggested that in the early 1980s some 60 per cent of all emigrants went to the UK, with 14 per cent going to the USA and 15 per cent to other countries.[13] The decade of the 1980s marked an important transition in emigrant patterns. Net emigration from Dublin was slightly higher than the national average, principally because many industries in the city had closed. The occupational and social profile of emigrants was more similar to the national population than in the past: indeed those with professional qualifications or managerial position experience were slightly more likely to leave. Almost half (42 per cent) quit a position in Ireland, offering evidence that dissatisfaction with a job, or with pay or promotional prospects, was increasingly a determining factor. Almost 30 per cent of those graduating in 1988 left Ireland, including 48 per cent of graduating engineers.[14] The 1980s emigration is commonly described as a brain-drain, an image promoted by the 1987 song, 'Flight of the Earls', performed by the Wolfe Tones, a folk group, but the term was also used by nineteenth-century nationalists when writing about emigration. Many of the 1980s emigrants, however, had similar profiles to earlier generations. More than two-thirds of male emigrants from north Donegal, west Cork and south Kerry were construction workers. Emigrants from Northern Ireland at this time also fell into two distinct categories: well-educated men and women, and the unskilled and unemployed, many of whom later returned home having failed to secure employment in Britain.[15] The 1980s saw the arrival of an estimated 50,000 'illegal', undocumented immigrants to the United States, a country where Irish emigrant networks had atrophied.[16]

Return and Inward Migration

Statistics on net immigration and emigration capture only part of the story – the numbers who actually experienced migration were much greater. During

---

12 E. Delaney, 'Placing Post-war Irish Migration in Britain in a Comparative European Perspective, 1945–1981', in Bielenberg, *Irish Diaspora*, 334–5.

13 National Economic and Social Council (NESC), *The Economic and Social Implications of Emigration* (Dublin: 1991), 14.

14 B. Halpin, 'Who are the Irish in Britain? The Evidence from Large-scale Surveys', in Bielenberg, *Irish Diaspora*, 89–107; I. Glynn, P. Mac Einrí and T. Kelly, *Irish Emigration in an Age of Austerity*, (Cork: University College Cork, 2013), 10–12.

15 F. Fosythe and V. Booroah, 'The Nature of Migration between Northern Ireland and Great Britain: A Preliminary Analysis based on the Labour Force Surveys, 1986–88', *Economic and Social Review*, 23, 105–27.

16 M.Corcoran, *Irish Illegals. Transients between Two Societies*, (Westport, CT: Greenwood, 1996).

the nineteenth century, Irish emigrants to the USA had a very low rate of return, perhaps because they had no difficulty finding an Irish wife in the United States. Emigration to Britain was more short-term; until the 1960s, gangs of young workers from Donegal or Achill Island travelled to harvest potatoes in Scotland. By the 1950s, Dublin construction workers were moving freely between Britain and Ireland in response to the local building cycle. Christmas and summer holidays brought the return of thousands of emigrants, often to save the turf or make hay. As the Irish economy improved in the 1960s, emigration and return (not just for short holidays) became more pronounced. Between 1971 and 1981, 176,000 people left Ireland but 280,000 arrived/returned. In the 1980s, 400,000 left, but 192,000 arrived. However it is only in recent decades, through more detailed Census questions and the annual Irish Labour Force Survey that we have begun to capture the full extent of these movements, and it appears that migration/return migration has become more common in recent decades. In 1987 over 10 per cent of residents in Ireland could be characterised as 'long-term migrants' – either Irish-born who had lived abroad for over one year, or foreign-born but resident in Ireland for a long time. By 1996, 13 per cent of the population were long-term migrants and by 2011, this figure had risen to almost 20 per cent of the population – 892,000 people, including 400,000 Irish-born men and women, who had lived outside Ireland for at least a year.

Net immigration in the 1970s was dominated by returning emigrants and their families, and by some immigration from Northern Ireland. Corcoran argues that during the 1970s 'many of the newly-created jobs went to returned emigrants who brought with them skills and experiences while Irish youth continued to seek work abroad'. Many of these immigrants appear to have been construction workers.[17] Many returning emigrants were in their thirties, others were nearing retirement age, and one study concluded that they were probably attracted back to Ireland by better job prospects.[18] In the 1990s, professional occupations, such as medicine and construction were over-represented among returning emigrants. By the turn of the century, returning emigrants were outnumbered by immigrants from EU accession states, whose ages and occupational profiles were an uncanny mirror of Irish emigrants to Britain in the 1950s: construction workers, domestic servants, hotel workers, along with significant numbers of nurses and doctors. Transnational

17 M. Corcoran, 'The Process of Migration and the Reinvention of Self', 303; NESC, *Emigration*, 78.
18 F. X. Kirwan, 'Recent Anglo-Irish Migration – the Evidence of the British Labour Force Surveys', *Economic and Social Review*, 13 (1982), 202–3.

migration continues, regardless of whether the economy is booming or in recession, though economic circumstances determine the numbers entering and leaving Ireland and the destinations of those who leave.

Female Emigrants

One of the distinguishing features of nineteenth-century Irish emigration was the almost equal numbers of men and women who left. Irish women were more likely to migrate, independently of their family, than any other nationality. Long-term gender parity masks significant short-term fluctuations. More men than women emigrated during the Second World War; this was reversed in the immediate post-war years, because women did not require work permits, whereas men did. Men were in the majority during the 1950s, and again in the early 1980s, because male employment in Ireland was falling, whereas the numbers of women in employment were rising. During the 1960s, as net emigration fell steadily, women were in the majority while more men than women returned in the 1970s. Since the 1920s, women have constituted the majority of Irish-born residents in Britain, and this trend has increased since the 1960s. In 1991 there were roughly six Irish women for every five Irish men in Britain. Women were less likely to return home than men, perhaps because they had established families in Britain, or had found rewarding careers and enjoyed comfortable lifestyles. Jackson reported the bewilderment of many married women teachers and nurses who returned home in the 1960s on discovering that married women continued to be barred from jobs in the public service. (This ended in the early 1970s.)[19]

Writings on Irish emigration, both in the nineteenth and twentieth centuries, often suggested that women were different. Descriptions of emigration as 'liberating' or 'escapology', were much more commonly applied to women than to men.[20] Commentaries on emigration in twentieth-century Ireland tended to distinguish between women and men. Women's motives for emigrating were questioned: 'the flight of the girls' conjured up an image of escape. While there was an acknowledgement, however grudging, that men emigrated to seek work, women were often seen as emigrating in search of glamour and excitement, thus leaving the Irish countryside denuded of

19 J. Jackson, *Report on the Skibbereen Social Survey* (Dublin: Human Sciences Committee, 1967), 44–6.

20 M. E. Daly, 'Irish Women and the Diaspora, why they Matter', in D. A. J. MacPherson and M. Hickman (eds.), *Women and Irish Diaspora Identities. Theories, Concepts and New Perspectives* (Manchester: Manchester University Press, 2014), 22–4.

marriageable women, and threatening the very survival of the rural population. Such strictures were rarely applied to men – many of whom would have
fled abroad to escape the tyranny of life as an 'assisting relative' on a family
farm, or in a family business. Women were frequently represented as vulnerable and thus in need of protection, being notably prey to sexual exploitation.
Such fears, though possibly exaggerated, cannot be totally dismissed, given
that in the 1950s many 15-year-old girls went to work in England without
any adult supervision and often without their parents knowing their address.
Significantly when Irish civil servants debated the merits of appointing a welfare officer at the Irish embassy in London in the 1950s, the appointee was
always envisaged as catering only for women. The message of female vulnerability was reinforced by those British Catholic charities that supported
single women who became pregnant, and which were not slow to vent their
criticism of these women to Irish churchmen and politicians. The moralising
mindset is perhaps best epitomised by a British Ministry of Labour official
who claimed that Irish girls were either very good or very bad: there was
no middle way.[21] Did emigration offer women an opportunity to triumph
over the cultural, religious and economic barriers that they faced in Ireland,
or did women remain bound by family responsibilities and expectations?
Gender is important, but the distinctions should not be overstated. Young
single female emigrants in the mid-twentieth century were expected to send
money home to their families, as were the men. Women left at an earlier
age than men – often under parental pressure – because there were fewer
jobs at home. And although emigration undoubtedly gave women better
career opportunities – especially in nursing – the gendered nature of British
and American society constrained their lives, though less onerously than in
Ireland. Irish-born women in Britain had better prospects of marrying than
if they remained at home, were less likely to remain single than emigrant
men, and fewer returned home in the 1970s. Whether this was for family reasons or because they were content in their careers remains to be established.
Breda Gray writes of the tensions that many 1990s female emigrants experienced between a career and life in Britain, and the continuing demands on
them from Ireland from parent(s) and family.[22] However, to fully understand

---

21 S. Lambert, 'Irish Women's Emigration to England, 1922–1960: The Lengthening
of Family Ties', in A. Hayes and D. Urquhart (eds.), *Female Experience: Essays in Irish
Women's History*, (Dublin: Irish Academic Press, 2000), 152–7; M. E. Daly, *The Slow
Failure. Population Decline and Independent Ireland, 1920–1973* (Madison, WI: University of
Wisconsin Press, 2006), quotation at 283.
22 B. Gray, '"Generation Emigration": The Politics of Transnational Social Reproduction
in Twenty-first Century Ireland', *Irish Studies Review*, 21 (2013), 20–36.

the impact of gender, we need more formal comparisons between male and female emigrants.

Welfare and Vulnerability

While PFI (Pregnant from Ireland), the designation accorded to emigrating single pregnant women, was one exclusive to women, vulnerable emigrants were by no means exclusively female. The Irish state provided minimal assistance to would-be or actual emigrants, in contrast to Italy, which provided pre-emigration counselling and support services abroad from the late nineteenth century. This laissez-faire attitude was partly a legacy of the Union, because Britain made no aftercare provision for British citizens who emigrated. After independence, successive politicians and civil servants justified the neglect of Irish emigrants by asserting that the government did not wish to do anything to encourage emigration. Irish emigrants in the USA gave rise to relatively few welfare issues until the 1980s, but visas excluded disadvantaged immigrants. However, with free movement to Britain, and the low cost of travel, the position there was quite different, and Britain became a favoured destination for those rejected by their families, for those who found it impossible to find a job in Ireland, for husbands who had abandoned wives and children, for ex-prisoners, for mixed-race Irish and for the former inmates of reformatories, industrial schools, mother and baby homes, Magdalen homes and psychiatric hospitals. Migration offered an escape from gossip and social stigma, and provided testimony to the shortcomings of Ireland's welfare services. Vulnerable emigrants, though a minority, remain a feature of emigrant Irish in the twenty-first century. In the mid-1980s, 15–17 per cent of recent immigrants to London sought assistance from the main Irish community centres or service centres, whether because of poverty, lack of accommodation or the difficulty faced by those with poor education in finding work.[23] Despite sustained lobbying by Catholic charities and Irish community associations, successive Irish governments refused to provide any substantial assistance to emigrants or support groups until the closing years of the twentieth century. Whether living in Britain, or in the USA, Irish immigrants in need had to call on support from local Irish networks, local authorities (in Britain), and from the Catholic Church. They could not rely on their government.

23 NESC, *The economic and social implications of emigration*, 166–9.

The Politics of Migration[24]

Before 1922, most Irish nationalists regarded emigration as an adverse consequence of Union with Britain, and it was widely believed that emigration would cease after independence. Successive governments expressed their determination to provide Irish citizens with attractive living conditions that would make emigration unnecessary. However, Irish governments had limited power to determine either the volume or destination of emigrants. Nevertheless, in the 1920s, and again in the 1950s, they refused to permit assisted passage schemes to Canada or Australia to be offered to Irish citizens, despite strong pleas from the Catholic hierarchy in Australia that they should do so in order to renew the numbers of Irish Catholics in the Australian population. By contrast the government of Northern Ireland encouraged Commonwealth emigration, notably the £10 fare to Australia, valuing this as a reflection of a common heritage. Of the 94,000 emigrants from Northern Ireland between 1922 and 1937 (migrants to Britain or Ireland are not included), half went to Canada, almost one-third to the USA and the remainder to Australasia. During the 1950s, 57 per cent of Irish emigrants to Canada were from Northern Ireland.[25] Northern Ireland did not regard emigration, whether to Britain or the Commonwealth, as a political or cultural issue; the population of Northern Ireland was rising, whereas the population of independent Ireland was falling until 1961. In the Republic however, continuing emigration called into question the merits of independence, and this was most evident with the record numbers leaving in the 1950s. In August 1961, when the Census revealed that the population of independent Ireland had fallen to 2.8 million, the lowest figure on record, the *Belfast Newsletter* reported this story under the headline, 'Fleeing Irish and East Germans'. They noted that the numbers leaving the Republic of Ireland were greater than the numbers leaving East Germany, which in the latter case had prompted the construction of the Berlin Wall.

In August 1951 Taoiseach Éamon de Valera attracted headlines in Ireland, and throughout England, when he claimed that fifty emigrants in Birmingham were living in one house, fifteen of them in a single room and, in addition, that work was available in Ireland in conditions that were 'infinitely better' for their health and morals.[26] Although many emigrants in war-damaged Britain

---

24 This section draws on Daly, *The Slow Failure*.
25 Trew, *Leaving the North*, 39.
26 Daly, *The Slow Failure*, 270–2.

were living in grossly overcrowded conditions, his speech ignored the realities of rural and urban squalor in Ireland, as well as the huge discrepancies in pay and employment prospects between Britain and Ireland. His speech caused gross offence among the Irish in Britain, and exposed emigrants to anti-Irish ridicule. In 1948, the first inter-party government established a Commission to examine the causes of Ireland's continuing emigration and low marriage rate. It eventually reported in 1954, concluding, somewhat reluctantly, that economics was the major factor. This economic argument was clearly acknowledged in 1958 in the foreword to *Economic Development* – a blueprint for a new economic development programme, which stated bluntly:

> After 35 years of native government, people are asking whether we can achieve an acceptable degree of economic progress. The common talk among parents in the towns as in rural Ireland, is of their children having to emigrate as soon as their education is complete in order to be sure of a reasonable livelihood.[27]

The resurgence of emigration in the 1980s was also seen as reflecting national failure. The 1991 NESC report noted the 'deeply felt Irish sensitivity' regarding emigration. This report, which was markedly sharper in focus (and took much less time) than the 1950s Commission, concluded that emigration was 'a symptom of relative economic underdevelopment'.[28] In 1958, and again in the 1980s, the high rate of emigration prompted a reassessment and a redirection in economic policy and, on both occasions, this exercise resulted in a fall in emigration.

For successive governments occasional speeches decrying emigration were overridden by the pragmatic consideration that emigration eased many short-term problems. This was especially during the Second World War, when neutral Ireland, suffering from high unemployment because construction and many manufacturing industries were short of supplies, agreed to cooperate with the British authorities in recruiting Irish workers for Britain's war industries. This cooperation enabled the Irish authorities to restrict emigration by rural workers who were needed to ensure supplies of food and turf. It was also seen as facing up to the inevitable and as offering a pragmatic means of alleviating mass unemployment. Similar pragmatism is evident when the Catholic Church and other interests demanded that the government prevent the emigration of women aged under 16 years, in order to protect them from

---

27 *Economic Development* (Dublin: Department of Finance, 1958), 5.
28 NESC, *The Economic and Social Implications of Emigration*, 15.

alleged moral dangers. The government recognised that most of these young women emigrated with the permission, and often with the encouragement, of their family. Restrictions would be, therefore, unpopular and, indeed, unenforceable unless passport controls were introduced between Britain and Ireland and, even more problematically, for Northern Ireland. In the 1960s however, when the USA was revising its immigration regulations and removing ethnic quotas, hubris about the growing Irish economy and a belief that emigration had been consigned to history, meant that Ireland failed to lobby for measures to secure a continuing quota for Irish emigrants. Whether political representations would have been effective is not certain, but no effort was made to prevent the abolition of the Irish quota. The consequences of US immigration reform became most apparent in the 1980s, when the combination of a booming US economy and stagnation in Ireland, resulted in significant 'illegal' or 'undocumented' Irish immigrants. This problem was partly addressed by the issuing of several rounds of special visas via lotteries, the so-called Donnelly and Morrison visas, of which 40 per cent went to the Irish, though in fact many successful applicants were not to be found among the 1980s undocumented. Dowling suggests that in the decade following the award of these visas, 'the Irish experienced a renaissance in the United States. However, undocumented immigration did not cease and the newer arrivals were overlooked, because the problems appeared to have ended.'[29]

Identities and Belonging: Religion, Nationalism and Ethnicity

'Traditionally Irish identity has been forged by three factors in Ireland and in America: nationalism, Catholicism, and either language (in Ireland), or Democratic Politics in the United States – all these factors were challenged from the 1960s.'[30] Catholicism has served in multiple ways to define Ireland's migrant communities and their identity, yet it is also a problematic determinant in that it excludes many migrants; a majority of the forty million Americans claiming Irish descent are Protestant.[31]

Since the mid-nineteenth century, Irish migrants have included male and female, Catholic and Protestant religious. Some ministered to the Irish abroad; others focused on bringing Christianity, schooling and medical care

---

29 Dowling, 'Irish America', 564–9. Corcoran, *Irish Illegals*, 131.
30 Dowling, 'Irish America', 556.
31 J. J. Lee, 'Introduction: Interpreting Irish America', in Lee and Casey (eds.), *Making the Irish American*, 38.

to Africa and Asia. Ireland's religious emigrants were one element in the over-supply of professionals in Ireland – the country produced more priests and nuns (and doctors) than were needed there. In the early 1960s, 10 per cent of boys who sat their school Leaving Certificate entered a seminary.[32] In 1960, 94 priests ordained for Irish dioceses were sent abroad on loan to foreign dioceses because they were not needed at home. A further 141 men were ordained for foreign dioceses – 75 for the USA and Canada and 50 for Britain and 53 were ordained for missionary societies and 139 for religious orders and congregations, the latter serving both in Ireland and overseas.[33] No similar statistics exist for lay brothers or nuns, but it is probable that similar pro-portions emigrated. Many emigrant religious came from poorer, less advan-taged families than those who remained in Ireland. Missionary orders such as SMA, the Society for African Missions, provided free secondary schooling and professional training for men and women whose families could not afford to educate them.

Ireland's 'spiritual empire' – the term was obviously designed to contrast with Britain's military / political empire – was celebrated at the 1932 Eucharistic Congress and again in 1961 during the Patrician Year. Dr Richard Downey, Archbishop of Liverpool, dubbed 'the doyen of the Kerry gang of priests in the Liverpool archdiocese',[34] described the Eucharistic Congress as 'Ireland's family reunion'. Although the numbers of returning migrants were much lower than originally expected because of the onset of the 1930s depression, an estimated 20,000 pilgrims travelled from the USA, with the overwhelming majority being of Irish descent. A similar number came from Britain. Contact between the clergy of Ireland's diaspora and Ireland probably increased in the 1950s with long-distance air travel. Many priests and bishops of Irish birth or ancestry combined a trip to Rome with a visit to Ireland. Some came to recruit seminarians and postulants (trainee nuns). In Australia and the USA, the continuing emigration of Irish religious sustained an identity with Ireland in communities several generations removed from Ireland. Catholic schools and parishes promoted Irish dancing, music and sports, as well as some sense, however vague, of Irish history. And yet, an absence of new Irish migrants, along with the arrival of migrants of other nationalities, and greater eth-nic diversity among the Catholic clergy, as well as the disruption caused to

---

32 Figures from 'The Modern Missionary Movement', in D. Fennell (ed.), *The Changing Face of Catholic Ireland*, (London: G. Chapman, 1968), 138–9.
33 *Hibernia*, 22 April 1961.
34 J. Belchem, *Irish, Catholic and Scouse. The history of the Liverpool Irish 1800–1939*, (Liverpool: Liverpool University Press, 2007), 298.

Church authority following Vatican II, resulted in a loss of Irish influence within American and Australian Catholicism.

The mid-1960s marked the peak in the numbers of Irish-born religious serving overseas. When the numbers entering religion began to decline in the late 1960s, the impact was first felt among those ordained for service overseas; ordinations for foreign dioceses fell from 120 in 1966 to 44 by 1970, whereas the numbers ordained for service in Ireland remained stable.[35] Independence for former colonies was replicated within the Catholic Church, as foreign bishops gave way to native-born clergy. By the 1970s, Ireland's links with developing countries had evolved from missionary activity to disaster relief and development aid, with charities such as Gorta and Concern providing new outlets for migrant activism in developing countries.[36]

The relationship between Catholicism and the Irish in Britain was more complex. Many Irish-born clergy served in Britain, often on loan from their Irish diocese, and the English hierarchy included men of Irish ancestry, but Hickman has suggested that Catholic schools did not promote a sense of Irishness. Indeed they sought to inculcate a British patriotism because of the fraught history of Catholicism in Britain.[37] In the 1950s the influx of Irish immigrants put considerable pressure on the English Catholic Church to provide sufficient churches, schools and teachers to support the growing numbers, and to meet the welfare needs of Irish emigrants. The English hierarchy was conscious of the religious and moral shortcomings of the Irish in England – the proportion failing to attend mass regularly, or the pregnant single women seeking assistance from Catholic charities, and they were not slow in complaining to the Irish hierarchy. By the late 1950s, the Irish Church had created a network of emigrant chaplains, who ministered to motorway workers, hotel workers and other groups deemed in need of special assistance. But disputes between the two hierarchies persisted; the Irish clergy tended to view Irish emigrants as a distinct group, whereas the English hierarchy was keen to integrate them into the English Catholic community.[38] Tensions between the British and Irish hierarchies reflect wider issues of identity. American

---

35 *Irish Catholic Directory* 1933, 590–649.

36 K. O'Sullivan, 'The Search for Justice. NGOs in Britain and Ireland and the New International Economic Order, 1968–82', in *Humanity. An International Journal of Human Rights, Humanitarianism and Development*, 6 (2015), 173–87.

37 M. Hickman, *Religion, Class and Identity: The State, the Catholic Church and the Education of the Irish in Britain* (Aldershot: Ashgate, 1995).

38 A. E. C. W. Spencer, *Arrangements for the Integration of Irish Immigrants in England and Wales* (Dublin: Irish Manuscripts Commission, 2011).

identity did not conflict with maintaining a sense of being Irish and Catholic; in Britain – the former colonial power – this was more problematical.

Race, Ethnicity and Class

Hickman and Walter claim that the Irish in Britain have been invisible, despite constituting Britain's largest source of migrant labour for over 200 years and Britain's largest ethnic minority.[39] This invisibility reflects the complexity of being Irish in Britain, a category that included both Anglo-Irish families whose history had straddled the two islands for centuries as well as Ulster Unionists. In Liverpool and Glasgow the political/denominational divisions of Irish history were recreated, through associations such as the Orange Order, Catholic processions, and through sport. Irish-America has celebrated its part in the struggle for Irish independence, which has been duly recognised in Ireland. However the contribution made by the Irish in Britain, and their efforts to influence British public opinion in favour of a settlement with Dáil Éireann, has only recently been acknowledged.[40] Once the new state was securely established, involvement in republicanism dwindled in both Britain and the USA, though it never entirely disappeared. The 1939 IRA bombing campaign in Britain witnessed 120 separate incidents, culminating in an explosion in Coventry that killed five people and injured over a hundred. Britain introduced the Prevention of Violence Act, giving the Home Secretary power 'to deport, exclude and detain any persons who he was satisfied were engaged in the IRA campaign', and requiring 'all Irish citizens' to register with the police. Given these political tensions, and the fact that the Irish immigrants to Britain included Ulster unionists, members of Anglo-Irish families, and Irish nationalists, it is not surprising that for many Irish in Britain in these years, 'being Irish became a more personal and less political matter for many people navigating the contradictory pressures of national identity, religious injunctions, nostalgia and ambition'.[41]

The all-party anti-Partition campaign of the 1940s and 1950s tried to involve Irish organisations in Britain, the United States and Australia, with limited success. Expressing support for a united Ireland was not controversial in the USA – indeed the cause often attracted token support from Irish-American politicians, including a young senator from Massachusetts, John F. Kennedy,

---

39 Hickman and Walter, *Discrimination and the Irish Community in Britain*, 7.
40 M. Moulton, *Ireland and the Irish in Interwar England* (Cambridge, 2014); Belchem, *Irish, Catholic and Scouse*, 263–96.
41 Moulton, *Ireland and the Irish in interwar England*, 306–20; quotation at 280.

who, however, showed no inclination to uphold this position when he became president. Irish-American involvement in republican activities after 1922 was restricted to a small, unrepresentative, if occasionally vocal, minority. The ending of mass migration to the United States in the 1930s meant that Irish-America was dominated by second-, third- and fourth-generation Irish. The 572,000 Irish-born in the USA in 1940, fell to 251,000 by 1970; by then almost one-in-three Irish-born Americans was over 70 years of age.[42] Physical and generational distance and military service helped to promote a hyphenated Irish-American identity that viewed Ireland nostalgically. In the 1950s, the GI Bill gave many Irish-Americans an undreamed-off opportunity to secure a college education, and economic prosperity saw Irish-Americans taking up middle-class occupations, and moving from traditional ethnic communities in the inner city to the suburbs, with a consequent weakening of ethnic identities.

The story in Britain or, more specifically, England, because few twentieth-century emigrants went to Scotland, is different. In 1911 there were 375,000 of Irish birth living in England and Wales; by 1971 there were 950,000. The post-war surge in Irish immigrants coincided with the beginnings of mass emigration from the West Indies and the Indian sub-continent. In 1951 there were 100,000 residents from the New Commonwealth (Africa, Asia, West Indies) and that number had quadrupled by 1961 and was destined to rise further as 136,000 Commonwealth immigrants arrived that year. Although Irish immigrants constituted the largest single immigrant cohort in the 1950s, they were not included in the 1962 Commonwealth Immigration Act, or subsequent legislation. Irish immigrants undoubtedly suffered discrimination, with some landladies specifying 'no coloured, no Irish', and they were victims of ethnic stereotypes about 'drunken Paddies'. Irish-born nurses were often denigrated as TB carriers, who would infect English patients with the disease, whereas most Irish nurses with TB contracted the disease in England.[43] Ultimately, however, the colour of their skin protected them.[44]

The 1948 British Nationality Act gave Irish-born residents in Britain a status similar to UK citizens. They were entitled to vote in elections, change jobs or residence as they wished, and this also helped to promote their invisibility.

42 K. Kenny, *The American Irish: A History* (London: Longman, 2000), 223, 228.

43 A. MacLellan, 'Victim or Vector? Tubercular Irish Nurses in England 1930–1960', in C. Cox and H. Marland (eds.), *Migration, Health and Ethnicity in the Modern World* (Basingstoke: Palgrave Macmillan, 2013), 104–25.

44 P. Clark, *Hope and Glory. Britain 1900–1990*, (London: Penguin, 1996), 325; K. Paul, *Whitewashing Britain. Race and Citizenship in the Post-war Era* (Ithaca: Cornell University Press, 1997), 132.

Surveys of housing and occupational profiles, prompted by a growing aware-ness of racial discrimination, presented data showing that Irish immigrants were disadvantaged. Nonetheless, the Irish were not covered under the terms of British Race Relations Acts. However, the formation of the Commission for Racial Equality (CRE), and an emerging awareness of race and ethnic-ity enhanced the sense that the Irish constituted a distinct ethnic group, and prompted campaigns for their housing and employment and other social indi-cators to be monitored by the CRE. A report published in 1997 by the CRE highlighted the disadvantages faced by the Irish in Britain, among them poor health, inferior housing, increasing isolation, racial stereotyping and harass-ment by police or by neighbours.[45] In 1991, the NESC report on emigration concluded that 'unlike the United States, Irish immigrant integration into Britain contains few clear-cut success models'.[46] This was probably an over-statement but at the time the successful Irish in Britain were also invisible.

Race and ethnicity also had an impact on Irish-Americans. Their dispersal to the suburbs was partly a response to growing prosperity; partly a flight from the cities in reaction to black migration. Suburbanisation plus black migration combined to weaken the influence of the parish in sustaining Irish culture. Social life in suburbia was less centred on the parish, with the country club and other non-ethnic middle-class associations being more significant. McGreevy shows how parishes that were once Irish, Italian or Polish lost their ethnic identity under the pressure of black immigration into northern cities.[47] As the ethnic composition of parishes became more diverse, so too did the parish schools. A growing number of Irish parents opted for public schools for their children. In Boston, in the 1970s, proposals to 'bus' children in public schools from their neighbourhood to achieve a greater racial bal-ance, prompted bitter and often militant protests in Irish neighbourhoods. Tensions over race fractured the long-established links between Irish-America and the Democratic Party.[48]

By the 1960s the Irish government was primarily interested in the USA as a source of tourist income, as a market for goods and as a source of for-eign direct investment. Irish-Americans were potentially a lucrative tourist market and would be the mainstay of CIE coach tours, Jury's Irish Cabaret

45 Hickman and Walters, *Discrimination and the Irish Community in Britain*.
46 NESC, *The Economic and Social Implications of Emigration*, 215.
47 J. McGreevy, *Parish Boundaries. The Catholic Encounter with Race in the Twentieth Century Urban North*, (Chicago: Chicago University Press, 1996).
48 J. A. Lukas, *Common Ground. A Turbulent Decade in the Lives of Three American Families* (New York: Random House, 1985).

and the Bunratty, County Kerry, medieval banquet. However a report by the Irish consul-general in New York in the late 1950s concluded that Irish-American economic influence remained limited. Membership of Irish organisations was falling, he noted, and was overwhelmingly blue-collar while the influence of more prosperous Irish-Americans was 'scattered and valueless'. The most successful Irish-Americans were many generations removed from Ireland, and perhaps for this reason the Irish embassy welcomed the publicity attracted by Cecil Woodham-Smith's history of the Famine, *The Great Hunger*, hoping that it would strengthen Irish-American identification with Ireland.[49]

In Britain, Irish ballrooms (The Galtee Mor, or the Thirty-Two club in Cricklewood, north London, for example), county associations, the GAA and Comhaltas Ceoltóirí Éireann (=Irish Traditional Music Society) reinforced a sense of Irishness. Irish showbands toured England during Lent, when Irish dance halls closed down. The National University of Ireland Club, a mecca for immigrant graduates, and the Irish Club in Eaton Square, London, attracted a more middle-class community. The *Irish Post*, founded in 1970, became the newspaper of the Irish in Britain, though the local Irish newspapers were also important links to home. But the strongest bonds were probably created by visits to Ireland, and, in contrast to Irish-America, these were often annual family visits. Bronwen Walters and Patrick Joyce have eloquently captured the importance of summer holidays in Ireland for the British-born children of immigrants. Yet Walters also noted the reluctance of these second-generation Irish children to speak about these holidays outside their immediate family or Irish community, and she drew attention to the complex issues that summer holidays in Ireland presented for children of mixed-race backgrounds.[50]

The outbreak of sustained violence in Northern Ireland in 1969 had a major impact on Irish communities both in Britain and the United States. The nationalist Social Democratic and Labour Party (SDLP), the Northern Ireland Civil Rights Association (NICRA), and both Provisional and Official Sinn Féin followed the traditional path to the United States in search of financial support. Older republican networks were resuscitated and new organisations emerged, including NORAID, founded in 1970 and which effectively became the American wing of the Provisional IRA. Noraid became involved in fund-raising, organising protests against visiting British politicians, and

49 Daly, 'Nationalism, Sentiment and Economics', in Kenny (ed.), *New Directions*, 272–6.
50 B. Walters, 'Transnational Networks across Generations: Childhood Visits to Ireland by the Second Generation in England', in M. Gilmartin and A. White (eds.), *Migrations. Ireland in a Global World* (Manchester: Manchester University Press, 2013), 17–35. P. Joyce, 'The Journey West', *Field Day Review*, 10 (2014).

campaigning against British policy in Northern Ireland. It was never a large organisation: most of the early members were veteran Irish-born republicans, but the hunger strikes of the 1980s saw the emergence of a younger, more diverse, Irish-American support and leadership. Noraid used the GAA, trade unions, and county associations to extend its network. The Irish government was caught between Noraid, the Irish National Caucus, who lobbied the US Congress on behalf of Sinn Féin, and the diplomatic and political might of the British government. However, Irish diplomats in the USA, and successive Irish governments worked patiently (often in association with the SDLP), to re-establish links with Irish-American politicians, and to garner support for the government's policy on Northern Ireland. The first significant achievement was on St Patrick's Day 1977 when four leading Irish-American politicians – soon dubbed the Four Horsemen – issued a joint statement appealing to all Americans not to promote or support organisations engaged in violence. The story of Irish-America and the Northern Ireland Peace Process does not belong here, yet it is evident that without a significant Irish diaspora in the United States, and a continuing identification of some Irish-American politicians with Ireland, Northern Ireland would never have attracted such a degree of international, especially US, attention.[51] The establishment of the Ireland Fund in 1976 provided a focus for affluent Irish-Americans to engage with Ireland.

The Northern Ireland Troubles had a much more serious impact on the Irish in Britain. Bombing campaigns by the IRA resulted in 124 deaths, of which 70 were civilians.[52] The 1974 Prevention of Terrorism Act (an updated version of the 1939 Act), was passed as an emergency response to bombs in Birmingham, that killed 21 people and injured 184. The six Irishmen hastily convicted of the Birmingham bombings were eventually shown to be innocent, but only after serving many years in prison. This miscarriage of justice was only one of a number perpetrated against the Irish in Britain. The impact of events in Northern Ireland was especially pronounced in Scotland, where both republican and loyalist paramilitaries attracted support.

Political violence, whether it took place in Britain or in Northern Ireland, made life difficult for the Irish in Britain, even for those who were long-term residents. One woman who had been in England for more than thirty years described how her neighbours of five or six years' standing, suggested that she

51 A. J. Wilson, *Irish America and the Ulster Conflict, 1968–1995*, (Belfast: Blackstaff, 1995).
52 D. McKitterick, S. Kelters, B. Feeney, *Lost Lives: The Stories of the Men, Women and Children who Died as a Result of the Northern Ireland Troubles* (Edinburgh: Mainstream, 1999), tables 13 and 14.

should 'go back to where you came from'. In common with many other Irish residents, she decided 'it was best to put my head down, and keep my mouth shut – it was better to say nothing at all'.[53] The 1998 Good Friday Agreement and Ireland's economic boom improved the self-confidence and standing of the Irish in Britain, though the lack of recognition given to Tony Blair's Irish ethnicity, as the son of a Donegal mother, suggests that the contrast between ethnic awareness in Britain and the USA survives.

The coincidence in the 1980s of a resurgence in emigration to the US, the emergence of new networks there campaigning on behalf of Irish undocumented immigrants, and a new consciousness among the Irish in Britain of their status as a distinct ethnic group, all helped to make Irish-based politicians and civil servants more conscious of Irish migrants. The new organisations established by the Irish in Britain in recent decades owe much to second-wave feminism, being far less likely than their predecessors to be male-dominated, and much less deferential than their forerunners in lobbying successive Irish governments for assistance for Irish communities overseas and for voting rights in Ireland to be accorded to emigrants. In 1992 Fianna Fáil and the Progressive Democrats agreed to support a constitutional amendment to give emigrants voting rights in Seanad, European and Presidential elections, though emigrant lobby groups were divided about these proposals; and in the event, nothing came of this initiative. In 1995, President Mary Robinson addressed both houses of the Oireachtas (the first such address by a President of Ireland) on the subject of the Irish diaspora. The subsequent creation of the Irish Abroad Unit in the Department of Foreign Affairs, and the appointment in 2014 of a junior Minister for the Diaspora, reflected greater awareness within government of the Irish worldwide.[54] It may be no coincidence that this increased awareness has coincided with Ireland becoming a country of immigration.

Conclusion

While migration has been a critical force in shaping twentieth-century Ireland, its impact has been complex and contested. It has been, and it remains, both a force for change and a conservative force. Emigration provided a safety

---

53 As quoted in C. Dunne, *An Unconsidered People. The Irish in London* (Dublin: New Island, 2003), 84.
54 M. E. Daly, *The Irish State and the Diaspora*, NUI Centennial, O'Donnell Lecture, 2008, (Dublin: NUI, 2009), 13. Similar proposals were endorsed in the Constitutional Convention in 2014: www.constitution.ie/ (accessed 1 July 2015).

valve for poor, unemployed Irishmen and women, and for those who were frustrated by the restrictions of Irish life. Yet emigrant letters, gifts from those abroad and first-hand experiences brought rural Ireland into contact with the values and lifestyles of British and American cities. Most migrants were young and single; the majority left as individuals, not as part of a family group. Yet while emigration divided families, it may also have ensured their survival. Remittances were a vital source of income for many Irish households until at least the 1970s, given the low level of welfare and pension payments in Ireland. Remittances from migrants now working in Ireland fulfil a similar role in Eastern Europe, the Philippines and elsewhere. Irish families were large, and the emigration of non-inheriting children on family farms was essential to enable one favoured son to inherit the land, to marry and to reproduce in the next generation. Indeed without emigration it is probable that Irish family size would have fallen several decades before it did. Family networks were also essential in facilitating emigration – providing information and access to jobs and short-term accommodation. The relative balance between male and female emigrants and the social networks created through the Catholic Church, sport, or Irish ballrooms, helped to replicate the 'Irish family' overseas, though the rate of endogamy fell in the later twentieth century.

Emigration involved the departure of working-age adults, resulting in a high rate of dependency – children and the elderly. Graduate emigration – which has become increasingly significant in recent decades, involves Ireland paying the costs of third-level education without reaping the benefits and this also applies to immigrant graduates settling in Ireland. While most emigrants in the early twentieth century left because they were unable to find work, there is growing evidence since the 1980s of a willingness to emigrate if working and living standards fail to match those perceived to be available elsewhere.[55]

The increasing use of the term diaspora, as 'a framework for understanding the world created by migration',[56] reflects a greater awareness of the importance of migration both in personal and national/transnational terms. Migration – whether from or into Ireland – raises questions about what it means to be Irish – a category that potentially includes those born and continuing to live in Ireland, Irish-born emigrants, immigrants who have settled in Ireland, and the forty or sixty million elsewhere who allegedly claim Irish

---

55 Irish emigration post-2008 was significantly higher than Italy, Spain or Greece, which were also seriously hit by recession, Glynn et al., *Irish Emigration* 114–15.
56 K. Kenny, *Diaspora. A Very Short Introduction* (Oxford University Press, 2011), 109.

Table 13 *Net Emigration*

	Ireland		Republic of Ireland		Northern Ireland	
	Census	Vital Stats	Census	Vital Stats	Census	Vital Stats
1831–41						
1841–51		1235				
1851–61	1328	1226				
1861–71	1209	772	946	584	253	
1871–81	688	621	523	380	165	
1881–91	733	771	593	553	139	
1891–01	452	434	386	347	66	
1901–11	329	346	259	240	70	
1911–26	498	276	398	187	100	
1926–36	225		169	177	56	35
1936–46	225		186	187	39	
1946–51	160		129	112	31	
1951–61	494		405	400	89	
1961–71	186		129	170	57	38
1971–81	0		−108	−100	108	111
1981–91	259		210	202	49	47
1991–01	−115		−122	−86	7	3
2001–11	−386		−349	−407	−37	−38

(*Source*: 'Vital stats' refers to the population as estimated from births and deaths statistics.)

ancestry. They reflect different definitions of Irishness that have undoubtedly changed in recent decades. Lee asks 'how many' of the self-styled thirty or forty million Irish-Americans 'allow their lives to be influenced by the fact'.[57] Applications for Irish citizenship by those of Irish descent were largely motivated by a wish to have employment and residency within the EU. In the 1980s the largest cohort of applications came from South Africa and Zimbabwe, and fewer than 4,000 have applied for a certificate of Irishness, a programme now discontinued.[58] Instrumentality is characteristic of both migrants and the Irish government, though efforts to harness the Irish diaspora have had mixed results. Relatively effective – if at times problematic – during the campaign for Irish independence, and again in resolving the Northern Ireland conflict but they have proved less so with their contribution to economic development, though emigrant remittances provided essential support for many families at a time when Irish welfare payments were parsimonious (see Table 13). Continuing emigration after 1914, despite the achievement of

57 Lee, 'Interpreting Irish America', in Lee and Casey (eds.), *Making the Irish American*, 38.
58 M. E. Daly, 'Irish Nationality and Citizenship since 1922', *IHS*, 32 (May, 2001), 377–407.

political independence and, more recently, the achievement of living standards that are among the highest in the world, can be seen as a reflection of the centrality of migration in Irish history. The significant immigration into Ireland in the closing years of the twentieth century has further enhanced and complicated Ireland's migration history.

18

Broadcasting on the Island of Ireland, 1916–2016

ROBERT J. SAVAGE

Introduction

On Easter Monday, 24 April 1916, Irish Republicans launched a rebellion against British rule in Ireland and occupied a number of buildings in central Dublin. Irish Volunteer Fergus O'Kelly found himself inside the General Post Office, along with leading figures of the rising including Patrick Pearse, James Connolly and Joseph Plunkett. O'Kelly had joined the Volunteers in 1913 and was assigned to a signalling company where he received training in wireless transmitting and Morse code. His training was put to use that Easter Monday when he was instructed by Plunkett to take a group of men from the General Post Office to seize the School of Wireless Telegraphy at the corner of Sackville, later O'Connell, Street and Abbey Street. O'Kelly and his men were ordered to secure the building and do everything they could to make operational a wireless transmitter that had been decommissioned at the start of the Great War. Led by O'Kelly, a group of rebels, including the well-known Abbey, and later Hollywood, actor, Arthur Shields, electrician Sean O'Connor, and Marconi operator David Burke, broke into the school and began resuscitating a 1.5 kilowatt ship-to-ship transmitter.

While Burke worked on the transmitter, O'Kelly and his men made his way to the roof of the building and struggled to erect an aerial. Sniper fire from British positions grew intense, killing one of O'Kelly's colleagues and forcing him and his men to withdraw. The aerial was eventually erected under cover of darkness and O'Kelly sent word to the General Post Office that the transmitter was operational. Many years later he was interviewed by the Bureau of Military History and explained:

> On reporting to H.Q. that the transmitting apparatus was operating, a message was sent over by James Connolly, commanding the Dublin area, for broadcast transmission. As the receiving apparatus could not be got to

operate correctly, it was not possible to get in direct touch with any station or ship but the message was sent out on the normal commercial wavelength in the hope that some ship would receive it and relay it as interesting news. As far as I can remember, the first message announced the proclaiming of the Irish Republic and the taking over of the city by the Republican Army. A later message stated that the British troops had attacked and had been repulsed and that the positions were still held by the Republican forces.[1]

Heavy shellfire from the gunboat *Helga* positioned on the River Liffey eventually forced O'Kelly and his men to withdraw altogether from the school. They struggled down narrow stairs and through back alleys to get the bulky transmitter back to the General Post Office, thinking it might be used again. However the transmitter was soon abandoned and later destroyed in the fire that consumed the building.

In his classic study, *Understanding Media* (1964), Marshal McLuhan, the Canadian 'guru' of media studies, defines the rebel's desperate transmission as the world's first 'broadcast'. He notes that by 1916 wireless was already being used in the maritime world as ship-to-shore 'telegraph': 'The rebels used a ship's wireless to make, not a point-to-point message, but a diffused broadcast in the hope of getting word out to some ships that would relay their story to the American press.'[2] Although the insurgents failed to inform the world of the history unfolding around them, 'broadcasting' as we know it today was born.[3]

This chapter will trace the uneven evolution of more traditional broadcasting in the Irish Free State (from 1949 the Republic of Ireland), and Northern Ireland during the twentieth century. Radio and television proved transformative in both parts of Ireland, with television in particular becoming a destabilising force that helped undermine a conservative consensus that had taken deep root in both jurisdictions. To understand how this happened the chapter will first explore how radio stations in Dublin and Belfast were established to project the political and cultural ideologies of their respective states. Radio Éireann and BBC Northern Ireland were established in the wake of devastating political violence that shaped the states established on both sides of the new border. These emerging stations were conservative,

1 Fergus Kelly, Witness Statement 351, Bureau of Military History, Military History Archives, Cathal Brugha Bks, Dublin.
2 R. J. Savage, *Irish Television, the Political and Social Origins*, (Cork: Cork University Press, 1996), 1.
3 See C. Morash, *A History of the Media in Ireland* (Cambridge University Press, 2010), for a detailed account of how news of the rebellion was clandestinely transmitted via telegraph, 125–30.

inward-looking institutions that promoted deference to authority and to governments desperately longing for stability and legitimacy. Radio Éireann and BBC Northern Ireland were both heavily influenced by political authorities anxious to present an image of two distinct 'nations', one uniquely Gaelic, the other defiantly British. For decades, broadcasting officials in both jurisdictions were careful to avoid controversy with religious, cultural and, especially, political elites. When television began broadcasting from Belfast in 1953 and Dublin in 1961, the defining conservatism of these societies was already beginning to erode. Television helped accelerate that erosion and became an active agent in provoking political, cultural and social change throughout the island. Simply put, broadcasting proved transformative, enabling citizens' access to and engagement with a more 'modern' world. By the end of the 1960s radio and especially television began a process that undermined the power of institutions that had long dominated Irish life.

Radio in an Independent Ireland

James Joseph Walsh was an ardent and somewhat eccentric republican from Bandon, West Cork who had a keen interest in radio or 'wireless broadcasting'. He joined the Irish Republican Brotherhood as a young man and like many of his generation was drawn to the political separatism of Sinn Féin and to the Gaelic revival that became popular at the start of the twentieth century. He helped establish the Cork City Corps of the Volunteers in 1913 and was active in promoting the Gaelic Athletic Association in the city. Walsh earned a reputation as an excitable revolutionary and was sometimes incapable of controlling his unbridled enthusiasm for the cause. He once famously declared 'the day an Irish Republic was formed, the landlords would be put against the wall and there would be an end to landlordism once and for all'.[4] In Cork he worked for the Post Office as a telegraph operator but was dismissed for his radical republican rhetoric that his supervisors found unsettling.

Walsh was an active participant in the 1916 Easter Rising and was in the General Post Office during the rebellion. He knew Fergus O'Kelly and at one point helped O'Kelly and his colleagues with the radio transmitter when it was moved into the General Post Office. According to his autobiography, *Recollections of a Rebel,* once the rising started he realised the authorities had not occupied the centre of telephone communications in the city located near Dublin Castle. A man who never missed an opportunity to stress his own importance, Walsh

4 R. Pine, *2RN and the Origins of Irish Radio*, (Dublin: Four Courts Press, 2002), 53.

explains that 'without instructions, I proceeded to exploit the possibilities of Telegraphic contacts. Representing myself as Superintendent X, I had no difficulty in getting in touch with overseers in Cork, Limerick, Galway and Wexford ... In this way Connolly, Pearse and their associates, knew how matters stood in the country'.[5] Walsh does not reveal if he explained to the rebel leaders that Dublin was alone, that no other city had risen, and that the rebellion was doomed.

Walsh was sentenced to death by firing squad for taking up arms against the King but had his sentence commuted to penal servitude. Once in gaol the defiant prisoner refused to wear a prison uniform and instead wrapped himself in a blanket. (IRA prisoners in Northern Ireland's Long Kesh Prison would emulate his 'blanket protest' in the 1970s and 1980s.) In spite of his ardent republicanism, Walsh later became a prominent figure in Cumann na Gaedheal, the faction of Sinn Féin that supported the 1921 Anglo-Irish Treaty. He was appointed to a Cabinet position, becoming the Irish Free State's first Postmaster General in what was initially designated the Irish Post Office. His title was later changed to Minister of Posts and Telegraphs when the department was renamed. As was the case in Britain, the Post Office was charged with overseeing the establishment of an indigenous radio service.

Tasked by the Dáil with determining how radio should be set up in the Irish Free State, Walsh unilaterally decided that it was best to follow the model of the newly formed British Broadcasting Company. The BBC was set up in 1923 when a number of companies involved in manufacturing wireless equipment formed a consortium to oversee the establishment of radio stations throughout the United Kingdom. Walsh decided to set up what he defined as the Irish Broadcasting Company. On his own initiative, and to the consternation of many Dáil Deputies, he placed advertisements in the national press in the summer of 1923 requesting parties interested in being part of the proposed IBC to contact his department. Subsequently, Walsh introduced to the Dáil a White Paper on broadcasting, which claimed that the relatively short history of radio revealed clearly the challenges faced in establishing broadcast stations. He had examined the British and American models for broadcasting and he declared, 'In America, and elsewhere, where broadcasting has been conducted as a private enterprise, a multiplicity of companies has been found to lead to chaos and confusion and to inefficient service.'[6] Believing that the

---

5 J. J. Walsh, *Recollections of a Rebel*, (Tralee: The Kerryman Press, 1944).
6 White Paper on Wireless Broadcasting (1923), quoted in Robert J. Savage, *The Origins of Irish Radio*, unpublished Master of Arts thesis, University College Dublin (1982), 32.

licensing of dozens of stations in the United States had created a hectic and incoherent landscape for the medium, he was convinced that following the American model would cause untold headaches for his department. Looking to London, he proposed bringing together a number of private Irish companies involved in broadcasting to form a consortium that would be licensed by his department. Walsh argued that 'all experience has proven that there must be unified control in broadcasting if the public are to get an efficient service' and later explained that his proposal 'follows as closely as circumstances will permit the English model'.[7]

Walsh certainly did not please his colleagues in the Dáil, many of whom were upset with the autocratic nature of his planning. Some complained that he was moving too quickly once he revealed that he had already opened up negotiations with, and gained agreement from, various firms 'to work out a system of broadcasting in the Irish Free State under license from the Post Office'.[8] Believing that the new medium of radio had tremendous potential, many deputies sought more time to examine the implications of broadcasting. Walsh, however, rejected criticism that he was moving too rapidly, making it clear to all that he regarded his scheme as wise, rational and workable. He insisted on implementing it quickly.

The Postmaster General's arrogance provoked the wrath of many Dáil Deputies. As debate developed, the issue of Irish broadcasting became even more complicated when rumours of certain irregularities among members of the proposed IBC began to circulate. Allegations of 'influence peddling' were made against a Dáil Deputy, Darrell Figgis, claiming that he had lobbied on behalf of an unqualified and highly suspicious company that was to be part of the proposed IBC.[9] (It transpired that the company in question had only recently been formed, had no experience in wireless broadcasting and had shadowy connections to Figgis, a determined advocate for Walsh's scheme.) Much to the chagrin of Walsh, the Dáil established a Special Committee on Wireless Broadcasting to consider his White Paper and to explore how radio should be introduced into the Irish Free State. The Committee took its time examining Walsh's proposal and called dozens of witnesses before issuing an exhaustive 600-page report that firmly rejected the central thesis of the Postmaster General's plan.

---

7 Savage, *Irish Television*, 2.
8 Ibid., 2–3, the companies that joined to form the BBC were all involved in the broadcasting industry, this was not the case for the proposed IBC.
9 Ibid., 3–4, also Pine, *2RN*, 79–94.

The Special Committee maintained that radio had enormous potential for Ireland, and argued that it was simply too important to be entrusted to a private consortium, even if that consortium was licensed and overseen by the Post Office. The Committee furthermore recommended that in order to protect what was considered an important national asset, radio should be established and run by Walsh's department. The concept of radio as a public service had now become part of the debate, and Dáil Deputies determined that radio should do more than simply entertain listeners. A consensus emerged that radio should also inform, educate and 'uplift' its audience with 'serious' programming. The Dáil committee proposed that the national radio station be financed through a combination of sources: license fees, a tax on the import of receivers and a limited amount of commercial advertising. The Cumann na nGaedheal government accepted the recommendations of the Special Committee and instructed Walsh to make arrangements for establishing a national radio service.[10]

This decision did not go down well with the volatile Postmaster General who still believed his own proposal was best for the country and his department. He made it clear to the Dáil that he resented the Committee's conclusions and argued strenuously that the Post Office was not at all suited to oversee a national radio service. Walsh was also concerned that politicians would interfere and try to exploit radio for their own political advantage. He angrily challenged his colleagues in the Dáil: 'If this House determines that the Post Office must differentiate between rival organ grinders, rival tenors and people of that kind, and even rival politicians who want to get control and preferential treatment, we will be able to do it at a price and it will be a very dear price.'[11] But a decision had been made, and Walsh reluctantly accepted the reality of supervising Ireland's radio service, which was designated 2RN. He left politics a short time later, disillusioned with W. T. Cosgrave's government and still upset that his proposal for an Irish Broadcasting Company had been rejected. Before resigning his office he warned 2RN's first director that 'it would be safe to steer clear as far as possible of religion and politics'.[12] Because successive broadcasting officials took up this advice over the next four decades, Irish radio failed to develop critical news and current affairs broadcasting that addressed political, religious or social issues until well into the 1960s.[13]

10 Ibid., 4–5.
11 Ibid., 5.
12 See B. Lynch, 'Steering Clear: Broadcasting and the Church, 1926–1951', *New Hibernia Review*, 4 (2000), 28.
13 See the author's interview with broadcaster and historian John Bowman on this point in *Éire-Ireland*, 50 (Spring/Summer 2015), 224–6.

The new radio station began broadcasting via a fairly primitive transmitter from Dublin on New Year's Day 1926. From the outset the station embraced the conservative ethos of the Irish Free State and supported the rhetoric of the Gaelic revival. Ironically, just as radio in much of the world was emerging as a transnational medium that reached across national boundaries, the fledgling Irish station was looking inwards, committed to protecting and supporting what was regarded as a frail national culture. The co-founder of the Gaelic League, and future President of Ireland, Douglas Hyde, delivered the inaugural address at the opening of the new radio service. His choice as speaker highlights the cultural imperatives of the day. Hyde's words captured the sense of anxiety shared by many cultural nationalists concerning the future of indigenous culture and the plight of the native language in the newly established Irish Free State. Decades earlier, his address 'the Necessity for de-Anglicizing Ireland' had served as a call to arms for the Gaelic revival. In his opening remarks, some of which echoed Robert Emmet's speech from the dock in 1803, Hyde told listeners that Irish radio 'was a sign to the whole world that a great change has come about when we can take our place among the nations of the world and make this wireless instrument work in our own language like every other country'.[14] While he welcomed the opportunity that the new technology offered the nation, he once again warned in graphic terms that 'foreign', especially English, influence threatened ruin:

> There were two tides in Ireland – one of them coming in on this side of Ireland and the other going out on the west coast. The tide of Gaelic was ebbing there and leaving behind a bare, cold, ugly beach in its wake. The fine Gaelic water had ebbed away and was replaced by the mud, slime and filth of English.[15]

A committee that included John Reith, later Lord Reith, the man most responsible for establishing the BBC as the world's premiere public broadcasting service, appointed Séamus Clandillon as director of the new Irish station.[16] Not only a manager and director, Clandillon was also a renowned singer; in radio's formative years he performed regularly with his wife, Maighréad Ní Annagáin, to the annoyance of some listeners. 2RN operated on a shoestring budget but slowly started to expand its reach; a second station opened in Cork

---

14 Opening address of 2RN, Douglas Hyde, 1 January 1926. My thanks to Nollaig Mac Congáil for the translation.
15 Ibid.
16 D. Bell 'Proclaiming the Republic: Broadcasting Policy and the Corporate State in Ireland', in *Broadcasting Policy and Politics in Western Europe*, 8 (1985), 27 and Pine, 2 RN, 138.

in 1927, and the service covered most of the country when a new transmitter was built in the midlands along the River Shannon in 1932. Renamed Radio Athlone in 1932, it became Radio Éireann in 1937 – all the while being staffed by civil servants and operated by the Department of Posts and Telegraphs.

The autonomy, and many would argue creativity, of Radio Éireann was constrained by its role as part of the Department of Posts and Telegraphs and staffing by civil servants for over thirty years. In its formative years, Radio Éireann was starved of funds and depended on the Department of Finance for support. That department was unimpressed with the needs of radio, believing there were more compelling priorities to which the new state should attend. This funding difficulty was especially true when the Minister of Finance, the notoriously frugal Ernest Blythe, also served as Minister for Posts and Telegraphs. Radio was certainly not one of his priorities, a belief made clear by his decision to siphon off tax revenue collected from the importation of receivers. These funds had been earmarked to help support Radio Éireann but, recognising a valuable revenue stream, Blythe diverted them to the national budget. In these early years Ireland's national radio service was understaffed, under-financed and unpopular. When Fianna Fáil came to power in 1932, a modest effort was made to improve the service. A new Director, T. J. Kiernan, was appointed, and by 1937 the number of listeners – or at least those willing to pay their license fee – exceeded 100,000. Under Kiernan, a number of new initiatives were begun, with an increase in outside broadcasts and greater coverage of games played by the Gaelic Athletic Association.

As Taoiseach, Éamon de Valera recognised radio as an important resource and exploited it successfully on a number of occasions. His Saint Patrick's Day address, 'The Ireland that we dreamed of', broadcast on Radio Éireann in 1943 is, perhaps, his most often-quoted speech.[17] In it he articulated his hope that Ireland would become comfortable in embracing 'frugal comforts' and its rural heritage and cultural traditions. At the conclusion of the Second World War, de Valera again took to the airwaves to respond forcefully and with great dignity to Winston Churchill's scathing denunciation of Ireland's wartime policy of neutrality. His address proved popular with the majority of citizens who supported Ireland's position as a non-belligerent during the conflict.

De Valera hoped to use radio to reach out to the Irish Diaspora in North America but was frustrated by technical difficulties in trans-Atlantic

---

17 M. Moynihan (ed.), *Speeches and Statements by Éamon de Valera 1917–1973* (Dublin: Gill & Macmillan, 1980), 466.

broadcasting and by the lack of popularity of short wave radio. Still, he understood the importance of radio and slowly devoted additional resources to the fledgling service. By 1947, in spite of the economic crisis that would undermine his government, Radio Éireann had become more professional. The director was now able to hire a professional news staff to collect and broadcast domestic and international news – an initiative that ended the practice of pilfering newspapers and other radio stations for information. Even a modest increase in funding meant that scriptwriters could be hired and a symphony orchestra assembled for music programmes. In one of its more innovative initiatives, in the 1950s Radio Éireann underwrote the cost of archivists who travelled the countryside to collect traditional music and folklore. Over time efforts were made to develop new programming that would be more appealing to listeners, but such initiatives met with mixed results. Irish language broadcasts had already moved on from didactic language instruction to commissioning short plays to build new audiences. However, surveys conducted by Radio Éireann made it clear that very few listeners were tuning into these broadcasts.[18]

Controversy remained almost non-existent on Ireland's national radio service since the civil servants who staffed the station failed to develop programming addressing complex political, religious or social issues. Officials in Radio Éireann were keen to avoid conflict; any inadvertent political or religious tensions that emerged were handled quietly behind the scenes by senior civil servants who avoided ruffling any political or ecclesiastical feathers.[19] Although Radio Éireann became part of the social and cultural landscape of Ireland, it remained a prisoner of the civil service. There was certainly a perception by critics that Radio Éireann lacked the imagination to engage listeners in a meaningful way because government employees staffed it. This perception began to change when the Broadcasting Act was passed in 1960, creating an independent, though government appointed, public authority that was responsible for overseeing both radio and television.

In spite of modest improvements in programming, listeners increasingly looked elsewhere for their listening choices, discovering their ability simply to turn the dial and receive programmes from powerful transmitters in Britain and the continent. The BBC began broadcasting from Belfast in 1923 and, combined with powerful transmitters on 'mainland' Britain, this enabled

---

18 RTÉ Written Archives, 105/58, no. 1, *Listenership Surveys*. Four were conducted in the 1950s, two in 1953 and one each in 1954 and 1955.

19 R. J. Savage, *A Loss of Innocence? Television and Irish Society 1960–1972*, (Manchester: Manchester University Press, 2010), 171–2.

listeners to enjoy British broadcasts. Advances in radio receivers meant that by 1945 many Irish listeners were tuning into other stations, including American Armed Forces Radio and Radio Luxemburg. These broadcasters could reach across the Irish Sea and find an Irish audience attracted to popular, especially American, music.

Radio in Northern Ireland

Northern Ireland's first station, designated 2BE, began broadcasting in 1924. When a Royal Charter formally established the British Broadcasting Corporation in 1927, the Belfast station was incorporated into what became BBC Northern Ireland. In its formative years BBC Northern Ireland relayed national programmes produced in London and only slowly began to develop regional programming of its own. Recent research, however, has highlighted the work of a number of innovative producers and writers of drama who left their mark on the BBC in Belfast during these formative years. A young Tyrone Guthrie got his start writing radio plays and having them broadcast in Belfast, and he later emerged as one of the most influential theatre directors of his generation. While at the Belfast station he wrote pioneering drama specifically for radio, and his innovative broadcasting techniques helped him become a producer at the Scottish National Theatre in 1926. After his departure the Northern Ireland station continued to excel in radio drama. The playwright Denis Johnson came to Belfast in 1936 as a researcher and radio producer, enjoying successes such as the critically acclaimed *Lillibulero* (1938) that dramatised the siege of Derry.[20]

From the outset, however, broadcasting in Northern Ireland was strongly influenced by the uneven power structure characterising life in the province. Officials in BBC NI accepted Unionist domination of political life and proved remarkably deferential to that powerful political establishment. Many, possibly most, Catholics, therefore, regarded BBC NI as a medium dominated by Protestants and were inclined to tune into Radio Éireann for news and entertainment. Until the appointment of Waldo Maguire in 1965, directors or controllers of the BBC in Belfast came from outside Northern Ireland. On arrival they were quickly accepted into the unionist community and schooled in the peculiarities of life in a deeply divided society. Many became comfortable in Belfast, including Gerald Beadle, an Englishman who arrived in Northern

---

20 G. McIntosh, 'Tyrone Guthrie and the BBC in Belfast', *Éire-Ireland*, 50 (Spring/Summer 2015).

Ireland in 1926 after setting up a radio service for the BBC in Durban, South Africa. Like many directors who followed him, he quickly adapted to his new home in Belfast, becoming one of the power brokers of the Unionist establishment. Directors of BBC NI were welcomed into Belfast's exclusive Ulster Reform Club, dominated by the great and the good of the province. There, broadcasting officials enjoyed dinners, drinks, billiards and card games with leading Unionist politicians and businessmen. Beadle became so embedded in the Unionist establishment of Belfast that he wrote to the BBC's Managing Director in London suggesting BBC Northern Ireland should make official its position as the voice of the province: 'I am sure that our position here will be strengthened immensely if we can persuade the Northern Government to look upon us as their mouthpiece.'[21]

BBC Northern Ireland defined itself as decidedly British, and senior staff underscored this assumption (or self identification) on a number of occasions. Directors of BBC NI made it quite clear that they regarded Northern Ireland as an integral part of the United Kingdom and, to that end, they worked to maintain a British façade for the province. Senior staff did not tolerate any reference to divisions within northern society, and directors insisted that broadcasting officials in Belfast and London present Northern Ireland as a loyal Protestant province. Programmes from London that stumbled into the minefield of Irish history or that made reference to the disaffected minority or politics provoked Unionist outrage. George Marshall learned this shortly after he arrived in Belfast as director. He had worked at the BBC in Edinburgh before arriving in Northern Ireland to take up the position in 1932. Only three years later in 1935, ferocious sectarian rioting in Belfast scarred the city and underscored for him the danger of collaborating with 'the enemy' south of the border. In the midst of the crisis, the Unionist press revealed that he was collaborating with Radio Éireann on the development of programmes that could be broadcast in both jurisdictions. He quickly cancelled these plans when news of the initiative provoked vehement protests and excited denunciation from political leaders and the Unionist press. Marshall learned that the BBC in Northern Ireland needed to avoid even the appearance of being soft on the 'constitutional question' explaining 'broadcasting should not precipitate civil strife'.[22]

---

21 R. Cathcart, *The Most Contrary Region, The BBC in Northern Ireland 1924–1984* (1984), 37.

22 H. R. Cathcart and Michael Muldoon, 'The Mass Media in Twentieth- century Ireland', in J. R. Hill (ed.), *A New History of Ireland, VII, Ireland 1921–1984,* (Oxford University Press, 2003), 685.

The deference of Belfast's BBC officials to the Unionist establishment explains the decision of senior management to agree to Prime Minister Lord Craigavon's demand that it stop reporting results of Gaelic Athletic Association games. Broadcasting officials accepted his complaints that the Sunday announcements 'were hurting the feelings of the large majority of people in Northern Ireland'.[23] At times, the BBC in Belfast appeared as zealously Unionist as the Unionist politicians and their supporters – as when Marshall bizarrely attacked London's network programme titled *The Irish* that was broadcast throughout the United Kingdom. Because the programme addressed life on both sides of the border, the director wrote to London to protest both the title and the content of the broadcast. He chastised London on the grounds that the title was 'highly undesirable'. It linked 'under one name two strongly antipathetic states with completely different political outlooks. There is no such thing today as an Irishman. One is either a citizen of the Irish Free State or a citizen of the United Kingdom of Great Britain and Northern Ireland. Irishmen as such ceased to exist after the partition'.[24] Led by the Unionist government at Stormont, BBC NI largely ignored the nationalist community and Gaelic culture, and regarded the country south of its border as a foreign nation.

During the Second World War regional programming was curtailed throughout the United Kingdom, and broadcasting from London dominated the BBC. But once the war ended, the Labour government of Clement Attlee sought to decentralise the network and encouraged regional broadcasting. A 1946 government White Paper called for Scotland, Wales and Northern Ireland to develop formal Advisory Councils that would be 'broadly representative of the general public of the region' with members chosen 'for their individual qualities and not as representatives of particular interests'. George Marshall complied with a request to nominate members for such a Northern Ireland Advisory Council and submitted his list to London, telling the Director-General, 'I have consulted numerous people, including the Prime Minister (Brookeborough) and I think my list is a representative one. You will note that I have included three Nationalists, which I would say, is about the right proportion.'[25] He seemed oblivious to the reality that choosing just three members from the nationalist community for a council of twenty was

---

23 G. McIntosh, *The Force of Culture, Unionist Identities in Twentieth-Century Ireland* (Cork: Cork University Press, 1999), 82–3.

24 P. Scannell and D. Cardiff, *A Social History of British Broadcasting, vol. 1 1922-1939, Serving the Nation* (Oxford: Wiley-Blackwell, 1991), 288.

25 Cathcart, *Most Contrary Region*, 139.

hardly representative. In general, little attention was paid to the nationalist community even though it made up roughly a third of the population of Northern Ireland.

The devolution of broadcasting became popular and in 1951 a parliamentary committee addressed the need for increased autonomy in Scotland, Wales and Northern Ireland. The committee proposed that each of these regions replace their advisory councils with broadcasting councils that would give substantial autonomy to the regions. The committee proposed that each region should have the power to develop its own programmes and make decisions concerning finance, accommodation and the hiring of staff.[26] Although the BBC in London hoped to encourage regional broadcasting and substantial autonomy for each 'nation' of the United Kingdom, Unionists in Belfast were alarmed. Many were concerned that regional programming would mean nationalist involvement and they feared that such a change would inevitably touch upon the deep divisions within Northern Ireland. Prime Minister Brookeborough, alarmed that Belfast would be cut off from Britain, worried that a vital link with British culture would be lost.

Andrew Stewart, who became the regional director at the Belfast station in 1948, took the unusual step of attending a Cabinet meeting at Stormont to urge ministers to reject the autonomy being offered by London. He warned ministers that involving the nationalist community in broadcasting decisions would be a grave mistake: participation would lead to conflict, argument and ultimately embarrassment for the Stormont parliament. In the end, Brookeborough and his cabinet agreed with Stewart and rejected London's offer of autonomy. Unionist determination to cultivate and protect a British image for Northern Ireland meant that devolution could not be tolerated.[27]

Although Unionists remained sensitive to any perceived slight from broadcasters, some in BBC Northern Ireland sought carefully to develop more inclusive regional broadcasts in the post-war period. Broadcasting House in Belfast did so by trying to create an Ulster identity that would set Northern Ireland apart from England, Scotland and Wales, all the while not undermining its 'Britishness'. Talented Ulster writers including Sam Hanna Bell, W. R. Rodgers and John Hewitt were recruited to produce material for listeners

26 Ibid., 164. See also A. Briggs, *The History of Broadcasting in the United Kingdom, Volume V Competition,* (Oxford University Press, 1995), 669–70.
27 For an insightful consideration of the early development of broadcasting in Northern Ireland, see M. McLoone, 'The Construction of a Partitionist Mentality: Early Broadcasting in Ireland', in M. McLoone (ed.), *Broadcasting in a Divided Community, Seventy Years of the BBC in Northern Ireland* (Belfast: QUB, Institute of Irish Studies, 1996).

that would reflect on life in Northern Ireland. Bell proved especially adventurous by making use of mobile recording equipment supplied by London to travel throughout the Ulster countryside, interviewing ordinary people from both communities. By 1949, some 260 outside broadcasts had been collected, edited and transmitted, allowing listeners to hear a variety of Ulster voices and offering a unique perspective of life in Northern Ireland's towns, cities and rural areas.[28] (As noted, Radio Éireann had launched a similar initiative south of the border, thereby building an impressive archive of folklore and music.)

While these initiatives in BBC Northern Ireland were intended to make its service more inclusive, most nationalists continued to view the BBC as overly sympathetic to the Unionist community and much too focused on representing a culture that was not theirs. Unionists continued to marginalise the nationalist community and its culture, remaining determined that the sole image of Northern Ireland presented to the outside world would be a British one. Any suggestion that Northern Ireland was Irish was considered offensive. Management at the BBC in Northern Ireland remained wary of upsetting the Unionist establishment and continued to show a remarkable degree of deference to its political sensibilities. The station employed few Catholics and featured little cultural programming that could be defined as Gaelic or Irish.[29] Such deference, however, came under tremendous pressure when television was introduced to Northern Ireland.[30]

Television in the Irish Republic

The Republic of Ireland was one of the last countries in Europe to establish an indigenous television service. Throughout the 1950s animated debates took place within government about how television should be structured, financed and introduced to the nation. Debate also centred on what should and should not be broadcast on an Irish television station. Once again, the Department of Posts and Telegraphs played a major role in shaping the debate and influencing the establishment of what became Telefís Éireann.

---

28 Cathcart, *Most Contrary Region*, 156 and Morash, *A History of the Media in Ireland*, 137–8.
29 Ibid., 80.
30 It should be emphasised that in spite of the reluctance of the Unionist establishment in Belfast to be associated with Gaelic or Irish culture, the BBC in London was keen to feature Irish producers, writers, poets and actors in programming on its national network. See Emily Bloom, ' "Channel Paddlers" 1950s Irish Drama on the British Airwaves', *Éire-Ireland*, 50 (Spring/Summer 2015).

The Secretary of the Department of Posts and Telegraphs, Leon Ó Broin, emerged as a powerful figure in these debates. He proved a wily and resourceful civil servant, impressed by BBC's programmes and its commitment to public service broadcasting. Ó Broin had spent time in the United States and the United Kingdom familiarising himself with commercial television. Regarding commercial networks and their programmes as the vulgar antithesis of public service broadcasting, he became a determined advocate of public service television. Ó Broin was convinced that Ireland should emulate the BBC.

Beginning in the mid-1950s proposals began to come across his desk from a variety of American and European entrepreneurs. These businessmen promised to provide Ireland with television at little or no cost if they could exploit the country's geographic position by setting up commercial radio stations that would broadcast directly into the United Kingdom. Charles Michelson, a Romanian exile living in Paris, and Gordon McLendon, a flamboyant Texan, both travelled to Ireland to sell their proposals to a Television Commission set up to explore bringing TV to Ireland. The Commission heard testimony from a wide range of experts, including Leon Ó Broin who urged members to reject the commercial proposals from foreign corporations. He pointed out that their desire to broadcast directly into Britain from Ireland violated international broadcasting conventions. He also argued convincingly that television could nurture and support Ireland's culture, pointing out that it should do more than simply entertain viewers with crude American and British programmes. Ó Broin was a pragmatist, understanding that as a poor nation with a small population Ireland could not hope to build a public broadcasting service like that of the BBC. He therefore argued for the establishment of a hybrid television service that would be overseen by a public authority and financed by both license fees and advertising. The Taoiseach Seán Lemass accepted this notion of a commercial public service, and Telefís Éireann began broadcasting on New Year's Eve 1961.

The first Director-General of Telefís Éireann was an Irish-American technocrat with extensive experience in commercial television. Edward Roth had worked for American networks before setting out as a hired hand to build television stations in Peru and Mexico. He arrived in Ireland to be told, in explicit terms, that Irish television should pay for itself and that it could not under any circumstances run a deficit or become a drain on the national exchequer. Roth succeeded in getting the service 'on air' and, in its early years, Telefís Éireann relied on a steady diet of inexpensive American 'canned' programmes, including many comedies and westerns. Telefís Éireann slowly built up its own material that included popular dramas and informative news and current affairs programmes.

The new television service caused much consternation for Fianna Fáil governments in its first decade of broadcasting. News and current affairs programming in particular, aroused controversy on a number of occasions by questioning the tactics, decisions and policies of government ministers wholly unaccustomed to being challenged by brash young men and women who were determined to use the medium to hold politicians accountable. Seán Lemass, often regarded as Ireland's great moderniser, learned to his chagrin that the television service he had helped establish could create major political headaches. He famously defined television as 'an instrument of public policy', suggesting that it was an arm of the government – which it most certainly was not. His menacing statement represented the frustration of a politician realising that the modernisation he encouraged – to boost the economy and stem emigration – inevitably would mean a new type of broadcast media that would not defer to the political establishment.

On the cultural front, critics lambasted the station's transmission of foreign – especially older American – programmes, and demanded that resources be concentrated on producing quality Irish material.[31] The Irish language struggled unsuccessfully to find a voice on television. Broadcasting officials had little time for the language lobby whose demands were viewed as unrealistic. Edward Roth and his successors argued that Irish language programmes were unpopular with the majority of viewers, who would simply switch stations and watch British television when these programmes came on. Critics within the language lobby countered by blaming the poor quality of the Irish language programmes for the failure to draw an audience. Other critics demanded the new television service support a wide range of cultural initiatives and enlist the services of Irish writers, artists and musicians in its programmes. Telefís Éireann responded by arguing that the station was operating on a limited budget and that developing quality material was time-consuming and expensive. As the 1960s progressed and Telefís Éireann began to gain confidence, popular, innovative, indigenous programming gradually made its way into Irish television. Irish language material slowly found a degree of traction but only gained a sense of security and support when, in

31 Roddy Flynn has written about Telefís Éireann's reliance on 'canned' programmes in its early formative years. See his essay 'It is against the Basic Concepts of Good Government to Subject our People to Rosemary Clooney at the Public Expense: Imported Programming on Early Irish Television', *Éire-Ireland*, 50 (Spring/Summer 2015).

1996, an Irish language television station began broadcasting from the west of Ireland. In this respect television followed the path laid out by radio twenty-five years earlier when the Irish language station, Raidió na Gaeltachta, had begun broadcasting from County Galway in 1972.

Religious authorities became increasingly un-nerved by a medium that broadcast programmes they regarded as vulgar and even obscene. The Archbishop of Dublin, John Charles McQuaid, tried and failed to insert a specially-trained priest, Joseph Dunn, onto the public authority that oversaw the new broadcasting service. Ironically, innovative religious programming was successfully developed by a number of Dublin Diocesan priests, including Dunn. This charismatic priest, who had been refused appointment to the broadcasting authority, established Ireland's first independent television production company, *Radharc*, in 1961. Dunn and his colleagues succeeded in creating interesting, often compelling, documentaries. *Radharc's* programmes could be cleverly subversive as they addressed issues of social justice and challenged the status quo both at home and abroad.

The deference that had characterised the relationship between Radio Éireann, the political establishment and the Catholic Church evaporated once the Broadcasting Authority Act became law in 1960. Passage of the act meant that older unofficial 'back channel' networks between politicians, the Catholic Church and broadcasting officials in the civil service were undone. Before 1960, McQuaid could work behind the scenes with senior civil servants and ministers to ensure that nothing broadcast would offend the church. But once legislation had set up the independent Radio Éireann Authority, the archbishop found he could no longer quietly pick up the phone to complain about a particular programme – and accept deference. Politicians also found that their complaints made directly to broadcasters would be publicised on the airwaves or in the press, causing them embarrassment and further public controversy.[32]

Throughout the 1960s a series of incidents provoked the wrath of the powerful elites in Irish society, including the Catholic Hierarchy. Many of these controversies have been chronicled over the years by a number of historians and cultural critics.[33] One of the most famous incidents, known as the 'bishop and the nightie' episode, unfolded live on television in 1966.

---

32 See Savage, *A Loss of Innocence?*, 52–90.
33 See, especially, J. Horgan, *Broadcasting and Public Life* (Dublin: Four Courts Press, 2004); L. Fuller, *Irish Catholicism Since 1950* (Dublin: Gill & Macmillan, 2002); and G. Byrne with D. Purcell, *The Time of My Life* (Dublin: Gill & Macmillan, 1989).

On Gay Byrne's celebrated *Late Late Show*, a quiz contestant revealed that she might not have been wearing a nightdress on her wedding night. The Bishop of Clonfert, Dr Thomas Ryan, denounced the episode as indecent and claimed that it showed the moral decay television was spreading throughout Ireland. Ryan's comments were covered extensively in the national press, and RTÉ felt compelled to issue an apology. However the bishop and the church were widely ridiculed for over-reacting to a mildly provocative entertainment programme. The episode illustrated a real disconnect between urban and rural Ireland – but also between a profoundly conservative church and a society that was slowly becoming more secular, or more 'modern' in its orientation.[34]

Gay Byrne deserves much credit for his uncanny ability to address taboo subjects on both television and on his popular daytime radio programme broadcast from 1973 to 1998. As an impressive mediator, he provided a popular and accessible forum for the discussion of a wide array of controversial topics.[35] His programmes deftly handled wide-ranging discussions about sensitive issues including clerical celibacy, domestic violence, infanticide, alcoholism and discrimination against Travellers.[36] They also helped promote debate about the role of women in Irish society and provided an important forum for the Irish Women's Liberation Movement in the early 1970s.[37]

However, RTÉ's contribution to the modernisation of Irish society was not simply Byrne's handiwork. A range of editors, producers, managers and writers developed a sophisticated broadcasting culture that enhanced Irish life. John Bowman, perhaps Ireland's best-known television journalist, was a pioneer in news and current affairs broadcasting. He became something of an institution in Irish broadcasting, especially when reporting on elections and the complex politics of the country. His astute observations, encyclopaedic knowledge of Irish politics, and incisive questioning of political operators of all stripes proved an asset to RTÉ, providing tremendous public service to the nation. He has commented incisively on the history of RTÉ and still (2016) continues to make an impact on broadcasting and public life.

---

34 The Irish broadcasting service was initially known as Telefís Éireann or TÉ, this designation was later changed to Raidió Telefís Éireann or RTÉ in 1966.
35 *The Corkman*, 12 December 1969.
36 L. Pettitt, *Screening Ireland, Film and Television Representation*, (Manchester: Manchester University Press, 2000), 169–70.
37 See A. O'Brien, 'Not in the Hot Seat: The Impact of Women on Broadcasting', in *Éire-Ireland*, 50 (Spring/Summer 2015).

Television in Northern Ireland

Television had a profound effect on politics and society in Northern Ireland. Until the outbreak of 'the Troubles' in 1969, the BBC in Northern Ireland existed in a veritable cocoon, with London tending to ignore Northern Ireland and leaving BBC NI to its own devices. The insulated regional station based at Broadcasting House in Belfast failed to develop a critical backbone and, as noted, remained alarmingly deferential to the Unionist establishment.

One particular episode speaks to the dysfunctional broadcasting culture that characterised Northern Ireland before 'the Troubles' shattered the province's isolation. This featured the irreverent television presenter Alan Whicker, who arrived from London in 1959 to report on life in the province. His initial report for the popular programme *Tonight*, broadcast on the national network, horrified the Unionist establishment. It appeared to characterise life in Northern Ireland's capital city as little more than legalised gambling and sectarian graffiti, overseen by armed policemen on the streets of Belfast. The programme provoked howls of protest from indignant Unionists, who denounced Whicker and his crew for recklessly slandering the good people of the province. Waldo Maguire, the controller for BBC NI, felt compelled to issue what Whicker characterised as a 'craven apology' to the people of Northern Ireland. Whicker had planned to film ten short features from Northern Ireland, but protests from outraged Unionist politicians, and the failure of broadcasting officials in London to support him, forced the project's cancellation. Following that controversy, BBC's London crews generally avoided the province and viewed Northern Ireland as a bizarre and isolated backwater of the United Kingdom. This shunning of Northern Ireland lasted until the outbreak of sustained political unrest ushered in 'the Troubles'.[38]

Television in Northern Ireland became a destabilising force only when national and international news crews descended on the province to address the campaign for civil rights, the backlash and brutality it provoked from the police and the subsequent slide into near chaos in the summer of 1969. Those who took to the streets to demand the vote in local elections, to call for an end to gerrymandering, and to protest against discrimination in housing and employment fully understood television's power to garner publicity for their cause. Many had recently viewed BBC news and current affairs programming from London that reported on the civil rights marchers in the

38 R. J. Savage, *The BBC's Irish Troubles, Television, Conflict and Northern Ireland* (Manchester: Manchester University Press, 2015), 18–22.

American south. They understood the strategy of Martin Luther King Jr and watched televised reports of peaceful Black American civil rights protesters being attacked by angry police using truncheons, water cannons and attack dogs. From 1968, the tactics of King and his followers began to be successfully employed within the United Kingdom. Viewing the parliament at Stormont as irreformable, the Northern Ireland Civil Rights Association used television to force London to intervene and address the long-held grievances of the Catholic community.

One particular march in Londonderry gained the civil rights campaign international attention and sympathy, while profoundly damaging the image of the Stormont government. On 5 October 1968, civil rights leaders defied a ban on marching issued by William Craig, the province's uncompromising Minister of Home Affairs. In the ensuing march, the Royal Ulster Constabulary attacked demonstrators, beating helpless protesters with batons and dousing them with water cannon. Gerry Fitt, MP for West Belfast, and three Labour MPs who had travelled from London to Derry in a show of solidarity with the marchers, experienced police violence first hand. Fitt, with blood streaming down his face, was transported by ambulance to a nearby hospital for medical attention.

The event might have gone largely unnoticed but for the perseverance of RTÉ cameraman Gay O'Brien and sound technician Eamon Hays, who filmed the attack. Their sensational footage captured the violence as it unfolded and made its way onto the BBC programme, *Twenty-Four Hours*. The incident, viewed widely on British television, caused uproar in the Westminster Parliament – an uproar exacerbated by the Unionist government's ill-timed firm statement of support for the police action.[39] That statement, juxtaposed with images of frenzied truncheon-wielding policemen clubbing peaceful civil rights marchers, badly damaged the credibility of the O'Neill government. These images were featured on international news networks, embarrassing a British government that was becoming increasingly uneasy with developments in the province and with the slow pace of reform at Stormont.

After being summoned to Downing Street and directed to address the grievances of the civil rights campaigners, Prime Minister Terence O'Neill announced a set of long overdue reforms on 22 November 1968. This initiative was designed to mollify both the British prime minister and moderates

---

39 Memorandum by the Prime Minister, 14 October 1968, Cab/4/1406, PRONI.

in the civil rights organisation. The proposed reforms, however, provoked anger and opposition from hardliners within his Ulster Unionist party and from more zealous loyalists outside the party, especially the Rev. Ian Paisley and his followers. In these circumstances O'Neill grasped the necessity of going directly to the people and used television to make his pitch. In his famous 'Ulster at the crossroads' speech, he told civil rights leaders 'your voice has been heard, and clearly heard. Your duty now is to take the heat out of the situation'.[40] The appeal was widely hailed as successful and helped usher in a short period of calm. This was the first, and one might argue, the only occasion in which the Unionist government at Stormont had taken advantage of television's power.

People's Democracy, the left-wing group that had its origins in Queen's University Belfast, dismissed the 1968 reforms as both too little and too late. Deciding to embark on a contentious march from Belfast to Derry on New Year's Day 1969, the group knew that its tactics would provoke a backlash from militant loyalists. At Burntollet Bridge, a few miles from Derry, several hundred loyalists – including off-duty members of the detested 'B-Specials', an auxiliary, exclusively Protestant police force – ambushed the march. Television cameras recorded the ensuing mayhem and the subsequent enthusiastic welcome marchers received in Derry. Images of these protests were picked up by international news agencies and transmitted around the world, competing with televised reports of the war in Vietnam and civil rights actions in American cities. A beleaguered Terence O'Neill resigned shortly afterward, again using television – but now to portray himself as a courageous victim of intolerance.

O'Neill was replaced by the ineffective James Chichester-Clark, a prime minister who fared badly on television. Despite his struggles to present himself as a confident leader, this Anglo-Irish aristocrat conveyed merely incompetence and bewilderment. His confused, harried image was unsettling, particularly under the unforgiving lens of television cameras that chronicled his calamitous tenure as prime minister while the province descended into disorder.

BBC reporting of the ensuing unrest caused tremendous unease in London. Labour and Conservative governments alike grew increasingly concerned with the violence – and with the damage these television reports had on Great Britain's image overseas. In August 1969, news crews filmed the rioting in Derry and Belfast, and then chronicled the arrival of the army onto

---

40 Savage, *The BBC's Irish Troubles*, 34–5. And see the chapter by Paul Bew and John Bew in this volume.

the smouldering streets of Belfast. As the Provisional IRA began its campaign of bombings and shootings and the security forces responded aggressively, BBC reporting unnerved governments in Belfast and London by questioning the policies, tactics and decisions of those in authority. Civil, political and military leaders reacted with fury to critical reporting that maintained that heavy-handed British policies were alienating the Catholic community and encouraging that minority to support the IRA.

One episode in the long and tortured history of 'the Troubles' underscored the power of television: the remarkable coverage of Bloody Sunday, the killing of thirteen protesters in Derry by the British Army in January 1972. The event itself enraged and radicalised an already alienated Catholic community while boosting enormously the ranks of the IRA. But the graphic images provided by television cameras succeeded in undermining a narrative London had been keen to present at home and, especially, abroad since the outbreak of 'the Troubles'.

In conjunction with the searing images recorded by BBC NI cameraman Cyril Cave and sound technician Jim Deeney, John Bierman's vivid reports of excited British soldiers amidst the dead and dying on the streets of Derry proved devastating to British policy in Northern Ireland. The images heavily damaged the international reputation of the United Kingdom. Since the outbreak of violence the British government had maintained that its army was a fair-minded peacekeeper, struggling to keep warring factions apart while determined to root out terrorists hell-bent on wrecking the province. After Bloody Sunday such a narrative was unsustainable. Watching BBC film rebroadcast on American networks, Donald Tebbit, a senior diplomat in the British Embassy in Washington DC, registered his horror to his London Foreign Office superiors. He wrote grimly that he feared the propaganda war was lost, that images of the carnage conveyed by television cameras in Derry had undone years of careful work. Tebbit warned, 'There is, we think, a real danger that unless we step up our propaganda effort, the myth that Northern Ireland is another British Colonial war will get firmly implanted in the American mind.'[41]

Relations between broadcasters and successive British governments continued to be marred by controversy. The 1976 confrontation between Roy Mason and senior BBC officials in Belfast underscored the fraught relationship that lasted throughout the 1970s and 1980s. Shortly after arriving in Belfast in the

41 Ibid., 95.

autumn of 1976 the newly-appointed Secretary of State for Northern Ireland forcefully attacked the BBC, arguing that television coverage of the unrest inflamed the violence. Mason denounced the BBC Board of Governors and senior editorial and managerial staff from London and Belfast at a dinner that had been arranged to welcome him to Belfast at the elegant Culloden Hotel, situated near Belfast. During what one observer defined as the 'second battle of Culloden', Mason condemned the work of the BBC as irresponsible and called for the imposition of censorship. The new Secretary of State declared to the assembled governors and officials that broadcasters were undermining the work of the security services, and described the BBC's coverage of the conflict as 'appalling'. He threatened to cut funding and punish the institution by making unspecified changes to its charter.

British governments looked to Dublin and were sympathetic to the censorship that had been put in place by Taoiseach Jack Lynch. His government had fired the entire RTÉ Authority in 1972 after it paraphrased an interview with a senior member of the IRA. Section 31 of the Broadcasting Act was then deployed to keep any organisation defined as subversive off the air. Despite protests, censorship remained in place in the Irish Republic until the peace process gained momentum in 1994.

When Margaret Thatcher came to power in the United Kingdom in 1979, she shared Mason's antipathy towards the BBC and resented its coverage of Northern Ireland. After a number of broadcasts that she considered undermined British security efforts in the province, she determined that the BBC was out of control and had to be reined in. The Prime Minister introduced formal censorship in 1988 by introducing the infamous 'broadcasting ban'. But her efforts to deny the IRA the 'oxygen of publicity' were ultimately unsuccessful, only highlighting the tenacity of her enemies and the contempt she felt for the freedom of the press. BBC television and independent television companies such as Thames TV chronicled thirty years of murder, mayhem, controversy and political paralysis. In the 1990s television also addressed the compromises and the uneasy peace that led to the 1998 Belfast Agreement. Throughout the conflict, governments in Belfast, Dublin and London tried with varying degrees of success to control, shape and censor broadcasts, provoking serious questions about censorship in democratic societies. Since 1998 and the apparent end of 'the Troubles', television in Northern Ireland has settled back into its more traditional role of entertainment – and of informing viewers about news from around the world, while reporting on more mundane events at home.

Conclusion

A century has elapsed since Fergal O'Kelly and his colleagues first tried to broadcast the proclamation of an Irish Republic to the world. O'Kelly and his fellow volunteers could hardly have imagined the impact of broadcasting on Irish life throughout the twentieth century. Radio and television broadcasting helped transform the island, north and south, especially during the second half of the century. Broadcasting had expanded exponentially by the twenty-first century as new networks and channels offered greater competition to both RTÉ and the BBC. In the Irish Republic traditional television and radio networks have come under tremendous pressure from market forces and governments keen on introducing greater competition. The advent of satellite radio and television has increased the options available to audiences throughout the island. The Internet, mobile 'smart' phones and advanced digital technology have made for a crowded broadcasting landscape in which technology competes for attention by providing access to an overwhelming amount of information. Writing from this congested, hectic environment, we can now begin to sense how access to information, entertainment and the news of the world altered Irish life, especially from the 1960s into the new millennium. Initially, broadcasting sought to define the 'nations' that emerged on each side of the border, providing each with an identity. However, that identity has evolved to challenge the narrow, defensive, insular states that struggled to assert themselves a century ago. We can only imagine where an increasingly globalised broadcast media is going in this new millennium and how it might further affect society on both sides of the border.

19

Popular Culture in Ireland, 1880–2016

PAUL ROUSE

Introduction

The forces that shaped Irish popular culture between 1880 and 2016 were many and complex.[1] Divides over politics and identity were influential, and so was the protean conflict, both real and imagined, between 'tradition' and 'modernity'. Other important factors included religion, the spread of associational culture, the rise of youth culture, the media, technological change, the growth of disposable income and globalisation. By examining the forces that shaped the evolution of popular culture in Ireland after 1880, this chapter seeks to offer an insight into the nature of that culture.

1880–1920

From large-scale public entertainments to private, domestic ones, popular culture in Ireland in the 1880s was shaped by the multiple influences that had forged its evolution. Most obvious, most ostentatious and most politicised, was the influence of a British imperial culture that, by the 1880s, was everywhere to be seen in Ireland. The influence of the Empire on music, theatre, books and newspapers was widespread and appeared to contemporary observers to be growing stronger. This flourishing imperial culture suggested an

---

1 There is an unending debate about what precisely is meant by 'popular culture'. Indeed, even the meaning of both words unto themselves is the subject of an extended discourse. For this chapter – given its scale – I have chosen to be as flexible as possible. Seeking to impose rigid definitions between, for example, elite and popular culture creates a binary opposition that is unconvincing, not because such opposition does not exist, but because it breaks down too often. For this reason alone, I use both terms – and all others – within a wider historical framework where popular culture (including music, drink, dance, fashion, cinema, television, sport, media and more) in Ireland is shaped by multiple influences, local, national and international.

Ireland that 'seemed little more than a province in the empire of Victorian taste'.[2] In sport, for example, the later decades of the nineteenth century saw the rise in Ireland of sports codified in England, including cricket, rugby football, soccer, tennis and much else. That Ireland was a venue for international touring teams from across the Empire in all of these sports underlined an imperial culture that extended around the globe. At many such sporting and other public occasions, the bands of the British army held a wide popular appeal. The arrival of the lord lieutenant of Ireland at sports events – and indeed at all manner of public occasions – brought the crowd to their feet and the playing of 'God Save the Queen'. Such displays of loyalty, against the backdrop of the Union Jack billowing on Irish winds, were unexceptional – this was true for cities from Cork to Belfast, but also in Irish country towns such as Enniscorthy in County Wexford where ostentatious identification with Empire was real.[3] In short, the 'Britishness' of large swathes of Irish popular culture was undeniable.

Many Irish nationalists were entirely comfortable with this culture of Empire; indeed, they immersed themselves in it as and how they wished, regardless of any supposed association with Britishness; they did not consider their Irishness necessarily compromised by their cultural choices. Others, though, saw things entirely differently and increasingly sought to push people to choose 'Irish' culture, not merely as well as 'British' culture, but instead of it. The case for such substitution was brilliantly set out by Douglas Hyde, the son of a Church of Ireland clergyman, in his seminal 1892 lecture, 'The Necessity for De-Anglicising Ireland'. Hyde spoke of the need to 'teach ourselves not to be ashamed of ourselves', and claimed that Ireland 'can never produce its best before the world as long as it remains tied to the apron-strings of another race and another island'. He continued:

> We must create a strong feeling against West-Britonism, for it – if we give it the least chance, or show it the smallest quarter – will overwhelm us like a flood, and we shall find ourselves toiling painfully behind the English at each step following the same fashions, only six months behind the English ones; reading the same books, only months behind them; taking up the same fads, after they have become stale there, following them in our dress, literature, music, games, and ideas, only a long time after them and a vast way behind. We will become, what, I fear, we are largely at present, a nation of imitators,

2 F. S. L. Lyons, *Culture and Anarchy, 1890–1939* (Oxford University Press, 1979) 8.
3 C. Tóibín (ed.), *An Homage to Enniscorthy,* (Wexford: Wexford Library Service, 2010), esp. 347.

the Japanese of Western Europe, lost to the power of native initiative and alive only to second-hand assimilation.[4]

Hyde was central to the founding of the Gaelic League, established in 1893 to promote the revival of Irish as a spoken language and reaching possibly 40,000 members in 671 nationwide branches by 1908.[5] As well as organising language classes, the League ran local and national festivals drawing large crowds to hear music, song and recitations, and to view dances, all presented as authentically Gaelic and now essential to Irish nationhood. The Gaelic League aimed to shift the cultural choices of those men and women who, as Hyde described them, spent their time 'protesting as a matter of sentiment that they hate the country which at every hand's turn they rush to imitate'.[6]

Afloat on ideas of cultural nationalism, some saw in the promotion of an 'Irish' popular culture the possibility of furthering the project of national liberation. In practical terms, this had partly driven the establishment in 1884 of a uniquely Irish sporting institution: the Gaelic Athletic Association (GAA). This institution promoted games described as 'Irish native games' and bathed them in ideas of Irishness, What ensued was a struggle for sporting supremacy between rival sporting organisations in the social, cultural and political context of late nineteenth-century Ireland. The GAA sought from the beginning to make Irish people choose between 'Irish laws' and 'English laws', and between 'native' and 'foreigner'. This was a potent rhetorical flourish in the divided politics of Ireland, notwithstanding its eschewing of history for propaganda. Beyond the GAA, the divisions within Ireland continually manifested themselves across popular culture. They could be seen in street ballads and parades, in romantic melodramas played at theatres and in the patriotic stories published in the press and in books.[7] A narrow political reading of culture in 1880s Ireland, understanding it as conflict between Britishness and Irishness, is misleading. The presentation of the clash between, say, rugby football and Gaelic football as simply rooted in opposing political or cultural beliefs – the 'Gael' versus the 'Shoneen' – was not grounded in reality. Rather, it can be understood 'as a conflict between two modes of thought: those who saw as imperative the expression of nationality through sport and those

---

4 D. Kiberd and P. J. Matthews (eds.), *Handbook of the Irish Revival: An Anthology of Irish Cultural and Political Writings 1891–1922* (Dublin: Abbey Theatre Press, 2015), 42–6.

5 D. Dickson, *Dublin: The Making of a Capital City* (London: Profile Books, 2015), 406.

6 D. Kiberd and P.J. Matthews (eds.), *Handbook of the Irish Revival*, 42–6. See also the chapter by Brian Ó Conchubhair in this volume.

7 See, for example, Marie-Louise Legg, *Newspapers and Nationalism: The Irish Provincial Press, 1850–1892* (Dublin: Four Courts Press, 1999).

who were swayed by personal conviction and social context'.[8] In this respect, the complexities, nuances, even the contradictions, of how people thought and behaved in Ireland are everywhere apparent and across popular culture. Indeed, popular culture demonstrated the extent to which the great majority of Irish people drew from its offerings as they saw fit, apparently regardless of the politics of identity. There were, to this end, no contradictions perceived by people who skated on rinks in Dublin to the tunes of British army bands and then fought in rebellion against that same army, as did the Easter week revolutionary, Joseph Mary Plunkett.[9] Or, if such contradictions were perceived, they were overcome by men and women who were notably fluid and eclectic in their cultural choices.

Disentangling the motives behind, and the meaning of, the decisions that people made in their cultural choices is fraught with difficulty. Popular culture in Ireland before the Great War was dynamic, defined not by boundaries but by change. This can be seen, for example, in the manner in which the social and cultural life of Ireland was transformed by the spread of associational culture. There had been a great diversity of clubs in existence from the eighteenth century, but the transformation of the late nineteenth century was the manner in which such clubs became less and less the preserve of an elite. In Ireland, the extraordinary growth of clubs in the last quarter of the nineteenth century was a marker of an unfolding societal shift in the balance of power. For Ireland's rising, expanding middle class and for people who were dragging themselves out of extreme poverty, assuming positions of authority in clubs was a signal moment. The social revolution in Ireland that flowed from the Land War of 1879 – rapidly shifting ownership of the land from gentry to peasant farmers – was given eloquent expression in the men and women who came to dominate Irish clubs. In essence, this is a story rooted in democratisation. The capacity of the elite to create in culture a platform for the display of wealth and exclusivity remained unchanged, but sheer weight of numbers swamped all but the most select activities. The ambitions of the wealthy to resist this process, or to control it, were unsuccessful and stand as a reminder of the limitations of elite power. From cycling to farming, Ireland's club world was extensive and so were the events those clubs organised.[10] This

---

8 L. O'Callaghan, *Rugby in Munster: A Social History* (Cork: Cork University Press, 2011), 164.

9 *Irish Times*, 15 April 2015.

10 J. Kelly and R. V. Comerford (eds.), *Associational Culture in Ireland and Abroad* (Dublin: Irish Academic Press, 2015) and B. Griffin, *Cycling in Victorian Ireland* (Dublin: Nonsuch Press, 2006).

process was well-captured in the words of a contemporary commentator who wrote of a sporting event in rural Ireland in the 1880s: 'Over the hedges and across the fields, from all directions the people poured.'[11]

By the 1880s, music societies – including many choral groups – flourished in Ireland; some 22 such societies had been established between 1841 and 1867, and many more followed every decade. Initially, such clubs had been dominated by 'upper-class Protestants', but increasing prosperity saw 'the rising merchant and middle-classes … take the lead in cultivating the arts'.[12] Part of this lead involved providing classical music to people of limited disposable income. To this end, the Ulster Hall in Belfast was opened in 1862 and could hold up to 3,000 people – it was intended that among these would be people previously 'virtually excluded from every entertainment which would improve or elevate their moral and intellectual character'.[13] A further popular dimension was the establishment of civilian bands, who could be found in every Irish country town – and in many rural areas – by the 1880s. As well as adapting the music of regimental bands, civilian bands mixed patriotic airs such as 'God Save Ireland' and 'The Wearing of the Green', with popular tunes like 'When the room's going round about it's time to gang way'.[14]

Bands and the music they played were associated with causes from temperance to politics, with the rebel songs of nationalists matched by loyalist ballads. Street ballads were printed and sold on the street in support of all manner of patriotic causes – and none. Songs and tunes continued to be handed down through the generations with songs from outside Ireland absorbed into folk tradition. The way music was shared, however, was transformed by technology. The first recording of Irish traditional music was undertaken at the Feis Ceoil of 1897 and initiated a process that expanded to allow for commercial recording. This process brought Irish music to a new audience – particularly in America. The popularity of Thomas Moore's *Irish Melodies* – notably songs such as 'The Last Rose of Summer' and 'Oft in the Stilly Night' – was manifest and new stars such as John McCormack found fame not just as live performers, but also as recording artists. The capacity to buy music and to listen to it at home also saw the music of other countries sold in Ireland from the first decades of the twentieth century.[15]

---

11 *Celtic Times*, 2 April 1887.
12 A. Fleischmann, 'Music and Society, 1850–1921', in W.E. Vaughan (ed.), *A New History of Ireland VI: Ireland Under the Union, 1870–1921* (Oxford University Press, 1995), 500–22.
13 A. Fleischmann, 'Music and Society, 1850–1921', 500–22, 503.
14 P. Rouse, *Sport and Ireland: A History* (Oxford University Press, 2015), 182.
15 C. Morash, *A History of the Media in Ireland* (Cambridge University Press, 2010), 99–103.

Irish popular culture was shaped by other technological changes, notably in transport. The expansion of the rail network and then the rise of the motor car facilitated the development of an island-wide culture. On a local level the bicycle became central to widening the circle of engagement. Among the many changes facilitated was the growth of holidaying and day-tripping, increasingly available to the growing numbers of Irish people with disposable income. Easier travel facilitated the growth of Irish seaside towns from Portrush, County Antrim, to Kilrush, County Clare, with the accompanying spread of 'seaside entertainment' such as Punch and Judy, and minstrel shows, donkey rides and other activities, now caught for posterity on newly-invented picture postcards.

The revolution in the media was at least as important as that in transport. In Ireland in the second half of the nineteenth century, the abolition of stamp duty and enhanced printing technology facilitated the production of cheaper newspapers. Improved rates of literacy – by 1881, 75 per cent of the Irish population was literate and this percentage continued to climb in the succeeding decade – offered new sections of the population as potential readers and the consequence was an explosion in the number of newspapers published in Ireland. Some of these newspapers promoted the creation of a national identity, where popular culture was wrapped in a discourse on political independence, land ownership, the promotion of domestic industry, the revival of the Irish language and the reclamation of a distinctive Irish historical narrative. Other newspapers were imported from Britain and distributed by rail across Ireland. They were part of a torrent of 'cheap periodicals and serialized fiction being imported from London'.[16]

Newspapers of every kind brought stories from around the world and facilitated cultural change in Ireland. A fine example of this was the tales from across the world of dangerous stunts and thrilling feats of speed undertaken by men and women in newly-invented cars, motorcycles and airplanes. As well as long articles written by dazzled journalists, new technology allowed for these feats to be shown in photographs. There were, in 1913, photographs in the Irish press of Adolphe Pégoud, a French airman who gave exhibitions of upside-down flying at an airshow in Surrey, carried in the Irish papers. Having been strapped into his Bleriot monoplane, he made a perpendicular dive from 3,000 feet and gradually turned the plane until the chassis came on top, before later righting it.[17] Such feats were much admired by the Irish public. Seaplane

---

16 D. Dickson, *Dublin: The Making of a Capital City*, 390.
17 *Irish Independent*, 19 August 1913.

races took place up and down the Irish Sea. One such race, for a prize of £5,000 offered by the *Daily Mail*, ended with a crash at Loughshinny, near Skerries in north Dublin. The following day, the pilot returned to the site of the crash where he was mobbed by spectators, including a reported fifty female autograph-hunters.[18]

In this, and in so much else, the Irish were part of cultural exchange that extended far beyond the United Kingdom. Waves of new crazes broke across Irish towns, some lingered, others disappeared. In 1920, Aodh de Blacam, Sinn Féin's arch propagandist, described the Free State that would be made in Ireland and imagined that it would be 'a medieval fragment in the modern world'.[19] Influential Irish Unionists would also look to the past for visions of the future and, just as de Blácam did, imagine that their world would be defined by their religion. The difficulty was that the modern world did not permit of such isolation, and all-out resistance to global and modernising influences would prove futile. The popular culture of urban Ireland reveals the manner in which globalising trends had been re-making social life throughout the nineteenth century and into the early twentieth century. Towns across Ireland had been reshaped by the building of skittle alleys and shooting galleries, Turkish baths and swimming pools, and so much else that formed part of international trends.[20] The words, images and ideas that were circulating in books, newspapers and other prints sold on stalls or available in libraries, reading rooms, and club and society houses, were drawn from across the world. Public houses, coffee shops and tearooms revealed a diversity of life that could not be corralled within the narrow ambitions of those who saw the past, present and future in stripes of green and orange. And all the while, as new modes of behaviour developed, they were either absorbed into older traditions or displaced them, before being displaced or re-ordered themselves, in turn. Indeed, throughout these decades – and through later ones – the new, the old, the invented and re-invented blended together, or were pushed together to serve the interests of commerce, tourism or simple pleasure.

---

18 *Irish Independent*, 18 July 1913.
19 M. Walsh, *Bitter Freedom: Ireland in a Revolutionary World, 1918–1923* (London: Faber and Faber, 2015), 17.
20 The Irish Historic Towns Atlas series brilliantly chronicles the changed entertainments of urban Ireland through the centuries. For a short overview, see A. Byrne, 'Entertainments, Memorials and Societies', in H. B. Clarke and S. Gearty (eds.), *Maps and Texts: Exploring the Irish Historic Towns Atlas* (Dublin: Royal Irish Academy, 2013), 236–56.

Against continuity and change, the extent to which the state could control – even shape – popular culture remained a moot point. Repeated legislative forays often revealed the challenges of any attempt at control. Legislation was conditioned by, among other things, the need for public order and by perceptions of the public good – in essence, the desirability of social control. The power of organised religion was obviously important in this regard. Key pieces of legislation were introduced or redrawn on foot of campaigns driven by a succession of religious organisations: a good example of this is the campaign to keep Sundays free from various forms of popular culture. Addressing midday mass in Ballybricken Church in early November 1915, Canon Furlong, the parish priest, condemned reports that one of the cinemas in Waterford was to open on Sunday evening. He denounced this as a move 'to secularize the Sunday', one that was part of a wider trend that saw Sunday being undermined by 'public sports and amusements', against the wishes of both Catholics and Protestants. Canon Furlong called on the congregation to display their displeasure:

> You are not going to allow the character of the city to be tainted; you are not going to allow the reputation of your city to be destroyed, but, on the contrary, you will use your entire efforts and your influence to preserve the good character of the City of Waterford, and to maintain God's rights in His claim upon the observance of Sunday.[21]

The difficulty was, of course, that frequenting public houses, going to cinemas and music halls, and attending sports grounds and other entertainments was precisely how increasing numbers of Irish people – north and south – wished to spend their Sundays at that time and in the decades that followed.

The struggle for Sunday was as nothing compared to struggles over sex or 'filth'. The Irish mainstreet was a site for the distribution of pornography. In the middle of the Great War, for example, a man was prosecuted for distributing indecent photographs after he handed an envelope containing three photographs to another man on Patrick Street in Cork. His action came to the attention of the Ancient Order of Hibernians, the police were then called, the offender was charged under Section 3 of the Indecent Advertisements Act, 1889 and was sentenced by magistrates to one month's imprisonment.[22] During the war – and, indeed, before and after – accounts written by members

---

21 *Cork Examiner*, 10 November 1915.
22 *Irish Times*, 2 November 1915.

of the Irish Women Patrols offered vivid portraits of the streets of Dublin in the night-time:

> The whole locality of Sackville Street between 9.30 and 11.30 pm appears to be one great low saloon where young girls, soldiers, sailors, and civilians loiter about. It goes to one's heart to see how very young most of the girls are; also to see how drunk many of them are. The awful boldness of these men and girls appalls one. They accost one another without apparently any shame, and more times than I can count I have turned my flashlight onto dark doorways and corners in laneways and disclosed scenes that are indescribable.[23]

This report was endorsed by the suffragettes Anna Haslam and Mary Hayden who noted the 'destruction' of large numbers of 'innocent, but perhaps giddy, girls' on the streets and lanes of Dublin.[24] The 'destruction' was not limited to Dublin and took many forms. A lingering dispute near Tuam, County Galway began with a young woman being tarred for her 'friendship' with an English soldier and her attackers were, in turn, assaulted by her father. A ballad was immediately written detailing the events and was sung locally.[25]

Here – and across Irish popular culture generally – alcohol was the lubricant to so much of what happened. Public houses were to be found in numbers on every significant street in urban Ireland. As well, they were the focal point of village life and were scattered across the countryside in numbers that were completely at odds with the country's declining population.[26] Alcohol consumption crossed divides of class and identity and geography. Its most spectacular impact could be seen in the country's jails and asylums, where a significant percentage of the inmates had been convicted of alcohol-related crimes. It was also essential to the success of the country's great music halls – from the Alhambra in Belfast in the 1870s through the music halls of Dublin and Cork, such as the Star of Erin. Such halls, where food and alcohol were sold to those who came to see comedians, acrobats, and singing and dancing acts that came to Ireland on a circuit that extended throughout the United Kingdom, were routinely condemned by those who saw them as vulgar dens of licentiousness, However, they were immensely popular in the years before and after the Great War.[27] During those years, moving pictures were part of

---

23 *Irish Times*, 18–19 October 1915.
24 *Irish Times*, 18–19 October 1915.
25 *Freeman's Journal*, 19 January 1915.
26 Of further significance was the enduring tradition of illicit distilling.
27 H. White and B. Boydell (eds.), *The Encyclopedia of Music in Ireland* (Dublin: UCD Press, 2013), 853–4.

the running order of music halls, but such was their success that stand-alone cinemas quickly emerged and later thrived in the inter-war years.[28] The music hall – once arguably the most successful form of popular entertainment in urban Ireland – declined after the Great War and then disappeared. Its fate offers a timely reminder of the changing patterns of popular culture.

1920–1945

What happens to popular culture when an island is sundered into two states? The creation of Northern Ireland and what ultimately became the Republic of Ireland offers a comparative framework to examine the relationship between popular culture and national identity. Irish popular culture was inevitably coloured by the legacy of a political settlement that emerged from a civil war in the new Irish Free State, which ensured that a sizeable minority of the population in Northern Ireland would never be reconciled to their new status, and guaranteed that Britain retained part of its oldest colony, but with no obvious benefit accruing from that retention. Sometimes the legacy of conflict was manifest only in the assertions of politicians stoking the fires of their own tribes; sometimes it was evidenced in the enduring cultural traditions of marching, music and balladeering; and sometimes it exploded into violence and mayhem as war again was fought over Ireland.

What the political settlement offered was a new context in which old traditions could now assert themselves. There was nothing new in the pageantry of political parades, for example, with the marching season seeing loyalist organisations demonstrate publicly in a tradition that dates back to 1778 at least. The high point of the season was the 12 July commemoration of the Battle of the Boyne (1690), initiated by the Orange Order, with 'mini-twelfths' held in the weeks beforehand. There had been periodic attempts to ban certain parades in the nineteenth century, but the formation of Northern Ireland gave official sanction to the tradition. Around all of this, religion wrapped itself like bindweed – north and south. There could be no denying the manner in which the popular culture of both Irelands was intimately bound up with religion. In Northern Ireland the manner in which city, town and countryside were devoid of formally organised cultural events on Sundays was most striking; in the Irish Free State, the imagery of the Catholic Church was everywhere to be seen – allied with the practical involvement of priests in just about every public pursuit.

28 Denis Condon, *Early Irish Cinema, 1895–1921* (Dublin: Irish Academic Press, 2008).

The manner in which both states sought to shape popular culture within their respective boundaries was often similar. There was agreement that radio should be licensed, for example. Radio broadcasts in Northern Ireland began with BBC transmissions in 1924, initially within a 50-mile radius of Belfast, and expanded after 1936. Across Britain the Reithian BBC promoted the idea of a national culture – 'making the nation as one man'. This presented obvious problems in Northern Ireland where the BBC walked a tightrope balancing the promotion of official culture against the reality of diversity of the state. The upshot was occasional programmes of Irish traditional music alongside a firm decision not to broadcast the results of GAA matches, apparently after the intervention by Prime Minister Lord Craigavon. Ultimately, the governing principle of those who ran BBC Northern Ireland was to avoid offending Unionist sensibilities.[29]

The national radio service licensed by the Irish Free State under the auspices of its Department of Posts and Telegraphs – and known from its launch in 1926 as 2RN, from 1933 as Radio Athlone, and from 1937 to 1966 as Raidió Éireann – was a clear copy of the BBC. At the heart of its ambition lay the promotion of the Irish language, Irish literature, traditional Irish music and Gaelic games. In time, radio moved far beyond this narrow remit but, from the very beginning, it was far more than a mere extension by another means of Irish traditional culture. The very fact of its existence as a new medium sitting in the corner of a room brought change to Irish popular culture. Writers such as Tom Murphy, Brian Friel and Frank McCourt saw Irish radio as 'a modernizing force with liberating effects', stimulating imaginations and enabling 'vicarious experience of foreign cultures'.[30]

The flashpoint of Catholic moral outrage in the Irish Free State was the country's dance halls, which were condemned as dens of vice where all manner of licentiousness thrived. The beginnings of mass motoring only increased these concerns. Reclining front seats and spacious back ones were understood to present too ready an opportunity to those who lived at home with their parents. In 1931, the Catholic Primate of All-Ireland Cardinal McRory condemned 'the parking of cars close to dancehalls in badly lighted village streets or on dark country roads. Cars so placed are used … by young people for sitting out in the intervals between dances'.[31] His fellow bishop Dr Thomas

---

29 G. McIntosh, *The Force of Culture: Unionist Identities in Twentieth Century Ireland* (Cork: Cork University Press, 1999), 72–82. And see the chapter by Robert Savage in this volume.
30 E. Morgan, 'Question Time: Radio and the Liberalisation of Irish Public Discourse after World War II', in *History Ireland*, 9 (Winter, 2001), 38–41.
31 L. Blaney, *The Motor Car and Ireland* (UCD: Doctoral thesis, 2015), 158. I would like to thank Leanne for permission to use the material drawn from her thesis.

O'Doherty, Bishop of Galway condemned what was now referred to as 'Joy-riding' – the manner in which men and women headed off into the dark in a car: 'Evil men – demons in human form come from outside the parish and outside the city to indulge in this practice. They lure girls from the town to go for motor drives into the country, and you know what happens ... it is not for the benefit of the motor drive. It is for something infinitely worse.'[32] The certainty that the new Free State was a cesspit of immorality – confirmed in the Catholic mind by the growing love of jazz – brought pressure on the state to act. The conclusions of the Carrigan Committee (named after the chairman) in a 1931 never-published report were that 'the moral condition of the country has become gravely menaced by modern abuses, widespread and pernicious in their consequences, which cannot be counteracted unless the laws of the state are revised and consistently enforced so as to combat them'.[33] The outcome of this moral panic was the Public Dance Halls Act, 1935 which was designed to make it extremely difficult to hold a dance without the sanction of the police, the judiciary and the clergy. The reality was that it was one thing to make the law but quite another to ensure that people changed their habits.

The battle to save people from themselves extended to the written word in the south of Ireland – though, again, not in the north. The Censorship of Publications Act, 1929, in the Irish Free State saw the establishment of an Irish Censorship Board with the power to ban books it considered to be, inter alia, 'indecent'. This was expanded upon as meaning 'suggestive of, or inciting to, sexual immorality or unnatural vice or likely in any other similar way to corrupt or deprave'. The number of books banned over the years that followed underlined the extraordinary breadth of that definition as the Board went about its work with an uncommon relish.[34] Some of the books banned were straightforward pornography, but others were books by authors such as Ernest Hemingway, George Orwell, John Steinbeck and Graham Greene, which were considered classics in countries around the world and by the early 1950s, the number of banned books averaged some 600 per year. A certain liberalisation process began slowly in the second half of the 1950s when two successive Justice Ministers, James Everett and Oscar Traynor, appointed Censorship Boards that adopted a less narrow view of what constituted

---

32 L. Blaney, *The Motor Car and Ireland*, 158.
33 J. Smyth, 'Dancing, Depravity and All That Jazz: The Public Dance Halls Act of 1935', in *History Ireland*, 1, (Summer, 1993), 51–4, 52.
34 P. Martin, *Censorship in the Two Irelands, 1922–1939* (Dublin: Irish Academic Press, 2006), 193–8.

appropriate reading material for the citizens of a republic. Eventually, the Censorship of Publications Act 1967 limited the period of prohibition orders of books to twelve years and allowed for the immediate sale of over 5,000 previously banned books.[35]

On a more mundane level, Irish people sought in popular culture an every-day escape from the demands of work and of family – and found such escape in the associational culture of Ireland where the number of clubs increased decade after decade. This can be seen in the growth of literary, dramatic, cho-ral and debating societies, and can be observed most obviously in the growth of clubs engaged in sport. Clubs were established across numerous sports – including hockey, tennis, cycling, boxing, athletics and golf – in association with businesses (dozens of company teams affiliated to the Munster branch of the IRFU and many competed in the Shannon Development Cup), with political organisations (the quasi-fascist Blueshirts established boxing clubs and hurling teams in the 1930s), as well as the usual establishment of clubs based on locality and on networks of friendship. In Gaelic games, too, there was substantial and sustained growth. Between 1924 and 1945, the number of GAA clubs doubled from 1,000 to reach more than 2,000. By 1960 they had increased again to reach 2,850. The ambition of the founders of the GAA to establish a club in every Catholic parish on the island was largely met and the association was also buttressed by the playing of a myriad of street leagues and factory leagues all across the country.[36] That those who played the game were almost exclusively Catholic and nationalist revealed the manner in which politics continued to shape sport.

This was revealed also in the place of soccer in the Irish Free State. For some who had fought for Irish freedom, the notion that what they considered to be the game of the English soldiers should now prosper drew frenzied dis-gust. The imagined Ireland of their struggle for freedom was supposed to cast off anything that was not native, but precisely the opposite happened. Soccer had initially spread through Belfast in the 1880s, before spreading to Dublin in the 1890s and filtering out into country towns, partially assisted by the number of Britsh army teams that competed. Now, in the 1920s, a concerted effort was made by those who ran soccer to spread the game outside the cit-ies. The Leinster Football Association noted how their 'propaganda work' in provincial towns had provoked interest to the point where soccer was prov-ing 'immensely popular'. In particular, the visits of Dublin clubs to 'remote

35 D. Ferriter, *Transformation of Ireland* (London: Profile Books, 2005), 533–5 and 609.
36 P. Rouse, *Sport and Ireland*, 280.

15. Barry McGuigan arrives home in Clones, County Monaghan, to a tumultuous welcome after becoming World Featherweight champion, 1985.

provincial towns' had played a great role in 'the propagation of the game in the Saorstát'. The foundation of clubs was ultimately driven by the establishment of new local league and cup competitions, including the Connacht Cup and the Waterford and District Association Football League in the 1920s and 1930s.[37] The result was a bitter rhetorical dispute and the exchange of insults on an epic scale. There is, for instance, the newspaper columnist for the *Southern Star* newspaper, who lumped soccer, non-Irish music and dancing, and other non-Gaelic pursuits into a tirade which condemned those Irish people with 'their inferiority complex, those children of tyrants who disguise their nationality and are always kowtowing to the English garrison and aping English ways, propagating English games and dances....'[38] The denunciation proved unavailing as soccer continued to spread; for many people, political symbols were an irrelevance and were incidental to their engagement with popular culture.

What facilitated the growth of clubs and allowed, indeed, the wider spread of multiple aspects of popular culture was the growth in disposable

37 P. Rouse, *Sport and Ireland*, 280.
38 D. Toms, *Soccer in Munster: A Social History, 1877–1937* (Cork: Cork University Press, 2015), 110.

income. There remained many people in Ireland who were mired in desperate poverty, but for those who had a stable job there was the prospect of entertainment. There was, for example, the bank officials of Dublin who, in 1919, travelled out to Tallaght for a picnic, complete with egg-and-spoon races, weight-throwing competitions, relay races and sprints. After a tea on the grass, the eighty-strong picnic party retired to a local ballroom for music and song.[39] A similar picnic in Cork saw thirty-four bank officials head out from the city to Ringabella on the last Sunday in August 1919. Along the beach, they played cricket, while others took to the water for a swim. There was also the hint of romance in the air: a report of the outing in the *Irish Banking Magazine* remarked that some members 'went on what appeared to be a voyage of discovery, judging from the length of time they were absent from the main party'.[40] In towns across Ireland, bank officials organised and held picnics and car-drives, and dances. They also established their own premises for socialising. In November 1921 an Irish Bankers' Club opened in Dublin (another followed later in Belfast). The club boasted a bar, a billiards room, a card room, a dining room and a reading room. Among the regular entertainments provided was a conjuror called 'Presto' who made packs of cards and an egg disappear. On the same night as 'Presto', members were entertained by performances from the Rathmines Choral and Musical Society.[41]

That this was a profoundly middle-class culture is readily apparent, but the growth of other forms of entertainment crossed class. The growth of the cinema in Ireland showed how Irish cities and towns were being reshaped by new forms of popular culture. In this instance, the building of iconic cinemas in Dublin included the Savoy (1929) and the Carlton (1937) on O'Connell Street and the Adelphi on Middle Abbey Street (1938). In Belfast, too, the cinema thrived with the opening of Classic Cinema on Castle Lane (1923). This was a phenomenon repeated across Ireland, where country towns saw the development of purpose-built cinemas, including the Tonic in Bangor, County Down and the Ritz in Athlone, County Westmeath. The 1930s saw an increase in the number of films made in Ireland – north and south – but it was usually imported films that dominated, with international stars such as Charlie Chaplin, Clark Gable and Joan Crawford hugely popular on both sides of the border. Despite the censorship which denied people the opportunity

---

39 *Irish Banking Magazine*, July 1919.
40 *Irish Banking Magazine*, August 1919.
41 *Irish Banking Magazine*, January 1923.

of seeing films such as *Gone With The Wind* (1939), 'cinema was probably the most popular form of entertainment for working people'.[42]

1945–1970

In the 1930s, Conrad Arensberg's celebrated study of life in the west of Ireland had presented a complex, multilayered society where age-old traditions had been shifted by 'the breath of the outer world'.[43] This breath swept more change in the years after the Second World War. It is a crude cliché to paint Ireland as some sort of uncultured backwater mired in the Dark Ages up to the 1950s. There were aspects of Irish life that were undoubtedly stultifying, but rural Ireland was not unchanging and isolated, nor were its people ignorant or resentful of modernity. The scale of emigration from Ireland, alone, forged a deep connection to the great cities of the Western world and an understanding of life there. The years after the Second World War saw that understanding deepen, driven as it was by a range of different forces.[44] The arrival of electricity transformed how people lived, so did the rise of the motor car and a media revolution that brought the arrival of television.

Nothing illustrated the challenge to old visions of Ireland more clearly than the arrival of television. Across the Western world after the Second World War, society was changed by the arrival of television. In 1955, BBC television broadcasts began in Northern Ireland and this was followed in 1959 by Ulster television. In the south of Ireland, during the late 1950s around 30,000 homes on the east coast and in border areas had TV sets and were receiving signals from British television stations.[45] The potency of the new medium was immediately understood. Opening Teilifís Éireann on 31 December 1961, the President of Ireland, Éamon de Valera, concluded his speech: 'Never before was there in the hand of man an instrument so powerful to influence the thoughts and actions of the multitude.' De Valera acknowledged its potential to build up the character of people, but also the potential for 'decadence and disillusion'. Whether for education or the pursuit of decadence, the lure of television was such that within two years of the opening of Teilifís Éireann 44

42 B. McEvoy, *World Cinema 4: Ireland* (Wiltshire, 1989) 38.
43 C. Arensberg, *The Irish Countryman* (London: MacMillan, 1937), 146.
44 For a brilliant study of the complexities of migration and its impact on society, see Mary Gilmartin, *Ireland and Migration in the Twenty-First Century* (Manchester: Manchester University Press, 2015).
45 D. Ferriter, *Transformation of Ireland*, 601–2.

per cent of Irish homes had a television; by 1966 this had grown to 54 per cent and by the end of the decade television had reached 76 per cent of homes.[46] In the decades that followed, television became the central conduit for popular culture in Ireland.

Television facilitated the growing reach of American culture, as did Hollywood movies. Impossibly attractive men and women driving impossibly modern cars shaped the desires of people of all classes and its reach was such that the President of Ireland, Seán T. O'Kelly asked to be provided with a modern large American car (a Chrysler Windsor eight-passenger Saloon), even though it was much more expensive than the European cars on sale.[47] The growth of Americana contributed to the diversity of popular culture in post-World War II Ireland. That war, itself, cast its own shadow as music, films and comic books told and retold stories of war from the real-life Dambusters to the fictional *Biggles*. Such stories were a central part of British popular culture through the 1950s and 1960s and thrived also in Ireland. This was a culture which reached far beyond loyalist communities. Brian Inglis, in his memoir *Downstart*, recalls a life lived in Dublin almost as if Irish independence had never manifested itself. For others, support for Manchester United and love of the Beatles sat easily beside ballad sessions where 'Sean South of Garryowen' was eulogised in song as a new Republican martyr, killed in an IRA assault on Brookeborough Police Station in County Fermanagh on 1 January 1957.

By that date, popular culture in Ireland was being changed by the rise, internationally, of youth culture. This culture of 'rock 'n' roll, jiving, teenpics, horror comics and romance magazines spread across Ireland, helped, notably, by cinema.[48] This was a process where 'mass market distribution of popular culture products placed American culture as the central reference point for modernity'.[49] This was not a simple matter of Irish teenagers aping global trends: it also meant the assertion of a new mode of behaviour in an Irish context. An example is the manner in which, by the end of the 1950s, the Fleadh Cheoil had become a focal point of youth culture in Ireland.

---

46 C. Morash, *A History of the Media in Ireland*, 172–81.
47 L. Blaney, *The Motor Car and Ireland*, 277.
48 E. O'Leary, *Teenagers, Everyday Life and Popular Culture in 1950s Ireland* (Doctoral Thesis, NUIM, 2013), 10–12.
49 E. O'Leary, *Teenagers, Everyday Life and Popular Culture in 1950s Ireland*, 87.

16. Youths playing cards, Falls Road area of Belfast, 1970s.

The Fleadh Cheoil was originally conceived in 1951 by Comhaltas Ceoltóirí Éireann as a music festival with competitions for music, song and dance. Local fleadhanna were held across the country and the National Fleadh immediately became established as a yearly exhibition of traditional music. An initial attendance of 1,500 grew rapidly through the decade. Spontaneous sessions in public houses and on the streets quickly became a distinctive feature of the Fleadh, drawing in a progressively younger audience. It also became synonymous with drunkenness and there were occasional public order problems through the late 1950s. If the Fleadh Cheoil was in many respects a repackaging of traditional culture, an entirely new craze swept the country in the second half of the 1950s. This was the era of bands such as The Clipper Carlton, The Dixies, Brendan Bowyer and others. These 'showbands' offered a heady mix of rock 'n' roll hits, country-and-western sentimentality, novelty numbers and routines. It was an extraordinary phenomenon. At their peak, there were an estimated 700 showbands touring the country and playing in more than 1,100 ballrooms and dancehalls.[50]

Alcohol, perhaps inevitably, was a central part of the night's entertainment. Geoff Brooks of the Brook Brothers recalled an Irish ballroom tour in the early 1960s: 'We turned up at half past seven or eight o'clock. By half past ten we were getting really worried because there was nobody there ... By eleven o'clock everybody poured in, arriving by cars, buses, on their bikes and everything. They had been at the pub.'[51] There were up to 500,000 members of the Pioneer Association in Ireland at its highpoint in the 1950s, but the culture of drinking in every class and in every community was real.[52] It was a culture that gathered momentum in the 1960s, with alcohol consumption increasing dramatically, buoyed by a growth in disposable income. In the 1960s, the average Irish person had increased their alcohol intake by 25 per cent over previous decades. Wine consumption rose by 59 per cent and beer consumption increased by 17 per cent. Modern advertising campaigns saw alcohol products deliberately targeted at women, with Bacardi rum and Smirnoff vodka both making huge inroads into the Irish market in ways that would have been unimaginable ten years previously. In eight years during the 1960s, admissions to psychiatric hospitals for drink-related illnesses rose from 404 to 2,015.[53] In drink, as in so much else, the

---

50 N. O'Connor, *Bringing It All Back Home: The Influence of Irish Music at Home and Abroad* (Dublin, 1991); F. Vallely, *The Companion to Irish Traditional Music* (Cork: Cork University Press, 1999); V. Power, *Send 'Em Home Sweatin': The Showband Story* (Dublin: Kildanore, 2000); *Ceol*, vols. I, II and III, *passim*.

51 C. Holohan, 'Every Generation has its Task: Attitudes to Irish Youth in the Sixties' (Doctoral Thesis, UCD, 2009), 126.

52 D. Ferriter, *A Nation of Extremes: The Pioneers in Twentieth-century Ireland* (Dublin: Irish Academic Press, 1999), 191.

53 D. Ferriter, *Ambiguous Republic: Ireland in the 1970s* (London: Profile Books, 2012), 581 and *The Transformation of Ireland*, 594.

17. Two men drinking in a pub in Downpatrick, County Down, 1970s.

change that was evident by the end of the 1960s accelerated in the decades that followed.

1970–2016

In the 1920s, W. B. Yeats had noted that the vision of creating an Irish-Ireland had been rooted in the desire to avoid being swept into what he called 'the filthy modern tide'. By the 1970s Irish people were throwing themselves into that tide with considerable abandon. A prime example of this related to sex. The 1960s marked the beginning of a sexual revolution in Ireland, even if its nature was limited. In Northern Ireland, the increased sexual freedom of 1960s London was not replicated in Belfast and beyond, even if the ready availability of contraception did suggest at least the possibility of promiscuity.

Ultimately, changes in sexual practices in Ireland were rooted in wider changes across Irish popular culture – it was what the then Archbishop of Dublin, Dermot Ryan, called, in a 1979 pastoral letter, the 'corruption of the young', itself a consequence of 'the modern era of enlightenment and

permissiveness'.[54] As ever, the focus of much of this 'culture of permissiveness' was music. There was nothing new about complaints of behaviour of
Irish people around music venues and the growth of discos and nightclubs
from the 1970s gave another venue for licentiousness. The arrival of disco in
Ireland is also a reminder of how people do not necessarily just adopt what
has come from elsewhere unchanged, rather they reshape it to fit the circumstances of their lives. For instance, the Stringfellows disco in the Offaly town
of Tullamore may have copied a name and much music from the original
Peter Stringfellow's nightclub in London – and shared also a reliance on drinking and dancing – but there was also difference. Stringfellows in Tullamore
was filled with men and women who had decanted from buses across the
midlands and their world was not that of metropolitan London. The wildness
of Irish country towns on Saturday night was a wildness that was markedly
different to that of city streets.

In general, the diversity (even unique qualities) of Ireland's music scene
in the 1970s and 1980s bore testimony to the range of forces that moulded
popular culture. From the 1960s, ballad singers and groups had prospered
through increased interest in traditional Irish music and the general global
increase in folk singers across Western society. The Chieftains travelled
widely with their instrument-based renditions of traditional music, while
The Dubliners enjoyed similar success with a more ballad-based approach.
Christy Moore was to the fore of musicians who began playing traditional
music, before moving towards the mainstream. Right at the heart of the
Irish mainstream remained the showbands and country-and-western stars,
both of which continued to fill out dance halls and other venues until the
1980s. Some – such as the extraordinary Joe Dolan whose legendary live
shows stretched into the new millennium – lasted even longer than that.
And no one did international mainstream quite as magnificently as the
Irish: the finest proof of this was the continuing success in the Eurovision
Song Contest which Ireland won for the first time through Dana in 1970.
Johnny Logan then won it twice in the 1980s, before four further successes
in five years followed in the early 1990s. Not content with simply winning
the competition, the Eurovision also became the platform from which the
Irish unleashed Riverdance, which became a global sensation. The inter-
marriage of imported musical styles with traditional Irish music influences
brought a 'Celtic' sub-genre of rock music-produced bands such as Horslips
in the 1970s. More interestingly, an innovative fusing of punk rock, ballad

---

54 *Irish Times*, 28 November 2009.

and traditional music in the 1980s brought great success to The Pogues, a London-Irish band whose singer, Shane MacGowan, was acclaimed as the leading songwriter of his generation.[55]

Ultimately, increased globalisation further facilitated the creation of a music market that transcended national boundaries. In Ireland, this brought the popular triumph of American music from James Taylor to Taylor Swift, but it also offered the best Irish musicians an international arena. The arrival of Van Morrison, Rory Gallagher and Phil Lynott in the late 1960s and early 1970s gave Ireland a credible position in the global rock firmament. All three enjoyed acclaim as international artists, with Morrison's 1969 album 'Astral Weeks' accepted as a classic. His position in Irish popular music stood second only to that of U2, whose multi-million selling albums and ground-breaking world tours marked them out as one of the biggest rock bands in the world from the mid-1980s. These were just a few of the top bands that enjoyed a national and international profile: others included the Boomtown Rats and Thin Lizzy. In a real sense, the most interesting bands to come out of Ireland in the 1970s and 1980s were from Northern Ireland. The Derry rock group, The Undertones, shot to fame with their classic 1978 single, 'Teenage kicks'. The Undertones had clearly been influenced by the bands of northern England, while their fellow northerners, Stiff Little Fingers, were part of the punk scene of the late 1970s. Inspired by attending a Belfast concert played by a visiting English band, The Clash, they began to make punk records about life in Belfast, mixing the personal with the political and the socially aware.

Stiff Little Fingers mined the Troubles in Northern Ireland for their finest song 'Alternative Ulster', but popular culture more usually reflected and reinforced existing divides. Sports clubs and associations were segregated along confessional lines. Similarly there was a clear denominational divide to where people lived, ate, drank and socialised. This divide could be crossed, but it most usually was not. The marching season remained a focus of particular conflict, but the broader targeting of people based on their cultural choices was also common.

The murals painted on the gable-ends of houses and elsewhere throughout Northern Ireland offered a fascinating insight into the mindset of conflict. Mural painting began in Belfast around 1908 with the creation of murals in honour of 'King Billy'. They were thereafter usually painted as part of 'the twelfth' celebrations. Republican mural painting blossomed during the 1981 hunger strikes and were often a celebration of armed struggle, drawing

---

55 Nuala O'Connor, *Bringing It All Back Home.*

18. The Ballroom of Romance at Glenfarne, County Leitrim. Dance halls were hugely popular in rural Ireland from the 1930s to the 1970s.

motifs from Irish history and mythology. Republican murals also drew heavily from the global pantheon of rebels and anti-heroes. There were, for example, murals of Frederick Douglass, Martin Luther King, Ché Guevara, Nelson Mandela and Malcolm X. For their part, loyalist murals also began to take on something of an international perspective, including portraits of Ulster Scots famous in America such as Davy Crockett and President James Buchanan. In the new millennium, it is striking that murals are funded by the state through the Arts Council of Northern Ireland as part of a re-imagining Communities Programme.[56]

---

56 J. Vannais, 'Mainstreaming Murals', in *Fortnight*, 385 (May, 2000), 21–2; B. Rolston, ' "The Brothers on the Walls": International Solidarity and Irish Political Murals', in *Journal of Black Studies*, 39, (January 2009), 446–70; T. Crowley, 'The Art of Memory: The Murals of Northern Ireland and the Management of History', in *Field Day Review*, 7 (2011), 22–49.

The role of religion in Irish popular culture was evidenced by an outpouring of religious fervor in the mid-1980s. In July 1985, in the small West Cork village of Ballinspittle, some people believed that the statue of the Virgin Mary in the Marian Shrine had come alive. News of the moving statue in Ballinspittle was reported first by the local, then the national and finally the international press. Initially hundreds and then thousands of people began congregating around the shrine every evening at dusk. Within a month, one-quarter of a million people had made their way to Ballinspittle. Hymns were sung and prayers recited. Many claimed to have seen the statue move. Through the summer and into the autumn the crowds kept coming to pray at the shrine and await a visitation from the Virgin Mary. Minor miracles were reported. One woman was claimed to have been cured of deafness; a stroke victim was said to have been cured of paralysis. Crowds also began to congregate at Marian shrines all across Ireland. Indeed, a certain mass hysteria swept villages and towns and even cities. As the weeks passed, other statues in other parishes were also said to have moved. Even while it lasted, many Irish people considered the phenomenon to be entirely ludicrous. Eventually, it retreated in importance – though not entirely as crowds still flocked to Ballinspittle through to the summer of 2015.[57] However, rather than emphasising the enduring importance of the Catholic Church in the Republic of Ireland, the 'moving statues' actually denoted a people in the midst of a profound identity crisis. The country was in the throes of far-reaching social and cultural change and was not coping particularly well with the implications of that change: the overt official Catholicism so symbolic of the 1950s had been undermined by social change in the 1960s. In the early decades after independence as the state tried to carve out an identity for itself, Catholicism was central to that identity. That Catholicism was now in retreat – and that retreat was hastened by repeated scandals of child sexual abuse from the early 1990s – but it was not clear what authority could or would fill the vacuum.

All the while, the commercialisation of leisure reshaped popular culture. There was nothing new in people attempting to package and sell cultural experiences. The 1950s, for instance, had seen the establishment of a whole range of literary and musical festivals across the country including the Wexford International Opera Festival, the Cork International Choral and Folk Dance Festival, the Cork International Film Festival, and the Dublin International Theatre Festival. Every subsequent decade brought expansion in the range of festivals, summer schools and other events aimed at showcasing Irish culture.

---

57 *Cork Examiner*, 22 July 2015.

These proved a significant draw, while the broader positioning of Ireland as a cultural oasis saw the country's cultural heritage play a central role in the experiences of the 7 million tourists who were visiting the country by 2013. In that year overseas tourists made 3.7 million visits to cultural or historic sites, 4 million visits to country houses or castles, 1.8 million visits to museums and galleries, 1.7 million visits to heritage and interpretive centres, 1.6 million visits to public gardens and 1.5 million visits to monuments.[58] For many tourists, equally, visiting Irish pubs to listen to Irish music was a major attraction. It was an attraction that, in the new millennium, people across the world could enjoy as the 'Irish pub' emerged as a truly global brand, a venue that sat beside MacDonalds as a ubiquitous presence in major (and minor) cities around the world. That Guinness remained connected in the global mind to Dublin was intimately linked to this phenomenon.

Ideas of the Irish capacity to party were given free rein during the Celtic Tiger. In the later years – even as the Irish economy was experiencing a huge downturn – this party shaded into an excess that was crass. From the purchase of designer handbags to the acquisition of holiday homes, frequently abroad, the triumph of conspicuous consumerism was real. The story of the Celtic Tiger is not just the story of champagne and helicopters, however: excess tells only part of the story. Between the mid-1990s and the mid-2000s, the number of young people living in Ireland with disposable income brought an exuberance that filled cities and towns with an uncommon energy. Communities across Ireland that had been devastated by inter-generational poverty and emigration were changed as stable, well-paid employment allowed people to enjoy a social life bouncing with good cheer. Not everybody prospered – some remained mired in deep poverty – but for many people new cultural experiences were made possible by the boom. From foreign holidays to fine dining, tens of thousands of Irish people – including those who behaved with restraint and proportion – enjoyed a lifestyle that was new and vibrant and a welcome relief from years of grind. And yet, when the froth is stripped away, people continued to live much as they always had – many simply indulged themselves more in the vices they already enjoyed. To this end, it is notable that alcohol consumption increased by 47 per cent in Ireland during the 1990s and increased again in the new millennium. The consumption of illegal drugs also grew in scale – as did the levels of crime associated with it.[59] Against that,

---

58 M. Duncan and P. Rouse, *Creating Ireland: Research & the Role of the Humanities and Social Sciences in Ireland* (Dublin Irish Research Council, 2014) 39.

59 Ferriter, *Transformation of Ireland*, 668.

the numbers volunteering to help at sports clubs and for other community-based cultural activities grew, and there were many more people deriding those who spent obscene sums of money on trophy consumer goods than there were people in the queue to purchase such goods.

The death of the Celtic Tiger – brought down by a mixture of hubris, greed and incompetence – coincided with a dramatic shift in popular culture. The growth of smartphones and their almost ubiquitous use in Ireland had immediate and far-reaching influence. In general, the spread of Internet-based technologies after the new millennium had begun to change the way people lived, from shopping to listening to music. After 2010, the popularity of the smartphone revolutionised aspects of how Irish people communicated with each other. The hyper-connectivity of smartphones facilitated the spread of social media and the manner in which it reshaped popular culture was only in its infancy by 2016. The role of the smartphone in facilitating popular protest, in driving new media and in the consumption of news, and in the almost instant creation of celebrity (however fleeting) were just three ways in which smartphones changed how people lived. This democratisation of access to extended networks of communication was a change as dramatic as it was unforeseen. In the process, institutions that long appeared fundamental to popular culture – notably newspapers, television stations and record companies – faced the choice of immediate and profound adaptation, or ruin. It was a further reminder of the manner in which popular culture shifts and shifts again, and shifts in ways that are sometimes radical.

Conclusion

Popular culture in Ireland contains aspects that are uniquely Irish, but the modern history of popular culture in Ireland is unique only in certain parts. Much of Irish popular culture is shared with that of other societies. Universal impulses, the history of Ireland within what was once the British Empire, and an international cultural exchange where political and geographic borders are increasingly permeable ensure that influences from outside Ireland have been essential in the making of that culture. Irish popular culture in 2016 was dramatically (though not completely) different to that of 1880. The importance of the Internet, television, radio, motor cars and planes in the new millennium illustrated the shift in popular culture wrought by technological change. And yet, beyond such change, the fundamentals of certain aspects of culture remained essentially unchanged. To this end, the importance of drinking and music and sport, for example, was everywhere apparent in the 1880s, just as remained the case in 2016. No amount of repackaging across the decades can disguise this essential truth. Similarly, wealth remains essential to the making of popular culture in Ireland: the capacity of people with money to shape the world as they have wished (at least in part) is everywhere to be seen in popular culture. Equally, modern popular culture is the product of both the accretion of change and the deepening of traditions over time. In this, popular culture reflects broader trends in society: commercialisation, growth in disposable income, and revolutions in education and health, for example, have all served to create the conditions for popular culture to change. This change has seen new fads (often, in reality, old ones refashioned for a new age) thriving in urban and rural areas; sometimes they endured, changing the social life of the inhabitants, while on other occasions they simply disappeared, leaving little or no trace. Ultimately, none of what we see around us in a new millennium was inevitable. This was true for previous centuries and remains true in the age of the Internet. The Internet – and digital technologies in general – have served to quicken and deepen Irish exposure to global culture, just as happened across the world. In Ireland, American popular culture is the dominant feature of this globalisation, but there are many other influences and many more are on the way. It is this combination of global trends and unique, localised aspects that has made, remade and will continue to make Irish popular culture.

20

Irish Foreign Policy: 1919 to 1973

MICHAEL KENNEDY

Introduction: In Pursuit of the National Interest

In constructing their foreign policies, all states seek to protect defined national interests. In Ireland's case, these encompass ensuring the state's development and survival as a recognised independent entity in an anarchic international order whilst supporting moves to regulate the chaos of the global system through international organisation. Independent Ireland's foreign policy sought to protect and enhance the state's place amongst the nations and concurrently make the relations between states peaceful and non-violent. Dublin consistently emphasised that Ireland could, and would, take part in international life on its own terms, free from British influence. Defined collectively, Ireland's national interests were the pursuit and protection of international sovereignty in a stable world order.[1]

In other words, Ireland was fearful that its hard-won independence would not be acknowledged, that internationally it would be seen as little more than an adjunct of Britain, and that Irish independence could be overwhelmed by any global war into which Ireland would be sucked regardless. Neutrality in the Second World War became the paramount expression of Ireland's desire to follow its own destiny in world affairs, and to take decisions based on its own judgement. Neutrality was not a foreign policy of isolation, but a policy which sought to safeguard Ireland's independence within a war zone. Based on pure realpolitik, it sought to ensure Ireland's survival through the careful management of relations with the belligerents, as global war raged around Ireland.[2]

---

1 Full details, and copious documentation for what follows, can be found in the texts and appendices of each volume of the Royal Irish Academy's *Documents on Irish Foreign Policy, 1919–57* (hereafter *DIFP*) which currently run from 1919 to 1957 (10 vols., Dublin, Royal Irish Academy 1998–2016) series.
2 See R. Fanning, 'Raison d'État and the Evolution of Irish Foreign Policy', in M. Kennedy and J. M. Skelly (eds.), *Irish Foreign Policy, 1919–66. From Independence to Internationalism* (Dublin: Four Courts Press, 2000), 308–26.

As the Second World War showed, Irish foreign policy makers were conscious of the state's geographic position. Geographic location in the context of the European balance of power and the North Atlantic sea lanes impacted strongly on how Ireland was treated by its more powerful neighbours after 1922. To the east was Britain, an established global power. To the west, Ireland had a maritime frontier on the Atlantic sea lanes – the western approaches – which Britain needed to control for its own security.[3] Control of these sea lanes, and the territory of independent Ireland itself, was vital to any continental enemy seeking to confront Britain and for Britain's own defence. Dublin also realised that Irish airspace was vital to Britain's defence and to the new technology of transAtlantic aviation that Britain was in competition to develop with the United States, Ireland's neighbour and rising global power to the west. Irish governments knew from these geopolitical and strategic realities that Ireland was not an isolated island behind an island off the coast of Europe, but a potential strategic centrepiece to a Great Power war in Europe and an important geographic link between the Old World and the New. The awareness of such geopolitical realities, taken in conjunction with Dublin's political relationship with London, dominated Irish foreign policy in the twentieth century.[4]

The Second World War is often seen as a dividing point in Ireland's twentieth-century external relations, but senior officials developing Ireland's post-war foreign policy saw continuity with the experiences at the League of Nations in the 1920s and 1930s, as well as more recent experiences with the post-war Marshall Plan.[5] United Nations membership came in 1955 after a nine-year wait caused by a Cold War-related Soviet veto on Ireland's application in 1946. The United Nations provided a significant forum for independent-minded action by Ireland. Had Ireland not taken its first steps in the international order in the inter-war League of Nations and the Commonwealth

---

3 The case is laid out in its classic form in H. J. MacKinder, *Britain and the British Seas* (Oxford University Press, 1907). See also G. R. Sloan, *The Geopolitics of Anglo-Irish Relations in the 20th Century* (London: Leicester University Press, 1997).

4 Few Irish policymakers outside the military and diplomatic nexus understood the realities of Ireland's island position. One who did was Colonel Dan Bryan, wartime head of Ireland's military intelligence directorate G2. His 'Fundamental factors affecting Saorstát Defence Problem' (University College Dublin Archives, Bryan Papers, P71/8) shows a unique geopolitical awareness of Ireland's international position.

5 See J. M. Skelly, *Ireland and the United Nations* (Dublin: Four Courts Press, 1997) and B. Whelan, *The Marshall Plan and Ireland* (Dublin: Irish Academic Press, 2000).

it would not have developed the reservoir of diplomatic skill to later capital-ise on the opportunities of United Nations membership.[6]

From the late-1950s European integration saw international economics and trade temper Dublin's hitherto politically motivated world view. Ireland had begun to open its economy in the late-1950s and eventual EEC membership was expected to fuel export-led economic growth. Whereas from 1919 to the late-1950s the singular stance of emphasising independence and sovereignty was the objective of Ireland's foreign relations, from the late 1950s the goal changed to viewing Ireland's destiny as being within a group of like-minded states seeking ever-closer union. Sovereignty would be shared, but it would be Ireland's choice to do so. Pooling sovereignty within an integrated Europe allowed Ireland to take an international perspective that was more global than that of an island nation on Europe's western seaboard.[7] Ireland achieved EEC membership in 1973. This was the culmination of over a decade of foreign policy re-orientation where the primacy of British–Irish relations made way for relations with Western Europe. The international sovereignty painstak-ingly developed and so jealously guarded in the inter-war years was traded for access to the European market and the greater collective power of a common European approach to world affairs.

The Foreign Policy of Independence

On 21 January 1919, as the Anglo-Irish War began, the members of the newly established Dáil Éireann passed a Declaration of Independence and sought international recognition for their separatist Irish parliament in Dublin.[8] They saw Ireland as an ancient mother country long under British domination now calling out to its diaspora and appealing to other subject nations seeking inde-pendence. As the Dáil took its first steps on the international stage, Irish for-eign policy emerged as a mixture of international propaganda and nationalist politics. The Dáil sent envoys to Paris to seek both international recognition as well as Ireland's admission to the post-war Versailles peace conference.[9]

---

6 Though published in 1969, D. W. Harkness's *The Restless Dominion* (Dublin: Gill & Macmillan, 1969) remains the best account of Ireland's Commonwealth heyday in the 1950s. For an account of Ireland's role in the League of Nations see M. Kennedy, *Ireland and the League of Nations* (Dublin: Irish Academic Press, 1996).

7 See M. J. Geary, *An Inconvenient Wait: Ireland's Quest for Membership of the EEC, 1957–70* (Dublin: Institute of Public Administration, 2009).

8 See *DIFP* I no. 1 for the text of the Declaration of Independence. It is also available online at www.difp.ie.

9 The development of Irish foreign policy from 1919 to 1932 is covered in G. Keown, *First of the Small Nations* (Oxford University Press, 2016).

Neither goal was achieved. The mission to Paris became Ireland's first diplomatic mission and a hub for disseminating Irish propaganda across Europe. There was no diplomatic tradition to draw on here. The young men and women who became Ireland's first diplomats were without training in the skills of diplomacy and were envoys by accident. The Dáil then sent envoys to rally the Irish diaspora to Ireland's independence struggle and to fundraise for the Dáil. A high-profile mission to America, headed by President of Dáil Éireann, Éamon de Valera, aimed at uniting Irish-American opinion and bringing United States public and Congressional pressure to bear on Britain to grant independence to Ireland. The mission succeeded in fund-raising and making the Irish cause visible to the Irish community in the United States, but its practical successes in gaining official support for Irish independence were limited.

British–Irish negotiations began after a truce in the Anglo-Irish War on 11 July 1921. On 11 October 1921 Irish and British negotiating teams commenced talks which culminated in the Anglo-Irish Treaty of 6 December 1921.[10] The Treaty provided not for the Republic of Ireland proclaimed in 1916 and fought for since the Rising, but for an 'Irish Free State' as a self-governing dominion within the British Commonwealth. By December 1921 Ireland had already been partitioned into Northern Ireland and Southern Ireland by the 1920 Government of Ireland Act. Though theoretically all-Ireland, the 1921 Treaty would apply only to twenty-six of the thirty-two counties of the island of Ireland. Dáil Éireann split over the terms of the Treaty. The split was not over partition, but over an oath of allegiance to the British monarch included in the Treaty by Britain with the preservation of its empire in mind. To many in Ireland the oath was an impediment to true Irish independence. To others, the oath and dominion status were tolerated as the Treaty gave the freedom to achieve freedom.

The 1921 Treaty was meant to be the high point of Dáil Éireann diplomacy. Instead diplomacy had, through the Treaty, shattered the Republic and provided an inauspicious birth to the Irish Free State. Outright civil war over the Treaty broke out in June 1922 and lasted to May 1923.[11] Sinn Féin foreign policy had failed and independent Ireland was born in civil war as the Irish Free

---

10 A comprehensive documentary account of the negotiation of the 1921 Treaty and the text of the Treaty itself is contained in *DIFP* I. The only narrative account remains Frank Pakenham's, Lord Longford's 1935 *Peace by Ordeal* (London: Jonathan Cape, 1935).
11 For a contemporary overview of Irish foreign policy on the eve of the Civil War, see Minister for Foreign Affairs George Gavan Duffy's 21 June 1922 memorandum 'The position of Ireland's Foreign Affairs at date of general election, 1922' (*DIFP* I, no. 299).

State, with at best partial independence on a partitioned island, and at worst Dominion status within the British Empire.

Inter-war Foreign Policy

Once the Irish Free State was formally established on 6 December 1922 independent Ireland achieved an acknowledged international persona. The immediate foreign policy goal of the pro-Treaty Cumann na nGaedheal government headed by W. T. Cosgrave was to win international support for the Irish Free State. The critical constituencies here were the Irish-American community and the wider Irish diaspora. Dublin did not want Ireland to appear internationally as a 'failed state' born in civil war. Securing Professor Timothy Smiddy's recognition as Irish Minister Plenipotentiary to the United States was a major objective towards achieving this end. Smiddy's July 1924 accreditation made the Irish Free State the first dominion to appoint a diplomatic representative independent of Britain.[12] This was a major success for Dublin in pursuing an independent foreign policy. Ireland now sought to show the world that it was a truly sovereign independent state. However, it was not to the recently independent states of eastern and central Europe that Ireland looked, nor the wider Irish diaspora, or movements seeking independence from Britain within the British Empire. Instead, Ireland looked rather to the United States of America, the established states of Western Europe and to the Commonwealth and the League of Nations.[13]

From 1922 to 1949 the Irish Free State was a reluctant member of the Commonwealth. It hoped to develop its unwanted dominion status to redesign the Commonwealth away from an imperial body towards a grouping of like-minded independent sovereign states. Commonwealth reform became a hallmark of Cumann na nGaedheal foreign policy. At the 1923 Imperial Conference, Irish diplomats began devising plans to reform Dominion status. Their intention to bring about radical change was dramatically illustrated at the 1926 Imperial Conference in actions which led to the Balfour Declaration. This declared each Dominion internationally equal to Britain. Further reforms diminishing Britain's role as the controlling force over the Commonwealth followed in the later 1920s and led on to the Statute of Westminster (1931). The Statute ensured the domestic sovereignty of the

---

12 See B. Whelan, *United States Foreign Policy and Ireland. From Empire to Independence, 1913–29* (Dublin: Four Courts Press, 2006).

13 Bilateral relations developed slowly. Missions were opened in Washington in 1924 and in the Holy See, Paris and Berlin in 1929, Madrid in 1935, Rome in 1938 and Ottawa in 1939.

Dominions and allowed a Dominion to repeal legislation passed for it by Westminster.[14] The Statute thus enabled the revision and ultimate repeal of the Anglo-Irish Treaty. Here the beneficiaries were not Cosgrave's Cumann na nGaedheal but de Valera's Fianna Fáil, who came to power in 1932. Where Cumann na nGaedheal sought to make the Treaty workable through reform, Fianna Fáil sought to reform it out of existence. There was, however, greater unanimity of approach between both parties over the role of the League of Nations in Irish foreign policy.

Ireland joined the League of Nations on 10 September 1923. League membership gave Ireland a stage from which it could act as a good international citizen. It represented value for money by allowing Irish diplomats to meet the representatives of over fifty states through one diplomatic mission in Geneva. Ireland would otherwise have had no relations with many states with which it had much in common as a new, small and comparatively weak member of the system of states created after the First World War. Irish League policy sought to demonstrate the state's international sovereignty and its belief in the League ideal of a peaceful international system. Despite British protest, the registration of the 1921 Treaty as an international treaty at Geneva in July 1924 achieved both purposes. Having unsuccessfully sought election to the League's Council in 1926, Ireland began to engage actively with the League's yearly assemblies during the late 1920s. In these years the 'good international citizen' role of Irish League membership became more apparent as Ireland promoted the League's role in developing international order and collective security. By the early 1930s Cosgrave's government had overcome any international notions that independent Ireland might be a failed state. It had secured Ireland's place as an active member of the League of Nations, a role which received peer approval in Ireland's election to the League Council in 1930.[15] In the Commonwealth it had ensured that the Dominions were well on the way to achieving ultimate international sovereignty. Despite these successes, closer to home there were difficult issues as yet unresolved.

Dublin's initial Northern Ireland policy of non-recognition foundered amongst the more pressing military considerations of the Civil War.[16]

---

14 The blueprint for Ireland's attitude towards dominion status in the late 1920s can be found in the 2 November 1926 memorandum 'Existing anomalies in the British Commonwealth of Nations' (See *DIFP* III, no. 55).

15 Ireland served on the League of Nations Council from 1930 to 1933.

16 For greater detail on Dublin's attitude to Northern Ireland see C. O'Halloran, *Partition and the Limits of Irish Nationalism* (Dublin: Gill & Macmillan, 1987) and M. Kennedy, *Division and Consensus, the Politics of Cross Border Relations in Ireland, 1925–69* (Dublin: Institute of Public Administration, 2000).

A policy of peaceful co-existence was adopted in late 1922 as the Irish Free State began to prepare for the Boundary Commission promised by the 1921 Treaty to revise the North–South border. From 1922 to 1924 Dublin developed its case for maximum border revision. The leaking of the Commission's report in the British Conservative-leaning *Morning Post* newspaper showed that the Commission proposed only minor alterations to the Irish Free State/Northern Ireland boundary. The leak brought about the collapse of the Commission. Emergency talks between the Irish, British and Northern Ireland governments led to an agreement on 3 December 1925 to suppress the Commission's report, to retain the existing boundary and to cancel certain Irish debts owed to Britain under the Treaty. Dublin's relationship with Northern Ireland entered a state of cold war until the first shoots of cross-border cooperation began during the Second World War and in the 1950s through the Erne Hydro-Electric Scheme, the joint running of the Great Northern Railway and the Foyle Fisheries Commission. After 1925 the two prime ministers of partitioned Ireland would not meet again until 1965.[17]

The first change of government in Dublin following independence took place in 1932 as Fianna Fáil, led by de Valera, came to power. In addition to becoming President of the Executive Council, de Valera took on the External Affairs portfolio. He was the dominant intellectual force behind Irish foreign policy from the 1930s to the late 1940s and built his vision of Ireland acting independently in world affairs on the achievements in the Commonwealth and at the League of Nations by Cumann na nGaedheal. The removal of the Oath of Allegiance and the retention of land annuities, repayments hitherto given to Britain under the Land Acts of the late nineteenth and early twentieth centuries, by the new government began a fundamental restructuring of British–Irish relations.[18] London responded by placing tariffs on Irish exports to Britain, triggering a trade conflict that lasted to 1938 known as the 'Economic War'.[19]

The negotiation of a 'coal-cattle pact' trade agreement in 1934 marked an improvement in British–Irish relations. There was little movement until Malcolm MacDonald became Dominions Secretary in late 1935. The death of

---

17 When Seán Lemass and his Northern Ireland counterpart Terence O'Neill met in Belfast.
18 For greater detail on de Valera's relationship with the Department of External Affairs in the 1930s, see M. Kennedy, ' "Nobody Knows and ever Shall Know from Me that I have Written It". Joseph Walshe, Eamon de Valera and the Execution of Irish Foreign Policy, 1932–8', *Irish Studies in International Affairs*, 14(2003), 165–83.
19 The enduring classic account of Anglo-Irish relations in the 1930s remains D. McMahon's *Republicans and Imperialists* (New Haven: Yale University Press, 1984).

19. De Valera chairs the League of Nations Council, 1932.

King George V, the accession of King Edward VIII and attempts to renegotiate the 'coal-cattle pact' dominated British–Irish relations through early 1936. A further concern was the place of the British monarch in the new Irish constitution being drafted in Dublin. In the winter of 1936 the British constitutional crisis surrounding King Edward VIII's abdication impinged upon British–Irish relations. De Valera used the abdication to introduce the Constitution (Amendment No. 27) Bill, 1936 and the Executive Authority (External Relations) Bill.[20] The former ended the functions of the British monarch in relation to internal affairs in the Free State. The latter gave authority for the continued exercise by the monarch, on the advice of Dublin, of functions relating to Ireland's external relations. The passage of these Acts was a milestone in five years of comprehensive revision of British–Irish relations. They made possible the external association of the Irish Free State with the Commonwealth, an often misunderstood relationship that was to last until Ireland left the Commonwealth in 1949. The swift enactment of the new Constitution of Ireland, Bunreacht na hÉireann, on 29 December 1937 cleared the way for de Valera to move towards the resolution of remaining differences with Britain.

20 This Act was colloquially referred to as the External Relations Act.

20. (i) De Valera with President Lyndon Johnston 1964.

The future relationship between Britain and Ireland in the now imminently expected European war was the spur that led to substantial British–Irish negotiations in January 1938. These produced the April 1938 Anglo-Irish Agreements which covered defence, finance and trade.[21] De Valera hoped for movement during the talks on ending partition, but his hopes were in vain. However the trade agreement ended the Economic War and the financial arrangement resolved British–Irish debts arising out of the 1921 Treaty. These two agreements concerned events in the past; for the future of British–Irish relations in wartime the defence agreement was paramount. By handing over to Ireland three British-controlled defended anchorages, the defence agreement ended the residual British military presence in Ireland outside Northern Ireland.[22] The return of these 'Treaty Ports' enabled Dublin to declare neutrality in September 1939 as Dublin was now in sole control of all the state's territory.

21 See *DIFP* V, no. 175 for the text of these agreements.
22 The 'Treaty Ports' of Cobh, Berehaven and Lough Swilly had been retained by Britain under the defence annex to the Anglo-Irish Treaty of 1921.

20. (ii) De Valera with President de Gaulle, 1968.

The 1938 defence agreement and growing concern about British–Irish relations in time of war highlight a further fundamental change in late-1930s Irish
foreign policy: Ireland had been moving away from the League of Nations
since 1936. Back in 1932 the League of Nations gave de Valera unparalleled
involvement with events on the international stage. De Valera was a firm
supporter of the League and the League was central to Irish foreign policy
in the first half of the 1930s as it was a vehicle for international cooperation
and was seen by de Valera as a motivating force for global peace and security.
Ireland's Permanent Delegate to the League of Nations, Seán Lester, took on

20. (iii) De Valera with Lady Mountbatten and Jawaharlal Nehru, Prime Minister of India.

the unenviable office of League of Nations High Commissioner in the Free City of Danzig from 1934 to 1937.[23] He tried to keep local Poles and Nazis apart and offered those who would listen the evidence of what Nazism would lead to in Europe. Few took other than cursory notice of Lester's warnings.

As Europe moved to war the League offered the best available hope for international stability in an increasingly unstable world. Ireland's belief in the need for a stable international order can be seen in Dublin's support for international non-intervention during the Spanish Civil War of 1936 to 1939. The war in Spain also had a significant domestic agenda. For the first time de Valera faced domestic political discontent over a foreign policy issue. Significant elements of public opinion supported General Franco's Nationalist forces which were perceived as standing against the atheistic communism of the Republicans. Despite this, Ireland supported the Anglo-French Non-Intervention Committee from its inception in August 1936 and restricted the transit of Irish volunteers travelling to Spain to fight on either side in

23 See P. McNamara, *Seán Lester, Poland and the Nazi takeover of Danzig* (Dublin: Irish Academic Press, 2009).

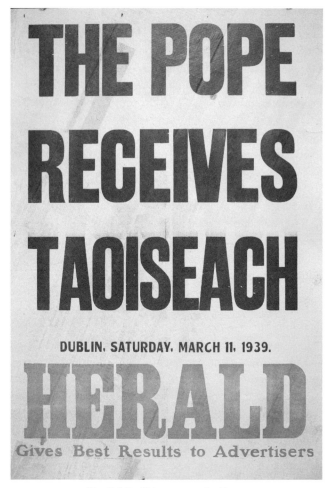

20. (iv) De Valera meets the Pope.

the Civil War.[24] The League's weak response to the 1935 Italian invasion of Abyssinia finally led Dublin to conclude that the League and its collective security system was of little practical value to Ireland in protecting the state in the event of war. Though de Valera remained a supporter of the League, his post-1936 speeches on international relations indicated that Ireland was moving towards neutrality in any future global conflict.

24 For the foreign policy implications to Ireland of the Spanish Civil War see D. Keogh, *Ireland and Europe: 1919–89* (Cork: Cork University Press, 1989), ch 3.

The Crisis Years of the Second World War: 1939–1941

De Valera believed that Ireland would only suffer by involvement in any great power clash. To de Valera neutrality was not a matter of morals, it was a matter of survival. Irish military preparations for the Second World War began too late and the state was almost defenceless when war broke out in September 1939.[25] In the autumn of 1938 External Affairs and military intelligence (G2) began a series of secret talks with the British security services on cooperation and counter-espionage in time of war.[26] Geopolitics and the vicissitudes of war saw Irish neutrality tempered by a certain consideration for Britain, even though the public face of neutrality remained one of strict impartiality. The maintenance of workable relations between neutral Ireland and belligerent Britain was a central theme of wartime foreign policy. Despite later commentators arguing that such talks implied Ireland was non-belligerent rather than neutral, government, diplomats and military in Ireland during the Second World War saw Ireland as a neutral state and would not have recognised the term non-belligerent as applicable to Ireland's position.[27]

From September 1939 to December 1941, and in particular during the summer of 1940, an invasion of Ireland by either Britain or Germany was a real possibility in the context of an invasion of the neighbouring island.[28] Britain invaded Iceland to deny it to Germany in the summer of 1940, and there was every possibility Ireland was next. British and German military planners drew up theoretical invasion plans for Ireland. Neutrality, hitherto aspirational, had to be implemented in practice. Ireland did not wish to be dragged unwillingly into war. However poorly prepared, Dublin emphasised that Ireland would defend itself militarily against any invading forces. It was expected that the

---

25 The historiography of neutrality is worthy of a chapter in its own right. R. Fisk's magisterial *In time of war: Ireland, Ulster and the Price of Neutrality, 1939–45* (Dublin: Gill & Macmillan, 1983) remains a key account, but with the increasing availability of declassified material not available to Fisk it is showing its age. C. Wills, *That Neutral Island: A Cultural History of Ireland during the Second World War* (London: Faber and Faber, 2007) is also essential reading for those seeking to understand 'Emergency Ireland'.

26 See E. O'Halpin, *Defending Ireland* (Oxford University Press, 1999) and M. Kennedy, *Guarding Neutral Ireland* (Dublin: Four Courts Press, 2008).

27 The numerous memoranda and position papers prepared by Dr Michael Rynne, the Legal Adviser at the Department of External Affairs during the Second World War bear this out. They can be found online on www.difp.ie and in *DIFP* VI and VII.

28 For a detailed account of Irish military preparations at this time see M. Kennedy and V. Laing (eds.), *The Irish Defence Forces 1940–49: The Chief of Staff's Report* (Dublin: Irish Manuscripts Commission, 2011).

Defence Forces could only fight for twenty-four hours before external assistance was required. Preventing invasion and preserving neutrality and independence became the overriding themes of Irish foreign policy from 1939 to 1945. Neutrality was not a fixed ideological position; it was a flexible response to a global war in which Ireland sought no part.

British Prime Minister Neville Chamberlain's resignation and replacement by Winston Churchill on 10 May 1940 saw British–Irish relations, already tense during the Phoney War, take a turn for the worse. Churchill rejected Ireland's neutrality. The fall of France and British losses in the Battle of the Atlantic increased the threat to Ireland of a British invasion to deny Ireland to Germany. Ireland was on the frontline of the Battle of the Atlantic, the longest battle in the Second World War, from September 1939 to May 1945. The Second World War was fought in Ireland's coastal seas and skies.[29]

Former Dominion Secretary Malcolm MacDonald arrived in Dublin on 17 June 1940 talking up a German invasion and offering early Irish unity in return for immediate Irish participation in the war. The MacDonald offer was firmly rejected by Cabinet decision. De Valera believed that Dublin's entry on the Allied side at Britain's request would lead to civil war in Ireland. He placed the maintenance of Ireland's international sovereignty and neutrality above any vague British offer to end partition. In the post-war years, Northern Ireland Prime Minister Lord Brookeborough suggested that Northern Ireland might in the summer of 1940 have been willing to consider Irish unity if de Valera joined the war.[30] But de Valera was also mindful of Britain's empty First World War promise of Home Rule for Ireland at the war's end if John Redmond and the Irish Parliamentary Party would agree to the suspension of the 1914 Home Rule Act for the duration of the conflict.

Though top-level relations were increasingly fraught, British–Irish defence talks in May 1940 agreed a strategy to counter a German invasion of Ireland. However Edouard Hempel, the German Minister to Ireland, emphasised that Germany had no intention of violating Ireland's neutrality. German armed forces nevertheless, and despite Irish protests, continually disregarded Ireland's neutrality, undertaking sporadic attacks on Irish territory and infrastructure and mounting unsuccessful intelligence operations in Ireland. The most difficult aspects of Irish–German relations concerned these operations and the use of the radio transmitter at the German legation. Though all German

---

29 See M. Kennedy, *Guarding Neutral Ireland* (Dublin: Four Courts Press, 2008) for a full account of Irish foreign policy in the context of the Battle of the Atlantic.

30 The remark was made to the Canadian High Commissioner to the United Kingdom, Norman Robertson.

spies in Ireland were ultimately rounded up and the legation transmitter was impounded, such German activities remained a problem for Dublin until 1945. Irish–German relations were tested to the limit in December 1940 when Germany attempted to fly in extra staff into Ireland for her mission in Dublin. Knowing them to be spies, de Valera refused permission and the Defence Forces went on alert expecting the refusal to become a pretext for immediate invasion.[31]

In retrospect, by January 1941 the worst of the war was over for Ireland, though this was not obvious at the time. Political and economic pressure on Ireland from London continued, but Germany's decision to invade Russia in July 1941 changed the nature of the war in Europe and made Ireland's position somewhat less difficult.[32] Neutrality could now accommodate limited quiet cooperation with Britain. This cooperation was not viewed by Dublin as covert involvement in the war; rather Dublin could expand the boundaries of neutrality as required.[33] There was nothing unusual in this approach, it was an attitude adopted by all neutrals in relation to their geopolitical realities. Yet London never accepted Ireland's right to remain neutral. The early summer of 1941 saw Britain's last attempt at introducing conscription in Northern Ireland. Dublin managed to wield sufficient influence over Britain directly, and through her allies, to have London drop the proposal. The final occasion when overt British pressure was placed on Ireland to abandon neutrality was Churchill's 8 December 1941 'now or never' telegram to de Valera calling on Ireland to regain her nationhood by joining the war. Churchill did not view the telegram as the basis of a deal on partition. Sent in the aftermath of the entry of the United States into the Second World War, it was not seriously entertained by de Valera either as an opportunity for abandoning neutrality or for ending the partition of Ireland.[34]

The United States Minister in Dublin, David Gray, viewed Ireland's neutrality with growing disdain. His relationship with de Valera was fraught and through his close personal relationship with the Roosevelts, Gray's anti-Irish

---

31 Frederick Boland, Assistant Secretary at the Department of External Affairs in 1940, referred to these developments as 'one of the sharpest crises' in Irish wartime relations with Nazi Germany. See Kennedy, *Guarding*, 179.

32 For a contemporary German view on the impossibility of invading Ireland with ease see J. Mallmann Showell, *Fuehrer Conferences on Naval Affairs* (London: Greenhill Books, 2005).

33 See *DIFP* VII, no. 76 'Help given by Irish Government to the British in relation to the actual waging of the war' for a comprehensive May 1941 list of covert Anglo-Irish wartime cooperation.

34 See *DIFP* VII, nos. 154, 155, 157, 158, 159 and 160 for both contemporary and 1950 accounts of this perpetually intriguing development.

opinions circulated through the White House and the State Department.[35] As British propaganda against Irish neutrality rose through 1940 and 1941, Washington also increased pressure on Ireland to abandon neutrality. Yet from January 1942 to the end of the war in Europe in May 1945, with the exception of the lead-up to D-Day, Ireland mattered little to the Allies, as the partition of Ireland allowed the British and American armed forces to benefit strategically from Ireland through the territory of Northern Ireland. Irish protests during 1942 that the stationing of United States forces in Northern Ireland amounted to American approval of partition were met with incredulity in Washington. The State Department responded that it could not be expected to put Irish concerns ahead of Allied strategic war aims. Irish diplomats were unable to make in-roads into the increasingly pro-British mindset in the United States. The earlier unsuccessful wartime mission of Frank Aiken, the Minister for the Coordination of Defensive Measures, to the United States in 1941 in search of arms and supplies merely hardened top-level American opinion against Ireland.[36]

Ireland and the Holocaust

By early 1943 de Valera was receiving telegrams from prominent Jewish personalities in Ireland and overseas to make representations in Berlin on behalf of Jews in danger in occupied Europe.[37] From Irish diplomatic correspondence, it is clear that there was general knowledge of the deportation and incarceration of European Jews in concentration camps in Poland and the east of Europe. Precise knowledge of their fate in these camps is less clear, though the names Bergen-Belsen, Birkenau and Auschwitz appear in telegrams between Dublin and the Irish legation in Berlin. Through late 1943 and into 1944, Dublin inquired from Berlin whether Jews in certain occupied countries and in Germany were exempt from deportation if they held neutral visas. The reply was that such documentation would afford no protection. External Affairs also intervened on behalf of a small number of Jews in Germany and France in an attempt to get them visas to leave occupied or

---

35 Gray's vitriolic Dublin memoirs were published in edited form as *A Yankee in de Valera's Ireland* with an introduction by Paul Bew (Dublin: Royal Irish Academy, 2012). They have not improved with age.

36 Aiken's visit is covered in *DIFP* VII, No. 40 and in a more embellished form in the memoirs of Ireland's wartime Minister to Washington Robert Brennan, *Ireland Standing Firm* (Dublin: University College Dublin Press, 2002 edition).

37 For a more detailed account of Irish–Jewish relations and the Holocaust, see D. Keogh, *Jews in Twentieth Century Ireland* (Cork: Cork University Press, 1998).

German territory. It was again to no avail; contacts between the Irish legation in Berlin and German officials resulted in Dublin being told that this was an internal matter for the German government. A further 1944–1945 attempt, agreed by de Valera, to bring a group of German Jewish children temporarily to Ireland in advance of their departure for the United States was also fruitless, though a small number of Jewish children did arrive in a none-too-welcoming Ireland in 1948.

D-Day and the End of the War

In the run up to D-Day (6 June 1944) the Allies sought to isolate Ireland in a series of moves that began with the 'American note' of 21 February 1944 which called for the expulsion of Axis diplomatic representatives from Dublin.[38] To de Valera, this was outside interference attacking Irish neutrality: a foreign power could not tell Ireland how to conduct its affairs. As the crisis waned, from March 1944 until Operation Overlord was launched on 'D-Day', measures were implemented jointly by the Allies and Ireland to close off Ireland to the outside world in order to reduce the possibility of information on the invasion of Europe leaking from Ireland. An example of how neutral Ireland's covert relations with the Allies had developed was that the weather forecast which permitted the Supreme Allied Commander, General Eisenhower, to give the go ahead for Overlord came from Blacksod lighthouse on Ireland's Atlantic coast.[39]

De Valera never publicly explained the rationale behind his 2 May 1945 visit to the German Minister Edouard Hempel's residence on the occasion of Hitler's death to offer his condolences.[40] The visit gave rise to widespread international condemnation. De Valera later explained privately that he acted out of respect for Hempel and out of courtesy to the German nation. Placing the visit in context offers some explanation for de Valera's ill-conceived action. Fearing the destruction of the German legation archives, American Minister to Ireland David Gray sought an assurance from de Valera that the building would be handed over to the Allies before the cessation of hostilities. On 30 April 1945 de Valera told Gray that, as a neutral, Ireland would not hand the legation over. External Affairs felt that Gray was being mischievous in his

---

38 For the text of the note see *DIFP* VII No. 369 and for context see O'Halpin, *Defending Ireland* and Kennedy, *Guarding*.
39 See Kennedy, *Guarding*, for further details.
40 The nearest he came was in a private letter to Ireland's Minister to Washington, Robert Brennan. See *DIFP* VII, No. 590.

handling of the transfer. The Taoiseach was displeased and angry. After his encounter with Gray, and against the advice of senior diplomats, de Valera, on the afternoon of 2 May 1945, visited Hempel. The German legation was finally handed over to the Irish authorities on the morning of 10 May 1945; the Allies took over the premises that afternoon.

The Spectre of Communism and the Cold War

Churchill roundly criticised Ireland's neutrality in his VE day speech. De Valera's reply was mature and dignified; yet it was immediately old news compared to the problems of peace.[41] Irish foreign policy now entered a period of change and reorientation as Ireland emerged from the Second World War fully aware that the threat from Nazism and Fascism was being replaced by that from the Soviet Union and Communism. Facing into the post-war world Ireland cast itself as internationalist, culturally part of the Western European Christian tradition and friendly towards the United States. The late 1940s are often seen as a vacuum period in Irish foreign policy, but they were nothing of the kind as during these years Ireland sought to adjust to the new normalcy of the unstable armed peace of the Cold War.[42] The transition to peace would present significant issues for Irish foreign policy makers.

Immediate post-war foreign policy dealt with problems hanging over from the Second World War. The most significant were, first, explaining to the Allies that there were no sizable German assets in Ireland; second, seeking compensation for German air attacks on Irish territory; third, undertaking the release of German internees in Ireland, and; finally, dealing with the fate of former Axis diplomats in Dublin. Further concerns included the position of Irish nationals who had fought in the Allied forces. Related to this was how to deal with Defence Forces deserters, an unknown number of whom had subsequently joined the Allied armies. Dublin stressed that legislative action against these men was taken because they had deserted the Irish Defence Forces and not because they had fought with the Allies.[43]

A further pressing question was the arrival of displaced persons from Europe in Ireland. There was a particular need to guard against the landing in Ireland of any individuals sought by the Allies. It was not in Ireland's interest

---

41 The text can be found in M. Moynihan (ed.), *Speeches and Statements by Eamon de Valera 1917–73* (Dublin: Gill & Macmillan, 1980), 470–7.

42 This transition to peace is the main theme of *DIFP* IX.

43 It remains unclear how many of these deserters actually joined the Allied forces. Much publicised Irish records show only the numbers who deserted. There are no accurate

to harbour possible war criminals. The Department of Justice also remained opposed to opening up general immigration to Ireland. This was particularly so in respect of Jews. Tánaiste and Minister for Industry and Commerce Seán Lemass refused to allow refugees into Ireland simply on humanitarian grounds. For Lemass, refugees had to have the specific skills that Ireland needed for economic modernisation. Both Industry and Commerce and Justice were forced to modify their restrictive policies. De Valera's policy towards refugees was somewhat more liberal. He favoured the admission of at least 10,000 refugees to Ireland. Nevertheless there was very limited immigration to Ireland in the post-war years. Answers to Dáil questions on the number of 'aliens' entering Ireland showing annual figures in the low hundreds and a cumulative 1951 figure for the period 1939 to 1950 inclusive being given as 1,934.[44]

The end of the war brought the renewal of traditional bilateral relations with Britain and the United States. The Labour government that came to power in Britain after the 1945 election was expected by Dublin – on no very clear grounds – to display less commitment to Northern Ireland. Such hopes were not fulfilled. The differing paths taken by Dublin and Belfast during the Second World War ensured that the two Irish jurisdictions were further apart in 1945 than in 1939.[45] Ireland's relations with the United States were dominated by the position of the United States Minister to Ireland, David Gray. By 1945 he was effectively *persona non grata* in Dublin. However, Ireland's Minister to the United States, Robert Brennan, lacked the high-level contacts in Washington to undermine Gray's influence and the Truman administration did not replace Gray until 1947.[46] Irish–American relations remained raw. It took the emergence of the Cold War and the appointment of John Hearne as Ireland's first Ambassador to Washington in 1950 for Irish–American relations to improve.

The most significant change in Ireland's post-war foreign relations was the 1946 appointment of Joseph Walshe as Ireland's Ambassador to the Vatican.[47]

records, by definition of where these men deserted to. See Michael Kennedy, 'Wrong to Assume All Deserters were Allied Veterans' (*Irish Times*, 15 February 2012) and Bernard Kelly, *Returning Home: Irish Ex-servicemen after the Second World War* (Dublin: Irish Academic Press, 2012).

44 *Dáil debates*, vol. 126, 4 July 1951, answer to parliamentary question by Minister for Justice Gerald Boland.

45 See Kennedy, *Division and Consensus*, and D. Kennedy, *The Widening Gulf: Northern Attitudes to the Independent Irish State* (Belfast: The Blackstaff Press, 1988).

46 See T. R. Davis, *Dublin's American Policy: Irish-American Diplomatic Relations, 1945–1952* (Washington, DC: CUA Press, 1998).

47 See D. Keogh, *Ireland and the Vatican. The Politics and Diplomacy of Church–State Relations, 1922–60* (Cork: Cork University Press, 1995).

Walshe was the first Irish diplomat to hold a posting at ambassadorial level. Secretary of the Department of External Affairs since 1922, he had directed Irish foreign policy for almost a quarter of a century. Walshe believed that the Vatican was a crucial actor in international affairs with whom Ireland as a Catholic country had a special relationship. Walshe was succeeded as Secretary by Frederick Boland, a career diplomat who had long been marked out as Walshe's successor. Boland's background in economics and finance was soon put to good use. From summer 1947 he became the driving force in Ireland's participation in the European Recovery Program.

Ireland remained a member of the League of Nations until its dissolution in 1946 but was not a founding member of the United Nations in 1945. Indeed it was Ireland's Seán Lester, who, as Deputy Secretary General, safeguarded the League from attempts by Secretary General Joseph Avenol in 1940 to hand it over to Vichy France. Lester became the League's last Secretary General in 1940 and safeguarded its spirit of international cooperation through the darkest days of democracy to hand it over intact to the United Nations in 1946. For his sterling efforts, he was comprehensively ignored by the founding states of the United Nations and forgotten, until relatively recently, in his native Ireland.

Many Irish diplomats were initially sceptical of the United Nations, considering that it would discriminate against formerly neutral states and that it was unlikely to facilitate an independent voice for the small states who would be reduced to obeying the great powers in the new international organisation. Nevertheless, de Valera was pleased when Britain and the United States intimated their support for Irish membership of the United Nations. Ireland's UN application, however, was vetoed by the Soviet Union in August 1946. Explanations for this ranged from the argument that Dublin lacked diplomatic relations with Moscow, to incorrect suggestions that Ireland had been pro-Axis during the war. More pragmatically Moscow knew that Ireland would be a pro-Western voice in the General Assembly in a period where the United Nations was dominated by the growing divide between East and West. For the following nine years Ireland endured a frustrating wait to enter the United Nations and in effect became a hostage to Cold War politics. Powerless, Ireland depended on a package deal between the Superpowers in 1955 to enter the United Nations.[48]

---

48 The 'pre-history' of Ireland's United Nations membership is covered in D. McMahon, ' "Our mendicant vigil is over." Ireland and the United Nations, 1946–55', in M. Kennedy and D. McMahon (eds.), *Obligations and Responsibilities: Ireland and the United Nations 1955–2005* (Dublin: Institute of Public Administration, 2005), 5–24.

Meanwhile Ireland had acceded to the International Civil Aviation Organisation (1944), the Food and Agriculture Organisation (1946) and the World Health Organisation (1948). It was a long-serving member of the International Labour Organisation (ILO), which became a United Nations specialised organisation in 1946. Thus Ireland engaged, as far as Cold War realities allowed, with elements of the United Nations system.

After failing to gain membership of the United Nations, the July 1947 Anglo-French invitation to participate in the Conference on European Economic Cooperation (CEEC) brought a new sense of purpose to Irish foreign policy.[49] The CEEC, which was to draw up an inventory of European needs for recovery to present to the United States, allowed Ireland to become involved again in mainstream European multilateral relations. It also required concentration on international economic and financial matters which had hitherto been outside the remit of Ireland's foreign relations. Minister for Industry and Commerce, Seán Lemass, not de Valera, represented Ireland at the opening of the CEEC conference. He reminded his audience that Ireland was a small economy which could play only a limited role in European economic recovery. Heavily protected by tariffs and reliant on agriculture, Ireland presented itself as a small state whose economy had remained underdeveloped for historical political reasons.

Since 1922 Ireland had remained tied economically and financially to Britain. The state held large sterling balances in London from which it funded its non-sterling imports by buying dollars. In August 1947 sterling ceased to be convertible against the dollar and Ireland, as a member of the sterling area pool, was forced to negotiate with Britain to maintain a supply of dollars to buy American imports. The economic and financial crisis of late 1947 demonstrated that the Department of External Affairs and the all-powerful Department of Finance had fundamentally different views of Ireland's place in the international economic system. External Affairs personnel attending the Havana conference that led to the formation of the General Agreement on Tariffs and Trade looked to develop a specifically Irish viewpoint towards the international monetary and financial system. The Department of Finance, by contrast, maintained that Ireland was best served by maintaining a close relationship with the Treasury in London. It was a difference of opinion that

---

49 See B. Whelan, *The Marshall Plan and Ireland* (Dublin: Irish Academic Press, Dublin, 2000).

would continue in the coming decades as Ireland slowly Europeanised its foreign policy and aimed for membership of the EEC.[50]

The Inter-Party Government of 1948 to 1951 continued the process of postwar change in Ireland's foreign relations. Comprising five parties: Fine Gael, the Labour Party, Clann na Poblachta, Clann na Talmhan and the National Labour Party, it held office from February 1948 to June 1951.[51] Led by John A. Costello of Fine Gael, the government suffered from the strains to be expected within a broad administration. Clann na Poblachta leader and former 'Chief of Staff' of the illegal Irish Republican Army, Seán MacBride, chose the External Affairs portfolio. For the first time in sixteen years control of Ireland's foreign policy was out of de Valera's hands and the head of government was not also the Minister for External Affairs. MacBride dominated the foreign policy of the Inter-Party Government and his choice of External Affairs demonstrated his desire to follow in de Valera's footsteps. MacBride, however, was new to international affairs and this was reflected in his idiosyncratic handling of Ireland's foreign policy. MacBride's inexperience made him vulnerable to alarmist reports regarding Ireland's position in the deepening East–West struggle. Disturbed on his second day in office by a report that the Italian left-wing press was claiming that the Inter-Party Government represented a leftwards shift in Ireland's outlook, MacBride instantly instructed that a message of Ireland's 'filial devotion' to the Holy See be sent to Pope Pius XII. Similarly when it seemed that a Socialist/Communist electoral alliance was heading for victory in the 1948 Italian general election MacBride used Irish government channels and his contacts with the Irish Catholic hierarchy to transfer over £50,000, close to €2,000,000 in 2016 figures, to Vatican contacts to support the election campaign of the Italian Christian Democratic party. MacBride sought to demonstrate how good a Catholic statesman he was by often seeking the opinion of the most powerful Catholic cleric in Ireland, Archbishop of Dublin John Charles McQuaid, on foreign policy issues. McQuaid regularly advised both Costello and MacBride, and a strong strain of Catholicism permeated the foreign policy of the Inter-Party Government.

50 See R. Fanning, *The Irish Department of Finance, 1922–1958* (Dublin: Institute of Public Administration, 1978).
51 The chaotic foreign policy of the Inter-Party Government is covered in *DIFP* IX and the most authoritative account is D. McCullagh's *A Makeshift Majority. The First Inter-Party Government, 1948–51* (Dublin: Institute of Public Administration, 1998). See also McCullagh's *The Reluctant Taoiseach. A biography of John A. Costello* (Dublin: Gill & Macmillan, 2010).

MacBride's initial dynamism was seen in his visit to Washington DC in May 1948 to negotiate with United States authorities on the financial provisions earmarked for Ireland under the European Recovery Programme (ERP). American policy makers maintained that countries such as Ireland that had suffered little or no war damage should receive loans rather than grants under the ERP. The 'Loans versus Grants' question was the primary issue facing Ireland over Marshall Aid. Ireland wished to avail of the ERP and play its part in the recovery of Western Europe, but Dublin protested its inability to repay Marshall Plan loans. Ireland was eventually to receive $18 million dollars of grants under Marshall Aid in addition to $130 million dollars of loans.

Costello's apparently off-the-cuff announcement in Canada on 7 September 1948 that Ireland was to leave the Commonwealth and that the External Relations Act of 1936, which set out Ireland's 'external association' with the Commonwealth, would be repealed, became the single foreign policy action by which the Inter-Party Government would be remembered.[52] Observers had little doubt that the External Relations Act was to be repealed; the question was when and how. No one expected Costello's announcement that the repeal of the External Relations Act was imminent and that Ireland's formal departure from the Commonwealth and the declaration of the Republic of Ireland would follow. What to the Irish authorities was a matter of altered legal language and expression regarding the Crown was for Britain a matter of deep political and economic significance. The impact upon Britain of Costello's announcement in Canada was far greater than Dublin expected. There would be consequences for Ireland and the loss of trade preferences and freedom of movement to Britain were hinted at. However, Canada, Australia and New Zealand encouraged restraint. Ireland and Britain ultimately agreed that there should be an orderly Irish departure from the Commonwealth.

Anglo-Irish talks in January 1949 accordingly covered practical, legal and political relations between Britain and Ireland consequent on the declaration of the Republic of Ireland. At the same time the British discussed with the Northern Ireland government the maintenance of the constitutional position and the territorial integrity of Northern Ireland within the United Kingdom following the declaration of the Republic of Ireland in April 1949. The Irish government could only watch as in June 1949 Westminster passed the Ireland Act and created a permanent Unionist veto on Irish unity.

---

52 See I. MacCabe, *A Diplomatic History of Ireland 1948–49. The Republic, the Commonwealth and NATO* (Dublin: Irish Academic Press, 1991).

The enhancement of partition in British law coincided with the development of a more aggressive anti-partitionism by the Inter-Party Government. At no time did MacBride or his officials attempt to understand the Unionist position in Northern Ireland. MacBride aspired to bring partition to an end during his term of office and defined a united Ireland as the primary goal of Irish foreign policy. He constantly raised internationally what became known derisively as the 'sore thumb' of partition. In the context of a world recovering from global war this won Ireland few friends and led to a deterioration of relations with Northern Ireland.

Despite its pro-Western outlook, Ireland was unenthusiastic about joining the various post-war collective security pacts proposed by the Western Allies. Joining a pact of which Britain was a member would mean acceptance of British military forces stationed in Northern Ireland. In the spring of 1949 MacBride privately indicated to the American government that Ireland agreed with the aims of NATO and would be prepared to join the alliance if Washington first persuaded Britain to end partition. This gamble failed. It underestimated the strength of Anglo–American relations and did not recognise Ireland's low strategic value to the Western Allies. NATO had sufficient access to facilities in Northern Ireland. The legacy of Ireland's wartime neutrality was compounded in some American eyes by Ireland's refusal to join NATO, and the outbreak of the Korean War in June 1950 led to some in Washington questioning where Ireland really stood in relation to the Cold War and support for the West.

In sharp contrast to Ireland's refusal to join NATO, in 1948 MacBride enthusiastically seized the opportunity for Ireland to become a founder member of the Council of Europe.[53] Ireland also warmly welcomed the May 1950 initiative of France and Germany to pool their coal and steel industries in what would in 1951 become the European Coal and Steel Community. Ireland subsequently joined the European Payments Union, although her currency linkage to sterling at parity, and membership of the sterling area, remained paramount. Ireland's main international currency and trade links remained with Britain. In the summer of 1949 sterling's devaluation against the dollar topped the agenda of British–Irish relations. As Ireland had a dollar deficit and only limited capacity to earn dollars, and because Ireland's foreign currency reserves were in sterling, British devaluation threatened Ireland's foreign

---

53 See M. Kennedy and E. O'Halpin, *Ireland and the Council of Europe. From Isolation towards Integration* (Strasbourg: Council of Europe Publishing, 2000).

economic interests. Yet when devaluation finally came on 18 September 1949, Dublin received only very limited advance notice from London.

Ireland was now outside the United Nations, NATO and the Commonwealth. With Marshall Aid coming to an end, Dublin had, apart from bilateral relations with fifteen states, only its membership of the Council of Europe and a range of European and international technical organisations to connect it to the international system. MacBride's attempts to internationalise partition and to bring about Irish unity by persuading the international community to act had failed. By the time the Inter-Party Government fell in 1951 Ireland had become increasingly isolated internationally.

Ireland's Heyday at the United Nations

When Fianna Fáil returned to power in 1951 Frank Aiken[54] replaced MacBride as Minister for External Affairs. The new minister was an acolyte of de Valera's and consciously modelled his approach to foreign policy on that of his Taoiseach. Aiken's first term as Minister, from 1951 to 1954, saw serious attempts to overcome the mismanagement of foreign relations under MacBride's term of office. Ireland sought to appeal to the United States in the Cold War and to play down the excesses of MacBride's adventurism.

Aiken left office in 1954 having steadied the foreign policy process and brought in a new Cold War normalcy in the wake of MacBride's overenthusiasm. Despite this, Ireland lacked a voice in international affairs. This would arrive when admission to the United Nations in December 1955 provided Ireland with a major opportunity to play an activist international role. Strongly influenced by Taoiseach John A. Costello, Liam Cosgrave, Minister for External Affairs in the 1954 to 1957 Second Inter-Party Government, ensured that Ireland's United Nations policy was influenced by the American and British Cold War agenda. The three principles on which this policy was based were, first, commitment to the United Nations Charter, second, the non-association of Ireland with bloc voting, and, third, the preservation of Christian civilisation. The tension between the second and third principles resulted in Ireland taking on a generally pro-Western, anti-Communist and pro-Christian alignment in the General Assembly.[55]

---

54 While there is no single-author biography of Aiken, B. Evans and S. Kelly (eds.), *Frank Aiken: Nationalist and Internationalist* (Dublin: Irish Academic Press, 2014) amply covers Aiken's long and at times controversial career.

55 J. M. Skelly, *United Nations*, remains the most authoritative account of Ireland's early years at the UN. Sadly, there is no comparable account for later years, though Kennedy and McMahon, *Obligations and Responsibilities*, covers some of the key areas.

On Fianna Fáil's return to office in 1957 Frank Aiken adopted a different approach. He prioritised the first and second principles and Ireland became more independent-minded in the General Assembly. Under Aiken, Ireland's United Nations delegation gained a reputation for principled action. In July 1957 Aiken proposed military disengagement from central Europe to defuse Cold War tensions. The following year he put forward a similar plan for disengagement in the Middle East. In 1957 Aiken supported discussion in the General Assembly of the representation of the People's Republic of China in the United Nations. This caused anger in Washington and in Irish Catholic circles in the United States. Yet Aiken's action was fully in accord with Ireland's belief that all states should be represented in the United Nations and paralleled de Valera's views on the admission of the Soviet Union to the League of Nations in 1934. Aiken also used the United Nations to promote decolonisation, generating tension with Ireland's European neighbours, particularly France and Portugal. He demanded self-determination for Algeria in 1957, attracting the ire of France. Ireland backed the UN General Assembly's Declaration on the Granting of Independence to Colonial Countries and Peoples in December 1960. It took a strong anti-apartheid stance against South Africa in the mid-1960s.

By the early 1960s Ireland had become more considerate of its Western neighbours while seeking to maintain an independent position that appealed to the Third World. Thus the US and Western European Group supported the election of Irish Ambassador to the United Nations Frederick Boland as President of the 1960 General Assembly. They also backed Ireland's election to the Security Council for a half-term (1962) in 1961 and backed Irish resolutions leading to the Nuclear Test Ban Treaty.

Peacekeeping

Taking on the obligations and responsibilities of UN membership, Ireland contributed to United Nations peacekeeping operations from 1958. In 1958 and 1959 small groups of Defence Forces officers deployed with the UNOGIL and UNTSO observer missions in Lebanon and along the Israeli–Egyptian border. In the summer of 1960 Ireland was asked to contribute to Opération des Nations Unies au Congo (ONUC), a large-scale mission to maintain law and order in the newly independent Congo. Ireland was chosen as a contributor due to its activist UN policy and its non-membership of Cold War military alliances. The mission, which began as a peacekeeping mission and ended in outright war was a step into the unknown for the Irish Defence Forces. It saw

Irish military forces, that had not seen active service since the Irish Civil War of 1922–1923, go into action in late 1961, with Indian and Swedish units, under the UN flag in an ultimately unsuccessful attempt to end the secession of the Congolese province of Katanga from Congo.[56]

The actions in Katanga, including the vigorous defence of an almost open location at the mining town of Jadotville by the 150-strong A-Company of the 35th Infantry Battalion, and the earlier deaths of nine soldiers in an ambush at Niemba in Northern Katanga in November 1960 revealed that better training and modern equipment were required if Ireland was to remain involved in peacekeeping. Though Commandant Pat Quinlan's forces at Jadotville ultimately were forced to surrender when their ammunition and water ran out, Quinlan got all his men out of Jadotville with only minor injuries. Twenty-six Irish soldiers lost their lives serving with ONUC by the time the mission concluded in 1964. These men were remembered for their sacrifice, yet it took until the 1990s for the Defence Forces to recognise A-Company's bravery and Quinlan's leadership and skills.

Another indication of Ireland's rising middle power role in the United Nations was the secondment of Conor Cruise O'Brien, head of the United Nations Section in the Department of External Affairs, as the Special Representative of the United Nations Secretary General in Katanga province in 1961 and the concurrent appointment of Lieutenant General Seán MacEoin, Chief of Staff of the Irish Defence Forces, as Force Commander of ONUC.

MacEoin was a safe pair of hands to oversee ONUC after the removal of the headstrong Swedish General Carl von Horn. O'Brien's was a much more volatile appointment. He interpreted his mission as being to end Katanga's secession and, with UN Secretary General Dag Hammarskjöld's authorisation, initiated a military plan to do so in September 1961 (Operation Morthor). The plan failed and O'Brien was blamed for acting outside his orders. Archive documents show conclusively that he did not do so and that he was unfairly blamed by Hammarskjöld. Hammarskjöld flew to Congo to try to engineer a peace settlement and was killed in mysterious circumstances in a plane crash during this mission. O'Brien ultimately resigned, writing his account of the period in *To Katanga and Back*, a strongly polemical work that was highly

---

56 Katanga's secession would ultimately end in 1963, as a result of further United Nations military operations. For more detail on Ireland's military involvement with the United Nations in Congo, see M. Kennedy and A. Magennis, *Ireland, the United Nations and the Congo* (Dublin: Four Courts Press, 2014).

critical of the UN and that remains an essential source for one of the United Nations' murkiest and most destructive chapters.[57]

Involvement in ONUC built on the smaller UNTSO and UNOGIL deployments and inaugurated a strong commitment to UN peacekeeping within Ireland. Ireland established a niche for itself in the UN with peacekeeping. Even before the last Irish contingents were withdrawn from the Congo in 1964, Irish peacekeepers were despatched to Cyprus as part of the UNIFCYP (United Nations Interim Force in Cyprus) keeping Greek and Turkish Cypriots from clashing. This was a policing mission, a very different kind of mission to what had become a war in Katanga. Peacekeeping became a defining element of Irish foreign policy. ONUC and UNIFCYP showed Ireland's commitment to United Nations peacekeeping and were added to in 1978 by another highly visible and dangerous deployment to Lebanon with UNIFIL.[58]

The Long Road to Europe

Irish engagement with European integration in the 1950s was limited to observation from the sidelines. Ireland remained economically on the periphery of Europe, with its industries sheltering behind protective tariff barriers. While Europe enjoyed a post-war economic boom, Ireland stagnated. Ireland's economic failures through the 1950s led to a critical self-evaluation. By the end of that decade, export-led growth and significant capital investment were seen to be the dual engines of possible Irish economic recovery. The protected Irish economy, in particular, its dominant agricultural sector, would be opened up. Ireland embraced free trade and competition and joined the International Monetary Fund and the World Bank in 1957.

Seán Lemass's term as Taoiseach from 1959 to 1966 encompassed a concentrated period of relatively significant growth. Ireland's new export-led economic policy began to produce results. Gross National Product grew by over 4 per cent in 1959 and 1960.[59] Ireland needed to expand its foreign

---

57 C. C. O'Brien, *To Katanga and Back: A UN Case History* (London: Hutchinson, 1962).

58 Although somewhat cursory and journalistic (as befits the style of its author), R. Smith, *Under the Blue Flag* (Dublin: Gill & Macmillan, 1980) gives an accessible overview of Ireland's post-Congo involvement with United Nations peacekeeping, concluding with Ireland's engagement with UNIFIL in Lebanon.

59 See J. Horgan, *Seán Lemass, the Enigmatic Patriot* (Dublin: Gill & Macmillan, 1997) for the early years of the Europeanisation of Irish foreign policy. Geary's *Inconvenient Wait* remains the best overall account of Ireland's entry into the EEC. The semi-official D. J. Maher, *The Tortuous Path. The Course of Ireland's Entry into the EEC 1948–73* (Dublin: Institute of Public Administration, Dublin, 1986) lives up to its name, though it is an essential account.

trade further. Lemass, a former advocate of protectionism, now believed that Ireland's economic regeneration could only come about by expanding foreign trade into Europe and joining the EEC. Europe moved to the centre stage of Irish foreign policy. Lemass was particularly keen on EEC plans to develop a Common Agricultural Policy (CAP) as its price guarantees and export subsidies would suit the agriculturally dominated Irish economy.

When Britain sought EEC membership in 1961, so important was British-Irish trade that Ireland immediately followed. Ireland applied for full EEC membership in July 1961. Ireland's economic shortcomings were evident and associate membership of the EEC was raised by the European Commission but ruled out by Lemass as suggesting that Ireland was economically underdeveloped. EEC admission was also drawn into question because Ireland was not a member of NATO. The state's non-membership of military alliances would complicate future European plans for foreign policy and defence cooperation. When accession negotiations began in October 1962 Lemass visited the capitals of the Six to emphasise that Ireland was sufficiently economically developed to join the EEC and that Ireland's military neutrality and non-membership of NATO were not obstacles to entry. Lemass's diplomacy broke the deadlock. The EEC Council of Ministers agreed to open entry negotiations with Dublin on the basis of full membership.

In January 1963 French President General de Gaulle raised doubts over Britain's suitability for EEC membership and vetoed London's application. The French President did not veto Ireland's application, but with its main trading partner apparently destined to remain outside the EEC there was no point in Ireland going it alone. British–Irish relations, so sensitive since 1921 and difficult during the Second World War, had improved considerably by the 1960s. An Anglo-Irish Free Trade Area which came into being in 1966 was evidence of this changed relationship. So too were regular summit level meetings between Irish Taoisigh and British Prime Ministers from the early 1960s. With Britain, Ireland tried to reactivate its application in May 1967, but de Gaulle again was unmoved. For the foreseeable future EEC membership was out of reach. Ireland would have to adopt a 'wait and see' attitude towards Europe.

Following de Gaulle's resignation in April 1969, Community enlargement became possible, but there would be no overnight Irish accession. Patrick Hillery[60] became Minister for External Affairs in 1969, replacing the United Nations-focused Frank Aiken and signalling Dublin's determination to

---

60 See J. Walsh, *Patrick Hillery. The Official Biography* (Dublin: New Island, 2008).

achieve EC membership.[61] After the agreement of the Six at The Hague in December 1969, entry negotiations began in June 1970, with face-to-face negotiations between Ireland and the Commission getting underway in September 1970. As a result of The Hague Summit's decisions to complete the Common Market, and take steps towards creating a European Monetary System and bringing about greater foreign policy coordination between member states, the Europe that Ireland was negotiating to join was a much more advanced entity than the original Common Market. The concerns facing Ireland were the five-year transitional measures for industry and agriculture, and the complex questions of the Common Agricultural Policy and the Common Fisheries Policy. The final negotiating session took place in January 1972 and Ireland's EC accession followed on 22 January 1972.

Membership of the EC involved participation in a nine-member European customs area with free trade between members and a common external tariff. Ireland would deconstruct its tariff walls and trade restrictions and accept free trade and globalisation. The hope was that by joining the EC, Ireland could belatedly join the post-war boom. Ireland obtained transitional arrangements under which it could gradually dismantle its own trade protection system between 1973 and 1977. Through a special protocol to the accession treaty, Ireland was also able to maintain aids and incentives to industrial development. Ireland would thus participate in a progressive manner with the EC's customs union.

From its first interaction with European integration in the 1920s in the guise of the Briand Plan, Ireland had been cautious about pooling sovereignty, and instead had favoured a Europe of the states through to the early 1960s.[62] On its own, Ireland was a small country, independent certainly but with little power to influence global events. In acceding to the EC, Ireland was sharing sovereignty, pooling it rather than losing it. Membership reduced dependence on the British market; it gave Ireland access to European export markets and a role in shaping EEC policies.

Ireland's accession to the European Communities required a change in the Constitution and so the matter was put to a popular vote via a referendum on 10 May 1972 and 83 per cent of the electorate endorsed membership. Ireland duly entered the Community on 1 January 1973. There was neither ceremony nor flourish in Dublin or Brussels to reflect the greatest change in Ireland's

---

61 The family of integration schemes including the European Economic Community (the 'Common Market') now being known collectively as the European Communities.
62 The text of Ireland's response to the Briand Plan can be found in *DIFP* III, no. 390.

sovereignty and international relations since independence. Ireland was now a member of the largest trading bloc in the world and of an economy that was the second richest to the United States of America.

Northern Ireland: The First Years of the Troubles

As well as seeking membership of the EEC, 1960s Irish foreign policy had seen Ireland for the first time taking a direct interest in Japan, China and Asia. This focus on the Far East was a direct result of policies of export-led economic growth. The war in the Nigerian province of Biafra in the late-1960s saw Ireland take a direct interest in African affairs and the development of a foreign aid programme.[63] But catastrophic events closer to home in Northern Ireland were to re-emerge in the late-1960s to distract from this global focus and become the primary focus of Ireland's foreign relations for the next three decades.

Dublin had failed to engage in substantive dialogue with Belfast since the unsatisfactory outcome of the Boundary Commission in 1925. Beyond regularly calling for the ending of partition Dublin had nothing approaching a 'Northern Ireland policy'. Few attempts were made to recognise mutual North–South interests. Low-profile secret contacts occurred between North and South, but they were largely at a civil service level and covered technical cross-border matters such as railways and electricity generation.[64] After 1959 Lemass proposed freeing North–South trade. The unilateral reduction of tariffs by Dublin on some exports from Northern Ireland followed. With the arrival of the more liberal Terence O'Neill, who became Prime Minister of Northern Ireland in 1963, Lemass's gestures were reciprocated and a carefully managed rapprochement in non-contentious areas commenced. This led to the first meeting of a Taoiseach and a Northern Irish Prime Minister since 1925 when Lemass visited O'Neill at Stormont in January 1965. O'Neill made the return visit to Dublin in February 1965. These efforts to normalise relationships were short-lived. O'Neill's modest efforts to introduce civil rights reforms to address Catholic grievances provoked opposition within his own Unionist Party and a violent response from loyalists. When Lemass's successor, Jack Lynch, met O'Neill for talks in December 1967 and January

---

63 See K. O'Sullivan, *Ireland, Africa and the End of Empire* (Manchester: Manchester University Press, 2014).

64 See Kennedy, *Division and Consensus* and Stephen Kelly, *Fianna Fáil, Partition and Northern Ireland, 1926–1971* (Dublin: Irish Academic Press, 2013).

1968 the situation in Northern Ireland was deteriorating. In April 1969 O'Neill resigned.

Through 1968 and 1969 the northern civil rights campaign's peaceful protests were violently attacked by loyalists, who suspected a nationalist agenda to the civil rights movement. Dublin, Stormont and Westminster were unprepared for the widespread rioting in Derry's Bogside and in Catholic areas of Belfast that erupted during August 1969. Dublin unsuccessfully warned London of the prospect of violence in Northern Ireland in the summer of 1969. The improvement of British–Irish relations in the 1960s did not stretch to Northern Ireland affairs. London instead saw Northern Ireland as an internal United Kingdom matter and said all was under control. The rioting and the burning of Catholic homes in autumn 1969 led to over 3,000 Catholic refugees from Derry and Belfast fleeing south for safety. Stormont was shown internationally to be incapable of managing the escalating crisis.

On 13 August 1969 Lynch announced that Dublin could 'no longer stand by and see innocent people injured and perhaps worse'. Ireland brought the growing violence to the attention of the United Nations and advised against the deployment of the British army to restore peace and order in Northern Ireland. British troops were deployed shortly afterwards. The attempt to internationalise the Northern Ireland crisis at the United Nations failed. Dublin realised that Western Europe and the United States were not prepared to intervene in what they saw as a British domestic matter. Fractures in Lynch's Cabinet came now to the surface. Hardliners viewed the Northern Ireland crisis as an opportunity to remove Lynch, whom they despised for lacking 'Republican' credentials, and they sought to use the crisis to achieve national unification. Demands grew for Irish military intervention and to arm Northern nationalists for their own self-defence. Lynch maintained a moderate line and rejected the use of force to solve inter-communal differences in Northern Ireland.

Lynch maintained that Dublin would not use force to solve the crisis and proposed a federal, unified state. He remained consistent in his efforts to seek a peaceful solution to the Troubles. He had to try to alleviate the sufferings of northern Catholics, minimise the radicalisation of the nationalist community, denounce IRA and loyalist violence, and, especially, prevent the Troubles from spilling over the border. He sought to persuade London that Dublin had a special interest in Northern Ireland, and that its advice on managing the crisis was valuable. This was rejected by London, even though the British government recognised Lynch's role as a moderating force. Dublin now worked closely with the recently-founded Northern Ireland Social Democratic and

Labour Party (SDLP) led by Gerry Fitt and John Hume, but its input on unfolding events in Northern Ireland was limited.

Violence increased in Northern Ireland in 1971 as the Provisional IRA intensified their attacks. The loyalist response targeted Catholic areas of Belfast, leading to a further 7,000 Catholic refugees fleeing south of the border. Stormont introduced internment without trial in August 1971 in an attempt to disrupt the IRA's campaign. National and international outrage followed 'Bloody Sunday' on 30 January 1972, when British paratroopers opened fire on a nationalist protest in Derry, killing thirteen people. Lynch temporarily recalled the Irish Ambassador to the United Kingdom from London. In a furious popular reaction to Bloody Sunday, the British embassy in Dublin was burned down.[65]

The British government suspended Stormont and introduced direct rule from Westminster. Edward Heath's Conservative government explored power-sharing in Northern Ireland. The result was the Sunningdale Agreement of December 1973 which created a short-lived, power-sharing executive comprising the main constitutional parties in Northern Ireland. It also envisaged a Council of Ireland with executive powers to deal with cross-border issues. The Executive was brought down by loyalist protests and a strike which paralysed Northern Ireland in May 1974 and the killing and bombing continued. (For more on the British–Irish reaction to the Northern Troubles, see the chapter in this volume by Paul and John Bew.)

Conclusion

Judged by the hopes of the early decades of independence, Irish foreign policy in the half century from 1919 to 1973 achieved considerable successes. Ireland's 'place amongst the nations' was secured by the mid-1920s. The state had begun to project itself outwards via the League of Nations and the United Nations. Bilateral relations, membership of international organisations and the stance adopted by Ireland, be it neutrality, independent-minded activism or even a presence at the conference table in multilateral relations, all reinforced the perception that Ireland was an independent international entity. The achievement of EEC membership a little over half a century after first emerging on the world stage as a Dominion in the British Empire marked the triumph of Irish foreign policy after the uncertainties of the formative years of the state.

---

65 See D. Williamson, *Anglo-Irish Relations in the Early Years of the Troubles*, 1969–72 (London: Bloomsbury, 2016).

However, to claim that Ireland's foreign policy was successful is a very broad-brush conclusion. Too often the self-satisfied, comfortable argument that, particularly at the United Nations, Ireland punched above its weight internationally fits an international self-image of a helpful, concerned Ireland. Ireland survived, Ireland looked after itself, and its fear of empires and encumbering alliances led it to follow a very singular stance which did bring with it international recognition. But there is a less positive side to be recalled.

Ireland was not particularly generous internationally from the 1920s to the 1970s. Foreign aid policy had made some small advances directly after the Second World War, but did not really establish itself until the late 1960s. Ireland, too, was notably insensitive to the plight of international refugees, arguing that until it could look after its own, it could not be expected to look after others. In fact, Ireland could not look after its own citizens in need internationally. The overseas adoption of Irish infants, undertaken for financial gain by Catholic Church agencies, with the knowledge of the Department of External Affairs, is an indictment of Irish society in the thirty years after the Second World War.[66] A stronger concern for human rights would emerge from the 1970s.

Neutrality was the diplomacy of pure survival during the Second World War, but it has more recently also been seen as selfish, inward-looking and immoral. Many forget that Ireland was only neutral until invaded, the latter being a nightmare scenario which, in no small part due to the skills of Irish diplomats, did not materialise. Recent debates have played down or ignored the real possibility of civil war in Ireland were Dublin to have willingly entered the conflict on the side of the Allies.[67] Neutrality post-war could be perceived as allowing Ireland a free ride in European security, particularly after MacBride's juvenile handling of NATO membership. However, since 1958 United Nations peacekeeping has ensured Ireland as a neutral plays a valuable international military role not initially open to many European states.

Perhaps the greatest failure of Ireland's foreign relations between 1919 and 1973 was towards Northern Ireland. Whether Northern Ireland was even part of Irish foreign policy was unclear. There was a complete lack of constructive

---

66 Official correspondence from the Department of External Affairs and the Department of Justice on the overseas adoption of Irish infants is contained in *DIFP* IX and *DIFP* X. For a narrative account see M. Milotte, *Banished Babies: The Secret History of Ireland's Baby Export Business* (Dublin: New Island, 1997).

67 See, for example, B. Girvin, *The Emergency: Neutral Ireland 1939–45* (Dublin: Gill & Macmillan, 2006) or T. Ryle Dwyer, *Behind the Green Curtain: Ireland's Phoney Neutrality during World War II* (Dublin: Gill & Macmillan, 2009).

thinking in Dublin when it came to Northern Ireland. The same tired anti-partitionist mantras were trotted out *ad nauseam*, as was the argument that since Britain had created partition, it could end it. Except for a brief moment in the 1960s there was no attempt to understand the Northern Ireland Unionist mindset. In reality Dublin also had little time for the plight of nationalists in Northern Ireland. Attempts to internationalise partition were a resounding and embarrassing failure and it took a decade of the Troubles for Dublin to convince London that Ireland had a role in Northern Ireland affairs. This was codified by the 1985 Anglo-Irish Agreement. The successes of Irish diplomacy in the 1970s and 1980s in Britain and the United States in creating a basis for a peaceful solution in Northern Ireland in the 1990s and drawing financial and popular support, in the United States in particular, away from the terrorism of the Irish Republican Army stand in marked contrast to the lacklustre approach of the previous 50 years.

Thus, the successes and failures of Irish foreign policy show a mixed balance sheet overall. It is the mark of a mature state that these can be reflected in the study of its foreign relations. International relations and diplomatic history developed late as fields of study in Ireland; it was not until the 1970s that either subject found a place, in other than cursory form, in the country's universities. This was also a result of the great secrecy with which Irish foreign policy was conducted; students could not study a field that gave little about itself away. Public opinion was often indifferent to Ireland's foreign relations and meaningful debate was stultified. There has since the 1990s been much more openness in official circles about the history and conduct of Ireland's foreign relations. A transparency now exists that would be both unthinkable and undesirable to those who made and executed Ireland's foreign relations between 1919 and 1973.

Those two pioneering generations of diplomats and their political and military counterparts had no prior structures or core cadre officials with which to create Ireland's foreign policies. With no prior structures, they yet gave Ireland an international role and voice. Modified by later concerns for human rights, development aid and environmental issues, their hopes and goals still resonate nearly one hundred years later in the core values of Ireland's foreign policies and as the foundations of independent Ireland's international outlook.

PART IV

*

THE LONG VIEW, IRELAND 1880–2016

21

The Family in Ireland, 1880–2015

LINDSEY EARNER-BYRNE

Take any family, living on a farm, that was born in the [eighteen] 'seventies or 'eighties. The father and mother live to a ripe old age and by the time they die even the youngest of the family is grown up. The family may well consist of six or seven. Of that one or two may at once be taken as having emigrated. Another may, if there is money enough, take up medicine – and will probably go the same way. Another enters the Church. On the farm finally there will be left a couple of brothers and a sister and as long as the mother at least is alive there will be little prospect of either of these brothers marrying. By the time they are free to marry they will have no desire to marry. . . . So they live on together, all unmarried; and of the entire family there may be the one married in Dublin.[1]

The picture of the 'typical Irish family' born in the 1870s–1880s that political economist, James Meenan painted for his 1933 audience represents the dominant narrative constructed about the 'Irish family' and its pathology between 1880 and the 1960s.[2] First, when contemporaries referred to the Irish family it was a rural farming unit they conjured; second, these families were understood to be created by marriage yielding several offspring; third, family members clung together until the surplus children were dispersed and the heir and dowry recipient were selected. Finally, emigration, religious life, the professions and/or the cities took care of the rest of the brood. Several things were implicit in this narrative: families were developed on the premise of emigration, upward mobility for one chosen member (via the professions) was aspired to, urbanisation absorbed the only eligible party – the one member destined to regenerate the family had to do so in the city – and, finally,

---

1 J. Meenan, 'Some Causes and Consequences of the Low Irish Marriage Rate', *Statistical and Social Inquiry Society of Ireland*, 15 (1932–33), 19–27, 26.
2 M. E. Daly, *The Slow Failure: Population Decline and Independent Ireland* (Madison, WI: University of Wisconsin Press, 2006), 3–4.

waiting and subservience condemned the remaining offspring to celibacy and the original farm unit to extinction. This was no happy tale; this was the story of crisis. The Irish family was deemed inherently dysfunctional by almost all commentators until the 1970s (and arguably beyond), because the fate of the family was wedded, in the contemporary mind, to the decline of rural Ireland.[3]

Even a cursory glance at the voluminous commentary on the Irish family between 1880 and 2016 indicates that it has been constantly under the social and cultural microscope. Contemporaries at any given juncture have counted, fretted over, lamented *and* eulogised the Irish family. However, as David Fitzpatrick has argued: 'The notion that depopulation was a consequence of "racial decay", exhibited in the avoidance of marriage as well as the ubiquity of emigration, was a propagandist construct of the later nineteenth century.'[4] Indeed, Donna Birdwell has suggested that this ' "gloom-and-doom" ethos', that pervaded all discussions of the Irish family and much of Irish scholarship on the subject, 'is itself a phenomenon worthy of examination'.[5] The exceptional behaviour that the Irish exhibited in relation to marriage and family formation, combined with mass and persistent emigration, fuelled real (and ultimately substantiated) fears about the decline of rural life – a way of life that had become symbolic of the 'real' Ireland.

While the debate about pre-famine marriage and the impact of the Great Famine (1845–1851) is hampered by the lack of concrete evidence, studies of local parishes in which church records survive indicate that prior to the mid 1840s marriage rates in certain parts of the country were between 40 to 60 per cent higher than the 1864 rate.[6] Furthermore, between the legal registration of Irish marriages in 1864 and the 1880s, the marriage rate in Ireland declined by 20 per cent, while the average European rate fell by only 7.5 per cent.[7] S. H. Cousens pinpoints the 1870s as pivotal in the establishment of fairly universal marriage patterns throughout the country because during this

---

3 Arensberg and Kimball's study of 1930s County Clare is an exception; they painted a picture of a stem family system that facilitated strong social cohesion. C. M. Arensberg and S. T. Kimball, *Family and Community in Ireland* (Clare: Clasp Press, 2001 [1940, 1968]).

4 D. Fitzpatrick, *Oceans of Consolation: Personal Accounts of Irish Migration to Australia* (New York: Cornell University Press, 1994), 547.

5 D. Birdwell, 'The Early Twentieth-century Irish Stem Family: A Case Study from County Kerry', in M. Silverman and P. H. Gulliver (eds.), *Approaching the Past: Historical Anthropology through Irish Case Studies* (New York, 1992), 205–35, 228.

6 According to McCarthy the records of Knockainy in County Limerick, which date back to 1820, indicate a marriage rate of 7 per 1,000. M. D. McCarthy, 'Some Family Facts in Ireland Today', *Christus Rex*, 5 (1951), 46–64, 55.

7 Meenan, 'Some Causes and Consequences of the Low Irish Marriage Rate', 20.

decade the west of Ireland came into line with the rest of the country as the marriage age increased and the marriage rate declined.[8] The Irish marriage situation remained remarkably stable until the 1960s; between 1870 and 1970 Ireland had one of the lowest marriage rates in the world. By the 1930s, Northern Ireland was also a 'demographic freak', having experienced a 'surge in celibacy' with 25 per cent of women and 22 per cent of men aged 45 years remaining unmarried.[9]

'The Land of Stem Families': Family Structure, Size and Surrogates

Both Birdwell and Patrick Clancy noted that Ireland has been portrayed in sociological and anthropological literature as 'the land of stem families'[10] well into the twentieth century.[11] Birdwell defined the five main features of the stem family as unitary inheritance, son inheritance, heir marriage, the co-residence of three generations, and the dispersal of non-inheriting siblings.[12] The classic reading of the Irish situation was that each of these components led to a slow marriage chain dependent on patience, obsequiousness, sexual abstinence and emigration.[13] Ireland seemed to 'float in a timeless void',[14] in fact it was quite explicitly framed as somehow beyond history by Conrad Arensberg and Solon Kimball in their seminal study of County Clare in the 1930s.[15] However, several case-studies have revealed that variables such as region, class and farm/family size influenced the degree to which families adhered to the tenets of the stem family system. Prior to 1911, most elderly people were cared for at home by their children. However, this situation

8 S. H. Cousens, 'The Regional Variations in Population Changes in Ireland, 1861–1881', *The Economic History Review*, 17 (1964), 301–21, 320.

9 L. Kennedy, K. A. Miller and B. Gurrin, 'People and Population Change, 1600–1914', in L. Kennedy and P. Ollerenshaw (eds.), *Ulster Since 1600: Politics, Economy, and Society* (Oxford University Press, 2012), 58–73, 67.

10 Birdwell, 'The Early Twentieth-century Irish Stem Family', 205.

11 P. Clancy, 'Demographic Changes and the Irish Family', in *The Changing Family* (Dublin: Family Studies Unit, UCD, 1984), 1–38.

12 Birdwell, 'The Early Twentieth-century Irish Stem Family', 210.

13 D. McLaughlin, 'Women and Sexuality in Nineteenth Century Ireland', *The Irish Journal of Psychology*, 15 (1994), 266–75.

14 Birdwell, 'The Early Twentieth-century Irish Stem Family', 205.

15 Arensberg and Kimball, *Family and Community*; Gibbon and Curtin have queried the universal nature of the stem system arguing that it was most prevalent among the medium-sized farm. P. Gibbon and C. Curtin, 'The Stem Family in Ireland', *Comparative Studies in Society and History*, 20 (1978), 429–753; See, D. Fitzpatrick, 'Irish Farming Families before the First World War', 339–74; P. Gibbon and C. Curtin, 'Irish Farm Families: Facts And Fantasies', 375–380.

would have lasted for only a limited period of a family's life cycle because the late age of marriage meant grandparents were older than their European counterparts.[16] Three generational households represented approximately 12–14 per cent of family groupings at any one time. Birdwell's study of households in Ballyduff, County Kerry, revealed that the bigger the farm the more likely the family was to deviate from the 'ideal' of unitary inheritance, while smaller farmers had a greater tendency to bequeath the farm to one son.[17] Furthermore, Liam Kennedy's study of four areas in Donegal, Tipperary and Meath indicates that primogeniture was not necessarily the predominant practice of inheritance in post-Famine Ireland.[18] He confirms that the larger the farms and the greater the assets, the more likely parents were to try to achieve equity in inheritance or gifts to children.

The gender aspect of inheritance was also less ideological than practical: sons were undoubtedly the preferred heirs, but when there was no suitable male, daughters could and did inherit.[19] Birdwell argues that the stem system was inherently flexible because the ideal was to ensure the 'preservation of the farm-family nexus' with the coequal values of the integrity of the farm and the integrity of the family being creatively balanced against one another in each successive generation.[20] Moreover, there is plenty of evidence to suggest that the Irish were creative in forming surrogate families through a network of celibate siblings, uncles, aunts and fosterage.[21] While much potentially divisive 'human congestion' in the home was dealt with by absorption into the religious orders or onto the many emigrant vessels,[22] many family disputes also ended up before the courts.

The behaviour of those who did not marry must be seen in the light of those who *did*: once the Irish married they had almost enough children to compensate for those who did not and for the thousands who emigrated

---

16 M. E. Daly, 'The Irish Family since the Famine: Continuity and Change', *Irish Journal of Feminist Studies*, 3 (1999), 1–21, 11.

17 Birdwell, 'The Early Twentieth-century Irish Stem Family', 213.

18 L. Kennedy, 'Farm Succession in Modern Ireland: Elements of a Theory of Inheritance', *The Economic History Review*, 44 (August 1991), 477–99, 486.

19 Kennedy notes this was more often on small holdings which would tally with the fact that heirs were harder to find for these holdings. Kennedy, 'Farm Succession', 495.

20 Birdwell, 'The Early Twentieth-century Irish Stem Family', 229.

21 T. Guinnane, *The Vanishing Irish: Households, Migration and the Rural Economy in Ireland 1850–1914* (Princeton, NJ: Princeton University Press, 1997); E. Leyton, *The One Blood: Kinship and Class in an Irish Village* (Toronto: University of Toronto Press, 1975), 27–8.

22 D. Fitzpatrick, 'Class, Family and Rural Unrest in Nineteenth-century Ireland', in P. J. Drudy (ed.), *Ireland: Land, Politics and People* (Cambridge University Press, 1982), 37–75, 65.

from each generation. The crude birth rate in Ireland had declined since the Famine: in 1935 it was 19 per 1,000 of the total population, compared to 28 in the 1870s and (approximately) 32 in the 1840s. However, the decline in the births per 1,000 married women aged 15–44 was merely 11 per cent. In other words, the decline in the crude birth rate was as a result of a smaller proportion of married women at child-bearing ages.[23] There was a significant negative correlation between the marriage rate and the fertility rate: families tended to be larger in the counties with the lowest marriage rates and this persisted in independent Ireland until 1961.[24] However, after 1921, the high birth rate in Northern Ireland was achieved by a lower marriage age and a higher marriage rate. Thus a similar birth rate masked quite different marital fertility rates in the two states: the difference is starkly revealed when one considers that the rate of children under 5 years of age per 100 married women aged 15–44 years was 122 in the Republic and 91 in Northern Ireland and 61 for England and Wales.[25] While Northern Ireland could boast the highest birth rate in Europe by the mid 1960s, this was sadly offset by the ignominious distinction of also having the highest infant mortality rate.[26]

Ireland had a high marital fertility rate until the late twentieth century, however family size was in slow decline by 1911. There were regional differences, but the most important variables were class and religion: the 1911 census reveals that professional couples had smaller families, and Protestant professional couples even smaller still.[27] By 1951, in the Republic, families of eight or more children had declined by 50 per cent since 1911, while families of six or seven children had declined by a third in the same period.[28] The Irish Catholic church was certainly anxious about the trend towards smaller families. In 1951 Father Cathal Daly – the future Archbishop of Armagh and Cardinal – warned about the spread of 'the contraception mentality', which, he argued, was 'fanned by the hot air of contemporary decadence with its

23 R. C. Geary, 'The Future Population of Saorstát Éireann and Some Observations on Population Statistics', *Statistical and Social Inquiry Society of Ireland*, 15 (1935–1936), 15–33, 19.
24 Daly, 'The Irish Family since the Famine: Continuity and Change', *Irish Journal of Feminist Studies*, 3 (1999), 1.
25 McCarthy, 'Some Family Facts in Ireland Today', 60.
26 D. Urquhart, 'Marriage, Fertility, and Breaking the Moral Code', in Kennedy and Ollerenshaw (eds.), *Ulster Since 1600*, 246–59.
27 C. Ó Gráda and N. Duffy, 'The Fertility Transition in Ireland and Scotland, *c*. 1880–1930', in S. J. Connolly, R. A. Houston and R. J. Morris (eds.), *Conflict, Identity and Economic Development: Ireland and Scotland, 1600–1939* (Preston: Carnegie Publishing, 1995), 92.
28 B. Walsh, 'Marriage in Ireland in the Twentieth Century', in A. Cosgrove (ed.), *Marriage in Ireland* (Dublin: College Press, 1985), 132–50, 142.

21. Bath night, Ballyfermot, Dublin, 1950s.

sexual licence, companionate marriage, emancipation of women, rejection of motherhood'.[29] However, by the 1970s marital fertility among Protestants in both the Republic and Northern Ireland was approximately two-thirds that of Catholics, irrespective of class or occupation.[30] Nonetheless, Mary E. Daly and Ciaran McCullagh argue that Catholicism is an 'inadequate' explanation for these differences: by the middle of the twentieth century Irish marital fertility was significantly higher than in other Catholic countries, such as Spain, Portugal or Austria.[31] Moreover, the Irish were perfectly capable of ignoring these teachings, when it was deemed necessary. For example, all clerical exhortations to marry younger and more often, fell on deaf ears.

29 Rev. C. B. Daly, 'Family Life: The Principles', *Christus Rex*, 5, (1951), 1–19.
30 L. Kennedy, K. A. Miller and B. Gurrin, 'People and Population Change, 1600–1914', in Kennedy and Ollerenshaw (eds.), *Ulster Since 1600*, 58–73; C. Ó Gráda and B. Walsh, 'Fertility and Population in Ireland, North and South', *Population Studies,* 49 (1995), 226.
31 C. McCullagh, 'A Tie that Binds: Family and Ideology in Ireland', *The Economic and Social Review* 22 (April 1991), 199–211; Daly, 'The Irish Family since the Famine', 1; M. E. Daly, 'Marriage, Fertility and Women's Lives in Twentieth-century Ireland', *Women's History Review*, 15 (2006), 571–85, 582.

22. Maguire family, 1960.

A notable attribute of Irish marriages until the late 1950s was a considerable age gap. For example, in 1946, in the case of half of the couples marrying, the age gap between husband and wife was greater than five years and for
a quarter it was more than ten years.[32] Perhaps this age gap 'accentuated male
dominance' and impacted on family planning.[33] In the late 1940s one Dublin
wife recalled: 'I think that it was really sinful that I was allowed to marry as
ignorant and as innocent as I was about the whole matter.'[34] Protests such
as this indicated a growing sense that people should be informed about sex,
inevitably leading to greater sexual autonomy and empowerment in relation
to fertility control. Nonetheless, before the availability of the contraceptive
pill, family planning required negotiation and male cooperation – were these
two things less likely to occur when the husband was so much older than his
wife?[35] In 1968 Ethna Viney acknowledged this difficulty: 'the rhythm method
is unworkable in a marriage where communication between husband and

---

32 Walsh, 'Marriage in Ireland in the Twentieth Century', 137.
33 Daly, 'Marriage, Fertility and Women's Lives', 582.
34 Humphreys, *New Dubliners: Urbanization and the Irish Family* (London: Routledge and
Kegan Paul, 1996), 139.
35 K. Fisher, ' "She was Quite Satisfied with the Arrangements I Made": Gender and Birth
Control in Britain 1920–1950', *Past and Present*, 169 (2000), 161–93.

23. Gaines family, 1957.

wife is not good'.[36] The decline in fertility coincided with the decline in matchmaking in the 1960s, rapid urbanisation and the narrowing of the age gap, all of which indicated a shift towards a more companionate marriage.

The Irish attitude to marriage and family formation made sense when seen as a communal response to Irish social realities and cultural expectations. Family was not construed along narrow nuclear lines, but was understood to encompass the wider kinship network, including those who had long since left Ireland and set up home elsewhere. Consider, for example, the history of Irish emigrant remittances: how else does one explain this global network other than as a manifestation of a wider understanding of family?[37] 'Moira' left Waterford in 1942 at the age of 14 years 'leaving the bed she shared with two sisters for a single bed in war-torn London'. In 2004, she recalled: 'I wasn't forced to come but I don't remember anybody saying I shouldn't. . . . I helped

36 E. Viney, 'Women in Rural Ireland', *Christus Rex*, 22 (1968), 333–42, 338.
37 Between 1847 and 1889 remittances of approximately £34 million per annum were sent to Ireland from North America (excluding dollar bills sent in letters). In 1932 alone they were £4 million, despite the US depression and by the end of the Second World War, they had increased to £9 million, by the 1950s Irish official statistics record a total of £11–12 million. Daly, 'The Irish Family since the Famine', 6.

24. Waterford, *c*.1890.

my family in Ireland when they needed it, I sent parcels and money when they had nothing, but it isn't remembered now or spoken about.'[38] Revolutionary leader and socialist, James Connolly, considered this practice proof that the Irish family was infected by a 'greedy mercenary spirit'. However, historian J. J. Lee was more sanguine, regarding the family as 'unconscious victims of their own collective values'.[39] Emigration was built into the ethos of family life. Irish families had many dependent children to provide for, with more than one-third of married men in the Irish Free State having three or more dependent children, almost double the proportion in England and Wales. In Northern Ireland the level of dependency was only slightly lower.[40] This situation was further exacerbated by the fact that young people had particularly poor employment prospects in most of Ireland. Women's employment

38 R. Ingle, 'They Won't be Home for Christmas', *Irish Times*, 4 December 2004.
39 J. Connolly, 'Woman', in *The Reconquest of Ireland* (Dublin, 1915), 225–6. Cited in M. Fogarty, L. Ryan and J. Lee, *Irish Values and Attitudes: The Irish Report of the European Value Systems Study* (Dublin: Dominican Publications, 1984), 114.
40 Daly, 'The Irish Family since the Famine', 4.

(married and single) steadily declined from the 1850s until there was a surge in the 1980s. It is hardly surprising that a distinguishing feature of Ireland's emigration statistics was gender equality: by 1926 Ireland was unique among developed countries due to its excess of males in the population caused, principally, by higher female emigration.[41]

'The Vanishing Irish': The Family, Pessimism and Urbanisation

Pessimism about the Irish family was a constant theme throughout the period and at certain historical moments it dominated social discussions regarding Ireland's future. In the 1950s this despair turned to panic as Britain offered large numbers of Irish young people viable economic alternatives. As Enda Delaney observes, Rev. John A. O'Brien's 1954 best-selling *The Vanishing Irish* captured the general sense of 'malaise and despondency associated with emigration in the 1950s'.[42] It also reflected the tendency to connect emigration with declining marriage rates and the death of rural Ireland. O'Brien opened his apocalyptic publication with the declaration: 'While Ireland has not formally disowned wedlock, her children enter into it so seldom and so late that the Irish nation is slowly but surely vanishing from the face of the earth.'[43] In this extraordinary collection of essays each writer connected Ireland's depopulation with unwilling bachelors and fleeing women. The portrayal of the Irish bachelor was everywhere unflattering: he was impotent, old-fashioned, gauche, pathetic and primitive. Admittedly, since the 1880s bachelors had been criticised for their status in many European countries in which the birth rate was declining; however, in Ireland there was a particularly harsh tone to the ridicule.[44] O'Brien cited a letter published in the *Times Pictorial* from an Imelda of Dundrum in Dublin, which linked emigration, Irish bachelors, religion and Irish marriage rates in a particularly vivid diatribe:

> Can anyone deny that the bachelors of Ireland are a toothless, gummy, shifty lot, as crude as you'll find them anywhere and with more feeling for an old

---

41 Walsh, 'Marriage in Ireland in the Twentieth Century', 136.
42 E. Delaney, 'The Vanishing Irish?: The Exodus from Ireland in the 1950s', in D. Keogh, F. O'Shea and C. Quinlan, *The Lost Decade: Ireland in the 1950s* (Cork: Mercier Press, 2004), 80–86, 81.
43 J. A. O'Brien (ed.), *The Vanishing Irish: The Enigma of the Modern World* (London: W.H. Allen, 1954), 15–45, 16.
44 K. Stomberg Childers, 'Paternity and the Politics of Citizenship in Interwar France', *Journal of Family History* 26 (2001), 90–111; M. Quine, *Population Politics in Twentieth-Century Europe: Fascist Dictatorships and Liberal Democracies* (London: Routledge, 1996).

pipe than for a woman who might help each one to a better life? ... The women of Ireland are a sorely tried lot. Virtue is preached at them from every corner – and I am talking here about the Church – but what national happiness can one expect if the women of the country are being frustrated.... I pity the poor Irish women over 40 or 50 who are unable to make a new start in life.[45]

Kevin Devlin's denunciation of the 'single and selfish' confirmed this picture, for him courtship Irish-style was an 'endurance test' in which 'placid lovers have travelled hopefully for so long that they seem to have lost all interest in arriving'.[46]

While it is easy to dismiss much of this writing as little more than hysteria, it touched on many of the fears troubling contemporaries: did the low marriage rate really indicate a rejection of rural Ireland?[47] If marriage was a 'vote of confidence in oneself and in the future',[48] then clearly young Irish people had lost faith in Ireland.[49] In a 1952 special edition of *Christus Rex* on 'The Rural Family', article after article declared the imminent death of the Irish family, assaulted by materialism, working mothers, birth control and divorce.[50] As the employment rate of married Irish women remained relatively static and low until the 1970s,[51] and birth control and divorce were both prohibited, what did these fears really represent? All these concerns emanated from the underlying belief that rural life was key to fostering the *right* kind of family life and the fear that rural life was dying.[52] Rev. H. Murphy's fear was commonplace: '[I]n the highly organized society of today family life is not flourishing ... one of the most important causes of this degradation is the increasingly urban character of modern civilization.'[53] The characteristics of the Irish urban family appeared alien and threatening to 'traditional' Ireland. Humphreys' study of Dublin families in the 1950s would have provided little comfort to the rural doomsayers:

> Dubliners worry about job security, not land. Parents seek their sons' betterment by social and occupational rise and their daughters' social rise by marriage, rather than homestead continuity and status stability. Savings go into

45 J. O'Brien, 'The Road Ahead', in O'Brien (ed.), *The Vanishing Irish*, 220–240, 231.
46 K. Devlin, 'Single and Selfish', *Christus Rex*, 6 (1952), 223–31, 224.
47 A. Ussher, 'The Boundary between the Sexes' in O'Brien (ed.), *The Vanishing Irish*, 150–63.
48 J. D. Sheridan, 'We are Not Dead Yet', in O'Brien (ed.), *The Vanishing Irish*, 177–92, 184.
49 Delaney, 'The Vanishing Irish', 85.
50 Rev. H. Murphy, 'The Rural Family: The Principles', *Christus Rex*, 6 (1952), 3–20.
51 F. Kennedy, *Cottage to Crèche: Family Change in Ireland* (Dublin: Institute of Public Administration, 2002), 63.
52 Murphy, 'The Rural Family', 6.
53 Ibid.

education rather than dowries, and children outstrive parents in ambition. Filial piety fosters achievement of higher status, not acceptance of ascribed status. Extreme parent reverence gives way to respectful familiarity.[54]

What was probably most troubling about Humphreys' study for those who feared an urban take-over was that he found happy families in which 'both sexes can and, as a rule, do achieve full social adulthood at an earlier age than the country people, and have better chances for social advancement to boot'.[55] Nor did he subscribe to the view that these shifts in family life would necessarily lead to secularisation, although he conceded it was a distinct possibility.

It was acknowledged that generations of men were being condemned to infantalisation by a social system that denied them independence or respect until, or if, they married. The folklorist, Caoimhín Ó Danachair opined that to 'see a young man of twenty-one or twenty-two guided and directed by his father is an unedifying sight, to see a "boy" of fifty ordered about by a doddering parent is distasteful in the extreme'.[56] Frequently, these middle-aged offspring were not remunerated for their labour: if they were lucky they received 'pocket-money', and even children that worked outside the homestead often had their wages claimed by their parents.[57] Humphreys believed this resulted in: 'maternal possessiveness, especially of sons; in the young men, a sense of inferiority (often covered by aggressiveness); feigned indifference to women; overt preference for male companionship and for sports, drinking and contention'.[58] While Hugh Brody's 1960s study of a community of 436 people in Connemara unearthed 131 people he adjudged as 'chronically sexually isolated: none of these people has a sexual partner in the house or the neighbourhood, and none can realistically expect to find one'.[59] Women were depicted as the drivers of departure, leading the 'big drift to towns and cities' resulting in too many women in urban areas and too few in rural ones.[60] By the end of the nineteenth century, as female economic redundancy increased, they were fleeing to urban Ireland, the convent or England with a basic education tucked under their arm.[61] Throughout these debates Irish

---

54 A. J. Humphreys, 'Migration to Dublin: Its Social Effects', *Christus Rex*, 9 (1955), 192–99, 198.
55 A. J. Humphreys, *New Dubliners: Urbanization and the Irish Family*, 35.
56 C. Ó Danachair, 'The Irish Family in Tradition', *Christus Rex*, 16 (1962), 185–96.
57 Daly, 'The Irish Family since the Famine', 6.
58 Humphreys, 'Migration to Dublin: Its Social Effects', 196.
59 H. Brody, *Inishkillane: Change and Decline in the West of Ireland* (London: Jill Norman & Hobhouse Ltd, 1973), 88.
60 McCarthy, 'Some Family Facts in Ireland Today', 50.
61 D. Fitzpatrick, 'The Modernisation of the Irish Female', in P. O'Flanagan, P. Ferguson and K. Whelan (eds.), *Rural Ireland 1600–1900: Modernisation and Change* (Cork University

young people were portrayed as impotent and helpless, but also selfish and materialistic. They were at once unwilling to sacrifice themselves for the sake of rural Ireland or the Irish family, but also the victims of selfish parents clinging to the reins of domestic power.

The explanation for Ireland's marital and fertility patterns lies in the confluence of various social, economic and cultural factors. Inheritance does not explain it alone, nor does the idea of the sexually gauche and reluctant Irish bachelor, or the overbearing mother, or the fear of the wife and mother-in-law encounter. Each of these explanations made up the meat of social commentary and have preoccupied many an anthropologist, sociologist and historian since. However, on some level and in certain situations each of these factors probably played a role and touched on deep social tensions and cultural sensitivities. De Cleir articulated the central dilemma for modern Ireland – rising living standards led to rising expectations (fuelled by emigration), which were hard to satisfy in rural Ireland as it then was: 'Immoral films and dollar aid, Sunday news-rags and Morris Minors, all come together in the same parcel. We must realise that many of the forces which make possible our comfortable way of living are the forces which make difficult the development of a healthy family amongst us.'[62]

Family Life: Gender, Morality and the Family

It is generally accepted that the 'match' and dowry system was widespread in Ireland by the 1880s, irrespective of religion or geography, reflecting the centrality of land and property to the understanding of the family.[63] While Northern Ireland urbanised in the 1920s, much earlier than independent Ireland, Elliot Leyton documented arranged marriages and an association with love matches and disharmony in rural Northern Ireland in the 1960s.[64] The match ensured that the status quo was maintained in relation to class and social status and, crucially, that any dowry was commensurate with both families' expectations and needs. Thus the chosen children were unlikely to have had much direct say in whom their marriage partner would be, although

Press, 1987), 162–80, 176; C. Clear, '"Too Fond of Going": Female Emigration and Change for Women in Ireland, 1946–1961', in D. Keogh, F. O'Shea and C. Quinlan (eds.), *The Lost Decade: Ireland in the 1950s* (Cork: Mercier Press, 2004), 135–46.

62 S. de Cleir, 'Marriage and the Family in Irish Life', *Christus Rex*, 6 (1952), 303–13, 308.

63 D. Fitzpatrick, 'Marriage in Post-famine Ireland', in Cosgrove (ed.), *Marriage in Ireland*, 116–31, 122.

64 Leyton, *The One Blood*, 32.

there is evidence that they could exercise a veto.[65] Parents, however, could exert considerable pressure. For example, in the early 1900s Edith Newman's Church of Ireland mother, who did not like her father's choice of groom, 'was locked in her bedroom "until she came round"'.[66] A marriage had many vested interests and the process had to be handled sensitively, particularly the installation of the new bride into her mother-in-law's home.[67] If this relationship was not a positive one, much misery ensued and there was considerable social commentary on the difficulties of this dynamic. In the late 1960s Viney and Leyton, writing about the Republic and Northern Ireland respectively, noted that the general social sense was that a mother-in-law and wife sharing a kitchen was 'an intolerable strain'.[68] The new wife had to manage domestic diplomacy, she was generally held responsible for the fertility of the union, and she became increasingly financially dependent on her husband as economic opportunities through selling eggs, butter and other products became more limited.[69] Joanna Bourke observes that a male child, in particular, was an important 'long-term investment' because he kept the land in the family and his wife's dowry added much to the family's resources.[70] In 1933, Meehan believed the widowed mother delayed many a rural marriage because she relied on her son's financial support.[71] This theory was still current in 1951, when McCarthy argued: 'The nexus between celibacy and the support of the aged is very evident.'[72] While in the 1960s, Brody described the tortured relationship between a widow and her son: the widow relied on her son 'John' and in their frequent rows he would threaten to go to England. She was often to be seen 'looking down the road, seeing if there was any sign of John's black car', fearing he had abandoned her.[73]

The transition into married life throughout rural Ireland was probably assisted by the division of labour within the home, which mitigated against 'a life of unrelenting and demanding proximity'.[74] The division of labour in

65 Fitzpatrick, 'The Modernisation of the Irish Female', 169.
66 E. Newman Devlin, *Speaking Volumes: A Dublin Childhood* (Belfast: The Blackstaff Press, 2000), 20.
67 Ó Danachair, 'The Irish Family in Tradition', 191; Humphreys, *New Dubliners*, 20; Brody, *Inishkillane*, 114.
68 Viney, 'Women in Rural Ireland', 336; Leyton, *The One Blood*, 26.
69 J. Bourke, *Husbandry to Housewifery: Women, Economic Change, and Housework in Ireland, 1890–1914* (Oxford: Clarendon Press, 1993), 263.
70 Ibid., 272.
71 Meenan, 'Some Causes and Consequences of the Low Irish Marriage Rate', 24.
72 McCarthy, 'Some Family Facts in Ireland Today', 49.
73 Brody, *Inishkillane*, 123.
74 Ibid., 111. For Northern Ireland, see Leyton, *The One Blood*, 25–38.

25. Clonbrock, County Galway, *c*.1901.

rural farming families was associated with each gender's social status, if either sex did a task associated with the other they were belittled or suspected by the community. According to Ó Danachair, if a woman was a poor housekeeper 'the neighbours were sorry for him but their sympathy was mixed with a feeling that he should have chosen a more efficient woman'. Likewise if a woman must assume a managerial role on the farm due to her husband's incompetence or 'worse still, if he was idle or shiftless or a drunkard' the community had a way of showing their disapproval of his failings.[75]

The idea of gender roles remained remarkably static throughout Ireland between the 1880s and 1970s. Mothers were mediators, and while a mother could be accused of 'domination by affection',[76] this was a passive power as her husband remained the head of the household, ultimately in charge of the domestic purse strings. He might have been generous or benevolent in practice, but it was still within his gift. The distribution of familial resources and marital fertility rates reveal the general subordination of women's needs

75 Ó Danachair, 'The Irish Family in Tradition', 189.
76 Humphreys, *New Dubliners,* 20.

and interests. The less food there was in a family, for example, the less food the wife received. For practical reasons she might have considered feeding the breadwinner was in her long-term interests, but it was assumed she would generally eat last and least.[77] Daly has also observed that running water, which hugely reduced the burden of women's domestic chores, appeared much less appealing to rural homes than electricity to supply their radios, many of which were bought instead of domestic labour-saving devices.[78]

The husband was not only the 'breadwinner', but also the public/political representative of the family until 1922 and 1928, when equal suffrage was introduced in the Irish Free State and Northern Ireland respectively. The Catholic Church's main argument against universal suffrage centred on the idea of these gender roles, as David Barry explained in 1909 in the *Irish Ecclesiastical Record*:

> while the wife has her well-recognised sphere of influence and authority in the domestic sphere of influence and authority in the domestic circle, the final word, even in that circle, rests with the husband, for he is the head of his wife, as Christ is of the Church ... she has only a consultative and not a definitive voice.... Catholic principles give no countenance to the movement for extending the franchise to women ... because the movement is a retrograde one, tending to supplant their position of real superiority by one of nominal equality.[79]

This line of argument was trotted out throughout the twentieth century to condemn birth control, married women's employment and divorce.[80] Even Humphreys' urbanised new Dubliners expressed similar ideas in the late 1940s. John and Joan Dunn were a 'typical' artisan family in Dublin and epitomised the new modern marriage in which couples were 'pals'.[81] Joan explained:

> Everybody in the family is much more closely knit now than they used to be. And that is especially true of husbands and wives. Today they are much closer than they ever were in my parents' day.... There is no doubt about it,

---

77 Ample sources confirm this practice. C. Cameron, *How the Poor Live* (Dublin, 1904), 11; T. W. T. Dillon, 'The Social Services in Éire', *Studies,* 34 (1945), 331.

78 M. E. Daly, '"Turn on the Tap": The State, Irish Women and Running Water', in M. Gialanella Valiulis and M. O'Dowd (eds.), *Women and Irish History* (Dublin: Wolfhound Press, 1997), 206–19, 208.

79 D. Barry, 'Female Suffrage from a Catholic Standpoint', *Irish Ecclesiastical Record,* 26 (September 1909), 295–303, 301–3.

80 See, for example, J. Newman, 'Socio-political Aspects of Divorce', *Christus Rex,* 23 (1969), 5–14. In relation to birth control see, T. E. Flynn, 'The Moral Argument against Birth Control', *The Dublin Review*, 173 (1923), 243–62; F. Hanna, 'Family Life: The Facts', *Christus Rex,* 5 (1951), 20–45, 38.

81 Humphreys, *New Dubliners,* 92.

then the women were the slaves to the men. . . . They simply did the drudgery of the housework and the men kept a tight hold on the purse. . . . The father was really the boss the other was subject to him . . . and I think many of the mothers were afraid of their husbands.[82]

Nonetheless, John evoked religious teachings as rationale for the fact that when there was a disagreement the father should decide: 'I think that is right and proper and as it should be. Even according to the teaching of the Church, the father is the one who should have the final say in a case like that.'[83] Similarly, writing in the Roman Catholic periodical *Christux Rex* in 1959, Ita Meehan asserted that 'motherliness is essential to the harmony of family life, the life of the community and the life of nations'.[84]

Families were regarded as fundamental to the transmission of religious teachings, practices and values, and the bulwark against religious dilution, hence the resistance to 'mixed marriages' by the main denominations. Thus, Irish marriages tended to be endogamous – like married like in terms of class and faith throughout the island of Ireland.[85] In 1908, the Catholic decree *Ne Temere* specified that partners had to agree in writing that their future offspring would be raised in the Roman Catholic faith and this was deeply resented by the Protestant churches.[86] In Northern Ireland marriage even between different Protestant denominations was frowned upon well into the twentieth century.[87] By 2001, only 10 per cent of marriages in Northern Ireland were inter-religious.[88]

'[A] moral institution that possesses inalienable and Imprescriptible Rights': The Family, the State and the Churches

The history of state involvement in family life in many senses began in the 1830s with the introduction of the national school system and the Poor Law.[89] There were complex ways in which this system supported/controlled poor families including institutionalisation, assisted emigration, food, clothing,

82 Ibid., 122.
83 Ibid., 99.
84 I. Meehan, 'Woman's Place in the Community', *Christus Rex*, 13 (1959), 90–102, 94.
85 Fitzpatrick, 'Marriage in Post-famine Ireland', 122.
86 D. Ó Corráin, *Rendering to God and Caesar: The Irish Churches and the Two States in Ireland, 1949–73* (Manchester: Manchester University Press, 2007), 184–91.
87 Leyton, *The One Blood*, 11.
88 *Northern Ireland Life and Times Survey*, 2001, cited in M. Hill, *Women in Ireland: A Century of Change* (Belfast: The Blackstaff Press, 2003), 189.
89 V. Crossman, *The Poor Law in Ireland, 1838–1948* (Dundalk: Dundalgan Press, 2006).

training, medical care and temporary shelter. The reality of the aged and infirm in the country's workhouses prompted calls for an old age pension, which was finally introduced in 1908 and embraced with gusto in Ireland.[90] The pension often represented the only source of reliable income in poorer households and resulted in greater household co-residence.[91] The Poor Law then began to focus on other cohorts such as impoverished mothers and children, and unmarried mothers. The Poor Law Act of 1889, for example, gave guardians control over deserted children and 'children whose parents were deemed to be unfit, either by reason of mental or physical incapacity or on account of "vicious habits" or "mode of life" '.[92]

While school attendance was not compulsory until 1892, there was considerable social and religious pressure to send one's children to school. Irish children became rapidly literate in English and for many families this enhanced their chances of successful emigration.[93] However, the school represented quite an intrusion into family life and autonomy. Children were no longer freely available to work for the family economy and outside influences had much easier access to the home via the classroom.[94] Children could be monitored: their bodies became maps of the home, indicators of neglect, abuse or anti-social values. Poorer families were more vulnerable to intervention, separation and / or incarceration for child neglect. Whatever about the benefits of school for children, Tony Fahey convincingly argues that compulsory attendance 'shifted the power of judgement about the issue from the arena of the family to the realm of public authorities'.[95] The Children's Act, 1929, extended the grounds for committal to an industrial school to include non-attendance at school, poverty and neglect. This mechanism became the vehicle for the greatest violation of the family unit; through it thousands of children were

---

90 C. Ó Gráda, ' "The Greatest Blessing of All": The Old Age Pension in Ireland', *Past and Present,* 175 (2002), 124–61.

91 T. Guinnane, 'The Poor Law and Pension in Ireland', *Journal of Interdisciplinary History,* 24 (1993), 271–91.

92 V. Crossman, 'Cribbed, Contained and Confined? The Care of Children under the Irish Poor Law, 1850–1920', *Éire-Ireland: An Interdisciplinary Journal of Irish Studies,* 44 (Spring/ Summer, 2009), 37–61, 55.

93 M. E. Daly, ' "The Primary and Natural Educator?": The Role of Parents in the Education of their Children in Independent Ireland', *Éire-Ireland* 44 (Spring/Summer, 2009), 194–217, 97; D. Fitzpatrick, ' "A Share of the Honeycomb": Education, Emigration and Irishwomen', *Continuity and Change,* 2/1 (1986), 217–34.

94 A. Ireland, 'Records of Pupils in National Schools: Samples from the Records of the National Archives of Ireland', *Irish Archives,* 20 (2013), 16–26.

95 T. Fahey, 'State, Family and Compulsory Schooling in Ireland', *The Economic and Social Review,* 21 (1992), 369–95, 392.

committed to the brutalising industrial school system.[96] Poverty was the greatest threat to family unity on the island of Ireland. In the south of Ireland, the first investigative commission into the industrial system in 1936 noted that poverty and neglect provided the grounds for 90 per cent of committals.[97]

Neil C. Fleming observed that the education system in Northern Ireland was 'the product of two centuries of inter-denominational antagonism and tension between interest groups and the state'.[98] After partition in 1921, segregation became further entrenched, despite the state's modest efforts to diminish denominational control and foster an inclusive Northern Ireland.[99] Crucially, the demands of the various religious groups led the government to bow to pressure and satisfy 'short-term demands at the cost of long-term political and social stability'.[100] In effect, the education system solidified religious, and thus cultural, differences within the community. Particularly after the Second World War, when intermediate education was provided to all, the majority of people in the state would spend fifteen years being educated/inculcated apart.[101] Hence in the North the potential for education to challenge segregationist instincts of the average home went unrealised and children were reared and schooled on a diet of fear and suspicion of the 'other' in their community.

Despite the deep religious and political differences that divided the island, the understanding of the family as a conservative, rural, Christian and patriarchal unit was broadly shared.[102] In the Free Irish State, the official response to the family was influenced by the dominance of the Roman Catholic church and, in particular, Catholic social teaching which was particularly wary of state intervention in family life. In 1925, when introducing the proposal to prohibit private member bills for divorce, the President of the Executive Council and head of the government, William T. Cosgrave explained to the Dáil: 'I consider that the whole fabric of our social organisation is based upon the sanctity of the marriage bond and that anything that tends to weaken the

---

96 L. Earner-Byrne, 'Child Sexual Abuse, History and the Pursuit of Blame in Modern Ireland', in K. Holmes and S. Ward (eds.), *Exhuming Passions: Memory and the Uses of the Past in Australia and Ireland* (Dublin: Irish Academic Press, 2011), 51–70.

97 *Commission of Inquiry into the Reformatory and Industrial School System 1934–1936: Report* (Dublin, 1936), 10.

98 N. C. Fleming, 'Education since the Late Eighteenth Century', in Kennedy and Ollerenshaw (eds.), *Ulster Since 1600*, 211–27, 211.

99 Ibid., 218–20.

100 Ibid., 221.

101 D. H. Akenson, *Education and Enmity: The Control of Schooling in Northern Ireland 1920–1950* (Newton Abbot, 1973), 165.

102 L. McCormick, *Regulating Sexuality: Women in Twentieth-century Northern Ireland* (Manchester: Manchester University Press, 2009), 8.

binding efficacy of that bond to that extent strikes at the root of our social life.'[103] These sentiments were given added validity in the 1937 Constitution of Ireland, which recognised 'the family as the natural primary and fundamental unit group of Society, and as a moral institution possessing inalienable and imprescriptible rights, antecedent and superior to all positive law'.[104] The male breadwinner/female carer ideal was enshrined in that document with the declaration: 'the State, recognised that by her life within the home, woman gives to the State a support without which the common good cannot be achieved.'[105] Finola Kennedy points out that while the first Dáil of 1919 had pledged to protect the well-being of children, the 1937 Constitution switched the focus to the family and 'the rights of the family as a unit and on to the protection of the family from intervention by the State, rather than on the rights of individual members of the family'.[106]

In Northern Ireland the government had little financial room to dictate policy, but as the British welfare state developed it struggled to keep pace as 'for political reasons it was considered impossible to ask Northern Irish people to accept inferior services'.[107] However, it was not until after the Second World War that the old Poor Law system was replaced by the welfare state, principally in the form of Family Allowances and a National Health Service. The latter was the most successful element of the Northern Irish welfare system and, as Peter Martin has noted, even the Roman Catholic Church, which had opposed tamer health initiatives in the south, accepted the NHS with only 'token complaints'.[108] However, the Northern Irish state was not inclined to use the welfare state to subsidise large families, which tended to be Catholic. Nonetheless, it was not able to weight family allowances in favour of smaller families due to accusations of anti-Catholic bias and Unionist fears that Northern Ireland would lose ground compared to Britain.[109]

In both jurisdictions, unemployment assistance/benefit introduced under various pieces of legislation throughout the 1920s and 1930s, represented a significant support for families. Its introduction underscored the state's responsibility for families that could not secure sufficient employment to survive and

---

103 'Private Bills for Divorce', *Dáil Debates,* 11 February 1925, vol. 10, no. 2, col. 158.
104 Article 41.1.1, *Constitution of Ireland* (Dublin, 1937).
105 Article 41.2.1.
106 Kennedy, *From Cottage to Crèche,* 123.
107 P. Martin, 'Social Policy and Social Change since 1914', in Kennedy and Ollerenshaw (eds.), *Ulster Since 1600,* 308–24, 310.
108 Ibid., 316.
109 Ibid., 318.

26. Family group, Waterford *c*.1923.

the rate was paid according to the number of dependents.[110] Assisting families to secure adequate housing also increasingly became a concern for the state, although in independent Ireland the state's record was particularly poor. The 1926 census offered a bleak view of the housing situation, in particular, high-lighting that Ireland did not fare well in comparative terms: 27.7 per cent of the population of the Free State lived in overcrowded conditions, whereas in Northern Ireland, Wales and England the percentages dropped to 18.1, 7.2 and 9.8 per cent respectively.[111] The 1944 Interim Report on Housing in Northern Ireland indicated that 24 per cent of rural houses were overcrowded and another 11 per cent were 'totally unfit houses'.[112] In 1947, the Rural Survey of Northern Ireland reported that one-third of families lacked 'sufficient money to purchase the necessities of life' and that 'the principal cause of poverty'

---

110 M. Cousins, *The Birth of Social Welfare in Ireland 1922–1952* (Dublin, 2003), 60.
111 Chapter 5: 'Housing', *Census of Population, General Reports, 1926, Vol. X* (Dublin: Stationery Office, 1934), 58, 61.
112 Mogey indicated that the situation was actually worse than the Interim Report. J. M. Mogey, *Rural Life in Northern Ireland: Five Regional Studies Made for the Northern Ireland Council of Social Service* (Oxford University Press, 1947), 207.

was 'the number of dependent children'. It concluded with the hope that 'family allowances may soon be introduced and, if they are sufficiently generous, they will do much to abolish this cause of poverty'.[113]

In the early 1940s both states contemplated a form of family allowances. The main champion of the legislation in the Dáil noted that the measure recognised that 'there should be no penalty for exercising a Christian man's right to marry and raise a family, in so far as the community can help it'.[114] The policy was also informed by gendered expectations of the family; for example, it was made payable to the father because, as the responsible Minister explained, 'we should not depart in the slightest from the principle that the father is the head of the family'.[115] However, Caitriona Clear argues that in reality many fathers signed the right of collection over to their wives, a reminder that policy and practice often differed.[116] Under the 1964 Guardianship of Infant's Act, men had to share guardianship of any children born within marriage with their wives. This was not the result of a desire to introduce the concept of gender equality into the home, but rather because of a series of disputes between the parents of mixed faith marriages regarding the religion of their children.[117] A combination of fears regarding the father's position and his grip on the family farm delayed the introduction of a succession act to prevent a man from disinheriting his wife and children. However, as one deputy in the Dáil remarked: 'In a country such as ours which recognises the very special position of the family as a moral institution ... freedom to disinherit one's wife and children is a paradox which cannot be defended on any ground.'[118] The Succession Act of 1965 entitled a surviving spouse to a proportion of the estate irrespective of the will.

In Northern Ireland the issue of guardianship was defined by the Guardianship of Infants Act, 1886 until the passing of the Children (Northern Ireland) Order, 1995, which outlined that legal parental responsibility for children was vested equally and permanently in both spouses if they were married to each other at the time of the child's birth.[119] The 1886 Act required the courts to consider the welfare of the child, the behaviour of the parents,

113 Ibid., 220.
114 James Dillon, *Dáil Eireann Debates*, 23 November 1943, vol. 92, col. 88.
115 Cited in F. Kennedy, *From Cottage to Crèche*, 218.
116 C. Clear, 'Women in de Valera's Ireland 1932–48: A Reappraisal', in G. Doherty and D. Keogh (eds.), *De Valera's Irelands* (Cork: Mercier Press, 2003), 104–14, 114.
117 C. O'Connor, 'Mixed Marriage "a Grave Injury to Our Church": An Account of the 1957 Fethard-on-Sea Boycott', *The History of the Family*, 13 (2008), 395–401.
118 Cited in Kennedy, *From Cottage to Crèche*, 227.
119 K. O'Halloran, *Family Law in Northern Ireland* (Dublin: Gill & Macmillan, 1997), 77–9.

and the wishes of the mother and father, when deciding issues of guardianship. However, subsequent case-law revealed that the common-law *prima facie* right of the father to custody of his legitimate children was not in fact challenged. While legislation enabled mothers to challenge this right in England and Wales in 1925 and in 1971, this was not enacted in Northern Ireland. As divorce was available in the North, the common-law assumption had a much greater impact there than in independent Ireland, and the northern courts routinely awarded custody to fathers on this basis until the 1990s.[120]

Behind Closed Doors: Domestic and Sexual Abuse in the Irish Family

A common theme in much of the public discourse was the idea that the family was vital to maintaining moral standards and social cohesion. McCullagh argues that the family played a 'key role in the ideology of Irish society', in order to mask or contain deep tensions within and between families regarding land, exploitation of family labour and the emergence of the stem family system.[121] To this list we should add gender tensions. Only when a comparative study is carried out can we assess if the Irish family was a more violent institution than its English, French or Italian counterparts, but there were culturally specific pressures on the family in Ireland. The high number of substitute families, brothers and sisters living together for a lifetime, the many people denied the status of full social adulthood until the 1960s, the lack of birth control or divorce, and the high level of female financial dependence on men – usually older men. This is not to suggest that these factors made the Irish family a more violent domain, but they offer an essential context when considering how violence may have manifested itself and how it may have been perceived, approached and resolved.

Carolyn Conley has demonstrated that in the late nineteenth century family violence was the second largest category to come before the courts, with nearly a quarter of all homicides involving family members.[122] Property was the ultimate source of power in Ireland, little wonder then that it featured so prominently in familial assault and murder cases that made it to the courts.[123]

---

120 Ibid., 34–8.
121 McCullagh, 'A Tie that Binds: Family and Ideology in Ireland', 200–5.
122 C. A. Conley, *Melancholy Accidents: The Meaning of Violence in Post-Famine Ireland* (Oxford, Lexington Books, 1999), 51–89, 83.
123 Conley, *Melancholy Accidents*, 51–89; P. M. Prior, *Madness and Murder: Gender, Crime and Mental Disorder in Nineteenth-Century Ireland* (Dublin, Irish Academic Press, 2008).

However, there was a general social acceptance of a certain level of violence in hierarchical relationships until at least the 1980s, which meant that such violence was often not perceived as a crime and often went unrecorded in the official domains of justice. Parents and teachers were expected to physically punish errant children (courts were still prescribing it until the 1950s),[124] and the husband and wife relationship was implicitly understood in a similar framework, hence husbands who beat their wives were considered justified if 'provoked'.[125] Thus in 1974 the barrister of a husband who had beaten his pregnant wife could inform the judge: 'This assault happened after severe provocation.'[126] This was a view peddled by women as well as men and was probably absorbed and accepted by many an abused wife.[127] Furthermore, the wife, self-sacrificing by definition, if truly heroic was expected to tolerate domestic violence in order to keep her family intact,[128] and due to financial dependence was often left with little other option.[129] The story of familial violence is one of its gradual cultural unacceptability; this was a conflicted, painfully slow, and often contradictory process.

The first campaigners against domestic violence in the late nineteenth century sought to challenge the assumption that 'as male sexual urges were uncontrollable, male sexual transgressions were excusable'.[130] Elizabeth Steiner-Scott argues that the Irish Free State was not willing to 'accept new feminist theories about the nature of domestic violence' and so it 'continued

---

124 M. J. Maguire and S. Ó Cinnéide, ' "A Good Beating Never Hurt Anyone": The Punishment and Abuse of Children in Twentieth Century Ireland', *Journal of Social History*, 38 (Spring 2005), 635–52.

125 Bourke noted that 'excuses' for domestic violence in nineteenth-century increasingly evoked poor housework on the part of wives. J. Bourke, *Husbandry to Housewifery*, 267.

126 N. McCafferty, *In the Eyes of the Law* (Dublin: Poolbeg, [1971] 1987), 48, 51.

127 A 2005 study revealed that 1:7 women and 1:16 men had experienced 'severely abusive behaviour of a physical, sexual or emotional nature from an intimate partner'. See, *Domestic Abuse of Women and Men in Ireland: Report on the National Study of Domestic Abuse* (ESRI: Dublin, 2005).

128 D. Urquhart, 'Irish Divorce and Domestic Violence, 1857–1922', *Women's History Review*, 22 (2013), 820–37, 826.

129 Steiner-Scott points out that this was an age-old dilemma for women in violent marriages. Crossman notes the workhouse was the chief refuge of poorer victims of domestic abuse in nineteenth-century Ireland. Wealthier women could, and did, file for divorce on grounds of cruelty until 1925. E. Steiner-Scott, ' "To Bounce a Boot off Her Now and Then": Domestic Violence in Post-famine Ireland', in M. Gialanella Valiulis and M. O'Dowd (eds.), *Women and Irish History* (Dublin: Wolfhound Press, 1997), 125–43, 143; Crossman, 'Cribbed, Contained and Confined?', 60; Urquhart, 'Irish Divorce and Domestic Violence, 1857–1922', *Women's History Review*, 22 (2013), 829–30.

130 S. McAvoy, 'Sexual Crime and Irish Women's Campaign for a Criminal Law Amendment Act, 1912–35', in M. Gialanella Valiulis (ed.), *Gender and Power in Irish History* (Dublin: Irish Academic Press, 2009), 84–100, 86.

to emphasise that the problem stemmed largely from an abuse of alcohol, not power'.[131] As with child abuse and neglect, wife beating was framed as a working-class problem. The cultural idea of the family as a primary unit of society afforded a selective policy of avoidance and interference depending on the 'type' of family in question. Undoubtedly, middle-class women were also the victims of violence in the home, but respectability hid them from prying eyes.[132] For working-class women it was the fear of the authorities that kept them quiet: they feared their children would be taken into 'care'.[133]

The Second Wave Women's Movement, which emerged in the early 1970s, played a crucial role in raising awareness of previously 'hidden' or taboo issues.[134] Several pieces of legislation introduced in the 1970s recognised the realities of violence within the family, for example, the Family Law (Maintenance of Spouse and Children) Act in 1976, which allowed for a husband to be barred from the family home. However, official resistance remained when it came to extending the definition of rape to include marital rape. It was not criminalised in the Criminal Law (Rape) Act of 1981, because it was feared that it would interfere with the 'intimate affairs of married people'.[135] The Criminal Law (Rape) (Amendment) Act 1990 made rape within marriage a crime; however, this piece of legislation continued to treat the victims of rape as suspect. Moreover, court cases continued to reveal the social and legal tendency to consider violent stranger rape as the most serious form of rape thus, implicitly, imposing a hierarchy in which the raped wife or partner was at the bottom of the scale.[136] The UK and Northern Ireland criminalised marital rape in 1992.[137]

Several studies in the late 1970s and 1980s revealed that there was 'a high degree of violence within marriages, families and households' in Northern Ireland.[138] In 1993, writing about Derry, Eithne McLaughlin noted the

---

131 Steiner-Scott, 'To Bounce a Boot off Her Now and Then', 143.
132 Urquhart, 'Irish Divorce and Domestic Violence, 1857–1922', 829–30.
133 K. C. Kearns, *Dublin's Lost Heroines: Mammies and Grannies in a Vanished City* (Dublin: Gill & Macmillan, 2004), 15, 81–93.
134 L. Connolly, *The Irish Women's Movement: From Revolution to Devolution* (London: Palgrave Macmillan, 2002), 90.
135 Minister for Justice, Sean Doherty, 'Criminal Law (Rape) Bill, 1980: Second Stage', *Seanad Éireann Debate*, 1980, 5: 14, col. 1337.
136 M. Anderson, 'Lawful Wife, Unlawful Sex – Examining the Effect of the Criminalization of Marital Rape in England and the Republic of Ireland', *Georgia Journal International & Comparative Law*, 27 (1998), 139–66.
137 The first conviction did not come until July 2002. 'First Marital Rape Conviction Recorded', *Irish Times*, 19 July 2002.
138 L. McShane and J. Pinkerton, '"The Family" in Northern Ireland', *Studies: An Irish Quarterly Review*, 75 (Summer, 1986), 167–76, 174.

prevalence and general sanction of verbal aggression by husbands, and the fear among women that this could result in physical violence:

> although domestic violence is officially illegal, it nevertheless remains socially sanctioned in a number of ways: the reluctance of the police on the ground to intervene in a domestic dispute; the same reluctance on the part of neighbours; the idea that the wife's behaviour provoked the husband; the perceived privacy of what passes between husbands and wives.[139]

Furthermore, the violence of the divided North added several dimensions to domestic violence: men had easier access to firearms, were likely to seek protection from membership of a paramilitary organisation, and were protected by a general community reluctance to involve the police.[140]

Incest was criminalised in Ireland and Britain under the Punishment of Incest Act of 1908 and this remained the guiding piece of legislation in the Republic of Ireland until 1995. Sarah-Anne Buckley has noted that in 1922 in Britain and Northern Ireland, legislators addressed impediments to the prosecution of incest by ceasing the hearing of cases in camera (closed court) and reclassifying incest as a felony.[141] However, in independent Ireland incest was legally treated as a misdemeanour and cases continued to be heard in camera. This had several implications: obviously, incest was not treated as seriously in terms of crime and punishment,[142] but also any public knowledge of and discussion relating to the issue was seriously impeded by the official silence. The removal of incest from public discourse increased the cultural tendency to see the family as a site of inviolate privacy about which no tales could be told.

It was the Kilkenny incest case in the early 1990s that is generally regarded as pivotal in changing public views on familial violence in the Republic.[143] Harry Ferguson situates this response in the context of the collapse of 'family centred ideology' that had hitherto resulted in the state's unwillingness to intervene in family life.[144] Indeed, a running theme through much of the

---

139 E. McLaughlin, 'Women and the Family in Northern Ireland: A Review', 553–68, 565.

140 Ibid., 565; M. McWilliams and J. McKiernan, *Bringing it Out in the Open: Domestic Violence in Northern Ireland* (Belfast: HMSO, 1993).

141 S. Buckley, 'Family and Power: Incest in Ireland, 1880–1950', in A. McElligott, L. Chambers, C. Breathnach and C. Lawless (eds.), *Power in History. From Medieval Ireland to the Post-Modern World* (Dublin: Irish Academic Press, 2011), 185–206, 186, 190. See chapter by her in volume 3 of CHI.

142 Buckley, 'Family and Power: Incest in Ireland', 197.

143 This involved the sexual abuse of a daughter by her father over a 16-year period. See, C. McGuinness, *The Report of Kilkenny Incest Investigation* (Dublin, 1993).

144 H. Ferguson, 'Abuse Inquiries and the Report of the Kilkenny Incest Investigation: A Critical Analysis', *Administration*, 41 (Winter 1993–1994), 385–410, 391.

professional debates on child abuse, incest and family violence was that the constitutional protection of the family had inhibited professionals and authorities when dealing with vulnerable children or women. In her report into the Kilkenny incest case, Justice Catherine McGuinness suggested that 'the very high emphasis on the rights of the family in the Constitution may consciously or unconsciously be interpreted as giving a higher value to the right of parents than to the rights of children'.[145] However, as noted, when it wished to do so the state proved more than capable of removing thousands of children from their family home to industrial schools. The answer is more complex and rests at the heart of the cultural reluctance to interrogate heterosexual relations, patriarchal understandings of sex, and the status of men and women within the family home and an implicit class bias when dealing with the family unit.

Reimagining the Irish Family: Lone-Parenting, Same-Sex and Divorce

By the end of the 1960s the Republic of Ireland had urbanised. In 1926, 1 in 6 farmers in the western region did not marry and secure an heir, by 1979 that was the case with 1 in 3 farmers.[146] In 1973, Hugh Brody portrayed a rural Ireland in which the familial tables had turned and rural parents now both feared and depended more on their children. Brody declared: 'Areas of competence have been freshly conceived. Sons quickly cease to be "boys" in the west of Ireland today.'[147] The percentage of marriages in which brides and grooms were of the same age had doubled between 1946 and 1979 representing 13.2 per cent of unions,[148] and the fertility rate of those that married between 1961 and 1981 declined by 38 per cent.[149] By 1986, 60 per cent of housewives lived in urban Ireland.[150]

Daly argues that 'Ireland's fertility revolution' coincided with the introduction of the contraceptive pill in the 1960s (it was available as a 'fertility regulator'), and an increase of married women in the workforce.[151] Irish families

---

145 Cited in Kennedy, *From Cottage to Crèche,* 123.
146 D. F. Hannan, *Displacement and Development: Class, Kinship and Social Change in Irish Rural Communities* (Dublin: The Economic and Social Research Institute, 1979), 196.
147 Brody, *Inishkillane,* 125.
148 P. Clancy, 'Demographic Changes and the Irish Family', in P. Clancy (ed.), *The Changing Family* (Family Studies Unit, UCD, 1984), 1–38, 12.
149 Walsh, 'Marriage in Ireland in the Twentieth Century', 140.
150 L. Collins, *The Irish Housewife – A Portrait* (Dublin: Irish Consumer Research, 1986), 7.
151 Daly, 'Marriage, Fertility and Women's Lives in Twentieth-century Ireland', 582.

were talking about limiting their families, but legal and gender inequality remained key obstacles. As one woman explained to Dorine Rohan in the late 1960s: 'We have had four children in five years, and we don't want any more for the moment – but my husband is very decent, he uses the withdrawal method.'[152] The Family Planning Act, 1979, legalised birth control for married couples, and several surveys indicated a predominance of 'natural methods' or no family planning among married couples until at least the late 1980s.[153] In 1986 the majority of Irish housewives surveyed believed that contraception was an 'acceptable and desirable thing', but there remained nostalgia for 'the idea' of the very large family.[154] Northerners also continued to express a marked preference for large families, with 85 per cent believing three to four was the ideal number of children.[155] In May 1962, the *Belfast Telegraph* described the North's attitude to family planning as 'befogged and confused by prejudice and muddled thinking'.[156] While legally accessible since the 1930s, birth control was only normalised and integrated in the general health services with the extension of the 1967 National Health Service Amendment (Family Planning) Act, in 1969. This Act permitted local authorities to provide contraception on social as well as medical grounds with no restrictions regarding marital status. In explaining the increased acceptance of contraception in the 1960s, Greta Jones points to the increased participation of married women in the workforce and the decline in marriage age.[157] The 1967 Abortion Act was not extended to Northern Ireland due to a strong opposition campaign.[158] Abortion remains highly restricted on the island of Ireland.

While marital fertility declined, unmarried fertility gradually increased throughout the twentieth century in the north and south of Ireland. These pregnancies were often hidden by absorbing the baby into the wider family, usually as the child of a married sister, sending the mother to a Magdalen asylum or a mother and baby home or on the boat to England.[159] In the 1950s

---

152 D. Rohan, *Marriage Irish Style* (Cork: Mercier Press, 1969), 67.

153 C. J. Carr, 'A Family Planning Survey', *Journal of the Irish Medical Association*, 73 (1980), 340–1.

154 Collins, *The Irish Housewife*, 64.

155 McShane and Pinkerton, ' "The Family" in Northern Ireland', 171.

156 *Belfast Telegraph*, 28 May 1962. Cited in L. McCormick, ' "The Scarlet Woman in Person": The Establishment of a Family Planning Service in Northern Ireland, 1950– 1974', *Social History of Medicine*, 21 (2008), 345–60, 350.

157 G. Jones, 'Marie Stopes in Ireland – The Mother's Clinic in Belfast, 1936–47', *Social History of Medicine*, 5 (1992), 443–58, 274–76.

158 McCormick, 'The Scarlet Woman in Person', 346.

159 L. Earner-Byrne, ' "Moral Repatriation": The Response to Irish Unmarried Mothers in Britain, 1920s–1960s', in P. Duffy, (ed.), *To and From Ireland: Planned Migration Schemes c. 1600–2000* (Dublin: Geography Publications, 2004), 155–73; C. Rattigan, ' "Done to

one observer noted: 'illegitimate births are frequently concealed, and young unmarried mothers are usually hurried out of the country "with a 10 pound note and the parental injunction not to show their faces at home again" '.[160] Ó Danachair explains that the most precious commodity a family had was its 'good name' and 'many people were quite ready to sacrifice the individual'.[161] In the late 1960s Leyton observed similar communal pressure in a rural Protestant town in Northern Ireland, noting that men were regarded as responsible for controlling the sexual behaviour of their wives, daughters and sisters, and pregnancy outside marriage was considered to 'lower individuals in the eyes of the community'.[162]

In the 1970s and 1980s various socially constructed issues were renegotiated and reformulated culturally and legally; for example, the status of the unmarried mother and the concept of illegitimacy.[163] The ideal of family life jarred with the realities for many people and the emergence of a new media meant that there was a forum and willingness to 'investigate' society. From this process emerged a new narrative of 'Irish hypocrisy' and the treatment of the unmarried mother became symbolic of this discourse.[164] Unmarried mothers had been treated in a very similar fashion in both parts of Ireland – condemned, isolated and institutionalised[165] – and the fertility rates outside marriage increased along similar lines in both states, rising approximately from 3 per cent to 15 per cent.[166] By the late 1970s the unmarried mother was either opting to keep her child (adoption rates collapsed by the end of the 1980s) or abort: a study in 1984 estimated that by 1981, 73.6 per cent of all pregnancies conceived outside marriage were terminated abroad.[167] The Status of Children Act, 1987 abolished the legal concept of illegitimacy and, Fahey argues, completed a 'normative revolution', which, 'signalled a new

Death by Father or Relatives"': Irish Families and Infanticide Cases, 1922–1950', *The History of the Family*, 13 (2008), 370–83; E. Farrell, '*A Most Diabolical Deed': Infanticide and Irish Society, 1850–1900* (Manchester: Manchester University Press, 2013); McCormick, *Regulating Sexuality*.

160 M. Frances Keating, 'Marriage-shy Irishmen', in O'Brien (ed.), *The Vanishing Irish*, 173–75.

161 Caoimhín Ó Danachair, 'The Family in Irish Tradition,' *Christus Rex*, 16 (1962), 185–96.

162 Leyton, *The One Blood*, 21.

163 Law Reform Commission, *Report on Illegitimacy* (Dublin: Law Reform Commission, 1982).

164 M. J. Maguire, 'The Changing Face of Catholic Ireland: Conservatism and Liberalism in the Anne Lovett and Kerry Babies Scandals', *Feminist Studies*, 27 (Summer, 2001), 335–58.

165 McCormick, *Regulating Sexuality*; L. Earner-Byrne, *Mother and Child*, 172–220.

166 McShane and Pinkerton, ' "The Family" in Northern Ireland', 172.

167 M. Nic Ghiolla Phádraig, 'Social and Cultural Factors in Family Planning', *The Changing Family* (Dublin: Family Studies Unit, UCD, 1984), 58–97, 79.

acceptance of sex and reproduction outside wedlock and reduced the importance historically accorded to marriage as the gateway to family formation'.[168]
Indeed, the unmarried mother was no longer alone, several other categories
of single-parent families emerged, a reality recognised by the introduction of
the Lone Parent's Allowance in 1990.[169] Similarly, in Northern Ireland in 1981
while families with dependent children represented 61 per cent of all families,
only 20.6 per cent of families fitted the male breadwinner, housewife and
children model.[170]

However, despite allies in the media and women's movement, the social
response to the unmarried mother remained ambivalent.[171] Abbey Hyde
noted that throughout the 1980s and 1990s the unmarried mother, while no
longer consistently portrayed as a 'moral danger', was repeatedly framed as a
'social problem' and a drain on the welfare system.[172] While expressed in different terms, the idea that the single mother undermined the 'legitimate family' continued to hold sway. In 1984, the Catholic Bishop of Limerick, Kevin
NcNamara articulated this fear, while attempting to change the tone in relation to the unmarried mother and her child: 'Their needs, however, can and
should be met on the basis of individual rights without resorting to the radical solution, the implications of which would be enormous, of substituting
a completely new understanding of what constitutes a family.'[173] More generally this concern was often framed in the fear of the emergence of 'man-
less families'.[174] In December 1997, AMEN Support Services was founded to
provide support for male victims of domestic abuse and to campaign for the
greater inclusion of men and men's experiences in the formulation of relevant social policy and legislation.[175] One of its main campaigns was in relation
to fathers' rights, particularly following a divorce.

While divorce had always been available in Northern Ireland, it was socially
unacceptable and faced opposition from all religious groups. It was reformed

---

168 T. Fahey, 'The Family in Ireland in the New Millennium', in L. Connolly, (ed.), *The
     'Irish' Family* (London and New York: Routledge, 2014), 54–69, 58.
169 A. Hyde, 'Marriage and Motherhood: The Contradictory Position of Single Mothers',
     Irish Journal of Feminist Studies, 2 (July 1997), 22–36, 24.
170 McShane and Pinkerton, ' "The Family" in Northern Ireland', 169.
171 For a contemporary medical example of that ambivalence see also, B. Powell,
     J. Dockeray and E. Swaine, 'Unmarried Mothers: A Survey of 200 Presenting for Ante-
     natal Care', *Irish Medical Journal,* 75 (1982), 248–49.
172 Hyde, 'Marriage and Motherhood', 24.
173 K. McNamara, *The Family Today* (Dublin: Irish Messenger, 1984), 7.
174 *Irish Times*, 9 November 1994.
175 www.amen.ie/Papers/110909_unmarried_fathers_IT.htm (accessed 23 September
     2015).

and simplified in 1979,[176] and divorce rates increased considerably from the 1990s.[177] In the Republic, divorce became the lightning rod for the defenders of the status quo in relation to 'family values'.[178] The first referendum in 1983 was resoundingly defeated, largely, it has been argued, because of a widespread fear that women and children would be the chief casualties.[179] Following this referendum, Bishop McNamara called on the traditional family to assert itself in a battle of values: 'if they feel at war with an anti-family culture that seems all the time to grow more strident.... [T]hey must make it clear to those who command the power and influence in society that a strong constituency exists for the support and defence of family values'.[180] The No-Divorce Campaign slogan during the 1995 campaign amalgamated various fears regarding the traditional family succinctly: 'Hello Divorce, Goodbye Daddy'. This referendum was passed, but only just, and Carol Coulter convincingly argued it was because of 'social and demographic change, rather than [any] ideological challenge to the anti-divorce arguments'.[181]

Conclusion

Between 1880 and 2015 Irish families underwent significant changes in terms of demography, policy and meaning, leading to alterations in the role, identity and expectations of their members. The momentum and interconnection of these developments reflected broader changes in relation to class, economics, state intervention, religion, gender and sexuality. In 1984, a survey of Irish values, revealed, 'It is clear ... that hell, the devil, mortal sin, and fear of damnation have all taken a bad beating.' However, it also reaffirmed that 'Ireland remains an outstandingly religious country', summing up a process of change that was anchored in the continuity of certain core values about kinship and faith, but that had enabled significant changes in values and behaviour.[182] This is a point sociologists, who have done so much to elucidate the Irish family, continue to remind us. In her recent volume on the subject Linda Connolly observes, '[T]raditional forms of family life ... continue and

---

176 McShane and Pinkerton, ' "The Family" in Northern Ireland', 172.
177 Hill, *Women in Ireland,* 189.
178 J. Newman, 'Socio-political Aspects of Divorce', 5–14, 7.
179 C. Hug, *The Politics of Sexual Morality in Ireland* (New York: Macmillan Press, 1999), 46.
180 McNamara, *The Family Today,* 21.
181 C. Coulter, ' "Hello Divorce, Goodbye Daddy": Women, Gender and the Divorce Debate', in A. Bradley and Maryann Valiulis (eds.), *Gender and Sexuality in Modern Ireland* (Massachusetts, 1997), 275–98, 287, 295.
182 Fogarty, Ryan, Lee, *Irish Values and Attitudes,* 105, 8.

27. Men embracing following the results of the 2015 referendum on marriage equality.

are sustained alongside new family forms emerging in contemporary Ireland, suggesting that in reality a complex tension exists between tradition, modernity and postmodernity.'[183] In 2013 Ireland continued to have one of the highest fertility rates among the twenty-seven EU states and the lowest crude rate of marriage,[184] however, almost 25 per cent of Irish children are currently raised in one-parent families, double the EU average.[185] In 2015 Irish people became the first to vote for equal marriage rights for same-sex couples. Irish primary school children are currently taught that there is no one type of family more privileged than any other through the 'Different Families, Same Love' campaign.[186] Though it would be misleading to give the impression that this plurality of vision in relation to the Irish family is uncontested, nonetheless it is legally and democratically enshrined.[187]

183 Connolly, 'Locating the Irish Family', 34.
184 http://ec.europa.eu/eurostat/statistics-explained/index.php/Fertility_statistics (accessed 20 January 2016).
185 Ibid., 18, 25, 27.
186 www.into.ie/lgbt/EducationalResources/ (accessed 23 September 2015).
187 In 2005, same-sex partnerships were legalised in Northern Ireland.

22

Institutional Space and the Geography of Confinement in Ireland, 1750–2000

CATHERINE COX

From the mid-eighteenth century, secular and evangelical philanthropists, social reformers, and later, penologists and public officials sought to convince legislators and elites of the efficacy of institutions as reformative sites. In these places, they argued, a range of concerns linked to the social dislocation and poverty associated with modernisation could be 'cured'. While Great Britain was one of the centres of this reforming intellectual ferment, this was a transnational exchange of ideas, part of a much broader pattern of development across the Western world and in colonial contexts. By the late nineteenth century, the landscapes of most countries were dotted with workhouses, prisons, lunatic asylums, hospitals, and reformatory and industrial schools. In seeking to understand this phenomenon, scholars alight on, and accord different weight to, a range of factors. These include: changing Enlightenment philosophies of, and mechanisms for, the management of public administration and welfare economics; alarmist fears of a 'disordered' society related to fundamental changes in economics and work practices; and changing social relations, usually associated with and articulated as 'class'.[1]

Until the 1970s most histories of institutional development were 'written as a narrative of reform', assumed the humane intent of reformers, and adopted a teleological approach. The revisionism of the 1970s, informed by political rights-based movements forced a radical re-think. New studies argued that these institutions were strategies of power, reflecting not only the state's

---

1 D. Rothman, *The Discovery of the Asylum* (Boston: Little Brown, 1971); M. Foucault, *Discipline and Punishment* (New York: Pantheon, 1978); M. Foucault, *Madness and Civilization* (1967); M. Foucault, *Birth of the Clinic* (London: Tavistock, 1973); A. Scull, *Museums of Madness* (London: Allen Lane, 1979); M. Ignatieff, *A Just Measure of Pain: Penitentiaries in the Industrial Revolution, 1780–1850* (New York: Pantheon Books, 1978); G. Stedman Jones, *Outcast London* (London: Penguin, 1971); S. L. Schlossman, *Love and the American Delinquent: The Theory and Practice of 'Progressive' Juvenile Justice, 1825–1920* (Chicago: University of Chicago Press, 1977).

authority but also class power.[2] These 'social control' models were in turn criticised as overly schematic, assuming the state exercised a monopoly of authority and conceiving of 'all social relations ... in the language of subordination'.[3] By the mid-1980s scholars were endeavouring to provide ballast to the humanitarian crusade on one hand or the 'conspiratorial rationality' of a ruling class on the other. Subsequent histories of institutions have chipped away at claims that there existed unanimity in support of a disciplinary ideology among political and social reforming leadership. These argue for greater 'agency' and resistance among the poor, contending that the state was not the only source of 'sanctioning' power. There were those among the poor, it is suggested, who differentiated themselves from the 'undeserving', the 'criminal' and the social and moral deviant within their own social grouping.[4]

In some respects, research on institutions in Ireland has followed this trajectory. There is an early body of literature mapping the development of individual institutions and the politics of welfare reform. Often commissioned administrative histories, many of these books are positivistic, uncovering with nationalist pride the precocious arrival of institutions to Ireland and the contribution that Irish reformers made to international debates on the efficacy of institutions. At a time when historians privileged Irish political history, these studies were important in marking out institutions as sites worthy of research. From the 1970s, Oliver MacDonagh, and R. B. McDowell, among others, complicated the paternalistic narrative, arguing that the state's intrusion into welfare and social arenas reflected British endeavours to control an unruly, violent and revolutionary population. Their work was concerned with the high politics of colonial administration rather than debates as to the nature and dynamics of class power and social relations.[5]

Mirroring developments in social history, the rate of publications on institutions increased from the 1980s. With growing interest in 'histories from below', more attention was given to marginalised groups such as children and the mentally ill. Histories also revealed the importance of sectarianism

---

2 See note 1.
3 M. Ignatieff, 'State, Civil Society and Total Institutions: A Critique of Recent Histories of Punishment', in S. Cohen and A. Scull (eds.), *Social Control and the State. Historical and Comparative Essays* (Oxford: Martin Robertson, 1983), 75–105; G. Stedman Jones, 'Class Expression versus Social Control. A Critique of Recent Trends in the Social History of Leisure', *History Workshop* 4 (1977), 162–70.
4 Ignatieff, 'State, Civil Society and Total Institutions', 90; N. Ó Ciosáin, *Ireland in Official Print Culture 1800–1850* (Oxford University Press, 2014), 91–107.
5 O. MacDonagh, *States of Mind: Two Centuries of Anglo-Irish Conflict, 1780–1980* (London: Pimlico, 1992); R. B. McDowell, *The Irish Administration 1801–1914* (London: Routledge and K. Paul, 1964); S. Palmer, *Police and Protest in England and Ireland, 1780–1850* (Cambridge University Press, 1988).

in the foundation of institutions.[6] A growing interest in women's history, which sought to recover women's contribution to Ireland's political and social history, revealed lay and religious women's philanthropic activity, much of which assumed an institutional character.[7] With notable exceptions, the nineteenth century was the focus of these investigations, reflecting, as discussed below, a readier availability of accessible archival records. The influence of MacDonagh is evident in many, including Jane Barnes's and Mark Finnane's accounts of the introduction of the industrial school and lunatic asylum systems to Ireland.[8] Thus, in different ways, the publications of the 1980s moved the history of institutions from the margins to the centre of specific, if very different, historical deliberations. While engaging with the concerns of Irish academia, scholars were influenced by international debates within their respective fields. Both Finnane and Barnes questioned the humanitarian foundational myths and endeavoured, with varying degrees of success, to move beyond administrative histories. In a response to the 1980s critique of 'top-down' histories, Finnane wrote an important article in which he argued for greater analysis of familial contexts and agency 'in reconstructing the place of incarceration in modern societies'.[9] Since then, scholarly and public interest in the history of psychiatry and of psychiatric institutions has continued apace with micro-studies of lunatic asylum districts revealing how institutions operated with, and were responded to, in local contexts.[10]

The institutions of the Irish Poor Law were once relatively neglected, except when considered in the context of the politics of famine relief.

6 J. Robins, *The Lost Children. A Study of Charity Children in Ireland 1700–1900* (Dublin: Institute of Public Administration, 1987); J. Reynolds, *Grangegorman: Psychiatric Care in Dublin Since 1815* (Dublin: Institute of Public Administration, 1992); E. Malcolm, *Swift's Hospital: A History of St Patrick's Hospital, Dublin, 1746–1989* (Dublin: Gill & Macmillan, 1989).

7 M. Luddy and C. Murphy (eds.), *Women Surviving: Studies in Irish Women's History in the 19th and 20th Centuries* (Dublin: Poolbeg Press, 1990); M. Luddy, *Women and Philanthropy in Nineteenth Century Ireland* (Cambridge University Press, 1995). See also D. Fitzpatrick, 'Women, Gender and the Writing of Irish History', *Irish Historical Studies*, 27 (1991), 267–73.

8 J. Barnes, *Irish Industrial Schools, 1868–1908. Origins and Development* (Dublin: Irish Academic Press, 1989); M. Finnane, *Insanity and the Insane in Post-Famine Ireland* (London: Croom Helm, 1981).

9 M. Finnane, 'Asylums, Families and the State', *History Workshop Journal*, 20 (1985), 134–48, 134.

10 C. Cox, *Negotiating Insanity in the Southeast of Ireland, 1820–1900* (Manchester: Manchester University Press, 2012); A. McCarthy, 'Hearths, Bodies and Minds: Gender Ideology and Women's Committal to Enniscorthy Lunatic Asylum 1916–25', in A. Hayes, and D. Urquhart (eds.), *Irish Women's History* (Dublin: Irish Academic Press, 2004), 115–36; O. Walsh, '"The Designs of Providence": Race, Religion and Irish Insanity', in J. Melling and B. Forsythe (eds.), *Insanity, Institutions, and Society, 1800–1914: A Social History of Madness in Comparative Perspective* (London and New York: Routledge, 1999), 223–42.

Local studies of workhouses were published but in the 1990s there was a reawakening of *famine* studies among academics. This was fuelled by the sesquicentennial of the Great Famine in the mid-1990s and influenced by Cormac Ó Gráda's pioneering research. Since then, as part of a shift internationally within Poor Law and welfare studies, historians have interrogated the post-Famine period, the recipients and mechanisms of relief, and the local implementation of national policy.[11] An institution that remains relatively underexplored by historians, however, is the prison. Criminologists and sociologists have published widely on the Irish prison system, with most focusing on the main personalities and structures of administration, whereas historians have tended to examine political imprisonment and individual prisons.[12]

In recent years, Ireland's institutions have come under sustained scrutiny. Since the 1990s research, especially on the twentieth-century history of industrial schools and Magdalen asylums, has coincided with, and was arguably prompted by, a national debate on historical institutional abuse of children and of vulnerable women. Currently, academics seem to be as captivated by institutions as the contemporary advocates once were. With some exceptions, most academic analyses have been pursued by scholars other than historians, who feel constrained by limited access to and by the nature of the primary sources. Nonetheless, historians were, and continue to be, involved in various official inquiries. Much of the research demonstrates an understandable desire to apportion blame; to identify the structures – state and religious – that allowed perpetrators to evade punishment and to uncover what was peculiar about the Irish experience of an almost global enthrallment with the 'institution'. Among scholars working on Irish material, this has prompted a revitalisation of theoretical frameworks

---

11 V. Crossman, *Poverty and the Poor Law in Ireland, 1850–1914* (Liverpool: Liverpool University Press, 2013); O. Purdue, 'Poor Relief in the North of Ireland, 1850–1921', in V. Crossman and P. Gray (eds.), *Poverty and Welfare in Ireland, 1838–1948* (Dublin: Irish Academic Press, 2011), 23–36.

12 T. Carey, *Mountjoy: The Story of a Prison* (Dublin: Collins Press, 2000); P. Carroll-Burke, *Colonial Discipline: The Making of the Irish Convict System* (Dublin: Four Courts Press, 2000); S. McConville, *Irish Political Prisoners 1848–1922: Theatres of War* (London: Routledge, 2003); W. Murphy, *Political Imprisonment and the Irish, 1912–1921* (Oxford University Press, 2014); I. O'Donnell and F. McAuley (eds.) *Criminal Justice History: Themes and Controversies from Pre-Independence Ireland* (Dublin: Four Courts Press, 2003); E. O'Sullivan and I. O'Donnell, *Coercive Confinement in Ireland: Patients, Prisoners and Penitents* (Manchester: Manchester University Press, 2012); C. M. Quinlan, *Inside Ireland's Women's Prisons. Past and Present* (Dublin: Four Courts Press, 2011); C. Reidy, *Ireland's 'Moral Hospital': The Irish Borstal System, 1906–1956* (Dublin: Irish Academic Press, 2009).

that identify metanarratives and situate power within specific authoritarian bodies, notably the state and the Catholic Church. The sociologist, Paul Sargent, deployed Foucauldian biopower in his work on industrial and reformatory schools, while James Smith, a literary critic, argued for an Irish architecture of confinement under which 'favoured responses to perceived social and moral deviancy' reflected 'esteemed conservative Catholic moral values'.[13]

This chapter offers an overview of themes identified in histories of Ireland's experience of the institution from the mid-eighteenth to the end of the twentieth century. It focuses on institutions that made claims to reformative capacities, that embodied the work of specific groups of social reformers, and that were, it is argued, shaped by 'similar economics of time' and 'order of surveillance and control'. Underpinning their establishment and operation were contested attitudes towards poverty that ranged from blaming the poor to regarding them as having a legitimate claim on relief.[14] When examined collectively, certain commonalities emerge across the various types of institutions and different geographical contexts. Admission to these sites was facilitated through the legal system as well as informal mechanisms and most of these institutions – state and philanthropic – were subject to some national inspection. There are, however, 'dangers in neglecting the distinctiveness of each of these realms',[15] conflating populations and ignoring regional differences. While some characteristics suggest uniformity, expressions of entitlements to relief differed not only across various institutional models but also between them and within varying regional contexts. Whether public and centrally-funded or voluntary institutions, criteria for relief, often based on religious belief, economic circumstance, and social position, were also defined by the moral state of prospective recipients. These institutions were core constituents of *both* welfare and criminal justice provision in Ireland for the period considered.

---

13 J. Smith, *Ireland's Magdalen Laundries and the Nation's Architecture of Containment* (Manchester: Manchester University Press, 2007), xiii–xvi; P. Sargent, *Wild Arabs and Savages. A History of Juvenile Justice in Ireland* (Manchester: Manchester University Press, 2013). For prisons, see E. O'Sullivan and I. O'Donnell, 'Coercive confinement in the Republic of Ireland. The Waning of a Culture of Control', *Punishment and Society*, 9 (2009), 29.

14 A. Gestrich, S. King and L. Raphael, 'The Experience of Being Poor in Nineteenth and Early-twentieth-century Europe', in A. Gestrich, S. King and L. Raphael (eds.), *Being Poor in Modern Europe: Historical Perspectives 1800–1940* (Bern: Peter Lang, 2006), 17.

15 A. Scull, 'Power, Social Control, and Psychiatry: Some Critical Reflections' in S. Armstrong and L. McAra (eds.), *Perspectives on Punishment. The Contours of Control* (Oxford University Press, 2006), 197–216.

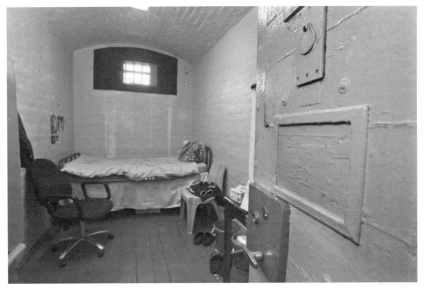

28. Interior of prison cell, Mountjoy Prison, Dublin, 1980s.

Institutional Landscapes

The contexts for the introduction of these institutions to Ireland varied, reflecting local and international circumstances. Throughout the eighteenth and early nineteenth centuries, prompted by an increasing concern with a range of economic and social issues, legislation was enacted in areas such as public health, law and order, and prison reform. The Irish parliament and, after Union in 1800, Westminster were variously, scholars argue, compensating for a weak voluntary sector, a neglectful local elite, and poor local government while also seeking to bind Ireland more closely to Britain.[16] In the early 1700s, for the Irish, as for most European poor, there was no 'legally defined Poor Law system' such as the English Elizabethan Poor Law. The problem of Irish poverty was, however, a vexatious issue, repeatedly commented on in travel writing and the subject of numerous parliamentary inquiries. With a view to addressing it and deterring vagrancy, punitive workhouses and houses of industry were established in the 1700s.[17] A formal and more comprehensive

16 V. Crossman, 'The Growth in the State in Nineteenth-century Ireland', in J. Kelly (ed.), *The Cambridge History of Ireland. Volume 3: Ireland, c.1730–c.1880* (Cambridge University Press, 2018).
17 Robins, *The Lost Children*, 15–55.

poor law system was introduced under the 1838 Irish Poor Relief Act. One of the most extensive state-funded programmes of institutional intervention, it was based on the 'New' Poor Law of 1834, which dismantled the old paro-chial-based system in operation in England and Wales. Rejecting 'indiscrimi-nate' relief, regarded as expensive, corrupt and inefficient, poor law relief was based on the workhouse model, underpinned by the doctrine of 'less eligibil-ity', with the poor divided into the 'deserving' and 'undeserving'.[18] Financed through a local property tax, the new workhouses catered for the 'deserving poor' – the destitute, the disabled and the aged – in normal economic con-ditions. From inception, the Poor Law and its workhouses were unpopular in Ireland, distrusted as a 'foreign' imposition unsuited to Irish conditions.[19] Within a decade, the workhouses were engulfed by the Great Famine and soon became dreaded places, cementing their unpopularity.

In addition, specific population groups were increasingly differentiated within, and diverted from, general institutions into new specialist establish-ments as campaigners and officials redefined models of provision. This can be traced to the eighteenth-century treatment of children and the insane. By the end of that century, the Dublin workhouse had been re-designated as a Foundling Hospital with the 'general poor' redirected to the Dublin house of industry.[20] In a similar vein, social reformers criticised, as out of step with changing philosophies on the treatment of insanity, the practice of incarcerat-ing the insane in non-specialists institutions. In advocating for change, they drew on the theories of Philip Pinel, Benjamin Rush and the Tuke family's York Retreat, England.[21] In Ireland, this culminated in the 1817 act that introduced a public asylum system. Several phases of institutional expansion followed, increasing the numbers and size of asylums. By 1904, there were twenty-two across Ireland, with 16,537 beds, though many were overcrowded.[22]

In the same period, prisons were championed as a response to the ending of transportation to the American colonies, anxieties about criminality asso-ciated with economic and demographic change, and disquiet about capital and corporal punishment. The late eighteenth-century prison reformers who visited Ireland – John Howard and Elizabeth Fry – were not only horrified at the systematic abuses in local gaols and bridewells, alongside their appalling

---

18 M. A. Crowther, *The English Workhouse System, 1834–1929. The History of an English Social Institution* (Athens, GA: University of Georgia Press, 1983).
19 P. Gray, *The Making of the Irish Poor Law* (Manchester: Manchester University Press, 2009).
20 Robins, *Lost Children*, 12–17; 29.
21 Cox, *Negotiating Insanity,* 1–6.
22 Finnane, *Insanity*, 227.

lack of hygiene, but were critical of the ineffective nature of existing forms of prison punishment.[23] This reforming zeal, alongside the emerging penological theories then circulating through the Western world, culminated in the 'invention' of the modern prison in the mid-nineteenth century. The apex of prison reform in Ireland is associated with the establishment of Mountjoy (1850) (see Illustration 28). It was based on Pentonville, opened in London in 1842, which in turn had been shaped by penal theories associated with the Eastern State Penitentiary in Philadelphia. The architectural design of each allowed for separate cellular confinement and the implementation of the 'separate system', modified in each context.[24] The separate system at Mountjoy was further adjusted when Sir Walter Crofton, Chairman of the Convict Prisons (Ireland) from 1854, introduced the 'intermediate' or mark system.[25] A focus on reward characterised this system, distinguished it from the English, and proved of considerable interest to international penologists and prison congresses.[26] The convict system, centred on Mountjoy, operated in parallel with a network of local prisons. In 1878, the General Prisons Board was established to manage both convict and local prisons.[27]

The prison environment was repeatedly identified as inappropriate for young, especially, first-time offenders, who, it was assumed, would become hardened criminals through association with adult prisoners. Jeremiah Fitzpatrick, the first inspector-general of prisons, was a particularly vocal critic of the practice of confining children. By the 1850s, the debate on juvenile criminality was a global one, with extensive commentary on the presence on city streets of apparently unsupervised young people who were either actively involved in criminality or in danger of becoming so.[28] Observers associated juvenile criminality with the large number of Famine orphans confined in prisons and workhouses or to be found wandering, and argued that there was a particular urgency about the 'problem' in Ireland. While sympathetic to

23 R. Porter, 'Howard's Beginning: Prisons, Disease, Hygiene'; A. Summers, 'Elizabeth Fry and Mid-Nineteenth Century Reform', in R. Creese, W. F. Bynum and J. Bearn (eds.), *The Health of Prisoners* (Amsterdam: Rodopi, 1995), 5–26, 83–101.
24 Carey, *Mountjoy*, 53–5; W. J. Forsythe, *The Reform of Prisoners 1830–1900* (London: Croom Helm, 1987).
25 E. Dooley, 'Sir Walter Crofton and the Irish or Intermediate System of Prison Discipline', in O'Donnell and McAuley (eds.), *Criminal Justice History*, 196–213.
26 L. Goldman, *Science, Reform and Politics in Victorian Britain. The Social Science Association, 1857–1886* (Cambridge University Press, 2002), 158–9.
27 Carey, *Mountjoy*, 124.
28 P. Cox and H. Shore, *Becoming Delinquent: British and European Youth 1650–1950* (Aldershot: Ashgate, 2002); H. Ellis, *Juvenile Delinquency and the Limits of Western Influence 1850–2000* (Houndmills: Palgrave Macmillan, 2014).

Famine orphans, the Irish prison inspectors, and other contributors, repeatedly stressed 'the great social peril' in failing to 'take timely and effective measures to root up, in each individual case, the seed-plot of crime, and thus prevent the growth of the whole tree of adult criminality'.[29] They supported the industrial and reformatory schools for children, hoping industrial schools would compensate for the failure to provide industrial training in Charter Schools and in workhouses.[30] These campaigners again drew inspiration from continental and American 'experiments' as well as from institutions in Britain.[31] Crofton, an influential advocate, visited many of these and through his involvement in the British Social Science Association met Mary Carpenter, an important figure in the English National Reformatory Union, which supported these schools.

Modelled on the English version, reformatory schools were introduced to Ireland in 1858. Industrial schools followed in 1868 during Crofton's tenure as 'special commissioner of prisons and reformatory schools' (1868–1869). Industrial schools became the larger of the two systems; by 1872, fifty-two had been certified, catering to 4,251 children. A public bias in support of girls' schools was evident immediately; of the fifty-six operating in 1880, thirty-five were for girls. In the north-east, the expansion of the Ulster linen industry from the 1870s provided young girls with employment opportunities, and there, industrial school provision for boys received more 'prompt attention'.[32] The delay in legislating for these schools in Ireland has been ascribed to anxieties concerning their management and religious ethos.[33] In England, the industrial school movement was closely associated with Evangelicalism, which placed spiritual reflection at the centre of moral reform.[34] In Ireland, there was intense confessional rivalry in the 1850s and 1860s related to the consolidation of the churches. Roman Catholic orphanages expanded while organisations such as the Anglican Irish Church Mission became more active, leading to conflict.[35] Given the heightened position accorded to spirituality within

29 W. H. Pim, *On the Importance of Reformatory Establishments for Juvenile Delinquents* (Dublin: Hodges and Smith, 1854), 8.
30 Barnes, *Irish Industrial Schools*, 15; K. Milne, *The Irish Charter Schools 1730–1830* (Dublin: Four Courts Press, 1997).
31 Sargent, *Wild Arabs*, 13; Barnes, *Irish Industrial Schools*, 22.
32 U. Convery, "Locked in the Past": An Historical Analysis of the Legal Framework of Custody for Children in Northern Ireland', *Journal of European Criminology*, 11 (2014), 251–69, 257.
33 Sargent, *Wild Arabs*, 13.
34 Goldman, *Science, Reform and Politics*, 44.
35 M. Luddy, *Women and Philanthropy in Nineteenth Century Ireland* (Cambridge University Press, 1995), 38–41.

both lay and religious theories of reformation, institutions were viewed with suspicion and monitored for evidence of proselytising, especially those that were state-run with predominantly Church of Ireland managing boards.[36] In this context, Roman Catholic MPs and clergy sought assurances that industrial and reformatory schools would be managed according to confessional divisions. As a result, religious bodies, predominantly, but not exclusively, Catholic sisters and brothers, became responsible for their management.

By the turn of the twentieth century, most reformatory schools had closed down or were re-certified as industrial schools.[37] The only reformatory established in the north-east was the Malone Reformatory for Protestant Boys (1860). Una Convery contends that Catholic children from that region were sent to schools in the south.[38] Following the 1895 Gladstone Committee, which was established in response to intense criticism of the prison system, a further category of institution, the borstal, was devised for young offenders. At the time, the only institution of its kind in Ireland was established in Clonmel, County Tipperary in 1906 catering for offenders aged between 16 and 21 years. While there were intermittent calls for a state-run borstal for young women, these were never realised in independent Ireland although in Northern Ireland a wing of Armagh Gaol was designated a borstal for girls in 1954.

Religious philanthropy was extremely influential in institutional development and frequently the impetus behind initiatives was anxiety around proselytising, especially of children. This is evident in the development of orphanages but also of specialist provision; the Christian Brothers and Sisters of St Dominic were the first to establish homes for 'Deaf and Dumb' children in Cabra, Dublin, while the Sisters of Charity assumed control of the North Dublin Union Auxiliary workhouse in 1892, which eventually became a home for 'mentally defective' children.[39]

Most institutions were directly funded through a form of local, usually property-based, taxation and received grants from the Treasury and/or capitation grants; this included the religious-managed industrial and reformatory schools. The administrative structures overseeing them were similar in several respects. For most, there was a national inspectorate based at Dublin Castle, while local committees, boards of governors and/or religious

---

36 J. Robins, 'Religious Issues in the Early Workhouse', *Studies*, 57 (1968), 54–66; P. M. Prior and D. V. Griffiths, 'The Chaplaincy Question: The Lord Lieutenant of Ireland versus the Belfast Lunatic Asylum', *Éire-Ireland*, 33 (1997), 137–53.

37 Barnes, *Irish Industrial Schools*, 74.

38 Convery, 'Locked in the Past', 257.

39 J. Robins, *From Rejection to Integration. A Centenary of Service by the Daughters of Charity to Persons with a Mental Handicap* (Dublin: Gill & Macmillan, 1992).

bodies managed individual institutions. Local structures and personnel were extremely important in determining regimes.[40] The Magdalen asylums operated more independently, and most were exempt from inspection, but the acceptance of state funding opened institutions up to state scrutiny. The quality of inspections varied and was dependent on the character and energy of inspectors. Nonetheless, there was a legislative requirement to regularly visit institutions – usually annually – to produce published reports and, among other matters, investigate mismanagement, outbreaks of epidemic disease, and inmates' deaths.

An influential cohort of penologists, doctors, reformers, public servants, and others, who laid claim to specialist expertise and created differentiated professional identities and organisations, promoted the growth of institutions. In the nineteenth century, those working on Ireland participated in the Social Science Association's congresses and the International Penal and Penitentiary Congresses, contributing to the transnational exchange of ideas that advocated for institutions as solutions to social problems. Lawrence Goldman has argued that these were 'men with schemes, blueprints for change, ideas for social improvement' as well as harbouring ambitions for 'group-advancement' inspired by 'professional commitments and experience'.[41] Crofton was one such figure, not simply because his theories on juvenile and adult penal reform contributed to the English and Irish debates but because he was a vehicle for the translation of models of institutional reform across the European continent and further afield.[42]

These 'visionaries' often became career public servants, specialists in their field, moving across national inspectorates and bringing with them their zeal. Sir George Plunkett O'Farrell MD, for example, was a local government inspector and medical commissioner of prisons, and from 1887 he was an inspector of reformatory and industrial schools and was appointed to the lunacy inspectorate in 1890. He was also a member of the General Prisons Board.[43] Medical men, such John Lentaigne, the inspector of both reformatory and industrial schools, featured prominently on inspectorates, indicating not only the pathologisation of behaviours but also the medicalisation

---

40 Cox, *Negotiating Insanity*, 240; Crossman, *Poverty and the Poor Law*, 228.

41 Goldman, *Science, Reform and Politics*, 13.

42 L. Goldman, 'Crofton, Sir Walter Frederick (1815–1897)', *Oxford Dictionary of National Biography*: www.oxforddnb.com/view/article/65325 (accessed 14 October 2015); Goldman, *Science, Reform and Politics*, 160, 165–6.

43 R. F. C. Burnard (ed.), *Catholic Who's Who and Year Book* (London: Burns & Oates, 1908), 308; Barnes, *Irish Industrial Schools*, 99; Cox, *Negotiating Insanity*, 51.

of solutions.[44] Lentaigne and others conceived of reformatories and industrial schools as moral hospitals for the 'bodily and psychological reform' of children to allow their return to 'normal' patterns of growth.[45] Towards the end of the nineteenth century, the pathologising of behaviours became more explicit especially in relation to 'repeat offenders', such as single women with more than one child, who were increasingly constructed as irredeemable, chronic or 'mental defectives'.[46]

Advocates for institutions sought the isolation of their populations, regarding them as morally and at times physically contaminating. This is especially true in the case of the Magdalen asylums; from the eighteenth century, philanthropists, often female, pursued rescue work focusing on 'saving' single mothers from sliding into lives of immorality and 'containing' the moral and medical contagion associated with prostitution. Philanthropists of all denominations established Magdalen asylums and opened institutions throughout the Western world from the mid-eighteenth century. Estimates suggest that by 1900, there were more than 300 in England and over 20 in Scotland.[47] Located on Leeson Street, the earliest opened in Dublin in 1766. It was intended for 'penitents' – young, Protestant women, some of whom were pregnant – who were expected to spend between eighteen months and two years within the institution to allow for their complete 'reformation'. Except for the Ulster Female Penitentiary, founded on a non-denominational basis in 1820, these lay institutions were reluctant to admit women regarded as hardened prostitutes and it seems that most early inmates did not engage in prostitution.[48] As female religious orders became significant forces in the Irish voluntary sector, religious orders took over most asylums.[49] Protestant-run institutions were mainly confined to Dublin and to the north-east.

Isolating inmates from their communities allowed, advocates argued, the subjects of reform – children, prisoners, single mothers, the mentally ill – to

---

44 E. Leaney, 'Lentaigne, John Francis O'Neill', in J. McGuire and J. Quinn (eds.), *Dictionary of Irish Biography*, vol. 5 (Cambridge University Press, 2009), 453–4.

45 I. Miller, 'Constructing Moral Hospitals: Childhood Health in Irish Reformatories and Industrial Schools, c.1851–1890', in A. Mac Lellan and A. Mauger (eds.), *Growing Pains: Childhood Illness in Irish History, 1750–1950* (Dublin: Irish Academic Press, 2014), 105–22.

46 M. Luddy, 'Moral Rescue and Unmarried Mothers in Ireland in the 1920s', *Women's Studies*, 30 (2001), 801; L. McCormick, *Regulating Sexuality. Women in Twentieth-century Northern Ireland* (Manchester: Manchester University Press, 2009), 63–4.

47 F. Finnegan, *Poverty and Prostitution. A Study of Victorian Prostitutes in York* (Cambridge University Press, 1979); L. Mahood, *The Magdalenes. Prostitution in the Nineteenth Century* (London: Routledge, 1990).

48 Luddy, *Women and Philanthropy*, 110–12; 13, also note 56.

49 Luddy, *Prostitution and Irish Society 1800–1940*, 78–82.

be removed from external sources of contamination, thus ensuring the success of the distinct 'reformative' models. The sources of contamination were criminal or morally unhealthy environments. These included the working-class family, an institution increasingly identified as a source of pathology. Thus, the reformatory theories and visions of lay and religious social reformers, national inspectors, legislators and public servants converged, implying a unanimity around different models of reform that was not always present. It was not envisaged that institutional populations would become permanent or even long-term residents, or that they would be readmitted. Such inmates were 'chronic' or irredeemable, a long-term drain on the public and private purse, and emblematic of failure. The situation in the reformatory/industrial schools and the Magdalen asylums was slightly different. The children were obliged to leave aged 16 but many had been admitted at a young age. While women in Magdalen asylums in the nineteenth century were not encouraged to leave, they could do so if they wished and some subsequently re-entered.[50]

Broader support for, and a shared belief in the efficacy of, institutions as remedies for specific social 'ills' fuelled further expansion. Local officials and merchants recognised the economic benefits and opportunities that large institutions provided. Such was the extent of public support for the new industrial schools that the state imposed a series of checks on new certifications between 1875 and 1879.[51] Likewise, there was very active support from landlords, magistrates and other local elites for the expansion of the number of lunatic asylums in the 1860s.[52] This enthusiasm was tempered when the financial cost, especially the drain on the local taxpayer, was revealed. Nonetheless, there was considerable support for institutions as solutions to social problems and as emblems of a progressive society.

In many instances, institutions were regarded as preferable to non-institutional interventions even when the latter were facilitated under legislation. For example, the 1868 Industrial School Act did not mandate complete residential care. Children could be boarded with their parents or 'responsible adults', but school managers seldom used that provision as it entailed returning children to the households identified as morally polluting. In response to concerns for the protection of the moral well-being of orphaned and illegitimate children in workhouses, their boarding out was permitted under the 1862 Poor Law Amendment Act. This was unpopular among Poor Law

50 Luddy, *Prostitution and Irish Society*, 107.
51 Barnes, *Irish Industrial Schools*, 49–50.
52 Cox, *Negotiating Insanity*, 39–45.

guardians and the numbers of children in workhouses consistently outnumbered those in foster homes.[53] Poor Law guardians later increased outdoor relief though those in the north-east provided less.[54]

The failure of institutions to provide aftercare, especially for young and older ex-residents, some of whom had spent decades within these institutions, is striking. By the end of the nineteenth century, industrial schools were attracting considerable criticism for this failure, as well as for the social stigma attached to former inmates and the tendency of these factors to contribute to renewed institutionalisation during adult life. For ex-prisoners the growth of discharged aid groups was faltering while there was no formal structure of support for patients released from lunatic asylums until the twentieth century.[55] For some, notably women convicted of infanticide, release was contingent on an undertaking to emigrate while reformatory and industrial school children were also encouraged to move abroad.[56] Conor Reidy has argued that the Borstal Association of Ireland supported offenders after release from the Clonmel, but this was relatively unusual. Overall, aftercare supports were not developed until much later, if at all.

Twentieth-century Continuities?

By the late nineteenth and early twentieth centuries, patterns of institutional development in Ireland deviated from many other European countries in several ways. During the early decades of the twentieth century the numbers held in some institutions – notably prisons – declined. Others, notably psychiatric hospitals, grew steadily and, in the view of some commentators, unremittingly. The multiplication and diversification of institutional models that took place elsewhere during the twentieth century did not occur in Ireland. Instead, officials continued to rely on older models, often eschewing new approaches. Endeavouring to understand these patterns, most research focuses on the Irish Free State and identifies a specifically Catholic 'culture of confinement' that reflected, but was not identical to, a deference to the Roman Catholic hierarchy and to the Catholic Church's social teaching. This work argues for a shared understanding among social reformers,

---

53 V. Crossman, 'Cribbed, Contained and Confined? The Care of Children under the Irish Poor Law, 1850–1920', *Éire-Ireland*, 44 (2009), 37–61.

54 Crossman, *Poverty and the Poor Law*, 63–100; Purdue, 'Poor Relief in the North of Ireland', 23–36.

55 Cox, *Negotiating Insanity*, 153–60.

56 P. Prior, *Madness and Murder. Gender, Crime and Mental Disorder in Nineteenth-Century Ireland* (Dublin: Irish Academic Press, 2008), 215–7.

welfare and medical professionals, civil servants and members of the Catholic Church on the best approach to promoting psychological and moral well-being. With a few exceptions, conspicuously less attention has been paid to Northern Ireland, to other denominational practices and philosophies of welfare, or to dissenting and competing models.

In the first decades of the twentieth century, the British Liberal government's welfare reforms signalled a shift towards a more collectivist and interventionist approach to relief that provided welfare supports – such as the Old Age Pension – outside residential, institutional contexts. Institutions, however, remained at the core of many welfare models; for example, although the Irish Free State government abolished the deeply unpopular Poor Law system in 1923 the old workhouses continued to operate as county homes.[57] In Northern Ireland, workhouses were not abandoned until the introduction of the National Health Service in 1948. For child welfare, the most significant Liberal intervention was the 1908 Child Act, which consolidated the state's power to interfere in cases of 'child neglect'. While not eschewing institutional models, it circumscribed removals to them.[58] Nonetheless, in response to an increase in child poverty associated with the decline of the Belfast economy, new industrial schools were opened in the north-east.[59]

After partition, many of the models – usually English – from which Irish institutions derived, underwent a process of change. From 1933, the English and Welsh reformatory and industrial schools were phased out with the introduction of Approved Schools and Remand Homes. It is important to note, however, that the changes did not prompt the closure of institutions or the rejection of that model. Following the American example, the 1933 English Act collapsed the industrial and reformatory schools into a single system of Approved Schools representing for Schlossman 'only a modest alteration of the status quo' with some 'new' institutions located in the same buildings.[60] Subsequently, psychiatric and probation services and personnel were introduced, as the populations were increasingly pathologised and conceived as being of inferior mental organisation. Similar services were

57 M. Cousins, *The Birth of Social Welfare in Ireland, 1922–1952* (Dublin: Four Courts Press, 2003).

58 J. Stewart, 'Children, Parents and the State: The Children Act 1908', *Children and Society*, 9 (1995), 90–9.

59 Convery, 'Locked in the Past', 257.

60 S. Schlossman, 'Delinquent Children: The Juvenile Reform School', in N. Morris and D. J. Rothman (eds.), *The Oxford History of the Prison: The Practice of Punishment in Western Society* (Oxford University Press, 1998), 343.

not introduced to the schools of independent Ireland.[61] Within the Northern Ireland Ministry of Home Affairs, there was little enthusiasm for the 1933 Act. There, mirroring general education policy, by 1925 the state had taken control of Protestant-run schools while religious orders continued to operate Catholic ones. Most clauses of the 1933 English Act were included in the 1950 Children and Young Peoples Act, but the management structures of Catholic and Protestant schools remained unchanged. It is unclear, Convery argues, to what extent the structural and nomenclature changes of the 1950s introduced significant reforms to the schools' ethos, function and regimes.[62]

In the Irish Free State, when proposals for reform were mooted, institutions criticised and alternative mechanisms proposed, the official response was to insist that the models in use elsewhere were not suited to Irish circumstances and that the state could not afford expensive alternatives. In examining officials' responses, scholars identify a deeply-held conviction among relevant actors that religious-run institutions provided a model of care based on spiritual and moral welfare that was preferable to those in operation elsewhere and that the state should not interfere. In 1950, for example, the Minister for Justice, Seán MacEoin, commenting on the relatively small number of probation officers and psychiatrists employed in the prison services, observed that 'in this country, where the influence of religion is very strong, our need for the services of these people is not great'.[63] Smith argues that in the 1940s and again in the 1960s, there was considerable support within the Department of Justice for the proposals of John Charles McQuaid, the Archbishop of Dublin, that the of remand homes for young adult women (16–21 years) was best resolved by recourse to the services of female, religious bodies. St Mary's Magdalen Asylum on Gloucester Street, Dublin, run by Our Sisters of Our Lady of Refuge, provided this service under the 1960 Criminal Justice Act (see Illustration 29).[64]

Further analysis is required as to whether and how financial supports materially affected on people's ability to avoid institutions. However, in the context of poor economic performance and comparatively low standards of living, alongside an apparently rigid and homogeneous culture, the southern

---

61 J. Conrad, *Crime and its Corrections. An International Survey of Attitudes and Practices* (California: University California Press, 1965), 93–5.

62 Convery, 'Locked in the Past', 259–60.

63 Cited in S. Kilcommins, I. O'Donnell, E. O'Sullivan and B. Vaughan, *Crime, Punishment, and the Search for Order in Ireland* (Dublin: Institute of Public Administration, 2004), 51.

64 Smith, *Ireland's Magdalen Laundries*, 68, 70–1. The Dáil debates on the 1960 bill included discussions of services for boys and Protestant-run institutions, Parliamentary Debates Dáil Éireann, vol. 180, no. 7, col. 873, (23 March 1960).

29. Exterior of entrance to Sisters of Charity Magdalene Laundry, Sean McDermott [formerly Gloucester] Street, Dublin.

state was dilatory in providing supports that diminished vulnerability to institutionalisation.[65] Social attitudes towards behaviours regarded as 'deviant', especially among the poor, were also unforgiving. Luddy contends that

65 Luddy, 'Moral Rescue', 807; M. Cousins, 'Sickness, Gender and National Health Insurance', 1920s to 1940s', in M. Preston and M. ÓhÓgartaigh (eds.), *Gender and Medicine in Ireland 1700–1950* (Syracuse: Syracuse University Press, 2012), 169–88, 170; M. E. Daly,

the Irish Free State considered a mother – single or married – to be 'morally obliged to support her child' but was slow to introduce welfare mechanisms to assist her.[66] In 1930 the Illegitimate Children (Affiliation Orders) Act was enacted to force fathers to contribute to the support of illegitimate children but, as Earner-Byrne and Luddy show, much of the discussion of the Act centred around protecting men's reputations and shielding them from blackmail. The Act did little to improve the social or financial position of mothers. By 1950, the Adoption Society of Ireland reported that, out of 200 cases before the courts, in only two had paternity been sucessfully established and the men found solvent.[67]

With few supports, single mothers continued to enter county homes, much to the annoyance of local authorities who insisted their presence dissuaded the 'respectable poor' from entering. Single mothers also approached charities and other institutions, including the Magdalen asylums, many of which had opened before the establishment of the state. Some of these boarded out children. By the 1920s, however, more women were entering private maternity homes or emigrating.[68] The census returns from 1901 and 1911 indicate that most Magdalen asylums surviving into the twentieth century, in both jurisdictions, accommodated relatively small numbers, with notable exceptions, mainly run by the Good Shepherd Sisters. Luddy and Smith contend that in the twentieth century, the 'reformative' function of the Magdalen asylums was replaced with a carceral one, reflecting a more assertive Catholic culture of containment in independent Ireland. Then, first time 'offenders' often ended up in mother and baby homes while those in Magdalen asylums were 'repeat offenders'.[69] The Protestant-run institutions in Northern Ireland were smaller.[70] There, those that continued to operate changed their names and functions. By the time it closed in the 1990s, the Good Shepherd institution in Belfast included a home for the 're-education of problem girls, a hostel for broken families and a home for unmarried mothers'.[71]

' "Oh Kathleen Ni Houihan, your Way's a Thorny Way". The Condition of Women in Twentieth Century Ireland', in A. Bradley and M. G. Valiulis (eds.), *Gender and Sexuality in Modern Ireland* (University of Massachusetts Press, 1997), 102–26.

66 Luddy, 'Moral Rescue', 798; L. Earner-Byrne, *Mother and Child: Maternity and Child Welfare in Dublin, 1920s–1960s* (Manchester: Manchester University Press, 2007), 187.

67 Luddy, 'Moral Rescue', 813; Earner-Byrne, *Mother and Child*, 179.

68 Luddy, 'Moral Rescue', 799–800; L. Earner-Byrne, 'The Boat to England: An Analysis of the Official Reactions to the Emigration of Single Expectant Irishwomen to Britain, 1922–1972', *Irish Economic and Social History*, 30 (2003), 52–70.

69 Luddy, 'Moral Rescue', 802–3; Smith, *Ireland's Magdalen Laundries*, 136.

70 Luddy, *Prostitution and Irish Society*, 78–82; McCormick, *Regulating Sexuality*, 50–3.

71 McCormick, *Regulating Sexuality*, 77–9.

The 'panic' in the 1920s and 1930s among Roman Catholic and Protestant clergy and rescue societies over rising illegitimacy rates prompted the establishment of mother and baby homes. Managed and staffed by religious orders, these catered specifically for single mothers. The Sisters of the Sacred Heart of Jesus and Mary opened the first at Bessboro in Cork, having been granted the site by the Bishop of Cork in 1921, followed by the Sean Ross Abbey in County Tipperary (1930) and a third, Manor House in Castlepollard, County Westmeath (see Illustration 30). Other examples are the Regina Coeli Hostel in Dublin run by the Legion of Mary and the Irish Church Mission's Bethany Home in Rathgar for Protestant women.[72] Though many predated the Act, the homes, Smith argues, were registered under the 1934 Maternity Homes Act and received state payments.[73] In advocating for these institutions, the Department of Local Government and Public Health stressed the need for an alternative to county homes, which were regarded as degrading and morally corrupting. Special institutions, it was contended, provided the ideal environment for the mother's rehabilitation. Highlighting the class dimension of discussions, Earner-Byrne observes that the special homes were intended for the 'better type of girl', the county homes for the 'poorest class'.[74]

Institutions for single mothers did not provide women with mechanisms to keep their children and who were often transferred to orphanages that were run by the same religious orders within the same complexes, or to industrial schools. Women in mother and baby homes tended to remain there until their children were old enough to be transferred. The introduction of legal adoption in 1952, following a sustained, acrimonious campaign, facilitated the adoption of 'illegitimate' children within six to eight weeks of birth, allowing mothers to leave the homes sooner.[75] The fate of the children born in these institutions was bound up with ambivalent attitudes towards adoption and the removal of children for 'informal' foreign adoption.[76]

When policy relating to state-managed institutions for the first fifty years of independence is assessed, the picture that emerges is one of neglect (see Illustration 31). For example, inspectors of Irish mental hospitals published

---

72 Luddy, 'Moral Rescue', 801.
73 Smith, *Ireland's Magdalen Laundries*, 52.
74 Earner-Byrne, *Mother and Child*, 183–9.
75 Earner-Byrne, *Mother and Child*, 189.
76 R. Gilligan, 'The "Public Child" and the Reluctant State?', *Éire-Ireland*, 44 (2009), 265–90; M. Maguire, *Precarious Childhood in Post-Independence Ireland* (Manchester: Manchester University Press, 2009).

30. Exterior of Sean Ross Abbey Industrial School, Roscrea, County Tipperary.

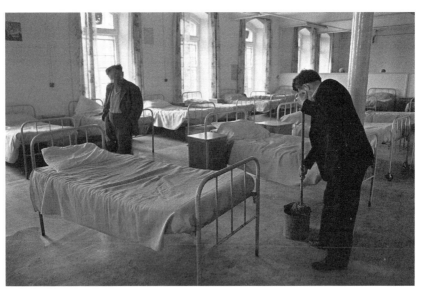

31. Interior of Our Lady's Psychiatric Hospital, Cork, *c.* 1980.

annual reports on an irregular basis while the quality of inspection at other institutions was extremely poor. These institutions, however, were not ignored. There were numerous official and unofficial investigations into mental hospitals in the decades after independence, yet these produced limited change in spite of vocal support from campaigning journalists and committed public servants.[77] This neglect, alongside the state's distrust of international psychiatric and psychological theories, especially those of a eugenic nature, however, halted the proliferation of new institutions such as occurred in England and Wales under the 1913 Mental Deficiency Act. Alternative, separate, specialist facilities for people, especially the young, with mental disabilities were slow to emerge.[78] Meanwhile, psychiatric treatment remained centred on older institutions. The populations of residential psychiatric hospitals were large; in 1961, there were 7.5 psychiatric beds per 1,000 in the Republic, 4.5 in Northern Ireland, 4.6 in England and Wales, 2.3 in the Netherlands, and 4.3 in the US.[79] The shift towards treating mental illness in general hospital units occurred later than in Britain and America – the first general hospital psychiatric unit was opened in Waterford in 1967 – although in Sweden and Denmark, similar changes also date to the 1960s.[80]

In the field of criminal justice, David Garland has maintained that from the late nineteenth century to the 1970s, a 'penal welfarist' approach, combining punishment with rehabilitation, shaped international policy and had cross-party consensus across the Western world. This was then replaced with a punitive 'culture of control' characterised by high rates of imprisonment.[81] Criminologists query the

---

77 *Report of the Commission on Relief of the Sick and Destitute Poor including the Insane Poor* (Dublin: Stationery Office, Saorstát Eireann, 1927); *Report of the Commission of Inquiry on Mental Illness* (Dublin: Stationery Office, 1966); *The Psychiatric Services. Planning For the Future. A Report of the Study Group on the Development of the Psychiatric Services* (Dublin: Stationery Office, 1984); *A Vision for Change. A Report of the Expert Group on Mental Health Policy* (Dublin: Staionery Office, 2006); M. Viney, 'Psychiatry and the Irish', *Irish Times* (30 October 1963); 'No Room to Move', *Irish Times* (23 October 1963); 'The Opening Door', *Irish Times* (24 October 1963); 'Patients with a Purpose', *Irish Times* (25 October 1963); 'Change for Revolution', *Irish Times* (26 October 1963); 'Psychiatry and the Irish', *Irish Times* (30 October 1963). H. Connolly, 'The Scandal of the Mental Hospitals', *Magill* (1 October 1980).
78 D. Walsh and A. Daly, *Mental Illness in Ireland, 1750–2002: Reflections on the Rise and Fall of Institutional Care* (Dublin: Health Research Board, 2004), 33.
79 Walsh and Daly, *Mental Illness*, 33, 46, 69.
80 A. H. Rosenthal, *Social Programs of Sweden: A Search for Security in a Free Society* (Minneapolis, MN: University of Minnesota Press, 1967), 58; S. S. Furman, *Community Mental Health Services in Northern Europe* (Bethesda, MD: National Institute of Mental Health, 1965).
81 D. Garland, *Punishment and Welfare: A History of Penal Strategies* (Aldershot: Gower, 1985), 5; D. Garland, *The Culture of Control. Crime and Social Order in Contemporary Society* (Oxford University Press, 2001), 27–8.

suitability of Garland's theories and periodisation to Ireland. The new Northern Ireland state inherited a small and depleted 'prison estate', while subsequent efforts at reform were complicated by the political context and by the impact of political prisoners.[82] In independent Ireland the small prison population, along with a conservative approach within the Department of Justice, ensured that prison policy was 'a marginal area'.[83] Between 1926 and 1971, there were fewer than 1,000 prisoners per year. Consequently, many older prisons were closed and by the late 1950s only Limerick, Portlaoise and Mountjoy, alongside St Patrick's Detention Centre, remained. Most prisoners, 60 per cent in 1950, were serving short sentences of less than three months. The decline in the number of female prisoners was especially remarkable; in 1971, there was a daily average of less than twenty-four.[84] In seeking to contextualise rates of imprisonment, O'Donnell and O'Sullivan, and Damien Brennan, among others, argue that ignoring the punitive character of other institutions, especially psychiatric hospitals, masks the true size of the confined population in independent Ireland before the 1970s.[85]

Demands to close various 'welfare' institutions gathered momentum from the 1970s. In 1970, the Committee on the Reformatory and Industrial Schools, chaired by Justice Eileen Kennedy, recommended the closure of the Republic's industrial school system. At that point, there were twenty-nine certified schools holding 2,000 children – there was capacity for 3,750. The Kennedy Report described the schools and the 1908 Child Act as out-dated, and failing to incorporate modern 'psychological' approaches to child welfare. Kennedy recommended that the schools be replaced with 'group homes which would approximate as closely as possible to the normal family unit'.[86] In Northern Ireland, the Children and Young Persons (Northern Ireland) Act, passed in 1968, was hurried through to avoid the welfare-oriented approaches under development in England as part of the Children and Young Persons Act (1969). The 1969 Act would disband the English Approved School system in 1973 replacing it with locally administered community homes with education services.[87] The 1968 Northern Ireland Act, in contrast, re-enforced many of the clauses of the 1950 Children and Young Peoples Act.[88]

82 S. McConville, *Irish Political Prisoners 1920–1962* (London: Taylor and Francis Ltd, 2013), 373–426.
83 O'Sullivan and O'Donnell, *Coercive Confinement*, 43–4; M. Rogan, *Prison Policy in Ireland. Politics, Penal Welfarism and Political Imprisonment* (London: Routledge, 2011), 34–41.
84 O'Sullivan and O'Donnell, *Coercive Confinement*, 5, 21, 25.
85 D. Brennan, *Irish Insanity 1800–2000* (London: Routledge, 2014).
86 *Reformatory and Industrial Schools System: Report* (Dublin: Stationery Office, 1970), 2–4, 7, 12.
87 Convery, 'Locked in the Past', 261; J. Conrad, *Crime and its Corrections* (Berkeley: University of California Press, 1965).
88 Convery, 'Locked in the Past', 261.

In the Republic, legislative change to welfare provision for single mothers was sought from the late 1960s, and forced through following the Commission on the Status of Women, a United Nations initiative which reported in 1973 – the year of the accession to the European Economic Community. The Commission's report shaped the 1974 Social Welfare Act, which introduced direct payment to women of children's allowance while payments to single mothers were introduced in 1973.[89] The rhetoric around single motherhood, especially relating to the perceived threat of benefit fraud and teenage pregnancies, however, remained critical. Family planning provision throughout Ireland was slow to develop and the social reality of being pregnant and single in Ireland was difficult, at times life-threatening.[90] In terms of institutions, the last Magdalen asylums were closed in the 1990s in both jurisdictions.

The movement away from the institutional treatment of psychiatric patients and towards higher levels of tangible official support for care in the community, took place later in the Republic. In 2002, only 41 per cent of all psychiatric hospital admissions were to general units while 3,891 patients remained in psychiatric hospitals.[91] The final decision to close the older generation of psychiatric institutions was taken in 2006. The institutions of the criminal justice system, however, grew. Increases in the size of the prison population from the early 1970s led to the opening of new prisons for adult males and a women's prison. The pattern has continued; in August 2014 the rate of imprisonment in Ireland was 88 per 100,000 representing a 400 per cent increase since 1970. A huge proportion of these committals were for twelve months or less.[92]

'Archipelago' Populations?

Recently, populations have attracted institutionalised attention from scholars, revealing the economic, class, religious and moral values that underpinned definitions of 'deserving' and who in society was, and was not, identified as worthy of, or amenable to, reform, rehabilitation and relief. The gendered nature of the institutions exposes how specific forms of aberrant behaviour were

---

89 F. Kennedy, *Cottage to Crèche. Family Change in Ireland* (Dublin, Institute of Public Administration, 2001).

90 See J. Horgan, 'Did the Media Exploit Granard?', *Irish Times* (1 March 1984), 10; M. Cowley, 'Parents did not Know Ann Lovett was Pregnant', *Irish Times* (22 February 1984), 1; F. Gartland, 'Church Said Ann Lovett's Death Due to "Immaturity"', *Irish Times* (27 December 2014), 13. L. McCormick, 'The Scarlet Woman in Person', 345–60.

91 Walsh and Daly, *Mental Illness*, 33, 46, 69.

92 Irish Penal Reform Trust, Facts and Figures: www.iprt.ie/ (accessed 15 October 2015).

associated with concepts of masculinity and femininity. While structural and legislative frameworks formally defined the economic, geographic and religious divisions among 'deserving' and 'undeserving' poor, managers of state and philanthropic institutions adjudicated on the 'moral state' of recipients determining access to support accordingly. This is especially clear in institutions where religious bodies had greater autonomy, but also occurred in state institutions irrespective of whether they were managed by religious or lay bodies. As outlined earlier, relatively few of the nineteenth-century Magdalen asylums and other rescue homes, for example, catered for 'hardened women'. In contrast to their English counterparts, Irish reformatory and industrial schools generally admitted 'pre-delinquent' juveniles especially those 'in danger' from 'immoral influences' due to absent or corrupting parents. Children convicted of offences were committed to local prisons because school managers refused to accept them.[93] Sargent contends that this was a product of the religious pre-occupation with managing bodies, in particular preserving young girls from sexual corruption.[94] Within workhouses, Poor Law guardians regarded prostitutes – the less 'deserving' – as corrupting influences, and instituted controversial policies to separate them from other inmates. Attitudes towards single mothers, whom guardians did not believe to be prostitutes varied, with some arguing that these women were victims of seduction and, as mothers, suffered hardship, often finding themselves unable to force the fathers to support their children.[95]

Throughout our period, institutional populations were poor, economically vulnerable and distinguished by their working-class status, though it should be noted private, fee-paying institutions are underexplored.[96] At the time of admission, most inmates were in poor nutritional condition.[97] With the exception of the post-Famine workhouse population, which became dominated by transient night-lodgers, the households from which they emerged, or were removed, were normally established although social commentators and reformers did not regard them as stable.[98] During the nineteenth and

93 Sargent, *Wild Arabs*, 13; Carey, *Mountjoy*, 142.
94 Sargent, *Wild Arabs*, 93–4.
95 Crossman, *Poverty and the Poor Law*, 182–86; Crossman, 'The New Ross Workhouse Riot of 1887: Nationalism, Class and the Irish Poor Laws', *Past and Present*, 179 (2003), 135–58.
96 A. Mauger, 'Great Class which Lies between: Provision for the Non-pauper Insane in Ireland, 1830–1900', unpublished PhD thesis, University College Dublin (2013); E. Malcolm, *Swift's Hospital. A History of St. Patrick's Hospital, Dublin, 1746–1989* (Dublin: Gill & Macmillan, 1989).
97 C. Ó Gráda, 'The Heights of Clonmel Prisoners, 1845–1849: Some Dietary Implications', *Irish Economic and Social History*, 18 (1991), 24–33; Barnes, *Irish Industrial Schools*, 65–6; Cox, *Negotiating Insanity*, 217.
98 Crossman, *Poverty and the Poor Law*, 198–225.

twentieth centuries, a significant proportion of the adult population of psy-chiatric hospitals emerged from local settled households. Most were single men who had resided in the family home, hinting at the protection marriage provided against institutionalisation. The Ryan Commission (2000–2005), in its inquiry into twentieth-century industrial schools, found that 75 per cent of their witnesses were removed from two-parent households, with most living with their parents or extended family members.[99]

In both centuries, admissions were frequently secured through the crimi-nal justice system, revealing how the values of society and attitudes towards poverty and the poor were inscribed into legislation. Most patients were admitted to lunatic asylums under the 'Dangerous Lunatic' legislation (1838; 1867) until it was eventually replaced in 1945, when the concept of volun-tary admissions was introduced. The impact of the 1847 Vagrancy Act can be traced in the numbers committed to prisons but the 'crime of begging' also featured prominently among admissions to industrial schools. Barnes found that in 1882, 73.1 per cent of children committed were 'found begging'. There were allegations that parents and guardians sent children out in the expectation that the police would send them to industrial schools. And mag-istrates struggled to differentiate between habitual beggars (punishable under the Vagrancy Act), and other categories, including those who were neglected by parents.[100] During the twentieth century, children were committed to the industrial schools under the School Attendance Act (1926) and the Children Act (1929).

Studies of Magdalen asylums emphasise the 'voluntary' nature of admis-sions during the nineteenth century. Smith, however, found that in twentieth-century independent Ireland, women were also admitted through the criminal justice system. Of significance for him are those women convicted under the 1949 Infanticide Act. Among his sample of 211 convictions between 1926 and 1964, 42 per cent were sent to Magdalen asylums, demonstrating, Smith has claimed, that 'these women passed seamlessly from direct state jurisdiction into the control of the religious congregations'. The remaining women – the majority – were discharged, committed to prisons, or found guilty but dis-charged on their own recognisance or to families. Only five were committed

---

99 *Final Report of the Commission to Inquire into Child Abuse, 2000–2005*, vols I–V (Dublin, Stationery Office, 2009) (hereafter *CICA*). Initially the Commission heard from '1,090 witnesses who applied to give oral evidence of abuse they experienced in Irish institu-tions', *CICA*, vol. 1, 3.

100 Barnes, *Irish Industrial Schools*, 64–5.

to mental hospitals.[101] Recent studies also suggest that residents were bartered between different institutions depending on local institutional provision, eligibility criteria, and evolving ideas of expertise. In the mid-nineteenth century, sustained campaigns by asylum medical staff and inspectors sought the transfer of the insane from workhouses to neighbouring lunatic asylums as sites of relevant expertise. Enthusiasm for the policy waned, however, as staff and officials, struggling with overcrowded institutions, became resentful of 'chronic' patients that came from the workhouses.[102] In the twentieth century, the official inquiries into the industrial schools and Magdalen asylums highlighted the movement of people between different institutions.[103]

Close examination of the routes into institutions reveals the frequency with which family members and neighbours, with the support of the structures of law and order, and welfare personnel, initiated approaches to both compulsory and 'voluntary' admission mechanisms. McCormick noted that in the twentieth century, relatives often brought young women to institutions, while women who have described their experiences have attested that relatives placed considerable pressure upon them to enter institutions and relinquish their babies.[104] Children were removed to the industrial schools in response to requests from parents and on the advice of the National Society for the Prevention of Cruelty to Children, while family members initiated most legal procedures to admit relatives to lunatic asylums.[105] The involvement of families and neighbours in committals seems to support Ignatieff's argument that constructions of deviance and deserving operated across society and were not confined to the state or, in the Irish case, the churches. Such behaviours, however, need to be understood in the context of the paucity of alternative, meaningful, non-institutional therapeutic and welfare provisions, and the cacophony of lay and religious expertise advising on the efficiency of institutions.

101 Smith, *Ireland's Magdalen Laundries*, 63, 195.

102 D. Durnin, 'Intertwining Institutions: The relationship between the South Dublin Union workhouse and the Richmond Lunatic Asylum, 1880–1911', unpublished MA thesis, UCD (2010).

103 *Report of the Inter-Departmental Committee to Establish the facts of State involvement with the Magdalen Laundries* (2013): www.justice.ie/en/JELR/Pages/PB11000256 (accessed 15 September 2015).

104 McCormick, *Regulating Sexuality*, 50; *Les Blanchisseuses de Magdalen* (France 3, 1998).

105 Sargent, *Wild Arabs*, 18; T. Feeney, ' "Church, State and the Family": The Advent of Child Guidance Clinics in Independent Ireland', *Social History of Medicine*, 25 (2012), 848–62, 850; S. A. Buckley, *The Cruelty Man: Child Welfare, the NSPCC and the State in Ireland, 1889–1956* (Manchester: Manchester University Press, 2013); The Ryan Commission concluded that 'The extent of the ISPCC involvement ... can be stated as significant', *CICA*, Executive Summary, 17.

Inside the Institutions

With the exception of prisons and borstals, throughout the nineteenth and twentieth centuries officials, social reformers and other advocates stressed the importance of recreating the domestic household – or rather the middle-class ideal of this – within institutions to facilitate reformation. The rhetoric, however, contrasts starkly with assessments which suggest that life 'inside institutions was always bleak'.[106] Between 1912 and 1914, for example, one female patient, writing from Wexford District Lunatic Asylum, Enniscorthy Asylum, made repeated references to the bleak, cold interior.[107] Patients in other asylums made similar comments.[108] Uncovering the voices and experiences of people in institutions is difficult; the necessary sources for such an endeavour – letters, memoirs and diaries – are ephemeral and are by their nature highly subjective.[109] Recent official inquiries into institutional abuse – the Inter-Departmental Committee into the State's Involvement with the Magdalen Laundries (McAleese Committee, 2011–2013) and the Commission to Inquire into Child Abuse (Ryan Commission, 2000–2005) – have been of some help, collating vital oral testimony from 'survivors' – a contested term. Nonetheless, the terms of reference of these enquiries shaped the collection of such testimonies and only a portion of residents – a self-selecting group – submitted evidence.

In seeking to write histories of 'life inside', historians are often reliant on source material that relates to the administration of institutions. Staff, not residents, authored records explicitly concerned with inmates. These are mediated sources, requiring careful negotiation and reflection.[110] For scholars interested in the twentieth century, there are additional challenges. Where the sources have survived and are available through official channels, material with identifying details falls under data protection legislation. Many official archives apply a one-hundred-year rule, while few facilitate 'academic access' as is the case in other jurisdictions. The abuse scandals of the 1980s and 1990s

---

106 O'Sullivan and O'Donnell, *Coercive Confinement*, 5.
107 Wexford County Archive, IE WXCA/P326, The Archive of St Senan's Psychiatric Hospital, Enniscorthy, letters to Mr [John] Redmond, 1912–1914.
108 H. Greally, *Bird's Nest Soup* (Dublin: Figgis, 1971).
109 T. Hitchcock, 'A New History from Below', *History Workshop Journal*, 57 (2004), 294–8; M. Lyons, *The Writing Culture of Ordinary People in Europe, c.1860–1920* (Cambridge University Press, 2013).
110 J. Andrews, 'Case Notes, Case Histories and the Patient's Experience of Insanity at Gartnavel Royal Asylum, Glasgow, in the Nineteenth Century', *Social History of Medicine*, 11 (1998), 255–81.

produced additional barriers. Just as the files of government departments were becoming available, many were recalled from repositories, sometimes for legal purposes such as redress schemes. Meanwhile, the religious orders that were responsible for managing institutions have become more wary of researchers.

Nonetheless, specific themes recur with some regularity within these varied records. At the core of the original reformative and disciplinary models in each institutional context were education and work (intended to train and rehabilitate), and religious and spiritual welfare. In many cases, however, institutional practices deviated from the ideal, differed across each system and between institutions, with local management committees and personnel shaping regimes. Within the industrial schools, the standards of education, identified as central to their foundation as training environments, were declining in the late nineteenth century and were poor in the twentieth. The Ryan Commission reported that standards were inferior to those in the 'ordinary' school system although the industrial schools received the national school grant and teachers were paid at the same rate. Generally, education ended at sixth class and it was noted that girls were often removed from classrooms to complete domestic chores.[111] The 1936 Cussen Report had recommended that industrial school children be sent to local national schools to facilitate integration, but by the 1960s this had occurred in only a few girls' schools. In the case of the Clonmel Borstal, rehabilitation and training was increasingly neglected, and by 1940 there was little to distinguish the borstal from a prison.[112]

The meaning of work was repeatedly redefined and became bound up in the economic functioning of institutions. Prisoners' labour, which at the start of the nineteenth century provided prisons with income, later became essential to Crofton's reformative system. With the shift in penal theories in the late nineteenth century, it became explicitly punitive. In nineteenth-century lunatic asylums, patients worked on wards and farms. Displaying a willingness and ability to perform tasks was evidence of recovery, opening up the potential for discharge. Work was claimed as central to the redemptive aims of the Magdalen asylums and most orders operated laundries in both centuries. The lack of inspection of these became a matter of concern in the 1890s and briefly, between 1907 and 1914, they were inspected under the 1901 Factory

---

111 *CICA*, Executive Summary, 24.
112 Reidy, *Moral Hospital*, 223–7.

and Workshop Act.[113] While Mahood maintains that laundries were essential for generating income – the women were not paid – McCormick notes that the Protestant-run Edgar Home regarded the profits as secondary to the potential the laundries provided for saving souls. It was argued that laundry work trained women for work in domestic service, though how many subsequently entered service is unclear.[114]

Mortality rates in nearly all the institutions were shockingly high, consistently outstripping rates within the general population, especially among babies born in institutions.[115] The sanitary conditions in the buildings were poor, made worse by faulty sewerage systems, assisting in the spread of dysentery and diarrhoea. The poor nutritional condition of many residents at the time of admission and, in some institutions, the bad quality of the food, made residents more susceptible to disease and infection. These unhealthy physical environments allowed chronic diseases – often tuberculosis – to thrive. For some residents, institutional diets constituted an improvement and, in some contexts, diet was intended to be part of the therapeutic and reformative models.[116] Published nineteenth-century dietaries suggest that meals were monotonous, with high starch contents. The quality of the food and provision of adequate nourishment was dependent on local managers' willingness to spend, levels of corruption and the rigour with which contractors' supplies were inspected.

The majority of residents admitted in the nineteenth century spent months rather than years within institutions. Most single mothers, who usually had only one child, left workhouses after several months, seldom returning. Lunatic asylum patients were typically discharged within twelve months – often sooner for women – though rates of recidivism were high. However, cohorts of long-stay residents and 'recidivists' who, in the case of lunatic asylums were regarded as problematic, in time 'clogged up' systems contributing to overcrowding and raised expenditure. Because of problems with source material, it is unclear to what extent these patterns continued into the

---

113 Luddy, *Prostitution and Irish Society*, 101.
114 Mahood, *The Magdalenes*, 87; McCormick, *Regulating Sexuality*, 73–5; Luddy; *Prostitution and Irish Society*, 98–9; A. Enright, 'Antigone in Galway', *London Review of Books*, 37 (17 December 2015), 11–14.
115 Earner-Byrne, *Mother and Child*, 199–201. In March 2017, the Commission of Investigation into Mother and Baby Homes released the results of test excavations carried out at Bon Secour Mother and Baby Home, Tuam, Co Galway. The excavations found significant quantities of human remains with age-at-death ranging from approximately 35 foetal weeks to 2 to 3 years in underground chambers. These date from the timeframe relevant to the operation of the institution.
116 Cox, *Negotiating Insanity*, 210–12; Miller, 'Constructing Moral Hospitals'.

twentieth century. Smith argues that the length of time women remained in Magdalen asylums increased as the institutions became more carceral.[117] While there was a legal obligation to release industrial school children at 16 years, some young women were subsequently transferred to Magdalen asylums. For psychiatric patients, time spent in institutions increased during the first half of the twentieth century. This was reversed following the implementation, in 1947, of the 1945 Mental Health Act, which in turn placed hospital capacity under severe pressure. New therapeutic, drug-based regimes also led to the diversion of patients to other institutions.[118]

Nineteenth-century advocates for institutions claimed that the emotional well-being of adult and child residents would be fostered through the replication of domesticity and by paying close attention to spiritual welfare. Individual institutional managers and staff, lay and religious, were expected to act *in loco parentis* to adults as well as to children, providing the necessary moral as well as physical supports. Through regular communications with key staff members – chaplains and medical officers among others – residents would reflect on, and renounce, previous behaviours. It is extremely difficult to ascertain whether this was realised in nineteenth-century institutions. The need to manage high levels of overcrowding in, and the expanding size of, nineteenth-century lunatic asylums, for example, suggests that a pattern of regular communication between asylum superintendents and individual patients was difficult to maintain. By the end of the nineteenth century, in most institutions, personalised contact with staff and the domestication of environments was replaced by a more rationalised system and increasingly institutions were criticised for prioritising discipline, routine and the need to reduce expenditure over the well-being of residents. The failure to attend to the emotional life of residents, especially children, featured repeatedly in the twentieth-century inquiries.[119] Whether residents in Irish institutions created the emotional communities or networks, such as the homo-social groupings found in prisons elsewhere, remains to be explored.[120] Cultures of bullying and abuse among children have been uncovered in recent inquiries.

---

117 Smith, *Ireland's Magdalen Laundries*, 81–2, 136; Luddy, 'Moral Rescue', 802–3.

118 F. Byrne, 'Madness and Mental Illness in Ireland: Discourses, People and Practices, 1900 to *c*.1960', unpublished PhD thesis, UCD, (2011), 226–7.

119 *Reformatory and Industrial Schools System. Report* (Dublin: Stationery Office, 1970) (hereafter *Kennedy Report*), 10–11; *CICA*, vol. III, 393–4.

120 P. O'Brien, *The Promise of Punishment. Prisons in Nineteenth-Century France* (Princeton, NJ: Princeton University Press, 1982).

Since the late 1990s there has been what Harry Ferguson describes as an 'endless stream of controversies and inquiries involving the abuse of children in institutional care' throughout the Western world.[121] Most studies locate the beginnings of this in Ireland to the 1990s, when RTÉ, the national television service, aired the 'States of Fear' (1999) documentary, exposing abuse in industrial schools. Since then, numerous documentaries and investigations have revealed harrowing accounts of sexual and physical abuse in industrial schools and Magdalen asylums, bringing them to a larger public. The oral testimonies that frequently feature in documentaries and publications added significantly to previous, often ignored, survivors' memoirs and testimonies, some of which had circulated for at least a decade.[122] Peter Tyrrell, who was in Letterfrack Industrial School in the 1920s and 1930s, tried repeatedly to have his experiences heard and was not only ignored but accused of 'working on the blackmail ticket' by a Christian Brother in 1953.[123] These accounts are replete with descriptions of punitive regimes and physical and sexual assaults: Tyrrell described the 'frightening' 'screams and shouts' of beaten boys, while Paddy Doyle, who was in a school in Wexford in the 1950s and 1960s, recounted being both sexually and physically assaulted.[124] Despite its compelling nature, as Diarmuid Whelan observes, the testimony of survivors has repeatedly been dismissed.[125]

These revelations which in the Republic focused on sites run by religious bodies, mainly Catholic, became part of a crisis within the Catholic Church globally relating to its mismanagement of clerical sex abuse. In response to them, governments initiated numerous commissions of inquiries, Taoisigh issued several apologies, and redress schemes were

---

121 H. Ferguson, 'Abused and Looked After Children as "Moral Dirt": Child Abuse and Institutional Care in Historical Perspective', *Journal of Social Policy*, 36 (2007), 123.

122 'Early days in Letterfrack. Memories of an Industrial School by Peter Tyrrell', *Hibernia* (June 1964); P. Doyle, *The God Squad* (Dublin: Raven Arts Press, 1988); G. M. Flynn, *Nothing to Say. A Novel* (Dublin: Ward River Press, 1983); M. Rafferty and E. O'Sullivan, *Suffer the Little Children: The Inside Story of Ireland's Industrial Schools* (Dublin: New Island, 1999); P. Touher, *Fear of the Collar: My Terrifying Childhood in Artane* (Dublin: O'Brien Press, 2001); P. Tyrrell, *Founded on Fear*, ed. D. Whelan (Dublin: Irish Academic Press, 2006). Also, P. Bourke Brogan, *Eclipsed* (Galway: Salmon Publishing, 1994) and J. Goulding, *The Light in the Window* (Dublin: Poolbeg Press, 1998) for staff memoirs.

123 Tyrrell, *Founded on Fear*, 43.

124 Tyrrell, *Founded on Fear*, 108–9; Doyle, *The God Squad*, 51–7.

125 Tyrrell contributed to Tuairim's 1960s investigations but his testimony was not included in *Some of Our Children: A Report on the Residential Care of the Deprived Child in Ireland by a London Branch Study Group* (London: Tuairim, 1966); Tyrrell, *Founded on Fear*, 38–9, 341.

established.[126] Some religious orders issued apologies while others were slow to acknowledge the extent of their culpability.[127]

The most recent inquiry in the Republic, under Judge Yvonne Murphy, announced in 2015, was prompted, in part, by Catherine Corless's work on the deaths of babies in the mother and baby home at Tuam, County Galway between 1925 and 1961. It is tasked with examining institutions that catered for pregnant single women. That commission is particularly concerned with the high infant mortality rates, allegations that vaccination trials were performed, and with the 'placement' of children with families in Ireland and abroad.[128] Commentators have demanded a commission of inquiry into psychiatric hospitals, though notably the institutions of the criminal justice system have not elicited similar levels of public outrage. Relatively absent from current studies is the abuse of boys in the Kincora Boy's Home, Belfast, which was revealed in the 1970s. There were allegations – then and later – of a cover-up and state and MI5 collusion resulting in two inquiries in 1982 and 1984.[129] The Inquiry into Historical Institutional Abuse in Northern Ireland, established to examine allegations of child abuse between 1922 and 1995 in numerous institutions, including those of the criminal justice and education systems, published its findings in January 2017. The inquiry concluded that children had been emotionally, physically and sexually abused while in institutional care in Northern Ireland. In relation to Kincora, the inquiry established that thirty-nine boys were abused during their time there, that the 1974 police investigation into allegations of abuse was 'inept and inadequate' but that there was no evidence that 'security agencies were complicit in the abuse'.[130] The inquiry also examined the 'child migrant programme', which sent children to Australia and the activities of Father Brendan Smyth, Norbertine Order, who abused children over a forty-year period.[131]

126 L. Earner-Byrne, 'Child Sexual Abuse, History and the Pursuit of Blame in Modern Ireland', in K. Holmes and S. Ward (eds.), *Exhuming Passions: Memory and the Pressures of the Past in Australia and Ireland* (Dublin: Irish Academic Press, 2011), 51–70.

127 *CICA*, vol. 1, 15–28.

128 Mother and Baby Homes Commission of Investigation Terms of Reference: www.mbhcoi.ie/MBH.nsf/page/Terms%20of%20reference-en (accessed 15 September 2015).

129 E. McCann, 'MI5's Murky Role in Kincora Scandal yet to be Exposed', *Irish Times* (24 July 2014): www.irishtimes.com (accessed 10 October 2015).

130 'Historical Institutional Abuse Inquiry: 'Widespread abuse' in children's homes', BBC News (January 2017): www.bbc.com/news/uk-northern-ireland-38685157 (accessed 17 April 2017).

131 Detailed information on the work of the Inquiry into Historical Institutional Abuse is available on their website: www.hiainquiry.org.

The success of, and responses to, these enquiries have been mixed. The United Nations Committee Against Torture, amongst others, criticised the McAleese Committee for adopting adversarial legal models and according the evidence of religious orders and state agencies greater significance than that of survivors.[132] The state, in particular Michael Woods, Minister for Education (2000–2002), was criticised for entering financial agreements in 2000 that favoured the religious orders. Nonetheless, the findings of the inquiries highlighted important lessons, useful for other states currently facing similar revelations. The inquiries demonstrate the dangers resultant from failures to maintain meaningful levels of inspection and placing too much confidence in cohorts and organisations with authority: the impact individual personalities, staff members and management committees had in cultivating abusive and brutalising environments; how survivors can themselves replicate abusive behaviours inside and outside institutions; and the harsh attitudes towards poverty within a society that frequently conceived of the poor and vulnerable as semi-criminal. There is also agreement that residents of the institutions were vulnerable to abuse not only because of their poverty but, as Ferguson puts it, because they carried additional moral and social taints.[133] Reaching an understanding as to *why* rather than *how* these institutions became sites of abuse and why testimonies from survivors and contemporary knowledge of the regimes were ignored in Ireland, in Europe, and elsewhere for so long remains challenging.

Conclusion

Referring to the Magdalen asylums, Smith argues that currently they exist in the public mind at 'the level of a *story* (cultural representation and survivor testimony) rather than history (archives records and documentation)'.[134] While there are problems with Smith's dichotomy, his observation has some weight. The contemporary debate on the twentieth-century history of institutions, in particular those intended for children and single mothers, has become the lens through which the longer history of institutions is now analysed. Studies exemplify other interpretative tensions; on one hand, authors eulogise the reformative and charitable impetus that informed their establishment and their 'Irish' pedigree, yet, on the other hand label them as institutions of

132 'McAleese Report Leaves Questions Unanswered', *Irish Examiner* (19 February 2014).
133 Ferguson, 'Abused and Looked After Children as "Moral Dirt"', 137.
134 Smith, *Ireland's Magdalen Laundries*, xvi–xvii.

'social control'.[135] There is also an assumption that with the passing of most of these institutions, the class-based responses to poverty, sexuality, criminality, alcoholism and household 'disorder' revealed in this literature have also been consigned to history. Yet, the entrenched nature of cultural divisions between deserving and undeserving poverty is still evident in current debates on the 'new' homeless in the post-crash economy of Ireland. Institutions continue to be used to contain populations that society is ambivalent about, notably direct provision accommodation centres for asylum seekers.

Most of the literature reviewed examines developments in Ireland within a British Isles context. These have uncovered important patterns as to the nature and the limitations of nineteenth-century central government and the variety of local institutional practices within and across systems. It remains unclear where Ireland can be situated within broader debates on the 'rise of the institution' outlined earlier. Whether the United Kingdom is the most useful comparator, especially during the twentieth century, is also open to debate. The National Health Service, the welfare model adopted in Britain after the Second World War, differed from those in operation in other parts of Europe, as did the relationship between the state and the churches. Linking Ireland's history of institutions to that of other European countries may prove revealing and may challenge claims to an exceptional Irish experience.

As with all fields of research, there are lacunae, some of which are a consequence of the problems with source material. With some important exceptions, existing studies tend to privilege independent Ireland's history, often focusing on Catholic-run institutions.[136] These emphasise the shared support among state and religious bodies for models of welfare based on Roman Catholic ideals and structures. This narrative requires further nuancing and development, not only to uncover alternative and dissenting models, if such existed, but also to gain a better understanding of the philosophical underpinnings of the models proffered within Catholicism.[137] McCormick's finding of 'considerable unity across the religious and political spectrum' in relation to female sexuality in Northern Ireland is in this respect important.[138] The

---

135 Reidy, *Ireland's 'Moral Hospital'*.

136 N. Meehan, 'Church and State and the Bethany Home', *History Ireland,* supplement, 18 (2010), 1–10.

137 S. Riordan, ' "Storm and Stress": Richard Devane, Adolescent Psychology and the Politics of Protective Legislation 1922–1935', in C. Cox and S. Riordan (eds.), *Adolescence in Modern Irish History* (Houndmills: Palgrave Macmillan, 2015), 129–50.

138 McCormick, *Regulating Sexuality*, 14.

paucity of research on Northern Ireland generally is striking and interesting; it would seem events there are analysed only in so far as they relate to that jurisdiction's troubled political history. Overall, a better understanding of the complex relationship between institutional and non-institutional welfare provision and support is required.

23

A Short History of Irish Memory in the Long Twentieth Century

GUY BEINER

On the cusp of the twentieth century, Ireland was obsessed with memorialisation. This condition reflected a transnational *zeitgeist* that was indicative of a crisis of memory throughout Europe. The outcome of rapid modernisation, manifested through changes ushered in by such far-reaching processes as industrialisation, urbanisation, commercialisation and migration, raised fears that the rituals and customs through which the past had been habitually remembered in the countryside were destined to be swept away. The future of memory was deemed uncertain.

Preoccupation with memory is pervasive in the writing of the period. It is apparent, for example, in the philosophy of Henri Bergson – namely in *Matter and Memory* [*Matière et mémoire* (1896)], the psychology of Sigmund Freud (as evident in several of his landmark essays) and, perhaps most famously, in Marcel Proust's classic novel *À la récherche du temps perdu* (1913–1927), originally translated as *Remembrance of Things Past*.[1] Writing in the early-twentieth century, the sociologist Émile Durkheim maintained that group identity requires a sense of continuity with the past.[2] This embryonic notion of social memory

---

1 R. Terdiman, *Present Past: Modernity and the Memory Crisis* (Ithaca and London: Cornell University Press, 1993). See also relevant chapters in S. Radstone and B. Schwarz (eds.), *Memory: Histories, Theories, Debates* (New York: Fordham University Press, 2010): K. Ansell-Pearson, 'Bergson on Memory', 61–76; R. Terdiman, 'Memory in Freud', 93–108; M. Wood, 'Proust: The Music of Memory', 109–122.

2 É. Durkheim, *The Elementary Forms of the Religious Life*, translated by J. W. Swain (London: G. Allen & Unwin, Ltd, 1915). See also W. Gephart, 'Memory and the Sacred: The Cult of Anniversaries and Commemorative Rituals in the Light of The Elementary Forms', in N. J. Allen, W. S. F. Pickering and W. W. Miller (eds.), *On Durkheim's Elementary Forms of Religious Life* (London and New York: Routledge, 1998), 127–35; B. A. Misztal, 'Durkheim on Collective Memory', *Journal of Classical Sociology*, 3, (1 July 2003), 123–43. It is disappointing that a Durkheimian study of Irish national identity failed to pick up on the significance of memory; see J. Dingley, *Durkheim and National Identity in Ireland: Applying the Sociology of Knowledge and Religion* (New York: Palgrave Macmillan, 2015).

would later be developed by his disciple Maurice Halbwachs, who coined the term collective memory ('la mémoire collective'). By calling attention to the social frameworks in which memory is framed ('les cadres sociaux de la mémoire'), Halbwachs presented a sound theoretical model for understanding how individual members of a society collectively remember their past.[3] The impression that modernisation had uprooted people from tradition and that mass society suffered from atomised impersonality gave birth to a vogue for commemoration, which was seen as a fundamental act of communal solidarity, in that it projected an illusion of continuity with the past.[4]

Ireland, outside of Belfast, did not undergo industrialisation on a scale comparable with England, and yet Irish society was not spared the upheaval of modernity. The Great Famine had decimated vernacular Gaelic culture and resulted in massive emigration. An Irish variant of *fin de siècle* angst over degeneration fed on apprehensions that British rule would ultimately result in the loss of 'native' identity. The perceived threat to national culture, articulated in Douglas Hyde's manifesto on 'The Necessity for De-Anglicising Ireland' (1892), stimulated a vigorous response in the form of the Irish Revival (see Chapter 8, this volume by Ó Conchubhair). The flourishing of home-grown literary production was dubbed by William Butler Yeats 'The Celtic Twilight' for its creative engagement with myths from a distant quasi-historical past. In addition, the Gaelic League set out to revive the Irish language and the Gaelic Athletic Association (GAA) reinvented traditional sportive games. By participating in popular commemorative rituals, such as the annual parades for the Manchester Martyrs (three Fenians who had been convicted and executed for killing a policeman during a prisoner rescue operation in England), nationalists of all shades endorsed a Fenian cult of political martyrdom, which was also expressed in the singing of ballads, such as the anthemic 'God Save Ireland'.[5]

---

3 Written in the interwar period, the seminal writings of Halbwachs were only translated into English at a much later date; see M. Halbwachs, *The Collective Memory* (New York: Harper & Row, 1980); M. Halbwachs, *On Collective Memory* (Chicago and London: University of Chicago Press, 1992).

4 For a sociological discussion of commemorative ceremonies as a 'compensatory strategy' of modernity, see P. Connerton, *How Societies Remember* (Cambridge University Press, 1989), 41–71.

5 G. Beiner, 'Fenianism and the Martyrdom-Terrorism Nexus in Ireland before Independence', in D. Janes and A. Houen (eds.), *Martyrdom and Terrorism: Pre-Modern to Contemporary Perspectives* (Oxford University Press, 2014),199–220 (esp. 200–7); O. McGee, '"God Save Ireland": Manchester-Martyr Demonstrations in Dublin, 1867–1916', *Éire-Ireland*, 36, (2001), 39–66.

Elsewhere in Europe, civic cults of anniversaries were introduced by modern states through such ceremonies as the inauguration of Bastille Day in the French Third Republic (1880), the commemoration of the Magyar Millennium in Hungary (1896), and the marking of Bismarck's death in Germany (1898).[6] Similarly, in 1897 the Diamond Jubilee of Queen Victoria was celebrated in Ireland not only by Protestants but also by large numbers of the Catholics, who seemed willing to participate in British imperial memorial culture.[7] Anxieties over such displays of popular loyalism mobilised nationalists, who in 1898 orchestrated numerous celebrations of the centenary of the 1798 Rebellion in a massive demonstration of counter-hegemonic remembrance. The overwhelming success of the centennial commemorations and the subsequent boom of what has been labelled 'statuomania', in reference to the enthusiasm in which communities throughout Ireland rushed to erect monuments to the United Irishmen, can be attributed above all to the agency of local '98 Clubs. These were typically dominated by school teachers, parish priests, newspaper editors and local politicians, who mediated between the political demands of a metropolitan nationalist leadership based in Dublin and London and the grassroots expectations for recognition of provincial folk memory, facilitating what can be labelled regeneration, or reinvention, of tradition.[8]

As a 16-year-old youth, James Joyce was among the crowd of 100,000 who attended the main centenary event in Dublin on 15 August 1898 and witnessed the ceremonial laying of the foundation stone for an intended monument in honour of the 'father of Irish republicanism', Theobald Wolfe Tone. In *A Portrait of the Artist as a Young Man* (1916), he irreverently recalled this moment as a 'scene of tawdry tribute'. In 1903, the rituals of nationalist commemoration were reaffirmed in the centenary of the execution of the republican martyr Robert Emmet, which was celebrated in Dublin with yet another massive procession. Joyce, however, would look back at the unfulfilled promise to construct a monument on Stephen's Green ('where Wolfe Tone's statue was not'), which would instead become the site of a memorial arch for the

---

6 E. Hobsbawm, 'Mass-Producing Traditions: Europe, 1870–1914', in E. Hobsbawm and T. Ranger (eds.), *The Invention of Tradition* (Cambridge University Press, 1983), 263–307.
7 J. H. Murphy, *Abject Loyalty: Nationalism and Monarchy in Ireland During the Reign of Queen Victoria* (Washington, DC: Catholic University of America Press, 2001). For similar reactions to royal visits in the early-twentieth century see S. Pašeta, 'Nationalist Responses to Two Royal Visits to Ireland, 1900 and 1903', *Irish Historical Studies*, 31124 (1999), 488–504.
8 G. Beiner, *Remembering the Year of the French: Irish Folk History and Social Memory* (Madison, WI: University of Wisconsin Press, 2007), 243–75.

soldiers of the Royal Dublin Fusiliers who fought in the Boer War. Joyce's compulsion to capture in *Ulysses* (1922) the minutiae of life on the streets of Dublin at the turn of the century produced a literary monument to a city on the verge of change that embodies the very essence of the modernist crisis of memory.[9]

The young generation that participated in the commemorations of the centenary of the United Irishmen was schooled on veneration of memory.[10] The graveside oration delivered by Patrick Pearse at the funeral of the veteran Fenian Jeremiah O'Donovan Rossa on 1 August 1915 encapsulated their belief in the regenerative power of remembrance of the dead: 'Life springs from death and from the graves of patriot men and women spring living nations.'[11] Many of the events that took place in the revolutionary decade between 1912 and 1923 were subject to instant mythologising. Above all, 1916 stands out as a cornerstone of twentieth-century Irish memory. Both nationalists and unionists re-adapted familiar motifs from historical traditions that pivoted on themes of trauma and triumph in order to construct evocative memories of blood sacrifice, which were quickly adopted as foundation myths by the ascendant political cultures of twentieth-century Ireland: the Easter Rising for nationalist Independent Ireland, and the Battle of the Somme for Unionist Northern Ireland.[12]

Revolutions characteristically entail the replacement of commemorative iconography associated with the previous regime. Moreover, partitions localise and intensify conflicts over the symbols of national memory. A contemporary comparison can be found in Central Europe by considering the partition of the Austro-Hungarian empire, following the Trianon Peace Treaty (1920). In a resentful reaction to the condescending policies of Magyarisation, Hungarian monuments were defaced and replaced with local nationalist memorials in the newly established states of Czechoslovakia and the Kingdom of Serbs, Croats and Slovenes, as well as in the province

---

9 L. Gibbons, ' "Where Wolfe Tone's Statue Was Not": Joyce, Monuments and Memory', in I. McBride (ed.), *History and Memory in Modern Ireland* (Cambridge University Press, 2001), 139–59. For essays on the many aspects of memory that appear in the works of Joyce, see O. Frawley and K. O'Callaghan (eds.), *Memory Ireland*, vol. 4: *James Joyce and Cultural Memory* (Syracuse: Syracuse University Press, 2014).

10 R. F. Foster, *Vivid Faces: The Revolutionary Generation in Ireland, 1890–1923* (London: Allen Lane, 2014), 289 and 328.

11 *Collected Works of Pádraic H. Pearse*, vol. 5: *Political Writings and Speeches* (Dublin, Cork and Belfast: The Phoenix Publishing Co., 1916), 133–7.

12 G. Beiner, 'Between Trauma and Triumphalism: The Easter Rising, the Somme, and the Crux of Deep Memory in Modern Ireland', *Journal of British Studies*, 46, (2007), 366–89.

of Transylvania, annexed by Romania. In response, irredentist monuments were erected in the truncated Kingdom of Hungary, planting an embittered memorial legacy which would return to haunt Central European politics.[13] After the partition of Ireland, nationalist commemoration was banned in Northern Ireland while Orange celebrations of the twelfth of July, considered intolerable to the minority Catholic population, were adopted as state holidays. In southern Ireland, a purge of the markings of loyalist heritage resulted in the destruction of 'Big Houses' and the removal of imperial monuments.[14] The forcefulness of this memorial iconoclasm, a phenomenon that can be labelled 'de-commemoration', was tempered by ambivalence over how independence had been achieved.

Commemoration of the Irish Revolution was stifled by bitter contentions.[15] Whereas in Northern Ireland remembrance of the Great War was accorded pride of place within authorised Unionist culture, the governments of independent Ireland (who claimed to be the heirs of the rebels of 1916) were far less keen to commemorate the tens of thousands of Irishmen who had enlisted in the British army with the encouragement of the Irish Parliamentary Party.[16] The disapprobation shown towards southern veterans, who wished to commemorate the Great War, was mirrored by the alienation of northern nationalists from Remembrance Day commemorations, which were conducted in Northern Ireland purely as Unionist events.[17] Commemorative paralysis was

---

13 G. Beiner, ' "No, Nay, Never" (Once More): The Resurrection of Hungarian Irredentism', *History Ireland*, 21, (2013), 40–4.

14 J. S. Donnelly, Jr, 'Big House Burnings in County Cork During the Irish Revolution, 1920–21', *Éire-Ireland*, 47, (2012), 141–97; T. Dooley, 'The Destruction of the Country House in Ireland, 1879–1973', in J. Raven (ed.), *Lost Mansions: Essays on the Destruction of the Country House* (Basingstoke and New York: Palgrave Macmillan, 2015), 44–62; Y. Whelan, 'The Construction and Destruction of a Colonial Landscape: Monuments to British Monarchs in Dublin before and after Independence', *Journal of Historical Geography*, 28, (2002), 508–33.

15 D. Fitzpatrick, 'Commemoration in the Irish Free State: A Chronicle of Embarrassment' in McBride (ed.), *History and Memory*, 184–203.

16 K. Jeffery, *Ireland and the Great War* (Cambridge University Press, 2000), 107–43; N. C. Johnson, *Ireland, the Great War, and the Geography of Remembrance* (Cambridge University Press, 2003); C. Switzer, *Unionists and Great War Commemoration in the North of Ireland 1914–1939* (Dublin: Irish Academic Press, 2007), esp. 106–20; J. Turpin, 'Monumental Commemoration of the Fallen in Ireland, North and South, 1920–60', *New Hibernia Review*, 11, (2007), 107–19.

17 J. Leonard, 'Facing "the Finger of Scorn": Veterans' Memories of Ireland and the Great War', in M. Evans and K. Lunn (eds.), *War and Memory in the Twentieth Century* (Oxford and New York: Berg, 1997), 59–72; T. Canavan, 'The Poppy My Father Wore: The Problems Facing Irish Nationalists in Commemorating the Two World Wars', in E. Bort *Commemorating Ireland: History, Politics, Culture* (Dublin: Irish Academic Press, 2004), 56–67.

particularly noticeable with regard to the Civil War, which had shaped the political fault lines of Irish politics and remained too controversial to be properly remembered in public.[18] Struggles over ownership of nationalist traditions were apparent in the alternative memorial ceremonies held at Theobald Wolfe Tone's grave in Bodenstown, as well as at numerous local sites of memory, each of which contested official commemoration by the state.[19]

Memoirs of the War of Independence were bestsellers in the early years of the state and their authors, such as Dan Breen, Tom Barry and Ernie O'Malley, became celebrities.[20] A great number of reminiscences of those who had participated in the struggle for Irish independence were compiled by government officials behind closed doors. In accordance with the Army Pensions Acts (1923 and 1953) and the Military Service Pensions Acts (1924, 1934 and 1949), applicants for state pensions were required to give their personal testimonies to the Department of Defence. Realising the historical value of such recollections, a specially designated Bureau of Military History collected between 1947 and 1957 a total of 1,773 witness statements and supplementary materials from veterans of separatist military organisations. These accounts, which reflect how the events were recollected after three decades, touched on sensitive issues. They were therefore kept out of the public eye and only released in the early twenty-first century.[21]

Folk memory was considered less controversial. However, concerns were raised about the survival of Ireland's rich oral traditions. Transformations in rural social practices brought a decline in the custom of evening gatherings in *céilí* (visiting) houses, which were described by American anthropologists in the 1930s as 'the seat of traditional lore and entertainment'.[22] The sense that tradition was doomed to pass away served as a catalyst for the collecting of folklore and for developments in its study. The founding of the Folklore of Ireland Society in 1927 was followed by the establishment of an

---

18 A. Dolan, *Commemorating the Irish Civil War: History and Memory, 1923–2000* (Cambridge University Press, 2003).

19 A. Dolan, 'An Army of Our Fenian Dead: Republicanism, Monuments and Commemoration', in F. McGarry (ed.), *Republicanism in Modern Ireland* (Dublin: UCD Press, 2003), 132–44.

20 D. Breen, *My Fight for Irish Freedom* (Dublin: Talbot Press, 1924); E. O'Malley, *On Another Man's Wound* (London: Rich & Cowan, 1936); T. Barry, *Guerilla Days in Ireland* (Dublin: Irish Press, 1949).

21 The Bureau of Military History Collection was publicly launched in 2003 and has since been made available online: www.bureauofmilitaryhistory.ie. The phased release of the Military Service Pensions Collection commenced in 2014: www.militaryarchives.ie/collections/online-collections/military-service-pensions-collection.

22 C. M. Arensberg and S. T. Kimball, *Family and Community in Ireland*, 3rd ed. (Ennis, County Clare: Clasp Press, 2001), 186.

Irish Folklore Institute (1930), which was replaced in 1935 by the Irish Folklore Commission. Under the directorship of James Hamilton Delargy [Séamus Ó Duilearga], specially trained folklore collectors were sent throughout the thirty-two counties on the island to document oral traditions. They recorded and transcribed the repertoire of storytellers and singers of local renown, many of whom no longer had a ready audience. A preference was shown towards Irish-speaking rural areas and long narrative tales (*scéalaithe*) were generally favoured over shorter folk history accounts (*seanchas*). By the time the commission was disbanded in 1970, its collections included 1,746 volumes of manuscripts.[23]

In addition, a Schools' Folklore Scheme organised in 1937–1938 by the Irish Folklore Commission, in collaboration with the Department of Education and the Irish National Teachers' Organisation, involved some 100,000 children from 5,000 primary schools in the twenty-six counties of the Irish Free State. Well over half a million manuscript pages were written by the participating pupils, who collected accounts of traditions in their local communities, often from older family members. The Schools' Scheme, which showed more willingness to record traditions in English, reached many areas that had not been covered by the official folklore collectors.[24] The ambitious extent of folklore collecting in Ireland is comparable to the United States Federal Writers' Project, created in 1935 as part of the New Deal. During the Great Depression, historians, teachers, authors and librarians were employed by the Works Progress Administration (WPA) to write local ethnographic accounts and to take down life histories, including the reminiscences of former slaves.[25] These two contemporary projects shared a democratic belief that memories of common people living in purportedly backward areas had intrinsic historical value and were well worth preserving as a cultural resource for a modern nation. It should also be acknowledged that folk memory, as expressed in traditional forms of storytelling and vernacular commemoration, never fully died away and re-adaptations of folk history continued to persist through the twentieth century.[26]

23 M. Briody, *The Irish Folklore Commission 1935–1970: History, Ideology, Methodology* (Helsinki: Finnish Literature Society, 2007).
24 Ibid., 260–70.
25 See J. Hirsch, *Portrait of America: A Cultural History of the Federal Writers' Project* (Chapel Hill: University of North Carolina Press, 2003); David A. Taylor, *Soul of a People: The WPA Writer's Project Uncovers Depression America* (Hoboken, NJ: Wiley, 2009).
26 H. Glassie, *Passing the Time in Ballymenone: Culture and History of an Ulster Community* (Philadelphia: University of Pennsylvania Press, 1982); G. Beiner, 'The Decline and Rebirth of "Folk Memory": Remembering "The Year of the French" in the Late Twentieth Century', *Éire–Ireland*, 38, (2003), 7–32; R. Cashman, *Storytelling on the Northern Irish Border: Characters and Community* (Bloomington: Indiana University Press, 2008), 233–56.

Segregated commemoration of the First World War would continue also in regards to commemoration of the Second World War. In Northern Ireland, Catholic war veterans were again excluded from the official narrative of war remembrance. The neglect for over half a century to honour the achievement of James 'Mick' Magennis, the only serviceman from Northern Ireland to be awarded a Victoria Cross in the war, is a telling example of how a Catholic war veteran from west Belfast did not fit into the dominant narratives of unionist or republican memory.[27] The southern state was altogether unwilling to recognise the many thousands of volunteers who defied Ireland's policy of neutrality and joined the effort to defeat Nazi Germany (including some 5,000 members of the Irish Defence Forces, who were branded deserters).[28] Meanwhile, state commemorations of the Easter Rising continued annually and reached a climax in 1966.

The golden jubilee of 1916 was marked with parades, pageants, renaming of streets and buildings, dedication of memorial sites – most notably the Garden of Remembrance in Dublin city centre and the museum exhibition at Kilmainham Gaol, commissioning of artworks, issue of commemorative stamps and the production of films. Television was introduced as a new media for remembrance in the eight-part drama series *Insurrection*, directed by Louis Lentin, which was broadcast twice on Teilefís Éireann and was enthusiastically received by viewers. Éamon de Valera, the 84-year-old president (who was re-elected for another term that year) was at the centre of the state ceremonies, as the last surviving commandant of the Rising. None the less, the official commemorative programme shied away from nostalgic romanticised pastoral visions of Ireland, associated with de Valera, in favour of applauding the economic development identified with the modernising policies of the then Taoiseach Seán Lemass (also a veteran of the Rising). The government was determined to overcome political rifts and to avoid any celebration of violence, going as far as banning the playing of rebel songs on Radio Éireann. However, a committee of oppositional Republicans, chaired by another veteran, Joseph Clarke, defiantly mounted an alternative commemorative programme. The wives and sisters of prominent 1916 rebels were particularly vocal in their criticism of the official celebrations. Outside of organised commemoration, the most spectacular event of the fiftieth anniversary was the blowing up by the IRA of Nelson's Pillar, which had stood directly opposite the GPO – the main site of the 1916 commemoration. This illegal act of

27 G. Woodward, *Culture, Northern Ireland, and the Second World War* (Oxford, 2015), 1–2.
28 R. Doherty, *Irish Volunteers in the Second World War* (Dublin: Four Courts Press, 2002).

de-commemoration fulfilled the drive to obliterate remnants of earlier commemorative culture and symbolically brought violence back on to the centre stage.[29]

In June 1966, the prime minister of Northern Ireland Terence O'Neill attended a Great War commemoration in France for the 36th (Ulster) Division, which had been heavily recruited from the original Ulster Volunteer Force. He was called back home upon receiving news of a sectarian murder committed by a newly-revived paramilitary Ulster Volunteer Force (UVF). That year, permission given to northern nationalists to commemorate the Easter Rising's fiftieth anniversary provoked a loyalist counter-demonstration headed by Rev. Ian Paisley, who was determined to re-assert Unionist control over remembrance in the public sphere. A few years later, Conor Cruise O'Brien argued that the commemorations of 1916 in 1966 triggered the militant revival of the IRA, which allegedly led to the uncontainable outburst of violence in 1969.[30] Even though the attribution of the outbreak of the Northern Irish conflict primarily to republican rituals of remembrance was a polemical exaggeration, the government of the Republic of Ireland promptly put an end to the annual military parades. Commemorative embarrassment was evident over the next decades and was particularly noticeable in the absence of official events during the seventy-fifth anniversary of the Easter Rising in 1991.[31]

Nationalists in Northern Ireland, which in 1972 was put under Direct Rule, found in remembrance a powerful medium to counter official narratives. With the popularisation of psychoanalytical discourse, memories of violence were intrinsically regarded as traumatic. When British paratroopers opened fire on a civil rights march in Derry on 30 January 1972, killing 13 people and injuring 14 (one of whom was to subsequently die of his wounds), the Catholic community at large underwent a collective trauma, which was soon politicised. Outrage was channelled into grassroots commemoration after the Widgery Tribunal accepted the government's denial of misconduct. Subversive remembrance of Bloody Sunday was ritualised in annual memorial parades and was expressed through a wide array of

29 R. Higgins, *Transforming 1916: Meaning, Memory and the Fiftieth Anniversary of the Easter Rising* (Cork: Cork University Press, 2012); M. McCarthy, *Ireland's 1916 Rising: Explorations of History-Making, Commemoration & Heritage in Modern Times* (Farnham and Burlington: Ashgate, 2012), 187–273; see also M. E. Daly and M. O'Callaghan (eds.), *1916 in 1966: Commemorating the Easter Rising* (Dublin: Royal Irish Academy, 2007).

30 C. C. O'Brien, *States of Ireland* (London: Hutchinson, 1972), 150.

31 D. Kiberd, 'The Elephant of Revolution Forgetfulness', in M. Ní Dhonnchadha and T. Dorgan (eds.), *Revising the Rising* (Derry: Field Day, 1991), 1–20.

cultural representations, including literature and drama, cinema, sculpture, murals and countless memorabilia.[32]

In the second half of the twentieth century, there was a noticeable shift in the dominant international paradigm of commemoration, which moved from celebration of victors to remembrance of victims. Adoption of the Holocaust as a cosmopolitan memory of human rights gave cultural trauma a privileged status that could yield political dividends.[33] This development was not lost on northern nationalists. The republican prisoner protest against the withdrawal of Special Category Status for convicted paramilitary members, which culminated in the hunger strike of 1981, became a memorial landmark. The funeral of IRA hunger-striker Bobby Sands in 1981 was attended by 100,000 people and the ten prisoners who starved to death were remembered as martyrs in annual commemorations, memorials and several feature films. Their memory was carefully stage-managed by the leadership of the provisional republican movement as a source of political legitimisation (although the leadership has since been criticised in a number of memoirs).[34]

In an age of growing globalisation, Irish memory was inherently transnational. For most of the twentieth century, there was a continuous outflow of disillusioned emigrants who left Ireland in search of a better life abroad. Disregarding the actual conditions of unemployment and dearth that were left behind, Irish diaspora communities sustained romanticised images of the homeland, continuing patterns of nostalgia from the nineteenth century that were especially prevalent among Irish-Americans.[35] The often sentimental ways in which the 'auld sod' was remembered abroad were communicated in letters home, which in turn influenced local memories. Globalisation

32 S. Dunn, 'Bloody Sunday and Its Commemoration Parades', in T. G. Fraser (ed.), *The Irish Parading Tradition: Following the Drum* (New York: St. Martin's Press, 2000), 129–41; P. Hayes and J. Campbell, *Bloody Sunday: Trauma, Pain and Politics* (London and Ann Arbor: Pluto Press, 2005); G. Dawson, *Making Peace with the Past? Memory, Trauma and the Irish Troubles* (Manchester: Manchester University Press, 2007), 87–205; T. Herron and J. Lynch, *After Bloody Sunday: Ethics, Representation, Justice* (Cork: Cork University Press, 2007); A. Blaney, 'Remembering Historical Trauma in Paul Greengrass's *Bloody Sunday*', *History and Memory*, 19, (2007), 113–38; B. Conway, *Commemoration and Bloody Sunday: Pathways of Memory* (Basingstoke and New York: Palgrave Macmillan, 2010).

33 See D. Levy and N. Sznaider, 'Memory Unbound: The Holocaust and the Formation of Cosmopolitan Memory', *European Journal of Social Theory*, 5, (2002), 87–106; D. Levy and N. Sznaider, 'The Institutionalization of Cosmopolitan Morality: The Holocaust and Human Rights', *Journal of Human Rights*, 3, (2004), 143–57.

34 S. Hopkins, 'The Chronicles of Long Kesh: Provisional Irish Republican Memoirs and the Contested Memory of the Hunger Strikes', *Memory Studies*, 7, (2014), 425–39.

35 J. P. Byrne, 'Cultural Memory, Identity, and Irish-American Nostalgia', in O. Frawley (ed.), *Memory Ireland*, vol. 2: *Diaspora and Memory Practices* (Syracuse: Syracuse University Press, 2012), 49–60.

contributed to the reinvention of traditions in Ireland, as in the importation of Americanised Saint Patrick's Day celebrations.[36] A developing Irish heritage industry, catering for tourists as well as for an internal market, assumed an increasingly dominant role in promoting commercialised national and local presentations of the past.[37] Generically berated as 'theme parks' that blatantly distort factual history, commemorative heritage came to play a key role in representing memory, often serving as a gateway to more rigorous historical explorations.[38] The fascination of Irish cinema with the past has been even more influential in reaching large audiences and shaping popular historical consciousness. The most striking example is Neil Jordan's *Michael Collins* (1996), which sparked a heated public debate on the War of Independence and the Civil War.[39]

The century ended with a worldwide revival of obsessive preoccupation with memorialisation, which has been described as a 'memory boom of unprecedented proportions'.[40] Echoing the apprehensions of the previous *fin de siècle*, postmodern critics maintained that connections with the past were about to be irrevocably severed. As put by the French historian Pierre Nora, in introducing his seminal concept of *lieux de mémoire*, 'we speak so much of memory because there is so little of it left'.[41] On this background, the 1990s in Ireland evolved into a commemorative decade, which centred

36 M. Cronin and D. Adair, *The Wearing of the Green: A History of St. Patrick's Day* (London and New York: Routledge, 2006), 210–23.

37 D. Brett, *The Construction of Heritage* (Cork: Cork University Press, 1996); N. C. Johnson, 'Framing the Past: Time, Space and the Politics of Heritage Tourism in Ireland', *Political Geography*, 18, (1999), 187–207; E. Zuelow, *Making Ireland Irish: Tourism and National Identity since the Irish Civil War* (Syracuse: Syracuse University Press, 2009), 136–77.

38 R. F. Foster, *The Irish Story: Telling Tales and Making It Up in Ireland* (London and New York: Allen Lane, 2001), 23–36. Cf. G. Beiner, 'Commemorative Heritage and the Dialectics of Memory', in M. McCarthy (ed.), *Ireland's Heritages: Critical Perspectives on Memory and Identity* (Aldershot and Burlington: Ashgate, 2005), 55–69.

39 R. Barton, *Irish National Cinema* (London and New York: Routledge, 2004), 130–56. For additional discussion of the role of history in the film *Michael Collins*, see L. Gibbons, 'Framing History: Neil Jordan's *Michael Collins*', *History Ireland*, 1, (Spring 1997), 47–51; B. McIlroy, 'History without Borders: Neil Jordan's *Michael Collins*', in J. MacKillop (ed.), *Contemporary Irish Cinema: From The Quiet Man to Dancing at Lughnasa* (Syracuse: Syracuse University Press, 1999), 22–8; R. Merivirta, *The Gun and Irish Politics: Examining National History in Neil Jordan's Michael Collins* (Bern and New York: Peter Lang, 2009).

40 A. Huyssen, *Twilight Memories: Marking Time in a Culture of Amnesia* (New York: Routledge, 1995), 1–9. See also J. Winter, 'Notes on the Memory Boom: War, Remembrance, and the Uses of the Past' in Duncan Bell (ed.), *Memory, Trauma and World Politics: Reflections on the Relationship between Past and Present* (Basingstoke and New York: Palgrave Macmillan, 2006), 54–73; D. W. Blight, 'The Memory Boom: Why and Why Now?', in P. Boyer and J. V. Wertsch, *Memory in Mind and Culture* (Cambridge University Press, 2009), 238–51.

41 P. Nora, 'Between Memory and History: Les Lieux de Mémoire', *Representations*, 26 (1989), 7–24 (quotation at 7). For a sociological study of contemporary culture as an agent

on the sesquicentenary of the Great Famine and the bicentenary of the 1798 Rebellion. Affluence as well as politics played key roles in the burgeoning of commemoration.

Public remembrance of the Famine had previously been observed largely through muted commemoration, which should not be mistaken for silence, as the catastrophe of the Great Hunger [*An Gorta Mór*], commonly referred to in folklore as *An Drocshaol* [the Bad Times], was always a significant point of reference within Irish culture. Perhaps, the most noteworthy project of the centennial was a questionnaire circulated in 1945 by the Irish Folklore Commission to its full-time and part-time collectors, through which thousands of pages were collected that demonstrated (alongside other relevant accounts in the previously mentioned folklore collections) how the Famine was remembered in oral traditions.[42] In conditions of economic stagnation, few resources were available to fund commemoration in the 1940s. In contrast, the hundred-and-fiftieth anniversary, which benefitted from the prosperity of the Celtic Tiger, was characterised by its monumentality. Community initiatives, private fundraising and substantial government support (to the total of one million pounds, allocated over three years), facilitated across Ireland and the Irish diaspora the erection of Famine monuments, which exhibited a range of varying complexities and aesthetic qualities.[43]

---

for loss of memory see P. Connerton, *How Modernity Forgets* (Cambridge University Press, 2009).

42 R. McHugh, 'The Famine in Irish Oral Tradition', in R. D. Edwards and T. D. Williams (eds.), *The Great Famine: Studies in Irish History 1845–52* (Dublin: Lilliput Press, 1994; orig. ed. 1957), 389–436; C. Póirtéir, *Famine Echoes* (Dublin: Gill & Macmillan, 1995). For an historical method to analyse this material, which distinguishes between three levels of memory: global, popular and local, see N. Ó Ciosáin, 'Approaching a Folklore Archive: The Irish Folklore Commission and the Memory of the Great Famine', *Folklore*, 115, (2004), 222–32.

43 *Ireland's Famine: Commemoration and Awareness* (Dublin: Famine Commemoration Committee, Department of the Taoiseach, 1995), esp. 56–60; D. Mullan, *A Glimmer of Light: An Overview of Great Hunger Commemorative Events in Ireland and Throughout the World* (Dublin: Concern Worldwide, 1995). For critical analysis see M. Kelleher, 'Hunger and History: Monuments to the Great Irish Famine', *Textual Practice*, 16, (2002), 249–76; P. Gray, 'The Memory and Commemoration of the Great Irish Famine', in P. Gray and K. Oliver, *The Memory of Catastrophe* (Manchester: Manchester University Press, 2004), 46–64; M. E. Daly, ' "History à la Carte?": Historical Commemoration and Modern Ireland' in Bort (ed.), *Commemorating Ireland*, 34–55; J. Crowley, 'Constructing Famine Memory: The Role of Monuments', in N. Moore and Y. Whelan (eds.), *Heritage, Memory and the Politics of Identity: New Perspectives on the Cultural Landscape* (Aldershot and Burlington: Ashgate, 2007), 55–67; E. Mark-FitzGerald, *Commemorating the Irish Famine: Memory and the Monument* (Liverpool: Liverpool University Press, 2013), esp. 57–95. For commemoration in the United States see M. C. Kelly, *Ireland's Great Famine in Irish-American History: Enshrining a Fateful Memory* (Lanham, MD: Rowman & Littlefield, 2014), 151–93.

Even though sesquicentennial commemorations of the Famine, which had continued in its enormity at least until 1850, should rightly have continued into the end of the century, the specially formed interdepartmental Government Commemoration Committee (based in the Department of the Taoiseach) shifted its attention towards the end of 1997 to the next planned commemorative programme. The two-hundredth anniversary of the 1798 Rebellion was identified as a 'project of significant national importance' and accordingly the bicentenary was commemorated through a staggering volume of commemorative activities that amounted, according to official estimates, to over one thousand events. In light of the breakthrough in the Northern Ireland peace process, which resulted in the signing of the Good Friday Agreement in 1998, the government maintained that 'attention should shift from the military aspects of 1798 and be directed towards the principles of democracy and pluralism which the United Irishmen advocated'.[44]

Outside Dublin, a large concentration of commemorative programmes took place around County Wexford, a main arena of the rebellion, including the opening of a National 1798 Centre in Enniscorthy. Numerous events were also held in other counties across Ireland and in Irish communities abroad. The most remarkable aspect of the bicentenary was the series of successful commemorations organised in Northern Ireland, notably in counties Antrim and Down, where the United Irish rebels had been predominantly Presbyterian. The centenary in Ulster in 1898 had resulted in de-commemorative riots, in which Protestant loyalists attacked nationalist celebrations, but the new political climate in 1998 was conducive to more inclusive commemoration that crossed, at least to some extent, the sectarian divide.[45] The extensive involvement of a number of historians in the commemorations aroused controversy, with critics arguing that so-called 'post-revisionist' historical interpretations downplayed the extent of sectarian violence and overlooked atrocities committed during the rebellion. In comparative perspective, the debate in Ireland was considerably less divisive than the 'historian's feud' that had raged in

---

44 For documentation on the government's involvement in the commemorations see *Government's 1798 Commemoration Committee National Programme* (Dublin: Department of the Taoiseach, 1998); statement by the Taoiseach, Dail Éireann Debates, vol. 493, 3 July 1998; the 1798 Commemoration Committee's mission statement (April, 1997) published in *Freedom of Information Act, 1997: Guide to the Functions and Records of the Department of the Taoiseach – Sections 15 and 16 Reference Book* (Dublin: Department of the Taoiseach, 1998), 25; 1798 Commemoration Office strategy statement in *Strategy Statement for the Department of the Taoiseach for the Years 1998–2000* (Dublin: Department of the Taoiseach, 2001), 43–4.

45 P. Collins, *Who Fears to Speak of '98? Commemoration and the Continuing Impact of the United Irishmen* (Belfast: Ulster Historical Foundation, 2004), 84–154.

France during the bicentenary of the French Revolution and the accusations levelled at Irish 'commemorationist history' may have been overstated.[46]

The century closed with the bicentenary of the passing of the Act of Union, which marked a historical event of major significance but did not ignite too much public interest, even among Unionists. The bicentenary of Robert Emmet was recalled in 2003 with the issue of a number of new biographies of the pre-eminent heroic icon of modern Irish memory.[47] Concurrently, Irish historical studies, and Irish studies in general, caught up, albeit after a characteristic delay, with the surge in the study of memory that was already prominent in other countries since the late-1980s. Critical engagement with memory contributed towards moving Irish historiography and academic discourse beyond the revisionist debate, which had by then run its course.[48]

The developments in Irish commemoration in the 1990s opened the way for redress of previous neglect. Back in 1967, the historian F. X. Martin observed that 'outside of the Six Counties [of Northern Ireland], it is difficult to find men and women who will acknowledge that they are children of the men who were serving during 1916 in the British Army, the R.I.C. [Royal Irish Constabulary], the D.M.P. [Dublin Metropolitan Police], and Redmond's Irish National Volunteers'. Martin denounced this 'Great Oblivion' as 'an example of national amnesia'.[49] Three decades later, the dedication of the Island of Ireland Peace Park by the battlefield of Messines in Flanders, which was unveiled by the Irish president Mary McAleese in conjunction with Queen Elizabeth II and the Belgian King Albert II at a Remembrance Day ceremony on 11 November 1998, signalled a rediscovery of interest in the memory of Irish participation in the First World War. The laying of a wreath at the cenotaph

---

46 R. F. Foster, 'Remembering 1798', in McBride (ed.), *History and Memory*, 67–94; T. Dunne, *Rebellions: Memoir, Memory, and 1798* (Dublin: Lilliput Press, 2004), 130–48. Cf. G. Beiner, 'Commemorating "Ninety-Eight"', in 1998: A Reappraisal of History-Making in Contemporary Ireland' in T. Botherstone, A. Clark and K. Whelan (eds.), *These Fissured Isles: Ireland, Scotland and British History, 1798–1848* (Edinburgh: John Donald Publishers, 2005), 221–41. For the French controversy see S. L. Kaplan, *Farewell, Revolution*, vol. 1: *The Historians' Feud, France, 1789/1989* and vol. 2: *Disputed Legacies, France, 1789/1989* (Ithaca and London: Cornell University Press, 1995).

47 G. Beiner, 'The Legendary Robert Emmet and His Bicentennial Biographers', *The Irish Review*, 32 (2004), 98–104.

48 The landmark publication that signalled new-found interest in memory was the outcome of the conference of Irish historians in Britain, which was held during the bicentenary of 1798; see I. McBride (ed.), *History and Memory in Modern Ireland* (Cambridge University Press, 2001). Since then, there have been numerous publications in the field. For critical discussion of the state of the arts see G. Beiner, 'Probing the Boundaries of Irish Memory: From Postmemory to Prememory and Back', *Irish Historical Studies*, 39, (2014), 296–307.

49 F. X. Martin, '1916: Myth, Fact, and Mystery', *Studia Hibernica*, 7 (1967), 68.

outside Belfast City Hall by the first Sinn Féin Lord Mayor of Belfast, Alex Maskey, on the anniversary of the Battle of the Somme in 2002, encouraged northern republicans to engage with what had previously been considered an exclusively Unionist memory.

The Irish National War Memorial Gardens in Islandbridge (on the outskirts of Dublin city centre) hosted on 1 July 2006 a state commemoration of the ninetieth anniversary of the Battle of the Somme, which was attended by President McAleese, the Taoiseach Bertie Ahern, as well as delegates from Northern Ireland. After years of neglect, this grandiose memorial site (which was designed by the illustrious architect of British Great War commemoration, Edward Lutyens, but upon completion in 1939 had not been treated to an official opening) was finally restored to its original role. The marked enthusiasm with which the RTÉ Radio 1 broadcasts of the 2008 Thomas Davis lecture series on Ireland and the Great War were received by the general public revealed the growing emergence of interest in what was now labelled as 'Our War'.[50]

The new commemorative inclusiveness was epitomised in the historic visit of Queen Elizabeth II to Ireland in May 2011 (the first royal visit since independence). Over the course of the visit, wreath-laying ceremonies took place at the Irish National War Memorial Gardens, as well at the Garden of Remembrance on Parnell Square (dedicated to the memory of the 1916 Rising). In a further gesture of conciliation, the queen also visited the GAA stadium at Croke Park, where in 1920 Crown forces had opened fire on a Gaelic football match killing 14 civilians in what would be remembered by nationalists as the original Bloody Sunday. This visit heralded the countdown towards the 'Decade of Centenaries', which promised to air the memory of the Great War, to reappraise the Easter Rising, to confront silenced memories of the Civil War, and to recognise other hitherto neglected events, such as the Dublin Lock-out of 1913.

Despite the brimming self-confidence displayed in the commemorations of the 1990s and the energetic preparations for the centenary of 1916, Irish memory at the turn of the twentieth century is once again in desperate need of regeneration. A veneer of sophistication disguises the stark reality that the officially-sanctioned representations of memory displayed in the public

---

50 A. Rigney, 'Divided Pasts: A Premature Memorial and the Dynamics of Collective Remembrance', *Memory Studies*, 1, (2008), 89–97; J. Horne (ed.), *Our War: Ireland and the Great War* (Dublin: Royal Irish Academy, 2008); K. Jeffery, 'Irish Varieties of Great War Commemoration', in J. Horne and E. Madigan, *Towards Commemoration: Ireland in War and Revolution, 1912–1923* (Dublin: Royal Irish Academy, 2013), 117–25.

sphere tend to feature a very narrow share of the diversity of historical experiences. Women are mostly excluded from the memorial meta-narratives, as are a wide range of alternative memories that pertain to ethnic, gender and class identities that do not conform to a perceived hegemonic mainstream. Irish social remembrance faces the imperative of coming to terms with glaring omissions that have long been repressed in public, but were often remembered in private. Under further exploration, it transpires that the history of Irish memory is riddled with social forgetting.

The uncovering of how the Irish government during the 1930s and the 'Emergency' had been unwilling to permit entry to Jewish refugees seeking to escape Nazi persecution, was regarded in 1998 as a historical precedent from which a moral lesson could be learned for the absorption of asylum seekers. It follows that the exclusion of minorities, not least the indigenous minority of Travellers, from national memory, begs redress.[51] Many other such *lieux d'oubli* (to re-adapt Nora's term) await acknowledgement. There are no monuments or memorial sites for the deadly influenza epidemic of 1918–1919, which had an impact that exceeded that of the much-commemorated Anglo-Irish War.[52] Likewise, recollections of the tuberculosis that afflicted countless families in Ireland are remembered in private, but have not yet entered public memory.[53] Notwithstanding the secularisation and liberalisation of Irish society, memories of homosexuality have yet to become part of the mostly heterosexual, if not asexual, Irish story.[54] These are but a few glaring examples of lacunae. Above all, the shocking revelations of institutional and clerical abuse have compelled Irish culture to grapple with finding means to ethically recall painful memories that defy sentimental remembrance of the recent past.[55]

---

51 D. Keogh, *Jews in Twentieth-Century Ireland: Refugees, Anti-Semitism and the Holocaust* (Cork: Cork University Press, 1998); K. Goldstone, '"Now You See Us, Now You Don't": Reflections on Jews, Historical Amnesia and the Histories of a Multi-Ethnic Dublin', *Translocations: Migration and Social Change*, 4, (2008), 102–9; M. Ó hAodha, 'Reconfiguring the Traveller Self: Cultural Memory and Belonging', in Frawley (ed.), *Memory Ireland*, 185–96.

52 C. Foley, *The Last Irish Plague: The Great Flu Epidemic in Ireland* (Dublin: Irish Academic Press, 2011), 137–52; I. Milne, 'Through the Eyes of a Child: "Spanish" Influenza Remembered by Survivors', in A. Mac Lellan and A. Mauger, *Growing Pains: Childhood Illness in Ireland, 1750–1950* (Dublin: Irish Academic Press, 2013), 159–74.

53 G. Simon, 'Cure, Superstition, Infection and Reaction: Tuberculosis in Ireland, 1932–1957', *Oral History*, 32, (2004), 63–72; S. Kelly, 'Stigma and Silence: Oral Histories of Tuberculosis', *Oral History*, 39, (2011), 65–76.

54 D. Cregan, 'Remembering to Forget: Queer Memory and the New Ireland', in Frawley (ed.), *Memory Ireland*, 184–94.

55 E. Pine, *The Politics of Irish Memory: Performing Remembrance in Contemporary Irish Culture* (Basingstoke: Palgrave Macmillan, 2011), 18–51; J. M. Smith, *Ireland's Magdalen Laundries*

Northern Ireland, in its somewhat deceptively labelled 'post-conflict' state, is rife with unsettled memories. During the Troubles the divided communities cultivated their own sites of communal memory and often showed hostility towards rival commemorations. Terrorist attacks could assume a de-commemorative purpose. The bombing of a Remembrance Day ceremony at Enniskillen on 8 November 1987 by the Provisional IRA, which left 11 dead and 63 injured, was a deliberate assault on what was considered a distinctly Unionist ritual of commemoration.[56] Similarly, the attack on 16 March 1988 on the funeral of the 'Gibraltar Three' (a team of Provisional IRA volunteers, who had been killed by the SAS) at the republican plot in Belfast's Milltown cemetery by the loyalist gunman Michael Stone, who killed three of the mourners and injured another 50, violated a hallowed ritual of nationalist remembrance.[57] The principle of 'parity of esteem' laid down by the Good Friday Agreement bestowed recognition on two rival traditions of incompatible historical memory, without finding effective ways to put them in constructive dialogue with each other. The murals on the walls of separate Catholic and Protestant neighbourhoods in Northern Ireland continue to display images of conflicting memories.[58] Moreover, Orange parades, celebrated annually in the July marching season repeatedly show potential to inflame sectarian conflict, as in the Drumcree standoffs in Portadown in the late 1990s, which deteriorated into riots.[59]

Many families in Northern Ireland retain unbearably painful memories of loss and grief.[60] Reflections of trauma have found cultural expressions in literature and in the performing and visual arts.[61] The state authorities, however,

and the Nation's Architecture of Containment (Notre Dame, IN: University of Notre Dame Press, 2007).

56 D. McDaniel, *Enniskillen: The Remembrance Sunday Bombing* (Dublin: Wolfhound Press, 1997); H. Robinson, 'Remembering War in the Midst of Conflict: First World War Commemorations in the Northern Irish Troubles', *Twentieth Century British History*, 21, (2010), 80–101.

57 J. Smyth, 'Milltown Cemetery and the Politics of Remembrance', in J. Smyth, (ed.), *Remembering the Troubles: Commemorating, Constructing and Contesting the Recent Past in Northern Ireland* (Notre Dame, IN: University of Notre Dame Press, 2017), 165–78.

58 M. Forker and J. McCormick, 'Walls of History: The Use of Mythomoteurs in Northern Ireland Murals', *Irish Studies Review*, 17, (2009), 423–65; B. Rolston, ' "Trying to Reach the Future through the Past": Murals and Memory in Northern Ireland', *Crime, Media, Culture*, 6, (2010), 285–307.

59 D. Bryan, *Orange Parades: The Politics of Ritual, Tradition, and Control* (London and Sterling, VA: Pluto Press, 2000).

60 D. McKittrick, *Lost Lives: The Stories of the Men, Women, and Children Who Died as a Result of the Northern Ireland Troubles* (Edinburgh: Mainstream, 1999); S. McKay, *Bear in Mind These Dead* (London: Faber and Faber, 2008).

61 F. Barber, 'At Art's Edge: Post-Conflict Memory and Art Practice in Northern Ireland' in Frawley (ed.), *Memory Ireland* vol. 3, 232–46; S. Lehner, 'The Irreversible and

have encountered difficulties in coming up with an acceptable policy for 'dealing with the past' and have been unable to institute inclusive commemoration of the victims of the Troubles. Models of 'truth and reconciliation' that were implemented in post-Apartheid South Africa and in Latin America have been deemed unsuitable, with Unionists, in particular, complaining that their social memory is not being adequately accommodated. It is quite possible that conflicts over memory of the Troubles will continue for a long time, as in Spain, where the memory of the Civil War of 1936–1939 remains an irreconcilable bone of contention in current political debate.[62]

There are clearly many significant recollections that have yet to be incorporated into public constructions of Irish memory. The promise of progress lies not so much with the authorities, whose ability to coordinate remembrance has proved to be limited and has always been contested, but more with the innovative memory work undertaken by individuals and community groups. Contemporary literature, theatre and film, as well as television and radio documentaries, are dealing creatively and working through some of these issues and have been facilitating meaningful interactions with memories of events that had hitherto been overlooked in public debate. New-found interest in oral history and the ongoing digitalisation of archival collections are producing resources for deeper understandings of the past and are stimulating the development of new methods for the study of memory. These initiatives are set to instigate an overhaul of Irish social and cultural memory, which will inevitably necessitate the rewriting of the history of the turbulent twentieth century.

Irrevocable: Encircling Trauma in Contemporary Northern Irish Literature', in ibid., 272–92.
62 B. Hamber (ed.), *Past Imperfect: Dealing with the Past in Northern Ireland and Societies in Transition* (Derry/Londonderry: INCORE, 1998); B. Graham and Y. Whelan, 'The Legacies of the Dead: Commemorating the Troubles in Northern Ireland', *Environment and Planning D: Society and Space*, 25, (2007), 476–95; M. B. Smyth, *Truth Recovery and Justice after Conflict: Managing Violent Pasts* (Oxford and New York: Routledge, 2007); K. Simpson, *Unionist Voices and the Politics of Remembering the Past in Northern Ireland* (Houndmills and New York: Palgrave Macmillan, 2009); K. Simpson, *Truth Recovery in Northern Ireland: Critically Interpreting the Past* (Manchester: Manchester University Press, 2009).

24

Catholicism in Ireland, 1880–2015: Rise, Ascendancy and Retreat

DAITHÍ Ó CORRÁIN

Introduction

In the nineteenth and twentieth centuries Catholicism was a defining element of Irish national identity and the terms Catholic and Irish were virtually synonymous for three-quarters of the population. The identification of faith and nationalist political identity, first harnessed by Daniel O'Connell, strengthened during successive efforts to end the Union and emerged triumphant in independent Ireland. Catholicism was also a core element of national identity in France, Spain and Italy but identification alone did not prevent a steady decline in church allegiance in those countries. Ireland was different because, aside from the absence of an anti-clerical left wing, the Catholic Church played a significant role in the struggle for political independence and in the subsequent state-building project. Partition reinforced the association of political allegiance and religious affiliation on both sides of the border after 1920. In retrospect, the first four decades of independent Ireland were an exceptional era. For the first time in centuries, the Irish Catholic Church found itself without a rival institution or even 'a dialectical sparring partner' and it consequently enjoyed unprecedented influence and power.[1]

Under the leadership of ultramontanist Cardinal Paul Cullen from 1852 until 1878, the Irish Catholic Church assumed a form that it maintained, remarkably, for over a century.[2] This was characterised by a strong allegiance to Rome; a vast institutional presence through control of Catholic education, health and welfare homes; a disciplined clergy under episcopal control; and a thriving 'spiritual empire' abroad. The exceptional popular piety of twentieth-century Ireland sprang from Cullen's success in standardising

---

1 P. Connolly, 'The Church in Ireland since Vatican II', *The Furrow* 30 (December 1979), 760.
2 See C. Barr, 'The Re-energising of Catholicism, 1790–1880', in *The Cambridge History of Ireland* Volume III (Cambridge University Press, 2018).

Irish devotional and liturgical life along Roman lines. As the Irish became the most practising Catholics in the world, with a busy calendar of church and devotional attendance, paradoxically they 'corresponded more closely to the British Protestant churchgoing mid-Victorian norm'.[3] A vastly expanded pastoral infrastructure of newly built churches was matched by swelling numbers of vocations as religious life became a means of upward mobility in Irish society. Between 1851 and 1901 the number of priests increased from about 2,500 to 3,700 and the number of religious sisters from 1,500 to 8,000.[4] The Cullenite model that evolved was 'a peculiarly Irish hybrid of Tridentalism, Folk religion and Victorian puritanism'.[5] It also fostered, however, a pervasive culture of clericalism that lies at the heart of the unprecedented crisis in which the Catholic Church is now mired. This championed a clerical elite, institutional loyalty, conformity, anti-intellectualism and resistance to change.

The power of religion peaked in the 1950s by which time the Catholic Church had become a lazy monopoly, the legacy of which is proving to be its greatest burden. The decline in the authority and pre-eminent position of the Catholic Church, the rise of secularism and the beginnings of the effort to dismantle legislative and constitutional support for a Catholic ethos can be traced to the early 1960s. Although identification with Catholicism and religious practice in Ireland remained atypically high and set Ireland apart from other parts of Western Europe, survey evidence since the 1970s has revealed dramatic change in the nature and practice of being Catholic. The inability of the institutional Church to respond to a rapidly changing Ireland prompted one commentator to ask in the early 1980s if Irish Catholicism was dying.[6] As elsewhere, scandal has engulfed the Catholic Church in Ireland since the 1990s. Yet despite the dramatic failure of leadership and the loss of power, credibility and moral authority of the institutional Church, 84.2 per cent of Irish people described themselves as Catholic in the 2011 census. This suggests that despite a steep decline in institutional observance Catholicism remains an integral, if increasingly elusive, aspect of Irish identity.

---

3 S. Gilley, 'Catholicism, Ireland and the Irish diaspora', in S. Gilley and B. Stanley (eds.), *The Cambridge History of Christianity: Vol. 8 World Christianities c. 1815–c.1914* (Cambridge University Press, 2006), 253.
4 E. Larkin, 'The Devotional Revolution in Ireland, 1850–1875', *The American Historical Review* 77 (1972), 626, 651.
5 L. Fuller, *Irish Catholicism since 1950: The Undoing of a Culture* (Dublin: Gill & Macmillan, 2002), xxix.
6 P. Kirby, *Is Irish Catholicism Dying? Liberating an Imprisoned Church* (Dublin: Mercier Press, 1984).

Church and Nation, 1880–1920

In an influential study, David Miller has charted the efforts of the Catholic Church to remain on terms with both the 'state' (the British government) and the 'nation' (the Catholic population) in the final decades before independence.[7] In return for advancing its interests, the Church was prepared to bestow its legitimacy on state and nation alike. For all Christian churches no concern was more supreme than the sensitive area of education, control of which was perceived as essential if faith and values were to be transmitted to future generations. William Walsh, archbishop of Dublin from 1885 to 1921 and the pre-eminent Irish prelate, played a pivotal role in securing equality of educational treatment for Catholics at all levels. His crowning achievement was the establishment of the National University of Ireland in 1908 which met Catholic concerns.

The Catholic Church was not neutral between state and nation, however. It backed nationalist aspirations in the belief that the nation would eventually supplant the British imperial state. This required considerable political dexterity and moral and theological ambiguity on the matter of rebellion. From the 1880s until 1916, a majority of the nation was represented by the Irish Parliamentary Party (IPP) which sought Home Rule. As Alvin Jackson has shown (see above Chapter 3), the spectre of a southern parliament helped to unify Ulster Protestants of various political shades whose political, religious and economic interests were intertwined with the Union itself. An informal but highly effective clerical-nationalist alliance, cultivated by Parnell, was disrupted by the IPP split. It re-emerged, however, when the party was reunited under Redmond in 1900. There were limits to the political influence of the Church just as there was a variety of political standpoints within the hierarchy and among the clergy. Church authority was accepted in matters deemed to be within the ecclesiastical domain such as education. But where politics was concerned the Church had little choice but to demonstrate that it was of and with the people. To do otherwise would alienate the laity – a lesson learned during the Land War (1879–1882). For this reason, Archbishop Walsh was concerned for the plight of the workers during the 1913 Lockout, though he successfully opposed a scheme to send their children to England when it raised the spectre of proselytism. Ireland's small urban working class was not divorced from religious belief and practice in contrast to large segments of the same class in Europe.

---

7 D. W. Miller, *Church, State and Nation in Ireland, 1898–1921* (Dublin: Gill & Macmillan, 1973).

The third Home Rule crisis between 1912 and 1914 demonstrated the limitations of the hierarchy's political influence. John Redmond largely ignored its concerns about the financial and educational aspects of the measure. His acceptance of partition in 1914 alienated the northern bishops and their flocks who feared their interests would suffer under a Unionist government in Belfast. For Bishop Patrick McKenna of Clogher partition was 'repugnant to every patriotic Irishman no matter what his political views'.[8] This was the beginning of a rupture with the IPP as the Church adapted itself to an Irish political landscape profoundly altered by an inoperative Home Rule measure, disenchantment with the First World War and the aftermath of the 1916 Rising. The Catholic Church's traditional abjuration of violence, so evident in its largely ineffective response to Fenianism in the 1860s, was moderated by caution in 1916. Strikingly, twenty-two of the thirty-one Catholic bishops and auxiliaries remained silent, including Archbishop Walsh. Bishops and clergy were sensitive to the transformation of public opinion occasioned by the ill-conceived government policy of executions, arrests and internment. The Church's alignment with majority nationalist opinion, embodied in the new nationalism of Sinn Féin, was demonstrated during the massive protest campaign against conscription in 1918 which the hierarchy declared was 'against the will of the Irish nation'. During the War of Independence clerical opposition focused on the violent methods employed but not on the goal of independence.

Catholicism Triumphant, 1920–1960

After the founding of the Irish Free State the Catholic Church was more secure and more confident than at any previous time; it had little to fear from rival churches and enjoyed close links with the state. The situation was very different in Northern Ireland. The 'traditional Catholicism' of twentieth-century Ireland, which has attracted widespread comment, generally refers to the period before the 1960s when the Church's approach to the laity was authoritarian, prescriptive and dogmatic.

The Irish Free State

A majority of Catholic Ireland supported the Anglo-Irish Treaty, which granted a significant measure of self-government but not a republic and could not prevent civil war. The Catholic Church played an important role in securing popular legitimacy for the fledgling Irish Free State. Prompted by

---

8 *Derry Journal*, 9 June 1916.

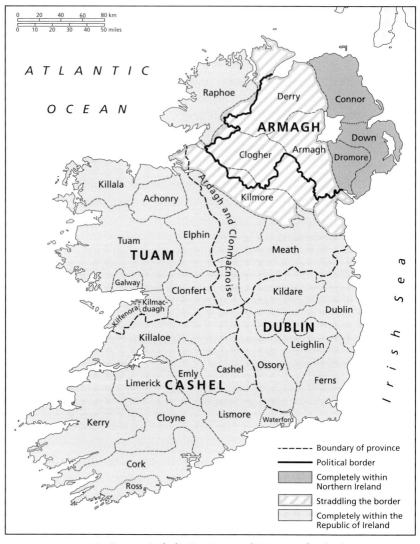

MAP 2. Roman Catholic Provinces and Dioceses of Ireland.

the government, the hierarchy strongly condemned the anti-Treaty side in October 1922. The bishops expressed horror at the destruction and loss of life and maintained that 'no one is justified in rebelling against the legitimate government ... set up by the nation and acting within its rights'.[9] A sense of cultural identity constitutes a bonding power in most societies. In the aftermath of the conflict, Catholicism and the reification (if not active use) of the Irish language provided a sense of shared identity and cohesion clearly distinct from Protestant England.[10] This may explain why remarkably little hostility was shown to the Church even by republicans threatened with excommunication during the civil war. Parish missions 'served as instruments of reconciliation in communities that had been deeply divided' by the conflict.[11] Similarly, the celebrations of the centenary of Catholic emancipation in June 1929 allowed the Free State to project an image of a country that was united, Irish, Catholic and free.[12]

During the uncertainties of the 1920s, the Church offered the new state continuity, stability and an extensive organisational infrastructure with over 13,000 clergy and religious. In return, a relatively penurious government allowed the Church to consolidate and extend its institutional presence in the realms of education, health and welfare with minimal interference – a pattern which persisted until the 1960s. This suited the state as religious labour was cheap or free and the capital costs were met by fundraising from the flock. The well-established nineteenth-century archetype of denominational pillarisation in these spheres continued as before and differed sharply from most European countries. After 1922 the Department of Education had limited power over the management of primary and secondary schools which remained vested in the Catholic and Protestant clergy. The state paid the salaries of teachers but its influence was largely restricted to control of the curriculum and an inspection system to ensure minimum teaching standards.[13] Church authorities flexed

---

9 Pastoral letter issued by the Archbishops and Bishops of Ireland, 10 October 1922 published in the *Irish Times*, *Irish Independent* and *Freeman's Journal*, 11 October 1922.

10 P. Corish, *The Irish Catholic Experience: A Historical Survey* (Dublin: Gill & Macmillan, 1985), 244.

11 B. McConvery, 'The Redemptorists and the Shaping of Irish Popular Devotion, 1851–1965', in H. Laugerud and S. Ryan (eds.), *Devotional Cultures of European Christianity, 1790–1960* (Dublin: Four Courts Press, 2012), 52.

12 G. McIntosh, 'Acts of "National Communion": The Centenary Celebrations for Catholic Emancipation, the Forerunner of the Eucharistic Congress', in J. Augusteijn (ed.), *Ireland in the 1930s: New Perspectives* (Dublin: Four Courts Press, 1999), 87.

13 S. Ó Buachalla, *Education Policy in Twentieth Century Ireland* (Dublin: Wolfhound Press, 1988), 60–1.

their muscles when the Vocational Education Act (1930), which provided continuation and technical education for 14- to 16-year-olds, was viewed as a threat to primary schools and to the curriculum of secondary schools. The hierarchy sought and secured the place of religious instruction in the vocational system, as well as clerical representation on local vocational education committees.[14] So modest was the state's role in education before the 1960s that General Richard Mulcahy, Minister for Education from 1954 to 1957, likened his function to a 'plumber' who 'will take the knock out of the pipes and will link up everything'.[15]

The Catholic Church and the Northern Ireland State

Despite the creation of northern and southern states, all the major Christian Churches continued to function as all-Ireland bodies. This was not without its challenges as Church members lived and Church institutions functioned in two states with very different cultural, economic and political milieu. Catholics accounted for 34 per cent of the population of Northern Ireland. Their experience before the 1960s was marked by a sense of being in but not of the state, where 'their religion *was* their politics'.[16] Antagonism initially characterised relations between Church authorities and the Northern Ireland administration, which was fond of depicting the Catholic population as disloyal. Two Catholic dioceses (see map on p. 730) – Down and Connor and Dromore – are located entirely within Northern Ireland and four others (Armagh, Clogher, Derry and Kilmore) straddle the border. Their bishops opted out of the Education Act (Northern Ireland) 1923, which introduced local authority involvement in the funding and management of schools, at the price of receiving significantly lower state funding. Finance and control of schools therefore posed a perennial dilemma for the bishops who deeply resented the inadequate financial provisions for their voluntary schools, full control of which they zealously defended. After the Second World War, the opportunities occasioned by the welfare state saw the northern Catholic bishops adopt a more pragmatic approach as they moved from highlighting the injustice of the state to injustices within in. There was never any question that

---

14 See M. Clarke, 'The Response of the Roman Catholic Church to the Introduction of Vocational Education in Ireland, 1930–1942', *History of Education*, 41, 4 (2012), 477–93.
15 *Dáil Debates* clix, 1494 (19 July 1956).
16 M. Elliott, 'Faith in Ireland, 1600–2000', in A. Jackson (ed.), *The Oxford Handbook of Modern Irish History* (Oxford University Press, 2014), 177.

the political border would compromise the religious unity of the Catholic Church whose map image remained an all-Ireland one.[17]

A Catholic Habitus

The Irish Free State was not a theocracy but Catholicism was 'effectively transformed into a civil theology'.[18] That the political culture had a pronounced Catholic ethos was inevitable given the Catholic educational formation of a majority of successive generations of Irish elites in politics, business and public service, and the extraordinary level of religious homogeneity. The 1926 census revealed that Catholics comprised 93 per cent of the population; before partition they accounted for 73 per cent. As Tom Inglis has argued, a Catholic habitus – a way of thinking and acting in conformity with a systematic view of the world – permeated all social classes, and religious capital facilitated the acquisition of economic, political or social capital.[19] And so, during the first fifty years of independence both church and state leaders, irrespective of political party, shared a desire to develop the country according to a philosophy of Catholic nationalism. As a result, the coming to power of Fianna Fáil under de Valera in 1932 was characterised by continuity in church–state relations, and 'their lordships took to Fianna Fáil as prodigals who had finally given up their errant ways'.[20] The new government demonstrated its loyalty to Catholicism during the thirty-first Eucharistic Congress, an international showpiece of global Catholicism, held in Dublin in June 1932. Unlike France or Italy, no anticlerical party emerged in Ireland and this reflected the failure of left-wing politics to develop.

Until the 1960s there was an informal consensus between political and religious leaders. Although keen to avoid confrontation, ministers did not always submissively dispose as the bench of bishops proposed. For example, diplomatic relations were opened with the Vatican in 1929 despite the known opposition of the hierarchy. Similarly, the views of bishops who participated in the Banking Commission in 1938 and the Commission on Vocational Organisation in 1943 were dismissed by the state. There was a concern too

17 See D. Ó Corráin, *Rendering to God and Caesar: The Irish Churches and the Two States in Ireland, 1949–73* (Manchester: Manchester University Press, 2006).

18 D. V. Twomey, *The End of Irish Catholicism?* (Dublin: Veritas, 2003), 33.

19 The term 'habitus' was coined by the French anthropologist Pierre Bourdieu; T. Inglis, *Moral Monopoly: The Rise and Fall of the Catholic Church in Modern Ireland* (Dublin: UCD Press, 1998), 11–12.

20 M. P. McCabe, *For God and Ireland: The Fight for Moral Superiority in Ireland, 1922–1932* (Sallins: Irish Academic Press, 2013), 240.

for the constitutional rights of religious minorities. In 1931 the government rejected attempts to veto, on religious grounds, the appointment of Letitia Dunbar-Harrison, a Protestant and Trinity College graduate, as county librarian in Mayo. Much ink has been spilled over the 'mother and child' debacle in 1951 as a demonstration of government pusillanimity in the face of episcopal pressure. This was arguably less a church–state crisis than an internal government one. Firmer leadership on the same issue by Fianna Fáil two years later negated the misgivings of the medical profession and clumsy episcopal impulses to embed certain Catholic principles in social legislation.[21] If anything, the 'mother and child' controversy brought public scrutiny to bear on the role of the Church, which came to be increasingly questioned.

Significant elements of the Catholic moral code were enshrined in law, particularly in the areas of sexual morality and family relations. Conservatism defined most aspects of Irish life between the 1920s and 1950s. For this reason, the censorship of films (1923) and publications (1929), the prohibition of divorce (1925) and a ban on the importation and sale of contraceptives (1935) were broadly favoured by all the Christian Churches. Pope Pius XI's encyclical *Quadragesimo anno* (1931) warned of the dangers of excessive state power and reinvigorated the Catholic social movement through its emphasis on solidarity and subsidiarity. It became a common theme in the pronouncements of the Irish bishops until the Second Vatican Council. The most important manifestation of the new Catholic social teaching in this period was Muintir na Tíre (people of the countryside), a community development organisation founded by Father John Hayes in 1931, which played an important role in the emergence of the discipline of sociology in Ireland.[22]

There has been a tendency to overstate the influence of Catholic social teaching on de Valera's 1937 constitution. Recent legal scholarship has emphasised the extent to which the document in fact reflected secular values such as respect for individual rights and separation of church and state.[23] Famously, article 44.2.1 recognised 'the special position' of the Catholic Church as the guardian of the faith professed by the great majority of citizens. Such recognition was common in Catholic countries. But 'apart from massaging episcopal *amour propre*', the 1937 constitution did not establish the Catholic Church or

---

21 The classic treatment of this episode is J. H. Whyte, *Church and State in Modern Ireland, 1923–1970* (Dublin: Gill & Macmillan, 1971).

22 See M. Tierney, *The Story of Muintir na Tíre 1931–2001: The First Seventy Years* (Tipperary: Muintir na Tíre, 2004).

23 See G. Hogan, 'De Valera, the Constitution and the Historians', *Irish Jurist*, 40 (2005), 293–320.

describe it as the one true church and recognised other churches to the chagrin of Cardinal Joseph MacRory, Catholic archbishop of Armagh and primate of all-Ireland from 1928 to 1945.[24] Instead it guaranteed not to endow any religion. The 'special position' clause was deleted with minimum fuss in a constitutional referendum in 1972 under the shadow of the Northern Ireland Troubles.

Hothouse Catholicism

Between the 1920s and the 1950s the institutional Church was at its most dominant and devotional practices by a devout and deferential laity, in addition to weekly attendance at Mass, were at their most visible and numerous. These activities included benediction, membership of confraternities and sodalities, pilgrimages, parish missions, processions, the rosary, stations, novenas, reading devotional literature (which was available in abundance), devotion to the Sacred Heart, the cult of the saints and their relics, and Marian devotion. Though well-established before independence with, for example, great Irish interest in Lourdes (which helped revive the Marian shrine of Knock in the 1930s), Marianism was particularly prevalent during the 1950s prompted by Pius XII's proclamation of the Assumption in 1950 and the Marian year in 1954 to mark the centenary of the definition of the Immaculate Conception. James Donnelly argues that the upsurge in Marianism was a defensive strategy to combat changing social and sexual mores and anti-Christian forces.[25] Television displaced the family rosary and in the public realm Marian sodalities such as the Sodality of Our Lady, which in the 1940s boasted 250,000 members, went into sharp decline after the Second Vatican Council.[26] So too did the Legion of Mary, a lay Catholic organisation founded by Frank Duff in 1921 which focused on spiritual and social welfare (for example it addressed social problems such as homelessness and prostitution). In an Irish context it was a rare example of autonomous mobilisation by the faithful, for which Duff encountered opposition from the Dublin diocesan authorities.[27] Donnelly contends that some rosary enthusiasts redirected their energies towards the charismatic movement in the 1970s and towards the cult of Padre

---

24 J. J. Lee, 'From Empire to Europe: The Irish State 1922–73', in M. Adshead, P. Kirby and M. Millar (eds.), *Contesting the State: Lessons from the Irish Case* (Manchester University Press, 2008), 43.

25 J. Donnelly, 'The peak of Marianism in Ireland, 1930–60', in S. Brown and D. W. Miller (eds.), *Piety and Power in Ireland, 1760–1960: Essays in Honour of Emmet Larkin* (Belfast: Notre Dame Press, 2000), 252–83.

26 J. Donnelly, 'Opposing the "Modern World": The Cult of the Virgin Mary in Ireland, 1965–85', *Éire-Ireland*, 40 (2005), 193–4.

27 See F. Kennedy, *Frank Duff: A Life Story* (New York: Continuum Publishing, 2011).

Pio in the 1980s.[28] The showing of a film about Padre Pio to schoolchildren is believed to have inspired the first incident of moving Marian statues in the mid-1980s.

At an official level, the absence of civic ceremonial resulted in a reliance on Catholic ceremonial such as special Masses for the opening of the Dáil and other occasions.[29] Visitors to Ireland, both lay and clerical, marvelled at the extent to which Irish life was imbued with the language, symbols and rituals of Catholicism. But some, such as the American writer Paul Blanshard, criticised the cultural and social domination of the Catholic Church.[30] Despite legislative and moral protectionism, this period was a time of vigilance and fortress Catholicism. The menace of atheistic communism loomed large during the 1930s and became an all-consuming struggle during the papacy of Pius XII (1939–1958).[31] At home, Saor Éire (a radical left-wing republican group) and a sister organisation, the Republican Congress, were condemned in 1931; while abroad there was great Irish interest in the Spanish Civil War, concern for the persecuted church in Hungary and Poland in the early years of the Cold War, and the collection by the hierarchy of £60,000 before the Italian general election in April 1948.[32] Sermons and pastorals warned relentlessly of a litany of corrupting influences which threatened Ireland's moral purity: proselytism, evil literature, indecent Hollywood movies, immodest dress, courting in public, excessive drinking, secularism, materialism, and 'leakage of the faith' among Irish emigrants (many of whom fell away from religious practice). Dancehalls, or more accurately the opportunities they afforded for sexual immorality, were a clerical obsession. Patrick Kavanagh's fictional character Tarry Flynn, poet and bachelor farmer, greatly admired the Catholic religion 'because it kept girls virtuous until such time as he'd meet them'.[33] A prudish emphasis on subduing the passions of the flesh, a focus on sin and a pessimistic view of salvation were integral to the religious culture of the time

---

28 Donnelly, 'Opposing the "Modern World" ', 201–21.

29 M. Nic Ghiolla Phádraig, 'The power of the Catholic Church in the Republic of Ireland', in P. Clancy, S. Drudy, K. Lynch and L. O'Dowd (eds.), *Irish Society: Sociological Perspectives* (Dublin: Institute of Public Administration, 1995), 609.

30 Paul Blanshard (1892–1980) wrote a number of books which enjoyed an international circulation: *American freedom and Catholic power* (1949), *Communism, democracy and Catholic power* (1951), *The Irish and Catholic Power* (1953) and *Freedom and Catholic Power in Spain and Portugal* (1962).

31 E. Duffy, *Saints & Sinners: A History of the Popes* (New Haven and London: Yale University Press, 2001), 352.

32 D. Keogh, 'Ireland, the Vatican and the Cold War: The Case of Italy, 1948', *Historical Journal*, 34 (1991), 931–52; Whyte, *Church and State*, 89–90, 166–7.

33 P. Kavanagh, *Tarry Flynn* (London: Penguin, 1978), 11.

32. 31st International Eucharistic Congress, 1932: Mass on O'Connell Bridge.

(and depicted by Irish writers from James Joyce to John McGahern). The fear of losing eternal salvation, brilliantly evoked in Frank O'Connor's short story *First Confession*, led to a high attendance at confession.[34] Before the 1970s there was little hierarchical concern for public ethics and morality.[35]

Until the Second Vatican Council, Irish Catholicism was 'characterised by a legalistic moral theology, a highly centralised, authoritarian institution and a sentimental spirituality'.[36] In spite of the hothouse climate, there were, as Louise Fuller notes, dissenting voices which found an outlet in two pioneering journals: the *Furrow*, founded in 1950, and *Doctrine and Life*, launched in 1951.[37] When introducing *Doctrine and Life*, the Dominican provincial stated that its aim was to initiate people into a deeper understanding of their faith which 'never became for them a personal conviction'.[38] Both journals communicated the ideas of European theologians and Catholic intellectual thought to Irish readers. This ensured that Catholic Ireland was not completely unprepared for the new thinking and renewal of the Second Vatican Council. Throughout the 1950s contributors warned repeatedly that Irish Catholicism was less secure than it appeared in the face of the rising tide of secularism. In 1959 one priest cautioned that an increasingly middle-class Ireland was 'trying to make do with a peasant religion ... and we must have a religion to fit our needs'.[39] This observation underscored the bizarre absence of theology in Ireland, a country which lacked a critical Catholic philosophical tradition in public discourse and produced not a single Catholic philosopher of European stature in the modern era. The prohibition of a theology faculty was a condition of the hierarchy's support for the establishment of the National University of Ireland in 1908. Perhaps ironically, Trinity College became the first university to introduce a theology degree for non-divinity students in 1979. Only in the twenty-first century did religious studies become a subject on the secondary school curriculum. As one commentator put it, 'Ireland must be the only

34 F. O'Connor, 'First Confession', in *My Oedipus Complex and Other Stories* (London: Penguin, 2005), 23–30.
35 J. J. Lee, 'Society and Culture', in F. Litton (ed.), *Unequal Achievement: The Irish Experience, 1957–1982* (Dublin: Institute of Public Administration, 1982), 11.
36 Twomey, *Irish Catholicism*, 56.
37 See Fuller, *Irish Catholicism*, 82–8; J. Horgan, 'The *Furrow*: navigating the rapids, 1950–77', in M. O'Brien and F. Larkin (eds.), *Periodicals and Journalism in Twentieth-Century Ireland* (Dublin: Four Courts Press, 2014), 173–86.
38 Foreword by T. E. Garde, *Doctrine and Life*, 1 (February 1951), 2–3 cited in L. Fuller, 'Critical Voices in Irish Catholicism: Reading the Signs of the Times', *Studies* 100 (2011), 479.
39 John C. Kelly, 'Solid Virtue in Ireland', *Doctrine and Life* 9 (October–November 1959), 120, cited in Fuller, *Irish Catholicism*, 61.

country in the world where lay Catholics were effectively excluded for a century from the option of achieving theological literacy.'[40]

Irish Catholicism in Transition, 1960–*c*.1990

Modernisation was the zeitgeist of the 1960s and a changing economic, political and social landscape gradually dissolved the protectionist walls that surrounded Irish Catholicism. A variety of factors combined to transform Irish society and the place of religion within it. From the premiership of Seán Lemass onwards, political elites were no longer so deferential and the state prioritised economic growth over the simpler Catholic nationalist vision of Irish society that had prevailed since independence. Another major instrument of modernisation was the establishment of a national television service in December 1961. The expansion of the market and the media in subsequent decades 'ushered in a new habitus that was based on liberal-individualism, materialism and consumerism, the very things against which the Church had preached so vehemently for generations'.[41] The shift from a culture of self-denial to one of self-indulgence was spectacularly evident during the Celtic Tiger era. It was belatedly recognised in the 1960s that the extension of educational opportunity was a central aspect of national economic development. This had profound consequences for a people used to unquestioning belief in their clergy. Yet another important stimulus of modernisation was the women's movement. The Second Vatican Council (1962–1965) and its aftermath revealed a sclerotic church institution in Ireland and a hierarchy more comfortable preserving rather than renewing its magisterium. To compound matters, vocations went into inexorable decline from the late 1960s.

Television

As Robert Savage notes (see Chapter 18, this volume), Ireland was one of the last countries in Western Europe to gain an indigenous television service. There was great anxiety at the challenge this posed to the Church's authority as well as the potential moral dangers of foreign programming.[42]

40 P. Kirby, 'The Catholic Church in Post-Celtic Tiger Ireland', in J. Littleton and E. Maher (eds.), *Contemporary Catholicism in Ireland: A Critical Appraisal* (Dublin: Columba Press, 2008), 29.

41 T. Inglis, 'Individualism and Secularisation in Catholic Ireland', in S. O'Sullivan (ed.), *Contemporary Ireland: A Sociological Map* (Dublin: UCD Press, 2007), 68.

42 R. Savage, *Irish Television: The Political and Social Origins* (Cork: Cork University Press, 1996), 108–10.

33. Archbishop John Charles McQuaid with schoolgirls at the centenary celebrations of High Park convent, Drumcondra. 1953.

The Catholic hierarchy had been slow to utilise the potential of the radio. High Mass on Sundays was not broadcast on a regular basis until 1948 and the daily broadcast of the Angelus was not inaugurated until 1950; both were at the prompting of John Charles McQuaid, the formidable archbishop of Dublin from 1940 to 1972, who appointed a priest as his own liaison with Radio Éireann.[43] The hierarchy did not enjoy the same degree of informal influence after the implementation of the Broadcasting Authority Act (1960) which established the new television service and removed broadcasting from direct government control. The speed and force of television's impact on Irish society far exceeded that of the cinema and the radio. With the relaxation of the laws on censorship, programmes such as the *Late Late Show*, an amalgam of American talk-show, light entertainment and current affairs, facilitated the questioning of traditional structures of authority that over time reduced the influence of and deference towards priests, bishops and even popes. Two contentious episodes in 1966 illustrated the new climate. In February Thomas Ryan, bishop of Clonfert, was ridiculed for criticising as indecent a quiz for

43 M. Gorham, *Forty Years of Irish Broadcasting* (Dublin: Talbot Press, 1967), 180–1, 195.

married couples in which Eileen Fox could not remember the colour of her nightdress on her honeymoon as she had not worn any. The following month a student called Bishop Michael Browne of Galway a 'moron' and the cathedral in Galway a 'ghastly monstrosity'.[44] The *Late Late Show* was the most watched and sometimes the most contentious programme on Irish television; it acted as 'mid-wife to contemporary Irish liberalism'.[45]

Broadening Access to Education

In 1965 *Investment in Education*, an OECD study of Ireland's long-term educational needs, revealed that just one-quarter of those leaving primary education continued to second level. The compelling case for reform was not lost on Lemass who oversaw an unprecedented period of educational expansion by appointing a succession of dynamic and assertive ministers: Patrick Hillery, George Colley, Donagh O'Malley. The most singular advance was the introduction of free post-primary education from the 1967 school year. Ironically, just as the number of school children began to increase, the number of vocations began to decline. John Walsh has revised the cordial characterisation of church–state interaction in this period put forward by earlier studies by revealing the 'profound suspicion and hostility with which Catholic bishops and managerial authorities greeted far-reaching educational reform' which undermined their hegemonic control.[46] Although the denominational character of schools remained unaltered, a new balance of power in education had been achieved in which the enhanced influence of the state in education was accepted with varying degrees of reluctance.[47] The replacement of one- and two-teacher schools with larger central schools, as recommended by *Investment*, illustrated the new reality. A public clash between Colley and Bishop Browne of Galway did not deter the Department of Education and by 1973, 1,100 small schools had closed. In Northern Ireland the 1968 Educational Act proposed grants of 80 per cent and public representatives on school management committees. Overwhelmingly supported by the Catholic laity, the financial imperative compelled the Catholic bishops to accept a position they

44 R. Savage, *A Loss of Innocence? Television and Irish Society, 1960–72* (Manchester: Manchester University Press, 2010), 207.

45 M. Earl, '*The Late Late Show*, Controversy and Context', in M. McLoone and J. MacMahon (eds.), *Television and Irish Society* (Dublin: RTE, 1984), 113 cited in L. Pettitt, *Screening Ireland: Film and Television Representation* (Manchester University Press, 2000), 166.

46 J. Walsh, 'Ministers, Bishops and the Changing Balance of Power in Irish Education 1950–70', *Irish Historical Studies* 38 (2012), 109; the older studies are Whyte, *Church and State* and Ó Buachalla, *Education Policy*.

47 Walsh, 'Ministers, Bishops and the Changing Balance of Power', 125.

34. The removal of the remains of Archbishop Byrne, archbishop of Dublin, from Clonliffe Church, Drumcondra to St Mary's Pro-Cathedral, Marlborough Street, a distance of around 2.3 km. through the centre of Dublin, 1940.

had resisted since 1923. There was also a growing interest in integrated education in Northern Ireland, something which notably predated the Troubles.

The Women's Movement

The changing position of women was crucial in modernising Ireland, particularly from the 1970s onwards. Irish women challenged the patriarchal nature of Irish society and traditional church teaching on birth control and on the natural role of woman as mother and home-maker. Several commentators have noted that the Irish mother played a vital role in the development and transmission of Irish Catholicism from generation to generation, and in maintaining the prestige in which the clergy were held. Once women were able to access alternative sources of power through the workplace and public life, a central pillar of the Church's ideological control was removed.[48]

48 See Inglis, *Moral Monopoly*, 178–200; B. Fallon, *An Age of Innocence: Irish Culture, 1930–1960* (Dublin: Gill & Macmillan, 1998), 185–6.

35. Archbishop McQuaid with nuns at the High Park convent of the Sisters of Our Lady of Refuge. The convent also contained a Magdalene laundry.

The introduction of various equality directives following Irish entry to the European Economic Community further empowered Irish women and brought the country more into line with its liberal Western European neighbours. Religious life was no longer one of the few means for women to access positions of power and responsibility.

The Second Vatican Council and its Implications

The Second Vatican Council generated an expectation of change in the religious sphere which was ultimately unfulfilled. In his opening address, John XXIII sought *aggiornamento*, the bringing of the Church up to date through the inner renewal of the Church, the unity of Christians, and the opening of the Church to the contemporary world. The proceedings between October 1962 and December 1965 were extensively reported by the world media. Catholic Ireland greeted the key deliberations – on the nature of the Church as the people of God, the collegiality of the bishops and lay participation in the mission of the Church – with optimism. By the Council's conclusion, four constitutions, nine decrees and three declarations had scrutinised every aspect of Church life and transformed the Catholic Church. While the fundamentals of faith remained immutable, their adaptation to, and presentation in, the modern world did not. The Irish bishops were not in the van of *aggiornamento* and took a very limited part in the Council sessions. The Irish ambassador to the Holy See described their attitude as 'the reverse of exuberant'.[49] The Irish hierarchy was wary of change lest it undermine their magisterium or endanger the faith and morals of the laity. This was reflected in episcopal pronouncements following the conclusion of the Council. Bishop William Philbin of Down and Connor warned against any suggestion that the Church could be 'cut adrift from its moorings by the Vatican Council' and McQuaid reassured a congregation that 'no change will worry the tranquillity of your Christian lives'.[50]

The alterations to liturgy, church governance, theology, and ecumenism led to fractious division along progressive/traditional lines in North America and Europe but not in theologically impoverished Ireland, where the local implementation was legalistic, begrudging and narrow. Vincent Twomey puts it more strongly: 'unthinking to the end, a provincial and submissive Church simply and obediently carried out the instructions coming from Rome that unintentionally but effectively dismantled their own, deeply cherished version of Catholicism'.[51] The use of the vernacular in the Mass was introduced on 7 March 1965 and sanctuaries were reordered to face the congregation. The Council led to the creation of a spate of new episcopal commissions, including, among others, Liturgy (1964), Missions (1968) and Justice and Peace (1969). A Catholic Communications Institute of Ireland was established in Dublin in 1969. A number of third-level institutions also came into being such as the Mater Dei Institute of Education in 1966 and the Milltown Institute of Philosophy and Theology two years later. Apart from participation as readers and ministers of the Eucharist from 1973, the laity remained on the margins of the Irish Church. The failure to permit women to play a significant role at all levels of decision-making within the Church continued; it took years before a dialogue was opened between the conference of priests and the hierarchy; and, unlike other countries, the Irish Church refused for decades to introduce the permanent diaconate.

---

49 Ó Corráin, *Rendering*, 203.
50 Ibid., p. 206. On McQuaid, see J. Cooney, *John Charles McQuaid: Ruler of Catholic Ireland* (Dublin: Gill & Macmillan, 1999); F. X. Carty, *Hold firm: John Charles McQuaid and the Second Vatican Council* (Dublin: Columba Press, 2007).
51 Twomey, *Irish Catholicism*, 35.

The Second Vatican Council did not bring about any immediate change in interdenominational relations in Ireland. Official contact came to fruition slowly in the decade after 1963 as a result of international factors such as the rapprochement between Rome and Canterbury and, in the Irish context, low key ecumenical moves and the galvanising impact of the Northern Ireland Troubles. Unofficial local level contact between the churches helped to overcome their mutual ignorance of one another. No issue poisoned inter-church relations more than mixed marriages (between a Catholic and usually a Protestant) and the Catholic Church's insistence under the *Ne Temere* decree that the children of such unions be raised as Catholics. The Church of Ireland viewed this as an instrument of slow strangulation, particularly in the Republic, where it was demographically weak. It was the root cause of the ugly Fethard-on-Sea boycott in 1957 when the local Church of Ireland community in a small County Wexford village was ostracised.[52] The Second Vatican Council brought about a new attitude towards inter-church marriage in a *motu proprio* entitled *Matrimonia mixta* in 1970. It consciously recognised the Christian faith of other Churches but the obligations incumbent on the Catholic partner to do all in their power to raise children in the Catholic faith remained. The implementation of *Matrimonia mixta* in Ireland was complicated by the Troubles in Northern Ireland and by Pope Paul VI's decision to let national episcopal conferences decide on the precise form of the promise. Catholic bishops in Switzerland, France, Germany and the Benelux accepted in principle that they could no longer insist on all children being Catholic. By contrast, the Irish Episcopal Conference was coldly juridical.[53]

Misconceptions of a religious war in Northern Ireland provided the most pressing rationale for ecumenical entente at the end of the 1960s. Eric Gallagher and Stanley Worrall make the interesting assertion that had the Troubles occurred ten years earlier, the Churches would have taken sides as they did during the Home Rule crisis.[54] The Troubles forced Church leaders to question whether they were prisoners of the cultural and political polarities of Irish life, and in part responsible for the anguish in Northern Ireland. This resulted in the first official inter-church meeting at Ballymascanlon, County Louth in September 1973. The tendency in media circles to evaluate the progress of ecumenical dialogue in terms of the resolution of the Northern Ireland problem did a great disservice to both. Eric Gallagher captured the

---

52 See Ó Corráin, *Rendering*, 93–7, 186–8.
53 Ibid., 188–91.
54 E. Gallagher and S. Worrall, *Christians in Ulster, 1968–1980* (Oxford University Press, 1982), 38.

paradox of ecumenical advance against the background of the Troubles: 'the leaders of our Churches are probably – even certainly – having more contacts ... than ever before. And at the same time the rank and file never had less and they never wanted less'.[55] Political violence posed particular difficulties for the Catholic Church. As Oliver Rafferty has observed, it was 'locked in a herculean struggle' with the Republican movement 'over the symbols and identity of northern Catholic life'.[56] Its sustained condemnation of violence had little impact and its actions were often misunderstood by the government resulting in a weak ability to influence the political agenda. Ganiel and Dixon suggest that over the course of the Troubles religion was, socially and politically, more important for Protestants than for Catholics.[57]

In 1986 Seán Freyne, theologian and biblical scholar, suggested that the Second Vatican Council had 'made almost no impact on Irish Catholicism apart from a few cosmetic changes to the liturgy ... because the questions the Council sought to grapple with had never been seriously posed in this country'.[58] This focuses attention on the quality of episcopal leadership. Oliver Rafferty suggests that in recent years 'it has become something of a fashion among retired bishops to lament that Vatican II was not fully implemented in Ireland. But who was responsible for its implementation if not these same prelates?'[59] The Vatican system of appointment of bishops with little input by the local church has attracted criticism given the tendency to select 'the "safe" man and the orthodox mentality, for which the Church is paying in Peter's Pence today'.[60] Other appointees have had very limited pastoral experience; many others had, as one historian puts it, 'excellent negative minds'.[61] Although religious orders have changed the way in which they exercise leadership and authority since the Council, this was not replicated in the institutional Catholic Church. During the long pontificate of John Paul II there was a 'disheartening return to an ethos of control and infallibility' as

55 E. Gallagher, 'Interdenominational trust' in *Doctrine and Life*, 23 (1973), 228.
56 O. Rafferty, 'Northern Catholics and the Early Years of the Troubles', in O. Rafferty (ed.), *Irish Catholic Identities* (Manchester: Manchester University Press, 2013), 356.
57 G. Ganiel and P. Dixon, 'Religion in Northern Ireland: Rethinking Fundamentalism and the Possibilities for Conflict Transformation', *Journal of Peace Research*, 45 (2008), 421–38.
58 Introduction to H. Küng, *Church & Change: The Irish Experience* (Dublin: Gill & Macmillan, 1986), 10.
59 O. Rafferty, 'The Catholic Church in Ireland and Vatican II in Historical Perspective', in N. Coll (ed.), *Ireland & Vatican II: Essays Theological, Pastoral and Educational* (Dublin: Columba Press, 2015), 24.
60 Fallon, *Age of Innocence*, 196.
61 D. Keogh, 'The Catholic Church in Ireland since the 1950s', in L. Woodcock Tentler (ed.), *The Church Confronts Modernity: Catholicism since 1950 in the United States, Ireland and Quebec* (Washington, DC: Catholic University of America Press, 2007), 105.

the legacy of the council was 'dismantled bit by bit, with significant teachings modified out of existence by a thousand qualifications'.[62] This approach to Church governance was demonstrated in 2011 when a new translation of the missal was introduced by the Vatican with little prior consultation with priests or people, many of whom protested at the stilted language used.

Missionary Activity

The focus on developments in Ireland should not obscure the remarkable level of missionary endeavour, both male and female, during the late nineteenth and twentieth centuries whether following the British Empire into Africa and Asia, the Maynooth Mission to China (founded in 1916) or serving the Irish diaspora from Birmingham to Brisbane. Paul Cullen helped shape a transnational Irish 'spiritual empire' by having 'Hiberno-Roman' bishops appointed to every English-speaking national church in the British Empire.[63] Cullen's 'episcopal imperialism' was complemented by his recognition of the need to ensure that lay emigrants were as 'assiduous in the practice of their faith as those who remained'.[64] Mass migration from Ireland involved all denominations and the nineteenth-century missionary movement was therefore not confined to Catholic missionaries. Unlike Irish Catholics who, as Donald Akenson remarks of New Zealand, 'simply refused to go away', Irish Protestants had largely vanished as a category of self-identification by the mid-twentieth century if not before.[65]

The half century to 1960 was 'the golden age of Irish missions'.[66] From the 1920s the number of Irish Catholic clerical and religious missionaries increased steadily until the 1970s when they plateaued at about 6,000 spread across Africa, Asia and Latin-America – the largest contribution per capita of any country.[67] In 2014 there were 1,600 Irish missionaries.[68] Missionary activity laid the basis for concern with the developing world from the 1960s. It paved the way for NGOs such as Concern, established in 1968; Trócaire, the Irish

---

62 B. Hoban, 'How did it come to this?', *Studies*, 101 (2012), 401–2.

63 C. Barr, ' "Imperium in Imperio": Irish Episcopal Imperialism in the Nineteenth Century', *English Historical Review* 123 (2008), 611–50.

64 S. Roddy, 'Spiritual Imperialism and the Mission of the Irish Race: The Catholic Church and Emigration from Nineteenth-century Ireland', *Irish Historical Studies* 38 (2013), 600–19.

65 D. H. Akenson, *Half the World from Home: Perspectives on the Irish in New Zealand, 1860–1950* (Wellington: Victoria University Press, 1990), 196.

66 Gilley, 'Catholicism', 258.

67 On this see E. Hogan, *The Irish Missionary Movement: A Historical Survey, 1830–1980* (Dublin: Gill & Macmillan, 1992).

68 *Irish Independent*, 19 October 2014.

Catholic Church's official overseas development agency founded in 1973 (with its distinctive Lenten collection boxes); and Goal established in 1977. 'The missionaries' work and that of the aid agencies that followed in their footsteps, became an extension of Irish values of Christianity, justice and peace, and their expression on the world stage.'[69]

Falling Vocations

Remarkably, according to the 1961 census there were more religious (the vast majority being Catholic) in Ireland (15,323) than civil servants (14,695).[70] For the first time in the twentieth century, a decline in the total number of priests, brothers and nuns was recorded in 1968.[71] Since then the power of the Church has waned due to the drying up of vocations. Without the human resources to staff the myriad of hospitals, welfare homes and schools the Church's institutional presence inevitably contracted. Depleted ranks, increased running costs, greater state involvement, professionalisation of services, new management structures and a post-Vatican II reassessment of their mission prompted a withdrawal of religious. For example, the ratio of religious to lay teachers dropped from 18.9 per cent of trained primary school teachers in 1965–1966 to 4.6 per cent in 1992.[72] In September 2014 only ten religious, half of them women, served as principals of post primary schools compared to 104 in 1991.[73] The day-to-day input into the religious ethos of schools has all but disappeared. The move away from the traditional ministries of education and healthcare towards pastoral and social ministries was facilitated by a post-Vatican II change in the mode of community life as smaller groupings of three to five religious replaced the traditional practice of living in large convents and monasteries.

This transformation did not arrest the slide in vocations, however. Between 1966 and 2006 vocations to all forms of religious life fell from 1,409 to 53, a decline of 96 per cent. This was most acute among religious orders, some of which are destined to disappear. The number of vocations to brothers' orders fell from 173 to 1, to clerical religious orders from 390 to 15, and to

69 K. O'Sullivan, '"Ah Ireland, the Caring Nation": Foreign Aid and Irish State Identity during the long 1970s', *Irish Historical Studies* 38 (2013), 481.

70 T. Fahey, 'Religion and prosperity', *Studies* 90:357 (2001), 39, note 1. Priests and religious working in hospitals and schools were recorded under those categories.

71 *A Survey of Vocations in Ireland, 1971* (confidential report submitted to the hierarchy in June 1971), 3.

72 M. Nic Ghiolla Phádraig, 'The Power of the Catholic Church in the Republic of Ireland', in P. Clancy, S. Drudy and L. O'Dowd (eds.), *Irish Society: Sociological Perspectives* (Dublin: Institute of Public Administration), 607–8.

73 B. Convery, 'Religious in education', *Reality* (September 2014) cited in E. Woulfe, 'Religious life in Ireland today', in Coll (ed.), *Ireland & Vatican II*, 219.

sisters' orders from 592 to 9.[74] In 1967 there were 29,984 religious in Ireland, the majority women. By 2000 the total was 16,046 (10,987 sisters, 4,134 clerical religious and 925 brothers) with just 24 male and 21 female new entrants.[75] The decline in the number of female vocations was a sharp reversal of the gender balance of earlier decades. Although there was a similar drop in numbers of religious in other western European countries, *fin-de-siècle* Ireland still had a significantly higher proportion of religious per head of the general population of 0.38 per cent; the corresponding figure for Italy was 0.205, Belgium 0.190 and Spain 0.171.[76] However, just over two-thirds of Irish religious were aged 60 or over. It is hardly surprising then that in 2015 the number of religious had declined further to 8,279 (6,282 sisters, 1,412 clerical priests and 585 brothers).[77] The magnitude of the post-Vatican II decline in vocations to religious orders was not unique to Ireland. There was a similarly rapid decline in North America and Western Europe. For instance, between 1965 and 1995 female religious in France declined by 44 per cent and male religious by 68 per cent; the respective figures in Britain were 43 per cent and 82 per cent.[78]

The contraction in the number of diocesan clergy in Ireland was not as drastic or as swift as in other Catholic countries. In France the number of ordinations fell from 646 in 1965 to 99 in 1977, whereas in Ireland the respective decline was from 282 to 141.[79] However, by the late 1990s, as for religious orders, falling ordinations had reached crisis point with deaths, withdrawals and retirements far outstripping new entrants. Between 1966 and 2006 the number of diocesan vocations fell from 254 to 28, a decline of 89 per cent.[80] In 2012 there were just 12 vocations, the lowest number on record. This recovered modestly in 2015 when 17 seminarians began their training for Ireland's twenty-six dioceses.[81] During the 1990s seminaries in Dublin, Thurles, Kilkenny, Waterford and Carlow closed; only the national

---

74 *Vocations in Ireland, 1971*, 7; *Irish Catholic Directory* (hereafter *ICD*) *2016*, 329.

75 *Irish Catholic Directory 2001* (hereafter *ICD*), 282.

76 E. Maxwell, 'Apostolic Religious Life in Ireland and Western Europe', in M. J. Breen (ed.), *A Fire in the Forest: Religious Life in Ireland* (Dublin: Veritas, 2001), 58–60.

77 J. Weafer, 'Statistical Profile of Religious Personnel in Ireland', in Breen (ed.), *Fire*, 31; Diocesan returns, *ICD 2016*.

78 R. Stark and R. Finke, 'Catholic Religious Vocations: Decline and Revival', *Review of Religious Research* 42 (2000), 125–45.

79 S. Tippett-Spirtou, *French Catholicism: Church, State and Society in a Changing Era* (Basingstoke: Macmillan, 2000), 142; *Vocations in Ireland, 1971*, 7; *ICD 1978*, 325. Of the 141 ordained in 1976–1977, 57 were ordained for Irish dioceses, 17 for foreign dioceses, 55 for religious orders and 12 for missionary societies.

80 *Vocations in Ireland, 1971*, 7; *ICD 2016*, 329.

81 *ICD 2001*, 282: www.catholicbishops.ie / 2015 / 08 / 24 / seventeen-seminarians-commence-priesthood-studies-saint-patricks-college-maynooth / (accessed 13 June 2016).

seminary in Maynooth remains. At a parish level, an aging and declining cohort of priests have increasing demands on their time and energy. In 2015 there were 1,966 active priests assigned to parish ministry, a fall of 1,010 since 2000 and almost half the 1961 total of 3,702.[82] The average age of an Irish priest in 2015 was 64. The future looks bleak. By 2020 the Dublin archdiocese will, by its own estimate, barely have one priest for each of its 199 parishes.[83] In many dioceses, parishes are now clustered. Greater lay ministry will be required to sustain the Church into the future when there may be no ordained minister to conduct services. It makes more glaring Dermot Lane's observation that the most serious deficiency in the decades since the Vatican Council was the failure to activate the priesthood of the laity as outlined in conciliar documents and more recent ones such as the *Vocation and Mission of the Laity* (1988).[84]

Declining Levels of Orthodox Religious Belief

Even in the early 1960s, survey evidence revealed an incipient but unmistakeable change of religious outlook. Bruce Biever, an American Jesuit, conducted an elaborate survey of Catholic attitudes towards religion and clerical authority in Dublin in 1962. This captured the prominent role of religion and the clergy in everyday life but signposted a more challenging future for the Church. Although 88 per cent of the sample agreed that the Church was the greatest force for good in Ireland, a striking 83 per cent of those who had completed secondary education disagreed with this proposition.[85] Biever suggested that the Irish priest faced a dilemma. An emerging educated class, as yet unrepresentative of the general population, demanded more sophisticated answers to modern-day problems than the platitudes that had satisfied their parents. But at the same time, he was confronted by the 'suspicious gaze' of the many people in rural areas 'who were hostile to change in whatever form'.[86] Change was not confined to Dublin, however. The Limerick Rural Survey, a pioneering sociological investigation commissioned by Muintir na Tíre, revealed higher personal expectations driven by the economic growth of the 1960s, the attractions of urban life and a more individualistic pursuit of fulfilment.[87]

---

82 *ICD 1962*, 653; *ICD 2001*, 284; *ICD 2016*, 329.

83 P. McGarry, 'All Churches in Ireland in Need of "Reality Check"', *Irish Times*, 24 May 2015.

84 D. Lane, 'Vatican II: The Irish Experience', in Liam Bergin (ed.), *Faith, Word and Culture* (Dublin: Columba Press, 2004), 63.

85 B. Biever, *Religion, Culture and Values: A Cross-Cultural Analysis of Motivational Factors in Native Irish and American Irish Catholicism* (New York: Arno Press, 1976), 226–7.

86 Ibid, 278.

87 J. Newman (ed.), *The Limerick Rural Survey, 1958–1964* (Tipperary: Muintir na Tíre, 1964).

In a climate of rapid social and cultural change, the extension of secondary education produced a population no longer willing to accept dictation on issues considered matters of individual conscience. This was evident in the Irish response to *Humanae Vitae*, Pope Paul VI's contested encyclical in 1968, which reaffirmed traditional Church opposition to artificial means of birth control. Internationally, many Catholic theologians dissented publicly from its teaching. This occasioned a crisis of authority for the global Church. Unlike episcopal conferences in other countries, the Irish hierarchy did not issue pastoral guidelines which would have given priests some flexibility in the confessional, where many committed Catholics were torn between allegiance to Church teaching and marital or health responsibilities to control fertility. Many came to regard artificial contraception, no longer a taboo subject, as morally acceptable. But clerical dissent was not entertained. In Cork Father James Good was suspended from priestly duties for describing the encyclical as a 'major tragedy' that would be rejected by Catholic lay people.[88] The hierarchy misjudged the public reaction which questioned the authority of the bishops to pronounce on such a subject. Much institutional credibility was lost twenty years before the sexual scandals of the 1990s.

The quietly shifting sands of Catholic Ireland were exposed during the 1970s. *A Survey of Religious Practices, Attitudes and Beliefs in the Republic of Ireland, 1973–4*, a four-volume sociological study commissioned by the Catholic Communications Institute of Ireland, confirmed that Ireland topped the church-going charts with 90 per cent observance of weekly Mass.[89] By contrast, attendance at Mass in France fell by 10 per cent per annum between 1971 and 1975.[90] But numbers at Mass were not an accurate index to the spiritual health of a Church and the Irish survey disclosed a significant disparity between High Mass attendance and a rate of weekly Communion of just 28 per cent. This suggested that for some Sunday observance was a matter of social conformism or convention rather than conviction. Furthermore, the young were losing interest: 30 per cent in the 21 to 25 age category and 25 per cent of young single men and women in the 18 to 30 age bracket had abandoned the minimal obligations of weekly Mass and annual sacraments. The survey forecast that many parents of the next generation would not return

---

88 *Irish Times*, 30 July 1968; L. Fuller, 'Religion, Politics and Socio-cultural Change in Twentieth-century Ireland', *The European Legacy* 10 (2005), 50.

89 This study by Máire Nic Ghiolla Phádraig was based on a random sample of 2,600 adults. It was published by Research and Development Unit, Catholic Communications Institute of Ireland, Dublin in 1975.

90 M. P. Gallagher, 'What Hope for Irish Faith?', *The Furrow* 29 (1978), 616.

36. Pope John Paul II arriving in Ireland on a visit in 1979, the first ever by a pope to the country.

to religious practice with marriage and middle age.[91] The analysis of attitudes was even more disconcerting. The survey revealed a serious absence of internalised faith, notwithstanding impressive church attendance and concluded that

> the beliefs and practices of the majority of Catholics are insufficiently interiorised ... not personally examined and tested and then affirmed or rejected.

91 Connolly, 'The Church in Ireland since Vatican II', 757.

Irish religious practice is sustained to an inadmissible extent by rule and law, social custom and a sense of duty, a framework of authority and sanction rather than by a personal commitment of mind and heart so that such belief or faith is extremely vulnerable in a rapidly changing society.[92]

This prompted one priest to write of Ireland's 'spiritual malnutrition' and the danger not of unbelief but of shallow belief.[93]

A survey by Mícheál Mac Gréil, SJ, of adults in Dublin in 1977 confirmed the growing gulf between the orthodox teaching of the Vatican and the beliefs of the faithful in respect of artificial contraception (63 per cent disagreed that it was always wrong), celibacy (46 per cent agreed that priests should be allowed to marry), the role of women in the Church and homosexuality (43 per cent agreed that it should be decriminalised).[94] Another study found that barely more than half fully accepted belief in the devil and hell, a sign that the habitual fear of eternal damnation was waning.[95] In important aspects of Church teaching the orthodox view had become a minority one. All of the many survey findings indicated that the higher the levels of urbanisation and educational attainment, the lower the level of orthodox religious belief, acceptance of Church teaching and attendance at confession.

Against this background, the three-day papal visit in 1979 was less a celebration of Catholic Ireland than an unsuccessful attempt to slow down the inroads made by materialism and secularism. In one of the great public events in the modern history of Irish Catholicism, an estimated 2.7 million people greeted Pope John Paul II in Dublin, Drogheda, Galway and Limerick. Almost one-third of the population gathered to hear the pontiff celebrate mass in the Phoenix Park, Dublin on 29 September in an event that dwarfed the 1932 Eucharistic Congress. Nearly a quarter of a million young people greeted the Pope in Galway and heard him warn that 'the religious and moral traditions of Ireland, the very soul of Ireland, will be challenged by temptations that spare no society in our age' before famously declaring: 'Young people of Ireland, I love you.' Likewise, in Limerick he challenged his audience to choose between 'giving excessive importance to economic growth and material possessions' or fidelity to 'the things of the spirit'.[96] The size of the crowds, the charisma of the pontiff, and the general excitement generated by

---

92 Ibid.

93 Gallagher, 'What Hope for Irish Faith?', 608.

94 M. Mac Gréil, *Prejudice and Tolerance in Ireland: Based on a Survey of Intergroup Attitudes of Dublin Adults and Other Sources* (Dublin: College of Industrial Relations, 1977), 411.

95 M. Nic Ghiolla Phádraig, 'Religion in Ireland: Preliminary Analysis', 120.

96 *The Pope in Ireland: Addresses and Homilies* (Dublin: Veritas, 1979), 46, 77.

the visit could not disguise the fact that secularisation may have been belated in Ireland but it was gathering pace.

The papal visit took place just two months after the passage of the Family Planning Act. For much of the twentieth century Ireland was unique among Western countries in not permitting abortion, contraception or divorce. The hierarchy held the traditional line on these issues, but for the first time in November 1973 openly acknowledged that the state should not be the guardian of private morality: 'There are many things which the Catholic Church holds to be morally wrong and no one has ever suggested, least of all the Church herself, that they should be prohibited by the State.'[97] In Britain and America change in this sphere occurred over a century but in Ireland this was telescoped into a much shorter time span. Seven bruising 'moral issue' constitutional referenda on abortion and marriage were held between 1983 and 2002. They were preceded by the legalisation of contraception in 1979, as a result of a Supreme Court ruling in the McGee case, with further extensions in 1985 and 1992. The insertion of an ambiguously worded pro-life amendment in 1983 was carried by a two to one majority in a poll of only 54 per cent. In the wake of the 'X' case, which permitted the risk of suicide by the mother as grounds for abortion, three concurrent referenda in 1992 affirmed freedoms of travel and information about abortion services but not the risk of suicide as grounds to allow an abortion. The latter position was reaffirmed in a further referendum in 2002. Garret FitzGerald recalled that concerns about property rights and pressure from the pulpit led 63 per cent to reject divorce in 1986.[98] But a significant minority dissented from Church teaching and nine years later divorce was narrowly approved. The so-called liberal agenda pursued during this tumultuous period was a reflection rather than a cause of change. As Nic Ghiolla Phádraig has noted, accompanying these campaigns was 'a growing coolness between the government and the hierarchy' and little prior church–state consultation, something unimaginable in earlier decades.[99]

Irish Catholicism in Crisis, 1990s to the Present

Since the 1990s the religious landscape in Ireland has changed dramatically. While there is little evidence of out and out secularisation, Irish religiosity

97 *Irish Times*, 26 November 1973.
98 G. FitzGerald, *All in a Life: An Autobiography* (Dublin: Gill & Macmillan, 1991), 631.
99 Nic Ghiolla Phádraig, 'The Power of the Catholic Church in the Republic of Ireland', 611–12.

has changed significantly. Traditionally, the sociology of religion has been dominated by the debate around secularisation – the 'process by which religious institutions, actions and consciousness lose their social significance'.[100] The secularisation thesis claims that the diminishing importance of religion in social and individual life is a consequence of an inherent tension between modernity and religion. Differences in the degree of secularisation between generations have been linked to changes brought about by increased levels of education, urbanisation, individualism, social mobility, greater female participation in the labour market and a decline of community.[101] There are several versions of secularisation theory. Some emphasise abandonment of church membership; others focus on measuring traditional institutional forms of religious expression with church attendance the most widely used indicator of attachment; while a more recent approach argues in favour of the privatisation of religion. The thesis has been challenged by persistently high levels of religiosity in the United States. European churches were more likely to be 'lazy monopolies', while their American counterparts were constantly subject to aggressive competition for 'market share'.[102]

Changing Religiosity

Attitudinal research reveals a divergence in Ireland between high levels of belief and declining formal religious practice. In 2008 the European Values Study (EVS) found that 92 per cent of Irish respondents believed in God, a decline of just 5 per cent since 1981.[103] Even in countries with very low participation in Church religion, there was ample evidence of the durability of some form of religious orientation. For example, 72 per cent in Britain expressed a belief in God in 1999.[104] Mac Gréil found that six of every seven Irish respondents reported some level of 'closeness to God'.[105] There was a high level of belief in heaven (80 per cent) and life after death (74 per cent), although both had declined by about ten per cent since 1981.[106] By contrast, between 1974 and

100 B. Wilson, *Religion in Sociological Perspective* (Oxford University Press, 1982), 149.
101 V. Malesevic, 'Ireland and Neo-Secularisation Theory', *Irish Journal of Sociology* 18 (2010), 23.
102 T. Fahey, 'Religion and Prosperity', 44.
103 M. J. Breen and C. Reynolds, 'The Rise of Secularism and the Decline of Religiosity in Ireland: The Pattern of Religious Change in Europe', *The International Journal of Religion & Spirituality in Society* 1 (2011), 195–212.
104 T. Fahey, 'Is Atheism Increasing? Ireland and Europe Compared', in E. Cassidy (ed.), *Measuring Ireland: Discerning Values and Beliefs* (Dublin: Veritas, 2002), 61.
105 M. Mac Gréil, *Pluralism & Diversity in Ireland: Prejudice and Related Issues in Early 21st Century Ireland* (Dublin: Columba Press, 2011), 462.
106 Breen and Reynolds, 'The Rise of Secularism'.

2008 there was a sharp decrease in attendance at weekly Mass (from 91 to 43 per cent), monthly Holy Communion (from 66 to 43 per cent) and monthly confession (from 47 to 9 per cent).[107] Mac Gréil's study revealed significant differences in weekly Mass attendance by age cohort (19.7 per cent of 18–25-year-olds attended compared to 83.1 of those over 71), location (29.5 per cent in urban areas with a population of over 100,000 but 62.7 per cent in rural Ireland) and educational attainment (75.7 per cent of those with primary education or less compared to 34.1 with third-level education). For all that, the rate of weekly Mass attendance in Ireland in 2008 was higher than other areas surveyed: Northern Ireland came a close second at just over 40 per cent, while the rate in Spain was 18.6 per cent.[108] However, the age profile of formal religious practice suggests that decline is gathering pace. One of the most striking findings was that confession was 'dying out', a further indication of the erosion of the Church's ideological power. According to Mac Gréil, one-third of Catholics never go to confession, only 28 per cent go 'several times a year', and just under half of 18- to 40-year-olds have given up going altogether.[109]

While surveys help map changes in religious belief and behaviour, they do not reveal the meaning of being Catholic in contemporary Ireland. To this end, Inglis constructed a typology based on a qualitative study of contemporary Irish identities in 2003–2005 and EVS data. He proposes four types of contemporary Irish Catholic for whom personal belief and institutional belonging remain important but to varying degrees. Orthodox Catholics are loyal members of the institutional Church. Creative Catholics mix and match beliefs and practices from Catholic and other religious menus in a type of 'smorgasbord Catholicism'. Cultural Catholics identify less with the institutional Church but strongly with their Catholic heritage and tradition. They may go to Mass, receive the sacraments and send their children to Catholic schools but no longer see the Church as a spiritual or moral force in their lives. Lastly, individualist Catholics identify themselves as Catholics but do not believe in some of the Church's fundamental teachings.[110] It should be noted that the social basis of religious practice in contemporary Ireland has yet to be examined in detail.

107 Mac Gréil, *Pluralism & Diversity*, 447.
108 *Practice and Belief among Catholics in Northern Ireland: A Summary of Data from the International Social Science Programme Religion III (2008–9) Survey for Northern Ireland & Ireland in a Comparative Perspective*.
109 Mac Gréil, *Pluralism & Diversity*, 448–9, 454.
110 T. Inglis, 'Catholic Identity in Contemporary Ireland: Belief and Belonging to Tradition', *Journal of Contemporary Religion* 22:2 (2007), 205–20.

An Altered Religious Landscape

Census data for the 20-year period from 1991 to 2011 reveals an evolving religious landscape in Ireland.[111] Four significant trends can be discerned. First, there has been a steady decrease in the share of the population who describe themselves as Catholic. The proportion was 91.6 per cent in 1991, 88.4 per cent in 2002, 86.8 per cent in 2006 and 84.2 per cent in 2011. Although the latter was the lowest proportion recorded, it was offset by population growth so that at 3.86 million the number of Catholics in 2011 was the highest since records began. In terms of nationality 92 per cent were Irish. Poles with 110,410 Catholic adherents and 49,761 UK citizens accounted for over half of all non-Irish Catholics; there were also sizeable numbers of Lithuanian (29,313) and Filipino-born (10,810) Catholics.[112] Despite the recent arrival of these non-Irish Catholics, Roman Catholicism had the lowest annualised growth rate of religions in Ireland between 1991 and 2011. It should be borne in mind that the census does not measure practice (unlike the Irish language) and offers no quantification of the number of lapsed members of a particular denomination.

Second, an increasing number identify as being of no religion. Between 1991 and 2011 this jumped from 66,270 to 269,811 – a fourfold increase. In 2002 this category exceeded the number of Church of Ireland adherents, traditionally the second largest religious grouping. In addition, in 2011 the religion of 72,914 individuals was not stated. Between 1991 and 2011 there was a sizeable proportionate increase in the number of atheists, which grew from 320 to 3,905, and agnostics, which increased from 823 to 3,521.[113] Those with no religion or atheist or agnostic had higher levels of education than the general population and were concentrated in Dublin. In the present century there has been a visible increase in mind–body publishing, adherence to alternative spiritualties and New Age practices, as well as growing syncretism.[114] According to Heelas and Woodhead, this represents a movement away from 'the institutionally and doctrinally-focused religiosity of recent centuries and towards a looser and more inner-directed spirituality, less easily measured by organisational affiliation or assent to particular principles'.[115]

---

111 Since 1951 censuses are generally held every five years. The census planned for 2001 was postponed until April 2002 due to an outbreak of foot and mouth disease. The most recent census took place on 24 April 2016, the results of which had not been released at the time of writing.

112 Census 2011: Profile 7, 52.

113 Ibid., 47.

114 For a useful overview, see L. Cox, 'Current Debates: New Religion(s) in Ireland', *Irish Journal of Sociology* 18 (2010), 100–11.

115 P. Heelas and L. Woodhead, *The Spiritual Revolution: Why Religion is Giving Way to Spirituality* (Oxford University Press, 2005) cited in ibid., 102.

Third, the Church of Ireland and Presbyterian Church have made a marked demographic recovery.[116] Since 1881 the recorded size of both denominations declined at each census. A nadir was reached in 1991 when just 89,187 Church of Ireland adherents and 13,199 Presbyterians were enumerated. But in April 2011 there were 134,365 members of the Church of Ireland, an increase of 45,178 adherents or 51 per cent since 1991; in the same period the number of Presbyterians doubled to 24,600.[117] Immigration played an important role in this recovery. The position of Methodists is more complex. A pattern of long-term decline was reversed between 1991 and 2002 when the number grew from 5,037 to 10,033. The increase was sustained in 2006 when 12,160 adherents were returned but fell to 6,842 in 2011. Some of the difference may be due to a change in the format of the census questionnaire. In 2011 there was no specific field for Methodist, unlike the censuses of 2002 and 2006. Some 41,161 persons described their religion simply as Christian in 2011.

Lastly, as a consequence of immigration from Africa, Asia and Eastern Europe, there has been a significant increase in the non-Catholic population and a growing variety of migrant religions. This has been facilitated by the constitutional guarantee of religious freedom. In percentage terms, the fastest growing religion has been Orthodox Christianity with an annualised growth rate of 27.4 per cent between 1991 and 2011. Orthodox Christians increased from 358 in 1991 to 20,798 in 2006 before doubling to 45,233 in 2011.[118] Four out of five of Ireland's Orthodox Christians were non-Irish. The largest nationalities were Romanian (26 per cent) and Latvian (12.5 per cent).[119] Orthodox Christians were mainly concentrated in Dublin and adjoining counties. The next fastest growing religion was Apostolic and Pentecostal which increased from 285 adherents in 1991 to 8,116 in 2006 and 14,043 in 2011.[120] This represents an annualised growth rate of over 21.5 per cent. Almost 64 per cent of the Apostolic and Pentecostal members lived in the greater Dublin area and over 60 per cent were of African ethnicity. African Pentecostal churches in Ireland are one of the few migrant religions to have benefitted from a book-length study.[121] The largest and most widespread group is the Redeemed Christian Church of God, which in 2012 had

---

116 The census uses the category Church of Ireland (including Protestant) as distinct from Presbyterian or Methodist.

117 Census 2011: Profile 7, 47.

118 Ibid, 47.

119 Ibid, 52.

120 Ibid, 47.

121 A. Ugba, *Shades of Belonging: African Pentecostals in Twenty-First Century Ireland* (Trenton, NJ: Africa World Press, 2009).

118 parishes of various sizes in the Republic and had, with the exception of Roscommon, at least one parish in each county.[122] Nonetheless, according to the leading scholar of African Pentecostal churches in Ireland, it is 'difficult to foresee the eventual transformation of the ghettoised universal of Ireland's African Pentecostals and their full integration into the majority society and culture'.[123]

Most notably, Islam has become the third largest religious group behind Roman Catholicism and Anglicanism. Ireland's Muslim community grew twelvefold from 3,875 persons in 1991 to 49,204 in April 2011 or from 0.1 per cent of the population to 1.1 per cent.[124] The majority of Muslim respondents claimed Asian (40.4 per cent) and African (21.4 per cent) ethnicity. This ethnic and denominational diversity has resulted in a variety of mosque associations and Muslim organisations in Ireland. Over half (52 per cent) of all of Ireland's Muslims were concentrated in Dublin. According to one recent study, 'as yet, Muslims in Ireland have not claimed their place in Irish society' and much will depend on how the second generation of Muslims engage with an Irish identity.[125] The Hindu population increased from 953 in 1991 to 10,688 in 2011, a tenfold increase.[126] They were largely an immigrant community with 80 per cent declaring themselves to be of Asian (other than Chinese) ethnicity. The number of Buddhists in Ireland increased from 986 in 1991 to 8,703 in 2011, of which over one-third were Irish by nationality.[127] There were 6,149 Jehovah's Witnesses in 2011, an increase of 19 per cent since 2006.[128] The Jewish religion recorded 1,984 persons in 2011, a slight increase over 2006. This religion was never numerous in Ireland and its highest recorded figure was 3,907 in 1946.[129]

Italy offers a pertinent example of a shift from a monopolistic Catholic religious culture to an unprecedented level of religious pluralism.[130] The Italians no longer subscribe *en masse* to the institutional Church but retain 'a generic

---

122 www.irishchurches.org/members/redeemed-christian-church-of-god.
123 A. Ugba, 'African Pentecostals in Twenty-first Century Ireland: Identity and Integration,' in B. Fanning (ed.), *Immigration and Social Change in the Republic of Ireland* (Manchester: Manchester University Press, 2007), 182.
124 Census 2011, Profile 7, 47.
125 O. Scharbrodt, T. Sakaranaho, A. Hussain Khan, Y. Shanneik and V. Ibrahim, *Muslims in Ireland: Past and Present* (Edinburgh University Press, 2015), 217.
126 Census 2011: Profile 7, 47. For a brief overview of Hindus in Ireland, see S. Skuce, *The Faiths of Ireland* (Dublin: Columba Press, 2006), 86–109.
127 See Skuce, *Faiths of Ireland*, 110–29.
128 Census 2011: Profile 7, 47.
129 Ibid.
130 See E. Pace, 'Achilles and the Tortoise: A Society Monopolized by Catholicism Faced with an Unexpected Religious Pluralism', *Social Compass* 60 (2013), 315–31.

sense of affiliation'.[131] The arrival over several decades of large numbers of immigrants transformed Italy's religious geography. Religions other than Catholicism account for 3.5 per cent of the population. This includes historically established communities such as Jews and the Protestant churches as well as the religions of immigrants. Islam has outstripped all other non-Catholic religious groups to become Italy's second religion.[132] Ireland presents a similar pattern of uneven but concurrent secularisation and new forms of religiosity. Sociological and ethnographic research on new religions in Ireland is yet in its infancy, let alone the study of the development of a second generation of Irish citizens of Islamic, Orthodox, Pentecostal faiths.[133] A recent study suggests that Ireland has become post-Catholic in the sense of moving beyond 'the once-dominant monopoly of the institutional Catholic Church to a mixed religious market' with a variety of contending types of Christianity and other religions.[134]

The changing religious landscape has contributed to a growing demand by parents and the state for a school system better aligned with the needs of a now culturally and religiously diverse population and a plurality of models of provision.[135] The Irish primary school system is quite unusual in the Anglophone world with 96 per cent of schools under denominational control. Some 2,841 (89.65 per cent) of the approximately 3,169 primary schools are under the patronage, management and ownership of the Catholic Church; in addition, about half of post-primary schools are under denominational control.[136] There were, in addition, 174 Church of Ireland schools, 17 Presbyterian, 1 Methodist, 1 Jewish, 1 Quaker and 2 Islamic schools. In the future there will be a wider choice of school types and less religious patronage. To this end, a *Forum on Patronage and Pluralism in the Primary Sector* reported in 2012 and policies to implement its recommendations are being devised.[137]

---

131 E. Pace, 'A Peculiar Pluralism', *Journal of Modern Italian Studies* 12 (2007), 90.

132 Ibid., 94.

133 For a recent survey, see O. Cosgrove, L. Cox, C. Kuhling, *Ireland's New Religious Movements* (Newcastle-upon-Tyne: Cambridge Scholars, 2011).

134 G. Ganiel, *Transforming post-Catholic Ireland: Religious Practice in Late Modernity* (Oxford University Press, 2016), 43.

135 According to the 2011 census, there were 14,769 primary school children, 14,478 secondary school pupils and 4,690 children aged less than one year of no religion; 8,322 Muslim children of primary school age and a further 3,582 of secondary school age.

136 *Forum on Patronage and Pluralism in the Primary Sector: Report of the Forum's Advisory Group* (April 2012), 29.

137 Ibid; *Forum on Patronage and Pluralism in the Primary Sector: Progress to Date and Future Directions* (July 2014). For a discussion of the complexities involved see D. Tuohy, *Denominational Education and Politics: Ireland in a European Context* (Dublin: Veritas, 2013), 259–89; K. Kitching, 'Governing "Authentic" Religiosity? The Responsibilisation of Parents beyond Religion and State in Matters of School Ethos in Ireland', *Irish Journal of Sociology* 21 (2013), 17–34.

Thinning Pews

A number of reasons for an increasing detachment from the institutional Church can be advanced. Atypically high participation rates may simply be converging with other European and Western countries, many of which went through periods of declining churchly religion. For example, Callum Brown has documented how abruptly Britain became more secular in the early 1960s.[138] Unquestionably, the number with a genuine faith commitment has shrunk. Commentators have pointed to the failure to evangelise a new generation as 'the great drama of contemporary Irish Catholicism'.[139] Understanding of the basic tenets of Catholicism has become so poor that even in seminary training a propaedeutic year – an introductory year before formal studies begin – is being introduced because of the impoverished levels of faith development.[140] Second, the church in contemporary Ireland has little influence over public opinion, the state and the media. Indeed the latter has become the chief supplier of alternative value systems and new forms of conformity. The media has also provided an intense critique of religious institutions which were once above public scrutiny. Some commentators have identified a form of 'secular fundamentalism' in the Irish media.[141] Investigative journalism played a major role in uncovering clerical sexual scandals and televised documentaries such as 'Suing the Pope' (BBC 2002) and 'Cardinal Secrets' (RTÉ 2002) prompted the establishment of inquiries. Marie Keenan has noted that in Ireland the coverage of clerical sexual abuse led to the emergence of a new and powerful media template: Brendan Smyth (a Norbertine order priest sentenced to twelve years' imprisonment) and the paedophile priest.[142] The dangers of false allegations and trial by media (sometimes without basic fact-checking) were exposed when RTÉ's 'Mission to Prey' (2011) defamed an innocent Catholic priest in what the director-general of RTÉ admitted was one of the gravest editorial mistakes ever made by the broadcaster. The Irish Church has yet to develop a coherent media strategy. Third, adherence to Church teaching on social and moral matters such as abortion, pre-marital sexual relations and same-sex relations has sharply declined. The percentage of non-marital births grew from 4 per cent in 1977

---

138 C. Brown, *The Death of Christian Britain* (London: Routledge, 2001), 175–6.

139 Kirby, 'The Catholic Church in Post-Celtic Tiger Ireland', 25–6.

140 J. Littleton, 'Being a Catholic in Ireland Today', in Littleton and Maher (eds.), *Contemporary Catholicism*, 17.

141 D. Kiberd, 'Ireland after *aggiornamento*', *Studies* 101 (2012), 438.

142 M. Keenan, '"Them and Us": The Clergy Child Sexual Offender as "Other"' in T. Flannery (ed.), *Responding to the Ryan Report* (Dublin: Columba Press, 2009), 192–4.

to 31.4 in 2005; the number of divorced Catholics in 2011 was 64,798, a rate of 3.6 per cent (the rate for the general population was 4.2 per cent).[143] Most spectacularly, in May 2015 a referendum on same-sex marriage was approved by 62 per cent. How people live out their Catholic identity has become, as Anderson and Lavan contend, an individual matter that consists of believing in Church teachings regarding beliefs but not obeying Church rules on how to practice this faith.[144] Fourth, for an increasing number, Catholicism is part of a socio-cultural identity expressed at key rites of passage such as baptism, marriage and last rites. In 1999–2000, the EVS found that over 90 per cent of the Irish population thought such religious ceremonies important. Even among the non-affiliated in other countries, there was an emphasis on a religious ceremony, particularly at death.[145] It may become increasingly difficult to measure the extent to which church membership becomes merely nominal and religious practice a matter of social convention or cultural ritual. Lastly, the clerical sex abuse scandals and the Church's inadequate response have been intensely corrosive.

Scandal

Since the early 1990s the Catholic Church in Ireland has been besieged by scandals too numerous to itemise. The first wave of sexual scandal involved paternity cases. In 1992 Catholic Ireland was shocked to discover that Éamonn Casey, Bishop of Galway, had secretly fathered a child with an American woman, Annie Murphy, in the 1970s and used Church funds to support her. Shortly afterwards, it emerged that Fr Michael Cleary, a media figure well-known for his defence of traditional Catholic values, had fathered two children with his housekeeper, Phyllis Hamilton. Both Casey and Cleary had introduced the Pope in Galway in 1979. For an institution so preoccupied with questions of sexual morality the consequent loss of standing was swift. By 1999 among the Catholic European countries examined in the EVS, Ireland had on average the lowest level of trust in the Church.[146] Far more destructive

---

143 B. Hilliard, 'Family', in O'Sullivan (ed.), *Contemporary Ireland*, 88; Census 2011: Profile 7, 51.

144 K. Anderson and A. Lavan, 'Believing in God but Not Obeying the Church: Being A Catholic in Ireland and Poland in the 1990s', in B. Hilliard and M. Nic Ghiolla Phádraig (eds.), *Changing Ireland in International Comparison* (Dublin: Liffey Press, 2007), 213.

145 Fahey, 'Is Atheism Increasing?', 63; T. Fahey, B. Hayes and R. Sinnott, *Conflict and Consensus: A Study of Values and Attitudes in the Republic of Ireland and Northern Ireland* (Dublin: Institute of Public Administration, 2005), 51–2.

146 S. Donnelly and T. Inglis, 'The Media and the Catholic Church in Ireland: Reporting Clerical Child Sex Abuse', *Journal of Contemporary Religion* 25 (2010), 12.

and larger in scale due to the extensive involvement of the Church in welfare provision, as outlined by Catherine Cox (see Chapter 22 this volume), was the emotional, physical and sexual abuse of vulnerable children by a minority of clergy and religious. This was revealed in a cascade of harrowing inquiry reports: Ferns (2005), Ryan (2009), Murphy (2009) and Cloyne (2011) among others. These revealed a failure of leadership, hypocrisy and a dysfunctional authoritarian institutional culture more concerned with avoiding scandal and secrecy than protecting the vulnerable. As Judge Yvonne Murphy found when investigating allegations of child sexual abuse by priests in the Dublin archdiocese between 1975 and 2004, the preoccupations of church authorities

> at least until the mid-1990s, were the maintenance of secrecy, the avoidance of scandal, the protection of the reputation of the Church and the preservation of its assets. All other considerations, including the welfare of children and justice for victims, were subordinated to these priorities. The archdiocese did not implement its own Canon Law rules and did its best to avoid any application of the law of the State.[147]

This echoed the findings of similar investigations in the archdiocese of Boston.

The betrayal of trust has undermined the credibility and moral authority of the institutional Church in Ireland and globally. The scale of clerical abuse may have appeared greater because decades of crimes were investigated in a relatively short period of time. The institutional Church does not stand indicted alone. The Irish state and society were complicit by their failure to safeguard the marginalised in the industrial school and Magdalen asylum. As in the US, the Irish Church responded by first developing child protection guidelines in 1996. This was followed five years later by the establishment of a child protection office (now the National Board for Safeguarding Children in the Catholic Church in Ireland) and a pastoral directive on clerical child abuse in 2011 called *Towards Healing and Renewal*. The commissioning of an independent study *Time to Listen: Confronting Child Sexual Abuse by Catholic Clergy in Ireland* (2003) to understand the impacts of and responses to clerical child sex abuse was the first of its kind in the global Church.[148] The scandals have overshadowed the invaluable work of priests, religious and Catholic

---

147 *Report by Commission of Investigation into Catholic Archdiocese of Dublin* (2009), part 1, ch. 1.15.
148 B. Conway, 'Religious Institutions and Sexual Scandals: A Comparative Study of Catholicism in Ireland, South Africa and the United States', *International Journal of Comparative Sociology* 55 (2014), 331.

voluntary organisations such as the Society of St Vincent de Paul (which in 2014 had 10,500 members) to ameliorate economic hardship and social ine-quality.[149] However, over the longer term the scandals were 'just the final act in a long play of structural transformations' which has denuded the power and influence of the Church.[150]

Conclusion

The Catholic Church in Ireland is in the maelstrom of its gravest crisis in centuries. As an institution, it labours under the challenge of coping with the past and salvaging its precarious position to find a relevant role in con-temporary Ireland. Catholicism is no longer an integral part of Irish identity in a society that has become increasingly heterogeneous, secular, ethnically diverse and religiously indifferent. Greatly diminished not just in membership but in authority and influence, the Irish Catholic Church could experience extreme contraction, as has occurred in France. Yet, despite Catholicism's many travails, there is still a significant critical mass of believers in Ireland. This holds the promise (and historians make at best unreliable prophets) of continued vigour within a more pluralist environment. In 1994 Grace Davie, a sociologist, advanced the concept of 'believing without belonging' which has been widely cited ever since.[151] More recently she updated this model and prefers the concept of 'vicarious religion', where an active minority main-tains the faith for the occasional use of the many.[152] The resilience and size of that active minority in an Irish Catholic context depends on effective Church leadership which must do more than simply manage decline. It must ensure institutional reform, a real sharing of authority at all levels, a new evangelism, an energetic theological culture, adaptation to the spiritual demands of the present age and, above all, a rediscovery of its core Christian mission.

149 B. Lawlor and J. Dalton (eds.), *The Society of St Vincent de Paul in Ireland: 170 Years of Fighting Poverty* (Dublin: New Island Books, 2014), xx.
150 Inglis, 'Individualism and Secularisation', 68.
151 G. Davie, *Religion in Britain since 1945: Believing Without Belonging* (Oxford: Blackwell, 1994).
152 G. Davie, *The Sociology of Religion* (London: Sage, 2007), 143.

25

Art and Architecture in Ireland, 1880–2016

PAULA MURPHY

Introduction

Historians of art, whatever their period of study, invariably make claims for
the discovery of innovation, variety, difference and novelty. Some experience
of newness – no matter what form it might take – seems essential to validate
the dedicated research. Throughout the history of art, new painting styles,
new sculptural shapes and new architectural configurations appear – displays
of virtuosity alternating with manifestations of classical restraint. However,
despite any inherent novelty, these remained the standard methods of visual
artistic expression created by traditional practitioners: painters, sculptors and
architects. It is only in the twentieth century that these traditions are questioned and that innovation is more prevalent than at any other time. With
hindsight it was obvious that art had been static for centuries. While painting,
sculpture and architecture do not disappear in the course of the twentieth century, they become less exclusive and are augmented by performance, installation, sound, time-based and many more innovative methods of expression.
Sculpture – in its 'expanded field'[1] – might be identified as the pivotal art form.
The traditional definition of practitioners by category became contentious,
as the makers of art chose to be known as artists, permitting them ultimate
freedom in their means of expression, rather than being identified with a single art form. In the course of the twentieth century long-standing accepted
conventions in art were not just questioned but overturned.

Innovation

In 1982, Cork artist Danny McCarthy (b. 1950) threw empty bottles of
Jameson whiskey from O'Connell Bridge into the River Liffey in Dublin in a

---

1 Rosalind Krauss, 'Sculpture in the Expanded Field', *October*, 8 (Spring, 1979), 30–44.

37. Danny McCarthy: *One-hundred bottles for James Joyce*, 1982.

performance art work to commemorate James Joyce. Exactly a hundred years earlier, in 1882, the long-awaited national monument commemorating Daniel O'Connell had been unveiled – just a stone's or even a bottle's throw away – at the south end of O'Connell Street, then known as Sackville Street. The *O'Connell Monument* was and remains a traditional commemorative work – heroic in presentation; conservative in style; classical in several of its elements; conventional in material; and, intentionally, permanent. O'Connell, the work of Irish-born, London-based sculptor John Henry Foley (1818–1874), was to be encountered in this statuesque form by future generations – *ad infinitum*. Everything about the McCarthy artwork, *One-hundred Bottles for James Joyce*, differed from its neighbouring sculpture, particularly in the artist's use of ready-made objects and in the ephemeral, time-based aspect of the work. While no memory of the event was intended to endure on O'Connell Bridge, an element of continuity – the continuation of the performance – prevailed in the return of the bottles when it occurred, as had been requested by way of a message inside each bottle. O'Connell, in his bronze likeness, was look-ing down on a new form of artistic expression. In less than a hundred years the nature of art had changed or, perhaps more appropriately, developed to incorporate new forms, cutting-edge methods, imaginative materials, novel displays and differing expectations.

38. John Henry Foley: the O'Connell Monument, Dublin, 1882/83.

Art in Western Europe generally in the period 1880–2016 is defined by innovation and although Ireland is no outsider in this, in the earlier decades Irish art was slow to manifest particular new influences, and the Irish establishment – artistic and political – was often unwilling to accept new tendencies in art. The now familiar example of this is in connection with so-called Abstract Art – the rejection of the representation of the known world

39. Mainie Jellett: *Decoration*, 1923.

in art and specifically recognisable objects. This most significant development
in the early twentieth century did not immediately find acceptance in Ireland.
Mainie Jellett's (1897–1944) notorious abstract cubist painting *Decoration*
(1923, NGI), exhibited in Dublin in 1923, was greeted with the derision that
often accompanied new forms of artistic expression – particularly in France
since the mid-nineteenth century. If in France rejection served more immediately as the herald of acceptance, however, it was not necessarily the case
that this would follow in Ireland. Non-representational art did not really find

acceptance in Ireland until the mid-century, notably when Patrick Scott (1921–2014) began to show his minimalist abstract work in Dublin in the 1960s. The work of Jellett and Scott is not without similarities, often, but not exclusively, geometric in form and spiritual in content.

Irish art at the turn of the century was largely dominated by developments in France. The new movements there, Naturalism, Realism and Impressionism, had by then found favour with the French public and beyond, and modernity was widely accepted as a new norm in painting. The work of the post-Impressionists, however, continued to be controversial, as would be the modernist styles that developed from their work in the early decades of the twentieth century. While Irish paintings of the period show naturalist, realist and post-Impressionist tendencies, there is a curious absence of any manifestation of Impressionism. There is evidence of the loose, sketchy brushwork so associated with the style, but the vibrant colour and exhilarating light are absent. The seriousness and solemnity in the work of painters Osborne and Hone, Henry and Yeats has no connection with the attractive *légèreté* of impressionist paintings.

Walter Osborne (1859–1903), who was in Pont Aven in Brittany in 1883, several years before Gauguin arrived there, employs a form of sympathetic realism to paint scenes in Brittany (*Apple Gathering, Quimperlé,* 1883, NGI) and in Dublin (*Life in the Streets, Musicians,* 1893, HLG); Nathaniel Hone the younger (1831–1917), much travelled and, pertinently, to the Forest of Fontainebleau, paints sombre land- and seascapes which sit comfortably with the work of the Pre-impressionist painters of the Barbizon School. Sincerity and integrity are dominant characteristics in the work of these two artists. Paul Henry (1876–1958) shows realist and post-impressionist influences in his well-known and ultimately constant paintings of the west of Ireland (*Leenane, 1913,* Ulster Museum); Jack Yeats's (1871–1957) work suggests more contemporary influences than those of Henry, notably that of Expressionism. His vigorous early realist style (*Bachelor's Walk, In Memoriam,* 1915, NGI) and perhaps more significantly his later energetic expressionist paintings (*Man in a Train Thinking,* 1927, priv. coll.) saw him anointed as the first Irish Modernist of international standing.

That Yeats had political sensitivity is evident in much of his work, and to contend that the politics of the period in Ireland dictated the serious, less experimental nature of painting at the time has some basis. The political position of Ireland in the decades prior to and immediately after the turn into the twentieth century was one of increasing nationalism, as limited independence seemed likely to become more than just an aspiration. Modernity was foreign and therefore threatening and unwelcome. There is something

40.   Walter Osborne: *Apple Gathering, Quimperlé*, 1883.

undesirably pragmatic about the preference for Irish subject matter treated in a respectful manner.

The inevitable co-existence of contradictory affiliations that are the result of colonisation are witnessed in the many Irish artists working in England and carrying out imperial commissions, sometimes for locations in Ireland. William Orpen (1878–1931) and John Lavery (1856–1941) were both society painters in London and considered rather more as British than Irish artists.

41. Jack Yeats: *Man in a train thinking*, 1927.

Both were appointed official war artists during the First World War, Lavery concentrating on the war effort in England and Orpen, in France, on life at the front. Similarly associated, in Ireland, sculptor John Hughes (1865–1941) was commissioned to carry out commemorative monuments for Dublin to William Gladstone and Queen Victoria, both of which works he thought – incorrectly as it turned out – would serve to make his name.[2] Both monuments were to prove controversial and the former, which was never to find a location in the Irish capital, was offered instead to Gladstone's hometown, Hawarden in Wales, where it was erected in 1925. The Victoria monument was unveiled in the forecourt of Leinster House, then home to the Royal Dublin Society, in 1908. However, in 1924 the building was acquired to house the Irish parliament, and, with many imperial monuments being destroyed or decommissioned in Dublin in the first half of the twentieth century, Queen Victoria was removed from her pedestal in 1948, in advance of the signing of the Republic of Ireland Act in December of that year.

The extent to which the burden of their location is evident in the work of these artists can be witnessed in a comparison with the paintings of their

2 P. Murphy, *Nineteenth-Century Irish Sculpture, Native Genius Reaffirmed* (New Haven: Yale University Press, 2010), 219.

42. John Hughes: the Queen Victoria Monument, 1908.

contemporary Roderic O'Conor (1860–1940), who, having spent time study-ing in Antwerp and Paris, readily resisted the pull of his native Ireland and instead immersed himself in French art circles, in French subject matter and in French light, in Paris and its environs, in Brittany (*La Ferme de Lezaven, Finistère*, 1894, NGI) and in Provence.

Like O'Conor, designer and architect Eileen Gray (1878–1976) left Ireland to study initially in London and then in Paris, where she finally established herself in 1906. Her furniture (*Bibendum Chair*, 1926), for which she was best known, and her houses in the south of France (*E-1027*, 1924) were at the cutting-edge of contemporary design. These two Irish artists were not on the sidelines of Modernism in France, but were actively engaged in the French art world – O'Conor, for example, sitting on the jury of the prestigious Parisian Salon d'Automne in 1908, an exhibition that included work by Modigliani, Braque and Matisse; Gray, a member of the Union des Artistes Modernes, a group of Modernist designers in France founded in 1929, and an exhibi-tor in Le Corbusier's *Pavillon des Temps Nouveaux* in the Paris International Exposition in 1937. Rooted in France and French art, these two artists appear to have had little influence in Ireland.

43. Eileen Gray: E-1027, 1924.

Influence

While one might expect the artistic link with England, and London in particular, to have significance for Irish artists in these turn-of-the-century decades,
in fact it was Paris to which they aspired. Irish artists had long been in the
habit of travelling to study abroad and in the course of the nineteenth century had more success in acquiring fame and recognition if they established
their studios in London, rather than Dublin. Beyond the capital of the British
Empire, Rome, the source of international Neoclassicism, had been a draw in
the early century. However, by the closing decades Paris was the undisputed
centre of the European art world and – according to the headmaster of the
Dublin Metropolitan School of Art (later NCA; NCAD) – the place where
artists were made, or so W. B. Yeats recounted in an anecdote in 1906. Yeats,
along with many other protagonists, was being interviewed in connection
with an inquiry into art education in Dublin at the time.[3] It is evident from

3 *Report of the Committee of Inquiry into the work carried out by the Royal Hibernian Academy
and the Metropolitan School of Art, Dublin* (Dublin and London: His Majesty's Stationery
Office, 1906).

the interviews generally that Paris was then the preferred choice for Irish artists. Among those who travelled there, most had studied first in Dublin or at the Belfast School of Art and subsequently in London (Westminster Art School; South Kensington Schools; Slade School of Fine Art), before making their way to Paris, where they studied variously at the École des Beaux Arts, in the private academies, in the museums (notably the Louvre and the Musée du Luxembourg) and the commercial galleries. In the late nineteenth and early twentieth century these included painters William Leech (1881–1968), Beatrice Glenavy (née Elvery 1883–1970), Mary Swanzy (1882–1978), Mainie Jellett, Evie Hone (1894–1955) and Norah McGuinness (1901–1980); and sculptors John Hughes, Oliver Sheppard (1865–1941), Mervyn Lawrence (1868–1961) and Rosamond Praeger (1867–1954) and Irish-American Andrew O'Connor (1874–1941).

The French capital would remain a draw for Irish artists with a later group travelling there after the mid-century, including architect Robin Walker (1924–1992, subsequently of Scott, Tallon, Walker), who was there in the later 1940s, and painters Louis Le Brocquy (1916–2012) and Michael Farrell (1940–2000), the latter moving with his family to live in Paris in 1971. But by then New York had supplanted Paris as the centre of artistic innovation and Irish artists' interests and loyalties were redirected across the Atlantic.

However, it was not exclusively a matter of Irish artists making their way out of the country. Experience and new influences gathered from foreign artists visiting the country had been a significant factor in the development of Irish art for centuries. At the outbreak of the Second World War, the London-based White Stag group, established by Basil Rákóczi (b. London, 1908–1979) in 1935, relocated to Ireland, where they were to prove influential. Rákóczi had strong Irish connections by way of his mother.[4] The surrealist-related imagery (Rákóczi, *Child Flying*, 1943, priv. coll.) of the group met with considerable success, such was the novelty witnessed in the work when it was exhibited in Dublin. If Surrealism in Ireland is more particularly associated with the quirky paintings of northern artist Colin Middleton (1910–1983), and the sculpture of fellow northerner F. E. McWilliam (1909–1992), who established his career in London, it is Pat Scott, who was most immediately associated with the White Stag group, exhibiting with them in Dublin and deriving motifs from their work for his own paintings.

Scott, who trained and worked initially as an architect, and whose architectural background continued to inform his art, was already on the road – in

4 S. B. Kennedy, *The White Stag Group* (Irish Museum of Modern Art, 2005), 44, footnote 2.

44. Patrick Scott: *Gold Painting 34*, 1965.

a Klee-like manner – to creating abstract work and, in his own modest way, to becoming Ireland's leading Modernist painter. This was confirmed when Alfred Barr, director of the Museum of Modern Art in New York (MOMA), purchased a Scott painting for the collection in 1958.[5] Scott was to develop a Minimalist abstract style (*Gold Painting* series, begun 1964), influenced by American Minimalism – experienced, less on the ground in the US, but more locally in Dublin in an exhibition, *Art USA Now*, at the Municipal Gallery of Modern Art in 1964. Minimalism was to manifest itself in Irish sculpture a little later – with such definitive examples of the work by Michael Bulfin (b. 1939. *Reflections*, 1975) and John Burke (1946–2006. *Red Cardinal*, 1978) located

---

5 *Woman Carrying Grasses* (1958). A. Dunne, *Patrick Scott* (Dublin: Liberties Press, Dublin) 61.

45. Gerda Frömel: *Sails*, 1970, at former Carroll's building (now DkIT), Dundalk.

on the plaza of the former Bank of Ireland Headquarters (1968–1978) on Dublin's Baggot Street. Designed by Ronnie Tallon (1968–1978) of Scott, Tallon, Walker, the dark geometric architectural edifice is intentionally enlivened by the abstract coloured steel forms.

Since the ancient world, sculpture has had an important relationship with architecture, usually by way of its use in completing a building. The simple unadorned nature of Modernist architecture saw sculpture located in the vicinity of, rather than on the building. Tallon's success in adapting sculpture to architecture had already been evident in his choice of Dublin-based Czech artist Gerda Frömel (1931–1975) to create a work for his Carroll's Cigarette Factory building (now DkIT) in Dundalk in 1970. Frömel's kinetic stainless steel *Sails* (1970), silver in colour, is positioned in a shallow pool outside the low-lying factory building. The gentle movement of three tall slim forms creates an intricate play of light, as they reflect the sky and one another, while in turn throwing their reflection onto the pool. These modern abstract sculptures, which concentrated on form for its own sake, were a decisive break with the established tradition of representational and commemorative public work.

While Modernist tendencies in art were fairly well established in Ireland by the 1970s, there was still something tentative about them. The numbers of artists involved were relatively small and therefore the manifestations of the different twentieth-century styles, from the early Cubism and Expressionism to the later Pop and Op Art and all that happened in between, were only scarcely evident in the exhibitions of the work of Irish artists. Academic styles prevailed with the public generally and with other than a small number of enlightened patrons – notably Basil Goulding and Gordon Lambert, both of whom were keen patrons of the avant-garde and formed important collections of contemporary art. With no national gallery of modern art, the public had little opportunity to become versed in modern art movements. And with little experience of Modernism, they were about to be introduced to post-modern practices that were beginning to make their appearance.

Brian O'Doherty (b. 1928) has worked as an artist, critic, writer and teacher in the US since the late 1950s. Trained in medicine in Dublin, Cambridge (UK) and Harvard (US), his early medical and scientific studies can be seen to have influenced his art in different ways throughout his career. Also known by the name of Patrick Ireland between the years 1972 and 2008, he activated this new identity in a performance work (*Name Change, 1972*), which was a protest against the killings on Bloody Sunday in Derry. In a single artwork he introduced performance and time-based art to Ireland. Other alternate identities were to be used by O'Doherty, but none with such political intent, and he was to continue to use this name until such time as peace was established in Northern Ireland.[6] O'Doherty / Ireland's art practice has taken many forms. A conceptual and installation artist, he became an important figure on the international stage and, in his early practice, was more widely known in the US than in Ireland. While employing paint, 3D form and, in particular, drawing in his work, O'Doherty / Ireland moves beyond their traditional usage to new methods of presentation, notably in his *Rope Drawings*, which use line and colour to create a work that is at once a sculpture and an installation. His early inspiration resides in the work of Marcel Duchamp (1887–1968), whom he met in New York on his arrival there. Duchamp is widely acknowledged as the most influential artist in the development of Western art in the twentieth century, establishing complete and independent creative freedom for artists. That O'Doherty / Ireland was immediately similarly influential in Ireland is less obviously the case. There were other artists closer to home that might be claimed to have had more impact.

---

6 D. Moos, 'Narrative of the Name', in C. Kennedy and G. Jackson (eds.), *Beyond the White Cube, A Retrospective of Brian O'Doherty/Patrick Ireland* (Dublin: Dublin City Gallery the Hugh Lane, 2006), 83–6.

46. Brian O'Doherty: *Name Change*, 1972.

The constant reference to Paris and New York in discussion of influences in Irish art in the twentieth century ignores the place of German Expressionism in the development. Expressionism was evident in the work of Jack Yeats early in the century and would reappear, in opposition to abstract painting, in the 1960s in the work of a group known as the Independents, including Michael Kane (b. 1935), Charles Cullen (b. 1939) and Brian Bourke (b. 1936). However in its 'neo' form in the 1970s and 1980s, Expressionism – revived in Germany in the work of Anselm Kiefer (b. 1945), Georg Baselitz (b. 1938), Jörg Immendorff (1945–2007) and others – inspired a particularly dark and violent variant of the style in Ireland. Artists included Brian Maguire (b. 1951), Mick Mulcahy (b. 1952) and Patrick Graham (b. 1943), who produced mostly large, aggressively painted, murky canvases. Much of their art addresses issues of politics and nationalism, social concerns, and – as the role of the Catholic Church in Ireland came under scrutiny – issues of religion and sexuality (Patrick Graham, *My Darkish Rosaleen (Ireland as a Young Whore)*, 1982, priv. coll.).

Neo-expressionist painting appeared to dominate the avant-garde art scene in Ireland in the early 1980s. This was largely the work of male artists. Few women engaged with this form of artistic expression, Eithne Jordan (b. 1954) being a notable exception. Yet a considerable number of Irish women artists were active at the time. Rejecting the ferocity of Neo-Expressionism, these women discovered other forms of artistic communication, ultimately liberating Irish art from the use of traditional materials and breaking the boundaries between the distinctive categories of art practice. It is not that painting and sculpture had not been interrelated previously in Irish art. Michael Farrell, for example, had used shaped canvas and incorporated 3D elements into his paintings in the 1970s (*Pressé* series). Even Patrick Graham's Neo-expressionist paintings suggested a relief sculptural element in his tortured use of mixed media on torn canvas. However, the terms sculpture and painting remain relevant in these instances.

The work of Patricia McKenna (b. 1951), Maud Cotter (b. 1954), Alanna O'Kelly (b. 1955), Alice Maher (b. 1956), Dorothy Cross (b. 1956) and Kathy Prendergast (b. 1958), all born within a few years of one another, challenges specific categorisation. Several of these women encountered the use of traditional materials in their art education and commenced their careers in painting or sculpture, yet by the end of the 1980s all of them were employing new materials and new processes for making art. This was to position them as the most innovative and most influential artists in Ireland by the close of the century. They were attracted, in particular, by natural, and ultimately, ephemeral materials, as a result of which some of their early work no longer exists.

47. Michael Farrell: *Pressé Politique*, 1972.

Why such materials? Multiple reasons emerge – the reaction against the male-dominated painting of the time; the expressive content of their work; the colossal cost of traditional materials. New art materials, such as corrugated cardboard, hair, fabric, found objects, were much cheaper than bronze or marble, oil paint and canvas. These women did not hail from wealthy Anglo-Irish backgrounds like Jellett, Hone and several of their contemporaries in the early part of the century.

Once more Germany had an influential role, notably Joseph Beuys (1921–1986) and German-born American artist Eva Hesse (1936–1970). Sculptor, performance and conceptual artist, Beuys, who used many different materials in his work and specifically fat and felt, exhibited and lectured in Ireland on different occasions in the 1970s and 1980s. His *Irish Energies* (1974, peat briquettes and Kerrygold butter) was included in a sculpture exhibition in Dublin in 1975.

Hesse, a pioneering mixed-media artist, used several new materials including latex, cheesecloth and fibreglass, the last of which was to form the basis of Deborah Brown's (b. 1927) abstract work in the 1970s. In the aftermath of Hesse's early death, retrospective exhibitions of her work were held in several locations, including the Guggenheim Museum in New York in 1972/1973 and the Whitechapel Art Gallery in London in 1979, making her art practice more widely known.

Many of these Irish women artists were using different aspects of their lives as the basis of their work, exploring what it was to be an Irish girl/woman/daughter/lover/mother. The materials often had a domestic impetus or family association. Alanna O'Kelly's installation in the Project Arts Centre, Dublin, in 1981, *Barriers*, comprised a series of large wooden posts from her native County Wexford; Alice Maher gathered wild brambles from her childhood home in Tipperary for her work, *Cell*, in Kilmainham Gaol in 1991; Kathy Prendergast used a baby's bonnet, a cotton reel and three generations of human hair in her two-piece work *The End and The Beginning I and II* (1997, Arts Council). Dorothy Cross explicitly addressed gender and sexuality in its Irish context in *Ebb*, an installation of individual and partnered works in the Douglas Hyde Gallery in 1988, in which she used wood, bronze, fabric, photographs, wallpaper and found objects. The works are now long since dispersed and few of them survive (*Shark Lady in a Ball Dress*, bronze, 1988, HLG). Patricia McKenna's *Grey House* (1993/1994) is also no longer extant. Part of a series titled *Marking the Land* (1990–1998), this was a site-specific installation in an abandoned farmhouse in a remote part of County Cavan, the county that was home to her parents. The house itself, the artist's activity within and the participation of the local community all formed part of the artwork, which existed for 12 months.

Art – since Duchamp's notorious *Fountain* (1917, ready-made porcelain urinal) – could now be made out of anything and the lasting nature of art, made in materials that endure, was being called into question. These women would proceed to have careers of considerable significance in Ireland, and, notably, in the case of Prendergast and Cross, outside the country. Cross's *Virgin Shroud* (1993, cowhide, muslin, satin, wood, plaster and iron), forms part of the collection of Tate Modern, purchased by the Patrons of New Art in 1995. Prendergast's *City Drawings* (IMMA), a series of exquisitely fragile drawings of capital cities begun in 1992, were exhibited at the Tate in 1997, and the gallery has since acquired later map work by her, including *Lost* (1999, digital print on paper) and *Black Map Series (America North Central)* (2009, ink on printed map). The practice of several of these women artists would expand into video, performance and sound work. O'Kelly made use of the

48. Kathy Prendergast: *The End and The Beginning I and II*, 1997. Human hair and wooden spool.

haunting sound of keening in a work that developed out of her time spent at the Women's Peace Camp located outside the US Air Force Base at Greenham Common in Berkshire, England, in 1986 (*Chant Down Greenham Common*). Cross later ventured into the world of opera, notably directing a production of Pergolesi's *Stabat Mater* in a remote slate quarry grotto on Valentia Island in County Kerry in 2004.

The use of non-traditional mixed media in art in Ireland was not the exclusive domain of women artists at this time. Brian O'Doherty, working in the

782

US, had already been exploring a range of new material, as had James Coleman (b. 1941), who was based in Milan and largely making use of slide projection (*Slide Piece*, 1972/1973) and video. Work by both artists was included in the third ROSC exhibition. Among the next generation, Philip Napier (b. 1965), who was born in Belfast, was to employ a wide range of materials and processes in his examination, through the 1990s, of subject matter related to the northern Troubles.

Irishness

Art in Northern Ireland is integral to any discussion of Irish art, while also requiring some separate consideration. The Northern subject or The Troubles, for example, was pivotal in the career of many artists in the last decades of the twentieth century. The conflict, played out on television news across the world, generated increased knowledge of and interest in matters Irish. The progressive participation of Irish artists in international art exhibitions, evident in this period, may or may not have been related. The resulting work necessarily has a significant role in any examination of Irishness in Irish art.

The need to identify what is Irishness and how it is manifest has been something of a constant in writing on Irish art in the twentieth century – a search for the existence of some inherent Irish expression, separate from that of British art. Yet in the early decades of the period under discussion here, Irish art was an offshoot of British art. The artistic relationship between England and Ireland was particularly strong through the nineteenth century. The South Kensington School dictated art education in Ireland until the end of the century.[7] Irish artists spent periods of study in England, London particularly, and participated in exhibitions across the UK. Several Irish painters and sculptors had established prominent careers in London, becoming leading British artists.

Early attempts to identify or project Irishness tended to have recourse to early Irish art – specific examples of which occurred at the nineteenth-century international art and industry shows known as Great Exhibitions or World's Fairs, exhibitions that purported to be about progress! Copies of Irish High Crosses were sent to the first of these exhibitions held at the Crystal Palace in London in 1851, the Paris show in 1867 and subsequently several

---

7 J. Turpin, *A School of Art in Dublin since the Eighteenth Century* (Dublin: Gill & Macmillan, 1995). See ch. 10.

American exhibitions, notably the Chicago Columbian in 1893. Who would have thought that, more than a hundred years after their first outing, this spectacle would be revisited, when, for ROSC '67, it was proposed that there would be an accompanying display of Irish art. Yet again in incongruous circumstances – on this occasion an exhibition of international contemporary art – the Irish High Cross was selected to perform the role of promoting Irishness. This appeared to suggest that, at the time, Irishness was only to be found in Early Celtic art.

What is meant by this problematic term Irishness? In 1984 the contemporary art journal *Circa* devoted an issue to the topic, questioning its very existence and/or relevance and certainly recognising the introspective nature of the label and its complexity in a divided country.[8] If a professed form of identity, then Irishness is most obviously manifest in subject matter rather than in style, notably in the work of Irish artwork that has a political purpose – discernible in the '98 and 1916 commemorative imagery and in work responding to the Northern Troubles. Even the extensive use of the west of Ireland as subject matter in painting in the early twentieth century was made to serve political motivation. Paul Henry, James Humbert Craig (1877–1944) (*Going to Mass*, 1939, Crawford Art Gallery) and Charles Lamb (1893–1964) (*Gathering Seaweed*, 1944, HGL), all of whom were born in Ulster, produced images of the western seaboard that formed part of a very particular type of Irish landscape painting. However, these paintings also served as propagandist imagery, suggesting an area of the country that might be identified – incorrectly – as being largely untainted by British rule in Ireland. Seán Keating (1889–1977), who hailed from Limerick, and was even to paint himself as a wild man of the West, used the location for recognisably nationalist political images (*Men of the West*, 1915, HLG).

Representations of Ireland in the guise of a woman – Éire, Mother Ireland – proliferated across Ireland at the end of the nineteenth century with the commissioning of monuments to commemorate the Manchester Martyrs (executed in 1867) and the centenary of the 1798 Rebellion. The monuments incorporate traditional Irish symbolic motifs such as the Celtic cross, harp and shamrock. There is nothing innovative about these sculptures, but rather they are academic or primitive in style, with no hint of the existence of modern styles in art at the turn of the century. Less art works and more political statements, these commemorative monuments were intended to rally the public to the nationalist cause, to serve as markers for political manifestations.

8 *Circa*, 14, January/February 1984.

49. Humbert Craig: *Going to Mass*, 1939.

By contrast, Friedrich Herkner's (1902–1986) representation of Éire on the façade of the Irish pavilion at the New York World's Fair in 1939 had none of the trappings of the Celtic past and the youthful woman suggested instead a modern country rather than one that was clinging to its distant heritage. This may have been the result of the commission being given, not as might have been expected to an Irish-born sculptor steeped in local lore, but to the newly-appointed professor of sculpture at the NCA, only recently arrived in Ireland from Austria. Later such imagery finds the women depicted engaged in society rather than hailing from legend or serving as symbols. F. E. McWilliam's non-partisan bronze sculptures, *Women of Belfast*, modelled in the 1970s, capture the vulnerability of women living in that city at the time, unexpectedly caught in a bomb blast as they went about their daily lives. However, this was to ignore the active participation of women in the Troubles on both sides of the conflict.

Promotion of things Irish – prevalent in art in Ireland throughout much of the nineteenth century – was further stimulated by the Home Rule crisis of the 1880s. This marks the start of the movement identified as the Celtic Revival, which is most particularly associated with literature. While

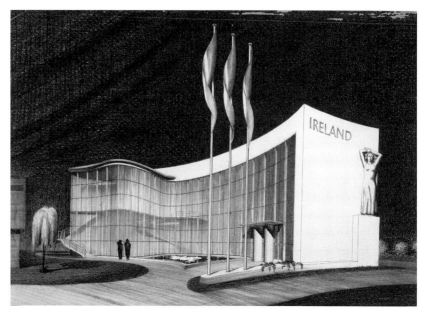

50. Michael Scott: Irish Pavilion, New York World's Fair, 1939, with Friedrich Herkner's *Éire* on the facade.

51. F. E. McWilliam: *Woman in a Bomb Blast*, 1974. Bronze.

52. Loughrea Cathedral, interior view.

many Protestant nationalists, notably Lady Gregory, were leading activists in the Celtic Revival movement, the association with Catholicism was prevalent. Irish freedom was at the core of the movement and it was a free Catholic nation that was being proffered, by contrast with its Protestant neighbour. The neo-gothic St Colman's Cathedral, Cobh, County Cork, built at the end of the century, is replete with images of early Irish saints, carvings depicting the history of the Catholic Church in Ireland (J. A. O'Connell, *Daniel O'Connell presenting Ireland with Catholic Emancipation,* 1895–1896, carved wall panel), and carved decorative shamrock patterning throughout.

However, it is the Cathedral of St Brendan at Loughrea, County Galway (1898–1902) and the Honan Chapel, Cork (1915–1916) that are key buildings of the Celtic Revival – treasure houses of both fine art, and arts and crafts work. Loughrea Cathedral includes sculptural work by Michael Shortall (1868–1951, relief carvings depicting the life of St Brendan), stained glass from An Túr Gloine (a cooperative stained-glass studio established in Dublin in 1903 by Sarah Purser (1848–1943)) and banners and vestments from Dun Emer (a craft studio and press founded in Dublin in 1902 by Evelyn Gleeson (1855–1944), and the Yeats sisters, Lily (1866–1949) and Elizabeth (1868–1940), sisters of Jack Yeats). Smaller in scale, the Neo-Hiberno-Romanesque Honan Chapel, dedicated to St Finbarr, is a similar showcase for early twentieth-century Irish design in its furnishing and vestments, mosaic floor and stained-glass windows (Harry Clarke, 1889–1931, who was a member of An Túr Gloine).

Nationalism favoured the use of indigenous subject matter and symbols, rejecting any weakening of the re-establishing and promotion of Irish identity by way of the infiltration of modern trends in art. This rejection continued well into the twentieth century. If, before Independence in 1922, the projection of Irish elements in art could be identified with the spurning of any association with English artistic expression, post-Independent art production in Ireland remained similarly controlled. The political and the art establishment were at one. A 1932 publication, *Saorstát Éireann, Irish Free State Official Handbook*, with essays on Irish history, culture and commerce, was illustrated with paintings by Keating, Maurice MacGonigal (1900–1979), Harry Kernoff and others who addressed Irish subject matter. The design of the front cover suggested a medieval Celtic manuscript and one of Paul Henry's Connemara landscape paintings served as frontispiece.

Éamon de Valera, whose Fianna Fáil party was elected to office in the same year, was a dominant figure in the political arena for many decades to come. His conservative Catholic views, his lack of interest in the arts generally and his entrenched nationalism left no room for experimental art. Equally, or perhaps even more powerful and influential than de Valera, was the uncompromising reactionary John Charles McQuaid, Archbishop of Dublin and Primate of Ireland for three decades, from 1940 to 1972. It is unsurprising that art associated with the Catholic Church flourished at the time. The mostly conservative religious ethos was exemplified in the 1942 controversy, when Dublin Corporation's Advisory Committee refused the gift of Georges Rouault's painting *Christ and the Soldier* (1930) for the Municipal Gallery of Modern Art. The modern interpretation of the subject matter was considered blasphemous and unacceptable at the time.

The predominance of church art was nothing new. The proliferation of commissions for church building and sculpture that was established in the course of the nineteenth century after the gaining of Catholic Emancipation (1829), continued into the twentieth century. In the case of religious architecture, the buildings were intended to be identifiably church-like, as a result of which revivalist church architecture prevailed (Mullingar Cathedral, County Westmeath, 1931–1936, William H. Byrne and Son). In 1954 such was the Archbishop McQuaid's objection to the modernity evident in the selected design in an architectural competition for a parish church in Clonskeagh, Dublin, that he reversed the decision in favour of a non-prize-winning

53. Ronnie Tallon: Church of Corpus Christi, Knockanure, Co. Kerry – with view of Oisín Kelly's *Last Supper* (1962) through glass entrance front.

entry.[9] It was not until the Second Vatican Council (1963) demanded a more participatory involvement of the church-going congregation that Catholic church design was modernised and integrated space replaced the lofty separateness of the traditional buildings. Ronnie Tallon's design for the Church of Corpus Christi at Knockanure, County Kerry (1959–1964), a box-like glazed structure, epitomised the shift in taste, and Modernist architectural design was soon encountered in churches across the country (Church of St Aengus, Burt, County Donegal, Liam McCormack, 1967; St Fintan's Church, Sutton, Dublin, Andrew Devane, 1973).

Tallon's Knockanure Church allows sculpture a key position. Oisín Kelly's (1915–1981) life-size teak relief of the *Last Supper* (1962) has a prominent location directly inside the glazed entrance front and is, therefore, visible from outside the building. The extensive use of glass suggested, erroneously as it turned out, a new openness in the Catholic Church. Patronage for religious work was important for Irish sculptors at the time and there were exhibitions and competitions, national and international, in religious art. The new

9 E. Rowley, 'Transitional Modernism: The Case of 1950s Church Architecture in Dublin', in E. Keown and C. Taafe (eds.), *Irish Modernism* (Bern: Peter Lang, 2010).

54. Michael Biggs: detail of Proclamation text, Arbour Hill Cemetery.

buildings that were the result of the Constitution on the Sacred Liturgy (1963) required new church furnishings, simpler and less sumptuous than what had been usual. Michael Biggs (1928–1993) and Patrick McElroy (1923–2008) are names particularly associated with these new forms (Sisters of Mercy Convent Chapel, Cookstown, County Tyrone, altar by Biggs; crucifix and tabernacle by McElroy, 1965). But most sculptors in the mid-century produced religious sculpture of a narrative or decorative nature.

If the landscape imagery of the West and the religious art of Catholic Ireland are both manifestations of conservatism in Irish art, so too is the commemorative work associated with the Rising and Independence. Statues and paintings of heroic Irish leaders are mostly academic in style and uninspiring in character. The mid-centenary celebrations in 1966 failed to inspire any interesting new work, serving largely only to revisit what had already been created. One of the most impressive works to be completed at that time was Michael Biggs's hand-carved text of the Proclamation, in both Irish and English, forming a memorial wall at Arbour Hill Cemetery, Dublin, to commemorate the executed leaders of the Rising who are buried there. The fact that, in 2014/ 2015, public money was being thrown at the centenary celebrations – which form part of a programme of commemorations known as the Decade of Centenaries (1912–1922) – will inevitably result in a range of work that is by turn safe and uncomplicated, as well as some that is experimental.

Until the advent of the Northern Troubles, politics in Ireland was a vehicle for artists in the form of commemorative portraiture, whereby the protagonists were represented for posterity (John Lavery, *Love of Ireland – Michael Collins Lying in State*, 1922, HLG; Albert Power, *Seán MacDiarmada*, 1940, Kiltychogher, County Leitrim). The Northern conflict was to prove more directly inspiring for artists, as their work reflected, in an overt or subtle manner, the reality and uncertainty of life in the North. This specifically Irish subject is particularly, but not exclusively (for example, Michael Farrell, *Pressé Politique* series, 1972; Shane Cullen (b. 1957), *Fragmens sur les Institutions Républicaines IV*, 1993–1997, IMMA), associated with Northern artists, who were working across a wide range of art practices, from painting and sculpture to installation, performance, sound, text, still photography and video. The School of Art in Belfast, which became a faculty of the Ulster Polytechnic in 1971 and subsequently of the University of Ulster, was the first of the art institutions in Ireland to offer post-graduate degrees in Fine Art, introducing a more pluralistic and interdisciplinary approach to art teaching. The programme has produced many award-winning graduates, including Scottish sculptor/sound artist Susan Philipsz, who won the prestigious Turner Prize in 2010.

One of the influential and inspiring teachers in the art school since the mid 1970s has been Scottish-born performance artist Alastair McLennan (b. 1943), who began teaching there after his move to Belfast in 1975. His own art has taken various forms, much of it live art and all of it politically or socially motivated. *Body of (D)earth 1969–1996*, an installation in the Project Arts Centre, Dublin, in 1997, and among the works that represented Ireland at the Venice Biennale in the same year, incorporated the recitation of the names of all of the people killed in Northern Ireland since the start of the Troubles.

The art of the Troubles has tended to be non-sectarian – other, that is, than the usually blunt mural painting. The walls of Belfast and Derry have been replete with hectoring and propagandist imagery. The visual response of artists has been more balanced – displaying an apparent unwillingness to take sides. This does not prevent them exploring every possible aspect of the Troubles: religious extremism (Rita Duffy (b. 1959), *Segregation*, 1989, oil painting); helicopter surveillance (Locky Morris (b. 1960), *Town, Country, People*, 1986, mixed media); disguise (Jack Pakenham (b. 1938), *Picking the Masks 1*, 1986, oil painting); conflict (John Kindness (b. 1951), *Monkey and Dog*, 1986, ceramic sculpture); death (Paul Seawright (b. 1965), *Sectarian Murder* series,

55. Philip Napier: *Gauge* – installed in derelict dwelling, Glenfada Park, Bogside, Derry, 1997.

1987–1988, photograph and text); borders (Willie Doherty, *At the End of the Day*, 1994, video); prison (Rita Donagh (b. 1939), *Long Meadow*, 1982, oil painting); individuals (Philip Napier, *Ballad No. 1, (View of Bobby Sands)*, 1992–1994, mixed media, motor and sound, National Museums of Northern Ireland).

Although the experience of Bloody Sunday, 30 January 1972, was a motivating force for artists to engage with the Troubles, explicit reference does not really emerge in the work until the 1980s. Rita Donagh was using maps in her work in the 1970s to reference the contrived and contested space that formed Northern Ireland. Deborah Brown, who had a studio in the centre of Belfast in the early 1970s, began to use barbed wire in her fibre-glass works at that time (*Barbed Wire I*, 1972, HLG). However, Donagh, Brown and Pakenham were an older generation of artists. In the case of the younger generation, the conflict was part of their lives from their teenage years and some among them will scarcely even have remembered a time of peace. For the 25th anniversary of Bloody Sunday, Philip Napier, who was only a child when the original event took place, created a two-part installation in Derry, in the Orchard Gallery and in a derelict housing estate in the Bogside. *Gauge*, 1997, consisting of a series of audio speakers communicating words of apology and suspended from weighing scales, questioned the nature and weight of such expressions of regret. In the light of the calls for an apology from the British government for the events of Bloody Sunday, this apposite work underlines the ambiguity encountered in the different ways of saying 'I'm sorry'.

Napier's work is the result of a very different relationship with Britain to that of Irish artists working earlier in the century. If the landscape imagery of the west of Ireland has to do with expressions of Irishness and serving as a response to the long history of colonialism, *Gauge* is concerned with contemporary history and political responsibility. Language is a particular feature of the art of the Troubles. The universal reach of the content of Napier's work found it exhibited at the Apartheid Museum in Johannesburg in 2006 and in Robben Island prison in 2010 in advance of the publication of the findings of the Saville inquiry into the Bloody Sunday shootings.

Institutions

The display of one section of Napier's *Gauge* in a non-gallery space was not unusual at the end of the twentieth century, when artists sought to move beyond both the formal gallery and the 'white cube', seeking instead a location that was rich with character. Since the 1980s several artists have chosen to exhibit their work in disused and/or derelict buildings that have no artistic connections. This enables the artist to engage with an environment that ultimately forms part of their work, rather than to make use of the traditional and authoritative exhibition space that confirms the naming of the work as art.

The development of new spaces for the display of art in Ireland in the course of the twentieth century had a profound effect on the development of art practice. By the end of the century several new national and local galleries had been established and commercial galleries had become a recognised location for the display of new national and international art. In addition new exhibition groups had been formed, new art associations were instituted, new working spaces for artists were opened, new educational opportunities were available and the teaching of art history had commenced.

Hugh Lane (1875–1915)[10] instigated the display of modern art in Ireland, when he opened the Municipal Gallery of Modern Art in temporary premises in Dublin's Harcourt Street in 1908. While the National Gallery of Ireland

---

10 B. Dawson (ed.), *Hugh Lane, Founder of a Gallery of Modern Art for Ireland* (London: Scala Publishers, 2008).

(1864) made old master paintings available to the public, there had been no permanent display of the work of modern artists. Lane had formed a collection of largely French nineteenth-century work, which included paintings by Boudin, Pissarro, Morisot and Degas. Key works such as Manet's *Music in the Tuileries Gardens* (1862), Monet's *Lavacourt under Snow, c.*1878–1881), Renoir's *Les Parapluies* (*c.* 1881–1886) and Rodin's *Age of Bronze* (1876–1877) were among those on display. Praise for the initiative and for the collection included the comment that 'the pictures are of our own time'.[11] This apt comment may have referred to the fact that many of the artists were still alive. However, the comment also pertains to the subject matter, which resulted from the requirement of modern artists in the late nineteenth century that they would depict the world they knew – the modern world.

The unwillingness of Dublin Corporation to establish a permanent home for the collection at the time was controversial and resulted, in the aftermath of Lane's early death when the *Lusitania* was torpedoed off Cork in 1915, in a long drawn out dispute with the National Gallery in London about ownership of Lane's bequest. While the Municipal Gallery of Modern Art finally opened in Charlemont House on Dublin's Parnell Square in 1933, it was nearly 60 years before a national museum of modern art would be established in the city. The Irish Museum of Modern Art, located like the Municipal Gallery in a historic building, was opened in the Royal Hospital at Kilmainham in 1991. The museum houses a permanent collection, much of which has derived from substantial donations by such perceptive collectors as Gordon Lambert (1919–2005). However, it is the continuously changing programme of temporary exhibitions in all media that are of particular significance. The exhibitions showcase the work of living artists of national and international repute, while also reinvigorating the careers of Irish artists now dead, such as for example the Modern Irish Masters series in the twenty-first century, which has included Gerda Frömel in 2015 and Patrick Hennessy (1915–1980) in 2016.

It must not be thought that, in the intervening decades between Hugh Lane's efforts in the early century and the creation of IMMA at its close, no modern or avant-garde art was shown in Ireland. There were several small galleries, mostly commercial, that supported contemporary art, both national and international. Trinity College Dublin was inspired to open such a gallery in 1978. For many years its Douglas Hyde Gallery was the main location for new art in all its variety and to see work by international artists of

---

11 *Irish Times*, 25 January 1908.

56. Irish Museum of Modern Art – view of courtyard.

repute. Commercial galleries began to proliferate in the mid-century with the Dawson (1944–1978) and Hendriks (1956–1989) in Dublin being replaced eventually by the Taylor (1978), Kerlin (1988), Rubicon (1995), Green on Red (1997), and many more. The Fenderesky Gallery, which opened in Belfast in 1983, continues today, joined by the Golden Thread (1998) and many others. In 1978 the Orchard Gallery and the Triskel Arts Centre opened in Derry and Cork respectively.

Not only did/do all of these commercial galleries showcase contemporary trends in art, they did/do so in 'white cube' spaces, which is in marked contrast to the purpose-built or adapted buildings of earlier centuries. In addition to national and municipal collections in Dublin, the Crawford Art Gallery in Cork, founded in 1818, is housed in the former Custom House. All of these buildings, including the Ulster Museum in Belfast, have followed the international trend of museum expansion in the early twenty-first century and had ultra-modern extensions attached to the building. These extensions were necessarily intended to expand the display area of the gallery and/or to facilitate more retail and social activity. Smart shops and fine cafés became essential in the museum world in the late twentieth century and Ireland was quick to follow suit.

These galleries and other institutions, notably the Royal Hibernian Academy (RHA) established in 1823, hosted temporary group exhibitions – another opportunity for the display of contemporary art, although not always of a very modern nature. If the RHA – academic and traditional in outlook through much of the twentieth century – served the art establishment, the Irish Exhibition of Living Art (IELA, 1943–1987), was intended to be its antithesis. Often referred to as the Salon des Refusés of Irish art, it was formed, like that iconic French salon (1863), as a result of RHA jury rejection of, among other works, Louis le Brocquy's scarcely avant-garde, but certainly Modernist painting *The Spanish Shawl* (1941, priv. coll.). The founding members of the IELA included Jellett, who was particularly outspoken about the dominance of conservatism at the RHA, Hone and Norah McGuinness (1901–1980), who would become president of the group after Jellett's death in 1944. The intention was not to focus exclusively on new developments in art, but rather, as they indicated at their inaugural meeting, to show 'a comprehensive survey of significant work, irrespective of School or manner, by living Irish artists'.[12] This afforded another platform for artists to display their work beyond the monopolising RHA. However, the extent to which the IELA was an open platform is evident in the fact that many artists showed both there and at the RHA.

Nearly a quarter century after the first IELA exhibition, the ROSC exhibitions were instituted to introduce the Irish public and Irish artists to contemporary developments in art that were taking place outside the country. This was the brainchild of architect Michael Scott who was something of a maestro in the art world. The continuing absence of a museum of modern art at the time and the inadequate awareness in Ireland of international trends in art prompted the instigation of a series of exhibitions of contemporary art from around the world. Money was put in place, juries were formed, artists were selected. The first of the exhibitions was held in 1967 on the premises of the Royal Dublin Society (RDS) in a usually bleak space that had been transformed by Pat Scott into an ethereal installation. The work on display was not all up-to-the-minute – work by long-established artists such as Picasso and Miro, for example, was included in the show – but the exhibition in its entirety matched the first IELA for excitement and public comment (for and against). Much of the criticism had to do with the exclusion of Irish artists from the exhibition or was in the 'that's not art' vein. In reality, although novel in content, the work remained largely painting and sculpture. It was not until later

---

12 R. Coulter, 'Hibernian Salon des Refusés', in *Irish Arts Review*, 20, (autumn, 2003), 81.

57. Louis Le Brocquy: *The Spanish Shawl*, 1941.

ROSC exhibitions (six exhibitions were held between 1967 and 1988) that new processes in art would be displayed to the Irish public.

The new media and new processes were also apparent eventually at new award shows sponsored by philanthropic corporate entities. These awards and their attendant publicity were valuable for artists, in much the same way as the Carroll Awards (Carroll's Cigarettes) had been at the IELA earlier in the century. The latter recognised innovative work, such as, for example, Ian Stuart's (1926–2013) metal *Black Man*, made after a visit to New York and

797

58. ROSC '67 – view of exhibition.

awarded the first prize for sculpture in 1965. The GPA (Guinness Peat Aviation) Emerging Artist exhibition/award commenced in 1981 and by the time of its demise nearly ten years later was recognised as an exhibition arena for video, conceptual and installation art. In the aftermath of the opening of IMMA, two further such initiatives were launched, the Glen Dimplex (1994–2001) and the Nissan Public Art Project (1997–2001). The former was instigated to recognise achievement and development in an artist's work (Irish artist working anywhere or non-Irish artist showing work in Ireland); the latter was to enable the realisation of a public artwork. Dorothy Cross was shortlisted for the GPA in 1986 and for the Glen Dimplex in 1995. Her winning entry for the Nissan in 1999, *Ghost Ship*, was the most successful work in the short life of the award. The work encapsulated so much of what was new in art at the close of the twentieth century – a ready-made, transient, time-based installation. The ghostly presence of the decommissioned ship in Dun Laoghaire harbour, where it was moored in the autumn/winter of 1999, was also topically engaged with the subject of memory – an echo of the once familiar sight of manned light-ships on the Irish sea.

Memory was particularly evident in the proliferation of Famine commemoration across the country, work that was mostly of a conventional nature. However, Alanna O'Kelly chose a different approach to the remote monumental public form and won the first Glen Dimplex award in 1994 for her mixed media work *The Country Blooms: A Garden and a Grave* (1992, video, still photography, text, sound). The work is at once personal (emigration) and universal (hunger in Ireland and everywhere). Elements of the series were shown, along with the work of 15 other Irish artists at the École Nationale Supérieure des Beaux-Arts de Paris in 1996, as part of the multi-venue cultural festival L'Imaginaire Irlandais. As the French journal *L'Express* pointed out at the time, history haunted the exhibition, with O'Kelly exploring the more distant past and Shane Cullen and Willie Doherty among those exploring more recent events in their work. If this event in France was something of a one-off, Irish artists have in recent decades had a more constant platform for their work in Paris in the Centre Culturel Irlandais, which hosts artists' residencies and mounts regular exhibitions.

More than a decade before the French exhibition a showcase of Irish culture had taken place in London, where exhibitions of Irish art were scarcely frequent, but somewhat more habitual, particularly at the turn into the twentieth century. Exhibitions of Irish art were held in London in 1888 (at Olympia), in 1904 (at the Guildhall, organised by Hugh Lane), and in 1913 (at the Whitechapel). In 1980, a festival of Irish culture, titled A Sense of Ireland, was held in different venues. The art exhibitions included solo shows of work by Jack Yeats (at Theo Waddington), who was dead more than two decades at the time, and Pat Scott (at Annely Juda), who was very much alive. Several group exhibitions proposed different interpretations of Irish art: Without the Walls at the Institute of Contemporary Arts (ICA), The Delighted Eye (painting and sculpture of the 1970s) at Earlham Street Gallery, and The International Collection (mostly abstract work) at the Round House Gallery. The Delighted Eye was just that, a selection of artworks that tended to support the long-held and more traditionally lyrical, romanticised sense of Ireland – paintings by Tony O'Malley (1913–2003), Seán MacSweeney (b. 1935), Brian Bourke (b. 1936), Patrick Collins (1910–1994) and others. The ICA show, in keeping with the venue, projected a more cutting-edge view of contemporary Irish art. Several of the selected artists would represent Ireland again in France in 1996, notably a young Alanna O'Kelly, who in 1980 was just out of art school. Curated by art critic Dorothy Walker (1929–2007), the show did not shy away from the Northern Troubles, in spite of the ongoing IRA campaign in Britain, notably in installation work by Noel Sheridan (1936–2006) and Brian King (b. 1942).

Interpretation

Temporary exhibitions of Irish art held in Ireland or elsewhere generated reviews, as a result of which the locations for and approaches to writing on art in Ireland developed over the century. The range of publishing outlets and the nature of the published content was varied. Descriptive, historical and critical approaches were augmented in the 1980s by new theoretical methods, among them feminist, psychoanalytical, socio-economic and structuralist. If, in the early century exhibition reviews were largely confined to newspapers and to religious journals, such as the *Father Mathew Record* (1908–1967), the *Capuchin Annual* (1930–1977) and *The Furrow* founded in 1950, more specifically art-focused journals appeared later including the *Irish Arts Review* (commenced 1984, ongoing) and *Circa* (1981–2011), the latter concentrating on contemporary art.

In addition to exhibition reviews, exhibition catalogues, particularly those that accompanied themed exhibitions, began to incorporate writing of a more questioning nature. For example, the publication that accompanied the series of five exhibitions exploring Irish Art of the Eighties, held in the Douglas Hyde Gallery in 1990/1991, is less a catalogue and more a series of essays contextualising the art within contemporary issues of identity, gender, politics and more. Similarly, books on Irish art published at the turn into the twentieth century were less accepting of the traditional view of Irish art as having been undermined by British colonialism and more interested in understanding exactly what constituted Irish art.

One of the major publications on Irish art in the early twentieth century was Walter Strickland's *A Dictionary of Irish Artists*, published in two volumes in 1913/1914. Strickland, then Registrar of the National Gallery, produced a biographical study of painters, sculptors and engravers. These were mostly artists of the nineteenth century and earlier, as Strickland did not include living artists. This remained a standard source of reference on Irish art until the Royal Irish Academy's five-volume publication *Art and Architecture of Ireland (AAI)* in 2014, for which the initiators were awarded the RHA Gold Medal 2015.

These five volumes were made possible by the establishing and development of the teaching of Art History in Ireland in the second half of the century. The subject was added to the academic programme in the Arts Faculty of University College Dublin (UCD) in 1965 and Trinity College Dublin (TCD) just a year later, at the instigation of Françoise Henry (1902–1982) and Anne Crookshank (1927–2016) respectively. In the decades since the subject was initiated in the two Dublin universities, Cork University (UCC) and, for a time, Queen's University Belfast also introduced Art History to their syllabus, in addition to Visual Studies augmenting the teaching programmes at art colleges. The numbers of students taking the subject have grown substantially since the first intake in UCD in 1965 and, with strong post-graduate numbers, there has been significant increase in research into Irish art. The *AAI* involved the whole of the community of writers on Irish art across the country north and south, many of whom were graduates in Art History from Irish universities, as well as those writers outside the country who engaged with Irish art.

Industry: Architecture

In addition to not including the biographies of any living artists in his dictionary, Strickland did not consider the life and work of any architect, alive or dead, either. The *AAI* redressed this omission, devoting an entire volume to architecture. In 2015, Irish architects have considerable international standing. Husband and wife team O'Donnell and Tuomey were awarded the prestigious Royal Gold Medal for 2015 by the Royal Institute of British Architects (RIBA), where their work was described as inventive and their buildings as beautifully crafted. If this award might seem to suggest little more than a continuation of the close artistic relationship between Britain and Ireland, the reality is that this is very much an international award, with the medal previously awarded to such architectural luminaries as Le Corbusier (1953), Frank Gehry (2000) and I. M. Pei (2010). O'Donnell and Tuomey were being positioned at the very top of their profession. Their work in Ireland includes the Ranelagh Multi-denominational School in Dublin (1998), the Glucksman Gallery in UCC (2004) and the Lyric Theatre in Belfast (2011), all of which are award-winning buildings. In London they recently completed the Saw Swee Hock Students' Centre (2014), at the London School of Economics. They are an inspiration to upcoming architects not only because of their buildings but also because of their continuing involvement in education, as teachers in the UCD School of Architecture.

The teaching of architecture in Ireland was fragmented and even insubstantial until the Faculty of Engineering and Architecture was established in 1909 in UCD, where, inevitably the headship of the faculty has oscillated between traditionalist and Modernist architects. Training also became available in the course of the twentieth century at the Dublin Institute of Technology and in Belfast at Queen's and Ulster University (UU), and in Limerick, Waterford and Cork. Oisín Kelly, sculptor and teacher of art at secondary level, disliked the

59. The Lyric Theatre, Belfast, O'Donnell + Tuomey, 2011.

elitist differentiation between the terms artist and craftsman, believing in the functionality of all art. This is particularly applicable to architecture, with its inherent utilitarian purpose. Architects are as occupied with designs for dwellings as they are with more theatrical structures. Unable to work in isolation, they require the involvement of builders and engineers to realise their designs. Developments in architecture are necessarily associated with changing modes of existence, evolving economic circumstances and technological advances.

Industrial development in Ireland, for example, prompted a huge number of new buildings across the country. Factories, transport hubs (bus stations, airports), office buildings, social housing, leisure sites (cinemas, swimming baths), media outlets, hospitals, all of which afforded the opportunity for projecting new architectural styles. The new structure, built to house the designated government department encapsulated the extent of the industrial progress at that time in its design, materials and decoration. The Department of Industry and Commerce (1935–1942), on Dublin's Kildare Street, was designed by Cork architect James Rupert Boyd Barrett and constructed by John Sisk and Sons. The austere steel-frame building, with its clear lines and Art Deco detailing, is confirmed in its designation by the relief sculptures on the façade. The work of

60. J.R. Boyd Barrett: Department of Industry and Commerce, Kildare Street, 1935–42, with sculptures by Gabriel Hayes, 1942.

Gabriel Hayes (1909–78), these sculptures depict, in a vigorous realist style, developing Irish industries, including aviation, electricity, cement and tobacco. More emphatically and more ornately Art Deco in style is the earlier D'Olier Street headquarters of the Dublin Gas Company (1928–1930) by Robinson and Keefe.

Simultaneously in the early century the International Style became evident in house building – white, flat-roofed villa-type houses, a series of which were built by architects Clifford and Newenham in the suburbs of Limerick City in the 1930s – and more publicly in Dublin airport (1937–1942, Desmond Fitzgerald and the OPW). The latter, awarded an RIAI Gold Medal in 1943, is curved in form, with stepped ends, external spiral staircases, and balconies open (initially) to the airfield. In spite of the attention given to the novelty of the airport building, it was Busáras (1944–1953, Michael Scott), the Le Corbusier-inspired bus terminus and office block on Store Street/Beresford Place, Dublin, that gained recognition as the first significant modern building in the city. Michael Scott was a pivotal figure in the art world in Ireland in the twentieth century, encouraging and facilitating modern approaches in art and architecture. As President of the AAI he invited several inspirational speakers to Ireland, including, in 1936, Walter Gropius of the Bauhaus, who lectured on contemporary trends in architecture.

Shortly before his success with the Busáras building, Scott had adapted the International Style for the purpose of projecting Irishness in his design for the Irish pavilion at the New York World's Fair in 1939. In keeping with the theme of the fair, 'the World of Tomorrow', the shamrock form of Scott's steel, concrete and glass building, was only visible from the air. The modernity of the building was augmented by Herkner's modern interpretation of Mother Ireland on the façade. However, inside the pavilion, the work on display, by, among others, Oliver Sheppard (*Cúchulainn*, bronze sculpture), Seán Keating (Ardnacrusha murals) and Evie Hone (*My Four Green Fields*, stained-glass), was more traditionally Irish. When, in 2000, Tom de Paor was Ireland's first representative at the Venice Biennale of Architecture, his *N3* pavilion reprised the traditional/modern juxtaposition, employing peat briquettes as innovative building material.

The building of 'office blocks' took off from the mid-century – the label aptly describing what are the aggressively block-like structures necessitated by the changing working environment of the corporate world. Making substantial use of glass, the bright, often open-plan Modernist buildings remain very much of their time. Typical examples are the Bord Fáilte headquarters, Baggot Street, Dublin (1959–1963, Robin Walker) and RTÉ's Administration building (1965–1967, Ronnie Tallon), both by Scott, Tallon, Walker architects. Such buildings were intended to exemplify the modern attitude of the organisation housed within. Inevitably controversy ensued in some instances, with height (Liberty Hall, 1958–1963, Desmond Rea O'Kelly), conservation (ESB headquarters, 1962–1970, Stephenson Gibney and Associates) and aesthetics (Civic Office building, 1962–1979, Sam Stephenson) among the concerns that prevailed.

More varied approaches to architectural design are evident towards the turn of the century, noticeably in museum design. It might be expected that innovation would manifest itself in an art environment. The refurbishment of the Royal Hospital at Kilmainham to house IMMA (Shay Cleary Architects, inaugurated 1991), the extension of the Model Arts Centre and Niland Gallery in Sligo (McCullough Mulvin, completed 2000) and the newly built Gallery of Photography in Dublin's Temple Bar (O'Donnell and Tuomey, completed 1996) are among the many new exhibition spaces in Ireland. While the designs often reflect the contemporary interest in sculpi-architecture and the interiors are frequently flexible to facilitate changing exhibitions, the display spaces continue to incorporate the minimal ideology identified in Brian O'Doherty's *Inside the White Cube: The Ideology of the Gallery Space*, published in 1976.

Like O'Doherty, Irish-born architect Kevin Roche (b. 1922) has lived and worked in the US since he moved there in 1948 to study with Ludwig Mies van der Rohe. Roche, who studied architecture in UCD, has had a stellar career in the States, where he was awarded the Pritzker Architecture Prize in 1982. His work includes the refurbishment of several sections of the Metropolitan Museum of Art in New York, notably the acclaimed Sackler Wing housing the Egyptian Temple of Dandur. The influence of his Ford Foundation Headquarters in New York (1963–1968) is evident in Irish office block design, but Roche has only one building in Ireland, the National Convention Centre (1998–2010), a late commission in his career. The untimely date of the commission saw the building of what is an awkward, seemingly toppling structure in Dublin's Dockland coinciding with the demise of the financial boom in Ireland known as the Celtic Tiger. There appeared to be a fateful irony about the design. The structure is in marked contrast with the gracefulness of the new bridge that was constructed to cross the Liffey approaching the Centre. The work of Spanish architect Santiago Calatrava (b. 1951), the bridge, dedicated to Samuel Beckett, was opened in 2009.

Calatrava is among the internationally renowned contemporary architects who integrate sculpture and architecture and who work across the two forms. The architectural designs of Polish-American Daniel Libeskind (b. 1946), who also has work in Dublin (Bord Gáis Energy Theatre, Grand Canal Square, 2010), are often similarly influenced by sculpture. These Irish commissions to internationally renowned architects Calatrava and Libeskind in the first decade of the twenty-first century form part of the heady times associated with economic growth that was experienced in Ireland at that time. However, in the aftermath of the crash that inevitably followed, not all commissions were realised. English sculptor Anthony Gormley's (b. 1950) colossal metal figure, the winning entry in an international competition in 2007 for a proposed sculpture in Dublin Docklands, was cancelled in 2009.

Inference

There was excitement about work by celebrated artists being erected or displayed in Ireland – and why not? Calatrava, Libeskind and Gormley are big names in the world of art. Naming and claiming have a role to play in Irish art and architecture. Ireland claims architect Kevin Roche, sculptor Augustus Saint-Gaudens (1848–1907) and painter Francis Bacon (1909–1992), all of whom were born in Ireland, but who lived elsewhere and fulfilled their careers outside the country. The bequest of Bacon's studio to Dublin's Municipal Gallery in 1998 was a huge impetus for the gallery and much has been made of it since. But Bacon, who was born in Dublin and lived much of his childhood and teenage years in Ireland, moved to London in 1926 and spent most of his working life there. Irish-born, London-raised, American-based painter Sean Scully (b. 1945) rediscovered his long-lost Irish connection in the twenty-first century. The extent of the interest in writing him into the story of Irish art is evident in the numerous exhibitions of his work that have been held in different venues in Ireland in recent years.

The desire for international recognition for Irish artists, for the work of Irish artists to form part of international displays, for Irish art to be acknowledged on the international stage has long been prevalent. In 1885, the then President of the RHA, portrait painter Sir Thomas Jones, encouraged students who wanted to make a name for themselves to leave Ireland and head for London.[13] This focus on international recognition suggests a sense of inferiority and is not immediately recognised as a concern in other countries. Yet, in the case of impressionist painting in the 1880s, it was the Americans, rather than the French, who were the early patrons. In the aftermath of the success of impressionist work in the US, the French began to buy. Validation came from outside the country. There is nothing amiss about seeking to be acknowledged on the international stage. Irish artists are participating in international group exhibitions across the world, notably at the biennials in Venice and Sao Paolo and the German quinquennial at Kassel, Documenta. Kathy Prendergast received considerable attention in 1995, when she won the coveted Premio 2000 Best Young Artist Award at the Venice Biennale in that year. Her mixed media work at the exhibition included the *City Drawings*, *200 Words for Lonely* (pillow and text), and *Untitled* (a child's knitted jumper and a heart beat mechanism). The award was seen as a launching pad for a successful international career,[14] as could already be identified by that of earlier winner (1990) British-Indian sculptor Anish Kapoor. This was a significant achievement for Prendergast and yet another indication of the central place of women in art in Ireland. From Jellett and Hone in the early century to the mixed-media practitioners in the 1980s and 1990s, women have often been the driving force in the introduction of new practices and processes.

13 *Irish Builder*, 1 May 1885.
14 *Irish Times*, 13 June 1995.

61. Duncan Campbell: *It for Others*, 2014.

Among the new practices that prevail, photography, video and film have been foregrounded in the twenty-first century. Dublin-born practitioner Duncan Campbell (b. 1972) was awarded the Turner Prize in 2014 for his montage *It For Others*, a 50-minute film that was admired for its dedication to exploring 'the construction of value and meaning'.[15] Campbell's focus on the past sees him making use of archive material. He has made use of Irish material in *Bernadette* (2008) and *Make it new John* (2009) – respectively, politician Bernadette Devlin and celebrity car manufacturer John DeLorean – both of which works have to do with Northern Ireland.

More contemporary politics has been the terrain for Anthony Haughey, whose *Settlement* project (2011) explores the fallout from the financial crash a few years earlier. In a series of haunting photographic and video works, Haughey captures the ghost estates that have resulted from the bursting of Ireland's 'property bubble' – evidence of the way in which landscape imagery can be seen to continue in Irish art to incorporate a political impetus.

The work of Haughey, Campbell and fellow video artist Gerard Byrne (b. 1969) did not form part of the exhibition of Irish art, purporting to be the Art of a Nation, at the Mall Galleries in London in 2015. Claiming to celebrate

15 Turner Prize 2014 winner announcement press release.

the story of Irish art from 1900 to the present day, the selection of work was restricted by the collections from which the exhibition was drawn and the show tended to perpetuate the romantic notion of Irish art as the poetry of vision. Much of the work in the exhibition was drawn from the Allied Irish Bank (AIB) collection, assembled over nearly three decades – a collection that, with the collapse of the Irish economy in 2008, transferred in part to the Crawford Art Gallery. The banks were major sources of patronage in the second half of the twentieth century, as the Catholic Church had been before them. Artists require their work to be purchased and, in the aftermath of the financial collapse, the reality is that there is little patronage for art. The banks are not buying art, nor are the art museums. The second decade of the twenty-first century is a quiet period for artists. While, at the time of the London exhibition, the historic nature of the collection that the bank had amassed was widely hailed, its continuity noted and the range of artists and themes applauded, it remained unremarked that, with scant patronage of contemporary art today, and no such collection being formed, the mounting of an exhibition of the art of the twenty-first century in a hundred years time might not prove to be so straightforward nor the artwork so readily obtainable.

Afterword

The main sources used for this text have been the *Art and Architecture of Ireland* (vol. 2, Nicola Figgis, *Painting 1600–2000*; vol. 3, Paula Murphy, *Sculpture 1600–2000*; vol. 4, R. Loeber, H. Campbell, E. Rowley, L. Hurley, J. Montague, *Architecture 1600–2000*; vol. 5, P. Murray & C. Marshall, *Twentieth Century*, 2014); and books by Fionna Barber (*Art in Ireland since 1910*, 2013); Enrique Juncosa and Christina Kennedy (*The Moderns, The Arts in Ireland from the 1900s to the 1970s*, 2011); Liam Kelly (*Thinking Long. Contemporary Art in the North of Ireland*, 1996); S.B. Kennedy (*Irish Art and Modernism 1880–1950*, 1991); Brian P. Kennedy (*Dreams and Responsibilities, The State and the Arts in Independent Ireland*, 1990). Full details of these publications are indicated in the bibliography.

26

Endword: Ireland Looking Outwards, 1880–2016

EUNAN O'HALPIN

Introduction

In July 1963, just a fortnight after President John F. Kennedy's tumultuous visit to Ireland, *Time* magazine's cover proclaimed a 'New spirit in the ould sod', carrying a drawing of a benign Taoiseach Seán Lemass accompanied by a leprechaun pulling back a shamrock-embroidered green curtain to reveal a power plant.[1]

Almost a decade later, Sir Con O'Neill, the austere Foreign Office grandee who led the negotiations culminating in British entry to the European Economic Communities (EEC), presented a BBC television programme on European economic modernisation. He was filmed in Sweden, observing the balance between rural and urban, agricultural and industrial development. The programme then moved to Ireland, whose people 'sixty years ago' although 'desperately poor ... seem to have chosen to make the most of life as it was, to cultivate the dignified arts of poetry, leisure, conversation', despite the consequence of underdevelopment and mass emigration. The script continued: 'Pan over Irish country side to reveal O'Neill toiling up hill towards cam[era] ... rusty wheel. ... Horses in field. ... Gorse. ... Countryside – pan L[eft] to O'Neill talking to Irish farmer: "How are the potatoes coming?" ... "No frost?"'. The script continued: 'Man cutting peat. Monks walking along street in Galway. ... Old Irish ruin: "Over the last century millions of Irishmen left Ireland to look for work and prosperity elsewhere"'. Then came the switch: 'Zoom in to factory chimneys. ... "Nowadays even the Irish are turning away from their old life". Nose of Boeing 707 turning on tarmac at Shannon Airport – pan ... to Aer Lingus sign on tail ... Pan ... to sign "Industrial Estate"'. Then "they are changing, modernising, industrialising – and pretty successfully". Pull out from chimneys to Computer Bureau sign'.

---

1 *Time*, 12 July 1963.

Both of these clichéd presentations reflected international perceptions of Ireland as a state undergoing marked and dramatic changes in its economic policies, ambitions and fortunes. O'Neill avoided parallel observations on Northern Ireland, 'quite another kettle of fish', where his first cousin Terence had been a mildly reformist prime minister in Belfast from 1963 to 1969.[2] In May 1972, of course, the entire system of provincial government in Belfast had just been suspended indefinitely, and Northern Ireland was in the midst of its bloodiest-ever year of conflict. That strife was to some degree a function, and was to become also a cause, of Northern Ireland's chronic economic weakness as a peripheral province of the United Kingdom.

Almost five decades later, Belfast's once-mighty shipyards endure a vestigial afterlife as the 'Titanic Quarter', a tourist attraction commemorating the world's most famous shipping disaster. The challenges facing those attempting to modernise Northern Ireland's economy were encapsulated in the fates of Jeff Agate, chief of the multinational Du Pont, then Derry's largest employer, murdered on a Provisional IRA whim in 1976, and of the DeLorean sports car, whose slapdash manufacture the British government, desperate to increase cross-community employment in divided Belfast in the late 1970s, were persuaded to bankroll by a plausible Detroit insider. DeLorean's gull-winged calamity has also had a cinematic afterlife as a time machine in the aptly titled *Back to the Future*, more than can be said for plans for the modernisation, expansion and diversification of Northern Ireland's industrial base. In the same era of EEC membership, independent Ireland developed what is reputedly the world's most export-oriented and open economy. How has all this come about?

Two Irelands

Consideration of Ireland's changing perspectives on and interactions with the wider world since the 1880s presents difficulties. Two Irelands emerged in 1921, one an independent state and the other a province of the United Kingdom. Northern Ireland neither distinctly influenced nor was much influenced by Britain's wider conduct of international affairs, until the province itself became partly a foreign policy problem for Britain following the outbreak of the Troubles in 1969. In areas of economic and trade policy, furthermore, Northern Ireland accepted rather than determined the United

2 O'Neill papers, MS Eng 6064, fols. 28–30, BBC television script for programme to be broadcast 29 May 1972.

Kingdom position, although there was often an element of special pleading. Even then, however, because London's main point of official contact with Belfast was the Home Office, the North's case on economic and industrial issues had to be made by the home secretary, whose voice naturally carried less weight in such spheres.[3] In matters such as railways, customs, animal disease control, and aspects of policing, Belfast and Dublin managed quietly to get along reasonably well without any external intervention. Other issues – the maintenance of a common travel area for the British Isles, and Irish adherence to sterling until 1979 – were unobtrusively managed by the relevant Irish and British departments and agencies at official rather than ministerial level.[4]

Reviewing the interplay of the national and international, the local and the global, for the two Irelands, we should recognise that there is no contradiction between increased public awareness of events, ideas and cultures outside a community, state or nation, and the pursuit of culturally, politically and economically isolationist, protectionist and even nativist policies. The emergence of the Gaelic League with its ambitious agenda for Gaelic regeneration, and other more enduringly successful forms of cultural nationalism such as Gaelic sports, were predicated partly on the apprehension that native Irish culture was mortally threatened by the modernising impetus and global reach of the late Victorian Anglophone British empire.[5] In the economic sphere, similarly, people are as likely to be alarmed as inspired by developments outside their borders. The idea of a self-sufficient island which would manufacture whatever it needed for itself, and feed its own people before exporting its agricultural surplus to pay for necessary imports of goods and commodities which Ireland did not possess, attracted the enthusiastic support of late Victorian separatists. It was, conversely, anathema to Ulster Unionists, who saw their future in manufacturing for Britain and the empire. The Home Rule leadership, on the other hand, by 1900 had no great economic vision for Ireland: under a Dublin legislature, it would be in everyones' interests that things should tick over much as before, although with reduced taxation on licensed vintners and other deserving groups, and a consequent reduction in Irish public spending.

---

3 P. Canning, *British Policy Towards Ireland, 1921–1941* (Oxford University Press, 1985), 211–18; K. Bloomfield, *A Tragedy of Errors: the government and misgovernment of Northern Ireland* (Liverpool: Liverpool University Press, 2007), 2–16; see, e.g. Home Secretary R. A. Butler memorandum on the grievances of Shorts Brothers and Harland and Wolff about British defence procurement, 25 Feb. 1963, CAB/129/112: TNA.

4 M. Kennedy, *Division and Consensus: the Politics of Cross-Border Relations in Ireland, 1925–1969* (Dublin: Institute of Public Administration, 2000).

5 T. Bartlett, *Ireland: A History* (Cambridge University Press, 2010), 346.

Independent Ireland's engagement with the outside world and development of a functional foreign policy was complicated by three factors: the fact that Northern Ireland remained a part of the United Kingdom, a source of nationalist grievance and practical complications because of the land border; Ireland's overwhelming dependence on Britain as an export market, trading partner and default absorber of Ireland's large labour surplus; and Ireland's location, shielded to the east by Britain from mainland Europe and to the west by three thousand miles of Atlantic ocean.

Angela Bourke's work reminds us that the railways, the telegraph and the burgeoning local press of the late nineteenth century did not change rural Ireland overnight.[6] But we know that throughout Ireland, mass emigration forged strong familial links with the new world, and that improved communications and increased literacy facilitated the rapid interchange of news, ideas and resources. Ireland also benefitted from the philanthropy of the Scottish-American Andrew Carnegie, whose trust paid for over eighty new public libraries on the island from the late 1890s onwards. The local and national press indicates considerable engagement with international affairs generally, more so perhaps than elsewhere in the British Isles. Before independence, such matters were addressed largely through an imperial prism, but addressed they were. After independence, the revolutionary turmoil which swept Europe, the rise of Bolshevism, and the growth of anti-colonial movements were all covered, while cinema newsreels brought world affairs before peoples' eyes. The League of Nations provided a welcome element of theatre and a sense that Ireland had taken its place amongst the nations of the world. In addition, as W. B. Yeats explained to an Indian journalist during the 1930s, there was a lively interest in colonial conflict: 'the Sinn Féin movement here and the papers dramatise your movement. So Irishmen know more about your movement than Englishmen'.[7] Adherence to neutrality during the 'Emergency' of 1939–1945 owed nothing to public ignorance of the issues at stake. So far from viewing the Second World War uncomprehending inside 'Plato's cave' as described by F. S. L. Lyons, the Irish watched from the sidelines, shielded from most of the horrors by geography, as informed and fortunate observers: it was not as if Mullingar would have enlisted *en masse* had they only known about the Holocaust.[8] Independent Ireland experienced

6 A. Bourke, *The Burning of Bridget Cleary: A True Story* (London: Penguin, 1999), 7–10.
7 Oral History Transcript Shri Durga Das Acc. No. 96 (27 December 1971); New Delhi, Nehru Memorial Library (NML).
8 F. S. L. Lyons, *Ireland since the Famine* (London, 1971; revised edn., London: Weidenfeld and Nicolson, 1973), 557–8.

an economic winter and widespread deprivation, a few acts of aerial and maritime violence, an internal security crisis, the loss of over one hundred seamen engaged in carrying goods to and from the state, and acute short-ages of imported raw materials: a Tipperary bird-dealer lamented a pair of goldfinches, 'splendid singers and they died with the hunger. I was unable to get canary seed for them during the war years and they refused to eat anything else and I was heartbroken after them'.[9] But the public, divided on the great issues, were well versed in them despite censorship which rendered newspapers, in the words of a British intelligence chief, 'dull and insipid'.[10] The Irish instead got their war news from the belligerents' English language radio services; from British newspapers which travellers brought across the border or from Britain; from friends or family amongst the many thousands who journeyed over the border or across the Irish Sea to work in or fight for the United Kingdom; and, in coastal areas, from the evidence of their own eyes and ears.[11]

After 1945 the gradual growth in broadcast media meant that Irish people in both jurisdictions had access to a widening range of international as well as Irish news. Northern Ireland benefitted from the development of regional United Kingdom radio and television services. The latter could also be received in other parts of the island long before Dublin's national television service began broadcasting in December 1961. Consequently it is hardly true that the public in either Irish jurisdiction were markedly less well-informed about or exposed to discourse about the world outside the British Isles than those living on the British mainland.

Factors other than the print and broadcast media helped to form the Irish worldview after 1918. The Catholic Church, often excoriated as the *fons et origo* of social conservatism and the perpetuator of Irish backwardness, was amongst the most ultramontane in the world (ironically, its glum accept-ance of the reforms of the Second Vatican Council of 1962–1965 contributed to its decline in authority). A related influence was Catholic and Protestant

---

9 C. Ó Gráda, *A Rocky Road: The Irish Economy since the 1920s* (Manchester: Manchester University Press, 1995), 7–18; P. Rigney, *Trains, Coal and Turf: Transport in Emergency Ireland* (Dublin: Irish Academic Press, 2010), 59–100; Michael Patterson to Sheehy, 1 April 1949, Tom Sheehy papers, P34/6/6: Tralee, Kerry County Archives.

10 Quoted in E. O'Halpin, *Defending Ireland: the Irish state and its enemies since 1922* (Oxford University Press, 1999), 211.

11 D. Ó Drisceoil, *Censorship in Ireland, 1939–1945: Neutrality, Politics and Society* (Cork: Cork University Press, 1996); C. Wills, *That Neutral Island: A Cultural History of Ireland dur-ing the Second World War* (London: Faber, 2007), 135–46, and 206–10; M. Kennedy, *Guarding Neutral Ireland: The Coast-Watching Service and Military Intelligence, 1939–1945* (Dublin: Four Courts Press, 2008), 308–11.

missionary activity in Asia and Africa. Orders such as the Missionary Society of St Columban, and the Medical Missionaries of Mary relied on home support, and every Catholic and Protestant parish and school was mobilised to assist missionary activities.[12] The spread of communism posed particular challenges: in 1958 the Columbans published '. . . *but not conquered*', an account of the suffering of their priests and parishioners at the hands of Chinese communists. Yet by the 1980s American-backed elites that oppressed the poor, and global capitalism, had taken the place of communism as the Satan which younger Columbans believed threatened the world.[13] The late 1960s saw the beginnings of a powerful development aid movement. Africa Concern was the first such Irish Non-Governmental Organisation (NGO), being joined by others which, although nominally secular in ethos, retained an emphatically episcopal capacity to moralise and to excoriate whilst constantly arguing for greater state aid and support for themselves. In Northern Ireland from the 1940s, equally, United Kingdom agencies such as Save the Children, Christian Aid and Oxfam blurred but never fully sundered the lines between confessional and secular community engagement with support for the developing world.

The Irish constitution, Bunreacht na hÉireann, enacted in 1937 has often been attacked for its allegedly excessively Catholic nature and an inherent parochialism. Yet the constitution's non-binding Catholic adornments notwithstanding, it was drawn up after review of a wide range of national constitutions and contemporary international legal scholarship, and in matters such as religious freedom (article 44) was unusually and courageously explicit for its time in recognising not only the Catholic and various Protestant faiths but Judaism. It was republican and secular in spirit, distinguishing clearly between church and state, in contrast to the United Kingdom constitution, where in 2016 mitre, crown and legislature remain fused.[14] Article 29, which until 1982 caused such difficulties in north/south and Anglo-Irish relations because it blocked extradition for offences with a political dimension, was not a get-out clause for republican terrorism: it simply attached the constitution generally to recognised principles of international law.[15]

---

12 M. Purcell, *To Africa with Love: The Life of Mother Mary Martin, Foundress of the Medical Missionaries of Mary* (Dublin: Gill & Macmillan, 1987); George Hook interview with Bibi Baskin, *Newstalk Radio 106*, Dublin, 3 September 2015.

13 B. T. Smyth (ed.), '. . . *but not conquered': communist China through the eyes of six Columban missionaries* (Dublin: Browne & Nolan, 1958); S. McDonagh, *The Greening of the Church* (London: Geoffrey Chapman, 1990).

14 M. Kennedy, *Ireland and the League of Nations 1923–1946: international relations, diplomacy and politics* (Dublin: Irish Academic Press, 1996); G. Hogan, *The Origins of the Irish Constitution, 1928–1941* (Dublin: Royal Irish Academy, 2012), 215–27.

15 E. O'Halpin, *Defending Ireland*, 326–8.

The Irish economy underwent three radical transformations in the wake of partition in 1921: first, with the adoption of a haphazard variety of protectionism and of state economic activism in its first decades; second, with the development in the late 1950s of an export-led growth strategy based largely on foreign direct investment; and third, with the painful but profitable adjustment to EEC membership from 1973 onwards.

The new state, hugely reliant on agricultural exports to Britain, struggled to build its economy. The Minister For Agriculture Patrick Hogan sought improved quality in agricultural produce in the 1920s not to find new markets, but to increase the value of sales to Britain. His efforts were viewed very positively: in 1931 the Bank of England supplied the Hungarian prime minister with a detailed brief on 'agriculture in the Irish Free State', including relevant legislation concerning 'the control and stimulation of agricultural production'.[16] But cleaner eggs and leaner bacon alone could not solve Ireland's problems of underdevelopment, unemployment and emigration. The gradual adoption of industrial protectionism from the late 1920s onwards was undertaken not in ignorance but in full knowledge of the changing world outside: indeed, one commentator in 1927 complained that the Cosgrave government was making inadequate use of 'the strongest weapon [in] ... the Treaty ... people are beginning to despair generally and to regard the possibility of industrial revival as quite hopeless'.[17] All the First World War victors favoured free trade, like international solidarity against aggression, solely to the extent that such approaches suited their existing economic and strategic interests. France and Britain each located free trade within imperial and colonial trading blocs protected by tariffs, and on terms which impoverished rather more than they enriched many of the far-flung territories and non-white peoples whom they ruled.[18] The 'white dominions' of Australia, New Zealand, Canada and, incongruously given its population make-up, South Africa, naturally fared rather better within the British imperial system than did colonies and dependencies. At times their leaders were disposed to preach to Ireland on the virtues of imperial economic cooperation, but by 1945 they themselves had largely been 'de-dominionised' in both economic and strategic terms: even Australia, the most supine interwar dominion, had experienced

---

16 Copy of Sir William Goode to Count Bethlen (prime minister of Hungary), 17 May 1931, OV81/1: London, Bank of England archives.
17 S. P. Campbell, 'Give Ireland A Chance for Economic Independence', *Honesty*, v, no. 118, 28 May 1927, 19–20.
18 In 2015 Indian prime minister Modi backed calls for British reparations for 200 years of economic despoliation. *The Guardian*, 24 July 2015.

what historian David Day has termed 'the great betrayal' at Britain's hands. By contrast, contiguity ensured that the empire's least loyal and least grateful dominion remained both a favoured trading partner and the dominion best defended by British arms.[19]

Belfast had fewer policy choices to make than Dublin after 1921 regarding industrial and agricultural protection, foreign trade, and foreign investment.[20] Ulster politicians were aggrieved that, as a loyal British province, she received less attention from the dominions than did the Free State. This remained so even when the upstart de Valera came to power in 1932 determined to dismantle the 1921 treaty. Northern Ireland benefitted from integration in the British economy, but during the interwar years that economy was itself beset by acute difficulties that disproportionately impacted upon its Celtic extremities. Up to 1939 the province had only limited success in harnessing opportunities for preferential trading within the empire. The Canadian prime minister Mackenzie King, a profound believer in the imperial ideal, irritably noted an Ulster Unionist tendency towards 'too much Empire and loyalty' in discussing economic and trade issues. The real problem was that the empire had little appetite for what Northern Ireland had to sell.[21]

Arthur Griffith's nostrum of economic self-sufficiency was replicated in many new states across the world. Unlike new European and Asian states before and after the Second World War, however, in Ireland protectionism did not lead to the expropriation of foreign interests, to laws demanding the transfer of majority ownership to Irish citizens, or still less the systematic exclusion of ethnic or religious minorities from participation in commercial life. Where the new state took over existing enterprises this was largely due to the withdrawal or failure of British firms.[22] Land redistribution, often a defining feature of newly created states, was handled with kid gloves. In the immediate aftermath of civil war, key issues were addressed through the 1923

---

19 *The Times*, 4 August 1933; K. Tsokhas, 'De-dominionisation: The Anglo-Australian experience, 1939–1945', *The Historical Journal*, 37 (1994), 861–83; D. Day, *The Great Betrayal: Britain, Australia and the onset of the Pacific War, 1939–42* (Oxford University Press, 1988).

20 Memorandum by minister of commerce, 4 March 1959 CAB/4/1097: PRONI.

21 P. Ollerenshaw, 'Businessmen in Northern Ireland and the Imperial Connection, 1886–1939', in K. Jeffery (ed.), *'An Irish Empire'? Aspects of Ireland and the British Empire* (Manchester: Manchester University Press, 1996) 183–4; Mackenzie King diary, 3 August 1932: www.bac-lac.gc.ca/eng/discover/politics-government/prime-ministers/william-lyon-mackenzie-king/Pages/search.aspx.

22 M. Ó Fathartaigh, *Irish Agriculture Nationalised: The Dairy Disposal Company and the Making of the Modern Irish Dairy Industry* (Dublin: Dairy Products Industry, 2015), 16–36.

Land Act. Thereafter, large landowners sank or swam depending on the profitability of their holdings. In 1925 a British army officer reported how his father Colonel J. Grove White of Doneraile had 'been nominated against his will' and elected in the Cork County Council elections. 'That a landlord, a retired British officer, an ex-High Sheriff and Deputy Lieutenant, should be able to get a vote ... is by no means an isolated case. It is a sign of the times.'[23]

The emergence of a policy of haphazard protectionism nevertheless attracted British criticism, particularly from manufacturers accustomed to easy access to the Irish market. Lionel Curtis, wet-nurse to his imagined British imperial constitution, hankered for the recasting of the Anglo-Irish Treaty of 1921 to create a genuine British Isles free trade area. In 1933 Curtis hoped the more malleable Cosgrave would return to office and 'think it worthwhile in the plenitude of his power and in the interests of agriculture to defy the bootmakers, biscuit-makers and various other interests that have forced Ireland into protection'.[24] This criticism was based not on missed opportunities for Irish economic modernisation, but rather on Ireland's failure to accept that her future lay simply in feeding Britain at prices set by the consumer.

De Valera's victory in the snap 1933 election, a mandate for his 'economic war' against Britain on the issue of the land annuities, destroyed Curtis's hopes. Initially regarded in London as sheer folly – *The Times* opined that 'there can be no hope of any kind of prosperity' in Ireland, which 'is bleeding to death', while de Valera held office – despite the damage inflicted on agricultural trade with Britain, the dispute strengthened him domestically, and also attracted international attention.[25] The economic war also yielded a major political and geo-strategic dividend, the 1938 Anglo-Irish agreement which revised the 1921 Treaty and gave Ireland sole control of her ports and defensive facilities. That made neutrality possible, just as the defence rights which Britain retained in the treaties in which she solemnly recognised the complete independence of her mandate territories Iraq (in 1930) and Egypt (1936) inevitably saw those supposedly sovereign states dragged unwillingly into the Second World War. Protection enabled the creation of indigenous industries which, at least in the short term, reduced imports, enhanced the national skill base, and provided increased manufacturing employment. But it never addressed the problem that Ireland remained hugely dependent on

---

23 Report by Major M. F. Grove White, 22 July 1925, WO32/3515: TNA.
24 Lionel Curtis to Tom Jones, 5 January 1933, MS Curtis 89 fol. 76: Bodleian Library, Oxford. Curtis (1872–1955) had been a key British advisor during the 1921 Treaty negotiations.
25 *The Times*, 6 December 1933.

imports of raw materials and goods she could never make, and that she needed to export her agricultural produce. Furthermore, the protected enterprises were inherently inefficient, focused solely on the small, captive domestic market. This problem was to bedevil the sector until its virtual disappearance following EEC membership in the 1970s.[26]

New states generally sought to bypass old masters when seeking technical guidance on industrialisation and development: even before the advent of Hitler, Britain fretted at the insatiable demand for German expertise and technology in Middle and Near Eastern countries adjoining the empire such as Egypt, Persia, and Afghanistan while British industry sulked at the loss of potential markets. London looked askance at the Cosgrave government's use of the German firm Siemens to construct the Shannon hydro-electric scheme, a prestige project initially viewed as a cross between a white elephant and a Trojan Horse: in 1926 the British security agency MI5 heard that 'the Shannon Valley is absolutely stiff with Boche', and later noted how 'from then onwards several industries were started or developed' with German assistance.[27] In the 1930s European firms provided expertise and capital for various new enterprises, public and private. Innovations in sugar processing, turf harvesting and industrial alcohol production initiated with the aims of import substitution and rural job creation were considerably influenced by developments in Belgium, Germany, the Soviet Union and Czechoslovakia.[28]

Even as protectionism took root, foreigners – even Jews – with capital and know-how were welcomed. British manufacturers established Irish subsidiaries to circumvent tariffs, although the government was anxious to diversify the pattern of foreign ownership: one entrepreneur found de Valera 'cordial to the project of bringing Canadian capital. . . . He mentioned particularly' that Ireland 'had not a single cement plant and is entirely dependent on imports for this commodity'.[29] The state relied on the privately owned Bank of Ireland to ensure the solvency of the financial system, and it and other banks took their cues from London.[30] Similarly, until the 1970s, the Irish Stock Exchange operated like a Dickensian sub-branch of the London Stock Exchange.

26 J. Haughton, 'The Historical Background', in J. O'Hagan (ed.), *The Economy of Ireland: Policy and Performance of a Small European Country* (London: St Martin's Press, 1995), 30–2; G. Murphy, *In Search of the Promised Land* (Cork: Mercier Press, 2009).

27 *Honesty*, 1, 6, (4 April 1925), 7–9; [illegible], Belfast, to MI5, 9 February 1926, KV4/ 279: TNA; E. O'Halpin (ed.), *MI5 and Ireland, 1939–1945: The Official History* (Dublin: Irish Academic Press, 2003), 37–8.

28 C. S. Andrews, *Man of No Property* (Dublin and Cork: Mercier Press, 1982), 137–55.

29 Memorandum by GEJ [unidentified], 20 May 1935, OV81/1: London, Bank of England archives.

30 C. Ó Gráda, *Ireland: A New Economic History 1780–1939* (Oxford University Press, 1993), 372–3.

Continued dependence on British ideas and practice was particularly marked in central administration. The Department of Finance, established under British tutelage in 1922, proved more papist than the Pope in its adherence to a conservative, risk-averse approach to economic affairs, in its imposition of corruption-free procedures on local authorities, and in its insistence on meritocratic apolitical recruitment (a departure from, *not* a continuation of, practice under British rule, where political favouritism had been a marked characteristic of recruitment and preferment).[31] This undoubtedly aided the new state in reputational terms. But prudence often seemed synonymous with paralysis. When Fianna Fáil attempted to identify alternative methods of funding industrialisation to those offered by the risk-averse banks, through the establishment of a Banking Commission in 1934, almost all its members were economic conservatives who saw no reason to restructure the financial system to suit Irish conditions.[32] The one international expert selected, the Swedish economist Per Jacobsson, had in fact been quietly suggested by the Bank of England, ostensibly because he had an Irish wife but really because he was utterly in thrall to the bank's Sir Otto Niemeyer.[33] Niemeyer told the fawning Jacobsson that 'the trouble with the Irish is that they have the vaguest ideas as to what banking means, though very practical ideas on the subject of tick [credit]'.[34] The commission duly produced a 'steady as she goes' report that could have been written in Threadneedle Street. The establishment of an independent Central Bank, for many states a keystone of sovereignty, occurred in 1942 only as an unavoidable consequence of wartime neutrality. Even then, Ireland remained tied to sterling until it launched its own tradable currency, the Punt, in 1979.[35] The Punt later entered the ERM (European Exchange Rate Mechanism), an uncomfortable see-saw experiment in monetary sovereignty which was eventually succeeded by adoption of the Euro in 1999.

What finished industrial protection was not simply its inherent costliness and inefficiency, but radical changes in how the Western world operated during the economic, political and social reconstruction that followed the Second

---

31 R. Fanning, *The Irish Department of Finance, 1922–1958* (Dublin: Institute of Public Administration, 1978); E. O'Halpin, *The Decline of the Union: British Government in Ireland 1892–1920* (Dublin: Gill & Macmillan, 1987), 95–7.

32 J. J. Lee, *Ireland 1912–1985: Politics and Society* (Cambridge University Press, 1989), 199–200.

33 Niemeyer to Harvey, 26 July and Harvey to Brennan (Department of Finance, Dublin), 30 July 1934, OV81/1: Bank of England archives,

34 Niemeyer to Jacobsson, 22 Jan. 1935, OV81/1: Bank of England archives.

35 E. Drea, 'The influence of Henry Parker-Willis and the Federal Reserve on the Institutional Design of the Irish Currency Act 1927', *The Historical Journal*, 58 (2015), 855–75.

World War. That was largely driven by the United States through its promotion of Western European economic cooperation, modernisation and consolidation underpinned by the Marshall Plan. Ireland was initially suspicious lest she risk her good name as a chaste neutral by accepting gifts from overbearing Yanks. When she overcame her scruples, it transpired that the Americans, far less forgiving of wartime neutrality than the British, would offer only very limited funds, almost all as loans with a 'rather measly' $18 million in grants.[36] The aid which Ireland received was, nevertheless, extremely significant in terms of strengthening Irish technical and analytical skills, while the process also highlighted the inadequacies and backwardness of the administrative system in areas such as national statistics which were essential components of policy-making. Irish participation in the Organisation for European Economic Cooperation (OEEC, later OECD) exposed officials to very uncomfortable comparative data, which grew worse as the 1950s progressed. At the political level there was much hand-wringing about increased emigration; within the bureaucracy, ideas based on hard information about the Irish and other economies began to germinate. This resulted in a new departure in economic policy, quietly initiated in 1956, and encapsulated in 1958 in the First Programme for Economic Development and the accompanying white paper *Economic Development*, involving the pursuit of foreign investment to build export-oriented industries, a reduction in dependence upon the British market for agricultural goods, and a gradual erosion of import tariffs so that Ireland could join the new world of free trade.[37] 1959 saw a significant decision to increase the school leaving age on a phased basis, a hesitant first step in a relatively ambitious investment in social capital through enhanced education and training, largely informed by OECD advice.[38]

Despite the initial success of *Economic Development* in terms both of economic growth and improved public morale, it was only a necessary preliminary to joining the Common Market. That was an imperative if, as expected, the United Kingdom entered. The failure of the first two British applications for membership in 1961 and 1967 afforded Ireland extra time, utilised quite effectively, to prepare for European economic integration. By 1972, when a referendum on accession took place, there was a clear divide between agricultural interests, pressing for membership since the late 1950s, and domestic industry and the trade union movement, who rightly feared the employment

---

36 Murphy, *In Search of the Promised Land,* 50–71.
37 Ibid., 304–6.
38 J. Walsh, *The Politics of Expansion, the transformation of educational policy in the Republic of Ireland* (Manchester: Manchester University Press, 2009), 66–99.

consequences. The republican movement, in 1972 presumably still impatiently awaiting a reply to Sinn Féin's indignant 1967 letter warning Prime Minister Harold Wilson not to bully Ireland into membership, opposed entry to a capitalist construct which would destroy Irish sovereignty and draw her into the Cold War, an hysterical analysis which still has some currency in left-wing circles.[39] In the short term, fears about domestic industry were amply justified: it was decimated. But this was more than replaced by vastly more efficient export-oriented industries, largely foreign owned; by a major rise in farm incomes; and by massive European infrastructural and social investment.[40] As in the United Kingdom, despite initial foot-dragging EEC membership also engendered radical advances in women's rights, employment law and other policy areas where Ireland had fallen far behind since 1945. Justin Keating, who led the Labour Party's campaign against membership, soon became a persuasive Europhile precisely on socialist grounds.[41]

That EEC accession was to prove a turning point for independent Ireland scarcely needs elaboration: it wrought the transformation of the economy, the reorientation of agricultural production away from dependence on the British market, a rapid and continuous improvement in living standards, the explicit pooling of sovereignty in areas of economic, social and environmental policy, and greatly enhanced status in the wider world. EEC membership had a major long-term impact on Irish relations with the United States, and as part of the world's largest trading bloc Ireland became party to negotiations on issues of global consequence.[42] For Northern Ireland, an underdeveloped province physically separate from Great Britain, United Kingdom EEC membership proved a less noteworthy development.

Between 1935 and 1945 rearmament and war had given Ulster's industries a sustained boost, but peace had put an end to that. In 1955 British Foreign Secretary Harold Macmillan thought 'Their industrial problems are not unlike those of Scotland. . . . Diversification (. . . not to rely only on shipyards

---

39 M. de Burca to Prime Minister Harold Wilson, 10 July 1967, PREM13/2732 TNA; A. Coughlan, *The Common Market: Why Ireland should not join* (Dublin, 1972).

40 M. E. Daly, *The Slow Failure: Population Decline in Independent Ireland, 1923–1973* (Madison, WI: University of Wisconsin Press, 2006), 231–3.

41 E. O'Halpin, 'Labour and the Making of Irish Foreign Policy 1973–77', and S. Collins, 'Labour and Europe: From No to Yes', in Paul Daly, Rónán O'Brien and Paul Rouse (eds.), *Making the Difference? The Irish Labour Party 1912–2012* (Cork: Cork University Press, 2012), 142–6 and 154–5.

42 G. FitzGerald, *All in a Life: An Autobiography* (Dublin: Gill & Macmillan, 1991), 146–77; E. O'Halpin, 'Labour and the Making of Irish Foreign Policy', 144–5 and see the chapters by Girvin, Kennedy and O'Hagan elsewhere in this volume.

and linen) are their best hope.'[43] Throughout the 1960s Stormont ministers were apprehensive about plans to join the EEC, and sensed threats in
increased British consumption of Irish produce and in the principle of free
movement of labour, which could have 'serious implications in places such as
Londonderry'.[44] In February 1971, disturbed at the course of the EEC accession talks, they discussed seeking 'more direct representation on the United
Kingdom negotiating team' to protect Ulster's interests, Con O'Neill evidently being an inadequate safeguard.[45] After 1973, efforts to attract inward
investment were greatly hampered by political violence, resulting in the
depletion of industrial employment. It had all been so different at the turn
of the twentieth century, when modern industries were what distinguished
north-east Ulster from the rest of the island.

Ireland and the World

A small and poor new state, independent Ireland had only very limited representation abroad. Its first diplomatic missions were in London, Washington,
Berlin, Geneva and Paris (1923). Until 1946, when a mission was opened in
Australia, there were none outside North America and Europe. In 1961 Nigeria
became the first African state to house an Irish embassy, initially mainly to look
after Irish missionaries, and despite strong personal connections between the
first generations of Indian and Irish independence fighters, it was only in 1964
that an embassy was established in New Delhi, the first Irish mission in Asia.[46]

League of Nations membership debunked the paternalistic British argument that Britain should speak for the empire as a whole. Ireland's approach
galvanised the other dominions to varying degrees, with Canada most energised. This produced the paradox that the empire's least enthusiastic dominion became the driver of imperial reform that culminated in the 1931 Statute of
Westminster which placed dominions unequivocally on a par with the United
Kingdom.[47] Representation at Geneva facilitated contact with a host of other

---

43 P. Catterall (ed.), *The Macmillan Diaries: The Cabinet years, 1950–57* (London: Pan
Macmillan, 2003) 11 March 1955, 414.
44 Northern Ireland Prime Minister Terence O'Neill to Prime Minister Sir Alec Douglas-
Home, 22 November 1963 PREM11/4874: TNA; Cabinet meeting, 8 June 1967, CAB4/
1574; PRONI.
45 Cabinet social and economic affairs committee meeting, 2 February 1971, CAB/4/1551/
21: PRONI.
46 K. O'Malley, *Ireland, India and Empire: Indo-Irish radical connections, 1919–1964*
(Manchester: Manchester University Press, 2008).
47 N. Mansergh, *The Unresolved Question: The Anglo-Irish Settlement and Its Undoing 1912–72*
(New Haven, CT: Yale University Press, 1991), 268–78.

small post-Versailles states within and beyond Europe which had escaped from colonial or imperial control, and which professed themselves fervent adherents of the League's founding principles of a law-bound international system maintained through collective security and the peaceful settlement of dispute, although all harboured ambitions to undo their existing inherited borders, and all adopted protectionist and sometimes nativist economic policies underpinned by resentment of ethnic minorities which League membership tempered only superficially.

Ireland adopted a rational small state approach – for instance supporting calls for radical armaments reductions – which periodically irritated the United Kingdom, her strategic guarantor in any general conflict. Shortly after taking power in 1932, de Valera availed of the goodwill accumulated by the Cosgrave government's sober contributions to secure the presidency of the League's 1932 general assembly, which provided a pulpit from which he could preach to the world at large, articulating the principles which Ireland and many other small states argued must govern international affairs. Not once did he raise Ireland's bilateral grievances with Britain. The sophistication of the Irish approach to diplomatic discourse from 1923 onwards gained Ireland credit in the dominions and the wider international community; such goodwill was to be sorely needed during the Second World War, when Irish neutrality became a very sore point across the world.

Northern Ireland's loyal participation in the conflict brought wartime privation, and considerable civilian fatalities and destruction from aerial bombing. Her ports and airfields, as well as its industries, made a significant contribution to the United Kingdom's war effort, particularly as regarded the defence of her Atlantic lifeline. Once they had seen off Churchill's impetuous and far-fetched proposal to facilitate a postwar united Ireland in return for independent Ireland's joining the war, the Belfast government earned long-term political credit in London, not only with Churchill but with the Labour government of Clement Attlee which succeeded him in July 1945, and with the United States for which it became an important military staging post and training ground. The arrival of American troops occasioned particularly ill-judged protests from Dublin which further damaged Ireland's standing with the United States.[48] The republican movement, under the lash in both Irish

---

48 J. Bowman, *De Valera and the Ulster question 1917–1973* (Oxford University Press, 1982), 246–52 and see the chapter by Kennedy in this volume.

jurisdictions after May 1940, proved an inept Nazi fifth column in terms of planned sabotage and espionage alike.[49]

When the war ended, many neutrals and various Central and South American states coerced into belligerency by the United States were invited to join the new United Nations Organisation (UN). Ireland was not. This was, perhaps, not as great a blow as might appear: it spared Ireland the necessity of participation in the Korean war (unlike Sweden and India, for example, both stalwarts of what became known as the Non-Aligned Movement). But it also intensified a sense of disconnection from the wider world which had germinated during wartime neutrality.[50] When, a decade later, eighteen more countries joined the UN, the British foreign secretary noted fatalistically that 'this means admitting a lot of trouble-makers (like Ireland)'.[51] He was right: although Ireland's first General Assembly contribution in September 1956 was impeccably Western and Christian in tone, things changed when Fianna Fáil returned to office in 1957 with Frank Aiken as Minister for External Affairs. Hitherto a cautious minister, Aiken was energised by decolonisation, the Cold War, and the threat of nuclear warfare. His approach, scented with a whiff of 'holier than thou' seldom absent from Irish public interventions in international affairs, saw his delegation pursue issues on a non-partisan basis, offending in turn most European colonial powers, the United States, Britain, China, the Soviet Union and even India. Ireland also became an advocate for and advisor to emerging states.[52] An American report noted Ireland's 'unusually active role' – although 'firmly anti-Communist', 'on several occasions [Ireland] has taken a position which diverges sharply from that of other western nations' – but when an Irishman was elected president of the 15th General Assembly in 1960 despite 'the Soviet bloc's drive to obtain the office', this was seen as a Western victory. Furthermore, as Ireland sought foreign investment and prepared to apply for EEC membership in parallel with Britain, Taoiseach Seán Lemass made it clear that the state would eschew policies at the UN incompatible with those of the bloc she aspired to join. EEC membership,

49 O'Halpin, *Defending Ireland*, 245–52.
50 Wills, *That Neutral Island*, 7–14.
51 Catterall (ed.), *The Macmillan Diaries*, 28 October 1955, 498.
52 J. M. Skelly, *Irish Diplomacy at the United Nations, 1945–1965: National Interests and the International Order* (Dublin: Irish Academic Press, 1997); CREST, current intelligence weekly summaries, CIA RDP7900927A0019000090001-3, 16 Oct. 1958, and CIA RDP7900927A002600050001-9, 11 February 1960: United States National Archives Records Administration (NARA); N. Dorr, *Ireland at the United Nations: memories of the early years* (Dublin: Institute of Public Administration, 2010), 54; *Challenges and Opportunities Abroad: White Paper on Foreign Policy* (Dublin, 1996).

not decolonisation, was the only foreign policy item on Fianna Fáil's agenda during the 1961 general election, proposed alongside further industrialisation as the means of reversing population decline.[53]

An American intelligence document described 'the decision to apply for full membership' as 'the most significant step away from neutrality ... Dublin has shown few of the qualms of Sweden, Switzerland or Austria about becoming entangled in an arrangement with heavy political significance'.[54] In fact, one of the conundrums of Irish EEC/European Union membership since 1973 has been her ability to avoid any defence commitments within an institution envisaged essentially as a means of enhancing Western European security. Instead, Ireland from 1958 onwards committed her exiguous defence forces primarily to UN operations. The loss of Irish troops in disasters such as at Niemba in the Congo had the effect not of souring but of enhancing public support for Irish participation: it was somehow nobler for Irish soldiers to die ill-equipped and ill-led in the cause of peace rather than of war. International service has remained a lifeline for the military, providing an important public rationale for the maintenance of defence forces whose primary though some-what disagreeable task since 1922 has been to prevent a takeover by militant republicanism.[55]

Irish UN policy during the various international crises of the Cold War era was generally constructive and, from 1972, was developed in close consul-tation with European partners.[56] There have been exceptions. In September 1969 Jack Lynch's government made a gauche attempt to involve the UN in the emerging Northern Ireland conflict; and in May 1982 during the Anglo-Argentine Falklands war, Taoiseach Charles Haughey abruptly reversed Ireland's diplomatic position.[57] This act of spite against Margaret Thatcher's government would have been farcical – though domestically popular – rather than serious, had not Ireland happened to hold the chair of the UN Security Council at the time.[58] As when Ireland attempted to flaunt the 'sore thumb' of partition at the Council of Europe in 1950–1951, a body composed mainly

53 Daly, *The Slow Failure*, 219–21.
54 NARA, CREST, CIA RDP7900927A0033000800001-8, Weekly Intelligence Summary, 7 September 1961.
55 O'Halpin, *Defending Ireland*, 270–3.
56 K. O'Sullivan, *Ireland, Africa and the End Of Empire: Small State Identities in the Cold War, 1955–75* (Manchester: Manchester University Press, 2012), 158–81.
57 J. Walsh, *Patrick Hillery: The Official Biography* (Dublin: New Island, 2008), 178–89.
58 M. Lillis, 'Mr Haughey's dud Exocet', *Dublin Review of Books* issue 21: www.drb.ie/essays/mr-haughey-s-dud-exocet (accessed 3 May 2016).

of states which had been almost crushed by war, despoliation and genocide, such behaviour was an aberration rather than the norm.[59]

In 1948 Seán MacBride, a recent convert to constitutional politics, became Minister for External Affairs. He appeared to think that the United States might intervene to end partition, but the idea that any American government could be persuaded to pressurise their closest geo-strategic ally on the Northern Ireland issue was absurd. In 1949 Washington saw Ireland not as a wronged state, but as an extremely lucky one which, protected from the ravages of war by the Allies, had publicly mourned Hitler in 1945, and which now presumed to lecture a shattered world on the overwhelming immorality and injustice of partition. The view within the Beltway was that Ireland's sole international virtue was its pronounced Catholic and rural character, which made it an unlikely seed bed for communism. When MacBride located Irish refusal to join the new North Atlantic Treaty Organisation (NATO) on the narrow ground of partition – 'Ireland was strongly in favour of the Atlantic Pact and would have liked to join in signing it' – the United States simply noted the point. MacBride subsequently sought American arms – 'under present conditions Ireland was unable to defend itself' although 'his people had the will to defend themselves against Communist aggression' – while his successor Frank Aiken proposed a bilateral defence pact.[60] In 1954 Minister for External Affairs Liam Cosgrave said Ireland might contribute to European defence by joining the Western European Union, but the British foreign secretary 'sugg[este]d NATO' instead: 'he c[oul]dn't do that'.[61] Unaware of such contacts, the Irish public saw military neutrality elevated to an absolute moral from being a contingent policy. Ireland remained profoundly anti-communist, and for a decade after 1945, the need to protect Christianity from the Soviet menace held pride of place in politicians' utterances. But after Ireland joined the UN, a significant distinction began to emerge between affairs in Europe – where communist bullying of the Catholic Church, and brutal repression of revolts in East Germany and Hungary, naturally drew criticism – and what was happening in Africa and Asia.

During the 1960s Irish attitudes towards the United States underwent a marked change. This was despite the election of the charismatic Irish-American John F. Kennedy as president in 1960, the shocks of the Berlin Wall

---

59 M. Kennedy and E. O'Halpin, *Ireland and the Council of Europe* (Strasbourg: Council of Europe publishing, 2000).

60 'Memorandum of conversation with Minister for External Affairs Mr Seán MacBride ...', 13 March 1951, Dean G. Acheson papers: Truman Presidential Library.

61 Informal notes of cabinet meeting, 25 January 1955, CAB195/13: TNA.

in 1961 and the Cuban missile crisis of 1962, and awareness of Soviet repression in Eastern Europe. The most influential factor at play was probably the spirit of civic protest internationally engendered by the Vietnam war. The Irish public could identify with what appeared increasingly as a Vietnamese struggle for national self-determination against foreign domination, rather than a valiant American-backed attempt to stem the Red tide in the Far East.

By the early 1980s Washington had replaced Moscow as the focus of what one American diplomat termed Irish contempt 'on virtually every issue in international relations'.[62] It became possible for Irish people at once routinely to denounce American imperialist interventions across the developing world, to demand that the United States intervene in the affairs of the United Kingdom on Northern Ireland, and to expect preferential treatment for Irish immigrants to the United States on foot essentially of historic ties and of being white and English-speaking. This was despite the crucial contribution of America to economic modernisation since the 1950s – in 2015 Ireland was reportedly the 'number one destination in the world' for American foreign investment – and despite the United States' central role in the Northern Ireland peace process.[63]

For a century British officials and Irish separatists shared a largely misplaced belief about the potency of a unitary Irish-American political bloc. In 1915 the British ambassador in Washington listed forces who opposed American assistance for Britain: 'Irish and German organisations, assisted by the Catholic Church, are working together … the Jews, as a rule, are with them.'[64] Yet the succeeding half century was to show that, while Irish-America could be a good source of funds for Irish extremists, it could deliver almost nothing at national political level. The Irish issue was simply not important enough, before or after 1921, to attract sustained interest; furthermore, the United Kingdom, from 1917 America's closest ally, would greatly resent any outside intervention or mediation in her internal affairs. Although Irish republicans continued to preach their cause and raise money in New York, Boston and other east coast cities, at intergovernmental level there was almost nothing to be done.[65] When the Second World War broke out the Roosevelt administration was deeply unsympathetic to Irish neutrality, which they believed threatened Atlantic security as well as British interests. It was left to the inept

62 G. Dempsey, *From the Embassy: A US Foreign Policy Primer* (Dublin: Liffey Press, 2004), 18–19.
63 *The Irish Times*, 5 March 2015.
64 British ambassador, Washington, to London, 21 July 1915, CAB37/132: TNA.
65 B. Whelan, *United States Foreign Policy and Ireland from Empire to Independence 1913–1929* (Dublin: Four Courts Press, 2004), 310–48.

Irish minister in Washington to argue Ireland's case while simultaneously plaintively begging favours from Washington: in 1940 he absurdly assured an incredulous State Department official that Britain would 'not resent' an American plea for mercy for two IRA bombers 'but would regard it as the act of a friend'.[66] Irish diplomacy in the United States, run from an embassy with at most four diplomats and a handful of consulates, remained at best cautious and diffident until the mid-1970s. By then, two things had changed: the Northern Ireland Troubles had attracted international interest, and the British government was itself applying pressure on Washington to stop guns and dollars reaching the IRA; and, as President Ford was told, 'an excellent beginning in intensifying the US-Irish dialogue was made during Ireland's EC six-month presidency from January to June 1975', contrary to expectations, and this had important ramifications for American/EC relations.[67] St Patrick's Day 1977 saw a declaration by senior Irish-American politicians of the need to find a peaceful way forward in Northern Ireland. These 'Four Horsemen' included Thomas P. 'Tip' O'Neill and Edward Kennedy, amongst the most powerful figures in the legislature, who could exert pressure selectively on the administration on Irish issues. The possibility that had respectively inspired and haunted Irish and British imaginations for almost a century gradually became a reality: intelligent Irish diplomacy finally found means of harnessing Irish-American political sentiment effectively on the Northern Ireland issue. This was a setback alike for Britain and for militant republicanism, because it provided a legitimate middle way for Irish-American leaders between unthinking support for Irish terrorism and glum acquiescence in the line historically favoured by American policy-makers – which was that relations with the United Kingdom always trumped lesser matters such as Britain's internal difficulties in Northern Ireland.[68] The long-term consequence was that Northern Ireland became an accepted part of the American foreign policy agenda rather than the absolute no-go area which it had been since 1917, to Britain's considerable discomfiture. This was demonstrated particularly during the Reagan and the Clinton presidencies of the 1980s and 1990s, in American brokerage of the Good Friday Agreement of 1998, and

---

66 J. P. Moffat journal, 1 February 1940. MS1407, vol. 44: Houghton Library, Harvard, MA.

67 Presidential Country file for Europe/Canada, box 7, folder Ireland 2, Kissinger brief for President Ford, 2 September 1975: Gerald R. Ford Library, University of Michigan; E. O'Halpin, 'British intelligence, PIRA and the Early Years of the Northern Ireland troubles', in P. Maddrell (ed.), *The Image of the Enemy: Intelligence Analysis of Foes since 1945* (Washington, DC: Georgetown University Press, 2015), 162–91.

68 A. Sanders, *Inside the IRA: Dissident Republicans and the War for Legitimacy* (Edinburgh: Edinburgh University Press, 2011), 168–89, argues the contrary.

in Washington's continued interest in the peace process. Overt reciprocation was never sought, although in 1981 Charles Haughey was happy to assure Tip O'Neill that Ireland would support conservationists on the International Whaling Commission: 'I am proud … that in a very real sense we have been pioneers in this field.'[69] Another of the horsemen, Senator Daniel Patrick Moynihan of New York, was unimpressed by Ireland's reluctance to open an embassy in Israel: 'What the hell is this all about? I will be seeing [taoiseach] Reynolds when? … Would some blunt talk be of use? … I could say something worse but not in writing.' The Irish offered a soothing explanation, but an embassy was still a few years off.[70] Successive governments, underpinned by public opinion and the imperatives of the beef export trade to the Middle East, have been consistently pro-Palestinian and critical of Israel. One delicate point in Irish–American relations has been American use of Shannon airport for military transports, on which successive Irish governments have said as little as possible. This became a significant domestic political issue: in 2008 the American embassy in Dublin reported that the creation of a cabinet committee on human rights policy will 'increase noise levels for a short time' on the Shannon issue, 'but things should soon return to normal'.[71]

A Hybrid People

In 1898 the *Skibbereen Eagle*, an obscure west Cork newspaper, acquired an international reputation for bumptiousness with its declaration, when condemning the brutality of Czarist expansionism, that it would henceforth keep a sharp eye on the emperor of Russia. The *Eagle*'s perspective was determinedly imperial: what was at stake was not the unhappy fate of the various, mainly Muslim, peoples forced to accept Moscow's rule, but Russian advances which might threaten Britain's Indian empire, where truth, liberty, justice and land for the people were apparently in abundance. Just as the *Eagle* spread its imperialist wings, another strand of Irish journalism was taking flight. The Boer War, coming just as the 1798 centenary invigorated popular nationalism, saw concerted nationalist demonstrations of sympathy with the

---

69 Haughey to O'Neill, 16 April, Tip O'Neill papers, folder 23/4, and folder 22/5, 19 May 1981: Boston College.
70 Moynihan note to Steve Rickard, undated [1993], and Michael Collins (Embassy of Ireland) to Rickard, 13 October 1993, Daniel Patrick Moynihan papers, box 327, folder 9: Library of Congress.
71 https://wikileaks.org/plusd/cables/08DUBLIN603_a.html, United States embassy, Dublin, to Washington, 4 November 2008 (accessed 30 August 2015).

Afrikaaner rebels and a fluctuating campaign against enlistment in the British army. Arthur Griffith, just returned from South Africa, played a prominent part in this agitation. Fellow-feeling with white European colonists seeking economic, cultural and political freedom from British rule undoubtedly came naturally to him and other early separatists; engagement with the political aspirations of indigenous colonial peoples was not to occur until the First World War, and even then it was opportunistic rather than principled.[72]

The same was true regarding the humanitarian work of the Irish consular official Roger Casement, later to die on a British scaffold, in the Belgian Congo and in Peru. Casement's shocking reports to the Foreign Office were lauded not as anti-colonial tracts, but as indictments of the barbarous behaviour of Belgians and Peruvians towards indigenous peoples. Irish newspapers applauded Casement's efforts, but drew no wider lessons about colonialism.[73] Copies of Casement's findings were solemnly dispatched by the Foreign Office to colonial governors so they could warn off their itinerant labouring classes from accepting 'employment in South America'.[74]

The conceit that the Irish were themselves a hybrid people, a kind of bridge between colonised and colonisers, has roots alike in imperialist and separatist traditions. As early as 1901, the arch-imperialist Rudyard Kipling created the street urchin Kim, an orphan son of Irish parents. With 'every unknown Irish devil in the boy's blood', Kim unconsciously spans the divide between the Indian peoples and their British rulers, appreciating the range, diversity and complexity of Indian civilisation while doing the secret work of empire.[75] Like Kipling, Indian and other nationalists associated Irishness with an innate rebelliousness. In 1932 Bombay police chief, Sir Patrick Kelly, had an embarrassing encounter with a female terrorist of good family whom he asked ' "What is the need of your joining the movement"? I said: "Look Mr Kelly it is not your business. You are an Irishman. What do you feel about it?" He kept mum.'[76] Even British ministers saw parallels: in 1941 Leo Amery, Secretary of State for India, termed Nehru 'a blend of Hitler and de Valera but on a more cultivated plane'.[77] Subhas Chandra Bose, who fled India in 1941 and established links with Germany and Japan in hopes that they would free

---

72 B. Nelson, *Irish Nationalists and the Making of the Irish Race* (Princeton, NJ: Princeton University Press, 2012), 121–47.
73 *Irish Times*, 16 July 1912; *Irish Independent*, 29 July 1912.
74 *Irish Examiner*, 8 August 1912.
75 Rudyard Kipling, *Kim* (London: Macmillan, 1901).
76 Mrs GMS Captain Oral History Transcript, Accession Number 271 (15 March 1968) NML.
77 Amery papers AMEL 7/35, diary, 26 July 1941; Churchill College Cambridge Archives.

his country from British rule, was particularly inspired by Irish revolution-ary example (he lauded de Valera and Cosgrave alike in the 1930s, and seems not to have been troubled by partition). In 1943 Bose's outlandish claim of Irish recognition for his Japanese-controlled government-in-exile was imme-diately denied by Dublin, but retained currency in Indian nationalist circles.[78] Ireland and India – though not, curiously, Pakistan or Bangladesh, the even-tual products of the hurried, arbitrary and unfair British-orchestrated parti-tion of India in 1947 – have since retained a vague amity based on connections between separatist elites made in the aftermath of the First World War, and there are clear parallels in the nationalist, statist and dynastic mentalities of the once near-hegemonic Fianna Fáil and Congress parties, each now threat-ened with electoral extinction.[79]

During the First World War anti-colonial movements from across the British and Czarist empires began to interact, encouraged by German and Turkish agents. By 1918 Irish separatism had become unequivocally anti-colonialist where Britain was concerned (if separatist leaders also had res-ervations about European or American colonialism, they kept these to themselves). Colonial separatists drew inspiration from the 1916 Rising and the subsequent independence struggle.[80] But the new Irish state was a white dominion and eschewed contact with other separatists within the empire, although anti-treaty republicans maintained links, facilitated to an extent by the Communist International.

From 1919 the growth of anti-colonialism was compounded by the spread of Bolshevik ideology across Europe and the world. Yet Marxism had little appeal for the Irish revolutionary leadership, and even the trade union move-ment was largely immune. Fellow-feeling with other nationalities seeking liberation from British imperial domination had virtually no impact on Irish foreign policy until the era of initial Irish activism in support of decolonisa-tion at the United Nations from the late 1950s to the early 1960s. In the 1920s Irish leftists did join the communist-controlled League Against Imperialism,

78 O'Malley, *Ireland, India and Empire*, 100–05; E. O'Halpin, *Spying on Ireland: British Intelligence and Irish Neutrality During the Second World War* (Oxford University Press, 2008), 234; L. A. Gordon, *Brothers Against the Raj: A Biography of Indian Nationalists Sarat and Subhas Chandra Bose* (New York: Columbia University Press, 1990), 502.

79 K. Jeffery, 'Introduction', in K. Jeffery (ed.), *'An Irish Empire: Aspects of Ireland and the British Empire* (Manchester: Manchester University Press, 1996), 9; S. Chandra Bose, *The Indian Struggle 1920–1942* (London: Asia Publishing House, 1964), 326; J. Cleary, 'Postcolonial Ireland', in K. Kenny (ed.), *Ireland and the British Empire* (Oxford University Press, 2004), 251–88.

80 Report of interdepartmental committee on bolshevism as a menace to the British empire, n.d. (1921): India Office records (IOR), L/PS/10/866: British Library (BL).

which British intelligence was 'watching very closely indeed'.[81] De Valera visited its offices while in Berlin in 1928 to attend a meeting of the inoffensive Interparliamentary Union, where he asked 'what are the moral rights of a State which has built itself up by force and maintains itself on the necks of conquered peoples?' He opposed any resolution which 'would seem to imply that the existing States are founded on right and justice, and that their present boundaries should be perpetuated. (*Applause.*)'.[82] The London police feared cultural as well as political intermingling: one dance organised by the communist-controlled Indian Freedom League was attended by some Indians, 'several negroes and a number of young men and women (mainly Irish)'.[83] But when he took charge of foreign policy in 1932, de Valera's contributions at the League of Nations focused on the rights and responsibilities of individual states in the international system, rather than on the problem of colonialism: to do otherwise would only antagonise Britain, whose agreement would be central to the ending of partition.

By and large colonial injustice generated greater criticism outside than within Irish corridors of power. The republican women's organisation Cumann na mBan noted the death of the Indian separatist hunger striker Jatindranath Das in 1929, asking 'shall we in Ireland leave India to fight alone? … Hasten the revolution by joining the Irish Republican Army, Cumann na mBan and Sinn Féin'. The writer and philosopher AE (George Russell) assured a visitor in 1931 that 'I believe in the spiritual message of India and that your country will become free before long and nothing can stop it', although he was disappointingly vague about how this would happen. Asked his views on Gandhi, George Bernard Shaw simply offered the gnomic reply 'Well, I am myself a minor Mahatma.'[84]

Ireland's relative official reticence on colonial issues until she joined the UN in 1955 was perhaps for the best. Ireland had contributed disproportionately to the expansion and maintenance of empire in the eighteenth, nineteenth and early twentieth centuries, and latterly Irish Catholic and Protestant missionaries had vigorously expanded their spiritual and compassionate activities very largely within the British imperial fold. In India the Connaught Rangers

81 Vickery (IPI) to Peel (India Office), 20 December 1927 and 12 Apr. 1928, L/PJ/12/268: BL, IOR.
82 SIS to IPI, 22 March 1929 KV2/515; TNA; de Valera speech, 28 August 1928, in *Compte Rendu de al XXVme Conférence* (Lausanne, 1928), 453–4.
83 Extract from police report, 4 February 1931, L/PJ/12/260; BL, IOR.
84 Undated flyer [1930], Elgin O'Rahilly ephemera in author's possession; Oral History Transcript Shri Durga Das Acc. No. 96 (27 December 1971); Nehru Memorial Library, Delhi.

acquired a reputation for harsh and racist treatment of locals before a chaotic mutiny in 1920 in protest at British excesses in Ireland saw the regiment abruptly converted in Indian eyes from brutal oppressors to fellow-sufferers at imperial hands (one mutineer jailed in 1920 later re-enlisted in the British army, spending most of the Second World War as a prisoner in Germany).[85] Two of the three most excoriated British officials in interwar Indian nationalist memory – Sir Charles Tegart and Sir Michael O'Dwyer – were Irish, and the third, Brigadier Reginald Dyer, was Irish-educated. A Scottish colleague recalled Tegart's 'characteristically Irish make-up. . . . He loved freedom for himself as he did for others . . . few were better constituted than he to understand what the mind of the bomb- and pistol-wallah was blindly groping after', but Indians regarded him as a brute.[86]

Recent research has confirmed that after independence as before it, thousands of Irish served without qualms throughout the empire in military, police, civil, legal and commercial roles. Britain's greatest expert on colonial subversive interconnections between 1915 and 1965 was Philip Vickery, like Tegart a Trinity College Dublin man.[87] To the final days of British imperial rule, Irish newspapers carried advertisements for the Palestine Police and other colonial forces, and Irish people featured prominently as judges, officials and policemen from the Seychelles to Cyprus to Hong Kong. The 'Ulster generals' of the Second World War were joined by many thousands recruited from independent Ireland (amongst them the executed Kevin Barry's closest university friend, who became a Royal Air Force doctor and honorary medical advisor to Queen Elizabeth II).[88] Brigadier Bill Magan from Westmeath, one of the ablest practitioners and finest chroniclers of colonial counter-subversion, and of two thousand years of his Irish family history, died only in 2010.[89] One way

85 M. Silvestri, *Ireland and India: Nationalism, Empire and Memory* (Basingstoke: Palgrave Macmillan, 2009), 176–207; T. G. Fraser, 'Ireland and India', in Jeffery (ed.), *'An Irish Empire'?*, 90; A. Babbington, *The Devil to Pay: the Mutiny of the Connaught Rangers, India, July 1920* (London: Pen and Sword Books, 1991); S. Gannon, 'The formation, composition, and conduct of the British section of the Palestinian Gendarmerie, 1922–1926', *Historical Journal*, 56 (December 2013), 997–1006; S. O'Connor, *Irish Officers in the British Forces, 1922–45* (Basingstoke: Palgrave Macmillan, 2014).

86 Tegart Mss, Eur c235, p. 46, BL, quoting Sir David Petrie on Tegart.

87 O'Malley, *Ireland, India and Empire*, 5; BL, IOR, L/PJ/12/39.

88 D. O'Donovan, *No More Lonely Scaffolds: Kevin Barry and his time* (Dublin: Glendale Press, 1989), 184–5.

89 H. O'Shea, *Ireland and the End of the British Empire: the Republic and its Role in the Cyprus Emergency* (Manchester: Manchester University Press, 2015). William Magan's works are *Umma-More: The Story of an Irish family* (Salisbury: Element Books, 1983); *An Irish Childhood* (Edinburgh: Pentland Books, 1996); *Middle Eastern Approaches: experiences and travels of an intelligence officer 1939–1948* (Salisbury: Michael Russell, 2001); and *Soldier of the Raj* (Salisbury: Michael Russell, 2002).

and another, Paddy carried more than his fair share of Kipling's 'white man's burden'.

Communist Russia, Nazi Germany, Fascist Spain

After independence, electoral politics was dominated by two parties representing essentially the 1922/23 civil war winners and losers, both of which were broadly democratic in outlook, with a small and largely rural Labour Party. Only Labour had obvious foreign social democratic exemplars. Ultramontane communism never took root despite fitful encouragement from Moscow. In the mid-1920s the IRA had spied for Soviet intelligence in Britain, France and the United States, but for money rather than for ideological reasons.[90] In the 1930s Moscow sent the occasional pittance, and a swathe of peremptory, cryptic and ill-informed secret directives to Irish communists: start 'building united front with the Republican masses from below, winning them over to our standpoint'; arrange a 'mighty demonstration and city strike' in Belfast following sectarian violence; and during a Dublin transport strike, 'organise contacts IRA ranks workers defence'.[91] The high tide of communist efforts to capture the IRA came with the 1934 Republican Congress, a dismal failure lovingly mythologised by its leading figure Peadar O'Donnell.[92]

Communists later attempted to mobilise Irish migrants in Britain through the Connolly Association, but very few were interested – one of the paradoxes of the Irish diaspora is how disengaged from Anglo-Irish issues were most Irish who settled in Britain.[93] In Northern Ireland, communism made some headway within the trade unions, but even Marxism could not seduce the working classes from visceral sectarian politics. In the early 1960s Marxist intellectuals did influence the leadership of the republican movement. Some suspected a Soviet masterplan, a suggestion dismissed out of hand by one of those involved.[94] From the early 1960s some leftist republicans periodically sought Soviet money and weapons, but Moscow's involvement was limited and opportunist.[95] The truth was that the Soviet Union, like Wilhelmine and

90 T. Mahon and J. J. Gillogly, *Decoding the IRA* (Cork: Mercier Press, 2008).
91 Decodes of Shields [to Pollitt?], 5 April 1932, Comintern (Berlin) to Pollitt, 20 October 1932, Pollitt to Comintern (Berlin), 6 January 1933, and Pollitt to Dublin, 10 April 1933 HW17/72: TNA.
92 D. Ó Drisceoil, *Peadar O'Donnell* (Cork: Cork University Press, 2001), 70–94.
93 E. Delaney, *The Irish in Post-War Britain* (Oxford University Press, 2007), 185–95.
94 R. H. W. Johnston, *Century of Endeavour: A Biographical & Autobiographical View of the Twentieth Century in Ireland* (Dublin: Maunsell and Co., 2003).
95 B. Hanley and S. Millar, *The Lost Revolution: The Story of the Official IRA and the Worker's Party* (Dublin: Penguin Ireland, 2010), 519–42.

Nazi Germany in earlier decades, had little strategic interest in that isolated island, although after meeting Taoiseach Charles Haughey during a refuelling stop in Shannon in 1989 the last Soviet leader Mikhail Gorbachev told the Politburo 'such a nice and friendly meeting! And even in an hour it was clear we could do so much, just by being attentive to this little country'.[96] The residual republican left was forced to seek other gallant allies in Europe and beyond, its courtship of North Korea being the most exotic. Even during the Cold War, American and British intelligence characterised the Provisional IRA's significant Eastern bloc and Middle Eastern links as essentially pragmatic, and discounted the practical importance of Marxist republican groups and their foreign associations.[97]

For a few years the 'Blueshirts', led by the disgruntled bombast General Eoin O'Duffy, with black berets, marching songs, a straight-armed salute, an appetite for street conflict and a fixation with the communist menace, gave Ireland a flavour of what mainland Europe was experiencing. O'Duffy's embarrassing union in 1934 with the Cosgrave party responsible for consolidating Irish democracy quickly fell apart. He became a political irrelevance, although he mustered 700 followers in a farcical foray to fight against communism in the Spanish Civil War in 1937. By contrast, a far smaller cohort of Irish communists and leftist republicans who joined the Spanish republic's International Brigades have, perhaps justly, entered folklore as righteous heroes.[98]

In the late 1930s the IRA leadership reached an understanding with Nazi Germany intended to facilitate German war aims, including intelligence-gathering and sabotage, in return for the ending of partition following British defeat.[99] This disastrous liaison, established by Irish emigrés in the United States, arguably marked the high point of ectopic republican influence on Irish affairs. From the 1940s onwards, the republican diaspora's role was to provide money, weapons and succour, rather than to set the republican agenda (by the mid-1960s, as American security agencies noted, there was an ideological disconnect between the fervent anti-communism of

---

96 Margaret Thatcher Foundation Archive: www.margaretthatcher.org (accessed 1 June 2014), translation of unofficial Politburo minute, 13 April 1989.

97 E. O'Halpin, 'The Geo-politics of Republican Diplomacy in the Twentieth Century', in M. Bric and J. Coakley (eds.), *From Political Violence to Negotiated Settlement: The Winding Road to Peace in Twentieth-Century Ireland* (Dublin: UCD Press, 2004), 81–98 and 'British Intelligence, PIRA and the Early Years of the Northern Ireland Crisis', 213–48; Hanley and Millar, *The Lost Revolution*, 489–90, 540–2.

98 F. McGarry, *Eoin O'Duffy: A Self-Made Hero* (Oxford University Press, 2005), 283–315.

99 O'Halpin, *Defending Ireland*, 245–52.

Irish-American IRA supporters, and the indigenous republican movement which they were expected to finance). The Nazi interlude became an embarrassment in the postwar decades, particularly once republicanism sought to present itself essentially as the Irish arm of a worldwide left-wing challenge to Western capitalism rather than as the ideologically flexible movement it has always been.

Until the 1970s unionism and loyalism had less reason to seek friends outside the British Isles, although the Orange Order provided a significant reservoir of goodwill and support for Ulster in many commonwealth countries. In 1966 the Reverend Ian Paisley received an honorary doctorate from the fundamentalist Bob Jones University in South Carolina, a reflection of Bible Belt sympathy for Ulster Protestants. Dr Paisley later became an occasional colourful contributor in the European Parliament (1979–2004), which although part of an entity which he affected to despise gave him a trans-national platform. Loyalist paramilitaries, like republicans, looked abroad for help in Canada, South Africa, and even the United States.[100] Mainstream unionists also made some efforts to put their case in the United States and elsewhere and, particularly as the peace process gathered steam in the 1990s, received sympathetic hearings within the American policy system.

★ ★ ★

The two Irelands have followed very different paths since the 1880s, in economic and political terms alike. Then the future appeared to belong to Ulster, with its modern industries, integration into the British economy, and imperial reach. The route of industrial protectionism pursued by Dublin from the 1920s to the 1950s was made possible by, and to an extent was a proof of, independence. But it also demonstrated its own acute limitations, particularly after 1945. Prosperity and a dilution of dependency on the United Kingdom came not through political and economic isolationism, but through trade and international cooperation from the late 1950s onwards. Independent Ireland could make choices which radically altered her economic fortunes; Northern Ireland could not.

Irish pretensions to being a natural bridge between the colonised and the colonisers do not square with the history of Irish involvement in Britain's colonial past, any more than contemporary republicanism's progressive international associations can easily be reconciled with republicanism's past

---

100 S. Bruce, *The Red Hand: Protestant paramilitaries in Northern Ireland* (Oxford University Press, 1992), 157–71.

external friendships with the Kaiser, with Hitler, and, during the Cold War, with the Soviet Union. The process of European integration since 1973, so far from promoting convergence and homogeneity on the island, has pushed the two Irelands further apart. The industries which epitomised Ulster's progress in the 1880s are all but gone and have not been adequately replaced – a failure for which London, not Belfast, should be blamed. While her agricultural sector has benefitted from EEC membership, Northern Ireland is largely sustained by the British taxpayer rather than through the fruits of her own enterprise. By contrast, for all Ireland's financial woes since 2007, a combination of EU grants and supports, and foreign direct investment greatly intensified by EEC membership, has transformed the economy from unbalanced dependency on the nearest neighbour to one which trades worldwide. Yet Ireland remains myopic towards its own history in the international system since 1921, whether this be regarding Irish enthusiasm for spreading Christianity amongst peoples who coped without it for millennia, or Irish participation in the last decades of British colonialism, or how Ireland's external security has relied entirely on unsolicited and unacknowledged Anglo-American protection, or how the state has pursued its interests in the global economy whatever the consequences for less developed states and peoples.

The last 50 years have also produced a geopolitical paradox: republicans and unionists both look to Washington almost as much as to London and Dublin to help resolve Northern Ireland's incessant quarrels, the Irish economy is hugely dependent on American investment, and American cultural penetration the length and breadth of the island is unarguable. Yet the decades since the Vietnam war have seen the mainstreaming of anti-Americanism in Irish discourse on international affairs. So much for the argument that he who pays the piper, calls the tune.

Bibliography

Introduction: Ireland 1880–2016: Negotiating Sovereignty and Freedom

Gearóid Ó Tuathaigh

Aldous, Richard (ed.), *Great Irish Speeches* (London, 2007).

Bardon, J., *A History of Ulster* (Belfast: Blackstaff Press, 1992).

Bew, P., *Conflict and Conciliation in Ireland 1890–1910: Parnellites and Radical Agrarians* (Oxford University Press, 1987).

Ideology and the Irish Question: Ulster Unionism and Irish Nationalism 1912–1916 (Oxford University Press, 1994).

Ireland: The Politics of Enmity 1789–2006 (Oxford University Press, 2007).

Bielenberg, A. and R. Ryan, *An Economic History of Ireland since Independence* (London: Routledge, 2013).

Bielenberg, A., 'Exodus: The Emigration of Southern Irish Protestants during the Irish War of Independence and the Civil War', *Past and Present*, 218 (February 2013), 199–233.

Bowman, T., *Carson's Army: The Ulster Volunteer Force 1910–1922* (Manchester: Manchester University Press, 2007).

Brady, C. (ed.), *Interpreting Irish History: The Debate on Historical Revisionism 1938–1994* (Dublin: Irish Academic Press, 1994).

Buckland, P., *The Factory of Grievances: Devolved Government in Northern Ireland, 1921–1939* (Dublin: Gill & Macmillan, 1979).

Campbell, F., *Land and Revolution: Nationalist Politics in the West of Ireland 1891–1921* (Oxford University Press, 2005).

The Irish Establishment 1879–1914 (Oxford University Press, 2009).

Clark, S., *Social Origins of the Irish Land War* (Princeton, NJ: Princeton University Press, 1979).

Connolly, L. and T. O'Toole, *Documenting Irish Feminisms: The Second Wave* (Dublin: Woodfield Press, 2005).

Corish, P., *The Irish Catholic Experience: A historical survey* (Dublin: Gill & Macmillan, 1985).

Daly, M. E., *Industrial Development and Irish National Identity 1922–1939* (Dublin: Gill & Macmillan, 1992).

The Slow Failure. Population Decline and Independent Ireland 1920–1973 (Madison, WI: University of Wisconsin Press, 2006).

Industrial Development and Irish National Identity 1922–1939 (Dublin: Gill & Macmillan, 1992).

Sixties Ireland: Reshaping the Economy, State and Society (Cambridge: Cambridge University Press, 2016).

Delaney, E., *Demography, State and Society: Irish Migration to Britain 1921–1971* (Liverpool: Liverpool University Press, 2000).

Devlin, P., *Yes, We Have No Bananas: Outdoor relief in Belfast 1920–1939* (Belfast: Blackstaff Press, 1981).

Dunne, T. (ed.), *The National University of Ireland 1908–2008* (Dublin: UCD Press, 2008).

Elliott, M., *The Catholics of Ulster: A history* (London: Allen Lane, 2000).

Hepburn, A. C., *A Past Apart: Studies in the History of Catholic Belfast, 1856–1956* (Belfast: Ulster Historical Foundation, 1996).

Fanning, R., 'Britain's Legacy: Government and Administration', in P. J. Drudy (ed.), *Ireland and Britain since 1922* (Cambridge University Press, 1986).

Farrell, M., *Northern Ireland: The Orange State* (London: Pluto, 1980).

Ferriter, D., *Judging Dev* (Dublin: Royal Irish Academy, 2007).

Occasions of Sin: Sex and Society in Modern Ireland (London: Profile Books, 2012).

Ambiguous Republic. Ireland in the 1970s (London: Profile Books, 2012).

A Nation and not a Rabble: The Irish Revolution 1913–1923 (London: Profile Books, 2015).

Fitzpatrick, D., *The Two Irelands 1912–1939* (Oxford University Press, 1998).

Follis, B., *A State under Siege: The Establishment of Northern Ireland, 1920–1925* (Oxford University Press, 1995).

Ford, A., J. McGuire and K. Milne (eds.), *As by Law Established: The Church of Ireland since the Reformation* (Dublin: Lilliput Press, 1995).

Foster, R. F., *Luck and the Irish: A Brief History of Change 1970–2000* (London: Allen Lane, 2007).

Vivid Faces: The Revolutionary Generation in Ireland 1890–1923 (London: Allen Lane, 2014).

Fuller, L., *Irish Catholicism since 1950: The Undoing of a Culture* (Dublin: Gill & Macmillan, 2004).

Garvin, T., *Between Two Worlds* (Dublin: Gill & Macmillan, 1989).

1922: The Birth of Irish Democracy (Dublin, Gill & Macmillan, 1996).

Nationalist Revolutionaries in Ireland 1858–1928 (Oxford University Press, 1987).

News from a New Republic: Ireland in the 1950s (Dublin: Gill & Macmillan, 2010).

Girvin, B., and G. Murphy (eds.), *The Lemass Era: Politics and Society in the Ireland of Seán Lemass* (Dublin: UCD Press, 2005).

Harris, M., *The Catholic Church and the Foundation of the Northern Ireland State* (Cork: Cork University Press, 1993).

Hart, P., *The I.R.A. at War 1916–1923* (Oxford University Press, 1993).

Hennessey, T., *Northern Ireland: The Origins of the Troubles* (Dublin: Gill & Macmillan, 2005).

Horne, J. and J. Madigan (eds.), *Towards Commemoration: Ireland in War and Revolution, 1913–1923* (Dublin: RIA, 2013).

(eds.), *Our War: Ireland and the Great War* (Dublin: RIA, 2008).

Howe, S., *Ireland and Empire: Colonial Legacies in Irish History and Culture* (Oxford University Press, 2001).

Inglis, T., *Moral Monopoly: The Rise and Fall of the Catholic Church in Modern Ireland* (2nd edn., Dublin: Gill & Macmillan, 1998).

Jackson, A., *The Ulster Party. Irish Unionists in the House of Commons, 1884–1911* (Oxford University Press, 1989).

Ireland 1798–1998 (Oxford: Blackwell, 1999).

Jacobsen, J. K., *Chasing Progress in the Irish Republic* (Cambridge University Press, 1994).

Jeffery, K., (ed.), *An Irish Empire? Aspects of Ireland and the British Empire* (Manchester: Manchester University Press, 1996).

Kennedy, K. A., T. Giblin and D. McHugh (eds.), *The Economic Development of Ireland in the Twentieth Century* (London and New York: Routledge, 1988).

Kennedy, M., *Ireland and the League of Nations 1919–1946* (Dublin and Portland, OR: Irish Academic Press, 1996).

Goodbye to Catholic Ireland (London: Sinclair-Stevenson, 1997).

Kennedy, M. and J. M. Skelly (eds.), *Irish Foreign Policy 1919–1966* (Dublin: Four Courts Press, 2000).

Keogh, D., F. O'Shea and C. Quinlan (eds.), *The Lost Decade: Ireland in the 1950s* (Cork: Mercier Press, 2004).

Kiberd, D. and P. J. Mathews (eds.), *Handbook of the Irish Revival: An Anthology of Irish Cultural and Political Writings 1891–1922* (Dublin: Abbey Theatre Press, 2015).

Laffan, M., *The Partition of Ireland, 1911–1925* (Dundalk: Dublin Historical Association, 1983).

The Resurrection of Ireland. The Sinn Féin Party 1916–1923 (Cambridge University Press, 1999).

Lane, F. and D. Ó Drisceoil (eds.), *Politics and the Irish Working Class 1830–1945* (Basingstoke: Palgrave Macmillan, 2005).

Lee, J. J., *The Modernisation of Irish Society, 1848–1918* (Dublin: Gill & Macmillan, 1973).

Ireland, 1912–1985 (Cambridge University Press, 1989).

Maher, D. J., *The Tortuous Path: The Course of Ireland's Entry into the EEC, 1948–1973* (Dublin: Institute of Public Administration, 1986).

Mathews, P. J., *Revival: The Abbey Theatre, Sinn Féin, the Gaelic League and the Co-operative Movement* (Cork: Cork University Press for Field Day, 2003).

Maume, P., *The Long Gestation: Irish Nationalist Life 1891–1918* (Dublin: Gill & Macmillan, 1999).

McCabe, I., *A Diplomatic History of Ireland, 1948–49: The Republic, the Commonwealth and NATO* (Dublin: Irish Academic Press, 1991).

McDowell, R. B., *Crisis and Decline: The Fate of the Southern Unionists* (Dublin: Lilliput Press, 1997).

McGarry, F., *The Rising. Ireland: Easter 1916* (Oxford University Press, 2010).

McGarry, J., and B. O'Leary, *The Northern Ireland Conflict: Consociational Engagements* (Oxford University Press, 2004).

McGarry, J., and B. O'Leary, *Understanding Northern Ireland: Colonialism, Control and Consociation* (London: Routledge, 2009).

McMahon, D. (ed.), *The Moynihan Brothers in Peace and War 1909–1918: Their New Ireland* (Dublin: Irish Academic Press, 2004).

McMahon, T. G., *Grand Opportunity. The Gaelic Revival and Irish Society, 1893–1910* (Syracuse: Syracuse University Press, 2008).

Miller, D. W., *Church, State and Nation in Ireland, 1898–1921* (Pittsburgh, PA: University of Pittsburgh Press, 1973).

Moody, T. W. and J. C. Beckett, *Queen's Belfast 1845–1949: The History of a University* (London: Faber and Faber, 1959).

Mulholland, M., 'Political Violence', in R. Bourke and I. McBride (eds.), *The Princeton History of Modern Ireland* (Princeton, NJ: Princeton University Press, 2016).

Mulholland, M., *The Longest War* (Oxford University Press, 2002).

Murphy, G., *In search of the Promised Land: The Politics of Post-War Ireland* (Cork and Dublin: Mercier Press, 2009).

Nevin, D., (ed.), *Trade Union Century* (Cork and Dublin: Mercier Press, 1994).

Nic Pháidín, C. and S. Ó Cearnaigh, (eds.), *A New View of the Irish Language* (Dublin: Cois Life, 2008).

Ó Cuív, B., (ed.), *A View of the Irish Language* (Dublin: Government Stationery Office, 1969).

Ó Doibhlin, D., (eag.) *Duanaire Gaedhilge Róis Ní Ógáin* (Dublin: An Clóchomhar, 1995).

Ó Gráda, C., *Ireland. A New Economic History 1780–1939* (Oxford University Press, 1994).

O'Brien, C., (ed.), *The Shaping of Modern Ireland* (London: Routledge & Kegan Paul, 1960).

O'Connor, E., *Syndicalism in Ireland, 1917–23* (Cork: Cork University Press, 1988).

  A Labour History of Ireland, 1824–2000 (2nd edn., Dublin, UCD Press, 2011).

O'Dowd, M., and V. Valiulis (eds.), *Women and Irish History: Essays in Honour of Margaret McCurtain* (Dublin: Wolfhound Press, 1997).

Owens, R. C., *A Social History of Women in Ireland* (Dublin: Gill & Macmillan, 2005).

Pašeta, S., *Before the Revolution: Nationalism, Social Change and Ireland's Catholic Elite, 1879–1922* (Cork: Cork University Press, 1999).

Patterson, H., *Class Conflict and Sectarianism: The Protestant Working-class and the Belfast Labour Movement, 1868–1920* (Belfast: Blackstaff Press, 1980).

Phoenix, E., *Northern Nationalism: Nationalist Politics, Partition and the Catholic Minority in Northern Ireland 1890–1940* (Belfast: Ulster Historical Foundation, 1994).

Prager, J., *Building Democracy in Ireland. Political order and cultural integration in a newly independent nation* (Cambridge University Press, 1986).

Puirséil, N., *The Irish Labour Party 1922–73* (Dublin: UCD Press, 2007).

Rouse, P., *Sport and Ireland: A History* (Oxford University Press, 2015).

Savage, R., *A Loss of Innocence? Television and Irish Society* (Manchester: Manchester University Press, 2010).

Skelly, J., *Irish Diplomacy at the United Nations 1945–1965: National Interests and the International Order* (Dublin: Irish Academic Press, 1997).

Stanford, W. B., *Faith and Faction in Ireland Now* (Dublin and Belfast: APCK, 1946).

Townshend, C., *The Republic. The Fight for Irish Independence, 1918–1923* (London: Allen Lane, 2013).

  Easter 1916: The Irish Rebellion (London: Allen Lane, 2005).

Walker, B. M., *Ulster Politics: The Formative Years, 1868–1886* (Belfast: Ulster Historical Foundation, 1989).

Whelan, B., *Ireland and the Marshall Plan 1947–1957* (Dublin: Four Courts Press, 2000).

White, J., *Minority Report: The Protestant Community in the Republic of Ireland* (Dublin: Gill & Macmillan, 1975).

White, R. W., *Ruairí Ó Brádaigh: The Life and Politics of an Irish Revolutionary* (Indianapolis, IN: University of Indiana Press, 2006).

Whyte, J. H., *Church and State in Modern Ireland 1923–1971* (Dublin: Gill & Macmillan, 1971).

Wohl, R., *The Generation of 1914* (Cambridge, MA: Harvard University Press, 1979).

1 Radical Nationalisms, 1882–1916

Matthew Kelly

Primary, including printed primary sources

Daly Papers, University of Limerick.

Colonial Office papers: CO 904/12, August 1912; CO 904/88.

CO 904/12, November 1910, TNA

Irish Freedom 1911–14

McGarrity Papers, McCartan to McGarrity, 4 September 1910, 6 January 1911, Ms 17457/8–9, National Library of Ireland

Yeats, W. B., *The Poems* (London: Macmillan, 1994).

Secondary works

Arrington, L., 'Socialist Republican Discourse and the 1916 Easter Rising: The Occupation of Jacob's Biscuit Factory and the South Dublin Union Explained', *Journal of British Studies*, 53 (2014), 992–1010.

Brasted, H., 'Indian Nationalist Development and the Influence of Irish Home Rule, 1870–1886', *Modern Asian Studies*, xiv (1980), 37–63.

Bull, P., 'A Fatal Disjuncture, 1898–1905: Sinn Féin and the United Irish League', in R. Phelan (ed.), *Irish-Australian Studies: Papers of the Seventh Irish-Australian Conference* (Sydney, 1994), 37–51.

Callanan, F., *The Parnell Split, 1890–91* (Cork: Cork University Press, 1992).

Cronin, M., 'Parnellism and Workers: The Experience of Cork and Limerick', in F. Lane and D. Ó Drisceoil, *Politics and the Irish Working Class, 1830–1945* (Basingstoke: Palgrave Macmillan, 2005).

Crossman, V., *Local Government in Nineteenth-Century Ireland* (Belfast: Institute of Irish Studies, 1994).

Curtis, K., *P. S. O'Hegarty (1879–1955): Sinn Féin Fenian* (London: Anthem Press, 2010).

Flanagan, F., *Remembering the Revolution. Dissent, Culture and Nationalism in the Irish Free State* (Oxford University Press, 2015).

Foster, R. F., *Modern Ireland 1600–1972* (London: Allen Lane, 1988).

Vivid Faces. The Revolutionary Generation in Ireland (London: Allen Lane, 2014).

Gailey, A., *The Death of Kindness: The Experience of Constructive Unionism, 1890–1905* (Cork: Cork University Press, 1987).

Gantt, J., *Irish Terrorism in the Atlantic Community, 1865–1922* (Basingstoke: Palgrave Macmillan, 2010).

Gladstone, W. E. G., *Special Aspects of the Irish Question* (London: J. Murray, 1892).

Glandon, V., *Arthur Griffith and the Advanced Nationalist Press, 1900–1922* (Bern: Peter Lang, 1985).

Greaves, C. D., *The Life and Times of James Connolly* (London: Lawrence and Wishart, 1961).

Kelly, M., 'The Irish Volunteers: A Machiavellian Moment?', in C. G. Boyce and A. O'Day (eds.), *The Ulster Crisis 1885–1921* (Basingstoke: Palgrave Macmillan, 2006).

The Fenian Ideal and Irish Nationalism, 1882–1916 (Woodbridge: Boydell Press, 2006).

'The *Irish People* and the Disciplining of Dissent', in J. McConnel and F. McGarry (eds.), *The Black Hand of Irish Republicanism* (Dublin: Irish Academic Press, 2009).

'Irish Nationalism', in D. Craig and J. Thompson (eds.), *Languages of Politics in Nineteenth-Century Britain* (Basingstoke: Palgrave Macmillan, 2013).

'Irish Nationalist Opinion and the British Empire in the 1850s and 1860s', *Past & Present*, 204 (August 2009), 127–54.

Lane, L., *The Origins of Modern Irish Socialism* (Cork: Cork University Press, 1997).

Lyons, F. S. L., *Charles Stewart Parnell* (Glasgow: William Collins, 1977).

Culture and Anarchy in Ireland 1890–1939 (Oxford University Press, 1979).

Marley, L., *Michael Davitt: Freelance Radical and Frondeur* (Dublin: Four Courts Press, 2007).

Marx, K., *Later Political Writings* (Cambridge University Press, 1996).

Mathews, P. J., *Revival. The Abbey Theatre, the Gaelic League and the Co-operative Movement* (Cork: Cork University Press, 2003).

Matthew, H. C. G., *Gladstone 1809–1898* (Oxford University Press, 1997).

McConnel, J., *The Irish Parliamentary Party and the Third Home Rule Bill Crisis* (Dublin: Four Courts Press, 2013).

'John Redmond and Irish Catholic Loyalism', *English Historical Review*, CXXV (February 2010), 83–111.

McCracken, D. P., *The Irish pro-Boers, 1877–1902* (Johannesburg: Preskor, 1989).

McGee, E., '"God Save Ireland": Manchester Martyrs Demonstrations in Dublin, 1867–1916', *Éire-Ireland*, 36, (Fall–Winter 2001), 39–66.

O'Callaghan, M., *British High Politics and a Nationalist Ireland. Criminality, Land and Law under Forster and Balfour* (Dublin: Irish Academic Press, 1994).

O'Hegarty, P. S., *The Victory of Sinn Féin* (Dublin: Talbot Press, 1924).

O'Keefe, T. J., 'The 1898 Efforts to Celebrate the United Irishmen: The '98 Centennial', *Éire-Ireland*, 28 (1992), 51–73.

Parfitt, R., '"Oh, What Matter, When for Erin Dear We Fall?": Music and Irish Nationalism, 1848–1913', *Irish Studies Review*, 23 (2015), 480–94.

Pašeta, S., *Irish Nationalist Women, 1900–1918* (Cambridge University Press, 2013).

'Nationalist Responses to Two Royal Visits to Ireland, 1900 and 1903', *Irish Historical Studies*, xxxi (November 1999).

Regan-Lefebvre, J., *Cosmopolitan Nationalism and the Victorian Empire. Ireland, India and the Politics of Alfred Webb* (Basingstoke: Palgrave Macmillan, 2009).

Rooney, W., 'Recent Irish Literature', *Prose Writings* (Dublin, 1909).

Steele, K., *Women, Press and Politics during the Irish Revival* (Syracuse: Syracuse University Press, 2007).

'Constance Markievicz's Allegorical Garden: Feminism, Militancy, and the Press, 1909–1915', *Communication Abstracts*, 24 (2001), 195–296.

Townend, P., 'Between Two Worlds: Irish Nationalists and Imperial Crisis, 1878–1880', *Past & Present*, 194 (February 2007), 139–74.

Townshend, C., *Easter 1916* (London: Allen Lane, 2005).

Urquhart, D., *Women in Ulster Politics 1890–1940* (Dublin: Irish Academic Press, 2000).

Wheatley, M., *Nationalism and the Irish Party. Provincial Ireland 1910–1916* (Oxford University Press, 2005).

Whelehan, N., *The Dynamiters: Irish Nationalism and Political Violence in the Wider World, 1867–1900* (Cambridge University Press, 2012).

2 Home Rulers at Westminster, 1880–1914

Conor Mulvagh

Primary sources

Dublin

National Library of Ireland

James Bryce, Memorandum of meeting with Henry Campbell Bannerman, 9 Dec. 1905, MS 11,011

Redmond-Kettle correspondence, Redmond papers, MS 15,199/6, NLI.

Trinity College Archives

John Dillon to T.P. O'Connor, 27 Nov. 1913, MS 6740/213: TCD archives.

UCD archives

'A memoir by Eoin MacNeill, c. 1932/3', Eoin MacNeill papers, IE LA1/G/372

Healy papers, IE P6/A/24/45

Redmond-Kettle correspondence, IE LA35/135

London

British Library

Gladstone – Katharine O'Shea correspondence, 1882–88 Add. MS 44,269

Add. MS 44,771, ff 1–2: BL.

Printed primary sources

[Anon.], *The Repeal of the Union Conspiracy, or Mr Parnell, M.P., and the I.R.B.* (London: William Ridgway, 1886).

Birrell, A., *Things Past Redress* (London: Faber and Faber, 1937).

Brock, M. and E. (eds.) *H. H. Asquith, Letters to Venetia Stanley* (Oxford University Press, 1982).

Churchill, W. S., *The World Crisis, 1911–1918, Vol. I* (London: Odhams, 1938).

Cooper, B., *The Tenth (Irish) Division in Gallipoli* (London: H. Jenkins, 1918).

Healy, T. M., *Leaders and letters of my day* (2 vols, London: Frederick A. Stokes, 1928).

Hocking, J., *Is Home Rule Rome rule?* (London: Ward Lock and Co., 1912).

O'Brien, W., *An Olive Branch in Ireland and its history* (London: Macmillan, 1910).

O'Connor, T., *The Parnell Movement: Being a History of the Irish Question from the Death of O'Connell to the Suicide of Pigott* (London: K. Paul Trench and Co., 1889).

O'Shea, K. (Mrs C. S. Parnell), *Charles Stewart Parnell; His Love Story and Political Life*, 2 vols. (New York: G. H. Dovan, 1914).

Parnell, A., *The Tale of a Great Sham* (ed. Dana Hearne) (Dublin, 1986).

Wemyss Reid, T., *Life of the Right Honourable William Edward Forster,* 2 vols. (London: Chapman and Hall, 1888).

Secondary works

Bew, P., *Conflict and Conciliation in Ireland, 1890–1910: Parnellites and Radical Agrarians* (Oxford University Press, 1987).

   Enigma: A New Life of Charles Stewart Parnell (Dublin: Gill & Macmillan, 2011).

Craig, F. W. S., *British Electoral Facts, 1832–1987* (5th edn., Aldershot: Palgrave Macmillan, 1989).

Fanning, R., *Fatal Path: British Government and Irish Revolution, 1910–1922* (London: Faber and Faber, 2013).

Ferriter, D., *A Nation and Not a Rabble: The Irish Revolution, 1913–1923* (London: Profile, 2015).

Foster, R. F., *Vivid Faces: The Revolutionary Generation in Ireland, 1890–1923* (London: Allen Lane, 2014).

Garvin, J. L., *The Life of Joseph Chamberlain, volume II, 1885–1895: Disruption and Combat* (London: Macmillan, 1933).

Jackson, A., *Ireland, 1798–1998: Politics and War* (Oxford: Blackwell, 1999).

   Home Rule: An Irish History, 1800–2000 (Oxford University Press, 2003).

Jackson, D. M., *Popular Opposition to Irish Home Rule in Edwardian Britain* (Liverpool: Liverpool University Press, 2009).

James, R. R., *Rosebery: A Biography of Archibald Philip, Fifth Earl of Rosebery* (London: Weidenfeld and Nicolson, 1963).

Jenkins, R., *Gladstone: A Biography* (New York: Random House, 1995), 526–31.

Keyes, M., *Funding the Nation: Money and Nationalist Politics in Nineteenth Century Ireland* (Dublin: Gill & Macmillan, 2011).

King, C., 'The Recess Committee, 1895–6', *Studia Hibernica*, 30 (1998/1999), 21–46.

Lyons, F. S. L., *The Irish Parliamentary Party, 1890–1910* (London: Faber & Faber, 1951).

   John Dillon: a biography (London: Routledge and K. Paul, 1968).

   Charles Stewart Parnell (London: Collins, 1977).

   'John Dillon and the Plan of Campaign, 1886–90', *Irish Historical Studies*, xiv, 56 (September, 1965), 313.

Lyons, J. B., 'Charles Stewart Parnell and his Doctors', in D. McCartney (ed.), *Parnell: The Politics of Power* (Dublin: Wolfhound Press, 1991).

Matthew, H. G., *Gladstone, 1875–1898* (Oxford University Press, 1995).

Maume, P., 'MacDonnell, Antony Patrick', in J. McGuire and J. Quinn (eds.), *Dictionary of Irish Biography*, 9 vols. (Cambridge University Press, 2009).

McCartney, D., 'Parnell's Manifesto "To the People of Ireland", 29 November 1890', in P. Travers and D. McCartney (eds.), *Parnell Reconsidered* (Dublin: UCD Press, 2013), 197–203.

O'Brien, C. C., *Parnell and his Party, 1880–1890* (Oxford University Press, 1957).

O'Brien, J. V., *William O'Brien and the Course of Irish Politics, 1881–1918* (Berkeley, CA: University of California Press, 1976).

O'Callaghan, M., *British High Politics and a Nationalist Ireland: Criminality, Land and the Law under Forster and Balfour* (Cork: Cork University Press, 1994).

O'Rahilly, A., *Winding the Clock: O'Rahilly and the 1916 Rising* (Dublin: Lilliput Press, 1991).

Thornley, D., *Isaac Butt and Home Rule* (London: MacKibbon and Kee, 1964).

Wheatley, M., *Nationalism and the Irish Party, Provincial Ireland 1910–1916* (Oxford University Press, 2005).

3 The Origins, Politics and Culture of Irish Unionism, *c.*1880–1916

Alvin Jackson

Primary sources

London

British Library
Balfour Papers, Add.Ms. 49773, 49830, 49849

Belfast

William Johnston Diary, Public Record Office of Northern Ireland D.989.

Printed secondary sources

Armour, W. S., *Armour of Ballymoney* (London: Duckworth, 1934).

  Facing the Irish Question (London: Duckworth, 1935).

  Ulster, Ireland, Britain: A Forgotten Trust (London: Duckworth, 1938).

Baldwin, S., *This Torch of Freedom: Speeches and Addresses* (London: Books for Libraries Press, 1935).

Beerbohm, M., *Fifty Caricatures* (London: William Heinemann, 1913).

Bullock, S., *Thomas Andrews: Shipbuilder* (Dublin: Maunsell, 1912).

Dodds, E. R., *Missing Persons: An Autobiography* (Oxford: 1977).

Ewald, A. C., *The Life of Sir Joseph Napier, Bart., Ex-Lord Chancellor of Ireland, From His Correspondence* (London: Longmans Green, 1887).

Falls, C., *The History of the Thirty Sixth (Ulster) Division* (Belfast: McCaw, Stevenson and Orr, 1922).

Fisher, J. R., *The End of the Irish Parliament* (London: E. Arnold, 1911).

Johnston, W., *Nightshade: A Novel* (London: Richard Bentley, 1857).

MacKnight, T., *Ulster as it is* (London: Macmillan, 1896).

Marsh, C., *Brief Memories of Hugh McCalmont, First Earl Cairns* (London: James Nisbet, 1885).

Monypenny, W. F., *The Two Irish Nations: An Essay on Irish Home Rule* (London: John Murray, 1913).

Porter, J., *Life and Times of Henry Cooke DD, LLD* (London: John Murray, 1875 edition).

Smith, C. F., *James Nicholson Richardson of Bessbrook* (London: Longmans Green, 1925).

Waddell, H., *John Waddell* (Belfast: Belfast Newsletter, 1949).

Whiteside, J., *Essays and Lectures: Historical and Literary* (Dublin: Hodges, Smith and Foster, 1868).

  Early Sketches of Eminent Persons (Dublin: Hodges, Smith and Foster, 1870).

Young, R., The 'Fermanagh True Blue', *The Orange Minstrel or Ulster Melodist: consisting of Historical Songs and Poems* (Londonderry: privately printed 1832).

Secondary works

Bell, P. M. H., *Disestablishment in Ireland and Wales* (London: S.P.C.K., 1969).

Bew, J., *The Glory of being Britons: Civic Unionism in Nineteenth Century Belfast* (Dublin: Four Courts Press, 2008).

Biggs-Davison, J., and Chowdharay-Best, G., *The Cross of Saint Patrick: The Catholic Unionist Tradition in Ireland* (Bourne End: Kensal Press, 1984).

Blackstock, A., *Loyalism in Ireland, 1789–1829* (London: Boydell Press, 2007).

Bowen, D., *The Protestant Crusade in Ireland, 1800–1870: A Study of Protestant-Catholic Relations between the Act of Union and Disestablishment* (Dublin: Gill & Macmillan, 1978).

Bowman, T., *Carson's Army: The Ulster Volunteer Force, 1910–22* (Manchester: Manchester University Press, 2008).

Buckland, P., *Irish Unionism I: The Anglo-Irish and the New Ireland, 1885–1922* (Dublin: Gill & Macmillan, 1972).

Irish Unionism II: Ulster Unionism and the Origins of Northern Ireland, 1886–1922 (Dublin: Gill & Macmillan, 1973).

Colley, L., *Britons: Forging the Nation, 1707–1837* (New Haven: Yale University Press, 1992).

Connolly, C., 'Completing the Union: The Irish Novel and the Moment of Union', in M. Brown, P. Geoghegan, and J. Kelly (eds.), *The Irish Act of Union, 1800: Bicentennial Essays* (Dublin: Four Courts Press, 2003).

Connolly, C., *A Cultural History of the Irish Novel, 1790–1829* (Cambridge University Press, 2011).

Corbett, M. J., *Allegories of Union in Irish and English Writing* (Cambridge University Press, 2000).

D'Alton, I., *Protestant Society and Politics in Cork, 1812–44* (Cork: Cork University Press, 1980).

Dibble, J., *Charles Villiers Stanford: Man and Musician* (Oxford University Press, 2002).

Fitzpatrick, D., *'Solitary and Wild': Frederick MacNeice and the Salvation of Ireland* (Dublin: Four Courts Press, 2011).

Foster, J. W., *Forces and Themes in Ulster Fiction* (New Jersey: Rowman and Littlefield, 1974).

Foster, R. F. and Jackson, A., 'Parnell and Carson', in *European History Quarterly*, 39, 3 (July 2009).

Gibbon, P., *The Origins of Ulster Unionism: The Formation of Popular Protestant Politics and Ideology in Nineteenth Century Ireland* (Manchester: Manchester University Press, 1975).

Hempton, D., and Hill, M., *Evangelical Protestantism in Ulster Society, 1740–1890* (London: Routledge, 1992).

Hill, J. R., 'Ireland without Union: Molyneux and his Legacy', in Robertson, J., (ed.), *A Union for Empire: Political Thought and the Union of 1707* (Cambridge University Press, 1995).

From Patriots to Unionists: Dublin Civic Politics and Irish Protestant Patriotism, 1660–1840 (Oxford University Press, 1997).

Holmes, F., *Henry Cooke* (Belfast: Christian Journals Limited, 1981).

Hoppen, K. T., *Elections, Politics and Society in Ireland, 1832–1885* (Oxford University Press, 1984).

Hughes, K., *The Scots in Victorian and Edwardian Belfast: A Study in Elite Migration* (Edinburgh: Edinburgh University Press, 2013).

Hutchison, I. A. G., *A Political History of Scotland* (Edinburgh: John Donald, 2003).

Jackson, A., *The Ulster Party: Irish Unionists in the House of Commons, 1884–1911* (Oxford University Press, 1989).

    Home Rule: An Irish History, 1800–2000, paperback edition (London: Phoenix, 2004).

    Two Unions: Ireland, Scotland and the Survival of the United Kingdom, 1707–2007 (Oxford University Press, 2012).

    'Unionist Politics and Protestant Society in Edwardian Ireland', *Historical Journal*, xxxiii, 4 (1990).

    'Unionist Myths, 1912–85', *Past & Present*, 136 (August 1992).

Jackson, D., *Popular Opposition to Irish Home Rule in Edwardian Britain* (Liverpool: Liverpool University Press, 2009).

Kanter, D., *The Making of British Unionism, 1740–1848: Politics, Government and the Anglo-Irish Constitutional Relationship* (Dublin: Four Courts Press, 2009).

Kidd, C., *Union and Unionism: Political Thought in Scotland, 1500–2000* (Cambridge University Press, 2008).

Leersen, J., *Remembrance and Imagination: Patterns in the Literary and Historical Representation of Ireland in the Nineteenth Century* (Cork: Cork University Press, 1996).

MacCormack, W. J., *The Pamphlet Debate on the Union between Great Britain and Ireland, 1797–1800* (Dublin: Four Courts Press, 1995).

Maguire, M., 'The Organisation and Activism of Dublin's Protestant Working Class, 1883–1935', *Irish Historical Studies*, xxix, (1994), 65–87.

McBride, I., *The Siege of Derry in Ulster Protestant Mythology* (Dublin: Four Courts Press, 1997).

McClelland, A., *William Johnston of Ballykilbeg* (Belfast: Ulster Society, 1990).

McHugh, D., 'Family, Leisure and the Arts: Aspects of the Culture of the Aristocracy in Ulster, 1870–1925', PhD thesis (University of Edinburgh, 2011).

McMinn, J. R. B., *Against the Tide: J. B. Armour, Irish Presbyterian Minister and Home Ruler* (Belfast: Ulster Historical Foundation, 1985).

Pole, A., 'Landlord Responses to the Irish Land War, 1879–82', PhD thesis (Trinity College, University of Dublin, 2006).

Raponi, D., 'British Protestants, the Roman Question, and the Formation of Italian National Identity, 1861–75', PhD thesis (University of Cambridge, 2009).

Savage, D. C., 'The Irish Unionists, 1867–86', *Eire-Ireland*, 2 (1967).

Shields, A., *The Irish Conservative Party, 1852–1868: Land, Politics and Religion* (Dublin: Irish Academic Press, 2006).

Thompson, F., *The End of Liberal Ulster: Land Agitation and Land Reform, 1868–86* (Belfast: Ulster Historical Society, 2001).

Urquhart, D., *The Ladies of Londonderry: Women and Political Patronage* (London: I. B. Tauris, 2007).

Walker, B. M., *Ulster Politics: The Formative Years, 1868–1886* (Belfast: Ulster Historical Foundation, 1989).

Whelan, I., *The Bible War in Ireland: The 'Second Reformation' and the Polarisation of Protestant-Catholic Relations, 1800–40* (Madison, WI: University of Wisconsin Press, 2005).

Wright, J. J., '"The Perverted Graduates of Oxford": Priestcraft, "Political Popery", and the Transnational Anti-Catholicism of Sir James Emerson Tennent', in Whelehan, N., (ed.), *Transnational Perspectives on Modern Irish History* (London: Routledge, 2015), 127–48.

4 Irish Land Questions, 1879–1923

Terence Dooley

Manuscripts

Dublin

National Archives

Financial agreements between the Irish Free State government and the British government, 12 February 1923 Dept of Taoiseach files, S3459

Bureau of Military History: Witness statement of Sean McNamara, WS 1072: www.bureauofmilitaryhistory.ie/reels/bmh/BMH.WS1072.pdf#page=8.

UCD Archives

Blythe papers, P24/174: P. Hogan, 'Report on the Land Purchase and Arrears Conference of 10–11 April 1923', 17 April 1923

Monaghan Museum

'A short sketch of the life of Thomas Toal' (Unpublished MS, Monaghan County Museum)

Minutes of Monaghan County Council, 7 January 1917: Monaghan County Museum.

London

The National Archives

Inspector General's monthly report, January 1918: CO 904

Police reports 1919–21, CO 904 series, part iv

Primary printed sources

Dáil Debates

Dundalk Democrat

Freeman's Journal

Irish Times

An Irish Priest [Father Thomas Conefrey], *A short history of the land war in Drumlish in 1881* (Dublin: James Duffy and Co., 1892).

Childers, E., *The Constructive Work of Dáil Eireann* (Dublin: Talbot Press, 1921).

Griffith, A., *Economic Salvation and the Means to Attain It* (Dublin: Whelan, n.d.).

Healy, T. M., 'Review' of Pomfret, *The struggle for Land*, in *Studies*, 19, (December 1930).

MacFhionnghail, L., [Laurence Ginnell], *The Land Question* (Dublin: James Duffy and Co., n.d. [1917]).

O'Brien, W., *An Olive Branch in Ireland and its History* (London: Macmillan, 1910).

Report of the Estates Commissioners for the Year from 1 April 1920 to 31 March 1921.

Royal Commission on Congestion in Ireland, [Cd 4007], HC 1908, xliii, 178.

Seanad Debates.

Wyndham-Quin, W. T., Earl of Dunraven, *The Crisis in Ireland, an Account of the Present Condition of Ireland and Suggestions towards Reform* (Dublin: Hodges Figgis, 1905).

Secondary printed works

Augusteijn, J., *From Public Defiance to Guerrilla Warfare: The Experience of Ordinary Volunteers in the Irish War of Independence, 1916–21* (Dublin: Irish Academic Press, 1996).

Bew, P., *Ireland: The Politics of Enmity 1789–2006* (Oxford University Press, 2007).

'Sinn Féin, Agrarian Radicalism and the War of Independence', in D.G. Boyce (ed.), *The Revolution in Ireland, 1879–1923* (Dublin: Gill & Macmillan, 1988), 217–35.

Bull, P., *Land, Politics and Nationalism: A Study of the Irish Land Question* (Dublin: Gill & Macmillan, 1996).

'The Significance of the Nationalist Response to the Irish Land Act of 1903', *Irish Historical Studies*, 26 (May, 1993), 283–305.

'The Formation of the United Irish League, 1898–1900: The Dynamics of Irish Agrarian Agitation', *Irish Historical Studies*, 33 (November 2003), 404–23.

Campbell, F., 'Irish Politics and the Making of the Wyndham Land Act, 1901–03', *The Historical Journal*, 45, (December 2002), 755–73.

Clark, G., *Everyday Violence in the Irish Civil War* (Cambridge University Press, 2014), 36–44.

Coffey, L. A., *The Planters of Luggacurran, Co. Laois: A Protestant Community, 1879–1927* (Dublin: Four Courts Press, 2006).

Comerford, R. V., 'The Land War and the Politics of Distress, 1877–82', in W. E. Vaughan (ed.), *A New History Of Ireland VI: Ireland under the Union II, 1870–1921* (Oxford University Press, 1996), 26–52.

Cosgrove, P., 'Irish Landlords and the Wyndham Act', in T. Dooley and C. Ridgway (eds.), *The Irish Country House: Its Past, Present and Future* (Dublin: Four Courts Press, 2011).

Cronin, M., *Agrarian Protest in Ireland, 1750–1960* (Dublin: Studies in Irish Social and Economic History, 2011).

Curtis, L. P., 'Ireland in 1914', in W. E. Vaughan (ed.), *Ireland under the Union*.

'Landlord Responses to the Irish Land War, 1879–87', *Éire-Ireland*, Fall/Winter (2003), 134–88.

Davies, J. C., 'Towards a Theory of Revolution', *American Sociological Review*, 27 (1962), 5–19.

Donnelly Jr, J. S., 'Big House Burnings in County Cork during the Irish Revolution, 1920–21', *Eire-Ireland*, 47 (Fall/Winter 2012), 141–97.

Donnelly, J. S., *The Land and the People of Nineteenth-century Cork* (London: Routledge and Kegan Paul, 1975).

Dooley, T., *The Decline of the Big House in Ireland* (Dublin: Wolfhound Press, 2001).

'The Land for the people': The Land Question in Independent Ireland (Dublin: UCD Press, 2007).

The Decline and Fall of the Dukes of Leinster, 1872–1948 (Dublin: Four Courts Press, 2014).

'Land and Politics in Independent Ireland: The Case for Reappraisal', *Irish Historical Studies*, xxxiv (November 2004), 175–97.

Dooley, T., and McCarthy, T., 'The 1923 Land Act: Some New Perspectives', in M. Farrell, J. Knirck and C. Meehan (eds.), *The 1920s: Ireland's Formative Decade* (Dublin: Irish Academic Press, 2015), 150.

Drumlish Land War Centenary 1881–1981 Commemorative Booklet (Drumlish: County Longford, 1991).

Geary, L. M., *The Plan of Campaign* (Cork: Cork University Press, 1986).

Gribbon, H. D., 'Economic and Social History, 1850–1921' in W. E. Vaughan (ed.), *A New History Of Ireland, Vol. vi, Ireland under the Union Part 2, 1870–1921* (Oxford University Press, 1996).

Hart, P., *The IRA and its Enemies: Violence and Community in Cork, 1916–23* (Oxford University Press, 1998).

Hopkinson, M., *Green against Green: The Irish Civil War* (Dublin: Gill & Macmillan, 1988), 45.

Jackson, A., *Col. Edward Saunderson: Land and Loyalty in Victorian Ireland* (Oxford University Press, 1995).

Home Rule: An Irish History 1800–2000 (Oxford University Press, 2003).

Jordan, D., *Land and Popular Politics in Ireland: County Mayo from the Plantation to the Land War* (Cambridge University Press, 1994).

Kennedy, E., *The Land Movement In Tullaroan, County Kilkenny, 1879–1891* (Dublin: Four Courts Press, 2004).

Kolbert, C. F., and O'Brien, T., *Land Reform in Ireland: A Legal History of the Irish Land Problem and its Settlement* (Cambridge University Press, 1975).

Lane, F., 'Rural Labourers, Social Change and Politics in Late Nineteenth-century Ireland', in F. Lane and D. Ó Drisceoil (eds.), *Politics and the Irish Working Class, 1830–1945* (Basingstoke: Palgrave Macmillan, 2005), 113–39.

Lucey, D. S., *Land, Popular Politics and Agrarian Violence in Ireland: The Case of County Kerry, 1872–86* (Dublin: UCD Press, 2011).

Lyons, F. S. L., 'The Aftermath of Parnell, 1891–1903', in W. E. Vaughan (ed.), *A New History Of Ireland, Vol. vi, Ireland under the Union Part 2, 1870–1921* (Oxford University Press, 1996).

Maguire, W. A., *The Downshire Estates in Ireland 1801–1845: The Management of Irish Landed Estates in the Nineteenth Century* (Oxford University Press, 1972).

Moran, G., 'Matthew Harris, Fenianism and Land Agitation in the West of Ireland', in F. Campbell, and T. Varley (eds.), *Land Questions in Modern Ireland* (Manchester: Manchester University Press, 2013), 218–37.

Ó Gráda, C., *Ireland: A New Economic History, 1780–1939* (Oxford University Press, 1995).

'The Investment Behaviour of Irish Landlords 1850–75: Some Preliminary Findings', *Agricultural History Review*, 23 (1975), 139–55.

Ó Tuathaigh, G., 'Irish land questions', in F. Campbell, and T. Varley, (eds.), *Land Questions in Modern Ireland* (Manchester: Manchester University Press, 2013).

O'Riordan, A., *East Galway Agrarian Agitation and the Burning of Ballydugan House, 1922* (Dublin: Four Courts Press, 2015).

Pomfret, J. E., *The Struggle for Land in Ireland, 1800–1923* (Princeton, NJ: Princeton University Press, 1930).

Purdue, O., *The Big House in the North of Ireland: Land, Power and Social Elites, 1878–1960* (Dublin: UCD Press, 2009).

Regan, J., *The Irish Counter-revolution 1921–1936: Treatyite Politics and Settlement in Independent Ireland* (Dublin: Gill & Macmillan, 1999).

Reilly, C., *The Irish Land Agent 1830–1860: The Case of King's County* (Dublin: Four Courts Press, 2014).

Strokestown and the Great Irish Famine (Dublin: Four Courts Press, 2014).

Reilly, C. J., 'The Burning of Country Houses in Co. Offaly during the Revolutionary Period, 1920–3', in T. Dooley and C. Ridgway (eds.), *The Irish Country House: Its Past, Present and Future* (Dublin: Four Courts Press, 2011), 110–33.

Solow, B. L., *The Land Question and the Irish Economy, 1870–1903* (Cambridge, MA: Harvard University Press, 1971).

Tebrake, J., 'Irish Peasant Women in Revolt: The Land League Years', *Irish Historical Studies*, 28 (1992), 63–80.

Tynan, E. P., 'War Veterans, Land Distribution and Revolution in Ireland 1919–1923' (unpublished PhD thesis, NUI Maynooth 2012).

Vaughan, W. E., *Landlords and Tenants in mid-Victorian Ireland* (Oxford University Press, 1994).

5 Social Conditions in Ireland 1880–1914

Caitriona Clear

Printed Primary Sources

Newspapers

Anglo-Celt
Belfast Newsletter
Cork Examiner
Derry People & Donegal News
Dundalk Democrat
Fermanagh Herald
Freeman's Journal
Kerry Sentinel
Leitrim Observer
Limerick Leader
Longford Leader
Munster Express
Nenagh Guardian
Western People
Westmeath Examiner

Government Publications

22nd Detailed Annual Report of the Registrar-General for Ireland 1885 (Dublin, 1886), 9–15
28th Detailed Annual Report of the Registrar-General for Ireland 1891 (Dublin, 1892)
31st Detailed.......1894 (1895)
37th Detailed......1900 (1901)
47th Detailed......1910 (1911)
51st Detailed......1914 (1915)
Census of Ireland 1881, General Report 19–25, and Table 18, 108–9; and county breakdown Vols I–IV
Census of Ireland 1891: General Report, tables of sickness in Poor Law Superintendent Registrars' Districts 1891
Census of Ireland 1901, General Report, 22–28 and Table 19, 115–16; county breakdown, Vol I–IV
Census of Ireland 1911 General Report
Available at: www//histpop.org/ohpr/servlet.

Secondary Works

Beckett, J. C. (ed.), *Belfast: The Making of the City* (Belfast: Appletree Press, 1983).

Bielenberg, A., *Cork's Industrial Revolution 1780–1870: Development or Decline?* (Cork: Cork University Press, 1991).

Bourke, J., *Husbandry to Housewifery: Women, Housework and Economic Change 1890–1914* (Oxford University Press, 1993).

'The Health Caravan: Domestic Education and Female Labour in Rural Ireland', *Eire-Ireland* 24 (1989), 21–38.

Bradley, M., *Farm Labourers: Irish Struggle 1900–1976* (Belfast: Athol Publications, 1996).

Carbery, M., *The Farm by Lough Gur* (London 1937: new edition, Cork: Mercier Press, 1973).

Carroll, L., *In the Fever King's Preserves: Sir Charles Cameron and the Dublin Slums* (Dublin: A. and A. Farmar, 2011).

Chuinneagáin, S., *Catherine Mahon: First Woman President of the INTO* (Dublin: INTO Publications, 1998).

Clarkson, L. and Crawford, E. M., *Feast and Famine: A History of Food and Nutrition in Ireland 1500–1920* (Oxford University Press, 2001).

Clear, C., *Nuns in Nineteenth-century Ireland (*Dublin: Gill & Macmillan, 1987).

*Women of the House: Women's Household Work in Ireland 1922–1961 (*Dublin: Irish Academic Press, 2000).

Social Change and Everyday Life in Ireland 1850–1922 (Manchester: Manchester University Press, 2007).

Colum, M., *Life and the Dream* (London: Macmillan, 1947).

Cox, P., and Hobley, A., *Shopgirls: The True Story of Life behind the Counter* (London: Hutchinson, 2014).

Cullen, L. M., *An Economic History of Ireland since 1660* (London: Batsford, 1972).

Cunningham, J., *Labour in the West of Ireland: Working Life and Struggle 1890–1914 (*Belfast: Athol Publications, 1995).

Czira, S. (née Gifford), *The Years Flew By: Recollections of Sidney Gifford Czira* (Galway: Arlen House, 2000).

Daly, M. E. et al. (eds.), *Dublin's Victorian Houses* (Dublin: A. & A. Farmar, 1998).

de Cléir, S., 'Bhí bród as sin i gcónaí; cruthaitheacht agus cultúr na mban i dtraidisiún fheisteas Oileáin Arainn' *Béascna: iris béaloideasa agus eitneolaíochta* 1 (2002), 85–100.

Dunlevy, M., *Dress in Ireland* (Cork: Cork University Press, 1999).

Dwork, D., *War is Good for Babies and Young Children: A History of the Infant and Child Welfare Movement in England 1891–1918* (London: Tavistock, 1987).

Fahey, T., 'Nuns in the Catholic Church in Ireland in the Nineteenth Century', in M. Cullen (ed.) *Girls Don't Do Honours: Irish women in Education in the 19th and 20th Centuries* (Dublin: Women's Education Bureau, 1987), 7–29.

Fallon, R., *A County Roscommon Wedding 1892: The Marriage of John Hughes and Mary Gavin* (Maynooth: Maynooth Local History Series 2004).

Farmar, T., *Patients, Potions and Physicians: A Social History of Medicine in Ireland* (Dublin: A & A Farmar, 2004).

Fealy, G., (ed.) *Care to Remember: Nursing and Midwifery in Ireland* (Cork: Mercier Press, 2005).

Feehan, J., *Farming in Ireland: History, Heritage and Environment* (Dublin: University College Dublin Press, 2003).

Ferguson, K., *Lessons in Cookery and Housewifery* (Dublin: Leabhairíní na Seamróige, 1900).

Fraser, M., *John Bull's Other Homes: State Housing and British Policy in Ireland 1883–1922* (Liverpool: Liverpool University Press, 1996).

French, P., *Prose, Poems and Parodies of Percy French* (Dublin: Talbot Press, 1973).

Gailey, A., 'Changes in Rural Housing 1600–1900', in P. O'Flanagan et al. (eds.), *Rural Ireland 1600–1900: Modernisation and Change* (Cork: Cork University Press, 1987).

Grace, D., *Portrait of a Parish: Monsea and Killdiernan Co. Tipperary* (Monsea: Relay Press, 1996).

Griffin, B., *Cycling in Victorian Ireland* (Dublin: Nonsuch, 2006).

Healy, J. N., *Percy French and his songs* (Cork: Mercier Press, 1966).

Healy, M., *For the Poor and for the Gentry: Mary Healy Remembers Her Life* (Dublin: Geography Publications, 1989).

Jacobs, D., and Lee, D., (eds.), *Made in Limerick: History of Industries, Trade and Commerce* (Limerick: Limerick Civic Trust, 2003).

Jones, G., *Captain of All These Men of Death: The History of Tuberculosis in Nineteenth and Twentieth-century Ireland* (Amsterdam: Rodopi, 2001).

Jones, M., *The Other Ireland; Changing Times 1870–1920* (Dublin: Gill & Macmillan, 2011).

Kearns, J., *Dublin Tenement Life: An Oral History* (Dublin: Gill & Macmillan, 1995).

Kelly, M., 'Down Memory Lane: The Tea Travellers', *Cathair na Mart: journal of the Westport Historical Society*, 15 (1995), 66–69.

Kennedy, L., and Ollerenshaw, P. (eds.), *An Economic History of Ulster 1820–1939* (Manchester: Manchester University Press, 1985).

Kinmonth, C., *Irish Country Furniture 1700–1950* (New Haven: Yale University Press, 1993).
Irish Rural Interiors in Art (New Haven: Yale University Press, 2006).

Lacy, B., *Siege City: The Story of Derry and Londonderry* (Belfast: Blackstaff Press, 1990).

Lane, F., 'Music and Violence in Nineteenth-century Cork: The "Band Nuisance" 1879–82', *Saothar: journal of the Irish Labour History Society* 24 (1999), 17–31.

Lane, P., 'The Organization of Rural Labourers 1870–1890', *Cork Archaeological & Historical Society Journal,* 10 (1995), 159–60.

Laverty, M., *Never No More: The Story of a Lost Village* (London: Longmans, 1942).

Lee, J. J., 'Railways in the Irish economy', in L. M. Cullen (ed.), *The Formation of the Irish Economy* (Cork: Mercier Press, 1976).

Loudon, I., *Death in Childbirth: An International Study of Maternal Care and Maternal Treatment* (Oxford University Press, 1992).

Magray, M.P., *The Transforming Power of the Nuns: Women, Religion and Cultural Change in Ireland 1750–1900* (Oxford University Press, 1998).

Malcolm, E., and Jones, G., (ed.) *Medicine, Disease and the State in Ireland 1650–1930* (Cork: Cork University Press, 1999).

McCarthy, M. J. F., *Priests and People in Ireland* (London: Hodder & Stoughton, 1902).

McKay, E., 'The Housing of the Rural Labourer 1880–1916', *Saothar: Journal of the Irish Labour History Society,* 17 (1992), 27–39.

Messenger, B., *Picking up the Linen Threads: A Study in Industrial Folklore* (Belfast: Blackstaff, 1980).

Ó Gráda, C., *Ireland: A New Economic History 1780–1939* (Oxford University Press, 1994).

O'Brien, J. V., *Dear, Dirty Dublin: A City in Distress 1890–1914* (Berkeley: University of California, 1982).

O'Flanagan, P., Ferguson, P. and Whelan, K. (eds.) *Rural Ireland 1600–1900: Modernisation and Change* (Cork: Cork University Press, 1987).

Owens, R. C., *Smashing Times: A History of the Irish Women's Suffrage Movement 1889–1922* (Dublin: Attic Press, 1984).

Rains, S., *Commodity Culture and Social Class in Dublin 1850–1916* (Dublin: Irish Academic Press, 2010).

Redington, J., *The Economic Cookery Book* (Dublin: M.H. Gill, 1905).

Robins, J., *The Miasma: Epidemic and Panic in Nineteenth-century Ireland* (Dublin: IPA, 1995). *Nursing and Midwifery in Ireland in the Twentieth Century* (Dublin: Institute of Public Administration, 2000).

Sayers, P., *Peig* (An Daingean: Eagrán An Sagart, 1998).

Scanlan, P., *The Irish Nurse: A Study of Nursing in Ireland 1718–1981* (Leitrim: Drumlin Press, 1991).

Sexton, R., *A Little History of Irish Food* (Dublin: Gill & Macmillan, 1988).

Smithson, A. P., *Myself and Others – and Others* (Dublin: Talbot Press, 1944).

Turner, M., *After the Famine: Irish Agriculture 1850–1914* (Cambridge University Press, 1996).

Urquhart, D., *Women in Ulster Politics 1890–1940* (Dublin: Irish Academic Press, 2000).

Ward, M., *Unmanageable Revolutionaries: Women and Irish Nationalism* (Dingle: Brandon Press, 1982).

6 The Irish Literary Revival

Roy Foster

Primary printed sources

Arnold, M., *On The Study of Celtic Literature and Other Essays* (London: Macmillan, 1910).

Birrell, A., *Things Past Redress* (London: Faber, 1937).

Boyd, E. A. (ed.), *Standish O'Grady: Selected Essays and Passages* (Dublin: Talbot Press, n.d.).

Boyd, E. A., *Ireland's Literary Renaissance* (Dublin: Maunsell, 1916).

Colum, M., *Life and the Dream* (Garden City, NY: Doubleday, 1947).

De Blacam, Aodh, *A First Book of Irish Literature, Hiberno-Latin, Gaelic, Anglo-Irish, From the Earliest Times to the Present Day* (Dublin: Talbot, n.d. [1935?]).

Gregory, Lady A., *Our Irish Theatre* (1913) reprinted in D. Kiberd and P. J. Matthews (eds.), *Handbook of the Irish Revival: An Anthology of Irish Cultural and Political Writings 1891–1922* (Dublin: Abbey Theatre Press, 2015), 158.

Eglinton, John., Yeats, W. B. and Larminie, A. C., *Literary Ideals in Ireland* (London: T. Fisher Unwin, 1899).

Moran, D. P., 'The Battle of Two Civilizations', in *The Philosophy of Irish Ireland* (1905), extracted in Seamus Deane et al., *The Field Day Anthology of Irish Writing* (Derry: Field Day Publications, 1995), II, 554.

Ryan, W. P., *The Irish Literary Revival: Its History, Pioneers and Possibilities* (privately printed, London 1894; reprinted by Lemma Publishing, New York, 1976).

Synge, J. M., 'Le Mouvement Intellectuel Irlandais', in *L'Européen*, 31 May 1902; reprinted (translated by Michael Egan) in D. Kiberd and P. J. Matthews (eds.), *Handbook of the Irish Revival: An Anthology of Irish Cultural and Political Writings 1891–1922* (Dublin: Abbey Theatre Press, 2015), 68–72.

Tynan, K., *The Wandering Years* (London: Constable, 1922).

Yeats, W. B., *Autobiographies* (London: Macmillan, 1955).

'The Poetry and Stories of Miss Nora Hopper', reprinted in J. Eglinton, W. B. Yeats and A. C, Larminie, *Literary Ideals in Ireland* (London: T. Fisher Unwin, 1899).

'Samuel Ferguson', in *Irish Fireside*, 19 October 1886.

Secondary printed sources

Berlin, I., *Russian Thinkers* (London: Allen Lane, 1978).

Brown, T., 'Cultural Nationalism 1880–1930', in S. Deane et al (eds.), *Field Day Anthology*, II, *The Field Day Anthology of Irish Writing* (Derry: Field Day Publications, 1995), 516–59.

Campbell, M., *Irish Poetry under the Union, 1801–1924* (Cambridge University Press, 2013).

Chaudhury, J. M., *Yeats, the Irish Literary Revival and the Politics of Print* (Cork: Cork University Press, 2001).

Connolly, C., *A Cultural History of the Irish Novel, 1790–1829* (Cambridge University Press, 2011).

Cullen, F. and Foster, R. F., (eds.), *Conquering England: Ireland in Victorian London* (London: National Portrait Gallery, 2005).

Deane, S., Introduction to 'Poetry 1890–1930', in Deane, S., et al. (eds.), *The Field Day Anthology of Irish Writing*, II (Derry: Field Day Publications, 1991), 720–23.

Ellmann, R., *Eminent Domain: Yeats among Wilde, Joyce, Pound, Eliot and Auden* (Oxford University Press, 1967).

Ferris, I., *The Romantic National Tale and the Question of Ireland* (Cambridge University Press, 2002).

Foster, J. W., *Irish Novels 1890–1940: New Bearings in Culture and Fiction* (Oxford University Press, 2008).

Fictions of the Irish Revival: A Changeling Art (Syracuse, NY: Syracuse University Press, 1987).

Foster, R. F., 'Thinking from Hand to Mouth: Anglo-Irish literature, Gaelic nationalism and Irish politics in the 1890s', in Foster, R. F., *Paddy and Mr Punch: Connections in Irish and English History* (London: Allen Lane, 1993), 262–80.

W. B. Yeats, A Life: Volume I, The Apprentice Mage 1865–1914 (Oxford University Press, 1997).

'Protestant Magic: W.B. Yeats and the Spell of Irish History', in *Paddy and Mr Punch*, op. cit.

'Yeats at War: Poetic Strategies and Political Reconstruction', in *The Irish Story: Telling Tales and Making it Up in Ireland* (London: Allen Lane, 2001), 58–79.

Vivid Faces: The Revolutionary Generation in Ireland 1890–1923 (London, Allen Lane, 2014).

Frayne, J. P., (ed.), *Uncollected Prose by W. B. Yeats*, vol I (London: Macmillan, 1970).

Garrigan Mattar, S., *Primitivism, Science and the Irish Revival* (Oxford University Press, 2004).

Kelly, M.J., *The Fenian Ideal and Irish Nationalism 1882–1916* (Woodbridge: Boydell Press, 2006).

Kiberd, D., *Inventing Ireland: The Literature of the Modern Nation* (London: Jonathan Cape, 1995).

Kiberd, D., and Matthews, P. J., *Handbook of the Irish Revival* (Dublin: Abbey Theatre, 2015).

Lyons, F. S. L., *Ireland since the Famine* (London: Collins, 1973).

Monk Gibbon, W., *The Living Torch* (London: Macmillan, 1937).

O'Halloran, C., *Golden Ages and Barbarous Nations: Antiquarian Debate and Cultural Politics in Ireland c.1750–1806* (Cork: Cork University Press, 2004).

Steele, K., (ed.), *Maud Gonne, Nationalist Writings 1895–1946* (Dublin: Irish Academic Press, 2004).

Steele, K., *Women, Press and Politics during the Irish Revival* (Syracuse, NY: Syracuse University Press, 2007).

Trumpener, K., *Bardic Nationalism: The Romantic Novel and the British Empire* (Princeton, NJ: Princeton University Press, 1997).

7 The Culture War: The Gaelic League and Irish Ireland

Brian Ó Conchubhair

Printed primary works

'The Irish Industrial and Social Revival', *The Tablet*, 31 October 1908.

Annual Report of the Gaelic League, 1901 (Dublin: Gaelic League, 1901).

Brooks, S., 'The New Ireland: VI. The Gaelic League', *The North American Review*, 188 (1908), 268.

Connolly, J., 'The Language Movement,' *The Workers' Republic*, 1 October 1898.

Secondary works

Anderson, P., *A Zone of Engagement* (London: Verso, 1992).

Augusteijn, J., *Patrick Pearse: The Making of a Revolutionary* (Houndmills: Basingstoke, Palgrave Macmillan, 2010).

Biletz, F. A., 'The Irish Peasant and the Conflict between Irish Ireland and the Catholic Bishops 1903–10', in S. J. Brown and D. W. Miller (eds.), *Piety and Power in Ireland 1760–1960: Essays in Honour of Emmet Larkin*, (Notre Dame, IN: University of Notre Dame Press, 2000).

Biletz, F. A., 'Women and Irish Ireland: The Domestic Nationalism of Mary Butler', *New Hibernia Review*, 6 (2002).

Billings, C., 'First Minutes: An Analysis of the Irish language within the Official Structures of the Gaelic Athletic Association, 1884–1934', *Éire-Ireland*, 48, (2013).

Brown, Terence, 'British Ireland', in E. Langley (ed.) Culture in Ireland: Division or Diversity? (Belfast: Institute of Irish Studies, The Queen's University of Belfast, 1991), 72.

Byrne, F. J., (ed.) *The Scholar Revolutionary* (Shannon: Irish University Press, 1967).

Collins, K., *Catholic Churchmen and the Celtic Revival in Ireland, 1848–1916* (Dublin: Four Courts Press, 2002).

Comerford, R. V., 'Nation, Nationalism and the Irish language', in T. Hachey and L. J. McCaffrey (eds.), *Perspectives on Irish Nationalism* (Lexington, KY: University of Kentucky Press, 1989).

Cormier, J. J., 'Blocked Mobility and the Rise of Cultural Nationalism: A Reassessment', *International Journal of Politics, Culture, and Society*, 16, (2003), 525–49.

Cormier, J., and Couton, P., 'Civil Society, Mobilization, and Communal Violence: Quebec and Ireland, 1890–1920', *The Sociological Quarterly*, 45, (2004).

Cronin, M., 'Projecting the Nation through Sport and Culture: Ireland, Aonach Tailteann and the Irish Free State, 1924–32', *Journal of Contemporary History*, 38 (2003).

Dean, J. F., *Riot and Great Anger: Stage Censorship in Twentieth-century* Ireland (Madison, WI: University of Wisconsin Press, 2004).

Delaney, P., 'D. P. Moran and the *Leader*: Writing an Irish Ireland through Partition', *Éire-Ireland*, 38 (2003), 189–211.

Dobbins, G., 'Whenever Green Is Red: James Connolly and Postcolonial Theory', *Nepantla*, I, (2000), 605–648.

Dowling, M., *Traditional Music and Irish Society: Historical Perspectives* (Burlington, VT: Ashgate Publishing, 2014).

Dunleavy, J. and Dunleavy, G., *Douglas Hyde: A Maker of Modern Ireland.* (Berkeley, CA: University of California Press, 1991).

Dunlevy, M., *Dress in Ireland* (London: B. T. Batsford, 1989).

Foley, C. E., *Step Dancing in Ireland: Culture and History* (Burlington, VT: Ashgate Publishing, 2013).

French, B. M., 'Linguistic Science and Nationalist Revolution: Expert Knowledge and the Making of Sameness in Pre-Independence Ireland', *Language in Society*, 38 (November 2009), 607–25.

Garvin, Tom, *Nationalist Revolutionaries in Ireland 1858–1928* (Dublin: Gill Books; New edition, 2005).

Gordon Bowe, N., and Cumming, E., *The Arts and Crafts Movements in Dublin and Edinburgh 1885–1925* (Dublin: Irish Academic Press, 1998).

Grote, G., *Torn Between Politics and Culture: the Gaelic League, 1893–1993* (Munster: Waxman, 1994).

Helland, J., *British and Irish Home Arts and Industries 1880–1914* (Dublin: Irish Academic Press, 2007).

Kelly, M., *The Fenian Ideal and Irish Nationalism, 1882–1916* (Woodbridge: Boydell and Brewer Ltd, 2009).

'… and William Rooney Spoke in Irish', *History Ireland*, 15 (2007), 30–34.

Kennelly, James J., 'The "Dawn of the Practical": Horace Plunkett and the Cooperative Movement', *New Hibernia Review*, 12 (2008), 64.

Keogh, D., *Jews in Twentieth-century Ireland* (Cork: Cork University Press, 1998).

King, C., 'The Early Development of Agricultural Cooperation: Some French and Irish Comparisons', *Proceedings of the Royal Irish Academy*, 96, C, (1996).

Mac Aonghusa, P., *Ar Son na Gaeilge: Conradh na Gaeilge 1893–1993* (Baile Átha Cliath: Conradh na Gaeilge, 1993).

Oireachtas na Gaeilge, 1897–1997 (Dublin: Conradh na Gaeilge, 1997).

MacPherson, D., *Women and the Irish Nation: Gender, Culture and Irish Identity, 1890–1914* (Houndmills, Basingstoke: Palgrave Macmillan, 2008).

Mathews, P. J., *Revival: The Abbey Theatre, Sinn Féin, The Gaelic League and the Co-operative Movement* (Notre Dame, IN: University of Notre Dame Press, 2003).

'A Battle of Two Civilizations?' *Irish Review* 29 (2002).

Maume, P., *D. P. Moran* (Dundalk: Dundalgean Press, 1995).

McCartney, D., 'Hyde, D. P. Moran and Irish-Ireland', in F. X. Martin (ed.), *Leaders and Men of the Easter Rising, Dublin 1916* (Ithaca, NY: Cornell University Press, 1967), 43–54.

McDiarmid, L., *The Irish Art of Controversy* (Ithaca, NY: Cornell University Press, 2005).

McElligott, R., '1916 and the Radicalization of the Gaelic Athletic Association', *Éire-Ireland*, 48 (2003).

McGee, O, *Arthur Griffith* (Dublin: Irish Academic Press, 2015).

McMahon, T. G., *Grand Opportunity: The Gaelic Revival and Irish Society, 1893–1910* (Syracuse: Syracuse University Press, 2008).

Mokyr, J., and Ó Gráda, C., 'Poor Getting Poorer? Living Standards in Ireland before the Famine,' *Economic History Review*, 41 (1988), 209–35.

Murray, D., *Romanticism, Nationalism and Irish Antiquarian Societies, 1840–80* (Maynooth: Maynooth Monographs, 2000).

Murray, P., 'Irish Cultural Nationalism in the United Kingdom State: Politics and the Gaelic League 1900–18', *Irish Political Studies* 8 (1993), 55–72.

Ní Mhuircheartaigh, E., and Mac Congáil, N., *Drámaí Thús Na hAthbheochana* (Dublin: Arlen House Press, 2009).

Nic Congáil, R., '"Fiction, Amusement, Instruction": The Irish Fireside Club and the Educational Ideology of the Gaelic League', *Éire-Ireland*, 44 (2009), 91–117.

Nic Pháidín, C., *Fáinne an Lae Agus an Athbheochan* (Dublin: Cois Life Teo, 1998).

Ó Baoighill, P., *Cardinal Patrick O'Donnell 1856–1927* (Baile na Finne: Foilseacháin Chró na mBothán, 2008).

Ó Cathasaigh, A., *An tAthrú Mór: Scríbhinní Sósialacha le Pádraic Ó Conaire* (Dublin: Coiscéim, 2007).

Réabhlóid Phádraic Uí Chonaire (Dublin: Coiscéim, 2007).

Ná Bac Leis: Rogha as nuachtán reibiliúnach (Dublin: Coiscéim, 2015).

Ó Cearúil, P., *Aspail ar son na Gaeilge: Timirí Chonradh na Gaeilge 1899–1923* (Dublin: Conradh na Gaeilge, 1995).

Ó Conchubhair, B., 'An Gúm and the Irish Language Dust-Jacket', in Sisson, E., and King, L., (eds.), *Negotiations: Modernity, Design and Visual Culture in Ireland, 1922–1992* (Cork: Cork University Press, 2011), 93–113.

Fin de Siècle na Gaeilge: Darwin, an Athbheochan agus Smaointeoireacht na hEorpa (Indreabhán: An Clóchomhar, 2009).

'The Gaelic Font Controversy: The Gaelic League's (Post-Colonial) Crux', *Irish University Review*, 33 (2003), 46–63.

Ó Cuív, B., 'The Gaelic Cultural Movements and the New Nationalism', in K. B. Nowlan (ed.), *The Making of 1916: Studies in the History of the Rising* (Dublin: Stationery Office, 1969), 1–27.

Ó Fearáil, P., *The Story of Conradh na Gaeilge* (Dublin: Conradh na Gaeilge, 1975).

Ó Murchú, M., *Cumann Buan-Choimeádta na Gaeilge: tús an athréimnithe* (Dublin: Cois Life Teo, 2001).

Ó Siadhail, M., *Stair Dhrámaíocht na Gaeilge: 1900–1970* (Indreabhán: Cló Iar-Chonnacht, 1993).

Ó Siadhail, P., *An Béaslaíoch: Beatha agus Saothar Phiarais Béaslaí (1881–1965)* (Dublin: Coiscéim, 2007).

Ó Súilleabháin, D., *Na Timirí i Ré Tosaigh an Chonartha 1893–1927* (Dublin: Conradh na Gaeilge, 1990).

Ó Tuathaigh, G., 'The Irish-Ireland Idea: Rationale and Relevance', in E. Longley, (ed.), *Culture in Ireland*, (Belfast: Institute of Irish Studies, QUB, 1991).

'The Position of the Irish Language', in T. Dunne (ed.), *The National University of Ireland, 1908–2008: Centenary Essays* (Dublin: UCD Press, 2008), 33–46.

O'Connor, B., *The Irish Dancing: Cultural Politics and Identities, 1900–2000* (Cork: Cork University Press, 2013).

O'Donnell, M. L., 'Owen Lloyd and the De-Anglicization of the Irish Harp', *Éire-Ireland*, 48 (2013), 155–75.

O'Kelly, H., 'Reconstructing Irishness: Dress in the Celtic Revival, 1880–1920', in J. Ash and E. Wilson (eds.), *Chic Thrills: A Fashion Reader* (London: Harper Collins, 1992).

O'Leary, P., *Gaelic Prose in the Irish Free State, 1922–1939* (University Park: Penn State University Press, 2004).

The Prose Literature of the Gaelic Revival, 1881–1921: Ideology and Innovation (University Park: Penn State University Press, 2005).

O'Rourke, K., 'Property Rights Innovation: Creamery Diffusion, Politics and Economy in Pre-1914 Ireland', *European Review of Economic History*, 11 (2007), 395–417.

Pašeta, S., 'Nationalist Responses to Two Royal Visits to Ireland, 1900 and 1903', *Irish Historical Studies*, 31 124 (1999).

Rouse, P., 'The Politics of Culture and Sport in Ireland: A History of the GAA Ban on Foreign Games, 1884–1971, Part One: 1884–1921', *International Journal of the History of Sport*, 10 (1993), 342–43.

Sheehy, J., *The Rediscovery of Ireland's Past: The Celtic Revival 1830–1930* (London: Thames and Hudson, 1980).

Steele, K., *Women, Press, and Politics During the Irish Revival* (Syracuse: Syracuse University Press, 2007).

Tierney, M., *Eoin MacNeill: scholar and man of action, 1867–1945* (Oxford University Press, 1980).

Trotter, M., *Ireland's National Theaters: Political Performance and the Origins of the Irish Dramatic Movement* (Syracuse: Syracuse University Press, 2001).

Uí Chollatáin, R., *An Claidheamh Soluis agus Fáinne an Lae 1899–1932* (Dublin: Cois Life Teo, 2004).

'*An Claidheamh Soluis*: A Journalistic Insight to Irish Literary Reviews in the Revival Period 1899–1932', *Proceedings of the Harvard Celtic Colloquium*, 23 (2003), 284–98.

Uí Fhlannagáin, F., *Fíníní Mheiriceá agus an Ghaeilge* (Dublin: Coiscéim, 2008).

Walsh, T., 'The Revised Programme of Instruction, 1900–1922', *Irish Educational Studies*, 26 (2002), 127–43.

Waters, M., 'Peasants and Emigrants: Considerations of the Gaelic League as a Social Movement', in D. Casey and R. Rhodes (eds.), *Views of the Irish peasantry, 1800–1916*, (Connecticut: Archon Books, 1977).

Wheatley, M., *Nationalism and the Irish Party: Provincial Ireland 1910–1916* (Oxford University Press, 2005).

Whyte, J. H., *Catholics in Western Democracies: A Study in Political Behaviour* (Dublin: Gill & Macmillan, 1981).

8 Ireland and the Great War

David Fitzpatrick

Manuscripts

Belfast

Public Record Office Northern Ireland

Belfast Chamber of Commerce, Minutes of Council Meeting, 7 September 1914: D1857/1/AB/8

Dublin

National Archives of Ireland

File on women's national service in CSO, Registered Papers (RP) 3950/1922

National Library

Report of recruiting meeting in Chief Secretary's Office (CSO), Newspaper Cuttings Books (NCB), vol. 48

Brennan Papers, MS 26191

Parsons Papers, MS 21278

London

The National Archives

Abstract of enlistment: NS 1/84, National Archives, Kew.

Primary printed works

Carnegie United Kingdom Trust, *Report on the Physical Welfare of Mothers and Children*, vol. iv, *Ireland* (Dublin: CUKT, 1917).

General Annual Reports of the British Army (including the Territorial Force from the Date of Embodiment) for the Period from 1st October, 1913, to 30th September, 1919, prepared by Command of the Army Council, 9, in House of Commons Papers, 1921 (Cmd. 1193).

Hanna, H., *The Pals at Suvla Bay, being the Record of "D" Company of the 7th Royal Dublin Fusiliers* (Dublin: E. Ponsonby, 1917).

Kerr, S. P., *What the Irish Regiments have Done* (London: T. Fisher Unwin, 1916).

Lavery, F., (comp.), *Irish Heroes in the War* (London: Everett, 1917).

Lucy, J. F., *There's a Devil in the Drum* (London: Faber, 1938).

Mac Giolla Choille, B., (ed.), *Intelligence Notes, 1913–16, Preserved in the State Paper Office*, (Dublin: Stationery Office, 1966).

MacDonagh, M., *The Irish at the Front* (London: Hodder and Stoughton, 1916).

   The Irish on the Somme (London: Hodder and Stoughton, 1917).

Saorstát Éireann, Department of Industry and Commerce, *Census of Population, 1926*, vol. X, *General Report* (Dublin: Stationery Office, 1934).

Statistics of the Military Effort of the British Empire during the Great War, 1914–1920 (London: War Office, 1922).

Walker, J., (ed.), *War Letters to a Wife* (Staplehurst, Kent: Spellount, 2001; 1st edn., 1929).

Secondary works

Aan de Wiel, J., *The Irish Factor, 1899–1919: Ireland's Strategic and Diplomatic Importance for Foreign Powers* (Dublin: Irish Academic Press, 2008).

Arthur, M., *Symbol of Courage: A History of the Victoria Cross* (London: Sidgwick and Jackson, 2004).

Bowman, T., *The Irish Regiments in the Great War: Discipline and Morale* (Manchester: Manchester University Press, 2003).

Burke, D., (ed.), *Irish Jesuit Chaplains in the First World War* (Dublin: Messenger Publications, 2014).

Butler, A. G., *The Australian Army Medical Services in the War of 1914–1918*, vol. iii (Canberra: Australian War Memorial, 1943).

Callan, P., 'Recruiting for the British Army in Ireland during the First World War', in *Irish Sword*, xvii (1987), 42–56.

Casey, P. J., 'Irish Casualties in the First World War', in *Irish Sword*, 20 (1997), 193–206.

Clear, C., 'Fewer Ladies, More Women', 161–2, in John Horne (ed.), *Our War: Ireland and the Great War* (Dublin: Royal Irish Academy, 2008), 157–70.

Cousins, C., *Armagh and the Great War* (Dublin: History Press, 2011).

Demisko, L. S., 'Morale in the 16th (Irish) Division, 1916–18', in *Irish Sword*, 20 (1997), 217–33.

Denman, Terence, *Ireland's Unknown Soldiers: The 16th (Irish) Division in the Great War, 1914–1918* (Dublin: Irish Academic Press, 1992).

   A Lonely Grave: The Life and Death of William Redmond (London: Irish Academic Press, 1995).

   'The Catholic Irish Soldier in the First World War: The "Racial Environment"', in *Irish Historical Studies*, 27 (1991), 352–65.

Doherty, R., and Truesdale, D., *Irish Winners of the Victoria Cross* (Dublin: Four Courts Press, 2000).

Downes, M., 'The Civilian Voluntary Aid Effort', in D. Fitzpatrick (ed.), *Ireland and the First World War* (Dublin: Trinity History Workshop, 1986), 27–37.

Dunwoody, J., 'Child Welfare', in D. Fitzpatrick (ed.), *Ireland and the First World War* (Dublin: Trinity History Workshop, 1986), 69–75.

Erickson, E. J., *Ordered to Die: A History of the Ottoman Army in the First World War* (Westport, CN: Greenwood Press, 2001).

Fitzpatrick, D., *Politics and Irish Life: Provincial Experience of War and Revolution, 1913–1921* (Dublin: Gill & Macmillan, 1977).

(ed.), *Ireland and the First World War* (Dublin: Trinity History Workshop, 1986).

'Militarism in Ireland, 1900–22', in T. Bartlett, and K. Jeffery (eds.), *A Military History of Ireland* (Cambridge University Press, 1996), 379–406.

'Home Front and Everyday Life', in John Horne (ed.), *Our War: Ireland and the Great War* (Dublin: Royal Irish Academy, 2008), 131–42.

'The Logic of Collective Sacrifice: Ireland and the British Army, 1914–1918', in *Historical Journal*, 38 (1995), 1,017–30.

'Irish Consequences of the Great War', in *Irish Historical Studies*, 39, (2015).

Grayson, R. S., *Belfast Boys: How Unionists and Nationalists fought and died Together in the First World War* (London: Continuum, 2009).

Gregory, A. and Pašeta, S. (ed.), *Ireland and the Great War: 'A war to unite us all'?* (Manchester: Manchester University Press, 2002).

Harris, H., *The Irish Regiments in the First World War* (Cork: Mercier Press, 1968).

Hennessey, T., *Dividing Ireland: World War I and Partition* (London: Routledge, 1998).

Horne, John (ed.), *Our War: Ireland and the Great War* (Dublin: Royal Irish Academy, 2008).

Jeffery, K., *Ireland and the Great War* (Cambridge University Press, 2000).

Johnstone, T., *Orange, Green and Khaki: The Story of the Irish Regiments in the Great War, 1914–18* (Dublin: Gill & Macmillan, 1992).

Kitchen, J. E., *The British Imperial Army in the Middle East* (London: Bloomsbury, 2014).

Leonard, J., 'Getting them at last: The I.R.A. and Ex-Servicemen', in D. Fitzpatrick, (ed.), *Revolution? Ireland 1917–1923* (Dublin: Trinity History Workshop, 1990), 118–29.

'Survivors', in J. Horne (ed.), *Our War: Ireland and the Great War* (Dublin: Royal Irish Academy, 2008), 209–23.

Niall, B., *Mannix* (Melbourne: Text Publishing, 2015), 146–9.

O'Flanagan, N., 'Dublin City in an Age of War and Revolution, 1914–1924' (M.A. Thesis, University College, Dublin, 1985).

Orr, Philip, *The Road to the Somme: Men of the Ulster Division tell their Story* (Belfast: Blackstaff Press, 1987).

Pennell, C., *A Kingdom United: Popular Responses to the Outbreak of the First World War in Britain and Ireland* (Oxford, 2012).

Perry, N., (ed.), *Major General Oliver Nugent and the Ulster Division, 1915–1918* (Stroud: Sutton Publications, 2007).

'Nationality in the Irish Infantry Regiments in the First World War', in *War and Society*, 12 (1994), 83–94.

'The Irish Landed Class and the British Army, 1850–1950', 322, in *War in History*, 18 (2011), 304–32.

Reilly, E., 'Women and Voluntary War Work', in A. Gregory and S. Pašeta (ed.), *Ireland and the Great War: 'A war to unite us all'?* (Manchester: Manchester University Press, 2002), 49–72.

Sandford, S., *Neither Unionist nor Nationalist: the 10th (Irish) Division in the Great War, 1914–1918* (Manchester: Manchester University Press, 2014).

Sheen, J., *Tyneside Irish: 24th, 25th and 26th and 27th (Service) Battalions of the Northumberland Fusiliers* (Barnsley: Pen and Sword Books, 1998).

Taylor, P., *Heroes or Traitors? Experiences of Southern Irish Soldiers returning from the Great War, 1919–1939* (Liverpool: Liverpool University Press, 2015).

Tierney, M., Bowen, P., and Fitzpatrick, D., 'Recruiting Posters', in David Fitzpatrick (ed.), *Ireland and the First World War* (Dublin: Trinity History Workshop, 1986), 47–58.

Walsh, F., 'Irish Women in the First World War', PhD Thesis (Trinity College, Dublin, 2015).

Yeates, P., *A City in War-time: Dublin, 1914–18* (Dublin: Gill & Macmillan, 2011).

9 Revolution, 1916–1923

Fearghal McGarry

Augusteijn, J., *From Public Defiance to Guerrilla Warfare. The Experience of Ordinary Volunteers in the Irish War of Independence 1916–1921* (Dublin: Irish Academic Press, 1996).

  The Irish Revolution, 1913–23 (Basingstoke: Palgrave Macmillan, 2002).

  'Coolacrease', *History Ireland*, 17 (2009), 56–57.

Borgonovo, J., *Spies, Informer, and the 'Anti-Sinn Féin Society': the Intelligence War in Cork City, 1920–1921* (Dublin: Irish Academic Press, 2007).

  The Dynamics of War and Revolution: Cork City, 1916–1918 (Cork: Cork University Press, 2013).

Campbell, F., *Land and Revolution. Nationalist Politics in the West of Ireland 1891–1921* (Oxford University Press, 2005).

Clark, G., *Everyday Violence in the Irish Civil War* (Cambridge University Press, 2014).

Coleman, M., *County Longford and the Irish Revolution, 1910–1923* (Dublin: Irish Academic Press, 2003).

  'Violence against Women in the Irish War of Independence, 1919–1921', in D. Ferriter and S. Riordan (eds.), *Years of Turbulence: The Irish Revolution and its Aftermath* (Dublin: University College Dublin Press, 2015).

Costello, F., *The Irish Revolution and its Aftermath 1916–1923. Years of Revolt* (Dublin: Irish Academic Press, 2003).

Dáil Éireann, Minutes of Proceedings, 1919–1921, vol. 1 (Dublin: Stationery Office, n.d.).

Dolan, A. *Commemorating the Irish Civil War. History and Memory, 1923–2000* (Cambridge University Press, 2003).

Dooley, T., *'The Land for the People'. The Land Question in Independent Ireland* (Dublin: University College Dublin Press, 2004).

Fanning, R., *Fatal Path. British Government and Irish Revolution 1910–1922* (London: Faber and Faber, 2013).

Farry, M., *The Aftermath of Revolution. Sligo 1921–23* (Dublin: University College Dublin Press, 2000).

Ferriter, D., *A Nation and not a Rabble. The Irish Revolution 1913–1923* (London: Profile Books, 2015).

Fitzpatrick, D., *Politics and Irish Life, 1913–1921: Provincial Experience of War and Revolution* (Dublin: Gill & Macmillan, 1977).

The Two Irelands 1912–1939 (Oxford University Press, 1998).

'Irish Consequences of the Great War', *Irish Historical Studies*, 39 (2015).

'Protestant depopulation and the Irish Revolution', *Irish Historical Studies*, 38 (2013), 643–670.

Foster, G., *The Irish Civil War and Society. Politics, class and conflict* (Basingstoke: Palgrave Macmillan, 2015).

Foster, R. F., *Modern Ireland 1600–1972* (London: Allen Lane, 1988).

W. B. Yeats: A Life. II: The Arch-Poet 1915–1939 (Oxford University Press, 2003).

Vivid Faces. The Revolutionary Generation in Ireland 1890–1923 (London: Allen Lane, 2014).

Garvin, T., *1922. The Birth of Irish Democracy* (Dublin: Gill & Macmillan, 1996).

Nationalist Revolutionaries in Ireland, 1858–1928 (Oxford University Press, 1987).

Gerwarth, R., and Horne, J., (eds.), *War in Peace: Paramilitary Violence in Europe after the Great War* (Oxford University Press, 2012).

Grayson, R. S. and McGarry, F., (eds.), *Remembering 1916: The Easter Rising, the Somme and the Politics of Memory in Ireland* (Cambridge University Press, 2016).

Gregory, A., '"You Might as Well Recruit Germans": British Public Opinion and the Decision to Conscript the Irish in 1918', in A. Gregory and S. Pašeta (eds.), *Ireland and the Great War: 'a war to unite us all'?* (Manchester: Manchester University Press, 2002).

Griffith, K. and O'Grady, T., *Curious Journey. An Oral History of Ireland's Unfinished Revolution* (Cork: Mercier Press, 1988).

Harnett, M., *Victory and Woe* (Dublin: University College Dublin Press, 2002).

Hart, P., *The I.R.A. and its Enemies. Violence and Community in Cork 1916–1923* (Oxford University Press, 1998).

The I.R.A. at War, 1916–1923 (Oxford University Press, 2005).

Heffernan, B., *Freedom and the Fifth Commandment: Catholic Priest and Political Violence in Ireland, 1919–21* (Manchester: Manchester University Press, 2015).

Hopkinson, M., *Green against Green: The Irish Civil War* (Dublin: Gill & Macmillan, 1988).

The Irish War of Independence (Dublin: Gill & Macmillan, 2000), 199.

Howe, S., 'Killings in Cork and the Historians', *History Workshop Journal* (2014).

Jeffery, K., *1916. A Global History* (London: Bloomsbury, 2015).

The British Army and the Crisis of Empire, 1918–22 (Manchester: Manchester University Press, 1984).

Kalyvas, S., *The Logic of Violence in Civil War* (Cambridge University Press, 2006).

Kenny, K., (ed.), *Ireland and the British Empire* (Oxford University Press, 2006).

Kissane, B., *The Politics of the Irish Civil War* (Oxford University Press, 2005).

Knirck, J., *Imagining Ireland's Independence. The Debates over the Anglo-Irish Treaty of 1921* (Lanham, MD: Rowman & Littlefield, 2006).

Kostick, C., *Revolution in Ireland: Popular Militancy 1917–1923* (Cork: Cork University Press, 2009).

Laffan, M., *The Resurrection of Ireland. The Sinn Féin Party 1916–1923* (Cambridge University Press, 1999).

Lee, Joe, *Ireland, 1912–1985: Politics and Society* (Cambridge University Press, 1989).

Leeson, D.M., *The Black and Tans. British Police and Auxiliaries in the Irish War of Independence* (Oxford University Press, 2011).

Lynch, R., 'Explaining the Altnaveigh Massacre', *Éire-Ireland*, 45 (2010), 184–210.

The Northern IRA and the Early Years of Partition, 1920–1922 (Dublin: Irish Academic Press, 2006).

Manela, E., *The Wilsonian Moment: Self-Determination and the International Origins of Anticolonial Nationalism* (New York: Oxford University Press, 2007).

McConnel, J., *The Irish Parliamentary Party and the Third Home Rule Crisis* (Dublin: Four Courts Press, 2013).

McGarry, F., *The Abbey Rebels of 1916. A Lost Revolution* (Dublin: Gill & Macmillan, 2015).

The Rising. Ireland: Easter 1916 (Oxford University Press, 2016 edn.).

Eoin O'Duffy. A Self-Made Hero (Oxford University Press, 2005).

McGaughey, J., *Ulster's Men. Protestant Unionist Masculinities and Militarization in the North of Ireland, 1912–1923* (Montreal: McGill-Queen's University Press, 2012).

McMahon, P., *British Spies and Irish Rebels. British Intelligence and Ireland 1916–1945* (Suffolk: Boydell Press, 2008).

Meagher, T. J., 'Irish America Without Ireland: Irish-American Relations with Ireland in the Twentieth Century', in N. Whelehan (ed.) *Transnational Perspectives on Modern Irish History* (London: Routledge, 2014).

Mitchell, A., 'Alternative Government: "Exit Britannia" – the formation of the Irish National State, 1918–21', in J. Augusteijn (ed.), *The Irish Revolution 1913–1923* (Basingstoke: Palgrave Macmillan, 2002).

Morash, C., *A History of the Media in Ireland* (Cambridge University Press, 2010).

Murphy, P. B., *Patrick Pearse and the Lost Republican Ideal* (Dublin: James Duffy, 1990).

Murphy, W., *Political Imprisonment and the Irish, 1912–1921* (Oxford University Press, 2014).

Nelson, B., *Irish Nationalists and the Making of the Irish Race* (Princeton, NJ: Princeton University Press, 2012).

Ó Ruairc, P.O., *Truce: Murder, Myth and the Last Days of the Irish War of Independence* (Cork: Mercier Press, 2016).

O'Callaghan, J., *Revolutionary Limerick. The Republican Campaign for Independence in Limerick, 1913–1921* (Dublin: Irish Academic Press, 2010).

O'Faolain, S., *Vive Moi! An Autobiography* (London: Sinclair-Stevenson, 1993 edn.).

O'Halpin, E., 'Counting Terror: Bloody Sunday and The Dead of the Irish Revolution' in D. Fitzpatrick (ed.), *Terror in Ireland 1916–1923* (Dublin: The Lilliput Press, 2012).

O'Hegarty, P.S., *The Victory of Sinn Féin*, (new edn. Dublin: University College Dublin Press, 2015).

O'Malley, E., *The Singing Flame* (Dublin: Anvil, 1978).

On Another Man's Wound (Boulder, Colorado: Roberts Rinehart, 1999 edn.).

O'Malley, K., *Ireland, India and Empire: Indo-Irish Radical Connections, 1919–64* (Manchester: Manchester University Press, 2008).

O'Neill, T. P., (ed.), *Private Sessions of the Second Dáil* (Dublin, 1972).

Pašeta, S., *Irish Nationalist Women, 1900–1918* (Cambridge University Press, 2013).

Prager, J., *Building Democracy in Ireland. Political Order and Cultural Integration in a Newly Independent Nation* (Cambridge University Press, 1986).

Regan, J., *Myth and the Irish State* (Dublin: Irish Academic Press, 2014).

Ryan, L., ' "Drunken Tans": Representation of Sex and Violence in the Anglo-Irish War, 1919–21', *Feminist Review*, 66 (2000), 73–95.

Silvestri, M., *Ireland and India: Nationalism, Empire and Memory* (Basingstoke: Palgrave Macmillan, 2009).

Sweetman, R., 'Who Fears to Speak of Easter Week? Antipodean Irish Catholic Responses to the 1916 Rising', in R. O'Donnell, (ed.), *The Impact of the 1916 Rising. Among the Nations* (Dublin: Irish Academic Press, 2008).

Taylor, P., *Heroes or Traitors? Experiences of Southern Irish Soldiers returning from the Great War 1919–1939* (Liverpool: Liverpool University Press, 2015).

Townshend, C., *The British Campaign in Ireland 1919–1921. The Development of Political and Military Policies* (Oxford University Press, 1975).

Political Violence in Ireland. Government and Resistance since 1848 (Oxford University Press, 1983).

'Historiography: Telling the Irish Revolution', in J. Augusteijn (ed.), *The Irish Revolution 1913–1923* (Basingstoke: Palgrave Macmillan, 2002).

'The Irish War of Independence. Context and Meaning', in C. Crowe (ed.), *Guide to the Military Service Pensions Collection* (Dublin: Óglaigh na hÉireann, 2012).

The Republic. The fight for Irish Independence (London: Allen Lane, 2013).

'The Irish Railway Strike of 1920: Industrial Action and Civil Resistance in the Struggle for Independence', *Irish Historical Studies*, 22 (1979).

Walsh, M., *The News from Ireland: Foreign Correspondents and the Irish Revolution* (London: I.B. Tauris, 2011).

Bitter Freedom. Ireland in a Revolutionary World 1918–1923 (London: Faber & Faber, 2015).

Wheatley, M., *Nationalism and the Irish Party: Provincial Ireland, 1910–1916* (Oxford, 2005).

Whelehan, N., (ed.), *Transnational Perspectives on Modern Irish History* (London: Routledge, 2014).

Wilson, T., ' "The Most Terrible Assassination that has yet Stained the Name of Belfast": The Mcmahon Murders in Context', *Irish Historical Studies*, 37 (2010), 83–106.

Frontiers of Violence. Conflict and Identity in Ulster and Upper Silesia 1918–1922 (Oxford, 2010).

10 Politics, Economy, Society: Northern Ireland, 1920–1939

Susannah Riordan

Akenson, D. H., *Education and Enmity: The Control of Schooling in Northern Ireland 1920–50* (Newton Abbot: David and Charles, 1973).

Bardon, J., *A History of Ulster* (Belfast: Blackstaff Press, 1992).

Bew, P. and Norton, C., 'The Unionist State and the Outdoor Relief Riots of 1932', *Economic and Social Review*, 10 (1979).

Bew, P., Gibbon, P., and Patterson, H., *Northern Ireland 1921–2001: Political Forces and Social Classes* (London: Serif, 2002).

Buckland, P., *The Factory of Grievances: Devolved Government in Northern Ireland 1921–39* (Dublin: Gill & Macmillan, 1979).

'A Protestant Parliament and a Protestant State: Regional Government and Religious Discrimination in Northern Ireland, 1920–1939', in A. C. Duke and C. A. Tamse (eds.), *Britain and The Netherlands: Volume VII Church and State Since the Reformation: Papers Delivered to the Seventh Anglo-Dutch Historical Conference* (The Hague: Martinus Nijhoff, 1981).

A History of Northern Ireland (Dublin: Gill & Macmillan, 1981).

'A Protestant state: Unionists in government, 1921–39', in D. George Boyce and Alan O'Day (eds.), *Defenders of the Union: A Survey of British and Irish Unionism Since 1801* (London: Routledge, 2001).

Edwards, A., *A History of the Northern Ireland Labour Party: Democratic Socialism and Sectarianism* (Manchester: Manchester University Press, 2009).

Farrell, M., *Northern Ireland: The Orange State*, 2nd edn. (London: Pluto Press, 1980).

Fionnuala O'Connor, *In Search of a State: Catholics in Northern Ireland* (Belfast: Blackstaff Press, 1993).

Follis, B. A., *A State Under Siege: The Establishment of Northern Ireland 1920–1925* (Oxford: Clarendon Press, 1995).

Harkness, D. W., *Northern Ireland since 1920* (Dublin: Helicon, 1983).

Harris, M., *The Catholic Church and the Foundation of the Northern Irish State* (Cork: Cork University Press, 1993).

Hennessey, T., *A History of Northern Ireland 1920–1996* (Houndmills: Palgrave, 1997).

Hopkinson, M., 'The Craig-Collins pacts of 1922: Two Attempted Reforms of the Northern Ireland Government', *Irish Historical Studies*, 27 (1990), 147–9.

Kennedy, M., *Division and Consensus: The Politics of Cross-Border Relations in Ireland, 1925–1969* (Dublin: Institute of Public Administration, 2000).

Laffan, M., *The Partition of Ireland 1911–1925* (Dublin Historical Association, 1983).

Lewis, M., 'The Fourth Northern Division and the Joint-IRA Offensive, April–July 1922', *War in History* 21 (2014).

Phoenix, E., *Northern Nationalism: Nationalist Politics, Partition and the Catholic Minority in Northern Ireland 1890–1940* (Belfast: Ulster Historical Foundation, 1994).

Rankin, K. J., 'The Provenance and Dissolution of the Irish Boundary Commission', Working Papers in British-Irish Studies, 79 (Dublin: Institute for British-Irish Studies, University College Dublin, 2006).

Ruane, J., and Todd, J., 'Irish nationalism and the conflict in Northern Ireland', in D. Miller (ed.), *Rethinking Northern Ireland* (Harlow: Addison Wesley Longman, 1998).

Stewart, A. T. Q., *The Narrow Ground: The Roots of Conflict in Ulster*, 2nd edn. (London: Faber and Faber, 1989).

Walker, G., *A History of the Ulster Unionist Party: Protest, Pragmatism and Pessimism* (Manchester: Manchester University Press, 2004).

Whyte, J. H., *Interpreting Northern Ireland* (Oxford University Press, 1990).

Wilson, T., *Ulster: Conflict and Consent* (Oxford: Basil Blackwell, 1989).

11 Politics, Economy and Society in the Irish Free State, 1922–1939

Anne Dolan

Printed primary sources

The Anglo-Celt
Irish Independent
The Irish Statesman

Irish Press

Leitrim Observer

Dáil Debates

Andrews, C. S., *Man of No Property* (2nd edn., Dublin: Lilliput Press, 2001).

Colum, P., *The Road Round Ireland* (New York: Macmillan, 1927).

Dail Eireann, official report, 2, col. 49 & 71 (8 December 1922).

Hogan, J., *Could Ireland become Communist? The Facts of the Case* (Dublin: Cahill, 1935).

McCourt, F., *Angela's Ashes* (London: HarperCollins, 1996).

O'Faolain, S., *The Irish* (3rd edn., London: Vintage Books, 1980).

Pritchett, V. S., *Midnight oil* (London, 1973 edn.).

   Dublin (London: Bodley Head, 1967).

Russell, G., (AE), 'Lessons of Revolution', *Studies*, 12 (March 1923).

Statistical Abstract 1938, 1939 (Dublin: ISPO, 1938, 1939).

Taylor, A., *To school through the fields: an Irish country childhood* (Brandon: 1988).

Secondary works

Bartlett, T., *Ireland: A History* (Cambridge University Press, 2010), 445.

d'Alton, I., '"A Vestigial Population"? Perspectives on Southern Irish Protestants in the Twentieth Century', *Éire-Ireland*, 44 (Fall–Winter, 2009), 14.

Dooley, T., *'The Land for the People': The Land Question in Independent Ireland* (Dublin: UCD Press, 2004).

Dunphy, R., *The Making of Fianna Fáil Power in Ireland 1923–1948* (Oxford University Press, 1995).

Ferriter, D., *The Transformation of Ireland 1900–2000* (London: Profile Books, 2004), 758–9.

Fitzpatrick, D., *The Two Irelands 1912–1939* (Oxford University Press, 1998).

Foster, R. F., *Modern Ireland 1600–1972* (2nd edn., London: Penguin, 1989).

Fuller, L., *Irish Catholicism since 1950* (Dublin: Gill & Macmillan, 2002).

Garvin, T., *Preventing the Future: Why was Ireland so Poor for so Long* (Dublin: Gill & Macmillan, 2004).

Geertz, C., *The Interpretation of Cultures* (New York: Basic Books, 1973).

Hobsbawm, E., *Age of Extremes: The Short Twentieth Century 1914–1991* (London: Michael Joseph, 1995 edn.).

Hogan, G., 'De Valera, the Constitution and the Historians', *Irish Jurist*, 40 (2005), 293–320.

Hoppen, K. T., *Ireland since 1800: Conflict and Conformity* (London: Routledge, 1989).

Kennedy, F., *Cottage to Crèche: Family Change in Ireland* (Dublin: Institute of Public Administration, 2001).

Laffan, M., *The Resurrection of Ireland* (Cambridge University Press, 1999).

Lee, J. J., *Ireland 1912–1985: Politics and Society* (Cambridge University Press, 1989).

Lynch, P., 'The Social Revolution that Never Was', in D. Williams (ed.), *The Irish Struggle 1916–1926* (London: Routledge and Kegan Paul, 1966).

Lyons, F.S.L., *Ireland since the Famine* (2nd edn., London: Weidenfeld and Nicolson, 1973).

Mazower, M., *Dark Continent: Europe's Twentieth Century* (London: Allen Lane, 1998).

McGarry, F., *Eoin O'Duffy: A Self-made Hero* (Oxford University Press, 2005).

O'Connor, F., *My Father's Son* (3rd edn., Belfast: Blackstaff Press, 1994).

Ó Gráda, C., *Ireland: A New Economic History 1780–1939* (Oxford University Press, 1994).

O'Hegarty, P. S., *The Victory of Sinn Féin* (2nd edn., Dublin: UCD Press, 1998), 91.

O'Higgins, K., *Three Years Hard Labour* (Dublin: Cahill, 1924).

O'Neill, T. P., and Lord Longford, *Éamon de Valera* (London: Hutchinson, 1970).

O'Rourke, K., 'Ireland and the Bigger Picture', in D. Dickson and C. Ó Gráda (eds.), *Refiguring Ireland* (Dublin: Lilliput Press, 2003).

Regan, J. M., *The Irish Counter-revolution 1921–1936* (Dublin: Gill & Macmillan, 1999), 383.

Titmuss, R., *Poverty and Population* (2nd edn., Basingstoke: Palgrave Macmillan, 2002).

12 Neutrality and Belligerence: Ireland, 1939–1945

Philip Ollerenshaw

Manuscripts

Public Record Office of Northern Ireland
Diary of Sir Basil Brooke, 12 August 1940. D/3001/D/31
Cabinet Meeting 21 May 1941, CAB 4/475
Report of the Ulster Unionist Council for 1941, D1327/20/2/24

Printed Primary Works

Belfast Telegraph
Bristol Evening Post
Irish Independent
Irish Times
Londonderry Sentinel
Manchester Guardian
The Times
Northern Ireland House of Commons Debates
Dáil Debates

Secondary Works

Bew, P. and Patterson, H., *Seán Lemass and the Making of Modern Ireland* (Dublin: Gill & Macmillan, 1982).

Canning, P., 'Another Failure for Appeasement? The Case of the Irish Ports', *International History Review*, 4 (1982).

Connolly, T., 'Irish Workers in Britain during World War II', in B. Girvin and G. Roberts (eds.), *Ireland and the Second World War: Politics, Society and Remembrance* (Dublin: Four Courts Press, 2000).

Cullen, M., 'Women, Emancipation and Politics, 1860–1984', in J. R. Hill (ed.), *A New History of Ireland, Vol. VII: Ireland 1921–84* (Oxford University Press, 2003), 877–79.

Daly, M. E., 'The Modernization of Rural Ireland, *c*.1920–c1960', in D. Dickson, and C. Ó Gráda (eds.), *Refiguring Ireland: Essays in Honour of L. M. Cullen* (Dublin: Lilliput Press, 2003).

    The Slow Failure: Population Decline and Independent Ireland, 1920–1973 (Madison, WI: University of Wisconsin Press, 2006).

Delaney, E., 'Irish Migration to Britain, 1939–1945', *Irish Economic and Social History*, 28 (2001).

Doherty, R., 'Irish heroes of the Second World War', in B. Girvin and G. Roberts (eds.), *Ireland and the Second World War: Politics, Society and Remembrance* (Dublin: Four Courts Press, 2000).

Donohue, L. K., *Counter-Terrorist Law and Emergency Powers in the United Kingdom, 1922–2000* (Dublin: Irish Academic Press, 2001).

Dunphy, R., *The Making of Fianna Fáil Power in Ireland, 1923–48* (Oxford University Press, 1995).

Evans, B., *Seán Lemass: Democratic Dictator* (Cork: The Collins Press, 2011).

    Ireland during the Second World War: Farewell to Plato's Cave (Manchester: Manchester University Press, 2014).

    'The Iron Man with the Wooden Head? Frank Aiken and the Second World War', in B. Evans and S. Kelly (eds.), *Frank Aiken: Nationalist and Internationalist* (Dublin: Irish Academic Press, 2014).

    'Coercion in the Irish Countryside: The Irish Smallholder, the State, and Compulsory Tillage 1939–45', *Irish Economic and Social History*, 38 (2011), 1–17.

Fallon, B., *An Age of Innocence: Irish Culture, 1930–1960* (Dublin: Four Courts Press, 1998).

Fanning, R., *The Irish Department of Finance, 1922–58* (Dublin: Institute of Public Administration, 1978).

Girvin, B., *Between Two Worlds: Politics and Economy in Independent Ireland* (Dublin: Gill & Macmillan, 1989).

    The Emergency: Neutral Ireland, 1939–45 (London: Macmillan, 2006).

    'Economic Policy, Continuity and Crisis in de Valera's Ireland, 1945–61', *Irish Economic and Social History*, 38 (2011).

Haughton, J., 'The Historical Background', in J. W. O'Hagan, (ed.), *The Economy of Ireland: Policy and Performance of a European Region* (Dublin: Gill & Macmillan, 2000).

Hayes, A., (ed.), *Hilda Tweedy and the Irish Housewives' Association: Links in the Chain…*, (Dublin: Arlen House, 2011).

Hayes-McCoy, G. A., 'Irish Defence Policy, 1938–51', in K. Nowlan and T. D. Williams (eds.), *Ireland in the War Years and After, 1939–51* (Dublin: Gill & Macmillan, 1969).

Inman, P., *Labour in the Munitions Industries* (London: HMSO and Longmans, Green & Co, 1957).

Kavanagh, C., 'Irish and British Government Policy towards the Volunteers' in B. Girvin and G. Roberts (eds.), *Ireland and the Second World War: Politics, Society and Remembrance* (Dublin: Four Courts Press, 2000).

Kelly, A., 'Catholic Action and the Development of the Irish Welfare State in the 1930s and 1940s', *Archivium Hibernicum*, 53 (1999).

Kennedy, K., 'The Roots of Contemporary Irish Economic Development', in D. Dickson, and C. Ó Gráda (eds.), *Refiguring Ireland: Essays in Honour of L. M. Cullen* (Dublin: Lilliput Press, 2003).

Kennedy, K., Giblin, T., and McHugh, D., *The Economic Development of Ireland in the Twentieth Century* (London: Routledge, 1988).

Keogh, Dermot, *Twentieth Century Ireland: Nation and State* (Dublin: Gill & Macmillan, 1994).

Longley, E., 'From Cathleen to Anorexia: The Breakdown of Irelands', in *The Living Stream: Literature and Revisionism in Ireland* (Newcastle-upon-Tyne: Bloodaxe Books, 1994).

Lucey, C., 'The Beveridge Report and Éire', *Studies*, 32 (1943), 37.

Lyons, F. S. L., *Ireland Since the Famine* (London: Fontana edition, 1973).

Meenan, J., *The Irish Economy since 1922* (Liverpool: Liverpool University Press, 1970).

'The Irish Economy during the War', in K. Nowlan and T. D. Williams (eds.), *Ireland in the War Years and After, 1939–51* (Dublin: Gill & Macmillan, 1969).

Mogey, J. M., *Rural Life in Northern Ireland* (Oxford University Press, 1947).

Murphy, J. A., 'Irish Neutrality in Historical Perspective', in B. Girvin and G. Roberts (eds.), *Ireland and the Second World War: Politics, Society and Remembrance* (Dublin: Four Courts Press, 2000).

Nolan, A., ' "A Most Heavy and Grievous Burden", Joseph Walshe and the Establishment of Sustainable Neutrality, 1940', D. Keogh and M. O'Driscoll (eds.), *Ireland in World War 2: Neutrality and Survival* (Cork: Mercier Press, 2004).

Ó Beacháin, D., *Destiny of the Soldiers: Fianna Fáil, Irish Republicans and the IRA, 1926–73* (Dublin: Gill & Macmillan, 2010).

Ó Drisceoil, D., *Censorship in Ireland, 1939–1945: Neutrality, Politics and Society* (Cork: Cork University Press, 1996).

' "Keeping the Temperature Down"; Domestic Politics in Emergency Ireland', in D. Keogh and M. O'Driscoll (eds.), *Ireland in World War 2: Neutrality and Survival* (Cork: Mercier Press, 2004).

Ó Gráda, C. and O'Rourke, K., 'Living standards and growth', in J. W. O'Hagan, (ed.), *The Economy of Ireland: Policy and Performance of a European Region* (Dublin: Gill & Macmillan, 2000).

Ó Longaigh, S., 'Emergency Law in Action, 1939–45', D. Keogh and M. O'Driscoll (eds.), *Ireland in World War 2: Neutrality and Survival* (Cork: Mercier Press, 2004).

O'Connor, S., 'Irish Identity and Integration within the British Armed Forces, 1939–45', *Irish Historical Studies, 39* (2015).

O'Halpin, E., *Defending Ireland: The Irish State and its Enemies since 1922* (Oxford University Press, 1999).

'MI5's Irish Memories: Fresh Light on the Origins and Rationale of Anglo-Irish Security Liaison in the Second World War', in B. Girvin and G. Roberts (eds.), *Ireland and the Second World War: Politics, Society and Remembrance* (Dublin: Four Courts Press, 2000).

'Irish Neutrality in the Second World War', in N. Wylie (ed.), *European Neutrals and Non-Belligerents during the Second World War* (Cambridge University Press, 2002).

Ollerenshaw, P., *Northern Ireland in the Second World War: Politics, Economic Mobilisation and Society, 1939–45* (Manchester: Manchester University Press, 2013).

Parker, H. M. D., *Manpower: A Study of War-time Policy and Administration* (London: HMSO and Longmans, 1957).

Patterson, H., 'Brian Maginess and the Limits of Liberal Unionism', *Irish Studies Review*, 25 (2000).
 'In the Land of King Canute: The Influence of Border Unionism on Ulster Unionist Politics, 1945–63', *Contemporary British History*, 20 (2006).

Privilege, J., 'The Northern Ireland Government and the Welfare State, 1942–8: the Case of Health Provision', *Irish Historical Studies*, 39 (2015), 439–59.

Quadragesimo Anno: On Reconstruction of the Social Order, 1931:
http://w2.vatican.va/content/pius-xi/en/encyclicals/documents/hf_p-xi_enc_19310515_quadragesimo-anno.html (accessed 2 October 2017).

Roberts, G., 'The British Offer to End Partition, June 1940', *History Ireland*, 9 (2001), 5–6.

Williams, T. D., 'Ireland and the War', in K. Nowlan and T. D. Williams (eds.), *Ireland in the War Years and After, 1939–51* (Dublin: Gill & Macmillan, 1969).

Wills, C., *That Neutral Island: A Cultural History of Ireland during the Second World War* (London: Faber & Faber, 2007).

Woodward, G., *Culture, Northern Ireland and the Second World War* (Oxford University Press, 2015).

13 Stability, Crisis and Change in Post-war Ireland
1945–1973

Brian Girvin

Manuscripts

London
The National Archives

Elizabeth Bowen, 'Notes on Ireland' June 1945 DO/130/65

'Sir Gilbert Laithwaite to Sir Percival Liesching 16 May 1950: PREM 8/1222 pt 2

Maffey memorandum on meeting with de Valera 26 July 1947, 3 August 1946, DO35/2096

Dublin
UCD Archives

Fine Gael papers: 'Cumann na nGaedheal/ Fine Gael General Purposes Committee, 14 November 1945 39/1/2; P39/MIN/4

MacEntee papers, P 67

De Valera papers, P150

Lemass speech to Federation of Irish Manufacturers 11 February 1947 P150/2736

Aiken papers, P104

National Archives

Documents on the Report of the Committee on Vocational Organisation Department of the Taoiseach S.13552

Meeting in Taoiseach's office 11 November 1956: DT, S 15281/A

'Aide Memoire for governments of the Six and Seven' 26 June 1959, S. 15281R DT. S.7985B
(Lynch correspondence with women's groups)
Aide memoire for Commonwealth Relations Office, 19 September 1959 S. 15281S
Department of Health memorandum 17 July 1948 S. 12064A
Justice to Taoiseach's office, 15 May 1947, S.137101
Memorandum by John J. Hearne: 'The Kingsmere Conversation' '(The Taoiseach and
Prime Minister Mackenzie King)' 9 September 1948, DFA/10/P12/5
Department of External Affairs memorandum for cabinet 26 October 1947 S. 14002A
Note by MacBride for cabinet 6 April 1951 S. 14997D
Note by Lemass for de Valera 10 January 1947 with additional material prepared by Industry
and Commerce, DT: 97/9/720.

National Library
Owen Sheehy Skeffington Papers, Fethard-on-Sea file Ms 40,515/8

Trinity College
Report by Stanley Lyons on visit to Britain 4 November 1948 March Papers, MS 8306/8/1

Dublin Diocesan Archives
McQuaid Papers

Printed Primary Sources

Blanshard, P., *Catholic Power in Ireland* (London: Derek Verschoyle, 1954).
Böll, H., *Irish Journal* (Evanston, Illinois: Marlboro Press/Northwestern, 1998) original
German ed. 1957.
Dáil Debates.
Gleas: A Monthly Bulletin Issued by Fianna Fáil 47.
Hogan, J., *Elections and Representation*, (Cork: Cork University Press, 1945).
O'Faolain, S., 'The Dáil and the bishops' *The Bell* 17 (June 1951), 6–7.

Secondary Works

Barry, F., 'Foreign Investment and the Politics of Export Profits Relief 1956', *Irish Economic
and Social History,* XXXVIII (2011), 54–72.
Barton, B., 'Relations between Westminster and Stormont during the Attlee Premiership',
Irish Political Studies, 7 (1992), 1–20.
Bew, P., *Ireland: The Politics of Enmity 1789–2006* (Oxford University Press, 2007).
Bielenberg, A. and Ryan, R., *An Economic History of Ireland since Independence* (London:
Routledge, 2013).
Biever, B. F., *Religion, Culture, and Values: A Cross-Cultural Analysis of Motivational Factors in
Native Irish and American Irish Catholicism* (New York: Arno Press, 1976).
Blanchard, J., *The Church in Contemporary Ireland* (Dublin: Clonmore & Reynolds, 1963).

Carey, S., *Social Security in Ireland, 1939–1952: The Limits to Solidarity* (Dublin: Irish Academic Press, 2007).

Coogan, T. P., *De Valera: Long Fellow, Long Shadow* (London: Hutchinson, 1993).

Crowe, C., Fanning, R., Kennedy, M., Keogh, D., O'Halpin, E., and O'Malley, K., (eds.), *Documents on Irish Foreign Policy: Volume IX 1948–1951* (Dublin: Royal Irish Academy, 2014).

Cullen, C., and Ó hÓgartaigh, M. (eds.), *His Grace is Displeased: Selected Correspondence of John Charles McQuaid* (Dublin: Merrion, 2013).

Evans, B., *Seán Lemass: Democratic Dictator* (Cork: The Collins Press, 2011).

Evans, B., and Kelly, S. (ed.), *Frank Aiken: Nationalist and Internationalist* (Dublin: Irish Academic Press, 2014).

Ferriter, D., *Judging Dev: A Reassessment of the Life and Legacy of Éamon de Valera* (Dublin: Royal Irish Academy, 2007).

Finn, T., *Tuairim, Intellectual Debate and Policy Formulation: Rethinking Ireland, 1954–1975* (Manchester: Manchester University Press, 2012).

Gallagher, M., *The Irish Labour Party in Transition 1957–82* (Dublin: Gill & Macmillan, 1982). *Irish Elections 1948–77: Results and Analysis* (London: Routledge, 2009).

Geary, M. J., *An Inconvenient Wait: Ireland's Quest for Membership of the EEC, 1957–73* (Dublin: Institute for Public Administration, 2009).

Girvin, B., 'Ireland and the Marshall Plan: A Cargo Cult in the North Atlantic?', in R. T. Griffiths (ed.), *Explorations in OEEC History* (Paris: OECD, 1997), 61–72.

Between Two Worlds: Politics and Economy in Independent Ireland (Dublin: Gill & Macmillan, 1989).

'The State and Vocational Education 1922–1960', in J. Logan (ed.), *Teachers' Union: The TUI and its Forerunners* (Dublin, 1999), 62–92.

From Union to Union: Nationalism, Democracy and Religion in Ireland (Dublin: Gill & Macmillan, 2002).

'Did Ireland Benefit from the Marshall Plan?: Choice, Strategy and the National Interest in Comparative Context', in T. Geiger and M. Kennedy, (eds.), *Ireland, Europe and the Marshall Plan* (Dublin: Four Courts Press, 2004), 182–220.

'The Treaty of Rome and Ireland's Developmental Dilemma', in M. Gehler, (ed.), *From Common Market to European Union Building. 50 Years of the Rome Treaties 1957–2007* (Wien: Böhlau Verlag, 2009), 573–95.

'Contraception, Moral Panic and Social Change in Ireland, 1969–79', *Irish Political Studies, 23* (2008), 555–76.

'Economic Policy, Continuity and Crisis in de Valera's Ireland 1945–61', *Irish Economic and Social History,* XXXVIII (2011), 36–53.

'Lemass's Brainchild: The 1966 Informal Committee on the Constitution and Change in Ireland, 1966–1973', *Irish Historical Studies* 38 (2013), 406–21.

Girvin, B. and Murphy, G. (eds.), *The Lemass Era* (Dublin: University College Dublin Press, 2005).

Horgan, J., *Noel Browne: Passionate Outsider* (Dublin: Gill & Macmillan, 2000).

Keane, E., *Seán MacBride: A Life* (Dublin: Gill & Macmillan, 2007).

Kearns, K.C., *Ireland's Arctic Siege: The Big Freeze of 1947* (Dublin: Gill & Macmillan, 2011).

Kennedy, M., and O'Halpin, E., *Ireland and the Council of Europe: From Isolation Towards Integration* (Strasbourg: Council of Europe, 2000).

Keogh, D., *Jack Lynch: A Biography* (Dublin: Gill & Macmillan, 2008).

MacDermott, E., *Clann na Poblachta* (Cork: Cork University Press, 1998).

Mair, P., 'De Valera and democracy', in T. Garvin, M. Manning and R. Sinnott (eds.), *Dissecting Irish Politics: Essays in Honour of Brian Farrell* (Dublin: UCD Press, 2004), 31–47.

Manning, M., *James Dillon: A Biography* (Dublin: Wolfhound Press, 1999).

McCullagh, D., *A Makeshift Majority: The First Inter-Party Government, 1948–51* (Dublin: Institute of Public Administration, 1998).

    The Reluctant Taoiseach: A Biography of John A. Costello (Dublin: Gill & Macmillan, 2010).

McKee, E., 'Church–State Relations and the Development of Irish Health Policy: The Mother-and-Child Scheme, 1943–53', *Irish Historical Studies* 25 (1986), 159–94.

Meehan, C., *A Just Society for Ireland: 1964–1987* (London: Palgrave Macmillan, 2013).

Murphy, G., *In Search of the Promised Land: The Politics of Post-War Ireland* (Cork: Mercier, 2009).

Ó Corráin, D., *Rendering to God and Caesar: The Irish churches and the two states in Ireland, 1949–73* (Manchester: Manchester University Press, 2006).

O'Halpin, E., ' "A Greek Authoritarian Phase"? The Irish Army and the Irish Crisis, 1969–70', *Irish Political Studies,* 23 (2008), 475–90.

O'Sullivan, E., and O'Donnell, I., *Coercive Confinement in Post-Independence Ireland: Patients, Prisoners and Penitents* (Manchester: Manchester University Press, 2012).

O'Sullivan, K., *Ireland, Africa and the End of Empire* (Manchester: Manchester University Press, 2012).

Puirséil, N., *The Irish Labour Party 1922–73* (Dublin; University College Dublin Press, 2007).

Rice, B., ' "Hawks Turn to Doves": The Response of the Post-Revolutionary Generation to the "New" Troubles in Ireland, 1969–1971', *Irish Political Studies,* 30 (2015), 238–54.

Walsh, J., *Patrick Hillery: The Official Biography* (Dublin: New Island, 2008).

    The Politics of Expansion: The Transformation of educational policy in the Republic of Ireland, 1957–72 (Manchester: Manchester University Press, 2009).

Whelan, B., 'Ireland, the Marshall Plan and the United States: Cold War Concerns', *Journal of Cold War Studies,* 8 (Winter 2006), 63–94.

Whelan, D. (ed.), *Founded on Fear* (Dublin: Irish Academic Press, 2006).

Whyte, J. H., 'Ireland: Politics Without Social Bases', in R. Rose (ed.), *Electoral Behaviour: A Comparative Handbook* (New York: Free Press, 1974), 619–52.

    Church and State in Modern Ireland 1923–1979, 2nd edn (Dublin: Gill & Macmillan, 1980).

14 Ireland Transformed? Modernisation, Secularisation and Conservatism since 1973

Brian Girvin

Primary sources

Ireland

National Archives of Ireland

'Basis of Irish Foreign Policy' 30 April 1973, Department of Foreign Affairs (DFA), 2005/145/2349

Conference of Heads of Missions, Policy Issues – EEC Aspects, 16–19 April 1973, DFA 2005/145/2349

European Monetary System, DT2009/135/427–28

Lynch to Cosgrave 8 December 1971, DT2003/16/533

Minutes of the All-Party Committee on the implications of Irish unity, DT2004/21/506

'Memorandum on Ireland's Constitutional difficulties in implementing certain proposed conventions between Member States of the European Community' prepared by the Attorney General's Office, February 1975, DT 2006/40/366

'Eight-Amendment of the Constitution' Department of Justice, 2013/98/28

'Consequences of British Withdrawal from the Community', 24 February 1975, DFA 2006/130/8, Dept., of Trade, 2006/133/296

Fitzgerald to Cosgrave 24 January 1975, DFA 2006/130/6 'Report of Inter-Departmental Group on Economic Consequences for Ireland of Withdrawal from the European Communities' 23 January 1975

'Family Planning and Contraception' 13 December 1977, DT, 2008/148/217

UCD Archives

Fianna Fáil Parliamentary Party minutes P176

National Library of Ireland

Brendan Corish Papers

UCC Archives

Annual Report of Fertility Guidance Company Ltd., 1970/71: Keery Papers, Box 54

Printed Secondary Works

Commission of Investigation, *Report into the Catholic Archdiocese of Dublin* (July, 2009) http://www.childabusecommission.ie/

European Commission, Brussels, *Behaviour and Attitudes, Eurobarometer 84* (Brussels: European Commission, 2015).

Challenges and Opportunities Abroad: White Paper on Foreign Policy (Dublin: Government Publications, 1996).

Mahon Tribunal: *The Final Report of the Tribunal of Inquiry into Certain Planning Matters and Payments (2012):* www.oireachtas.ie/parliament/media/committees/archivedcommittees/cnranda/The-Final-Report-Mahon.pdf.

Market Research Bureau of Ireland, *Éire Inniu: An MRBI Perspective on Irish Society* (MRBI, 1987).

Moriarty Tribunal: www.moriarty-tribunal.ie/asp/detail.asp?objectid=310&Mode=0&RecordID=545.

Report of the Joint Committee of Inquiry into the Banking Crisis, 2013.

Report of the Joint Committee of Inquiry into the Banking Crisis, Volume 1: Report Findings and Recommendations (Dublin: Houses of the Oireachtas, 2016).

Secondary Works

Buckley, A. M., 'The Primacy of Democracy over Natural Law in Irish Abortion Law: An Examination of the C Case', *Duke Journal of Comparative & International Law 9* (1998), 275–309.

Devenney, A. D., ' "A Unique and Unparalleled Surrender of Sovereignty": Early Opposition to European Integration in Ireland, 1961–72', *New Hibernia Review / Iris Éireannach Nua* 12 (2008), 15–32.

Dooge, J., and Barrington, R. (ed.), *A Vital National Interest: Ireland in Europe 1973–1998* (Dublin: Institute for Public Administration, 1999).

Fahey, T., Hayes, B. C., and Sinnott, R., (eds.), *Conflict and Consensus: A Survey of values and attitudes in the Republic of Ireland and Northern Ireland* (Dublin: Institute of Public Administration, 2005).

Fahey, T., Russell, H., and Whelan, C. T. (eds.), *Best of Times? The Social Impact of the Celtic Tiger* (Dublin: Institute of Public Administration, 2007).

Ferriter, D., *Judging Dev* (Dublin: Royal Irish Academy, 2007).

FitzGerald, R., and Girvin, B., 'Political Culture, Growth and the Conditions for Success in the Irish Economy', in B. Nolan, P. J. O'Connor and C. T. Whelan, (eds.), *Bust to Boom? The Irish Experience of Growth and Inequality* (Dublin: Institute of Public Administration, 2000), 268–85.

Foster, R. F., *Luck and the Irish: A Brief History of Change 1970–2000* (London: Allen Lane, 2007).

Franklin, M., Mackie, T., and Valen, H. (eds.), *Electoral change: Responses to Evolving Social and Attitudinal structures in Western Countries* (Cambridge University Press, 1992).

Gallagher, M., 'The Earthquake that Never Happened: Analysis of the Results', in M. Gallagher, and M. Marsh (eds.), *How Ireland Voted 2007* (Houndmills, Basingstoke: Palgrave Macmillan, 2008), 78–104.

'Societal Change and Party Adaptation in the Republic of Ireland, 1960–1981', *European Journal of Political Research,* 9 (1981), 269–85.

Gallagher, M. and Sinnott, R. (ed.), *How Ireland Voted 1989,* (Galway: Centre for the Study of Irish Elections, 1990).

Girvin, B., 'The Campaign', in M. Laver, P. Mair and R. Sinnott (eds.), *How Ireland Voted: The Irish General Election 1987* (Swords, Co. Dublin: Poolbeg Press, 1987), 9–29.

'Nationalism and the Continuation of Political Violence in Ireland', in A. F. Heath, R. Breen and C. T. Whelan (eds.), *Ireland: North and South* (Oxford University Press, 1999), 369–400.

'Ireland: More Referendums Anyone?', in C. Carbone (ed.), *National Politics and European Integration: From the Constitution to the Lisbon Treaty* (London: Edward Elgar, 2010), 126–43.

'Church, State and Society since 1960', *Éire-Ireland*, 43 (2008), 179–204.

'Contraception, moral panic and social change in Ireland, 1969–79', *Irish Political Studies,* 23 (2008), 555–76.

'Before the Celtic Tiger: Change Without Modernisation in Ireland 1959–1989', *The Economic and Social Review,* 41 (2010), 349–65.

Girvin, B. and Murphy, G., (eds.), *Continuity, Change and Crisis in Contemporary Ireland* (London: Routledge, 2010), 1–18.

Hanafin, P., 'Same Text, Different Story: Reinterpreting Irish Constitutional Identity', *Bullán: An Irish Studies Journal,* 4 (1998), 103–19.

Hesketh, T., *The Second Partitioning of Ireland: The Abortion Referendum of 1983* (Dun Laoghaire, County Dublin: Brandsma Books, 1990).

Holmes, M., (ed.), *Ireland and the European Union: Nice, Enlargement and the future of Europe* (Manchester: Manchester University Press, 2005).

Horgan, J., *Mary Robinson: An Independent Voice* (Dublin: O'Brien Press, 1997).

Kennelly, B., and Ward, E., 'The Abortion Referendums' in M. Gallagher and M. Laver (eds.), *How Ireland Voted 1992* (Dublin: Folens/PSAI Press, 1993), 115–34.

Leahy, P., *Showtime: The Inside Story of Fianna Fáil in Power* (Dublin: Penguin, 2009).

MacGréil, M., *Prejudice and Tolerance in Ireland* (Dublin: College of Industrial Relations, 1977).
    Prejudice in Ireland Revisited (Maynooth: Survey and Research Unit, 1996).
    Pluralism & Diversity in Ireland: Prejudice and Related Issues in Early 21st Century Ireland (Dublin: Columba Press, 2011).

Market Research Bureau of Ireland, 'Religious Practice and Attitudes Towards Divorce and Contraception among Irish Adults', *Social Studies,* 3 (1974), 276–85.

Marsh, M., and Cunningham, K., 'A Positive Choice, or Anyone But Fianna Fáil?' in M. Gallagher and M. Marsh (eds.), *How Ireland Voted 2011: The Full Story of Ireland's Earthquake Election* (London: Palgrave Macmillan, 2011), 172–204.

Marsh, M., and Mitchell, P., (ed.), *How Ireland Voted 1997* (Boulder, Colorado: Westview Press, 1999).

McGraw, S. D., *How Parties Win: Shaping the Irish Political Arena* (Ann Arbor, MI: Michigan University Press, 2015).

Meehan, C., *A Just Society for Ireland? 1964–1987* (London: Palgrave Macmillan, 2013).

Murphy, G., *Electoral competition in Ireland since 1987: The Politics of triumph and despair* (Manchester: Manchester University Press, 2016).

Penniman, H.R., (ed.), *Ireland at the Polls: The Dáil Elections of 1977* (Washington, DC: American Enterprise Institute, 1978).

Puirséil, N., *The Irish Labour Party 1922–73* (Dublin: University College Dublin Press, 2007).

Wall, M., 'Ireland and the European Economic Community, 1973–1977' unpublished PhD thesis, National University of Ireland, Cork (2011).

Whelan, C. T. (ed.), *Values and Social Change in Ireland* (Dublin: Gill & Macmillan, 1994).

Whelan, K., 'Policy Lessons from Ireland's Latest Depression', *The Economic and Social Review*, 41 (2010), 225–54.

Wilson-Davis, K., 'Irish Attitudes to Family Planning', *Social Studies,* 3 (1974), 262–75.

15 War and Peace in Northern Ireland: 1965–2016

Paul Bew and John Bew

Manuscripts

London, The National Archives

Anglo Irish Agreement, 1985: PREM 19/1548, PREM 19/1549, PREM 19/1550, PREM 1551 PREM 19/1550 and PREM 19/1551

Sir Richard Hopkin's report, 1939, T 160/550/6563/021/1

Memorandum by Merlyn Rees, 12 December 1975, CAB 134/3921

Report from Sir R. Armstrong, CAB 164/615

Thatcher's comments on Irish affairs, 3 Nov. 1981, 3 July 1985, PREM 19/816, PREM 19/1550: TNA

Primary Printed Works

Newspapers and magazines

Hibernia
Daily Telegraph
Belfast Telegraph
Irish Times
Irish Edition, Philadelphia, PA.
Sunday Times
Sunday Tribune

Memoirs and Media Reports

Adams, G., interview with Nick Stadlen, *The Guardian*, 12 September 2009.
  Before the Dawn: An Autobiography (Dingle: Brandon press, 2001).

Baxter, L., Devlin, B., Farrell, M., McCann, E., and Toman, C., 'People's Democracy: A Discussion Strategy', in *New Left Review 55* (May/June 1969).

Bew, J., 'Newly Released State Papers for 1984', in *Irish Times*, 30 December 2014.

Callaghan, J., *A House Divided: The Dilemma of Northern Ireland* (London: Collins, 1973).

Crossman, R. H. S., *Diaries of a Cabinet Minister*, iii, 1968–70 (London: Hamish Hamilton, 1977).

Devlin, P., *The Fall of the Northern Ireland Executive*, (Belfast: P. Devlin, 1975).

Donnelly, C., 'Brothers in the Lord: The DUP MP and LVF frontman', *Slugger O'Toole.com*, 11 December 2006.

Faulkner, B., *Memoirs of a Statesman*, (London: Weidenfeld and Nicolson, 1978).

Mallon, Seamus, Interview on BBC Talkback, reported as 'Seamus Mallon: Sinn Féin "played John Hume like 3lb trout"', 28 Dec. 2015: www.bbc.co.uk/news/uk-northern-ireland-35115892.

Moloney, E., 'So, Was The IRA Defeated, Or Not?' *The Broken Elbow*: https://thebrokenelbow.com/2015/07/29/so-was-the-ira-defeated-or-not/.

Phoenix, E., 'Paisley's Paramilitary Links', *Irish Times*, 20 December 2007.

  'Minutes Show How Fr Faul And Prior Paved way to Hunger Strike Resolution', *Irish Times*, 30 December 2011.

Wilson, H., *The Labour Government 1964–70*, (London: Penguin Harmondsworth, 1974).

Secondary Sources

Bell, G., *Troublesome Business, the Labour Party and Ireland* (London: Pluto Press, 1982).

Bew, J., 'Introduction', to D. W. Miller, *Queen's Rebels: Ulster Loyalism in Historical Perspective* (Dublin: Gill & Macmillan, 2007 edn.).

Bew, J. and Frampton, M., 'Debating the "Stalemate": A Response to Dr Dixon', *The Political Quarterly*, 83 (April–June 2012), 277–282.

Bew, J. and Frampton M., and Gurruchage, I., *Talking To Terrorists: Making Peace in Northern Ireland and the Basque Country* (New York: Columbia University Press, 2009).

Bew, P., 'The Role of the Historical Adviser and the Bloody Sunday Tribunal', *Historical Research*, 199 (February 2005).

"The Blind Leading the Blind"? London's Response to the 1969 Crisis', *History Ireland*, 4 (July / August 2009).

Bew, P. and Patterson, H., *Seán Lemass and the Making of Modern Ireland*, (Dublin: Gill & Macmillan, 1982).

Branch, T., *The Clinton Tapes: A President's Secret Diary* (New York: Simon and Schuster, 2009).

Burton, F., *The Politics of Legitimacy: Struggles in a Belfast Community* (London: Routledge and Kegan Paul, 1978).

Carter, C., and Barrett, D., *Northern Ireland Problem* (Oxford University Press, 1962).

Edwards, O. D., *The Sins of our Fathers: Roots of Conflict in Northern Ireland* (Dublin: Gill & Macmillan, 1970).

Grey, S., *The New Spymasters* (London: St Martins Press, 2015).

Hanley, B., *The Lost Revolution: The Story of the Official IRA and the Workers' Party* (London: Penguin Harmondsworth, 2010).

Hennessey, T., *The Origins of the Troubles* (Dublin: Gill & Macmillan, 2005).

Ingram, M., and Harkin, G., *Stakeknife: Britain's Secret Agents in Ireland* (Dublin: O'Brien Press, 2004).

Lawrence, R., *The Government and Politics of Northern Ireland: Public Finance and Public Services, 1921–64* (Oxford University Press, 1965).

Lillis, M., and Goodall, D., 'Edging Towards Peace', *Dublin Review of Books*, 13 (Spring, 2010), 1–20.

Matthews, C., *Tip and the Gipper: When politics worked* (New York: Simon and Schuster, 2013).

Mawhinney, B., *Just a Simple Belfast Boy* (London: Biteback Publishing, 2013).

McCleery, M., *Operation Demetrius* (Manchester: Manchester University Press, 2015).

Moore, C., *Margaret Thatcher: The Authorised Biography, vol 2 Everything She Wants* (London: Allen Lane, 2015).

Mulholland, M., 'Assimilation versus Segregation: Unionist Strategy in the 1960s', *Twentieth Century British History*, 11, (2000), 284–307.

Ó Dochartaigh, N., *From Civil Rights to Armalites: Derry and the Birth of the Troubles* (Cork: Cork University Press, 1997).

O'Malley, P., *Biting at the Grave: The Irish Hunger Strikes and the Politics of Despair* (Boston: Beacon Press, 1991).

Patterson, H., *Ireland's Violent Frontier: The Border and Anglo-Irish Relations* (Houndmills: Palgrave Macmillan, 2013).

Smith, W. B., *The British State and the Northern Ireland crisis, 1969–73* (Washington, DC: The United States Institute of Peace Press, 2011).

Smyth, J., 'A Discredited Cause? The IRA and Support for Political Violence', in A. O'Day and Y. Alexander (eds.), *Ireland's Terrorist Trauma: Interdisciplinary Perspectives* (Basingstoke: Palgrave Macmillan, 1989), 101–23.

Smyth, P., and Hennessey, M., (eds.), 'Anglo-Irish Agreement', *Irish Times*, 14 November 2015.

Spencer, G., *The British and Peace in Northern Ireland: The Process and Practice of Reaching Agreement* (Cambridge University Press, 2015).

Stothard, P., *30 Days: A Month at the Heart of Blair's War* (London: Element press, 2009).

Ware, J., 'Collusion Cuts Both Ways', *Standpoint* (November 2015).

Warner, G., 'The Falls Road Curfew revisited', *Irish Studies Review*, 4 (August, 2006).

16 The Irish Economy 1973 to 2016

John O'Hagan

Bradley, J., and Best, M., *Cross Border Economic Renewal: Rethinking Irish Regional Policy,* (Centre for Cross Border Studies, March 2012).

Bradley, J., 'Economic Development: The Textile and Information Technology Sectors', in J. Coakley and L. O'Dowd (eds.), *Crossing the Border: New relationships between Northern Ireland and the Republic of Ireland* (Dublin: Irish Academic Press, 2006).

Carswell, S., *Anglo Republic: Inside the Bank that Broke Ireland* (Dublin: Penguin Ireland, 2011).

Donovan, D. and Murphy, A. E., *The Fall of the Celtic Tiger: Ireland and the Euro Debt Crisis* (Oxford University Press, 2013).

Haughton, J., 'Historical Background', in J. O'Hagan and C. Newman, *The Economy of Ireland: National and Sectoral Policy Issues* (12th edn., Gill & Macmillan, Dublin 2014).

'Growth in Living Standards and Output', in J. O'Hagan and C. Newman, *The Economy of Ireland: National and Sectoral Policy Issues* (12th edn., Gill & Macmillan, Dublin 2014).

Nyberg, P., *Misjudging Risks: Causes of the Systemic Banking Crisis in Ireland* (Dublin: Government publications, 2011).

O'Hagan, J., and McIndoe-Calder, T., 'Population, Employment and Unemployment', in J. O'Hagan and C. Newman, *The Economy of Ireland: National and Sectoral Policy Issues* (12th edn., Gill & Macmillan, Dublin 2014).

O'Hagan, J. and Newman, C., (ed.), *The Economy of Ireland: National and Sectoral Policy Issues* (12th edn,), Gill & Macmillan, Dublin 2014.

www.crossborder.ie/pubs/2012-economic-report.pdf.

www.economist.com/blogs/economist-explains/2013/11/economist-explains-4.

17 Migration Since 1914

Mary E. Daly

Primary Printed Sources

Commission on Emigration and Other Population Problems, 1948–54. (Dublin: Government Publications, 1955).

Economic Development (Dublin: Department of Finance, 1958).

Fennell, D., (ed.). *The Changing Face of Catholic Ireland* (London: G. Chapman, 1968).

Irish Catholic Directory, 1933.

Secondary Works

Barritt, D., and Carter, C., *The Northern Ireland problem. A Study in Group Relations* (Oxford University Press, 1962).

Belchem, J., *Irish, Catholic and Scouse. The history of the Liverpool Irish 1800–1939*, (Liverpool: Liverpool University Press, 2007).

Bielenberg, A., 'Exodus: The Emigration of Southern Irish Protestants during the War of Independence and the Civil War', *Past and Present*, 218 (2013).

Bielenberg, A. (ed.), *The Irish Diaspora*, (Harlow: Longman: 2000).

Bordo, M., Taylor, A. M., and Williamson, J. G. (eds.), *Globalization in Historical Perspective* (Chicago: University Chicago Press, 2005).

Chiswick, B. R. and Hatton, T. J., 'International Migration and the Integration of Labor Markets', in M. Bordo, A. Taylor, A and J. Williamson (eds.), *Globalization in Historical Perspective* (Chicago: University Chicago Press, 2003), 65–120.

Clark, P., *Hope and Glory. Britain 1900–1990*, (London: Penguin, 1996).

Corcoran, M.J., *Irish illegals. Transients between Two Societies,* (Westport, CN: Greenwood, 1996).

Corcoran, M., 'The Process of Migration and the Reinvention of Self: The Experiences of Returning Irish Emigrants', in K. Kenny (ed.), *New Directions in Irish-American history*, (Madison, WI: University of Wisconsin Press, 2003).

Courtney, D., 'A Quantification of Irish Migration with Particular Emphasis on the 1980s and 1990s', in A. Bielenberg (ed.), *The Irish Diaspora*, (Harlow: Longman, 2000).

Daly, M. E., 'Irish Nationality and Citizenship since 1922', *IHS*, 32 (May, 2001), 377–407.

'Irish Women and the Diaspora, Why they Matter', in D. A. J. Macpherson and M. Hickman (eds.), *Women and Irish Diaspora Identities. Theories, Concepts and New Perspectives* (Manchester: Manchester University Press, 2014).

'Nationalism, Sentiment and Economics: Relations between Ireland and Irish America in the Post-war Years', in J. J. Lee and M. Casey (ed.), *Making the Irish American. History and heritage of the Irish in the United States,* (New York: New York University Press, 2006).

The Irish State and the Diaspora, NUI Centennial, O'Donnell Lecture, 2008, (Dublin: NUI, 2009).

The Slow Failure. Population Decline and Independent Ireland, 1920–1973, (Madison, WI: University of Wisconsin Press, 2006).

Delaney, E., 'Placing Post-war Irish Migration in Britain in a Comparative European Perspective, 1945–1981', in A. Bielenberg (ed.), *The Irish Diaspora*, (Harlow: Longman, 2000).

The Irish in Post-war Britain, (Oxford University Press, 2007).

Dowling, L. A., 'Irish-America, 1940–2000', in J. J. Lee and M. Casey (ed.), *Making the Irish American. History and Heritage of the Irish in the United States,* (New York: New York University Press, 2006).

Dunne, C., *An Unconsidered People. The Irish in London* (Dublin: New Island, 2003).

Earner-Byrne, L., 'The Boat to England: An Analysis of the Official Reactions to the Emigration of Single Expectant Irishwomen to Britain, 1922–1972', *Irish Economic and Social History*, 30 (2003), 52–70.

Fosythe, F. and Booroah, V., 'The Nature of Migration between Northern Ireland and Great Britain: A Preliminary Analysis based on the Labour Force Surveys, 1986–88, *Economic and Social Review*, 23, 105–27.

Gilmartin, M. and White, A., (eds.), *Migrations. Ireland in a Global World* (Manchester: Manchester University Press, 2013).

Glynn, I., Mac Einrí, P. and Kelly T., *Irish Emigration in an Age of Austerity* (Cork: University College Cork, 2013).

Gray, B., ' "Generation Emigration": The Politics of Transnational Social Reproduction in Twenty-first Century Ireland', *Irish Studies Review*, 21 (2013), 20–36.

Halpin, B., 'Who are the Irish in Britain? The Evidence from Large-scale Surveys', in A. Bielenberg (ed.), *The Irish Diaspora*, (Harlow: Longman, 2000), 89–107.

Hart, P., 'The Protestant Experience of War and Revolution in Southern Ireland', in R. English and G. Walker (eds.), *Unionism in Modern Ireland* (London: Macmillan, 1996).

Hickman, M. and Walters, B., *Discrimination and the Irish Community in Britain* (London: Commission for Racial Equality, 1997).

   Religion, Class and Identity: The State, the Catholic Church and the Education of the Irish in Britain (Aldershot: Ashgate, 1995).

Joyce, P., 'The Journey West', *Field Day Review*, 10 (2014).

Kenny, K. (ed.), *New Directions in Irish-American history*, (Madison, WI: University of Wisconsin Press, 2003).

   The American Irish: A History (London: Longman, 2000).

   Diaspora. A Very Short Introduction (Oxford University Press, 2011).

Keogh, D., *Jews in Twentieth-century Ireland: Refugees, Anti-semitism and the Holocaust*, (Cork: Cork University Press, 1998).

Kirwan, F. X., 'Recent Anglo-Irish Migration – the Evidence of the British Labour Force Surveys', *Economic and Social Review*, 13, 1982.

Lambert, S., 'Irish Women's Emigration to England, 1922–1960: The Lengthening of Family Ties', in A. Hayes and D. Urquhart (eds.), *Female Experience: Essays in Irish Women's History* (Dublin: Irish Academic Press, 2000).

Lee, J. J., 'Introduction: Interpreting Irish America', in J. J. Lee and M. Casey (ed.), *Making the Irish American. History and heritage of the Irish in the United States,* (New York: New York University Press, 2006).

Lukas, J. A., *Common Ground. A Turbulent Decade in the Lives of Three American families*, (New York: Random House, 1985).

MacLellan, A., 'Victim or Vector? Tubercular Irish Nurses in England 1930–1960', in C. Cox and H. Marland (eds.), *Migration, Health and Ethnicity in the Modern World*, (Basingstoke: Palgrave Macmillan, 2013), 104–25.

McGreevy, J., *Parish Boundaries. The Catholic Encounter with Race in the Twentieth-century Urban North*, (Chicago: Chicago University Press, 1996).

Moulton, M., *Ireland and the Irish in Interwar England* (Cambridge University Press, 2014).

National Economic and Social Council (NESC), *The Economic and Social Implications of Emigration* (Dublin: 1991), 14.

O'Brien, M., 'Transatlantic Connections and the Great Depression', in K. Kenny (ed.), *New Directions in Irish-American history*, (Madison, WI: University of Wisconsin Press, 2003), 78–97.

O'Sullivan, K., 'The Search for Justice. NGOs in Britain and Ireland and the New International Economic Order, 1968–82', in *Humanity. An international journal of human rights, humanitarianism and development*, 6 (2015), 173–87.

Paul, K., *Whitewashing Britain. Race and Citizenship in the Post-war Era* (Ithaca: Cornell University Press, 1997).

Spencer, A. E. C. W., *Arrangements for the Integration of Irish Immigrants in England and Wales* (Dublin: Irish Manuscripts Commission, 2011).

Trew, J., *Leaving the North. Migration and Memory: Northern Ireland 1921–2011* (Liverpool: Liverpool University Press, 2013).

Walters, B., 'Transnational Networks across Generations: Childhood Visits to Ireland by the Second Generation in England', in M. Gilmartin and A. White (eds.), *Migrations. Ireland in a Global World* (Manchester: Manchester University Press, 2013), 17–35.

Wasserstein, B., *Vanishing Diaspora: The Jews in Europe since 1945* (London: Hamish Hamilton, 2006).

Wilson, A. J., *Irish America and the Ulster Conflict, 1968–1995* (Belfast: Blackstaff Press, 1995).

18 Broadcasting on the Island of Ireland, 1916–2016

Robert J. Savage

Manuscripts

Dublin

Kelly, Fergus, Witness Statement 351, Bureau of Military History, Military History Archives, Cathal Brugha Barracks, Dublin.

RTÉ Written Archives, 105/58, no. 1, *Listenership Surveys*.

Belfast

Memorandum by the Prime Minister, 14 October 1968, Cab/4/1406, PPRONI Public Record Office of Northern Ireland.

Secondary Works

Bell, D., 'Proclaiming the Republic: Broadcasting Policy and the Corporate State in Ireland', in *Broadcasting Policy and Politics in Western Europe*, 8 (1985).

Bloom, E., ' "Channel Paddlers" 1950s Irish Drama on the British Airwaves', *Éire-Ireland*, 50 (Spring/Summer 2015).

Briggs, A., *The History of Broadcasting in the United Kingdom, volume V: Competition* (Oxford University Press, 1995).

Byrne, G., with Purcell, D., *The Time of My Life* (Dublin: Gill & Macmillan, 1989).

Cathcart, R., *The Most Contrary Region, The BBC in Northern Ireland 1924–1984* (Belfast: The Blackstaff Press, 1984).

Cathcart, R. and Muldoon, M., 'The Mass Media in Twentieth Century Ireland', in J. R. Hill (ed.), *A New History of Ireland, VII, Ireland 1921–1984*, (Oxford University Press, 2003).

Flynn, R., 'It is against the Basic Concepts of Good Government to Subject our People to Rosemary Clooney at the Public Expense: Imported Programming on Early Irish Television', *Éire-Ireland*, 50 (Spring/Summer 2015).

Fuller, L., *Irish Catholicism Since 1950* (Dublin: Gill & Macmillan, 2002).

Horgan, J., *Broadcasting and Public Life* (Dublin: Four Courts Press, 2004).

Lynch, B., 'Steering Clear: Broadcasting and the Church, 1926–1951', *New Hibernia Review*, 4 (2000).

McIntosh, G., *The Force of Culture Unionist Identities in Twentieth-Century Ireland* (Cork: Cork University Press, 1999).

'Tyrone Guthrie and the BBC in Belfast', *Éire-Ireland*, 50 (Spring/Summer) 2015.

McLoone, M., 'The Construction of a Partitionist Mentality: Early Broadcasting in Ireland', in M. McLoone (ed.), *Broadcasting in a Divided Community. Seventy Years of the BBC in Northern Ireland* (Belfast: Institute of Irish Studies, QUB, 1996).

Morash, C., *A History of the Media in Ireland* (Cambridge University Press, 2010).

Moynihan, M., (ed.), *Speeches and Statements by Éamon de Valera 1917–1973* (Dublin: Gill & Macmillan, 1980).

O'Brien, A., 'Not in the Hot Seat: The Impact of Women on Broadcasting', in *Éire-Ireland*, 50 (Spring/Summer 2015).

Pettitt, L., *Screening Ireland, Film and Television Representation,* (Manchester: Manchester University Press, 2000).

Pine, R., *2RN and the origins of Irish Radio*, (Dublin: Four Courts Press, 2002).

Savage, R. J., *Irish Television, the Political and Social Origins,* (Cork: Cork University Press, 1996).

    A Loss of Innocence? Television and Irish Society 1960–1972, (Manchester: Manchester University Press, 2010).

    The BBC's Irish Troubles, television, conflict and Northern Ireland (Manchester: Manchester University Press, 2015).

    'Interview with John Bowman', *Éire-Ireland*, 50 (Spring/Summer 2015), 224–6.

    The Origins of Irish Radio, unpublished Master of Arts thesis, University College Dublin (1982).

Scannell, P., and Cardiff, D., *A Social History of British Broadcasting, vol. 1 1922–1939, Serving the Nation* (Oxford: Wiley-Blackwell, 1991), 288.

Walsh, J. J., *Recollections of a Rebel*, (The Kerryman Press: Tralee, 1944).

19 Popular Culture in Ireland, 1880–2016

Paul Rouse

Printed Primary Sources

Celtic Times
Cork Examiner, 22 July 2015
Freeman's Journal, 19 January 1915
Irish Banking Magazine, July 1919
Irish Banking Magazine, August 1919
Irish Banking Magazine, January 1923
Irish Independent, 18 July 1913
Irish Independent, 19 August 1913
Irish Times, 18–19 October 1915
Irish Times, 2 November 1915
Irish Times, 28 November 2009

Secondary Works

Arensberg, C., *The Irish Countryman* (London: Macmillan, 1937).

Blaney, L., *The Motor Car and Ireland* (PhD thesis, UCD, 2015).

Byrne, A., 'Entertainments, Memorials and Societies', in H. B. Clarke and S. Gearty (eds.), *Maps and Texts: Exploring the Irish Historic Towns Atlas* (Dublin: RIA, 2013), 236–56.

Condon, D., *Early Irish Cinema, 1895–1921* (Dublin: Irish Academic Press, 2008).

Crowley, T., 'The Art of Memory: The Murals of Northern Ireland and the Management of History', in *Field Day Review*, 7 (2011), 22–49.

Dickson, D., *Dublin: The Making of a Capital City* (London: Profile Books, 2015).

Duncan, M. and Rouse, P., *Creating Ireland: Research and the Role of the Humanities and Social Sciences in Ireland* (Dublin: Irish Research Council, 2014).

Ferriter, D., *A Nation of Extremes: The Pioneers in Twentieth-century Ireland,* (Dublin: Profile Books, 1999).

    The Transformation of Ireland (London: Profile Books, 2005).

    Ambiguous Republic: Ireland in the 1970s (London: Profile Books, 2012).

Fleischmann, A., 'Music and Society, 1850–1921', in W. E. Vaughan (ed.), *A New History of Ireland VI: Ireland Under the Union, 1870–1921* (Oxford University Press, 1995), 500–22, 500.

Gilmartin, M., *Ireland and Migration in the Twenty-First Century* (Manchester: Manchester University Press, 2015).

Griffin, B., *Cycling in Victorian Ireland* (Dublin: Four Courts Press, 2006).

Holohan, C., 'Every Generation has its Task: Attitudes to Irish Youth in the Sixties' (PhD Thesis, UCD: 2009).

Kelly, J., and Comerford, R. V. (eds.), *Associational Culture in Ireland and Abroad* (Dublin: Four Courts Press, 2015).

Kiberd, D., and Matthews, P. J. (eds.), *Handbook of the Irish Revival: An Anthology of Irish Cultural and Political Writings 1891–1922* (Dublin: Abbey Theatre, 2015).

Legg, M.-L., *Newspapers and Nationalism: The Irish Provincial Press, 1850–1892* (Dublin: Four Courts Press, 1999).

Lyons, F. S. L., *Culture and Anarchy, 1890–1939* (Oxford University Press, 1979).

Martin, P., *Censorship in the Two Irelands, 1922–1939* (Dublin: Irish Academic Press, 2006).

McIntosh, G., *The Force of Culture: Unionist Identities in Twentieth Century Ireland* (Cork: Cork University Press, 1999).

Morash, C., *A History of the Media in Ireland* (Cambridge University Press, 2010).

Morgan, E., 'Question Time: Radio and the Liberalisation of Irish Public Discourse after World War II', in *History Ireland*, 9 (Winter, 2001), 38–41.

O'Callaghan, L., *Rugby in Munster: A Social History* (Cork: University Press, 2011).

O'Connor, N., *Bringing It All Back Home: The Influence of Irish Music at Home and Abroad* (London: BBC books, 1991).

O'Leary, E., *Teenagers, Everyday Life and Popular Culture in 1950s Ireland* (PhD Thesis, NUIM, 2013).

Power, P., *Send 'Em Home Sweatin': The Showband Story* (Dublin: Mercier Press, 2000).

Rolston, B., '"The Brothers on the Walls": International Solidarity and Irish Political Murals', in *Journal of Black Studies*, 39, (January, 2009), 446–70.

Rouse, P., *Sport and Ireland: A History* (Oxford University Press, 2015).

Smyth, J., 'Dancing, Depravity and All That Jazz: The Public Dance Halls Act of 1935', in *History Ireland*, 1, (Summer, 1993), 51–4.

Toibín, C., (ed.), *An Homage to Enniscorthy*, (Wexford: Wexford Library Service, 2010).

Toms, D., *Soccer in Munster: A Social History, 1877–1937* (Cork: Cork University Press, 2015).

Vallely, F., *The Companion to Irish Traditional Music* (Cork: Cork University Press, 1999).

Vannais, J., 'Mainstreaming Murals', in *Fortnight*, 385 (May, 2000), 21–2.

Walsh, M., *Bitter Freedom: Ireland in a Revolutionary World, 1918–1923* (London: Faber & Faber, 2015).

White, H. and Boydell, B. (eds.), *The Encyclopedia of Music in Ireland* (Dublin: UCD Press, 2013).

20 Irish Foreign Policy: 1919 to 1973

Michael Kennedy

Brennan, Robert, *Ireland Standing Firm* (Dublin: UCD Press, 2002 edition).

Davis, T. R., *Dublin's American Policy: Irish-American diplomatic relations, 1945–1952* (Washington, DC: CUA Press, 1998).

Dorr, N., *Ireland at the United Nations: Memories of the Early Years* (Dublin: Institute of Public Administration, 2010).

Evans, B. and Kelly, S. (eds.), *Frank Aiken: Nationalist and Internationalist* (Dublin: Irish Academic Press, 2014).

Fanning, F., 'Raison d'État and the Evolution of Irish Foreign Policy', in M. Kennedy and J. M. Skelly (eds.), *Irish Foreign Policy, 1919–66. From Independence to Internationalism* (Dublin: Four Courts Press, 2000).

Fanning, R., *The Irish Department of Finance, 1922–1958* (Dublin: Institute of Public Administration, 1978).

Fisk, R., *In time of war: Ireland, Ulster and the price of Neutrality, 1939–45* (Dublin: Gill & Macmillan, 1983).

Geary, M., *An Inconvenient Wait: Ireland's Quest for Membership of the EEC, 1957–1973* (Dublin: Institute of Public Administration, 2009).

Girvin, B., *The Emergency: Neutral Ireland 1939–45* (Dublin: Gill & Macmillan, 2006).

Gray, D., *A Yankee in de Valera's Ireland* (Dublin: Royal Irish Academy, 2012).

Harkness, D., *The Restless Dominion* (Dublin: Gill & Macmillan, 1969).

Horgan, J., *Seán Lemass, the Enigmatic Patriot* (Dublin: Gill & Macmillan, 1997).

Kelly, K., *Returning Home: Irish Ex-servicemen after the Second World War* (Dublin: Irish Academic Press, 2012).

Kelly, S., *Fianna Fáil, Partition and Northern Ireland, 1926–1971* (Dublin: Irish Academic Press, 2013).

Kennedy, D., *The Widening Gulf: Northern Attitudes to the Independent Irish State* (Belfast: The Blackstaff Press, 1988).

Kennedy, M., *Ireland and the League of Nations* (Dublin: Irish Academic Press, 1996).

'Wrong to Assume all Deserters were Allied Veterans', *Irish Times*, 15 February 2012.

Division and Consensus: The Politics of Cross-border Relations in Ireland, 1925–1969 (Dublin: Institute of Public Administration, 2000).

'"Nobody Knows and Ever Shall Know from Me that I Have Written It". Joseph Walshe, Éamon de Valera and the Execution of Irish Foreign Policy, 1932–8', *Irish Studies in International Affairs*, 14 (2003), 165–83.

Guarding Neutral Ireland (Dublin: Four Courts Press, 2008).

Kennedy, M. and Laing, V., *The Irish Defence Forces 1940–1949. The Chief of Staff's reports* (Dublin: Irish Manuscripts Commission, 2011).

   and O'Halpin, E., *Ireland and the Council of Europe. From isolation towards integration* (Strasbourg: Council of Europe Publishing, 2000).

   and Skelly, J. M., *Irish Foreign Policy 1919–1966* (Dublin: Four Courts Press, 2000).

Kennedy, M., Crowe, C., Fanning, R., Keogh, D. and O'Halpin, E. (eds.), *Documents on Irish Foreign Policy, I – X (1919 to 1957)* (Dublin: Royal Irish Academy, 1998 to date). See also www.difp.ie.

Keogh, D., *Ireland and Europe* (Cork: Cork University Press, 1990).

   Ireland and the Vatican. The Politics and Diplomacy of Church–State Relations, 1922–60 (Cork: Cork University Press, 1995).

   Jews in Twentieth Century Ireland (Cork: Cork University Press, 1998).

Keown, G., *First of the Small Nations* (Oxford University Press, 2016).

Magennis, A., *Ireland, the United Nations and the Congo* (Dublin: Four Courts Press, 2014).

Maher, D. J., *The tortuous path. The Course of Ireland's Entry into the EEC 1948–73* (Dublin: Institute of Public Administration, Dublin, 1986).

Mallmann Showell, Jak, *Fuhrer Conferences on Naval Affairs* (London: Greenhill Books, 2005).

MacKinder, H. J., *Britain and the British Seas* (Oxford University Press, 1907).

McCabe, I., *A Diplomatic History of Ireland 1948–49: The Republic, the Commonwealth and NATO* (Dublin: Irish Academic Press, 1991).

McCullagh, D., *A Makeshift Majority. The First Inter-Party Government, 1948–51* (Dublin: Institute of Public Administration, 1998).

   The Reluctant Taoiseach. A Biography of John A. Costello (Dublin: Gill & Macmillan, 2010).

McMahon, D., *Republicans and Imperialists: Anglo-Irish Relations in the 1930s* (New Haven: Yale University Press, 1984).

   '"Our Mendicant Vigil is Over." Ireland and the United Nations, 1946–55', in M. Kennedy and D. McMahon (eds.), *Obligations and Responsibilities: Ireland and the United Nations 1955–2005* (Dublin: Institute of Public Administration, 2005).

McNamara, P., *Seán Lester, Poland and the Nazi Takeover of Danzig* (Dublin: Irish Academic Press, 2009).

Milotte, M., *Banished Babies: The Secret History of Ireland's Baby Export Business* (Dublin: New Island, 1997).

Moynihan, M. (ed.), *Speeches and Statements by Éamon de Valera 1917–73* (Dublin: Gill & Macmillan, 1980).

O'Brien, Conor Cruise, *To Katanga and Back: A UN Case History* (London: Hutchinson, 1962).

O'Halloran, C., *Partition and the Limits of Irish Nationalism* (Dublin: Gill & Macmillan, 1987).

O'Halpin, E., *Defending Ireland* (Oxford University Press, 1999).

O'Sullivan, K., *Ireland, Africa and the End of Empire: Small State Identity in the Cold War* (Manchester, Manchester University Press, 2012).

Pakenham, Frank, *Peace by Ordeal* (London: Jonathan Cape, 1935).

Ryle Dwyer, T., *Behind the Green Curtain: Ireland's phoney neutrality during World War II* (Dublin: Gill & Macmillan, 2009).

Skelly, J. M., *Irish Diplomacy at the United Nations: National Interests and the International Order* (Dublin: Irish Academic Press, 1997).

Ireland and the United Nations (Dublin: Four Courts Press, 1997).

Sloan, G. R., *The Geopolitics of Anglo-Irish Relations in the 20th Century* (London: Leicester University Press, 1997).

Smith, R., *Under the Blue Flag* (Dublin: Gill & Macmillan, 1980).

Tonra, B., Kennedy, M., Doyle, J. and Dorr, N. (eds.), *Irish Foreign Policy* (Dublin: Gill & Macmillan, 2012).

Walsh, J., *Patrick Hillery. The official biography* (Dublin: New Island, 2008).

Whelan, B., *The Marshall Plan and Ireland* (Dublin: Irish Academic Press, 2000).

United States Foreign Policy and Ireland. From Empire to Independence, 1913–29 (Dublin: Four Courts Press, 2006).

Wills, C., *That Neutral Island: A Cultural History of Ireland during the Second World War* (London: Faber and Faber, 2007).

Wylie, P., *Ireland and the Cold War: Recognition and diplomacy 1949–1963* (Dublin: Irish Academic Press, 2006).

21 The Family in Ireland, 1880–2015

Lindsey Earner-Byrne

Printed Primary Sources

Barry, D., 'Female Suffrage from a Catholic Standpoint', *Irish Ecclesiastical Record*, 26 (September, 1909), 295–303.

Cameron, C., *How the Poor Live* (Dublin: John Falconer, 1904).

Census of Population, General Reports, 1926, Vol. X, Housing (Dublin: Stationery Office, 1934).

Commission of Inquiry into the Reformatory and Industrial School System 1934–1936: Report (Dublin, 1936).

Dáil Éireann Debates, 'Private Bills for Divorce', 11 February 1925, 23 November 1943, vols. 10, 92.

Daly, Rev. C. B., 'Family Life: The Principles', *Christus Rex*, 5, (1951), 1–19.

Debates, Seanad Éireann (1980), 5.

de Cleir, S. 'Marriage and the family in Irish Life,' *Christus Rex*, 6 (1952).

Devlin, K., 'Single and Selfish', *Christus Rex*, 6 (1952), 223–31.

Dillon, T. W. T., 'The Social Services in Éire', *Studies,* 34 (1945).

Domestic Abuse of Women and Men in Ireland: Report on the National Study of Domestic Abuse (Dublin: ESRI, 2005).

Flynn, T. E., 'The Moral Argument against Birth Control', *The Dublin Review*, 173 (1923), 243–62.

Geary, R. C., 'The Future Population of Saorstát Éireann and Some Observations on Population Statistics', *Statistical and Social Inquiry Society of Ireland*, 15 (1935–36), 15–33.

Hanna, F., 'Family Life: The facts', *Christus Rex*, 5 (1951), 20–45.

Humphreys, A. J., 'Migration to Dublin: Its Social Effects', *Christus Rex*, 9 (1955).

Law Reform Commission, *Report on Illegitimacy* (Dublin: Law Reform Commission, 1982).

McCarthy, M. D., 'Some Family Facts in Ireland Today', *Christus Rex*, 5 (1951), 46–64.

McGuinness, C., *The Report of Kilkenny Incest Investigation* (Dublin: HMSO, 1993).

McNamara, K., *The Family Today* (Dublin: Irish Messenger, 1984).

McWilliams, M., and McKiernan, J., *Bringing it Out in the Open: Domestic Violence in Northern Ireland* (Belfast: HMSO, 1993).

Meenan, J., 'Some Causes and Consequences of the Low Irish Marriage Rate', *Statistical and Social Inquiry Society of Ireland*, 15 (1932–33).

'Woman's Place in the Community', *Christus Rex*, 13 (1959), 90–102.

Murphy, Rev. H., 'The Rural Family: The Principles', *Christus Rex*, 6 (1952), 3–20.

Newman, J., 'Socio-political Aspects of Divorce', *Christus Rex*, 23 (1969), 5–14.

Ó Danachair, C., 'The Irish Family in Tradition', *Christus Rex*, 16 (1962), 185–96.

http://ec.europa.eu/eurostat/statistics-explained/index.php/Fertility_statistics (accessed 20 January 2016).

www.amen.ie/Papers/110909_unmarried_fathers_IT.htm (accessed 23 September 2015).

www.into.ie/lgbt/EducationalResources/ (accessed 23 September 2015).

Viney, E., 'Women in Rural Ireland', *Christus Rex*, 22 (1968), 333–42.

Secondary Works

Akenson, D. H., *Education and Enmity: The Control of Schooling in Northern Ireland 1920–1950* (Newton Abbot, 1973).

Anderson, M., 'Lawful Wife, Unlawful Sex – Examining the Effect of the Criminalization of Marital Rape in England and the Republic of Ireland', *Georgia Journal of International & Comparative Law*, 27, (1998), 139–66.

Arensberg, C. M., and Kimball, S. T., *Family and Community in Ireland* (Clare: Clasp Press, 2001 [first edition, 1940]).

Birdwell, D., 'The Early Twentieth-century Irish Stem Family: A Case Study from County Kerry' in M. Silverman and P. Gulliver (eds.), *Approaching the Past: Historical Anthropology through Irish Case Studies* (New York: Columbia University Press, 1992).

Bourke, J., *Husbandry to Housewifery: Women, Economic Change, and Housework in Ireland, 1890–1914* (Oxford: Clarendon Press, 1993).

Brody, H., *Inishkillane: Change and Decline in the West of Ireland* (London: Jill Norman and Hobhouse Ltd, 1973).

Buckley, S., 'Family and Power: Incest in Ireland, 1880–1950' in A. McElligott, L. Chambers, C. Breathnach and C. Lawless (eds.), *Power in History. From Medieval Ireland to the Post-Modern World* (Dublin: Irish Academic Press, 2011), 185–206.

Carr, C. J., 'A Family Planning Survey', *Journal of the Irish Medical Association*, 73 (1980), 340–1.

Clancy, P., 'Demographic Changes and the Irish Family', in P. Clancy (ed.), *The Changing Family* (Dublin: Family Studies Unit, UCD, 1984), 1–38.

Clear, C., 'Women in de Valera's Ireland 1932–48: A Reappraisal' in G. Doherty and D. Keogh (eds.), *De Valera's Irelands* (Cork: Mercier Press, 2003), 104–14.

'"Too Fond of Going": Female Emigration and Change for Women in Ireland, 1946–1961', in D. Keogh, F. O'Shea and C. Quinlan (eds.), *The Lost Decade: Ireland in the 1950s* (Cork: Mercier Press, 2004), 135–46.

Collins, L., *The Irish Housewife – A Portrait* (Dublin: Irish Consumer Research, 1986).

Conley, C. A., *Melancholy Accidents: The Meaning of Violence in Post-Famine Ireland* (Oxford: Lexington Books, 1999).

Connolly, L., *The Irish Women's Movement: From Revolution to Devolution* (London: Palgrave Macmillan, 2002).

Coulter, C., ' "Hello Divorce, Goodbye Daddy": Women, Gender and the Divorce Debate', in A. Bradley and M. Valiulis (eds.), *Gender and Sexuality in Modern Ireland* (Massachusetts: University of Massachusetts Press, 1997), 275–98.

Cousens, S. H., 'The Regional Variations in Population Changes in Ireland, 1861–1881', *The Economic History Review*, 17 (1964).

Cousins, M., *The Birth of Social Welfare in Ireland 1922–1952* (Dublin: Four Courts Press, 2003), 60.

Crossman, V., *The Poor Law in Ireland, 1838–1948* (Dundalk: Dundalgan Press, 2006).

'Cribbed, Contained and Confined? The Care of Children under the Irish Poor Law, 1850–1920', *Éire-Ireland*, 44 (Spring/Summer, 2009), 37–61.

Daly, M.E., ' "Turn on the Tap": The State, Irish Women and Running Water', in M. Valiulis and M. O'Dowd (eds.), *Women and Irish History* (Dublin: Wolfhound Press, 1997), 206–19.

'The Irish Family since the Famine: Continuity and Change', *Irish Journal of Feminist Studies*, 3 (1999), 1–21.

Slow Failure: Population Decline and Independent Ireland (Madison, WI: University of Wisconsin Press, 2006).

'Marriage, Fertility and Women's Lives in Twentieth-century Ireland', *Women's History Review*, 15 (2006), 571–85.

' "The Primary and Natural Educator?": The Role of Parents in the Education of their Children in Independent Ireland', *Éire-Ireland* 44 (Spring/Summer, 2009), 194–217.

Delaney, E., 'The Vanishing Irish?: The Exodus from Ireland in the 1950s', in D. Keogh, F. O'Shea and C. Quinlan, *The Lost Decade: Ireland in the 1950s* (Cork: Mercier Press, 2004), 80–6.

Earner-Byrne, L., 'Moral Repatriation': The Response to Irish Unmarried Mothers in Britain, 1920s–1960s', in P. Duffy (ed.), *To and From Ireland: Planned Migration Schemes c.1600–2000* (Dublin: Geography Publications, 2004), 155–73.

'Child Sexual Abuse, History and the Pursuit of Blame in Modern Ireland', in K. Holmes and S. Ward (eds.), *Exhuming Passions: Memory and the Uses of the Past in Australia and Ireland* (Dublin: Irish Academic Press, 2011), 51–70.

Fahey, T., 'The Family in Ireland in the New Millennium', in L. Connolly (ed.), *The 'Irish' Family* (London and New York: Routledge, 2014), 54–69.

'State, Family and Compulsory Schooling in Ireland', *The Economic and Social Review*, 21 (1992), 369–95.

Farrell, E., *'A Most Diabolical Deed': Infanticide and Irish Society, 1850–1900* (Manchester,: Manchester University Press, 2013).

Ferguson, H., 'Abuse Inquiries and the Report of the Kilkenny Incest Investigation: A Critical Analysis', *Administration*, 41 (Winter 1993–1994), 385–410.

Fisher, K., ' "She was Quite Satisfied with the Arrangements I Made": Gender and Birth Control in Britain 1920–1950', *Past and Present,* 169 (2000), 161–93.

Fitzpatrick, D., 'Class, Family and Rural Unrest in Nineteenth-century Ireland' in P. J. Drudy (ed.), *Ireland: Land, Politics and People* (Cambridge University Press, 1982), 37–75.

'Marriage in Post-Famine Ireland' in A. Cosgrove (ed.), *Marriage in Ireland* (Dublin: College Press, 1985), 116–31.

'The Modernisation of the Irish Female', in P. O'Flanagan, P. Ferguson and Whelan, K. (eds.), *Rural Ireland 1600–1900: Modernisation and Change* (Cork: Cork University Press, 1987), 162–80.

Oceans of Consolation: Personal Accounts of Irish Migration to Australia (New York: Cornell University Press, 1994).

'Irish Farming Families before the First World War', *Comparative Studies in Society and History*, 25 (1983), 339–74.

'"A Share of the Honeycomb": Education, Emigration and Irishwomen', *Continuity and Change*, 2 (1986), 217–34.

Fleming, N. C., 'Education since the Late Eighteenth Century' in Kennedy and Ollerenshaw (eds.), *Ulster Since 1600*, 211–27.

Fogarty, M., Ryan, L. and Lee, J., *Irish Values and Attitudes: The Irish Report of the European Value Systems Study* (Dublin: Dominican Publications, 1984).

Frances Keating, M., 'Marriage-shy Irishmen', in O'Brien (ed.), *The Vanishing Irish*, 173–75.

Gibbon, P., and Curtin, C., 'The Stem Family in Ireland', *Comparative Studies in Society and History*, 20 (1978), 429–53.

'Irish Farm Families: Facts and Fantasies', *Comparative Studies in Society and History*, 25 (1983), 375–80.

Guinnane, T., *The Vanishing Irish: Households, Migration and the Rural Economy in Ireland 1850–1914* (Princeton, NJ: Princeton University Press, 1997).

'The Poor Law and Pension in Ireland', *Journal of Interdisciplinary History*, 24 (1993), 271–91.

Hannan, D. F., *Displacement and Development: Class, Kinship and Social Change in Irish Rural Communities* (Dublin: The Economic and Social Research Institute, 1979).

Hill, M., *Women in Ireland: A Century of Change* (Belfast: The Blackstaff Press, 2003).

Hug, C., *The Politics of Sexual Morality in Ireland* (New York: Macmillan Press, 1999).

Humphreys, A. J., *New Dubliners: Urbanization and the Irish Family* (London: Routledge and Kegan Paul, 1966).

Hyde, A., 'Marriage and Motherhood: The Contradictory Position of Single Mothers', *Irish Journal of Feminist Studies*, 2 (July 1997), 22–36.

Ingle, R., 'They Won't be Home for Christmas', *Irish Times*, 4 December, 2004.

Ireland, A., 'Records of Pupils in National Schools: Samples from the Records of the National Archives of Ireland', *Irish Archives*, 20 (2013), 16–26.

Jones, G., 'Marie Stopes in Ireland – The Mother's Clinic in Belfast, 1936–47', *Social History of Medicine*, 5 (1992), 443–58.

Kearns, K. C., *Dublin's Lost Heroines: Mammies and Grannies in a Vanished City* (Dublin: Gill & Macmillan, 2004).

Kennedy, F., *Cottage to Crèche: Family Change in Ireland* (Dublin: Institute of Public Administration, 2002).

Kennedy, L., 'Farm Succession in Modern Ireland: Elements of a Theory of Inheritance', *The Economic History Review*, 44 (August 1991), 477–99.

Kennedy, L., Miller, K. and Gurrin, B., 'People and Population Change, 1600–1914', in L. Kennedy and P. Ollerenshaw (eds.), *Ulster Since 1600: Politics, Economy, and Society* (Oxford University Press, 2012), 58–73.

Leyton, E., *The One Blood: Kinship and Class in an Irish Village* (Toronto: University of Toronto Press, 1975).

Maguire, M. J., 'The Changing Face Of Catholic Ireland: Conservatism and Liberalism in the Anne Lovett and Kerry Babies Scandals', *Feminist Studies*, 27 (Summer, 2001), 335–58.

Maguire, M. J., and Ó Cinnéide, S., '"A Good Beating Never Hurt Anyone": The Punishment and Abuse of Children in Twentieth-Century Ireland', *Journal of Social History*, 38 (Spring 2005), 635–52.

Martin, P., 'Social Policy and Social Change since 1914', L. Kennedy and P. Ollerenshaw (eds.), *Ulster Since 1600*.

McAvoy, S., 'Sexual Crime and Irish Women's Campaign for a Criminal Law Amendment Act, 1912–35', in M. Valiulis (ed.), *Gender and Power in Irish History* (Dublin: Irish Academic Press, 2009), 84–100.

McCafferty, N., *In the Eyes of the Law* (Dublin: Poolbeg, 1987).

McCormick, L., *Regulating Sexuality: Women in Twentieth-century Northern Ireland* (Manchester: Manchester University Press, 2009).

'"The Scarlet Woman in Person": The Establishment of a Family Planning Service in Northern Ireland, 1950–1974', *Social History of Medicine*, 21 (2008), 345–60.

McCullagh, C., 'A Tie That Binds: Family and Ideology in Ireland', *The Economic and Social Review* 22 (April 1991), 199–211.

McLaughlin, E., 'Women and the Family in Northern Ireland: A Review', *Women's Studies International Forum*, 16 (1993), 553–68.

McLoughlin, D., 'Women and Sexuality in Nineteenth-Century Ireland', *The Irish Journal of Psychology*, 15 (1994), 266–75.

McShane, L. and Pinkerton, J., '"The Family" in Northern Ireland', *Studies: An Irish Quarterly Review*, 75 (Summer, 1986), 167–76.

Mogey, J. M., *Rural Life in Northern Ireland: Five Regional Studies Made for the Northern Ireland Council of Social Service* (Oxford University Press, 1947).

Newman Devlin, E., *Speaking Volumes: A Dublin Childhood* (Belfast: The Blackstaff Press, 2000).

Nic Ghiolla Phádraig, M., 'Social and Cultural Factors in Family Planning', *The Changing Family* (Dublin: Family Studies Unit, UCD, 1984), 58–97, 79.

Ó Corráin, D., *Rendering to God and Caesar: The Irish Churches and the Two States in Ireland, 1949–73* (Manchester: Manchester University Press, 2007), 184–91.

Ó Gráda, C., '"The Greatest Blessing of all": The Old Age Pension in Ireland', *Past and Present*, 175 (2002), 124–61.

Ó Gráda, C. and Walsh, B., 'Fertility and Population in Ireland, North and South', *Population Studies*, 49 (1995).

Ó Gráda, C. and Duffy, N., 'The Fertility Transition in Ireland and Scotland, c. 1880–1930', in S. J. Connolly, R. A. Houston and R. J. Morris (eds.), *Conflict, Identity and Economic Development: Ireland and Scotland, 1600–1939* (Preston: Carnegie Publishing, 1995).

O'Brien, J. A. (ed.), *The Vanishing Irish: The Enigma of the Modern World* (London: W.H. Allen, 1954).

O'Connor, C., 'Mixed Marriage "A Grave Injury to our Church": An Account of the 1957 Fethard-on-Sea Boycott', *The History of the Family*, 13 (2008), 395–401.

O'Halloran, K., *Family Law in Northern Ireland* (Dublin: Gill & Macmillan, 1997).

Powell, B., Dockeray, J. and Swaine, E., 'Unmarried Mothers: A Survey of 200 Presenting for Ante-natal Care', *Irish Medical Journal*, 75 (1982), 248–49.

Prior, P. M., *Madness and Murder: Gender, Crime and Mental Disorder in Nineteenth-Century Ireland* (Dublin: Irish Academic Press, 2008).

Quine, M., *Population Politics in Twentieth-Century Europe: Fascist Dictatorships and Liberal Democracies* (London: Routledge, 1996).

Rattigan, C., ' "Done to Death by Father or Relatives": Irish Families and Infanticide Cases, 1922–1950', *The History of the Family*, 13 (2008), 370–83.

Rohan, R., *Marriage Irish Style* (Cork: Mercier Press, 1969).

Sheridan, J. D., 'We Are Not Dead Yet' in O'Brien (ed.), *The Vanishing Irish*, 177–92.

Steiner-Scott, E., ' "To Bounce a Boot off Her Now and Then": Domestic Violence in Post-famine Ireland', in M. Valiulis and M. O'Dowd (eds.), *Women and Irish History* (Dublin: Wolfhound Press, 1997), 125–43.

Stomberg-Childers, K., 'Paternity and the Politics of Citizenship in Interwar France', *Journal of Family History*, 26 (2001), 90–111.

Urquhart, D., 'Marriage, Fertility, and Breaking the Moral Code', in L. Kennedy and P. Ollerenshaw (eds.), *Ulster Since 1600: Politics, Economy, and Society* (Oxford University Press, 2012), 246–59.

'Irish Divorce and Domestic Violence, 1857–1922', *Women's History Review*, 22 (2013), 820–37.

Ussher, A., 'The Boundary between the Sexes' in O'Brien (ed.), *The Vanishing Irish*, 150–63.

Walsh, B., 'Marriage in Ireland in the Twentieth Century', in A. Cosgrove (ed.), *Marriage in Ireland* (Dublin: College Press, 1985), 132–50.

22 Institutional Space and the Geography of Confinement in Ireland, 1750–2000

Catherine Cox

Primary Sources

Wexford County Archive: letters to John Redmond, 1912–14: The Archive of St Senan's Psychiatric Hospital, Enniscorthy.

Printed Primary Sources

A Vision for Change. A Report of the Expert Group on Mental Health Policy (Dublin: Stationery Office, 2006).

Connolly, H., 'The Scandal of the Mental Hospitals', *Magill*, 1 October 1980.

Cowley, M. 'Parents did not Know Ann Lovett was Pregnant', *Irish Times*, 22 February, 1984.

Doyle, P., *The God Squad* (Dublin: Raven Arts Press, 1988).

Final Report of the Commission to Inquire into Child Abuse, 2000–2005, vols. I–V, (Dublin: Stationery Office, 2009).

Flynn, G. M., *Nothing to Say. A Novel* (Dublin: Ward River Press, 1983).

Irish Penal Reform Trust, Facts and Figures: www.iprt.ie/prison-facts-2 (accessed 15 October 2015).

McCann, E., 'MI5's Murky Role in Kincora Scandal Yet to be Exposed', *Irish Times* (24 July 2014).

Mother and Baby Homes Commission of Enquiry: Terms of Reference: www.mbhcoi.ie.

Pim, W. H., *On the Importance of Reformatory Establishments for Juvenile Delinquents* (Dublin: Hodges and Smith, 1854).

Reformatory and Industrial Schools System: Report (Dublin: Stationery Office, 1966).

Report of the Commission of Inquiry on Mental Illness (Dublin: Stationery Office, 1966).

Report of the Commission on Relief of the Sick and Destitute Poor including the Insane Poor (Dublin: Stationery Office, 1927).

Report of the Inter-Departmental Committee to establish the facts of State Involvement with the Magdalene Laundries, 2013): www.justice.ie.

The Psychiatric Services. Planning For the Future. A Report of the Study Group on the Development of the Psychiatric Services (Dublin: Stationery Office, 1966).

Tyrrell, P., 'Early Days in Letterfrack. Memories of an Industrial School', *Hibernia* (June, 1964). *Founded on Fear*, ed. D. Whelan (Dublin: Irish Academic Press, 2006).

Viney, M., 'Psychiatry and the Irish', *Irish Times*, 30 October 1963; 'No Room to Move', *Irish Times*, 23 October 1963; 'The Opening Door', *Irish Times*, 24 October 1963; 'Patients with a Purpose', *Irish Times*, 25 October 1963; 'Change for Revolution', *Irish Times*, 26 October 1963.

Secondary Works

Andrews, J., 'Case Notes, Case Histories and the Patient's Experience of Insanity at Gartnavel Royal Asylum, Glasgow, in the Nineteenth Century', *Social History of Medicine*, 11 (1998), 255–81.

Barnes, J., *Irish Industrial Schools, 1868–1908. Origins and Development* (Dublin: Irish Academic Press, 1989).

Bourke Brogan, P., *Eclipsed* (Galway: Salmon Publishing, 1994).

Brennan, D., *Irish Insanity 1800–2000* (London: Routledge, 2014).

Buckley, S. A., *The Cruelty Man: Child Welfare, the NSPCC and the State in Ireland, 1889–1956* (Manchester: Manchester University Press, 2013).

Burnard, R. F. C. (ed.), *Catholic Who's Who and Year Book, 1908* (London: Burns & Oates, 1908).

Byrne, F., 'Madness and Mental Illness in Ireland: Discourses, People and Practices, 1900 to *c.*1960', unpublished PhD thesis. (UCD, 2011).

Carey, T., *Mountjoy: The Story of a Prison* (Dublin: Collins Press, 2000).

Carroll-Burke, P., *Colonial Discipline: The Making of the Irish Convict System* (Dublin: Four Courts Press, 2000).

Conrad, J., *Crime and its Corrections. An International Survey of Attitudes and Practices* (Berkeley: University California Press, 1965).

Convery, U., 'Locked in the Past': An Historical Analysis of the Legal Framework of Custody for Children in Northern Ireland', *Journal of European Criminology*, 11 (2014), 251–69.

Cousins, M., *The Birth of Social Welfare in Ireland, 1922–1952* (Dublin: Four Courts Press, 2003).

'Sickness, Gender and National Health Insurance, 1920s to 1940s', in M. Preston and M. Ó hÓgartaigh (eds.), *Gender and Medicine in Ireland 1700–1950* (Syracuse: Syracuse University Press, 2012), 169–88.

Cox, C., *Negotiating Insanity in the Southeast of Ireland, 1820–1900* (Manchester: Manchester University Press, 2012).

Cox, P., and Shore, H., *Becoming Delinquent: British and European Youth 1650–1950* (Aldershot: Ashgate, 2002).

Crossman, V., *Poverty and the Poor Law in Ireland, 1850–1914* (Liverpool: Liverpool University Press, 2013).

'The Growth in the State in Nineteenth-century Ireland', in J. Kelly (ed.), *The Cambridge History of Ireland. Volume 3: Ireland, c.1730–c.1880* (Cambridge University Press, 2018).

'The New Ross Workhouse Riot of 1887: Nationalism, Class and the Irish Poor Laws', *Past and Present*, 179 (2003), 135–58.

'Cribbed, Contained and Confined? The Care of Children under the Irish Poor Law, 1850–1920', *Éire-Ireland*, 44 (2009), 37–61.

Crowther, M. A., *The English Workhouse System, 1834–1929. The History of an English Social Institution* (Athens: University of Georgia Press, 1983).

Daly, M. E., ' "Oh Kathleen O'Houlihan, Your Way's A Thorny Way". The Condition of Women in Twentieth Century Ireland', in A. Bradley and M. Valiulis (eds.), *Gender and Sexuality in Modern Ireland* (Massachusetts: University of Massachusetts Press, 1997), 102–26.

Dooley, E., 'Sir Walter Crofton and the Irish or Intermediate System of Prison Discipline' in O'Donnell and McAuley (eds.), *Criminal Justice History*, 196–213.

Durnin, D., 'Intertwining Institutions: The relationship between the South Dublin Union workhouse and the Richmond Lunatic Asylum, 1880–1911' (unpublished MA thesis, UCD, 2010).

Earner-Byrne, L., *Mother and Child: Maternity and Child Welfare in Dublin, 1920s–1960s* (Manchester: Manchester University Press, 2007).

'Child Sexual Abuse, History and the Pursuit of Blame in Modern Ireland', in K. Holmes and S. Ward (eds.), *Exhuming Passions: Memory and the Pressures of the Past in Australia and Ireland* (Dublin: Irish Academic Press, 2011), 51–70.

'The Boat to England: An Analysis of the Official Reactions to the Emigration of Single Expectant Irishwomen to Britain, 1922–1972', *Irish Economic and Social History*, 30 (2003), 52–70.

Ellis, H., *Juvenile Delinquency and the Limits of Western Influence 1850–2000* (Houndmills: Palgrave Macmillan, 2014).

Enright, A., 'Antigone in Galway', *London Review of Books*, 37 (17 December 2015), 11–14.

Feeney, T., ' "Church, State and the Family": The Advent of Child Guidance Clinics in Independent Ireland', *Social History of Medicine*, 25 (2012), 848–62.

Ferguson, H., 'Abused and Looked after Children as "Moral Dirt": Child Abuse and Institutional Care in Historical Perspective', *Journal of Social Policy*, 36 (2007).

Finnane, M., *Insanity and the Insane in Post-Famine Ireland* (London: Croom Helm, 1981).

'Asylums, Families and the State', *History Workshop Journal*, 20 (1985), 134–48.

Finnegan, F., *Poverty and Prostitution. A Study of Victorian Prostitutes in York* (Cambridge University Press, 1979).

Fitzpatrick, D., 'Women, Gender and the Writing of Irish History', *Irish Historical Studies*, 27 (1991), 267–73.

Forsythe, W. J., *The Reform of Prisoners 1830–1900* (London: Croom Helm, 1987).

Furman, S. S., *Community Mental Health Services in Northern Europe* (Bethesda, Md.: National Institute of Mental Health, 1965).

Garland, D., *Punishment and Welfare: A History of Penal Strategies* (Aldershot: Gower, 1985). *The Culture of Control. Crime and Social Order in Contemporary Society* (Oxford, 2001).

Gartland, F., 'Church said Ann Lovett's Death due to "Immaturity"' *Irish Times* (27 December 2014).

Gestrich, A., King, S., and Raphael, L., 'The Experience of Being Poor in Nineteenth and Early-twentieth-century Europe', in A. Gestrich, S. King and L. Raphael, (eds.), *Being Poor in Modern Europe: Historical Perspectives 1800–1940* (Bern: Peter Lang, 2006).

Gilligan, R., 'The "Public Child" and The Reluctant State?', *Éire-Ireland*, 44 (2009), 265–90.

Goldman, L., *Science, Reform and Politics in Victorian Britain. The Social Science Association, 1857–1886* (Cambridge University Press, 2002).
'Crofton, Sir Walter Frederick (1815–1897)', *Oxford Dictionary of National Biography*: www. oxforddnb.com/view/article/65325 (accessed 14 October 2015).

Goulding, J., *The Light in the Window* (Dublin: Poolbeg Press, 1998).

Gray, P., *The Making of the Irish Poor Law* (Manchester: Manchester University Press, 2009).

Greally, H., *Bird's Nest Soup* (Dublin: Figgis, 1971).

Hitchcock, T., 'A New History from below', *History Workshop Journal*, 57 (2004), 294–8.

Horgan, J., 'Did the Media Exploit Granard?', *Irish Times* (1 March 1984).

Ignatieff, M., *A Just Measure of Pain: Penitentiaries in the Industrial Revolution, 1780–1850* (New York: Pantheon Books, 1978).
'State, Civil Society and Total Institutions: A Critique of recent Histories of Punishment', in S. Cohen and A. Scull (eds.), *Social Control and the State. Historical and Comparative Essays* (Oxford: Martin Robertson, 1983), 75–105.

Kennedy, F., *Cottage to Crèche: Family Change in Ireland* (Dublin: Institute of Public Administration, 2001).

Kilcommins, S., O'Donnell, I., O'Sullivan, E., and Vaughan, B., *Crime, Punishment, and the Search for Order in Ireland* (Dublin: Institute of Public Administration, 2004).

Leaney, E., 'Lentaigne, John Francis O'Neill', in J. McGuire and J. Quinn (eds.), *Dictionary of Irish Biography*, vol. 5 (Cambridge University Press, 2009).

Luddy, M., *Women and Philanthropy in Nineteenth-Century Ireland* (Cambridge University Press, 1995).
'Moral Rescue and Unmarried Mothers in Ireland in the 1920s', *Women's Studies*, 30 (2001).
and Murphy C., (eds.), *Women Surviving: Studies in Irish Women's History in the 19th and 20th Centuries* (Dublin: Poolbeg Press, 1990).

Lyons, M., *The Writing Culture of Ordinary People in Europe, c.1860–1920* (Cambridge University Press, 2013).

MacDonagh, O., *States of Mind: Two Centuries of Anglo-Irish Conflict, 1780–1980* (London: Pimlico, 1992).

Maguire, M., *Precarious Childhood in Post-Independence Ireland* (Manchester: Manchester University Press, 2009).

Mahood, L., *The Magdalenes. Prostitution in the Nineteenth Century* (London: Routledge, 1990).

Malcolm, E., *Swift's Hospital: A History of St Patrick's Hospital, Dublin, 1746–1989* (Dublin: Gill & Macmillan, 1989).

Mauger, A., 'Great Class which Lies between: Provision for the Non-pauper Insane in Ireland, 1830–1900' (unpublished PhD thesis, University College Dublin, 2013).

McCarthy, A., 'Hearths, Bodies and Minds: Gender Ideology and Women's Committal to Enniscorthy Lunatic Asylum 1916–25' in A. Hayes and D. Urquhart (eds.), *Irish Women's History* (Dublin: Irish Academic Press, 2004), 115–36.

McConville, S., *Irish Political Prisoners 1848–1922: Theatres of War* (London: Routledge, 2003).

  Irish Political Prisoners 1920–1962 (London: Taylor and Francis Ltd., 2013).

McCormick, L., *Regulating Sexuality. Women in Twentieth-century Northern Ireland* (Manchester: Manchester University Press, 2009).

  '"The Scarlet Woman in Person": The Establishment of a Family Planning Service in Northern Ireland, 1950–1974', *Social History of Medicine*, 21 (2008), 345–60.

McDowell, R. B., *The Irish Administration 1801–1914* (London: Routledge and K. Paul, 1964).

Meehan, N., 'Church and State and the Bethany Home', *History Ireland*, supplement, 18 (2010), 1–10.

Miller, I., 'Constructing Moral Hospitals: Childhood Health in Irish Reformatories and Industrial Schools, *c.*1851–1890', in A. Mac Lellan and A. Mauger (eds.), *Growing Pains: Childhood Illness in Irish History, 1750–1950* (Dublin: Irish Academic Press, 2014), 105–22.

Milne, K., *The Irish Charter Schools 1730–1830* (Dublin: Four Courts Press, 1997).

Murphy, W., *Political Imprisonment and the Irish, 1912–1921* (Oxford University Press, 2014).

Ó Ciosáin, N., *Ireland in Official Print Culture 1800–1850* (Oxford University Press, 2014).

Ó Gráda, C., 'The Heights of Clonmel Prisoners, 1845–1849: Some Dietary Implications', *Irish Economic and Social History*, 18 (1991), 24–33.

O'Brien, P., *The Promise of Punishment. Prisons in Nineteenth-Century France* (Princeton, NJ: Princeton University Press, 1982).

O'Donnell, I., and McAuley, F. (eds.), *Criminal Justice History: Themes and Controversies from Pre-Independence Ireland* (Dublin: Four Courts Press, 2003).

O'Sullivan, E., and O'Donnell, I., *Coercive Confinement in Ireland: Patients, Prisoners and Penitents* (Manchester: Manchester University Press, 2012).

  'Coercive Confinement in the Republic of Ireland. The Waning of a Culture of Control', *Punishment and Society* 9 (2009).

Palmer, S., *Police and Protest in England and Ireland, 1780–1850* (Cambridge University Press, 1988).

Porter, R., 'Howard's Beginning: Prisons, Disease, Hygiene', in R. Creese, W. F. Bynum and J. Bearn (eds.), *The Health of Prisoners* (Amsterdam: Rodopi, 1995), 5–26.

Prior, P., *Madness and Murder. Gender, Crime and Mental Disorder in Nineteenth-Century Ireland* (Dublin: Irish Academic Press, 2008).

Prior, P. M. and Griffiths, D. V., 'The Chaplaincy Question: The Lord Lieutenant of Ireland versus the Belfast Lunatic Asylum', *Éire-Ireland*, 33 (1997), 137–53.

Purdue, O., 'Poor Relief in the North of Ireland, 1850–1921', in V. Crossman and P. Gray (eds.), *Poverty and Welfare in Ireland, 1838–1948* (Dublin: Irish Academic Press, 2011), 23–36.

Quinlan, C. M., *Inside Ireland's Women's Prisons. Past and Present* (Dublin: Four Courts Press, 2011).

Rafferty, M., and O'Sullivan, E., *Suffer the Little Children: The Inside Story of Ireland's Industrial Schools* (Dublin: New Island, 1999).

Reidy, C., *Ireland's 'Moral Hospitals': The Irish Borstal System, 1906–1956* (Dublin: Irish Academic Press, 2009).

Reynolds, J., *Grangegorman: Psychiatric Care in Dublin Since 1815* (Dublin: Institute of Public Administration, 1992).

Riordan, S., ' "Storm and Stress": Richard Devane, Adolescent Psychology and the Politics of Protective Legislation 1922–1935', in C. Cox and S. Riordan (eds.), *Adolescence in Modern Irish History* (Houndmills: Palgrave Macmillan, 2015), 129–50.

Robins, J., *The Lost Children. A Study of Charity Children in Ireland 1700–1900* (Dublin: Institute of Public Administration, 1987).

From Rejection to Integration. A Centenary of Service by the Daughters of Charity to Persons with a Mental Handicap* (Dublin: Gill & Macmillan, 1992).

'Religious Issues in the Early Workhouse', *Studies*, 57 (1968), 54–66.

Rogan, M., *Prison Policy in Ireland. Politics, Penal Welfarism and Political Imprisonment* (London: Routledge, 2011).

Rosenthal, A. H., *Social Programs of Sweden: A Search for Security in a Free Society* (Minneapolis: University of Minnesota Press, 1967).

Rothman, D., *The Discovery of the Asylum* (Boston: Little Brown, 1971).

Sargent, P., *Wild Arabs and Savages. A History of Juvenile Justice in Ireland* (Manchester: Manchester University Press, 2013).

Schlossman, S., *Love and the American Delinquent: The Theory and Practice of 'Progressive' Juvenile Justice, 1825–1920* (Chicago: University of Chicago Press, 1977).

'Delinquent Children: The juvenile reform school', in N. Morris and D. J. Rothman (eds.), *The Oxford History of the Prison: The Practice of Punishment in Western Society* (Oxford University Press, 1998).

Scull, A., *Museums of Madness* (London: Allen Lane, 1979).

'Power, Social Control, and Psychiatry: Some Critical Reflections', in S. Armstrong and L. McAra (eds.), *Perspectives on Punishment. The Contours of Control* (Oxford University Press, 2006), 197–216.

Smith, J., *Ireland's Magdalen Laundries and the Nation's Architecture of Containment* (Manchester: Manchester University Press, 2007).

Some of Our Children: A Report on the Residential Care of the Deprived Child in Ireland by a London Branch Study Group (London: Tuairim, 1966).

Stedman Jones, G., *Outcast London* (London: Penguin, 1971).

'Class Expression versus Social Control. A Critique of Recent Trends in the Social History of Leisure', *History Workshop* 4 (1977), 162–70.

Stewart, J., 'Children, Parents and the State: The Children Act 1908', *Children and Society*, 9 (1995), 90–9.

Summers, A., 'Elizabeth Fry and Mid-Nineteenth Century Reform' in R. Creese, W. F. Bynum and J. Bearn (eds.), *The Health of Prisoners* (Amsterdam: Rodopi, 1995), 5–26.

Touher, P., *Fear of the Collar: My Terrifying Childhood in Artane* (Dublin: O'Brien Press, 2001).

Viney, M., 'Psychiatry and the Irish', *Irish Times*, 30 October 1963; 'No Room to Move', *Irish Times*, 23 October 1963; 'The Opening Door', *Irish Times*, 24 October 1963; 'Patients with a Purpose', *Irish Times*, 25 October 1963; 'Change for Revolution', *Irish Times*, 26 October 1963; 'Psychiatry and the Irish', *Irish Times*, 30 October 1963.

Walsh, D., and Daly, A., *Mental Illness in Ireland, 1750–2002: Reflections on the Rise and Fall of Institutional Care* (Dublin: Health Research Board).

Walsh, O., ' "The Designs of Providence": Race, Religion and Irish Insanity' in J. Melling and B. Forsythe (eds.), *Insanity, Institutions, and Society, 1800–1914: A Social History of Madness in Comparative Perspective* (London and New York: Routledge, 1999), 223–42.

23 A Short History of Irish Memory in the Long Twentieth Century

Guy Beiner

Primary Sources

The Bureau of Military History Collection available online: http://www.bureauof militaryhistory.ie.

Military Service Pensions Collection: www.militaryarchives.ie/collections/online-collections/military-service-pensions-collection.

Printed Primary Sources

1798 Commemoration Office Strategy Statement in *Strategy Statement for the Department of the Taoiseach for the Years 1998–2000* (Dublin, 2001).

Arensberg, C. M., and Kimball, S. T., *Family and Community in Ireland*, 3rd edn. (Ennis, County Clare: Clasp Press, 2001).

Barry, T., *Guerilla Days in Ireland* (Dublin: Irish Press, 1949).

Breen, D., *My Fight for Irish Freedom* (Dublin: Talbot Press, 1924).

Collected Works of Pádraic H. Pearse, vol. 5: *Political Writings and Speeches* (Dublin, Cork and Belfast: The Phoenix Publishing Co., 1916).

Durkheim, É., *The Elementary Forms of the Religious Life*, translated by J. W. Swain (London: G. Allen & Unwin, 1915).

Government's 1798 Commemoration Committee National Programme (Dublin: Department of the Taoiseach, 1998).

Ireland's Famine: Commemoration and Awareness (Dublin: Famine Commemoration Committee, Department of the Taoiseach, 1995).

O'Malley, E., *On Another Man's Wound* (London: Rich & Cowan, 1936).

The 1798 Commemoration Committee's Mission Statement (April, 1997) published in *Freedom of Information Act, 1997: Guide to the Functions and Records of the Department of the Taoiseach – Sections 15 and 16 Reference Book* (Department of the Taoiseach: Dublin, 1998).

Secondary Works

Barber, F., 'At Art's Edge: Post-Conflict Memory and Art Practice in Northern Ireland', in O. Frawley (ed.), *Memory Ireland, vol. 3: Diaspora and Memory Practices* (Syracuse: Syracuse University Press, 2012), 232–46.

Barton, R., *Irish National Cinema* (London and New York: Routledge, 2004).

Beiner, G., 'Commemorating "Ninety-Eight" in 1998: A Reappraisal of History-Making in Contemporary Ireland', in T. Brotherstone, A. Clark and K. Whelan (eds.), *These Fissured Isles: Ireland, Scotland and British History, 1798–1848* (Edinburgh: John Donald Publishers, 2005), 221–41.

'Commemorative Heritage and the Dialectics of Memory', in M. McCarthy (ed.), *Ireland's Heritages: Critical Perspectives on Memory and Identity* (Aldershot and Burlington: Ashgate, 2005), 55–69.

Remembering the Year of the French: Irish Folk History and Social Memory (Madison, WI: University of Wisconsin Press, 2007).

'Fenianism and the Martyrdom–Terrorism Nexus in Ireland before Independence', in D. Janes and A. Houen (eds.), *Martyrdom and Terrorism: Pre-Modern to Contemporary Perspectives* (Oxford University Press, 2014), 199–220.

'The Decline and Rebirth of "Folk Memory": Remembering "The Year of the French" in the Late Twentieth Century', *Éire – Ireland*, 38 (2003), 7–32.

'The Legendary Robert Emmet and His Bicentennial Biographers,' *The Irish Review*, 32 (2004), 98–104.

'Between Trauma and Triumphalism: The Easter Rising, the Somme, and the Crux of Deep Memory in Modern Ireland', *Journal of British Studies*, 46 (2007), 366–89.

'"No, Nay, Never" (Once More): The Resurrection of Hungarian Irredentism,' *History Ireland*, 21 (2013), 40–4.

'Probing the Boundaries of Irish Memory: From Postmemory to Prememory and Back', *Irish Historical Studies*, 39 (2014), 296–307.

Blaney, A., 'Remembering Historical Trauma in Paul Greengrass's *Bloody Sunday*,' *History and Memory*, 19 (2007), 113–38.

Blight, D. W., 'The Memory Boom: Why and Why Now?', in P. Boyer and J. V. Wertsch (eds.), *Memory in Mind and Culture* (Cambridge University Press, 2009), 238–51.

Brett, D., *The Construction of Heritage* (Cork: Cork University Press, 1996).

Briody, M., *The Irish Folklore Commission 1935–1970: History, Ideology, Methodology* (Helsinki: Finnish Literature Society, 2007).

Bryan, D., *Orange Parades: The Politics of Ritual, Tradition, and Control* (London and Sterling, VA: Pluto Press, 2000).

Byrne, J. P., 'Cultural Memory, Identity, and Irish-American Nostalgia', in O. Frawley (ed.), *Memory Ireland, vol. 2: Diaspora and Memory Practices* (Syracuse University Press, 2012), 49–60.

Canavan, T., 'The Poppy My Father Wore: The Problems Facing Irish Nationalists in Commemorating the Two World Wars' in E. Bort, *Commemorating Ireland: History, Politics, Culture* (Dublin: Irish Academic Press, 2004), 56–67.

Cashman, R., *Storytelling on the Northern Irish Border: Characters and Community* (Bloomington: Indiana University Press, 2008), 233–56.

Collins, P., *Who Fears to Speak of '98? Commemoration and the Continuing Impact of the United Irishmen* (Belfast: Ulster Historical Foundation, 2004).

Connerton, P., *How Societies Remember* (Cambridge University Press, 1989), 41–71.

How Modernity Forgets (Cambridge University Press, 2009).

Conway, B., *Commemoration and Bloody Sunday: Pathways of Memory* (Basingstoke and New York: Palgrave Macmillan, 2010).

Cregan, D., 'Remembering to Forget: Queer Memory and the New Ireland', in O. Frawley (ed.), *Memory Ireland, vol. 2: Diaspora and Memory Practices* (Syracuse University Press, 2012), 184–94.

Cronin, M., and Adair, D., *The Wearing of the Green: A History of St. Patrick's Day* (London and New York: Routledge, 2006).

Crowley, J., 'Constructing Famine Memory: The Role of Monuments' in N. Moore, and Y. Whelan, *Heritage, Memory and the Politics of Identity: New Perspectives on the Cultural Landscape* (Aldershot and Burlington: Ashgate, 2007), 55–67.

Daly, M. E., '"History à la Carte?" Historical Commemoration and Modern Ireland', in E. Bort, *Commemorating Ireland: History, Politics, Culture* (Dublin: Irish Academic Press, 2004), 34–55.

and O'Callaghan, M., (eds.), *1916 in 1966: Commemorating the Easter Rising* (Dublin: Royal Irish Academy, 2007).

Dawson, G., *Making Peace with the Past? Memory, Trauma and the Irish Troubles* (Manchester: Manchester University Press, 2007).

Dingley, J., *Durkheim and National Identity in Ireland: Applying the Sociology of Knowledge and Religion* (New York: Palgrave Macmillan, 2015).

Doherty, R., *Irish Volunteers in the Second World War* (Dublin: Four Courts Press, 2002).

Dolan, A., 'An Army of Our Fenian Dead: Republicanism, Monuments and Commemoration' in F. McGarry (ed.), *Republicanism in Modern Ireland* (Dublin: UCD Press, 2003), 132–44.

Commemorating the Irish Civil War: History and Memory, 1923–2000 (Cambridge University Press, 2003).

Donnelly, Jr, J. S., 'Big House Burnings in County Cork During the Irish Revolution, 1920–21', *Éire-Ireland*, 47 (2012), 141–97.

Dooley, T., 'The Destruction of the Country House in Ireland, 1879–1973', in J. Raven (ed.), *Lost Mansions: Essays on the Destruction of the Country House* (Basingstoke and New York: Palgrave Macmillan, 2015), 44–62.

Dunn, S., 'Bloody Sunday and Its Commemoration Parades' in T. G. Fraser (ed.), *The Irish Parading Tradition: Following the Drum* (New York: St. Martin's Press, 2000), 129–41.

Dunne, T., *Rebellions: Memoir, Memory, and 1798* (Dublin: Lilliput Press, 2004).

Fitzpatrick, D., 'Commemoration in the Irish Free State: A Chronicle of Embarrassment', in I. McBride (ed.), *History and Memory in Modern Ireland* (Cambridge University Press, 2001), 184–203.

Foley, C., *The Last Irish Plague: The Great Flu Epidemic in Ireland* (Dublin: Irish Academic Press, 2011), 137–52.

Forker, M., and McCormick, J., 'Walls of History: The Use of Mythomoteurs in Northern Ireland Murals,' *Irish Studies Review*, 17 (2009), 423–65.

Foster, R. F., 'Remembering 1798', in I. McBride (ed.), *History and Memory in Modern Ireland* (Cambridge University Press, 2001), 67–94.

The Irish Story: Telling Tales and Making It Up in Ireland (London and New York: Allen Lane, 2001), 23–36.

Vivid Faces: The Revolutionary Generation in Ireland, 1890–1923 (London: Allen Lane, 2014).

Frawley, O. and O'Callaghan, K., (eds.), *Memory Ireland, vol. 4: James Joyce and Cultural Memory* (Syracuse: Syracuse University Press, 2014).

Gephart, W., 'Memory and the Sacred: The Cult of Anniversaries and Commemorative Rituals in the Light of The Elementary Forms' in N. J. Allen, W. S. F. Pickering and W. W. Miller (eds.), *On Durkheim's Elementary Forms of Religious Life* (London and New York: Routledge, 1998), 127–35.

Gibbons, L., '"Where Wolfe Tone's Statue Was Not": Joyce, Monuments and Memory', in I. McBride (ed.), *History and Memory in Modern Ireland* (Cambridge, 2001), 139–59.

'Framing History: Neil Jordan's *Michael Collins*,' *History Ireland*, 1 (Spring 1997), 47–51.

Glassie, H., *Passing the Time in Ballymenone: Culture and History of an Ulster Community* (Philadelphia: University of Pennsylvania Press, 1982).

Goldstone, K., '"Now You See Us, Now You Don't": Reflections on Jews, Historical Amnesia and the Histories of a Multi-Ethnic Dublin', *Translocations: Migration and Social Change*, 4 (2008), 102–9.

Graham, B., and Whelan, Y., 'The Legacies of the Dead: Commemorating the Troubles in Northern Ireland,' *Environment and Planning D: Society and Space*, 25 (2007), 476–95.

Gray, P., 'The Memory and Commemoration of the Great Irish Famine' in P. Gray and K. Oliver (eds.), *The Memory of Catastrophe* (Manchester: Manchester University Press, 2004).

Halbwachs, M., *The Collective Memory* (New York: Harper & Row, 1980).

On Collective Memory (Chicago and London: University of Chicago Press, 1992).

Hamber, B., (ed.), *Past Imperfect: Dealing with the Past in Northern Ireland and Societies in Transition* (Derry / Londonderry: INCORE, 1998).

Hayes, P. and J. Campbell, *Bloody Sunday: Trauma, Pain and Politics* (London and Ann Arbor: Pluto Press, 2005).

Herron, T., and Lynch, J., *After Bloody Sunday: Ethics, Representation, Justice* (Cork: Cork University Press, 2007).

Higgins, R., *Transforming 1916: Meaning, Memory and the Fiftieth Anniversary of the Easter Rising* (Cork: Cork University Press, 2012).

Hirsch, J., *Portrait of America: A Cultural History of the Federal Writers' Project* (Chapel Hill: University of North Carolina Press, 2003).

Hobsbawm, E., 'Mass-Producing Traditions: Europe, 1870–1914' in E. Hobsbawm and T. Ranger (eds.), *The Invention of Tradition*, (Cambridge, 1983), 263–307.

Hopkins, S., 'The Chronicles of Long Kesh: Provisional Irish Republican Memoirs and the Contested Memory of the Hunger Strikes,' *Memory Studies*, 7 (2014), 425–39.

Horne, J., (ed.), *Our War: Ireland and the Great War* (Dublin: Royal Irish Academy, 2008).

Huyssen, A., *Twilight Memories: Marking Time in a Culture of Amnesia* (New York: Routledge, 1995).

Jeffery, K., *Ireland and the Great War* (Cambridge University Press, 2000).

'Irish Varieties of Great War Commemoration', in J. Horne and E. Madigan, *Towards Commemoration: Ireland in War and Revolution, 1912–1923* (Dublin: Royal Irish Academy, 2013), 117–25.

Johnson, N. C., *Ireland, the Great War, and the Geography of Remembrance* (Cambridge University Press, 2003).

'Framing the Past: Time, Space and the Politics of Heritage Tourism in Ireland', *Political Geography*, 18 (1999), 187–207.

Kaplan, S., *Farewell, Revolution, vol. 1: The Historians' Feud, France, 1789/1989 and vol. 2: Disputed Legacies, France, 1789/1989* (Ithaca and London: Cornell University Press, 1995).

Kelleher, M., 'Hunger and History: Monuments to the Great Irish Famine,' *Textual Practice*, 16 (2002), 249–76.

Kelly, M. C., *Ireland's Great Famine in Irish-American History: Enshrining a Fateful Memory* (Lanham, MD: Rowman & Littlefield, 2014).

Kelly, S., 'Stigma and Silence: Oral Histories of Tuberculosis,' *Oral History*, 39 (2011), 65–76.

Keogh, D., *Jews in Twentieth-Century Ireland: Refugees, Anti-Semitism and the Holocaust* (Cork: Cork University Press, 1998).

Kiberd, D., 'The Elephant of Revolution Forgetfulness', in M. Ní Dhonnchadha and T. Dorgan (eds.), *Revising the Rising* (Derry: Field Day, 1991).

Lehner, S., 'The Irreversible and Irrevocable: Encircling Trauma in Contemporary Northern Irish Literature' in M. Ní Dhonnchadha and T. Dorgan (eds.), *Revising the Rising*.

Leonard, J., 'Facing "the Finger of Scorn": Veterans' Memories of Ireland and the Great War', in M. Evans and K. Lunn (eds.), *War and Memory in the Twentieth Century* (Oxford and New York: Berg, 1997), 59–72.

Levy, D., and Sznaider, N., 'Memory Unbound: The Holocaust and the Formation of Cosmopolitan Memory', *European Journal of Social Theory*, 5 (2002), 87–106.

'The Institutionalization of Cosmopolitan Morality: The Holocaust and Human Rights,' *Journal of Human Rights*, 3 (2004), 143–57.

Mark-FitzGerald, E., *Commemorating the Irish Famine: Memory and the Monument* (Liverpool: Liverpool University Press, 2013).

Martin, F. X., '1916: Myth, Fact, and Mystery,' *Studia Hibernica*, (1967), 7–126.

McBride, I., (ed), *History and Memory in Modern Ireland* (Cambridge University Press, 2001).

McCarthy, M., *Ireland's 1916 Rising: Explorations of History-Making, Commemoration & Heritage in Modern Times* (Farnham and Burlington: Ashgate, 2012).

McDaniel, D., *Enniskillen: The Remembrance Sunday Bombing* (Dublin: Wolfhound Press, 1997).

McGee, O., '"God Save Ireland": Manchester-Martyr Demonstrations in Dublin, 1867–1916,' *Éire-Ireland*, 36 (2001), 39–66.

McHugh, R., 'The Famine in Irish Oral Tradition', in R. D. Edwards and T. D. Williams, *The Great Famine: Studies in Irish History 1845–52* (Dublin: Lilliput Press, 1994; orig. edn. 1957), 389–436.

McIlroy, B., 'History without Borders: Neil Jordan's *Michael Collins*', in J. MacKillop (ed.), *Contemporary Irish Cinema: From The Quiet Man to Dancing at Lughnasa* (Syracuse: Syracuse University Press, 1999), 22–28.

McKay, S., *Bear in Mind These Dead* (London: Faber & Faber, 2008).

McKittrick, D. et al., *Lost Lives: The Stories of the Men, Women, and Children Who Died as a Result of the Northern Ireland Troubles* (Edinburgh: Mainstream, 1999).

Merivirta, R., *The Gun and Irish Politics: Examining National History in Neil Jordan's Michael Collins* (Bern and New York: Peter Lang, 2009).

Milne, I., 'Through the Eyes of a Child: "Spanish" Influenza Remembered by Survivors', in A. Mac Lellan and A. Mauger (eds.), *Growing Pains: Childhood Illness in Ireland, 1750–1950* (Dublin: Irish Academic Press, 2013), 159–74.

Misztal, B. A., 'Durkheim on Collective Memory,' *Journal of Classical Sociology*, 3 (1 July 2003), 123–43.

Mullan, D., *A Glimmer of Light: An Overview of Great Hunger Commemorative Events in Ireland and Throughout the World* (Dublin: Concern Worldwide, 1995).

Murphy, J. H., *Abject Loyalty: Nationalism and Monarchy in Ireland During the Reign of Queen Victoria* (Washington, DC: Catholic University of America Press, 2001).

Nora, P., 'Between Memory and History: Les Lieux de Mémoire,' *Representations*, 26 (1989), 7–24.

Ó Ciosáin, N., 'Approaching a Folklore Archive: The Irish Folklore Commission and the Memory of the Great Famine,' *Folklore*, 115 (2004), 222–32.

Ó hAodha, M., 'Reconfiguring the Traveller Self: Cultural Memory and Belonging' in O. Frawley (ed.), *Memory Ireland, vol. 2: Diaspora and Memory Practices*, 185–96.

O'Brien, C. C., *States of Ireland* (London: Hutchinson, 1972), 150.

Pašeta, S., 'Nationalist Responses to Two Royal Visits to Ireland, 1900 and 1903', *Irish Historical Studies*, 31 (1999), 488–504.

Pine, E., *The Politics of Irish Memory: Performing Remembrance in Contemporary Irish Culture* (Basingstoke: Palgrave Macmillan, 2011), 18–51.

Póirtéir, C., *Famine Echoes* (Dublin: Gill & Macmillan, 1995).

Radstone, S., and Schwarz, B. (eds.), *Memory: Histories, Theories, Debates* (New York: Fordham University Press, 2010).

Raven, J. (ed.), *Lost Mansions: Essays on the Destruction of the Country House* (Basingstoke and New York: Palgrave Macmillan, 2015).

Rigney, A., 'Divided Pasts: A Premature Memorial and the Dynamics of Collective Remembrance,' *Memory Studies*, 1 (2008), 89–97.

Robinson, H., 'Remembering War in the Midst of Conflict: First World War Commemorations in the Northern Irish Troubles', *Twentieth-Century British History*, 21 (2010), 80–101.

Rolston, B., '"Trying to Reach the Future through the Past": Murals and Memory in Northern Ireland,' *Crime, Media, Culture*, 6 (2010), 285–307.

Simon, G., 'Cure, Superstition, Infection and Reaction: Tuberculosis in Ireland, 1932–1957', *Oral History*, 32 (2004), 63–72.

Simpson, K., *Truth Recovery in Northern Ireland: Critically Interpreting the Past* (Manchester: Manchester University Press, 2009).

   Unionist Voices and the Politics of Remembering the Past in Northern Ireland (Houndmills and New York: Palgrave Macmillan, 2009).

Smith, J., *Ireland's Magdalen Laundries and the Nation's Architecture of Containment* (Notre Dame, IN: University of Notre Dame Press, 2007).

Smyth, J. 'Milltown Cemetery and the Politics of Remembrance' in J. Smyth (ed.), *Remembering the Troubles: Commemorating, Constructing and Contesting the Recent Past in Northern Ireland* (Notre Dame, University of Notre Dame Press, 2017).

Smyth, M. B., *Truth Recovery and Justice after Conflict: Managing Violent Pasts* (Oxford and New York: Routledge, 2007).

Switzer, C., *Unionists and the Great War: Commemoration in the North of Ireland 1914–1939* (Dublin: Irish Academic Press, 2007).

Taylor, D. A., *Soul of a People: The WPA Writer's Project Uncovers Depression America* (Hoboken, NJ: Wiley, 2009).

Terdiman, R., *Present Past: Modernity and the Memory Crisis* (Ithaca and London: Cornell University Press, 1993).

Turpin, J., 'Monumental Commemoration of the Fallen in Ireland, North and South, 1920–60,' *New Hibernia Review*, 11 (2007), 107–19.

Whelan, Y., 'The Construction and Destruction of a Colonial Landscape: Monuments to British Monarchs in Dublin before and after Independence,' *Journal of Historical Geography*, 28 (2002), 508–33.

Winter, J., 'Notes on the Memory Boom: War, Remembrance, and the Uses of the Past' in Duncan Bell (ed.), *Memory, Trauma and World Politics: Reflections on the Relationship between Past and Present* (Basingstoke and New York: Palgrave Macmillan, 2006), 54–73.

Woodward, G., *Culture, Northern Ireland, and the Second World War* (Oxford University Press, 2015).

Zuelow, E., *Making Ireland Irish: Tourism and National Identity since the Irish Civil War* (Syracuse: Syracuse University Press, 2009).

24 Catholicism in Ireland, 1880–2015: Rise, Ascendancy and Retreat

Daithí Ó Corráin

Primary Printed Sources

Forum on Patronage and Pluralism in the Primary Sector: Report of the Forum's Advisory Group (2012, 2014).

www.catholicbishops.ie/2015/08/24/seventeen-seminarians-commence-priesthood-studies-saint-patricks-college-maynooth/ (accessed 13 June 2016).

www.irishchurches.org/members/redeemed-christian-church-of-god (accessed 13 June 2016).

Irish Catholic Directory

Kavanagh, P., *Tarry Flynn* (London: Penguin, 1978).

O'Connor, F., 'First Confession', in *My Oedipus Complex and Other Stories* (London: Penguin, 2005), 23–30.

Pastoral letter issued by the Archbishops and Bishops of Ireland, 10 October 1922 and published in *Irish Times*, *Irish Independent* and *Freeman's Journal*, 11 Oct. 1922.

Practice and Belief among Catholics in Northern Ireland: A Summary of Data from the International Social Science Programme Religion III (2008–9) survey for Northern Ireland & Ireland in a comparative perspective.

Report by Commission of Investigation into Catholic Archdiocese of Dublin (Dublin: Stationery Office, 2009)

The Pope in Ireland: Addresses and Homilies (Dublin: Veritas, 1979).

Secondary Works

Akenson, D. H., *Half the World from Home: Perspectives on the Irish in New Zealand, 1860–1950* (Wellington: Victoria University Press, 1990).

Anderson, K., and Lavan, A., 'Believing in God but not Obeying the Church: Being a Catholic in Ireland and Poland in the 1990s', in B. Hilliard and M. Nic Ghiolla Phádraig (ed.), *Changing Ireland in International Comparison* (Dublin: Liffey Press, 2007).

Barr, C., ' "Imperium in Imperio": Irish Episcopal Imperialism in the Nineteenth Century', *English Historical Review*, 123 (2008), 611–50.

Biever, B., *Religion, Culture and Values: A Cross-Cultural Analysis of Motivational Factors in Native Irish and American Irish Catholicism* (New York: Arno Press, 1976).

Blanshard, P., *American freedom and Catholic power* (Boston, MA: Beacon Press, 1949).

The Irish and Catholic Power (Boston, MA: Beacon Press, 1953).

Breen, M. J., and Reynolds, C., 'The Rise of Secularism and the Decline of Religiosity in Ireland: The Pattern of Religious Change in Europe', *The International Journal of Religion & Spirituality in Society*, 1 (2011), 195–212.

Brown, C., *The Death of Christian Britain* (London: Routledge, 2001).

Carty, F. X., *Hold Firm: John Charles McQuaid and the Second Vatican Council* (Dublin: Columba Press, 2007).

Clarke, M., 'The Response of the Roman Catholic Church to the Introduction of Vocational Education in Ireland, 1930–1942', *History of Education*, 41 (2012), 477–93.

Connolly, P., 'The Church in Ireland since Vatican II', *The Furrow*, 30 (December 1979).

Conway, B., 'Religious Institutions and Sexual Scandals: A Comparative Study of Catholicism in Ireland, South Africa and the United States', *International Journal of Comparative Sociology*, 55 (2014).

Cooney, J., *John Charles McQuaid: ruler of Catholic Ireland* (Dublin: Gill & Macmillan, 1999).

Corish, P., *The Irish Catholic Experience: A Historical Survey* (Dublin: Gill & Macmillan, 1985).

Cosgrove, O., Cox, L. and Kuhling, C., *Ireland's New Religious Movements* (Newcastle-upon-Tyne: Cambridge Scholars, 2011).

Cox, L., 'Current Debates: New Religion(s) in Ireland', *Irish Journal of Sociology*, 18 (2010), 100–11.

Davie, G., *Religion in Britain since 1945: Believing Without Belonging* (Oxford: Blackwell, 1994).

The Sociology of Religion (London: Sage, 2007).

Donnelly, J. S., 'The Peak of Marianism in Ireland, 1930–60', in S. Brown and D. W. Miller (ed.), *Piety and Power in Ireland, 1760–1960: Essays in Honour of Emmet Larkin* (Notre Dame, IN: University Notre Dame Press, 2000), 252–83.

'Opposing the "Modern World": The Cult of the Virgin Mary in Ireland, 1965–85', *Éire-Ireland*, 40 (2005), 193–4.

Donnelly, S., and Inglis, T., 'The Media and the Catholic Church in Ireland: Reporting Clerical Child Sex Abuse', *Journal of Contemporary Religion* 25:1 (2010).

Duffy, E., *Saints & Sinners: A History of the Popes* (New Haven, Yale University Press, 2001).

Earl, M., '*The Late Late Show*, Controversy and Context', in M. McLoone and J. MacMahon (eds.), *Television and Irish Society* (Dublin: RTE, 1984).

Elliott, M., 'Faith in Ireland, 1600–2000', in A. Jackson (ed.), *The Oxford Handbook of Modern Irish History* (Oxford University Press, 2015).

Fahey, T., 'Is Atheism Increasing? Ireland and Europe compared', in T. Cassidy (ed.), *Measuring Ireland: Discerning Values and Beliefs* (Dublin: Veritas, 2002).

'Religion and Prosperity', *Studies* 90 (2001).

Fahey, T., Hayes, B., and Sinnott, R., *Conflict and Consensus: A Study of Values and Attitudes in the Republic of Ireland and Northern Ireland* (Dublin: Institute of Public Administration, 2005).

Fallon, B., *An Age of Innocence: Irish Culture, 1930–1960* (Dublin: Gill & Macmillan, 1998).

FitzGerald, G., *All in a Life: An Autobiography* (Dublin: Gill & Macmillan, 1991).

Fuller, L., *Irish Catholicism since 1950: The Undoing of a Culture* (Dublin: Gill & Macmillan, 2002).

'Religion, Politics and Socio-cultural Change in Twentieth-century Ireland', *The European Legacy* 10 (2005).

'Critical Voices in Irish Catholicism: reading the signs of the times', *Studies* 100 (2011).

Gallagher, E. and Worrall, S., *Christians in Ulster, 1968–1980* (Oxford University Press, 1982).

Gallagher, M.P., 'What Hope for Irish Faith?', *The Furrow* 29 (1978).

Ganiel, G., *Transforming post-Catholic Ireland: Religious Practice in Late Modernity* (Oxford University Press, 2016).

Ganiel, G., and Dixon, P., 'Religion in Northern Ireland: Rethinking Fundamentalism and the Possibilities for Conflict Transformation', *Journal of Peace Research*, 45 (2008), 421–38.

Gilley, S., 'Catholicism, Ireland and the Irish Diaspora', in S. Gilley and B. Stanley, (eds.), *The Cambridge History of Christianity: vol. 8 World Christianities c. 1815-c.1914* (Cambridge University Press, 2006).

Gorham, M., *Forty Years of Irish Broadcasting* (Dublin: Talbot Press, 1967).

Heelas, P., and Woodhead, L., *The Spiritual Revolution: Why Religion is Giving Way to Spirituality* (Oxford University Press, 2005).

Hilliard, B., 'Family', in S. O'Sullivan (ed.), *Contemporary Ireland: A Sociological Map* (Dublin: UCD Press, 2007).

Hoban, B., 'How Did it Come to This?', *Studies*, 101 (2012).

Hogan, E., *The Irish Missionary Movement: A Historical Survey, 1830–1980* (Dublin: Gill & Macmillan, 1992).

Hogan, G., 'De Valera, the Constitution and the Historians', *Irish Jurist* 40 (2005), 293–320.

Horgan, J., '*The Furrow*: Navigating the Rapids, 1950–77', in M. O'Brien and F. Larkin (eds.), *Periodicals and Journalism in Twentieth-Century Ireland* (Dublin: Four Courts Press, 2014), 173–86.

Inglis, T., *Moral Monopoly: The Rise and Fall of the Catholic Church in Modern Ireland* (Dublin: UCD Press, 1998).

'Individualism and Secularisation in Catholic Ireland', in S. O'Sullivan (ed.), *Contemporary Ireland: A Sociological Map* (Dublin: UCD Press, 2007).

'Catholic Identity in Contemporary Ireland: Belief and Belonging to Tradition', *Journal of Contemporary Religion* 22 (2007), 205–20.

Keenan, M., "'Them and Us": The Clergy Child Sexual Offender as "Other"' in T. Flannery (ed.), *Responding to the Ryan Report* (Dublin: Columba Press, 2009), 192–4.

Kennedy, F., *Frank Duff: A life Story* (New York: Continuum Publishing, 2011).

Keogh, D., 'The Catholic Church in Ireland since the 1950s', in L. Woodcock Tentler (ed.), *The Church Confronts Modernity: Catholicism since 1950 in the United States, Ireland and Quebec* (Washington, DC: Catholic University of America Press, 2007).

'Ireland, the Vatican and the Cold War: The Case of Italy, 1948', *Historical Journal* 34 (1991), 931–52.

Kiberd, D., 'Ireland after *Aggiornamento*', *Studies*, 101 (2012).

Kirby, P., *Is Irish Catholicism Dying? Liberating an Imprisoned Church* (Dublin: Mercier Press, 1984).

'The Catholic Church in post-Celtic Tiger Ireland', in J. Littleton and E. Maher (eds.), *Contemporary Catholicism in Ireland: A Critical Appraisal* (Dublin: Columba Press, 2008).

Kitching,K., 'Governing "Authentic" Religiosity? The Responsibilisation of Parents beyond Religion and State in Matters of School Ethos in Ireland', *Irish Journal of Sociology* 21 (2013), 17–34.

Küng, H., *Church & Change: The Irish Experience* (Dublin: Gill & Macmillan, 1986).

Lane, D., 'Vatican II: The Irish Experience', in L. Bergin (ed.), *Faith, Word and Culture* (Dublin: Columba Press, 2004).

Larkin, E., 'The Devotional Revolution in Ireland, 1850–1875', *The American Historical Review*, 77 (1972).

Lawlor, B., and Dalton, J., (ed.), *The Society of St Vincent de Paul in Ireland: 170 Years of Fighting Poverty* (Dublin: New Island Books, 2014).

Lee, J. J., 'Society and culture', in F. Litton (ed.), *Unequal Achievement: The Irish Experience, 1957–1982* (Dublin: Institute of Public Administration, 1982).

'From Empire to Europe: The Irish State 1922–73', in M. Adshead, P. Kirby and M. Millar (eds.), *Contesting the State: Lessons from the Irish Case* (Manchester: Manchester University Press, 2008).

Lennonn C. (ed.), *Confraternities and Sodalities in Ireland: Charity, Devotion and Sociability* (Dublin: Columba Press, 2012).

Littleton, J., 'Being a Catholic in Ireland today', in J. Littleton and E. Maher (eds.), *Contemporary Catholicism in Ireland: A Critical Appraisal* (Dublin: Columba Press, 2008).

Mac Gréil, M., *Prejudice and Tolerance in Ireland: Based on a Survey of Intergroup Attitudes of Dublin Adults and Other Sources* (Dublin: College of Industrial Relations, 1977).

Pluralism & Diversity in Ireland: Prejudice and Related Issues in early 21st Century Ireland (Dublin: Columba Press, 2011).

Malesevic, V., 'Ireland and Neo-secularisation Theory', *Irish Journal of Sociology*, 18 (2010).

Maxwell, E., 'Apostolic Religious life in Ireland and Western Europe', in M. J. Breen (ed), *A Fire in the Forest: Religious Life in Ireland* (Dublin: Veritas, 2001), 58–60.

McCabe, M. P., *For God and Ireland: The Fight for Moral Superiority in Ireland, 1922–1932* (Sallins: Irish Academic Press, 2013).

McConvery, B., 'The Redemptorists and the shaping of Irish popular devotion, 1851–1965', in H. Laugerud and S. Ryan (eds.), *Devotional Cultures of European Christianity, 1790–1960* (Dublin: Four Courts Press, 2012).

McGarry, P., 'All Churches in Ireland in Need of "Reality Check"', *Irish Times*, 24 May 2015.

McIntosh, G., 'Acts of "National Communion": The Centenary Celebrations for Catholic Emancipation, the Forerunner of the Eucharistic Congress', in J. Augusteijn (ed.), *Ireland in the 1930s: New Perspectives* (Dublin: Four Courts Press, 1999).

Miller, D. W., *Church, State and Nation in Ireland, 1898–1921* (Dublin: Gill & Macmillan, 1973).

Morrissey, T., *William J. Walsh, Archbishop of Dublin, 1841–1921: No Uncertain Voice* (Dublin: Four Courts Press, 2000).

Newman, J., (ed.), *The Limerick Rural Survey, 1958–1964* (Tipperary: Muintir na Tíre, 1964).

Nic Ghiolla Phádraig, M., 'The Power of the Catholic Church in the Republic of Ireland', in P. Clancy, S., Drudy, K., Lynch and L. O'Dowd (eds.), *Irish Society: Sociological Perspectives* (Dublin: Institute of Public Administration, 1995).

'Religion in Ireland: Preliminary Analysis', *Social Studies: Irish Journal of Sociology* 5 (1976).

Ó Buachalla, S., *Education Policy in Twentieth-Century Ireland* (Dublin: Wolfhound Press, 1988).

Ó Corráin, D., *Rendering to God and Caesar: The Irish Churches and the Two States in Ireland, 1949–73* (Manchester: Manchester University Press, 2006).

'"Resigned to Take the Bill with its Defects": The Catholic Church and the Third Home Rule Bill', in Gabriel Doherty (ed.), *Cork Studies in the Irish Revolution: The Home Rule Crisis 1912–14* (Cork: Mercier Press, 2014), 185–209.

'Archbishop William Joseph Walsh', in Eugenio Biagini and Daniel Mulhall (eds.), *The Shaping of Modern Ireland: A Centenary Reassessment* (Sallins: Irish Academic Press, 2016), 110–23.

O'Sullivan, K., ' "Ah Ireland, the Caring Nation": Foreign Aid and Irish State Identity during the long 1970s', *Irish Historical Studies* 38 (2013).

Pace, E., 'A Peculiar Pluralism', *Journal of Modern Italian Studies* 12 (2007).

'Achilles and the Tortoise: A Society Monopolized by Catholicism Faced with an Unexpected Religious Pluralism', *Social Compass* 60 2013), 315–31.

Pettitt, L., *Screening Ireland: Film and Television Representation* (Manchester: Manchester University Press, 2000).

Rafferty, O., 'Northern Catholics and the Early Years of the Troubles', in O. Rafferty (ed.), *Irish Catholic Identities* (Manchester: Manchester University Press, 2013).

'The Catholic Church in Ireland and Vatican II in historical perspective', in N. Coll (ed.), *Ireland & Vatican II: Essays Theological, Pastoral and Educational* (Dublin: Columba Press, 2015).

Roddy, S., 'Spiritual Imperialism and the Mission of the Irish Race: The Catholic Church and Emigration from Nineteenth-century Ireland', *Irish Historical Studies* 38 (2013), 600–19.

Savage, R., *Irish Television: The Political and Social Origins* (Cork: Cork University Press, 1996).

A Loss of Innocence? Television and Irish Society, 1960–72 (Manchester: Manchester University Press, 2010).

Scharbrodt, O., Sakaranaho, T., Hussain Khan, A., Shanneik, Y., and Ibrahim, V., *Muslims in Ireland: Past and Present* (Edinburgh: Edinburgh University Press, 2015).

Skuce, S., *The Faiths of Ireland* (Dublin: Columba Press, 2006).

Stark, R., and Finke, R., 'Catholic Religious Vocations: Decline and Revival', *Review of Religious Research* 42 (2000), 125–45.

Tierney, M., *The Story of Muintir na Tíre 1931–2001: The First Seventy Years* (Tipperary: Muintir na Tíre, 2004).

Tippett-Spirtou, S., *French Catholicism: Church, State and Society in a Changing Era* (Basingstoke: Palgrave Macmillan, 2000).

Tuohy, D., *Denominational Education and Politics: Ireland in a European Context* (Dublin: Veritas, 2013).

Twomey, D. V., *The End of Irish Catholicism?* (Dublin: Veritas, 2003).

Ugba, A., 'African Pentecostals in Twenty-first Century Ireland: Identity and Integration,' in B. Fanning (ed.), *Immigration and Social Change in the Republic of Ireland* (Manchester: Manchester University Press, 2007).

   Shades of Belonging: African Pentecostals in Twenty-First Century Ireland (Trenton, NJ: Africa World Press, 2009).

Walsh, J., 'Ministers, Bishops and the Changing Balance of power in Irish Education 1950–70', *Irish Historical Studies* 38 (2012).

Weafer, J., 'Statistical Profile of Religious Personnel in Ireland', in M. J. Breen (ed), *A Fire in the Forest: Religious Life in Ireland* (Dublin: Veritas, 2001).

Whyte, J. H., *Church and State in Modern Ireland, 1923–1970* (Dublin: Gill & Macmillan, 1971).

Wilson, B., *Religion in Sociological Perspective* (Oxford University Press, 1982).

Woulfe, E., 'Religious life in Ireland today', in N. Coll (ed.), *Ireland & Vatican II: Essays Theological, Pastoral and Educational* (Dublin: Columba Press, 2015), 219.

25 Art and Architecture in Ireland, 1880–2016

Paula Murphy

Barber, F., *Art in Ireland since 1910* (London: Reaktion Books, 2013).

Coulter, R., 'Hibernian Salon des Refusés', in *Irish Arts Review*, vol. 20 (autumn, 2003).

Dawson, B., (ed.), *Hugh Lane, Founder of a Gallery of Modern Art for Ireland* (London: Scala Publishers, 2008).

Dunne, A., *Patrick Scott* (Dublin: Liberties Press, 2014).

Juncosa, E. and Kennedy, C. (eds.), *The Moderns, The Arts in Ireland from the 1900s to the 1970s* (Dublin: Irish Museum of Modern Art, 2011).

Kelly, L., *Thinking Long. Contemporary Art in the North of Ireland* (Kinsale: Gandon Editions, 1996).

Kennedy, S. B., *Irish Art and Modernism 1880–1950* (Belfast: Institute of Irish Studies, Queen's University, 1991).

Kennedy, B. P., *Dreams and Responsibilities, The State and the Arts in Independent Ireland* (Dublin: Arts Council, 1990, reprinted 1998).

Kennedy, S. B., *The White Stag Group* (Dublin: Irish Museum of Modern Art, 2005).

Krauss, R., 'Sculpture in the Expanded Field', *October*, 8 (Spring, 1979), 30–44.

Moos, D., 'Narrative of the Name', in C. Kennedy and G. Jackson (eds.), *Beyond the White Cube, a retrospective of Brian O'Doherty/Patrick Ireland* (Dublin: City Gallery the Hugh Lane, 2006).

Murphy, P., *Nineteenth-Century Irish Sculpture, Native Genius Reaffirmed* (New Haven: Yale University Press, 2010).

Report of the Committee of Inquiry into the work carried out by the Royal Hibernian Academy and the Metropolitan School of Art, Dublin (Dublin and London: His Majesty's Stationery Office, 1906).

Rowley, E., 'Transitional Modernism: The Case of 1950s Church Architecture in Dublin', in E. Keown and C. Taafe (eds.), *Irish Modernism* (Bern: Peter Lang, 2010).

Turpin, J., *A School of Art in Dublin since the Eighteenth Century* (Dublin: Gill & Macmillan, 1995).

26 Endword: Ireland Looking Outwards, 1880–2016

Eunan O'Halpin

Primary Sources

United Kingdom
London, British Library

Tegart Mss, Eur c235, p. 46, IOR, L/PJ/12/39: Police reports, IOR, L/PJ/12/260, 268

Report of interdepartmental committee on Bolshevism as a menace to the British empire, n.d. (1921): L/PS/10/866

Oxford, Bodleian Library

Sir Con O'Neill papers.
Lionel Curtis papers.

Cambridge University

Amery papers AMEL 7/35, diary, 26 July 1941; Churchill College.

London, The National Archives

Cabinet papers: CAB/129/112

SIS to IPI, 22 March 1929 KV2/515

Report by Major M.F. Grove White, 22 July 1925, WO32/3515 [illegible], Belfast, to MI5, 9 Feb. 1926, KV4/279

M. de Burca to Prime Minister Harold Wilson, 10 July 1967, PREM13/2732

Informal notes of cabinet meeting, 25 January 1955, CAB195/13

British ambassador, Washington, to London, 21 July 1915, CAB37/132

Comintern decodes, 1932, HW17/72.

Margaret Thatcher Foundation Archive, accessed via http://www.margaretthatcher.org, 1 June 2014, translation of unofficial Politburo minute, 13 April 1989.

Terence O'Neill to Prime Minister Sir Alec Douglas-Home, 22 Nov. 1963 PREM11/4874

London, Bank of England

OV81/ 1: Bank of England archives. London

Belfast

Memorandum by minister of commerce, 4 March 1959 CAB/4/1097: Belfast, Public Record Office of Northern Ireland Purcell.

Cabinet meeting, 8 June 1967, CAB4/1574.

Cabinet social and economic affairs committee meeting, 2 February 1971, CAB/4/1551/21.

Canada

Mackenzie King diary, 3 August 1932: www.bac-lac.gc.ca/eng/discover/politics-government/prime-ministers/william-lyon-mackenzie-king/Pages/search.aspx.

United States

Cabinet CREST, current intelligence weekly summaries, CIA RDP7900927A0019000090001-3, 16 Oct. 1958, and CIA RDP7900927A002600050001-9, 11 Feb. 1960, RDP7900927A0033000800001-8, Weekly Intelligence Summary, 7 September 1961: United States National Archives Records Administration (NARA)

Truman Presidential Library, MO, 'Memorandum of conversation with Minister for External Affairs Mr Seán MacBride …', 13 March 1951, Houghton Library, Harvard: Dean G. Acheson papers.

Gerald R. Ford Library, University of Michigan, MI Presidential Country file for Europe/Canada, box 7, folder Ireland 2, Kissinger brief for President Ford, 2 September 1975

Boston College, MA, Tip O'Neill papers, folder 23/4, and folder 22/5, Haughey to O'Neill, 19 May 1981.

Library of Congress, Washington DC, Moynihan note to Steve Rickard, undated [1993], and Michael Collins (Embassy of Ireland) to Rickard, 13 October 1993, Daniel Patrick Moynihan papers, box 327, folder 9.

https://wikileaks.org/plusd/cables/08DUBLIN603_a.html, United States embassy, Dublin, to Washington, 4 Nov. 2008 (accessed on 30 August 2015).

Ireland

Tom Sheehy papers, P34/6/6, Michael Patterson to Sheehy, 1 April 1949: Tralee, Kerry County Archives,

Bureau of Military History: Military Archives of Ireland

India

Transcripts Shri Durga Das Acc. No. 96 (27 Dec. 1971); New Delhi, Nehru Memorial Library (NML)

Oral History Transcript Shri Durga Das Acc. No. 96 (27 December 1971); Nehru Memorial Library, Delhi,

Printed Secondary Sources

Andrews, C. S., *Man of No Property* (Dublin: Mercier Press, 1982).

Campbell, S. P., 'Give Ireland a Chance for Economic Independence', *Honesty*, v, (28 May 1927), 19–20.

Catterall, P., (ed.), *The Macmillan Diaries: The Cabinet Years, 1950–57* (London: Pan Macmillan, 2003).

FitzGerald, G., *All in a Life: An Autobiography* (Dublin: Gill & Macmillan, 1991).

Kipling, Rudyard, *Kim* (London: Macmillan, 1901).

Magan, W., *An Irish Childhood* (Salisbury, 1996).

Smyth, B. T. (ed.), *'… but not Conquered': Communist China Through the Eyes of Six Columban Missionaries* (Dublin: Browne & Nolan, 1958).

Walsh, J., *Patrick Hillery: The Official Biography* (Dublin: New Island, 2008).

Secondary Works

Babbington, A., *The Devil to Pay: the Mutiny of the Connaught Rangers, India, July 1920* (London: Pen and Sword Books, 1991).

Bartlett, T., *Ireland: A History* (Cambridge University Press, 2010).

Bloomfield, K., *A Tragedy of Errors: The Government and Misgovernment of Northern Ireland* (Liverpool: Liverpool University Press, 2007).

Bourke, A., *The Burning of Bridget Cleary: A True Story* (London: Penguin, 1999).

Bowman, J., *De Valera and the Ulster Question 1917–1973* (Oxford University Press, 1982).

Bruce, S., *The Red Hand: Protestant Paramilitaries in Northern Ireland* (Oxford University Press, 1992).

Canning, P., *British Policy Towards Ireland, 1921–1941* (Oxford University Press, 1985).

Chandra Bose, S., *The Indian Struggle 1920–1942* (London: Asia Publishing House, 1964).

Cleary, J., 'Postcolonial Ireland', in K. Kenny (ed.), *Ireland and the British Empire* (Oxford University Press, 2004), 251–88.

Collins, S., 'Labour and Europe: From No to Yes', in P. Daly, R. O'Brien and P. Rouse (eds.), *Making the Difference? The Irish Labour Party 1912–2012* (Cork: Cork University Press, 2012), 154–5.

Coughlan, A., *The Common Market: Why Ireland should not join* (Dublin: Common Market Study Group, 1972).

Daly, M. E., *The Slow Failure: Population Decline in Independent Ireland, 1923–1973* (Madison, WI: University of Wisconsin Press, 2006).

Day, D., *The Great Betrayal: Britain, Australia and the Onset of the Pacific War, 1939–42* (Oxford University Press, 1988).

Delaney, E., *The Irish in Post-War Britain* (Oxford University Press, 2007).

Dempsey, G., *From the Embassy: a US foreign policy primer* (Dublin: Liffey Press, 2004).

Dorr, N., *Ireland at the United Nations: memories of the early years* (Dublin: Institute of Public Administration, 2010).

Drea, E., 'The influence of Henry Parker-Willis and the Federal Reserve on the institutional design of the Irish Currency Act 1927', *The Historical Journal*, 58 (2015), 855–75.

Fanning, R., *The Irish Department of Finance, 1922–1958* (Dublin: Institute of Public Administration, 1978).

Fraser, T. G., 'Ireland and India', in K. Jeffery (ed.), *'An Irish Empire?: Aspects of Ireland and the British Empire* (Manchester: Manchester University Press, 1996).

Gannon, S., 'The Formation, Composition, and Conduct of the British Section of the Palestinian Gendarmerie, 1922–1926', *Historical Journal*, 56 (December 2013), 997–1006.

Gordon, L. A., *Brothers Against the Raj: A Biography of Indian Nationalists Sarat & Subhas Chandra Bose* (New York: Columbia University Press, 1990).

Hanley, B. and Millar, S., *The Lost Revolution: The Story of the Official IRA and the Worker's Party* (Dublin: Penguin Ireland, 2010).

Haughton, J., 'The Historical Background', in J. O'Hagan (ed.), *The Economy of Ireland: Policy and Performance of a Small European Country* (London: St Martin's Press, 1995), 30–2.

Hogan, G., *The Origins of the Irish Constitution, 1928–1941* (Dublin: Four Courts Press, 2012).

Jeffery, K., 'Introduction', in K. Jeffery (ed.), *'An Irish Empire?: Aspects of Ireland and the British Empire* (Manchester: Manchester University Press, 1996).

Johnston, R. H. W., *Century of Endeavour: A Biographical and Autobiographical View of the Twentieth Century in Ireland* (Dublin: Maunsell and Co., 2003).

Kennedy, M., *Ireland and the League of Nations 1923–1946: International Relations, Diplomacy and Politics* (Dublin: Irish Academic Press, 1996).

    Division and Consensus: The Politics of Cross-Border Relations in Ireland, 1925–1969 (Dublin, 2000).

    Guarding Neutral Ireland: the Coast-Watching Service and Military Intelligence, 1939–1945 (Dublin: Four Courts Press, 2008).

    and O'Halpin, E., *Ireland and the Council of Europe* (Strasbourg: Council of Europe Publishing, 2000).

Lee, J. J., *Ireland 1912–1985: Politics and Society* (Cambridge University Press, 1989).

Lillis, M., 'Mr Haughey's dud Exocet', *Dublin Review of Books* issue 21: www.drb.ie / essays / mr-haughey-s-dud-exocet.

Lyons, F. S. L., *Ireland since the Famine* (London, 1971; revised edn., London: Weidenfeld and Nicolson, 1973).

Mahon, T. and Gillogly, J. J., *Decoding the IRA* (Cork: Mercier Press, 2008).

Mansergh, N., *The Unresolved Question: The Anglo-Irish Settlement and Its Undoing 1912–72* (New Haven: Yale University Press, 1991).

McDonagh, S., *The Greening of the Church* (London: Geoffrey Chapman, 1990).

McGarry, F., *Eoin O'Duffy: A Self-Made Hero* (Oxford University Press, 2005).

Murphy, G., *In Search of the Promised Land* (Cork: Mercier Press, 2009).

Nelson, B., *Irish Nationalists and the Making of the Irish Race* (Princeton, NJ: Princeton University Press, 2012).

Ó Drisceoil, D., *Censorship in Ireland, 1939–1945: Neutrality, Politics and Society* (Cork: Cork University Press, 1996).

    Peadar O'Donnell (Cork: Cork University Press, 2001).

Ó Fathartaigh, M., *Irish Agriculture Nationalised: the Dairy Disposal Company and the making of the modern Irish dairy industry* (Dublin: Dairy Products Industry, 2015), 16–36.

Ó Gráda, C., *Ireland: A New Economic History 1780–1939* (Oxford University Press, 1993).

    A Rocky Road: The Irish Economy since the 1920s (Manchester: Manchester University Press, 1995).

O'Connor, S., *Irish Officers in the British Forces, 1922–45* (Basingstoke: Palgrave Macmillan, 2014).

O'Donovan, D., *No More Lonely Scaffolds: Kevin Barry and his Time* (Dublin: Glendale Press, 1989).

O'Halpin, E., *The Decline of the Union: British government in Ireland 1892–1920* (Dublin: Gill & Macmillan, 1987).

    Defending Ireland: The Irish State and its Enemies since 1922 (Oxford University Press, 1999).

(ed.), *MI5 and Ireland, 1939–1945: The Official History* (Dublin: Irish Academic Press, 2003).

'The Geo-politics of Republican Diplomacy in the Twentieth Century', in M. J. Bric and J. Coakley (eds.), *From Political Violence to Negotiated Settlement: The Winding Road to Peace in Twentieth-Century Ireland* (Dublin: UCD Press, 2004).

Spying on Ireland: British Intelligence and Irish Neutrality During the Second World War (Oxford University Press, 2008).

'Labour and the Making of Irish foreign policy 1973–77', in P. Daly, R. O'Brien and P. Rouse (eds.), *Making the Difference? The Irish Labour Party 1912–2012* (Cork: Cork University Press, 2012), 142–6.

'British Intelligence, PIRA and the Early Years of the Northern Ireland Troubles', in P. Maddrell (ed.), *The Image of the Enemy: Intelligence Analysis of Foes since 1945* (Washington, DC: Georgetown University Press, 2015).

O'Malley, K., *Ireland, India and Empire: Indo-Irish Radical Connections, 1919–1964* (Manchester: Manchester University Press, 2008).

O'Shea, H., *Ireland and the End of the British Empire: The Republic and its Role in the Cyprus Emergency* (Manchester: Manchester University Press, 2015).

O'Sullivan, K., *Ireland, Africa and the End of Empire: Small State Identities in the Cold War, 1955–75* (Manchester: Manchester University Press, 2012).

Ollerenshaw, P., 'Businessmen in Northern Ireland and the Imperial Connection, 1886–1939', in K. Jeffery (ed.), *'An Irish Empire'? Aspects of Ireland and the British Empire* (Manchester: Manchester University Press, 1996). 183–4.

Purcell, M., *To Africa with love: The Life of Mother Mary Martin, Foundress of the Medical Missionaries of Mary* (Dublin: Gill & Macmillan, 1987).

Rigney, P., *Trains, Coal and Turf: Transport in Emergency Ireland* (Dublin: Irish Academic Press, 2010).

Sanders, A., *Inside the IRA: Dissident Republicans and the War for Legitimacy* (Edinburgh: Edinburgh University Press, 2011).

Silvestri, M., *Ireland and India: Nationalism, Empire and Memory* (Basingstoke: Palgrave Macmillan, 2009).

Skelly, J. M., *Irish Diplomacy at the United Nations, 1945–1965: National Interests and the International Order* (Dublin: Irish Academic Press, 1997).

Tsokhas, K., 'De-dominionisation: The Anglo-Australian Experience, 1939–1945', *The Historical Journal*, 37 (1994), 861–83.

Walsh, J., *The Politics of Expansion, the transformation of educational policy in the Republic of Ireland* (Manchester: Manchester University Press, 2009).

Whelan, B., *United States Foreign Policy and Ireland from Empire to Independence 1913–1929* (Dublin: Four Courts Press, 2004).

Wills, C., *That Neutral Island: A Cultural History of Ireland during the Second World War* (London: Faber, 2007).

Index